Y0-AGJ-878

The Nonprofit Management Handbook: Operating Policies and Procedures

Edited by Tracy Daniel Connors

John Wiley & Sons, Inc.

New York • Chichester • Brisbane • Singapore • Toronto

SUBSCRIPTION NOTICE

This Wiley product is updated on a periodic basis with supplements to reflect important changes in the subject matter. If you purchased this product directly from John Wiley & Sons, Inc., we have already recorded your subscription for this update service.

If, however, you purchased this product from a bookstore and wish to receive (1) the current update at no additional charge, and (2) future updates and revised, or related volumes billed separately with a 30-day examination review, please send your name, company name (if applicable), address, and the title of the product to:

Supplement Department
John Wiley & Sons, Inc.
One Wiley Drive
Somerset, NJ 08875
1-800-225-5945

This text is printed on acid-free paper.

Copyright © 1993 by John Wiley & Sons, Inc.

All rights reserved. Published simultaneously in Canada.

Reproduction or translation of any part of this work
beyond that permitted by Section 107 or 108 of the
1976 United States Copyright Act without the permission
of the copyright owner is unlawful. Requests for
permission or further information should be addressed to
the Permissions Department, John Wiley & Sons, Inc.,
605 Third Avenue, New York, NY 10158-0012.

This publication is designed to provide accurate and
authoritative information in regard to the subject
matter covered. It is sold with the understanding that
the publisher is not engaged in rendering legal, accounting,
or other professional services. If legal advice or other
expert assistance is required, the services of a competent
professional person should be sought.

Library of Congress Cataloging-in-Publication Data
The Nonprofit management handbook : operating policies and procedures
    / edited by Tracy Daniel Connors.
        p.   cm.
    Includes bibliographical references and index.
    ISBN 0-471-53702-0 (cloth) 0-471-15177-7 (paper)
      1. Corporations. Nonprofit—Management—Handbooks, manuals, etc.
    2. Corporations. Nonprofit—Finance—Handbooks, manuals, etc.
    3. Total quality management—Handbooks, manuals, etc.   I. Connors,
    Tracy Daniel.   II. Series.
    HD62.6.N662   1993   92-10811
    658′.048—dc20

Printed in the United States of America

10 9 8 7 6 5 4 3 2

The Nonprofit Management Handbook: Operating Policies and Procedures

NONPROFIT LAW, FINANCE, AND MANAGEMENT SERIES

To my wife
Faith Cottrell Raymond Connors
for over three decades of support, encouragement, and friendship.

About the Editor

Tracy Daniel Connors is president of the BelleAire Institute in Bowie, Maryland, a management communications and publishing organization. He has served in a variety of management positions in business, government, and philanthropic organizations. A captain in the Naval Reserve, he was voluntarily recalled to active duty six times since 1985, as director of Congressional and Public Affairs for the Space and Naval Warfare Systems Command and the Naval Sea Systems Command in Washington, D.C., and as Deputy Director of the Navy's Command Excellence and Leader Development Program. Other recent Navy assignments have included duties on the staff of the Chief of Naval Operations, where he served as the first Total Quality Leadership Public Affairs Officer, and at Naval District Washington. Other positions have included Director of Satellite Learning Services for the U.S. Chamber of Commerce; Congressional administrative assistant; corporate communications manager for a major electronics corporation; vice president of a national publishing corporation; and as an officer, board member, or professional staff director of numerous nonprofit organizations. He attended Jacksonville University, graduated from the University of Florida, and earned a Master of Arts Degree from the University of Rhode Island. He is also the editor of the *Volunteer Management Handbook, Nonprofit Organization Handbook, Financial Management for Nonprofit Organizations,* the *Dictionary of Mass Media and Communication,* and *Flavors of the Fjords: The Norwegian Holiday Cookbook.*

Contributors

Pamela G. Arrington, PhD, is a volunteer trainer for United Way/United Black Fund Management Services, Inc. She is an associate professor in Behavioral Sciences at Bowie State University, Maryland. For the past three years, Dr. Arrington has served as a consultant to the Department of Defense Task Force on Human Resource Management: Workforce 2000.

Jody Blazek, CPA, is a partner in the accounting firm of Blazek, Rogers & Vetterling in Houston, Texas, where she specializes in nonprofit clients. Since starting at KMPG Peat Marwick in 1969, her expertise has grown through experience as treasurer for the Menil Foundation and the Rothko Chapel and a variety of other affiliations. Ms. Blazek is highly regarded as a lecturer on nonprofit topics and is the author of *Tax and Financial Planning for Tax-Exempt Organizations: Forms, Checklists, Procedures,* published by John Wiley & Sons.

Barbara A. Burgess is a fund-raising and board development consultant with the firm of Staley/Robeson and a doctoral candidate in higher education administration at Kent State University, Ohio.

Ellen E. Chaffee, PhD, is Vice Chancellor for Academic Affairs for the North Dakota University System. She has been president of two national higher education professional associations and has written extensively on strategic management and total quality management.

Joseph E. Champoux, PhD, is a professor of management at The University of New Mexico. Dr. Champoux serves as a consultant to several public and private organizations. His consulting activities include the design of attitude surveys, management training, and development programs, training in total quality management, and organization assessments.

Constance Clark is founder and president of Clark Communications, a direct mail fund-raising consulting and creative services firm. She has created direct mail control packages for many organizations including the Smithsonian Institution Press and the National Easter Seal Society. Ms. Clark has also provided extensive consulting services to a variety of nonprofit organizations.

Barbara M. Cox, MA, has created innovative fund-raising programs, including building and endowment campaigns and special events for such clients as the NOW Legal Defense & Education Fund, The Council for Basic Education, the American Civil Liberties Union, the American Assembly, and the Public Education Association. She is co-founder of Doty & Cox, a consulting firm that provides fund-raising, marketing, board development, strategic planning, and capital campaign management services to gift-supported organizations.

Diane M. Disney, PhD, is director of the Research Center in Business and Economics at the University of Rhode Island, where she teaches management policy at the College of Business Administration. She has written and edited publications on employee benefits (particularly health policy), management, human resources, and governmental spending; in addition, she serves as book review editor of *Compensation & Benefits Management*.

Nan D. Doty has been honored for her work as a senior staff member of four United Way organizations and as Director of Marketing for Connecticut Deloitte & Touche. She is co-founder of Doty & Cox, a consulting firm which provides fund-raising, marketing, board development, strategic planning, and capital campaign management services to gift-supported organizations.

John P. Dreves, MPA, CFRE, is managing partner for the Washington, DC, office of Staley/Robeson/Ryan/St. Lawrence, Inc. During a 27-year fund-raising career, he has been chief development executive with four medical centers and a consultant serving national social service organizations, colleges, and universities, religious groups, and cultural institutions. A focus of his consulting work is fund-raising assessments; he has directed or been instrumental in assessing programs for 24 nonprofit organizations.

Erik D. Dryburgh, JD, CPA, is a partner in the law firm of Moerschbaecher & Dryburgh, where he specializes in nonprofit organizations, assisting them in becoming organized and obtaining tax-exempt status. He also works with nonprofit organizations regarding the tax and corporate issues that arise in operation, including private foundation, unrelated business income, and other issues.

Denise Gallaro, MA, has worked in the Office for Assessment of Student Learning and Development for the past four years. Her graduate work in the Behavioral Sciences has complimented the assessment office's interest in organizational change, goal setting, instrument development, setting standards, quality and effectiveness, and the impact on improvement.

Larry J. Geringer, MS, is manager of Continuous Quality Improvement for the Fabrication Division of The Boeing Company. Previously, he served as a manager of Continuous Quality for Boeing Support Services and as a senior instructor for the Boeing Commercial Airplane Group. He is a board member and serves as the treasurer for the nonprofit organization, Tacoma Rescue Mission.

Lenore B. Goldman, MBA, is a consultant to nonprofit, government, and business clients in strategic planning and organizational change. She specializes in organizations that want to link their social and financial goals. Ms. Goldman holds an MBA from the University of New Mexico's Robert O. Anderson Graduate School of Management.

Henry Goldstein, CFRE, has been serving nonprofit organizations since 1956. Since 1964, he has been associated with The Oram Group, Inc., a consulting firm. He is president and chief executive officer.

James M. Greenfield, CFRE, FAHP, is Senior Vice President of Development and Community Relations at Hoag Memorial Hospital Presbyterian, Newport Beach,

California. He is presently in his tenth year of service on the Board of Directors of the NSFRE Foundation. He is the author of *Fund-Raising: Evaluating and Managing the Fund Development Process,* published by John Wiley & Sons.

Bruce R. Hopkins, JD, LLM, is a practicing lawyer with Powers, Pyles & Sutter in Washington, DC, where he specializes in the representation of nonprofit organizations. He has served as Chair of the Committee on Exempt Organizations, American Bar Association; and President, Planned Giving Study Group of Greater Washington, DC. Mr. Hopkins is the series editor of Wiley's Nonprofit Law, Finance, and Management Series, and author of several books in that series.

Joseph R. Jablonski, MS, is president of Technical Management Consortium, Inc., a professional services firm based in Albuquerque, New Mexico. Mr. Jablonski serves clients throughout the United States and Canada and assists them in the design and implementation of corporate-wide quality systems. He speaks on the subject of quality and assists clients in successfully bidding for work with stringent quality requirements.

Eugene M. Johnson, PhD, MBA, is a professor of marketing at the University of Rhode Island. He has served as a consultant for a large number of business and nonprofit organizations and is a frequent lecturer. Dr. Johnson has done extensive research on services marketing and sales management and has published articles in *Nonprofit World, Banking,* and *Burroughs Clearing House,* as well as in a number of other publications.

Jeffrey D. Kahn, JD, is an attorney with Schnader, Harrison, Segal & Lewis in Philadelphia, Pennsylvania. He is a Volunteer Consulting Legal Advisor to the Nonprofits' Risk Management and Insurance Institution in Washington, DC, and is the author of various articles about legal issues relating to volunteer programs.

Michael E. Knight, PhD, has coordinated the nationally recognized Kean College Assessment of Student Learning Project for the past six years. Dr. Knight has made presentations at over 20 national conferences and has been a consultant to 40 nonprofit organizations and institutions.

Richard F. Larkin, CPA, MBA, is a senior manager in the Not-for-Profit Industry Services Group of Price Waterhouse. He is extensively involved in the development of accounting standards for not-for-profit organizations, is the chairman of the AICPA's Not-for-Profit Audit Guide task force, and is a member of the FASB Not-for Profit Accounting Issues task force. He is co-author of *Financial and Accounting Guide for Not-for-Profit Organizations, Fourth Edition,* published by John Wiley & Sons.

Charles E. Lawson, MPC, is one of the leading figures in the nonprofit field. He is the author of the NSFRE Glossary of Fund-Raising Terms, founder of the AAFRC Trust for Philanthropy, and a frequent lecturer and contributor to books and periodicals. In 1990, he was honored as Fund-Raiser of the Year by NSFRE in Connecticut.

D. Kerry Laycock, MS, is an organizational consultant serving industry, government, and nonprofit organizations. His practice is devoted to improving organizational effectiveness through planning, employee involvement, and quality management.

Lynn Lee, MA, MSA, has worked for 15 years in educational grant writing. Since 1988 she has been associated with Pyramid Associates, Inc., specializing in researching targeted funding sources, grant and proposal writing, and program planning.

Donald Lumsden, PhD, has coordinated the nationally recognized Kean College Assessment of Student Learning Project for over five years. He has made presentations at over 20 national conferences and has been a consultant to 40 nonprofit organizations and institutions.

Gay Lumsden, PhD, former director of Kean College's Freshman Center, has worked in the field of communications and advisement providing academic, social and personal guidance to new students. She has made presentations at national conferences and consulted with nonprofit organizations and institutions.

Mark D. Michaels, MPA, is president of People Technologies, a management consulting firm providing services in organization development, personnel management, and training to profit and nonprofit service organizations. Mr. Michaels also teaches courses in nonprofit management and performance management at Illinois Benedictine College, Lisle, Illinois.

Lynda S. Moerschbaecher, JD, MBA, is a consultant and lawyer in San Francisco, California, where she represents nonprofits organizations in consulting, legal work, publications, and seminars. She is the co-creator of the monthly publication *Charitable Gift Planning News,* is a member of the Exempt Organizations Committee of the American Bar Association Tax Section, and was a past Secretary/Treasurer of the Fund-Raising School.

Kenneth L. Murell, PhD, DBA, is presently on the faculty of management at The University of West Florida in Pensacola, Florida, and president of Empowerment Leadership Systems. In addition, he is a management consultant working both independently and with internationally recognized consulting organizations. He has extensive experience in Organizational Development and Management Development in improving organizational effectiveness and is working with numerous nonprofit agencies.

Lester A. Picker, PhD, is president of Pyramid Associates, Inc., consultants in philanthropy and marketing to charitable organizations, corporations, and foundations. Dr. Picker has authored more than 200 books and articles. He is a syndicated business columnist with *The (Baltimore) Sun,* and his articles focus on nonprofit marketing and management.

Elizabeth Power provides consulting services in the areas of managing change, implementing Total Quality Management (TQM), and instructional design in both the nonprofit and for-profit sector. She is best known for her work in helping people learn how to reduce resistance to change, become focused on process, and apply TQM concepts and skills in all areas of life. Her clients include Pike's Peak Mental Health Systems, Inc., and the Saturn Corporation.

Ruthie G. Reynolds, PhD, CPA, JD, is an associate professor of accounting in the School of Business at Howard University. She has conducted research in nonprofit accounting and management and has published articles in *Nonprofit World, The Woman CPA,* and *The ABC Theological Journal.* In addition, she has conducted seminars and workshops for accountants, board members, and administrators of nonprofit agencies throughout the United States.

Howard J. Rhine, MBA, is a consultant specializing in the nonprofit sector. He received his MBA from the Andreas School of Business of Barry University. He has previously authored a "Guide to Donor Management Software Products," which appeared in the *Journal of Taxation of Exempt Organizations.*

Lawrence A. Sherr, PhD, is a Chancellors Club Teaching Professor and Professor of Business at the University of Kansas. He teaches statistics and management science and has recently co-edited a monograph on Total Quality Management in higher education.

Sara H. Skolnick, BBA, CAE, has had over 25 years of experience in leadership positions of church, school, and community nonprofit organizations, including major fund-raising efforts. For the past 12 years, she has been a professional nonprofit association manager.

Janet L. Unger is president of Unger Consulting Services, based in Philadelphia, Pennsylvania, which provides services to nonprofit organizations in board development, strategic planning, affiliate relations, and volunteer management. She is the former manager of the U.S. Committee for UNICEF, Philadelphia Area Office. Ms. Unger has trained hundreds of individuals and organizations on volunteer development at local, regional, and national conferences.

Preface

This handbook is a comprehensive reference guide to the *policies* (guidelines, directives, rules, and courses of action) and *procedures* (established methods and proven best practices) now shared by a great majority of small and medium-sized nonprofit organizations.

Management of nonprofit organizations is steadily becoming more professional. Information is shared through a growing number of associations and periodicals enabling sector leaders to adapt these policies and procedures to fulfill the various missions of their organizations. Approaches that work are sorted out from those that generally do not. However, this process is often sporadic or subject to chance. The need for a convenient, comprehensive guide to the daily operation and management of nonprofit organizations gave rise to this handbook. The primary objective of this handbook is to compile the best of these proven approaches, in an accessible, readily adaptable format.

Operational policies and procedures are not static. They cannot be adopted and arbitrarily applied to a particular organization. If they are to be effective, they must be carefully adapted to the needs and realities of a specific organization. Second, internal and external environments change, just as the organization itself changes. Operational policies and procedures, once adapted and employed must be reviewed regularly to ensure that they continue to fulfill the functions for which they were intended.

The dynamic, evolving nature of all areas of nonprofit management policy and procedures requires constant review, assessment, renewal, and change. Outdated policies and procedures may become impediments to progress and the organization's ability to fulfill its mission. But how and where do we implement changes? In what direction should we move the organization? How do we organize for constant change and also bring about constant improvement in our services, products, and processes? How do we know what we can and should do to fulfill our public services mission in the face of dwindling resources and a more competitive environment?

Timely, rational change is a major benefit gained by those organizations adopting continuous quality improvement techniques and philosophies. Therefore, the handbook's second major objective is to provide a foundation that nonprofit organizations need to implement continuous quality improvement. Our contributors offer general guidance regarding the basic principles of quality as they apply to nonprofit organizations. They provide a framework for assessment, evaluation, and decision making for leaders and managers grappling with the challenges of achieving total quality (TQ).

Nonprofit organizations (or nonprofits, for short) are interested in quality because they see the relevance of successful industry quality models. This is the view of Dr. Curt Reimann, Director of the Malcolm Baldrige National Quality Award (NQA)

Program of the U.S. Department of Commerce, National Institute of Standards and Technology. "They feel there is a very close correspondence—even perhaps one-to-one correspondence—between the things that promote business effectiveness, and those that can be used to promote the effectiveness of the nonprofit organization." Whether government or business, profit or nonprofit, manufacturing or service, Reimann believes quality principles are applicable to all organizations.

Nonprofit organizations, like their corporate counterparts, are affected by global systems of economics and production. Organizations from all sectors of our economy are trying to establish quality as their "organizational culture." Nonprofits, like business and government, must adopt the principles and best practices of quality and continuous improvement, if they are to meet growing public service needs in the face of scarce resources. Because every element of our society is being forced to move in this new direction, TQ is not a trend likely to "fade away" when organizational leaders change or when press coverage wanes, as it inevitably will. Quality must become the basic culture within nonprofit organizations, just as it must become the way all U.S. organizations do business, if they expect to be successful.

One of the major challenges to effective development and implementation of total quality is getting the organization's leaders to recognize the crucial roles that leadership plays. Leadership demands personal involvement and knowledge of quality principles and best practices. Our contributors have stressed and outlined the new and different roles for leaders in the emerging quality organization. Quality concepts in this handbook are presented in ways that will facilitate their adaptation by nonprofit leaders to meet the specific needs in their organization.

Leaders of nonprofit organizations should treat the implementation of quality as an important new tool to take on important challenges facing their organization. "Don't treat quality as an 'off-line' program or thing—'we won't be able to do anything in quality until we all go off and get training in quality, put up signs on the wall, and charts.' Instead, tackle quality improvement within the framework of things you are trying to do well, now," Reimann recommends.

Some "generic" management information will appear in the handbook when needed for continuity, to ensure the work's utility, or to outline significant differences between nonprofit, business, or government management practices. The emphasis however, will be on policies and procedures that are specific to the effective management of nonprofit, voluntary action organizations, particularly those which focus on or support quality and continuous improvement initiatives and programs.

The handbook is designed for daily use as a guide for nonprofit leaders and managers who are seeking to implement those plans and policies required to bring about the excellence or quality transformation within their organization and to develop their own policy and practices manual, to draft policy statements, update management procedures, and establish more effective management systems.

The *Operational Policies and Procedures Handbook* has been divided into parts:

I. *Management and Organization.* A comprehensive overview of nonprofit management and organizational policies, with particular emphasis on continuous quality improvement.

II. *Human Resources.* Specific guidance is provided concerning the board of directors, staff and volunteer development, and managing today's volunteers in the training process.

   III. *Employee Compensation and Benefits.* Thorough coverage of such vital policy areas as effective personnel policies, performance evaluation and management, employee-related benefits, and compensation management.

   IV. *Fund-Raising.* All major areas of fund-raising policy needed by nonprofits are covered, including: annual giving, planned giving, capital fund appeals, special gifts, corporate support, grantsmanship, direct mail, donor software, and fund-raising assessment.

   V. *Marketing.* Customer focus is an essential component of a successful marketing program. Both are covered in this section.

   VI. *Consultants.* The functions and services of fund-raising and organizational development consultants for nonprofits are explained.

   VII. *Financial Management.* Explains the essential elements of nonprofit accounting, budgeting, and what managers must know about unrelated business income.

   VIII. *Laws and Regulations Governing Nonprofit Organizations.* Law, taxation, fund-raising regulations, lobbying and advocacy, and legal issues concerning volunteers are outlined in this section.

Throughout these sections, the handbook offers:

- Drafts of policies, procedures and statements specifically for nonprofits
- Management, quality and continuous improvement practices
- Established models for use by staff and volunteer managers
- Accepted techniques explained and illustrated
- Sample plans, forms, records, and reports specifically for nonprofits.

Our contributors represent a wide variety of professional backgrounds. They were selected for their demonstrated knowledge of specialized subject areas and for their day-to-day, real world experience with nonprofits. Their specialized expertise is the cornerstone of this work. The editors have worked closely with our contributors, reviewing and editing their manuscripts. However, each chapter is the work and viewpoint of the contributors.

Making an "enormous difference" has always been the challenge of the dedicated men and women, volunteer and professional, who lead our nonprofit, public service organizations. We have tried in this handbook to present the most successful operational policies and procedures, and to recommend those principles and practices of total quality that nonprofit leaders need to meet successfully the challenging demands of an uncertain future. Our national quality of life, from health care and culture, to recreation and religion, depends on whether leaders of nonprofit organizations can achieve levels of quality in the future that by today's standards would be considered extraordinary. We have prepared the handbook to provide what we believe represents the best of current management and leadership approaches to help ensure success in meeting the pressing demands of today. We have tried also to include the basic knowledge and understanding needed to fashion the new quality values and approaches required to conquer the challenges we know are our future.

TRACY D. CONNORS

Bowie, Maryland
October 1992

Acknowledgments

In the same spirit of service, dedication, and sharing that characterizes the leaders of our nonprofit organizations, the contributors to this handbook have devoted countless hours to their respective chapters. We thank these dedicated professionals for their willingness to share their experience and knowledge to help leaders and managers of nonprofit organizations provide a better quality of life for us all.

Others whose extraordinary efforts deserve special thanks and recognition, include:

Jim Greenfield, who not only prepared outstanding chapters, but identified other contributors and edited much of the fund-raising section. His support and contributions were invaluable.

Marla Bobowick, whose guidance and management were essential to this complex, long-term effort. Ably assisted by Tracy King, Marla was a constant resource and catalyst throughout the process.

Others to whom we extend deep gratitude for their special support and important contributions during this multi-year effort, include: Dr. Pamela Arrington, Joseph Bizup, Jody Blazek, Dr. James W. Browning, Dr. Joseph Champoux, Miriam F. Connors, Paul Dickson, Dr. Diane Disney, Larry Geringer, Dr. Carl Grant, Dr. Jeffrey A. Henson, Karen C. Henson, A. Scott Hults, III, Dr. Eugene Johnson, Dr. Michael Knight, Whitney McKindree Moore, Dr. Sterling Nichols, Jr., Captain Timothy O'Keefe, Dr. Curt Reimann, Captain Fred Reis, Commander Bruce Spiher, Janet Unger, and Alan Wheeler.

Contents

PART IV FUND-RAISING

PART ONE

Management and Organization

Total Quality Management

Ellen Earle Chaffee
North Dakota University System

Lawrence A. Sherr
University of Kansas

CONTENTS

1.1 WHY TOTAL QUALITY MANAGEMENT?

"Nobody's perfect."
"If it's not broken, don't fix it."
"Experience is the best teacher."
"That's good enough for government work."

These statements are all too prevalent in America. They represent attitudes that have brought much of the for-profit sector to its knees in the face of consumer revolts and international competition. The nonprofit sector, with its altruistic purposes and its dependence on voluntary patronage, has still less latitude for such laxity.

Calls for change, first sounded 40 years ago by such visionaries as W. Edwards Deming (1986) and Joseph M. Juran (1988, 1989), have finally reached the ears of America's industrial and government leaders. The new messages are:

> "Until we're perfect, we will continuously improve—which means forever."
> "If it's not broken, make it better."
> "Experience is the teacher of last resort—we have better methods."
> "In all work, in all organizations, we must strive constantly for the highest quality."

The messengers are leaders of Fortune 500 companies, federal departments of commerce and defense, and Congress; hundreds of lesser known business and government leaders; educators; and spokespersons for a growing number of voluntary associations throughout the land. They are proponents of Total Quality Management (TQM), and they know that nonprofit leaders stand to gain as much or more from TQM as leaders in any other kind of enterprise.

What are the benefits of TQM for nonprofit organizations?

> Constantly improved quality of services and products (which contributes directly to our national quality of life);
> Happy patrons and motivated volunteers;
> Greater productivity—more payoff per hour of effort;
> More services for less money;
> High staff morale.

The purpose of this chapter is to provide a brief introduction to TQM for nonprofit organizations. Total Quality Management is far more than simply a new set of management principles. It is a comprehensive way of life for an organization, and it is driven by an organization-wide, "all hands" commitment to continuously improve service to others. TQM includes a wide array of tools for solving any organizational problem. Other chapters in this book and the end-of-chapter lists of references address various elements of TQM, but the serious nonprofit leader will need to make a personal, lifelong commitment to learning about TQM not only from books but also from periodicals, seminars, and visits to other TQM organizations.

This chapter gives relatively detailed attention to the inner workings of organizations; some senior leaders may see these details as too "operational" for their attention. A fundamental premise of TQM is that quality *is* attention to appropriate detail. This does not mean that leaders necessarily become personally involved in such operations, at least not routinely. It means that leaders must understand why detail is so important, and they must learn to identify the details that require organizational attention. We cannot provide a list of "key details" because these vary not only from one organization to the next, but also over time within a single organization. TQM requires top-level commitment and top-level understanding of how the organization really works. The illustrations in this chapter should help senior leaders see why this is the case.

1.2 SYSTEMATIC IMPROVEMENT OF WORK PROCESSES

Understanding TQM requires recognizing that all work is part of a process. For example, fund-raising campaigns start with identifying goals and strategies; they then move into volunteer identification and training, go on to contacts with potential donors, and ultimately yield funds. Each of these stages involves many other series of steps, each of which can also be seen as a process. Each organization also has processes that produce season ticket sales, mailings of many kinds to different lists, the appointment of a staff person, a well-oriented board of directors, provision of a client service, the production of an event or a paycheck, and many more.

The idea that work is a process allows the development of effective improvement methods that can increase quality and productivity while also decreasing cost. As an analogy, consider the manufacturing organization. When completed gizmos arrive at the end of the production line, quality inspectors may examine each one. They remove any gizmo that has a defect (if they can detect it), and the imperfect gizmos go either to the scrap heap or back for rework. But what if the defect is not visible? What if the inspector is tired or distracted?

Some imperfect gizmos go to the consumer, who becomes unhappy. Whatever the cost of scrap and rework to the organization, the consumer ultimately pays for it and/or the firm goes out of business. Manufacturers are increasingly realizing a very important fact: quality cannot be inspected into a product at the end of the line. Relying on inspection involves cost to the consumers, dissatisfied consumers, and workers who cannot take pride in their work. The remedy is prevention: doing it right the first time and every time.

The analogy to nonprofit enterprise should be clear. Suppose random calls in a telethon are monitored and ineffective, even harmful, practices by the callers are discovered. How many potential donors have been lost? Will it ever be possible to change their attitude toward the organization? Will the ineffective caller, feeling unsuccessful, ever volunteer to help again?

The only way to prevent such calamities is to build quality into every step of every work process. In the telethon example, improving caller performance reverts to the caller-training program, which leads back to the calling strategy and the campaign goals. Ultimately, the goals and performance record of the organization itself are intrinsic to a successful campaign. Improving quality must address every step of every process in the organization, including those that make up the daily work of employees and managers.

(a) DEFINING A PROCESS TQM offers a wide array of tools for process improvement. For example, the flowchart helps people visualize the work process. Many organizations reimburse people for travel—a typical process. Exhibit 1.1 is a simplified, hypothetical version of one symphony's process. It is important to note that flowcharts usually show how the process *really* works, not how it is *supposed* to work. The only way to know how processes really work is to ask each person to explain his or her actions in the process, and these interviews often yield surprises.

For example, a physical facilities department wished to reduce its number of complaints about slow responsiveness to requests from other departments for facilities services (customers). The department manager's first surprise was how much time the

Exhibit 1.1.   Flowchart.

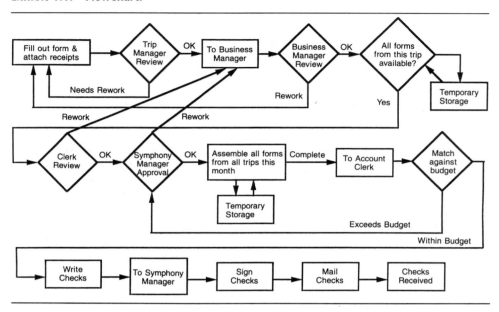

process really required—she thought it took an average of 10 days from request to completion, but, by examining recent events, she found it was 20 days. While interviewing the people who handled the process, she found that the department secretary automatically held all requests for 10 days before forwarding them to the facilities superintendent. Why? "That's what my predecessor told me to do." Calling the predecessor, now in retirement, the manager discovered that her own predecessor had ordered the 10-day delay because those requesting services often changed their minds about the services they wanted, during or after the facilities' work. The 10-day lag was a "cooling off" period to make sure the facilities' workers would do only the work that was actually wanted.

Although the travel-reimbursement process in Exhibit 1.1 is simplified, the first impression from just a brief glance is one of *complexity*. Are all those steps really needed just to repay travel expenses? A team of experienced symphony travelers and financial staff could identify steps that are redundant or that no longer serve a useful purpose—perhaps some steps were necessary before the symphony started managing with computers but now could be eliminated. The team members might determine whether each step adds value or only adds cost—a time cost or a financial cost. What steps generate a number of complaints? Where are the bottlenecks? Simply inviting serious analyses among a team of those involved in the process often generates improvements.

Other tools are also available. The cause-and-effect diagram (also called a fishbone diagram because of its underlying shape) is a good way to begin looking for less obvious improvements. Suppose the symphony members complain about inaccurate travel reimbursements. Without a process analysis, management might decide to add a final inspection by the controller—a new step in the process—before issuing the check. This remedy might reduce the errors (if the controller isn't busy with other matters), but it does not eliminate the cause of errors. It also increases costs. Having prepared a flowchart, the symphony would not be inclined to further complicate the process. Instead, the goal will be to prevent error, which requires identifying the causes of error.

Exhibit 1.2 presents a cause-and-effect diagram that the symphony improvement team could develop by brainstorming and reflecting on their own experience. They array their ideas in similar groups. In the "people" category, they note the possibility that error most frequently occurs with respect to those who travel least. In the "methods" category, they suspect that most travelers do not understand the travel reimbursement form. In the "machines and equipment" category, they suppose that the computerized system for matching travel claims against budget categories is not working properly and is causing "corrections" that reflect budget rather than the amount owed the traveler.

(b) COLLECTING DATA TO ANALYZE A PROCESS   Armed with these ideas, the team is in a position to look systematically for the root causes of error. They will do so by collecting data. They might interview travelers and financial staff regarding the nature and extent of their difficulties with the process, categorize the replies, determine which category has the greatest number of complaints, and use this information to refine the cause-and-effect diagram. They could also verify the accuracy of each check in a given month and trace each error back to its cause. They could determine how long it takes to complete each step, remembering that time is money because wasted time could be put to more productive uses. When the data identify a root cause of error, the team develops a recommendation for eliminating the cause.

To illustrate some of the additional tools in TQM, suppose that the symphony team reviewed actual experience with reimbursement checks over the past 12 months, to see whether errors were cyclical. They might graph the results either by the number of errors each month or the proportion of erroneous checks. Exhibit 1.3 is a run chart by number of errors; Exhibit 1.4 is a run chart by proportion of errors. Examining Exhibit 1.3, the

Exhibit 1.2.   Cause-and-effect diagram.

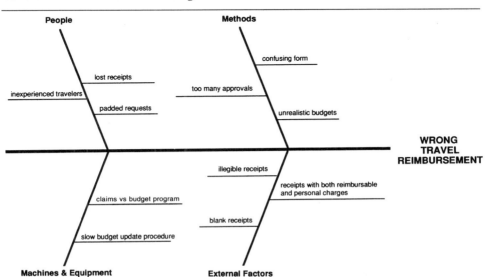

Exhibit 1.3.   Run chart for number of errors.

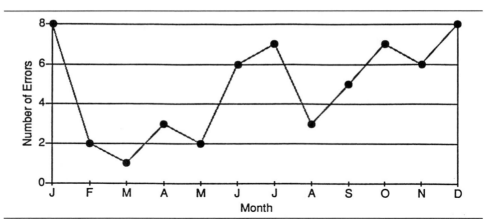

team notices that periods with a high number of errors correspond to the symphony's two touring seasons—early summer and late fall/Christmas. The more traveling is done, the more errors appear in the reimbursement checks. The team theorizes that something systematic is creating errors in the reimbursement process.

Looking at Exhibit 1.4, the team sees that its theory is borne out for the summer tour—the proportion of errors then is the same as in the spring, although the number of travelers is higher in the summer. However, it finds an exceptional increase in the late fall season. On further inquiry, the team discovers that the account technician was on leave during this period and a temporary person assumed his tasks. To prevent this kind of problem in the future, the team can look closely at what happens when the regular account technician is absent and take appropriate steps to ensure smooth functioning at such times.

The evidence of a "temporary person effect" signifies what is called a "special cause"; that is, this cause of error is not part of the routine procedure. Whenever a team discovers a special cause, its first task is to eliminate that cause. Most often, eliminating

Exhibit 1.4.   Run chart for error rate.

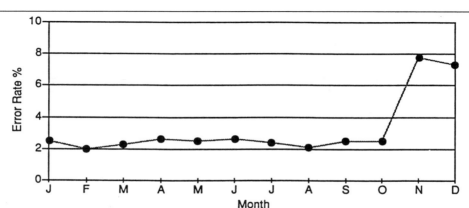

special causes does not create a perfect process. Errors continue to occur in the routine procedure. The causes for these errors are called "common causes."

TQM provides a simple statistical tool, called a control chart, that allows a team to see any patterns in the errors of a process. A control chart (an enhanced run chart) allows the team to calculate the expected error rate for a process and observe when the process yields results that fall outside the boundaries of the expected error rate. Results that fall randomly within the boundaries are due to common causes; those outside the boundaries are due to special causes.

Special causes and common causes require different kinds of treatment. Solutions to special causes typically involve isolating the special cause for a one-time fix, such as deciding not to use temporary personnel to perform certain duties. Solutions to common causes typically involve changing key elements in the process, such as eliminating an inspection. If an organization changes its voucher system because someone cheated, it is treating a special cause (one person cheated) as if it were a common cause (the voucher system was not cheat-proof). When an organization treats a problem with a common cause as if it had a special cause, it tends to waste time and energy, divert attention from central concerns, introduce even greater variability in the error rate, reduce productivity, and reduce morale. The greatest consequence is that the problem continues—the "solution" will not work. (The cheater finds new loopholes or begins to cheat on another process.)

Suppose an organization blames personnel who do not fill out a form properly, when the form itself is confusing. It might add inspection steps or training steps to the process, instead of clarifying the form and preventing the need for special inspections and training. When an organization treats a common-cause problem as if it had a special cause, the consequences include higher costs, more complexity, more variability, and lower morale. Again, the problem continues because the "solution" is inappropriate (inspections are never perfect, and personnel may forget the training).

The point of this discussion is that run charts such as those shown in Exhibits 1.3 and 1.4 are the initial step toward development of control charts, and control charts are extremely powerful tools for problem analysis and solution development. (For more on how to create and use control charts, see the statistical readings at the end of this chapter.)

Notice that Exhibit 1.4 shows a constant small error rate during most of the year—the times when the regular account technician was on duty. Common causes are the source of this error rate, and common causes are often difficult to detect. To avoid the extra time, cost, and hassle of producing erroneous travel reimbursement checks, the symphony team set out to identify the common causes.

The team learned, through talking with participants in the process, that error could come from the traveler, the business manager, the clerk, the symphony manager, or the account technician who matched requests against budgets via his computer program. Each of these people either created or amended the numbers that generated an individual's reimbursement check. The team identified all erroneous checks for the previous 3 months and traced each one through all its paperwork to find out where the error began. Compiling their results, they created the check sheet in Exhibit 1.5. To make the results easier to "see," they used the check sheet results to make the Pareto chart in Exhibit 1.6.

Noting high errors involving both the traveler and the symphony manager, and noting that these errors were the most frequent, the team reviewed the details of these requests

Exhibit 1.5. Check sheet.

Reason	Frequency
A. Traveler's request incorrect	卌
B. Manager changed request	卌 I
C. Request lost in assembly period for trip	I
D. Request lost in assembly period for month	II

and interviewed the individuals involved. They found that all these requests involved personal auto expenses, an unusual item for this symphony. The mileage reimbursement rate for the symphony was not included in the instructions that accompanied the reimbursement form, and everyone had a different idea about what the rate was. The problem was compounded by the fact that the symphony manager was so sure he knew the correct rate that he never returned the forms to the business manager—he just made his "correction" and forwarded the form to the account technician. The solution was to print the mileage reimbursement rate on the instruction sheet. As the team monitored travel checks for the next several months, they found the error rate dropped considerably. The team went on to look into the matter of lost forms.

(c) CONTINUOUS PROCESS IMPROVEMENT The process improvement illustrated in the preceding section may seem laborious, especially for an organization that is quite

Exhibit 1.6. Pareto chart.

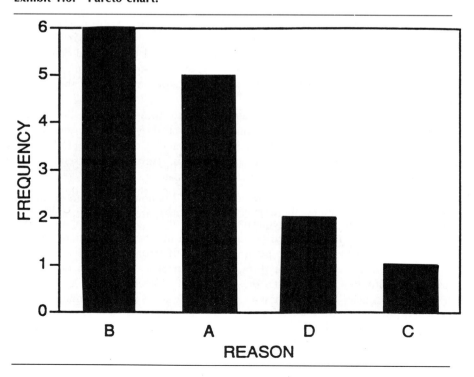

small or whose members do very little traveling. Travel reimbursement is only an example; improving that process may be important for one organization but not for another. Every organization has key processes that merit this kind of attention because improving them would substantially improve quality, increase productivity, and decrease cost.

As an example of a process that may seem innocuous but could be vitally important in many nonprofit organizations, consider the mailing of a solicitation letter. Errors could lead to incurring unnecessarily high printing and postage costs, missing potentially important recipients, and reducing the effectiveness of future mailings by sending someone the wrong letter.

One nonprofit group found that mailing alone (not including the processes for developing the letter, printing it, or selecting the target mailing list) required 13 steps, with four inspections. Even if the process is relatively effective in getting the right letter to the right person, it seems excessively complex. Considering the potential costs of error, the organization might decide that it needs many steps to guard against error. However, because complexity itself can be a significant cause of error, process improvement often involves simplification.

The nonprofit group might be proud to discover that the accuracy rate of each of its 13 steps is an impressive 99 percent. At this rate, however, the process yields a mailing that is only 88 percent accurate (the probability of a correct result in this example is found by taking .99 to the 13th power). The remaining 12 percent represents rework or scrap to the organization or, worst of all, the error is passed on to the customer. Ninety-nine percent is not good enough. Simply by reducing its 13 steps to 10, the organization can increase the mailing's accuracy rate to 90 percent. A surprising number of processes require far more than 13 steps. Sixty steps is not unusual in the payroll process; reducing to 40 steps creates a substantially more accurate process.

As the travel-reimbursement example illustrates, process analysis in TQM is essentially the same as rational problem solving: identify the problem, investigate to determine the root causes of the problem, and remove the causes. Going through this process is called "Plan, Do, Check, Act," also known as the Shewhart Cycle or the Deming Wheel. (The terms "cycle" and "wheel" indicate that the Plan-Do-Check-Act process is never ending: further improvements are always possible.) *Planning* is mapping the process and identifying root causes and potential solutions; *doing* is trying out a solution in a limited way; *checking* (or studying) is verifying that the solution removes the error; and *acting* is implementing the solution permanently if it has proven effective.

Process analysis shows that experience is not, after all, the best teacher of how to do things well. The missing link in that aphorism is the need to *analyze* experience to find out how to improve performance. Experience is *not* the best teacher—properly interpreted data can teach better.

With the travel-reimbursement example in mind, it is now possible to explain more fully what the other key elements of TQM are, why they are important, and how they benefit the organization.

1.3   THE BENEFICIARIES OF THE PROCESS

The key people in the process are its immediate beneficiaries. Some people, often employees or volunteers, benefit directly from improvements within and to a process. For example, the account technician no longer must deal with incomplete or inaccurate travel reimbursement requests. But often, benefits expand and ripple out far beyond those directly involved in the process. People, often clients or patrons outside the organization, will benefit from the end result of a process.

A person may be a beneficiary at some times and a service provider at others. The traveler is a service provider when completing the reimbursement form, but a beneficiary when the correct check arrives in timely fashion. Moreover, every organization has a great many beneficiaries, both within and outside. *A good process is one that delivers what the beneficiary needs, every time.*

Contrary to popular conception, organizations do not do well when their members mistakenly believe that the primary purpose is to stay in business, pay salaries, or generate a profit. Rather, organizations do best when they meet the needs of their beneficiaries (customers). Everything else the organization does must support that mission and will, in turn, benefit proportionately.

A central focus in using TQM is to determine who the organization's beneficiaries are and what they need. For whose benefit does an organization exist? Once a list is compiled, representatives of beneficiary groups can be asked what they need. Research should be done on their needs and expectations and their priorities among those needs and expectations. This research should be an ongoing organizational activity.

In general, beneficiaries tend to want three kinds of benefits (Levitt, 1983): more discretionary time, more discretionary money, and less hassle. Among external beneficiaries, for example, social service clients may object to long waits for their appointments (more time), patrons may want lower ticket prices or assurance of high impact for their contributions (more money for services, less on overhead), and clients may want accurate referrals and simple forms (less hassle). Internal beneficiaries may want more time to get caught up on their work or to plan ahead, more savings in productivity to free up funds for salary increases, and less hassle in the form of clear directions for their tasks.

These issues are central to all organizations: Who are our beneficiaries? What do they need? How do we know? Are we meeting their needs? How do we know? Answering these questions focuses an organization on serving its beneficiaries and on gathering data to ensure constant improvement in services.

1.4 THE PEOPLE IN THE PROCESS

The travel-reimbursement example is a typical quality-improvement project in TQM: an ad hoc team of people with diverse views and personal involvement in a process undertakes to improve it. Thus, process analysis highlights the value of personal involvement, the value of diverse roles, and the value of teamwork. Quality improvement projects also demonstrate the importance of empowerment and of training.

People working to improve quality must be involved—they must know how the process really works. Some of their knowledge will come from experience, but other information will come from their research as a team. Moreover, their involvement gives them a personal stake in improving the process, which increases their motivation to solve a quality problem and allows them to enjoy the fruits of their work.

When the team includes representatives of diverse roles (a cross-functional team), members can knowledgeably discuss what happens at various steps and why. They can explain their needs as beneficiaries of preceding steps and ask those who work later in the process about their needs. For example, a traveler, noting the long delay while all forms for a given trip are collected, can explain the need for timely reimbursement and ask what purpose the delay serves.

The value of teamwork is well-established in research, especially when a problem is complex and ambiguous—typical characteristics of many organizational processes. Compared with individuals, including managers, teams come up with more ideas and are better able to winnow them down to the best ideas. Moreover, teamwork helps people establish a shared sense of responsibility. This reduces the amount of stress felt by any one person, allows all team members to see how their work contributes to the whole, and builds relationships among them for other work.

The importance of empowering teams to effect change cannot be underestimated. Everyone has experienced the frustration of being asked for an opinion, only to have that opinion ignored. The more often this happens, the less likely team members will offer an opinion at all. TQM organizations cannot afford this withdrawal of involvement, and no organization can afford the alienation this causes. A primary role of leaders in TQM organizations is to encourage, support, and authorize the changes that a quality-improvement team (e.g., a Process Action Team) recommends. Leaders must still ask tough questions, such as: How do we know this will eliminate the problem? Will the solution affect our ability to control expenditures? When the team provides responsible answers, managers must implement the recommendations.

Organizations that have used TQM generally find that about 85 percent or more of the problems their teams identify are built into the process itself. That is, although people have a general tendency to go looking for someone to blame (the traveler pounds on the desk of the business manager), they have about an 85 percent chance of being wrong when they blame an individual. People are usually doing the best they can under the circumstances—only a change in the process, which usually must be authorized by management, can fix the problem.

Unfortunately, people often lack essential training. People may be underprepared in their basic knowledge and skills, often having no way of knowing how and why their organization wants them to perform their tasks. Moreover, participating effectively in quality-improvement teams requires knowing the philosophy and tools of TQM, basic statistics (helpful, but not critical in every case), and how to work effectively in teams. At its foundation, an organization is nothing more than a collection of people. The more knowledgeable and skilled each person is, the more effective the organization can be. That is why TQM organizations invest heavily in a continuous program of personnel training, education, and development.

Nonprofit organizations need to apply these proven concepts to volunteers as well as professional staff members, and it appears that they are moving rapidly toward doing so. According to management expert Peter Drucker (1989), nonprofits are recognizing that they have a special obligation to emphasize and improve volunteer satisfaction and productivity, precisely because volunteers are not working for pay. Interviewing business-people about why they engaged in volunteer activities, Drucker found that nonprofit service provides businesspeople with a greater sense of meaningful involvement, productivity, and challenge than they find in their paid work. Because these are among the benefits motivating volunteer participation and are direct consequences of TQM, non-profit leaders should include both staff and volunteers in their TQM activities and training, and should expect beneficial results with both groups. Effective participation on cross-functional teams will require both staff and volunteer comfort and familiarity with TQM principles and best practices.

1.5   SUMMARY OF KEY IDEAS IN TQM

The key ideas presented thus far are:

- Defining the needs of beneficiaries (customers);
- Committing to continuous quality improvement;
- Systematically improving work processes;
- Building quality into each process at every step;
- Preventing problems by eliminating their root causes;
- Collecting and using process data;
- Meeting the needs of beneficiaries;
- Empowering quality-improvement teams of diverse, involved personnel;
- Continuously training and educating.

Various authors on TQM have different ways of summarizing its key ideas. TQM can be simplified to two ideas: the technical system (process analysis) and the management system (beneficiaries and personnel). Some authors, such as Philip Crosby, are highly prescriptive in providing numerous lists and steps. Different organizations will relate well to different approaches to TQM. Despite the fact that most of the current literature on TQM arises from the for-profit sector (often, manufacturing organizations), nonprofit leaders should approach the literature with a healthy amount of confidence that it is proper to modify the various approaches to suit their own organization. More than anything else, TQM is a philosophy and "culture" about quality, people, and methods. It is hard for organizational leaders to go wrong in implementing TQM if they stick close to that philosophy.

The following list can be used as a guide to implementing TQM. An organization needs to:

1. Think *process*. Understand that all work is part of a process that may have "upstream" and "downstream" steps. All quality-improvement initiatives start with a recognition of this fact. Employees need to know how their work contributes to the process, and to understand that most failures are attributable to the process, not the employee.

2. Listen to customers. They are the judges of how well the organization is doing and where it needs to improve.

3. Serve as a benchmark for excellence. It is not enough to do as well as a parallel organization. Find, where feasible, those who perform a given process better than anyone else, and learn from them. Seek to exceed their level of performance and quality.

4. Improve the process. Understanding how work flows now is a vital step toward identifying areas and methods to achieve improvement.

   a. Change the process from a defect-detection mode to a defect-prevention mode.

   b. Involve the people who do the work, those who "own the process." They know where the problems are, they have excellent improvement ideas, and it is they, ultimately, who will implement or hobble the improvement.

   c. Make data-driven, fact-based decisions. Hunches may be effective in identifying an area that needs improvement, but they cannot analyze the nature, location, source, and magnitude of a problem, nor can they guide an effective search for solutions.

  5. Learn from experience—systematically! Using the Plan-Do-Check-Act cycle teaches what an organization needs to know—and do—to hit the quality target.

The U.S. Department of Commerce has provided a set of criteria that can also act effectively as a checklist for those wishing to assess their organization's use of TQM. Many organizations have begun to use the criteria on a regular basis, often annually, to help them see their progress. The criteria are associated with the Department's Malcolm Baldrige National Quality Award (NQA), authorized by Congress and privately funded to recognize the nation's leading TQM practitioners since 1989.

The following list is modified slightly to suit nonprofit enterprises, and the sequence is shifted so that the sections begin with the highest point value and end with the lowest. The point values indicate the relative importance of the sections, with a total of 1,000 possible points. The list could be adapted easily into a self-assessment tool for an organization.

(a) CUSTOMER (BENEFICIARY) SATISFACTION (300 POINTS)   Who are our beneficiaries? How do we determine our beneficiaries' current and future requirements and expectations? How do we provide effective management of our relationships with beneficiaries? How do we ensure continuous improvement of beneficiary relationship management? What are our standards governing direct contact between our internal beneficiaries (personnel) and our external beneficiaries (consumers, clients, patrons)? How are they set and modified? What explicit and implicit promises do we make to our beneficiaries? How do we promote trust and confidence in what we do? How do we handle complaints, resolve them, and use complaint information for quality improvement and prevention of problem recurrence?

(b) HUMAN RESOURCE UTILIZATION (150 POINTS)   How do our human resource plans support our quality leadership objectives? What are our principal short-term (1 to 2 years) and longer-term (3 to 5 years or longer) priorities? What means are available for all our personnel to contribute effectively to our quality objectives? What are the trends in personnel involvement? How do we decide what quality education and training are needed by our personnel, and how do we use the knowledge and skills they acquire? What types of quality education and training does each category of personnel receive? How do our recognition and performance measurement processes support quality improvement? How do we safeguard the health and safety of employees, ensure their comfort and physical protection, and maintain a supportive work environment? What are the trends in well-being and morale of our personnel?

(c) QUALITY ASSURANCE OF PRODUCTS AND SERVICES (140 POINTS)   How do we design and introduce new or improved programs and services to meet or exceed beneficiary requirements? How do we design processes to deliver according to the requirements? How do we control the processes that produce our programs and services, to ensure uniform high quality? How do we ensure that programs and services meet design plans or specifications? How do we continuously improve programs and services through improvement of processes? How do we assess the quality of programs, processes, services, and quality practices? How do we document and transfer information to support quality assurance, assessment, and improvement? How do we ensure, assess, and improve the quality of support services and processes? How do we ensure, assess, and improve the quality of materials, components, and services furnished by our suppliers?

(d) QUALITY RESULTS (180 POINTS) What are our trends in quality improvement, based on key program and service quality measures derived from beneficiary needs and expectations? How do our current quality levels compare with national averages and national leaders in comparable organizations, based on those key program and service quality measures? What are our trends in quality improvement, based on key measures of processes, operations, and support services? What are our trends in improving the quality of supplies and services furnished by other providers, based on key measures of program and service quality?

(e) LEADERSHIP (100 POINTS) What leadership, personal involvement, and visibility are shown by the top administrators in developing and maintaining an environment for quality excellence? What are the organization's quality values, how are they projected in a consistent manner, and how does the organization assess and reinforce adoption of the values throughout the organization? How does the organization integrate its quality values into day-to-day management of all units? How does the organization extend its quality leadership to the external community and integrate its responsibilities to the public for health, safety, environmental protection, and ethical practices into its quality policies and activities?

(f) INFORMATION AND ANALYSIS (70 POINTS) What is the organization's base of data and information used for planning, management, and evaluation of quality, and how are data and information reliability, timeliness, and access ensured? How does the organization analyze data and information to support its key quality leadership objectives in a timely manner?

(g) STRATEGIC QUALITY PLANNING (60 POINTS) What is the organization's strategic quality planning process for short-term (1 to 2 years) and longer-term (3 to 5 years or more) quality leadership and beneficiary satisfaction? What is the organization's approach to selecting quality-related competitive comparisons and world-class benchmarks to support strategic quality planning? What are the organization's principal quality priorities and plans for the short-term (1 to 2 years) and longer-term (3 to 5 years or more)?

Notice that, in each of the categories, the descriptive paragraphs raise key questions—they do not give definitive guidance about *how* the organization should answer the questions. This approach to assessing the use of TQM emphasizes again the fact that organizations need not use any particular TQM tool or follow the dictates of any special TQM author or consultant. Each organization must find its own most effective ways of answering these questions, with the TQM tools acting as suggestions that have been found to work well at various times in diverse organizations.

1.6   GETTING STARTED USING TQM

One of the advantages of TQM is that an organization can learn about it *while* doing it and *by* doing it. There is no need to learn about it first and then do it. One of the disadvantages of TQM is that *only* key organization leaders can do it—TQM does not work without top management dedication. Another disadvantage is that *there is no recipe for implementation*. This is a disadvantage from the standpoint that using TQM requires considerable effort and judgment, but that very flexibility is also a major component of the widespread successes organizations have had in using TQM.

Unlike many previous management innovations, TQM is not a step-by-step procedure. Rather, TQM is a well-equipped, well-stocked kitchen, complete with nutritional guides, cookbooks, and good food; there is no poison in this kitchen. An organization must decide what to make and how to make it. Does Greek food or Korean food best suit the culture of the group and its patrons? This final section is a guide to learning about TQM and trying it out.

(a) LEARNING MORE ABOUT TQM   Suggested references on TQM are provided at the end of this chapter. Many others are available, and those who become attuned to the key concepts of TQM will notice that business magazines, newspapers, and other popular sources often report on TQM users. A beginner should start with either Walton (1986) or Gitlow and Gitlow (1987). Walton's book is geared for the lay reader; the Gitlows' book is for those who are more technically inclined. Imai (1986) should be read next. Anyone who wants to be very active in using TQM should benefit from owning Imai's book and using it as a reference manual. The "how to" books by Berry (1991), Brassard (1989), and GOAL/QPC (1988) are also excellent references, but Imai's book provides the context for using them. For inspiration, Block (1987), DePree (1989), Shook (1990), or Townsend (1990) is recommended.

A valuable approach would be to set up an informal book club with others who are learning about TQM—ideally, but not necessarily, people in an immediate work group. All could read a chapter a week and spend an hour or so talking about what they have read: Does it apply to us? Do we need to translate it in order to make it useful in what we do? Do we agree with it? Do we see a way in which we could try to use it?

Is anyone in the local business community using TQM? If so, a visit should be arranged to ask what they are doing and how it is working for them. Users of TQM can be invited to join the book club. If they are clients, how can services to them be improved?

The number of community colleges and universities teaching TQM classes, using TQM in their own management, or both, is rapidly growing. If a postsecondary institution is located nearby, the business or engineering department or the continuing education division can be contacted to see whether the campus is involved in TQM. Knowledgeable faculty and administrators can be excellent resource people for nonprofit organizations.

(b) DOING TQM   How an organization begins to do TQM will depend in part on its circumstances. Has the chief executive officer made a clear commitment to TQM? Does the organization, a local business, or a nearby college have a TQM coordinator or trainer with whom beginners can work? How well-informed about TQM are the organization's staff members?

Assume the beginner is a person who is unsure of top-level commitment and whose colleagues are not yet well-informed. Even "going solo," this person can begin by thinking about work output (a letter completed, a form filled out, or whatever). The person who receives the work output is the beneficiary. A list of all beneficiaries can be developed. Each can be asked, "Are there some ways in which I could better meet your needs? Can I make your life simpler or pleasanter in some way?" The questioner may or may not be in a position to respond as the beneficiaries request but, if possible, should do so. If the time, dollars, or authority to respond are lacking, can their need be met in some other way that is within the questioner's power? Meanwhile, the questioner should remember what they asked for and look for opportunities to gain the time, dollars, or assistance needed. The single most powerful act a person or organization can take to move directly into TQM is to be constantly obsessed with defining and meeting the needs of the beneficiaries.

The work processes in which the organization participates can also be examined. Are we, or is someone close to us, engaging in work that may have been functional at one time but now seems useless? For example, one staff member realized that he had long been assuming that there must be some purpose behind a stack of computer printouts that the satellite agencies submitted every year. He had never figured out its purpose, so he asked around to see whether anyone used the information. When he found that the printouts had been replaced by a consolidated report generated centrally, he notified the satellites that they could stop producing and shipping the printouts. Are there some things that could be stopped or done more efficiently in some other way?

Finally, and by all means, an organization should look for others who share an interest in TQM and build a support network.

The more local support, the more can be done. Teamwork is essential in using TQM, and other interested, informed people are potential team members who can brainstorm together on major common problems. Would anything on the resulting list yield to immediate and obvious corrective action? If so, that action should be taken. Because some problems are more complex than they look and some solutions end up creating new problems, the organization should be sure that the change being considered does not fall into these categories.

It is important to pick a problem and make a commitment to work on it. The team might choose one that can be solved in a relatively short time, thus giving some early positive results. Or, the team might choose one that is pretty much confined to one department, to avoid having to persuade someone from another department to join the team until later, when TQM is more widespread in the organization. Another good reason for selecting a problem is that solving it would make the organization's work life much better. It is probably *not* advisable to select a problem that is enormous in scope and widespread in the organization. After TQM skills and confidence have been developed, such problems can be tackled.

After selecting a problem, the organization should put together a small team consisting of people whose work relates to the problem and who collectively represent the primary participants in the problem process. Effective teams usually have no more than seven members, but even a team of two can work well. Effective teams also seek to include a representative of the external beneficiaries, or customers, of the organization. It is beneficial, but not essential, to involve a TQM coordinator or trainer as the team's facilitator. If there is no access to such a person, one of the books mentioned earlier can be used as a guide to the improvement process.

Use of the Plan-Do-Check-Act cycle, one step at a time, will confirm that enough time is spent defining and analyzing the nature of the problem. A flowchart of the process and collection of data are essential. Teams normally meet for an hour a week, often using some time between meetings to collect data. The organization needs a clear sense of purpose, in order to recognize when the team has done its work and can be disbanded.

Another kind of TQM activity that can be undertaken is to systematically define who the beneficiaries are and find out what they need. It is vitally important to ask them, through interviews, surveys, or focus-group discussions. Some beneficiaries are able to state exactly what they need. Others cannot put their needs into words and it may be necessary to watch them or deliberately role-play their responsibilities. Their needs can be learned by paying close attention to any complaints they might register.

When identification of beneficiaries' needs involves changing a work procedure, the process-improvement cycle has swung round again. Is this something that can be remedied easily—say, the way a staff member answers the telephone? Or does it require a project-team approach?

In the end, whether in learning about TQM or doing it, it matters far less *how* it is started than *whether* and *when* it is started. When managers are enthusiastic about TQM, it is not enough to think of themselves only as beneficiaries who are eagerly awaiting someone else's use of TQM. Managers cannot possibly demand TQM from their staff without their own personal involvement. As W. Edwards Deming has put it so well, "The transformation is everybody's job."

SOURCES AND SUGGESTED REFERENCES

SOURCES CITED

Berry, Thomas H. 1991. *Managing the Total Quality Transformation.* New York: McGraw-Hill.

Block, Peter. 1987. *The Empowered Manager: Positive Political Skills at Work.* San Francisco: Jossey-Bass.

Brassard, Michael. 1989. *The Memory Jogger Plus + : Featuring the Seven Management and Planning Tools.* Methuen, MA: GOAL/QPC.

Deming, W. Edwards. 1986. *Out of the Crisis.* Cambridge: MIT Center for Advanced Engineering Study.

DePree, Max. 1989. *Leadership is an Art.* New York: Doubleday.

Drucker, Peter F. 1989. "What Business Can Learn from Nonprofits." *Harvard Business Review* (July–August), *67* (4): 88–93.

Gitlow, Howard S., and Gitlow, Shelly J. 1987. *The Deming Guide to Quality and Competitive Position.* Englewood Cliffs, NJ: Prentice-Hall.

GOAL/QPC. 1988. *The Memory Jogger: A Pocket Guide of Tools for Continuous Improvement.* Methuen, MA: GOAL/QPC.

Imai, Masaaki. 1986. *KAIZEN: The Key to Japan's Competitive Success.* New York: Random House.

Juran, J. M. 1988. *Juran on Planning for Quality.* New York: Free Press.

———. 1989. *Juran on Leadership for Quality: An Executive Handbook.* New York: Free Press.

Levitt, Theodore. 1983. "The Globalization of Markets." *Harvard Business Review* (May–June), *61* (3): 92–102.

Walton, Mary. 1986. *The Deming Management Method.* New York: Putnam.

READINGS ON TQM MANAGEMENT PRINCIPLES*

Bossert, James L. 1991. *Quality Function Deployment: A Practitioner's Approach.* Milwaukee: ASQC Quality Press. Quality Function Deployment (QFD) is a total quality process that provides structure to the cycle of developing new products or services with a primary focus on customer requirements. A straightforward description of how to use QFD.

Chaffee, Ellen E. and Sherr, Lawrence A. 1992. *Quality: Transforming Postsecondary Education.* ASHE-ERIC Higher Education Reports No. 3. Washington. DC: George Washington University. Expands on the ideas in this chapter and applies the ideas to colleges and universities.

Cornesky, Robert A., et al. 1990. *W. Edwards Deming: Improving Quality in Colleges and Universities.* Madison, WI: Magna Publications. The author, a dean at Edinboro University of Pennsylvania, provides higher education-related commentary, examples, and cases for each of Deming's 14 points. Stimulates ideas and notable in that it is among the first to relate TQM to higher education.

Garvin, David A. 1988. *Managing Quality: The Strategic and Competitive Edge.* New York: Free Press. Written for managers, elaborating the history and nature of the quality concept and illustrating its impact with a comparative study from industry.

Ishikawa, Kaoru. 1985. *What Is Total Quality Control?: The Japanese Way* (David J. Lu, trans.). Englewood Cliffs, NJ: Prentice-Hall. A basic and relatively comprehensive "how to" book on Total Quality Control characterized as "a thought revolution in management."

Scherkenbach, William. 1988. *The Deming Route to Quality and Productivity: Road Maps and Road Blocks.* Rockville, MD: Mercury Press/Fairchild Publications. Elaborates on each of Deming's 14 points, with insights drawn from the author's experiences at Ford Motor Company.

Scholtes, Peter R., et al. 1988. *The Team Handbook: How to Improve Quality with Teams.* Madison, WI: Joiner Associates, Inc. Has many useful ideas to help teams work together to make improvements.

Shook, Robert L. 1990. *Turnaround: The New Ford Motor Company.* Englewood Cliffs, NJ: Prentice-Hall. The Ford Motor Company story from its origins through the 1980 crisis, when Ford needed a federal bailout nearly as much as Chrysler. A cornerstone of the successful turnaround was the adoption of Total Quality Management.

Spanbauer, Stanley J. 1987. *Quality First in Education . . . Why Not?* Appleton, WI: Fox Valley Technical College Foundation. Fox Valley Technical College (FVTC) was among the first to teach TQM in its business continuing education program and has begun to use TQM, based on Philip Crosby's approach, in its own management. FVTC has adapted TQM for education in its Quality First program. Explains Quality First with illustrations from FVTC's experience.

Townsend, Patrick L. 1990. *Commit to Quality.* New York: John Wiley & Sons. The first five years of Total Quality at The Paul Revere Insurance Company. A good case history of service-industry implementation, full of applications ideas, but no statistical applications.

READINGS ON TQM STATISTICAL REASONING

Gitlow, Howard S., and Process Management International, Inc. 1990. *Planning for Quality, Productivity, and Competitive Position.* Homewood, IL: Dow Jones-Irwin. Places the seven new management tools of TQM in the context of the TQM concept, Deming's 14 points, and the seven traditional TQM tools. Explains how and when to use the seven new management tools.

Ishikawa, Kaoru. 1989. *Guide to Quality Control.* Asian Productivity Organization. (Available from UNIPUB, White Plains, NY.) The best seller in the area of basic statistical approaches for quality improvement. Originally written for factory foremen in Japan, but has much wider appeal.

---

*Unless otherwise indicated, the readings in this chapter are available through American Society for Quality Control, P.O. Box 3066, Milwaukee, WI 53201-3066 (800-248-1946).

Kume, Hitoshi. 1985. *Statistical Methods for Quality Improvement.* AOTS. (Available from UNIPUB, White Plains, NY.) A good book on statistical methods that are useful for manufacturing processes.

Statistical Quality Control Handbook. 1985. (Available from AT&T Technologies, Indianapolis, IN.) One of the classics on statistics for manufacturing processes; prepared for Western Electric personnel.

Wheeler, Donald J., and Chambers, David S. 1986. *Understanding Statistical Process Control.* Knoxville, TN: Statistical Process Controls. Probably the best book on the practical aspects of control charts. Written for engineers with little or no statistical training.

Implementing Total Quality Management: A Proven Strategy

Joseph R. Jablonski
Technical Management Consortium, Inc.

CONTENTS

This chapter offers a road map to implementing Total Quality Management (TQM) in a nonprofit organization. The end results of TQM are: increased service, productivity, and product quality; increased customer/client satisfaction; reduced costs, enhanced quality of work life, and improved competitive position.

2.1 OVERVIEW: IMPLEMENTATION APPROACH

TQM involves a five-phase process of implementation, as shown in Exhibit 2.1.

The schedule identifies a time frame and inter-relationships that must be maintained, throughout implementation, to ensure a smooth transformation from an organization's current status to its goal for the future.

2.2 PHASE 0: PREPARATION

Successful implementation of TQM begins with Phase 0, Preparation. It is termed Phase 0 because it precedes a building process involving the organization's Executive Director and upper-level managers, with the aid of a professional facilitator. In Phase 0, administrators obtain initial training, develop the organization's vision statement, set goals, and draft policies supporting the organization's strategic plan. Phase 0 concludes with a commitment of the resources that are necessary to plan the implementation of TQM. Phase 0 is unique in that it has a definite beginning and end. The later phases evolve over time and go on continuously. Exhibit 2.2 outlines the steps involved in preparation.

(a) DECISION TO CONSIDER TQM This decision can range from "Let's do it" to "Let's consider implementing TQM." It may be prompted internally—by an Executive Director who notices areas needing improvement—or externally. For example, Allen Berkowitz (1991), Director of Corporate Planning for the American Red Cross, has cited external pressures, "such as Congress, the Food and Drug Administration, and public and state governmental bodies," as the major force that motivates the agency he heads to change or improve its way of doing business. Regardless of the reason for the decision, training must follow.

(b) KEY ADMINISTRATIVE TRAINING A large faction, preferably the entire administrative staff, undergoes initial TQM training, either off-site or on the organization's

Exhibit 2.1.   TQM implementation overview.

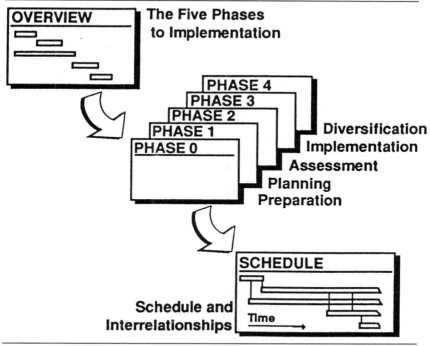

Source: Joseph R. Jablonski, *Implementing Total Quality Management: Competing in the 1990s* (Albuquerque, NM: Technical Management Consortium, 1990), p. 74.

Exhibit 2.2.   Phase O: Preparation.

▲   Decision to Consider TQM

—▲   Training of Key Executives

———▲   Development of Vision Statement

Development of Organizational Goals   ▲

Outline of Organizational Policy   ▲

Decision to Proceed   ▲

Commitment of
Initial Resources   ▲

Preparation of Speech   ▲

Source: Joseph R. Jablonski, *Implementing Total Quality Management: Competing in the 1990s* (Albuquerque, NM: Technical Management Consortium, 1990), p. 85.

premises. Off-site training is recommended whenever possible; the change of environment eliminates interruptions and encourages a change in attitudes. It is important that all upper-level personnel participate in the training concurrently, so they can better understand the benefits of TQM to their organization and gain the advantages of training interaction among their peers.

During this training, key administrators begin aligning their thinking with the philosophy of TQM. For some, TQM concepts may be new and their application may not be readily apparent. For this reason, a professional facilitator should encourage a high level of interaction. It is important to overcome the fear of change and to address individual resistance to this method of operating. These issues will surface later with staff members, and upper-level personnel must be prepared to deal with them.

It is also important to define and refine the terminology the organization will use. For instance, the resource approval and team empowerment entity for TQM might be called the Quality Committee or the Quality Council.* It is important to select and agree on terminology to which everyone can relate readily. Instituting consistent terminology becomes particularly important later, when downward deployment of TQM begins throughout the organization.

(c) STRATEGIC PLANNING   Every organization must have a purpose, a reason for being in business. (See Chap. 7.) This can be called the organizational mission. When considering the future of the organization, however, a different picture may be visualized by the administrators. This image can be referred to as the organizational vision— a statement of where the organization should be in the future. The vital link between the mission and the vision of the organization becomes the strategic plan. The strategic plan serves as a road map, guiding the organization toward the new, desired state.

Exhibit 2.3 shows the division of responsibilities and elements that is necessary to put an organizational strategic plan in place.

Strategic planning begins with a definition of the organizational vision. This vision translates into a set of organizational objectives. Some goals, such as "Recruit More Volunteers," are long-term and may take several years to be fully realized. Others, such as "Reduce the Number of Forms Currently in Use," may be short-term, with visible results sought almost immediately. Organizational goals translate into objectives, tasks and eventually into measurable parameters that are gathered by management and workforce personnel. Downward deployment of this important information conveys it to employees at all levels within the organization.

Follow-up actions and their results can then be communicated back through the hierarchy. A comparison is made between the expectations and the actual results obtained; the necessary adjustments are made so as to keep the organization on course. Feedback and communication among different levels within the organization maintain a constant alignment between the highest and lowest levels of the organization's personnel. The organizational vision communicates to all staff and volunteers what is valued, what is important, and where the organization is going. As Bill Copeland (1986) has explained, "You've removed most of the roadblocks to success when you've learned the difference between motion and direction."

---

* Other terms in use include Quality Management Board and Quality Management Group.

Exhibit 2.3. Division of responsibilities.

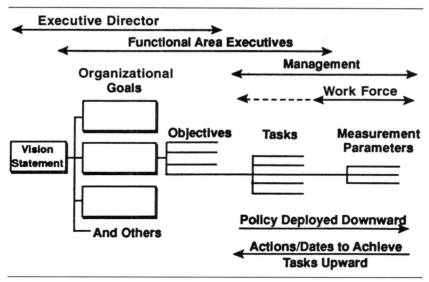

Source: Joseph R. Jablonski, *Implementing Total Quality Management: Competing in the 1990s* (Albuquerque, NM: Technical Management Consortium, 1990), p. 94.

(d) DEVELOPING THE VISION STATEMENT Developing the organization's vision statement is the first positive step toward TQM. Ideally, this takes place during a brainstorming session, typically off-site, with the aid of a trained professional facilitator. Here, via consensus, key administrators arrive at a brief, concise statement as to why the organization exists. It is normally expressed in terms of a commitment to quality, to increased responsiveness to customer/client requirements, and to becoming more effective. Exhibit 2.4 provides some examples.

The following techniques can help participants arrive at the vision statement:

1. Have each person brainstorm one ingredient or one term that is so important for the vision statement that, without it, a major point would be lost.
2. Draw the group to a prioritized list of things that should be embodied in the vision statement.
3. Use the prioritized list as an outline of the vision statement and have the group develop several versions of how the vision statement should read.
4. Allow everyone to eventually arrive at a final product through iteration and consensus.

The vision statement must be concise and easy to understand, so that everyone in the organization can relate to its meaning and his or her role in its success.

(e) DEVELOPING ORGANIZATIONAL GOALS The organizational goals must flow from the organization's vision statement. There may be many goals but, again, they

Exhibit 2.4. Examples of organization vision statements.

"We are the Aeronautical Systems Division, the center of excellence for research, development and acquisition of systems. We work together to create quality systems for combat capability to ensure we remain the best Air Force in the world and preserve the American way of like forever."

> United States Aeronautical Systems
> Division, Wright Patterson AFB, Ohio

"The policy of the Midwestern Steel Division of Armco is to provide products that conform to our customers' requirements and deliver them on time and at a competitive price. Our name must represent quality to our vendors, ourselves, and to our customers."

> Armco, Inc.
> Midwest Steel Division

"In order to improve quality we shall provide clearly stated requirements, expecting each person to do the job right the first time, in accordance with those requirements or cause the requirements to be officially changed."

> Bechtel
> Ann Arbor Power Division

"We shall strive for excellence in all endeavors. We shall set our goals to achieve total customer satisfaction and to deliver error-free competitive products on time, with service second to none."

> Burroughs

"We will deliver defect-free competitive products and services on time to our customers."

> IBM
> Research Triangle Park, Raleigh

"Milliken and Company is dedicated to providing products and services designed to be at a level of quality which will best help its customers grow and prosper. Its operational area (Research and Development, Marketing, Manufacturing, Administration, Services) will be expected to perform its functions exactly as written in carefully prepared specifications."

> Milliken

Source: Joseph R. Jablonski, *Implementing Total Quality Management: Competing in the 1990s* (Albuquerque, NM: Technical Management Consortium, 1990), p. 96–97.

---

must be concise. Exhibit 2.5 provides an example of an organization's goals. Their focus touches every aspect of the organization—from retraining personnel to maintaining a safe work environment.

The goals should be fluid, dynamic, and flexible over time. Goal 0, Implement TQM, may need to remain on the list indefinitely. TQM is a continuous process that goes on throughout the organization's life. If this goal were to be removed, it might imply that TQM is finished. Therefore, to avoid creating misconceptions in the minds of all personnel, this goal should be retained indefinitely.

(f) OUTLINING ORGANIZATIONAL POLICY A successful definition of policy accurately conveys to the work force the leaders' resolve to see TQM succeed. Senior leaders will form the "skeleton" of policy, determining what is important and what is not. The "body" takes shape as it is developed in Phase 1 by the Quality Council.

Exhibit 2.5. Organizational goals.

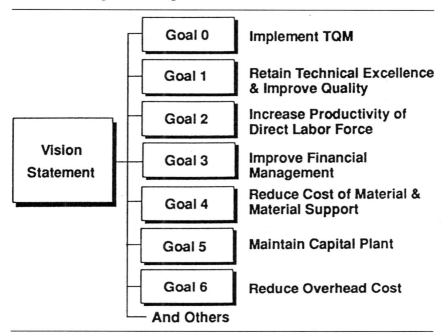

Goal 0	**Implement TQM**
Goal 1	**Retain Technical Excellence & Improve Quality**
Goal 2	**Increase Productivity of Direct Labor Force**
Goal 3	**Improve Financial Management**
Goal 4	**Reduce Cost of Material & Material Support**
Goal 5	**Maintain Capital Plant**
Goal 6	**Reduce Overhead Cost**

Source: Joseph R. Jablonski, *Implementing Total Quality Management: Competing in the 1990s* (Albuquerque, NM: Technical Management Consortium, 1990), p. 98.

The traditional system of rewards and recognition changes dramatically. Typically, staff and volunteers are rewarded for their individual accomplishments. The definition of accomplishment may expand to include people (and groups) who attempted to apply a TQM principle or use a TQM tool and fell short of expectations. This definition presents an opportunity to emphasize that something less than total "success" may be a step in the right direction; a person's (or group's) best efforts are recognized in a positive way.

Other policy issues include job security and management support. Workers need assurance that they will not lose their jobs as a result of a productivity gain realized through TQM. They need to understand that their skills will be applied to other areas within the organization. This point must remain separate and distinct from the organization's need to trim the payroll (or other resources) because of economic downturns.

Management support can be best conveyed by giving staff and volunteers an opportunity to be heard at the top. A review entity must be formed to prioritize suggestions for consideration by the Quality Council. The perceived fairness of this group plays a key role in whether members of the organization feel they have a pipeline to the top.

(g) THE DECISION TO PROCEED The sixth step in Phase 0 is a decision and a commitment of resources. After completing the previous five steps, the key leaders elect to pursue implementation of TQM. This is done by committing resources to accomplish part of Phase 1, Planning. At this point, other members of the organization become involved with TQM.

The importance of this decision to commit resources cannot be understated. The decision represents a potential pitfall, where many organizations fail. Without full commitment, the Executive Director proceeds on to Phase 1 without making it absolutely clear that an important, far-reaching decision has been made. It is critical to arrive at a clear decision and make the decision known—even if the decision is to scrap the whole idea.

(h) DELIVERY OF THE MESSAGE To effectively communicate the message on TQM, the Executive Director must do three things:

1. Know what the message is;
2. Believe in the message;
3. Deliver the message in person and circulate its text to all staff and volunteers, and appropriate media, after the presentation.

The basis of the message is the vision statement. The corporate speech shown in Exhibit 2.6 can be easily adapted to delivery of a nonprofit organization's message.

Belief in and delivery of the message are frequently overlooked. The person at the top must convey support for an initiative by promoting it personally. Two common errors are: delegating the communication responsibility to a subordinate, or using a routine communication mechanism, where the importance of the message can be easily lost.

Communication from the top of an organization is often routinely accomplished via memos. If the Executive Director uses that same mechanism to convey the importance of TQM, the impact will be diminished. Therefore, the Executive Director must communicate the message by some means that sets it apart from all other messages, and nothing works as well as his or her personal presence. As John Morley (1986) has said, "Three things matter in a speech: who says it, how he says it, and what he says, and of the three, the last matters least."

(i) TOP MANAGEMENT: THE ESSENTIAL INGREDIENT Top management commitment involves dedicating a substantial amount of the Executive Director's time to the TQM

Exhibit 2.6.   Example of a corporate speech.

I feel that each one of us at Technical Management Consortium (TMC) must promise Quality to our clients. This is a commitment of ongoing value by TMC. Our pledge is to provide error-free, interested, and knowledgeable service to each client throughout the service life cycle. This pledge applies to each and every employee. This pledge of QUALITY sets us apart from others whose goals are short-term versus our ongoing, long-term vision. In these days of mediocre service and lack of attention to detail, it is paramount for all of us to make this pledge and commitment of QUALITY to remind us of what our clients expect of us when they come to TMC.

> Joseph R. Jablonski
> President

Source: Joseph R. Jablonski, *Implementing Total Quality Management: Competing in the 1990s* (Albuquerque, NM: Technical Management Consortium, 1990), p. 102.

implementation process. Barry Miller (1991) attributes to top management commitment much of the success Delaware Valley Industrial Resource Center (DVIRC) has
had with a quality initiative:

> The DVIRC's Executive Director has assumed the necessary leadership role by exhibiting
> a commitment to Total Quality. In addition, more than in previous years, the Executive
> Director not only keeps staff well-informed of strategic planning issues, but works with
> staff to refine and improve our organization's mission.

2.3 PHASE 1: PLANNING

(a) PHASE 1 OVERVIEW During this phase, the detailed implementation plan is developed, the supporting structure is put in place, and resources are committed to accomplish implementation. Along with committing resources, another important decision
occurs—determining the strategy for implementing TQM. Exhibit 2.7 summarizes the
steps necessary to accomplish Phase 1. This phase continues to develop the foundation
on which success stories will be built later.

(b) STEPS IN THE PLANNING PHASE The following subsections describe the steps
involved in the planning process for TQM implementation.

(i) Selecting Quality Council members and a TQM Coordinator The first two steps of
the planning phase involve propagating the spirit of TQM beyond the upper-level
personnel. Individuals now brought into the improvement process include all Quality
Council members, as well as a TQM Coordinator. For the most part, members of the
Council will be selected from the existing organizational chart. The TQM Coordinator, however, will be hand-picked to serve as the "glue" that bonds together all aspects of this important initiative. The selection of this person should be done
carefully, because he or she maintains a prominent position near the top of the organization chart.

Exhibit 2.7. Phase 1: Planning.

▲ Select Quality Council Members

▲ Select TQM coordinator

       ▲ Train Corporate Council & TQM Coordinator

       ▲ 1st Quality Council Meeting

           ▲ Draft Implementation Plan

Approve Plan &

Commit Resources ▲

Identify Critical Processes & Objectives ▲

       Select Implementation Strategy ▲

         Support Services on Board ▲

Source: Joseph R. Jablonski, *Implementing Total Quality Management:
Competing in the 1990s* (Albuquerque, NM: Technical Management
Consortium, 1990), p. 108.

(ii) Training Council members not trained in Phase 0 are trained along with the TQM Coordinator. As in Phase O, this training includes an introduction to the principles and concepts of TQM, with exposure to the tools peculiar to TQM. To ensure a broad-based understanding of the management aspects, the TQM Coordinator should receive supplemental training on management and tools of TQM as well as facilitation. This knowledge will prove useful because the TQM Coordinator will facilitate meetings, advise all levels within the organization, and match consulting support with the specific needs of Process Action Teams (PATs). The traits to consider among candidates for the TQM Coordinator position appear in Exhibit 2.8.

(iii) First Quality Council meeting After the Quality Council members and the TQM Coordinator have been selected and trained, they proceed to their first Quality Council meeting. Specific items that should be discussed during this first meeting include the Council's charter, the division of responsibilities necessary to support the implementation plan, and a schedule of events. A sample agenda for this meeting is shown in Exhibit 2.9.

This meeting is the first opportunity to involve the work force and introduce them to the improvement process. One management technique is to invite a representative or two from the staff and volunteer corps to participate in Council proceedings, either as regular members or advisers on specific agenda items.

(iv) Drafting the Implementation Plan The TQM Implementation Plan involves the direct participation of all Council members and specific inputs from the work force. The overall coordination and integration task will be the responsibility of the TQM Coordinator. Active involvement of the organization's training representative is essential. The review, selection, and implementation of the training program will be the responsibility of the Training Department, with inputs from the Council, the work force and the TQM Coordinator.

Exhibit 2.8. Coordinator selection criteria.

---

1. A mix of personnel from different levels within the organization.
2. People who have credibility.
3. People with a track record of successfully introducing innovation and achieving organizational commitment.
4. People who are known to be team players and have the leadership capacity to bring together the thinking of the group.
5. People with good interpersonal and communication skills.
6. Volunteers! They must really want to do this.
7. People who have a strong personal belief in the participative ethic.
8. People who can constructively confront the status quo and still work effectively with those in positions of authority.
9. People who are self-secure and able to maintain clear thinking in conflict situations.
10. People who will be around for a while.

Source: Joseph R. Jablonski, *Implementing Total Quality Management: Competing in the 1990s* (Albuquerque, NM: Technical Management Consortium, 1990), p. 116.

Exhibit 2.9. Sample agenda for first Quality Council meeting.

❑ Call meeting to order
❑ Introduce Council members
❑ Introduce TQM Coordinator
❑ Review roles & responsibilities of Council members & TQM Coordinator
❑ Review draft charter
❑ Review upcoming schedule of events   <u>   Date   </u>
  Implementation Plan draft due   _____
  Implementation Plan approval   _____
  Selection of implementation strategy   _____
  Identification of critical processes & objectives   _____
  Support services on board   _____
  Speech preparation   _____
❑ Define division of responsibilities to prepare Implementation Plan
❑ Schedule next meeting
❑ Adjourn meeting

Source: Joseph R. Jablonski, *Implementing Total Quality Management: Competing in the 1990s* (Albuquerque, NM: Technical Management Consortium, 1990), p. 112.

(v) Approving the Implementation Plan Approval of the implementation plan transpires smoothly if everyone participates in its development. The difficulty comes in committing resources. It may require a reallocation of budgets within the organization, or a request for support from an affiliated organization. Regardless of how this is accomplished, it should be recognized that this is a long-term investment from which the organization can expect a substantial return.

(vi) Committing resources After the plan's approval, the next step is identifying the critical processes within the organization and their link to the organizational goals. The quantitative and qualitative tools of TQM—such as brainstorming, facilitation, and group dynamics—assist in this process.

(vii) Identifying Critical Processes and Objectives Next, the Council selects an implementation strategy that will be used to select problems for the Process Action Teams (PATs). Four basic approaches can serve this purpose:

1. The top-down approach;
2. Good ideas from staff and volunteers;
3. Customer/client suggestions;
4. Chronic problems.

The top-down approach provides a logical audit trail from the organization's vision statement, through goals, to objectives and assignment of PATs. PATs are assigned based on a demonstrated relationship between problem resolution and organizational objectives. Although this approach works from an accounting perspective, PAT support and personal commitment from the work force can be diminished because the ideas generally belong to someone else.

Supporting good ideas from staff and volunteers helps get them to "buy into" the improvement process. Work-force resistance can be reduced if the Council supports such ideas and provides the necessary resources to succeed.

A customer/client suggestion should not be ignored. Despite conventional wisdom, complaints are assets; they may bring to the surface opportunities for process improvement that have been overlooked by members of the organization. Because clients and customers understand their needs best, they can offer valuable input about areas within the organization that need improvement.

Chronic problems—those that have plagued an organization for as long as anyone can remember—cost money and time, and create frustration regularly. Because such problems are not remedied easily, it is advisable to wait for professional help and to achieve some preliminary successes in process improvement before tackling them.

(viii) Selecting Implementation Strategy   A summary of the four problem selection criteria and some pros and cons of each criterion are shown in Exhibit 2.10. The second and third options generally prove most effective. It is preferable to support the ideas of the work force and customers/clients first.

Two considerations help ease the burden of selecting problems to be addressed by PATs:

1. Offering a clear path to success for the first few problems addressed;
2. Establishing a quick turnaround time for gaining feedback from the things that do not go exactly as expected as well as from the successes.

(ix) Gathering support services   The top TQM individual within the organization, the TQM Coordinator, and a mix of consulting and training services are involved here. Organizationally, the TQM Coordinator resides at a level directly below that of the Executive Director. It is the full-time responsibility of the Coordinator, with the aid of others in support services, to serve as arms, legs, and adviser to the Council.

The TQM Coordinator plays a key role in developing and integrating the TQM Implementation Plan and aids in prioritizing suggestions for PATs, based on the Council's

Exhibit 2.10.   Problem selection criteria options available to the Quality Council.

Options	Pros	Cons
Top-down	Relates PAT assignments directly to organization's vision statement.	Risks overlooking compelling or more costly problems.
Good idea from work force	Supports and encourages more ideas from employees.	Those offering suggestions may feel overlooked if their idea is not selected.
Customer/Client suggestion	"The customer is always right."	Mechanism must be in place to provide feedback to organization.
Chronic problem	Everyone recognizes this is a long-term problem that must be resolved.	May be too difficult to tackle in the early phases.

Source: Joseph R. Jablonski, *Implementing Total Quality Management: Competing in the 1990s* (Albuquerque, NM: Technical Management Consortium, 1990), p. 121.

selected criteria. One responsibility is to closely coordinate the training portion of the Implementation Plan with the organization's training department. The TQM Coordinator also represents the organization in interface meetings involving other organizations and suppliers on issues related to TQM. As a regular participant in Council meetings, he or she will also serve as secretary.

Consulting services combine in-house and hired consultants. It should be the eventual goal of the organization to have the majority of this support accomplished by in-house talent.

Consulting services provide one-on-one aid to the TQM Coordinator, the Council, and middle-level staff in resolving TQM issues. Most of the coordinators' time will be spent helping the PATs better understand the use of specific TQM tools and how to apply them to specific goals.

The final support service is training. Early training can be accomplished by some form of contracted services, with in-house assistance. The preliminary phases require a heavy emphasis on concepts and principles. Later, training will shift to a focus on management and technical aspects.

(c) FORMING THE TEAM To successfully implement TQM in any organization, the existing organization hierarchy must be transformed into a team that will make TQM a reality. This renewed structure will become one of three team elements shown in Exhibit 2.11—the Quality Council, support services, and PATs.

(i) Quality Council The Quality Council consists of a leader and the organization's functional managers. In nonprofit groups, the leader is generally the Executive Director; functional managers are comprised of the remaining upper-level personnel. In

Exhibit 2.11. Team elements necessary to implement TQM.

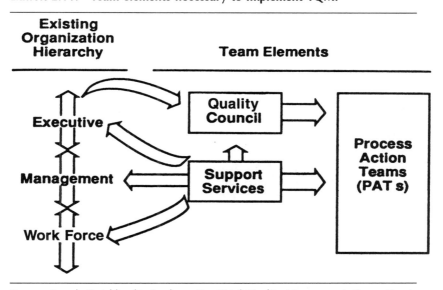

Source: Joseph R. Jablonski, *Implementing Total Quality Management: Competing in the 1990s* (Albuquerque, NM: Technical Management Consortium, 1990), p. 109.

essence, the Council includes those who actively participated in Phase 0. The Council now has responsibility for developing and implementing policy, developing and implementing the TQM plan, and creating, empowering, and supporting PATs. The Council reviews, analyzes, and improves processes within the organization with the aid of PATs and the advice of the TQM Coordinator.

The greatest responsibility of the Council is to remove barriers between functional entities within the organization and facilitate communication that will show support and overcome the resistance PATs will inevitably encounter. Council members are trained prior to creating the first PAT.

(ii) Process Action Teams (PATs)   Process Action Teams are chartered by the Council as a result of their having selected a process for improvement. Commonly, one member of the PAT will have suggested the idea being addressed. PATs include a mixture of personnel from all levels; the Council selects the exact composition. The PAT chooses one member—not necessarily the highest ranking individual on the team—to serve as its leader.

(iii) Support services   Support services are led by the TQM Coordinator, who helps to develop and integrate the TQM Implementation Plan and to prioritize suggestions for PATs. The TQM Coordinator is responsible for arranging for training and consulting services for personnel, as deemed necessary by the Quality Council.

(iv) Obstacles to implementation   Resistance to change is inevitable, even when change offers improvement. This resistance consists of a mixture of real and perceived difficulties, not only within the work force but in management as well. Whether real or imagined, such resistance must be met head-on with positive and enthusiastic support of TQM. Management's ability to overcome resistance early can help to eliminate much of the fear and anxiety associated with change.

One of the best vehicles to overcome resistance to change is awareness and orientation training for staff and volunteers. The organization's policy statement can also alleviate resistance. If tied directly to recognition and rewards, the policy statement(s) will convey a positive message throughout the organization. When developed properly and stated correctly, it can help staff and volunteers realize that benefits from TQM might include better working conditions, less frustration within the organizational structure, and, in some cases, financial rewards or bonus days off.

The Quality Council can contribute significantly to implementing TQM. When the Council acts correctly, its very presence conveys a message to staff and volunteers: "We're with you 100 percent." The Council can praise employees for merely suggesting a good idea. Further support is displayed by committing resources to charter new PATs. Most importantly, the Council removes barriers that impede solutions.

Some potential problems for Council consideration are listed in Exhibit 2.12. Solutions and approaches to resolving them are suggested.

(v) The need for consultants   The benefits from the application of consultants' expertise far exceed the cost. Their credibility and direct "hands-on" experience provide a faster and smoother transition toward Total Quality. Consultants have encountered and overcome the barriers and pitfalls of implementation; they possess detailed knowledge that will minimize problems.

Exhibit 2.12. Compilation of some likely resistance-to-change issues and how they might be overcome.

Potential/Probable Issues	Suggested Solution or Approach
Management doesn't care.	We now realize the importance and value of our work force. Through TQM, we wish to bring the work force into the decision-making process on issues affecting their careers and their tasks. Participative management is a foundational principle of TQM.
I don't believe TQM can work in our organization.	The principles and tools of TQM have been successfully applied throughout thousands of organizations. Our goal is to learn the basics of TQM so we can begin creating success stories within our own organization.
We do not have the resources to support this initiative.	The implementation of TQM *will* cause all of us to sacrifice precious time. We all will be doing double duty, but this investment will yield great dividends. This initiative will actually save us time and money in the long term and will make us more efficient in delivering our services.
There is no continuity of leadership to support this initiative.	Turnover at all levels is always a problem. If we demonstrate success early on and establish ourselves as being on track, no future staff will argue with our proven success, and we can continue the TQM process of improvement.

Source: Joseph R. Jablonski, *Implementing Total Quality Management: Competing in the 1990s* (Albuquerque, NM: Technical Management Consortium, 1990), p. 115.

It is important to select outside consultants carefully. Changing consultants partway into the TQM implementation process disrupts progress, which results in a substantial cost in time and money for the organization. More important, this action will be viewed as a discontinuity by personnel looking for a reason to circumvent this initiative. If upper-level staff members lose their credibility in this area, the costs can be tremendous.

2.4 PHASE 2: ASSESSMENT

The assessment phase consists of four steps: self-evaluation, organizational assessment, customer survey, and training feedback. All of these steps provide input for the TQM implementation process, feedback to management and the training department, and direct support for the organization's strategic plan. Each step occurs more than once, and some steps are repeated more frequently than others.

(a) SELF-EVALUATION Three basic surveys work well as self-evaluation tools. The survey developed by Philip Crosby (1984), a guru in the U.S. Total Quality movement, is intended for use in facilitated meetings. Everyone receives a copy of the form, completes it, and calculates his or her own bottom-line score. The facilitator gathers the results by a show of hands and summarizes them on a flip chart. The objective in conducting this exercise is to have everyone ultimately agree that there is room for improvement in the way the organization does business.

The Individual Survey Questionnaire in Exhibit 2.13 is used differently. A trained professional, usually a consultant with no vested interest in the outcome, administers this form. It is important that all personnel view the interviewer as a neutral party.

The questions are intended to help management better understand the work force's perceptions of TQM and the role those perceptions play in the implementation process. Staff and volunteer perceptions reflected by the surveys will influence how the organization spends training dollars. Everyone must be sensitized to his or her role in making this a successful initiative and must understand why it is being done.

A third effective self-evaluation tool is the Performax Systems International, Inc. Personality Profile System, which provides a means for understanding behavioral patterns. It is used most effectively during team-building exercises in the early stages, often during the first training session for PATs.

Behavior patterns include the way people think, feel, and act in daily situations. Recognizing the four behavior patterns in the Performax System helps both in organizational endeavors and in making TQM a reality. The four basic profiles are referred to as D, I, S, and C. Each specifies certain personality traits that are identifiable to the trained person.

Exhibit 2.13. Sample individual survey questionnaire.

---

1. What does this organization have to do to remain competitive in the future?
2. What types of initiatives are you currently addressing in your organization to improve the way you accomplish your goals?
3. What do you see as the reason for and benefit of TQM?
4. What are the most effective vehicles (formal and informal) to communicate information? (i.e., top-down, bottom-up)
5. If TQM is successful, what would it look like in your organization? How could you measure it?
6. What are the goals of your organization? What is your role in the implementation of these goals?
7. What is your role in bringing organizational products or services to the client/customer? (Research and development, operation, administration, etc.)
8. How does your organization differ from others in the same field? What are the strengths of your area? What are the weaknesses (things you'd like to change)?
9. What are the obstacles to implementing TQM?
10. What do you see as your role in the quality-improvement process?
11. What types of training or preparation would enhance your chances for success in this process?
12. Provide examples of the types of tools and techniques you have used in the implementation of TQM.
13. Describe the culture of your organization (things people value, concerns, issues, beliefs).
14. How do you determine customer/client satisfaction?
15. Management commitment is a prerequisite for productivity/quality improvement. How will you demonstrate your commitment to TQM?
16. Who are your customer/clients? (List them by name and organization/category/company.)

Source: Joseph R. Jablonski, *Implementing Total Quality Management: Competing in the 1990s* (Albuquerque, NM: Technical Management Consortium, 1990), p. 130.

For example, a high-D-profile person is characterized as a people mover, someone who tends to be impatient. The I personality tends to be disorganized and resists personal rejection. An S personality is characterized as a cooperative group worker who is fearful of risk taking. The C personality is creative and resistant to criticism of his or her ideas or work.

Most teams consist of a mix of individuals from each of the four personality types. When people understand the personalities comprising their group, a team forms more quickly, capitalizing on individual strengths. People who understand themselves and their co-workers tend to get along better and have greater success in working toward a common goal.

The Performax Personality Profile System serves as a valuable tool in implementing TQM. For more information about this system, contact Performax Systems International, Inc., P. O. Box 59159, Minneapolis, MN 55459-8247; 612-449-2824. Attn: Sandra Burk, Sales Administrator.

(b) ORGANIZATIONAL ASSESSMENT   An organizational assessment evaluates the current state of an organization and leads to positive, action-oriented recommendations for improvement. Factors contributing to the development of these recommendations include the organization's "vision" of where it wants to be, as well as the customer's/client's expectations. The organizational assessment process can account for numerous factors; it measures and quantifies variables that some consider immeasurable, such as an individual's beliefs.

One aspect of the organization on which the assessment can focus is organizational culture (Cooke, 1989). Culture can be described as thoughts, behavior, and beliefs that members of an organization have in common. Literature provides many definitions of culture, but Cooke and Rousseau (1988) have emphasized three central points:

1. Culture is something shared by members of an organization;
2. Values (what is important) and beliefs (how things work) are central components of culture;
3. Culture encompasses norms and expectations that influence the way members of the organization think and behave.

Assessing an organization's culture can be accomplished via personal interviews with the work force, a walk-through of an organization, a review of employee performance, and the administration of surveys. The Organizational Culture Inventory, or OCI™, developed by Cooke and Lafferty (1989), is frequently used.

The OCI, offered by Human Synergistics of Plymouth, Michigan, consists of 120 statements that measure 12 different cultural styles, or, more specifically, 12 sets of behavioral norms and expectations that might exist in an organization. Based on their responses to these items, individual members can develop a profile of their impressions of the organization's culture, using the Organizational Culture Profile.

Understanding the individual members' impressions of norms and expectations is an important step toward developing a picture of each section, department, division, or any other subculture of an organization.

Averages may be taken across all respondents (along all 12 categories) and plotted the very same way to yield a composite picture of the entire organization. Recent studies have shown that the "shape" of the resultant profile relates to such outcomes as the perceived quality of products and services and the supportiveness of quality within the organization's culture.

The results of such surveys can indicate whether an organization has a strong culture (high consensus among respondents regarding norms or values), a weak culture, or no culture at all (no consensus among respondents). The results can also show that the prevailing culture differs substantially from the values and norms members believe would contribute to organizational effectiveness.

For example, the work force might perceive that they are expected to simply "follow orders and not get involved," but that "participation in decision making" is critical for achieving continuous improvement and excellence in quality. If this conflict is present, such findings could explain low motivation, unmet goals, and dissatisfaction with the system. This type of information provides an important vehicle for organizational change and development.

After identifying disconnects or "gaps" between the organization's present culture and the desired culture, relevant recommendations to support TQM can be made to organizational executives. These insights provide tangible, measurable changes in the organization's fulfillment of its goals and support its vision more effectively. The results of an OCI play a key role in developing the strategic plan and provide direct input for the training plan.

For more information on the products and services available through Human Synergistics, contact: Human Synergistics, Inc., 39819 Plymouth Road, Plymouth, MI 48170; 313-459-1030.

(c) CUSTOMER/CLIENT SURVEY   The customer/client also provides an important assessment tool. It presents an opportunity to convey concern for satisfaction among people served by the organization. Exhibit 2.14 provides an example of a customer survey. Although any survey should be tailored to the organization's particular needs, it should always obtain certain basic information, such as: What are we doing right? and What can we improve on?

Because clients and customers cannot be expected to devote a great deal of time to completing such surveys, it can be helpful to use innovative approaches to gather pertinent information. As one option, the questions can be asked during a regular business meeting. If deficiencies in the organization's performance surface during the discussion, the client should be assured that the organization intends to correct them and to keep the client informed of progress in that area.

Customer/client surveys can be conducted anywhere in the TQM improvement process. For example, Terri Cole (1991), President of the Greater Albuquerque Chamber of Commerce, has explained that, in addition to an annual mailing to solicit feedback and suggestions from members, her organization conducts monthly member-to-member evaluations. According to Cole, "Each month, ten members are surveyed with respect to their perception of value of involvement in Chamber feedback, regarding programs and responsiveness of the Chamber to their needs."

Surveys should always be conducted and the results compiled before the Quality Council decides which implementation strategy to employ. At this point, the Council determines the criteria for selecting problems for resolution, and PATs are formed. Customer/client feedback, a crucial factor, may greatly influence the Council's selection of a strategy.

Exhibit 2.14. Sample customer survey.

---

1. Describe the attributes you look for when your agency requires the collection of [specialized] data.

   _____

   _____

2. Describe the attributes you look for when your agency requires an interpretative [specialized] study.

   _____

   _____

3. Do you believe that your District Office is trying to meet your needs?   (Y)   (N)
4. Please describe what singular factor came to mind, causing you to answer the preceding question as you did.

   _____

   _____

5. Identify any organizational/operational policies or procedures you feel have caused roadblocks to meeting your requirements.

   _____

   _____

6. Describe the attributes you find most desirable in those with whom you coordinate your program with the District (i.e., Project Chief, Chief of [Specialized] Investigations, District Chief, etc.).

   _____

   _____

7. Please provide an overall rating of your District Office's performance as a provider of professional [specialized] services. (Please circle one number only.)

   Poor   1   2   3   4   5   6   7   8   9   10   Excellent
8. Please describe what singular factor came to mind, causing you to rate your District Office as you did in the preceding question.

   _____

   _____

9. In one sentence or phrase, please summarize your opinion of your District Office.

   _____

   _____

10. Are there any additional comments or remarks you would like to make that would aid your District office in better meeting your needs in the future?

   _____

   _____

Source: Joseph R. Jablonski, _Implementing Total Quality Management: Competing in the 1990s_ (Albuquerque, NM: Technical Management Consortium, 1990), p. 134.

(d) TRAINING FEEDBACK Training feedback, the fourth and final step of the assessment phase, represents the first opportunity to view the perceptions of the training attendees and to evaluate the impact their training has had on the bottom line. Exhibit 2.15 shows a sample training survey. Like the customer survey, it should include two basic questions: How did we do? and How can we improve?

If initial training has been ineffective, these survey results will reveal where adjustments are necessary. Obtaining surveys from each training session should be routine; the survey results should be compiled and summarized by the training department

Exhibit 2.15. Sample training survey.

WORKSHOP CRITIQUE SHEET

Course: _____   Dates: _____

Instructor: _____

	Please Circle One			
	EXCELLENT	GOOD	FAIR	POOR
1. COVERAGE OF SUBJECT MATTER	A	B	C	D
2. ORGANIZATION OF SUBJECT MATTER	A	B	C	D
3. PRESENTATION OF SUBJECT MATTER	A	B	C	D
4. EXERCISES USED FOR SUBJECT MATTER	A	B	C	D
5. SUITABILITY OF INSTRUCTIONAL MATERIAL	A	B	C	D
6. LEVEL OF DIFFICULTY	A	B	C	D
7. LENGTH OF COURSE	A	B	C	D
8. EFFECTIVENESS OF INSTRUCTOR	A	B	C	D
9. APPLICABILITY OF SUBJECT MATTER TO THE JOB	A	B	C	D

10. RECOMMENDATION TO CO-WORKERS
(circle one):

      HIGHLY RECOMMEND   RECOMMEND   NOT RECOMMEND

COMMENTS ON STRONG POINTS OF COURSE:

_____

_____

COMMENTS ON WEAK POINTS OF COURSE:

_____

_____

WHAT WILL YOU DO DIFFERENTLY AS A RESULT OF HAVING ATTENDED THIS TRAINING SESSION? _____

_____

_____

SUGGESTED IMPROVEMENTS: _____

_____

_____

GENERAL COMMENTS ON COURSE: _____

_____

_____

Source: Joseph R. Jablonski, *Implementing Total Quality Management: Competing in the 1990s* (Albuquerque, NM: Technical Management Consortium, 1990), p. 146.

representative and the TQM Coordinator. The survey results should also be brought to the attention of the Council, because it governs some of the largest financial commitments of the decision to proceed into implementation.

(e) TRAINING RESULTS AND THE BOTTOM LINE People often overlook the relationship between training and the bottom line. Because training comprises a large part of the TQM budget, it is an important subject to address. Providing good training requires a four-level evaluation process:

1. Reaction—Were the trainees satisfied with the program?
2. Learning—What facts, techniques, skills, or attitudes did the trainees understand and absorb?
3. Behavior—Did the program change the trainees' behavior in a way that improves on-the-job performance?
4. Results—Did the program produce the desired results?

The work force's reactions to training, learning, and behavior are reflected to varying degrees in the training survey. (See Exhibit 2.15.) The fourth element, results, presents a more difficult challenge. Tangible results from training are provided to the Quality Council as feedback, confirming that the training investment is paying off. On-target training offers this important link to the bottom line, using its own structured evaluation system.

First, the organization's training program is assessed to determine a proper fit. Have objectives been clearly defined? How will value to the organization be assessed? Next, the evaluation instrument is designed. Finally, the individuals who will use the evaluation instrument must be made to realize how to derive the greatest benefit from it.

Managers learn to convey expectations and provide a foundation for follow-up. They identify and eliminate barriers that can sabotage training. Rewards and reinforcement for performance are established, and training needs and results are communicated to the training department.

2.5 PHASE 3: IMPLEMENTATION

Exhibit 2.16 summarizes the steps necessary to accomplish the implementation phase.

(a) ORGANIZATION FACILITATORS The first step involves the selection of the organization's facilitators, who will assist the TQM Coordinator. The facilitators will serve in the consulting/training role as part of the support services.

Exhibit 2.16. Phase 3: Implementation.

Source: Joseph R. Jablonski, *Implementing Total Quality Management: Competing in the 1990s* (Albuquerque, NM: Technical Management Consortium, 1990), p. 149.

After initial training, these in-house facilitators begin the transition away from a consultant-driven implementation process. Their first few sessions to train management and work-force personnel will be co-facilitated with the aid of the consultant, who fields the difficult questions and helps smooth over the rough spots.

Organization facilitators should be selected using standards similar to those used for the TQM Coordinator. Eventually, they will become the in-house experts, assuming increased responsibilities in interpersonal and problem-solving skills. Facilitators should represent all levels within the organization and should have credibility and a strong commitment to the organization's development.

Organization facilitators receive the same training as the TQM Coordinator: a two-week, intensive training evolution exposing them to a broad-based training experience. A mix of the principles, concepts, and tools of TQM is included.

As training proceeds, "specialists" emerge. Each person begins to identify with those topics he or she feels most comfortable with. Some will gravitate toward the more technical tools, such as control charts. Others may focus on presentation skills or on conducting personality profile exercises. The TQM Coordinator will schedule organization personnel, using the strengths and specialized skills of each.

(b) THE TQM LIBRARY   The TQM Library should contain relevant texts, periodicals, case studies, and audio and video tapes. Content selection should be based on the following considerations:

1. Making available relevant material that will aid in the TQM training process;
2. Serving as a ready resource to support the organization's facilitators, PATs, and other interested parties.

(c) MANAGEMENT AND WORK FORCE TRAINING   Group or large-scale training should begin only after the completion of necessary planning, the selection of terminology to be used, and the propagation of executive momentum throughout the organization. Exhibit 2.17 outlines a road map for the three kinds of training provided for employees.

Like the pieces of a puzzle, each element plays a specific role in the transition of the entire work force toward Total Quality. The most valuable aspect of the training approach is timing. Each session provides employees with just enough information so they can digest it, discover which facets of TQM they agree with, and identify those parts of TQM with which they feel uncomfortable. (Later training sessions will address these concerns.)

(i) Awareness training   Most personnel receive their first exposure to TQM through awareness training. This pivotal introduction plants the seed that TQM will benefit them. It should be brief (50 minutes maximum), polished, and well-organized. The training should address three basic concepts:

1. What is Total Quality Management?
2. Who has benefited?
3. How can it help members of the organization?

Exhibit 2.17.   Corporate-wide training to support TQM implementation.

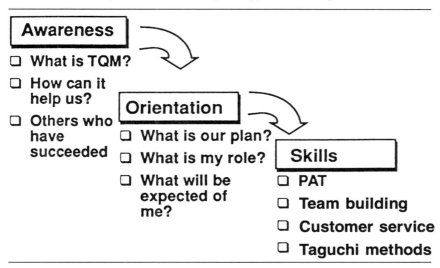

Source: Joseph R. Jablonski, *Implementing Total Quality Management: Competing in the 1990s* (Albuquerque, NM: Technical Management Consortium, 1990), p. 152.

(ii) Orientation training   Orientation training generally consumes about 3 to 4 hours. The work force learns of the organization's strategic plan to make Total Quality a way of life. To underscore its importance, senior persons from within the organization should play a key role in the presentation.

Beyond discovering the magnitude of the changes taking place, attendees should understand the following key points:

1. Top-level management is committed to the plan;
2. Everyone in the organization will be affected in a positive fashion;
3. Everyone contributes to the TQM process;
4. Exactly what will happen, and when.

(iii) Skills training   The third element in the training process, skills training, is based on individual needs, which become apparent as opportunities for improvement surface during the assessment phase.

This training can include such things as leadership training, group dynamics, team building, and even telephone-answering skills. In essence, much of skills training represents a continuation of the already planned and budgeted training initiatives. The difference is that TQM relates the continuation to the organization's strategic plan.

Skills training can be reviewed and updated each year. For example, the Personnel Director for the U.S. Olympic Committee explains that Division Directors in his organization use a performance appraisal instrument to measure specific criteria for each job. For a typist, for instance, the measurement would involve words typed per minute, accuracy, and so forth.

(d) PROCESS ACTION TEAM (PAT) TRAINING   PAT training consists of five basic parts:

1. Introduction and overview;
2. Information gathering;
3. Analysis and interpretation;
4. Packaging and presentation;
5. Follow-up.

The timing of each component of PAT training is vital. Each component should give trainees just enough information to act on. The work force should learn enough skills training so they can go forth and practice these skills with some mechanism in place for addressing questions and refining concepts for application to their specific process.

Each PAT member should have access to a specialist who addresses specific problems as they arise. The TQM Coordinator makes the support available; it consists of a mix of in-house and hired consultants. In the course of training, PAT members learn both technical and nontechnical tools, and they apply these tools using a structured problem-solving approach.

(i) Shewhart Cycle   One model for problem solving, or continuous process improvement, is the Shewhart Cycle, shown in Exhibit 2.18.

- P (Plan) represents the beginning, the early planning. TQM tools help identify an opportunity for process improvement, define the problem, identify the customer/ client, and pinpoint what quality characteristic is important for the process under study.

Exhibit 2.18.   The Shewhart Cycle.

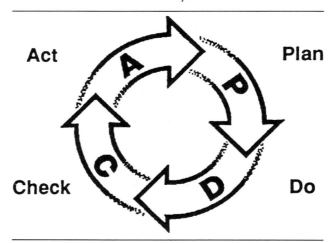

Source: Joseph R. Jablonski, *Implementing Total Quality Management: Competing in the 1990s* (Albuquerque, NM: Technical Management Consortium, 1990), p. 155.

- D (Do) follows, as solutions are developed to improve the process. After approving one solution, schedules and resource estimates for implementing the process improvement are prepared. Employee training ensures a smooth transition to the new, improved process.

- Check (C) identifies what has actually happened as a result of the changes. The same quality characteristics are measured and compared to the original, or benchmarked, values.

- Act (A) incorporates successful process improvements as work standards. Their success is applied to other, similar processes, and the organization addresses the question "What should we do next?"

(ii) PAT training PAT training has four parts:

- Introduction and overview—PAT members receive training in small groups. Each team is trained to address a specific process identified for improvement by the Quality Council. This training provides the initial occasion for creating a bond among cross-functional entities within the organization. Teamwork allows individual members to fulfill their potential. The skills taught include team building, brainstorming, interpersonal interaction, and understanding processes. Flowcharting serves as a powerful tool in understanding processes because it graphically depicts all of the steps, activities, and operations necessary to accomplish a goal. After completing this part of PAT training, participants have learned how to work toward process improvement as a team, flowcharting their process along the way.

- Information gathering—PATs learn to use the flowchart symbols to brainstorm opportunities for information that would allow them to quantify the performance of the existing process and identify numerical goals for process improvement. By the end of this training, each team knows how to gather and summarize the researched information in preparation for the next training session.

- Analysis and interpretation—Information acquired since the last training session is reviewed. Participants learn to extract usable information from their data, while applying some basic tools of TQM. These might include a tubular compilation of the data, a Pareto diagram, or a control chart. Information is presented in several different ways, to develop the most concise method for presentation to the Quality Council.

- Packaging and Presentation—The results of analysis and interpretation are reviewed, the information summarizing the best efforts is documented for review by the TQM Coordinator, and a brief summary of the recommendations is prepared for presentation during the next Council meeting. The training includes practicing the presentation with visual aides. PATs leave this forum ready to "sell" their ideas. Exhibit 2.19 illustrates a sample PAT report outline. When the PAT disbands, the TQM Coordinator keeps this report so others with similar processes can benefit from it in the future.

(e) FIRST SUCCESS STORY In the final implementation step, experienced PAT members brief new PAT members during the early stages of their training. Newcomers receive real-world feedback from their peers on the challenges and accomplishments

Exhibit 2.19.   Sample Process Action Team report outline.

1. OVERVIEW
   A. Executive Statement
   B. Team Purpose/Charter
      1. To make recommendations based on data collected and analyzed
      2. To ask for concurrence from Quality Council
      3. To continue to review and improve
II. INTRODUCTION (Background)
   A. Brief History
   B. Process Action Team Members
   C. PAT Objectives
III. PROCESS SELECTION
   A. Selection Process
      1. Brainstorming
      2. Flowchart
      3. Cause-and-effect diagram
   B. Project Description
IV. PROJECT IMPLEMENTATION
   A. What Data Collected?
   B. Where Data Collected?
   C. When Data Collected?
   D. How Data Collected?
   E. Who Collected the Data?
V. ANALYSIS AND RECOMMENDATIONS
   A. Process Changes
   B. Cost Savings
VI. CONTINUING IMPROVEMENTS
   A. PAT Schedule
   B. PAT Recommendations
   C. PAT Follow-up

Source: Joseph R. Jablonski, *Implementing Total Quality Management: Competing in the 1990s* (Albuquerque, NM: Technical Management Consortium, 1990), p. 160.

encountered only months before. The measure of success is based on how close the PATs come to meeting the performance parameter goal they themselves have developed.

Another measure is the learning experience taking place. In addition to the successes, people need to understand the pitfalls encountered and how to overcome such adversity. Revealing this information helps remove PATs' hesitation about venturing into the unknown. Whether successful or not, PAT members should know they have the full support of the Quality Council.

(f) HOW MUCH TRAINING IS REQUIRED?   It is important to consider the magnitude of training realized by each level within the organization. Exhibit 2.20 summarizes these results.

Although the specifics differ among organizations, this breakdown is widely applicable. Training is a key element in making TQM work. All members of the work force

Exhibit 2.20. Estimated initial training requirements necessary to implement TQM.

Layer within Organization	Type of Training			
	Principles and Concepts	Management Overview	Technical Overview	Specific Skills
Executive	2	2	.5	Days-Weeks
Management	1.5	1.5	.5	Days-Weeks
Work force	1	.5	.5	Days-Weeks

*All estimates are measured in days of training.

Source: Joseph R. Jablonski, *Implementing Total Quality Management: Competing in the 1990s* (Albuquerque, NM: Technical Management Consortium, 1990), p. 164.

must realize that their turn will come in the training process, and that they will be expected to contribute.

2.6 PHASE 4: DIVERSIFICATION

In this final phase of TQM implementation, the organization capitalizes on its experience and begins to invite others into the improvement process. Logical candidates for invitation include affiliated and component organizations and suppliers.

(a) INVOLVING OTHERS The first step in diversification involves inviting affiliated and component organizations into the TQM improvement process. The Quality Council provides a logical entry point for them. Senior managers view the organization and the function of the improvement process. The TQM Coordinator briefs senior management on the benefits of TQM, based on real-life experiences. It is advisable to establish credibility before expecting others to improve.

A walk-through of the organization that allows observing a PAT at work, and a review of recent success stories can help immensely. A team consisting of the TQM Coordinator, a facilitator, and the organization's Executive Director should plan to spend time at the PAT's facility, discussing the concept of TQM and their experiences with it.

(b) BRINGING SUPPLIERS ON BOARD Organizations moving toward TQM often reduce their number of suppliers significantly. In doing so, they tighten their bond with their remaining suppliers. For example, the Delaware Valley Industrial Resource Center, a nonprofit organization committed to reviving manufacturing in Pennsylvania, has experienced a change in supplier involvement since initiating a Total Quality program, as Barry Miller (1991) has explained: "As we strive to obtain better goods and services at a better price, we perform periodic assessments of our office-supplies suppliers, coffee-service supplier, cleaning-service supplier, our printers, and the other economic development organizations with which we work."

Shortly after introducing component or affiliated organizations to TQM, suppliers, vendors, and subcontractors should be brought on board. Tours of the organization, reviews of the Quality Council at work, and briefings by senior management should set the tone. In this way, suppliers learn how they can benefit from what the organization has done and learn how they, too, can realize savings and become more competitive in the marketplace.

(c) SUPPLIERS' DAY A "Suppliers' Day" provides a convenient opportunity for initiating two-way communication between the organization and its suppliers. Suppliers should be asked for feedback on what they've seen in the organization that may benefit them. More important, they should be encouraged to identify how TQM may help them. Some suppliers may be surprised to discover how the principles and tools of TQM have already been used to improve the quality of their delivered products and services because of actions taken earlier by PATs.

2.7   COSTS OF IMPLEMENTING TQM

Before an organization's leadership decides to implement TQM, research is done to aid the executives in deciding whether to commit the time and fiscal resources necessary to implement an organization-wide change process. The budget line items included in the cost of TQM implementation include the following:

- Off-site training;
- Travel and per-diem costs;
- Time away from the job;
- TQM Coordinator;
- Training aids;
- Facilities;
- Library materials;
- Consulting support;
- Course development.

(a) OFF-SITE TRAINING, TRAVEL, AND PER-DIEM COSTS Off-site training usually includes attendance at several public workshops where upper-level management gathers information to help in the decision-making process. The main travel and per-diem costs are airfare, food, and transportation. Registration fees are included in these expenses.

(b) TIME AWAY FROM THE JOB This can be the largest cost of implementation, based on how the organization accounts for work-force training time. At worst, it will include all of the workers' time spent being trained, attending PAT meetings, and working on PAT-related responsibilities. In most instances, time spent in awareness and orientation training can be justifiably included as an overhead item. PAT training and its associated responsibilities should be viewed as part of the work force's routine responsibilities.

(c) TRAINING AIDS These expenses include reproduction of training materials and purchase of binders, overhead transparencies, and assorted office supplies.

(d) FACILITIES Facilities expenses include rental fees for the training space, food, and audiovisual equipment. These fees are routinely part of the initial training expenses where training might be held at a remote location to remove the trainees from the daily flurry of the office.

(e) LIBRARY MATERIALS Expenses include the books, original training materials, video- and audio-based training, exercises, and texts for researching more sophisticated tools that may apply to the workplace in the future.

(f) CONSULTING SUPPORT This category includes the initial training and advisory services the organization will need to design the specific details of a quality system, conduct initial training, and coach the organization toward success.

(g) COURSE DEVELOPMENT Larger organizations typically invest in some form of tailoring for their training packages. This provides the advantage of presenting a consistent image and terminology that assists in communicating the message.

SOURCES AND SUGGESTED REFERENCES

Berkowitz, Allen. 1991. Interview. (Director of Corporate Planning, American Red Cross.)

Cole, Terri. 1991. Interview. (President, Greater Albuquerque Chamber of Commerce.)

Cooke, R. A. (Ed.). 1989. *Organizational Culture Inventory Leader's Guide.* Plymouth, MI: Human Synergistics, Inc.

Cooke, R. A., and Rousseau, M. D. 1988. "Behavioral Norms and Expectations: A Quantitative Approach to the Assessment of Organizational Culture." *Group and Organization Studies, 13:* 245–273.

Crosby, Philip B. 1984. *Quality Without Tears: The Art of Hassle-Free Management.* New York, NY: McGraw-Hill.

Jablonski, Joseph R. 1992. *Implementing TQM: Competing in the Nineties Through Total Quality Management.* Albuquerque, NM: Technical Management Consortium.

Miller, Barry. 1991. Interview. (Director of Manufacturing Services, Delaware Valley Industrial Resource Center.)

White, Rolf B. 1986. *The Great Business Quotations.* Secaucus, NJ: Lyle Stuart, Inc.

Building a Total Quality Culture

Joseph E. Champoux
The University of New Mexico

Lenore B. Goldman
Goldman Associates

CONTENTS

3.1 INTRODUCTION

This chapter describes how to build a total quality culture in nonprofit organizations. It also describes organization culture and its positive and negative contributions to organizations and their management. The discussion focuses on (1) the type of culture necessary for a successful quality-oriented nonprofit organization, (2) the amount of change needed to move an organization to that quality position, and (3) the role of leadership in causing the change. Many examples from nonprofit organizations are included.

(a) SUMMARY OF TOTAL QUALITY MANAGEMENT   Total Quality Management (TQM) is a philosophy and system of management built on work dating to the 1920s (Garvin, 1988). TQM includes a set of principles, tools, and techniques that help organizations manage for quality services, products, processes, and relationships. Although its roots are in manufacturing, it is a management system that can result in major improvements for any organization.

The goal of TQM is the management of quality. Although long-term cost reductions and increased profit often result, quality management is the focus of TQM. It readily applies to the management of service organizations, nonprofit organizations, and the internal processes of any organization or group. TQM focuses an entire organization on continuous improvement in its product or service.

TQM forces a total systems view of management that reaches well beyond the boundaries of the organization. It uses an understanding of interdependence with outside people and outside organizations, and among groups within the organization, to better manage its quality. The list of those stakeholders—groups with an interest in the organization's activities—is long. It includes employees, vendors, suppliers, donors, board members, volunteers, clients, customers, patrons, constituents, members, the community surrounding the organization, coalitions of which the organization is part, professional or trade associations, chapters of the organization, and competitors for the same funds or clients. (We refer to those served by a nonprofit organization as "clients" in the rest of this chapter.)

TQM can bring to an organization many benefits that do not directly result from other approaches to management. Managers (executive directors, managers, program directors, administrators, development directors) can expect lower costs of providing a service, doing research, starting a social issues campaign, or manufacturing a product. Service processes will function more dependably. Research will be more focused and cost-effective. Issues can be targeted and communicated more effectively. Products will have higher reliability.

Employee, board, and volunteer commitment to continuous quality improvement will increase. The results can be: more loyalty to the organization, improved funding potential, easier volunteer and board recruitment, and more lasting social change. TQM's assumption of high interdependence among many system parts to get continuous quality improvement can lead to better cooperation and clarity with outside contractors, suppliers, vendors, coalition partners, and the community.

TQM differs from other systems of management in the following specific ways. It is a way of managing that:

Is unlike what most organizations have done in the past;

Emphasizes a long-term commitment to continuous quality improvement;

Stresses that quality is everyone's job, not just that of the quality assurance department, the executive director, or the administrator;

Is intensely client-focused;

Requires that focus of all members of the organization.

TQM emphasizes cooperation among people in any unit that has adopted TQM and with people outside the unit. TQM also emphasizes high involvement in the work process. It assumes that people want high involvement in their work or that managers and supervisors can create that involvement.

TQM emphasizes communication in all directions—top-down, bottom-up, and laterally. This feature follows directly from the requirements of cooperation and high involvement. It also is a way in which TQM generates large amounts of information in the system. Many nonprofit organizations already have such communication systems. Some examples are those with experience using cross-departmental task forces; participative decision making; multicultural staffs, boards, volunteers, or clients; and a decentralized organization design.

Managers who adopt the TQM philosophy develop a long-term orientation, a view to the future. It is not the here-and-now that is important. The decisions made today by anyone in the organization must be made with the future in mind. Being good now is not enough. Being great is the goal, and it is reached through a passionate pursuit of continuous improvement. (See Chap. 7 for a broader discussion of Strategic Planning.)

(b) WHY TOTAL QUALITY MANAGEMENT FOR NONPROFIT ORGANIZATIONS? This section indicates the reasons nonprofit organizations should move toward TQM and describes some features found in many nonprofit organizations that will support such a move.

Peter Drucker's analysis of high-performing nonprofit organizations (Drucker, 1989, 1990) suggests they have many features that support a move toward TQM. The strongest supportive features are a mission focus, a client focus, and self-motivated volunteers.

A mission focus gives people in the organization a clear sense of direction and a reason for being. A strong client focus keeps the nonprofit organization concentrated on client needs. Both foci can remind members of the organization of the need to constantly improve what they offer to their environment. Self-motivated volunteers are a key instrument for nonprofit organizations' attaining their mission. They already want to do well. TQM can show them how to continuously do better.

Drucker's observations for high-performing nonprofit organizations should have been a reminder of the description of TQM given above. If an organization is not performing as well as it can, then TQM can help improve its performance in the following ways.

TQM's emphasis on continuous improvement of all processes in an organization will let nonprofit organizations do more with fewer, equal, or new dollars (Kotler and Roberto, 1989). The agitation to do more for nonprofit organizations' clients is consistent with the philosophies of those organizations and of their staff and volunteers. The involvement of everyone in continuous improvement can add challenge to employees' and volunteers' jobs. The long-run effect for nonprofit organizations is a highly committed corps of people who have an impassioned focus on mission and client.

3.2 ORGANIZATION CULTURE AND TOTAL QUALITY MANAGEMENT

(a) ORGANIZATION CULTURE Organization culture is an ideology and a set of values that guide and affect the behavior of members of the organization. Heroes, ceremonies, and rituals are part of an organization's culture. Some facets of an organization's culture are highly visible to both insiders and outsiders; other facets are less visible (Deal and Kennedy, 1982; Schein, 1985; Wilkins, 1983).

The following more extensive definition of organization culture offers the flavor of its elements and functions (Van Maanen and Schein, 1979):

> [A]ny organizational culture consists broadly of long-standing rules of thumb, a somewhat special language, an ideology that helps edit a member's everyday experience, shared standards of relevance as to the critical aspects of the work that is being accomplished, matter-of-fact prejudices, models for social etiquette and demeanor, certain customs and rituals suggestive of how members are to relate to colleagues, subordinates, superiors, and outsiders, and . . . some rather plain "horse sense" regarding what is appropriate and "smart" behavior within the organization and what is not.

Organization culture is the glue holding the system together and the motor moving it toward its goals.

Within the larger organization culture, subcultures develop around occupational groups—management, program, development, finance, quality assurance, and public relations. They also can develop around the founders of an organization, those who arrived after its founding, and the "true believers" in the mission of the organization. Decentralized organizations and geographically dispersed organizations all build different subcultures. TQM, however, asks managers to integrate those subcultures into a single quality-oriented culture.

(b) LEVELS OF ORGANIZATION CULTURE Insiders and outsiders can see an organization's culture at three different but related levels. Each level varies in degree of visibility to an observer. In decreasing order of visibility, the three levels are the physical artifacts, values, and basic assumptions of the culture.

The most visible part of an organization's culture is its physical characteristics or artifacts. Photographs about the history of the organization, open or closed office space, and the way people dress tell much about an organization's culture.

The values of the culture are the next level at which an organization's culture is evident. Outsiders have a hard time seeing such values. Insiders know the values but find it difficult to describe them. Only time with the organization lets a person learn about its values.

The last level at which an organization's culture can be seen is its basic assumptions. Often, these are unconscious values guiding the behavior of veteran organization members. Basic assumptions develop over the history of the organization. They deal with many aspects of relationships among people in the organization and relationships of the organization to its external environment. Newcomers have difficulty seeing the basic assumptions, but can learn them over time.

(c) SOURCES OF AN ORGANIZATION'S CULTURE An organization's culture develops from the surrounding societal culture, the effects of the early history of the organization, its mission, and the people it serves. A nonprofit organization may be founded by a person with a vision, a community facing a crisis, or a group of people sharing an interest. A founder or core founding group builds an organization to achieve the vision. The organization grows over time, developing a shared history along the way. Stories and parables told to new employees, volunteers, and board members carry parts of that history forward. Pieces of the history often are recorded and displayed as photographs or as a written history. Regular review of that history embeds the values of the founder, and the early group, into the cultural fabric of the organization.

The type of activity of the organization, or the industry it is in, also shapes its culture. It defines the work force from which the organization will draw. Many people in the work force already have been socialized to a set of values. They bring those values with them when they join the organization. Universities, trade unions, health care organizations, and orchestras draw from a base of professionals who have been socialized to their unique sets of values as part of their training.

An organization's ideology draws people who have certain values that become part of the organization's culture. The ideology of the National Rifle Association differs from that of the pacifist American Friends Service Committee. The gender character of the National Organization of Women and the Sigma Alpha Epsilon fraternity results in strong cultural contrasts. Sexual orientation influences the cultures of Reverend Lou Sheldon's Traditional Values Coalition and the National Gay and Lesbian Alliance. Class differences alter the frames of reference of the International Brotherhood of Teamsters and the Friends of the Santa Fe Opera.

The nature of the "business" decides with whom and how the organization must interact. It also defines the type of external environment the organization usually will face. That environment will vary in uncertainty, risk, and speed of feedback to the organization and its employees. The adaptation of the organization to its environment adds to the values and norms of its culture.

(d) FUNCTIONS AND DYSFUNCTIONS OF ORGANIZATION CULTURE An organization's culture serves several functions. It helps members of the organization adapt to changes in the organization's environment through commitment to its mission. The values and basic assumptions of the culture help integrate the internal processes of the organization by guiding individuals in their daily work activities. Nonprofit organizations, for example, have strong service-oriented values and basic assumptions. Those values tell members their mission is to serve, to protect, to champion, to enlighten, or to effect social change.

Unfortunately, an organization's culture also can be dysfunctional. An existing organization culture can constrain a strategic change, such as a shift to a TQM emphasis. Subcultures can increase conflict, communication difficulties, and differences in perception. An existing organization culture, and its subcultures, all can be a significant source of resistance to change. A social change nonprofit organization could view efforts to move toward TQM as interfering with its mission. "Unless we save the planet today, TQM won't even exist" could be a phrase heard in such organizations. Such resistance presents executive directors and managers with a major barrier when they are considering moving to a TQM system of management.

(e) ASSESSMENT AND DIAGNOSIS OF ORGANIZATION CULTURE Executive directors and managers are well advised to stand back and assess the culture of their organizations. The assessment will indicate what their culture looks like now and how much change it needs to move it to a new state (Wilkins, 1983). Exhibit 3.1 is a worksheet that can be used to do a culture assessment and diagnosis. The rest of this section describes the main steps in an assessment.

The first step is to examine the physical characteristics of the organization—its architecture, office layout, and interior decor, and how people dress. If there are

Exhibit 3.1.   Organization culture assessment worksheet.

Visible Artifacts

1. Physical Characteristics. Note the architecture, office layout, and interior decor, and how people dress. Are there any photographs? If there are, do they say anything about the history of the organization?

_____

_____

_____

_____

2. Behavior. Include interpersonal and verbal behavior. What is the interpersonal orientation of people toward each other? Do people use titles when referring to each other, or do they use first names?

_____

_____

_____

_____

3. Public Documents. What is said publicly about the organization? Include as public documents an annual report, press releases, internal newsletters, fund-raising campaigns, and so on.

_____

_____

_____

_____

Invisible Artifacts

4. Values. Identify espoused values separately from in-use values. Infer the values from activities given the most time in a typical week. What does the organization say it values? What do people appear to value, as shown by their actions?

_____

_____

_____

_____

5. Basic Assumptions. Infer these from aspects of people's behavior. Include personal thoughts and feelings as well.

_____

_____

_____

_____

_____

This exhibit was suggested by the discussion in E. H. Schein, *Organizational Culture and Leadership* (San Francisco: Jossey-Bass, 1985), and T. E. Deal and A. A. Kennedy, *Corporate Cultures* (Reading, MA: Addison-Wesley, 1982).

photographs, do they say anything about the organization's history? Many organizations have written histories of their beginnings. If these exist, what do they say about the organization's roots?

San Francisco's Shanti Project assessed their organization culture to prepare for a change in their clients' and community's needs. They had started as an organization that offered emotional aid to people with terminal illnesses. In the mid-1980s, a growing number of people dying of AIDS had no source of reliable help. The Emotional Support

Program became the focus of the Shanti Project's services. Their client focus became people with AIDS and their loved ones. Their culture assessment uncovered an ever present physical symbol—a box of tissues. Emotional succor, symbolized by the box of tissues, had become the most important way Shanti served its clients.

The second step is to watch people's behavior in the organization—both their interpersonal and their verbal behavior. Do people behave formally or informally toward each other? Do they use titles or first names when addressing each other? Do they interact freely across organizational levels? Do conversations focus on work-related matters or do they drift into discussions about personal matters? Behavior is a key source of information about both the espoused and in-use values of an organization.

The third step begins by examining documents the organization releases to the public—annual reports, press releases, internal newsletters, descriptions of fund-raising campaigns, and so on. What do those documents discuss? Do they talk mainly about the contribution of the organization through successful accomplishment of its mission? Or, do they talk mainly about the difficulties the organization has in raising funds or dealing with a shifting environment? (See Chap. 5.)

The values of the organization's culture can be readily inferred from the above assessment. Espoused values are the easiest to see; they are the values openly discussed or published about the organization's culture. In-use values are harder to identify; they must be inferred from behavioral and published information. If several people complete the assessment and diagnosis in Figure 3.1, agreement may emerge after some discussion. New employees are especially helpful with this step because they are actively learning the organization's culture and bring a fresh view to it.

It may be difficult to assess an organization's culture. Some nonprofit organizations change so rapidly that they look chaotic. Assessing any part of these organizations' culture can feel fruitless because it was so different a few months ago and a few months before that. Unexpected funding cuts, high staff turnover, court rulings, government regulations, Congressional budgeting, and shifting clients can leave a nonprofit organization reeling. Veteran staff often can help identify the permanent features of an organization's culture, but constant change may be a dominant characteristic in some nonprofit organizations. Defining the characteristics of a constantly changing culture is as important as defining the properties of more stable organization cultures (Vaill, 1989).

The last step in the worksheet is the most difficult, but it gets to the heart of an organization's culture. Veteran employees usually are unaware of basic assumptions; they have become almost second nature and are below the level of conscious thought. Discussion among both veteran employees and newcomers can help uncover them. Basic assumptions are the core of an organization's culture and the glue holding it together.

(f) FEATURES OF ORGANIZATION CULTURE THAT SUPPORT TQM Exhibit 3.2 shows some features of an organization culture that supports Total Quality Management. Such a culture has major elements of trust, cooperation, and caring. It supports high commitment to the organization, and high involvement of all employees, to get continuous quality improvement. TQM cultures strongly focus on customers or clients. Those cultures also regard conflict as a useful management tool for increasing information and solving problems. They reject fault-finding and blaming. They embrace decentralized decision making as a way of quickly reacting to clients' requirements (Allen and Kraft, 1984; Peters, 1988; Scott and Jaffe, 1989).

Exhibit 3.2.   Some features of an organization culture that support Total Quality Management.

_____	Caring—for employees, customers, clients, and donors
_____	Committed to continuous improvement
_____	Committed to a learning organization (training and continuous skill development)
_____	Committed to quality
_____	Customer-focused
_____	Desires to always do better than now
_____	Encourages all employees to interact directly with customers, clients, or donors
_____	Encourages cooperation among organization members and with customers, clients, and donors
_____	Encourages interaction across functions
_____	Feels constant agitation for improvement
_____	Flexible
_____	Not satisfied with the status quo
_____	Perceives problems and complaints as opportunities to do better
_____	Process-focused
_____	Questions decisions and actions
_____	Rejects simply finding fault or placing blame
_____	Trusting
_____	Uses conflict as a constructive problem-solving tool
_____	Values decentralized decision making
_____	Values dispersal of information throughout the organization
_____	Values self-examination to find ways of improving
_____	Values using teams to solve problems and make decisions

Many features of nonprofit organizations suggest that they have TQM-like values. Staff, volunteers, and board members usually have high commitment to serving their clients. The existing service commitment can be an excellent starting point for a non-profit organization to move toward TQM's client-driven focus on quality.

The results of the assessment and diagnosis of an organization's culture can be compared to the elements shown in Exhibit 3.2. The amount of change required by an organization to move toward TQM is a direct function of the difference between the two. The larger the difference, the greater the change the organization will need.

3.3   CHANGING AN ORGANIZATION'S CULTURE

(a) STEPS, PROCESSES, AND EFFECTS   Moving TQM into an organization is a major change for most organizations. People are asked to let go of old behaviors and learn new ones. The quality assurance department of a hospital is asked to let go of an inspection orientation to quality. People in service organizations are asked to focus on the quality of their processes, not just the delivery of a service. Scientists and engineers in research and development organizations are asked to attend not only to their scientific and engineering activities, but also to find ways of continuously improving the processes they use. All the above changes in behavior can be unsettling for many people.

Successful organization change begins with identifying the key people who must themselves change, if TQM is to be successful (Beckhard and Harris, 1987). Those same people can infuse the need for change in others throughout the organization. The type and amount of organization change required by TQM usually call for strong leaders in several places in the organization. Although leaders can be identified by title, leadership is a set of behaviors, no matter what the position or status.

Moving TQM into an organization will happen more quickly, and more effectively, if members of the organization are motivated to change. The motivation can come from a vision that TQM will let the organization be more effective in the future. It also can come from fear that the organization will fail if it does not begin to focus on quality.

Moving an organization toward TQM is a form of planned organization change (Beckhard and Harris, 1987; Burke, 1987; Lippitt, Watson, and Westley, 1958). Planned change requires managers to define the desired end-state of the organization, analyze and diagnose its present state, and manage the process of moving the organization from where it is now to where the manager wants it to be. Consultants or change agents, either from inside or outside the organization, often are part of planned change activities. Organization change consultants usually are behavioral science specialists who help managers do planned change.

Large-scale planned change uses three processes to start the change and move it to the desired end-state (Barczak, Smith, and Wilemon, 1987). First, the pattern-breaking process crumbles old behaviors as the organization separates from its past. This process forces a turbulent state on the organization and can be disconcerting to many people. The second process is experimenting—with new ideas, innovations, and thinking, and with behaving in new ways that support quality. Such experimenting has its eye on the basic mission and vision of the organization, often building on the organization's roots (Wilkins and Bristow, 1987).

The third process is visioning. This process gives organization members a clear focus for their activities. It also tells them about the future state of the organization and the important role of a quality orientation. The vision can come from the strategic plan, especially if there has been widespread involvement in its development. It also comes from the organization's leaders at all levels, who play a key role in infusing a vision of quality and continuous improvement. (See Chap. 5.)

A last phase in planned change activities focuses on stabilizing or institutionalizing the change. This phase also features ending the consultant–client relationship because the organization is ready to continue by itself. This phase is so important to a lasting change to TQM that a separate section treats it in detail later.

(b) STRATEGIES OF PLANNED ORGANIZATION CHANGE There are three generic strategies of planned organization change (Chin and Benne, 1969; Greiner, 1967). The *empirical–rational* change strategies induce change by logically arguing the value of the proposed change. These strategies are a form of persuasive communication, using arguments based on facts. They also assume people will act in their self-interest and change as needed, once persuaded of the value of the change. An example in moving toward TQM is the widespread practice of informing senior managers about TQM in awareness workshops. Such awareness training assumes it can start changing the home organizations of the managers.

Normative–reeducative strategies try to change an organization's culture by affecting the norms of behavior embedded in that culture. These strategies assume that social norms and values guide behavior in organizations. They use two different methods of getting change. The first method resocializes people to the new values, and the second directly changes social interactions in the organization. Both methods help build a vision of the desired future state of the organization.

Power–coercive strategies change an organization's culture by using influence approaches based on power or organizational authority. Some approaches depend on a powerful person's overcoming a weaker person. Others use the formal authority relationships of an organization and order the change into place. For example, the Department of Defense issued a directive ordering all military organizations and their contractors to put TQM into place. The directive began a massive national effort to move those organizations in a quality-oriented direction.

All organization change strategies need top management support to be effective. Although staff, the board, and external stakeholders can start a change effort, it requires top management involvement to succeed. Piecemeal approaches to change do not use all the resources of an organization in a cooperative mutual effort. Such change approaches will not get all the benefits of TQM because it is a transformation in values, perceptions, awareness, and behavior (Nicoll, 1984).

(c) RESISTANCE TO CHANGE   Because TQM differs strongly from more familiar ways of managing organizations, it often faces resistance to moving toward it. Resistance forms because of changes from a familiar way of managing an organization to a way that is unfamiliar to many people (Klein, 1976; Lawrence, 1954). The changes required by moving toward TQM also can change familiar patterns of social interaction. The latter is often a basic source of resistance to any organization change.

Resistance reactions take many forms. The forms common to moving toward TQM include not being cooperative with the change effort, directly sabotaging efforts to bring it into particular units, and becoming dysfunctionally argumentative about the value of TQM.

Resistance to change is not an irrational response to changes in social systems (Kotter and Schlesinger, 1979). Some people resist change in the move toward TQM because they perceive themselves losing something they value. Others resist change because they do not trust the person or persons pressing for the change or have a low tolerance for change.

Resistance to moving toward TQM in a nonprofit organization may be well grounded. Such change may alter services or processes in ways that can hurt clients' needs or sources of funding. In the private sector, better service often means more revenue and profit. In a nonprofit organization, improving quality may divert organization resources from clients or result in less revenue in the near future.

Taking risks in a well-planned quality change effort can bring unexpected results. The Children's Museum of Denver reduced dependence on a few foundations and large donors by taking an innovative approach to producing high-quality educational products and services for families. The strategy required learning new skills in business development, marketing, and management. Although resources were diverted from other museum activities, the change strategy brought new people to the museum, gave it a national profile, developed a broader base of contributors to its collection, and served families in exciting new ways (Simons, Miller, and Lengsfelder, 1984).

Other reasons for resistance to change give some hints about how to reduce resistance to moving an organization toward TQM. Those reasons include not having a common view about the value of the change or simply misunderstanding the goals of the change. In both cases, increasing the information about TQM and its value to the organization can help reduce the resistance.

Managers can view resistance to change as either a problem to solve or a signal to get more information about the resistance. The latter uncommon way of viewing resistance is recommended for change of the size implied by a move toward TQM. This approach asks managers to get more information from the sources of resistance, in order to better understand the reasons for resistance (Lawrence, 1954).

The alternate view treats resistance reactions as problems to solve. Managers often use the power–coercive approaches to change, to overwhelm opposition. Such approaches also have the side effect of increasing resistance to the proposed changes (Lewin, 1951).

The absence of resistance to change should not be viewed as good fortune. It may lead to a less effective move toward TQM than one in which the merits of the proposed change have been actively examined and discussed. The healthy examination of differences among those proposing and resisting the change to TQM could uncover possibly dysfunctional results for an organization (Albanese, 1970; Klein, 1976).

Exhibit 3.3 offers a checklist of guides for managing a change process in order to reduce resistance to change. Each tactic can work with the others toward managing the change to TQM with the least dysfunctional effects of resistance (Lawrence, 1954; Kotter and Schlesinger, 1979).

Early in the program, the key people affected by the proposed change to TQM should be involved in the change process. Such people need to learn about TQM—what it can do for the organization, and how it can help the organization work better. Such involvement is not participation for the sake of participation, but a true effort to use their knowledge about the organization to design an effective change effort.

Information about the change should be made widely available, in an understandable form. TQM might appear to many people to be just another management fad. Information can be in oral, written, audiotaped, or videotaped form.

The change to TQM should be supported by committing resources to the change effort. Such resources include information about TQM and training in using its tools and techniques. Resources also include time—the time of senior managers who discuss openly why the organization is moving toward TQM, and the time of employees who get information and training.

Programs of change to TQM often require the help of an outside consultant. (See Chap. 30.) Because TQM has its roots in manufacturing, many consultants and

---

Exhibit 3.3. Managing a change process to reduce resistance.

_____ Involve the key people affected by the proposed change early in the change program, to help develop it.

_____ Create methods for two-way communication of information and feelings about the change so it is understandable to all affected by the change.

_____ Commit adequate resources to the change effort.

_____ Select a change agent (consultant) with characteristics congruent with the target of change.

_____ Use symbols and ceremonies to mark departure from the past and a move toward the future.

examples of change programs come from that sector. In nonprofit organizations, it will be especially important to match the characteristics of the consultant with the characteristics of the target organization (Rogers, 1971). Such characteristics include the education, language, and values of the consultant. Education refers to basic credentials to be a TQM consultant. Language refers to linking the manufacturing roots of TQM and the daily language of nonprofit organizations. Values refer to the beliefs of the target organization and those of the consultant.

The last item in the checklist should not be treated lightly. Moving toward TQM can be such a major change for an organization that marking the departure from the past and the move to the future with a ceremony is entirely appropriate (Burke, 1987; pp. 118–119). The goal is to show all people in the organization that the business of the organization no longer will be done the way it was in the past.

(d) INSTITUTIONALIZING THE NEW ORGANIZATION CULTURE   Institutionalization is the process that sustains changes in an organization over time. For TQM, it means moving an organization to Total Quality Management and then holding it in that position. Institutionalization also includes socialization processes needed to teach successive generations of members of the organization about TQM (Goodman, Bazerman, and Conlon, 1984).

Institutionalized behavior has three characteristics: It is *persistent* behavior, *shared by two or more people* in reaction to the same event, that is *part of the cultural fabric* of the organization. The latter is clearly the result wanted by those trying to move their organizations toward TQM. They want the changes in their organizations to be lasting events.

The institutionalization process follows three phases. During the *acquisition* phase, people learn the desired new behavior. This phase is largely targeted by the planned organization change efforts described above. The *reinforcement* phase shapes the desired behavior into its final and enduring forms. Managers rely heavily on the organization's reward system for the motivational tools that let them shape behavior. Because nonprofit organizations often pay lower salaries and benefits than many private-sector organizations, their managers must use rewards creatively. The last phase, the *transmission* phase, is important for the long-term retention of the new behaviors. It socializes newcomers to the behaviors needed by Total Quality Management.

Institutionalization features two different but related levels of learning. The first focuses on the individual. People adopt the new behavior because they can easily do it or because it yields some specific results. If a person also values those results, he or she is highly likely to adopt the desired behavior.

The second level of learning is at the level of the whole organization. Here, the learning of the new behavior spreads from one or a few individuals to the behavior of the whole organization.

Three conditions must be present before learning can move from individuals to the entire organization. First, individuals must perceive others acting the new behavior. Second, they must share the belief that the new behavior is more right than the old. Third, they must believe that management will reward the new behavior. Those three conditions have clear implications for management actions to institutionalize TQM.

The physical setting of the organization must help social interaction and allow high visibility of others' behavior. Physical settings that do not let people see each other's behavior constrain institutionalization. The organization's communication system can overcome physical constraints. Nonprofit organizations with geographically dispersed locations, for example, can send information about TQM activities at one location to all others.

The degree of congruence between the new behavior and valued old behavior affects the shared belief that the new behavior is more right than the old. Cohesive groups and their norms play a role here. If those norms closely accord with the desired behavior, institutionalization happens fast. If they do not closely accord, the norms can act as a source of resistance to the change. Cohesive groups can strongly affect the adoption of behavior consistent with TQM. Nonprofit organization managers should analyze the norms of cohesive groups in their organizations to see whether they are in accord with or opposed to Total Quality Management.

The result of the institutionalization process is the persistence of the new behavior. An organization's socialization process and its reward system play key roles in reaching this result. The socialization process passes the new behaviors on to successive generations of employees. The reward system lets managers shape the behavior of newcomers and maintain the behavior of veterans. Both are major tools for institutionalizing TQM in any organization.

3.4 LEADERSHIP AND MANAGEMENT ROLES

(a) ARE LEADERSHIP AND MANAGEMENT THE SAME? This final section of the chapter discusses two important processes for moving an organization toward TQM. The two processes, leadership and management, play different, important, and complementary roles in that activity. (See also Chap. 5.)

Jennings (1960, 1974) long ago argued persuasively for a distinction between leadership and management in organizations. Scholars and historians had for centuries given special meaning to leadership. Managers did useful work for their organizations, but they did not play the same role as leaders. A summary of Jennings's view says: Leaders change human systems, managers maintain and control them.

This section builds on Jennings's arguments. It shows the key roles leaders and managers play at different points in an organization's move toward TQM.

(b) LEADERSHIP: MOVING TOWARD TOTAL QUALITY MANAGEMENT Earlier sections of this chapter described moving toward TQM as a major organization change for many organizations. Because of the amount of change normally required, leaders and leadership play major roles in the change process. Leaders can emerge at any level in a nonprofit organization, but the senior executive position of the organization is a key level. Whatever this person's title—executive director or manager—the role the person plays is one of a leader and is pivotal in successful moves toward TQM.

Jennings (1960, 1974) offered the "leadership mystique" as a way of viewing leadership. He identified the leadership mystique after many years of observing executives who had made major changes in their organizations. His research pointed consistently to three dimensions of leadership: a sense of mission, a capacity for power, and a will to survive and persevere.

A sense of mission is a vision of a future state for the organization. Leaders passionately hold to their visions. They energetically try to instill their visions in others around them, to move all of them forward toward the vision.

A capacity for power lets the leader get and use the power he or she needs to reach the mission and realize the vision. Such power can come from any source. Some power bases are in the leader as qualities of charisma and expert knowledge. Other bases are in the leader's organizational position (French and Raven, 1959). The latter bases of power can be the authority of a position and the right to reward or sanction behavior.

The will to survive and persevere expresses both the passionate pursuit of a vision and the intense personal sacrifice that often goes with that pursuit. In Jennings's words, it is ". . . a will to survive and persevere against a discourteous world of sometimes total opposition" (Jennings, 1974, p. 391). The will to survive and persevere clearly plays an important role in facing resistance to organization change.

Bass's transformational leadership theory offers a complementary view to that of Jennings (Avolio and Bass, 1987; Bass, 1985, 1990). This view of leadership features the three dimensions of charisma, individualized consideration, and intellectual stimulation.

Charismatic leaders excite their followers with a new vision of the future for the organization. Such leaders inspire others to transcend their self-interest and work well beyond their expectations of what they can do. Charismatic leaders have the personal qualities of high self-esteem and self-confidence.

Individualized consideration refers to the leader's high commitment to the development of subordinates, based on each person's unique combination of qualities, skills, and abilities. Such leaders thoroughly know their subordinates' abilities, needs, and desires. The leaders delegate decision-making authority and assign tasks that extend the subordinate beyond his or her current level. They also develop a mentoring relationship with their followers. This relationship lets the leader show everyone around the leader the type of job performance he or she expects.

Intellectual stimulation is the ability to build awareness of solutions to problems among subordinates and to change their beliefs about the future direction of the organization. This attribute of a transformational leader comes from brilliance and unequaled technical ability. Such leaders' use of intellectual stimulation includes managing images and symbols that show the leaders' vision of the future. Intellectual stimulation is more than stimulating thinking. It includes an emotional element that propels followers toward understanding their role in reaching the desired end-state the leaders envision.

Leaders, with the many qualities just described, play key roles in moving an organization from where it is now to a quality-based culture. Leaders have the vision, capacity, and perseverance to imbue followers with the pressing need to change to TQM thinking. They can show why the new vision is better than the old. They can garner the power needed to cause change. They have the charisma to attract a following. They have such thorough understanding of those who work for them that they can communicate how a quality-based organization will create future challenges that will be personally satisfying. Their intellectual stimulation ability lets them excite organization members to embrace quality thinking.

Managers play a critical role as well. Theirs is not usually a large role during the process of organization change, but their role increases when the organization is ready to institutionalize Total Quality Management.

(c) MANAGEMENT: INSTITUTIONALIZING TOTAL QUALITY MANAGEMENT Earlier, some key qualities of institutionalizing a new organization culture were discussed. The result of institutionalization is persistence of new behavior and transmission of the behavior to new members of the organization. Achieving persistence of behavior requires using the organization's reward system to reward or sanction behavior. Transmission of behavior requires developing and managing socialization processes within the organization. Both aspects of institutionalization are especially well-suited to roles for people who are managers but who may not be leaders (Bass, 1985).

Managers steer, guide, and direct organizations. They have as active a role in organization affairs as do leaders, but they focus on guiding an established system, not creating or changing it (Jennings, 1960, 1974). Managers can steer a quality-oriented organization with unswerving focus on the client, flexibility, and continuous improvement. A TQM-based culture asks managers to delegate decision-making authority and manage a decentralized organization. Such managers decentralize by using self-managing work teams at all levels (Lawler, 1990, 1991). Those teams are authorized to react to clients' needs and bring to TQM-based organizations the hallmark of response flexibility.

Managers actively use the organization's reward system to shape and guide behavior. They develop socialization processes that transmit the quality-based culture's values to all newcomers. Managers know they must build commitment to the organization's values among new hires—and build it fast—if there is to be no breakdown in their quality-oriented culture.

Everything just stated about managers in a TQM organization contributes to what managers should do to institutionalize and widely spread the values of their cultures. When done properly, managers' role has the same challenge and importance in institutionalizing TQM as does that of leaders.

SOURCES AND SUGGESTED REFERENCES

Albanese, R. 1970. "Overcoming Resistance to Stability." *Business Horizons, 13:* 35–42.

Allen, R. F., and Kraft, C. 1984. "Transformations That Last: A Cultural Approach." In J. D. Adams (Ed.), *Transforming Work: A Collection of Organizational Transformation Readings* (pp. 36–54). Alexandria, VA: Miles River Press.

Argyris, C. 1990. *Overcoming Organizational Defenses: Facilitating Organizational Learning.* Boston: Allyn & Bacon.

Avolio, B. J., and Bass, B. M. 1987. "Transformational Leadership, Charisma and Beyond." In J. G. Hunt, B. R. Baglia, H. P. Dachler, and C. A. Schriesheim (Eds.), *Emerging Leadership Vistas* (pp. 29–49. Lexington, MA: Lexington Books.

Barczak, G., Smith, C., and Wilemon, D. 1987. "Managing Large-Scale Organizational Change." *Organizational Dynamics, 16:* 23–35.

Bass, B. M. 1985. *Leadership and Performance Beyond Expectations* (pp. 43–43). New York: Free Press.

———. 1990. "From Transactional to Transformational Leadership: Learning to Share the Vision." *Organizational Dynamics, 18:* 19–31.

Beckhard, R., and Harris, R. T. 1987. *Organizational Transitions: Managing Complex Change.* Reading, MA: Addison-Wesley.

Beer, M., and Walton, A. E. 1987. "Organization Change and Development." In M. R. Rosenzweig and L. W. Porter (Eds.), *Annual Review of Psychology: Vol. 38* (pp. 339–367). Palo Alto, CA: Annual Reviews.

Burke, W. W. 1987. *Organization Development: A Normative View.* Reading, MA: Addison-Wesley.

Child, P., Diederichs, R., Sanders, F., and Wisniowski, S. 1991. "SMR Forum: The Management of Complexity." *Sloan Management Review, 33:* 73–80.

Chin, R., and Benne, K. D. 1969. "General Strategies for Effecting Changes in Human Systems." In W. G. Bennis, K. D. Benne, R. Chin, and K. E. Corey (Eds.), *The Planning of Change,* 3rd ed. (pp. 22–45). New York: Holt, Rinehart and Winston.

Connor, P. E., and Lake, L. K. 1988. *Managing Organizational Change.* New York: Praeger.

Deal, T. E., and Kennedy, A. A. 1982. *Corporate Cultures: The Rites and Rituals of Corporate Life.* Reading, MA: Addison-Wesley.

Drucker, P. F. 1989. "What Business Can Learn from Nonprofits." *Harvard Business Review* (July–August), *67*(4): 88–93.

———. 1990. *Managing the Nonprofit Organization.* New York: Harper Collins.

French, J., and Raven, B. 1959. "The Bases of Social Power." In D. Cartwright (Ed.), *Studies in Social Power* (pp. 150–167). Ann Arbor, MI: Institute for Social Research.

Garvin, D. A. 1988. *Managing Quality: The Strategic and Competitive Edge.* New York: Free Press.

Goodman, P. S., Bazerman, M., and Conlon, E. 1984. "Institutionalization of Planned Organizational Change." In B. M. Staw and L. L. Cummings (Eds.), *Research in Organizational Behavior: Vol. 2* (pp. 215–246). Greenwich, CT: JAI Press.

Greiner, L. E. 1967. "Patterns of Organization Change." *Harvard Business Review, 45:* 119–122, 125–130.

Hickman, C. R., and Sliva, M. A. 1984. *Creating Excellence: Managing Corporate Culture, Strategy, and Change in the New Age.* New York: New American Library.

Jennings, E. E. 1960. *An Anatomy of Leadership.* New York: Harper & Row.

———. 1974. "On Rediscovering the Leader." In J. W. McGuire (Ed.), *Contemporary Management: Issues and Viewpoints* (pp. 390–396). Englewood Cliffs, NJ: Prentice-Hall.

Klein, D. 1976. "Some Notes on the Dynamics of Resistance to Change: The Defender Role." In W. G. Bennis, K. D. Benne, R. Chin, and K. E. Corey (Eds.), *The Planning of Change,* 3rd ed. (pp. 117–124). New York: Holt, Rinehart and Winston.

Kotler, P., and Roberto, E. L. 1989. *Social Marketing: Strategies for Changing Public Behavior.* New York: Free Press.

Kotter, J. P., and Schlesinger, L. A. 1979. "Choosing Strategies for Change." *Harvard Business Review, 57:* 106–114.

Kupfer, A. 1988. "Managing Now for the 1990s." *Fortune,* September 26, pp. 44–47.

Lawler, E. E., III. 1990. "The New Plant Revolution Revisited." *Organizational Dynamics* (Autumn), 1990; 5–14.

———. 1991. "The New Plant Approach: A Second Generation Approach." *Organizational Dynamics* (Summer), 5–14.

Lawrence, P. R. 1954. "How to Deal with Resistance to Change." *Harvard Business Review* (May–June) *32:* 49–57.

Lewin, K. 1951. *Field Theory in Social Science.* New York: Harper & Row.

Lippitt, R., Watson, J., and Westley, B. 1958. *Dynamics of Planned Change.* New York: Harcourt, Brace.

Main, J. 1988. "The Winning Organization." *Fortune,* September 28, pp. 50–52, 56, 60.

Massarik, F. (Ed.). 1990. *Advances in Organization Development.* Norwood, NJ: Ablex Publishing Corp.

Nicoll, D. 1984. "Consulting to Organizational Transformations." In J. D. Adams (Ed.), *Transforming Work: A Collection of Organizational Transformation Readings* (pp. 157–169). Alexandria, VA: Miles River Press.

Peters, T. 1988. *Thriving on Chaos: Handbook for a Management Revolution.* New York: Harper & Row.

Rogers, E. M. 1971. *Communication of Innovations.* New York: Free Press.

Schein, E. H. 1985. *Organizational Culture and Leadership.* San Francisco: Jossey-Bass.

Scott, C. D., and Jaffe, D. T. 1989. *Managing Organizational Change: A Practical Guide for Managers.* Los Altos, CA: Crisp Publications.

Simons, R., Miller, L. F., and Lengsfelder, P. 1984. *Nonprofit Piggy Goes to Market.* Denver, CO: Children's Museum of Denver.

Vaill, P. B. 1989. *Managing as a Performing Art: New Ideas for a World of Chaotic Change.* San Francisco: Jossey-Bass.

Van Maanen, J., and Schein, E. H. 1979. "Toward a Theory of Organizational Socialization." In L. L. Cummings and B. M. Staw (Eds.), *Research in Organizational Behavior: Vol. 1* (p. 210). Greenwich, CT: JAI Press.

Wilkins, A. L. 1983. "The Culture Audit: A Tool for Understanding Organizations." *Sloan Management Review, 25:* 24–38.

Wilkins, A. L., and Bristow, N. J. 1987. "For Successful Organizational Culture, Honor Your Past." *Academy of Management Executives, 1:* 221–229.

CHAPTER FOUR

Problem Solving with Information and Analysis

Gay Lumsden
Donald Lumsden
Kean College of New Jersey

CONTENTS

4.1   DEVELOPING DATA FOR DECISIONS

(a) QUALITY DECISIONS AND THE NEED FOR INFORMATION   People who make quality decisions proceed on three premises. First, they must have facts to make good management decisions. Second, problems are solved at all levels of an organization and by combinations of people and teams, not unilaterally. Third, information is a source of power and of empowerment for people and for quality.

(i) Management by fact   It's a human trait to hold beliefs on the basis of anecdote, observation, and wishful thinking, but these do not constitute the information we use in fact-based decision making. W. Edwards Deming built the quality movement on the "need to base decisions as much as possible on accurate and timely data . . ." (Walton, 1986, p. 96). Constant improvement of quality requires constant information gathering and analysis about all aspects of the organization—suppliers, customers or clients, processes of production and delivery, and end products, to name but a few.

This is particularly true for nonprofit organizations, even though the concepts were originally developed in the corporate sector. In nonprofits, commonly organized for furthering the interests of a group of people or of a cause rather than for owners and profit, the "bottom line" is harder to read. The yearly report may reveal amounts of moneys acquired and spent and numbers of people served by a charitable organization, for example, but it will not measure processes, long-term benefits to the clients, or the satisfaction of volunteers. To understand these, all parts of the organization must continually gather and properly assess information and data through all stages of the processes.

(ii) Decision-making levels   In most nonprofit organizations, the boards of directors or trustees have enormous influence on management and direction. Depending on the size and complexity of the group, the board will provide advice and guidance to a chief administrative officer who directs a group of executive managers and volunteer leaders. The managers may direct middle managers, who in turn manage supervisors, who guide work teams and individual workers and, in many cases, numbers of service-providing volunteers.

Individuals and consultation.   At each of these levels, decisions are made. An individual may make them alone or in consultation with department chiefs or management teams. Each level has a range of formal and informal responsibilities and accountabilities.

It is very easy for people at the top to imagine that they have all of the important data and decision-making power. Wrong! History abounds with executives who made bad decisions—or no decisions—because they thought they knew it all or because their subordinates had "protected" them from critical information. Witness the *Challenger* disaster, where all the information was "in the computer!" In that instance, as in so many others, the vital information was little help when critical decisions should have been made.

Groups and teams. The importance of consultation and team problem solving to good decision making cannot be overemphasized. The greater the complexity of the problem, the greater the importance of team communication.

Four factors indicate the extent to which decision makers need to work in a group. The more information that is necessary and the more dispersed it is among various sources; the more complex the task; the more complicated the alternative paths to reach it; finally, the more obstacles in the path, the more group consultation will contribute to a better decision (Hirokawa, 1990, pp. 190–204).

It's easy to see why a team of people, working closely together, can handle the complexities of information and task better than an individual working alone. The small group can be seen as an information-processing system (Wilson and Hanna, 1990, p. 22). The members of the group provide increased quantity and variety of input. The skills and behaviors they use to process their input apply a range of experience and background, including culture, gender, status, education, and skill far beyond what one individual could assert. The richer the fuel of the input and the more powerful the engine of the processes, the stronger the yield and the more creative the outputs.

The quality, the quantity, the timeliness, and the availability of data and their use in critical analysis determine whether a decision will be well-founded, and this is true throughout an organization. Where information is unavailable, people are disempowered, problems are compounded, and decisions are poor. We are all frustrated regularly by some bureaucrats. Uninformed and alienated, they too often use noncooperation, or even sabotage, to assert their power through petty, but damaging, decisions or inaction.

(iii) Power in information At individual and at organizational levels, people need power. Power enables people to have some control in their lives, to affect the direction and consequences of their action. Human beings need that power.

There are many sources from which human beings draw their power—position and authority, personal credibility, expertise, and information. In purely practical terms, factual and solid information, when used well, gives people the ability to prevent mistakes and enables good decisions. At a more abstract level, information puts power into the hands of human beings, which is good news and bad news.

The bad news is twofold. First, information presents responsibility, and responsibility can be intimidating. Some people would prefer not to know too much; having information might cause them to see responsibilities they don't necessarily want to face or assume. People who operate on "What I don't know won't hurt me" may feel they have little control over their lives or their jobs; so what's the use in knowing?

On the other hand, some people who feel helpless may view information as a personal power source for controlling others, and they clutch their knowledge like the reins on a runaway horse. Such people, rather than give up an exhilarating bit of power, keep their subordinates and their superiors in the dark about facts that would help them make good decisions.

The extraordinarily good news is that these ills can be cured when information is shared openly. Like other forms of power, when information is shared, it multiplies the power of individuals and of the organization. Empowered people are informed people; they are energized people.

Information-empowered people have a stake in the gathering, analysis, and application of data at every level of their organization; they understand and participate in the vision of the organization; they know how their jobs impact on the fulfillment of that vision. Information becomes the lifeblood flowing through every organ of the body and making it grow.

(b) PRINCIPLES FOR GATHERING AND USING INFORMATION   Gathering and using information should be an ongoing process that is open to and participated in by all aspects of an organization. A few guidelines help to keep this process in perspective.

(i) All data are viewed as positive   There is no such thing as "bad news." No matter how disappointing the results may be from a survey of, say, client satisfaction, they are not bad news if they are useful for improving services.

A department in a state college, for example, found that its majors rated faculty advisement as "average." The department, which considered its involvement with students superior, was distressed. Follow-up surveys revealed that students were extremely happy with academic advisement, but they wanted more specific career advice than academic departments were geared to provide. The "bad news" provided the insight and impetus to create a "good news" advising program.

(ii) Information gathering is a cybernetic process   It is a process of constant feedback and adjustment. Like a thermostat—as opposed to a thermometer, which only records information—it uses the data to keep the system stable and in balance. More than that, it develops and improves the system.

A quality organization gathers data for formative rather than summative evaluation. It uses information to create approaches to constant improvement and development. Such data should be developmental in design and purpose. Unfortunately, our society typically has relied on summative evaluation; research has focused exclusively on deciding whether what has been produced is satisfactory. With a summative, terminal approach, when the report is issued, the research is over. Heads may roll, bonuses and promotions may be issued, and business goes back "as usual."

The Japanese principle of "*Kaizen,*" now being emulated in the United States, approaches data gathering as part of a cybernetic, developmental process of constant improvement. The assumption is that good can only get better with the right data and process.

(iii) Data and their consequences must be refinable   The process of building quality is one of constant questioning, learning, and changing. Every bit of information can be followed up, refined, and applied to the constant development of quality.

In a convalescent home, for example, a study revealed that meals met all levels of nutritional requirements. Further, they were appropriately prescribed for each patient's particular needs. The nutritionist was doing his or her job. The data, however, needed refinement and further investigation. Observers noted that many people simply could not or did not eat their food; it was poorly prepared, flavorless, unappetizing, cold.

To improve quality in this organization, data should have included surveys and interviews with the patients, the chefs and kitchen staff, and suppliers. The information should have been refined through creating flowcharts of the food provision process to determine what affected the condition of the food between its preparation and service. With such full information, something could have been done to make the food edible as well as nutritionally acceptable.

(iv) Information is attainable and accessible Useful data must be open, at least to those in the organization. Problems may go unrecognized—and unsolved—until they become impossible. If people don't know that a problem exists and they don't have the information to solve it, it can escalate into a monster.

One nonprofit organization was so horrified at some survey data that it "buried" the information in a file. Not only were the data excluded from a report, they also were not shared within the institution. They could have been used to solve a problem and to improve quality, but the personnel who needed to know them were disempowered and the problem continued to increase.

(v) Information must be purposeful and applicable In a quality organization, the whole point is to get information that can be used to make the organization work better. Information gathering, therefore, should start with pointed, clear questions; it should get answers that solve problems and help make decisions that advance the organization's goals of quality.

Some data gathering becomes nothing more than a fishing expedition. Out of excessive enthusiasm or inadequate planning, a survey gathers a truckload of irrelevant information. If someone has wallpapered a wall with computer printouts and says, "Hmm. We've got a lot of interesting data here!" the question ought to be, "Interesting to whom, in what context, and to what end?"

(c) CRITERIA FOR USEFUL DATA Useful information has specific qualities. The manner in which information is gathered, the type of information collected, its applicability, and its timeliness need to be considered to ensure its utility.

(i) Data must be gathered systematically If data are episodic, that is, gathered only on occasion and in relation to one event or another, they will not provide adequate information about the development and process of an issue. Systematically gathered data allow decision makers to make comparisons, to see development, to chart processes, to plan.

Systematic information collection requires planning ahead, using a repeatable process, and gathering data regularly. An organization might want to see how participants reacted to public workshops on political issues. If it does an ad hoc response form for one or two presentations, the information it gets will show no more than what participants thought of isolated instances; it will be limited in what it shows about the workshops program. If, however, the organization designs its assessment methods well in advance, tests and revises them, and then uses them systematically for a series of workshops, the information becomes useful for improving the service.

(ii) Data must be user-friendly Stacks and stacks of printouts rarely mean much to people who need the information. Even complex statistical studies can be converted into comprehensible language and easily understood graphs and visuals for decision makers' use.

(iii) Data must be reliable   Although there are statistical tests of reliability for studies that use quantitative data ("numbers studies"), these tests in effect simply measure the extent to which the data would be the same if the same studies were repeated. They measure consistency, in other words. Much information is nonstatistical but needs to be reliable, and people can apply rational tests of reliability that are, themselves, user-friendly.

To be reliable, information should come from appropriate sources; that is, it should be primary, credible, competent, and objective. It also should be user-generated and applied, and it should be consistent.

Primary sources are first sources rather than reported or hearsay (secondary) sources. If an organization wants to know whether a client is happy, it should ask the client. The source also must be credible: Is he or she trustworthy? Competent in the area? Is the source objective or is there a bias or vested interest behind his or her information?

It's also best if information is user-generated and applied. If the director of volunteers surveys his or her team and discovers that people want more direction, then the director can create a plan to fill that need. If someone else gathers the same information, there will be three problems. The survey likely will not touch the most pertinent issues because the outsider will not know what they are; the surveyor will not have the necessary knowledge base to analyze the information reliably; and, perhaps most importantly, the director and the team will have been detached from the process and hence will be disempowered and unmotivated to change.

(iv) Interpretations of information must be valid   Validity measures logical relationships between the question and the data and between the data and the conclusion drawn from it. In data gathering, validity can be judged in terms of goals, context, and the work to be done.

Questions to ask to test validity of information include: Does the information answer questions relating to goals? Is the language of questions pointed specifically, clearly, and unambiguously to the desired information? Is the connection between goals and questions sensible and clear? Are the conclusions reasonable and consistent? Are there factors that contradict either the information or the application of it?

For example, an organization for helping underprivileged children wants to know what appeals to present in magazine ads targeted at middle-class Americans. The organization surveys readers of its own publication to identify their values. The question "What are middle-class American values?" is not answered by their survey, because their readers' values may not be representative of the broader spectrum of the middle class. If the organization tries to apply the survey results to the writing of appeals, the ads will be based on invalid information and conclusions. Appeals based on this survey would only have validity targeted at the organization's own members or at very similar groups.

(v) Data must be timely   Timely means at the right time and on time. To be timely, the right questions must be asked at the moment when the issues are important and relevant. The results must then be analyzed and applied in time to accomplish the goals. This is another reason why quality requires constant, systematic, ongoing, instrumental information gathering that involves all parties in the process.

At one organization, research was done to evaluate a new program. That was fine, but the desire to compare the new program to an old one was frustrated. The old one simply had not been evaluated on the questions of interest in the new one. Some inferences could be made on related information, but they were very loose and inconclusive. That looseness could have cost the organization some crucial funding. Now the program is systematically studied and quality is constantly upgraded.

Exhibit 4.1 gives a checklist for evaluating the usefulness of data.

(d) TYPES OF INFORMATION It is tempting to view information purely as hard facts, but it's much more than that. Information includes quantitative data, to be sure, but it also includes qualitative and personal information.

(i) Quantitative information Quantitative information is data viewed in terms of numbers; those numbers may be actual counts (how many, how often, to what extent) or ratings of people's opinions, values, or attitudes. Usually, statistical tests are applied to determine the probability of an occurrence. Although a "quantitative" study often measures some quality, it doesn't probe qualities or attributes in depth.

For example, an organization has subjects rate their attitudes toward an issue before and after seeing a television documentary; the ratings are tested statistically to determine the probability that the subjects' attitude changes were caused by seeing the documentary. The study provides information about the extent and probability of attitude change, but that's all.

The advantages in quantitative data are that it is "hard": it's easy to work with, it's clear, and it doesn't muddy up the issues with opinion and extraneous information. The disadvantages are that it also can be simplistic, it can exclude important information, and it can be consciously or unconsciously distorted. After all, its interpretation still relies on human intellect, intuition, and ethics.

Many people are intimidated by quantitative data. Although statistics certainly can be sophisticated, complicated, dubious, or frightening, many treatments are simple, easy to use, and easy to interpret. When they are confusing, it's time to get a knowledgeable consultant to help out.

Exhibit 4.1. Checklist of criteria for useful data.

---

1. Data must be gathered systematically.
2. Data must be user-friendly.
3. Data must be reliable.
   —Are the sources primary, credible, competent, and objective?
   —Are the data user-generated and applied?
   —Are the data consistent?
4. Interpretations of information must be valid.
   —Does the information answer questions relating to goals?
   —Is the language of questions pointed specifically, clearly, and unambiguously to the desired information?
   —Is the connection between goals and questions sensible and clear?
   —Are the conclusions reasonable and consistent? Are there factors that contradict either the information or the application of it?
5. Data must be timely.
   —Are the right questions asked when the issues are important?
   —Are the results analyzed and applied in time to be useful?

(ii) Qualitative information Qualitative information refers to that which focuses more specifically on describing and analyzing the qualities of a situation. It's likely to rely more on human analysis and intuition than on statistics.

Qualitative methodologies include such approaches as case studies, anecdotal reports, and interviews, as well as critical analyses of documents or situations. In qualitative study, the point is to find insights that numbers cannot reveal. Its advantage is that it permits insightful, probing analysis and in-depth investigation; its disadvantages are that it can be limited in the numbers of cases it studies, limited to human intuition, and ill-defined. It's easy to overgeneralize from a few anecdotes and case studies or to bring personal biases to their interpretation. Ideally, qualitative and quantitative research work together to provide a more complete picture.

If an organization wanted to know how best to help an American Indian tribe with educating its members, for example, a quantitative study could reveal how many people on the reservation attended what schools and what level of education they have achieved. Other quantitative studies could reveal something about attitudes, socioeconomic conditions, and even cultural predispositions. (See Exhibit 4.2.)

To understand the situation fully, the organization would need to see these data in the context of qualitative information, through case studies; interviews with tribal members and educators; historical studies of events, processes, and people, through research

Exhibit 4.2.   Sample grid: information sources needed to design an effective program for American Indian (AI) educational opportunity.

Sources	Systems	Suppliers	Customers
Quantitative:			
Public records, tribal records	Numbers of schools, tribal schools, and colleges near	Numbers of AI teachers, non-AI teachers, AI support, non-AI support, AI administrators, non-AI administrators	Numbers and percentages attending elementary school, middle school, high school, college, postgraduate programs; graduating at each level
School assessment	School ratings (each school)	Teacher ratings (teachers, groups)	
Qualitative:			
Surveys and interviews: Personnel, teachers, students, families, tribal elders	School quality, educational process, orientation to helping students	Teaching quality, teacher preparation, teaching styles	Student achievements, student motivation, learning styles, distractions, life-styles, tribal traditions
Analysis: Stories, documents			
Legal code Federal Regulations	Legal system, effectiveness of Fed. Bureau of Indian Affairs		
Personal:			
Focus groups, community forums	Expert ideas, opinions, suggestions	Teacher ideas, opinions, suggestions	AI community ideas, opinions, feelings, suggestions

of legal and tribal documents; and much more. Even then, interpreting all these data becomes a very human, personal process.

(iii) Personal information Personal information is brought into the analyses of qualitative and quantitative data by individuals and, frequently, in team discussions or focus groups. It includes individual knowledge of facts; personal values, attitudes, and opinions; human intuition; insight; and skills in analysis and problem solving.

The disadvantages of personal information are that it, too, relies on human intellect and communication skill, and that discussion of it is time-consuming. Its advantage is that these sources of information feed the process through which individuals synthesize, create, and recreate the information and the analysis indispensable to a quality organization.

Exhibit 4.3 identifies the advantages and disadvantages of quantitative, qualitative, and personal information, using the format of a T-chart.

(e) SOURCES OF INFORMATION The specific sources of information are manifold, so it is easy to overlook possibilities. In gathering data, no possibility should be disregarded.

(i) Production reports Production reports are a typical source for departmental or organizational evaluation. Generally, they record quantities produced, funds raised, numbers of clients served, quantities of services designed or rendered, and so on. The numbers are useful for cost–benefit analyses and bottom-line justification.

Exhibit 4.3. Sample T-chart: Advantages and disadvantages of kinds of information.

	Advantages	Disadvantages
Quantitative Information Numbers, percentages, frequencies, surveys, questionnaires, lab studies.	Statistical analysis of probability provides general picture, "hard" data.	Statistics may be confusing or misleading; may not picture accurately.
	Provides "clean," neat method for studying abstract issues.	With wrong sample, it may not mean what it appears to mean.
	Can get information from large numbers of people.	Studies may lack validity for application.
Qualitative Information Anecdotal reports, case studies, interviews, critical analysis: documents, stories, myths, folklore, letters.	Allows probing, deep analysis of individual cases, sensitivity to specific issues. Provides a way of using insight to find truths.	Deals with limited samples of people or events; can't be generalized too far.
Personal Information Individual or group analysis, focus groups.	Provides a way for ideas, facts, opinions, feelings, and intuition to illuminate other data.	Can be biased, inaccurate, too absolute, or too vague.
	Can enrich discussion as people hear and build on others' ideas.	Can dominate other data, lead to decisions on the limited knowledge of individuals.

(ii) Financial reports   Financial reports provide bottom-line information that can help to assess the budget expenditures, cost accounting, economic processes, priorities, and effectiveness of the organization. These, too, should be seen in terms of reliability, validity, and consistency, and should be subjected to qualitative analysis.

(iii) Safety records   Safety records can reveal a lot about conditions, workers' attitudes, and processes. Usually, such records are of numbers and kinds of accidents, although studies can and should include questions about why, how, where, when, and under what conditions accidents occur, as well as how they are recorded and by whom.

(iv) Employee performance   Employee performance is, for individuals in an organization, frequently a critical source of information. Performance evaluations contain both quantitative and qualitative data, usually involving the supervisor's assessment and sometimes including the employee's self-assessment of performance.

Although performance evaluations often are summative, used exclusively for promotion and pay processes, they ought not to be. Employee performance, properly studied and used, ought to be developmental; the study can provide information that will help individuals and the organization to develop and improve.

(v) Employee studies   Employee studies can examine aspects of employees' experiences not included in the specifics of performance, safety, or production. They can look at people's perceptions of the organizational culture; how communication with superiors, peers, and subordinates is working for them; how they would like to improve working conditions, relationships, and products. Quality organizations look to their employees for ideas and insights, and they use and reward employees' suggestions.

(vi) Quality studies   Quality studies examine not only "how many" are served or produced, but "how well." They look at the actual quality of elements in the process or the product. A department would look at the quality of each step of its process as well as at the outcome.

For example, an environmental task force could examine the qualifications and accomplishments of its human resources, could observe and evaluate the task force's teamwork, could measure and evaluate the quality and effectiveness of media relations, and could examine not only the amount but also the quality of legislation the task force has influenced. Such information serves to evaluate final effectiveness and to help improve the process at each step.

(vii) Customers   Internal and external customers are important sources of information. Internal customers (or clients) are individuals, teams, or departments within the organization who are served by other in-house units. The public relations department, for example, is a client of the legal department, in that the lawyers tell the public relations people when and how an issue might have legal implications. In this instance, the public relations department can provide important information to the legal department about the promptness, clarity, and effectiveness with which it is being served.

External customers (or clients), those to whom the product or the service is delivered, should be a constant source of information to the organization. Are their expectations being met? Is the process they are experiencing comfortable, satisfactory, timely, and effective? Do they have ideas that could help the organization offer new or better products or services?

Exhibit 4.4.   Checklist of sources of information.

1. Production reports
2. Financial reports
3. Safety records
4. Employee performance appraisals
5. Employee studies
6. Quality studies
7. Customers, internal and external
8. Suppliers, internal and external
9. Consultants, internal and external
10. Studies of competitors

Many organizations today have special programs geared to elicit and act on ideas from users of their products or services. Who would be in a better position to see the possibilities?

(viii) Suppliers   Internal and external suppliers are as important as customers. The internal supplier, like the internal client, interacts within the organization. The duplicating room, as a supplier of copies, may have important information about the process through which it receives material from other departments (its clients or customers), and its personnel may have innovative ideas about how to improve the process.

(ix) Consultants   Consultants also are both internal and external; by the very nature of their services, they offer constant information to the organization. A range of departments, from legal to media, act as consultants to other departments in an organization. Indeed, any department may become a consultant when its reports or information become useful to some other area of the organization. As soon as it shares those data, it is in a position to consult with another area. Perhaps if every department viewed every other department as a possible consultant, the entire quality process would be improved.

(x) Studies of competitors   Studies of competitors or of similar organizations can provide important data about resources, services, funding, internal and external processes, and achievement of client satisfaction. If another organization is getting more funding, or more contributions, or is serving more clients with greater satisfaction, there are reasons and its "competitors" need to know both the facts and the reasons.

Exhibit 4.4 offers a checklist of the sources of information an organization uses.

4.2   ANALYZING AND APPLYING DATA FOR DECISIONS

Nobel prize winner Herbert A. Simon sees decision making as involving four interrelated parts of a process: intelligence, design, choice, and review (Simon, 1977). *Intelligence* is the state in which the need for a decision is recognized and information is gathered and analyzed; *design* is the period of identifying and analyzing possible solutions and decisions; *choice* is the process of selection; and *review* is the process of looping back, assessing the effectiveness of the decision, and identifying needs for modification or change.

These four categories will provide a model for the following discussions of the analysis and application of data. It's important to note, however, that this is not a purely linear model; although an individual or a team may engage in these activities as sequential steps, there also may be considerable overlapping and reversing as the decision approaches.

(a) INFORMATION AND ANALYSIS (INTELLIGENCE)   Gathering and analyzing information requires decisions about what to gather and how to present it in its most useful format.

(i) Information gathering as intelligence   People at all levels of the organization should constantly be involved in information gathering. In addition to the available pool of information, however, departments or outside consultants may go to any of the sources described in the previous section for the information needed to make a specific decision on a given problem. As the initial processes of problem-examination occur, new needs for information may instigate new research.

(ii) Organizing, displaying, and communicating information   It is essential to make information "user-friendly" so that people can work with it. The audience may be one person or many. Information for individual decision makers may be provided through a written report; for teams, it may be seen on overhead transparencies or flip charts. Later, decisions may be communicated by report or presentation to larger groups within or outside of the organization. For all of these information users, presentation makes the difference.

Visual messages can have great power. What is not understood from words may be comprehended from visual images. Proper presentation of information uses the viewers' senses more completely by giving both aural and visual stimuli. It keeps individuals' attention and focus on the information, and it eliminates extraneous information by keeping the data visible, brief, and clear. Whether the data are in a printed report, on overhead transparencies, or on a flip chart, small increments of information should be presented in large, easy-to-see, easy-to-read figures that vividly illustrate the necessary data.

There are two general categories of information display for problem solving and decision making. One category represents facts or conditions and the other facilitates analysis.

Ways to present facts or conditions include line or bar graphs, scatter diagrams, matrices, and grids. (See *graphic tools* in the Glossary.) These presentations are familiar territory and easy to read for almost anyone; because they enable the viewer literally to see the data, they make them vivid, clear, and memorable.

Exhibit 4.5 is a checklist of the criteria for creating an effective visual presentation.

A line graph displays the interaction between two things. Exhibit 4.6 is an example of a line graph; it illustrates the average number of clients served each day of the workweek. The numbers ascend on the vertical side of the graph, and the weekdays are indicated along the horizontal line. The points at which the number of clients served intersects with the days of the week are connected, and the result is a line that exhibits changes or trends.

Exhibit 4.5.   Checklist of criteria for presenting information visually.

1. Are the data clearly presented?
2. Is the presentation vivid and easy to read?
3. Are the data easily understood?
4. Are the data memorable?
5. Is the method of display (graph, chart, diagram) the best one for the data?

A bar graph is a different way of visualizing relationships; bars are drawn vertically or horizontally to demonstrate distinctions between units of time or categories. In Exhibit 4.7, a bar graph shows how funds raised by an organization in each quarter compare over each of four years; the Quarter 1 bars show that $35,000 was raised in 1989; $44,000 in 1990; $48,000 in 1991; and $50,000 in 1992. A bar graph can illustrate any comparisons, from numbers of minority students retained in different programs in a college, to quantities of cosmetics used by people in different economic classes.

A histogram, a particular variety of a bar graph, exhibits frequencies of occurrences.

A scatter diagram also shows relationships, once again by plotting the occurrence of one variable against another variable. In this instance, the plot is not marked with a line or bars, but stands by itself; the scattering or clustering of intersections shows the trends of the data.

Matrices and grids are extremely helpful. They provide the benefit of showing information in spatial relationships, a powerful aid both to understanding and to memory. A matrix may be computer-generated (via a "spread-sheet program" such as Lotus 1-2-3).

A grid can be handmade, to allow decision makers to logically organize information that might derive from various sources. A grid is set up so that variables that interrelate are labeled across the horizontal (top) and down the vertical (left side); each cell of the grid is filled with the relevant interacting information.

Earlier in this chapter, Exhibit 4.2 demonstrated, using an informational grid, the categories of data that an organization would have to see in interactive relationships

Exhibit 4.6.   Average number of clients per weekday.

Ave. No. Served

Weekday

March through July

Exhibit 4.7.   **Example of bar graph.**

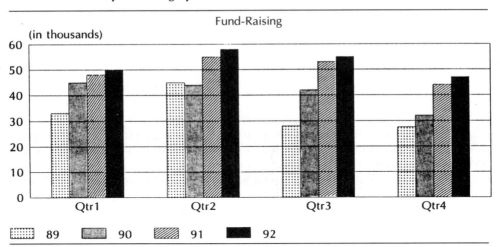

before it could make a decision on how to help an American Indian tribe create educational programs for its members. Filling in the grid would help the organization's team decide what information was needed, how to get it, and how to use it.

Ways to present information for analysis include checklists, flowcharts, Pareto charts, fish-bone diagrams, and T-charts. Each of these helps people to visualize components or processes in solving a problem and making decisions. Once again, the visualization process aids understanding, spurs insight, and aids memory.

Checklists are like grocery lists in several ways. They need to be generated by the people who are using them; somebody else's checklist may exclude important items. They need to be as complete as possible, and they need to be reworked into logical categories for further analysis. (A matrix can be helpful here.) In the process of analyzing and organizing the list, people begin to "see" things they didn't see before.

The checklists exhibited throughout this chapter might have started out by brainstorming possible points; those points became more useful when they were divided into sequential categories that could be "checked off" as a team worked through a problem.

The human tendency is to have faith in memory; people expect to retain and recall items as needed. Aids to recall are essential if the task is important. No matter how many previous times a flight crew has flown a particular type of aircraft, they are expected to use the checklist before each flight. History records a few fateful times when crews did not.

Flowcharts map out a process by showing yes/no alternatives for each decision point. Like checklists, they need to be complete and worked through step-by-step for comprehension and insight. Exhibit 4.19, at the end of this chapter, is a flowchart for tracking the decision-making process.

Pareto charts use graphing specifically to get a visual "fix" on what is important and what is not. If a manager wanted to know what events in the organization might be affecting absentee rates, for example, she or he might set up a Pareto chart via a bar graph that would show numbers of absences, say, following a holiday; numbers of absences following an organizational policy change; numbers of absences concurrent with supervisor vacations or leaves; and so on. The graph would demonstrate which issues, if any, seemed to be most related to the absences.

Fish-bone diagrams map relationships among causes and effects. They are especially useful when a team is brainstorming multiple variables and sequences that lie behind a problem or problems. In Exhibit 4.8, a fish-bone diagram demonstrates some of the causes and effects that might surface in a medical clinic's need for better access.

T-charts also are frequently used during a brainstorming session or in a decision-making sequence because they provide visual help in "seeing" two sides to an issue. The top of the T is labeled with each of two alternative views—the pros and cons; the benefits and costs; and so on. A line extends to the bottom of the sheet, and each column is filled in as people identify the opposing ideas or the facts.

Exhibit 4.3, shown earlier, uses a variation of a T-chart to compare the advantages and disadvantages of different kinds of information. This comparison can help people both to visualize the distinctions and to choose the best type of study to get the information they need.

(b) PROCESS FOR PROBLEM SOLVING AND DECISION MAKING (DESIGN) Thinking through problems, even with good information, is complex. It involves identifying and defining the problems, establishing criteria for acceptable solutions, and making decisions.

This section uses examples that refer to the problem of a free clinic positioned on a corner, next to a stoplight, on a major street. Disabled clients face difficult access through a back street and a long driveway, and the clinic access team needs to decide what to do about it.

(i) Identifying and defining the problem At this early stage of the process, decision makers need to look carefully at what the problem is, what kinds of questions will be raised in resolving it, and how the problem can be described.

Three kinds of questions have to be resolved as analysis proceeds. These overlap and intertwine, but they all lead to the decision.

Exhibit 4.8. Sample fishbone diagram: Causes and effects of access problem at a medical clinic.

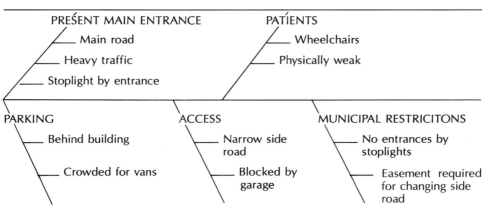

Policy questions are the broad questions that problem solving and decision making address: What is the problem? How can it be solved? What decision should be made?

The clinic faces these broad policy questions: What should the clinic do about wheelchair access? How should the clinic approach this issue? Embedded in the policy questions—and leading to their resolution—may be a dozen other questions that relate to facts or values.

Fact questions should be answerable by data: Is it true that . . .? What is the condition of . . .? It is essential, however, to bear in mind that most data are not incontrovertible. Most "facts" are probably true, or are true in a certain percentage of the cases, or are asserted to be true by experts; however, in most instances, even facts are debatable.

For the clinic, three fact questions might be: What is the law? How many disabled patients do we actually have? What physical conditions pertain to their access? The first question requires reference to the legal code; the second must have a definition and a count of the "disabled." The third requires a definition of "physical conditions," a flowchart of the steps that must be taken to get into the clinic, and a survey of patient opinions. As an inquiry proceeds, any number of questions of fact may surface and require answers.

Value questions are not so easy to answer, but they are important and easy to overlook—or, at a minimum, the answers are easy to assume. Such questions ask whether an idea or suggestion is moral, ethical, worthwhile, desirable. Often, people make assumptions about their own values, about others' values, or about the values underlying a policy decision.

As causes, effects, and solutions to a problem are probed, people need to ask such questions as: What is more important, A or B? What will be the effect, and will it be worth the cost? What cost is involved in human and social terms as well as economic terms? How will this affect the well-being of our constituency and of others?

Two obvious value questions for the clinic issue are: How important is the comfort of our disabled patients to us? How fair will a given decision be to everyone?

Analysis of fact and value questions proceeds throughout the entire process of intelligence, design, choice, and review. To clarify that sequence, in the intelligence stage of the clinic question, an individual might suggest that the two patients who have complained are chronic complainers and access is not a real problem. Another might suggest finding out how bad it really is (a question of fact) by asking other wheelchair patients to make a personal appraisal of the two patients' credibility. The question of value becomes: Would such an inquiry be ethical?

At the design stage of the decision-making process, a proposal might be made to station an assistant near the back entrance, to assist wheelchair patients. A question of fact might be: How much will that cost? A question of value might be: How will that action fulfill our priority for increasing patients' independence?

At the choice stage, a question of fact might be: How practical is widening the access road as compared to stationing an assistant? A question of value might be: How should we weigh the cost of each proposal against other ways of serving our patients?

Finally, at the review end of the process, a fact question might be: How effective is the implementation of our decision for increasing access? A value question might be: How worthwhile is this effort?

Describing the problem requires careful logical analysis. It should delve into the scope, the causes, the direct effects, and the tangential effects of the problem.

The scope of the problem refers to its breadth and depth. How many people, departments, etc., are affected by the problem? How frequently is this a problem? How serious is the problem? Questions like these will begin to get at scope analysis.

The causes often are multiple and are arrived at by hypothesizing and then testing them for validity. Analysis is facilitated with questions such as: Has the suggested cause happened every time before the effect, or are there exceptions? Did the suggested cause happen concurrently with other events? Could the other events be causes? Do other causes seem more probable? In looking for causes, decision makers are looking for something as close to fact as they can get; yet they have to settle for probable conclusions and, frequently, for multiple causes.

The clinic may have been spurred to action by two incidents in which wheelchair patients were blocked by cars along the narrow back road. Is the cause the narrowness of the road, its utilization by motorists, the skill of the patients in using their wheelchairs, the inattention of personnel, or some other variable? Some of these relationships are shown in Exhibit 4.8, the fish-bone diagram given earlier in this chapter.

There may be many effects and examining them involves looking at their quality as well as their quantity. Questions to ask might include: How extensive are these effects? Who is affected, to what extent, and under what circumstances? How serious are the effects? What is the harm of the effects? Are some of the effects desirable; if so, how do they weigh against the negative effects? Fact questions and value questions combine to infuse the issues.

Tangential effects are identified with similar questions by going outside of the immediate problem and looking at how the identified causes might be impacting on other issues, people, or events. Questions that help with this analysis could be: What else happens at the same time as the effect under study? Is the cause the same? How extensive, how serious, and how harmful are the tangential effects? Are some of the tangential effects positive or desirable?

Exhibit 4.9 is a checklist for identifying and defining a problem.

(ii) Establishing criteria   The next step in the design process, after the problem has been defined, is to establish criteria for a satisfactory solution. This step often is skipped because people think to themselves, "I'll know it when I see it." Relying on that assumption can produce a decision that overlooks an important issue and introduces more problems. Ways to establish the criteria for a good solution include establishing the ideal conditions, testing those conditions against reality, stating the criteria, and visualizing the best solution.

Establishing the ideal conditions can be done by projecting from each area of the defined problem what conditions would be like if the problem were solved. An ideal solution for the clinic would be to have wide, safe, direct access from the main road.

Testing the ideal against the real at this point is tentative; it simply means looking at the ideal conditions and modifying them where they obviously are impossible to achieve.

Suppose municipal regulations make it impossible to put a direct entrance into the clinic at the main road. An ideal solution might require two goals: get municipal regulations changed and create a direct entrance, or modify "direct entrance" to "accessible entrance close to the main street."

Stating the criteria should involve carefully phrasing and recording a list of all the criteria for the solution. Each criterion should contain only one objective and should

Exhibit 4.9.   Checklist for identifying and defining a problem.

1. Identify questions that have to be answered.
    —What information, facts, evidence, and proof must be found?
    —What questions of value must be debated?
    —What questions of policy and procedure must be decided?
2. Describe the problem.
    —What is needed that the present situation does not provide?
    —What is the scope (breadth, depth) of the problem?
    —How many people or units are affected? How frequently? How seriously?
3. Identify the cause(s) of the problem.
    —Has the suggested cause happened every time before the effect, or are there exceptions?
    —Did the suggested cause happen concurrently with other events?
    —Could the other events be causes?
    —Do other causes seem more probable?
4. Analyze the effects of the problem.
    —How extensive are the effects?
    —Who is affected, how, and how much?
    —How serious are the effects? How harmful?
    —Are some of the effects desirable? How do they weigh against the negative effects?
    —What are the tangential effects, if any?
    —What are their consequences? Positive? Negative?

be phrased unambiguously; each term should be clearly defined and understood. The list should be kept available for decision makers and, when choices are being made, the criteria should be applied to those choices.

Visualizing the best solution in place means getting a mental picture of how that solution would feel and look. Every member of a decision-making team needs to have that picture in mind, because it will be the foundation for each step of the problem-solving process from that moment on.

A checklist for establishing the criteria for a good solution appears as Exhibit 4.10.

(iii) Creating solutions   Creating solutions means just that. This is the stage when logical, left-brain activity recedes and artistic, right-brain activity takes over. The creative process may take decision makers far afield for a time, but, as it does, it may reveal realms of possibilities that a straight, linear, and rational process would surely miss. As the process continues, logical analysis kicks back in.

Many people are uneasy with the creative stage, feeling that it wastes time or is silly, or that they just are not creative. Those who get over that restraint discover their minds can reach farther than they ever suspected. It is critically important, therefore, that at this stage it be made acceptable and desirable to be playful, as an investment in the quality of materials on which the rational analysis later will work.

The following strategies for loosening up the creative process are presented here as part of the design of possible solutions. They are equally good for brainstorming facts or issues, locating values, unearthing possible problems and implementation methods, and developing feedback and review techniques in the problem-solving process.

Exhibit 4.10. Checklist for establishing criteria for a good solution.

1. Establish the ideal results from the solution.
2. Test the ideal against the real conditions of the problem.
3. State a list of criteria for the solution to meet.
   —Are criteria phrased clearly and unambiguously?
   —Does each criterion contain just one objective?
   —Does everyone understand and accept each criterion?
3. Visualize the best solution as being accomplished.
   —Can everyone "see" the solution?
   —Can everyone describe how the solution looks and feels?

Brainstorming, the "old faithful" of small-group techniques, can collect a lot of ideas quickly. To work effectively, however, the participants must adhere to a few rules. It helps to have a facilitator who will remind them when they lapse, and it's essential to have someone record the ideas as they emerge.

Brainstorming has energy and flow; a facilitator and a recorder should help the group keep the energy and ideation going. People need to generate ideas as quickly as possible, getting ideas from anywhere (including piggybacking on someone else's thought); there should be no judging or evaluating or owning a thought; wild and crazy ideas should be encouraged. Most importantly, when a painful silence strikes, people need to sweat it out. Silences are plateaus during which new levels of creativity may be reached. The best idea often emerges after a long and painful silence.

The checklist shown as Exhibit 4.11 is useful for generating solutions.

Exhibit 4.11. Checklist for generating solutions.

Setting the Stage
1. Make it okay to be crazy.
2. Agree that no judgment or criticism is allowed in the generating stage.
3. Keep the process going.
4. Suggest as many solutions as possible.
5. Keep the mood creative and energetic.

Guidelines for Brainstorming
1. Have someone facilitate and record ideas.
2. Generate ideas as quickly as possible.
3. Do not "own" ideas, good or bad.
4. Do piggyback ideas on a previous thought.
5. Do not evaluate any idea; bizarre or ridiculous is fine.
6. Sweat out the silences and plateaus until someone comes up with something.
7. After many ideas are on the list, winnow down.
   —Which ones might meet the needs in the problem?
   —Which ones might be feasible?
8. Start serious analysis of the few possibilities.
9. Continue with decision-making processes.

Nominal Group Technique (NGT) is similar to brainstorming. It will not create as many ideas as brainstorming because ideas are not generated as rapidly and because "piggybacking" and creativity are more limited. Because individuals put their ideas down initially in written form, however, NGT allows them to work with less risk; further, it permits maximum participation.

In NGT, each member of a group writes down ideas on cards, and then reads them aloud, one at a time, in a round-robin. A facilitator records each one on a flip chart. After all are recorded, the group discusses each idea in turn. Through this process, the group narrows possibilities to a few and discusses their relative merits. If the task is to establish a ranking of priorities or to make a final decision for one solution, the group completes the task with several multiple rankings and final votes.

Recently, a group of researchers developed a stepwise, structured process by which NGT can be used to facilitate discussion and "allow results from unit-specific NGT sessions to be combined into organization-wide solutions, without sacrificing any unit's needs . . ." (Thomas, McDaniel, and Dooris, 1989, p. 191).

The *delphi technique* is useful for involving people who cannot get to meetings, or a group that is too large for a meeting, in any or all stages of the decision-making process. To be effective, the delphi technique has to be carefully done. It is conducted by repeated mailings, tallying, analysis, and reporting of questionnaires. Individuals must know that their participation in the process is authentic. They must be motivated to respond and feel safe about doing so.

Questionnaires have to be carefully written and unambiguous. After initial responses, questionnaires need to be redrafted for emerging issues and distributed again. The process can be carried all the way through voting by multiple ranking, if necessary. Participants must be kept fully informed all the way through implementation and review of any decision in which they were involved in the delphi technique.

Group solutions can be generated by following the checklist in Exhibit 4.12.

Metaphorical thinking can be used at any stage of the creative process, but it is especially helpful if the individual or group is geared to using metaphors for creativity. A metaphor phrases a comparison between two things as if one thing were the other.

In a team frustrated by bureaucratic regulations, for example, a member might say, "These regulations are a boa constrictor, choking out the life of our organization." The metaphor has an interesting effect on listeners' minds: it helps them see relationships and "truths" they might otherwise not notice. The image of the boa is a reminder that the creatures wind themselves around and around the victim; they constrict and choke and consume; they are mindless in doing what their nature dictates.

To a team in this situation, the image clicks and goes further. Questions start arising: How can a boa be handled without harm? If you're caught in its grip, how do you get out? What is the nature of this particular boa? How can it be tamed? From there, a combination of information, creative thinking, and analytical thinking may generate original ideas and concrete solutions.

Fantasy chaining is a process identified by Ernest Bormann (1990, pp. 101–120) as something group members do spontaneously, when they seek release from tension and are working to create a sense of commonality. It is easy to understand if connected to memories of plays created with friends during childhood. "I'm the mother and you're the father and Tommy's the baby . . . and Woof is the monster." "Yeah, and the monster comes in. . . ." "It's the middle of the night. . . ." "And there's a moon. . . ."

The process is playful and creative, and adults do it, too. In a fantasy chain, someone starts off an idea—perhaps a metaphor, a comparison, a pun, a joke—and from

Exhibit 4.12.   Generating group solutions.

Nominal Group Technique (NGT)

1. Get each member to write ideas on cards.
2. Collect ideas round-robin, one at a time from each person.
3. Discuss each idea in order.
4. Narrow the list to the best set.
5. Proceed with critical analysis and choices.
6. Use multiple ranking for final voting.

Delphi Technique

1. Prepare a questionnaire and send to concerned individuals.
   —Will recipients feel safe about responding honestly?
   —Will recipients be motivated to respond?
   —Are questions clear and unambiguous?
2. Analyze responses, redraft questionnaires, and repeat the process in order to refine information.
3. Send out ballots, listing possible decisions, for multiple rankings; repeat until a decision is made.
4. Follow up with reports to all participants.
   —Is the report prompt and complete?
   —Is further reporting necessary?
   —How will participants be involved in the review process?

---

that cue the group's members create a series of fantasized events that chain out like a play or a story. As a "drama," the chain involves heroes, villains, plots, actions, settings, scenes. Like metaphorical thinking, it can trigger insights and possibilities that do not show up in any other way.

Exhibit 4.13 is a checklist for these various thinking processes.

A structured, applied use of metaphorical thinking and group fantasy is used in a group process called *synectics*. In this design, a person as a "client" presents a problem he or she needs to solve. A facilitator, who must be skilled in guiding groups, moves the problem solving through several specific stages. Participants, who may be drawn from anywhere within or outside an organization, have expertise in the problem area. They have one role: to generate ideas. To do that, they must have the skill and the expertise to question, probe, and understand the problem in depth. They also must be ready to move from critical thinking to creative thinking and then back to critical thinking, without mental blocks or self-consciousness.

After the client describes the problem and the group probes the issues until they are well-defined, the members use metaphors or fantasies to explore possible insights into the problem and its solution. The process helps to "reframe and trigger new associations that might stimulate novel solutions" (Jensen and Chilberg, 1991, p. 395).

Napier and Gershenfeld (1985, pp. 342–343) describe an instance in which a synectics group focused on a manager's problem with the poor performance—and low morale—of a long-time employee. In brainstorming the attributes of morale, the members listed the concept of "spirit"; spirit became a metaphor for morale. When the group listed the qualities and effects of alcoholic "spirits," this metaphor led to the fantasy of a supernatural spirit overlooking the department, and hence to critical analysis and application of the concepts that had emerged from the fantasy.

Exhibit 4.13.   Checklist for thinking processes, to generate solutions.

Metaphorical Thinking

1. State the objectives of thinking in metaphors.
   —To see comparisons between two ideas.
   —To find new insights from comparisons.
2. Brainstorm possible metaphors for some aspects of the problem.
3. "Piggyback" on metaphors; build on them.
4. Choose the best metaphor to carry further.
5. Examine all imaginable areas of comparison in the metaphor.
6. Look for insights into causes, effects, and solutions.

Fantasy Chaining

1. Someone's idea spontaneously starts an imaginative part of a drama (a joke, sarcasm, characterizing a person in the problem in some way, making a pun, relating the problem to some event, story line, or plot . . .).
2. Someone else builds drama on top of the first idea.
3. The group develops a chain of dramatic events in the discussion.
   —Someone in the problem may be characterized as a villain.
   —Someone may be characterized as a hero.
   —An imaginary plot develops.
   —A pattern of action and reaction develops in the story.
4. The group develops a shared symbology and insights from developing the drama together.
5. Possible solutions are generated as part of the plot and action of the drama.

Throughout the process of synectics, a group, facilitator, and client build a tightly woven sense of trust and cooperation. Almost inevitably, the group develops mutually held symbols and humor that hold the group together through stages of critical analysis and tough application.

Focus groups provide a way of getting the thinking of several people working together on a single issue. A focus group usually is drawn from a population of people concerned with the subject, and a series of questions is formulated to get them to focus on it. A facilitator asks the questions, probes for deeper and deeper insights, and keeps discussion on-track. A tape recorder and/or secretary records the discussion, and questionnaires or surveys may be used to get individual responses.

Focus groups were used, for example, to get students' feelings about a general education program in a college. The groups were led by trained upper-class students, to eliminate an "authority" presence. The participants were students currently finishing their series of general education courses. As the facilitators led the students through the discussion, some unexpected positives about the program emerged; so did some negatives and some excellent ideas. When the information was analyzed, the program directors had information that helped to identify the problems and to generate solutions that related directly to the people most concerned with the issue, the students.

Focus groups can be guided toward solutions by using the checklist shown as Exhibit 4.14.

Thinking through all the steps of the process is not always easy. Human beings are prone to an infinite number of *fallacies in thinking*, both as individuals and as groups.

Exhibit 4.14. Checklist for generating ideas through focus groups.

1. Identify and phrase questions that need to be answered by a specific population of people.
2. Select and train nonbiased, credible facilitators.
3. Invite groups of concerned participants.
4. Have facilitators conduct meetings with participants.
   —Use open questions to start discussion.
   —Guide discussion to get participants' honest feelings.
   —Use a tape recorder.
5. Analyze discussions to isolate the necessary information.
6. Provide participants with appreciation and positive feedback.

Some particularly stand out in the decision-making process, and being aware of them can help produce decisions that reflect wisdom and rationality:

- Assumptions about people, events, and causes underlie many decisions; decision makers can help each other identify assumptions by questioning how they arrive at conclusions and what the premises are for their conclusions.
- Generalizations, stereotypes, and biases crop up in thinking when people are not aware of them. It helps to examine general ideas for exceptions and sources. Careful treatment of these categories can avoid a lot of "-isms"—racism, sexism, classism, handicapism—and open a raft of unseen possibilities for solutions to problems.
- Cause-effect, or false-cause fallacies accept something as a cause only because it appears to happen prior to an effect. A lot of folklore, myth, bad science, and terrible decisions have come about because someone did not examine the relationship between causes and effects.

Language fallacies can throw off analysis at any point of a discussion. Language fallacies are numerous, but ambiguity and circumlocution might be considered paramount in decision making and organizations:

- Ambiguity allows two meanings into the same statement; it can be found in some memo that's on almost anyone's desk at any time. "The executive board requires that all directors come to the meeting Monday. Please RSVP." Is it required or not?
- Eliminating ambiguity from written language takes careful editing, and getting rid of it in oral language often takes feedback and rephrasing.
- Circumlocution takes a statement full-circle. "The reason for requiring all employees to file statements of residence is that statements of residence are required." Bureaucratese, and very unproductive. Eliminating circumlocution requires that the speaker or writer think about the logic of the thought and articulate the relationships among the premises, the facts, and the conclusion.

Ways of reducing fallacies are listed in Exhibit 4.15.

Exhibit 4.15.   Checklist of ways to reduce fallacies in thinking and talking.

1. Assumptions about people, events, causes.
   —What lies behind an action or event?
   —Why does that seem to be so? From background? Experience?
   —How can the assumption be checked?
2. Generalizations, stereotypes, and biases.
   —Is a person or event seen as representing a larger group of persons or events?
   —Has the person or event been interpreted as a separate individual?
3. False cause or fallacious cause–effect conclusions.
   —Have all possible causes been considered?
   —Could the "cause" be coincidence?
   —Could the "cause" be a co-effect of some other cause?
   —Could the "cause" be a symptom rather than a cause?
4. Ambiguity in statements.
   —Is there more than one critical term in a statement?
   —Do the two terms carry inconsistent meanings?
   —How can the statement be revised for a single direct meaning?
5. Circumlocution.
   —Does the statement seem to go in circles?
   —How can one idea be isolated and phrased so that it is clear?

Another entire area of problems can arise when people are involved in a close, cohesive group or team. As positive as that cohesiveness can be, it can block thinking badly.

This effect, called *groupthink,* is a serious problem for individuals working in groups. Janis (1983), in studying groups of presidential advisers over several years, identified groupthink as a closed process that sometimes happens when a group works closely together and develops a strong sense of cohesiveness, or when leaders are dominant and intolerant of deviant opinion. "Above all," says Janis (1989, p. 223), "there are numerous indications pointing to the development of group norms that bolster morale at the expense of critical thinking."

Groupthink is shown when people protect a leader from bad news, silence dissenters in the group, and guard their own minds from seeing information that could create dissension. They develop an illusion of being the right and moral ones, or the heroes who combat the villains, and of being invulnerable to outside forces. Their decisions are based on inadequate data and examination and are rife with danger.

Groupthink, ironically, might be particularly easy for nonprofit organizations to slide into, because nonprofits frequently have a very clear and altruistic vision of their mission. It would be so easy to feel "right" and cohesive about the group and to resist ideas that might disturb that feeling.

It's possible to guard against groupthink by agreeing, as a team, to share all information; to examine even the most controversial points of view and issues without censuring those who raise them; to be open to information and expertise from outside the group; and to have people play "devil's advocates" on issues. If members are aware of the pitfalls of groupthink and use constant feedback and review of their processes, they can develop rational, objective, and effective analyses.

Any manager facing the threat of groupthink should use the checklist shown as Exhibit 4.16.

(iv) Deciding on solutions (choices) When a range of possible solutions has been identified, the work of critical analysis begins. Critical analysis focuses on applying the previously established criteria and analyzing whether the solution actually solves the problem, how it can be implemented, what advantages and disadvantages it might provide, and how desirable it may or may not be. Finally, it requires making the actual decision.

Applying the criteria for an acceptable solution requires going back and reviewing them. If the process of gathering and analyzing the data, defining the problem, and generating solutions has changed the situation, then the criteria may have to be modified at this point. This is the time to do it, so that each stage of the next process is clearly defined in terms of those criteria.

Solving the problem is not quite as obvious as it appears. For each possible choice, decision makers must predict the outcome against each of the criteria they established at the onset for a solution; they need to see whether, in fact, the proposed step would solve the problem, or at least part of it. If it solves part of it, is it an important part? What would have to be sacrificed? When each solution is weighed against the others, which is the best?

Possible implementation of the proposed solution raises sticky practical issues. Discussion of these issues will center on several areas, including from whom or from what agencies cooperation will be required, and how probable their cooperation might be.

Implementation will hinge, also, on what resources (financial, physical, time, people) will be needed to implement the proposal. It is necessary to determine, as nearly

Exhibit 4.16. Checklist for recognizing and stopping groupthink.

1. Do members protect the leader from "bad" news?
   —Agree that all information will be shared;
   —Share responsibility for reporting and for making bad news useful to the group's success.
2. Do members disregard or silence anyone who raises a point of disagreement or information contradicting a group belief?
   —Agree that all points of view must be heard;
   —Encourage people to play "devil's advocates."
3. Do members refuse to even think about ideas or information that clashes with the group's point of view?
   —Assign each member to actively consider and debate all points of view and possibly relevant information;
   —Open discussion to understanding why someone might have a different point of view.
4. Do members assume their group is always morally right and could not make an ethically wrong decision?
   —Be careful to discuss ideas objectively;
   —Be careful to discuss values and ethics in issues.
5. Does group pressure keep members from expressing concerns about risks? Is there a feeling of group invulnerability to consequences?
   —Agree that all possible risks will be discussed openly;
   —Always look at the pros and cons of possible consequences.

as possible, to what extent those resources will be available and what an implementation team would have to do to procure them.

Finally, implementation of any plan will, in some way, affect other persons, agencies, aspects of the organization, and so on. The decision makers need to identify those impacts and how they can be handled.

Advantages and disadvantages of implementing the proposal create a third area of analysis. Sometimes, the decision to adopt a plan is on the basis (all other things being equal) of an extra advantage that it offers. Analysis should help to determine what advantages or disadvantages might occur as side effects of the plan, and whether they will accrue automatically. If the plan must be modified to gain an extra advantage, the decision makers need to know in what way and to what effect.

If extra advantages are to be gained, the decision could hinge on whether they can only be gained from the proposed solution, or whether, in fact, they might occur from other causes. How do the advantages weigh against disadvantages in this proposal and against the advantages of other proposals?

Disadvantages may or may not weigh heavily against a decision, depending on how serious they might be, whether they are unique to the proposal being considered or might result from some other cause anyway, and how they compare to the disadvantages of other proposals.

If serious disadvantages, the final question becomes whether they can be eliminated or managed by some revision of the proposal. If a revision handles the disadvantages, what other effect might it have?

At this point in the analysis, as discussion begins to center on comparative advantages and disadvantages, the questions turn increasingly to issues of values and ethical choices.

Desirability of the solution focuses on two sets of questions. The first compares the relative worth of probable outcomes. The second looks at value and ethical choices in terms of solution, implementation, and advantages or disadvantages. The discussion is based, therefore, not only on the preceding analyses but on the decision makers' ethics and value systems.

As the discussion turns on the probability that the solution will actually solve the problem, that it will be capable of implementation, and that advantages may accrue, the question becomes: Is it probable enough to make it worthwhile to do it? Or, is the goal so valuable that any possibility of effect is worth the effort? Here, values and goals really come into play, as the decision makers determine how desirable, how valuable, and how worthwhile the goals are in terms of what it will take to implement a given plan.

If implementing an expensive proposal might improve clients' quality of life for only a tiny amount, perhaps it isn't worth doing; the money might benefit them more in some other way. But what if the proposal would save a life? Several lives? A hundred lives?

How desirable, in other words, is the solution? Does it serve the vision of the organization? Does it serve the members and the constituency of the organization? Is it morally consistent with the values of the decision makers or of the organization as a whole?

By the time the above analyses are completed for each proposed solution, the possibilities have been limited to one or a very few solutions. At that point, the actual decision must be made.

Analysis of solution choices will benefit from the checklist shown as Exhibit 4.17.

Making the decision will depend, in part, on the structure of decision making in the organization. It may be up to one person, using the counsel of others; it may be up to a team, a board, or a special task force. When it's the decision of a group, the final

Exhibit 4.17.   Checklist for analyzing solution choices.

1. Does the solution meet the original criteria?
2. Will the solution solve all or part of the problem?
3. Will implementation be practical?
4. Will there be advantages (other than solving the problem) to the solution?
5. Will there be disadvantages to the solution?
6. Will the solution have desirable effects?

decision may rely on consensus, majority vote, or, in the case of several solutions, on multiple rankings.

Consensus decisions seem ideal: they require every member of the body to be in agreement. In practice, consensus decisions can take great expenditures of time and personal energy; sometimes consensus can be achieved, sometimes it cannot.

High-level executive teams in Japan will meet around-the-clock, using moral suasion, patience, and exhaustion to achieve full consensus on major decisions. The process can be harrowing, especially to people from more individualistic cultures, but it also gains greater commitment and conformity to the final decision than do other methods of decision making.

Majority vote, the method to which Americans are most accustomed, is the quick and easy way to decide between two alternatives or between a Yes and a No. If discussion has been thorough and everyone has had his or her say, most people are willing to accept a majority decision and go with it. Compared with a consensus decision, however, it leaves more people dissatisfied.

Multiple rankings is a common approach when there are several possibilities. The process may require several ballots. This process works similarly to the delphi technique. Members first rank the solutions from, say, one to ten. The ballots are tallied, and the solutions with the top rankings are identified. This eliminates several possible solutions, and members rank the isolated few remaining proposals. Again, the rankings

Exhibit 4.18.   Checklist for implementing and evaluating decisions.

1. Create an implementation plan.
   —What steps are required for each part of the plan?
   —How do the steps map out on a flowchart?
   —Who is responsible for each part?
   —What are the order and target dates for each step?
   —What problems might arise? What are contingency plans?
   —How will the implemented plan be evaluated? When?
   —What will the sources of funding be?
2. Implement the plan.
   —Is there regular overview and supervision?
   —Is management support strong and consistent?
   —Is the plan going according to the flowchart and schedule?
3. Get feedback on results.
   —Is data gathering going on constantly?
   —Is everyone involved in the plan also involved in the feedback?
   —Is everyone open to change and revision if based on good feedback and analysis?

are tallied and the top rankings are identified. It is possible at this point that a clear winner is in view; it is also possible that there is a two- or three-way tie.

At this point, members may discuss their reasons for and against the remaining proposals, and yet another ballot is taken. The process is a bit slow, but it works well for achieving something close to consensus while efficiently working through probably good solutions to find the "best" one.

(v) Implementing the plan   The final—but sometimes very difficult—steps are in creating a plan, implementing it, getting feedback on the results, and modifying the program.

Creating an implementation plan requires going back to each element of the design of the solution and working out several steps. The design of the plan needs to be exact, because the implementation is where the solution fails or succeeds.

A checklist and a flowchart are helpful in this procedure. (See Exhibits 4.18 and 4.19.) Initial checklisting should be based on the formula: Who will do what, when,

Exhibit 4.19.   Sample flowchart: the decision-making process.

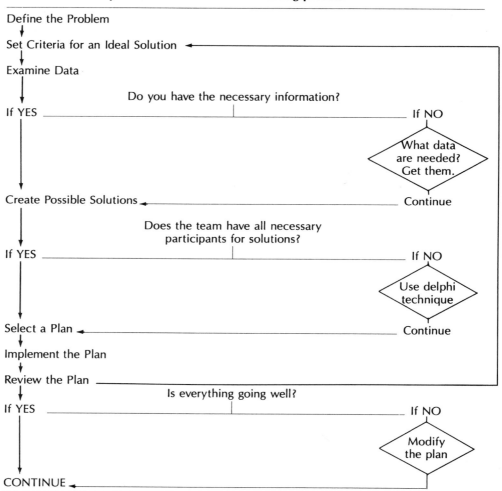

where, and from what funding sources? The planning should include an excruciatingly complete list of every step that needs to be taken for implementation and of all the persons responsible for each part. A flowchart should include the order and target date for each step and, where steps are concurrent, that fact should be indicated. The flowchart also should plot possible problems and alternatives, and should indicate contingency plans. Finally, the plan should include projected methods for reviewing and modifying the solution at specific times after its implementation.

Implementing the plan should flow naturally from the work that has been done; too often, it does not. Organizations often forget to overview and supervise the implementation, and the flowchart gets lost in the files. This is the time for the person in charge to set up a schedule for review and feedback from those involved in implementing the plan.

(vi) Getting feedback and modifying the plan (review) This final loop is essential to the effectiveness of the solution. Once again, asking questions and gathering data are involved, and the organization uses all the principles for good data gathering and analysis to find out how the solution is working. Everyone involved in the implemented plan should be part of generating and using the data to assess every part of the program. Measures, surveys, observations, studies—all need to be undertaken to determine whether the effect is as anticipated and what can be done to improve it.

4.3 SUMMARY

Quality decisions can be made only on the basis of quality information. Every part of an organization—suppliers, employees, consultants, customers—must be constantly involved in data gathering, analysis, and application to the improvement of the organization and the achievement of its vision and goals. Information empowers people and it enables good decisions.

Principles for gathering and using information include the following:

- All data should be seen as positive because they can be used for positive effects;
- Information gathering is cybernetic, in that information feeds the constant improvement of the process;
- Information must be attainable, accessible, purposeful, and applicable for people in the organization; it must be systematically and purposefully gathered; it must be user-generated and applied; and, for it to be applicable, it must be reliable, valid, and timely;
- Quantitative and qualitative studies should be used, together with personal information and interpersonal processing, to provide maximum insight into numbers, frequencies, and qualities of issues.

Information legitimately can come from a wide variety of sources, and it should be shared and displayed in comprehensible, easy-to-remember ways. Charts, graphs, and diagrams help people use data effectively in the processes of analysis.

Analyzing information for decisions will involve discussing questions of fact and of value as they impact on policy decisions. Decision making follows a nonlinear process of intelligence (data gathering), design (creation of solutions), choice (decision making), implementation, and review and modification of the plan.

Decision makers must define a problem facing them and establish criteria by which they will judge a solution. Designing solutions is a creative as well an analytical process, and participants can use a number of group strategies for opening up the creative process and generating several possible solutions before moving into critical analysis of them. Critical thinking, then, involves careful analysis of possible causes, effects, and solutions. People must determine whether a proposal solves the problem, whether it carries advantages or disadvantages, and whether it is desirable in terms of its effects and of moral and ethical values.

Decisions, whether on the basis of consensus, majority vote, or multiple rankings, must be implemented with a careful plan, a comprehensive overview, and support. The implemented proposal must, once again, involve all parties in the design, implementation, and use of feedback and review methods, to constantly improve the quality of the implementation.

SOURCES AND SUGGESTED REFERENCES

Bormann, E. B. 1990. *Small Group Communication: Theory and Practice,* 3rd ed. New York: Harper & Row.

Hirokawa, R. Y. 1990. "The Role of Communication in Group Decision-Making Efficacy, A Task Contingency Perspective." *Small Group Research, 21*(2): 190–204.

Janis, I. L. 1983. *Groupthink: Psychological Studies of Policy Decisions and Fiascoes,* 2nd ed. Boston: Houghton Mifflin.

————.1989. "Groupthink: The Desperate Drive for Consensus at Any Cost." In J. S. Ott (Ed.), *Classic Readings in Organizational Behavior.* Belmont, CA: Wadsworth.

Jensen, A. D., and Chilberg, J. C. 1991. *Small Group Communication Theory and Application.* Belmont, CA: Wadsworth.

Napier, R. W., and Gershenfeld, M. K. 1985. *Groups: Theory and Experience.* Boston: Houghton Mifflin.

Simon, H. A. 1977. *The New Science of Management Decision.* Englewood Cliffs, NJ: Prentice-Hall.

Thomas, J. B., McDaniel, R. R., Jr., and Dooris, M. J. 1989. "Strategic Issue Analysis: NGT + Decision Analysis for Resolving Strategic Issues." *The Journal of Applied Behavior Science, 25*(2): 189–200.

Walton, M. 1986. *The Deming Management Method.* New York: Putnam.

Wilson, G. L., and Hanna, M. S. 1990. *Groups in Context: Leadership and Participation in Small Groups,* 2nd ed. New York: McGraw-Hill.

C H A P T E R   F I V E

Leadership, Values, and the Nonprofit Organization

Elizabeth Power
EPower & Associates

CONTENTS

The transformation to Total Quality Management (TQM) requires commitment and action on the part of organization leadership. Leadership commitment drives involvement and functions in the emergent quality organization; characteristics of effective leaders, as well as personal and organizational values in relationship to quality, shape action. This chapter, through a combination of information and process questions offered for consideration by the reader, focuses on the concepts and practices in these areas that guide leadership development.

5.1 LEADERSHIP

(a) SENIOR LEADERSHIP INVOLVEMENT Who leads the organization? What does leadership mean? Because many nonprofit organizations provide public services or focus on the advancement of a special interest group, "followers" may in fact exercise more leadership potential and power than those in senior leadership positions, except for the day-to-day activities of running the organization. Leadership in this context includes, then, not only the body of people involved in the day-to-day management of the organization but also those who are affected by them. "Leadership" also means the attitudes, values, and actions involved in creating the outcomes of the organization.

The day-to-day senior leadership of a nonprofit organization recognizes influence as the "trim tab." Like the trim tab of an airplane, where as little as 2 percent of the surface area steers the aircraft, the influence of as little as 20 percent of the organization may be all that is required to change its course. This influence affects the organization from the top down and from the bottom up—and such influence in fact runs in both directions.

(i) Commitment and modeling When senior and top management commit to and model quality in their own offices and daily workings, staff and volunteers can more readily adopt new practices and processes: instead of being pushed, they are being led. Leadership actions are congruent with the values espoused.

Commitment emerges from belief in the process and the results it will yield. Without belief in the process first and the results second, the "faith" required to commit to action is absent. This faith gives the courage to act unswervingly when the changes required seem to cause doubt and disruption.

When leadership is observed actively striving to learn and to apply what has been learned, others involved in creating the results for which the organization strives will more readily perform in like manner. One means of accomplishing this top-down performance is to involve cross-functional groups (volunteers, CEOs, board members, and paid staff in the same sessions, for example) and top-level leadership in planning the education required for the transformation.

Followers model what leaders demonstrate: leaders must adopt TQM and act in ways that demonstrate their acquisition of the mindset and the skills required, if others are expected to follow.

(ii) Specific behavior demonstrating involvement How will senior leadership demonstrate involvement? Performance of the tasks in Exhibit 5.1, through response to the questions provided, should yield useful data.

Exhibit 5.1. Checklist for senior leadership involvement.

---

1. Identify internal and external followers.
   a. Who seeks and values input from senior leadership?
   b. Who seeks opportunities to ask the penetrating questions others may fear to pose?
   c. Who lends support when times are tough?
   d. Who refuses support and provides effective factual reasons for the refusal?
2. Talk with followers about their dreams for the organization.
   a. What do they want the organization to be doing 10 years from now?
   b. What are the most and the least creative actions they can envision the organization undertaking?
   c. If the organization had available funding (for a change), what would they do differently and for what reasons?
3. Identify followers' needs and desires, and clarify how to meet them in exchange for role performance.
   a. What do followers need to feel satisfied with their role?
   b. How can those needs be satisfied by the organization?
4. Build interpersonal bridges to all functions and levels within the organization.
   a. What are the names or labels of the functions and levels?
   b. When and where do they gather for support and exchange of information?
   c. How can levels of sharing information about common needs and accomplishments begin in an informal way in these locations?
   d. What would it take for senior leadership to be willing to risk sharing basic personal information with these functions and levels?
5. Talk about the organization's commitment to quality in everyday language.
   a. What is the worst way to talk about quality?
   b. How can the basic principles and best practices be related in such a way that the least knowledgeable learner can comprehend and use them?
   c. Where are quality basics being used in everyday practice within the organization so they can be discussed relevantly?
   d. What is the difference between talking about the commitment as it is versus as it is becoming?
6. Be personally involved as a learner and supporter in quality training and education.
   a. How many of the basic quality tools (such as fish-bone analysis, scatter diagram, five repetitions of asking and answering "What is the reason?") are used at least monthly in work assignments?
   b. When attending skill development classes, is it exclusively with others of the same level or with line staff and volunteers?
   c. Do you ask questions as a learner in classes?
   d. In what ways do you enable training and education as both a learner and supporter?
7. Learn basic quality skills and practice them daily.
   a. Of the responsibilities in your charge, which 20 percent consumes 80 percent of your time?
   b. By what process will you continue to identify and reduce variation and improve the processes used in your organization?
8. Listen to and answer honestly questions about changes.
   a. What are the short-term benefits of "disinformation"?
   b. How does deciding what to say before the questions are asked benefit the audience or the respondent?

Exhibit 5.1.   *(Continued)*

    c. What is the impact on resistance to change when senior leadership listens poorly, hedges, gives disinformation, or skirts issues?

  9. Be honest and play fair.

    a. How is the pool of winners increased by deception or withholding?

    b. If some win at the expense of others who must then be supported by other means, has the pool of winners increased?

    c. From what does the need to be dishonest or unfair come?

 10. Exercise a sense of vision; delegate, coach, advise, provide feedback; encourage new ideas and foster creativity: stress rethinking and reexamination of assumptions and how the use of intelligence may have been limited to this point.

    a. Who benefits if leadership is the only component of the organization pursuing the vision?

    b. What is risked by doing what's always been done?

    c. Has the organization discouraged the full use of individuals' abilities and the rethinking and reexamination of apparent assumptions?

 11. Communicate about the vision with fluency and confidence.

    a. What is the source of leadership's fire about the organization's vision, individually and as a group?

    b. Whose lives will be changed, and how, if the vision is achieved?

    c. Where is the background work that supports the belief that the vision can be achieved?

(b) FUNCTIONS OF LEADERSHIP IN THE QUALITY ORGANIZATION   There are five leadership functions that are basic to a successful transformation to quality. Because the adoption is basically an enculturation process, these functions must be exercised over time. The variability inherent in the early stages of adopting new behavior is reduced with practice. It is very important to embed and reward appropriately (without spreading the deadly disease Deming describes as "evaluation of performance, merit rating, ranking, or annual review") the acts connected with these functions in the daily life of leadership; people make mistakes when they are learning new skills.

(i) Lead rather than manage   In Dr. W. Edwards Deming's 14 points, this means helping people, machines, and processes to do a better job, and removing barriers to pride in workmanship (whether the work is volunteer or paid) for all levels of workers. Full implementation of Deming's concepts would include abolishing management by objectives (MBO) or numbers, including the annual or merit evaluations and ratings currently known to most organizations. (See Chap. 7 for additional discussion outlining the relationship between strategic planning and MBO.) MBO is unnecessary when quality (reduction in variation and constantly improving quality) is the target; annual ratings and evaluations reinforce fear and make the evaluation the focus of the work rather than the quality of the work itself. The quality of the work itself rates and evaluates the worker. "Work" may be a service rendered (often a less visible output or result), such as reduced distress from a crisis intervention call; or, it may be a product (a more visible output or result) such as gift baskets for donors or assembled publicity packets for attracting donors, volunteers, or clients.

Processes for defining the specific actions for leading rather than managing include:

1. Ask the workers.
   a. What can the organization do to help them do a better job?
   b. How can the equipment or other tools used in their work help them do a better job?
   c. What needs to happen, for them to be able to increase their pride in their work and in doing the work they do?
2. Identify systems in the organization.
   a. What parts are interrelated and dependent on each other?
   b. Where are processes and subprocesses completed, even if they yield information instead of product?
   c. How does work flow through the organization? What is the sequence, step-by-step, for each task?
   d. What are the logical geographical and functional groupings that make up the systems in the organization?

(ii) Act as the change initiator, agent, and target Leadership fulfills three roles simultaneously in relationship to change, when demonstrating actions that are congruent with values and modeling skills that are to be utilized in the transformation. Leadership *initiates changes* required for the quality transformation, *is the agent* helping implement those changes, and *is the target* of the effect of those changes, including all the human emotion that accompanies change and enhances resistance to it.

These changes occur and are made in arenas where leadership can choose to initiate changes and can influence those changes. As leadership liberates others to serve as initiators and agents of change in their areas of control and influence, workers more readily accept being targets for change.

We should recognize that changes occur along a continuum of risk, threat, and pressure in each of the political, technical, and social cycles of the organization during what Deming calls the "quality transformation."

Specific actions are driven by leadership's answers to questions such as these:

1. From the functions, levels, and systems identified earlier, in what areas of the organization do you have actual control and in what areas do you have influence?
2. What changes do the workers believe need to be initiated in these two areas? Of those, which do you have the power to initiate? To implement?
3. What changes do you believe need to be implemented?
4. Where are you the target of change; that is, during the transformation, what changes does the organization expect you to make?

(iii) Identify and focus needed organizational changes These changes require identification by outcome and by type. Three types of change are involved in the quality transformation:

- Developmental change, such as the establishment of rules and norms early on, is followed by periods of stability as the organization ages and matures, and then by adaptation for new growth. Developmental changes follow the life cycle of the organization and may be likened to a person's progression from infancy to old age. An effective strategy to bypass the deterioration of organizational aging is through innovating, pursuing TQM, and thinking creatively.

- Transitional changes normal to developmental change occur as changes enabling the transformation to TQM are made. These include grumbling and complaining associated with movement out of the comfort zone. Computerizing fund-raising, learning how to systematically identify and eliminate process waste, or physically rearranging the office layout to better meet growing organizational needs are some of the developmental processes that may move people out of their comfort zone.

- Transformational change is fundamental to the identity of the person, situation, or organization; it is movement to a never-before-known state from which there is no return. It seldom occurs unless new paradigms emerge, are recognized, and implemented.

Two of the most notable transformational changes in the for-profit business world in recent years were the divestiture of AT&T and the General Motors Saturn project. Both required complex and simultaneous changes in people, process, and product. Similar change is occurring in the nonprofit sector with the increasing activity by nonprofits to impact governmental processes. The leadership of the new republic of Lithuania, for example, established a nonprofit institute to support private efforts toward democracy. Another example of transformational change in the nonprofit world is found in new arrangements by insurers that allow policyholders to buy insurance specifically to benefit charities.

In many ways, the choice to implement TQM is now a part of the developmental process and represents a transition during specific developmental phases of an organization's life. It is, however, a transformational change for each individual organization because of its impact.

When an organization is aware of the types of change it is experiencing, responses formed to those changes will be more effective. Consider these questions throughout the transformation, to help differentiate types of changes:

1. Of the changes identified earlier, which are developmental, that is, which are in response to the specific stage of development in which the function, level, or system in need of change is found? (Think of life cycles to help identify these.)
2. What changes are occurring in response to the developmental process or within a particular stage of development? (For example, promotions are part of developmental change; firings or layoffs are transitional.)
3. Of those left, which are longer lasting and have less knowable outcomes that will irrevocably change the culture or process of the organization (transform it)?

(iv) Move from being result-driven to being process-driven   This move is imperative. When systems are in control—that is, when processes are continuously assessed and improved, variation is reduced, and efficiency is improved—the quality result becomes a natural by-product. (If the process is proper, the desired result—quality—will follow.) Quality results depend on having stable and capable processes, minimizing variation, and meeting and exceeding mutually defined customer/supplier expectations. Meeting these criteria helps eliminate the need for "annual ratings" and "evaluations," which actually amount to inspections of the processes within the organization instead of evaluations of the persons.

Leadership's unwavering commitment to "process first" demonstrates to followers that they are not being deceived. For example, if the commitment to quality is "lip service," then driving for quantity over quality when numbers falter during the transformation will unmask the hypocrisy, which is based on a fear that must be driven out. It takes additional time to identify the steps and flow of each process, determine the existing variation in the process, find the special or common causes of variation, and determine improvement steps—in other words, to conduct the "Plan, Do, Check, Act" cycle. All these activities involve personnel from the top down as each area works on its own processes. Leading the transformation to a quality organization will initially make *more,* not less, time.

Freeing up personnel or funds through increased efficiency attracts leadership to focus squarely on process instead of results. However, this focus may pose an ethical challenge. Changes made in the name of quality should not be used as justification to terminate workers. (Would you support or participate in a program being used to jeopardize your own security?) Workers can instead be retrained and refocused to increase the output of the organization, which increases the results. For example, if fundraising activities are streamlined, requiring fewer staff and volunteers to perform administrative tasks, could not staff and volunteers be "redeployed" to seek funds? If telephone calls "lost" because of system issues (transfer errors, long waits, finding the right person) decrease, more incoming calls can be processed, which might:

- Justify additional phone lines;
- Increase the need for staff and volunteers;
- Improve donor satisfaction;
- Add capability for fund-raising;
- Improve service image.

Specific leadership behaviors demonstrating focus on the process are suggested by the answers to the questions in Exhibit 5.2.

(v) Invite change When leaders use informal and formal processes to discuss change and its impact on everyone, levels of fear and resistance to change decrease.

Fear of loss of perceived power places leaders on one side of the pendulum, acting like victors toward personnel, who are at the other side of the pendulum, feeling like victims of change and of leaders. This creates the familiar "them and us" scenario; high levels of loss are the result.

The only balanced "win–win" position is for all within the organization to become choice makers through ongoing conscious effort; like a stilled pendulum, there is no polarization. The organization can then steer toward active fulfillment of its vision instead of bouncing from one conflict situation to another, fighting for survival.

Getting stuck in feelings and focusing on change as a problem can create fight-or-flight behavior. Decoupling, or separating the "feelings" of change from the "facts" of change, enables everyone to choose the viewpoint of problem or opportunity. Day-to-day life is a process with results, and, as individuals in an organization practice this skill, extreme variation in emotional and cognitive reactions to change is reduced, and

Exhibit 5.2.   Checklist for focus on process.

1. What behaviors can be demonstrated to reassure workers that increases in process efficiency *do not* equal elimination of jobs?
2. What are the "results" (outputs) the organization creates?
3. What inputs go into creating those results?
4. Through what processes must inputs move to become transformed into results or outputs?
5. As it becomes apparent that worker security is not being threatened by TQM implementation, ask workers to use TQM training to answer these questions:
   a. How long does it take (length of the process) for an input to become an output?
   b. Over time, what are the mean and the upper and lower control limits for this process?
   c. How much variation is there over time? How can it be reduced?
   d. What are the causes of variation above and below the control limits? Owners correct the special cause process and leadership addresses the common cause variation, which is paradoxical to most management practice.
   e. Through what steps does the input pass? How much do the actual steps vary over time? What are the names of the variant steps and how often is each engaged in and under what circumstances?
   f. How might resequencing, combining, eliminating, or revising impact the process by which inputs become outputs?
   g. In the resulting improvements, how can people, who might be eliminated otherwise, be utilized in ways that increase outputs?

stability—required for successful transformation—is increased. This is another example of proper process yielding desired results.

Leaders' open discussion of their own feelings as they go through the change will clarify the organization's key question with regard to the outcome of the change: Will it be a problem, from which flight or fight will result, or an opportunity, from which growth or goal achievement will result?

Leaders should build on this type of discussion with workers, talking about the feelings everyone could choose to associate with the change. While those impacted by change may be unable to choose the changes with which they are faced, they can choose their emotional responses—negative reactions (remembered more readily than positive) or (by choice and practice) more positive feelings. Leaders can support this choice by consistently using language that encourages choice instead of rebellion ("could" instead of "should," for example).

Inviting change is related to the ability to motivate oneself. In quality organizations, motivation for excellence comes from within; it is intrinsic. Most organizations, however, use extrinsic motivation, often in the form of punishment or shaming for failure to comply. This approach creates high losses because of the dynamics of the victim/victor relationship and the shame and fear instilled in workers. Intrinsic motivation promotes optimum system ability; the desire to "make a difference" and the pride in performance that come from within a person as the results of personal choices create passion. This passion is necessary: it liberates everyone to help overcome the resistance to change inherent in becoming a quality organization.

How will leaders act and what can result when change is invited rather than feared? Leaders' answers to the questions in Exhibit 5.3 help shape the outcome.

Exhibit 5.3.   Checklist for leaders' responses to change.

1. What power do you possess and to what extent can you give it away?
2. What would happen if you gave it up, as opposed to having it taken?
3. How would you behave if you shared your power with those involved in the processes for which you are responsible?
4. How much power do the people who are involved with a process really have? What control do they have over that process?
5. What emotions do you feel as you think through these questions?
6. If those involved in a process have a great deal of power through the actions they take with regard to the process, isn't it more beneficial to involve them in learning to be more effective in process management than to try and prove how much power you really have?
7. If people are to learn better stewardship of areas within their control, what would it take for you to let it be an opportunity instead of a problem?
8. When you face challenges or problems, how do you talk about them with your staff or board?
9. Under what circumstances do you own up to your fears and anxieties as well as to the excitement of working through a situation?
10. When you are motivating yourself or others, do you use words that imply lack of choice of compulsion to act, such as "should" and "got to"? Or do you use language that acknowledges the fact that choice still exists as to how to act, although the consequences may shift according to choices made?
11. How quickly can you fully remember a time when you were sad or angry as opposed to remembering and feeling a positive feeling, indicating the degree of choice you have about what you feel?
12. What would it take for you to be willing to practice remembering and recreating positive feelings more often?
13. If you are exercising more choice about how you think, feel, and act, what is happening to your power?

(c) CHARACTERISTICS OF EFFECTIVE LEADERS   When leaders are effective, colleagues and associates find stewardship of processes and tasks enjoyable. Everyone is rowing in the same direction. Recognition of the balances of power is evident. Leaders show genuine appreciation for services rendered by staff and volunteers, and gratitude for the opportunity to serve the organization is clear. The reciprocity of follower/leader and leader/follower becomes evident. The ability to focus on the changes incumbent in the process of implementing and adopting TQM and to manage through conscious choice is enhanced.

Driving all characteristics of effective leaders is the demonstration of the *principles of quality leadership,* outlined in the following subsections.

(i) Use modeling effectively   An effective leader sets an example by modeling desired processes, presenting a transparent self in areas where resistance exists, increasing awareness of ways in which stigma and shame are used to motivate, and refusing to continue those processes. The core use of shame in organizations denies the reality of the needs expressed by the persons being shamed, in essence asking those persons to believe a lie about themselves.

Such a process leads to denial, dishonesty, and deterioration through reinforcing addictive patterns and encouraging sabotage as a way of resolving the pain of being shamed.

Effective leaders learn about, identify, are sensitive to, and dismantle this approach where it exists in their organization; they recognize that the shamed shame others, modeling the organization's antithesis.

Modeling, or practicing what is preached, demonstrates commitment and reinforces others' commitment. Another function of leadership is establishing accountability for improvement efforts, such as assessing current quality levels and determining targets using factual criteria based on numbers instead of emotions (a classic example of separating feelings from facts, as described earlier). Measuring achievements against these criteria, plotting progress, and advancing the target for areas in need of improvement are other examples of modeling by effective leaders.

(ii) Have deep and honest self-knowledge   This is the most powerful principle of quality leadership. Fearless self-examination is required of effective leaders, to minimize leading to failure and to identify where leadership may be at risk for deterring adoption of improvements or changes. Leaders with addictive behavior (toward work, toward others' views or contradictory thinking, or involving any process or substance about which one has to lie), for example, can only lead organizations toward the externalized results of their addiction. These results show up in dishonesty, denial, and moral deterioration—all expressions of resistance to changes that will improve quality. Only fearless self-examination can begin to uncover areas where intervention in one's personal addictions is required. Where addiction of any sort exists, intervention is required to prevent creating failure and wounding others, neither of which is part of the suggested model of leadership.

Leaders should carefully consider the questions in Exhibit 5.4, as a measure of self-knowledge.

Exhibit 5.4.   Self-knowledge questionnaire for TQM leaders.

---

1. For the methodology chosen for implementing TQM, what are the areas of knowledge in which you are strong? Weak?
2. For the role you play in the transformation, which of your attitudes is most effective and which is most ineffective?
3. Based on what you have read and what you have heard, what personal or business values do you have that prohibit the implementation of TQM?
4. How threatened would others say you are about releasing power?
5. What logical cognitive errors might you have about quality or people? For example, if you think quality is the absence of defects, how can you hire persons with disabilities (defects)?
6. If you think reducing variation and increasing efficiency are ways in which you can justify lower head counts, how will that affect fear levels in your organization?
7. What skills do you have that support or distract from TQM?
8. If asked, could you list the job tasks (behaviors) required of you in supporting and implementing the transformation?
9. Under what circumstances do you lie or distort the truth even when the facts are presented to you?

Know your own areas of acceptance and resistance, your skills, and your needs for improvement, and act on them. Otherwise, your effectiveness becomes shallow and positional at best, and will be doomed to fall short before the transformation's maturation.

Identify leaders' and workers' personality types and styles, using tools such as the Myers–Briggs Type Indicator, to increase understanding and promote an ability to work effectively as a team.

(iii) Abandon competition and adopt collaboration Competition increases the pool of losers. Cooperation thinly veils the same process by requiring only the appearance of reciprocal commitment to creating situations where everyone wins.

Collaboration requires a deeper realization of the interdependence between customers and suppliers. The involvement of a person in the internal or external customer/supplier relationship leads to one of two outcomes, based on how inputs are transformed into inputs: either a larger pool of winners or a larger pool of losers.

Coming together to focus common energy on constantly and forever improving the components of those relationships (inputs, process, and outputs), and settling only for "win–win" outcomes for all—these are the essence of collaboration.

Like consensus, collaboration requires that all involved parties achieve specified levels of comfort before action is taken—without compromise, trades, or voting. To collaborate is to labor together for a common end. It relies on images of "community," inclusive and committed to the good of all, rather than "tribe," willing to play the game and allow some more "good" than others. Organizational tribes, exclusive and fearful of anything outside their domain, have highly rigid and inflexible boundaries that inhibit moving beyond cooperation into collaboration.

Tribal subcultures, complete with their jargon and dress codes, often exist within an organization; their vying for hierarchical superiority is inappropriate to the quality transformation.

Leaders must be aware of how their organization's answers to questions such as these might sound or look:

1. How would you know if the organization's active, overt position is "we and they," "we, as long as . . ." or "we," with regard to other organizations, clients, the community?

2. What is the cultural basis for "teams" in the United States? (Think of sports, and the variations in types.)

3. What is the reason self-interest is dominant in an "instant gratification" culture? (Think about how fast-food culture allows people to change their mind instantly about getting what they want.)

4. If delayed gratification is required to create long-term results, by what processes can people learn to support each other as the discomfort created by time increases? (Think through the ways in which adults help children learn to wait or be patient.)

5. What can be learned from groups such as the Society of Friends (Quakers) about consensus? (They have been using consensus decision making as an organizational tool for many years.)

6. Why is it so difficult to choose to refuse to compromise, trade, peddle influence, or vote, in achieving consensus (part of the Quaker tradition)?

7. If consensus is key in collaboration, by what process can increased consensus decision making be introduced in the organization? (Part of this is thinking through obvious and subtle differences among competition, cooperation, and collaboration.)

8. Specifically, how does consensus support the dismantling of competition (win–lose) and the building of collaboration (all win or no one plays)?

(iv) Know and advance those for whom one is responsible   TQM-based criteria for advancement or promotion (based on how the organization is structured) prohibit padding budgets, juggling results to compensate for anticipated changes, or undercutting others to cause oneself to appear more suitable for promotion. They focus instead on the application of TQM practice and process to the candidate's arena of influence. In fact, such criteria, like the Deming and Baldridge awards, focus more on the process than on the results, even though the latter invariably include reduced variation and increased quality and excellence.

Knowing, directing, developing, and advancing those for whom one is responsible displays truly effective leadership to all. Such behavior models confidence in one's own abilities. It also demonstrates self-esteem, appropriate personal transparency, and a commitment to growing leadership. The organization's growth and development are enhanced, and the cycle of good growth reaps many harvests internally and externally.

The following questions will help to identify those whom leaders should know and advance and will profile their potential for development and the structures and issues surrounding advancement:

1. Who are those for whom a leader is responsible and in what ways is the leader responsible for them?

2. What skills and abilities are present in those persons?

3. In this organization, what opportunities for advancement exist?

4. What steps are being taken to identify and enact advancement of these people?

5. How are the organization's leaders preventing development and advancement, and for what reasons?

6. What would it take for the leaders to choose a different position regarding those being prevented from advancement?

7. If the current organizational structure has limited opportunity for advancement, how can advancement structures be built in other ways?

(v) Project a clear vision   Leaders who are responsible for management should draft the quality vision. Once the initial vision is drafted, those who are key stakeholders (internal/external customer/suppliers) in bringing it into being should help distill the final vision. (See Chaps. 3 and 7.)

Buy-in, increased by involvement, may be attained by having functional work groups distill the organization's vision into one that reflects its achievement at the level of the processes for which they are responsible. This revision should be followed by a joint working session with organizational leaders, to define jointly the final vision. Clear differentiation in levels of responsibility for the decision, defined by role, is also required to facilitate the highest level of collaboration possible.

If the process of defining the vision is lengthy, it is useful for leaders and the functional work groups to meet together regularly for process checks. They should read all versions of the vision with care for tense, direction, and hedging, and make sure the vision contains a statement of outcome that fulfills the organization's reason for being.

A first-draft vision might be: "We want to try to help people do better for themselves." Do *what* better? How? Want to *try* or to *do* it? Which people? Do better by your definition or theirs? Who's the customer? How does this vision enable data collection?

A later draft might read: "Our vision is to use needs-based consulting and education to enable people and organizations we serve become more effective and productive on an ever increasing basis."

The development and communication of this vision should be accomplished as a product of the entire organization, not one person. This can be facilitated, for example, through proposing human interest stories that outline the involvement of all in the process of its creation. This supports buy-in: fear based on lack of knowledge about the process is reduced, a transparency of self is demonstrated in people's willingness to be interviewed and share honestly about the process, and effective personal change management is modeled through the willingness to look at the process as an opportunity instead of a problem.

When communicating the vision, leaders should try to couple it with one or more of the benefits that improving quality will create over time. Quality has the potential to do all of the following:

1. Preserve precious resources, human and monetary;
2. Please funding sources;
3. Satisfy customers and clients;
4. Empower and motivate workers;
5. Decrease costs (creating more available funding);
6. Reduce stress.

Quality organizations improve processes through quality measures taken not to reduce staff but to increase service capability through more effective utilization of resources (personnel, money, and time). The "over time" aspect, in too many organizations, reflects a tendency to believe everything can be done yesterday, instead of needing the actual years usually required. Some measurable gains occur within weeks, some take much longer. Setting, projecting, and pursuing the vision are the first steps.

Once the vision (the outcome of fulfilling the reason for being) has been established, the mission of the organization can be derived. The mission defines who the organization is, what the organization does, for whom it is done, and the reason it is done. From the mission, operative values (guiding principles) can be derived.

The following questions can help leaders identify and project a clear vision:

1. What is the organization's reason for being, the ultimate long-term outcome to be achieved by its efforts?
2. How have leadership, board members, staff, volunteers, suppliers, and consumers been involved in identifying this ultimate outcome or vision?

3. What behaviors are demonstrated that indicate the operative vision and the stated vision are in alignment?

4. Once the vision has been specified, by what means will it be publicized and its fulfillment explored?

5. What will leadership relate, to all involved, about benefits that should accrue from achieving TQM, and how are these benefits related to fulfilling the vision?

6. How will leadership actively encourage workers to utilize TQM in other areas of their lives and thus expand its benefits?

(vi) Make use of complaints *and* good ideas   Getting people across the organization involved in the transformation begins with listening.

Effective leaders characteristically listen to those having the strongest complaints or to groups that talk about the good ideas they have that never get implemented. Those groups (frequently the same people) can be:

- Invited to learn how to address and solve problems they identify;
- Educated with basic tools;
- Encouraged to assume ownership for the processes they use in their part of the organization.

Everyone in the organization, whether involved in delivering services, fund-raising, or creating products, will benefit from learning how to use the quality tools—checking sheets for gathering data; performing fish-bone analyses to identify potential inputs for problem outputs; using Pareto charts, scatter diagrams, and run charts. (The Crawford Slip Method is an excellent tool for quick generation of many ideas around a target question. An easily organizable and readily usable written record can be created through a process that is not unlike brainstorming.) Tracking process flow from input to output to reduce the number of steps required (such as in planning and implementing a fund-raising program) is a skill that will benefit everyone, from the newest volunteer to the chairperson of the board.

Learning how to implement the continuous improvement cycle ("Plan, Do, Check, Act") and to apply the tools for continuous improvement (eliminate, combine, reduce, resequence) are also musts for everyone.

These tools can be applied to the analysis of work flow (telephone calls, client process, fund-raising) in any nonprofit organization as readily as they can to any manufacturing process.

In learning to act out work roles, education in the quality tools mentioned above can be appropriately leveraged to decrease stress (through increasing ability to control processes, both good and bad) and improve the environment.

Process-related questions leaders should ask to identify areas for attention include:

1. In terms of the complaints heard within the organization:
   a. What are the top five?
   b. In whose area do they fall?
   c. Within that area, who is the person most interested in correcting problems?
   d. How much support and influence does that person have?

e. What might encourage/limit willingness of associates in that area to participate in learning and applying TQM as a pilot group?

2. In terms of the people who always have a good idea:

   a. Is there a concentration of those people?

   b. How much support and influence do they have?

   c. What might asking them to learn TQM tools, for use in shaping good ideas, do for them?

   d. How can their willingness to accept process boundaries in exchange for greater ability to implement good ideas be assessed (and improved)?

(vii) Provide adequate resources Effective leaders allow these groups paid training and problem-solving time; coach them as needed in using the tools; and, once improvements have been proposed, welcome meetings to hear their analyses of situations, their recommended improvements, and their cost–benefit analyses. For continuity, implementation teams need to include workers, process owners, and those who identified the improvement.

Remember the trim tab's influence; several group members spreading the word about leadership commitment to quality is a powerful use of positive influence. This commitment also is demonstrated through senior leaders' involvement in training, problem solving, and adoption of continuous improvement suggestions. Influence is increased because leaders have listened, employed suggestions, lowered fear, and demonstrated commitment to quality.

Resources (time, training, dollars) must be provided to improve quality throughout the organization. If leaders truly believe in what is being implemented, sufficient resources to accomplish the mission must be made available. If justification of resources is required, leaders should perform a quick study of the costs of injuries, illness, time away from work, and what would happen if those costs were reduced. (Exclude salaries as a source of study; include benefits used.) The cost of the unknowables— funding not obtained, worker and client dissatisfaction, board members who are inactive or not involved—should also be considered.

When considering training for implementation, leaders must recognize the trap of buying highly elaborate training for a limited or specialized group instead of easily usable hands-on tools everyone can use. This is not a six-month quick fix for one department; it is a long-term investment for the entire organization. Everyone should be trained to use quality tools and to prepare to measure gains over years. From the top down and the bottom up, training should be done when and where training is needed ("just-in-time" training, or "cascading" training, down level-by-level, with leaders at each step training those with whom they work).

Leaders should consider these concepts and questions prior to acquiring training:

1. Recognize common threads among Deming, Juran, Crosby, and others.

   a. What do the "quality gurus" agree on?

   b. How do the basis skills each suggests overlap?

2. Differentiate between skills used in product/service functions such as those performed by staff and volunteers, and those performed by more senior leaders and staff.

a. What is common, such as the existence of processes, between product/service industries? Management/support tasks?

b. What common skills can be employed by all in all areas? (Look at fish-bone problem-solving skills, flowcharts, Pareto charts, histograms, run charts, scatter diagrams, and control charts.)

c. Of the basic skills, which will be of most timely use most immediately?

3. Develop a long-range plan that includes monitoring the effectiveness and utilization of training acquired.

a. How will the organization know if it benefited from planned training?

b. By what method will it measure ongoing use of this training?

c. How will it encourage ongoing skill usage?

(viii) Identify and systematically remove barriers to excellence Stop using shame and punishment to motivate (scare) personnel. Encourage intrinsic motivation instead; quality work is done for the sake of accomplishment and the choices it enables each person to make. Focus on helping followers or people working for the organization to become the best they can be. Confront fear when it is found, because fear builds barriers instead of removing them.

Encourage pride in work, innovation, continuous improvement, and open communication. When reciprocal and equal communication occurs between leaders and associates, especially using language that "sells" instead of "tells," pride in work, excellence, and innovation are encouraged.

How can all of this happen? Exhibit 5.5 is a checklist of questions related to removing barriers to excellence.

Exhibit 5.5.   Identifying and removing barriers to excellence.

---

1. How can you support doing the work for the sake of the work? (Consider the impact of earlier performance ratings, annual evaluations, and merit raises.)

2. Under what circumstances are people told that the needs they perceive themselves as having are "wrong" or "bad"?

3. When, how often, and in what manner is gratitude expressed directly for identifying, planning, and implementing improvements that result in reduced variation and increased excellence in performance?

4. How prevalent is the use of slogans and exhortations instead of direct appreciation and involvement?

5. By what process is fear identified and addressed?

6. What are the three most mentioned fears in the organization, among leaders, workers, suppliers, and consumers? (Anonymous surveys may be required, with multiple questions to identify them.)

7. What actions are being taken to remove the need for fear around those issues? How is confidence built?

8. By what process is input about how the organization's performance can be improved sought from internal and external customers and suppliers?

9. What is the difference between "telling" and "selling," in terms of language?

(ix) Evaluate the quality values These values can be defined only after the vision and mission have been defined. The vision defines the outcome; values help define the guiding principles by which the organization operates day-to-day.

Values must be defined in terms of behaviors—observable actions that can be counted, for determination of presence and strength—rather than as "scores." For example, consider the value "We believe that the people feeling the effect of the problem are the best ones to solve it." Presence and strength of organizational commitment to the value as a guiding principle can be determined in part by counting:

- Problems that have been identified;
- Processes in which the problems exist;
- Owners (specific workers, staff, leadership) of those processes;
- Persons impacted by the problems in the process;
- Times those impacted (and owners) have been directly involved in identifying cause and effect, collecting data, and developing recommendations.

Remember to consider and assess the "unknown and unknowable"—those factors, such as good will, that are more qualitative than quantitative, yet are equally important. Harder (if not nearly impossible) to measure, they are critical indicators of the operative values of an organization.

Values and leadership are tightly intertwined and almost synonymous, because leaders' actions demonstrate (operationalize) the values they hold. Evaluation of action compared to values is a characteristic of effective leaders.

(x) Grow and sustain effective teams This is a key characteristic of effective leadership. To do this, the current work paradigm (frame of reference, or literal and symbolic pattern) must first be defined. Is it a vertical or horizontal structure? How are power and authority distributed? How are decisions made? What meaning do certain symbols or rituals have? These are the "guts" of the current paradigm.

What would an effective team look like? How would you know one if you saw it? What visible characteristics would it have? How would answers to the questions used to help identify the current work paradigm vary?

Leaders should define the operative values of such teams, what the behaviors by role would be, how they would progress over time by role, and what measurement techniques should be used to assess progress and strategies for supporting team development.

(xi) Promote relationships vital to the accomplishment of the organization's mission Effective leaders function as the organization's trim tab for a specific organizational level. They should promote, throughout the organization, relationships that strengthen the effect of the trim tab and make sure these relationships are aligned with the requirements for creating the open display and obvious effects of the quality value system (discussed below).

Effective leadership in the quality organization depends on followers' adoption of those in leadership positions. When followers recognize and acclaim leaders in response to visibly consistent displays of behavior, fulfilled functions, a level of involvement expected of followers, interlocked expectation and action, and steady implementation of TQM, the progress required for successful actualization of the quality organization occurs.

5.2 VALUES

(a) QUALITY VALUE SYSTEM   In nonprofits as in other organizations, values are the lever for organizational change. Values—operationalized by leaders at all levels in the organization to fulfill its vision, mission, and philosophy—become the foundation of all action designed to create the change. When values and actions are congruent (aligned), the disruptive impact of change is lessened; when incongruent, organizational dysfunction becomes apparent very quickly.

The "quality value system" consists of fundamental beliefs about the way the organization acts to fulfill its vision and mission in relation to the practices involved in Total Quality Management.

(i) Determining the values   Once the vision and mission have been solidified, the organization is in a position to define the values by which it should operate. Values are belief systems represented by behaviors and, as such, should connect vision/mission to the operative behavior of leaders. Leaders model the values they expect of followers.

In determining values, leaders should explore:

1. Overt and covert beliefs about people and their value;
2. Relationships, internal and external, to people and the environment;
3. Responsibility and accountability of individuals and of the organization;
4. Value of the organization's internal and external outputs;
5. What's fair and just;
6. Beliefs about how business is to be done;
7. How the organization acts on all of the foregoing.

What does the organization believe? The answer is found in what people say, public perceptions, press reports, complaints and compliments, and the dissonance among what the organization wants to believe, what people truly believe, and what is actually expressed. Only when differences are identified can they be reconciled.

These process questions can help to identify organizational values:

1. If we say that we value people, how do we demonstrate this value? How would strangers looking at our operation know that? What would it look like to them?
2. What do our records of longevity, turnover, complaints, absenteeism, and sick leave say about the experience of working here on staff or as volunteers?
3. What are the worst and best things ever said about the organization?
4. How does the organization treat internal and external customers and suppliers? How does it handle their concerns?
5. What would a new client, customer, or supplier perceive about the organization, based on how it feels and looks and how people act toward the newcomer?

6. Where does the organization stand with regard to accountability for actions impacting the community and the environment?

7. What is the action plan for implementing TQM? Is it in action?

(ii) Individual adoption and commitment Each individual, his or her adoption of and commitment to the organization's implicit and explicit values, and the organization's persona embody the relationship between values and actions.

Methods by which to enhance individual adoption of organizational values can be devised. They include articulation and publication of the organization's values through the following:

1. Discussion of a specific value at lunch meetings;

2. Articles in each month organizational newsletters, exploring how workers live out a value;

3. Training and education—in particular, team-building activities focusing on operationalizing the values;

4. Pocket cards.

(iii) Cycle of deepening enactment Leaders are responsible for operationalizing (acting in accord with) specific values known to support quality and for leveraging desired change by using these values to encourage responsive followers.

Responsive followers then expect and elicit continuing alignment of actions and values from leaders, thus encouraging and sustaining continuous improvement initiatives throughout the organization. This "cycle of deepening enactment" helps enculturate the values adopted by the organization.

Key in making TQM the culture and life blood of an organization is coping with the changes it brings. Organizational change has the same impact as personal change; only the number and degree of personalization of the "cells" in the "body" vary. The degree and expression of acceptance or resistance to change are directly related to the level of conscious choice making exercised by all persons involved.

Resistance to change, and therefore conscious choice making, is the biggest barrier to implementation of TQM in all organizations. This resistance is often based on fear of loss of the familiar ("the way we've always done business") or of loss of what is perceived to be personally or professionally advantageous, such as a perception of power over others.

The value system most effective in moving a nonprofit organization toward quality as a life-style is one that recognizes and uses the power of change appropriately to continue improving the organization's processes, production, and services—and the quality of life for those involved.

How can the organization promote greater awareness of and commitment to improved quality of life? Exhibit 5.6 offers some suggestions.

(iv) Continuous improvement process The assessment of how the values are serving as the basis for action and behavior should be treated like any other process: collect data on it, monitor variation, identify special and common causes, and correct and reduce variation.

Exhibit 5.6.   Checklist for promoting commitment to improved quality of life.

---

1. Develop human interest stories about the power of specific values.
    a. Who has gotten "fire in the belly" from the process?
    b. Where has the payoff occurred?
    c. Who thought they couldn't, but could?
2. Relate the impact of the values to the organization and the community, from the point of view of those impacted.
    a. Where have increases in efficiency occurred that positively impacted the ability to provide better and expanded services?
    b. How have the organization's improved public services resulted from the process of implementing TQM?
3. Have senior leaders address how they act based on values.
    a. How does senior leadership "walk the talk"?
    b. What is being done to communicate this?
    c. How can this be related to all involved as a positive expectation of their performance and behavior?
4. To identify behaviors for assessment and measuring, answer this question: What will it look like if a person in this organization, at this level and with this much history with the organization, is acting on the values?
5. Attend to the development of effective teams.
    a. What behaviors do you expect to see, at what levels of development, from internal and external customers and suppliers that are part of the organization's team?
    b. How will leadership make it possible for these behaviors to be sustained in the culture?
    c. By what process will leadership support team building and accommodate changes in teams?
6. Determine how the organization will know whether its values are in fact serving as the basis for action and behavior.
    a. How will you know whether core values are being acted on as demonstrated?
    b. Will extrinsic motivation or intrinsic motivation be used to encourage their demonstration (for example, encouraging choice or imposing fear)?
    c. What are the consequences of the lack of demonstration, and are they consistent with the values? (Explore what will happen if the values are not acted on.)

Perception soon becomes belief. However, informal and formal survey tools can quickly provide an assessment of how the organization sees itself and is seen with regard to how it acts on values.

If there is discrepancy between the values espoused and actions reflecting values, use the quality tools as part of the problem-solving analysis. For example, fish-bone analysis, the Crawford Slip Method of generating individual anonymous inputs around a target question, and asking "What is the reason?" or "Why?" five times to identify the root cause of a situation all are helpful.

Continuous improvement follows the "Plan, Do, Check, Act" cycle—planning the intervention to change the process, acting on it, checking to see the kinds of results it achieved, and then acting to make it part of the new process.

5.3 SUMMARY

Leadership and values are so closely intertwined that the definition of organizational values supports transformational leadership, and "change agent" leadership supports core values, which engages the cycle again. Any endeavor to achieve the transformation required by Total Quality Management includes attention to both components—leadership principles and core values—and recognizes their interrelationship and synergistic effect.

Both result from engaging process and allowing process to be guided rather than driven by content. Effective outcomes yield passion, commitment, and determination without increases in fear—and the diseases that prevent the maturing transformation.

Senior leaders' involvement, exercise of functions, acting out of characteristics, and deepening enactment of the organization's adopted values—all model the transformation of the person as the microcosm of the organization. As leadership embraces the changes and masters choices that increase acceptance of changes chosen to propel the transformation, followers will do likewise.

SOURCES AND SUGGESTED REFERENCES

Aviolo, B. J., and Bass, B. M. 1989. *Transformational Leadership, Charisma and Beyond.* Binghamton, NY: SUNY, Center for Leadership Studies Report.

Bennis, Warren G. 1966. *Changing Organizations.* New York: McGraw-Hill.

Bennis, Warren G., and Nanus, B. 1986. *Leaders.* New York: Harper & Row.

Burnside, R. M. 1989. "Visioning: Building Pictures of the Future." Paper presented at Second International Creativity Conference, Noordwijk, The Netherlands.

Covey, Stephen. 1989. *The Seven Habits of Highly Effective People.* New York: Simon & Schuster.

Crawford, C. C., Demidovich, John W., and Krone, Robert M. 1984. *Productivity Improvement by the Crawford Slip Method.* Los Angeles: USC, School of Public Administration.

dePree, Max. 1989. *Leadership is an Art.* New York: Doubleday & Co.

Doll, Russel. "Transcendentals: An Overlooked Factor in Leadership Research and Training." *Proceedings of the Twelfth Symposium on Psychology in the Department of Defense* (pp. 226–229). Colorado Springs, CO: USAF Academy.

Frankl, Victor. 1984. *Man's Search for Meaning.* New York: Simon & Schuster.

Gaier, Donna, and Holliday, Artis. 1988. "Achieving Quality in Nonprofits." *Nonprofit World,* 6(3): 22–24.

Juran, J. M. 1988. "Quality Leadership." *Proceedings of the Fourth National Forum on Human Resources Planning: Bringing the Private and Public Sectors Together* (pp. 11–15). Baltimore, MD: Department of Defense.

Krone, Robert. 1987. *Crawford Slip Method Bibliography.* Los Angeles: USC, Institute of Safety and Systems Management.

Lefton, R. E., Buzzotta, V. R., and Sherberg, M. 1982. *Improving Productivity Through People Skills: Dimensional Management Strategies.* Cambridge, MA: Ballinger.

Morton, G. L. 1987. "Working Together: Developing Collaboration Among Competing Organizations." *NonProfit World,* 5 (January–February): 15–17.

Peters, Thomas J. 1988. *Thriving on Chaos.* New York: Harper & Row.

Peters, Thomas J., and Waterman, Robert H., Jr. 1984. *In Search of Excellence.* New York: Warner Books.

Power, Elizabeth. 1990. *If Change Is All There Is, Choice Is All You've Got.* Brentwood, TN: EPower & Associates.

Sims, H. P., Jr. 1990. "Self-Managing Work Teams." *The Maryland Workplace, 12* (Summer): 3–5.

Tichy, Noel. 1983. *Managing Strategic Change.* New York: John Wiley & Sons.

Walton, Mary. 1988. *The Deming Management Method.* New York: Putnam.

Wonder, J., and Donovan, P. 1989. *The Flexibility Factor.* New York: Doubleday.

Zenger, J. H. 1985. "Leadership: Management's Better Half." *Training* (December): 45–53.

Empowerment and Teamwork in the Quality Organization

Denise Gallaro
Michael E. Knight
Gay Lumsden
Donald Lumsden
Kean College of New Jersey

CONTENTS

Developing strategies for ensuring quality—quality products, quality services—has been an evolving process. Assessment centers, quality control departments, quality circles, and self-managing teams are just a few of the strategies used by corporations to establish quality within their organizational structures.

Employees require the fulfillment of their needs for affiliation or association with other members in their group. They need to acquire the self-respect, self-confidence, and heightened levels of self-esteem that come as a result of a job well done; they need to know that they are competent.

These needs are basic, not only to employees of corporations or giant conglomerates, but also to employees of nonprofit organizations, societies, associations, and charitable organizations. Although different techniques have been employed, the overriding theme of the quality movement has been the use of employee empowerment and teamwork as essential tools for attaining quality.

Employees need to feel that they are in control of their future. They need the freedom to be creative and to be able to try innovative approaches to the accomplishment of tasks. They need to know that their contributions may make a difference.

When people are treated with the respect and dignity they deserve, in an open, honest environment structured around the organizational mission of quality, quality will be the result.

Material gains and monetary rewards may motivate people to do a good job, but treatment of employees with dignity and respect will sustain this motivation for longer periods of time and at a more intense level. All too often, we hear about a friend or relative who had a seemingly successful career complemented with appropriate monetary rewards—and was miserable. Basic human needs have to be attended to first. Money cannot be a substitute for a positive self-concept, autonomy, a feeling of competence, and self-respect.

Monetary rewards are usually not as great in the nonprofit sector as they are in manufacturing or other for-profit industries. This may be the primary reason why the quality principles of empowerment and teamwork should become essential elements for the nonprofit sector.

In nonprofit organizations, people work together cooperatively to build an integral whole. Individuals work in units and teams, interacting with other units and teams, to create the whole organization. At times, these individuals, teams, and organizations interact with individuals and teams in other organizations. All individuals and the teams on which they function need to take responsibility for their contributions to the organization.

6.1 EMPOWERMENT

To establish appropriate levels of responsibility and accountability, it is necessary to empower all members, including employees and volunteers, to move them to a greater degree of control. An essential element of self-esteem is locus of control. The degree of control expressed by individuals with high self-esteem is great; the degree of control expressed by those with low self-esteem is minimal. Empowerment increases control, enhances self-esteem, and allows people to create quality within an organizational structure.

According to Rosabeth Moss Kanter (1983), these four principles strategically strengthen (or empower) individuals:

1. Giving people important work to do on critical issues;
2. Giving people discretion and autonomy over their tasks and resources;
3. Giving visibility to others and providing recognition for their efforts;
4. Building relationships for others, connecting them with powerful people, and finding them sponsors and mentors.

(a) LOCUS OF CONTROL People with positive self-concepts have one widely accepted characteristic: they feel that they are, in a large measure, in control of their lives and that what they think and do will determine what happens to them. Conversely, those with low self-esteem feel they are controlled by fate and their actions will have little influence on their situations.

A somewhat similar analysis holds true for the willingness to take reasonable risks. Positive self-concepts allow people to assess a risk, to acknowledge the results of failure, and, if it does occur, to keep failure within the bounds of the task. They do not label themselves "failures" because of particular instances. A person with a negative self-concept will frequently avoid situations that held even the slightest risk, therefore limiting his or her opportunities for growth and learning. The fear of failure may be so great that a type of paralysis develops, preventing the exploration of new ideas and areas.

It is fairly common to see people who have been highly praised for a particular action repeating this action over and over in the belief that they have discovered success and simply have to repeat this formula to please others. Yet, they explore no other possibilities for success. One goal all supervisors should have for their workers is the development of sufficient self-confidence to enable them to take risks, explore new ideas, and recognize failure as a temporary "learning" state.

The many other facets of an individual can give firm answers to: Who am I? How important am I? How much control can I exercise? The manner in which people evaluate these many facets in themselves is strongly influenced by the other people in their lives and the images reflected by these people.

(b) CREATIVITY   The workplace needs to provide an environment that encourages people to try new, different, innovative, creative things. Exactly what kind of work environment will offer that encouragement?

Creativity is a vital component of successful problem solving, change management, and conflict resolution. Empowerment of people liberates every individual worker to express his or her ideas. An effective workplace will use the resources of each individual. It will listen to and rely on the people who are actually doing the work, and will benefit from their experience, knowledge, and enthusiasm.

Diversity leads to creativity and to the generation of ideas. Nonprofits should ask themselves what they know about their workers. What special talents do individuals possess? Are they eager to learn new techniques and new tasks? What special needs motivate workers?

Robert Burnside (1988), who manages Innovative projects at the Center for Creative Leadership, has said that, to achieve innovation, it is necessary to "manage the heart as well as the head of the organization." He summarizes research and proposes the following four-component model "as a guide for improving the climate for creativity":

- Goal clarity—. . . includes . . . the long-term goals of the organization, a clear shared vision, and the short-term goals and action employees are expected to take.
- Freedom—personal autonomy in reaching the goals that give full play to the individual's inner motivation.
- Resources—not only money and time, but information, and the assistance and cooperation of other people.
- Encouragement—. . . by managers is the least prevalent stimulant to creativity found in our research. It means, literally, "to give heart," to encourage employees to take risks in forming, sharing, and trying out new ideas. [p. 4]

(c) FULFILLMENT OF BASIC NEEDS   The process of empowerment entails the fulfillment of basic human needs. These needs include:

- Approval in the form of acceptance as an integral component of the organization;
- Association or affiliation needs as attained by membership in the organization;
- The sense of achievement or accomplishment that comes as a result of knowing that one's contribution makes a difference;
- Respect or esteem that originates from the knowledge that quality work has been accomplished;
- A sense of self-fulfillment at the realization of one's own competence.

These human needs can be satisfied by participation, and their satisfaction can be directly transformed into the intrinsic rewards of participation or involvement in important work decisions. Empowering individuals creates a workplace in which each member personally believes in creating his or her own vision for the future, based on the mission of the organization.

Only when first steps are taken can a broader circle be created. Attention to the implementation of these first critical steps is vital. The key to success lies in blending knowledge of the entire organizational structure, including teams (e.g., cross-functional teams) and individuals who have the pragmatic knowledge and realistic know-how that are essential for improvement and quality results. Organizational structures that foster empowerment of individuals create environments in which people are eager to suggest ideas for improvement. They are free to work in problem-solving groups and typically interact with others to lend their knowledge and expertise to the process of turning innovative ideas into realities.

(i) Reward systems   Salary and benefits are certainly primary components of any organization's reward system, but an understanding of what motivates people to work in the nonprofit sector requires additional analysis. A volunteer is obviously seeking some nonmonetary satisfaction. This suggests that managers should be attempting to find out what motivates the employees, the volunteers, and the managers themselves. A general analysis will yield only general suggestions; the factors that provide satisfaction to individuals are specific.

Another consideration regarding the reward system is what types and amounts of resources are available to the manager to distribute as rewards. If there are no additional resources to distribute and the manager does not control the type or level of compensation, the significant remaining factor is the job itself. How can the manager involve people in their work so that they are able to obtain greater satisfaction and develop a stronger commitment to their team and to the organization? Most leaders of modern management have a clear and consistent response—ASK THEM!!

Involvement and empowerment are among the most powerful tools available to any manager.

(d) SUCCESS   Success and failure result in different changes in behavior. The type of evaluation given by supervisors will have an impact on a worker's level of competence. Positive reinforcement, in the form of recognition and rewards, leads to high self-esteem. Employees who have low self-esteem develop self-consciousness, which impairs task performance. Lower expectations will be set and reduced effort will follow. Because achievement is determined in part by effort, a bleak cycle can result: reduced effort leads to poor performance, which leads to additional feedback to support feelings of worthlessness.

To break the cycle of failure and low self-esteem, cognitive processes must be altered. A self-fulfilling prophecy can be transposed to produce and incorporate positive expectations and results, in place of the normally negative connotations associated with the concept. Belief in oneself leads to increased performance. Workers and their supervisors alike should set attainable goals, reward accomplishments, and criticize the process or action, not the person. The supervisor can be compared to an athletic coach who takes responsibility for success, encourages education and training that lead to growth, and promotes actions that eliminate self-handicapping and self-defeating attitudes.

(e) SUPPORT   Empowerment implies giving people the support and authority needed to do their jobs effectively. The process of empowering individuals, teams, and organizations is the same at all levels. Authority is the key component: individuals must have the authority to participate in the design of their own training programs and to act when needed.

Maintaining the premise that, in order to gain power, one must give it away, the empowered individual is free to ask questions that are relevant to the successful achievement of personal and organizational goals. These questions include:

What does *support* mean?

Can I select my own training?

Can I visit our customers/clients?

Can I visit other offices or agencies that affect my work?

(i) Knowledge, skills, tools   People who are empowered have the ability to sense opportunities and to act while others hesitate. They have the knowledge, skills, and tools necessary for achieving quality. Training and education—the enhancement of technical skills as well as interpersonal skills—provide the essential tools required of the empowered individual. Workers who lack the authority, skills, and tools (information) to make decisions about their own work will perform tasks without knowing what or how their labors contribute to the entire picture.

Activities must be defined clearly so that each person knows what is expected of him or her. Workers should be able to see where their contributions fit into daily operations. Interpersonal skills—those skills aimed directly at the improvement of human interaction, such as listening skills, communicating skills, conflict management, and problem solving—are essential aspects of empowerment.

Empowered individuals thrive in and help cultivate an atmosphere where people at all levels think for themselves and manage their own work. Participation in this type of environment leads to a more rewarding, satisfying, and productive job. Respect for individuals' diverse talents leads to trust and a healthy working environment (Lumsden, Knight & Gallaro, 1989).

(f) HOW TO EMPOWER PEOPLE—SHARE THE POWER   Empowered people bring energy and commitment to their efforts. The question always is: How should power be shared? Final responsibility, after all, lies with management, and managers are apprehensive about giving away power that might affect their final responsibility. There *are* risks in empowering others, but there are greater risks in not doing so. A risk in empowering people might be that they will be too enthusiastic or that they will fail in a task. The risk in not empowering them is that members of an organization may become disillusioned, disappointed, and deenergized, and will—almost certainly—fail. How can empowerment happen?

1. Move information to lower levels. Information is power; it enables people to think and to act. One of the most alienating facts of life in organizations is the "need-to-know" premise for giving information. It is simple to inform people at all levels, and it is wise to provide opportunities for them to discuss the information and interpret it. They then become both informed and understanding.

Even if it appears they have no specific, immediate application for the information, they become the informed representatives of the organizational vision. Their power accrues to everyone's advantage.

2. Enhance ownership of the organizational processes and vision. Ask for the opinions of people as to how the organizational structure should work and what its vision should be; make those opinions important, act on them, respect them. Pride of ownership is power, and people will exercise that power for improvement.

3. Help empowered people to empower others; take empowerment all the way through the organization. Directly state organizational norms for providing information and explanation to volunteers and staff. Publicly set norms for soliciting opinions and ideas, and create ways to use, to recognize, and to reward those ideas. Make each person an "owner" of the organization and the vision.

(g) ACHIEVING QUALITY THROUGH EMPOWERMENT   Although one tends to seek a logical, linear sequence of events, a number of questions must be answered simultaneously about different aspects and conditions of a nonprofit organization. These questions appear in Exhibit 6.1.

(h) ENVIRONMENT   Organizational structures tend to disregard human relationships by using inappropriately or overusing competitive activities. This error can foster negative and damaging relationships.

According to W. Edwards Deming (1982), achieving a positive atmosphere of respect entails driving out fear in order to build a "climate of trust." People may be afraid to ask questions or take a position, even when they do not understand what the job is or what is right or wrong. People will continue to do things the wrong way, or to not do them at all. "It is necessary for better quality and productivity that people feel secure" (Walton, 1986, p. 35).

Cooperative working conditions can be expressed in the maxim of Max DePree (1989): "Every pitcher needs a great catcher." A pitcher receives signs from the catcher, but the catcher must be able to handle the pitch that is delivered. The circumstances constitute a mutual learning process in which individuals work together effectively.

Competition has been given great currency in our culture. It may have its place in the areas of team sports or in striving to reach personal or team goals, but most of the defense of competition is based on a series of myths that have developed. Some of those false assumptions are worth examining.

1. Competition builds character. There is no evidence to support this statement, but there is evidence that competition can limit growth in some areas. The pressure of competition may reveal personality flaws quickly and prevent successful completion of tasks.

2. Competition builds self-confidence and self-esteem. Competition often leads to insecurity and negative self-attitudes. Fear of failure is evident. We all know that not everyone can be a winner all the time.

3. Achievement, success, and motivation depend on competing with others. Cooperation facilitates achievement. The use of competition may decrease the quality of work and may not necessarily determine who is superior under a variety of conditions. Competitive motivation interferes with one's capacity for problem solving. Success in achieving goals does not depend on being better than others.

Exhibit 6.1. Checklist of environments for empowerment.

The following list of questions is designed to ensure that the nonprofit organization is providing an environment that fosters empowerment of employees. A positive response to each of these questions indicates a commitment to achieving quality through the empowerment of individuals.

1. Is collaboration promoted over competition? _____
2. Does this collaboration foster helpful relationships? _____
3. Are the hierarchical levels of the organizational structure not discernible by an outsider? _____
4. Are the needs of individuals important to success? _____
5. Do individuals' jobs draw on the employees' multiple talents? _____
6. Do workers know they are valued for their contributions? _____
7. Do management skills incorporate concern for the human needs of personnel? _____
8. When people are assigned responsibility, are they given the appropriate and corresponding authority? _____
9. Does every worker feel involved and accepted? _____
10. Does every worker realize that individual successes are successes for the organizational structure? _____
11. Do employees agree that, if the culture of the workplace is changed, there is an opportunity to enhance productivity and quality and to increase self-satisfaction? _____
12. Has the organization created an environment where people can become successful? _____
13. Can leadership originate in a variety of places? On a variety of levels? _____
14. Can a good idea originate with anybody? _____
15. Does planning include moving generalities to specific actions? _____
16. Is there an environment of mutual respect? _____
17. Are accomplishments recognized? _____
18. Does the individual understand his or her relationship to the entire system? _____
19. Are all workers encouraged to rethink their work? _____
20. Does the above checklist include both the director and the consumer (end user) of the organization's services? _____

4. Workers prefer competitive situations. As long as workers are "winning" and can demonstrate mastery of a task, they will prefer competitive situations. Cooperative situations better serve the majority.

5. To succeed in this highly competitive world, employees must be competitive. The vast majority of human interaction is cooperative, not competitive. Because we are social animals, cooperation (e.g., laws, behavior, trade) is a necessity.

Exhibit 6.2. Cooperative vs. competitive working environments.

Cooperative Conditions		Competitive Conditions
High sharing and helping	◄-----------------►	Attempts to mislead and obstruct
Worker interaction	◄-----------------►	Low interaction
Effective communication	◄-----------------►	Misleading or no communication
High acceptance and support	◄-----------------►	Low acceptance and support
Trusting atmosphere	◄-----------------►	Low trust
Coordination of efforts	◄-----------------►	Low or no coordination of efforts
High risk taking	◄-----------------►	Low risk taking
No comparison among workers	◄-----------------►	High comparisons among workers

Another way to view cooperation and competition is in terms of the working environment each creates. Exhibit 6.2 juxtaposes the conditions fostered by each.

(i) COMMUNICATION A clear vision and mission should be communicated to all levels of the work force. Open, honest, and consistent communication builds interpersonal relationships and a sense of "ownership." Candid communication on the part of leaders increases perceived leadership effectiveness.

An individual's self-esteem can be increased through a sense of belonging and an awareness of membership. Access to pertinent information is necessary to accomplish stated goals and objectives. When information is shared openly and consistently, no one can have doubts about his or her responsibilities and duties. A job well done becomes the by-product of effective communication, which, in turn, fosters increased self-esteem.

The dynamic interaction of effective communication can sustain motivation and enthusiasm. It can also lead to increased levels of trust, a greater commitment to the organizational structure, greater use of talents and skills, and a more flexible attitude toward change. A communication philosophy that encourages individuals to talk about issues and feelings is a prerequisite to empowerment.

(j) CHANGE AND EMPOWERMENT Flexibility is essential to adapt to an ever changing environment. The process of change must be continuous if it is to foster health and vigor within an organization. Change can create new perspectives, allow for exciting opportunities, and reaffirm the mission or vision of all members. The manner in which individuals and systems adapt to change facilitates or hinders empowerment of individuals.

(i) Adapting to a changing environment Many organizational structures or systems have refused to change. They have denied that change was necessary for revitalization or failed to realize that change was actually occurring—and they have perished.

(ii) Change strategies There must be motivation to embrace change. Time is needed to break down old habits and attitudes. Communication and trust by all involved in the change process can foster empowerment and ownership.

(iii) Novelty The novelty of work presented to individuals can be an important factor in sustaining enthusiasm during change. New and unique work experiences can bring about high interest and involvement. The novelty of an experience can become self-reinforcing, and this reinforcement can strengthen and maintain the behavior leading to learning. Many workers do not need extrinsic rewards to learn new skills. The experience of achieving a new skill is in itself a positive reinforcement that leads to continued enthusiasm and involvement.

Repetition, familiarity, or simplicity of an activity will reduce the enthusiasm and motivation to continue the task. Individuals may seek out other activities. The elevation of standards or performance can sustain interest and involvement, and empowered individuals themselves will increase the level of difficulty of their tasks as their learning and ability increase. Exhibit 6.3 suggest numerous ways to introduce novelty.

(k) EMPOWERING INDIVIDUALS When attempting to construct plans or to determine how individuals will contribute to a team, how the team will work with other teams, and how these processes will contribute to both the goals and the improvement of the processes of the organizational structure, it is essential to consider several basic premises associated with effective functioning.

Organizations often use the talents and skills of many people from whom leadership has not previously been sought. Empowerment means that each individual realizes the potential he or she possesses, and people are given options to examine their work and the work of their team so that they will function more effectively and productively.

In a group of empowered individuals, there is one consistent answer to the question: Whose organization is this? That answer is: MINE! (See Exhibit 6.4.)

Although it is commonly acknowledged that "people are our greatest asset," it is less common for this premise to be used as a basis for planning. The questions in Exhibit 6.5 should be addressed during further development of an understanding of the relationships among people, their work, and their places in the organization.

A problem in all organizations is the difficulty of involving individuals and creating in them feelings of ownership of their own work. If feelings of ownership do not exist, it is unlikely that employees or volunteers will obtain the satisfaction they desire. If they are disenchanted or discouraged with their work and see little possibility

---

Exhibit 6.3.   Checklist introducing novelty into work.

1. Can I vary the pattern or sequence of work to be done? _____

2. Can I alter the timing of production? _____

3. Can I modify the complexity of a task? _____

4. Can I rearrange old ideas to vitalize them? _____

5. Can I fit new ideas into an existing framework? _____

6. Can I move the task to a different setting? _____

7. Can I add constraints on achievement? _____

8. Can I introduce elements of cooperative or collaborative work into this task? _____

Exhibit 6.4. Checklist for empowering individuals.

Empowering individuals requires a careful consideration of the following questions:

1. Has "the individual" been included in the plans? _____

2. Does the organization believe that individuals want to perform well because they are seeking satisfaction from their work? _____

3. Is it important that all employees understand their contribution to the organization's goals? _____

4. Does the organization "care" for individual workers and does this "caring" improve productivity? _____

5. Will the organization invest the resources and training necessary to create a positive response to the questions listed above? _____

6. Is what the organization says consistent with what it does? _____

of influencing the direction of their positions, they are not likely to invest themselves and their energy in analyzing and planning. Lack of opportunity will create lethargy, which will lead to further diminished performance.

Empowered individuals will consistently be seeking ways to develop their potential through an analysis of their work, including the parts of their tasks that require interactions and cooperative efforts with others.

Enlightened self-interest is another significant force acting on individuals (and their work groups) and demonstrating the effects of empowerment. According to Peter

Exhibit 6.5. Checklist of individual work roles.

Can these questions be answered in the negative?

1. Does the job description of each position "pigeonhole" individuals? _____

2. Are opinions asked for when there is no intent to use them? _____

3. Is the supervisor expected to provide an answer to every question and leadership for every situation? _____

4. Are the first questions raised in planning sessions questions of accountability and measurement of performance? _____

Can these questions be answered in the positive?

1. Is the individual encouraged to make significant suggestions and participate in decision making? _____

2. Is the level of decision making comfortable for all individuals? _____

3. Does a person who has made suggestions receive feedback on how they have been used? _____

4. Are acceptance of risk and sharing of uncertainty encouraged and valued? _____

5. Are the first questions raised in planning sessions questions about methods for involving employees in exploring how the problems could be resolved? _____

Block (1987), the following issues describe how people will balance their needs and the needs of the organization.

1. **Meaning:** "We will engage in activities that have meaning to us and are genuinely needed. We will express our values about what we have to contribute."
2. **Contribution and service:** "We decide to do the things that we feel genuinely contribute to the organizational structure and its purpose."
3. **Integrity:** "All of us have the fear that we cannot maintain our integrity and still succeed."
4. **Positive impact on others' lives:** "It is in our self-interest to treat other people well. The organization is our primary meeting place, and we care deeply about the well-being of our colleagues."
5. **Mastery:** "We will simply learn as much as we can about the activity we are engaged in. We take pride and satisfaction in understanding our function."

DePree's (1989) description of the relationship between leaders and their people in both the for-profit and not-for-profit sectors demonstrates the need to have empowered, innovative, self-motivated workers:

> Leaders owe a covenant to the corporation or institution, which is, after all, a group of people. Leaders owe the organization a new reference point for what caring, purposeful, committed people can be in the institutional setting. Notice I did not say what people can do—what we can do is merely a consequence of what we can be. Corporations (or institutions), like the people who compose them, are always in a state of becoming. Covenants bind people together and enable them to meet their (overall) needs by meeting the needs of one another. We must do this in a way that is consonant with the world around us. [pp. 12 and 13]

6.2 EMPOWERING TEAMS AND TEAMWORK

A commonly and prominently displayed poster, issued by the Association for Quality Control, reads: "Quality—The Result of Teamwork." Organizational structures increasingly rely on teams, and much of the impetus to teamwork can be attributed to the quality movement. Indeed, the entire philosophy of empowerment and quality involves people working together intensively, to maximize individual and interactive capability.

Frances Hesselbein, former head of the Girl Scouts of America, demonstrated a commitment to this philosophy by replacing the typical pyramid with a circular management structure that emphasized the change in relationships and functioning from one of authority to one of collaboration. In addition, she encouraged each of the organization's 333 councils to define their mission and set their own agenda.

(a) HOW ORGANIZATIONS USE INNOVATIVE TEAM APPROACHES Small groups have been used in organizations for a very long time. Only recently, however, has their power been realized, and strategies for making them into teams have been developed. The possibilities for creating and using teams probably are endless, but some commonly used types stand out and are here to stay. These are:

Management and staff groups;
Quality circles;

Self-managing teams;

Creative or project teams;

Intra- or interorganizational task forces;

Governance groups.

Each has its purposes, its functions, its problems, and its solutions to those problems.

(i) Management and staff groups These teams are usually formed by administrative units or by levels of management or supervision. They meet on a regular basis (e.g., daily, weekly) to share information and make decisions. Frequently, these meetings involve the superior-rank person's providing the agenda, making reports, and asking for ideas or questions. These groups rarely achieve the qualities of a good working team, and become more like the infamous Pentagon briefings. Opportunities for empowering teams are rarely seized.

(ii) Quality circles Quality circles are groups of workers who work together to solve problems and make proposals. Originally, most quality-circle members were drawn from across an organization, although contemporary uses frequently are more specifically oriented. The purposes, according to consultant and trainer John Baird, ". . . are to improve quality, climate and participation" (Baird, 1982, p. 5). Quality circles are used at all levels, in all kinds of organizations. Members typically meet with an assigned leader and focus on improving quality in specific areas of concern.

Problems with quality circles have been: insufficient focus in their areas of concern, insufficient training for members and leaders, and insufficient resources and empowerment from the organization. For a period of time, quality circles were looked on as mechanisms for management's manipulation of workers by pretending to be interested in their ideas (reinforced by management's failure to follow up on whatever the circle proposed) or as an easy way for a lazy worker to get out of the department for a time.

Today, many organizations and workers are enthusiastic about quality circles because management is taking them more seriously; leaders and participants are being given team communication training; resources are being provided; circles are focusing on specific problems and carrying ideas through to the action stage with the support of management.

(iii) Self-managing teams Self-managing teams are people who work together in any area of an organization and who are responsible for all aspects of their task. They determine their own structure and working system; they make budget allocations, personnel decisions, and scheduling plans; they coordinate with other teams and departments; and they are directly responsible for their own success.

(iv) Project teams or creative teams These groups are comprised of several people who bring together very specific expertise to plan and complete a project. A creative team is a specific type of project team. A project team may be appointed by management in an organization or it could be a group of people who come together out of mutual interest in developing an answer to a problem. It may or may not have a designated leader and it probably works within very specific deadlines.

Problems in project teams can develop from conflict over resources, objectives, and approaches. The necessity to work together to bring a project to fruition, however, can create a strong sense of "teamness." Here again, a strong vision, freely shared expertise, and competent communication skills can make the team a success.

(v) Intra- or interorganizational task forces   Task forces are teams of people brought together to investigate and make reports or proposals on a given problem. Because the team membership may encompass more than one administrative unit in an organization (or even in multiple organizations), task forces are frequently referred to as *cross teams* (or cross-functional teams).

One important goal of cross-team efforts is to develop relationships that will enable workers to have a more complete understanding of the mission of the organization, how they contribute to that mission, and how they might contribute to the improvement of other workers.

Cross-team efforts encourage the assessment of performance from multiple viewpoints (e.g., clients, patients, consumers, employees, suppliers) to both assess current practices and seek new ways to improve service. These activities further empower people to the extent that they not only make recommendations but also use their authority to take active steps toward improvement.

Each team should analyze its own success in meeting its goals. An emphasis on collaborative efforts leads to increased identification with the organization and greater commitment to the team and the project.

Often, a task force is appointed; it may have a designated leader, and its work usually is intensive. Two organizations, or sections of one organization, sometimes create a task force comprised of two or more teams representing their respective areas.

The Environmental Defense Fund and McDonald's Corporation Task Force brought together a small team from each organization to investigate waste management issues and to make proposals to McDonald's. Over about a year of intensive work, the task force educated each other and themselves, gathered the necessary information, and made a proposal that was adopted by McDonald's—an unprecedented effort in cooperative action between corporate and nonprofit environmental interests.

The problem often faced by task forces, especially when they bridge organizations or departments, is lack of empowerment through resources, support, and authority. When appointing organizations select the task force members well, make a commitment to their work, and give the team full support and cooperation, a task force can create some incredible progress on seemingly insurmountable problems.

(vi) Governance groups and committees   These are internal groups of elected or, sometimes, appointed representatives. Their functions are to guide professional behavior and to protect the rights and responsibilities of their members and those whom they represent. Such groups meet regularly, and their numbers vary from a few on a committee to a large, legislative-type body. Usually, they follow parliamentary procedure in conducting their meetings, they are founded on a set of bylaws, and they have a set of elected officers.

Problems with governance groups are that they often are at odds with adversarial groups, thus taking time and energy; they move very slowly, as everything in democratic process generally does; and they rarely think of themselves or behave as "teams."

These characteristics are inherent in the process, but even a governance group can become a team when it articulates a clear vision or goal, incorporates the values and objectives of its constituency, and proceeds with solid teamwork. Strong leadership, from members as well as from the "leader," and the clear vision that makes any group a team are required.

(b) WHAT THE IDEAL, TOP-QUALITY TEAM IS LIKE For groups of people to become empowered teams, they must understand the traits of top-quality teams, must develop quality with individual members, and must develop themselves as team units.

(i) General team characteristics Dennis Kinlaw (1991), a consultant to NASA and many other organizations, identifies four areas of distinction in the way a superior work team functions. He says that such a team:

1. Achieves certain distinctive results;
2. Employs successfully certain kinds of informal work processes;
3. Develops in members certain kinds of feelings;
4. Develops leadership that focuses both on team development and on team performance.

The picture of a team that produces these four distinctive ways of doing things is complex. A British consulting group has put together a concept of the "superteam," based on extensive observation of work teams. Superteams, they say, "weave together a rich fabric of competencies, experience, attitudes and values which create a tightly woven, integrated cloth suitable for many purposes" (Hastings, 1986, p. 10). These consultants posit an incredible dynamism, commitment, cooperation, and vision within a superteam; they suggest that a fine team works well together and with the system, and that its members are never satisfied and won't take no for an answer.

(ii) Developing quality with individuals An effective team has effective members, people who bring special individual characteristics to their work. These include commitment, responsibility, leadership, motivation, diversity, and credibility.

Members must have *commitment* to the vision of the organization and to the mission of the team. They are willing to take responsibility both for their own work and for the effectiveness of the team as a whole. Their commitment is manifested in several ways.

A person who is committed to the team and to the vision will assume personal *responsibility* for team interactions and products. When necessary, this person represents the team, provides *leadership,* and is willing to make personal sacrifices for the sake of the team. Accounts of successful team experiences are full of anecdotes about people who sacrificed personal time and energy to get the job done.

Quality members work with *motivation* for themselves and they keep motivation high for others. Motivations start within the person; they are driven by needs and wants. An effective member will be motivated to see something accomplished; to derive satisfaction from interacting productively with others, and to attain rewards in his or her job.

An excellent team experience can reach members at all levels of need satisfaction. Working in a finely tuned team can satisfy a person's need for social contact and affiliation, build self-esteem, satisfy the human need for control over one's own work and destiny, and fulfill those less finite needs for creativity and growth through the challenges the team takes on and achieves.

Members who exercise leadership with commitment and motivation have one thing in common: they are empowered people who are fully involved in—who "own"—the goals and the process of their team.

Members of an effective team also bring *diversity* to the experience. Each individual has intrinsic characteristics that contribute to the depth and breadth to which a team may reach. These include differences in gender, culture, background, and experiences. A useful member both recognizes his or her own unique qualities and appreciates those of others. A mutual appreciation of member diversity occurs when people recognize the value that diversity brings to their team by enlisting the distinct skills and fields of expertise of each member. Some of the value, however, is in the point of view, the experience, the way of seeing that individuals develop because of their gender, their ethnic background, or their cultural or subcultural experiences.

To help develop a strong team, members must have *credibility* in the eyes of other team members. When team members perceive a person as credible, they are willing to trust, to rely on, and to interact with that individual. What makes a person credible in the eyes of others has been analyzed for years. The studies converge to suggest that the factors of competence or expertise, objectivity, trustworthiness (Whitehead, 1969), and coorientation (Tuppen, 1974) are paramount.

Competence or *expertise* in a work team is essential. Comembers need to see an individual as competent both in the specific area of his or her expertise and in thinking, analyzing, and communicating. Teamwork is so intense, and time and energy are so valuable, that people simply don't want to waste resources with others whose knowledge and skills are inadequate. This is one reason why teams should be carefully constituted and trained.

Objectivity is as important as credibility in a work team. Individuals need to be able to see issues and ideas from more than one side; they need to be able to suspend judgment and leave their biases behind. Even when other members agree with a person's biases, they may be leery of that individual's inability to transcend them in the interest of inquiry and fairness.

Trustworthiness, the foundation for any interpersonal or public relationship, is necessary to teamwork. Members need to trust each other on a number of levels: in confidentiality, so that communication can be open; in tolerance and support from others, in order to take risks in discussing ideas; in shared values, ethics, and each other's honesty, because their self-esteem, their accomplishments, and their jobs are mutually on the line.

People may tolerate lapses in competence or objectivity, but they will not develop interdependency in a team with someone they cannot trust.

Coorientation describes the feeling of similarity and identification that one individual has for another. A person's credibility will be strengthened by other team members' perceptions that the same understandings, the same orientation toward the mission and the team, are shared by that person. They may not all walk in the same moccasins, but they all are walking in the same direction.

(c) HOW A TEAM DEVELOPS QUALITY BY DEVELOPING ITSELF   A team does not just happen. It develops when individuals cooperate to transfigure their group into a team. "[E]very work group can become a work team," according to Kinlaw (1991, p. 12), "and every work team can become a superior work team."

(i) A shared team image Strong teams have a strong sense of who they are, of their identity and image. Groups develop a "syntality" that is to a group as personality is to an individual. Together, a team develops a sense of identity and direction. Members create, together, a shared vision, a shared sense of values, and shared teamwork expectations.

(ii) How to create a shared image A team has its own kind of energy, called "synergy," composed of the combined energies and motivations of the entire group. Together, syntality and synergy make the team much more than the sum of its parts. It has an identity of its own, to itself and to the outside system. That sense of who and what the group is helps members bond into a working unit and provides an image against which to measure the team's behavior and effectiveness.

Developing a strong identity is the result of intelligence, commitment, and hard work. Fortunately, the hard work is definable and direct.

Leadership—from leaders and members—can help create that sense of identity and will reinforce it as time goes on. Some specific ways to develop identity are:

1. Create connections among members. Invest time in getting to know each other personally and finding common threads and interests. Build on these as bonds.

2. Set norms for member behavior early. Give every member a chance to express preferences and concerns for ways of working; these will include everything from attitudes toward being on time to constraints on ways of presenting information. As a team, discuss the ideas and establish consensus about those that seem important to the group. State these as expected "norms" for team members' behavior and get people's confirmation that they will adhere to these norms. The norms not only help to avert unnecessary functioning problems, but they reinforce the team's sense of who it is.

3. Create fantasies, myths, and symbols with the team. (See Chapter 4 of this volume for creativity and fantasy-chaining techniques.) As discussions proceed, people will naturally use humor or imagination or metaphors to think aloud about the team. These can be built into mutually held symbols, and symbols help to hold together a common concept of what the team is.

   For example, if someone says in a meeting, "I feel like I need spikes on my shoes, we're climbing so many mountains," another person might respond, "Yeah! I've got my little pick and repel rope handy." A few more comments, and the team has an image of a carefully coordinated team of skillful climbers, mutually dependent on one another, scaling a difficult peak and determined to plant their flag at the top. The image becomes a metaphor for their entire experience, and the symbols become refined through frequent reference. Sooner or later someone says, "Wait a minute—I've got to get my spikes in," and everyone knows exactly what that means.

   This is not a technique that can be superimposed on a team; it is a strategy for developing "groupness" that can flow from what happens naturally, if people are allowed to explore their relationships and their ideas creatively.

(iii) A shared vision When group members do not understand a clear purpose for the team or they do not make a personal commitment to the goals, the group eventually ceases to function. When an individual has a clear "mental picture" of what she or he is striving for, both the goal and the steps to be taken are more vivid and more attainable

Visualizing a goal and strategies for achieving it helps individuals in their personal lives, in their professions, and in sports. Organizations are training people at all levels—sales, service, management; personal, physical, and psychological health—in techniques for visualizing where they are going. (See Chap. 5.)

The effect is, perhaps, most obvious in athletics. In a recent letter to *The New York Times Magazine,* Shane Murphy, of the Sports Science and Medicine Division of the United States Olympic Committee (Murphy, 1991), contended that "Interventions based on techniques like goal-setting, relaxation training, visualization and self-talk are effective in helping about 80 percent of athletes."

A work team, no less than an athlete, needs a vision of the goal and of how it will be reached. A shared vision is a mental picture that any member of the team can describe in terms of objectives and of feelings. It is related closely to the organizational vision for itself, but, more specifically, it is comprised of the sense of what the team is and what it is striving for. "Seeking" that goal ahead and "feeling" what it will be like to get there can motivate the team and help it act in concert to achieve the goal.

(iv) Developing a shared set of goals Developing a shared set of goals is itself a necessary goal. The process of reaching agreement on common goals provides additional opportunities to create ownership; develop problem-solving, communication, and decision-making skills; and, in general, demonstrate to employees that organizational leadership is serious in its commitment to empower the team. Exhibit 6.6 can aid in that process.

(v) How to create and nurture the team "vision" The following methods will help to create the vision:

1. When the goals have been set, discuss what the organization will be like when they are achieved. Take some time for members to describe what they will feel about it and how it will be for others who are concerned with it. If the project

Exhibit 6.6.   Checklist of strategies leading to shared goals.

1. Have we consciously sought multiple points of view?   _____

   —Have we solicited different perspectives on the activity/endeavor?   _____

   —Have we utilized surveys and group meetings to ensure a pluralistic
   point of view?   _____

   —Have techniques for wide involvement, such as the delphi method,
   been used to gain consensus or agreement?   _____

2. Have all potential impacts been considered?   _____

3. Have goals been described in terms of expected results?   _____

4. Have goals been weighted/ordered in terms of their individual significance?   _____

5. Are those who are doing the work making judgments about the
   appropriateness of the goals?   _____

6. Are the goals and objectives, and the priorities given to each,
   understood and accepted by all?   _____

or problem is one that can be put into a concrete visual image, all the better. Even if the end is very abstract, make it as mentally visual as possible.

2. As teamwork moves on, relate discussion to the vision when appropriate. As the process moves toward choosing decisions, it becomes especially important to look at them in terms of the goals and the vision.

3. Reinforce the vision by representing it to new team members, to associates, and to outside systems or authorities. Make the shared vision a part of the team image; in the earlier example, the mountain climbers are climbers who see a vision of their achievement at the top of their mountain. The particulars of the vision are determined by the problem, but the vision is contained in the objectives of the team itself.

(vi) Shared values and expectations To trust fully and cooperate with each other, members of a team have to understand some of their individual priorities and assumptions. Further, they must find a common, shared base of values and expectations that will affect their team transactions. (See Chap. 5.)

A *shared sense of values* does not necessarily mean that all members will see ethical issues in precisely the same light; in fact, diversity of membership ensures that they will not. What it does mean is that members work through their value assumptions and choices; important ethical standards are assumed to be mutually understood and accepted so that analysis and decision making can proceed without assault on individuals' sense of right and wrong.

Shared teamwork expectations involve high standards and norms for individual and team processes and performance. These include expectations of leader roles and behaviors and of leadership responsibilities of members.

Expectations of leader roles and behaviors seem to be high and specific in top-quality teams. Kinlaw noted that McDonnell Douglas reorganized its managers and supervisors "based on subordinates', peers', and superiors' perceptions of their abilities to lead." The first characteristic evaluated was: "Teamplayer: Unites others toward a shared destiny through sharing information and ideas, empowering others and developing trust" (Kinlaw, 1991, p. xvi).

Similarly, among the behaviors identified as characteristic of "superteam" leaders (Hastings, 1986, p. 83), these stand out:

A leader helps to develop and "sells" the team's vision to the parent organization and other systems;

A leader represents and gains support for the team and its vision;

A leader creates a quality climate within the team through his or her own behavior and attitudes.

These observations are consistent with those of Kinlaw (1991, p. xix) who observed that managers' jobs are shifting ". . . from managing by control to managing by commitment; from focusing on individual motivation and output to focusing on team motivation and output; and from traditional functions of planning, organizing, staffing, evaluating to the functions of coaching and facilitating."

Expectations of leadership responsibilities of members also are very high in good teams. Although "leadership" often has been thought of as "the leader's job" or "a managerial prerogative," it is not that way in an effective team. As with the designated leader, team members represent the team to other systems by the way they reflect and present the vision and the syntality of the team. Further, members expect one another constantly to fill roles that lead, motivate, instigate, facilitate, and support each other. Each team member must be alert to individual and team needs, must look for ways to meet them, and, in fact, should be ready to fill specific functions of the leader when necessary. Leadership is a shared function in a good team.

Leadership happens when an individual influences group members to develop healthy transactions about people's feelings as well as about the job the team is doing. Leadership requires skill and sensitivity in guiding and participating in these processes with the team.

(vii) How to establish shared values and expectations Among the first thing teams should do, when they are becoming acquainted as members, is explore what each member expects of the team. People need to look at expectations of leadership, of behaviors, and of structure, and these expectations should be clearly articulated. If, for example, several team members want or expect to receive a clear agenda a week before every meeting, this should become a norm and an expectation of the team. The designated leader or a delegated member then should assume the responsibility to see that it happens. The more thoroughly and clearly expectations are explored and norms are set, the fewer conflicts will arise in the future.

Related, but even more important, is an exploration of members' values. Much of this process necessarily will happen as the team develops, but an initial exploration of what people believe and value will provide a starting point for members to understand each other and to communicate clearly and empathically on value-laden issues. Exploring values can start with very direct questions and discussion: What do you think is important about the issues facing the team? What kinds of questions will we face about values? What kinds of ethical criteria will the team use to make value decisions?

Later, when the team inevitably faces conflicts among members or with other systems, understanding one another's expectations and values will make it easier to find ways to manage those conflicts.

(viii) Shared transactional and task processes of communication Communication is complex, dynamic, and essential. It also involves a certain amount of risk: every time a person communicates anything more personal than name–rank–serial number, he or she risks a range of possible harms. Communication might result in rejection, in giving the other person a weapon to use against the communicator, or in learning something about others or about oneself that would require adjustment and change. And human beings often are frightened of adjustment and change.

Communication in a team is compounded—in its complexity, in its challenge, and in its risk—by the numbers of members and the numbers of interactions with outside elements. Yet, communicating is what teams do. There must be trust and confidence and openness if that communication is to work. Trust and confidence are built by members' communicating those feelings to each other.

Actions and reactions that develop a climate of either supportiveness or defensiveness are *transactional processes*. They involve the transactions, negotiations, understandings, and effects that occur through communicating within the team. Actions and reactions that help or hinder information gathering, analysis, problem solving, decision making, and task achievement are part of *task processes*.

There are times when transactional and task processes seem mutually exclusive. Investing the time it takes to create positive working climates, for example, appears to take time from working on achieving the team's goal. However, both processes must work together. If transactions upset or alienate people, that will interfere with pursuing the task. If transactions help people to feel excited about their teamwork, that will advance the task. If task achievement is high, transactions will be easier and more rewarding; if the task is frustrating and seems unattainable, transactions between people will reflect that pain.

In a climate marked by openness and trust, where members are willing to take risks, to disclose information, and to support others in pursuit of common goals, the approach is cooperative, although team members understand competition and work with it when it is appropriate to goal achievement. The team can work with conflict and confrontation by keeping the climate supportive, and the team maintains a norm for constant assessment and improvement of its processes.

Such communication processes help to develop every aspect of team vision, team image, shared values, and expectations. They create, in the view of Blake, Mouton, and Allen (1987), a team culture. These theorists have identified two primary drives in a team culture: "concern for task" and "concern for people." The excellent team demonstrates a balance between them.

Concern for people is manifested through transactional process communication, which promotes positive transactions between and among human beings. Concern for task is manifested through task process communication behaviors, which help the team progress toward its goals. With these relationships in mind, it is useful to look at specific leadership behaviors in the context of transactions and task.

(ix) How to communicate through positive transactional processes   Every member of the team takes leadership responsibility for the transactional processes that make all this possible. Transactional process leadership behaviors that help to advance a supportive climate include:

1. Asking for and reminding others of norms for supportiveness, trust, and openness; making a positive climate an expectation for which everyone strives.
2. Encouraging the involvement of each member; asking for information, ideas, opinions, and feelings; supporting with agreement or open questions; confirming the other person as worthy through verbal and nonverbal support. (Nonverbal support can be expressed simply by leaning forward, nodding, or using "uh-hums.")
3. Encouraging trust and openness; taking risks, disclosing personal as well as professional information, and maintaining confidentiality and support for each other.
4. Helping people to manage conflict; stating the value of conflict for opening up issues; helping each side state the case; and negotiating compromises and approaches to management.
5. Helping people to support each other; looking for and stating commonalities and agreement; rephrasing confusing or negative statements and asking for confirmation that the rephrase is, in fact, acceptable; reinforcing positive behavior by showing agreement and satisfaction with it. Nonverbal communication that helps this process includes appropriate touching, supportive eye-contact, being sensitive

to territory and space relationships, and avoiding crowding people or using height or space for power.

6. Monitoring language to make it supportive; phrasing, and helping others with rephrasing, ideas; replacing blaming, manipulative, accusatory, or all-or-nothing statements with wording that focuses on the problem, rather than on the person, is supportive of others' rights, and qualifies opinions and positions.

7. Being assertive and helping others to be assertive; stating positions nondefensively, before the urge to be aggressive or to withdraw passively sets in; helping others to be assertive by sensing their needs and asking sensitive questions to get the statement made.

8. Listening interactively and empathically; concentrating on others' statements; asking clear and helpful questions; paraphrasing to confirm ideas, information, or feelings; giving nonverbal support; and tactfully bringing attention back to a speaker when someone else interrupts.

9. Working actively to change a defensive climate when it occurs; looking for the causes of the stress and calling attention to the damaging interactions; and negotiating change with other members.

(x) How to communicate for a positive task process   In an effectively functioning team, the task process is characterized by the use of an appropriate agreed-on structure, by flexibility and adaptability, and by clarity of goals and objectives. A team properly focused on its task has the ability and commitment to get and use necessary information and resources, and maintains a norm for openness to and practice of both creativity and critical analysis. Members use a variety of problem-solving and decision-making approaches, and constantly evaluate and reevaluate their progress. Every member of a fine team provides leadership through specific behaviors that move the task processes along. Task process behaviors include:

1. Facilitating clear and mutually accepted goals; suggesting, phrasing, confirming, and revising goal statements with team members.

2. Identifying needs for information and resources; asking for sharing of information; brainstorming on needs; and suggesting organized approaches to getting what's needed.

3. Assuring that labor is equitably and rationally shared; guiding discussion of individuals' skills, expertise, interests, and suggestions; helping to design a system and division for information gathering and analysis.

4. Making sure that everyone's information and ideas are shared; questioning and probing to get others to provide everything they can.

5. Providing information, analysis, and ideas; doing the homework of thinking through contributions; listening carefully and asking questions, to test the validity and reliability of evidence and reasoning.

6. Providing ethical and quality tests; asking questions to examine the value and acceptability of suggestions, decisions, and actions.

7. Orienting the team toward the task process; calling attention back when it wanders; providing summaries; suggesting next steps; checking consensus among members before going on to the next stage.

8. Being sure meetings are organized; calling attention to or asking for confirmation of meeting times and places; preparing and distributing agendas; record keeping and reporting; assignments; follow-up and evaluation of decisions or actions.

6.3 TEAMS IN SYSTEM RELATIONSHIPS

Like every other entity, teams do not exist on an island of autonomy. They function in relationship to multitudes of other entities. To understand the complexities of a team's processes and tasks, they have to be seen in terms of systems and subsystems.

A system is an interacting, interrelating, and interdependent arrangement of entities that take inputs (information, ideas, resources) and process them (through interpersonal transactions, creative and critical thinking, decision making) to produce outputs (goal achievement, decisions, products, services). In a closed system, such as an enclosed transistor, that's the end of it. In an open system—the type all human systems necessarily must be—there is a cybernetic process of feedback, evaluation, and change.

(a) A TEAM IS A SYSTEM IN ITSELF Team members interact and interrelate; they are dependent on each other for support and for doing the job. The members bring information (input) and they process it; then they produce the goal or the mission of the team (output). They are constantly in the process of feedback and change as they live within their system, but they do not function autonomously.

(b) A TEAM WORKS WITHIN AND INTERACTS WITH OTHER SYSTEMS The team essentially interacts with and interdepends on at least three other systems: the parent organization, related teams or organizations, and the public. The team becomes, therefore, a subsystem of the larger organization and a co-subsystem with other teams (and, in some instances, with other organizations). The ways in which relationships function are specific, in many ways, to specific teams; the principle can be seen, however, in terms of containing, overlapping circles and vectors of communication.

The team's relationship to other teams and organizational structures will be both simple and complex. Members may be drawn from different departments, and input from those departments may be important to the functioning of the team. Or, output, in the form of reports back to the department, may affect the functioning of the departmental system. Or, the team, in making recommendations for, say, safety regulations, may need to interact with and receive input from numbers of other teams and departments in the organization and then may make recommendations that will affect many others in the end. Sometimes, interdependency with one or more systems will conflict with other relationships.

In one organization, an overly enthusiastic president typically appointed two, three, or even four separate groups to study or act on the same issue. Usually, none of the teams knew about the others. When employees finally caught on to what was happening, they became irritated and discouraged. Although their organization gave them support and resources, the subsystems within it were disconnected and dysfunctional.

(c) A TEAM IS A SUBSYSTEM OF THE PARENT ORGANIZATION The parent organization provides the "charge" or the goal to the team; it may appoint the membership or it may delegate that task to a leader, to managers, or to departments. The parent organization may appoint a leader, or it may designate someone to convene the first meeting and leave the question of leadership up to the team to decide.

The team is responsible, ultimately, to the parent organization, but its members also may be responsible to represent and to report to other departments or organizations. In real terms, this means that members must fully understand the vision and the culture of both the larger system and the related systems. Finally, it should go without saying that the parent organization has responsibility to the team.

Unfortunately, organizations are only now becoming educated in this responsibility, and the work of many teams has been frustrated because management has failed them. The organization, to get the quality responses it wants from teams, must empower them by providing the information, resources, encouragement, and support they need; by allowing them time and room for failure as well as for success; and by granting them the authority to make decisions and to act. With any less than these forms of support, teams must work uphill all the way; they become exhausted, disempowered, and, finally, ineffective. With the empowerment, outstanding results can occur.

(d) A TEAM WORKS IN RELATIONSHIP TO PUBLIC AND COMMUNITY SYSTEMS The team as a whole almost inevitably works in relationship to other outside systems. These might include government agencies or bureaus with which the team must deal for information or authority; related nonprofit organizations with which teams must cooperate to achieve a goal; or related or adversarial corporate systems.

Individual team members, too, have a range of contacts with other systems that might impact on the team's interactions in some way; a person's family, church, or educational institution may influence his or her input into—and, therefore, the processing and output of—that person's team.

A team, then, is a system within systems, and it interacts with and interdepends on multiple other subsystems.

(e) HOW TO MAXIMIZE THE TEAM'S EFFECTIVENESS IN RELATION TO OTHER GROUPS AND AUTHORITIES Because it's a subsystem of a larger organization, a team interdepends on and interacts with other teams, with other subsystems (departments) of the organization, and with other outside systems and subsystems. Its effectiveness requires that it build trust and respect and that it achieve cooperation with other entities.

(i) Achieving trust and respect Achieving trust and respect from other teams and organizational systems is no different than achieving credibility with other individuals. The difference is that others are seeing the team as an entity; its vision and its image must, like individuals, communicate competence, objectivity, trustworthiness, and coorientation. When these characteristics are perceived in a team, other groups will be likely to cooperate in providing resources and in coordinating ventures.

(ii) Ways to build team credibility These approaches involve individual team members' actions as representatives of the team, as well as team decisions and interactions viewed from outside the team. The expertise, or competence, of individual members reflects the credibility of the team as a whole. Similarly, statements and actions, by members and by the team, that demonstrate objectivity and fair-mindedness lead others to see the team as objective; concrete demonstration of this characteristic may come through team members' ability to qualify their statements about issues, or to acknowledge others' points of view. If the team is seen to make a decision that allows others to share in its resources or its glory, that will increase its credibility as being objective and fair-minded.

Trustworthiness, too, is seen both in terms of members and of team syntality. If single members of the team are known to be dishonest or manipulative, the effect will be to tarnish the team. If, on the other hand, members are known to act ethically and the team is seen to make ethical decisions, then others will be able to trust the team.

Finally, an attitude of coorientation must be demonstrated by both individuals and the team as a whole. Other groups must perceive the team as a unit that shares their objectives and values. This requires that the team understand not only its own shared values, beliefs, and objectives, but also that it inquire into and understand those of related groups and systems. Other groups that have different orientations still need to see important areas of coorientation.

(iii) Team and member relationships A brief examination of a major league baseball team provides a view of teams and their relationships. Are only the players team members? What are the roles of the field manager and coaches? Of the general manager and owners? Do the bat boy and trainer contribute to the team's success? This simple analysis will undoubtedly give insight to the vast relational structure supporting a major league baseball team.

A similar analysis can be made of any work unit. In addition to the people who spend the majority of their time on-site at a particular office, others in the organizational structure provide support and service to the office. The obvious conclusion is that everyone within the system relies on everyone else in some clearly identifiable way. This realization highlights the need for shared goals and for the shared successes necessary to develop a total quality approach.

(f) HOW TO CREATE COOPERATIVE VENTURES WITH OTHER TEAMS AND TASK FORCES Creating a cooperative venture is challenging, but it can lead to incredible results. It requires demonstrating the credibility of individual members and of the team, and maintaining intensive, focused, analytical communication between teams. Successful cooperative ventures generally will follow these steps from conception to delivery:

1. Analysis leading to a cooperative venture starts with gaining understanding of the other group and its members' perceptions of its vision, image, goals, and individual and team ways of doing things.

2. Initiation should be a tentative and open contact, an invitation to the other group to explore ideas. When the proposed cooperation is between groups from two different organizations or associations, initial contacts and subsequent support should be at the highest level possible. A call from CEO to CEO can set the level of importance for the task and assure both teams of a high level of support.

3. An exploratory meeting should be held at which representatives of each team start with a tentative, careful exploration of goals, resources, and problems faced by each team.

4. More exploratory meetings, with part or all of each team present, may take some time, as members examine ways in which the two teams can work together to achieve mutual goals. At this point, the cooperative task force must go through the same process of developing a shared image, a shared vision, shared values and expectations, and task and transactional processes of communication. Meetings should be either in a location outside of the territory of both teams, or should alternate, so that neither always has the home court advantage. No matter how cooperative people are, their territory does affect their attitudes and their communication.

5. Developing group identity and a shared vision is a process that may take some time and may result in many lapses in communication. Where the team is a composite from two or more different organizations or associations, this process of working out a shared perspective is even more important and more difficult than it is for a cooperative effort between teams that both are subsystems of the same organization. In either case, members bring previously established team cultures and individual predispositions to the process, but, in the case of teams representing more than one parent organization, they also bring the larger organizational cultures into the new entity.

6. Setting out processes of information gathering and analysis, setting goals, and developing criteria for success (see Chapter 4) must be done early in the process and may take considerable compromise and negotiation. Members have to devote time to educating and being educated by each other about their respective organizational cultures and points of view.

7. The new team works out its relationship and methods of working with its parent organizations and related subsystems in each organizational structure. There must be considerable feedback between parent organization (or parent teams) and the new team.

8. The new team creates an agreement, in writing, that spells out the way the members intend to handle the entire process and the results of its cooperation.

9. As it progresses, the team uses transactional and task processes, together with feedback and assessment, to work out conflict or competition problems and to achieve a positive climate.

10. As the goal approaches, members negotiate the final steps of completing the project and presenting, writing, and/or publishing the results.

11. All members of the team, and the parent organization or organizations, should be responsible and acknowledged for the end results. A cooperative venture, when it is successful, not only accomplishes a goal that rarely could be accomplished alone but also creates a model for further cooperation within and between organizations. It is important, therefore, that organizational and public communication carry the results through to a positive and visible conclusion.

6.4   USING CYBERNETIC PROCESSES TO IMPROVE QUALITY

The foundation of quality management is a constant cybernetic process of feedback and adjustment from every part of the system. For any organizational structure, that means soliciting, gathering, and using feedback from suppliers, from every part of the system, from consumers, and from clients.

For the team, which is a subsystem of the organization, the process is the same. A top-quality team should use a constant feedback loop that involves its suppliers (the parent organization, outside resources), its team members (in their transactional and task processes), its customers or clients (the parent organization, other teams or departments, or organizational clients themselves), and its products (decisions, recommendations, and productivity).

In the cybernetic process, a team must first establish the climate for feedback, assessment, and change. Then it can involve feedback and analysis processes.

(a) ESTABLISHING A CLIMATE FOR FEEDBACK, ASSESSMENT, AND CHANGE There are two very important principles for establishing a climate in which the team wants feedback and uses it well. The process must be nonthreatening and team-generated.

"*Kaizen,*" the Japanese approach to the need for continuous improvement, suggests that there will be few "major" breakthroughs. There will, however, be innumerable opportunities to make small improvements. While these small improvements may not be significant by themselves, their cumulative effects can be powerful.

(i) Nonthreatening To be nonthreatening, any evaluation must be exclusively for the purpose of the team's self-improvement. It absolutely cannot be used by the parent organization for personnel evaluation, promotion, or pay-increase purposes. It cannot be used by any outside authority or system for evaluating or judging either the team or its members. To achieve that climate of safety and growth, any group that could use information "against" the team must make it credibly clear that it will not expect such information to be made available to it and, even if it were, that it would not use it for evaluation. Even one violation of this principle will create such mistrust and suspicion that all future efforts will be undermined.

(ii) Team-Generated For assessment to be team-generated, the members must "buy into" the process at the very beginning. Like all other human beings, team members must see how they will benefit, as individuals and as a team, from assessing their experience. They have to want to learn and apply that information. This happens only when the team, at the very beginning, discusses why, how, and to what effect they will use feedback processes. The team members themselves must set expectations that they will collect information on how they are doing, and they, as a team, have to decide what measures they will use, and when and how they will apply their results. When this happens, and *only* when this happens, the cybernetic process belongs to the team and serves its health and effectiveness.

(b) METHODS FOR ASSESSMENT Getting feedback from suppliers, customers, or clients of a team is essentially the same as gathering information at any other level of the organization. It can involve questionnaires, surveys, and quality studies of the team's resources or appointing authority, of team members, and of clients or customers of the team.

Even more critical to the team, however, is ongoing assessment of how it is actually working: How are the members functioning in their transactional and task processes?

These are some useful techniques for assessing what is happening in team transactional and task processes:

1. Feedback forms, which members regularly complete individually and analyze together. Feedback forms can focus on individuals' perceptions of: their own effectiveness or satisfaction; the climate in which the team is working; the team's processes and effectiveness; what has been accomplished; and the next steps to take.

2. Objective process observers and consultants, who observe and analyze the team's processes as it works together. Such a resource can then help the team evaluate the information and find ways to make it useful in improving its processes. A process observer may be an internal consultant from, say, the Training and Development Department, or an external consultant with expertise in small group/team communication, hired specifically to assist the team in developing effective process skills. Frequently, videotape and feedback instruments are used in conjunction with process observation and consulting.

(c) **IMPLEMENTING THE RESULTS OF FEEDBACK**   Only the team, acting *together,* can use feedback effectively. These are some of the methods:

1. Focus on the team's successes and accomplishments. Identify those processes that are working well and the positive feelings members have about the team's work. All teams do some things well; starting with this perspective provides a foundation on which to build future successes.

2. Discuss what the feedback means to the team. Is it valid? Was the technique used to gather it objective, complete, and consistent? Is the information supported by and consistent with other knowledge the team has of itself? Does it indicate important insights into the way the team is functioning?

3. Design a method for implementing the insights gained from the feedback. The method could be structural (changing the format, location, or times of meetings), constitutional (modifying the team's task, adding or deleting members, changing the leader), or transactional (changing specific communication behaviors, agreeing to be more assertive, more supportive, and so on).

4. Agree on a method for achieving the change, for example, getting outside support or resources, adopting new procedures, supporting and helping each other with behavioral changes.

5. Agree on times and methods for reassessing the issue to see whether it is resolved or improving. Simply repeating the original method of feedback and comparing it may be sufficient, or new evaluation methods may need to be added to the process.

6. Contract with each other to implement and support the changes and to be open in giving and receiving feedback in the process of improvement.

An example of this process could be a project team whose observer/consultant has noted that only three out of the seven members talked in any of the four meetings that were observed, and that those three were the people with the highest status in the team. In discussing these data, the team notes that this observation held over all four meetings, that it is objectively supported by videotape and the observer's notes, and that it is consistent with the members' own observations and evaluations. The assessment is, therefore, objective, complete, consistent, and supported.

Is it important? In discussing the subject, with the facilitation of the observer/consultant, suppose the four usually silent members speak up and reveal that there was information they needed to contribute previously, but they were intimidated by the status of the three verbal members. The information might have made a difference in the outcome of those meetings, but it was unavailable because of their silence. Yes; then it is important.

Suppose the more dominant three are shocked; they thought they had to talk because the others would not. At this point, the team and its observer would explore why the three members' status and behavior might be affecting transactions in the team, and how, together, all seven members might modify that behavior.

The feedback loop is not over. After working out ways of changing their transactions, the team members will have to practice their new behaviors and, at an agreed-on point in the near future, they again will assess their transactions to see whether they are working better. They might use feedback forms and discussion, or they might even bring their observer/consultant back in, depending on what they, as a team, feel they need to do at that point.

6.5 TROUBLESHOOTING FOR COMMON PROBLEMS

There are some problems that almost any team can run into. Some of these are system problems, involving organizational support or resources; some are teamwork problems and leadership problems.

(a) SYSTEM PROBLEMS Sometimes, a team is working in a context of an unsupportive or politically unhealthy system, and members become disheartened.

The first response, clearly, is to seek better support by contacts with the parent organization. This can require considerable energy from the leader and from members. The process involves making requests for meetings; holding meetings with management or related organizational structures, to explain the problems the team is facing; carefully preparing and presenting evidence to support the team's needs and the importance of its work; perhaps meeting with other organizations competing for resources or facing similar problems; and finally, and very importantly, providing written follow-up to record the points that have been made and any agreements that are to be implemented. The response takes careful preparation, a strong belief that the final goal is worth the effort, optimism that it can be done, and strong interpersonal communication skills.

Other responses can be simply to quit; to continue, but to give only minimum effort to the job; or to forge ahead with a "damn the torpedoes" attitude.

Quitting, or dismantling the team, may be the best decision when the organizational structure clearly has turned away from the goals, cut the resources, and alienated the team. Sometimes, it's better to cut losses and look for more positive ways to get the job done. Doing the job at the minimum is what happens when people are disenfranchised but stuck in one position. The situation is unhealthy for everyone; it is wasteful of team members' talents, time, and energy, and the results are nonproductive and inevitably hard on the team's self-esteem.

The forge-ahead approach can be surprisingly effective. People often work very well together in an "us-against-them/we'll-show-them" coalition. If the team is deeply committed to its vision and its syntality as a group is strong enough, it may be able to overcome all obstacles. In fact, one of the characteristics of a superior work-team experience is the members' comprehension that they triumphed over insurmountable odds (Kinlaw, 1991). Incredible commitment and mutual reinforcement and support are required but the outcome can be amazing.

(b) TEAMWORK PROBLEMS   When teams run into problems, they frequently fall into two broad categories of communication issues: problems in managing conflict, and problems in managing group cohesiveness and conformity.

(i) Conflict   Conflict may be perceived as stressful and to be avoided, but it is normal and inevitable and it can be healthy. A team needs to recognize the value of conflict, understand the sources of conflict, and recognize its options for managing conflict constructively.

Conflict is valuable: it can reveal issues that need to be resolved, it can cause people to deal with issues and to change behaviors, and it can stimulate creative thinking and problem solving.

As Warren Bennis (1989) has pointed out, "Organizations that encourage thoughtful dissent gain much more than a heightened air of collegiality. They make better decisions . . . the greater the initial disagreement among group members, the more accurate the results. With more disagreement, people are forced to look at a wider range of possibilities."

To manage conflict constructively requires an early decision to do so. At the beginning, teams need to acknowledge the probability that there will be conflict, and to agree that members will manage it cooperatively. As with many other working issues, a norm needs to be set for conflict.

Managing conflict requires, first, a choice of strategy. The team can try ignoring it, it can postpone acting on it, or it can confront it. Ignoring it may be feasible in the short term, and it may be the right choice if the team simply doesn't have time to work it through at that moment or if feelings are so volatile that a confrontation would result in serious damage.

Rarely does ignoring conflict make it go away, so postponement may be appropriate if it can't be handled immediately. Eventually, most conflicts need confrontation—the attention and cooperation of the team to convert them into positive influences on teamwork.

The sources of conflict can be resources, personal hidden agendas, differences in expectations and behavior styles, or differences of opinions. Conflict also can arise from personal differences in values.

Resource conflicts   When conflict is over resources—time, money, availability of personnel or of office support, and so on—it can arouse considerable competitiveness and irritation.

There are two options for confronting and managing resource issues. One is to get more resources through negotiation with the parent organization or with competing teams or departments; the other is to negotiate compromise and cooperative uses among team members.

Personal hidden agendas If one individual has a "hidden agenda"—his or her own unrevealed objective—then the pursuit of that agenda may block teamwork and cooperation. Other members of the team may have no idea what is behind the conflict; often, it is manifested simply by obstructionist behavior or manipulative actions by that one member, whose reasons are obscure.

If one member, for example, looks on the team as a route to promotion, that person will consider every idea primarily in terms of how it will look on his or her record. Although that person probably will not state ambition as a criterion, his or her objections to or support for an idea will be biased. A good idea may be blocked or a bad idea supported for no good reason, and team members may react in bewilderment or anger.

If the hidden agenda causes much obstruction and conflict, it eventually will have to be faced. To do that, members need to take an attitude that solving one member's agenda issue is to everyone's advantage—that the member's problem belongs, in fact, to everyone. In that spirit, a member can start examining the issue with a nonjudgmental, nonaccusatory, problem-oriented statement such as: "John, I keep feeling something is in the way when we discuss this idea. Is there something we should know about your position on it?" From there, careful questioning, support, probing of issues, and team discussion of ways to deal with the person's agenda can yield results.

Some hidden agendas are emotional; simply getting the acknowledgment and support of the team may be all the person needs. In other cases, the individual may want to attain a tangible objective, and team members can provide some suggestions or help in resolving the personal issue. Even where the team can be of no help at all, getting the hidden agenda out in the open where everyone understands it can make communication more open and effective.

Differences in expectations and behavior styles People enter a team experience with an entire set of expectations and ways of behaving, for example, they have expectations of the way people should treat each other, of the way leaders should behave, of the ways they and others should fulfill roles in the team, or of the ways meetings should be handled. They bring their habitual ways of acting into the experience as well: how they treat issues of time and responsibility, how they speak, how they listen, how they use and react to territory and space, and how they dress. People don't usually think about these expectations; they are just the foundation on which they proceed.

Expectations come from people's backgrounds. An individual's culture and ethnic background, gender, educational experience, work experience, stereotypes, and biases—all these affect his or her expectations. Conflict can arise when members of a team violate each other's expectations, often without even realizing they have done so.

For example, women frequently take a more cooperative, conciliatory, and interpersonal approach to group communication than do men. As a consequence, many females, in their first experiences with male teams, have been confused and alienated by what seemed to them excessive competitiveness among their teammates. (It should be noted that gender distinctions are changing rapidly.)

Another example is in expectations of formality. Some people come from cultures where respect for status and authority dictates a high degree of formality and concession to the position of the designated leader. When they find themselves deal-ing with other members whose behavior reflects a highly individualistic and non-conformist tendency to treat the leader as just one of the gang, conflict may result. The conflict may be reflected through passive withdrawal or outright confrontation, but it will be there either way.

Managing conflict caused by differences in expectations really starts with under-standing how deeply background can affect people's expectations and how strongly their behaviors can be affected. Understanding starts with respecting and appreciating those differences and shelving permanently a tendency to say, "Well, he really should . . ." or "The problem with her is . . . ." When the team approach is one that cherishes the di-versity of its members, expectation and behavior conflicts may be minor.

Where those differences create conflicts in teamwork, they can be managed by careful and supportive discussion of what expectations people bring to the group and why. From that discussion, the team can examine ways of setting norms that everyone can live with and can reach an agreement on how to help each other meet those norms.

For example, one member of a team may come from a large and noisy family in which the only way to be heard is to interrupt insistently; another member may come from a culture in which silence and respectfulness are highly regarded characteristics. Not only is the loud one going to be heard and the quiet one going to be isolated, but the entire team may find itself split between the extreme behaviors. A discussion of norms for speaking up, limiting the length of one's speech, listening to others, not interrupting, and asking others for their participation can lead to adopting new behaviors.

In an instance of this kind, the process of discussing why people behave as they do often yields a team approach to enforcing the new norms supportively. Such mutually understood cues may be nonverbal (for example, a raised eyebrow) or may use a word or two, such as "Time out!" These cues work because they happen through open dis-cussion and negotiation of norms. They belong to everyone, and they benefit everyone by benefiting teamwork.

Differences in opinion   When people discuss issues, ideas, and solutions, they dis-agree. Disagreement can get hot and adversarial and can lead to conflict. Such con-flict, however, allows an opportunity to examine both sides in depth. Managing it requires setting some norms or guidelines for advocacy and decision making, and it helps to set those norms early in the life of the team.

When two sides clash, the possibilities are to abide by majority decision, thus leav-ing some room for individuals to agree to disagree while the team as a whole commits to the final vote; or to present the arguments to a higher authority, a judge, who will make a final decision to which all parties are bound; or to try to achieve consensus or compromise.

In teamwork, any of these is a possibility, depending on the issues. Usually, a team must work toward agreement or finding a compromise with which all can live. To work through that process, the team, together, needs to: analyze all of the issues involved in each side, evaluate all of the information and evidence on each issue, determine what might be accomplished by each side and what is valuable or desirable about each posi-tion, and, finally, propose and discuss possible compromises. A negotiation process of give-and-take ensues.

In this process, members look for similarities and points of agreement; they seek ways to weaken disagreements through redefining the issues or the terms of the disagreement. They seek compromises. Eventually, they reach a point where everyone can agree on an overall picture, even if individual members have reservations about parts of it. They are then over the conflict and on their way to a decision.

The advantages of the process are obvious: thinking, analysis, and awareness come out of the interaction required to understand and compromise or decide between the two positions.

Differences in values Differences between people's values present the stickiest conflict of all. When other kinds of conflicts seem unmanageable, it often is because underlying values are at odds and people don't recognize the real source of their conflict. Many other conflicts, to be managed, eventually come down to finding out what the relevant values are and how they differ among members.

Some value conflicts cannot be managed in any way but to say "We cannot agree." A member whose top priority is making money will have a standing conflict with another member whose top priority is serving the poor. The values seem so antithetical that they cannot be compromised. In such cases, the team has to look for ways of making the interpretations and applications of the values acceptable to all parties. If the money person and the helper person can work together to find ways to make money that can be used for the poor, then perhaps they can shelve their differences for a time.

Often, value conflicts are not as serious as they seem. Once they are defined and discussed, members may find greater similarities than they had perceived. Discussing the differences between members in terms of source, definition, priorities, and consequences of their values can help with finding similarities and understanding differences.

Sources for people's values are family, culture, church, personal experience, friends, and authorities. When people examine and explain the sources of their values, they are enabled to examine the legitimacy and the potency of those values. That can open the discussion.

Definitions of values involve creating and defining the terms of the values. As people define and describe, they begin to see what is not, as well as what is, in the concept. The statement "I value human life," for example, has little meaning until the person starts defining the last two words.

Values come down to priority rankings when people approach an application of their values. An individual might value the goal of the team highly but discover that she or he values free time with the family more highly. That unseen difference in ranking could cause conflict with team members who see that member as not valuing the team and uncommitted to its goal. A discussion of value rankings, or possible choices among values, can yield much deeper understanding of the positions from which members are approaching the team, and where conflicts are.

Finally, team discussion of the ways in which members might manifest their values through actions can clarify what those values mean. For example, a team might be confused about a conflict that arises at the point of decision about a recommendation to establish a scholarship for the children of employees, because, up to that moment, everyone seemed to be in agreement about the value of higher education. Yet, some members would limit the team to acting on that value only through efforts at persuading employees to see education as important; others would see the value as one to be expressed through concrete, material action. When value conflicts can be isolated to differences of extent rather than differences of concept, negotiation can proceed to compromise and satisfactory action.

Some guidelines for managing conflict can be helpful:

1. Determine the source of the conflict:
   Resources?
   Personal agendas?
   Differences in expectations?
   Differences in style and personality?
   Differences of opinion?
   Differences in values?
2. Determine a strategy for managing the conflict:
   Ignore it?
   Postpone management of it?
   Confront it?

If confronting a conflict:

Agree, as a team, to manage conflict constructively and cooperatively;
Examine, as a team, ways to define the problem and to identify similarities and commonalities;
Examine ways to diminish differences;
Examine ways to compromise and negotiate agreement;
Select strategies the entire team can live with;
Agree to set norms or devise ways for members to help each other live with the agreed-on approaches;
Follow up by assessing how the team is doing with its conflict management strategy.

(ii) Cohesiveness and conformity problems   Sometimes, a team feels too good about itself. Members feel strongly cohesive; they share the vision, they share the image, they work well together, they believe they're "the best." All of these are positive characteristics—essentials, really, of a fine team—but they can lead to arrogance, to blocking out necessary information and ideas, and to pressures on members to conform. (See Chapter 4 for a discussion of "groupthink.")

To experience the best of cohesiveness and limit the worst of conformity, teams need to do the following:

1. Set a rule at the beginning that all information, good or bad, should be open for discussion by the team;
2. Set a rule at the beginning that any member can voice an objection, share information, or make a suggestion without being silenced or evaluated by another member;

3. Set a norm that it is O.K. to agree to disagree and still feel like and act like a team;

4. Keep the team process open to input from outside the group as well as from team members;

5. Set a norm and follow it for constant team assessment of its transactional and task processes;

6. Set a norm and follow it for constant use of feedback to improve transactional and task processes.

6.6 SUMMARY

Attitude makes the difference, expectations are everything and attention is all there is to get any project accomplished. —Robert Waterman (1987)

Waterman's statement provides a good overview for achieving empowerment and teamwork in any quality organizational structure.

(a) EMPOWERING INDIVIDUALS Possibly the two most significant characteristics of an effective, high-performing system are concern for people and a constant striving for improvement. As with most human activities, however, it is not sufficient to identify and support only the most important factors.

The successful manager understands the implication of Alfred North Whitehead's observation that all plans are conceived in generality but lived in detail. It is clear that successful implementation of a program to achieve quality requires attention to a number of broad principles and specific actions.

(b) EMPOWERING TEAMS Teams are used in a wide variety of formats because top-quality results come from empowered people working together to maximize their creativity and effectiveness. The ideal team develops a shared identity and image of itself, a shared vision of its goal, and shared values and expectations. It employs positive task and transactional processes that involve open, supportive, honest communication that makes it safe to gather and use information, think critically and creatively, and take risks that will enhance process and quality.

Teams need to work in an open system where a flow of feedback, information, and support feeds and enlarges on the work of the team. Troubleshooting in a team focuses on improving communication, managing conflict, and promoting cohesiveness while minimizing pressures to conform.

Two common statements are often heard during any new initiative: "Let's not reinvent the wheel" and "We should find out what others are doing." An examination of these perspectives provides an opportunity to develop the insight necessary to understand effective team functioning.

Although it is helpful to study what others are doing, each team must modify, adapt, and then adopt its own processes. This sequence might appear to be reinventing the wheel, but it is actually redesigning it to fit the needs of the specific team. Participants in this activity will "own" and act on a plan they create. Without "ownership," there is little or no commitment to any effort for identifying and improving weaknesses.

Recognizing the differences among successful quality teams does not preclude examining their similarities. The following consistent observations have been made by those who have studied these efforts:

1. The organizational culture plays the dominant role in determining the design and implementation of teams and teamwork.

2. Successful organizations or associations encourage and reward productive relationships as well as productive individuals.

3. A flat management structure minimizes the approval levels needed to act. Self-managing teams have and exercise responsibility, autonomy, and authority.

4. Sharing "success stories" within the system motivates others to examine their activities and explore new ways of working.

5. Data are collected only for predetermined needs. There are policies about what data will be collected, how and by whom, and who will analyze the data and make recommendations. By reducing threat and ensuring ownership, this approach increases efficiency and empowerment.

6. Expectations of quality at every level become a series of self-fulfilling prophecies. People will be influenced to act in the manner that is expected of managers as examples and role models; they will create the positive result not accomplished through exhortations.

7. Leadership emerges from unexpected sources in response to situations rather than through assigned positions. Good ideas don't care who has them.

8. The messenger is not killed! Actions supporting the statement that "There is no bad news" encourage people to identify problems and seek solutions in an open, collaborative manner. They won't identify and solve problems if they get punished for finding things out. The worst news is that no one is collecting and analyzing information about important team goals.

The process for developing teams and cross teams takes an extended period of time. All teams will not develop their competence and commitment at the same rate. These individual rates of development provide an opportunity for managers to reinforce cooperative work methods by reassuring the teams that comparisons of developmental rates are inappropriate and will not be made.

(c) EMPOWERING ORGANIZATIONS   Empowerment entails learning how to remove barriers to success while at the same time staying within the boundaries of the task and position. Robert Waterman, in his book, *The Renewal Factor* (1989), expresses this idea as "Congenial Controls." He believes that controls must reflect realities but not entangle the people doing the job. "Plans must be flexible and able to respond to a changing environment," thus allowing for innovative approaches. An organization must break down the barriers of structure and rigidity to enable all to see the larger picture and work within this expanded framework (Lumsden, Knight, & Gallaro, 1989). An organization's structure must be founded in and constructed by its people.

Deming (1982) refers to barriers to effective transformation (through quality principles) as "The Seven Deadly Diseases" (p. 97). Empowering individuals by creating a trusting environment in which all members are free to express themselves is a constructive method of breaking down barriers or combating the deadly diseases. Innovative

Exhibit 6.7. Checklist for creating empowerment and teamwork in quality organizations.

Managerial Roles

As a manager, do you:

1. Make yourself available to your people? _____

2. Consistently encourage cooperative efforts? _____

3. Provide clear and prompt feedback? _____

4. Minimize distractions (reports, meetings, and so on) for your people? _____

5. Model and expect good performance? _____

6. Encourage and develop your people's talents? _____

7. Respect ways of thinking, learning, and performing that are different from yours? _____

Organizational Characteristics

Does the organization provide for:

1. Ensuring that everyone understands and supports the mission? _____

2. Ensuring that everyone understands his or her contribution to the mission? _____

3. Valuing the employees and volunteers? _____

4. Making improvement part of everyone's work? _____

5. Recognizing that satisfying clients, patients, customers, and others, is the reason for the organization's work? _____

6. Regularly reviewing the goals, to be certain the needs of those served are being met? _____

7. Regularly collecting, analyzing, and using information about programs, services, and so on, to improve them? _____

8. Defining quality in a way that emphasizes enhancing the effectiveness of everyone's efforts? _____

9. Supporting people with the appropriate training, education, and development needed to do their work? _____

10. Recognizing and rewarding individuals' and groups' contributions? _____

11. Communicating clearly and frequently the value of innovation and creativity? _____

12. Making significant decisions at all organizational levels? _____

13. Routinely encouraging and praising innovation, reasonable risk taking, and creativity? _____

14. Open and trusting communication? _____

15. Emphasis on team activities? _____

16. Minimal rules, regulations, and structures? _____

17. Maximum cross-functional cooperation? _____

18. Time to develop organizational changes and people's participation? _____

19. The three most important aspects of empowering people and teams: Patience, Patience, and Patience? _____

ideas and novel tasks foster creativity while at the same time impeding the growth of malady within organizations. Exhibit 6.7 is directed toward creating empowerment.

SOURCES AND SUGGESTED REFERENCES

Baird, J., Jr. 1982. *Quality Circles: Leader's Manual.* Prospects Heights, IL: Waveland Press.

Bennis, W. 1989, December 31. The dilemma at the top: Followers make good leaders good. *The New York Times,* p. D.3.

Blake, R. B., Mouton, J. S., and Allen, R. 1987. *Spectacular Teamwork.* New York: John Wiley & Sons.

Block, P. 1987. *The Empowered Manager: Positive Political Skills at Work.* San Francisco: Jossey-Bass.

Burnside, R. M. 1988. "Encouragement as the Elixir of Innovation," *Issues & Observations, 8:* 1–6.

Deming, W. E. 1982. *Out of the Crisis.* Cambridge, MA: Massachusetts Institute of Technology Press.

DePree, M. 1989. *Leadership Is an Art.* New York: Doubleday.

Ellis, M. J. 1973. *Why People Play.* Englewood Cliffs, NJ: Prentice-Hall.

Hastings, C., Bixby, P., and Chaudhry-Lawton, R. 1987. *The Superteam Solution.* Aldershot, England: Gower Publishing Co.

Kanter, R. M. 1983. *The Change Masters: Innovation for Productivity in the American Corporation.* New York: Simon & Schuster.

Kinlaw, D. C. 1991. *Developing Superior Work Teams.* Lexington, MA: Lexington Books.

Lumsden, D., Knight, M., & Gallaro, D. 1989. "Assessing Learning Outcomes: Opportunities for Institutional Renewal." *Journal of Staff, Program and Organization Development, 7:* 181–185.

Murphy, S. 1991, August 4. "Letter to the Editor," *New York Times Magazine,* p. 8.

Scholtes, Peter R. 1988. *The Team Handbook: How to Use Teams to Improve Quality.* Madison, WI: Joiner Associates.

Sims, H. P., Jr., and Dean, J. W., Jr. 1985, Jan. "Beyond Quality Circles: Self-Managing Teams." *Personnel,* 20–32.

Tuppen, C. 1974. "Dimensions of Communicator Credibility: An Oblique Solution." *Speech Monographs, 41:* 253–266.

Walton, M. 1986. *The Deming Management Method.* New York: Putnam.

Waterman, R. 1987. *The Renewal Factor: How the Best Get and Keep the Competitive Edge.* New York: Bantam Books.

Whitehead, J., Jr. 1969. "Factors of Source Credibility," *Quarterly Journal of Speech, 54:* 59–63.

C H A P T E R   S E V E N

Strategic Planning and Management by Objectives

D. Kerry Laycock

CONTENTS

"Chesire Puss," Alice began, "Would you tell me please which way I ought to go from here?"

"That depends a good deal on where you want to get to," said the cat.

"I don't much care where . . .," said Alice.

"Then it doesn't matter which way you go," said the cat.

"—so long as I get somewhere," Alice added.

—Lewis Carroll

Like Alice, nonprofit organizations are asking questions about their future direction. These organizations see so much to be done, and they express a great passion to "get somewhere." Unfortunately, turning passion to consensus and articulating a clear direction are often difficult tasks for nonprofits. The Chesire Cat, a wise strategist, recognized that mapping out a plan is useless in the absence of a well-defined purpose.

Until recently, nonprofits operated in relatively stable environments. Funding and programming were fairly consistent from year to year. Public opinion was the concern of politicians, not nonprofit leaders. Today, all of that has changed. Human service organizations face burgeoning demands for services. Cultural and human service organizations face increasing public scrutiny. Government seeks to turn over more service delivery to nonprofits but is under intense fiscal and public pressure to reduce spending.

For example, health care providers are faced with increased government intrusion into what services are provided and how they are delivered. Hospitals and child welfare organizations must contend with new populations of sick and addicted children.

Most nonprofit organizations face intense pressure from other organizations and individuals who claim a right or responsibility to define the direction of the organization. For example, humane societies must contend with the often conflicting demands of animal rights advocates, professional breeders, local authorities, and a host of other groups. Arts organizations face a reconsideration of what is art and who decides.

Resources are increasingly difficult to obtain. Government has less to spend, corporations seek to support more programs that have direct business benefits, and foundations are overwhelmed by requests for funding. The degree of sophistication in fund-raising has increased, too. The funding environment is extremely competitive.

For most nonprofits, the world seems as chaotic as it did for Alice in her dream. For these reasons, leaders of nonprofit organizations increasingly are turning to strategic planning as a way to enhance organizational effectiveness and adapt to the rapidly changing world.

7.1 DEFINITION OF STRATEGIC PLANNING

Strategic planning is a comprehensive organizational process of adaptation through assessment, decision making, and evaluation. Strategic planning seeks to answer the most basic questions about why the organization exists, what it does, and how it does it. The result of the process is a completed plan that serves as a guide for organizational action for the next 3 to 5 years.

It may be an overstatement to say that the process is more important than the product, but, in turbulent times, planning offers a constructive approach to organizational learning. Planning team members often emerge from the process as highly knowledgeable and committed members of the organization. Their ability to contribute to the organization increases enormously. Developing a solid plan contributes to organizational effectiveness by helping members make the right decision now and in the future.

7.2 CHARACTERISTICS OF STRATEGIC PLANNING

Four factors distinguish strategic planning from other planning models and organizational improvement strategies:*

1. Strategic planning is fundamentally concerned with *adapting to a changing environment.* This external orientation focuses on recognizing and responding to the forces for change that exist *outside* the organization.

2. Strategic planning is *future-oriented.* During the course of planning, consideration is given to current problems only if these problems present a barrier to getting to a desired place in the future. Strategic planning is anticipatory rather than reactionary. Planners are more concerned with problems of the future than with those of today.

3. Strategic planning is *comprehensive.* It encompasses a wide range of factors, both internal and external to the organization. It requires an enormous commitment of time and energy and a willingness to struggle with difficult issues and divergent perspectives.

4. Strategic planning is a *consensus-building process.* Given the diversity of stakeholder interests that many nonprofits face, strategic planning offers a way to surface those needs and interests and to reach agreement on the future direction that best serves them.

7.3 PLANNING PARAMETERS

Exhibit 7.1 describes the parameters of the planning process. Planning begins with building a consensus about the desired future. This view should be expansive and not constrained by practicality. In other words, *vision* describes the world in an ideal

---

* Portions of the material contained in this chapter originally appeared in D. K. Laycock, "Are You Ready for Strategic Planning?" *Nonprofit World, 8* (5) (September–October 1990), 25–27.

Exhibit 7.1.   Strategic planning parameters.

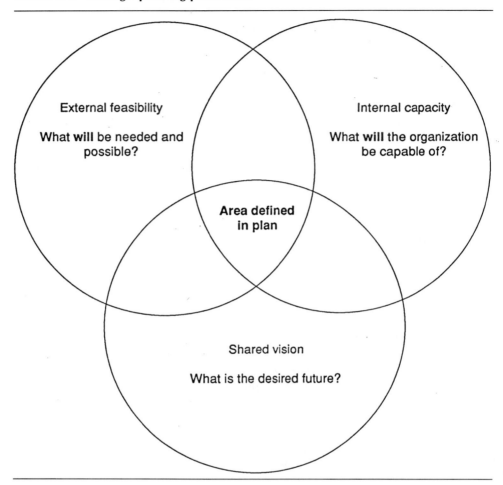

External feasibility

What will be needed and possible?

Internal capacity

What will the organization be capable of?

Area defined in plan

Shared vision

What is the desired future?

state. For example, the vision of an adoption agency may be a world in which all children are raised as permanent members of loving families. In this world, there are no residential institutions and no foster care.

This perfect world may never exist. The next broad area of investigation is the external environment. This inquiry seeks to answer questions about what is most needed and most likely. Every organization is faced with certain opportunities and challenged by certain barriers.

Besides the external barriers, there are questions of internal capacity. No organization can meet all needs. Which needs are met is often the result of defining what the organization does best.

The adoption agency may wish that all children had a permanent, loving home, but may see children with disabilities as the most critical need. In addition, the agency may have a staff that has special strengths in this area and, as a result, may decide to specialize in this one area and leave other children to other organizations. This decision is the agency's strategic position.

Thus, the strategic plan seeks to define the intersection of what is desired, most needed, and most possible. This clarity is critical to the success of nonprofit organizations. As Peter Drucker (1990) has suggested, "Non-profit organizations have no 'bottom line.'" They often consider the public services they provide as righteous, moral, and serving a cause, so they are often less willing to say, if it doesn't produce results, then maybe we should direct our resources elsewhere. "Non-profit organizations need the discipline of organized abandonment perhaps even more than a business does. They need to face up to critical choices" (pp. 10–11). Strategic planning is about the discipline and process of making those choices.

(a) PLANNING FOR QUALITY Nonprofit organizations have just begun to apply to their operations and services the principles of the quality revolution of manufacturing (Kennedy, 1991). But, unlike manufacturing organizations, nonprofits seldom have a physical product, and the measures of quality are not immediately apparent. On an automobile, one can measure fit, form, and finish; but how would an organization that serves the homeless define quality?

How an organization defines quality depends first on how it defines its mission. If the organization serving the homeless has as its mission the *relief* of suffering, then the number of beds and of meals served may be counted as indicators of quality. If the mission is the *prevention* of suffering, then the measures of quality are very different. Serving more people could, in fact, be an indicator of lack of success.

In today's competitive environment, with its growing demands for accountability, it is not enough to "get somewhere." The organization serving the homeless may see doing something, anything, for a group of people so much in need as "getting somewhere." But is it the best use of resources? Does it provide the greatest benefit? Is it what is most needed?

In nonprofit organizations, quality improvement begins with a clear sense of mission, but it asks another important question that is not mentioned above: How can we do it better? Quality improvement is a strategy for enhancing organizational effectiveness and may be considered further in relation to defining strategies.

(b) ASSESSING READINESS In recent years, strategic planning has become widely practiced in nonprofit organizations. For the most part, this trend has been very positive, and many would argue that it has had a significant positive impact on the health of nonprofit organizations. But strategic planning is not a panacea, and, in the rush to get involved in planning, many organizations fail to consider or ensure the appropriateness of the process for their situation.

Understanding the nature and definition of strategic planning, and asking a number of specific questions, will help define the appropriateness of its application. Exhibit 7.2 describes the assessment process.

(i) Stability Potential planners must ask whether the organization is stable. In other words, is the organization preparing for the future, or is it attempting to resolve a crisis? If the organization is in crisis, the crisis must be resolved. This is an immediate problem requiring an immediate response.

Exhibit 7.2.   Assessing readiness for strategic planning.

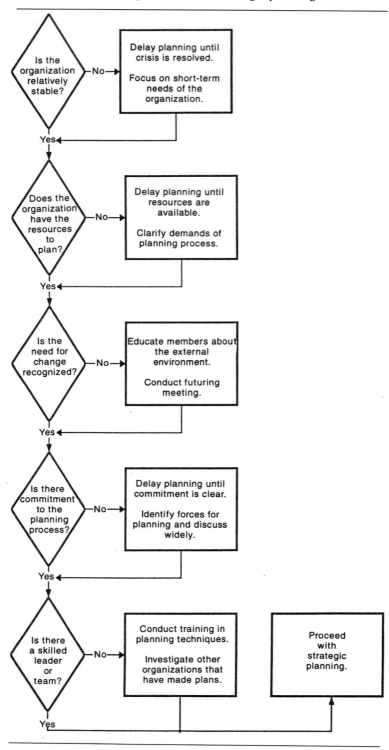

If the organization faces a major crisis, planning should be delayed until the crisis has passed. All efforts should be focused on stabilizing the organization. Once this is done, the organization may turn to the broader concerns of strategic planning.

(ii) Capability Potential planners must ask whether the organization is capable of undertaking the work of planning. Planning requires an enormous amount of time and, depending on the extent of research and the use of an outside consultant, money. Unless these resources are committed up-front, the planning process may become an unexpected drain on the organization, particularly in terms of human resources. Burnout and frustration can lead to a hastily completed plan or, worse yet, a failure to complete the plan at all.

Planners should assess and determine whether current operations are strong enough to endure the stress of directing resources, particularly board and staff time, toward planning. It is important that the organization be able to maintain present functions *and* plan for the future.

The board of directors should make a specific budget allocation for planning. This allocation is to cover the costs of materials, a consultant (if one is used), and research (for example, mailing a survey to members or service users). Organizations that are set up on a fund accounting basis will need to allocate staff time to planning. A significant commitment of staff time to planning can have an impact on the organization's overhead ratio.

An organization that lacks the capability to undertake this effort should help members understand the demands of planning and identify additional resources. Planning should be delayed until the organization can ensure that current operations will not be hindered.

(iii) Recognized need for change Planners must determine whether there is a recognized need for change. Do members of the organization have some awareness of a changing environment? Is there a leader with compelling ideas or a strong vision? Unless there is a strongly felt need for change, the resistance to change may overpower those attempting to move the organization forward. (See Chap. 3.)

If there is not such a need, planners can help the organization explore the external environment, perhaps by developing a *futuring* session without a specific commitment to developing a plan. This meeting is designed to explore the future of the organization and develop a consensus about the future and the impact of the organization. (This approach is discussed later in this chapter.)

Whatever approach is chosen, it is essential that formal planning be delayed until there is a strongly felt, compelling need for change.

(iv) Commitment to planning The fourth area of assessment, the degree of commitment to planning, is related to the recognition of the need to change. If the issues are well understood and a course of action is obvious, perhaps strategic planning is not the best use of time.

My experience suggests that there are few issues of this type. They may appear simple on the surface but are, in fact, very complicated. The responses to them require careful consideration of unintentional effects on other aspects of the organization. Frequently, individuals are very clear on an issue, but, as a group, there is a considerable degree of disagreement that must be resolved. Planners must help clarify the divergent views of the issues and assess whether the process is understood and supported by members of the board and staff.

Planning must begin with a clear commitment from the top of the organization. The chairperson or president of the board and the executive director should be involved in the process and act as its advocates. Organizations should be wary of allowing the process to be undertaken by a small, nonrepresentative group of individuals within the organization, without the support of other members. For example, a planning team comprised solely of staff, without board representation or support, or a planning team comprised of a small faction of the board who want to change the organization, would likely fail to get their plan implemented. Perhaps the most extreme example is when the planning is given over to a consultant, with little or no involvement of the organization members.

At best, these individuals are misguided, even though sincere in their interest to help the organization. At worst, they seek to politicize the organization, creating conflict and compromise rather than unity and consensus.

It is important to analyze not just the forces for change, but the forces for planning itself. Is the exercise perceived as valuable, or is planning being done merely to satisfy a major funder, an internal faction, or a key stakeholder?

If there are questions of commitment, planners should attempt to identify and address specific concerns. They should delay planning until the process is better understood and the participants are committed to it: Planners should help identify the driving forces for planning, and initiate discussion within the organization on the politics of planning. If the planning effort is being driven by a funder or other external stakeholder, a scaled-down approach that will satisfy the demand at less cost to the organization should be considered.

Developing a "plan to plan" may help build support for the process. This document provides a concise rationale for undertaking planning, clarifies roles of planning team members, outlines data requirements, and sets a timetable for completion.

(v) Level of skill Planners need to consider the level of skills in the organization. Strategic planning is not as complex as some make it sound. However, it does help to have someone who is familiar with the process, as well as a planning team that has clear roles and responsibilities. Perhaps most important is having someone to lead the process. This person needs both commitment and the organizational skills to pull the team together.

If there is not a clear leader who has sufficient familiarity with the planning process, the organization should consider delaying planning for a short period and should work with the executive director or a key board member to develop leadership for the planning process. A planning orientation for the staff and board can be conducted, and organizations that have completed plans can be investigated as a way to understand the process and commitments necessary.

(c) THE PLANNING TEAM AND MEMBER ROLES Planning is done by a committee comprised largely of board members, but may include staff, constituents, and a facilitator or consultant. The size of the team is a function of the size of the organization and the scope of planning. For small nonprofits undertaking their first planning effort, a group of about eight people probably would be most efficient.

In nonprofit organizations, strategic planning is largely a board function. The board is responsible for setting the direction of the organization (Houle, 1989; Carver, 1990). The full board should be updated frequently on the progress of the planning team and allowed to have input at any point in the process.

Staff members should be represented on the planning committee; generally, this is the executive director's function. In larger organizations, staff may provide support to the planning committee, help conduct research, and generate financial data.

A key aspect of strategic planning is that it is conducted by members of the organization—the people who know and care most about the organization. Often, nonprofits will turn to an outsider for help in planning. An objective person who has expertise in the planning process can make an enormous contribution. Consultants are expensive, but, in the long run, can save the organization time and money by defining an appropriate process and keeping it on track. The consultant is largely the process expert and the facilitator of meetings. The consultant is not the planner.

Many organizations will include key stakeholders in the planning process. A few stakeholders may be of such importance as to be made members of the planning team. Others will act as resources to the team, to be consulted on specific issues. (Stakeholders are discussed further in section 7.5(b).)

Clear role definitions are critical to the success of planning and should be discussed prior to the initiation of planning. Role definitions should be included in a plan-to-plan document.

Because planning is about change, it is an inherently political process (Benveniste, 1989). Choosing the members of the planning team is no small task. As discussed earlier, the group should be representative of the diversity of opinion in the organization.

7.4 THE PLANNING PROCESS: OVERVIEW

Exhibit 7.3 outlines the steps in the planning process. Many planning models exist, and the differences are often academic. Nonetheless, some consideration should be given to the needs of the organization and to tailoring the model to fit with those needs. The model in Exhibit 7.3 emphasizes strategic vision and stakeholder interests.

Each component of the planning process will be discussed in detail. Briefly, developing a vision of the desired future involves describing the world as it would be if the organization were successful. Thus, the planning process begins with ultimate ends and works backward to develop means.

The situation analysis attempts to look at external trends, stakeholder issues, internal issues, and organizational performance data, in order to identify potential barriers and means for realizing the desired future. The product of this analysis is a list of critical planning issues.

Mission refers to the development of a clear consensus about the purpose of the organization.

Directions are the basic divisions of resources. Broad organizational goals describe what the organization seeks to accomplish by allocating resources in each of these directions.

Strategies are the means for accomplishing these goals. Objectives describe specifically what each strategy is designed to accomplish. They are measurable outcomes of the strategy implementation and are written in terms of *when* and *how much*.

Exhibit 7.3.   The strategic planning process.

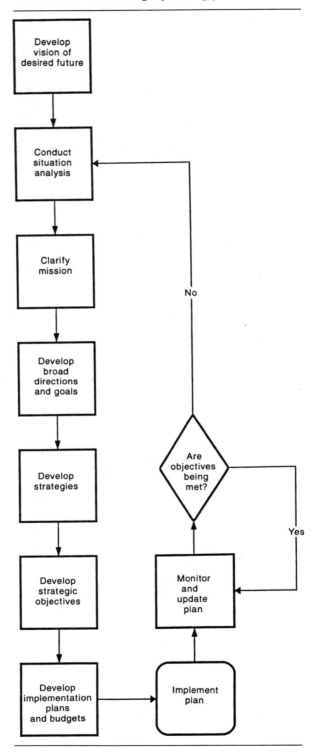

Exhibit 7.4. Elements of the strategic plan.

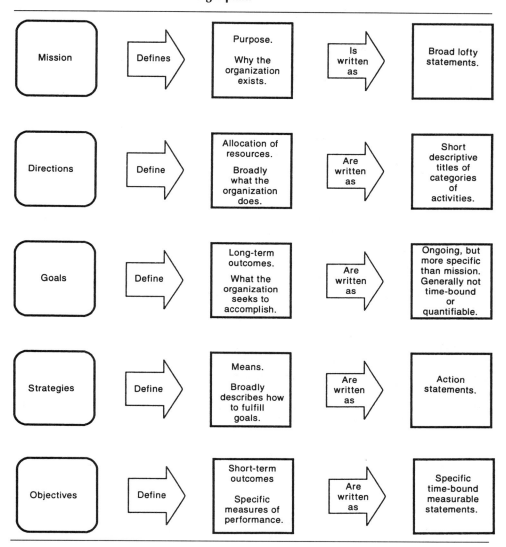

Implementation plans are basic assignments of responsibility and completion dates. They may be expanded into more specific operational plans, but these extend beyond the scope of strategic planning.

Finally, all plans must be periodically monitored and updated. Adjustments in the plan must be made in response to new information, changing conditions, and evaluations of present efforts.

Although Exhibit 7.3 represents the process as having very distinct phases, it is, in actuality, somewhat messier. My experience suggests that groups can become bogged down in defining what is a direction, a goal, a strategy, and an objective. These are not clear lines, and, in general, groups develop a feel for the distinctions only after having wrestled with them for a while. Like the turning of a lens, each level of planning provides greater clarity and specificity. Exhibit 7.4 provides some basic guidelines for constructing each phase of the plan.

7.5   THE PLANNING PROCESS: ASSESSMENT

(a) FUTURE VISION   Despite our best efforts, from palm reading to computer modeling, our ability to foretell the future is very limited. The future is uncertain because it has not happened yet, and some people feel threatened by this uncertainty. Strategic planners assume the future is never entirely knowable, and, as such, presents a great opportunity. Strategic planning is about being ready for the future, but it can be more: it can offer a means to move from anticipation to action, thus creating the future. (See Chap. 5.)

A vision statement describes the world as we want it to be. It may be possible for the planning team to reach a consensus without employing any specific techniques. A talented writer can capture the discussions of the group in a coherent statement to be shared with others within and outside the organization. These discussions should be held away from the pressures of everyday work. (A Saturday morning retreat often works well.) Exhibit 7.5 describes several areas of investigation for a more structured approach to futuring.

(i) Organizational values clarification   Formal discussions about vision should begin with a clarification of organizational values. Values and ethics are central to the existence of nonprofit organizations. American government grants special status to these organizations because they are thought to perform a public good. Current treatment of nonprofits is traceable to early notions of charity and the relationship between church and state (Hall, 1987). Being clear about what is meant by "good" is extremely important.

Clarifying values is a matter of coming to agreement about the basic beliefs that guide the organization. It is sometimes useful to analyze critical incidents in the organization's past as a way to surface and test these values.

(ii) Paradigm shifts   Futurist Joel Barker (1988) has recently popularized the notion of paradigms—sets of rules and assumptions about the way things are. Typically, they are so ingrained that they are unquestioned, perhaps even unspoken. Occasionally, an idea or concept can radically alter the dominant paradigm. Creating a vision requires examining the potential for new or emergent ideas to radically alter the way things are.

For example, until recently, our notion of what is best for developmentally disabled or emotionally impaired people was driven by what might be called the "institutional paradigm": creating bigger and better institutions was seen as the best way to provide for these people.

About 15 years ago, a new idea began to take hold: perhaps institutions were inherently harmful to these people. Today, the "community care paradigm" has largely replaced the "institutional paradigm." Governments and organizations that missed the impact of this single idea went on to build more buildings that now stand empty or have been converted to other uses.

Exhibit 7.5. Future vision.

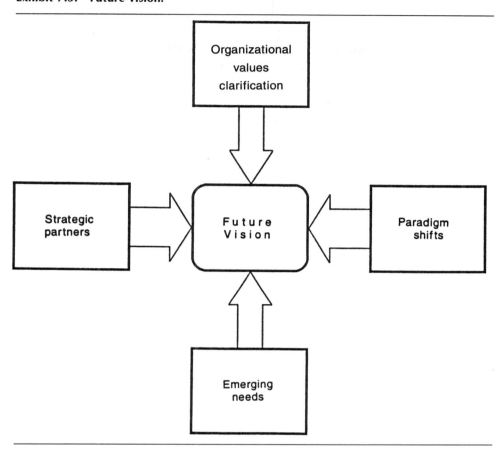

In developing a future vision, organizations need to ask: What ideas are being expressed, however wild, that could radically change the way we do business, and in what ways would the organization change?

(iii) Emerging needs Identifying emerging needs requires that the organization look at relevant areas of concern and analyze new, unmet needs. At this point in the planning process, needs identification is not intended to yield strategic responses, but rather to justify the continuation of the organization. Child welfare organizations may look to the burgeoning number of "crack"-addicted babies. A community arts agency or fund-raising organization may look to the movement away from federal and state funding of the arts and see a need to develop new sources of financial support. In this case, the vision might be for artists and arts organizations to be supported through private donations.

(iv) Strategic partners Developing a future vision may involve identifying strategic partners. No one organization can meet all needs. Identifying collaborators may be necessary to make the vision possible. For example, a community recycling program may see waste haulers, schools, and block clubs as important partners in their cause. A vision to bring them all together could make possible the improvement of the environment.

All of these concepts are brought together in the vision statement, a written statement that describes the future the group hopes to see. In addition, these discussions will have yielded important insights to be explored further in the situation analysis and developed into actual strategies.

(b) SITUATION ANALYSIS The situation analysis provides the data on which the planning team will make strategic decisions. The key components of the analysis are presented in Exhibit 7.6.

(i) Stakeholder audit A stakeholder audit is an analysis of the relationships that exist between an organization and key individuals or groups. Freeman (1984) defines a stakeholder as "any group or individual who can affect or is affected by the achievement of an organization's purpose." Stakeholders may be for or against the organization. They

Exhibit 7.6.   Situation analysis.

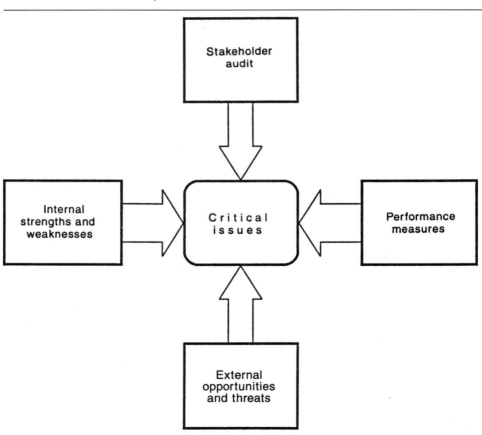

may be customers or suppliers, employees or outside special-interest groups. Stakeholder management assumes that understanding and managing these relationships are essential for organizational success.

Stakeholders will usually fall within one of four categories:

1. Individuals or organizations that control key resources needed by the organization;
2. Individuals or organizations that affect public perception of the organization;
3. Competing organizations;
4. Individuals or organizations served by the organization.

The stakeholder audit is a comprehensive look at both strategic partners and competitors. As such, it goes beyond futuring by examining, in depth, the nature of relationships and the opportunities for collaboration. The process is also intended to yield insights into competitive relationships.

The stakeholder audit seeks to answer a number of questions about these relationships, as detailed in Exhibit 7.7. The results are then used as a basis for strategy development.

Nonprofit organizations face significant pressures from outside stakeholder groups. In some cases, these demands are conflicting; in others, stakeholder groups may form coalitions to increase leverage on the organization. Nonprofit stakeholders include: donors, competitors, clients, volunteers, other nonprofits (particularly special-interest or political advocacy groups), and the state and federal governments.

The stakeholder audit can yield important strategic insights. For a rural county humane society, it changed the entire focus of the planning effort. Prior to conducting the audit, the humane society saw itself as serving the community. The audit suggested that the primary stake of the community was to have a place to dump unwanted animals, which seemed contrary to the humane society's purpose. The planning team began to see the disposal of unwanted animals as providing the community with a convenient alternative to spaying and neutering, and perhaps was actually contributing to the problem of unwanted pets.

The humane society realized that its most important stakeholder group was the animals. The society existed to serve them, and, at times, serving them put them in conflict with the community. The second most important stakeholder group consisted of members of the organization who shared a deep concern for the animals and provided financial support to the organization.

Exhibit 7.7.   Stakeholder audit questions.

1. Who are the key stakeholders?
2. What are their stakes, and in what ways do they judge the success of this organization?
3. Who are the most important stakeholders to whom this organization must respond?
4. For those stakeholders that can affect this organization, what is the strength of their influence?
5. For those stakeholders that are affected by this organization, what is their relative importance?
6. How well is this organization responding to these stakeholders?
7. What new strategies must this organization implement?

This insight brought forth many difficult issues for the organization, including whether to continue to accept all animals and to practice euthanasia. Nonetheless, the insights gained in the stakeholder audit provided focus for the entire planning effort and, in particular, helped clarify the mission. Exhibit 7.8 presents the stakeholder map for the rural county humane society. The strength or influence of each stakeholder group is indicated by the size of its circle; its importance is indicated by its circle's proximity to the organization.

The issues or concerns of the various stakeholders can vary significantly. Even within a constituent group, issues and concerns can vary. For example, funders' concern with fiscal accountability may be reflected in their willingness to provide support to the organization. Business donors may be concerned with how support of the nonprofit reflects on their own organizational image and the exposure they receive.

The planning group may be able to identify the stakes of the various stakeholder groups without further investigation; often, the stakes are well understood. When a stakeholder group is perceived as important but the planning team is uncertain about what the group's stakes are, a representative of the planning team should seek to clarify them by asking a representative of this stakeholder group.

Exhibit 7.8.   Stakeholder map, rural county humane society.

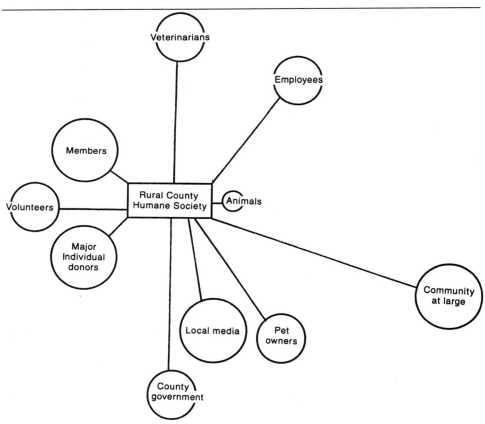

Exhibit 7.9. Business donor stakes.

	Performance Assessment		
Criterion	Good	Fair	Poor
Accountability	•		
Donor recognition	•		
Timely reporting		•	
Value to community	•		
Matching grants			•

Assessing how well the organization is performing can generally be accomplished through an educated guess. In most instances, if the criteria can be defined, the evaluation of performance will be relatively simple. Exhibit 7.9 provides an example of the criteria and evaluation of a single stakeholder group.

With a clear indication of who the key stakeholders are and what the issues are, members of the organization will have a better sense of how organizational success is defined. This insight provides a useful starting point for strategy development. In the example shown in Exhibit 7.9, the organization would want to develop strategies for leveraging large corporate gifts for additional matching grants.

(ii) Performance measures The stakeholder audit will yield an extensive list of criteria by which to measure the performance of the organization, but the list may not be complete nor will it provide sufficient focus. Many organizations are developing *critical measures of success,* which provide important data for strategic planning and are a key component of continuous quality improvement efforts.

These measures yield significant insight into overall organizational performance and provide a basis for analyzing internal strengths and weaknesses.

Exhibit 7.10 provides an example of critical measures of success for an organization concerned with finding permanent homes for difficult-to-adopt children.

(iii) External opportunities and threats During the course of the stakeholder audit, the planning team will have begun to examine external forces for change. During the assessment of opportunities and threats, the view broadens to encompass all aspects of the organization's external environment.

The process begins with an assessment of external needs. This discussion encompasses the emerging needs discussed in the development of the vision statement, but looks at the issues in the time frame of the plan, generally 3 to 5 years.

Exhibit 7.10. Critical measures of success.

Permanency Planning

1. Length of stay in temporary placement.
2. Number of changes in temporary placement.
3. Total number of permanent placements.
4. Number of permanent placements that continue until the child becomes an adult.
5. Average cost of permanently placing a child.

Exhibit 7.11.   Critical external trends.

Areas to Be Investigated

1. Sources of funding and support.
2. Political (tax, regulation, policy).
3. Volunteerism.
4. Demographics.
5. Technology (computers and other information technology).
6. Competition (for funding and in service-delivery areas).

Next, the organization looks at critical trends that will shape those needs and the organization's ability to meet them. In general, a nonprofit organization will need to investigate six areas, shown in Exhibit 7.11. Although not all-inclusive, the list indicates the common areas in which most nonprofit issues fall. (Organizations with special concerns may identify additional areas.) These issues are then categorized as: those presenting an opportunity that may be exploited by the organization, and those representing a threat to the organization's ability to fulfill its mission.

One way to involve more board members and ease the burden on the planning team members is to create small subcommittees to look at each of the relevant areas. In one organization, this was done as a way to not only explore the issues in depth, but to integrate new board members and create an opportunity for board and staff members to work side-by-side. The results were important insights into several key issues, enhanced by the differing perspectives of board and staff, and markedly improved board–staff relations.

In the past few years, an enormous volume of research has been conducted on the nonprofit sector (Hodgkinson, Lyman, and Associates, 1989; Powell, 1987; Van Til and Associates, 1990). A short visit to the library can yield a wealth of useful data. Ongoing subscriptions to publications such as *The Chronicle of Philanthropy, Nonprofit World, Nonprofit Management and Leadership,* and *Nonprofit and Voluntary Sector Quarterly* will provide an invaluable knowledge base for planning.

(iv) Internal strengths and weaknesses   By this point in the planning process, the internal strengths and weaknesses of the organization should be becoming clear. During this phase, the planning team will seek to assess the capability of the organization in terms of the need to address a threat or pursue an opportunity. Not all opportunities can or should be pursued. Understanding what the organization does well, and what it does not, will help to make these decisions. Exhibit 7.12 lists the areas of concern for internal assessments.

Exhibit 7.12.   Internal assessment.

Areas of Concern

1. Finances.
2. Human resources (staff, board, and volunteer knowledge and skills).
3. Marketing and public relations.
4. Service delivery.
5. Management policies and practices.

Exhibit 7.13. Critical issues list.

Private State-Wide Arts Fund-Raising Organization

1. How can this organization provide support to arts organizations that have lost all state funding and are threatened with closing?
2. How can this organization raise money to support arts organizations without competing against those same organizations?
3. How can this organization enhance public awareness of its activities?
4. Can this organization reduce overhead by sharing facilities with another, noncompeting organization?
5. Can this organization become the arts-funding adviser to small and midsize corporations that have small giving programs?
6. Can this organization expand the amount of funds available to arts organizations rather than redistribute existing monies?

(v) Critical issues list   The product of the situation analysis is a list of the critical issues that the organization must address in the course of developing the plan. These issues are often stated in the form of questions.

Coming to a consensus on which issues are critical can be a challenge to the planning team. Several issues will emerge clearly; others will overlap or seem uncertain. As a general rule, the final list should not exceed 12 issues. A longer list suggests that the group has failed to achieve sufficient focus and will get bogged down in the process of developing strategic responses.

One technique for generating this list is to have each member of the planning team list his or her top six issues, eliminate the redundancies, summarize the issues on flip chart, and look at the final list. Often, with just a bit of refinement, a consensus list will have emerged. Another technique is to assign to a single member the task of presenting a draft list to the group. Each member then comments in writing and a second draft is created. This procedure continues until the group reaches consensus on the list. Exhibit 7.13 presents an example of a critical issues list for an arts fund-raising organization.

(c) ASSESSMENT SUMMARY   At this point, the assessment phase of planning is complete. The planning team should have a clear vision of the world as it could be, an understanding of key stakeholders and their relationship to the organization, a clear understanding of organizational effectiveness, and a grasp of key trends and of the strengths and weaknesses of the organization. In other words, the team will have defined the areas contained in each of the three circles presented in Exhibit 7.1. The remaining work is to define the area of overlap and create the plan. If the assessment phase has been done well, the actual planning phase should proceed fairly smoothly.

7.6 THE PLANNING PROCESS: DEVELOPING THE PLAN

(a) MISSION STATEMENT   No other aspect of strategic planning is more important than writing the mission statement. All activities of the organization flow from this understanding.

The mission statement provides clarity of purpose and thus directs decision making about what programs to pursue. It is also a guide for action. Because it helps define the manner in which the organization will conduct its activities, it should be understood by all members of the organization.

By communicating purpose to the world, the mission statement helps attract needed resources (money and people). Research suggests that the primary reason individuals donate money and become volunteers is because they identify with the purpose of the organization. Exhibit 7.14 provides a list of questions that the planning team may consider in developing the mission statement.

(i) Writing a mission statement   The articulation of an organization's purpose into clear, concise language is achieved through the following steps:

1. Consensus seeking. The mission statement should reflect a broad consensus of the purpose of the organization. Working in a group, begin by identifying the key concepts or phrases that should by included. As a group, narrow the list by eliminating overlap and providing focus.

2. Generation of individual rough drafts. Allow each group member to generate and share a rough draft statement.

3. Assignment of the first draft. Groups have their limitations. Mission statements generated entirely by a group tend to be wordy, awkward, and sometimes difficult for others to comprehend. Assign the task of creating a first draft to one or two individuals and have them report back to the group at the next meeting. They may wish to begin with someone else's draft. The wordsmiths must incorporate the key concepts and phrases from the group's list into the first draft.

4. Editing. Less is more. Strive for economy of expression. Try to limit the mission statement to fewer than 40 words.

5. Full group review. Present the first draft to the full group for comment. If only minor changes are necessary, the group may settle on a working draft.

6. Repeating the process. If the first draft requires significant revision, send it back for more work by the writers, or reassign the task. Allowing other individuals a turn at writing helps build ownership.

7. Validating the mission. Throughout the planning process, periodically review the mission statement, answering these questions: Are our directions consistent with

Exhibit 7.14.   Guide for writing the mission statement.

Questions About Mission
1. Whom does this organization serve?
2. What are the basic needs that this organization fills?
3. Broadly speaking, how does this organization meet the needs of those it serves?
4. Is the area served geographically limited? If so, what is the area served?
5. What makes this organization unique?
6. What values does this organization seek to promote?
7. Who are the individuals who make up this organization? How does that affect its purpose?

our mission? If not, is our mission adequate? If the group determines that the mission statement is accurate, all planning should reflect the mission. If the proposed goals consistently fall outside the mission, perhaps the statement is too narrow and needs to be reevaluated. It may be useful to have external stakeholders review the mission statement.

Exhibit 7.15 presents guidelines for the writing of the actual mission statement.

(b) DIRECTIONS AND GOALS Directions describe the major areas of activity in the organization. Directions can be determined by defining the major categories of the budget or the basic divisions of labor in the organization. The planning process may or may not determine new directions for the organization.

Goals define in broad terms why the organization directs resources toward these activities. Goals also begin to define the outcomes of the organization.

Taken together, the mission statement, directions, and goals provide a complete picture of the organization's purpose, activities, and desired outcomes. Many planning models do not contain the directions and goals steps, and some might argue that they are unnecessary exercises. Although not mandatory, I believe these steps provide a greater degree of clarity than is possible with a mission statement alone.

Many mission statements are long, obtuse statements that have extensive lists of subpoints. If a camel is a horse designed by a committee, then these mission statements are strategic planning camels.

The approach presented here stresses conciseness and clarity, participation and consensus. Although these pairs are not mutually exclusive, a tension exists between them. Use of this approach and of the guidelines presented in Exhibit 7.15 can help resolve these competing aims. Exhibit 7.16 provides an example of a complete statement of mission, directions, and goals.

(c) DEVELOPING STRATEGIES There are no tricks to developing the strategic responses to the issues identified. Many sophisticated approaches to evaluating strategies exist, but few nonprofits will have the time and resources to conduct such research, and the results are not likely to be better than a well-considered approach selected by the group.

Brainstorming is perhaps the most effective approach for generating strategies. A group that has come this far in the planning process should have a deep grasp of the

Exhibit 7.15. Guidelines for writing a mission statement.

Qualities of a Good Mission Statement
- Is clear and concise.
- Is forward-thinking.
- Is a guide to action.
- Defines whom the organization serves.
- Is expressed in broad, nonquantifiable terms.
- Provides inspiration.
- Reflects a broad consensus.
- Is easily understood by people outside the organization.

Exhibit 7.16.   Rural county humane society—mission and goals.

Mission

> The Society is a community of people who believe that all life should be respected and whose mission is to promote responsible treatment of animals and be an advocate on their behalf.

Directions	Goals
Education	• Educate the community on responsible pet ownership and the humane treatment of animals.
	• Reduce pet overpopulation.
Direct Services	• Reunite lost pets with their owners as rapidly as possible.
	• Find homes for homeless animals.
	• Relieve animal suffering.
	• Reduce pet overpopulation without euthanasia.
Administration/Fund-Raising	• Provide the resources necessary to sustain our efforts.
	• Responsibly manage the allocation of resources and the coordination of the activities of the organization.

issues and should be able to generate many effective responses. Based on the premise that quantity will lead to quality, brainstorming is designed to generate as many ideas as possible. The key to its success is to defer judgment until the idea generation is exhausted. Exhibit 7.17 lists the basic rules of brainstorming.

(i) Selecting the right strategy   There is no way to be certain that the correct strategy has been chosen, but if the issues are well understood and sufficient time has been given to developing possible strategies, the planning team should be in a position to make effective choices. Having a consultant or facilitator who is not a member of the team is important at this point. The planning team is essentially engaged in problem solving and can easily become bogged down. The following process can help keep the group on track:

1. Maintain focus. The facilitator or team leader should clearly state the goal and relevant critical planning issues to be addressed.
2. Refresh the group data base. Review the issues and the key points that have been considered up to this point in the process. If resources permit, it is useful to have members of the team create a summary document for each of the planning issues. The discussion may begin with a brief presentation on the issue.
3. Encourage critical thinking and avoid criticism. Help the group learn to work with ideas rather than defend positions. Criticism merely seeks to find fault

Exhibit 7.17.   Brainstorming.

Basic Rules
1. Criticism of one another's ideas is prohibited.
2. Free wheeling and wild ideas are encouraged.
3. Quantity of ideas is sought.
4. Combining or modifying ideas is encouraged.

with others' ideas. Critical thinking looks for strengths and weaknesses and is focused on finding the best solution rather than winning the argument. Criticism makes people defensive of their ideas and less open to others' contributions.

4. Beware of groupthink. Some groups will become overly cautious of offending members and will avoid critical discussions. This reaction is perhaps more dangerous than defensive argumentation. The phenomenon of groupthink has been well studied, and many notorious examples of its effects exist (Zander, 1983). Planning teams may appoint a devil's advocate or bring in outsiders to help find faults that the group may have missed. Exhibit 7.18 presents the continuum of group decision making, from argumentative criticism to groupthink. Groups should strive for the midpoint: critical thinking.

5. Consider the consequences. The facilitator or team leader should push the group to consider all the possible consequences. An effective technique is to appoint members of the team as temporary representatives of key stakeholders and ask them to react to the strategy under consideration.

6. Summarize and test for consensus. Often, groups will extend the discussion of an issue far beyond the point of agreement. A good facilitator or leader will watch for emerging agreement and attempt to summarize what appears to be the decision. At this point, a show of hands is a useful indicator of how close the group is to agreement.

7. Work for consensus. Voting for the final decision should be avoided if possible. Taking a vote sets up winners and losers and, when it is time to implement the decision, it sets up supporters and dissenters. Working for consensus does not

Exhibit 7.18. Group decision making—selecting a strategy.

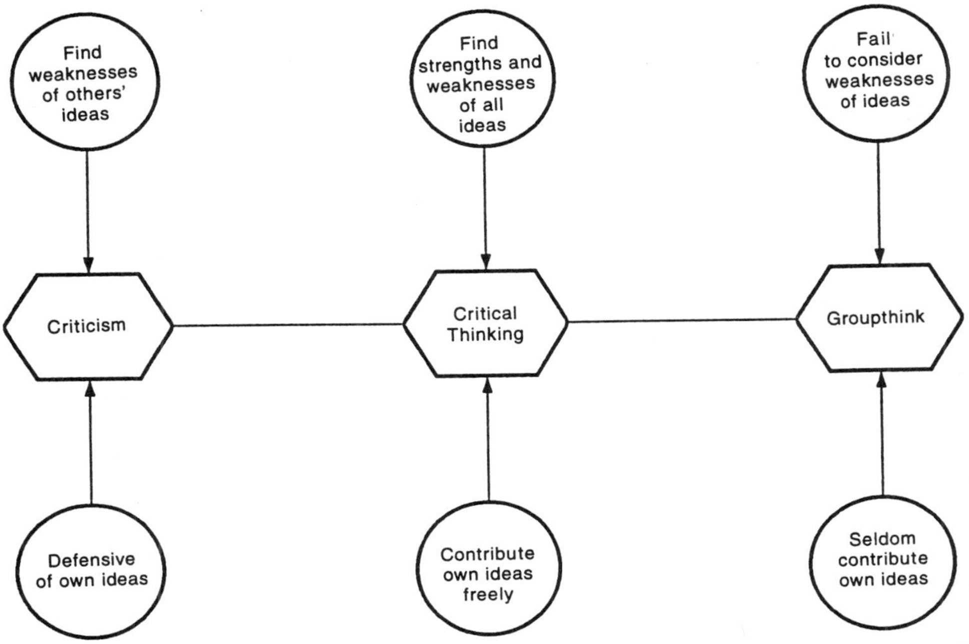

mean achieving unanimous agreement; it simply means that all members of the group can live with the decision.

An example of strategy development is provided by the state-wide arts fund-raising organization (Exhibit 7.13), which developed a strategy of targeting growing small and midsize corporations that did not have large corporate giving programs but wanted to make a contribution to the arts and culture. This strategy was chosen because (1) it provides additional money for the arts and does not simply redistribute existing funds; (2) it offers a way to raise money without competing with the arts organizations it serves (most of these arts organizations have not targeted small and midsize corporations); and (3) it offers these corporations a way to tap into arts-funding expertise without having to staff their corporate giving function. In other words, this strategy addresses four of the six critical issues presented in Exhibit 7.13.

(d) DEVELOPING STRATEGIC OBJECTIVES   As stated before, goals describe why resources are being committed to the basic directions of the organization; they begin to define what the organization seeks to accomplish. Strategies define how the goals will be accomplished. Objectives provide quantitative measures of success; they describe *when* and *how much.*

In the example above, the objective of targeting growing small and midsize corporations was to raise, in 3 years, $500,000 in new money for the arts in the state. There are some fairly sophisticated approaches to assessing the feasibility of such an objective. If time and money are available to conduct such research, perhaps it is worth doing. If not, the group should set a target that is judged to be challenging but attainable, and should monitor how well the organization is doing. These objectives may be specified in terms of hard numbers, percentages, or specific achievements, and should indicate the expected time for completion.

Adjustments can be made as the organization gains experience. The critical fact is that a target exists. Objectives are the most flexible aspect of the strategic plan and can change as a result of new information or changing conditions.

(e) DEVELOPING IMPLEMENTATION PLANS   It is not the responsibility of the planning team to carry out the strategic plan or even to specify the steps for implementation. Those are better left to the groups or individuals that have expertise or responsibility in the respective areas. Nonetheless, a strategic plan should provide some indication of who will be responsible for implementing major areas of the plan, when implementation is expected, about what it will cost, and, if appropriate, how much it will earn for the organization. A planning team cannot present a plan without attention being paid to the availability of resources to carry out the plan.

(i) Assignment of responsibility   It should be clear to readers of a strategic plan who is responsible for carrying out the plan's major aspects. This does not mean that all steps are detailed. It simply means thought has been given to the practicality of the strategy. Exhibit 7.19 provides an example of an implementation planning form that details the necessary information.

Strategies are listed in the first column. The second column indicates who has primary responsibility for implementation; this could be an individual or a committee comprised of board, staff, and volunteers. The third column is divided to show the

Exhibit 7.19.   Implementation planning form.

Strategy	Responsibility	Schedule		Resources Needed
		Start	Finish	

start and completion dates. The last column is for specifying needed resources—staff, board, and volunteer time and money.

(ii) Budgeting The implementation of the strategic plan cannot proceed without the necessary financial forecasting and control mechanisms. It is beyond the scope of this chapter to provide a detailed discussion of budgeting, but a few key points should be considered.

Budgets provide a means to determine the amount of financial resources necessary to carry out the plan; to allocate those resources in the appropriate amounts; to control the use of those resources; and to measure performance. In the budget, the entire plan comes together. Assuming that the planning assumptions are correct and the objectives are achievable, the budget will indicate whether the organization can reasonably support the plans it has set forth.

If the implementation plans have sufficiently detailed the needed resources and the objectives have sufficiently detailed the expected earnings, then the creation of a draft budget should be relatively easy. The estimates of earnings can be tested against historically reliable standards, but this is only a marginal indicator and cannot account for changes called for in the plan.

7.7 THE PLANNING PROCESS: MONITORING AND UPDATING THE PLAN

At a minimum, strategic plans should be reviewed and updated annually. Given the volatile environment of most nonprofits, updating should probably occur more often, perhaps even quarterly. In general, quarterly meetings should be for review of progress only, and major considerations of the plan should happen, at most, annually. Ideally, these sessions will not be the only times the plan is taken off the shelf, but they will allow reflection on the experiences to date in implementing the plan. The plan is not only an evaluation tool; it is a guide to action and should be consulted often in the ongoing operations of the organization.

During an update meeting, the planning team should spend 3 to 6 hours reviewing the performance of the organization against the specified objectives, considering changes in the situation of the organization, and altering the plan as necessary.

It is important to understand that a need for alterations is not a sign of a poor plan. More likely, it is an indicator of a healthy planning process. Despite the rational formality of the approach presented here, planners should become comfortable with the evolutionary nature of strategic planning. As Henry Mintzberg (1987) has suggested: "Virtually everything that has been written about strategy making depicts it as a deliberate process. First we think, then we act. We formulate, then we implement. The progression seems so perfectly sensible. Why would anyone want to proceed differently? . . . Strategies need not be deliberate—they can emerge" (p. 68).

If the organization is not performing as expected, the updating of the plan proceeds backward through the model. Perhaps the objectives were not realistic and should be scaled back a bit. Perhaps the strategy itself was faulty and should be changed. Perhaps the world has changed in a significant and unexpected way, causing the organization to reconsider everything from mission to strategies. There are no clear guidelines for conducting this assessment. As a rule of thumb, the planning team should question all aspects of the plan and be open to revision of any aspect of the plan that no longer seems appropriate.

7.8   TIME COMMITMENT TO PLANNING

There is no simple formula for how long it takes to complete a plan. It depends on the scope of the planning, the number of people on the planning team, the amount of work accomplished between planning meetings, and, frankly, the amount of time the organization is willing to devote to the process.

Groups have created effective plans in a single full-day retreat. The focus of these sessions is generally on clarifying mission and perhaps setting long-term organizational goals. Most efforts take longer, however. As a general guideline, planning team members should expect about 32 hours of work. Organizations with large staffs may be able to provide support to the planning team and reduce the actual time commitment of team members.

Planning meetings should be 2 to 6 hours in length. Shorter meetings do not allow sufficient time to discuss issues, and longer meetings produce diminishing returns. The recommended interval for planning meetings is every 2 weeks. This allows time to accomplish assignments and should prevent the team from losing momentum. Exhibit 7.20 presents an 8-meeting schedule, showing the element(s) of the plan covered at each meeting. This schedule assumes that a considerable amount of work will be done between meetings.

Exhibit 7.20.   Eight-meeting planning schedule.

Element of Strategic Plan	Team Meetings							
	1	2	3	4	5	6	7	8
Clarify vision	•							
Situation analysis		•	•					
Clarify mission				•				
Develop directions and goals				•	•			
Develop strategies					•	•		
Develop objectives							•	
Develop implementation plans								•

Between-meeting work includes many aspects of the situation analysis and the implementation planning/budgeting process. The latter are largely staff functions (where sufficient staff exists).

7.9   MANAGEMENT BY OBJECTIVES (MBO)

Linking staff performance to the strategic plan is essential to bringing the plan to fruition. This is especially important in large organizations, where staff may be largely removed from the planning process.

Management by objectives (MBO) was first introduced by Peter Drucker in the 1950s. It is, without a doubt, the most widely used management tool—and with good reason. Goal setting has been shown to be the most effective motivational tool (Locke and Latham, 1984). (For the purposes of this discussion on MBO, the terms "goals" and "objectives" are used interchangeably.) The MBO process varies from one organization to another. In some large corporations, MBO is often a complex, paper-intensive, time-consuming process that has little relationship to employee performance and evaluation. In others, it is a comprehensive approach to employee performance planning and evaluation.

The key to making MBO effective is to keep it simple. Karl Albrecht (1978) offered, perhaps, the most common-sense definition of MBO:

> Management by Objectives is nothing more—nor less—than an observable pattern of behavior on the part of the manager, characterized by studying the anticipated future, determining what payoff conditions to bring about for that anticipated future, and guiding the efforts of the people of the organization so that they accomplish these objectives while deriving personal and individual benefits in doing so [p. 20].

For the organization as a whole, the studying of the anticipated future is complete. Implementing MBO is about defining payoff conditions and guiding the efforts of the people in the organization. It represents an approach to managing for results. Exhibit 7.21 presents the basic steps in the MBO process.

(a) FOUR FACTORS CRITICAL TO SUCCESSFUL MBO

(i) Board commitment to strategic objectives   Successful completion of a strategic plan should ensure that this support is in place. It is mentioned here because MBO begins at the top of the organization. In nonprofits, this means the board of directors.

(ii) Collaborative goal setting   Central to MBO is the balancing of the need to meet organizational goals and individual goals. To accomplish this end, each employee meets with his or her manager to define the objectives for the individual job.

(iii) Periodic review and evaluation   Early approaches to MBO prescribed an annual review of performance. The turbulent nature of nonprofits requires a more frequent review schedule. The organization should review all goals and objectives at least semiannually and perhaps quarterly. During these reviews, progress should be measured, intervening circumstances should be noted, and, where necessary, goals, and objectives should be updated to reflect changing conditions and priorities. The annual

Exhibit 7.21. Management by objectives (MBO).

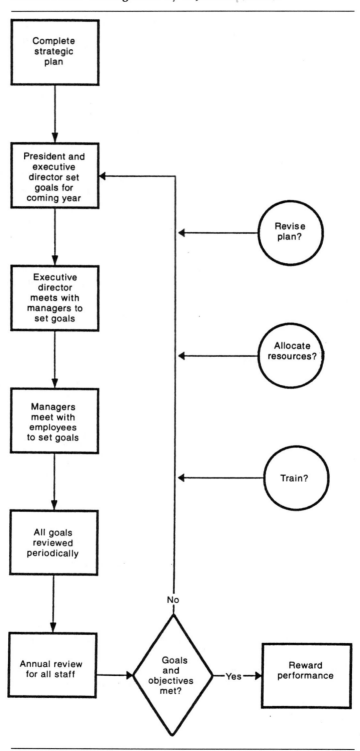

review should be an opportunity to evaluate performance against goals, and to begin planning for the next year's efforts. MBO processes that become limited to performance appraisal systems lose the motivational benefits of collaborative goal setting, which has been stressed in the discussion of both strategic planning and MBO.

(iv) Tied to rewards Perhaps the simplest truism of management is: What gets rewarded gets done. MBO offers a process to define and measure what gets done. It is up to managers and the board of directors to reward this performance. Recognition, and rewards should be linked to the strategic planning/MBO process.

(b) WRITING GOAL STATEMENTS THAT WILL MOTIVATE PERFORMANCE The positive effects of goal setting have been extensively studied. Having clear and challenging goals increases motivation and maximizes performance. Among the explanations for why goals improve performance, the following four appear most frequently:

1. Goals focus attention and effort. We are faced with endless options in our lives. Goals allow us to focus our attention and energy on relevant activities rather than on the endless irrelevant alternatives. This allows us to accomplish more with the same expenditure of energy.
2. Goals challenge us to perform at a higher level. Once we have committed to making an accomplishment, we are more likely to increase our effort and to seek out ways to improve our performance. In addition, we become more tenacious and are less likely to give up.
3. Goals give purpose to undesirable tasks. Knowing what we wish to accomplish can help us complete uninteresting and unpleasant tasks. The value of our effort is known to us, and these tasks are no longer viewed as unnecessary or avoidable.
4. Goals can enhance cooperation. Being clear about what we hope to accomplish allows others to make informed choices about whether to go along with us.

Employee goals and objectives should specify work outcomes, which can be specified in four ways.

1. Quality of service or production, such as customer satisfaction, the number of errors, or conformity to a standard.
2. Units of production, such as the quantity of products or number of clients served;
3. Time standards, such as predetermined deadlines, cycle time to complete a process, or service delivery time.
4. Money, such as budgets, income, and costs.

Exhibit 7.22 presents guidelines for writing goal statements for employees. (Goals should be related to the strategic plan.) These are the areas to which the organization has decided to direct its efforts and resources. Employee efforts should be aimed at accomplishing these ends.

MBO goals should be specific, measurable, and time-bound, in much the same manner as the objectives are in the strategic plan. The work outcomes described above will help define the nature of the goal statements.

Exhibit 7.22.   Goal-setting guidelines.

Characteristics of Effective Goals
- Related to strategic plan.
- Specific, measurable, and time-bound.
- Jointly set by the employee and his or her manager.
- Related to things over which the employee has control.
- Challenging, yet attainable.

Employees must understand and be committed to their goals, in order to perform them. The most effective way to ensure understanding and commitment is to have the employees participate in goal setting. Goals should be limited to areas or actions over which the employee has control.

The key aspect of motivating employees is to have challenging goals. The goals should seek to stretch employees beyond previous levels of performance.

7.10   CONCLUSION

Taken together, strategic planning and MBO offer a comprehensive approach to planning, organizing, and controlling organizational and individual performance. Some models prescribe an intermediate step of operational planning. In an effort to streamline the approach presented here, aspects of operational planning have been incorporated into both strategic planning and MBO.

This process integrates strategic management concepts, such as environmental scanning and stakeholder management, with mission clarification and planning techniques. The approach also integrates aspects of operational planning and human resource management.

Organizations that do not wish to undertake the entire process will find many aspects of the process independently useful. For example, stakeholder management is a critical need for many nonprofits and might represent an appropriate partial use of this approach. The most important point presented here is that each organization must understand its own needs for organizational improvement and select an approach that addresses those needs.

Done well, strategic planning can offer substantial improvements in individual and organizational performance. Done poorly, it can be an enormous waste of time and resources, leading to resentment and withdrawal from the organization. Only after the needs of an organization are assessed should the necessary commitment be developed and the approach adapted as necessary. The benefits are worth the investment.

SOURCES AND SUGGESTED REFERENCES

Albrecht, K. 1978. *Successful Management By Objectives: An Action Manual.* Englewood Cliffs, NJ: Prentice-Hall.

Barker, J. 1988. *Discovering the Future: The Business of Paradigms,* 2d ed. Lake Elmoy, MN: ILI Press.

Benveniste, G. 1989. *Mastering the Politics of Planning.* San Francisco: Jossey-Bass.

Carver, J. 1990. *Boards That Make a Difference.* San Francisco: Jossey-Bass.

Drucker, P. F. 1990. *Managing the Nonprofit Organization.* New York: HarperCollins.

Freeman, E. 1984. *Strategic Management: A Stakeholder Approach.* New York: Pitman.

Hall, P. B. 1987. "A Historical Overview of the Private Nonprofit Sector." In W. W. Powell (Ed.), *The Nonprofit Sector: A Research Handbook.* New Haven: Yale University Press.

Hodgkinson, V. A., Lyman, R. W., and Associates. 1989. *The Future of the Nonprofit Sector.* San Francisco: Jossey-Bass.

Houle, C. O. 1989. *Governing Boards.* San Francisco: Jossey-Bass.

Kennedy, L. W. 1991. *Quality Management in the Nonprofit World.* San Francisco: Jossey-Bass.

Locke, E. A., and Latham, G. P. 1984. *Goal Setting: A Motivational Techniques That Works!.* Englewood Cliffs, NJ: Prentice-Hall.

Mintzberg, H. 1987. "Crafting Strategy." *Harvard Business Review* (July–August), *65*:68.

Powell, W. W. (Ed.). 1987. *The Nonprofit Sector: A Research Handbook.* New Haven: Yale University Press.

Van Til, J., and Associates. 1990. *Critical Issues in American Philanthropy.* San Francisco: Jossey-Bass.

Zander, A. 1983. *Making Groups Effective.* San Francisco: Jossey-Bass.

P A R T   T W O

Human Resources

The Board of Directors

Barbara A. Burgess
Staley/Robeson

CONTENTS

8.1   WHAT THE BOARD IS AND WHAT IT DOES

Over the years, nonprofit boards have collected a full rack of descriptive tags that characterize styles of operation. One hears about power boards, token boards, working boards, money-raising boards, and hands-on boards. More than anything else, however, how a board operates relates to how well it understands its responsibilities and functions.

This chapter defines and describes the charge of a controlling or governing nonprofit board of directors in two ways. First, it describes the functions and responsibilities of a board generically. Second, it presents a concept of board development that will enable a board to fulfill its responsibilities effectively and, consequently, to evolve and mature.

(a) DEFINITION OF A NONPROFIT BOARD A nonprofit board of directors is the governing or policy-setting body that bears legal responsibility for the institution it serves. A board also plays a role in maintaining a system of decision-making checks and balances among three organizational branches: the administration, the board, and any constituency that has input into the workings of the organization. A nonprofit organization is required to have a voluntary or lay board of directors in order to get a state charter and qualify for Section 501(c)(3) tax status under the Internal Revenue Code.

(b) TYPES OF BOARDS Boards of directors are sometimes referred to as controlling boards because they are responsible for every major decision an organization makes. An organization can have other boards, such as auxiliary boards or associational boards, but these should not be confused with controlling boards. Auxiliary boards are created by the controlling board to execute a specific responsibility—most often, to raise money. Associational boards usually exist to increase membership and to act as a body that represents the needs and special interests of the general membership. A college alumni association is an example of this type of board.

8.2 PURPOSES OF A BOARD

Whether a nonprofit organization is a social service agency, an educational institution, a health care organization, or a cultural institution, its board will have the same basic charge. Functional differences among boards are more a matter of emphasis than of purpose. Generically, a board has three governing functions (Ingram, 1988):

> To preserve the integrity of the trust;
> To set policy;
> To support and promote the organization.

(a) TO PRESERVE THE INTEGRITY OF THE TRUST This function has two facets: overseeing the mission and preserving institutional autonomy.

(i) Overseeing the mission Nonprofit constitutions and governing bylaws usually begin with a statement of the organization's mission or purpose. As overseer of that mission, a board must make certain that everything the nonprofit does is true to it. A board fulfills this purpose by asking hard questions. Because asking questions is perhaps their most important task, members should never hesitate to request information about all facets of the institution's operations. Traditionally, boards involve themselves with financial activity more closely than they do with programs and services, because they are not usually experts in the services their organizations provide. To assess how well the mission is being fulfilled, however, a board must become familiar with *all* areas of the organization. Moreover, extraordinary expertise in the service delivery of the organization is not required in order to determine whether a program is meeting the mandates of the mission. The integrity of the institution rests on more than balanced books or well-managed assets; indeed, the integrity of an organization depends primarily on the fulfillment of its mission and public service.

(ii) Preserving institutional autonomy   Another aspect of preserving the integrity of the trust relates to preserving institutional independence. A board must weigh carefully decisions that could compromise the organization's ability to steer its own course. Complete independence is nearly impossible today because of strings attached to state and federal assistance. Nevertheless, a board must still reject pressures from special-interest groups that would compromise the organization's mission, or from public agencies or businesses that may try to exert undue influence. It is equally important for a board to protect the organization's autonomy through adoption of a clear policy for accepting gifts and grants that have donor restrictions.

(b) TO SET POLICY   The day-to-day administration of an organization is the charge of a chief administrator, but it is the role of the board to provide an operational framework. Most policy is proposed by administrators and presented to the board for questioning, discussion, and, ultimately, a vote of approval. The degree to which a board becomes involved in policy implementation varies among organizations, depending on the balance of strengths and the level of cooperation between the board and the administrative leadership.

Policy making should be grounded in the mission statement and other governing documents of the organization. It should also be preceded by research and input from those members of the organization who will be affected by the policy. Examples of policy decisions that typically require board approval include:

1. Change of the institution's name;
2. Approval of annual operating budgets;
3. Increases in fees for services;
4. Formal endorsement of fund-raising projects;
5. Staff promotions and salary increases;
6. Changes in program offerings or client services;
7. Endowment decisions;
8. Purchase or sale of property;
9. Risk management decisions.

(c) TO SUPPORT AND PROMOTE THE ORGANIZATION   Outside the boardroom, the directors' role changes from devil's advocate to chief advocate. Directors ask hard questions in the privacy of the boardroom, but in public they put aside their criticisms and promote the organization in every way possible. The board's external functions include bringing positive attention to the institution, supporting it financially, supporting the chief administrator, and introducing the organization to those who may be able to help it. In a word, these functions are ambassadorial.

8.3   THE DIFFERENCE BETWEEN FOR-PROFIT AND NONPROFIT BOARDS

Particularly when nonprofit organizations come under criticism, comparisons are frequently made between nonprofit and for-profit boards. Moreover, it is not uncommon for an uninitiated board member to think that a nonprofit board should mold itself in the image of a for-profit board. However, each is a distinctly different entity, and it is important for nonprofit administrators and board members to know the differences.

(a) FUNCTIONAL DIFFERENCES The most obvious difference between for-profit and nonprofit boards is that for-profit board members usually receive a stipend for their service, and members of nonprofit boards are volunteers. Moreover, for-profit board members normally are chosen for their professional expertise in an area that is directly related to the organization's endeavor; members of nonprofit boards are selected using a different, broader set of criteria, including that of representing a layperson's point of view. This is not to infer that nonprofit board members do not bring expertise to the board. The expertise they bring, however, is often intended to complement the expertise of the staff, not to replicate it.

Typically, nonprofit boards do not generally include staff or chief executive officers as voting members of the board, as do for-profit boards of directors, although in some states it is legal to do so. Frequently, the chief executive officer is an ex officio member without voting power.

(b) DIFFERENCES IN FOLLOW-THROUGH Conrad and Glenn (1986) noted several other differences between for-profit and nonprofit boards. Decisions of nonprofit boards tend to penetrate the organization more deeply and quickly, and carry more specific ramifications for day-to-day procedures; for-profit boards make decisions that many employees may never hear about. Similarly, nonprofit boards become more involved in the implementation of their decisions; they may even oversee and fund implementation themselves. For-profit boards, on the other hand, merely pass the decision on to the chief executive officer for appropriate delegation and implementation. Perhaps this practice accounts for another difference: for-profit boards generally do not have committees. A nonprofit's major work is often done in and by a variety of committees.

8.4 TEN RESPONSIBILITIES OF A BOARD

It is in the best interest of an organization to educate its entire staff about board functions and responsibilities. Senior administrators and staff members who interact with their boards should study the ten basic responsibilities of a board, given in this section. It is their job to steer and support the board in fulfilling those responsibilities. Before describing each one, it should be noted that authors who write about nonprofit boards have created myriad lists of board responsibilities. The list given here is a conglomerate of many lists and conventional board wisdom, but owes a special debt to Ingram (1988, 1990).

(a) SELECT, SUPPORT, AND EVALUATE THE CHIEF ADMINISTRATOR Because incompetent leadership can threaten an institution's very existence, a board's role in the hiring, evaluation, and termination of a chief administrator is perhaps the most critical responsibility a board has.

(i) Hiring the chief administrator The process of selection is difficult and time-consuming. The rewards of careful selection, however, are many: a well-chosen leader will oversee efficient operations, facilitate the development of sound programs, and enhance the organization's public relations and fund-raising activities. Even though search committees most often have nonboard members, the final authority to hire a new chief administrator rests with the board. Before voting to hire a candidate, a responsible board will be able to answer all the questions on Exhibit 8.1.

(ii) Supporting and evaluating the chief administrator   Once a board selects a chief administrator, it owes that individual its whole-hearted support and should refrain from meddling in day-to-day operations. This is not to say, however, that the board cannot express its opinion or disagree with the administrator's performance in the appropriate venue. Indeed, if a board member has a concern about the administrator's performance, that member should speak with the administrator directly. If the member is not comfortable with direct conversation, that concern should be discussed with the board chair, who, in turn, will discuss it with the administrator. In general, it is not appropriate to discuss the chief administrator's performance, among directors or anyone else, outside of a meeting at which the board chair is present. (See Chap. 13.)

When boards find themselves in disputes over a decision to terminate a chief administrator, they most likely have not conducted formal, annual evaluations. John Nason (1990) has suggested that the process for evaluating the performance of the chief administrator should begin with notification of evaluation and a request for the chief administrator to prepare a self-assessment. At the same time, the board should evaluate itself on how well it has supported the administration. A formal review should be conducted at least once a year and, to guarantee objectivity and candor, a consultant should facilitate the process periodically. Finally, the results of the evaluation should be shared with both the chief administrator and the entire board. When handled with sensitivity, evaluations can be constructive for both the organization and the individual(s) involved.

(iii) Terminating the chief administrator   If the hiring and evaluation process are executed well, a board should seldom have to terminate the chief administrator. When termination issues arise, the board should consult legal counsel immediately, to review the administrator's contract and to develop a procedural plan for the termination. Hasty, uninformed attempts to terminate often violate the contract or due process, and the organization as well as the board could be sued. Legal counsel minimizes this

---

Exhibit 8.1.   Checklist for hiring a new chief administrator.

1. Has everyone who will report directly to the new person had a chance to meet and react to the candidate?   _____

2. Have the candidate's references been thoroughly checked? Did they reveal caveats the board should know about and evaluate?   _____

3. Has the candidate seen and agreed to a complete, written job description?   _____

4. Have contract negotiations been thorough? Is the length of the contract clear and have conditions for termination been spelled out?   _____

5. Have all perquisites of the job been identified in writing and agreed to?   _____

risk and provides objectivity in a situation that is frequently fraught with subjectivity and highly charged emotions.

(b) REVIEW AND PROTECT THE MISSION OF THE ORGANIZATION Organizations with financial, operational, and image problems can often trace their troubles to the lack of focus that comes from not having and not communicating a clear institutional mission. Even clear missions need regular review and updating.

(i) Reviewing the mission If a board chair or board committee with planning responsibility does not initiate an annual mission review, the chief administrator should initiate it. The result of a mission review should be a short written statement that answers three questions about the organization (Bryson, 1989): Who are we? What do we do? Why do we do what we do? Every time the board makes a decision, it should ask itself: Is this decision in keeping with what we are all about?

Although a mission statement provides an anchor in the policy- and decision-making processes, it is not immutable. Consequently, annual reviews should consider whether changes in internal and external environments are rendering the mission, or parts of it, obsolete.

(ii) Changing the mission statement If a change in mission seems prudent and justified, the board should begin a revision process that includes representatives from all constituencies of the organization. When the process is complete, the administrator must follow up by making all publics aware of the change in mission.

When an organization considers a radical change in mission, the board should consult an attorney specializing in nonprofit law: major changes could impact the organization's state charter or gift endowment—and even, in some cases, place it in jeopardy.

(c) DRIVE THE ORGANIZATION'S PLANNING EFFORTS Once a mission has been defined, it is the board's job to motivate and oversee a planning process that results in a vision for the organization. Ongoing planning is necessary for the simple reason that things change. Shifts in demographic trends, changes in national standards of care, the development of new technology, and changes in societal needs are all conditions that affect a nonprofit's future. Ideally, and increasingly, it is a necessity that an organization look and plan ahead, anticipating change instead of dealing with it reactively. (See Chaps. 2 and 7.)

It is not a board's role to formulate plans, but it is its responsibility to insist that planning be undertaken. As planning occurs, the board should be kept informed and involved in discussions with the planners. Finally, the board should review formal plans while still in draft form, then vote on final adoption. The administration is responsible for providing the board with all information needed to perform this task effectively.

(d) SERVE AS FIDUCIARY REPRESENTATIVE OF THE ORGANIZATION The law is murky about the exact responsibilities of nonprofit board members, but legal precedent supports the ten responsibilities described in this chapter. In general, a board and its individual members are considered agents of a corporation and are liable for the actions of a nonprofit organization. This means that they can be sued collectively, as well as individually, for failure to carry out the duties of the organization. Although many states have passed legislation providing charitable or qualified immunity for directors and officers of nonprofit organizations, there are still areas where liability exists. Consequently, it is important for board members and chief administrators to act at all times in the best interest of the organization and to understand their legal duties. These duties are discussed in detail in a later section of this chapter.

(e) ENSURE THE FINANCIAL SOLVENCY OF THE ORGANIZATION   This responsibility has two facets: overseeing fiscal management and participating in fund-raising for the organization.

(i) Overseeing fiscal management   In the financial arena, board members routinely approve actions that can have a significant effect on the fiscal health of the organization. While details may be delegated to a board finance committee, the full board will need to approve operating budgets, loans, retrenchment plans, capital expenditures, fee increases, investments, property sales, salary and benefit packages, and funding for new programs and projects. It will also need to make risk management decisions regarding insurance and indemnification.

To tackle this responsibility competently, board members must understand fund accounting and review assiduously the monthly balance sheets, activity and expense statements, and statements of cash flow. In addition, they need to give thorough scrutiny to the auditor's annual report. Because fiscal *mis*management is no stranger to nonprofit organizations, board members have not only the right, but the responsibility, to question any expenditure and financial action the administration takes. The chief financial administrator must provide financial data to the board in a timely fashion and answer all questions. To ensure a system of checks and balances, external accountants and auditors should report directly to the board, not to the chief administrator (Dalsimer, 1991).

(ii) Participating in fund-raising   In plainest terms, a board has a responsibility to support every fund-raising endeavor the institution undertakes. That support comes in two ways: board endorsement of all fund-raising undertakings as the governing body of the organization, and individual financial support from every board member. In other words, fund-raising is not merely the responsibility of a development officer, a chief administrator, or a board's fund-raising committee. The commonly heard imperative "Give, get, or get off" may be coarse, but it is grounded in a sound, three-part rationale regarding fund-raising: it is an act of leadership that all prospective donors need for guidance in their own giving; it is an act of commitment that all constituents of the organization look to for reassurance of a caring board; and it is an act of faith and confidence in the institution, which all constituencies will use in assessing the health of the organization.

Everyone readily acknowledges that some members are capable of contributing more money than others. This variance gives rise to the question of how much a member should give. The answer is: Members should give as much as they can. It does not matter that, for some, the highest level they can manage is under $100 and, for others, it may be thousands of dollars. No matter what the total, the board should reflect 100 percent participation in the organization's annual giving program every year, in addition to supporting special campaigns authorized by the board. Board members and administrators should note that contributions of time and gifts-in-kind, while welcome and appreciated, should not count as support of the organization's fund-raising programs, for the simple reason that they do not show up as income on fund activity statements.

(f) SERVE AS AMBASSADOR AND SPOKESPERSON FOR THE ORGANIZATION To carry out this responsibility effectively, the board must be well informed about the organization and willing to promote it at every opportunity. This responsibility calls for circumspection in speaking against the institution in public. It also calls for individual members to take the initiative in finding opportunities to promote the organization and to be visible in supporting events sponsored by the organization, such as fund-raisers and public programs. Board members and administrators alike should recognize the special responsibility and influence that board members have in shaping the public image and awareness of the organization. Some board members will have a natural facility for carrying out this responsibility. Others will have the contacts and connections for doing it, but will need strong direction and support from the staff. It is the staff's responsibility to help channel and choreograph board activities in the public relations and fund-raising arenas. In this sense, the administration should view the board as a special donor constituency and cultivate individual member involvement in the same way as it would a major donor prospect.

(g) EVALUATE THE ORGANIZATION'S PROGRAM REGULARLY While its members may be laypersons, the board is responsible for making sure that the organization's programs are sound. The chief administrator should provide the board with a rationale and description of each program and service the organization provides. In response, a board should probe and question until it is satisfied that programs are being conducted in keeping with the mission, and in fulfillment of what the organization has promised the public. It is also the duty of a board to determine whether programs are meeting public needs and are being marketed effectively. Specific issues will vary according to the type of service the organization provides. Exhibit 8.2 offers a generic set of questions board members should ask in evaluating their organization's programs.

Just as board members often feel inadequate to the task of reviewing programs because of their lay status, staff members sometimes resist board involvement for the same reason. Both staff and board members need to bear in mind that, regardless of their lay status, board members are legally liable when an organization fails to provide a standard of care.

(h) COMMUNICATE THE COMMUNITY AND THE LAY PERSPECTIVE TO THE ORGANIZATION There is a special value in board members' perspective as laypeople. By offering their interpretation of the interests and perceptions of the community toward the organization, they provide a valuable perspective that the administration cannot possibly have, and they prevent an organization from viewing itself myopically. A well-chosen board will have broad community representation and expertise not found within the organization.

(i) IN INTERNAL CONFLICT, SERVE AS A FINAL COURT OF APPEALS Although it is not the role of the board to become involved in the administration of the organization, situations arise occasionally that cannot be settled by the administration and are brought to the board for resolution. If institutional policy is clear and comprehensive, these situations should be rare. Nevertheless, there will always be disgruntled

Exhibit 8.2.   Questions board members should ask about programs and services.

1. Do the programs offered have sufficient depth and diversity to meet the needs of both the current and potential client base? _____

2. What do the consumers of the organization's programs and services say about the organization? _____

3. What other measures of program success or failure (measures of effectiveness) are available? _____

4. How is successful performance rewarded? _____

5. What is the long-range plan for the program and service-delivery areas of the organization? What strategies have been developed to address the program's external threats and opportunities? _____

6. Are new approaches or new research in these programs and services recognized and adopted by the organization? _____

7. Is the institution representing its programs and services accurately in its promotional literature and reports to donors? _____

8. Are there audiences or populations not being served that should be? _____

9. How are fees determined and what is known about how the fees attract or deter new clients? _____

10. Are fee schedules and intake policies fair to all socioeconomic, racial, and ethnic groups? _____

11. How does the organization's service record match that of comparable institutions? _____

12. What is the rationale for a proposed new program and what are the resource requirements attached to it? _____

employees (or volunteers) who will fight institutional policies and there will always be dissatisfied clients who may make extreme demands. Moreover, even the best of administrations is not always right. When a dispute with potential for legal action is brought before a board, it is appropriate for the board to review the situation and decide whether to support or overrule the administration. It must be emphasized, however, that this should be an infrequent event, and a board should remand appeals that are not last-resort. Administrators can avoid board involvement in internal disputes by providing employees with clear, written personnel policy information and by establishing adequate grievance procedures for employees. Clients should receive written clarification of the terms of services provided. When disputes do come before the board, it should seek legal counsel regarding the particulars of its fiduciary and other responsibilities in the case at hand.

(j) SELF-ASSESS PERIODICALLY   With all the scrutiny a board gives an organization, it is only fitting that periodic self-assessment is in order. Too many boards become stagnant and passive—particularly when the administration is effective and there are few crises. Chief administrators often prefer passive boards; they give them freer reign. However, when crises occur and a board is not up-to-date on the administrative action, the administrator is vulnerable to criticism. Depending on the severity of a crisis, the administrator's job could be in jeopardy. Consequently, a chief administrator should eagerly promote an active board that knows and fulfills its responsibilities—one that shows and uses its strengths in times of crisis.

It is incumbent on a board to take a periodic critical look at itself, for the same reason that a mission has to be reviewed: things change. Terms of office end and new members come on board. New members may not be cognizant of the history and policy of the organization, or they may not understand their roles. Self-assessment alerts a board to gaps in understanding about vision, policy, procedure, and responsibility. It also identifies areas of disagreement about the performance of a committee, a chief administrator, or the staff. In addition, it gives a board member an opportunity to express constructive criticism. Finally, self-assessment identifies board members' perceptions of the strengths and weaknesses of the board in all ten areas of its responsibility.

Self-assessments should occur annually. The most common method for doing this is a formal assessment survey instrument that individual members complete confidentially. Surveys can be custom-designed, but both the Association of Governing Boards and Arthur Frantzreb (1988) have available instruments that offer tested reliability and validity. Once a survey has been completed, a meeting should be devoted to analyzing its results and determining how the weaknesses and points of disagreement shall be resolved in ways that strengthen the organization.

8.5 BOARD LEADERSHIP

Although nonprofit bylaws provide for and describe the functions of various board officers (secretary, treasurer, and at least one vice chair), the ultimate effectiveness of a board depends on the leadership of its chair and the relationship of the chief administrator to the board and its committee chairs. (See Chap. 5.)

(a) THE BOARD CHAIR When asked what board chairs do, the most frequent response is: "Preside at meetings." Although correct, the response is far from complete. The hardest work of a board chair is done outside the boardroom and involves two critical roles—organizational spokesperson and board executive.

(i) The chair as organizational spokesperson In this role, the chair must be prepared to handle inquiries from the media, community representatives, clients, and staff. Fortunately, these inquiries do not always happen in the face of adversity, but, no matter when they occur, the chair must be prepared either to speak or to decline comment. In this role, the chair presides at official functions of the organization, such as dedications, ground breakings, donor recognition events, and special ceremonies.

(ii) The chair as board executive In this role, the chair's chief responsibility is to provide leadership. Pohl (1990) has cited four ways in which a chair leads:

1. Defining objectives;
2. Outlining the year's work;
3. Delegating responsibility to members;
4. Making members feel as though they are doing the job.

As a leader, a board chair must be adept at facilitating communication among the board, the administration, and committees. It is essential that the chair's relationship with the chief administrator be grounded in mutual respect and trust. In this relationship, they should be able to speak candidly with one another and work through disagreements. It is the job of the chair to inform the chief administrator when board members do not approve of particular administrative actions or decisions. On the other hand, it is the function of the chair to help interpret and clarify for the board the administration's style and actions.

As board executive, a chair must oversee the activity of all board committees. Although it is not feasible for a chair to attend all committee meetings, he or she must stay in touch with committee chairs and diplomatically prod the sluggish ones to follow through on their goals and objectives. Overall, a board chair needs strong motivational talents and leadership skills, including a working knowledge of parliamentary procedure.

(b) THE CHIEF ADMINISTRATOR The chief administrator is the paid professional who has ultimate responsibility for running the day-to-day operations of a nonprofit organization. Although its titles may vary—president and executive director are the most common—the position carries specific responsibilities relating to the board: administrator as board informant, and administrator as board adviser.

(i) Administrator as board informant Although board members sometimes complain that administrator, inundate them with materials, the fact is that they could never be too well-informed. It is the chief administrator's primary duty to let board members know what is happening, whether the news is bad or good. Contacts should be frequent and should include conversations with the board chair several times a week. Notices of noteworthy activity must be sent to the full board between meetings. The chief administrator also ensures that minutes, financial statements, and reports are distributed well in advance of board meetings, in addition to reports presented at executive committee and full-board meetings. A very important chief administrative duty is to prepare and distribute a comprehensive annual report. The chief administrator also must inform the board about activity at competing organizations and about important trends or issues that could have an impact on the organization or the services it provides. A final responsibility related to keeping board members well informed is providing staffing for board committees and coordinating board committees with their internal counterparts.

(ii) Administrator as board adviser An administrator should proffer to the board opinions about such matters as expansion or retrenchment measures, new policy, changes in programs, or financial decisions. Although an administrator does not tell a board what to do, and a board is in no way bound to adopt offered recommendations, it is important to acknowledge that the administrator probably has the broadest and most professional perspective of most issues facing the organization; the administrator's opinions and advice deserve thorough consideration. On the other hand, in matters where the chief administrator truly feels indecisive, the administrator's responsibility is to acknowledge the indecision and seek the board's guidance.

(c) COMMITTEE CHAIRS It is frequently observed that the real work of a governing board takes place in committee meetings. If a board's committees are active, this is usually true. How active and effective a committee is rests squarely on its chair and the staff person assigned to work with it. Committee chairs have the same responsibilities for their committees as a board chair has for the full board.

Many committees never accomplish much because they are unclear about their purposes or do not know how to begin carrying them out. A good committee chair will overcome this inertia by taking the initiative to call meetings and by requesting appropriate staffing from the administration. If the chair is inert, two members of the committee may call a meeting without the chair. A designated staff member needs to work closely with the chair to prepare meeting agendas, to gather information and serve as resource persons for the committee, and to make meeting arrangements.

If a committee has been inactive when a new chair is appointed, the chair's first tasks are to review the committee's purpose with its members and to establish goals and objectives. Ideally, these will be integrated and coordinated with the goals and objectives of the whole board and of the other board committees.

All committee work is subject to the approval of the full board, and the chair is responsible for presenting committee reports at full board meetings or executive committee meetings. In making committee recommendations to the board, the chair must include dissenting opinions. Moreover, if the recommendation requires a full-board vote, the dissent must be permitted to present its point of view.

Committee chairs should prepare an annual written report of the committee's activity. Given the leadership skill required of the task, chairing committees provides an excellent training ground for higher positions on a board.

8.6 COMMITTEE FUNCTIONS

There are two types of committees: standing and ad hoc (also known as special committees). Both standing and ad hoc committees may establish subcommittees to deal with issues in a more focused way. Standing committees receive their charge from the bylaws, and function on an ongoing basis. Ad hoc committees, which are created by the board to address special issues that are not ongoing, are dissolved as soon as their charge has been expedited. Pohl (1990) cited five ways to establish committees:

1. A board chair can appoint a committee.
2. A board chair can nominate a committee to be approved by full-board vote.
3. The committee can be nominated from the floor.
4. The committee can be named as part of a motion.
5. The committee can be nominated by ballot.

(a) STANDING COMMITTEES   The number of standing committees a board has varies among boards. There is wisdom in keeping the number of standing committees on the lean side, particularly if the board is not large. A good practice is to have standing committees address ongoing issues, and handle everything else with subcommittees or ad hoc committees. The five standing committees that are prevalent among boards are described in the following subsections.

(i) Executive committee   Large boards and boards that transact a lot of business between full-board meetings need to have executive committees over which the board chair usually presides. Membership includes board officers and, sometimes, the chairs of standing committees. The responsibilities of an executive committee vary among organizations but usually include: making interim decisions for the board (to be ratified by the full board at its subsequent meeting); overseeing the long-range and strategic planning of the organization; and serving as a sounding board for new programs or policies that should come before the full board eventually. Minutes of executive committee meetings should be sent to the full board of trustees.

(ii) Finance committee   This committee works closely with an organization's chief financial officer and chief administrator in making recommendations to the full board about asset management, endowment investment, debt management, indemnification, and other aspects of risk management. The committee also oversees monthly financial statements and a proper audit. Members of this committee usually have experience in business and finance and can lend perspective to the institution in investment counseling and in budget planning. Other areas of responsibility that sometimes come within the purview of this committee include: overseeing the buildings and grounds of the organization, personnel policy management, and review of the cost effectiveness of programs.

(iii) Development committee   This committee, acting in concert with the chief development officer, has the responsibility of planning annual fund-raising programs and capital campaigns. Plans should address major donor cultivation and encourage the involvement of the organization's constituencies in the process. It is important to correct the popular misconception that development committees have the sole responsibility for raising funds. The whole board must participate in helping the organization raise its level of gift and grant income.

(iv) Program committee   The nature and responsibilities of program committees vary greatly according to the type of service a nonprofit organization provides. Schools will have academic policy committees to review the timeliness, effectiveness, marketability, and cost of the educational programs being offered. Social service agencies' and health care organizations' program committees will review the viability and effectiveness of their programs and services. Community organizations will review how well the programs are meeting the mandates of their funders. Cultural organizations will assess how well their offerings are being received by their publics. Regardless of the type of nonprofit, however, the role of the board's program committee is to become thoroughly familiar with the programs and services offered by the organization and to assess program needs in terms of the institutional mission, financing required, and future trends.

(v) Nominating/Membership committee   Most organizational bylaws charge a nominating or membership committee with the task of preparing a slate of candidates for membership and board offices. The committee is frequently appointed by the chair of the board, although appointments sometimes require full-board approval. It is an old saw that the nominating committee is the most powerful because it controls the slate and can "pack the court." Normally, terms of board membership are staggered, to prevent the nominating committee from making changes that are too radical. Moreover, the committee only has the power to nominate; final appointment to the board usually requires a membership or full-board vote. Nevertheless, because new membership is a key change agent, a nominating or membership committee can indeed influence the future of the board.

Another role of this committee—one that is most often neglected—involves stewardship of members. The purview of stewardship includes assessing the mix of characteristics and constituency representations on the current board and identifying future recruitment needs. Stewardship also involves recruiting new members effectively and educating them about the roles they will be expected to play when they come on the board. The means of fulfilling these responsibilities are discussed later in this chapter.

(b) AD HOC COMMITTEES Unlike standing committees, ad hoc committees are formed to carry out a specific charge and are dissolved as soon as that charge has been completed. Another difference is that ad hoc committees are more likely to have nonboard membership. For example, if a board chair names a search committee for a chief administrator, the committee may (and should) include members from a cross-section of constituencies, in addition to board members, so that the committee is representative of the organizational community. Another example of a board-initiated ad hoc committee that should include a cross-section of nonboard members is a strategic planning task force.

At the time they are formed, ad hoc committees should receive a specific statement of mission along with a deadline for accomplishing it. They report to the full board in the same manner as standing committees. Examples of charges given to ad hoc committees include: drafting a bylaws revision; planning a fund-raising event, or conducting a feasibility study for a new program. When an organization is running a capital campaign, the board can name a special committee, apart from the development committee, to conduct solicitation of board members.

8.7 INDIVIDUAL BOARD MEMBER RESPONSIBILITIES

Even if a board member holds no office and chairs no committee, he or she has important responsibilities to fulfill both in and out of the boardroom.

(a) IN-HOUSE RESPONSIBILITIES

(i) Preparing for meetings Adequate preparation involves reviewing the minutes, financial statements, and all reports received prior to meetings, and having a working knowledge of parliamentary procedure.

(ii) Attending board meetings regularly Each board member has been elected to represent and articulate a valuable point of view in discussions and votes.

(iii) Raising questions through the chair In the boardroom, constructive dissent should be welcome. If a pending action is unclear to a member or if a member opposes an action, he or she should speak out. If a member feels further information is necessary before a vote is taken, the information should be requested without hesitation.

(iv) Representing the entire organization   Board members often face the dilemma of having come from a particular faction of the organization and having to vote against that group's interests. The fiduciary and ethical responsibility of the member is to represent the entire institution—not an individual constituency. Although a board member can and should present any constituency's point of view during discussion, the greater good for the organization should ultimately influence an individual's vote.

(v) Voting ethically   Conflict of interest occurs when a board member has a relationship to a party who has a stake in a decision the board is about to make. If this is a temporary situation or a one-time conflict, the member can simply abstain from voting on the issue at hand. If the conflict is more permanent, the member must consider resigning from the board. Conflict of interest is discussed in detail later in this chapter.

(b) ROLE OUTSIDE THE BOARDROOM   Outside the boardroom, a board member's job is best characterized as ambassadorial, and, depending on a member's motivation and creativity, the ways and means of carrying out this role are limitless. Minimally, members should attend the organization's functions whenever possible, stay informed about programs and projects sponsored by the organization, and contribute to all fund-raising projects. Apart from fund-raising, individual board members have six roles to play outside the boardroom:

1. Taking the initiative to connect corporate funding contacts with the organization;
2. Taking the initiative to make foundation contacts for the organization;
3. Cultivating individual donors for the organization;
4. Helping to promote the organization's services and good reputation;
5. Supporting politicians and legislation favoring the mission of the organization;
6. Reporting all outside activity on behalf of the organization to the chief administrator or the development officer.

8.8   THE BOARD–STAFF RELATIONSHIP

As long as boards have existed, there has been controversy over where the line of board authority stops and that of administrative authority begins. It is easy to say that a board's job is to make policy and the staff's job is to execute it. However, most organizations do not enjoy a clear-cut distinction in their board–staff functions.

Balance is the key to good board–staff relationships. Conrad and Glenn (1986) used the image of a teeter-totter balancing on a fulcrum, to illustrate the concept of good board–staff relations. When the board is too involved, it weighs operations down and the staff is held up in the air. When the staff is too powerful and not working with the board, the board is held up in the air. When a board and its staff are in balance, the result is a dynamic tension: no one is weighed down nor left in the air; both board and staff are using each other's weight to achieve the desired balance.

There are times when it is appropriate for the board to become more involved in administrative affairs. Times of transition for the organization, times of crisis, and periods when there is no chief administrator in place are examples. As a general guideline, however, it is appropriate for a board to ask questions of its administration; when that board begins to answer its own questions, it is crossing the balance boundary.

8.9 LEGAL ISSUES RELATED TO BOARD MEMBERSHIP

As Tremper and Babcock (1990) have noted, legal liability for nonprofit organizations has been increasing to the point where charitable immunity affords little guarantee that an organization and its board cannot be sued. Boards must prepare themselves to deal with the possibility of legal suits. Risk insurance and indemnification are worthy options that can minimize liability, but the best protection is for the administrators and the board to let their decisions be guided by a sound knowledge of their fiduciary responsibilities. Those responsibilities fall into three categories: the standard of care, the duty of loyalty, and the duty of obedience. (See Chap. 35 and 37.)

(a) STANDARD OF CARE   A nonprofit board has a fiduciary responsibility to protect the assets of the organization. An organization's money, people, property, good will, and integrity are all considered assets. When a board member fails to protect them, the law considers the failure to be a breach in the duty of care. Consequently, a board member must always act in good faith and in the best interests of the organization. In making good-faith decisions, the member may rely on information prepared by officers of the organization, by legal counsel, and by a committee of the board. The member can assume, with reasonable certainty, that each source has acted responsibly and competently. However, because different states have varying degrees of protection for directors who delegate decision making to committees, board members and administrators are well-advised to check out the laws in their own state (Kurtz, 1988).

(b) DUTY OF LOYALTY   In the eyes of the law, board members owe the nonprofit organization the loyalty of placing its interests above all others. The preponderance of breach of loyalty suits occurs in two areas: conflict of interest and improper loans to board members.

(i) Conflict of interest   Conflict of interest occurs in two ways:

- When a board member makes decisions out of self-interest or in the interest of only part of the institution instead of for the common good of the whole organization;
- When an institution makes a transaction with a business or organization that has a financial connection with a board member or a board member's family.

When financial connections exist, it is incumbent on the board member to refrain from involvement in any decision making that is related to the connection.

To protect an organization from legal repercussions, its board should require board members to sign a written policy statement on conflict of interest when they join the board. Exhibit 8.3 presents a sample statement and questionnaire used by the National Center for Nonprofit Boards. Where it is unclear whether conflict of interest exists, the board can vote to decide, but the safest course of action is to seek legal counsel. Kurtz (1989) has suggested other ways for a board to avoid conflict of interest situations:

Exhibit 8.3. Policy on potential conflicts of interests.

The Board of Directors of the National Center for Nonprofit Boards has adopted the following policy designed to avoid any possible conflict between the personal interests of Board members or staff and the interests of the Center.

The purpose of this policy is to ensure that decisions about Center operations and the use or disposition of Center assets are made solely in terms of the benefits to the Center and are not influenced by any private profit or other personal benefit to the individuals affiliated with the Center who take part in the decision. In addition to actual conflicts of interest, board members and staff are also obliged to avoid actions that could be perceived or interpreted in conflict with the Center's interest.

Conflicts of interest may occur when the Center enters into transactions with not-for-profit organizations as well as those that are undertaken with profit making entities. The best way to deal with this problem is to make known one's connection with organizations doing business with the Center and to refrain from participation in decisions affecting transactions between the Center and the other organization. Such relationships do not necessarily restrict transactions so long as the relationship is clearly divulged and non-involved individuals affiliated with the Center make any necessary decisions.

Policy

1. *Directors.* Any member of the Board of Directors who may be involved in a Center business transaction in which there is a possible conflict of interest shall promptly notify the Chairman of the Board. The Trustee shall refrain from voting on any such transaction, participating in deliberations concerning it, or using personal influence in any way in the matter. The Trustee's presence may not be counted in determining the quorum for any vote with respect to a Center business transaction in which he or she has a possible conflict of interest. Furthermore, the Trustee, or the Chairman in the Director's absence, shall disclose a potential conflict of interest to the other members of the Board before any vote on a Center business transaction and such disclosure shall be recorded in the Board minutes of the meeting at which it is made. Any Center business transaction and such disclosure shall be recorded in the Board minutes of the meeting at which it is made. Any Center business transaction which involves a potential conflict of interest with a member of the Board of Directors shall have terms which are at least as fair and reasonable to the Center as those which would otherwise be available to the Center if it were dealing with an unrelated party.

2. *Staff.* Any staff member who may be involved in a Center business transaction in which there is a possible conflict of interest shall promptly report the possible conflict to the Executive Director. If the possible conflict involves the Executive Director, the possible conflict shall then be reported to the Chairman of the Board.

The Executive Director or, where applicable, Chairman, after receiving information about a possible conflict of interest, shall take such action as is necessary to assure that the transaction is completed in the best interest of the Center without the substantive involvement of the person who has the possible conflict of interest. (This does not mean that the purchase or other transaction must necessarily be diverted, but simply that persons other than the one with the possible conflict shall make the judgments involved and shall control the transaction.)

Each board member and senior staff member shall complete the attached questionnaire on an annual basis.

A written record of any report of possible conflict and of any adjustments made to avoid possible conflicts of interest shall be kept by the Executive Director or, where applicable, Chairman.

3. *Definitions.*

A. "Involved in a Center business transaction" means initiating, making the principal recommendation for, or approving a purchase or contract; recommending or selecting a vendor or contractor; drafting or negotiating the terms of such a transaction; or authorizing

Exhibit 8.3. *(Continued)*

---

or making payments from Center accounts. That language is intended to include not only transactions for the Center's procurement of goods and services, but also for the disposition of Center property, and the provision of services or space by the Center.

B. A "possible conflict of interest" is deemed to exist where the Director, or staff member, or a close relative, or a member of that person's household, is an officer, director, employee, proprietary, partner, or trustee of, or, when aggregated with close relatives and members of that person's household, holds 1% or more of the issued stock in the organization seeking to do business with the Center. A possible conflict is also considered to exist where such a person is (or expects to be) retained as a paid consultant or contractor by an organization which seeks to do business with the Center, and whenever a transaction will entail a payment of money or anything else of value to the official, member, to a close relative, or to a member of that person's household.

A "possible conflict of interest" exists when an individual affiliated with the Center has an interest in an organization which is in competition with a firm seeking to do business with the Center if the individual's position gives him or her access to proprietary or other privileged information which could benefit the firm in which he or she has an interest.

A "possible conflict of interest" exists when an individual affiliated with the Center is a trustee, director, officer or employee of a not-for-profit organization which is seeking to do business with or have a significant connection with the Center or is engaged in activities which could be said in a business contest to be "in competition with" the programs of the Center.

4. This policy statement shall be made available to each trustee and each person appointed to a Center position which regularly involves initiation, review or approval of significant Center contracts or other commitments. Such people will be asked to sign the attached acknowledgment concerning reporting of potential conflicts of interest.

I have read and understand the Center's policy on Potential Conflicts of Interest. I agree to report promptly any such interest which arises in my conduct of Center business and, in other respects, to comply with the policy and its procedures.

_____ (Signed)

_____ (Date)

Exhibit 8.3. *(Continued)*

CONFLICT OF INTEREST QUESTIONNAIRE
National Center for Nonprofit Boards

Name
_____

Office or Position Held
_____

In responding to these questions, please note that a "yes" answer does not imply that the relationship or transaction was necessarily inappropriate.

1. Are you an officer or director of any corporation with which the National Center for Nonprofit board has business dealings?

   Yes_____   No_____

   If the answer to the foregoing question is "yes," please list the names of such corporations, the office held and the approximate dollar-amount of business involved with the National Center for Nonprofit Boards last year.

   _____
   _____
   _____
   _____
   _____
   _____

2. Do you, or does any member of your family, have a financial interest in, or receive any renumeration or income from, any business organization with which the National Center for Nonprofit Boards has business dealings?

   Yes_____   No_____

   If the answer to the foregoing question is "yes," please supply the following information:

   a. Names of the business organizations in which such interest is held and the person(s) by whom such interest is held:

   _____
   _____
   _____
   _____
   _____

   b. Nature and amount of each such financial interest, renumeration or income:

   _____
   _____
   _____
   _____
   _____

3. Did you, or any member of your family receive during the past twelve months any gifts or loans from any source from which the National Center for Nonprofit Boards buys goods or services or with which the National Center for Nonprofit Boards has significant business dealings?

   Yes_____   No_____

Exhibit 8.3. *(Continued)*

If the answer to the foregoing questions is "yes," list such gifts or loans as follows:

Name of Source   *Item*   *Approximate Value*

_____

_____

_____

_____

_____

4. Were you involved in any other activity during the past year that might be interpreted as a possible conflict of interest?

Yes_____   No_____

If "yes," please describe:_____

_____

_____

_____

_____

_____

I certify that the foregoing information is true and complete to the best of my knowledge.

_____   _____
Date   Signature

Used by permission from the National Center for Nonprofit Boards, 2000 L St., NW, Suite 411, Washington, DC 20036; 202-452-6262.

1. Select a financially disinterested board;
2. Have a balance of power between the board and the chief administrator;
3. Have a policy that goes further than the law's requirements;
4. Have an attorney review the policy.

The last point is especially important. The law is becoming increasingly complex about conflict of interest, particularly because many board members serve on more than one board.

(ii) Loans Loans by the organization to its officers and board members are another source of breach of loyalty. Currently, 30 states ban such loans, but 20 others have at least a limited legal provision for making loans to officers and board members (Kurtz, 1988). A board should be reticent to make loans to employees or directors because, even when they are legal, they are likely to cause the organization negative public and legal scrutiny once they are disclosed.

(c) DUTY OF OBEDIENCE This duty is carried out simply by honoring the stated intentions of an organization's founders and donors. Aside from the ethics involved, organizations have a fiduciary responsibility to spend money received from gifts in a manner consistent with the wishes of the donor. If the donor's intent cannot be honored, or if it is not in the best interest of the organization to honor it, the gift should not be accepted. The best way to avoid litigation in this area is to weigh a donor's gift designation against the organization's mission as well as against the founders' intent. It is also important for the organization to adhere strictly to the organization's governing documents and tax code regulations.

It is not unheard of for nonprofit organizations to be called into court for failure to honor terms of endowment bequests made to them decades ago. Terms of bequests often stipulate that the remains of a trust or endowment revert to another party if its provisions are not met. Would-be inheritors are often alert to an organization's transgressions in this area and will go to court in attempts to gain control of the principal.

8.10 THE CONCEPT OF BOARD DEVELOPMENT

Board members frequently become discouraged because they struggle with board staff involvement issues, because they are not powerhouse fund raisers, or because they do not have an active committee structure in place. In the face of discouragement, it is especially helpful for a board to view itself as an evolving organism and adjust its expectations to its maturational level. It is also helpful for boards to realize that, as with maturing children, change does not occur without growing pains.

(a) MATHIASEN'S STAGES OF BOARD DEVELOPMENT Karl Mathiasen (1990) has described three developmental stages that nonprofit boards normally go through in the process of becoming a mature board.

(i) The organizing board In this first stage, boards either follow a visionary leader or are steeped in doing the actual hands-on work of the organization. If an organization succeeds at this stage, it will experience strains that will force a board to change. The succeeding board will need to become less of a cheerleading unit for the founder and take a stronger role in governance; the hands-on board may need to turn over its heavy operational involvement to a stronger chief administrator. Either way, transition will lead a successful board into the second stage.

(ii) The governing board At this stage, committee structures usually develop and the board–staff relationship becomes clearer. The board also begins to understand and accept its fund-raising role. Some boards remain in this stage forever, but if the organization grows and achieves widespread recognition, the board will evolve once again.

(iii) The institutional board In this final stage, a board has become larger, has many well-connected members, and focuses primarily on fund-raising. The governing activities are handled by a powerful executive committee. Although all boards do not fit these stages exactly, Mathiasen's model can help a board understand where it is in its evolution and lends insight into where the board is headed.

(b) STAGES OF INDIVIDUAL BOARD MEMBER DEVELOPMENT There are also stages in the involvement of individual board members. Conrad and Glenn's model of board member involvement and contributions (Exhibit 8.4) suggests that, if handled effectively, a board member's activity with the organization is also likely to evolve over

Exhibit 8.4. Conrad and Glenn's involvement–contribution ratio.

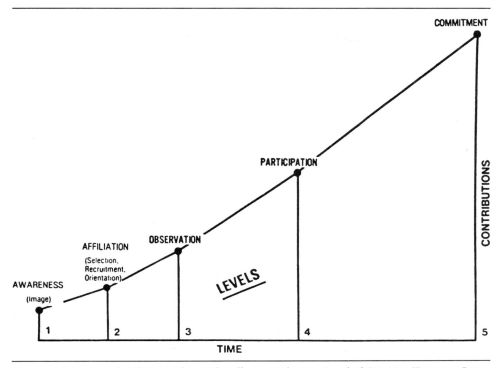

(*Source:* W. R. Conrad and W. E. Glenn, *The Effective Voluntary Board of Directors* (Downers Grove, IL: Voluntary Management Press, 1983), p. 197.) Reproduced by permission of W. A. Conrad.

time as the member goes through stages of awareness, affiliation, observation, participation, and commitment. It is the administration's job to track the progress and to nurture the development of individual board members.

8.11 ELEMENTS OF BOARD DEVELOPMENT

There are four major elements in the board development process: self-assessment and selection of board candidates; the recruiting process for new members; orientation of new members; and increased involvement of board members.

(a) SELF-ASSESSMENT AND SELECTION OF BOARD CANDIDATES As described earlier, the work of the nominating or membership committee sets the future course of the board. It is also the key change agent of the board.

(i) The board audit To carry out its tasks effectively, a nominating committee should conduct an annual board audit to help determine what desired characteristics current board members possess and what special-interest and constituency groups they represent. The literature on nonprofit boards contains many examples of grids or worksheets for conducting audits, but, to tailor an audit to its particular needs, an organization can create its own. Exhibit 8.5 illustrates a sample grid and lists the steps of an audit.

Exhibit 8.5.   Board membership audit worksheet.

Steps

1. Make a list of characteristics and skills needed in board members, prioritize them and enter them at the top of the grid columns.
2. List the names of current board members in the first column.
3. Assess each board member. Check (✓) the boxes to show characteristics and skills each board member has.
4. Determine when current members' terms expire, and project representation needs for 3 future years, to get a long-range perspective on recruiting.
5. Check (✓) the appropriate boxes to show the characteristics and skills that will have high priority in the new recruits who will replace the outgoing members.

Board Representation Audit

Name	Characteristics and Skills Needed								
Current members:									
New recruits:									
Year 1									
Year 2									
Year 3									

The best way to guarantee that a board will have a composition matching its needs is to view nominations as a long-term process. Last-minute nominations run the risk of selecting weak members or members whose strengths are not needed.

(ii) Identification of candidates In the short term, candidates should be very obvious: they will already be close to the organization through committee work and volunteer activity. Planning for the long term, however, requires early identification of prospective board candidates. The staff and all board members should report suggestions for future candidates to the nominating committee. Civic leaders who might have an interest in the service the nonprofit provides, volunteers serving on auxiliary boards, and donors to similar programs, are all possibilities. Accounting firms and advertising or public relations firms that have a sense of civic duty often encourage their executives to participate in nonprofit organizations and can be a source of skilled board members. Another important resource for identifying board candidates is community leadership programs.

(b) THE RECRUITING PROCESS It is one thing to identify candidates for board membership; inviting them to serve is another story. There is a correlation between time and success in recruitment: the more time spent recruiting a board member, the better that member will perform on the board. Ideally, the nominating committee should have a long-range plan for board recruitment that includes several years of cultivation of board candidates. The development committee and development officer should work with the nominating committee to make certain that potential board members are being cultivated.

In the shorter term, there are more immediate tactics to consider in effective recruiting. When it gets down to the time to issue the actual invitation to serve, there are eight guidelines for the process:

1. Always recruit in person. Recruitment by letter or telephone sends the message that membership is not very important.
2. Be honest about the current circumstances of the organization. Describe the problems and weaknesses of the organization as well as its strengths.
3. Clarify expectations about the recruit's financial obligations to the organization.
4. Explain exactly what serving entails. Discuss time commitment, meeting requirements, committee activity, and the need to attend organizational events.
5. Strategize the asking. A senior staff member, preferably the chief administrator, and a board member should do the actual recruiting. Decide where the candidate would be most comfortable.
6. Answer the "Why me?" question. Candidates need to get a sense of why they are wanted. Recruiters should explain specifically what the candidate personally can contribute to the organization.
7. Ask the candidate to think it over. At the invitational meeting, the recruiter should never accept an answer but should, instead, ask the candidate to take at least a week to think over the commitment. Responsible board membership is a serious commitment that is not made spontaneously.
8. Show the recruit around. If a recruit has not seen the organization's facilities or attended events where the fruits of the organization's labors can be seen, the administration should arrange it. It is critical that the candidate have a sense of

the organization he or she would represent as a board member. It is the responsibility of the administration to arrange and host on-site visits with candidates.

(c) ORIENTATION OF NEW MEMBERS   Board members frequently comment: "It seems like I just got the hang of things with this board in time for my term to end." Such remarks indicate that effective orientation has not occurred. With a proper introduction to the issues and procedures of the board, there is no reason why new members cannot begin contributing to the organization from the first day of their term.

Both the staff and fellow board members have roles to play in orienting a new board member. Although there is no one correct way to conduct orientation, there is one desired result—to make the new members feel welcome and acquaint them with the people and the work of the board. Following is a list of approaches to orientation that have served boards well:

1. The buddy system. Assign new board members to experienced board members who will make sure that new members get answers to questions.
2. The board manual. Give new members a board manual that outlines all board procedures and policies. Exhibit 8.6 shows a sample table of contents for a board manual.
3. Meeting minutes. Give new members copies of minutes of the previous year's meetings.
4. Social event. Host an introductory event to give the incoming members an opportunity to meet current members in a context outside of the boardroom.
5. Delegation of doable tasks. As soon as new members come on board, give each of them a task that is easy to carry out, to help get them invested in the organization from the start.
6. Orientation session. Host a formal orientation session at the facility, to give new members background information on committee issues, to explain board procedures, to answer questions, and to introduce them to staff.

(d) INCREASED INVOLVEMENT OF BOARD MEMBERS   Board development theory suggests that increasing member awareness and interest requires continuous nurturing. As the model in Exhibit 8.7 indicates, a board can mature, but it is never fully developed. As seasoned members move off the board, the uninitiated come into the cycle, each bringing different perspectives and experience, and each having different nurturing needs.

The chief ingredient in developing a board is good communication between staff and board. Although both the board and staff share the responsibility for good communication, it is the staff's responsibility to facilitate the exchange of information and to anchor efforts to increase member involvement. There are two complementary approaches to increasing board involvement: giving sincere, appropriate recognition to board members, and creating a sense of community. There are also many indirect ways to increase members' understanding of and involvement in fund-raising.

(i) Recognition   A critical factor in nurturing the commitment of board members is appropriate recognition of their efforts. For some members, "appropriate" means a simple thank-you note; for others, it means a formal public citation for contributions made to the organization. In all cases, "appropriate" means sincere recognition for

Exhibit 8.6. Sample table of contents for a board manual.

[In preparation of a board manual, the following sample table of contents provides a generic organizational outline. Content for the manual can be drawn from this chapter and existing documents of the organization.]

THE ABC NONPROFIT ORGANIZATION
BOARD OF DIRECTORS MANUAL
Table of Contents

I. An introduction that explains the scope of the manual.
II. A description of the purpose and functions of the ABC board.
III. A description of how the ABC board operates: how members are nominated, their terms of office, how officers are selected, when and where regular meetings occur, and how committees generally operate.
IV. A statement of attendance expectations for meetings and a description of events at which a board presence is called for—ceremonies, annual dinners, special events, and fund-raisers. This section might also include expectations regarding board member visits to the ABC facilities.
V. A list and explanation of the ten responsibilities of a board.
VI. A description of the charge of each ABC board committee.
VII. An explanation of the responsibilities of individual board members, placing special emphasis on the fact that all members have a role to play in the fund-raising area.

Suggested Appendices

The ABC organization's mission statement
Articles of Incorporation and Bylaws of ABC
A copy of the organization's conflict of interest policy
A sample meeting agenda
An explanation of fund accounting
The ABC organization's gift acceptance policy
Current facts about ABC (e.g., number of clients served, special program recognitions, program facts)
A brief history of the ABC organization

---

real contributions. It is the responsibility of the staff to make sure that board members' contributions are not taken for granted—particularly with those members who are consistently selfless and hard-working. Even among the most dedicated board members, burnout is a very real phenomenon. The staff must make it as easy as possible for these members to do their jobs and should give them all the credit for the results—even if 99 percent of the work was done behind the scenes by the staff.

In addition to staff recognition of board efforts, the board chair should pay attention to giving credit to the work of committees and individual members in full-board meetings. Finally, board members should be given the limelight in public events and media coverage, to strengthen their commitment and sense of identification with the organization.

(ii) Creating a sense of community People generally do not join boards for social reasons. Nevertheless, if people are strangers, they will not work together as well as they

Exhibit 8.7.   The board membership process.

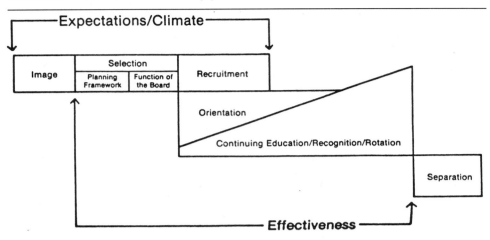

Source: W. R. Conrad and W. E. Glenn, *The Effective Voluntary Board of Directors* (Downers Grove, IL: Voluntary Management Press, 1983), p. 130.

will when they know and like one another. Having a sense of fellowship and community with the board is an important factor in getting members to show up for meetings and in influencing how deeply they will dig into their pockets for fund-raising projects. Having an occasional dinner after a meeting, or staging an annual event such as a golf or tennis outing just for board members and spouses or guests, may afford the opportunity for board members to form relationships with one another. Overnight board retreats also serve this purpose.

(iii) Fund-raising   Except for the rare member who has a decided talent for it, board members generally dislike fund-raising. "I hate asking for money" is a standard phrase. If members are enthusiastic about what the money will do for the organization, they are more willing to get involved in raising it. Some members simply need training, to gain confidence in their own ability to ask for gifts. Even the board members who have no hope of becoming good solicitors can develop more positive attitudes about fund-raising through indirect involvement with it. The following strategies help to increase the involvement of reluctant board members:

1. Have a board retreat, to consider mission and set goals. This will help members understand the purpose of fund-raising.
2. Have the board review and approve a written set of fund-raising policy guidelines. Those who attach a negative connotation to fund-raising will feel better about the integrity of the process.
3. Have board members meet major donors. It is inspiring to hear donors discuss why they give.
4. Make sure that members get recognition for whatever they do to help with fund-raising, even if their participation does not involve solicitation.

5. Develop a time-line of the history of the organization in a group setting, as part of a special meeting. This helps a board that is becoming more involved in fund-raising to understand how and why it has reached a point where it is important to focus on raising money.

6. As a "toe in the water" tactic, get board members involved in identifying donor prospects.

7. Have board members get close to the activities and the people who are supported by fund-raising.

8. Have the board take part in a phonathon with other volunteers, or have them lead pace-setting calling sessions. This will ease tentative solicitors into the process in a pleasant setting where they will have a lot of support.

9. Ask board members to help cultivate prospects by spending time with them. They can take prospects to lunch, visit them in their offices, or ask them to come to the board member's office. The purpose of the meetings is to educate the prospects about the work of the organization—not to solicit.

10. Do things that help board members get to know one another, as a way of increasing their commitment to the group and helping them to accept the fund-raising process more comfortably.

8.12 DEALING WITH RESISTANCE TO BOARD DEVELOPMENT

There are many reasons why board members may resist development. They may have served a long time under a strong chief executive who required nothing of them, and they may like their token status. Boards in transition from a controlling or organizing board status to governing board status may have members who are reluctant to give up their hands-on decision-making power to a stronger chief administrator. Other members might resist change when a previously non-fund-raising board decides it must become active in fund development.

Administrators and board members who are eager to improve their boards' performance need to develop long-term perspectives; change is not easy. The only rapid way to change a board is through crisis. Outside of crisis-motivated change, however, board development is a plodding process that happens through two approaches that have mutually dynamic effects on each other: triage and new membership.

(a) TAKING ADVANTAGE OF CRISIS The most dramatic changes occur on boards in times of crisis. Even the worst resisters will move when an organization is faced with critical survival issues such as a decision to close its doors, the termination of a chief administrator, the eruption of a scandal, or the threat of a lawsuit. In moments such as these, board members are often forced into making decisions that they would have stalled over had there been no crisis. There is a downside to crisis-motivated change: it is easier to make bad decisions in times of crisis.

(b) THE PRACTICE OF TRIAGE Like most voluntary groups, boards usually have three factions: those who perform up to or beyond expectations without prodding; those who would perform well if choreographed and educated; and those who will not respond to any intervention by staff and fellow board members. When a board is particularly inert and unresponsive to energizing efforts, it is best to retrench and to work only on the individual members in the second faction. Through personalized attention and the delegation of very clear, time-specific, and doable tasks (followed up, close on the heels of their completion, with recognition from the staff and the board chair), this faction will become more involved. Over time, this strategy will activate the majority of the board and, when this happens, those in the obdurate third faction will cycle off the board.

If a board's bylaws have a section that empowers the board to remove members for nonattendance at meetings, nonperforming members can be removed through those means. This does not usually occur in practice, however; most boards are reluctant to be so direct about "kicking off" a member. Moreover, some of the most ineffective board members seem to be those who attend meetings regularly but are not prepared to contribute to the business at hand.

(c) NEW MEMBERS AS CHANGE AGENTS Wise selection of new members is the most effective way to achieve positive change on a board because the minute one active new member arrives, the entire dynamics of the board changes. Because new members have not been mired in ongoing struggles over tough decisions, they arrive with fresh perspectives. Even one new member can change the whole political balance of a board, perhaps allowing the passage of policies that would have failed earlier. Sometimes the arrival of a new member is all that is needed to recharge burnt-out members. Thus, new members are indeed the key change agents for boards.

(d) FORMATS FOR ADDRESSING CHANGE There are times outside of crisis when boards recognize the need to change but are not certain how to go about it. In these cases, there are three basic formats for addressing change as a group: conducting a retreat, using a consultant, and conducting a bylaws review.

(i) Conducting a retreat If the majority of board members will commit a day or two of their time to sequestering themselves at a location away from the traffic of normal day-to-day business, a retreat can be a very effective way to get members to look at the board and the performance of individual members in a constructive and introspective fashion. To be effective, retreats should be well-planned and organized around a particular, predetermined charge. The following list suggests situations that may call for a retreat:

1. When a new administrator is hired, a board retreat can focus on clarifying board and administration roles and responsibilities.
2. When there is a major decision to make, such as a change in mission or program, a retreat can afford a board an opportunity to consider the issue thoroughly, in isolation from normal board business.
3. When an organization has a major conflict to resolve, and board and staff are willing to make good-faith attempts to resolve it, a board retreat can provide a time-limited format in which to negotiate a resolution.
4. When an organization is about to undertake a strategic planning process, a board retreat with selected staff members and constituency representatives can provide the means of reviewing the mission and identifying the strategic issues facing the organization.

5. When a board is considering a major fund-raising campaign and needs to get the entire board committed to it, a board retreat offers a forum for discussing the rationale and the case for the campaign.

In addition to being held in an out-of-the-way location, retreats should be facilitated by a person who is not connected with the organization and who will keep the agenda on track without being suspected of favoring a particular point of view. The agenda and format will vary according to the needs and the charge. It is wise to conduct a preliminary survey with open-ended written responses or to require every participant to do pertinent advance reading, to help everyone come to the retreat with a similar point of reference and sense of purpose. Good retreats need 3 to 6 months of planning so that appropriate arrangements can be made and relevant information can be gathered. Board members also need that much notice in order to block such a large chunk of time on their calendars.

(ii) Using a consultant Use of a board development consultant is an option that boards and administrators are using with increasing frequency. A consultant can be effective in fostering change within a board or change in the working relationship between the board and the chief administrator. Because consultants work from an external perspective and have a broad base of experience, they often have new ideas to offer when a board seems to be spinning in its tracks. Moreover, because they function outside the political climate of the organization, they can speak candidly to the chief administrator and board members without fear of reprisal or without being accused of harboring a hidden agenda. Finally, because consultants get paid for their point of view, their advice is often accepted by the full board more readily. The following list presents interventions that consultants commonly use to help boards:

1. They advise a new nonprofit organization about how to structure its board and they help prepare its documents.
2. They design board assessment instruments tailored to the circumstances of the organization, as opposed to using standardized instruments.
3. They conduct constituency research and interviews aimed at gathering information needed for the board to make important decisions or to plan strategically.
4. They present reorganization models and facilitate deliberations over a board restructuring process.
5. They work with individual board committees to forge statements of purpose and identify goals and objectives with action plans for implementation.
6. They facilitate planning processes and decision-making sessions.
7. They give workshops that address board members' involvement in fund-raising and the improvement of members' solicitation skills.
8. They facilitate retreats.

(iii) Bylaws review as change agent A bylaws review is an effective means of getting the board to focus on how it functions and to evaluate the individual responsibilities of board members. The advantage of this approach to change is that the decisions made are clear and enforceable by virtue of the revised document. The disadvantages are that a bylaws review will only be able to focus on structural and procedural matters, and that the process does not directly address member performance standards and desired characteristics of a performing member.

8.13 RESOURCES FOR CONTINUED BOARD DEVELOPMENT

One of the most well-known and well-established resources for information and services related to boards is the Association of Governing Boards of Universities and Colleges (AGB). This organization is a research clearinghouse for postsecondary and independent school trusteeship. It offers board mentoring services, publications on various aspects of boards, and a bimonthly magazine for member institutions.

In response to the proliferation of new nonprofits outside of the education arena, the AGB and Independent Sector secured grant funding for the creation of the National Center for Nonprofit Boards (NCNB) in 1988. This center does for non-education-related nonprofit boards what the AGB does for college and university boards. Through the NCNB, board members and administrators can find easy access to recent resources and educational materials about board roles and responsibilities. In addition to a newsletter and publications catalogues, NCNB offers board mentoring and retreat facilitation services at reasonable costs. Perhaps most valuable is NCNB's accessibility by telephone; inquiries regarding very specific board problems will either be answered over the telephone or directed to an appropriate source for response.

The increasing academic interest in the workings of the nonprofit sector has given rise to a number of research institutes and graduate programs in nonprofit management. Among the most notable of these are the National Center for Postsecondary Governance and Finance, at the University of Maryland, and the Case Western Reserve University Mandel School of Nonprofit Management. Nonprofit organizations can check with their own local institutions of higher education, for library and consulting resources.

In addition to university resources, The Foundation Center in New York City will provide a list of locations of its affiliate libraries around the nation. These libraries have materials on nonprofit board development and management as well as files of materials about local consultants. Independent Sector is another organization that serves as a clearinghouse of information for nonprofit initiatives and offers publications about boards of directors. Following is a list of resource centers for information on nonprofit boards:

The Association of Governing Boards of Universities and Colleges
One Dupont Circle, Suite 400
Washington, DC 20036
Telephone: 202-296-8400

The Foundation Center
7 East 54th Street
New York, NY 10022
Telephone: 212-620-4230

Independent Sector
1828 L Street, NW
Washington, DC 20036
Telephone: 202-223-8100

Mandel School for Nonprofit Management
Case Western Reserve University
11235 Bellflower
Cleveland, OH 44106
Telephone: 216-368-2290

National Center for Nonprofit Boards
2000 L Street, NW, Suite 411
Washington, DC 20036
Telephone: 202-452-6262

National Center for Postsecondary Governance and Finance
4114 CSS Building
University of Maryland
College Park, MD 20742-2435
Telephone: 301-405-5582

SOURCES AND SUGGESTED REFERENCES

Bryson, J. M. 1989. *Strategic Planning for Public and Nonprofit Organizations.* San Francisco: Jossey-Bass.

Conrad, W. R., and Glenn, W. E. 1986. *The Effective Voluntary Board of Directors.* Athens, OH: Swallow Press.

Dalsimer, J. P. 1991. "Understanding Nonprofit Financial Statements: A Primer for Board Members." Washington, DC: NCNB Governance Series.

Frantzreb, A. C. 1988. *Nonprofit Organization Individual Governing Board Audit.* McLean, VA: Arthur Frantzreb, Inc.

Ingram, R. T., et al. 1988. *Handbook of College and University Trusteeship.* San Francisco: Jossey-Bass.

Ingram, R. T. 1990. "Ten Basic Responsibilities of Nonprofit Boards." Washington, DC: NCNB Governance Series.

Kurtz, D. L. 1988. *Board Liability: Guide for Nonprofit Directors.* New York: Moyer Bell Ltd.

Mathiasen, K., III. 1990. "Board Passages: Three Key Stages in a Nonprofit Board's Life Cycle." Washington, DC: NCNB Governance Series.

Nason, J. W. 1990. "Board Assessment of the Chief Executive: A Responsibility Essential to Good Governance." Washington, DC: NCNB Governance Series.

Paltridge, J. G., White, F., and Ingram, R. T. 1986. "Self-Study Criteria for Governing Boards of Independent Colleges and Universities." Washington, DC: AGB.

Pohl, A. N. 1990. *Committees and Boards: How to Be an Effective Participant.* Lincolnwood, IL: NTC Publishing Group.

Tremper, C., and Babcock, G. 1990. "The Nonprofit Board's Role in Risk Management: More Than Buying Insurance." Washington, DC: NCNB Governance Series.

C H A P T E R N I N E

The Total Quality Approach to Staff Development and Training

Larry J. Geringer
The Boeing Company

CONTENTS

9.1   STAFF TRAINING AND DEVELOPMENT IN THE TOTAL QUALITY NONPROFIT ORGANIZATION

Standard subjects such as grant writing, donor development, fund-raising, and specific nonprofit curricula are part of staff training in typical nonprofit organizations (NPOs). However, a new Total Quality approach to staff development is steadily gaining favor and is being adopted by a growing number of NPOs. As shown in Exhibit 9.1, continuous quality improvement begins with education. The development of staff training in a Total Quality NPO will require not only a new set of courses, but a new approach to the overall process of staff development. In the past, many organizations approached employee training as an afterthought or a nice-to-have extra. In the new era of high-quality expectations in all areas of profit and nonprofit enterprises, staff development must take the highest priority. Changes in employee expectations and a changing operating environment for all organizations, including nonprofits, will cause effective leaders to reflect on the question: "Why quality improvement?" Some answers are shown in Exhibit 9.2.

As organizations prepare for Total Quality improvement, staff training and development issues must first be analyzed and then planned, coordinated, carried out, evaluated, and improved in a continuous process. New types of training are needed to support this process and to implement successful approaches to improvement throughout the organization. NPO leaders must recognize and meet the need to include employee training and development in every program plan and budget cycle. The changing environment shown in Exhibit 9.2 indicates a need to involve employees in the decision-making process.

In his book, *Thriving on Chaos,* Tom Peters (1987) summarizes involvement and training this way:

> The need for involvement—and flexibility—has an obvious corollary: Train and retrain. We must:
>
> —Invest in human capital as much as hardware.
>
> —Train entry level people; retrain them as necessary.
>
> —Train everyone in problem solving techniques to contribute to quality improvement.
>
> —Train extensively following promotion to the first managerial job; then train managers every time they advance.
>
> —Use training as a vehicle for instilling a strategic thrust.
>
> —Insist that all training be line-driven—radically so; all programs should consist primarily of input from the line, be piloted in several line locations, and be taught substantially by line people.

Exhibit 9.1.   Elements of a successful quality improvement process.

- Education and training
- Senior management commitment and involvement
- Employee participation
- Tracking of costs and benefits
- Positive attitude
- Appropriate strategy for implementation

Exhibit 9.2. Why quality improvement is needed in an NPO.

- Changing employee environment
  - —Better educated people at all levels
  - —Increased importance of environmental factors
  - —Ability and desire to be involved in decision making
  - —Expectation of enjoying work
- Changing client/customer environment
  - —Costs a primary consideration
  - —Intensified competition for volunteers and donors
  - —Demands for higher quality, reliability and accountability
- Changing nonprofit environment
  - —Major losses caused by lack of cost consciousness
  - —Quality improvement showing results elsewhere
  - —Increasing competition for time and money

Work-force training and constant retraining—and the larger idea of the work force as an appreciating (or depreciating) package of appropriate (or inappropriate) skills—must climb to the top of the agenda of the individual firm and the nation. Value-added will increasingly come through people, for the winners. Only highly skilled—that is trained and continuously retrained—people will be able to add value.

Consider doubling or tripling your training and retraining budget in the course of the next 24 to 36 months. Less serious consideration will mean a failure to come to grips with both the nature of the problem and the magnitude of the opportunity.

Peters gives perspective to staff training and development by emphasizing its importance in the agenda of the "firm and the nation." Every organization should honestly evaluate how it is responding to training needs. The need for a staff training and development strategy is critical to a Total Quality organization.

(a) TRAINING AND DEVELOPMENT SKILL ANALYSIS   NPOs should apply Peters's logical approach in analyzing their current and future training and development needs. The cost of training must be viewed as an investment in human capital. To properly consider an increase in the training budget, an organization should accomplish a training needs analysis.

A training needs analysis can be a simple matter of documentation and review of facts. To begin, an organization should document each skill needed to accomplish the mission of the organization, and then determine the current level of skill and ability of each person in the organization. The next question is: Where would the individual and the organization like to be in terms of skills and abilities? The final step is to establish the training and development curriculum necessary to reach the improved skill level. This process is similar to the following algebra problem:

Y = the current state of training and development;

Z = where the individual and the organization would like to be; and

X = the difference between Y and Z. To achieve the proper level of training, apply X. Therefore, if Y and Z are known values, we can solve for X.

Simply stated, you need to know where you are before you can begin to make meaningful staff training and development improvements.

Depending on the size and complexity of the organization, there may be a need to conduct a thorough task analysis. Deeper analysis is possible by examining individual job tasks.

Most jobs are divided into one or more tasks. In one method of task analysis, the individual employee and the supervisor, together, determine the following three levels:

1. *Basic understanding.* The person performing the task has demonstrated the skills and abilities necessary to perform the basic task. The person may require some supervision to satisfactorily complete the task.
2. *Mastery of the task* and associated skills. The person has mastered the task and performs it and all associated tasks without supervision.
3. *Ability to teach* the task to others. The person has demonstrated mastery of the task and has the ability to teach this task to others.

Using these three levels of task skill can help determine what training employees need and may point out some teaching capabilities inside the organization. The goal should be to move from basic understanding to mastery and then to an ability to teach the task to others. This approach supports Peters's admonition to make all training line-driven and line-tested. Additionally, because overhead and operating costs are always a concern to NPOs, a strategy for training and development can assist in the solution to this problem.

(b) A NEW MODEL FOR TRAINING AND STAFF DEVELOPMENT   To reduce the need for supervision and oversight, employees must reach levels of competency that utilize their ability and self-confidence to perform many functions as a self-managing, self-improving team. Old models of training need to be overhauled and should now include process-thinking and outcome-based approaches to staff development. Team-member training is essential for all members of the organization. Training and staff development approaches should contribute to the long-term growth and health of the organization. Leadership and cooperation courses should be included in the employee development curriculum.

9.2 FUNDAMENTAL TRAINING REQUIREMENTS FOR TOTAL QUALITY

To begin the process of staff training and development, every member of the Total Quality organization needs specific training classes and follow-up development in four quality fundamentals:

1. The principles of continuous quality improvement (Imai, 1986). An overview of how improvement must be a continuous process involving all employees.
2. Customer service, for both internal and external customers (Carlzon, 19). Clients and donors must be treated as valuable assets because each contact with a client, donor, or volunteer should be seen as a "moment of truth" that has the potential to make a permanent positive or negative impression.

3. Statistical process control tools (Deming, 1986; Juran, 1989; Scherkenbach, 1987). Basic statistical methods—learning to operate with facts and data—are critical for sustaining the drive to continuously improve.

4. Teamwork as a process and discipline (Scholtes, 1988). Learn the functions and major roles of an effective team. Team leaders and team members have to learn their roles and responsibilities if they expect to be effective.

In addition, fundamental principles of Total Quality must be addressed by the organization (see Exhibit 9.3). Other factors that can improve the competence of working individuals include:

- Education and training;
- A selection process that matches personality, education, and experience to the job's requirements;
- Work methods established to assure the highest and best use of resources;
- An opportunity to work in multi-skill jobs and to develop new skills;
- An assurance of safety and security on the job;
- A well-defined promotion or progression system;
- Leadership and supervision designed to develop the talents of the individual (Bradford and Cohen, 1984).

(a) SKILL DEVELOPMENT To establish an effective, holistic approach to the staff development process, three major areas of skill development should be addressed:

1. Technical skills needed to accomplish the work and to advance with technology (currently, fifth-generation technology and second-generation ability are engaging the technology);

Exhibit 9.3. The fundamental principles of Total Quality.

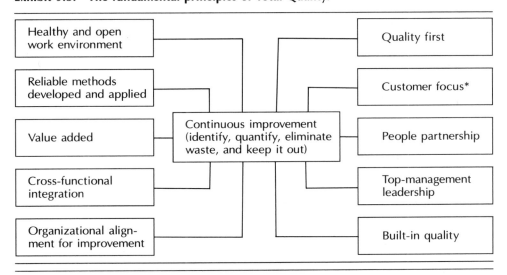

* Includes donors, clients, and volunteers.

2. Leadership, social, and managerial skills appropriate to the level of responsibility and the experience of the individual and the job;

3. Problem-solving and improvement skills focused on the job skill area, using extensive on-the-job teaching and coaching.

Training in these three areas should aim at improving the job to be done, which will require an analysis of the current positions and levels of training needed in each major skill area. This is a job for management, not outside training consultants: meaningful improvement comes from inside an organization.

A critical requirement of effective staff development and training is the clear commitment of top management to participate *first* in all new approaches to training. The leaders of the organization must be the role models; they have to learn to "talk the talk" and then must "walk the walk." In fact, one principle or approach to successful implementation of continuous quality improvement is the "management first" principle, which states that the top leaders of the enterprise will always be the first to learn and practice any new tool or improvement practice. Canon Corporation, a well-known Japanese company whose focus is on quality, uses these principles in its approach to training:

1. Develop basic training that is structured, practical, and reliable;

2. Combine training organized by level with training organized by function;

3. Make training part of the overall plan for human resources development;

4. Always provide follow-up systems so training can be linked to work results;

5. Focus training to support quality, cost, and delivery control;

6. Establish unified objectives for training at all levels;

7. Use the "story" training method, which combines classroom and on-the-job training;

8. Develop company teaching staff by using outstanding company personnel as teachers;

9. Establish standards for programs, so that differences in training opportunities do not develop between divisions or job functions. (Give everyone the opportunity to learn and improve.)

It is important that these principles be carefully studied; a plan for each of the principles should be developed. This approach adds substance and process to the development of staff members. These principles can easily be adapted to provide the outline of a staff training and development policy and perhaps even the framework for a policy manual.

(b) TEAMS AND TEAMWORK   Other approaches to training and development support the drive to improve quality and service. The approach of Orsburn et al. (1990) looks at the idea of improving through self-directed teams. The authors point out that there are training requirements both during and after the transition to self-direction and quality improvement, and the organization must provide intensive training in three critical areas:

- Technical skills. Technical cross-training, which allows team members to move from job to job within the team itself, is the foundation for the flexibility and

Exhibit 9.4. Functions of a facilitator.

- Acts as coach/consultant to the improvement team.
- Attends quality improvement team meetings.
- Provides feedback on team's process and progress.
- Provides postmeeting assessment to team leader.
- Interfaces with statistician, consultants, and specialists, as required.
- Ensures understanding of quality improvement team process.

productivity of the team as a whole. After a thorough review of all of the tasks performed by the team, individual team members receive training in the specific skills that will broaden their personal contributions to the overall effort.

- Administrative skills. Self-directed teams, as the name implies, perform many tasks formerly handled by supervisors. At first, the teams will need training in record keeping, reporting procedures, and other aspects of working within the larger organization. Later, depending on the team's charter, they will need to learn procedures for budgeting, scheduling, monitoring, and even hiring and evaluating team members. Typical team roles are highlighted in Exhibits 9.4 through 9.7.
- Interpersonal skills. With their broader responsibilities, members of a self-directed work team must communicate more effectively than conventional workers one-on-one, in groups, with each other, and with people outside the team. Conventional workers rely on their boss to ensure good communication, set priorities, and handle interpersonal conflict. The peers who make up a self-directed team must handle these critical, often explosive matters on their own, and, because these skills rarely come naturally, team members will need skill-building training in several areas. Day-to-day interactions can be chaotic unless team members master the basics of listening and giving feedback. Cooperative decision making within and among teams demands the skills of group problem solving, influencing others, and resolving conflicts. In short, every team member must learn to collaborate in getting the right information, sending the right information, and using that information to increase productivity.

(c) FEASIBILITY The focus here is on three broad categories of skills: technical, administrative, and interpersonal. A careful reviewing of these three categories makes it obvious that a general curriculum will be required to teach the skills to team members and to maintain the skills over time.

Exhibit 9.5. Functions of a team leader.

- Schedules team meetings.
- Guides meetings according to agenda.
- Encourages all team members to participate.
- Ensures efficient use of time by maintaining focus on specific problems or proposals and by keeping individuals working together.
- Helps team achieve goals through consensus.
- Keeps records of team information and progress.
- Has influence on team decisions equal to that of other team members.

Exhibit 9.6.   Functions of a team member.

- Identifies, analyzes, and solves chronic system problems.
- Identifies other improvement opportunities.
- Is committed to and fully involved in project.
- Is responsible for representing his or her organization.

All quality improvement approaches recommend teams and teamwork as a method to achieve continuous quality improvement, which means that there must be a corresponding training and development effort to begin and sustain team activity. There are six feasibility questions to ask, when deciding to implement self-directed teams:

1. Are the work processes compatible with self-directed teams?
2. Are employees willing and able to make self-direction work?
3. Can managers master and apply the hands-off leadership style required by self-directed teams?
4. Is the organization healthy or promising enough to support improved productivity without reducing the work force?
5. Will the organization's policies and culture in both corporate and field locations support the transition to teams?
6. Will the community support the transition to teams?

This feasibility process will need to be augmented with another question: Does the organization have a training and development process that will support a team-based operation? The initial and ongoing budget for teams can be sizable. Therefore, top managers must build in a training and development process that will maintain the skills of all team members.

The payback can be quite dramatic. Motorola Corporation claims a whopping $30 return on every $1 invested in training and employee development. It has established a Motorola University, with a full curriculum that begins with basic math, reading, and writing skills, and then advances to courses in all major job skills within the corporation. By first doing a training needs analysis that included testing for basic skills, Motorola learned that many of its employees did not have basic math and reading skills. It redesigned the curriculum to begin with the basics and build to more advanced training and education classes (Wiggenhorn, 1990). NPOs may need to evaluate basic reading and math skills among their staff and volunteers. (Because of its drive to improve quality, Motorola won the Malcolm Baldrige National Quality Award in 1988.)

Exhibit 9.7.   Typical team member activities.

Equal participation in:
- Defining the problem;
- Investigating causes;
- Implementing solutions—management presentations;
- Documenting and tracking implemented solutions.

9.3 THE MALCOLM BALDRIGE NATIONAL QUALITY AWARD CRITERIA

Another way to determine the best method of curriculum development is to learn how the best organizations in America measure up to national quality criteria. The skills of "Plan, Do, Check, Act," process thinking, using facts and data, using management planning and statistical tools, and cause-and-effect diagramming, among others, must all be learned. Fortunately, an outline for these skills is found in the Malcolm Baldrige National Quality Award Criteria, developed by the National Institute of Standards and Technology. The Application Guidelines for the Malcolm Baldrige National Quality Award provide an excellent starting point to determine staff development needs in both profit and nonprofit organizations. The front cover for the current application quotes President George Bush: "Quality management is not just a strategy. It must be a new style of working, even a new style of thinking. A dedication to quality and excellence is more than good business. It is a way of life, giving something back to society, offering your best to others." The guidelines, prepared by the U. S. Department of Commerce (National Institute of Standards and Technology, Route 270 and Quince Orchard Road, Administration Building, Room A537, Gaithersburg, MD 20899), can be requested for review and for use as a guide for training and self-evaluation, even though an organization does not intend to apply for the award. According to Dr. Curt Reimann, Director of the Malcolm Baldrige National Quality Award, about 12,000 guidelines were distributed in 1988, and about 65,000 in 1989. By 1990, the number had more than doubled, and distribution was over 250,000 in 1991. Although fewer than 100 organizations annually apply for the award, Reimann feels that most are using the application guidelines as a training document. A review of the categories of the award indicates that they apply to any organization, large or small, public or private, profit or nonprofit. They are universal requirements of any successful Total Quality organization. These are the seven categories of quality:

1. Leadership;
2. Information and Analysis;
3. Strategic Quality Planning;
4. Human Resource Development and Management;
5. Management of Process Quality;
6. Quality and Operational Results;
7. Customer Focus and Satisfaction.

(a) SUBCATEGORY REQUIREMENTS There are 28 subcategories and 89 separate items to address, in a self-audit format. These categories, subcategories, and items to address provide a substantial outline for a staff training and development plan. For example, many organizations have leadership courses, but how many have information and analysis, or strategic quality planning training? Similar questions can be asked concerning training and development in all of the categories and subcategories. Category 4, Human Resource Development and Management, specifically addresses Quality Education and Training in subcategory 4.3: "Describe how the company (NPO) decides what quality education or training is needed by employees and how it utilizes the knowledge and skills acquired; summarize the types of quality education received by employees in all employee categories."

(b) TWENTY-FIRST-CENTURY STRATEGY   Using the Malcolm Baldrige National Quality Award Criteria as a basis for staff development and training is a strategy that looks toward the year 2000. It may well require a culture change by traditional training managers, who must recognize that the NPO should fully prepare its leaders and staff for quality thinking. The National Quality Award Criteria will be very helpful in understanding what the strengths and weaknesses of any organization are as they relate to Total Quality. The criteria are straightforward and can be answered using three guidelines: the organization's *approach* to any of the categories, the *deployment* or implementation of the approach, and the *result* of the approach and its implementation. The Baldrige Award criteria represent the most complete checklist on quality improvement processes developed in America, and they are simple to apply to any nonprofit or service organization. There have been serious discussions on adapting the criteria to allow nonprofits an opportunity to compete for the award. In the meantime, even if an organization does not wish to win an award, the criteria are adaptable to any organization interested in assessing its own level of quality commitment. As stated previously, the seven categories of the Baldrige Award can be used as a roadmap to staff development. In fact, I recommend a staff development and training curriculum that includes each of the seven major categories.

(c) USING THE AWARD CATEGORIES AS A STAFF DEVELOPMENT AND CURRICULUM GUIDE   This section discusses how to use the Baldrige Award criteria as a guide to developing curriculum. I will outline each category and then discuss its key elements, pointing out the training that is indicated. This approach provides a number of training and staff development examples, but other training requirements may come to readers' minds for specific organizations. Each of the seven categories is equally important in constructing a balanced strategy for staff development and training in an NPO.

(i) Leadership   The category of *Leadership* includes a wide range of subjects for study: leadership values and vision, planning, assessment, review of quality plans and teams, communication, quality values, management systems, resource allocations, cross-functional management, and public responsibility. Some courses in current leadership theory are also appropriate. Contemporary ideas such as "management by wandering around" (MBWA), Deming's 14 points, Juran's breakthrough, team leadership, continuous quality improvement *(Kaizen),* "frontline leadership" (developed by Zenger-Miller Training Inc.), and other leadership-specific materials should be reviewed for inclusion as beginning guides to leadership training. Leadership training courses should be in the curriculum for premanagement and for all levels of management, to satisfy this category's criteria.

(ii) Information and Analysis   *Information and Analysis,* the second category, requires an understanding of data and "management by fact." The suggested curriculum includes: basic statistics/statistical process control, management information systems, data analysis, and problem-solving courses. This category should also address word processing and basic personal computer skills training. Facts and data analyses are critical to meeting the criteria for this category.

(iii) Strategic Quality Planning   *Strategic Quality Planning* suggests a need for training and development in: long-range and short-range planning techniques, world-class competitiveness, benchmarking, project management, time management, and sustaining quality leadership through priorities. The criteria are concerned with long-range thinking and the plans to achieve a strategy.

(iv) Human Resources Development and Management   An opportunity to train in the effective use of the human resources of the organization is offered in *Human Resources Utilization.* Staff training and development opportunities should include these topics: basic management processes, employee acquisition and retention, new employee orientation, facilitator, team leader, team member (see Exhibits 9.4 through 9.6), and self-managing teams. Other courses should cover: participative management practices, employee suggestion systems, employee recognition, coaching and counseling, people skills, interviewing skills, and employee survey techniques. Satisfying the criteria requires courses and measurement of the training results.

(v) Management of Process Quality   Category 5, *Quality Assurance of Products and Services,* includes a need to train in the "design and introduction of new or improved products and services." Every organization must have a process to determine the needs of its customers and clients as well as its relationship with suppliers. Employees should be familiar with an eight-step process called "departmental task analysis." These are the steps:

1. Review the mission statement of the organization and ensure that it is the current version and that all key personnel agree on its main tenets;
2. Determine the key customers of the organization;
3. Determine how information about key services and products is requested by the customers;
4. Identify activities to meet customers' requirements;
5. Determine the key suppliers to the organization;
6. Determine how requirements are communicated to suppliers;
7. Develop a customer/supplier interview–feedback system and a measurement system;
8. Identify defects and improvement opportunities.

A thorough understanding of departmental task analysis and organizational process analysis is needed by all members of the organization. There will also be a need to train staff and volunteers on quality audit, quality control methods, and analysis of business processes. Like departmental task analysis, business/organizational process analysis has a number of steps to learn:

1. Identify the process and assign responsibility or ownership;
2. Define the process boundaries, the start, the end, and the major parts;
3. Document the process flow and the time required to complete it;
4. Define control points and measurements of the process;
5. Communicate and implement changes to improve the process;
6. Measure and assess the impact of changes in the process;
7. Identify non-value-added activities.

Departmental task analysis and business process analysis training will help satisfy the criteria in Quality Assurance of Products and Processes.

(vi) Quality and Operational Results The category of *Quality Results* will require a knowledge of trends and measures to ensure that objective measures of improved quality show connections between quality improvement results and the improvement projects.

A word of caution here: Numerous "quality improvement" training and consulting groups are springing up, because many organizations, both profit and nonprofit, want to learn the discipline of quality. Choice of consultants should be based on past results, after talking to previous clients. (See Chap. 30.)

"Quality," like mathematics, chemistry, and language arts, is a discipline. Quality has been described as having three characteristics: fitness for use, as determined by the customer or user; fulfillment of required specifications, as determined by the designer; and value, as determined by the user or customer. An organization should be able to identify its key measures of quality, summarize trends in quality improvement, and compare operating quality levels with other similar organizations or benchmarks. To satisfy the Quality Results criteria, there is a need to understand statistical data and to be able to measure the quality of supplies and services furnished by various suppliers.

(vii) Customer Focus and Satisfaction The final category, *Customer Satisfaction,* delves into how customer service and satisfaction are handled. Nonprofits now recognize that everyone has customers. They are either the persons who directly receive the service, or the next persons in the process. An excellent reference for understanding user/customer satisfaction is *Moments of Truth,* by Jan Carlzon, Chief Executive Officer of Scandinavian Air Systems (SAS). Each time a person from an organization speaks to a client, volunteer, donor, or customer, that interaction is a "moment of truth," because there is an opportunity to show the client, volunteer, donor, or customer just how important (or unimportant) he or she is. Many other interesting ideas about service in Carlzon's book can be directly applied to NPOs.

How staff and volunteers are instructed about the importance of good relations with clients, volunteers, donors, and customers is critical to the success of the organization. All of the work force need training on the importance of customer satisfaction—the key to developing a healthy NPO. Therefore, all members of the organization must have a knowledge of customers' requirements and expectations. How does the organization determine current and future customer needs? (See Chapter 28.) How are customer relations handled? Is there a complaints system? Some interesting data about customer research that appeared in *Quality Digest* (September 1991), applies to donors, clients, volunteers, and friends. The data may give some insight to the critical nature of client/volunteer/donor/customer management.

A typical organization hears by mail or phone from only 4% of its dissatisfied customers. The other 96% just quietly go away, and 91% never come back. A survey to determine why customers quit found the following:

1. 3% move away
2. 5% develop other relationships
3. 9% leave for competitive reasons
4. 14% are dissatisfied with the service or product
5. 68% quit because of an attitude of indifference toward the person by a manager or some other employee.

On an average, a typical dissatisfied person (customer, donor, client, or volunteer) will tell eight to ten people about [a] problem. One in five will tell twenty people about the problem they had with the service or product. It takes twelve positive service incidents to make up for one negative incident. Seven of ten complaining clients/volunteers, donors/customers will do business with you again if you resolve the complaint in their favor. If you resolve it on the spot 95% will do business with you again. On an average, a satisfied complainer will tell five people about the problem and how it was satisfactorily resolved.

The average organization spends six times more to attract new customers/clients/donors/ volunteers than it does to keep old ones. Yet customer loyalty is in most cases worth ten times the price of a single business transaction. Organizations having low-quality service average only a 1% return on sales and lose market share at a rate of 2% per year. Organizations with high quality service average a 12% return on sales, gain market share at the rate of 6% per year (and charge significantly higher prices).

Leaders of nonprofits must realize that these factors apply to their organizations in an equally dramatic way—simply substitute donor/supporter/volunteer/client for customer. Employees need to know how to determine satisfactory methods of measurement and results. All employees need training and education on customer satisfaction trends. They should be able to compare customers' satisfaction with similar organizations to customers' view of their own. Gains and losses of clients/customers/volunteers/donors should be visible to all employees. Key service features should be identified to customers and employees as evidence that the organization is best suited to fill particular service or "market" needs. There must be a method of generating and assessing the organization's trends in gaining and losing clients/customers/volunteers/donors.

(d) APPLICATIONS FOR THE AWARD   The seven categories of quality identified in the National Quality Award provide an excellent staff development curriculum model for the 1990s and beyond.

The categories are divided into subcategories and may be translated to fit any organization. It seems readily apparent that any organization, profit or nonprofit, that applies the techniques outlined by the award application will be successful. Further, if the management and staff of an organization strive to demonstrate a quality approach, understand how that approach is deployed throughout the organization, and measure the results achieved from the approach and deployment, that organization will be successful in all of its efforts.

The Malcolm Baldrige National Quality Award is managed by: U. S. Department of Commerce, National Institute of Standards and Technology, Gaithersburg, MD 20899; telephone: 301-975-2036, telefax: 301-948-3716. The award is administered by the Malcolm Baldrige National Quality Award Consortium, Inc., P.O. Box 443, Milwaukee, WI 53201-0443; telephone: 414-272-8575, telefax: 414-272-1734; *or* P.O. Box 56606, Department 698, Houston, TX 77256-6606; telephone: 713-681-4020, telefax: 713-618-8578.

The managing organization in Gaithersburg, Maryland, can provide the most current application guidelines; the administering organizations in Milwaukee and Houston can provide access to information on quality in America and on U.S. organizations that are currently interested in improving quality of service and product. These groups should be seen as resources to all organizations throughout the country. Every manager should have a copy of the National Quality Award guidelines to assess his or her organization's ability to match the criteria of the seven categories of quality. *Single copies of the application and guidelines are available at no cost by calling or writing to the organizations listed above.* The guidelines give excellent advice on quality issues, and there are other considerations for staff development and training.

9.4 PARTICIPATORY MANAGEMENT

Participating in management is a necessary skill for members of all organizations, especially those who are developing teams and teamwork as a basic management approach. A number of ideas and processes clarify how to become more effective in leading and participating in teams. First, it can be demonstrated that leadership is not necessarily a skill, but more exactly is a deep sensitivity about people—their needs and motivations. The designated leader who operates in a directive, goal-giving, manipulating way contributes to the group's probable failure to become totally effective.

Top-down directives and forced goals can result in 10 percent or even 20 percent improvement; innovative team-based processes are capable of 80 percent to 100 percent

Exhibit 9.8. How to conduct a meeting.

BEFORE
- Plan for the meeting by identifying:
    —What problems or objectives are to be covered.
    —Who should attend.
    —What should come out of the meeting.
    —What activities will help get the desired results.
    —A time schedule (where and when).
- Develop and distribute an agenda:
    —Obtain a list of items from prospective attendees.
    —Put items in priority order.
    —Assign time limits to each item if necessary.

DURING
- Review the minutes.
- Follow the agenda in the meeting:
    —Move the meeting along promptly and smoothly to meet objectives.
    —Use the three P's as necessary.
    —Stick with meeting time schedules.
- Diagnose and intervene to correct interaction problems:
    —Remain sensitive to people's feelings.
- At the end of the meeting, clarify:
    —What has been discussed.
    —What is to be done.
    —Who is to do what.
    —When and where it's to be done.
- Set the agenda for the next meeting.
- Conduct meeting critiques on a regular basis.

AFTER
- Ensure follow-up by having minutes distributed promptly.
- Take follow-up actions.

improvement. However, people need to participate in decisions and be empowered to make such dramatic contributions. Teams or groups can improve themselves if they evaluate how they are doing and frankly discuss the good and bad features of their present operation: "How did we do at this meeting?" "What caused us to bog down?" "Do we have a team goal?" Exhibits 9.8 through 9.18 suggest helpful management procedures.

Exhibit 9.9. Personal analysis of listening habits.

Have you ever evaluated your listening habits? If you have, this will be a good review. If you have not, it will give you some insights that will help you increase your listening effectiveness. Be as honest with yourself as you can.

When you are in a communications situation where you have a listening responsibility do you:

	Most of the time	Occasionally	Seldom
1. Position yourself so that you can see and hear the other person or persons clearly?			
2. Try to keep an eye on what's going on elsewhere in the room?			
3. Continually reflect mentally on what the speaker is trying to say?			
4. Develop your response while the other person is speaking?			
5. Suspend judgment of the person's appearance and delivery?			
6. Interrupt frequently to be sure you make your point when you disagree or feel the need to challenge a statement?			
7. Examine your thoughts for prejudice and bias that may influence your reception of the other person's message?			
8. "Turn off" the other person because you dislike him or her?			
9. Keep your mind open to new ideas or variations of old themes that might be productive?			
10. React quickly and vigorously to certain words and phrases?			
11. Focus on the importance of the message and repeat key concepts and essential aspects of the information?			
12. Feel the need to have the last word?			
13. Listen to the feelings being expressed to better understand the other person's comments?			
14. Let your emotions such as anger, dislike, defensiveness, and prejudice influence your attention to the real message the other person is trying to convey?			
15. Maintain frequent eye contact with the other person?			
16. Assume you know what the other person is going to say before he says it?			

Checkmarks in any of the three columns may indicate a need to improve that listening responsibility.

Exhibit 9.10. Postmeeting assessment.

	Date				
	Disagree			Agree	
1. Were members prepared for the meeting?	1	2	3	4	5
2. Were ideas and viewpoints actively listened to and fully understood?	1	2	3	4	5
3. Were topics summarized before progressing to a new topic?	1	2	3	4	5
4. Were decision issues fully explored before reaching consensus?	1	2	3	4	5
5. Were problem-solving techniques used effectively?	1	2	3	4	5
6. Was the group discussion refocused when it strayed from the immediate topic?	1	2	3	4	5
7. Were the meeting and its action items summarized at the end of the meeting?	1	2	3	4	5
8. Was there a feeling of accomplishment at the end of the meeting?	1	2	3	4	5

Positive aspects of meeting and/or recommendations for improvement

(a) EVALUATION Occasional use of postmeeting evaluation and reaction blanks, when examined by the team, will stimulate thinking about the way the team is functioning. The end result will be solutions to such problems as resistance, cliques, failure to act, apathy, domination by one or a few members, and simple misunderstandings. This process can also lead to an understanding of what training and development are needed in the area of group processes. It is easy to talk about the new team culture, but operating on teams can be difficult if team members do not understand group dynamics.

(b) GROUP DYNAMICS A commonly understood phenomenon is the so-called "Ming" dynasty of group dynamics: forMING, storMING, norMING, and perforMING. In the forming stage, the team is coming together and getting acquainted. The storming stage is the most difficult but the easiest to predict: members determine how far to push the leader, and what the rules of the team are; they attempt to stake out their own territory and to develop relationships with other team members. After the storming stage, the team develops its own processes and norms. Finally, the team begins to perform.

Team leaders need to look for the signs of the team group dynamics and guide them as smoothly as possible to the performing stage. However, nearly 100 percent of all teams go through all stages before they become fully effective. A number of group dynamics subjects should be part of the development curriculum.

"Groupthink," and the "Abilene paradox" are two subjects that team leaders and members should be aware of. Groupthink describes a follow-the-leader thought process

Exhibit 9.11. Evaluating meeting effectiveness.

Team _____   Date _____

Fill out the evaluation sheet and then share your comments with the team. Check the more effective and less effective points of your participation in today's meeting. Then do the same for the team's overall performance.

Self	Team	More effective participation
		Listen attentively
		Ask for information and examples
		State agreement or disagreement
		Restate and paraphrase
		Give information and examples
		Encourage others
		Summarize; build consensus
		Ask for useful pause

Self	Team	Less effective participation
		Dominating the meeting
		Withdrawing from the meeting
		Interrupting others
		Sidetracking the discussion
		Putting others down
		Lack of preparation

- How well did you achieve the stated agenda outcomes?
- What agenda items do you want included in the next meeting?
- Briefly summarize any comments you wish to make about your participation or the team's performance.
- What, if any, changes would help to make the team's meeting more effective?

Exhibit 9.12. Meeting evaluation.

Team: _____   Date: _____

Responding: _____

	High	Medium	Low
• I feel I participated in the meeting	____	____	____
• I feel I could say whatever I wanted	____	____	____
• I feel we made progress toward our goals	____	____	____
• In general, the meeting went [comments]	____	____	____

Exhibit 9.13. Meeting preparation worksheet.

Meeting purpose:		Key people:		Time limit:
Team leader function	Useful techniques	Notes		Time estimate
I. Open the meeting	• Restate purpose • Review agenda			
II. Guide the process of the meeting Process steps:				
III. Summarize action items	• Action register • Prepare agenda			
IV. Summary and critique	• Meeting critique			
Points to remember				
• Maintain members' self-esteem • Focus on problems, not personalities	• Encourage participation • Ensure clear next step	• Value all ideas • Use tact		

Exhibit 9.14. Team meeting critique sheet.

Team: _____   Date: _____

Making team meetings effective is everyone's job. Through candid but constructive criticism, we can improve. If you feel your time was wasted, say so, but be fair—provide specific suggestions for improvement.

This meeting was:

( ) Productive

( ) Waste of time

( ) Okay—but could be improved

The next meeting could be improved by:

---

in which group members feel compelled to follow the lead of the ranking person on the team. Those who disagree with the leader's point of view are usually disregarded, even if they have a legitimate difference of opinion. Group members will make decisions to please the leader.

According to its author, Dr. Jerry Harvey, the "Abilene paradox" occurs when people go along with an idea or decision as a group, even when, individually, they don't believe the idea is correct. These and other subjects related to group dynamics should be part of the staff training curriculum.

9.5 COST OF QUALITY

According to many experts, especially Phillip Crosby (1979) and William Conway (1986), the "cost of quality" should be a topic for staff and employee development. Crosby and Conway state that every organization has "scrap, waste, rework, redundancy, work-arounds, extra inventory and many other costs" that do not show up on a balance sheet but most definitely are costs of quality. Another consideration is the cost of doing things that do not add value to the final output, product, or service of the organization. These costs can be measured and tracked to demonstrate the value of improved quality processes. Quality experts argue that many of the costs of poor quality are like the bottom of an iceberg; they cannot be seen, but they are there. An iceberg is very dangerous and not dealing with it can have disastrous results. Cost of quality is an important subject to include in the NPO curriculum.

Exhibit 9.15.　Team meeting planning worksheet.

Date: _____　　　　　Time: _____

Opening:

Subject:　　Time allotted:	Subject:　　Time allotted:
Subject:　　Time allotted:	Subject:　　Time allotted:
Subject:　　Time allotted:	Subject:　　Time allotted:
Subject:　　Time allotted:	Subject:　　Time allotted:

Closing:

Exhibit 9.16. Sample agenda.

Team:	Alpha Process Improvement

Date:	December 6, 1993

Location:	fourth floor, conference room 1

Time:	8:00 A.M.

Agenda:

8:00 A.M. • Opening
            Guest: John Dough, statistician
8:05 • Summarize and review last meeting . . . Bill
8:10 • Report on action items:
           • Memo to facilities . . . June
           • Last train to Abilene report . . . Jerry
8:25 • Discuss data from checksheets with John Dough (guest) . . . team
8:45 • Start identifying most likely causes (C&E diagram) . . . team
9:15 A.M. • Review action items assigned for next week
9:25 • Close
           • Summarize progress
           • Inputs for next meeting
           • Meeting evaluation

9.6 CONSULTANTS

In the development of any new approach to organizational improvement, there is the question of inside versus outside assistance to develop basic knowledge and an approach. (See Chap. 30.) Continuous quality improvement has its basis in statistics and process control; (Montgomery D.C., 1985) however, it is also concerned with humanware and teamwork as well as a keen understanding of customer and supplier relationships. Outside consultants may have limited usefulness to organizations just beginning to understand the quality message. However, most of what quality is about is neither deep nor mysterious. Quite the contrary, much of it is just good common sense. Unfortunately, quality can be overcomplicated to the point where some managers might begin to believe that Total Quality or continuous quality improvement is some sort of "magic" imported from the Far East and spoken of in "mystical" terms: *Kaizen*, Ishikawa diagrams, statistical process control (SPC), departmental task analysis (DTA), business process analysis (BPA), facilitation skills, Pareto diagrams and analysis, histograms, run charts, X-bar, upper and lower control limits, Hoshin planning, seven tools for problem solving and seven more for planning, "Plan, Do, Check, Act," the Deming wheel and the Deming prize, and the Malcolm Baldrige Award. Most of these terms and techniques typically associated with quality improvement can be

Exhibit 9.17.   Agenda form sheet.

Team: _____

Date:
Location:
Time:
Agenda:

Exhibit 9.18. Weekly activity report.

Team _____ Alpha Process Improvement _____

Date of meeting:
June 6, 1992

Location of meeting:
fourth floor, conference room 1

Team members		Guests
____ Don White	____ Jamie Blue	John Dough
____ Wil Black	____ _____	_____
____ Loni Brown	____ _____	_____
____ Pat Grey	____ _____	_____
A Tom Green	____ _____	_____
Facilitator	A Ian Gone	_____
		A = absent

Meeting summary:

Facilities is ready to move library; Abilene express is still in operation—need to

exercise care when boarding; John dough helped us analyze data on "100 Errors"

project; Pat reminded us that we need to look at our milestone chart and see

where diagram for "100 Errors"; meeting evaluation positive.

Action items:

Loni: Check with Facilities for date

Jamie: Bring backup data ("100 Errors")

Don: Bring milestone chart to next meeting

Prepared by:

Distribution: Team members   Carbon Copy: Walter Brennen, process owner
                Facilitator
                Recorder's book

learned through self-study and a step-by-step approach to understanding Total Quality. (Block, Peter 1981) *Flawless Consulting.*

9.7 CASCADE TRAINING AND DEVELOPMENT

Cascade training offers a useful approach to accomplishing training with internal resources. It can also be an excellent development tool because it reinforces the role of the manager as a teacher and developer. Cascade training is a top-down method of training from one level to the next; that is, a supervisor learns the skill or subject and then teaches it to his or her staff members. Ideally, top-level management learns first, and then "cascades" the training to the next level, with this process continuing until all members of the organization are trained in the skill or subject. Cascade training ensures that the subject is learned and taught by those who manage the organization. Those doing the teaching may need initial assistance from training professionals in course development and delivery.

(a) CURRENT SITUATION NPOs should begin by assessing the current state of knowledge in the organization—the training and development situation as it exists today. What type of strategy exists, if any, for the training and development currently used? They can then decide where the knowledge level needs to be and what strategy could and should be used.

(b) TARGET This effort describes establishing targets for staff training and development activities. What is the organization's unique situation, the NPO niche it wants to establish and maintain? What is realistic, achievable, and an improvement over the current situation? The targets should include goals for curriculum development and for the desired outcome of training courses and development processes.

(c) PROPOSAL The final steps will be to analyze the situation and target and then to develop a process to take the organization to the target area. The proposal will become a staff training and development roadmap for future goal achievement. The proposal is a strategy that tells what is needed to hit the designated target.

9.8 PURPOSE, PROCESS, PAYOFF

By reviewing its situation, establishing a target, and developing a proposal, an organization should be able to describe the "three Ps"; that is, it should now know its *purpose* for becoming a Total Quality NPO. By describing its *process* of staff training and development, it should clearly establish how it will use the Malcolm Baldrige National Quality Award criteria to establish training requirements. Finally, it should know the *payoff* of staff training and development strategy. If NPOs use the continuous quality approach and learn to employ its techniques, they will ensure their own success—the best possible payoff.

For tips on management, there is no better source than Deming's 14 points, shown in Exhibit 9.19.

Exhibit 9.19. Deming's 14 points.

1. Create and publish to all employees a statement of the aims and purposes of the company or other organization. The management must demonstrate constantly their commitment to this statement.
2. Learn the new philosophy, top management and everybody.
3. Understand the purpose of inspection, for improvement of processes and reduction of cost.
4. End the practice of awarding business on the basis of price tag alone.
5. Improve constantly and forever the system of production and service.
6. Institute training (for skills).
7. Teach and institute leadership.
8. Drive out fear. Create trust. Create a climate for innovation.
9. Optimize toward the aims and purposes of the company, the efforts of teams, groups, staff areas, too.
10. Eliminate exhortations for the work force.
11. a. Eliminate numerical quotas for production. Instead, learn and institute methods for improvement.
    b. Eliminate MBO (management by objectives). Instead, learn the capabilities of processes, and how to improve them.
12. Remove barriers that rob people of pride of workmanship.
13. Encourage education and self-improvement for everyone.
14. Take action to accomplish the transformation.

(*Source: The Deming Library,* Vol. 16, 1989).

SOURCES AND SUGGESTED REFERENCES

Arter, Dennis R. 1989. *Quality Audits.* Milwaukee, WI: ASQC Quality Press.

Blake, R., Mouton, J., and Allen, R. 1987. *Spectacular Teamwork.* New York: John Wiley & Sons.

Block, Peter. 1981. *Flawless Consulting.* San Diego Univ. Associates Inc.

Bradford, D. L. and Cohen, A. R. 1984. *Managing for Excellence.* New York: John Wiley & Sons.

Brassard, Michael. 1989. *The Memory Jogger Plus.* Methuen, MA: Goal QPC.

Buchholtz, S., and Ross, T. 1987. *Creating the High Performance Team.* New York: John Wiley & Sons.

Clemmer, Jim. 1990. *Firing on All Cylinders.* Toronto, Canada: Macmillan.

Crosby, Phillip B. 1979. *Quality Is Free.* New York: McGraw-Hill.

Deming, W. Edwards. 1986. *Out of the Crisis.* Cambridge, MA: MIT Press.

Feigenbaum, Armand V. 1983. *Total Quality Control.* New York: McGraw-Hill.

Harvey, Jerry. 1984. *The Abilene Paradox.* New York: McGraw-Hill.

Heskett, James L. 1986. *Managing in the Service Economy.* Cambridge, MA: Harvard Business School Press.

Imai, Masaaki. 1986. *Kaizen: The Key to Japan's Competitive Success.* New York: Random House.

Ishikawa, Kaoru. 1985. *What Is Total Quality Control? (The Japanese Way).* Englewood Cliffs, NJ: Prentice-Hall.

Kanter, Ronabeth Moss. 1983. *The Change Masters.* New York: Simon & Schuster.

Mohr, William, and Mohr, Harriet. 1983. *Quality Circles.* Reading, MA: Addison-Wesley.

Montgomery, Douglas C. 1985. *Introduction to Statistical Quality Control.* New York: John Wiley & Sons.

Nadler, Leonard, and Zeace, R. 1990. *Handbook of Human Resource Development,* 2nd ed. New York: John Wiley & Sons.

National Institute of Standards and Technology. 1990. "Malcolm Baldrige National Quality Award Criteria." Gaithersburg, MD: Author.

Peters, Tom. 1987. *Thriving on Chaos.* Alfred A. Knopf, NY.

Rosow, S., and Zager, R. 1988. *Training = The Competitive Edge,* San Francisco, CA: Jossey-Bass.

Sadler, Phillip. 1988. *Managerial Leadership.* Aldershot, England: Gower Publishing.

Scholtes, Peter R. 1988. The Team Handbook. Madison, WI: Joiner Associates, Inc.

Wiggenhorn, William. 1990. "Motorola U: When Training Becomes an Education." *Harvard Business Review* (July–August), Vol. 68 #4 pp. 71–83.

Volunteer Development: Individual and Organizational Considerations

Janet L. Unger
Unger Consulting Services

CONTENTS

10.1 DEFINE THE NEED FOR VOLUNTEERS

(a) DETERMINE HOW VOLUNTEERS CAN HELP ACHIEVE ORGANIZATIONAL GOALS

What is the organization's mission and how can it be achieved?

What are the organization's short-term and long-range goals?

How can volunteers help achieve those goals?

Answering these questions with full board and staff involvement is a vital first step in defining and communicating the appropriate role for volunteers in the organization.

Nonprofit leaders need to clearly articulate the mission of the organization and consistently work toward achieving that mission. The mission should "specify the purposes of the organization and the philosophy and values that guide it" (Bryson, 1989). The mission must be credible and inspirational if it is to foster enthusiasm for what the organization does and why it does it. John Carver (1990) has suggested that nonprofit leaders ask the question: "What will be different in the world because we do business?" A clear answer will be the mission.

Once the mission is accepted, the organization must work on its short- and long-term goals and define the human, physical (materials and space), and financial resources necessary to achieve those goals. Only when the organization is clear about where it is going, and the best ways to get there, will it be in a position to identify how volunteers can help achieve the desired goals. In some organizations, there would be no programs or services without volunteers. In others, volunteers are involved primarily with fund raising efforts. Each department and committee can begin to define how volunteers would help achieve their goals by asking:

What could more people with more skills do?

What top-priority objectives are not being met because there are not enough staff to work on these projects?

In the planning process, emphasis must be placed on understanding the details of every process used in the organization's operations. The people who are working on the planning process should be challenged to devise changes that will:

- Get the job done better;
- Get the job done faster;
- Get the job done less expensively;
- Get the job done in ways that are easier and more fun;

• Get the job done in ways that will make the recipient of the job results (the clients and customers) more satisfied.

(b) ASSESS THE COSTS AND BENEFITS OF HAVING VOLUNTEERS

What are the costs associated with having volunteers?

What benefits will the agency derive from utilizing volunteers?

Volunteers will bring both tangible and intangible benefits to the organization. "They also bring with them costs which an organization must be willing to bear if it is to maintain a strong and well qualified volunteer force" (Larkin and Smith, 1988).

The basic costs of bringing volunteers into the operation relate to the logistics of having more staff doing more work. Is there adequate work space? It is common to find nonprofit organizations that want to incorporate volunteers but simply lack sufficient space. What supplies and materials will volunteers need? Are there enough tools and equipment, desks, telephones, and computer terminals to do the job? Increased volunteer activity will also increase general operating expenses such as postage, printing, and telephone bills.

Although it is not paying for salaries, health insurance, vacation time and pension plans for volunteers, the organization needs to provide different kinds of benefits for them. If volunteers are working in the community and traveling on behalf of the agency, it may be necessary to cover their meeting and travel expenses. In most cases, it is helpful to have a policy that provides for reimbursement of volunteer travel and out-of-pocket expenses. Some volunteers will accept this offer; many others will not ask to have their expenses reimbursed. If the agency provides free parking for volunteers, they are reminded, every time they park in the lot, that the organization values and appreciates their efforts and has made it easier and less costly to volunteer. Thus, providing these benefits is a form of volunteer recognition.

From a legal perspective, there are risk considerations for both the volunteers and the agency. If a client is injured while being assisted by a volunteer, both the agency and the volunteer may be sued. There are additional risks: something may happen to volunteers in the course of providing service (Chapman, Lai, and Steinbock, 1984). It is always best to explore these concerns with the agency's insurance agent. The organization's general liability carrier may name volunteers as additional insured staff or it may be necessary to purchase a special volunteer liability policy.

The personnel expenses associated with volunteer participation include salaries and benefits for staff charged with volunteer management. Staff time and materials will be needed to plan and provide volunteer training as well as to conduct training for staff in working with volunteers. Nonprofit leaders must take into consideration the time and expenses that are associated with providing staff support to volunteer committees.

One must also plan to spend funds on volunteer recognition. These expenses will vary greatly, depending on how volunteers are recognized. Publicly acknowledging the contributions of volunteers can range from producing awards to preparing a formal recognition event.

To justify these expenses, one must anticipate a significant return on the investment and numerous benefits to accrue from involving volunteers. It has been well documented that "a person who volunteers is far more likely to be a financial contributor" (Independent Sector, 1987) to the same organization. Moreover, volunteers frequently donate materials to the projects that they are working on, and a significant value can be attached to the unreimbursed expenses incurred and generously donated by volunteers.

Many nonprofit and government employees find increased satisfaction and inspiration in working with volunteers. Improvements in morale are frequently seen as a result of the passion and commitment that enthusiastic volunteers bring to an organization. It is also important to realize that staff leadership and management skills will be enhanced by working with volunteers.

Significant intangible benefits that arise from increased volunteer participation are greater awareness of the organization and new connections that will evolve through volunteer contacts with individuals, agencies, and businesses throughout the community. The organization's image can be greatly enhanced when people speak positively with their friends and colleagues about their volunteer experiences.

Above all, volunteers can help the organization "accomplish its mission and provide services in the most cost-effective and compassionate manner possible" (Larkin and Smith, 1988). Increased volunteer participation will enhance the quality and level of service because more people will be providing more personalized services and expanding the program to serve more clients and customers.

(c) DEVELOP A PLAN FOR VOLUNTEER PARTICIPATION

What are the roles for volunteers?

What skills should volunteers have?

How many volunteers will be needed?

Once the organization decides to involve volunteers, it is essential to develop a plan that outlines the best ways to incorporate these new members of the team. In an effort to determine the needs and opportunities for volunteers, it is necessary to look at past, current, and future projects. If volunteers have been or are currently active, then it is helpful to start by defining the tasks that volunteers have done in the past and the work they are currently doing, to determine the successes and failures associated with those experiences. The next step in developing the volunteer participation plan is to define how volunteers could handle current needs that are not being met. Finally, the organization should identify new opportunities and challenges that could be addressed with the right volunteer assistance.

A great deal of flexibility and creativity is needed in designing roles for volunteers. Given the trend toward fewer long-term and more short-term project volunteers (J. C. Penney and VOLUNTEER, 1987), nonprofit agencies will need to break volunteer jobs down into small, manageable segments, for greater appeal to those people who want to make a limited commitment. Episodic volunteering does not necessarily imply that volunteers will come once and never return. Today's volunteers want to make a limited commitment and continue to have brief assignments that allow them the opportunity to serve as a volunteer as well as attend to their other life commitments. Most short-term project volunteers are willing to continue with repeated short-term efforts if they have a satisfying experience. The current volunteer climate demands that the volunteer participation plan be designed to accommodate short-term project volunteers and not be crippled by expecting overwhelming levels of responsibility from volunteers.

Many nonprofit organizations prepare job descriptions to help clarify volunteer roles. The volunteer job description outlines the job title, the duties and responsibilities, the skills and qualifications needed, and the minimum time commitment that would be acceptable for a particular role. Marlene Wilson (1976) recommended that, for the most responsible volunteer positions, the organization should "define broad areas of responsibility and authority" and "leave room for initiative and creativity" in how those responsibilities are carried out. She went on to explain that volunteers in less responsible, task-oriented positions will need to know "exactly what needs to be done and when."

Volunteer administrators who recruit people for various departments within a large institution often see a carefully crafted job description as an indication that the department staff are prepared to enroll a new volunteer. Job descriptions can serve as a tool for helping to target recruitment efforts and determining whether a prospective volunteer is qualified for a particular job.

To be useful, job descriptions must be written, reviewed, and updated regularly. Unfortunately, updating rarely occurs. Volunteer job descriptions can "turn people off" when they contain a list of overwhelming, rigid expectations. Prospective volunteers may react to this type of job description by feeling that the position cannot accommodate their interests and availability. Nonprofit leaders must realize that written volunteer job descriptions can be helpful to the organization for planning purposes but they seldom benefit the volunteer.

As noted by Tom Peters in his best seller, *Thriving on Chaos* (1987), the problem with job descriptions is that they "cover all the bases and limit the possibilities." Job descriptions confine what one is allowed to do. Peters goes on to say that job descriptions provide a "misleading comfort" that everything is clear and all of the details as to executing the duties and coordination among volunteers and employees are understood. Job descriptions do not tell a person how to do a job. What volunteers need, beyond a general outline of the role, are written standard operating procedures and good job training for the critical tasks they will be asked to perform.

Although it is true that volunteers should know what is expected of them before they accept a position, it is not always as necessary to have a formal job description as it is to have good communications that will lead to clear understandings between the volunteer and the organization. Flexibility is needed in working with people in general and volunteers in particular. Roles, expectations, and time commitments must be negotiated with each volunteer. This points to the importance of the volunteer interview. As a way of clarifying expectations, after the volunteer has signed on, some volunteer leaders draft a letter of understanding, which outlines the agreements made between the volunteer and the organization.

After identifying positions for volunteers, it will be necessary to determine the number of people who have particular skills needed to achieve the organization's goals. Projecting numerical goals for the volunteer participation plan can be difficult because of the varying nature of volunteer time commitments. However, it should be possible to make a reasonable approximation.

If the organization has never involved volunteers, it works well to pick the one program, unit, or department that is most likely to be successful at incorporating volunteers and use that as a model for gradually bringing more volunteers into the organization. It would be a mistake for an agency to plan on a sudden influx of volunteers. As noted by Deming (1986), "people that expect quick results are doomed to disappointment." However, with careful planning and targeted recruitment, volunteers will soon be calling to see how they can participate in the organization's programs.

10.2 PREPARE THE ORGANIZATION FOR VOLUNTEERS

(a) ESTABLISH ORGANIZATION-WIDE SUPPORT FOR VOLUNTEERS

> What type of support is needed for volunteers to be effective?
>
> What type of training will be needed for staff to work effectively with volunteers?

For volunteers to have an impact and to find personal satisfaction in their work, there must be an organization-wide commitment to support volunteers. This starts with the belief that, if given the proper training, volunteers can do many jobs that will help the organization. Volunteers can bring to the organization valuable skills and talents that may not be available among paid staff. Volunteers must be perceived as critical to the success of achieving the agency's mission and program goals.

(i) Board policies regarding volunteers Organizations that expect to rely heavily on volunteers to implement their programs and services should have a board policy statement that reflects the importance of properly incorporating volunteers. A good example comes from the American Red Cross (Larkin and Smith, 1988), which states, "No major initiative will go forward at any level of the organization without an assessment of its implications for volunteers and without appropriate and timely volunteer input." Top level commitment from the board of directors is critical to the long-term success of volunteer and employee team efforts.

(ii) The importance of top management support for volunteers The nonprofit executive must be committed to volunteer participation and must demonstrate this commitment through both words and actions. Top management must explain in meetings, and by other means, why volunteers are necessary and important to the organization and how inviting volunteers into the organization will require support from staff at all levels. In making the case for volunteers, nonprofit leaders need to focus on how volunteers will help the organization achieve its goals.

Paid and volunteer staff at all levels will be significantly influenced by the decisions and behaviors of the organization's leaders. Nonprofit executives must make not only a commitment in principle to establish a volunteer presence but also a personal commitment to work with and support volunteers. As noted by Ellis (1986), too often the executive becomes involved only "if and when something goes wrong." Top leaders must be accessible to have routine contact with volunteers. They must get to know the volunteers, encourage open communication with them, and listen actively to their suggestions.

The lead staff in the organization, whether paid or volunteer, need to create an environment that is welcoming and conducive to bringing people from the outside into the organization. The environment within the organization must encourage openness and cooperation. The agency needs to be an inviting place—a place to which volunteers want to come and where they find respect and appreciation.

The belief in the value of volunteers must permeate the organization. Nonprofit leaders must provide significant resources (time, money, and training) to properly involve volunteers throughout the organization. Comprehensive support for volunteers will enhance their experience and productivity.

Many large national organizations that rely extensively on volunteers at the local level may not have volunteers working at their national headquarters. This represents an inconsistent organizational philosophy. If local staff are expected to work in a volunteer-intensive operation, then the organization should maintain similar standards at the national and regional offices. Leaders of large national organizations must be mindful of the implications these staffing patterns will have in their work with paid and volunteer field staff.

(iii) Training staff to work with volunteers It is most helpful to think about volunteers as integral to the success of the organization rather than in the context of a "volunteer program." Unfortunately, the volunteer program is often perceived as a distinct and separate entity within the organization. Ideally, volunteers should be seen as members of the staff team, and all staff need to think about and plan how they can incorporate volunteers in helping to achieve their goals. All staff must have an appreciation for why the organization wants volunteers, what volunteers can do for the agency, and what the agency can do for the volunteers.

Training in volunteer development needs to be provided for staff at all levels of the organization, from the CEO to the custodian; it cannot stop with supervisors. Secretaries get a lot of information about volunteers over the telephone and they can significantly influence how someone feels about volunteering just by the way they greet and interact with volunteers on a daily basis. All staff must learn to treat volunteers with the same respect that they would accord anyone else associated with the organization. All staff must learn interviewing techniques, to elicit the personal interests and talents of the volunteers who are interested in working in their department. All staff must learn how to train, support, and coach the volunteers who work with them.

Staff members must understand that volunteers can be their peers and colleagues, their supervisors, or their subordinates. People should not feel threatened when a volunteer has greater knowledge and experience on a particular subject. The volunteer is there to help, not to compete for the staff position. It is helpful to treat new volunteers as one would treat a guest in one's home. Volunteers should be welcomed as people who are expected to stay a while, people who will gradually make themselves at home and become part of the nonprofit family.

(b) ESTABLISH VOLUNTEER RECORD KEEPING AND REPORTING SYSTEMS

What kind of records and reports will be needed to keep track of volunteers?

What information will management want and need with regard to volunteers?

(i) Standard components of a volunteer record keeping system The organization will need to establish information systems to keep track of its volunteers. Basic contact information can be maintained manually or on a computer. The level of recordkeeping that is needed beyond contact information will depend on the nature and level of volunteer involvement. In most cases, it is helpful to have new volunteers complete a volunteer profile, to help determine where the individual will fit best within the organization. The volunteer profile can range in complexity and level of detail, depending on the nature of the volunteer work.

Common information requested on a volunteer profile includes:

- Name;
- Current address and telephone number;
- Current and past employment;
- Current and past volunteer experience;

- Education;
- Type of involvement the volunteer is seeking;
- Motivation—why the individual wants to volunteer for this agency;
- Availability—when and how often the individual is available to volunteer;
- Skills, hobbies, and interests;
- Physical limitations;
- Emergency contact information;
- References.

Many of these items can be asked as open-ended questions. Regarding availability and type of involvement, it is usually easier for volunteers if a menu of options or choices is offered on the profile form.

It is helpful to maintain an individual file on each volunteer. The volunteer profile form and other pertinent information can be entered into that file. After the volunteer is placed, the organization should document the type of service performed by that volunteer. In a decentralized setting, volunteers may be asked to report—by telephone, by postcard, or by completing an evaluation form—on progress in their work or to signal when a project is complete. For special-event volunteers, there should be a record of the event in which the volunteer participated, the date of the activity, the role the volunteer filled, and, if relevant, the client(s) served by the volunteer. It usually works best if the responsibility for maintaining volunteer records is centralized within the organization.

It is also important to develop a system for tracking volunteers who leave the organization. An exit interview should be conducted with volunteers whenever possible, to determine the cause of a volunteer's departure and elicit suggestions about how his or her experience could have been enhanced. Nonprofits seldom learn of their volunteers' dissatisfaction. Like dissatisfied customers who do not return to a particular store, volunteers usually will not complain; they just do not return. If the organization is losing volunteers, it needs to understand why. One of the purposes of maintaining volunteer records is to signal trends in the level and nature of volunteer participation, which are useful for policy making and strategic planning. The volunteer leader should keep records of volunteer retention and make changes that will correct negative trends in the levels of volunteer involvement and satisfaction. Tracking the reasons why a volunteer stops participating may often shed light on organizational problems. As the competition for volunteers increases, the need to recognize and correct organizational weaknesses becomes critical.

Several computerized volunteer record keeping systems and volunteer/client matching programs are available on the market, and many custom-made programs have been developed using a data base program. Before selecting a software package, the organization should determine what its tracking needs are and the kind of reports that will be useful. It is helpful to check with colleagues to find out what problems or satisfactory results they have had with various computer software programs. It is expensive to reinvent the wheel.

(ii) Preparing management reports that measure the impact of volunteer participation
Successful volunteer participation cannot be measured by volunteer numbers alone. Too often, nonprofit organizations proudly count the number of volunteers who have passed through their system, with no serious regard for the impact these volunteers have had on helping the organization achieve its goals. Nonprofit organizations need to

eliminate volunteer management by numerical goals, get past counting hours and heads, and focus on the more significant measures of volunteer involvement. More attention has to be paid to the quality of the volunteer service. In shifting the emphasis away from quantity and moving to a concern for quality (Deming, 1986), volunteer leaders will be able to measure the true impact that volunteer participation is having on both the individual volunteers and the organizations they are serving. The following guidelines will be helpful:

What notable and measurable impacts have resulted from volunteer participation?

How satisfied are clients and customers with the services received from volunteers?

Are volunteer recruitment efforts more effective?

What are volunteers getting out of their experience?

Has volunteer satisfaction increased?

Has the performance of volunteers improved?

Is the organization more productive?

Many programs that match volunteers in providing direct, one-to-one service with clients, such as youth/adult companions or mentors, friendly visitors to the elderly, literacy tutors, and professionals providing technical assistance to nonprofit agencies, count a volunteer when he or she is "matched" with a client. The urge to be able to document success encourages this type of premature counting. There is no question that a lot of work goes into preparing a "match." But many matches are not successful for any number of reasons, ranging from poor chemistry to the volunteer's not being qualified or trained to handle the assigned duties. The number of clients satisfactorily *served* by volunteers (not just matched with volunteers) accurately reflects the organization's success with the mission. The goal in preparing and representing volunteer reports should be to document the successful accomplishment of the mission. It may be helpful to track the number of matches versus the number of successful matches each year, to quantitatively measure the organization's progress.

Although there is a basic need to maintain records to keep track of volunteers, there are also evaluation benefits to recordkeeping, and these can be much more important. Nonprofit managers and board members do not want or need to be burdened with excessive information. For the most part, nonprofit leaders should look for data that demonstrate improvements in the quality of services as a result of volunteer involvement. The opening line of a volunteer management report could read: "As a result of volunteer efforts, we can proudly report . . .". Top management and board leaders should evaluate the data that they currently receive, and redefine what volunteer-related information would be most meaningful and useful. The most important data are those that measure the quality of the service described by the mission.

(c) INSTITUTE CHANGES THAT WILL OPEN DOORS TO A WIDER RANGE OF VOLUNTEERS

How can the organization adapt and modify its practices to accommodate more volunteers?

Nonprofit organizations must create new opportunities for volunteers and seriously address the need to diversify the volunteer work force. It is not wise or practical to settle for the status quo and passively acknowledge that the profile of the volunteer sector is changing. There is too much competition for the precious time and talents of volunteers; nonprofit groups cannot ignore the need to make adjustments that will appeal to new volunteers.

Volunteer organizations need to recognize that they function in a multicultural world. If they are to meet their client and customer needs, they must engage a multicultural volunteer work force. This takes decisive action, targeted recruitment efforts, and conscious decisions on the part of top management to open the doors and expand volunteer opportunities to include new audiences. This may require sensitivity and cultural awareness training for current staff. However, enhanced cultural awareness is often best achieved when people have the opportunity to work together and get to know each other. Much respect can be gained and many barriers overcome when a cross-cultural mix of people has the opportunity to volunteer together and share a common experience.

It is also important to increase the agency's accessibility for disabled volunteers. Lack of ramps and elevators precludes some physically disabled people from sharing their talents as volunteers. A tape recorder is often all that is needed to enhance communication so that a blind or visually impaired person can become a volunteer. A nonprofit leader who establishes a climate of acceptance will find roles and opportunities for all kinds of volunteers. All it takes is the ability to identify an individual's strength, a bit of sensitivity, and personal attention to find the right spot for someone who is emotionally distressed or an individual who is mentally retarded. The emphasis should always be on the individual's ability, not his or her disability.

For some time now, it has been difficult for nonprofit agencies to find weekday (9:00 to 5:00, Monday through Friday) volunteers. These rare birds still exist and provide great strength and stability to many well-established nonprofit organizations, but they are gradually becoming extinct in the volunteer world. One reason for this, as noted by Ellis (1985), is that many agencies have not successfully approached the vast talent pool of prospective daytime volunteers—shift workers, weekend workers, and people who work on a contractual basis with flexible schedules. In addition to recruiting people who have nontraditional work hours, nonprofit organizations can extend their operating hours to include evenings and weekends. This will open the door to a whole new wave of working volunteers. In order to meet with evening and weekend volunteers, it may be necessary for the volunteer leader to establish a staggered work schedule. Creative nonprofit managers will also identify work that volunteers can do in their homes.

Volunteer diversity demands a climate of openness and inclusiveness. Nonprofit leaders need to consciously and conscientiously plan how they can make adjustments to accommodate the needs and interests of a wider range of volunteers.

10.3 DEVELOP A STRONG AND DIVERSE VOLUNTEER WORK FORCE

(a) RECRUITMENT

Is the organization recruiting volunteers from the total available population?

How can the organization find the volunteers it needs?

Often, what is perceived as a recruitment problem is actually an organizational problem relating to the agency's volunteer culture. The next time someone cries "We need more volunteers," instead of instantly identifying all the tried and true ideas for recruiting volunteers, that person should be asked what current barriers prohibit people from volunteering for this organization. Who might volunteer if the organization presented new volunteer opportunities or if there were modifications to existing roles? Is the organization too inbred? Instead of discussing recruitment techniques, what adjustments can this organization make in order to attract new volunteers? Volunteer recruitment will be much easier once the organization is prepared to accommodate new people in new ways.

(i) Recruiting specific target audiences Targeted volunteer recruitment involves determining the type of volunteer needed and then selectively marketing to qualified prospects. Some key questions for a targeted volunteer recruitment campaign are:

1. Based on the work that needs to be done, what qualities and skills are we looking for in volunteers?
2. Where can we find these people?
3. What is the best method for reaching out to the target audience?
4. What would motivate them to volunteer?

Targeted recruitment is aimed at specific segments of the community instead of the community at large. Target audiences might include homebound people, disabled people, retirees, minorities, religious groups, civic groups, students, or professionals.

If the organization knows that it wants young people helping, then people at the schools should be approached. There is always a heightened awareness of social issues on college campuses, and students are often looking for something to do off-campus. Moreover, many high schools and colleges require students to do a certain amount of community service work for school credits. The organization must be prepared to complete additional paperwork, such as references and evaluations, for students seeking credit for their volunteer work. In planning recruitment efforts for youth, it is important to consider what jobs would be most appropriate for high school or college students and to adapt work schedules to accommodate a student's schedules. Methods for reaching out to students include: disseminating recruitment materials on campus, placing ads in the college newspaper, having college volunteers talk about their experiences on the college radio station, and involving students in promoting volunteer opportunities to others at school assemblies. There also may be opportunities for younger students to help or for families with young children to share a volunteer experience together.

As their numbers grow, retirees become an increasingly rich source of volunteers who have wonderful skills and experience to share. Like students, retirees often have the time, the resources, or the need to be needed. As with any targeted market, it is helpful to involve current retired volunteers in planning how to reach out to their peers. Recruitment materials must present older people as vital, healthy, and active. These materials should be distributed in areas known to attract older people. In-person recruiting of older volunteers can be done through groups such as the American Association of Retired Persons or at retirement communities. Whenever possible, an organization should pass the word about volunteer opportunities at corporate preretirement planning sessions or ask a company to put a notice in mailings that are sent to retirees.

If an organization needs technically skilled volunteers, the appropriate professional association can be approached. Recruiters should not be afraid to ask professionals for their assistance, whether in public relations, accounting, law, architecture, engineering, or any other profession. A general appeal for volunteers would be wasteful of everyone's time and effort when it is known that specialized skills are required. Many professional associations have a community service arm that actively seeks to involve their members in volunteer service.

Recruitment aimed at increasing the number of minority volunteers will require enhanced publicity and outreach in the targeted minority community. Minority persons must be well represented in helping roles in marketing materials. The organization should meet with leaders in the targeted minority community, nominate members of the minority community to board and committee positions, and actively deliver services in the targeted community. If agency brochures are translated into different languages to attract minority volunteers, it will be necessary to have multilingual staff members available to respond to the people who call in for further information about volunteering.

In planning volunteer recruitment efforts, it is extremely important to remember that "the largest single reason people volunteer is because someone asks them" (Independent Sector, 1987). Posters, brochures, and print ads will all increase awareness of volunteer needs but it usually takes the personal touch of an agency representative to directly ask someone to become a volunteer. Direct appeals to prospective volunteers also work well because, in a personal meeting, recruiters are in a position to tailor their appeal to the personal needs and motivations of the individual.

It usually works best if the primary responsibility for recruitment belongs to the people who are in need of the volunteers. Leaders in the organization should work with these people and encourage them to consider the advantages that will accrue when they recruit volunteers from a broader and more diverse population.

(ii) Recruiting large numbers of volunteers   When the organization is planning a project that will require a large number of volunteers, it is more appropriate to make a general appeal to the public. These are the times when the organization may send out an open invitation and call for help. "We need volunteers. We need you." "Can you drive a car? We need your help." Although many studies have clearly documented that most volunteers are not recruited through the media (Hodgkinson and Lyman, 1989), short-term large-scale events do lend themselves well to mass media appeals for volunteers.

Even a call for large numbers of people will benefit from a campaign that is at least somewhat targeted.

Who are the people most likely to care about this cause?

Who are the people best suited to provide the help that is needed?

These and similar questions will target recruitment efforts more effectively. It is helpful to target large groups of potential volunteers through churches, synagogues, sororities, fraternities, corporate volunteer programs, scout clubs, and service clubs. It is also extremely valuable to utilize the resources and contacts that can be found through the local volunteer center.

(b) SCREENING AND PLACEMENT

How will the organization screen prospective volunteers?

How will the organization determine the best place for each new volunteer?

(i) Determining an individual's suitability, strengths, and interests Once individuals start responding to the organization's appeals for volunteers, someone will need to screen these people to determine who can help and in what ways. Screening is probably the most critical step in bringing volunteers into an operation. The interviewer needs to assess the individual's skills, interests, and abilities. Plenty of time needs to be devoted to each new individual to determine what he or she can offer and how his or her skills and experience can be utilized within the context of a particular organization.

This is also the best opportunity to skillfully ask questions and carefully listen to the answers, which will elicit the individual's personal motivation for choosing to volunteer for a given assignment. Time is needed, to understand the prospective volunteer's needs, interests, and motivations. A guide for using this information to match the volunteer's needs with the agency's opportunities is shown in Exhibit 10.1. An organization that is using volunteers benefits the volunteer as well as the recipient of the services being rendered. The benefits derived by volunteers cannot be underestimated.

The interview sets the tone, style, and pace of the volunteer's experience with the organization. If extra time is taken to get to know the individual, it tells the volunteer that he or she is important. If the volunteer is quickly passed over and told "We need you to help right away with a project that is going on in the next room," it can lead to the loss of a potentially good volunteer.

Exhibit 10.1. Volunteer placements that meet personal needs.

Volunteer's Motivation/Need	Recommended Placement/Position
Power and control	Interacting with people in authority or being in charge of a project
Personal relationships	Interacting frequently with other staff or the public
Public recognition and visibility	Representing the organization to the public at community events, or conducting speaking engagements
Accomplishments and achievements	Having responsibility for leading a team project or an opportunity to work independently
Creativity	Trying new things, starting a new program, taking risks
Security and stability	Working regularly on similar work assignments
Growth and development	Learning new skills and progressively taking on more difficult tasks
Fun	Interacting with others in a lively, exciting, fast-paced setting

Note: A proper placement that builds on the individual's personal motivations is a form of private volunteer recognition.

Depending on the nature of the volunteer position, the interviewer may be required to check references. Volunteers who serve in positions dealing with children may also be required to have a police check.

When an interviewer determines that the individual is not suited to volunteer for a particular position, the volunteer should be tactfully pointed in another direction. It is best to refer that individual to another volunteer group or to the local volunteer center, so that the person's interest in becoming a volunteer is not destroyed.

(ii) Matching individual abilities and preferences with agency needs The trick here is to find the right place for each person. For this symbiotic relationship to work best, care must be taken so that the volunteer's skills and personality mesh well with the job assignment. In a detailed discussion, the expectations of both the volunteer and the organization should be clarified.

Scheduling can be a problem, when trying to match the organization's needs with the availability of volunteers. However, it is usually possible to accommodate diverse schedules through a process of negotiation and a willingness to make adjustments. Volunteers who are placed in long-term assignments are likely to require ongoing negotiations because the needs and interests of both the individual and the organization will change over time.

Most volunteers who do not do well on their jobs have simply been misplaced. A common problem among volunteers is underplacement: giving someone an assignment that presents little or no challenge. On the other hand, if someone is incapable of doing a job, the volunteer manager has an obligation to try to find a more appropriate placement or for that person. It is important to follow up with each new volunteer within the first few weeks, to determine whether he or she is satisfied and feels properly placed in the assignment. Management must take responsibility for an improper volunteer placement because it is usually the result of ineffective interviewing techniques (Pearson, 1986). Volunteer leaders should keep track of misplacements because they may reveal that some staff members do not work well with volunteers.

(c) ORIENTATION AND TRAINING

How will the organization orient new volunteers?

How will volunteers be trained to do their job?

(i) Orienting new volunteers to the organization and to the program New volunteers need to develop a thorough understanding of the organization and the program in which they will be working. Examples of content matter to be covered in an orientation program are given in Exhibit 10.2. Orientation meetings should be as interactive as possible. Too often, volunteers are overloaded with factual information they will not remember. It is important that volunteers feel free to ask questions throughout the orientation, to break up the monotony of the factual presentations. Asking volunteers to explain what they understand about the client populations and the services that the organization provides can help to give volunteers an active role in the orientation meeting and to illuminate common misunderstandings and false assumptions about the program.

Many organizations provide regular volunteer orientation programs but some find it difficult to attract new volunteers to orientation sessions because of logistical

Exhibit 10.2.   Agenda for a generic volunteer orientation session.

Orientation should offer volunteers an overview of the organization. Whether in a formal group meeting or an informal individual discussion, nonprofit organizations need to present the following information to new volunteers:

1. History
2. Mission/Purpose
3. Goals and objectives
4. Client populations
5. Current programs and services
6. Future plans
7. Organizational structure:
    Major departments
    Relationships with other organizations
8. Policies and procedures:
    Example: Confidentiality with regard to client information
9. Benefits for volunteers:
    Training
    Expense reimbursements
10. Practical details:
    Where is the bathroom?
    Where do volunteers hang their coats or leave a briefcase or handbag?
    Where is the best place to park a car?
11. Tour of facility
12. Introductions to people with whom the volunteers will work

problems and the time commitments involved in getting people to attend these meetings. These organizations can combine the volunteer orientation with the initial interview and on-the-job training. This practice is acceptable, provided there are future opportunities for continuing education and training.

To supplement the in-person presentation, and for purposes of future reference, the new volunteers will need written materials that present basic facts about the organization. However, it is recommended that written information never substitute for direct communication with new volunteers. The agency must also be careful not to dump too much information on new volunteers all at once. Orientation and training should be gradual and ongoing processes.

Video tapes can be used to present background information on the organization in an exciting, lively, and visible manner; however, if not done well, videos can be deadly. Videos are helpful because, even if volunteers do not attend an orientation session, they can borrow the tape and watch it on a video player at home. A disadvantage is that videos provide no opportunity for interaction. They should never be considered a substitute for direct communication with volunteers.

A tour of the facility will make the program and operations come alive for volunteers. Too many volunteers and board members serve their organizations for years, before ever getting a tour of the facility. Providing a tour when volunteers are new gives them a greater appreciation for the organization's resources and a broader understanding of what is going on in the program. Tours should be conducted by knowledgeable and enthusiastic people—preferably veteran volunteers.

(ii) Training volunteers to do their job   Training is different from orientation in that it emphasizes what a volunteer needs to know for a particular assignment. Many volunteers get inadequate or improper training, which means that they frequently do not know when they have done their job correctly. As Deming (1986) pointed out, "It is very difficult to erase improper training."

When new volunteers join the organization, they should be provided with training that will develop or enhance the knowledge, skills, and attitudes that they need to do their job. Volunteers who will have direct contact with clients may need training that is designed to make them more aware of clients' needs and to elicit the attitudes and behaviors that are desired in working with a particular client group. Volunteers need proper training if the organization is going to count on them to identify problems, prevent problems, and offer constructive recommendations related to the work that they do.

In planning and designing volunteer training, it is always helpful to ask experienced volunteers to offer advice on how best to train new volunteers for a particular position. This can usually be accomplished through a combination of direct conversations with individuals, surveys, and focus group meetings with the experienced volunteers.

Unfortunately, because of the flexible nature of volunteer commitments, scheduling training sessions for volunteers and getting people to attend can be problems. In some cases, volunteer training is mandatory. In those situations where it is optional, it is necessary to make it clear how volunteers will benefit from the training and to make sure that it is a fun experience.

Standard operating procedures   In many situations, particularly those such as in emergency health care, travelers' aid, and crime victim assistance, written standard operating procedures must be available to the volunteer. Procedures are critical and cannot be left to chance. If left unwritten, they will drift as the truth drifts when playing Whisper Down the Lane. Volunteers in sensitive positions must have written instructions; they might even be asked to complete a checklist, to confirm that each critical step has been followed. This discipline can be beneficial because it forces the person to really examine each step in the process to which he or she is assigned and, often, to think of how a step might be eliminated or done better. Standard operating procedures should be living documents that will change as improvements are discovered. The constant review and evaluation of each step in a process will result in continuous improvement that is gratifying to the volunteer and beneficial to the organization and the recipients of its services.

Flowcharts that graphically demonstrate the chain of events can be extremely valuable in planning how to execute a special event. A volunteer who is filing would benefit from a written guide outlining the organization's filing system. A volunteer who will be driving people to medical appointments will need guidelines on the following points:

- Must seat belts be worn?
- Can the driver smoke?
- Should the driver play the radio?
- Should the driver take more than one person if someone has a contagious disease?
- What should the driver talk about to someone who is suffering from a terminal illness?

As these examples indicate, manuals, guidelines, and task descriptions will all serve to help train volunteers and will be useful as future reference tools.

Preservice training   Some nonprofit organizations require many hours of training before volunteers are allowed to serve clients. This is common for hotline volunteers who deal with people in crisis, or literacy tutors who need to learn how to teach an illiterate adult how to read. Preservice training ensures that all new volunteers have a common base of knowledge and skills to handle the job that they have agreed to do. Usually, during the preservice training, the organization will review standard operating procedures with the new volunteers. Whenever possible, it is helpful to build in client contact gradually, throughout the course of preservice training, by allowing new volunteers to shadow experienced volunteers.

On-the-job training   On-the-job training starts when someone explains the purpose and goals of the work unit. In addition to providing volunteers with the knowledge and skills that they need to carry out their work, volunteers must understand how their role or task fits into the overall picture.

Nonprofit leaders can train and coach volunteers on the job by demonstrating the work that needs to be done and the skills that need to be learned. The manager should also observe volunteers performing the task and provide feedback so that volunteers will know what they did well and how to improve further. An effective manager will use a volunteer's mistake as an opportunity for personal development. The supervisor should also make sure that volunteers have the tools and information necessary to do the job, that they have easy access to the standard operating procedures related to their job, and that they have opportunities to ask questions comfortably.

Continuing education   Programs should be in place to provide opportunities for continuing education and retraining, in order to constantly upgrade the skills necessary for volunteers to do their jobs better. This represents an investment in volunteers. Continuing education informs volunteers and helps them to improve the work they do on behalf of the agency. In-service training also serves as a motivating force for those people who wish to develop their skills through their volunteer work. It is one thing for an organization to have volunteers and it is an altogether different commitment for the organization to *develop* its volunteers. Volunteer development means making a commitment to help volunteers grow and learn with the organization by making sure that volunteers have the skills and training necessary to do their jobs. Nonprofit organizations will find constant improvement through constant education of their paid and volunteer staff.

Special event training   When volunteers will be working on a special event, it usually works best to conduct their training on the day of the event. The coordinator should build time into the day to provide for a general orientation and job training. For some events, it is possible to hold a preservice training session. However, it is often difficult to get project volunteers to attend the training if it means an extra time commitment on their part. Moreover, the lack of immediacy can dilute the impact of the training. It is critical that standard operating procedures be outlined in a very clear and concise manner for all special-event volunteers.

(d) PROVIDING SUPPORT AND LEADERSHIP FOR VOLUNTEERS

What kind of support is needed from the direct supervisor or team leader?

What is the role of the volunteer manager/leader?

(i) Role of the direct supervisor or team leader   The job of the nonprofit manager is to develop a strategic plan and lead the paid and volunteer staff through the successful execution of that plan in ways that provide job satisfaction, pride, success, and fun. It must be remembered that "people seek leadership, not management" (Zenger, 1985).

The direct supervisor must spend time with every volunteer, to properly understand individual needs. In this way, the supervisor will know what motivational buttons to push to inspire an individual to become more productive and to make him or her feel more a part of the team. People who are doing poorly will require individual help. An individual's need for support should be identified and addressed in a manner that is consistent with the nature and level of the volunteer's involvement with the organization. Most managers do not need a sophisticated performance evaluation system to identify a problem person, whether it is a paid or volunteer staff member. The manager does need to talk to and work with that person to determine whether he or she is misplaced or in need of special training.

Nonprofit leaders should be giving and getting feedback from volunteers on a regular basis. Frequent communication is beneficial in all instances, but it is particularly important with new volunteers or with volunteers assigned to a new task. The team leader can help volunteers do their job right by providing individual performance feedback that is timely and constructive.

Volunteers should be encouraged to ask for additional instruction when needed, to call attention to potential problems, and to report faulty equipment. Volunteers will have valuable suggestions for improving whatever work they are doing and they should be encouraged to solve problems. However, it will not work to simply listen to volunteers describe the obstacles to their success if the manager is not prepared to respond. The team leader should discuss suggestions with volunteers and, whenever possible, act on those suggestions (Harrington, 1987). This dialogue will help the organization achieve its mission and will, at the same time, make volunteers feel good about being there.

Managers often blame individuals for problems that are a result of structural faults within the system. Deming (1986) noted that a high percentage of organizational problems are usually within the system and not with the workers. It is vital that managers learn to identify and separate the system problems from the people problems. Volunteers can be held responsible only for that which they can control. Any violation of this principle will lead to frustrations, dissatisfaction with the job, and poor performance.

The nonprofit leader has a responsibility to improve organizational systems and to make it possible for everybody to do a better job with greater satisfaction (Deming, 1986). This means removing potential barriers to open and honest communication and providing the tools that are necessary to complete a job. It is the responsibility of management to discover and remove barriers that prevent volunteers from taking pride in their work. Volunteers can often tell the supervisor exactly what those barriers are, if they are encouraged to do so. Deming (1986) explained: "The aim of leadership is not merely to find and record the failures of men, but to remove the causes of failure; to help people do a better job with less effort."

Some nonprofit organizations have performance review systems by which everyone, paid and volunteer staff, receives a rating from his or her supervisor each year. As noted by Deming (1986), the effect of these reviews can be devastating. They can nurture short-term performance, build fear, and demolish teamwork. During these reviews, too much emphasis is placed on the negatives that people can do little to change, which leaves people feeling bitter and bruised. The performance of any individual is the result of a combination of many forces—the individual, the people with whom he or she works, the job, the tools, the clients and customers, the management, and the supervision. Reviews are often unfair because many of theses factors are beyond the control of the individual being evaluated, yet they have a tremendous influence on the evaluator's judgment.

Volunteers do not need performance evaluations as much as they need an opportunity to sit down with their team leaders and express the satisfactions and dissatisfactions they have encountered in their volunteer experience. The team leader should meet with every long-term volunteer at least once a year—not for criticism, but for help and understanding on the part of both the volunteer and the team leader. Volunteers may want to discuss the need for changes in their schedule, offer observations or recommendations about the way their work is being handled, discuss problems being encountered with other staff, or request a more (or less) responsible assignment. As things change with volunteers, the organization needs to be able to accommodate these changes or will risk losing good people.

The time spent on volunteer performance reviews would be spent more productively on detailed reviews of systems or processes used in pursuit of the organization's mission. When focus is placed on the jobs to be done rather than on the individual, there is less fear, more opportunity for constructive participation, and improved teamwork.

There is a real need for people to "know where they stand." This is best accomplished by immediate recognition for good work and immediate correction of work done poorly. Wherever possible, emphasis should be placed on evaluating the progress of the team rather than the performance of the individual. This does not diminish the importance of the individual volunteer; if anything, it will put more pressure on the individual to perform well because the entire group is watching and is dependent on him or her for success.

(ii) Delegating authority along with responsibility to volunteers   Volunteers need to be given the opportunity to do the job they have been asked to do, and to be able to do it to the best of their ability; to be given a chance to make choices and decisions; and to be trusted. Volunteers are not less competent than their paid staff counterparts and, in many cases, they bring new skills and experience to the job. If volunteers are asked to plan a special event, they should be allowed to suggest and follow up on making the necessary arrangements. If volunteers are preparing food for home-delivered meals, the volunteer leaders should participate in deciding what food will be served and how it will be prepared and packaged within any prescribed guidelines for health and nutrition purposes. Volunteers should be encouraged to feel the sense of ownership and responsibility that will result in greater commitment to the organization.

New volunteers need to be given increased responsibility gradually, so as not to overwhelm them. Initially, some volunteers may be reluctant to make decisions and offer suggestions, but that will change when they see that they are trusted and respected. There is always a danger—and often a tendency—to "burn out" good volunteers by relying on them too much. The organization should be careful not to push volunteers beyond what they are willing to give.

Too often, volunteers are limited in their authority to proceed in handling a problem and must check with paid staff for direction. Volunteers need to be empowered to resolve problems that arise in the course of doing their job, and they need to have the authority to take corrective actions. Nonprofit leaders must trust volunteers and be willing to share with volunteers their power as well as their responsibilities. Volunteers need to understand their levels of responsibility and authority, if they are to be held accountable for their actions. With the proper training and support and the opportunity to use their knowledge and skills, volunteers will prove themselves to be highly valuable members of the nonprofit team.

(iii) Responsibilities of the volunteer manager/leader   A successful volunteer manager/ leader needs to represent the interests of volunteers to others and to be an advocate for the full representation of volunteers throughout the organization. The volunteer administrator needs to "make sure that volunteers are involved in planning, problem-solving and decision-making" (Schindler-Rainman, 1989). The volunteer leader has the primary responsibility to see that the organization is making adjustments to involve a wider variety of volunteers. If volunteers are to be successfully incorporated into the organization's operations, the volunteer leader must actively demonstrate his or her belief in the full and creative potential of volunteer involvement by encouraging volunteers to work in the volunteer department.

In meetings with volunteers, the volunteer manager will hear people voice their frustrations at not being able to perform the job they would like to do. Volunteers often complain that they do not know what is expected of them from one day to the next and they are seldom given feedback on their work. Some volunteers will reveal that they never really learned to do their job. The volunteer manager will hear many complaints about supervisors and about equipment that needs to be repaired or replaced. Volunteers may feel powerless to change things. The volunteer leader should view these problems as opportunities to empower volunteers and to educate staff about how to work effectively with volunteers.

The volunteer leader has a critical role in dealing with both internal and external customers. The volunteer management team will not be effective if it focuses only on internal customers—the volunteers themselves and the staff who work with volunteers. An important role for the volunteer leader is to talk with the organization's clients. In developing a questionnaire for interviewing the people being served, questions might include: How do you rate the service this organization is providing? Do you feel the volunteers are trained well to provide you with the needed service? Are you treated with respect? What problems have you observed? Would you speak favorably about this organization to your friends and colleagues? The responses received should be tracked and used to address structural changes. This information will serve as a measure of success in dealing with the most important customers—the clients the organization is committed to serve.

(e) BUILDING EMPLOYEE/VOLUNTEER TEAMS

How can the organization build a sense of team spirit among employees and volunteers?

Why is interdepartmental cooperation so important?

(i) Developing a sense of team spirit by working toward common goals For volunteers and employees to work together successfully as a team, volunteers need to be seen as equal partners in the nonprofit system. Nonprofit leaders can support cooperative team behavior by involving the entire volunteer/employee team in planning, decision making, and problem solving, and by reinforcing successful group performance. Each department, unit, or committee needs to identify the most important contribution its team can make. The process of developing common goals will encourage commitment to achieving the organization's mission. "Much of the volunteer's sustaining and renewing motivation comes from seeing clear steps toward the group's goals and from successfully completing them one by one" (Schindler-Rainman, 1989). In a successful organization, team spirit is developed best by getting the job done and doing it well.

Team leaders should institute regular (monthly or quarterly) review meetings to evaluate progress on the jobs that need to get done, discuss whether goals are being met, and examine how the work might be improved. The group should ask itself the following questions:

Based on what we set out to do, what new problems and opportunities have developed that were not anticipated?

How can we exploit the opportunities?

How should be modify our course in order to get where we want to be?

Team review meetings will provide an opportunity for paid and volunteer staff to share information and ask each other questions. In order to get everyone's input, volunteers and employees need to feel that they can speak openly, and no one should be allowed to use these meetings for grandstanding. When the team meets to report on progress and problems, each volunteer and paid staff member should report on what he or she is doing to achieve the group's goals. Volunteers will feel that they are part of the team if they are encouraged to express concerns that impact their efforts in reaching the team goals. Combining the good ideas generated by both paid and volunteer staff will bring about the best possible solutions (Harrington, 1987) and will do much to improve team spirit. The nonprofit leader can use common goals to promote and reward effective teamwork.

Someone should briefly record the analyses and recommendations that are discussed in these review meetings. The team leader should also keep records that assess services being delivered so that the group can use this information to make continuous improvement in the structure and operations of their unit.

Some volunteers will not want to work with a team and do not work well with other individuals, but they may demonstrate exceptional achievements. The volunteer leader must identify these people and determine the best positions for them. Although they do their work independently, perhaps at home, these volunteers are still members of the larger team and, at appropriate times, should be given recognition.

One obstacle to incorporating volunteers into project teams relates to problems associated with time. Gretchen Stringer (1985) has pointed out that paid and volunteer staff "generally operate with different perceptions of time." A 20-hour project can be completed in a matter of days by a full-time paid staff member, but, depending on an individual's schedule, that same project could take weeks for a volunteer to complete. Perceiving time as a barrier will often lead paid staff to the conclusion that "I'd rather do it myself." However, with proper planning, this hurdle can easily be overcome and volunteers can become valuable members of the nonprofit team.

(ii) Interdepartmental cooperation   Nonprofit managers must coordinate the relationships among various departments within the organization to achieve optimal performance. It is essential that nonprofit leaders break down the barriers among departments so that people in development, finance, marketing, and direct service are all working together to anticipate, identify, and resolve problems that interfere with successful accomplishment of the overall mission.

Interdepartmental cooperation is needed to improve the quality of services to clients and to reduce costs. For a quality home-delivered meal to be received "on time," all of the following tasks must occur properly:

- Record intake information on client who is to receive meal;
- Order the food;
- Deliver the food;
- Ensure that refrigeration and cooking equipment are all in good repair;
- Contact volunteers to be ready when needed to prepare food;
- Give instructions to cooks and volunteers packaging food;
- Cook the meals and package them for distribution;
- Deliver the meals to homebound residents.

This simple example demonstrates how many interdependent tasks are associated with a common volunteer assignment. Each team of volunteers and employees must meet its time schedule if a high-quality, nutritious meal is to reach the homebound client within the specified time frame.

The example of the "on-time home-delivered meal" demonstrates the necessity of communication and cooperation across departmental lines and functions. Much of the work that volunteers are asked to do will cut across departmental lines. Volunteers and employees from the client intake unit, kitchen staff, case managers, purchasing department, maintenance personnel, and drivers must all work cooperatively with each other to continually improve the home-delivered meal system. This can be done by forming a project team that will include members from all the disciplines that are needed to get the job done. Successful project teams do much to break down the artificial barriers created by functional department delineations.

(f) RECOGNITION

Should volunteer recognition be private or public?

How can the organization reward individual and team efforts?

What kind of rewards should be given to volunteers?

(i) Private and public forms of volunteer recognition   "There needs to be substantial recognition for fairly mundane actions as well as for truly exceptional performance" (Peters, 1987). Too often, the private part of volunteer recognition is forgotten. It is important for nonprofit staff to remember the little things that will have a significant impact on volunteers. Big rewards for big efforts are a must, but numerous rewards for small acts are equally—if not more—important. Peer recognition is important, and celebration of small successes should become commonplace.

Recognition starts with informal reminders that volunteers are accepted as contributing members of the nonprofit team. Nonprofit leaders need to offer private recognition to volunteers on a regular basis. When a job is done well, the individual should be acknowledged immediately: "You did a great job." An appropriate "Thank you" will probably mean more to a volunteer than attending the annual recognition luncheon. Above all, volunteer recognition needs to be sincere, honest, and timely. Nothing does more damage than a phony pat on the back. Recognition must be genuine.

In some agencies, staff are badly overextended and appear too busy running programs to make time for recognition. If the organization does not have time for volunteer appreciation, it has no business involving volunteers in providing services. An organization that has asked private citizens to set aside time to serve their clients must acknowledge the value of these efforts by dedicating time to show appreciation to the volunteers. Acknowledging a volunteer's special efforts one month after the fact is often too late to have an impact. During the intervening weeks, a volunteer may have built up resentment that his or her contribution was not appreciated. Volunteers will remember when they are not properly thanked.

As eloquently stated by Larkin and Smith (1988), "Recognition is respect made visible." When publicly recognizing a volunteer, timing is less critical but it should not be too far removed from the individual's or team's accomplishment. An award ceremony should bring out pride and provide a good time for all. Beyond the motivational influence of those being recognized, this is also an opportunity to "parade and reinforce the kinds of behavior that the organization hopes others will emulate." (Peters, 1987). An organization should celebrate what it wants to see more of by showcasing individuals and groups that represent the foundation of the organization's success.

It is important to evaluate the annual recognition event by asking people to critique the procedures for picking volunteers who are recognized, asking volunteers how they felt about the food and the speakers, and carefully considering these comments in planning for the next annual event. What kind of recognition will have the most impact and be most memorable for volunteers?

Many nonprofit organizations make a point of offering public recognition for volunteers during National Volunteer Week, which is usually the third week in April. This is often a good way to get additional newspaper or television coverage. Public recognition will also demonstrate to the community at large that volunteers are important to the organization.

(ii) Rewarding individual and team efforts Timely recognition is critically important for both individual and group efforts. Individuals should be recognized immediately for their special contributions and accomplishments. The agency should recognize the importance of a volunteer's job as well as the quality of his or her performance. To have the greatest level of personal impact, whenever possible, recognition should take into consideration the motivations that an individual has for volunteering.

The most common forms of volunteer recognition are events, certificates, and letters of appreciation. A great deal of volunteer recognition involves rewards for length of volunteer service. This has its place, but much greater emphasis on recognition teamwork among volunteers and paid staff is needed. If the organization is trying to build team spirit, then most of the awards should go to teams of people rather than individuals. The committee, group, team, or department should be recognized when they reach a landmark. If a team completes a project successfully or a committee produces a wonderful fund raising event, it is time for the organization to celebrate and show its appreciation.

Everyone in the unit, whether volunteer or paid staff, who has worked to achieve a common goal should receive recognition. Paid staff also appreciate, need, and benefit from recognition beyond a salary. Too often, public volunteer recognition ceremonies only acknowledge volunteer contributions, to the obvious exclusion of the paid staff who have been an integral part of volunteer successes. This does not make for good team spirit. Broad-based volunteer recognition should encompass all levels of the organization, and rewards should be innovative. Some suggestions are given in Exhibit 10.3.

Business leaders stand to learn a great deal about motivation and recognition from those nonprofit leaders who have found ways to reward volunteers in meaningful ways that transcend the usual dependence on money. In both the nonprofit and business sectors, it is important to reward individuals and groups for improving systems, programs, or services, and for achieving results that significantly contribute to realizing the organization's mission.

Exhibit 10.3. Suggested methods of volunteer recognition.

	For the Individual	For the Team
Private:		
When	• Immediately following a significant contribution	• In the course of working on a project
How	• Say "You did a good job" • Send a thank-you note to the volunteer for a job well done • Send a letter of appreciation to the volunteers family • Attend to volunteer's concerns as they arise	• Peers recognize each other • Provide the team with a treat when it reaches a minor milestone
Public:		
When	• Annual event • National Volunteer Week	• Upon successful completion of significant task • Annual event
How	• Acknowledge an individual's contribution to their team • Ceremonies • Local newspaper coverage • Awards • Trinkets—mugs, pens, etc. • Certificates • Publish the volunteer's name and success in the agency newsletter • Promote volunteer to new position • Invite volunteer to speak at convention • Nominate volunteer for a local or national award • Create a Volunteer Hall of Fame	• Have a party or picnic • Newspaper or TV coverage • Awards • Team plaques • Group photo in newsletter • Sponsor a team trip • Treat group to lunch • Ceremonies • Group T-shirts • Team of the Year award • Invite a special guest to speak to the group

SOURCES AND SUGGESTED REFERENCES

Baker, William J., and Murawski, Kris. 1986. "A Method for Measuring Paid Staff Support for Volunteer Involvement." *Journal of Voluntary Action Research, 15*(3).

Brainerd, Susan. 1987–1988. "Creating an Organizational Climate to Motivate Volunteers," parts 1–3. *Nonprofit Times* (November 1987, January and February 1988).

Bryson, John M. 1989. *Strategic Planning for Public and Nonprofit Organizations.* San Francisco: Jossey-Bass.

Carver, John. 1990. *Boards That Make a Difference.* San Francisco: Jossey-Bass.

Chambre, Susan Maisel. 1987. *Good Deeds in Old Age: Volunteering by the New Leisure Class.* Boston: D. C. Health/Lexington Books.

Chapman, Terry S., Lai, Mary L., and Steinbock, Elmer L. 1984. *Am I Covered For . . .? A Guide to Insurance for Nonprofits.* CIGNA Companies.

Dailey, Richard C. 1986. "Understanding Organizational Commitment for Volunteers: Empirical and Managerial Implications." *Journal of Voluntary Action Research, 15*(1).

Deming, W. Edwards. 1986. *Out of the Crisis.* Cambridge, MA: MIT Center for Advanced Engineering Study.

Ellis, Susan J. 1985. "Daytime Volunteers: An Endangered Species?" *Journal of Volunteer Administration* (Spring).

Ellis, Susan J. 1986. *From the Top Down: The Executive Role in Volunteer Program Success.* Philadelphia: Energize Associates.

Harrington, H. James. 1987. *The Improvement Process.* New York: McGraw-Hill.

Hodgkinson, Virginia A., and Richard W. Lyman. 1989. *The Future of the Nonprofit Sector: Challenges, Changes and Policy Considerations.* San Francisco: Jossey-Bass.

Independent Sector. 1987. *Daring Goals for a Caring Society: A Blueprint for Substantial Growth in Giving and Volunteering in America.* Washington, DC: Author.

Kahn, Jeffrey D. 1985–1986. "Legal Issues Survey Results." *Journal of Volunteer Administration* (Winter).

Larkin, Frank, and Smith, Maria. 1988. *Volunteer 2000 Study, Volumes I, II, and III.* Washington, DC: American Red Cross.

Lynch, Rick, and Vineyard, Sue. 1991. *Secrets of Leadership.* Downers Grove, IL: Heritage Arts.

Macduff, Nancy. 1991. *Episodic Volunteering: Building the Short-Term Volunteer Program.* Walla Walla, WA: MBA Publishing.

McCurley, Steve. 1990. *Volunteer Management Policies.* Downers Grove, IL: Heritage Arts.

McCurley, Steve, and Vineyard, Sue. 1988. *101 Tips for Volunteer Recruitment.* Downers Grove, IL: Heritage Arts.

Pearson, Henry G. 1986. "Interviewing Volunteer Applicants for Skills." *Voluntary Action Leadership* (Summer).

Penney, J. C., Company, Inc., and VOLUNTEER—The National Center. 1987. *A National Profile: VOLUNTEERING.*

Peters, Thomas 1987. *Thriving on Chaos: Handbook for a Management Revolution.* New York: Harper & Row.

Saxon, John P., and Sawyer, Horace W. 1984. "A Systematic Approach for Volunteer Assignment and Retention." *Journal of Volunteer Administration* (Summer).

Schindler-Rainman, Eva. 1989. "Volunteers: An Indispensable Human Resource in a Democratic Society." In Tracy Daniel Connors (Ed.), *The Nonprofit Organization Handbook,* 2nd ed. New York: McGraw-Hill.

Stringer, Gretchen E. 1985. "Staff/Volunteer Relationship 'Perceptions.'" *Journal of Volunteer Administration* (Spring).

Vineyard, Sue. 1989. *Beyond Banquets, Plaques and Pins: Creative Ways to Recognize Volunteers,* 2nd ed. Downers Grove, IL: Heritage Arts.

Widmer, Candace. 1987. "Minority Participation on Boards of Directors of Human Service Agencies: Some Evidence and Suggestions." *Journal of Voluntary Action Research* (October/December).

Wilson, Marlene. 1976. *The Effective Management of Volunteer Programs.* Boulder, CO: Volunteer Management Associates.

Zenger, John H. 1985. "Leadership: Management's Better Half." *Training* (December).

CHAPTER ELEVEN

Managing Today's Volunteers in the Training Process

Pamela G. Arrington
Bowie State University Graduate School

CONTENTS

11.1 INTRODUCTION

The United States has been called a nation of volunteers. At last count, the U. S. had 98 million volunteers who put in 20.5 billion volunteer hours working for charitable causes (Reed, 1991). Donations of both time and money have increased dramatically since 1987: 23 percent more Americans are volunteering their time, and charitable contributions have increased by 20 percent (Reed, 1991).

Furthermore, the number of nonprofit organizations keeps multiplying even with government cutbacks in subsidies to their causes. This chapter discusses how nonprofit organizations can better implement their organizational goals by recruiting and managing today's volunteers in the agencywide training process.

11.2   TODAY'S VOLUNTEERS

Today's volunteers are remarkably different from volunteers 10 to 20 years ago. Traditionally, women who did not work outside the home comprised the majority of the nation's volunteers. Over the past 20 years, there has been a mass movement of women into the paid work force. Presently, more than 60 percent of women work outside the home (Hudson Institute, 1987), and a large majority of these women have family responsibilities. Volunteers no longer are primarily "empty-nesters" who have unlimited time to stuff envelopes and perform routine administrative tasks (Geber, 1991).

Of today's volunteers, 70 percent have full-time jobs, specialized skills, and family responsibilities (Geber, 1991). With the multiple roles that volunteers are engaged in, the amount of time they can devote to volunteer work is limited. However, many are committed to participate in community service activities, even if only on a limited basis.

Many of today's volunteers are looking for learning experiences that will sharpen current knowledge, skills, and abilities utilized in the paid work force, or will provide opportunities to gain new knowledge, skills, and abilities that may be used in the paid work force. The person–job match is imperative, as is constant improvement through learning (Connors, 1991). The meaningfulness and challenge of volunteer work assignments are important to today's professional and/or volunteer.

Generally, volunteers are highly skilled "knowledge" workers who have limited time to volunteer. They want to know they are contributing to the organization's long-range plan. The value of learning and growing on the job is also important to them; they want meaningful assignments that are congruent with their knowledge, skills, and abilities. Flexibility in completing volunteer projects is also a prerequisite.

11.3   HUMAN RESOURCE DEVELOPMENT

Nonprofit organizations continue to devote a significant amount of their resources to human resource development for their volunteers and paid staff. Like the public and private sectors, nonprofit organizations depend on human resource development to achieve their organizational goals.

Nadler and Nadler (1989) have defined human resource development as organized learning experiences (intentional/purposeful) provided by employers, within a specified period of time, to bring about the possibility of performance improvement and/or personal growth. Human resource development includes three activity areas: training, education, and development.

Training is defined as organized learning experiences centered around the employee's current position (Nadler, 1988). This training should increase the possibility of the employee's performing current job responsibilities better. Education is defined as learning experiences that prepare the worker to perform future job duties (Nadler, 1984). Developmental experiences are not necessarily job-related but they provide opportunities for professional development and growth.

11.4   USE OF VOLUNTEERS IN THE TRAINING PROCESS

One need not be on-site to accomplish a project, if the nonprofit is explicit in its guidelines for the project assignment. The degree of autonomy a nonprofit can afford a volunteer is crucial in the recruitment and retention of highly qualified volunteers. Volunteers who work full-time have little patience with any unwise demands on their time; a challenge for nonprofits is to manage the "knowledge worker" volunteer for productivity. Any assignment given to volunteers needs follow-up.

For example, suppose a nonprofit manager has a volunteer with instructional design skills who needs an assignment. An appropriate project would be to ask the volunteer to design a training program that will prepare volunteers to work on the organization's annual fund-raising campaign (Geber, 1991).

In another example, United Way/United Black Fund Management Services Incorporated recruits professionals with requisite skills to fill predetermined needs for its constituency. Potential volunteers complete a capability profile (see Exhibit 11.1). An annual needs assessment is conducted among United Way/United Black Fund member organizations, as announced in Exhibit 11.2.

Based on the reported member training/consulting needs, volunteers with commensurate areas of expertise are asked to provide professional services to the designated agency. United Way/United Black Fund Management Services Incorporated serves as a broker and makes the person–job match.

Although almost all of the volunteers work full-time, they are eager to participate in the service. Because many are starting their own consulting businesses, they see the service as a way to add up training credits for marketing purposes. Others have strong altruistic values and enjoy giving back to their respective communities. Some use the opportunity to gain experience in a new professional endeavor.

Four key steps can be employed to maximize volunteer output in the training process:

- Recruitment and selection;
- Orientation;
- Training;
- Performance appraisals.

As with recruiting and retaining paid staff, there needs to be a person–job match between training roles and responsibilities to be performed and the competencies and skills of human resource practitioners and/or volunteers.

(a) RECRUITMENT AND SELECTION The recruitment and selection of volunteers is the first step in effectively managing volunteers. Recruitment should involve the same amount of research, time, and strategizing that is required when seeking a million-dollar gift (Alexander, 1991).

Technology can assist in the recruitment and selection of volunteers. Data bases exist in which volunteers have recorded their areas of expertise and agencies have entered their mission, needs, and requests for services. Potential volunteers can go to the local library to identify a person–job match.

Nonprofits must prioritize their training needs around their mission. (See Chap. 2.) Once specific training projects are identified as necessary to the organizational mission, then volunteers with commensurate knowledge, skills, and abilities can be recruited, trained, or retrained. The selection, placement, and training of volunteers give everyone an opportunity to advance personal learning and contribute the best of personal talents (Deming, 1989).

Exhibit 11.1. Sample of volunteer application.

VOLUNTEER APPLICATION

NAME OF CONSULTANT: _____

ADDRESS: _____

TELEPHONE NUMBER—WORK: (___)_____ TELEPHONE NUMBER—HOME: (___)_____

The agencies served by Management Services, Inc. have expressed a number of needs for assistance. These may be categorized into the following key areas: AGENCY POLICY-MAKING, AGENCY ADMINISTRATION & MANAGEMENT, CORPORATE MANAGEMENT, FINANCE, MARKETING AND PUBLIC RELATIONS AND PERSONNEL. Please rank order the areas in which you have knowledge, experience, and demonstrated competence. For the first three choices, provide three references who can verify your expertise in the area noted. (NOTE: PLEASE PROVIDE A RECENT VITA OR RESUME WITH THIS APPLICATION . . . THANK YOU!)

AGENCY POLICY-MAKING_____
____ Board Organization and Structure
____ Policy Development
____ Planning and Goal Setting
____ Resource Allocation
____ Agency Evaluation

CORPORATE MANAGEMENT_____
____ Articles of Incorporation
____ By-Laws
____ Tax-Exempt Status
____ Tax Reporting

MARKETING AND PUBLIC RELATIONS_____
____ Community Analysis: Need for Agency Service
____ Cooperative Relationships with other agencies
____ Packaging the Agency's Story
____ Working with the Media

AGENCY ADMINISTRATION & MANAGEMENT_____
____ Decision-Making
____ Time Management
____ Problem Solving
____ Communication
____ Team Building
____ Program Evaluation

FINANCE_____
____ Management: bookkeeping, budget, payroll, indirect cost, cash flow, audit preparation
____ Fund Raising
____ Grantsmanship

PERSONNEL_____
____ Staff Development and Training
____ Wage and Salary
____ Staff Recruitment
____ Staff Performance Appraisal
____ Position Qualifications/Classification
____ Volunteer Recruitment, Training, Management
____ Volunteer/Paid Staff Relations

Exhibit 11.1.   *(Continued)*

PAGE TWO—VOLUNTEER APPLICATION

REFERENCES

	AREA #1_____	AREA #2_____	AREA #3_____
NAME _____	_____		
ADDRESS _____	_____		
PHONE _____	_____		
NAME _____	_____		
ADDRESS _____	_____		
PHONE _____	_____		
NAME _____	_____		
ADDRESS _____	_____		
PHONE _____	_____		

TIME AVAILABLE TO DO VOLUNTEER WORK

TIME OF DAY:	DAY OF WEEK:	TIME OF YEAR:	HOURS PER YEAR:
____ Morning	____ Monday	____ Winter	____ 10
____ Afternoon	____ Tuesday	____ Spring	____ 10–50
____ Evening	____ Wednesday	____ Summer	____ 51–100
	____ Thursday	____ Fall	____ You tell us ____
	____ Friday		
	____ Saturday		
	____ Sunday		

KIND OF VOLUNTEER JOB OF INTEREST (Rank order those of interest)

____ One-to-One Consulting

____ Organizational Diagnosis & Management of Volunteer Trainers Assigned to Case

____ Seminar Presentation (10–20 people)

____ Workshop Presentation (20 + people)

____ Evaluation of MSC Service to Agencies

____ Training of Trainers

____ Special Projects for MSC

WHERE/HOW DID YOU LEARN OF THIS VOLUNTEER OPPORTUNITY?

HAVE YOU BEEN REFERRED TO MSC BY: ____ ASTD

____ UNITED WAY

____ UNITED BLACK FUND

WORK HISTORY

Please attach a current resume to this application and respond to the following questions:

• Name of current employer: _____

• Name(s) of employers in past five (5) years

• Educational record:

Signed _____

Date _____

Exhibit 11.2.   Cover letter for annual survey of management needs.

UnitedWay·UnitedBlackFund
MANAGEMENT SERVICES INCORPORATED

ANNUAL SURVEY

TO: Executive Director of United Way, United Black Fund and other non-profit
         501 (C) (3) Agencies of the Washington Metropolitan Area.

FROM: Myrtle E. Johnson
        Executive Director

DATE: July 2, 1990

RE: Management services available to your agency.

   Each year we conduct a survey to ascertain the needs of your agency so that we may better assist you in meeting your management objectives. We would greatly appreciate it if you would take a few moments to complete the attached form.

   On one side, please suggest topics for workshops to be conducted at our facility. On the other side is an Agency Request for Services Application. Please complete it if you want management training, technical assistance, or consultation services provided at your individual agency at no cost. Please return the SURVEY to:

> United Way/United Black Fund
> Management Services Incorporated
> 1012 - 14th Street, N.W. / Suite 304
> Washington, D.C. 20005

   Thank you for assisting us. And, if you have questions you may call 347-4024. We look forward to serving you.

MEJ/ah
Attachment

Volunteers can be recruited and/or trained to assist nonprofit managers during the needs assessment step. The conduct of a needs assessment should be a very thorough and comprehensive activity. If an agencywide needs assessment is conducted, this part of the training process can be conducted once a year. Volunteers can be recruited and trained to conduct face-to-face interviews; develop questionnaires and accompanying cover letters; collect, organize, and analyze the data; and report the results. These data collection steps are necessary for a thorough and comprehensive needs assessment.

Increasingly, colleges and universities are requiring their students to complete an established number of hours in public service work. Many government-sponsored loans and grants for college students are "forgiven" based on the student's completing a set number of hours of community service.

Most graduate and professional school programs in adult education, human resource development, gerontology, and social work, as well as undergraduate programs in psychology and sociology, require students to complete hands-on field experiences. Graduate programs in areas commensurate with identified agency needs and goals can be tapped as resources for the training process. Other examples include management information, public administration, business management, facility management, and so on. Nonprofit leaders should involve local colleges and universities in the training process as potential resources.

Nonprofit organizations will find college students knowledgeable volunteers who complement their paid staff. Most college students possess the survey research skills required to conduct a needs assessment; at least, nonprofit managers may want to screen for these capabilities. Once identified, involving this group of volunteers in the strategic planning process seems appropriate. Nonprofit managers may invite volunteer professionals and students with a background in computer science to develop computer programming assistance for the needs assessment process. This would include designing and formatting survey instruments/questionnaires so data can be tabulated and analyzed using readily available software packages.

Colleges and universities also offer nonprofit organizations a wealth of human resource development services. Faculty volunteers can function as expert trainers and consultants in various subject areas, once these needs have been identified through the training process. Students can also volunteer as trainers and consultants.

For example, master's-level students in human resource development at Bowie State University in Bowie, Maryland, have served as volunteer consultants in the United Way/United Black Fund Management Services Project. Students' interests and skills were matched with identified organizational needs. Students then developed and delivered seminars, on topics such as stress management and team building, to paid staff and volunteers at Washington (DC) area nonprofits. This was a way to involve volunteers in the training process, particularly the design/development and delivery phases. The training request was the result of predetermined organizational needs.

The library, media, equipment, and facilities at colleges and universities are available to local nonprofits as resources and can be used to enhance their training process and practices. Local college and university departments of education and communications can be tapped to design, develop, and package educational videotapes for use by nonprofits, after course goals and objectives have been agreed on. University experts in the area of adult education can help nonprofits facilitate the writing of course outlines, goals, objectives, and lessons.

In addition, paid staff can avail themselves of credit and noncredit course offerings in subject areas that are critical to the mission of the nonprofit. The possible linkages between colleges and universities and nonprofits are limitless. For example, a needs assessment may reveal knowledge and skill gaps among staff that may be efficiently met through long-term education or development experiences at nearby colleges and universities.

After a needs assessment has been conducted, nonprofit managers can recruit and/or select volunteer trainers who have subject matter expertise and/or experience in the identified organizational need or mission. For example, United Way/United Black Fund Management Services Incorporated volunteer application form (Exhibit 11.1) asks the volunteer to identify the type of position that is of interest. Seminar presentation, workshop presentation, and training of trainers are three of the possible seven choices. More importantly, the volunteer is asked to specify the content area in which he or she would be able to volunteer. The content area is based on annual needs assessment data collected from agencies served by the management services corporation.

Under the United Way Loaned Executive program, volunteer training professionals from the business community become available to nonprofits. Particularly in the fund-raising arena, this program has an illustrious history. Senior executives spend up to a year with nonprofits, advising on a myriad of business needs in a consultative role. Training could be one such area. Like the management services corporation, the Washington (DC) Volunteer Clearinghouse provides training and consultation to nonprofits for negotiable fees.

In addition to possible partnership arrangements with colleges and universities, a wish list can be explored with area businesses through a request for service form, as shown in Exhibit 11.3. Nonprofits may want to utilize companies' physical and human resources; they need not call on local business leaders only for monetary contributions. Companies are anxious for their employees to become involved in community service projects. Sometimes, when a business is not initially willing to make substantive cash donations, for whatever reason, it will get involved with the nonprofit in other ways that are beneficial to both. This contact may lead to future contributions, once the corporation knows the nonprofit better.

(b) ORIENTATION Volunteer training should begin with an orientation to the organization. Volunteers should be appraised of the agency mission, financial operation, achievements, and long-range goals. United Way/United Black Fund Management Services Incorporated does not provide a structured orientation session for its volunteer consultants, but volunteers are required to come in for a structured interview during which the goals and objectives of the program, as well as the how, when, and where of the delivery of services, are explained. How the consultant's services will be evaluated is also presented. The interview, coupled with handouts such as a workshop survey (Exhibit 11.4), provide the volunteer with an orientation program. In addition, background information about the agency (Exhibit 11.5) is sent to the volunteer, for use in the planning process. The volunteer is encouraged to call and meet with the agency director to collect even more data, in order to affirm the diagnosis specified from the needs assessment conducted earlier. Official agreements are often made between the volunteer consultants and the agency they are servicing (Exhibit 11.6).

Exhibit 11.3.   Sample request for service form.

UNITED WAY · UNITED BLACK FUND
MANAGEMENT SERVICES INCORPORATED

AGENCY REQUEST FOR SERVICE

NAME OF AGENCY: _____

MEMBER OF (Check One):   UNITED WAY____   UNITED BLACK FUND____   OTHER____

ADDRESS: _____

TELEPHONE NUMBER: (___)_____

EXECUTIVE DIRECTOR/PRESIDENT OF AGENCY: _____

PRESIDENT/CHAIRPERSON OF AGENCY'S BOARD OF DIRECTORS: _____

NUMBER OF BOARD MEMBERS: _____   NUMBER OF PAID STAFF MEMBERS: _____

NUMBER OF REGULAR VOLUNTEER STAFF MEMBERS: _____

YEAR GROUP WAS FOUNDED: _____

PURPOSE OF THE ORGANIZATION: _____

_____

_____

FUNDING SOURCE(S)—CIRCLE THOSE WHICH APPLY:

SPECIAL EVENTS   SOLICITATION/DONATIONS   GRANTS

FEES FOR SERVICE   MEMBERSHIP FEES   OTHER: _____

ASSISTANCE REQUESTED—PLEASE CHECK THE CATEGORIES:

AGENCY POLICY-MAKING
____ board organization & structure
____ policy development
____ planning & goal setting
____ resource allocation
____ agency evaluation

CORPORATE MANAGEMENT
____ articles of incorporation
____ by-laws
____ tax-exempt status
____ tax reporting

MARKETING & PUBLIC RELATIONS
____ community analysis: need for agency service(s)
____ cooperative relationships with other agencies
____ packaging the agency story
____ working with the media

AGENCY ADMINISTRATION & MANAGEMENT
____ decision-making
____ time management
____ problem solving
____ communication
____ team building
____ program evaluation

FINANCE
____ management: bookkeeping, budget, payroll, indirect cost, cash flow, audit preparation
____ fund raising
____ grantsmanship

Exhibit 11.3.   *(Continued)*

PAGE TWO - AGENCY REQUEST FOR SERVICE

ASSISTANCE REQUESTED (Continued)

PERSONNEL

____ staff development & training	____ position qualification/classifications
____ wage and salary	____ volunteer recruitment, training, mgmt.
____ staff recruitment	____ volunteer/paid staff relations
____ staff performance appraisal	

THIS REQUEST IS MADE BY: _____. POSITION: _____

DATE OF REQUEST(S): _____

ADDRESS: _____

TELEPHONE NUMBER(S): _____

(c) PERFORMANCE APPRAISALS   Effectively managing volunteers in the training process includes making the right person–job match. Recruitment and selection, orientation, training, and performance appraisals enable nonprofits to maximize their volunteer productivity. (See Chap. 13.)

11.5   THE TRAINING PROCESS

(a) OVERVIEW   The training process involves four important phases: strategic planning, design and development, delivery, and evaluation. (The strategic planning phase includes conduct of a needs assessment.) These are the elements of the training process phases:

1. Strategic planning
   —Needs assessment
   —Annual training plan
   —Scheduling
   —Budgeting
2. Design and development
   —Job/Task analysis
   —Course objectives and lessons
   —Training of trainers
3. Delivery
   —Trainee preparation
   —Arrangement for training services
   —Conduct of training
   —Record keeping

Exhibit 11.4.   Sample workshop survey form.

UnitedWay·UnitedBlack Fund
MANAGEMENT SERVICES INCORPORATED

WORKSHOP SURVEY

Please list below topics/issues you wish to see addressed in a workshop setting:

1) _____

2) _____

3) _____

4) _____

5) _____

6) _____

7) _____

8) _____

PLEASE CHECK AS MANY THAT MAY APPLY!

I prefer a ____ Half-day session.   I prefer ____ Full-day sessions.

I find that ____ Mornings are better for me.   ____ Afternoons are better for me.

The day(s) of the week that works best for me are: ____ Mondays   ____ Tuesdays

____ Wednesdays ____ Thursdays ____ Fridays ____ All with at least two (2) Weeks notice.

NAME: _____   TITLE: _____

AGENCY: _____

ADDRESS: _____

TELEPHONE NO: _____

____ UNITED WAY AGENCY   ____ UNITED BLACK FUND AGENCY   ____ OTHER

————1012 - 14th Street, N.W./Suite 304, Washington, D.C. 20005 (202) 347-4024————

Exhibit 11.5.   Organizational policy statement.

UNITED WAY·UNITED BLACK FUND
MANAGEMENT SERVICES INCORPORATED

POLICY STATEMENT

The United Way/United Black Fund Management Services Incorporated was established in the fall of 1981, after months of collaborative planning by the United Way of the National Capital Area, the United Black Fund of Greater Washington, and the Washington Chapter of the American Society for Training and Development. MSI is designed to respond to management concerns of executives and boards of not-for-profit agencies. The corporation is supported by the United Way, the United Black Fund, and the American Society for Training and Development.

Consultation services are provided to agencies through the assignment of volunteer consultants. There is no fee for the services, and agencies are placed on a waiting list for service, based upon criteria determined by the MSI Board of Directors.

1. MANAGEMENT ASSISTANCE. MSI recognizes the need for sound, effective management of human service agencies to efficiently provide social services and programs. MSI is designed to strengthen the management core of agencies by providing volunteer consultants from business and industry, government and educational institutions, professional and civic organizations and associations.

   In support of agency autonomy and self-help, MSI encourages agencies to use to the fullest extent possible, their own initiatives for management assistance before requesting assistance from MSI.

2. AGENCY AUTONOMY. Participation in MSI by agencies is voluntary. Agencies have the right not to participate and to reject consultation recommendations.

3. TARGET MARKET. Management assistance is available to not-for-profit agencies located within the MSI service area. Agencies need not be members of the United Way or the United Black Fund.

4. CONFIDENTIALITY. The Management Services Incorporated is separate from the United Way and the United Black Fund; therefore, agencies are encouraged to discuss their problems and seek assistance. Confidentiality is essential to developing and maintaining trust and open communications with agencies. All information pertaining to the agency consultation engagement is considered confidential and will only be released upon the signed authorization of the agency.

5. CONSULTATION. Diagnosis and problem solving are part of the consultation process. Implementation of the recommended solutions is given equal emphasis. Both elements provide agencies with the maximum opportunity to apply new or modified management procedures to the operation of the agency. MSI stresses the importance of the "transfer of skills" to agencies as a result of the consultation engagement.

————1012 - 14th Street, N.W./Suite 304, Washington, D.C. 20005 (202) 347-4024————

Exhibit 11.6. Sample of contract with volunteer consultant.

UNITEDWAY·UNITEDBLACK FUND
MANAGEMENT SERVICES INCORPORATED

VOLUNTEER CONSULTANT
CONTRACT

This agreement is make by and between the United Way/United Black Fund Management Services Corporation, hereinafter termed "MSC" and _____, hereinafter called the volunteer consultant. The contract goes into effect on the _____ day of _____, 19_____.

MSC agrees to assign the volunteer consultant to _____ agency and the Volunteer Consultant agrees to see that the following task(s) are accomplished.

All administrative support, typing photocopying, etc. will be provided by United Way/United Black Fund Management Services, Inc. immediately upon request from the Volunteer Consultant.

The consultation is to begin by: DATE _____ and to be completed no later than: DATE _____.

The volunteer consultant agrees that he/she represents the United Way/United Black Fund Management Services Corporation and operates under the direction of the Executive Director during the time that this agreement is in effect. This contract can be terminated by either party with 30 days notice should either feel that it is not in their best interest to continue the relationship.

DATE _____

_____
Myrtle E. Johnson
Executive Director

DATE _____

_____
Volunteer Consultant

————1012 - 14th Street, N.W./Suite 304, Washington, D.C. 20005 (202) 347-4024————

4. Evaluation
—Volunteer and paid staff
—Trainers
—Assessment of program accomplishments
—Cost–benefit analyses

(b) STRATEGIC PLANNING It is possible for an organization to involve volunteers at all levels of management and decision making. Given the financial situation of most volunteer organizations, more emphasis on planning and evaluation and on the role training plays in those processes is needed. Although the financial situation of nonprofits has preoccupied planning initiatives (Olson, 1984), budget cutbacks provide an opportunity for nonprofit managers to emphasize the need for strategic planning in carrying out the organization's mission. Such a plan may well need to include training in efficiency techniques.

Strategic planning involves the vision of how the organization plans to meet its constituents' needs, based on analyses of both the external and internal environment—local, state, and national economic condition; work force demographics; financial portfolio of the organization; strengths and weaknesses of paid and volunteer staffs; and prioritizing of organizational needs and goals.

The training, education, and development functions for both volunteers and paid staff should be well integrated into any nonprofit strategic plan. All functional area managers should provide input into the training process and practices endorsed by the nonprofit. Their input should be reflected in any organizationwide planning document. Training must be more than a series of random events or activities. Instead, the human resource development program should be based on strategic planning, a systems approach.

Use of a systems approach to training and development enhances the organization's ability to focus training on the prevention of problems. When one is not always in a reactive mode of "putting out fires," energy can be devoted to creative and innovative proactive training. What is good for the human resource development area's strategic plan is good for the organizationwide strategic plan. Indeed, most organizations that adopt quality management principles will make sure training needs, action plans, and evaluation are thoroughly integrated throughout the organization's strategic plan.

The process ensures that training will be applied to ongoing projects and to projects that are to begin in the near future. If an experience is developmental, then the applicability to the achievement of organizational goals must be evident. The human resource development manager should make the connection explicit.

Key decision makers should gather at least once each year for a planning session. A good brainstorming exercise for this meeting, preferably off-site, is to consider agency problems. For each identified problem and need, solutions should be considered and resources identified. A facilitator will be needed for this planning session. Volunteers with expertise in group dynamics and group process skills should be recruited for this critical planning meeting. The discussion goals for a strategic planning session are:

• Problems and needs;
• Solutions;
• Resources;

Faculty at area colleges and universities can be tapped to identify a facilitator. In addition, during summer months and on weekends, college campuses may provide ideal facilities for a meeting site. Some nonprofit board members may volunteer their homes; vacation or beach homes provide a particularly relaxing setting, away from the agency. In addition, some corporations, like Xerox Corporation, donate space for off-site meetings. The Xerox International Training Center in Leesburg, Virginia, noted for its wooded landscapes complete with wild deer, is an example. More importantly, for actual training programs, such as orientation for new employees and staff retreats for team building, these same resources should be considered. For agencies involved in direct services, it is important to get paid and volunteer staff away from the office occasionally, especially for team-building training.

Agencies need to work these programs into the annual budgeting process—another reason why the human resource development planning process should be integrated into the nonprofit's total strategic planning process. As priorities for the agency are determined, training, education, and development for volunteer and paid staff should be given equal consideration alongside other agency needs.

(c) NEEDS ASSESSMENT Data collection and analysis are paramount to the planning process. Training outcomes must be based on organization needs or business needs. Key volunteer leadership and executives from the organization, and from similar organizations, must be surveyed. Performance appraisal data from volunteer and paid staff should be reviewed. Job descriptions should be broken down into key component parts. A job analysis based on job descriptions can be done using a structured staff interview closed-question format. Sample questions may include:

1. Rate yourself in quality of job performance on a scale of 1 to 10.
2. What systems and equipment do you use on the job?
3. What courses, programs, or training do you think you need, to help you do your job better?
4. What results do you want?
5. What are your strengths?
6. Name any weaknesses you perceive.
7. What are your personal goals?
8. What are your professional goals?
9. Are your personal and professional goals compatible?

Community involvement in the identification of priorities is recommended, and feedback should be incorporated into the planning process. After such a thorough analysis, the human resource development manager can better determine the knowledge, skills, and abilities required of paid and volunteer staff in order to accomplish organizational goals. The value of a comprehensive needs assessment in the training process cannot be overemphasized.

One of the reasons the needs assessment is so necessary to the strategic planning process is that it gives managers, clients, potential participants, paid staff, community leaders, and everyone who has an interest in the success of the organization an opportunity to provide input into the process that determines the training, education, and development experiences needed by paid staff and volunteers to implement organizational goals and objectives. (See Chap. 7.)

Training is not always the only answer. Changes in management styles may be necessary, or other organizational development efforts may be more appropriate solutions to problems identified as a result of the strategic planning and needs assessment phase. The benefit of this phase of the training process is the identification of appropriate solutions and resources for confirmed organizational needs. Volunteers with particular skills may need to be recruited. However, orientation must be provided to the newly recruited volunteers: they need to know how their work fits in with the work of the organization.

Returning volunteers need training or retraining programs in order to accomplish certain organizational goals. This type of needs assessment data can only be incorporated into the human resource development planning process if the human resource development manager is an integral player in the organizational planning process. An appropriate human resource development plan can then be implemented, based on the organization's needs, problems, change efforts, development objectives for work performance, personnel strengths and weaknesses, and career opportunities for volunteer and paid staff (Olson, 1984). This kind of goal setting is important for any organization.

Needs assessment data include all of the following:

- Organization needs;
- Organization problems;
- Change efforts;
- Work objectives;
- Personnel strengths;
- Personnel weaknesses;
- Career opportunities.

Needs assessment data are typically collected through the use of face-to-face interviews, confidential questionnaires, agency mission statement, financial statements, personnel records, output records, project costs and projected cost savings, quality improvement goals, logged reports, timeliness of the service rendered, written objectives and standards, and time factors. Needs assessment data should be "hard data," defined as quantifiable, easy to assign dollar values to, objective, and credible in the view of management.

(d) DESIGN AND DEVELOPMENT Most national voluntary organizations are large, complex, and highly decentralized (Olson, 1984). Levinson (1987) described training design needs of nonprofit organizations as including: small size, complex interpersonal environments, uncertain and unstable financial environments, a core value of altruism, strong belief in the value of what the organization does, and a large number of minority group members.

The design phase of the training process provides a means for the human resource development manager to gain valuable input and feedback from other managers while developing training programs for the organization. The person responsible for the design and development of the training programs should try to secure input and feedback at each critical step of the training process: the selection of goals and objectives, the selection of instructional strategies, delivery, and evaluation. These are the common training needs for nonprofit organizations:

- Orientation;
- Team building;
- Quality management.

Because of the interdependence of volunteers and paid staff, teamwork between the two groups is of paramount importance. Common technical-skills training includes: fund-raising, donor research and solicitation, efficiency techniques, and computer literacy. Volunteer and paid staff job descriptions should be reviewed as a key step in the training process. Volunteer trainers can be recruited to review job descriptions in order to determine course objectives. Once the training course is written, it is important to prepare the trainers or instructors. Volunteer human resource practitioners can be recruited for all of the roles and responsibilities required of the training process.

Course objectives should always be written in *measurable* terms, such as:

- Tell what the participant will do;
- Can be taught;
- Can be learned;
- Can be measured;
- Should emphasize a behavior to be modified;
- Show linkage to organizational goals;
- Follow job/task analysis;
- Relate to other objectives of the course;
- Specify conditions for learning to occur.

An example of a course objective is:

> After completion of a course on desktop publishing software, staff will be able to design and construct a fund-raising brochure using desktop publishing software.

(e) DELIVERY Geber (1991) has reported that many of today's volunteers are more receptive to the "lean" approach to training. According to research, when delivering training to adult audiences, interactive instructional methodologies should be considered. However, volunteers who work full-time are not particularly receptive to the group process dynamics (games, exercises, role plays, and so on) that most training specialists incorporate into structured learning experiences to illustrate key concepts. Instead, orientation delivered in printed media (handouts, workbooks, and so on) is preferred by this time-conscious audience. This is not to suggest these instructional strategies should not be included in the final training product developed by the volunteers involved in the training process. Volunteers with expertise in educational technology can develop and produce varied educational materials, such as video tapes, to be used in lieu of the traditional classroom format.

Hands-on training techniques are most helpful when trying to keep training activities to a minimum. As much factual information as possible should be delivered in the form of manuals, handouts, handbooks, or other training aids that can be referred to throughout the assigned project. Self-directed learning is a very appropriate instructional strategy, given the demographics of the typical volunteer.

Trainers should emphasize the need to participate in training activities. How else can the training be related to assigned projects? The trainer and/or human resource development manager must stress the fact that, without certain information presented in the training session, the volunteer will not be able to complete the assigned project in a satisfactory manner. This emphasis on job-related training should motivate the professional volunteer to find time to participate in agency training.

Volunteers are more willing to participate in training that is designed with this target group in mind. Volunteer training should be lean and mean—just the facts, with minimal group dynamics exercises. Team-building activities are important, but many of today's volunteers are not willing to commit time to activities outside of their assigned work project for the organization.

Depending on the skill levels of the volunteers, they may not require an intense training, in order to be effective in assisting paid staff who are responsible for writing and delivering training programs. The quality of instructors is crucial, but Levinson (1987) warns trainers who volunteer their expertise to nonprofits to remember that personal contact is a core nonprofit value and remains the favored mode of communication.

The readiness level of agency personnel is crucial to the training process. Paid and volunteer staff should be recognized for their contributions to the nonprofit's mission. Their participation in training, education, and development programs should be presented as a form of recognition for a job well done as well as an incentive for participation in future projects. Agency employees must be informed of the availability of training programs and materials. Nonprofit managers should ensure that training, education, and development programs are widely publicized to employees. Other nonprofits may be invited to participate, to help underwrite some of the costs and to introduce a different set of group experiences when agencies with similar constituents have an opportunity to compare experiences. Learning experiences must be reinforced back at the office.

Human resource managers need to keep records of staff and volunteers who participate in agency-related training, education, and development programs. These data should be included in annual performance appraisals and in the annual planning process. It is important to have measures of productivity for meaningful comparisons.

(f) EVALUATION Evaluation of training, perhaps the most overlooked step of the training process, is critical if nonprofit managers responsible for training participate in the agencywide strategic planning process. At this time, nonprofit managers responsible for human resource development need to be able to present program accomplishments in cost–benefit or return-on-investment terms.

The data that were collected to plan and to design and develop training should be revisited in order to assess program accomplishments and outcomes. Evaluation is a criterion at each step of the training process. Exhibit 11.7 provides an outline of the key categories and topics.

Nonprofit managers must evaluate the training process. If technical training has occurred—data base management, word processing, financial record keeping—has the error rate improved? What is the percent of tasks completed properly? Has efficiency improved? Are schedules being met? Has automation shortened task completion time? Did orientation training decrease the amount of break-in time for new employees? Has

Exhibit 11.7. Key evaluation data.

Hard data	*Examples of cost savings* (Continued)
Output	Variable costs
Cost savings	Fixed costs
Quality improvement	
Time savings	*Examples of quality improvement data*
	Error rates
Measures of output	Amount of rework
Money collected	Percent of tasks completed properly
Forms processed	Amount of variance from organizational prescribed
Clients served	standards
Applications processed	
Tasks completed	*Time savings possibilities*
Productivity	Time to project completion
Work backlog	Processing time
	Supervisory time
Examples of cost savings	Break-in time for new employees
Number of cost reductions	Training time
Project cost savings	Meeting schedules
Program costs	Efficiency
Operating costs	Late reporting
Overhead costs	Lost time days

training resulted in increased output? Is more money being collected? Is the work backlog reduced? Has productivity increased?

Nonprofit managers should ask the above questions in order to assess whether training has affected cost–benefit outcomes. Hard data of this type will show the governing board and senior managers the benefits of training.

The use of data to make decisions is probably the most important factor contributing to a Total Quality effort. The emphasis in continuous process improvement is to make decisions based on objective data (Biech and Danahy, 1991).

Exhibit 11.8. Tasks of managers responsible for human resource development.

1. Show how training is tied to organizational goals and priorities;   _____

2. Identify training outcomes;   _____

3. Document return on investment and cost of effectiveness of training;   _____

4. Evaluate training;   _____

5. Compare training results against training expectations;   _____

6. Develop data and methods to illustrate bottom-line impact of training;   _____

7. View training as a strategic investment;   _____

8. Learn management's current needs and priorities;   _____

9. Get sufficient resources allocated, to ensure employees are equipped to perform duties;   _____

10. Emphasize quality improvement.   _____

Evaluation should be viewed as necessary in order to provide input for planning. Hence, evaluation is another step in an open, continuous training process. Evaluation is a criterion at each step of the training process.

The data collected from the evaluation process provide input for the next planning session. Nonprofit managers should be able to show, in numerical terms, the bottom-line contribution of training, education, and development programs to the achievement of organizational goals. (See Exhibit 11.8.)

The nonprofit human resource development manager must be able to show the above data to nonprofit executive directors and board members. Measurement and evaluation of training are critical. Evaluation begins with the writing of measurable objectives; their written form is another example of the open and continuous nature of the training process.

11.6 VOLUNTEER RECOGNITION/INCENTIVES

Volunteers view volunteer work as a developmental activity through which they can gain skills and knowledge either to benefit them in their current careers or to enable them to try out new careers. Some professionals volunteer as a means to get ahead on their paid jobs. In either case, volunteers are interested in personal and professional growth activities and the satisfaction of doing well.

One of the major activities nonprofits have mastered over the years is volunteer recognition. Nonprofits have learned how to express appreciation to volunteers in tangible, concrete terms, such as: "You have contributed your expertise and x number of hours [or weeks] of your time. Because of you, many lives were affected in these ways: . . . ."

Volunteer recognition should begin with the organizational policy statements. Volunteers can be recognized in periodic communications from the board and managers. The use of internal periodicals can also reinforce the need for paid staff to support volunteer staff in a team effort. Peer recognition is important. Some agencies recognize their volunteers at an annual banquet or at regional breakfast meetings. Tokens of appreciation, such as engraved pewter mugs and certificates of recognition, are frequently presented to volunteers.

It is important to ask volunteers what kinds of recognition they appreciate. Depending on their reasons for volunteering, something other than a plaque or volunteer banquet may be appropriate—for example, a new assignment offering more visibility and responsibility, or a letter of appreciation to the volunteer's paid-job supervisor may be a more meaningful form of recognition than a plaque.

SOURCES AND SUGGESTED REFERENCES

Alexander, G. D. 1991. "Working with Volunteers." *Fund Raising Management, 12*(2): 62–63.

Biech, E., and Danahy, M. 1991. *Diagnostic Tools for Total Quality.* Alexandria, VA: American Society for Training and Development.

Connors, T. 1991. "Avoiding Quality Shock: Can Mere Mortals Achieve Perfection?" *The Observer,* July 15, pp. 3–9.

Deming, W. E. 1989. *Out of the Crisis.* Cambridge, MA: MIT Center for Advanced Engineering Study.

Deutsch, C. 1991. "In Motivation, Nonprofits Are Ahead." *New York Times,* July 14, p. 25.

Dobie, K. 1991. "The New Volunteers." *Vogue.* August, pp. 213–217.

Donaldson, L., and Scannell, E. 1986. *Human Resource Development: The New Trainer's Guide.* Reading, MA: Addison-Wesley.

Galer, D., and Holliday, A. 1988. "Achieving Quality in Nonprofits (Part 3)." *Nonprofit World,* (May/June), *3:* 22–24.

Geber, B. 1991. "Managing Volunteers." *Training.* (June), 22–23.

Ireland, T. 1991. "Fighting for Financial Support." Paper presented at Technical Trainers Conference, Department of the Navy, Arlington, VA; August.

Johnston, W., and Packer, A. 1987. *Workforce 2000: Work and Workers for the 21st Century.* Indianapolis, IN: Hudson Institute.

Levinson, D. 1987. "Training and Development for Nonprofits." *Training and Development Journal 41:* 80–82.

Lindsay, J. 1991. Informational interview, Volunteer Clearinghouse, Washington, DC; May.

Mills, G., Pace, R., and Peterson, B. 1989. *Analysis in Human Resource Training and Organization Development.* Reading, MA: Addison-Wesley.

Nadler, L. (Ed.). 1984. *The handbook of human resource development.* NY: John Wiley & Sons.

Nadler, L. 1988. *Designing Programs: The Critical Events Model.* Reading, MA: Addison Wesley.

Nadler, L. and Nadler, Z. 1989. *Developing human resources.* Reading, MA: Addison-Wesley.

Nelson, D. V., and Johnson, M. E. 1991. Informational interview, United Way/United Black Fund Management Services, Washington, DC; May.

Olson, E. A. 1984. "Volunteer Organizations." In L. Nadler (Ed.), *The Handbook of Human Resource Development.* New York: John Wiley & Sons.

Reed, J. 1991. "The New Volunteers." *Vogue.* August, pp. 213–217.

Designing Effective Personnel Policies

Diane M. Disney
University of Rhode Island

CONTENTS

12.1   INTRODUCTION

As nonprofit organizations grow, they need to deal with a range of employment-related issues often not considered at the organization's creation. This chapter is intended to help leaders of nonprofit organizations understand those issues from both managerial and legal perspectives. The chapter reflects insights gained from work with nonprofits specializing in a wide variety of public services, including social services, arts and culture, education, housing, health, and employment.

A major concern for all types of nonprofits is that their personnel policies will reflect their approach to dealing with their human resources. Therefore, the policies must be adopted by a vote of the board of directors and can be amended only by a similar vote. For the sake of efficiency, items at the procedural level are best left to the staff. Similarly, *policies* should not be amended frequently, because they are intended to provide a measure of stability to the employer–employee relationship; the staff, however, needs to have the authority and flexibility to amend *procedures* as circumstances warrant.

Another issue worth particular attention is that of employment at will. Until relatively recently, employers in the United States had wide latitude in the way they dealt with employees. In the famous words of a Tennessee judge in 1884, an employer could terminate an employee "for good cause, for no cause, or even for cause morally wrong, without thereby being guilty of legal wrong" (*Payne v. Western & Atlantic RR,* 81 Tenn. 507, 519). Customs have changed, however; employees' rights are now continually being expanded while employers' rights are being constrained. Perhaps just as important has been the change in societal expectations of behavior; individual workers are now much more likely to know and to assert their real and perceived rights than ever before, and juries tend to side with those individuals when cases are brought to court.

This chapter is designed to identify the basic elements that may be covered in a set of personnel policies and to highlight issues or problems that might arise within these elements. It may not reflect everything a given nonprofit might want to include; local laws, regional customs, personal preferences, or "that awful experience we had last year" might dictate the inclusion of a specific subsection. It does, however, address most of the standard items.

The format of the chapter (developed originally for a Federation of State Humanities Councils project) is to identify an element, present the reason(s) for its inclusion, and highlight the factors that policy makers should consider. Reading only the caveats given here might cause some dismay, but they are included to reinforce an awareness that we are an increasingly litigious society whose members are increasingly less reluctant to assert real and imagined "rights."

A few central guidelines warrant emphasis:

- A policy should be specific enough to provide guidance for consistent action in similar situations. It should not be so detailed as to suggest that any action other than the one named is exempt from its coverage.
- Any procedure outlined in the organization's personnel policy manual should be followed. Failure to follow its own processes leaves an organization liable to defeat, should a claim of unfair practice or arbitrary treatment be lodged.
- Policies (and their amendments) must bear their effective dates.
- Before adopting a set of personnel policies, a board would be well advised to consult a local attorney, to be assured that the proposed document complies with local laws and regulations.

Following these guidelines can help ensure that the resultant policies will provide a framework for communicating with employees efficiently and treating them in a fair and consistent manner. A further bonus is that the policies, in addition to protecting the nonprofit's legal interests, can save management time.

12.2 INTRODUCTION TO POLICIES

The introductory section sets the tone for the entire policy document, while limiting the policies to a particular time and organization.

(a) TITLE PAGE

Reasons for inclusion:
To identify the organization by name and address.
To provide the date when the policies take effect.
Caveats: None.

(b) DATE ON WHICH POLICIES TAKE EFFECT

Reason for inclusion:
To avoid confusion and unnecessary litigation.
Caveats: Individuals who feel aggrieved will use the set of policies that fits their needs. Undated sets invite misuse.

(c) WELCOMING STATEMENT

Reasons for inclusion:
To welcome each employee.
To state that amendments may be made from time to time.
To alert employees that the policy manual is not a contract guaranteeing employment for any specified period.
To explain who has the authority to make an employment contract and that such a contract must be in writing.
Caveats: One of the most rapidly growing areas of employment law during the 1980s involved the implicit contract. An employer may therefore wish to assert

within the policies the notion of employment at will. Should a board choose to have any written employment contracts, it should be particularly clear in each about the extent to which that contract supersedes the personnel policies.

(d) OVERVIEW OF NONPROFIT ORGANIZATION

Reason for inclusion:

To provide some sense of the organization's creation, funding, development, objectives, and structure.

Caveats: None, except that brevity can be a virtue.

(e) ORGANIZATION CHART

Reason for inclusion:

None, if the nonprofit is small and has no continuing projects or affiliations; otherwise, including a chart adds clarity.

Caveats: Attempting to account for every *person* can be fraught with peril; instead, the chart needs to reflect *functions* and reporting relationships.

(f) STATEMENT ON PRONOUN USAGE

Reason for inclusion:

To avoid upsetting people while avoiding the need to use grammatically cumbersome constructions such as "s/he" or "his or her."

Caveats: None.

12.3   KEY DEFINITIONS

The aim here is to set forth the *organization's meanings* for commonly used terms. "Full-time work," for instance, can be interpreted as involving 35, 37.5, 40, or some other number of hours, with lunch breaks variously included or excluded.

(a) KEY ABBREVIATIONS

Reason for inclusion:

To avoid confusion when abbreviations are used.

Caveats: Usual abbreviations include those for the nonprofit itself, those for any significant affiliated groups, and those for equal employment opportunity, affirmative action, and similar employment-related terms.

(b) CLASSIFICATIONS OF EMPLOYEES

Reasons for inclusion:

To enunciate the differences between full-time and part-time employees, which can result in differing compensation, benefits, or treatments.

To enunciate the differences between exempt and nonexempt employees, in accordance with the Fair Labor Standards Act (FLSA).

To enunciate the differences among employees, consultants, independent contractors, and volunteers.

To avoid repetition throughout the document.

Caveats: Failure to define terms can create the impression that all employees are entitled to all benefits and all have the same rights. Violations of the FLSA with regard to compensatory time can be a particular problem. In some nonprofit organizations, long-time volunteers have been known to believe that they have the same seniority rights as paid employees.

12.4 GENERAL MANAGEMENT POLICIES

Some issues are of such overarching managerial importance as to warrant highlighting at the beginning of the document.

(a) AUTHORITY OVER PERSONNEL MATTERS

Reasons for inclusion:

To specify that the board creates policies and may, from time to time, amend them in accordance with the procedures in the bylaws or the personnel policies themselves.

To specify the authority of the governing board of the nonprofit over the executive director, and the authority of the executive director over other employees.

Caveats: Spelling out such a policy can protect both the staff and the board members from embarrassing or troublesome actions stemming from an excess of emotion or an overstepping of authority.

(b) PERSONNEL FILES

Reasons for inclusion:

To describe what is kept in the personnel files.

To explain which people may have access to those files under what circumstances.

Caveats: Spelling out this policy can alleviate curiosity and set limits on access. It is important to note that state laws vary here. Connecticut and Illinois laws, for example, permit employees to add statements to their files if they disagree with the contents. In Michigan, access must be given "at reasonable intervals"; in Oregon, employees may receive certified copies of relevant portions of their records.

(c) EQUAL EMPLOYMENT POLICY

Reasons for inclusion:

To enunciate the nonprofit's commitment to equal employment opportunities.

To enunciate the policy against unlawful harassment.

To explain the procedure for addressing instances of job-related discrimination or harassment.

Caveats: When a nonprofit receives over $10,000 in federal funds, it must have an Equal Employment Opportunity (EEO) policy. If it has fewer than 50 employees, it is not required to have a written Affirmative Action (AA) plan. (Note: EEO and

Affirmative Action (AA) are *not* synonymous. Equal Employment Opportunity refers to giving equal consideration to all individuals in the pool for hiring, promotion, or other personnel actions. Affirmative Action refers to taking particular and definite steps to enlarging the pool—specifically, to include people with characteristics, such as race and sex, specified by the federal government.) State laws and nonprofit preferences may add requirements in this area.

(d) DRUG-FREE WORKPLACE

Reasons for inclusion:

To comply with the Federal Drug-Free Workplace Act of 1988.

To indicate the board's commitment to providing such a workplace.

Caveats: None.

(e) CONFLICT OF INTEREST

Reasons for inclusion:

To define conflicts of interest as related to employees.

To specify actions when such conflicts exist.

Caveats: Board members are covered by the bylaws; including this section here makes it clear that the principle applies to employees as well. A nonprofit that distributes funds is well advised to prohibit employees from serving on the boards of any current or prospective grant-seeking organizations.

(f) EMPLOYMENT OF RELATIVES

Reason for inclusion:

To forestall problems when board or staff members insist on hiring a relative.

Caveats: "Relative" needs to be defined. Hiring one, or having a staff member feel pressured to do so, can create serious morale and performance problems. Any policy in this area, of course, needs to recognize that employees might become relatives of each other or of board members through marriage.

12.5 EMPLOYMENT POLICIES

This section concerns the ways the organization defines and fills positions, as well as the overall guidelines for evaluating performance.

(a) JOB CREATION AND DESCRIPTION

Reasons for inclusion:

To enunciate the authority and the steps for creating a position.

To make it clear that there is a written description for every paid and volunteer position, and that such description is subject to review and revision when funds, time, or personnel changes warrant.

To describe the uses of job descriptions and specifications.

Caveats: Because job incumbents soon begin to do more of what they like and less of what they do not like, a typical description may soon bear little resemblance to the position originally filled. Periodic reviews of job descriptions help minimize problems in recruitment, promotion, compensation, and performance evaluation.

(b) RECRUITMENT

Reasons for inclusion:

To explain how and when job openings are posted internally.

To explain how, when, and where job openings are advertised externally.

To state who has the authority to participate in recruitment.

Caveats: Failure to let staff know of openings before the rest of the world does can cause morale problems by seeming to deny people the right to internal mobility; it can also cost money, because informed staff members can be helpful in identifying likely candidates or sources of candidates.

(c) EMPLOYEE SELECTION

Reasons for inclusion:

To reinforce the earlier statement on authority over personnel actions.

To make clear which person has the authority to make an offer of employment.

To specify any preemployment requirements such as a medical examination and the verification that a candidate is not an illegal alien.

Caveats: Failure to specify the authority to make an offer has been known to result in a situation where two different people thought they had been given a job and both showed up for work.

(d) PERFORMANCE REVIEWS

Reasons for inclusion:

To specify the purposes of reviews.

To indicate that informal reviews happen continually.

To specify the intervals for written reviews.

To indicate which people are involved in reviews and which general areas are to be considered.

To indicate the steps to be taken when an employee disagrees with an evaluation.

Caveats: Specifying the review procedure here makes it seem a more positive phenomenon than if the issue were to arise only when describing discipline or termination. Indicating that everyone is subject to review can alleviate some nervousness.

12.6 SCHEDULING POLICIES

A board cannot assume that employees automatically share its views on the use of time.

(a) WORK HOURS

Reasons for inclusion:

To specify standard working hours and breaks.

To reserve the right to change working schedules as circumstances dictate.

To specify requirements for recording the time worked.

Caveats: Because definitions of the standard workday and workweek vary widely, a board needs to provide its own definition, to avoid confusion (and recriminations). The difficulty of getting people to complete time sheets does not relieve the employer of having such records; having such a section in the personnel policies underscores the importance of time records.

(b) OVERTIME PROVISIONS

Reason for inclusion:

To clarify the eligibility for overtime pay, the procedure for earning it, and the formula for determining its amounts.

Caveats: Nonexempt employees must be paid overtime in accordance with the FLSA. Another potential problem is that an employee might do little during the day, stay late, and then demand overtime pay, if the organization does not have an authorization policy.

(c) FLEXTIME OPTIONS

Reason for inclusion:

To explain the circumstances under which a flexible schedule will be approved and the limits within which it may fall.

Caveats: Employers, particularly small ones, need to balance the requirement for maintaining regular business hours with the constraints imposed by domestic concerns in an increasingly diverse work force. At the same time, scheduling options cannot be seen to be violating fair employment practices.

(d) ATTENDANCE AT MEETINGS AND CONFERENCES

Reasons for inclusion:

To indicate how such attendance is authorized.

To indicate how expenses are reimbursed and how time demands are treated.

Caveats: Individuals should not be led to assume that they are free to attend anything they want and be paid for such attendance. The board needs to determine the way it will regard time spent away from home at professional conferences, when such time extends beyond a normal workday.

12.7 COMPENSATION AND EXPENSE POLICIES

(a) OVERVIEW OF COMPENSATION POLICIES

Reasons for inclusion:

To enunciate the reasons for having compensation policies.

To describe how compensation is tied to job descriptions and specifications.

To explain that total compensation includes both direct monetary compensation and indirect compensation in the form of benefits and leave.

Caveats: Because the amount spent on benefits continues to rise at a much faster rate than the amount spent on salaries or wages, employees need to have a sense of how much they really cost the employer. Failure to communicate on this issue can lead to real dissatisfaction when, for example, health insurance premiums rise so much as to preclude raises.

(b) PAYROLL POLICIES

Reasons for inclusion:

To specify when people will be paid, and what happens when a scheduled payday falls on a weekend or holiday.

To indicate the treatment of mandatory and voluntary payroll deductions.

To explain what employees should do if there is a payroll error.

Caveats: Wage and hour divisions of state labor departments may require that people be paid at certain intervals.

(c) COMPENSATION CHANGES

Reason for inclusion:

To clarify the connection between performance and compensation while indicating the role of budgetary constraints.

Caveats: Here, the debate between seniority and merit arises. Nonprofits are advised to avoid stating or implying that they will give cost-of-living raises; they should also make some provision for salary reductions in case of serious budgetary constraints.

(d) REIMBURSEMENT FOR EXPENSES

Reasons for inclusion:

To identify the types of job-related expenses for which employees may be reimbursed.

To describe the method by which such expenditures are authorized and reimbursed.

Caveats: Without an authorization policy, employees might incur expenditures for which the organization has neither the funds nor the intention to provide reimbursement. Rancor follows.

12.8 BENEFITS AND LEAVE POLICIES

This tends to be the longest single section in any set of personnel policies. Because of the rapidly changing nature of benefits plans and legislation, it is very important to relegate names of carriers and details of policies to separate documents.

(a) MANDATORY BENEFITS

Reasons for inclusion:

To list and describe (briefly) the benefits required by law (FICA, Medicare, unemployment insurance, workers' compensation, and others as required by state law).

To indicate who pays for each of these in what way.

Caveats: Employees often have no idea that some of these programs have a cost. Informing them of this reality can be helpful when budgetary constraints (or tax increases) limit the availability of funds for raises.

(b) VOLUNTARY BENEFITS

Reasons for inclusion:

To list and describe (briefly) the goods and services sponsored by the employer in the absence of any legal requirement (generally including such items as health insurance, disability insurance, pensions or savings plans, life insurance, dependent care, and educational reimbursement).

To indicate which source pays for each benefit, and how the payment formula is determined.

To indicate where copies of relevant documents (including summary plan descriptions) are located.

To enunciate the procedure for informing employees of the amounts accrued or spent for each of these items.

Caveats: Employees seldom have a clear idea of these costs, so it is important to explain the notions of deductibles, copayments, and vesting. As mentioned above, because benefits laws change so rapidly and carriers may change as well, details of coverage should be provided in separate documents.

(c) VACATION LEAVE

Reasons for inclusion:

To indicate the amount of paid vacation to which each category of employee is entitled annually.

To indicate the formula for accrual and the requirements for discharge of accrued vacation leave (including provisions for carrying vacation leave over into another year).

To indicate any possibilities for receiving pay instead of paid leave.

To describe the policy and authority for scheduling vacation leave.

To explain what happens when vacation periods include holidays, paydays, or periods of illness.

Caveats: Given budgetary and scheduling constraints, nonprofits are advised to minimize accrual and carryover options. Given the importance of having alert employees, boards are advised against allowing employees to forgo vacations. It might also be wise to point out that there is no federal law requiring the granting of any vacation leave.

(d) HOLIDAYS

Reasons for inclusion:

To specify the holidays recognized by the board as warranting paid leave.

To indicate the categories of employees entitled to such leave.

To specify procedures for pay or leave when a holiday falls on a weekend.

To indicate any special requirements that may restrict payment or scheduling of leave, such as the need to keep the office open.

Caveats: Standard holidays vary by state, and sometimes by municipality. Failure to require that people work the days before and after a holiday, to receive pay for that holiday, can result in an uncovered office.

(e) SICK LEAVE

Reasons for inclusion:

To enunciate clearly the purpose of sick leave and to indicate whether it may be taken for illness of a relative (or pet).

To indicate the amount of paid sick leave to which each category of employee is entitled to annually.

To indicate the formula for accrual and the requirements for discharge of accrued sick leave (including provisions for carrying sick leave over into another year).

To indicate any possibilities for receiving pay instead of paid sick leave.

To describe the notification requirements concerning sick leave.

To explain what happens when an employee becomes ill while away from the office on another form of paid leave.

To explain the relationship between sick leave and the organization's disability policies.

Caveats: Of all the areas of personnel management, this is the one of the most absurd; some employees regard sick leave as synonymous with vacation, and some use it for family matters. Whatever policy is chosen here, it should not promote lying.

(f) PARENTAL LEAVE

Reasons for inclusion:

To indicate the organization's willingness to provide unpaid leave (within limits) to an employee for the birth or adoption of a child.

To specify the timing, compensation, and reinstatement limits of such leave.

Caveats: The term "parental" is much more inclusive than either "maternity" or "paternity." Adoption requires emotional adjustment within the family, just as birth does.

(g) PERSONAL LEAVE

Reasons for inclusion:

To indicate the amount of paid personal leave to which each category of employee is entitled annually.

To indicate the formula for accrual and the requirements for discharge of accrued personal leave (including provisions for carrying personal leave over into another year).

To indicate any possibilities for receiving pay instead of paid personal leave.

To describe the notification and scheduling requirements concerning personal leave.

Caveats: Failure to put restrictions on the discharge of personal days can result in being short-staffed, particularly around holidays and proposal-writing time. Granting personal leave is a very effective way for avoiding religious leave, a category that can create as many accusations of discrimination as it avoids.

(h) OTHER FORMS OF PAID LEAVE

Reasons for inclusion:

To indicate the other reasons (if any) for which the organization will grant paid or unpaid leave (jury duty, military service, and bereavement).

To enunciate the circumstances under which such leave is granted and the reporting and scheduling requirements that result.

Caveats: The opening day of the baseball season has been know to coincide with requests for bereavement leave; in any event, the types of individuals whose death warrants such paid leave should be specified. (Some employees have been known to request bereavement leave for the death of pets.) Legal requirements help guide policies regarding jury and military leave. Compensatory time should be accrued with advance approval and discharged within a reasonable time (not to exceed a month); unregulated "comp time" can be a decided liability.

(i) BREAKS IN SERVICE

Reasons for inclusion:

To indicate the circumstance under which one may have a paid or unpaid leave from work, beyond the normal limits of vacation and sick leave.

To specify the compensation and benefits coverage that would result.

To indicate which individual(s) have the authority to grant such leave.

To clarify the effects on seniority.

Caveats: The Employee Retirement Income Security Act (ERISA) sets limits on breaks in service for pension purposes. State-run temporary disability plans may affect decisions here. Also, sabbatical leave may come under this heading.

12.9 EMPLOYEE CONDUCT

Some topics seem to be difficult for supervisors to broach with employees. Covering these in the personnel manual can help ensure consistent behavior and supervision.

(a) APPEARANCE AND DEMEANOR

Reasons for inclusion:

To enunciate the requirement that employees dress and behave professionally.

To indicate that failure to behave and dress as prescribed may result in disciplinary action.

Caveats: Although it is very unlikely that a nonprofit's employees will violate standards of decency or decorum, this section can provide a remedy should any decide to do so.

(b) APPROPRIATE CONDUCT

Reasons for inclusion:

To indicate the types of conduct deemed inappropriate and therefore unacceptable (such as falsifying records, extorting kickbacks from grantees, using obscene language, theft, disregarding safety regulations, insubordination, excessive use of the organization's telephones or facsimile machines for personal matters).

To indicate that the penalties for such actions may include discipline and dismissal.

Caveats: This section indicates some of the behaviors that merit disciplinary action or dismissal. It should be made clear that some do fall into the latter category, so as to avoid unnecessary recriminations or delays.

(c) TARDINESS AND ABSENTEEISM

Reasons for inclusion:

To reinforce the importance of prompt and regular attendance at work.

To indicate that violation of such guidelines may be grounds for discipline or dismissal.

Caveats: Employees sometimes have little regard for the effect that their lack of attention to work hours may have on other employees or on the organization's effectiveness or reputation. The "family" atmosphere engendered by some nonprofits' small size or by a dedication to a shared mission may make it possible for a worker to abuse the system yet difficult for the supervisor to correct the behavior. Having this policy can help by making it clear that the requirement is not an arbitrary one developed for a single situation.

(d) SMOKING

Reason for inclusion:

To indicate the organization's regulations concerning smoking on its premises or at its functions.

Caveats: A nonprofit may be located in a building designated a smoke-free by its owner or the local government.

(e) USE OF ORGANIZATION-OWNED EQUIPMENT AND MATERIALS

Reason for inclusion:

To identify the circumstances under which employees may use (or borrow) organization-owned equipment, the process for seeking authorization, and the limits on such use.

Caveats: This statement is designed to forestall misuse or overuse of equipment, without seeming to play favorites among the staff.

(f) POLITICAL ACTIVITIES

Reason for inclusion:

To explain the restrictions on use of nonprofit-owned equipment and nonprofit-paid time for political activities.

Caveats: Some states have laws limiting political activities at work, such as the placement of political literature in pay envelopes. Given the reliance on governmental funds among nonprofits, political involvement should not be a surprise; still, the organization needs to restrict use of its resources for such activities because of its nonprofit status and its receipt of public funds.

12.10 TERMINATION AND COMPLAINT RESOLUTION

A major caveat here is that overly detailed policies can often more readily be used *against* an organization than for it.

(a) TERMINATION

Reasons for inclusion:

To differentiate possible reasons for termination (voluntary and involuntary).

To reserve employment-at-will rights.

To indicate notice preferences and termination benefits (such as payment for accrued but unused vacation).

To describe the process of exit interviews.

Caveats: Itemizing causes for dismissal can create a legalistic nightmare, as the nonprofit (which had been fostering a "familylike" atmosphere) attempts to document undesirable behavior of the type mentioned in the policies. Meanwhile, the employee insists that the behavior was not covered by the policies' terminology. Any procedure spelled out here *must* be followed scrupulously.

(b) COMPLAINT RESOLUTION

Reasons for inclusion:

To outline the steps to be taken to resolve conflicts or misunderstandings.

To indicate that there will be no retaliation for following the steps to resolve a conflict or misunderstanding.

To make it clear that seeking conflict resolution will not by itself prevent or delay any announced disciplinary action.

Caveats: Employees should be encouraged to try to resolve conflicts in the smallest arenas possible; most issues can be resolved far short of a formal hearing. However, some small group should be established as a final point of appeal for serious issues. Establishing this outside the board itself will work toward insulating the board members from lawsuits.

To demonstrate how these guidelines can be applied, the Appendix to this chapter contains a sample set of personnel policies. As with any other document having legal consequences, however, these policies should not be adopted until an organization has checked with its attorney for their compliance with local laws and regulations.

APPENDIX: SAMPLE PERSONNEL POLICIES FOR A NONPROFIT ORGANIZATION

CONTENTS

Effective Date: _____

1. INTRODUCTION

1.1. Welcome to The Nonprofit Organization

All of us at The Nonprofit Organization (NPO) believe that our goals and those of our employees are closely related. Indeed, the success of NPO, to a great extent, is dependent on the success of the employees in meeting their own goals. We trust that your association with the NPO will be a mutually rewarding one.

We have prepared this personnel manual to answer some of the questions you might have regarding the NPO and its policies. Please read it carefully and retain it for future reference. From time to time, you may receive updates of individual sections, or of the entire document, should the Board (at its sole discretion) decide that some or all policies need changing. If you have any questions about any of the policies, please feel free to discuss them with the Executive Director.

This is not a contract guaranteeing employment for any specific amount of time. While we hope that your association with The Nonprofit Organization will be a long and happy one, either you or the NPO may terminate the relationship at any time, for any reason, with or without cause or notice.

It should be remembered that *NPO is a small organization.* Therefore, flexibility, initiative, and the willingness to be a "team player" are some of the characteristics important to all positions at The Nonprofit Organization.

Again, we welcome you to The Nonprofit Organization and express our sincere hope that your employment will be a fulfilling experience.

1.2. Overview of The Nonprofit Organization

Established in 19XX as a 501(c) (3) nonprofit corporation, The Nonprofit Organization (NPO) exists to develop, promote, and support programs in XYZ. Much of its funding comes from ABC, which is charged with [identification of charge].

While most of The Nonprofit Organization's funds come from ABC, additional monies are often available from state and local governmental agencies, other nonprofits or for-profit enterprises, and individual donors. Any of these might have operating guidelines which must be met by individual employees or the NPO as a whole.

NPO activities are overseen by a 24-member Board of Directors comprised of individuals with professional, academic, or general interest in [our charge]. Most of these directors are elected annually to specified terms by members of the NPO Corporation; some are appointed by [elected official]. Working together, these 24 individuals develop policies for their own operations and for the operations of the agency as a whole.

[Insert another paragraph about what the organization does.]

Effective Date: _____

2. KEY DEFINITIONS

2.1. The Board of Directors

2.1.1.   *Elected members* are those 20 individuals who are elected to positions on the Board at the annual meeting. Each person is limited to two consecutive three-year terms but may be reelected after an absence of one full year. All are volunteers who receive no compensation for their service as Board members. They may, however, receive meals or reimbursement for expenses incurred while engaged in authorized NPO business.

2.1.2.   *Appointed members* are those appointed to the Board by the [political official]. Here the members serve only as long as their appointing official remains in office. They have the same rights and restrictions as elected members.

2.1.3.   Guidelines for NPO Board members' conduct appear in the bylaws and such other policy documents as the Board may from time to time adopt.

2.1.4.   Hereafter, the organization may be identified as *The Nonprofit Organization,* or its name may be abbreviated as *NPO.*

2.2. Full-Time and Non-Full-Time Employees

2.2.1.   *Full-time employees* are those individuals hired to work a scheduled 35-hour workweek on a regular basis. These employees may be "exempt" or "nonexempt" as defined below. They are entitled to full participation in the NPO's benefits, as defined in subsequent sections.

2.2.2.   *Part-time employees* are those hired to work fewer than 35 hours a week on a regular basis. These employees may be "exempt" or "nonexempt" as defined below. They are entitled to full or prorated participation in the NPO's benefits, as defined in subsequent sections.

2.2.3.   *Temporary employees* are those individuals who are placed on the NPO's payroll with the understanding that their employment ceases when a particular assignment has been completed or a particular deadline has been reached. These employees may be "exempt" or "nonexempt" as defined below. They are entitled to participate only in the mandated benefits, as defined in Section 8.

Individuals hired from a temporary agency remain employees of that agency, not of The Nonprofit Organization, and are therefore not entitled to participate in any of the NPO's benefit programs.

2.3. Exempt and Nonexempt Employees

2.3.1.   *Exempt employees* are those whose work is at least 80 percent executive, administrative, or professional. In accordance with the Fair Labor

Standards Act, such individuals are not required to be paid overtime for working beyond 40 hours in a given week.

2.3.2.   *Nonexempt employees* are those who are covered by the Fair Labor Standards Act. They must be paid overtime at the rate of 1.5 times their regular rate for all work lasting beyond 40 hours in a given week. To qualify for such pay, the overtime work *must* be authorized in advance by the Executive Director or the appropriate supervisor. Compensatory leave is not an acceptable substitute for overtime pay.

2.4. Consultants and Volunteers

2.4.1.   *Consultants* are those individuals or groups hired on a contractual or fee-for-service basis. They are entitled to participate in none of the NPO's benefit programs. Their performance is reviewed in accordance with the provisions of their contract.

2.4.2.   *Volunteers* are those individuals recruited to participate in NPO programs because of their interest or acknowledged expertise in some aspect of [the charge]. They neither receive financial compensation nor participate in any of the NPO's benefit programs; they may, however, be eligible for reimbursement for authorized expenses incurred as part of their NPO involvement.

Effective date: _____

3. GENERAL MANAGEMENT POLICIES

3.1. Authority over Personnel Matters

3.1.1.   The *Board,* in consultation with the Executive Director and such others as deemed appropriate, shall create and promulgate personnel policies for the organization. [NOTE: Personnel policies are established by a vote of the Board of Directors, which may then delegate the policies' implementation.]

The Board has the authority to establish pay ranges for positions and to establish benefits policies.

Authority to hire and terminate the Executive Director rests with the Board's Executive Committee.

3.1.2.   The *Executive Director* has the responsibility to hire, supervise, evaluate, and terminate all other employees and consultants. The Executive Director works for the Board as a whole, but reports directly to the President.

The Executive Director has the authority to negotiate compensation levels with all employees, subject to the ranges approved by the Board.

3.1.3.   *Program or project directors* may from time to time be given responsibility by the Executive Director for identifying prospective employees or consultants and working with those who have been hired. All hiring, compensation, and termination decisions rest with the Executive Director.

3.2. Personnel Files

3.2.1.   The NPO retains a *personnel file* for each employee. This file will contain documentation regarding such aspects of the individual's employment as job descriptions, performance appraisals, beneficiary designation forms, letters of commendation, and disciplinary notices.

The Fair Labor Standards Act requires that the Board also retain all time sheets, work schedules, and wage rate tables for at least two years, and all payroll records and employment contracts for at least three years. For all nonexempt employees, the Board must also retain records showing name, social security number, address, birth date (if an employee is under 19), sex, occupation, and wage rate.

3.2.2.   You may *review your own personnel file.* If you wish to do so, contact the Executive Director to schedule an appointment. [NOTE: State laws vary here. Connecticut and Illinois laws, for example, permit employees to add statements to their files if they disagree with the contents. In Michigan and California, access must be given "at reasonable intervals." Oregon says that employees may receive certified copies of relevant portions of their records.]

3.2.3.   To *keep your personnel file up-to-date,* you should notify the Executive Director or other appropriate staff member of any changes in your name, telephone number, home address, marital status, dependents, beneficiary designations, educational attainments, and any other relevant factors.

3.3. Equal Employment Opportunity

3.3.1.   The Nonprofit Organization provides *equal employment opportunity* to all applicants and employees without regard to race, color, religion, sex, national origin, age, handicap, or veteran's status, in accordance with applicable federal and state laws. [NOTE: Some state laws add categories here, such as pregnancy, marital status, and political affiliation.]

This policy extends to all terms and conditions of employment, including hiring, placement, promotion, termination, leaves of absence, compensation, and training. In addition, the NPO will not use the services of any placement agency known to discriminate in its referrals on the basis of any of the characteristics mentioned above.

3.3.2.   The NPO prohibits *sexual harassment* of its employees by Board members, employees, contractors, and grantees. All employees should expect to work in an atmosphere free of unwanted sexual overtures or any unwelcome behavior which is personally offensive, which debilitates morale, or which otherwise interferes with working effectiveness.

The NPO will not tolerate situations wherein an employee is made to feel that submission to such advances is a term or condition of employment or where reaction to such treatment is used as a basis for decisions affecting the individual's employment. Offensive comments, innuendos, "jokes," and sexually oriented "kidding" are regarded as forms of sexual harassment.

3.3.3.   If you feel that you have suffered unlawful discrimination or sexual harassment, contact the Executive Director. If the Executive Director is the one you feel is discriminating or harassing, contact the NPO President.

3.3.4.   No form of *retaliation* is permitted for filing bona fide charges of illegal discrimination or harassment. Should such allegations prove groundless, however, disciplinary action may be taken against the complainant.

3.4. Drug-Free Workplace

3.4.1   The Nonprofit Organization adheres to the requirements of the *Drug-free Workplace Act of 1988.* Use of controlled substances is inappropriate behavior that subjects coworkers, grantees, visitors, and others unacceptable safety risks and undermines the NPO's operating effectiveness.

3.4.2.   *Reporting to work, or working* under the influence of a controlled substance (except with a physician's prescription) is prohibited. This prohibition extends to the NPO premises and to all other sites where an employee is engaged in NPO business.

3.4.3   The NPO prohibits *the criminal use, manufacture, distribution, dispensation, possession, or sale of a controlled substance* on any NPO-affiliated worksite. Such conduct is also prohibited outside scheduled working hours to the extent that NPO regards it as impairing the employee's ability to perform on the job or as threatening the reputation of The Nonprofit Organization.

3.4.4. Any employee *convicted of a violation* related to a controlled substance (or pleading no contest to such a charge) must notify the Executive Director in writing within five working days of the conviction or plea.

3.4.5. Employees wanting *information on locally available sources of substance-abuse counseling* should contact the Executive Director, who will make every reasonable effort to keep the request confidential.

3.4.6. Individuals who violate any aspect of this policy will be subject to *disciplinary action,* up to and including termination. The NPO may also require that an employee successfully complete a substance-abuse or rehabilitation program as a condition of further employment.

3.5. Health and Safety

3.5.1. The NPO tries to provide a *safe and healthful environment* for employees, grantees, visitors, and others while they are on Nonprofit Organization premises or attending NPO-sponsored programs.

3.5.2. The Executive Director is responsible for establishing *procedures and programs* that minimize the risk of personal injury to everyone using Nonprofit Organization facilities or equipment or attending NPO-sponsored functions.

3.5.3. All *employees are required* to follow the safety procedures that have been established. They are expected to report any potentially unsafe or hazardous conditions, or any injuries, to the Executive Director immediately.

3.5.4. Employees may be injured in the course of work and therefore have to be absent from work. If so, they are subject to the provisions of the State's *workers' compensation program* and are paid accordingly.

3.5.5. All employees share responsibility for personal safety and for the security of Nonprofit Organization property. Any untoward behavior by any visitor or suspicious person in the vicinity of The Nonprofit Organization premises or the location of any NPO-sponsored program should be reported to the Executive Director immediately.

3.6. Conflict of Interest

3.6.1. To avoid any action that could be interpreted as using their positions at the NPO unfairly, all employees shall refrain from *serving on the board of directors* of any organization or institution known to be or likely to become an applicant for NPO funds.

3.6.2. Employees shall not accept any *fees or other remuneration* from any organization or institution in conjunction with a project or program for which NPO funds are being sought or have been granted.

3.6.3. If an employee's *spouse or other immediate relative* (see Section 3.7.2) has any financial or managerial connection to a project or organization for which NPO funds are being sought or have been granted, that relationship must be disclosed before any proposal concerning that project or organization is reviewed. The employee then may not participate in or remain in the room during any discussion of the project or organization in question.

3.6.4.   All employees should strive to avoid conflicts of interest as well as the *appearance of any such conflict.*

3.7. Employment of Relatives

3.7.1.   Given the small size of The Nonprofit Organization, relatives of employees and Board members would almost inevitably find themselves in situations where NPO and private interests were in conflict. Therefore, it is the policy of NPO that *no immediate relative of an employee or a Board member* shall be employed by The Nonprofit Organization as long as the original employee or board member remains with the organization.

3.7.2.   *Immediate relatives* include parents, siblings, and children; people in those categories with a "step" or "in-law" relationship; and any other member of the employee's or Board member's immediate household, such as the "significant other."

3.7.3.   Should *employees marry each other* while working for the NPO, they may both remain employed so long as the Board does not perceive any conflict or the appearance of any conflict of interest. If such a conflict or the appearance thereof arises, the employees will be given an opportunity to decide which will leave The Nonprofit Organization. If the employees do not make this decision, the NPO reserves the right to select and terminate one of them with 30 days' notice. The same policy applies should a Board member and an employee become married.

Effective Date: _____

4. EMPLOYMENT POLICIES

4.1. Job Creation and Description

4.1.1. NPO shall develop and maintain a *written description* of the responsibilities, qualifications, and salary range for each of its positions. Responsibility for developing these shall rest with the Executive Director. (For the Executive Director's position, it shall rest with the NPO Executive Committee or be covered by the employment contract.)

4.1.2. The applicable *position description shall be discussed* with each individual upon hiring and during each annual performance review, as both a guide for performance and a means of identifying any needed changes.

4.1.3. Each position description shall be *formally reviewed* at least once every three years to determine any needs for revision. If you feel that yours might need revision at any other time, you should talk with the Executive Director about possible changes.

4.1.4. A copy of each individual's position description shall be kept in his or her *personnel file.*

4.1.5. When the Executive Director decides that a *position needs to be created,* that one needs to be changed in a significant manner, or that one needs to be abolished, the Executive Director will create or revise the affected position descriptions.

4.2. Recruitment and Selection

4.2.1. NPO's recruitment and selection activities are conducted to ensure the employment of the best qualified candidates. Therefore, they will be implemented in a manner consistent with providing equal employment opportunity, as discussed in Section 3.3.

4.2.2. When a position is created or when one becomes vacant, NPO *employees will be notified* before or at the same time as external recruitment begins. Qualified internal candidates will be encouraged to apply for openings, because NPO believes in staff development.

4.2.3. Within the organization, the *Executive Director must approve* all employment decisions (including recommendations for hiring, promotion, demotion, and other changes) before any commitments are made or any notification is given to an applicant or a current employee. This approval extends to issues of compensation and working hours.

4.2.4. The NPO will *check references* before making any hiring decisions.

4.2.5. For each new employee, NPO will provide an *orientation* to the organization, the work, and the coworkers.

4.3. Performance Reviews

4.3.1. NPO believes in providing *frequent feedback* so that employees can be recognized for good performance and informed of areas where improvement is necessary. Therefore, you can expect that your performance will be evaluated by the Executive Director or your supervisor on a continuing basis.

4.3.2. You will receive a *written performance evaluation* from the Executive Director after the first six months at The Nonprofit Organization and at least once a year thereafter. (The Executive Director's evaluation will be provided by the Board President, after consultation with the Executive Committee.) [NOTE: Other provisions may be made through an employment contract.]

All written performance reviews will be based on your performance in relation to your responsibilities. They will also take into consideration your demeanor, record of attendance, and demonstrated willingness to cooperate with colleagues in furthering the NPO mission.

Should you disagree with any items on your evaluation or feel that any information is incorrect, you are encouraged to discuss your concerns with the evaluato. If this discussion does not meet your expectations, you are entitled to have your written comments added to your personnel file.

Effective Date: _____

5. SCHEDULING POLICIES

5.1. Work Hours

5.1.1. The *regular workweek for full-time employees* is 35 hours, divided into five seven-hour workdays, Monday through Friday.

5.1.2. *Regular work hours for full-time employees* are from 9 A.M. to 5 P.M., with a one-hour unpaid lunch break, to be taken between 11:30 A.M. and 2:00 P.M. The specific meal time will be scheduled to ensure appropriate coverage of the office. Should such scheduling present difficulties, the Executive Director will designate times for meal breaks.

5.1.3. Work *schedules for part-time employees* will be arranged by the Executive Director.

5.1.4. Daily and weekly *schedules may be changed* from time to time by the Board or by the Executive Director to meet the changing needs of the organization. Any such changes will be announced as far in advance as possible.

[NOTE: State laws may specify breaks for nonexempt workers.]

5.2. Overtime

5.2.1. *Nonexempt employees* (see Section 2.3) are eligible for overtime pay for authorized work beyond 40 hours in a given regular workweek. This pay is to be calculated at the rate of 1.5 times each individual's normal hourly rate. It also is calculated weekly, meaning that working an "average" of 40 hours a week over several weeks does not obviate the need for overtime pay if, in any one of those weeks, the nonexempt employee works more than 40 authorized hours.

5.2.2. If you are a nonexempt employee, you will be paid at your *normal rate for work between the 35th and 40th hours* of work in a given week. Overtime pay begins after the 40th hour. [NOTE: Some states have tougher standards. In California, for example, a nonexempt employee must be paid time and-a-half for working more than 8 hours in a given day, and double-time for working more than 12 hours. Also, the 40-hour requirement is a legal one; however, a nonprofit *may* choose to start paying overtime at any hour short of 40 that it chooses.]

5.2.3. *Exempt* employees are not eligible for overtime pay, but, in some cases, may accrue compensatory time, as described in Section 9.10. For exempt employees, the standard workweek represents the minimum number of hours they are expected to work.

5.2.4. No payment for overtime work shall be made unless the work was *authorized in advance,* in writing, by the appropriate supervisor or the Executive Director.

5.2.5.   *All* employees are required to keep accurate *records of the time they work,* on the forms provided. These forms are to be submitted to the Budget Officer by noon each Monday.

5.3. Attendance at Meetings and Conferences

5.3.1.   The nature of NPO's business will, from time to time, require that staff members attend meetings and conferences outside the office. When such sessions occur *during normal working hours,* no special provisions are made, except that individuals are reimbursed for expenses as outlined in Section 7. When such sessions extend to time beyond normal working hours, the following guidelines pertain.

5.3.2.   In compliance with Department of Labor regulations, when a *nonexempt employee is required to make a one-day trip,* he or she is compensated for the time spent traveling to and from the assigned location (but not the time spent traveling between home and the airport or train station) and the time involved in actually working on the assignment. The time normally spent on meal breaks is not compensable.

5.3.3.   When a *nonexempt employee's travel extends overnight,* the only travel time that is compensable is that which overlaps the normal working schedule (even if the travel occurs on a weekend or holiday). When conference or meeting attendance involves work at the other site(s) that goes beyond normal working hours, those hours are compensable in accordance with Section 5.2.

5.3.4.   When an *exempt employee is required to attend a meeting or conference* that necessitates being away from home for more than two consecutive nights, he or she accrues four hours of compensatory time for each additional night he or she is required to be away. Such time is accrued when budgetary concerns require an extra night's travel to reduce airfare. (Scheduling convenience and airline preference are not seen as travel requirements.)

Effective Date: _____

6. COMPENSATION POLICIES

6.1. Overview

6.1.1. To attract and retain high-quality employees, NPO endeavors to pay salaries competitive with those offered by similar nonprofit organizations. This process involves setting *a compensation range for each position*. Each salary range is reviewed at least once every three years for possible adjustment.

6.1.2. Your *total compensation* at NPO reflects not only your salary or wages but also the various benefits that NPO offers (such as health insurance and paid vacation). It is possible that increases in the costs of benefits might from time to time limit the amount of money available for changes in direct compensation. To clarify such situations, the NPO will inform you each year of the change in your total compensation.

6.1.3. The Nonprofit Organization conforms to the compensation provisions of the Equal Pay Act of 1963 and Executive Order 11246.

6.1.4. Your *compensation will be reviewed* at least once a year. Factors to be considered include your performance, the NPO budget for the coming year, your responsibilities, and the recommendation of the Executive Director. If your salary is to be changed, the new amount will normally be effective at the beginning of the fiscal year.

6.2. Payroll Policies

6.2.1. NPO employees are paid by check on a *semimonthly basis,* usually on the fifteenth and the last days of the month. All required and voluntary deductions will be withheld automatically from your paycheck.

6.2.2. Should the scheduled *payday fall on a weekend or an NPO-observed holiday,* checks will usually be issued on the day before the weekend or holiday.

6.2.3. You will not receive a paycheck on time unless the Budget Officer has received your *completed timesheet* by the scheduled deadline.

6.2.4. You should review your paycheck for accuracy when you receive it. If you find an error, please report it to the Executive Director or the Budget Officer immediately.

6.2.5. If your paycheck is lost or stolen, notify the Budget Officer immediately so that a stop-payment order can be issued. If the check is cashed before such a stop-payment order can be issued, you alone will be responsible for the loss.

6.2.6. NPO does not normally provide payroll advances. However, if you have been an employee for at least a year, and if a payday would fall during your scheduled vacation, The Nonprofit Organization will advance an amount equivalent to your base salary, less the standard deductions. This amount, in turn, will be deducted from the payroll in question. To receive such an advance, you should complete the required form and return it to the Budget Officer at least one week before the start of the vacation.

Effective Date: _____

7. EXPENSE REIMBURSEMENT

7.1. Travel Expenses

7.1.1. If you are required to use *your automobile* on NPO business, you will be reimbursed at a mileage rate determined annually, plus expenses for tolls and parking. Reimbursement will not be provided for travel between your home and the office.

7.1.2. *Air fares* will be reimbursed at coach rates. Costs for alternative transportation on ground will be reimbursed at rates not more than the coach fare. If you make travel arrangements for non-NPO reasons, such as traveling by an indirect route or stopping over, you will be responsible for any extra charges.

7.1.3. If your air travel involves the accumulation of *frequent flyer miles,* you may credit them to your account.

7.1.4. If NPO business requires that you stay overnight away from home, The Nonprofit Organization will reimburse your for the cost of *reasonably priced accommodations.*

7.1.5. Normally, *meals away from home* will be at your expense. However, when you incur meal costs in direct connection with NPO business, you will be reimbursed according to the NPO schedule.

7.1.6. To secure reimbursement for any travel expense, you must complete a travel expense form and attach the relevant receipts within a month of completing the travel.

7.2. Other Expenses

7.2.1. *Membership fees* for professional and social organizations will normally be your responsibility.

7.2.2. The Nonprofit Organization will reimburse you for any fees involved with *conferences* you are required to attend.

7.2.3. You will be reimbursed for expenses incurred for telephone calls, supplies, postage, copying, and *other items* authorized by the Executive Director.

7.2.4. The *reimbursement procedure* here is the same as that for travel expenses.

Effective Date: _____

8. EMPLOYEE BENEFITS OTHER THAN LEAVE

8.1. Overview

8.1.1. The Nonprofit Organization provides a number of benefit programs designed to help you and your eligible dependents meet the expenses that may arise in connection with such matters as illness, disability, kin care, death, and retirement. This section of the manual highlights features of those programs required by law and those which NPO has chosen to sponsor. *Program details can be found in the summary plan description available from the Budget Officer.* Unless otherwise stated, all employees are covered by the mandatory programs, while only full-time employees are covered by the voluntary ones.

8.1.2. The NPO reserves the right, at its discretion, to change or terminate any of the nonmandatory programs or to require employee contributions toward any benefits. This right may be exercised regardless of financial necessity.

8.2. Mandatory Benefits

8.2.1. All NPO employees are covered by *Social Security and by Unemployment Insurance,* in accordance with federal law.

8.2.2. To help meet financial needs if you suffer a work-related injury or illness, NPO provides *workers' compensation insurance.* To make certain that your injury or illness is covered, you need to report it immediately to the Executive Director.

8.2.3. You are also covered by the state's *Temporary Disability Insurance program,* for which a monthly premium will be deducted from your paycheck. [NOTE: Availability and scope of coverage here differ by state.]

8.3. Flexible Benefit Options

8.3.1. If you are a full-time employee, you are eligible for *flexible spending accounts;* if you are a part-time employee, you may participate on a prorated basis, according to the percentage of a normal workweek you are employed. The flexible benefits plan conforms to the requirements of the Employee Retirement Income Security Act (ERISA).

8.3.2. NPO's flexible benefit plan allows you the option of paying your portion of the health care premium, the dental care premium, and your child care expenses with *pretax dollars.* This benefit means that the eligible amounts are deducted from your compensation before taxes are deducted; your tax bill may be lower as a result.

8.3.3. New employees are *eligible to participate* in the flexible plan within their first 31 days of employment; thereafter, an employee may join only during the open enrollment period in January. You may leave the flexible program only during January as well.

8.3.4.   The *dependent care assistance plan* (DECAP) allows you to deduct up to $5,000 a year in dependent care expenses on a pretax basis.

[NOTE: The language in this section is illustrative only. Each nonprofit should use language that reflects its own policy regarding benefit options, if any.]

8.4. Health Insurance

8.4.1.   NPO offers employees a *choice of major medical insurance* between an indemnity plan and a health maintenance organization. NPO pays 80 percent of the cost of individual coverage for a full-time employee, and 50 percent of the cost of individual coverage for a part-time employee who works a regular schedule of at least 17.5 hours a week. Other employees are not covered. [NOTE: An alternative is to pay $X per month toward the cost of health insurance.]

8.4.2.   Health insurance premiums to *cover your dependents* are your individual responsibility, but NPO will handle the transfer of premiums to the carrier.

8.4.3.   All employees are *eligible for coverage upon joining the payroll.* If you choose not to participate, you must wait until the next open enrollment period to add coverage.

8.4.4.   If you leave NPO or if your work schedule is changed so that you are no longer eligible for health insurance coverage, you and your eligible dependents may be able to *continue to participate* for up to 18 months at your expense. Continuing coverage may end, though, if you fail to make required payments, if NPO drops its plan, or if you join another health plan. Details on this option are available from the Budget Officer.

8.4.5.   NPO *requires that all full-time employees participate* in the health insurance plan or annually provide evidence of participation in another plan.

8.4.6.   If you receive your primary health insurance coverage from a policy other than NPO's, The Nonprofit Organization will pay the *copayment on the other policy,* so long as that amount does not exceed the amount that would have been paid had you remained with NPO's coverage. You will not receive the monetary equivalent of any unexpended health insurance fees in cash or in other benefits.

8.5. Dental Insurance

8.5.1.   NPO provides individual dental insurance for all full-time employees and pays half the premium for part-time employees who work a regular schedule of at least 17.5 hours a week.

8.5.2.   Dental insurance *benefits cease* when you leave The Nonprofit Organization.

8.6. Long-Term Disability Insurance

8.6.1.   NPO provides every full-time employee with insurance to cover *long-term disability.* This coverage, for which NPO pays the entire premium, is effective on the day each employee joins the payroll.

8.6.2.   *Coverage under this plan terminates* when you leave The Nonprofit Organization, unless you are receiving disability benefits at the time of termination, in which case the benefits continue as long as your qualifying disability continues.

8.7. Life Insurance

8.7.1.   All full-time employees are eligible to participate in The Nonprofit Organization's life insurance program, which offers *coverage for employees* but not for dependents.

8.7.2.   *NPO pays the premium* for a life insurance benefit of twice your annual salary, to a maximum of $50,000. Additional coverage in the same amount is provided for accidental death or dismemberment.

8.7.3.   Life insurance benefits terminate on the date your employment with The Nonprofit Organization ends.

8.8. Retirement Plan

8.8.1.   NPO offers *participation in [Retirement Plan]* to all full-time and part-time employees who work for the agency for at least 1,000 hours a year.

8.8.2.   When an eligible employee agrees to *contribute an amount equivalent to 5 percent of annual salary* to [Retirement Plan], NPO will contribute an equal amount. Employee contributions will be withheld from regular paychecks.

8.9. Educational Assistance

8.9.1.   NPO is interested in helping full-time employees develop their skills and upgrade their performance. To those ends, The Nonprofit Organization offers an educational assistance program to all full-time employees who have completed at least a year of service.

8.9.2.   NPO will reimburse you an amount equivalent to the state university's charges for up to *three academic credits per term* for courses (a) which are offered at an accredited postsecondary institution and (b) which are directly or reasonably related to your present position or are part of a degree program.

8.9.3.   *Costs will be reimbursed* only if (a) you receive approval from the Executive Director before enrolling, (b) you earn a grade of B or better, and (c) you supply the Budget Officer with evidence of having successfully completed the course.

Effective Date: _____

9. PAID AND UNPAID LEAVE

9.1. Holidays

9.1.1.   The NPO office is open Monday through Friday, except for the following *10 holidays:*
   a. New Year's Day
   b. Martin Luther King, Jr., Day
   c. President's Day
   d. Memorial Day
   e. Independence Day
   f. Labor Day
   g. Columbus Day
   h. Thanksgiving Day
   i. National Shopping Day (day after Thanksgiving)
   j. Christmas Day

9.1.2.   *Holidays falling on a Saturday* are normally observed on the preceding Friday, while those falling on a Sunday are normally observed on the following Monday. The Executive Director will post a schedule of the specific dates at the beginning of each January.

9.1.3.   Full-time employees will be compensated for each holiday, provided that they have worked *the regularly scheduled workdays immediately preceding and following the holiday.* Approved vacation or sick leave is regarded as a day worked for the purposes of holiday pay.

9.1.4.   *Part-time employees* who are normally scheduled to work on a day that is a holiday will be compensated at their regular rate for the hours on that holiday during which they would normally have worked. Part-time employees will not receive holiday pay if they were not normally scheduled to work on a holiday.

9.1.5.   *Temporary employees* are not eligible for holiday pay.

9.1.6.   *Nonexempt employees* who are required to work on an observed holiday will be paid their regular rate plus time-and-a-half for the hours actually worked on the holiday.

9.1.7.   *Exempt employees* who are required to work on an observed holiday will be eligible for one hour of compensatory time for every hour worked on the observed holiday (to a maximum of seven hours per holiday).

9.2. Vacation

9.2.1.   NPO believes that vacation time provides important opportunities for rest, recreation, and personal activities. Therefore, NPO grants annual paid vacations to all full-time and part-time employees, in varying amounts according to work schedule and length of service.

9.2.2.   For the *first five years of full-time employment,* an employee earns 10 vacation days per calendar year, accrued at the rate of 5/6 of a day per month. Thereafter, a full-time employee receives 15 vacation days a year, accrued at the rate of 1.25 days a month.

9.2.3.   *Part-time employees accrue vacation time* on schedules proportionate to those above; however, during the vacation period, they are paid only for hours they would normally be scheduled to work.

9.2.4.   *Newly hired employees* may take no paid vacation leave until they have worked at The Nonprofit Organization for six months. At that point, they are eligible to take one half of their first year's vacation.

9.2.5.   You may not *carry* more than five *vacation days into a subsequent year.* If you are working on a time-limited project, all accrued vacation must be taken before the scheduled end of the project.

9.2.6.   Employees are *required to use their earned vacation* time or lose it. There will be no payments made in lieu of vacation time, except that an employee leaving The Nonprofit Organization will be compensated for any accrued but unused leave at the time of termination.

9.2.7.   If an *NPO-observed holiday falls during your scheduled vacation,* you will be granted an alternative vacation day later.

9.2.8.   Vacations may be taken as individual days or in longer intervals, as long as the *periods have been approved in advance* by the Executive Director. Requests for vacation should be submitted at least two weeks in advance. For popular times, requests should be submitted earlier. If two requests are submitted concurrently, the Executive Director, in recognition of NPO requirements, will decide which will be granted.

9.2.9.   An employee who becomes ill during a scheduled vacation may not then apply sick days to that period.

9.3. Personal Days

9.3.1.   NPO provides full-time employees with up to *three days of personal leave a year* to deal with personal business, religious observance, and other matters of personal importance. Personal leave is accrued at the rate of one day for each four months of work per calendar year.

9.3.2.   Personal days may not be used to extend a scheduled vacation.

9.3.3.   You must give the Executive Director *written notice* of your intention to take a personal day (although you need not give the reason) at least one week before taking that day off, except in emergency situations. The Executive Director will consider Nonprofit Organization needs before granting that request; scheduled vacation time has priority. However, every effort will be made to accommodate requests for personal leave to observe holidays of religious significance.

9.3.4.   Personal days may be taken only after they have been accrued. They may not be *carried over* into a subsequent calendar year, and there shall be no payment for any personal days that have not been taken by the end of the calendar year.

9.3.5.   Personal leave may not be taken in units smaller than a half-day (3.5 hours).

9.4. Sick Leave

9.4.1.   NPO provides sick leave to encourage employees to take care of their health and to help alleviate the financial hardships that might accrue in its absence. Sick leave is not synonymous with vacation.

9.4.2.   Full-time employees *accrue* up to 10 days of paid sick leave per calendar year, at the rate of $5/6$ of a day per month. Part-time employees accrue sick leave on a prorated basis.

9.4.3.   Sick days may not be *carried over* into a subsequent calendar year, nor are payments made for any accrued but unused sick days at the end of a calendar year.

9.4.4.   If you are unable to work because of illness, you must *notify* the Executive Director by 9 A.M. on each day of your inability to work, unless you have been granted an official medical leave. Failure to notify The Nonprofit Organization will result in the day's being treated as unpaid leave.

9.4.5.   At any time, the Nonprofit Organization has the right to require a *statement from a physician* concerning your illness, its expected duration, and your ability to return to work.

9.4.6.   Employees are eligible to take sick leave after having worked at The Nonprofit Organization for three months. Any time taken off during the first three months will be treated as unpaid leave.

9.4.7.   If you have *exhausted your sick leave* but are still unable to return to work, you may request that your accrued vacation and personal days and compensatory time be discharged as sick leave. Should all of these be exhausted, you may request an unpaid leave of absence, or you may be eligible for coverage under the state's temporary disability program.

9.4.8.   Your regular pay and benefits continue while you are on approved sick leave.

9.4.9.   Time off for medical or dental appointments shall be charged to sick leave. Sick leave may not be taken in units smaller than two hours.

9.5. Bereavement Leave

9.5.1.   NPO will provide leave for work time missed due to the death of an immediate relative. For full-time employees, the maximum is three days with pay per bereavement; for part-time employees, the maximum is three scheduled workdays with pay per bereavement. For temporary employees, the maximum is three days without pay per bereavement.

9.5.2.   For the death of a relative other than one in the immediate family, the maximum paid leave is one day.

[NOTE: Nonprofit organizations might want to consider eliminating Sections 9.2 through 9.5, and replacing them with another policy which grants everyone 22 days a year to satisfy *all* demands for leave except those with which the government is involved, namely military and jury duty. Doing so could greatly simplify management—after people become accustomed to the new method. Putting holidays into this category would raise questions about letting everyone have keys to the office, or about running the heating or air-conditioning system for one person; therefore, holidays should probably remain separate.]

9.6. Parental Leave

9.6.1.   NPO will provide unpaid leave for up to 12 weeks for an employee following the birth or adoption of a child.

9.6.2.   Parental leave may not be taken more than once in any three-year period, or twice in any five-year period.

9.6.3.   During this leave, The Nonprofit Organization will continue health benefit coverage; however, no paid leave or seniority will accrue, nor will pension contributions be made. If an individual decides not to return to work after the end of the period of parental leave, he or she will be expected to reimburse the NPO for the cost of health coverage paid during the leave period.

9.6.4.   The NPO will make every reasonable effort to return the employee to the same position as that held before the leave; however, changing circumstances may render this impossible.

9.7. Jury and Witness Duty Leave

9.7.1.   All employees are allowed unpaid leave for answering a summons to appear as a witness in court.

9.7.2.   All full-time employees summoned to jury duty are allowed paid leave up to 15 working days per calendar year. They must turn over their jury stipend to The Nonprofit Organization.

9.7.3.   Part-time and temporary employees are given unpaid leave while serving on a jury.

9.7.4.   To qualify for jury or witness leave, you must give the Executive Director or the Budget Officer a copy of your summons and of your jury-discharge notice.

9.8. Military Leave

9.8.1.   Military leave permits employees to fulfill their military obligations as members of the U.S. Armed Forces, the National Guard, or the State Militia in accordance with federal and state laws.

9.8.2.   All full-time and part-time employees called to *active duty or to Reserve or National Guard training* will be granted leaves of absence without pay in accordance with federal and state laws. [NOTE: State laws vary here.]

9.9. Leaves of Absence

9.9.1.   Any full-time or part-time employee who has worked for The Nonprofit Organization for at least one year may request an *unpaid personal leave* for a period of up to 30 calendar days. This leave must be requested in writing at least two weeks prior to the planned beginning of the leave; if the leave is precipitated by an emergency, the request must be made by you or an immediate relative within three days of the beginning of the leave.

9.9.2.   Unpaid personal leave may be granted, at the discretion of the Executive Director, provided that it does not unduly disrupt NPO operations. *Such leave is not encouraged,* however, because the small size of the organization makes it difficult to shift responsibilities for very long. Such leave shall not commence until all accrued vacation and personal days have been discharged.

9.9.3.   If an unpaid leave is granted, The Nonprofit Organization will continue paying for health and life insurance, but paid leave and retirement benefits will not continue to accrue.

9.9.4.   *Reinstatement cannot be guaranteed* after an employee takes an unpaid personal leave, but every effort will be made to return the employee to the same or a comparable position. Budgetary constraints, the availability of temporary replacements, and the need to fill positions may each affect the reinstatement.

9.9.5.   After each seven years of full-time employment, the Executive Director will be eligible to apply for a two-month, paid leave for professional development, in accordance with guidelines adopted by the Executive Committee. After each seven years of full-time employment, the Associate Director will be eligible to apply for a one-month, paid professional leave, and other staff will be eligible to apply for a two-week, paid professional leave. All such leave is to be used for developmental activities related to the work of the Nonprofit Organization and must be approved by the Executive Committee. [NOTE: These numbers are merely illustrative, not recommended. Also, the Executive Director's leave arrangements would be covered by employment contract, if one existed.]

9.10. COMPENSATORY TIME

9.10.1.   Because *nonexempt employees* receive overtime pay, they generally do not accumulate compensatory time. The Executive Director, however, may grant some such leave in addition to overtime pay for extraordinary work on major projects.

9.10.2.   *Exempt employees* may accrue compensatory time for required work on holidays, at conferences, and on significant projects with impending deadlines. Each employee is required to keep accurate records of all such time accrued.

9.10.3. Compensatory time must be *taken within 30 days of its accrual.* None may be carried forward any longer. No payment is made for accrued but unused compensatory time.

9.10.4. An employee wanting to discharge compensatory time must submit a *discharge request* to the Executive Director. If there is a conflict, the Executive Director may extend the period during which the compensatory time can be taken.

9.11. Emergency Closing

9.11.1. This section creates an authorized paid absence when the NPO work schedule must be curtailed because of inclement weather or other emergency conditions.

9.11.2. When the Executive Director (to the extent possible, in consultation with the Board President) determines that the NPO must close, he or she will notify employees in accordance with established procedures. Full-time employees will be paid as if the agency remained open; part-time employees will be paid only if they had been scheduled to work during the closed hours. Temporary employees do not receive compensation.

9.11.3. Both exempt and nonexempt employees required to work during the closing will receive an hour of compensatory time for each hour of required work.

9.11.4. When the NPO remains open, employees who are *late to work* because of inclement weather or other natural disasters must notify the Executive Director of their difficulties at the start of the workday. At the Executive Director's discretion, they will be permitted to extend their work hours to compensate or they will be required to discharge the time from available vacation, personal, or compensatory leave.

9.11.5. When the NPO remains open, employees who are *absent from work because of inclement weather* or other natural disasters must notify the Executive Director at the start of the workday. The missed time will be charged to available vacation, personal, or compensatory leave.

Effective Date: _____

EMPLOYEE CONDUCT

10.1 Overview

10.1.1.   Working for The Nonprofit Organization involves demonstrating respect for the opinions and rights of others. As a member of the NPO team, you are expected to accept certain responsibilities and adhere to acceptable *principles of conduct.* Because your conduct reflects on The Nonprofit Organization and [its charge], you are encouraged to observe the highest standards of behavior at all times.

10.1.2.   Some of the types of behavior which the NPO considers inappropriate are as follows:

   a. Violating NPO's polices against discrimination and sexual harassment.
   b. Soliciting or accepting gratuities or consulting contracts from clients, applicants, or grantees.
   c. Excessive absenteeism or tardiness.
   d. Excessive, unnecessary, or unauthorized use of NPO facilities, supplies, or equipment (including the telephone and facsimile machine).
   e. Falsifying employment or other records.
   f. Using abusive, obscene, or threatening language or gestures.
   g. Theft.
   h. Disregarding safety regulations.
   i. Insubordination.
   j. Reporting to work intoxicated or under the influence of nonprescribed drugs, or otherwise violating the Drug-Free Workplace Act.

10.1.3.   Performance, conduct, or demeanor that becomes unsatisfactory will be subject to *disciplinary action up to and including dismissal.*

10.2. Smoking

10.2.1.   To provide a safe and comfortable working environment, several parts of the NPO facilities have been designated as *no-smoking areas.* Further, there shall be no smoking during a Board meeting in the meeting room itself, regardless of its designation at other times.

10.2.2.   Employees who smoke in areas designated as no-smoking areas will be subject to disciplinary action.

[NOTE: Some state and local laws might restrict smoking, as might some host institutions or landlords.]

10.3. Use of NPO-Owned Equipment and Supplies

10.3.1.   Employees are expected to use NPO equipment carefully and its supplies prudently.

10.3.2. In cases of obvious misuse, an employee may be expected to pay all or part of the replacement cost.

10.3.3. NPO's telephones are provided for Nonprofit Organization business. While employees might occasionally have a legitimate need to use an NPO telephone for personal matters, such calls are to be kept to a minimum, both in number and duration. Employees are expected to reimburse the Nonprofit Organization for any personal long-distance calls they make on NPO telephones.

10.3.4. Employees are expected to reimburse The Nonprofit Organization for any personal use of the NPO facsimile machine.

10.4. Political Activities

10.4.1. In all facilities, employees, volunteers, and Board members are prohibited from distributing literature about, or soliciting funds for, any candidate for public office.

10.4.2. In any outside work on behalf of a political candidate or party, you may not publicly represent yourself as providing any express or implied endorsement by The Nonprofit Organization.

10.4.3. If you choose to run for public office, your political activities may not be conducted in whole or in part from NPO facilities or with NPO materials.

Effective Date: _____

11. TERMINATION OF EMPLOYMENT

11.1. Retirement

11.1.1. If you plan to retire, you are expected to give NPO at least *three months' notice*. Doing so will not only permit the organization to make the necessary staffing adjustments but also enable the staff to process the paperwork necessary for a timely payment of retirement benefits.

11.1.2. The Nonprofit Organization reserves the right to extend an early retirement offer from time to time.

11.1.3. The Executive Director (or the Executive Committee) will hold an *exit interview* with each retiree, just as with all others leaving the organization. (See below.)

11.2. Termination for Reasons Other Than Retirement

11.2.1. Employment relationships with NPO are on an *at-will basis*. As mentioned in the manual's introductory section, "either you or the NPO may terminate the relationship at any time, for any reason, with or without cause."

11.2.2. If *you decide to leave NPO,* you are urged to provide notice at least two weeks before the termination date so that staffing patterns can be adjusted and your final pay can be calculated.

11.2.3. Each departing employee is normally scheduled for an *exit interview*. This session is intended to review eligibility for continuation of benefits and complete any required forms, to collect all NPO property in the individual's possession, and (as appropriate) to discuss the job-related experiences.

[NOTE: Unless a nonprofit organization wants to provide some form of job security, such as three warnings before discharge, it should *not* spell out details on procedures leading to termination. Nor should it use terms like "probationary" to mean a period of during which someone may be dismissed without cause; the implication is that there must be a specified cause at all other times.]

Effective Date: _____

12. COMPLAINT RESOLUTION

12.0.1.   For working relationships within the NPO to remain effective, efforts should be made to resolve misunderstandings and conflicts before serious problems develop.

12.0.2.   If a situation does not seem to be resolving itself, you are encouraged to discuss it with the other individual(s) involved. If that discussion does not resolve the situation, you are encouraged to discuss the matter with your immediate supervisor, and, if necessary, with the Executive Director. Normally, you will receive a response concerning the situation within five working days.

12.0.3.   If you are unsatisfied with the Executive Director's decision, you may submit your concern in writing to the Board-established appeals committee. This group will normally advise you of its decision within 15 working days; this decision shall be final. [NOTE: Establishing a special appeals committee can help insulate board members from lawsuits. This body may include people outside the organization.]

12.0.4.   The Nonprofit Organization does not tolerate any *retaliation* against any employees for following this complaint resolution process. However, the process should also not be construed as limiting or delaying the NPO's right to take disciplinary action (up to and including termination) against any employee if the NPO feels that such action is appropriate.

SOURCES AND SUGGESTED REFERENCES

Cascio, Wayne F. 1982. *Costing Human Resources: The Financial Impact of Behavior in Organizations.* Boston: Kent Publishing.

Gatewood, Robert D., and Feild, Hubert S. 1990. *Human Resource Selection,* 2nd ed. Chicago: Dryden Press.

Green, Ronald M., Carmell, William A., and Gray, Peter S. 1992. *1992 State-by-State Guide to Human Resources Law.* New York: Panel Publishers.

Kahn, Steven C., Brown, Barbara Berish, Zepke, Brent E., and Lanzarone, Michael. 1990. *Personnel Director's Legal Guide,* 2nd ed. Boston: Warren, Gorham & Lamont. (Supplements are available.)

London, Manuel, Bassman, Emily S., and Fernandez, John P. 1990. *Human Resource Forecasting and Strategy Development.* Westport, CT: Quorum Books.

Mobley, William H. 1982. *Employee Turnover: Causes, Consequences, and Control.* Reading, Ma: Addison-Wesley.

Pierce, Jon L., Newstrom, John W., Dunham, Randall B., and Barber, Alison E. 1989. *Alternative Work Schedules.* Boston: Allyn & Bacon.

Shepard, Ira Michael, Heylman, Paul, and Suston, Robert L. 1989. *Without Just Cause: An Employer's Practical and Legal Guide on Wrongful Discharge.* Washington, DC: Bureau of National Affairs.

Performance Evaluation

Mark D. Michaels
People Technologies

CONTENTS

13.1 THE PERFORMANCE MANAGEMENT SYSTEM

(a) CONTINUOUS IMPROVEMENT: THE PLANNING–EVALUATION–PLANNING CYCLE
Performance management is continuous improvement programming at the individual level. Like a continuous improvement team, the evaluator and employee ask: "What is our current status and how can we improve?" The question is just another way of describing the core strategy of performance management: planning and evaluation.

Continuous improvement methods include four steps: plan, do, study, and act (Deming 1986). Study, which is the testing phase, and act are synonymous with evaluation. When the systems are compared, as demonstrated in Exhibit 13.1, a complete cycle of "planning–evaluation–planning" emerges as defining both continuous improvement and effective performance management.

Unfortunately, many performance management programs misuse the planning phase of the cycle. Instead of planning the future, the supervisor emphasizes the past. Managing becomes like driving a car while looking only into the rear-view mirror. Evaluation provides a backward-directed view rather than a future-directed program.

For example, an agency may evaluate case workers based on their caseload levels. At Agency X, Joe maintained a caseload average of 40 clients throughout the past year, with a positive turnover of 30 percent. Jill maintained a caseload average of 30 clients, with a positive turnover of 50 percent. Jan maintained a caseload of 30 clients, with a 30 percent positive turnover.

Because of the agency's funding arrangement, the agency goal is a 40-client caseload with a 30 percent positive turnover rate for each case worker. Which case worker, Jill or Joe, will receive the higher evaluation? Joe; even though Jill was able to positively discharge 80 percent more clients than Joe.

By looking out the rear-view mirror, Joe's future will involve doing what he has always done. Jill's plans for the coming year will include building a larger caseload at the expense of her positive turnover rate. Jan will work harder to live up to Joe's standards.

When performance evaluation is linked with the continuous improvement, the results differ. The manager learns to look out of the car's front window. Even though Joe was on target, the manager looks ahead to where Joe and the agency can go. The past tells the manager that Joe can handle a caseload of 40 with a 30 percent turnover rate. Joe is told

Exhibit 13.1. The continuous improvement cycle.

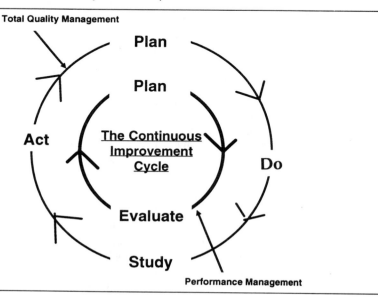

"Great job" and is asked: "How can you increase the positive turnover rate for your cases?" Jill is also told "Great job" and is then asked: "How can you increase your caseload while maintaining the positive turnover rate?"

The real pressure will be on Jan, who will be asked to find ways to increase both the caseload and the turnover rate. Luckily, the team environment that is a part of continuous improvement programs will provide Jan with training and ideas from both Joe and Jill.

The impact of this forward planning does not stop with the three caseworkers. Performance management systems are an integral part of the total management system. When properly used, they are a critical part of the larger, organizationwide continuous improvement program.

By continuing the caseload example, we can demonstrate this system connection. Successful implementation of the forward planning with the caseworkers will result in an increase in the organization's caseload capacity. This causes the agency to consider a new set of organizational options.

Assuming that the agency competes for its grant funds, the increased capacity will make the grant proposal more competitive. The agency can offer to handle a larger caseload where there are more potential clients; or, it could compete to take over the caseload from a weaker agency nearby. Other options are to move some of the saved funds into a developing program area, or to make the grant more competitive by laying off a caseworker—successfully doing more with less. The performance management system is directly impacting the strategic direction of the organization.

This impact is another example of the plan–evaluate–plan cycle of performance management. The original goals—the performance standards—were set by organizational strategy. Actual performance was evaluated, which resulted in changing organizational strategy (plans), changing standards, and so on.

(b) THE PERFORMANCE MANAGEMENT SYSTEM As with all systems, the performance management system can be understood in terms of inputs, process, outputs, and feedback. Exhibit 13.2, which displays the entire system with its major connections, shows that personal development, organizational strategy, and the human resource management systems are all affected by a well-functioning performance management system.

(i) System inputs An effective performance management system starts with information about the organization and individuals within the system.

Organizational inputs are the critical—and, most frequently, the forgotten—ingredients for a successful performance management system. The organizational inputs are the standards of performance originally determined by the organization as necessary to achieve its goals.

Consultants are frequently asked questions like "Should we evaluate tardiness on our forms?" The answer must be: "What impact does tardiness have on achieving your strategic plan? If your agency uses flex-time, evaluating tardiness is absurd."

To define the organizational inputs, ask: "What are we going to measure?" For instance, equal employment opportunity (EEO) is an important issue in nonprofits. Organizations that are really concerned with it will evaluate managers based on their record for hiring and providing equal opportunities for minorities in their work group. One of the best ways to make a performance management system effective is to evaluate managers on their use of the performance management system.

Exhibit 13.2.   The performance management system.

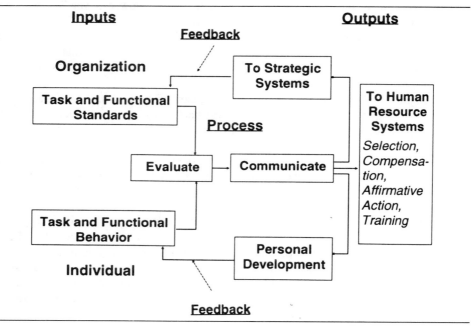

A number of organizations in both the private and nonprofit sectors use preprinted evaluation forms or checklists. These forms list behaviors such as tardiness, creativity, timeliness of work, and so on. The supervisor evaluates the worker on a scale ranging from poor to excellent.

Executives love the forms because they are an inexpensive way to fulfill a cumbersome management chore. Supervisors love them because they are quick and easy to complete. But the forms do not evaluate what is important to an organization, and they fail to provide real information about an individual's performance.

Consider having to rate someone's creativity on the job-based standard evaluation scale. To do the rating, the supervisor must ask what the organization means by the word creativity and what meeting the standards in that organization means. The preprinted forms do not include this information.

To be effective, the evaluation form—the organizational standards—must ask two questions:

- Do the standards evaluate what is important to our organization?
- Do the standards define various levels of performance in such a way that two people reading them will come to the same conclusions?

(A method for developing performance standards is described in section 13.2.)

The organizational inputs define what is wanted; the individual inputs define what is actually happening—that is, the individual inputs are the employee's behavior.

Behavior can be evaluated from two perspectives, task and function. Task performance looks at what is done. Is the job complete? Is the objective reached? What was the average caseload? Functional performance looks at how the job is done. Is it timely? Are there defects? Was the individual an effective team member?

According to Schneier and Beatty (1979), an effective performance management system will evaluate both task and function. The authors demonstrated their point with an example of a manager, who achieved his objective of reduced delivery time by using punitive supervision of subordinates.

Objectively gathering information about an individual's performance is difficult. Our observation skills are hindered by a number of inherent biases. The biases are caused by the way we process information: we filter out more than we take in.

Clear performance standards are the best defense against observation bias. Without such standards, the evaluator must make assumptions based on a personal value system. These assumptions are rarely shared with the subordinate or the organization.

Training evaluators is also critical to reducing bias. Training should include methods of behavior observation, techniques for avoiding typical evaluation biases, and feedback communication skills.

Exhibit 13.3 describes six major biases and some methods for avoiding them.

(ii) System process The act of evaluation is the process of comparing the individual's performance with the standards established by the organization. Clear standards simplify the evaluation process.

Exhibit 13.3. Performance assessment bias.

Bias	Precautions
Comparison error Employees are compared to each other instead of to the performance standards. Results in lowering evaluations of individuals whose work is almost comparable.	Spread out evaluations over the year. Use clear performance standards.
Judging a book by its cover Employees are evaluated based on conditions not related to job performance, such as dress.	Use clear standards. Provide method for evaluator to review historical performance data during evaluation.
Halo effect Total performance is over-looked in favor of recent achievements. Also, there is a tendency to rate an individual higher than deserved because he or she falls within a group of highly rated workers.	Provide method for evaluator to review performance data from entire evaluation period. Spread out evaluations over the year.
Self-emulation Employees who appear or act like the rater receive higher evaluations. Race and sex biases tend to show here.	Review aggregate evaluation data by organization and evaluator, to identify possible trend. Provide diversity sensitivity training to evaluators.
Central tendency, leniency, and strictness Based on the assumption that performance overall will statistically fall on a bell curve. Some evaluators and systems support average evaluations, some evaluators are generally lenient to be supportive, some start strict to allow for movement. In all cases, comparison with standards is ignored.	Use clear performance standards. Train evaluators to observe behavior. Review aggregate evaluation data by evaluator, to identify trend.

Evaluation is like piecing together a puzzle. One half of the puzzle defines the desired behavior. If the second half fits into the puzzle, the employee has demonstrated acceptable behavior.

A task example: A comptroller is required to make monthly financial reports to the board. During the past year, the comptroller made such reports in 10 out of the 12 months. The pieces do not fit.

A functional example: An employee is expected to resolve client complaints about agency services with little involvement from a supervisor. During the past year, the employee handled 20 complaints, bringing the supervisor in for help only once. The piece fits.

Communicating the evaluation results to the employee is also considered a part of the process. A well-conducted feedback session is a two-way communication where the evaluator observes the performance from the employee's perspective. The resulting new information often leads to changes in evaluation decisions, causing different pieces if the puzzle to fall in place.

(iii) System outputs　The most tangible output of a performance management system is a plan of action for a change in the employee's behavior. Under our continuous improvement model, this is a personal improvement plan. Plans can be both task-oriented, such as increasing caseload, and function-oriented, such as improving communication skills.

A number of other outcomes also develop. These outcomes provide feedback to the organization's strategy and human resource management systems.

The potential for strategy change is caused by information that develops from a review of one or more evaluations. The anticipated increase in caseloads described above is an example of the system in action.

Performance management systems affect most human resource management systems. Data from one or more evaluations provide the basis for determining training needs. The information is also used in succession planning and to validate the employee selection process. The output provides critical information on the success of affirmative action programming.

If the program is linked to the compensation system, the aggregate results will affect the budgeting and financial status of the organization. Even if the compensation link does not exist, the output can help identify compensation-related turnover problems.

(c) USE OF AUTOMATION TO ACCESS PERFORMANCE INFORMATION　The performance management system can provide data for continuous improvement activities. The problem becomes how to access the large quantities of data to make optimum use of the system.

Data acquisition is always a problem in continuous improvement programs. Performance management data are no exception. In most cases, the information is stored in an individual's personnel folder, never to be seen again unless there is a discipline problem.

Personnel files are manual human resource information systems. During the past decade, it became possible for the majority of organizations to automate their human resource information system (HRISystem). Many HRISystems now function on personal computers and cost under $1,000.

Automating personnel information into larger, relational data bases makes it possible to look for correlations that used to remain hidden in individual personnel folders.

Automating the human resource management function is a critical step toward being able to effectively use performance management information.

Most HRISystems include fields for performance review data. Unfortunately, the larger systems usually include a checklist-type system similar to the preprinted checklist. However, there are also a number of stand-alone performance systems that help the manager develop job descriptions and performance standards, and then track evaluations. The manager can correlate the data to identify performance problems or opportunities. Both management by objectives (MBO) and behaviorally anchored rating scale systems are available. The Personnel Software Census (Advanced Personnel Systems) maintains an updated list of available programs.

(d) TYPES OF PERFORMANCE MANAGEMENT SYSTEMS   There are four general categories of performance management systems: global, trait-based, effectiveness-based, and behavior-based.

Global evaluation systems contrast the total performance of an individual against either some standard or, more typically, other individuals. The most prevalent form of global evaluation is forced ranking: the supervisor is asked to rank employees from best to least best.

Forced ranking works when a single, clear objective defines a person's job. For instance, salespeople can be ranked based on sales quantity. In this case, forced ranking can be used for compensation planning.

However, forced ranking is a nightmare if there is any complexity to the job. On an old episode of the TV show "Cagney and Lacey," Cagney was asked to force-rank her fellow detectives for pay purposes. Cagney dreaded the task. In the end, she had little information to support her position when she ranked her partner second. Like Lacey, lower-ranked employees have a sense of being the worst performer, even when the performance differences may be very small.

Trait-based evaluations, developed by industrial psychologists during the 1940s, assume that there is a single list of personality traits that distinguish good from poor performance on the job, regardless of company. Most of the research over the intervening years has disproved the theory. Yet, trait-based evaluations, such as the preprinted forms, remain the most common evaluation system in the country.

Effectiveness-based systems measure task performance: Does the job get done? The oldest such system is the *work standards* evaluation. Work standards originated in industrial settings, but they are now used in service industries as well. A work standards evaluation establishes an output work level, such as 100 widgets per day or 60 discharges per month. The employee is then evaluated based on achieving or not achieving the standard.

Management by objectives (MBO) is a work standards system for managers. The manager is given a list of objectives to be reached in the coming evaluation period. Traditionally, the evaluation is based solely on whether the objectives are reached, regardless of what was done to reach them.

A number of management theorists criticize MBO as limiting the continuous improvement process. The feeling is that objectives place constrictions on creativity and the manager's willingness to change directions when necessary. Other criticisms include concern that the manager emphasizes achieving objectives at the expense of day-to-day activities. Others point to the problems that develop when the manager is not in complete control of the resources necessary to achieve an objective.

No one has found a suitable replacement for MBO. In fact, MBO methods are now being applied outside of management in such settings as educational development plans, development plans for the disabled, patient management plans, and so on. In management, only the name has changed. Many organizations now practice *action planning,* which is the objectives planning process from MBO systems. To enable more flexibility, the action plan has lost some of its connection to the strategic plan.

The conflict between MBO and continuous improvement can be resolved by assessing how objectives are used. Some objectives establish behavioral limits. An objective to sell 30 widgets this year will be limiting. However, other objectives can break down restraining walls. To "build the creative capacity of the work team" will be an invigorating objective.

A somewhat different approach is the *critical incident process.* Its purpose is to provide pure feedback to employees on their behavior. The supervisor maintains records of exceptional incidents, both good and bad, and reviews them periodically with individual employees. Critical incident reports can also be used to develop data for behavior-based systems.

Beginning in the 1960s, as a reaction to the weaknesses of effectiveness-based systems, a number of *behavior-based* systems were developed. These systems assess functional behavior.

The first major behavior-based system was the *assessment center.* An assessment center places a worker, usually a manager, into a simulated work situation. The typical environment is the "in-basket" exercise, but simulations are as varied as the creativity of assessors. Trained assessors observe the employee's behavior in the simulation. Some observations are based on set criteria; for others, the purpose is to provide pure feedback. If the center is used for developmental purposes, the employee will write a developmental plan based on the assessors' report.

Performance standards (behavior-anchored rating scales) improve on and customize the traditional checklist. Each scale includes an operational description of a behavior as performed in that organization. For instance, communication skills to be assessed may in one job, include written and oral presentations; only oral communications may be required in another position. Evaluation is done by comparing the individual's behavior with examples of acceptable and unacceptable behaviors listed with the description.

Both behavior-based systems are time-consuming, and development is expensive. Both require extensive job analysis, and the assessment center requires exceptional training of assessors.

Supervisors usually complain about the time necessary for evaluation using performance standards. Frequently, the supervisor will learn to skip the standards descriptions, providing inaccurate information to the employee. Various coding schemes have been developed to reduce this problem.

It is possible to mix and match evaluation systems for optimum effect. Schneier and Beatty (1979, September) believe that a mix of effectiveness-based and behavior-based systems is essential to creating an effective performance management system.

13.2 DEVELOPING THE PERFORMANCE MANAGEMENT SYSTEM

(a) DEVELOPING YOUR OWN SYSTEM Developing an effective performance management system is a major organizational undertaking. Implementation will change many of the agency's other systems, including its values and culture. For a small to medium-size nonprofit, creation of the system can take six months from start to full implementation (see Exhibit 13.4). Larger organizations can take even longer.

It is no wonder that purchasing preprinted evaluation forms is the most popular method for implementing the system; it is a quick and inexpensive procedure: Purchase and copy the form, hand it to the supervisors, and expect results.

Sometimes, to augment the system, supervisors are sent to a public training program on performance evaluation. By the time they leave the program, they are getting mixed messages about workable systems and program purpose. As a result, their attitude is that the form is only a vehicle to enhance communication between the employee and supervisor.

A more enlightened approach is for the human resource manager or a committee to gather forms from other agencies and cut-and-paste their way to a new form. The theory is: if it works at a successful organization, it should work here. At times, training is held in-house to help clarify the performance definitions on the new form. Often, such training sessions end in confusion because of disagreements over definitions in the form.

The reason the system works at Agency A but fails in Agency B is that Agency A addressed the critical issues being ignored at Agency B. Agency A took the time to identify the organization's inputs—the performance expectations—for meeting the agency's strategic plans. For the same system to work in Agency B, the agency must have the same strategic plan and culture.

An effective performance management system is a method for achieving the organization's strategic goals while providing the vehicle for continuous improvement. Implementation requires answering strategic questions specific to the organization. There are no "right" answers for these questions:

- *Should compensation be linked to the performance management system?* Linking pay to individual performance can negate team-building efforts. Failing to make the link when there are obvious performance differences can hurt morale.

Exhibit 13.4. Performance management system project plan (mixed systemwide and individual performance standards).

Task	Month					
	1	2	3	4	5	6
Establish system goals	→					
Conduct employee orientation meetings	→					
Train a task force	→					
Develop a list of job dimensions	→					
Develop performance standards	→					
Design an evaluation form	→					
Test the pilot system		→				
Evaluate and adjust the system						→
Train supervisors						→
Promote the plan to employees						→
Implement the system						→

- *Should individual performance standards be established for each position, or one set for all positions, or some combination?* A large organizational change may be accomplished by evaluating a broad group of organizationwide values. Maintaining quality and morale in a static environment may require more individualized attention.
- *Should different types of systems be used for different employee levels?* MBO may not be appropriate for nonexempt employees, and work standards may have no meaning to managers. The organization may be too small to manage multiple systems.
- *How should individuals be evaluated in terms of their teams?* An individualized performance management system can work against efforts at team building.
- *Should managers, employees, and/or others participate in developing the standards?* Who runs the organization? What are its trust levels? Does it want to build participatory structures?

Because no two agencies will have the same answers to these questions, no two systems will be exactly alike. Developing an effective performance management system is a process unique to each organization.

It may not be necessary to hire a consultant to help develop the system. Consultants are hired to design compensation systems, thus relieving employees of the task of determining salaries of peers. In developing a performance management system, the conflict of interest within staff is much less than with compensation planning. The only reasons for hiring a consultant are: (1) the organization lacks the expertise to design the system or (2) no one in the organization has time to coordinate the development of the system.

(b) DEVELOPING TASK STANDARDS   Task standards are much easier to develop than functional standards. Task standards come directly from the organization's strategic and long-term plans and its grant agreements.

Some form of management by objectives remains the best method for creating managerial task standards. On paper, this starts with the strategic plan and the board-produced annual plan. From the board plans, the CEO develops a list of objectives to be achieved by staff in the coming year. Objectives are assigned to and become the goals of department heads, according to their area of specialty. The same process is used by the department heads to develop work plans for supervisors.

In practice, the system is not run in such a top-down fashion. In fact, according to Tosi and Carroll (1970), one of the major benefits of MBO is that it enables subordinates' participation in the planning process. In practice, the system works in both directions at once. Usually, the CEO develops the work plan in a series of meetings with department heads, who usually are already meeting with their staff. The board may be the last group to see the plan. The result is a more free-flow negotiation over the resources necessary to achieve goals in the coming year.

(The reader is cautioned that an MBO system that is linked to an agency's strategic plan cannot be conducted in a vacuum. Annual management objectives must be agreed to before the budgeting process can begin.)

Either an MBO or a work standards system can be effective at the professional level. A fund raiser may have the goal of increasing revenues by at least 10 percent. A job placement counselor may be required to meet a work standard of maintaining an average caseload of 30 and a goal of increasing long-term placements 10 percent in the coming year.

Technical and other nonprofessional positions may work best under a work standards system; the standards can be incorporated into the job description. The evaluation system then refers to the job description for evaluative information.

Developing work standards is a job analysis process, and can be accomplished through the strategies described in Chapter 4.

Even nonprofessional positions can use a modified version of MBO as part of their evaluation. During the evaluation, the employee and supervisor develop an action plan for personal development. The plan may include such tasks as taking a course at a local college, or spending 30 hours in an upgraded position. The plan is evaluated during the year and at the end of the evaluation period, to determine whether the objectives were met and whether those objectives had an impact on reaching the developmental goal.

(c) DEVELOPING FUNCTIONAL STANDARDS Many certifying agencies recognize the effectiveness of performance standards and require their development for individual jobs. Performance standards appear similar to the trait-based checklist, but they overcome the biases built into the trait-based system in three ways:

- Performance standards use job analysis to clearly define the behavior being evaluated;
- Performance standards use job analysis to clearly define acceptable and unacceptable performance of the behaviors;
- Performance standards are unique to a given organization and/or job.

Historically, performance standards were developed by industrial psychologists who came in and observed behavior within a given organization. In the past few years, methods have been accessible to nonprofessionals to develop the ranking scales. The process is time-consuming, especially if a management or employee task force is involved, but in-house development saves cash resources. (There is a cost for the time given to task force involvement.) It also begins the supervisory training process, and increases organizational acceptance in the implementation phase. The general manager of a small telephone cooperative in Idaho admitted that setting up the performance management system has taken several hundred employee-hours. "But I wouldn't do it any other way." (Michaels, 1987).

Performance standards are usually developed for behavioral evaluation; however, they also work for task evaluation. If a work standard of 30 widgets a day is established, 35 widgets per day exceeds standards and any amount above that level is exceptional. However, it is not necessary to quantify performance that does not meet standards.

The following sections describe a participatory process for developing performance standards. It starts with the assumption that only one set of performance standards is being developed for the entire organization. Suggestions for developing systems in larger organizations are added later.

(i) Using in-house staff to develop performance standards First, the organization must assign responsibility for developing the performance standards. The project can be completed independently by a human resource manager or a CEO skilled in job analysis techniques. However, this person can expect a great deal of conflict and negotiation over standards definitions when implementing the system.

The conflict can be reduced by using a task force to develop the performance standards. The task force can include only managers, or managers and workers, depending on the culture of the organization. The more levels of the organization involved in the process, the greater the acceptance of the final product. Some organizations strongly believe that establishing standards is a managerial function, and they accept the necessary trade-offs.

When a task force is used, the CEO, human resource specialist, or an outside consultant, serves as the task force facilitator. The facilitator's role is to bring the decision process into the task force. The facilitator must be able to forgo the expert role.

(ii) The performance standards development process   The five steps described below should be used to develop performance standards.

Step 1. Create a list of job dimensions. This is a critical policy step because it answers the question: What do we want to measure? Activities essential to the success or culture of the organization that are ignored here will be ignored in employee performance.

Three methods can be used to create the list of job dimensions: (1) recognize the importance of the list as a policy issue by requesting the list from the board and/or CEO; (2) draw the list from the organization's mission statement and statement of values; or (3) develop the list by facilitating the exercise at the board level.

The job dimensions can be taken directly from the "Knowledge, Skills, and Abilities" section of a well-written job description and translated to standards for individual positions.

The third method begins by having each task force member independently list 6 to 10 activities that are performed by those to be evaluated—activities that the member believes are critical to successful performance. The task force is instructed to write complete, descriptive sentences, not single words like "communication." The sentences should not include judgmental terms. For instance:

Acceptable: Communicates both orally and in writing with staff and with clients from diverse populations.
Not acceptable: Effectively trains and motivates clients from diverse backgrounds so that they improve their personal hygiene habits.

In the second example, the adverb "effectively" is judgmental and the verb "improve" implies a successful outcome, making it judgmental as well.

The facilitator then uses the nominal grouping technique to develop consensus around a maximum of 10 job dimensions. This technique involves listing the suggestions from all task force members, eliminating duplicates, discussing activities that can be combined, and then achieving a consensus on a prioritization of the list.

Step 2. Develop examples of behavior for each job dimension. (Steps 2 through 5 should be done for each dimension independently.)

There are two ways to do this step. The first, more time-consuming way is to have supervisors maintain critical incident reports for 3 to 6 months. After reviewing these reports, the task force assigns the behavioral characteristics of each report to one or more job dimensions.

The second way is to ask the task force to list behavioral examples associated with the job dimension being discussed. The task force members should list answers to the following questions:

1. Think of a person who was an exceptional performer on this dimension. List behaviors that this person showed when performing this activity.
2. Think of a person who was a poor performer on this dimension. List behaviors that this person showed when performing this activity.
3. Think of a person who was not deficient when performing this dimension, but also did not excel. List behaviors that this person showed when performing this activity.

Task force members should be cautioned to think only in terms of the activity under question. An example can be given of a generally exceptional performer who is a poor performer in this one area. Task force members should be encouraged to use specific adjectives; words like "effective," "frequently," and "excellent" are too subjective for this process. Specifics should be used instead, like "never," "always," and "20 percent." (In Step 5, the facilitator will be required to help the task force replace subjective terms with specific adjectives.)

Step 3: Mix up the responses. Mix up the task force responses so that no one knows the behavioral level assigned by the authors. Away from the task force meeting, randomly list the descriptions on a separate paper for review by the task force members.

By performing this task outside of the meeting, the facilitator can remove duplicates and edit out statements that do not relate to the activity in question.

Step 4: Individually rating the behaviors. Provide each task force member with the randomized list of behaviors for the dimension under discussion and a copy of the performance standard worksheet shown in Exhibit 13.5. Have each task force member place each behavior into one of the five categories shown in the worksheet. Collect the results and create a report for the task force showing how many task force members assigned each behavior to each level.

As an example, one behavior under a communications-related scale might read: "Uses mixed media when making public presentations." Five task force members may place this under "meets standards" and five may place it under "exceptional."

Step 5: Facilitate consensus rating. Bring the task force together to discuss the differences in ratings, and facilitate a consensus rating for each behavior.

This step usually requires making subjective statements more specific. Sometimes, there will actually be a values difference that cannot be resolved. In that case, leave the specific behavior off the scale.

Exhibit 13.5.   Sample worksheet—Performance standards development.

Performance Standards Development Worksheet

Job Dimension _____

Unacceptable	Below Standards	Meets Standards	Exceeds Standards	Exceptional

When complete, each performance standard can be edited to look like those in Exhibit 13.6. Steps 2 through 5 can then be repeated for the remaining essential activities.

Task force members should do as much work as possible away from the task force meetings, saving meeting time for consensus-building discussions. Under this strategy, each standard should take about one hour of meeting time. Otherwise, facilitating consensus on a single standard can take two to three hours.

(iii) Development in larger organizations   Some successful evaluation systems consider each position according to its own job description. For example, hospitals in Illinois are required to develop performance standards for each job description as part of the certification process. For smaller organizations, this procedure is expensive and time-consuming. It also can be counterproductive in any organization that is going through a major change.

It is possible to mix organizationwide and individual performance standard scales in one form. Some agencies list about five agencywide performance standards and then develop specific standards on the department or job description level. This mixed standards method allows for flexibility within the organization and gives employees a chance to receive more personal performance feedback.

One way to develop the mixed system is to teach supervisors how to develop performance standards. Individual supervisors can then sit down with an employee or a

Exhibit 13.6. Sample form—Evaluation.

Evaluation Form

Employee _____ Position _____

Department _____ Years in position _____

Evaluation date _____

Part 1—Performance Standards

	Communication	Team Work	Job Aptitude	Job Attitude
Standard	The ability to transmit information and instructions both orally and in writing	The ability to participate in building consensus decisions and support team efforts	The ability to perform tasks assigned	The extent to which the employee shows motivation for the job
Unacceptable	Only explains problem once. Memos are difficult to read or understand. ☐	Argues for personal agenda and goals. Only performs personal work, and does not chip in when team goals are not met. ☐	Requires extensive coaching and support to perform tasks considered standard for position. ☐	Complains whenever assigned any task outside of own job description. ☐
Below	Problems explained through extensive questioning. Memos state point but lack supportive detail. ☐	Always takes position of central negative, but supports final decisions. Chips in but acts unsocial within the group. ☐	Asks questions about procedures without first checking available resources such as manual. ☐	Performs additional tasks which meet personal interests without complaint. ☐
Standard	Presentations are clear, needing only minimal clarification. Memos state point, lack detail. ☐	Participates with constructive ideas in team meetings. Backs up other team members' actions when asked. ☐	Performs standard duties without problem. Researches new problems before asking questions. ☐	Performs all tasks assigned without complaint. Shows specific job interest. ☐
Exceeds	Presentations use appropriate and varied media. Written materials are clear. ☐	Takes a facilitative leadership role, but doesn't share leadership. Gets others to help with problem solving and team tasks. ☐	Performs standard and new assignments without supervisory help, except for special circumstances. ☐	Seeks out new tasks that can expand personal growth. ☐
Exceptional	Presentations wow the listeners. Written materials are prepared with desktop publishing. ☐	Participates in and raises team process issues. Jumps in to support other team members, offers social support. ☐	Performs all assignments with ease. Instructs others in methods, Can function as lead person. ☐	Loves work and motivates others through positive spirit. ☐

Exhibit 13.6. *(Continued)*

Part 2—Task Evaluation

Step A: List critical tasks as described in the job description or major objectives from last year's evaluation. (Tasks must be described in terms of expected outcomes.)	*Step B:* Describe the observed outcomes or results for each task.	*Step C:* Identify differences between A and B.
Task 1:	Task 1:	Task 1:
Task 2:	Task 2:	Task 2:
Task 3:	Task 3:	Task 3:
Task 4:	Task 4:	Task 4:
Task 5:	Task 5:	Task 5:
Task 6:	Task 6:	Task 6:

Exhibit 13.6.   (*Continued*)

Part 3—Action Plan

INSTRUCTIONS

1. List goals relating to task differences and objectives differences. Goals may be corrective action to complete the task or fulfill the goal, or they may be directed at changes to the task or goal based on the information acquired during the evaluation period.
2. Write specific objectives to be done in the next evaluation period to achieve each goal.
3. Write planned follow-up and completion dates for each goal.

Goals	Objectives	Due Dates

This is to certify that the above evaluation was reviewed by both of us and that we are in agreement with regard to the above action plan as representing the critical actions which we will take during the coming evaluation period.

_____   _____   _____
Supervisor's signature   Employee's signature   Date

group of employees who share the same job description and jointly develop the non-standard performance standards.

Allowing supervisors to develop standards can improve communications between supervisors and subordinates and help to move decision making down into the organization. However, the system loses some of its reliability and credibility when the same job is done in different departments and the employees are evaluated on different performance standards.

A second strategy is to use multiple task forces for performance standards development. An organizationwide task force develops organizationwide performance standards. Cross-departmental task forces for agencywide positions can work with departmental task forces for specific departmental positions to develop the job-specific standards. The original task force serves as a steering committee during this process.

(d) THE EVALUATION FORM   There is no perfect evaluation form. Every organization creates its own, to meet its own information needs. If the form is associated with an automated record-keeping system, the form's design will have to relate to data input requirements.

Assuming that an agency is assessing both tasks and functional behavior, the form will include at least three major parts. One section, covering task performance, may be a place to review the previous year's objectives in an MBO system, or it may list specific work task requirements, for a work standards system.

A second section will include the functional performance standards. Usually, the performance standards are listed together, as in exhibit 13.6. However, some organizations have found it helpful to have supervisors review a checklist of behaviors exhibited by the employee, without knowledge of the rating for those behaviors. The information is then compiled in the human resource office to establish the actual performance level. The method is quicker for the supervisor and it reduces the supervisor's tendency to ignore the behavioral descriptions in favor of the rating scale. However, this system can reduce trust between the supervisor and the organization.

The third section will be the action plan for the coming evaluation period. If an MBO system is being used for managers, the action plan will include both organizational objectives and personal development objectives. For other employees, the form includes only personal development objectives.

Must the employee sign the form? Most forms require that the employee sign the form only to indicate that the form has been shown to and discussed with the employee. Agreement with the evaluation should never be required.

An employee's refusal to sign an evaluation form is not insubordination. The employer wants the signature as protection against claims that performance information was never shared with the employee. The same protection can be achieved by having a third party witness the employee's refusal and so indicate on the form.

(e) TESTING AND IMPLEMENTING THE SYSTEM   Keeping the spirit of continuous improvement, a new performance management system should not be implemented until it has been "studied." In this case, testing requires identifying a small group of employees and supervisors, placing them on the system, and assessing the results.

Medium-size nonprofits can test the system in one department; for smaller organizations, the test may have to be agencywide. Because, in both cases, the test should last only about three months, the agencywide test will still only be on a small percentage of the organization.

The organization should not link salary increases to performance until after the system is fully tested. If a merit plan is already in effect, pay increases should either be based on evaluations under the older system, or increases should be across-the-board until the new system is implemented.

It will not be possible to test the effectiveness of the system (whether it improves performance) in the trial period. The system can only be tested for reliability and acceptance.

(i) Reliability   When two people see an apple and call it an apple, there is reliability between their assessments. Similarly, if two supervisors look at the same information, they should make similar decisions about an employee's performance.

Reliability can be tested in several ways. One way is to have both supervisors and employees complete the evaluation form. Comparing the results then serves as a good starting point for discussion in the performance evaluation meeting.

To show reliability, the human resource manager or task force does a statistical analysis comparing the frequency of agreement between supervisor evaluations and employee self-evaluations. The higher the frequency of agreement, the more valid the system.

In like fashion, a supervisor and department head can perform parallel evaluations. Both must have access to the same employee information for this to work. Again, statistical analysis can establish reliability.

Reliability fails for two reasons: either the evaluator was not properly trained in observation, or the language on the form is not yet clear. Determining which is the real problem is achieved by interviewing supervisors and employees.

Reliability issues will most likely result in fine-tuning the performance standards.

(ii) Acceptance Acceptance can be assessed informally through interviewing employees or reviewing evaluation complaints. A more formal approach is to survey employees approximately one month after their evaluation.

Acceptance and reliability are closely related. If the employees believe the system is fair, they will accept it. If they reject the system, reliability should be looked at more closely. If reliability is high, the organization has other employee issues to deal with, such as trust and compensation levels, before the system will be accepted.

Once the system works, the following steps should be used to implement the program agencywide:

1. Before starting the project, inform all employees of the project and solicit volunteers for task forces. During the project, keep employees informed of task force actions. Allow observers into task force meetings.

2. Set a date for the switch to the new system.

3. Conduct in-depth supervisory training programs that include a clear explanation of the performance standards, skill development for observing behavior, a strategy for comparing observed behavior with standards, and communication skills development, including nondefensive feedback and counseling skills for the evaluation meeting. Employees can be invited into the training sessions.

4. Conduct employee meetings to explain the new system. Answer questions and concerns. Describe the task force process and testing results, particularly those relating to reliability and acceptance.

5. Switch over to the new system.

13.3 MANAGING THE PERFORMANCE MANAGEMENT SYSTEM

(a) GENERAL SYSTEM PROCEDURES Like a Rolls Royce, the best performance management system is worthless unless it is properly maintained. A preamble and related policies and procedures similar to the following should be included in the organization's personnel policy and procedure manual and then followed to ensure proper maintenance of the system.

Preamble. The performance management system is established to provide a vehicle for continuous improvement and growth for our employees. The system is not designed to be punitive. It is intended to act as a critical part of the forward-directed planning process by helping our employees grow through receipt of constructive positive feedback concerning their performance. At the same time, the performance management system provides the agency with information on the current capacity of the organization, enabling us to plan future activities more effectively. The performance management system will be managed in a manner that complies with our affirmative action plan and will not be used to discriminate against any employee on the grounds of race, sex, religion, national origin, or physical or mental handicap.

Starting the policies with a preamble establishes the purposes and limitations of the performance management system. The preamble tells the employees that the system exists for the benefit of both the employee and the organization. It also sets the tone for integration of the system into the organization's efforts toward quality transformation.

Policy 1. The performance management system was developed by a joint committee of employees and managers. This committee shall be responsible for the continuous improvement of the quality of the system. The committee shall establish policies that will allow it to continue indefinitely while providing for an orderly change in its membership. The committee shall review on request and periodically review at its own initiative the effectiveness of the performance management system and may propose, form time to time, to add, change, or eliminate agencywide work and performance standards. The committee will also act as the coordinating committee of departmental and cross-departmental committees established to develop standards not in use agencywide.

Instituting a method for system maintenance and change is critical to enabling the ongoing effectiveness of the system. This policy institutes the participatory development process recommended for the development of a performance management system. The committee is a continuous improvement team with a changing membership. The committee changes membership to avoid burnout of committee members and to maintain its credibility with the rest of the staff.

Procedure 1A. The committee shall consist of both management and nonmanagement staff members, in equal proportion. A chair, elected annually by the committee members, will have the responsibilities of calling meetings and ensuring that minutes are recorded and that employees are kept informed of committee actions.

The use of a joint committee is in keeping with the methodologies of continuous improvement programs. The chair's role has been limited to task-maintenance issues to maintain a consensus-making decision process.

Procedure 1B. The human resource director shall serve as facilitator to the committee. The human resource director shall have no vote on the committee and shall not participate in discussions outside of a facilitative capacity, except that the director may answer technical questions on request.

In traditional companies, the human resource director chairs committees like this one. The director's expertise is placed in a powerful position, generally hurting the participatory nature of the program. The committee is seen as the personnel manager's committee, resulting in reduced attendance and involvement. Because the work of the performance management committee affects more than just human resource systems, a broader chair representation is appropriate. Implementation of this procedure and any quality-based program may require that the human resource director receive facilitation skills training.

Procedure 1C. Decisions by the committee concerning changes in the performance management system shall be made by consensus. When consensus is not achieved, a three-fourths supermajority must be achieved to approve a decision.

The decision process is in keeping with continuous improvement programs.

Policy 2. New and promoted employees will be evaluated and will meet with their supervisor to review the evaluation during the last week of their first six months in their new position. After that time, employees will be evaluated and will meet with their supervisor to review the evaluation annually no later than two weeks following the employee's anniversary of hiring or last promotion.

It is important that probationary employees be informed of their evaluation before the end of their probationary period. Once the probationary period is over, their employment status is the same as that of regular employees with regard to benefits and rights to employment, even if it is subsequently determined that they failed to pass probation.

Many organizations evaluate all their employees on the same date. Such policies ensure that a halo-effect bias will impact the results. It is easier for supervisors to pay close attention to evaluations that are spaced out over time, rather than committing a large block of time to many evaluations.

Evaluations should not be allowed to drag on. Untimely evaluations reduce morale in subordinates and diminish the credibility of the system.

Procedure 2A. One month before the employee's anniversary date, the Human Resource Department will send both the supervisor and the employee notice of the pending evaluation, a copy of the previous year's evaluation, and a blank draft evaluation form. Upon receipt, the supervisor shall contact the employee to set up a meeting date to begin discussing the evaluation.

Through either an automated HRISystem or some other form of record keeping, the human resource manager maintains a tickler file of upcoming evaluation dates and due dates. The human resource manager sends out the original forms as stated, and follows up with reminders of due date two weeks and one week before the evaluations are due back.

Procedure 2B. The employee and supervisor shall both complete draft evaluation forms. The completed forms will be shared at the first evaluation meeting. A final completed form will be prepared by the supervisor and/or employee and signed by both at the end of or shortly following the evaluation meeting(s).

Employee self-evaluation has proven to be an excellent evaluation tool in many non-profits. Comparing evaluation forms provides an effective format for identifying and discussing performance problems in the evaluation meeting.

Procedure 2C. The supervisor will return the completed evaluation form to the human resource department no later than the due date. If the completed evaluation form is returned to the human resource management office late, the employee shall receive a pay raise equal to the rate paid for "exceeds standards" for his or her job classification, beginning with the pay period following the due date and continuing through one pay period past the time the evaluation is received. [Assumes a connection between the compensation and performance management systems.]

Employees should not be punished for the supervisor's failure to complete the evaluation in a timely manner. Establishing some sort of bonus system for the employee ensures that the supervisor will at least complete questionable evaluations in a timely manner. Supervisors who routinely complete late evaluations should have this fact noted as part of their own evaluation.

Policy 3. Both the supervisor and employee shall sign the evaluation form signifying that the evaluation was reviewed with the employee and that the action plan on the form was agreed to between the employee and the supervisor. Signing the form does not signify agreement with the evaluation by the employee.

By signing the form committing to the action plan, the employee establishes a contract for performance of work. Should a discharge situation arise, the "contract" can be raised by the employer as a positive defense under contract law as well as labor relations law.

Procedure 3A. If the employee refuses to sign the evaluation form because of disagreement with the evaluation, the supervisor shall request that the form be signed in front of a third party. The third party will then place a note on the form with his or her signature, stating that he or she witnessed that the employee refused to sign the form.

As noted earlier, failure to sign the evaluation form is not insubordination; signing the form protects the interests of the employer while possibly hurting the employee's interests. Usually, insubordination charges do not hold up in arbitration or administrative hearings. The employer's interests can be protected in other ways, such as using a third-party witness.

Procedure 3B. Evaluations are subject to the agency grievance procedure. However, the employee pay adjustment will be in accordance with the disputed evaluation unless and until the grievance is decided in the employee's favor. [Assumes compensation is related to the evaluation system.]

A performance management system that contains clear standards will show fewer appeals going through the grievance procedures. It is also easier to document performance under such systems because the arbitrariness and subjectivity have been reduced.

Procedure 3C. If the employee refuses to sign the evaluation form because of a disagreement over the contents of the action plan, the human resource manager shall be called in to act as a mediator between the supervisor and employee. If mediation fails, both the supervisor and the employee shall draw up separate proposed action plans. The plans will be reviewed by the Chief Executive Officer, who shall choose between the plans or prepare an alternative plan. The Chief Executive Officer's plan shall be considered the action plan for the coming evaluation period. Failure to comply with the action plan submitted by the Chief Executive Officer shall be treated in the same manner as if the plan had been drawn up and agreed to between the supervisor and the employee.

Supervisors with strong communication skills rarely have problems with the employee's signing of the contract. However, when an employee refuses to sign the action plan, it does not become a contract. This procedure takes advantage of recent experiments in mediation of MBOs while maintaining ultimate control with management.

(b) SUPERVISORY TRAINING Effective implementation of the performance management system requires training supervisors on how to use the system. Maintaining the system over time requires an ongoing training program to instruct new supervisors in the procedures, refresh supervisory evaluation skills, and bring supervisors up-to-date on changes in the system. The training program also provides a separate vehicle for receiving feedback on the system's effectiveness in the field.

Whether an initial training program or a refresher course, the program should consist of four topics:

1. Review of the current and anticipated changes in the policies and procedures.
2. Review of the agreed-to definitions of any unclear terms in the performance standards. This may include a discussion of how the participants are interpreting the standards and a review of grievance procedure decisions.
3. Skill development in performance observation. Observing and recording behavior are the most difficult parts of the observation process. Supervisors are being asked to perform a task for which psychologists and social workers train in graduate school. This section should include a review of observation biases and techniques for performance record keeping (such as critical incident files).
4. Communication skill development for conducting nondefensive, goal-oriented evaluation meetings. These skills include providing constructive feedback, active listening, conflict resolution, negotiation, decision making, and counseling.

A sample agenda from successful training sessions is shown in Exhibit 13.7.

(c) SUPPORTING CONTINUOUS IMPROVEMENT WITH PERFORMANCE MANAGEMENT DATA The performance management system describes how performance management effects many other areas of the organization. In this role, the system provides vital support for the continuous improvement process.

Exhibit 13.7.   Sample workshop agenda.

Performance Management for Supervisors—Workshop Agenda

8:30	Introductions, Icebreaker Exercise: Characteristics of Successful Evaluation Systems

9:00	Evaluating the Employee
	    Observation Skills
	    Documentation
	    Reducing Bias

10:00	Break
10:15	Evaluation Case Study Exercise
10:45	The Evaluation Meeting—An Overview
11:15	Conducting a Nondefensive Goal-Oriented Evaluation Meeting Step 1 Establishing Rapport
11:45	Lunch
12:45	Step 2 Describing Behavior
1:15	Step 3 Problem Solving
1:45	Step 4 Setting Performance Standards
2:15	Step 5 Follow-Up
2:30	Break
2:45	Performance Evaluation Role-Plays
3:30	Procedural Issues
4:30	Wrap-Up and Evaluation

The performance management program includes data for problem identification. Any trend in aggregate performance statistics is worth investigating. Often, the information identifies problems within the human resource management system. For instance, applying an fishbone cause-and-effect diagram to determine the cause of a performance drop in a job classification where turnover has been constant might reveal a need to change the selection or training programs.

Performance data should be consulted when performing cause-and-effect analyses on other quality issues as well. If there is a quality problem with a specific service, the problem may be caused by physical conditions. Discovering that there has been a concurrent drop in performance levels adds important information to the analysis.

Acquiring aggregate performance data is not easy. Usually, performance reports are placed in individual personnel files, never to be seen again. Finding the information can require a great deal of clerical work. Automated human resource information systems are very effective tools for making such data easily accessible without jeopardizing an individual's right to privacy.

(d) APPLYING CONTINUOUS IMPROVEMENT TO THE PERFORMANCE MANAGEMENT SYSTEM   When ignored, the best performance management system loses its effectiveness after three to five years. Standards change and even become irrelevant. The initial training wears off, resulting in disagreement over performance standard definitions. New supervisors remain untrained in using the system. Only by applying continuous improvement principles to the performance management system itself will the system remain vital.

Two performance indicators determine the quality of the performance management system: validity and reliability.

Validity tests the effectiveness of the system. It asks: Is the system improving performance?

Showing validity can be very difficult when performance is defined as the organization's achievement of its mission. Other factors, such as economic conditions, affect the same definition. To assess the system's support of the mission, the agency should review whether any given performance standard is still an effective contributor to achieving the mission.

It is possible to make a more detailed assessment of individual work and performance standards. The effectiveness of work standards can easily be checked. The manager should see whether the rate for exceeding standards goes up following a series of evaluations. If it does, the system works.

The validity of an MBO system is a little more complicated. It requires assessing the continued linkage between objectives and the organization's mission. The most common MBO problems happen when managers fail to take the system seriously and begin writing easily achieved goals. The CEO or human resource manager must track the goals that managers establish and intercede when the goals become too simplistic. On the other hand, when goals are out of line with the mission, it may mean that the mission should be changed.

Other MBO problem indicators include an increasing failure rate at goal achievement, late evaluations, and goal carryover for specific objectives.

It is easier to test the effectiveness of organizationwide performance standards. The manager looks for organizational outcomes associated with a standard and tracks changes in those outcomes. For instance, if there is a standard on client/customer service, the manager might look for a decrease in client complaints and/or an increase in complimentary letters. A management standard on equal employment opportunity can be correlated with reduced complaints and increased achievement of affirmative action goals.

Failing validity may indicate a need to change or drop a performance standard. If customer service is being evaluated and complaints are rising, the organization needs to identify a more effective set of behaviors than those being evaluated.

A standard may also be dropped when it is no longer an essential organizational activity. For instance, once a performance management program is firmly in place, it should not be necessary to evaluate managers on how they conduct their evaluations.

After the system has been running a while, reliability can be tested statistically. The statistical null-hypothesis is that the distribution of evaluation scores is not random. If the scores are random, then the system remains reliable. Any trend development in the data raises a red flag of caution. When scores become attracted to any one point—midpoint, low, or high—either rating biases are creeping into the system or the standards need changing, to reflect changing organizational conditions.

For example, a human resource manager may note that there is a strong tendency for supervisors to rate people high on creativity. This could be the result of a lack of understanding of the scale or a lack of importance (reliability) in the scale. Or, the trend may be the result of a recent agencywide training program on creativity. The last possibility validates the standard and the training program, while indicating a potential need to either drop or improve the standard.

13.4 CONCLUSION

In a workshop held in Flint, Michigan, on December 5, 1990. W. E. Deming stated: "Ninety-four percent of problems in organizations are system problems. Six percent have special causes such as the employee, the machine, a sudden change in work methods, or something unexpected in the work environment." Accordingly, quality transformation and continuous improvement programs are designed to adapt systems to current and future organizational needs. As a result, some now argue that performance management systems are outdated, because human performance will increase as a function of system performance.

Unfortunately, the argument fails on two points. First, performance management is the original continuous improvement program. Strategies for assessing system performance were first designed for assessing human performance. The continuous improvement methodology of "Plan, Do, Study, Act" has been used throughout the history of social sciences: it is the scientific method. In organizations, the method was simplified to the plan-evaluate-plan cycle.

Second, as system analysts know, change in any one part of a system will change the rest of the system, and the concurrent change is not predictable. As a result, ignoring the performance of one part of the system will guarantee failure of the entire system.

Creating an effective performance management program is a critical step toward building quality in nonprofit organizations. It must be done carefully and with an eye to the future, not the past. The successful system will consider both task and functional performance. It will provide the opportunity for continuous personal improvement— growth—as it provides essential information supporting the organizations's Total Quality Management program.

SOURCES AND SUGGESTED REFERENCES

Advanced Personnel Systems. 1988. *The Personnel Software Census,* Vol. 1. Roseville, CA: Author.

Babcock, Richard, and Sorensen, Peter, Jr. 1980. *Strategies and Tactics in Management by Objectives.* Champaign, IL: Stipes Publishing Co.

Baird, Lloyd S., Beatty, Richard W., and Schneier, Craig Eric. 1985. *The Performance Appraisal Sourcebook.* Amherst, MA: Human Resource Development Press.

Deming, W. Edwards. 1986. *Out of the Crises.* Cambridge, MA: MIT Center for Advanced Engineering Studies.

Latham, Gary P., and Wexley, Kenneth N. 1981. *Increasing Productivity Through Performance Appraisal.* Reading, MA: Addison-Wesley.

Michaels, Mark, 1987, Fall. "Putting Performance Management to the Test." *Rural Telecommunications, 6*(4).

Michaels, Mark, 1988. *The Performance Technologies Workbook.* Champaign, IL: People Technologies.

Michaels, Mark, 1990. "CEO Evaluation, The Board's Second Most Crucial Duty." *Nonprofit World, 8*(3).

Sample, John A. 1986. "The Use of Behaviorally Based Scales in Performance Appraisal." In *The 1986 Annual: Developing Human Resources.* University Associates.

Schneier, Craig E., and Beatty, Richard W. 1979, July. "Integrating Behaviorally-based and Effectiveness-based Methods." *The Personnel Administrator, 42* (7) pp. 65–72.

Schneier, Craig E, and Beatty, Richard W. 1979, August. "Developing Behaviorally-anchored Rating Scales (BARS)." *Personnel Administrator, 42* (8) pp. 59–68.

Schneier, Craig E., and Beatty, Richard W. 1979, September. "Combining BARS and MBO: Using an Appraisal System to Diagnose Performance Problems," *Personnel Administrator, 42.* (9) pp. 51–60.

Tosi, Henry L., and Carroll, Stephen. 1970, July–August. "Management by Objectives." *Personnel Administrator, 33.*

University Associates. 1986. "BARS: Developing Behaviorally-anchored Rating Scales." In *The 1986 Annual: Developing Human Resources,* Author.

CHAPTER FOURTEEN

Employment-Related Benefits

Diane M. Disney
University of Rhode Island

CONTENTS

14.1 OVERVIEW OF EMPLOYMENT-RELATED BENEFITS

As recently as the late 1970s, nonprofit organizations could use the term "fringe benefits" rather comfortably to describe those goods and services provided to employees in addition to basic salaries and wages. Indeed, even the customarily above-average amounts of paid leave were seldom costly, in light of the often modest salary levels.

Over the past half-century, however, the amount spent on employment-related supplements in the United States has risen at a rate 11 times more rapid than that of salaries and wages. The cost of health insurance premiums alone has been rising at double-digit rates for several years. Today, it is not uncommon for an employer to spend an additional amount equal to 40 percent of payroll, to cover benefits. The term "fringe" is clearly no longer appropriate.

(a) OBJECTIVES OF COMPENSATION SYSTEMS Before analyzing the details of benefit systems, one needs to understand that *total* compensation consists of both direct elements (salaries and wages) and indirect elements (goods and services purchased or provided by the employer on behalf of the employee). As a system, these compensation elements should be designed to satisfy both internal and external needs. The most obvious objectives are to attract, motivate, and retain employees who perform in ways congruent with the employer's needs. Meeting these objectives requires an awareness of two types of equity:

- *External equity,* a condition existing when the compensation rates are consistent with those of other, similar organizations;
- *Internal equity,* a condition whereby individuals feel that differences in compensation within an organization are justified by differences in performance, job requirements, or both.

The nonprofit manager must address both types of equity while coping with numerous constraints, including:

- The organization's financial resources;
- The internal labor market (including existing and proposed positions, their relationships, and the existence of unions);
- The external labor market (particularly the number and compensation patterns of competitors for employees);
- Employment-related laws (the Fair Labor Standards Act, the 1964 Civil Rights Act, the Equal Payment Act, and relevant state laws)
- The requirements of the Internal Revenue Service (IRS).

(b) FINANCIAL CONSIDERATIONS For employers in this country, the design and operation of a compensation system are complicated by the changing mix of direct and indirect compensation and the changing needs of an increasingly diverse work force. Nonprofits have faced additional challenges with the historically high amount of paid leave, the extension of social security coverage, and special provisions under the Employee Retirement Income Security Act (ERISA). Unfortunately, the typical nonprofit employer often continues to behave in the paternalistic mode of earlier times. Because the employer often does not keep the employee informed about the extent of his or her total compensation, it becomes increasingly difficult to manage costs, much less to justify any sharing of them.

At the beginning of this chapter it was mentioned that many employers currently spend another 40 percent *beyond* basic payroll costs just to cover benefits. That percentage can be misleading, unless one clearly understands the elements that are included. Exhibit 14.1 compares two individuals who work for the same employer: A is an hourly worker making the equivalent of $20,000 a year, and B is a salaried employee at the $50,000 annual level.

The first payments their employer must make are those mandated by law: Social Security and Medicare (generally listed as Federal Insurance Contribution Act (FICA) deductions), unemployment insurance tax, and workers' compensation. Together, these items cost the equivalent of approximately 11 percent of payroll. Several points are worth noting here. Until 1984, a nonprofit's participation in social security was optional and could be terminated at the organization's choice. Changes in the law, making social security mandatory, meant that many nonprofits saw their payroll costs increase with no commensurate increase in productivity. In fact, employees saw their

Exhibit 14.1. Comparison of benefit costs for two employees.

	Employee A	Employee B
Basic annual compensation	$20,000	$50,000
Mandatory benefits (FICA, unemployment insurance, workers' compensation)	$ 2,200	$ 5,500
Optional benefits (individual health and life insurance, 7.5% pension)	5,500	7,750
Total benefits	$ 7,700	$13,250
Benefits/Payroll	38.5%	26.5%

pay reduced by their own share of FICA, and the employers' share was paid with funds that might otherwise have been used for raises.

If each individual receives employer-paid individual health insurance, modest life insurance, and a modest contribution toward a pension (7.5% of annual pay), the benefits payments rise to an additional 38.5 percent of payroll for the hourly worker and an extra 26.5 percent for the salaried worker. In other words, employee A is actually costing the employer $27,700 a year and employee B, $63,250. Making them aware of this total cost can both improve morale and increase the likelihood of being able to control costs.

These direct payments, however, do not tell the whole story. As Exhibit 14.2 demonstrates, most employees receive pay for 52 weeks while actually working only 45 (or fewer) weeks. For the hourly worker, paid breaks need to be identified as a cost because they are generally mandated by state laws.

Exhibit 14.2 shows that the hourly employee receives $15,880 for time worked, and earns $11,820 for benefits and time *not* worked. Items totally unrelated to productivity, then, cost the equivalent of 74.4 percent of the amount paid for actual work. For the salaried employee, the figure is 46.2 percent. From the standpoint of both relative and absolute amounts, these costs cannot be ignored.

(c) KEY QUESTIONS IN BENEFITS MANAGEMENT To manage the indirect portion of compensation, then, the employer must develop strategies to cope with a number of issues:

- *Benefits design*—developing packages that meet both employees' and the employer's needs, particularly in view of changing family patterns and resource constraints.
- *Benefits communication*—letting employees know the details of their compensation and enlisting their aid in managing costs.
- *Governmental requirements*—avoiding discrimination in favor of highly compensated or "key" employees, while complying with frequently changing state and federal laws. (A further consideration here is that an employer's failure to

Exhibit 14.2. Comparison of total benefits costs and pay for time worked.

	Employee A	Employee B
Basic annual compensation	$20,000	$50,000
Pay for time not worked:		
Vacation, sick days, holidays	($ 2,692)	($ 6,730)
Rest periods, cleanup time	(1,428)	—
Pay for time worked	$15,880	$43,270
Total benefits cost	$11,820	$19,980
Benefits/Pay for work	74.4%	46.2%

satisfy governmental requirements can result in an additional tax burden for the employees.)

- *Group size*—finding insurance companies that will provide coverage to organizations with very few employees.
- *Rising costs*—developing procedures to deal with continuing increases in benefits costs; health premiums alone are expected to continue to rise by 25 percent or more a year.

One strategy for nonprofit organizations to follow in addressing these issues is to seek answers to the following five questions.

(i) What benefits are currently offered? Benefits fall into two categories: those that are required by federal or state law, and those that are not legally required but may be expected because of custom, contract, or the actions of competitors. As mentioned earlier, *required benefits* include social security, unemployment insurance, workers' compensation, and state-mandated programs (such as temporary disability insurance).

Optional benefits include health insurance for an employee, health insurance for the employee's dependents, dental insurance, vision care, life insurance, pensions (which may appear in a variety of forms), dependent care facility or subsidy, educational assistance, vacation pay, sick leave, paid holidays, sabbaticals, rest breaks, severance pay, meals, and health facilities. Employees (and even some employers) are often surprised to learn that there is no legal requirement to provide such commonly available benefits as paid sick leave; sharing that information can help make employees aware of their total compensation amounts.

Usually, an employer first provides mandatory programs, moves to health coverage and paid leave, and then adds pensions or life insurance, depending on the employee profile. Other benefits typically come later, as an organization grows or when it adopts a flexible plan. (One benefit that falls outside the compensation program but still operates to attract, motivate, and retain employees is that of flexible scheduling. An employer with flexibility in scheduling is likely to be flexible in compensation as well.)

(ii) What does the current package cost? Some costs here are *relative* in that they are tied to the amount of direct compensation; social security is the most obvious example. Allowing employees to shelter part of their income is a strategy for reducing the amount paid by employer and employee for such programs. The long-term effect, however, may be to reduce one's retirement benefit from social security.

Items with *fixed* costs (such as individual health insurance coverage) vary by number of employees per work category. It is important to know how many people are eligible for each benefit, how much the unit cost is, and what the probable increase will be for each of the next several years.

Shared expenses are those for which the employee pays a portion. Dependents' health coverage might fall in this category, as might the copayment for the employees' health insurance.

(iii) What do employees want? The typical benefits package was developed for a stereotyped family structure that no longer represents the majority of households. An employer cannot hope to know what employees *value* and what will motivate them, without asking the employees themselves. Any attempt at benefits design or redesign, therefore, should involve an employee survey.

(iv) What can the employer afford?   Because personnel costs are generally the largest expense of any nonprofit organization, any decision in this area can have a profound effect on the budget. The decision to add a benefit should be made only after careful consideration of the costs to continue it. It is extremely difficult to drop a benefit or to limit it to only one or two persons. (The urge to add paid holidays clearly needs to be curbed: the costs are very real, even if not immediately apparent.)

(v) How can the needs of the employer and the employee be met at the same time? Answering this question requires a balancing act. For some, the solution is to provide a flexible plan wherein everyone receives some core benefit (such as individual health coverage) and has some choice about others. For others, the best approach is to increase salaries enough to offset higher taxes and let workers make their own purchases. For still others, the preferred approach is to offer a set package and give employees the right to refuse items they do not want.

Managing benefits is an increasingly complicated task. The balance of this chapter is designed to help nonprofit managers by summarizing benefits-related laws, identifying useful resources, and defining key terms.

14.2   COMPENSATION- AND BENEFITS-RELATED LAWS

Many pieces of legislation touch on compensation in some way, but the framework for compensation in this country was provided in the 1930s by the Social Security Act and the Fair Labor Standards Act, both of which have been amended several times. From the benefits perspective, the major law remains the Employee Retirement Income Security Act of 1974 (ERISA), although the pace of benefits-related legislation has been accelerating in recent years.

(a) SOCIAL SECURITY ACT

(i) Overview   The county's most comprehensive piece of social legislation, the Social Security Act created the social security program, the federal–state unemployment insurance system, and various other governmental programs. The social insurance portions are funded through payroll taxes.

(ii) Major provisions   The following comments concern only the programs funded through payroll taxes:

- Participation is mandatory, even for nonprofit employers.
- Retirement benefits (income and Medicare coverage) are funded through provisions of the Federal Insurance Contribution Act (FICA), with each employer and employee paying the same percentage on the salary or wages received.

- Unemployment benefits are funded through a payroll tax paid by the employer. Four states also require that the employee contribute some amount. Because the unemployment program is managed on a state level, amounts and duration of payments vary.

Details on program eligibility, rates, and benefits are too numerous for this chapter.

(iii) Implications for nonprofit organizations

- Payroll tax amounts must be withheld from employees' wages, supplemented by the employer's share, and deposited in the appropriate account in a timely fashion. Failure to do so results in penalties.

- Employees must be given an accounting of the amount withheld for their FICA share. This must be done on the annual W-2 form given employees for income tax purposes.

- Nonprofits generally may choose, once a year, whether to pay the unemployment amount (1) as a flat tax on the first X dollars of each person's wages or (2) as a dollar-for-dollar reimbursement of amounts paid to former employees collecting benefits. An employer with high turnover would choose the former; an employer with little or no anticipated turnover would choose the latter.

- Given that nearly all nonprofit employees earn less than the social security wage cap, managers need to create budgets with the realization that the two mandatory programs will cost them perhaps an eighth more than each employee's nominal salary.

- Another reality is that the program's old-age benefits were never intended to provide an adequate income for retirement. Thus, as nonprofits (and their employees) mature, the importance of having some type of pension plan will grow.

(b) FAIR LABOR STANDARDS ACT

(i) Overview The FLSA established the minimum wage, maximum work hours, child-labor standards, and overtime pay requirements.

(ii) Major provisions

- Employees are exempt from overtime pay requirements if they hold bona fide administrative, managerial, or professional positions or if they work as outside sales representatives. Nonexempt employees *must* be paid at 1.5 times their normal hourly rate when they work more than 40 hours in a given workweek.

- Employees must be paid the federal minimum wage unless the state minimum wage is higher, in which case the latter applies. A student or "learner" wage may also be paid in some circumstances, after the employer has received the appropriate certificate from the Department of Labor.

- Children between the ages of 14 and 16 may be employed if the work is other than mining or manufacturing (which are not areas known for nonprofits) and if the work does not interfere with their education, health, or well-being.

- Independent contractors are exempt from FLSA provisions.

(iii) Implications for nonprofit organizations

- State and local governments have the option of granting nonexempt workers compensatory time instead of paying overtime. Private employers do not have a similar right. Also, the government views the workweek as the unit of measurement: Overtime is earned for each week separately. It is not legal to average a 30-hour week and a 50-hour week, declare them two 40-hour weeks, and thereby avoid paying overtime.
- To support decisions about overtime pay, employers must keep sufficiently accurate records of time worked. If these records are incomplete or missing, the *employee's* memory may be deemed sufficient to win a claim.
- The label of "independent contractor" or "consultant" cannot be used to avoid compliance with FICA and FLSA. Among the factors examined are the contractor's economic ties to the employer and the permanency of the relationship. In recent years, the Internal Revenue Service has looked much more closely at the use of such arrangements in the nonprofit sector.
- The nonprofit sector is not exempt from scrutiny for FLSA violations. In the past few years, libraries have been prosecuted for child-labor violations (too many hours) and even the Salvation Army has been accused of violating the minimum wage provisions.

(c) EMPLOYEE RETIREMENT INCOME SECURITY ACT

(i) Overview   ERISA is the major law governing the establishment, operation, and administration of employee benefit plans, specifically those concerning pensions and welfare (including health care, vacation benefits, dependent care, prepaid legal services, and educational assistance). It also covers the requirements for informing employees of their benefits and rights.

(ii) Major provisions   ERISA is a lengthy, highly complex piece of legislation. It does not require that any employer offer a pension or welfare benefit plan. Should an employer choose to offer a plan, however, that plan is subject to ERISA. In general:

- The Act covers requirements for reporting and disclosure, participation, vesting (the right to receive a benefit), funding, and fiduciary standards. It also covers tax provisions, presented as amendments to the Internal Revenue Code.
- ERISA is enforced by the Treasury Department (for participation, vesting, and funding matters) and the Labor Department (for reporting, disclosure, and fiduciary matters).

(iii) Implications for nonprofit organizations

- Pension and welfare plans cannot be established or operated for the exclusive or disproportionate benefit of highly compensated or "key" employees. (The complexity of the nondiscrimination rules precludes their presentation here.)
- Employers must give employees understandable information about their plans and benefits. Failure to do so results in fines.
- Employers must file annual IRS reports on forms from the 5500 series.

(d) CONSOLIDATED OMNIBUS BUDGET RECONCILIATION ACT

(i) Overview Essentially, this Act, referred to as COBRA, permits employees and their dependents (current and former), after certain events occur, to continue group health insurance coverage by reimbursing the employer for the amount of the coverage plus an additional 2 percent as an administrative fee.

(ii) Major provisions

- An employee who leaves or loses a job (for reasons other than gross misconduct) may continue group health insurance for up to 18 months by making the payments mentioned above. An employee whose hours are reduced to a level below that at which eligibility for coverage begins may continue the coverage in the same way. Someone ruled disabled under the Social Security Act is eligible for 29 months of continuation after job loss or reduction of hours.
- Some dependents are eligible for 36 months of continuation of certain events occur, such as divorce or legal separation from the covered employee.

(iii) Implications for nonprofit organizations

- Employers must amend the summary plan descriptions of their health insurance plans to advise employees of their COBRA rights. In addition, there are several notification requirements.
- Employers with fewer than 20 employees are exempt from COBRA but may be liable under COBRA-like state laws.

(e) OTHER RECENT BENEFITS LEGISLATION Since ERISA was passed in 1974, the pace of legislative action on compensation and benefits issues has quickened. Four major trends are discernible:

1. An increasing interest in ensuring that taxpayers will not subsidize the wealthy, evidenced in the requirements that benefit plans seeking tax breaks in turn not discriminate in favor of owners or the highly compensated;
2. Changes in regulations concerning the establishment and funding of Individual Retirement Accounts (IRAs) and pension plans for small employers;
3. Expanded requirements to help ensure solvency of pension plans;
4. Increased regulations affecting for-profit employers (such as those concerning employee stock ownership plans (ESOPs)).

Many changes have been designed to expand coverage and benefits; all have increased the system's complexity. This section highlights the major pieces of legislation and summarizes their main features.

(i) Tax Reform Act of 1976 A worker with a nonworking spouse can set aside $2,250 a year in an IRA.

(ii) Revenue Act of 1978 The Simplified Employee Pension was created for small employers. It also allowed employers to establish what became known as 401(k) plans, named after their relevant section in the Internal Revenue Code.

(iii) Economic Recovery Tax Act of 1981 The maximum deductible limit for an IRA was raised to $2,000 and IRAs were extended to all workers, even those covered by an employer-provided pension plan. ERTA also doubled the amount that could be contributed to a simplified employee pension (SEP) or a Keogh plan.

(iv) Tax Equity and Fiscal Responsibility Act of 1982 This Act restricted the maximum contribution and benefit limits for pension plans, permitted partial rollovers between IRA accounts, and limited the kinds of loans people could get from their pension plans without tax consequences. Keogh plans became subject to the same minimum age and service requirements as other pension plans.

(v) Deficit Reduction Act of 1984 Intended to close tax loopholes, this Act limited flexible benefit plans ("cafeteria" plans). The only benefits that could be included in a cafeteria plan without tax consequences were those specifically excluded from gross income by the Internal Revenue Code. These included health care benefits, group term life insurance, prepaid group legal services, dependent care, and educational reimbursement.

(vi) Retirement Equity Act of 1984 Designed to improve women's pension opportunities, this Act lowered the age at which an employee must be allowed to participate in a pension plan and lengthened the acceptable "break in service," the period during which one may leave work without losing pension credits. The law also specified that a worker could not waive survivor benefits without the spouse's written consent. (The intention here was to constrain a worker from choosing higher benefits during his or her own lifetime in exchange for coverage as long as either spouse survived.)

(vii) Tax Reform Act of 1986 "TRA 86" shortened vesting periods (generally to 5 years); restricted the ability of workers covered by an employer-sponsored pension to make tax-deductible contributions to an IRA; dropped the annual employee deferral in a 401(k) to $7,000; allowed small employers to defer part of a salary to a SEP; imposed a 10 percent penalty on funds withdrawn from an IRA before a person reaches age $59\frac{1}{2}$; and increased nondiscrimination rules.

(viii) Omnibus Budget Reconciliation Act of 1986 The Age Discrimination in Employment Act was amended to require employers to continue pension benefit accruals for workers over 65.

(ix) Omnibus Budget Reconciliation Act of 1987 Pension contributions for employers having defined benefit plans were increased, and restrictions on pension plan terminations were tightened.

14.3 BENEFITS-RELATED RESOURCES

Given the rapidly changing nature of employment-related benefits, a resource listing needs updating almost as soon as it is printed. Nonetheless, this section presents major types of resources that may be useful to nonprofit organizations.

(a) ASSOCIATIONS AND ORGANIZATIONS

(i) Association of Part-Time Professionals   This association publishes information on job sharing and on employers of part-time professionals. Its publication, *Employee Benefits for Part-Timers,* covers ways of prorating benefits. For further information, contact:

> Association of Part-Time Professionals
> 7700 Leesburg Pike
> Falls Church, VA 22043
> (703) 734-7975

(ii) Association of Private Pension and Welfare Plans   With members from large and small benefits consulting firms, investment firms, accounting firms, insurers, utilities, law firms, and other businesses, APPWP is a national association that lobbies Congress on benefits issues. It also helps members deal with governmental agencies and elected officials. In addition to an annual conference, it offers members a newsletter and a report on legislation and regulation. For more information, contact:

> Association of Private Pension and Welfare Plans
> 1212 New York Avenue, N.W.
> Washington, DC 20005
> (202) 289-6700

(iii) Bureau of National Affairs, Inc.   The BNA sponsors conferences and offers weekly and biweekly summaries of court cases, legislation, arbitration decisions, and other factors affecting benefits. On an affordable level for nonprofit organizations are BNA's many books, including the recently published third edition of Barbara Coleman's *Primer on ERISA.* For more information, contact:

> Bureau of National Affairs
> 1231 25th Street, N.W.
> Washington, DC 20037
> (202) 452-4276

(iv) Business Group on Health   Such groups can be found variously on state and city levels. They exist to share information and sometimes to lobby. Probably the best known is the Washington Business Group on Health, which produces *Business and Health,* a monthly journal. For more information, check local telephone books.

(v) The Conference Board   One of the most widely known providers of information about employment-related issues, the Conference Board bases its reports and conferences on actual practices. Representatives of over 2,500 organizations from business, academia, and government are connected through Conference Board activities. The organization has produced reports on such issues as retiree health care, family issues, and flexible benefits. One regular publication is *Across the Board.* For more information, contact:

> The Conference Board
> 845 Third Avenue
> New York, NY 10022
> (212) 759-0900

(vi) Employee Benefit Research Institute   A "nonprofit, nonpartisan, public policy research institution," EBRI sponsors policy forums and produces research reports and other publications on benefits-related issues. Its monthly report, *EBRI Issue Briefs,* examines benefits issues and trends. Of its many publications, one is particularly noteworthy: *Fundamentals of Employee Benefit Programs,* now in its fourth edition. This is an excellent primer on the subject. For further information, contact:

> Employee Benefit Research Institute
> 2121 K Street, N.W., Suite 600
> Washington, DC 20037-2121
> (202) 659-0670

(vii) Group Health Association of America   A national association representing prepaid health care programs (meaning Health Management Organizations, HMOs), GHAA provides information through publications on industry trends, regulatory trends, and legislative issues. Its library provides research help on matters concerning managed care plans. For more information, contact:

> GHAA Library Services
> 1129 20th Street, N.W.
> Washington, DC 20036
> (202) 778-3268

(viii) Health Insurance Association of America   A major trade association of commercial health and life insurers, HIAA provides information on cost containment approaches, benefit plan designs, financing insurance, and insurers that write policies for small employers. For more information, contact:

> Consumer Affairs
> Health Insurance Association of America
> 1025 Connecticut Avenue, N.W.
> Washington, DC 20036-3998
> (202) 223-7780

(ix) International Foundation of Employee Benefit Plans   Founded to foster an exchange of information about benefits, the Foundation sponsors conferences at the introductory and advanced levels; programs leading to certification as an employee benefits specialist (CEBS designation); books on such topics as cost containment and ERISA;

research reports; the quarterly *Employee Benefits Journal;* and various other publications on legislation, regulations, and benefits. The Foundation also has an extensive library on benefits-related topics. For further information, contact:

International Foundation of Employee Benefit Plans
18700 West Bluemound Road, P. O. Box 69
Brookfield, WI 53008-0069
(414) 786-6700

(x) Practising Law Institute Among PLI's many courses and conferences are several each year concerning employee benefit plans. The materials for these sessions are published in thick compendia for general purchase. In the 18-title tax law and estate planning series, for example, PLI offers a two-volume set, *Employee Welfare Benefit Plans.* Because the laws and regulations change so rapidly, the PLI publications are valuable for timeliness. For more information, contact:

Practising Law Institute
810 Seventh Avenue
New York, NY 10019
(212) 765-5700

(xi) U.S. Chamber of Commerce Of this organization's services, two seem particularly useful to nonprofit organizations: (1) the annual survey on employee benefits (quantity discounts available), and (2) the syndicated television show, "It's Your Business." For more information, contact:

Research Center, Economic Policy Division
U. S. Chamber of Commerce
1615 H Street, N.W.
Washington, DC 20062
(301) 468-5128

(xii) U.S. Government Printing Office Federal bookstores offer publications on wages and salaries, benefits, and various other human resource issues. Among these are *Handbook for Analyzing Jobs* and *Employee Benefits in Medium and Large Firms.* For more information, consult local telephone directories for the nearest federal bookstore or write:

Superintendent of Documents
U. S. Government Printing Office
North Capitol and H Streets, N.W.
Washington, DC 20401

(b) PUBLICATIONS AND PUBLISHERS Specific topics vary with journals and issues. A brief annotation is given for general recommendation of these sources.

(i) *Benefits Quarterly*   A publication (with refereed articles) of the International Society of Employee Benefit Specialists, through the International Foundation of Employee Benefit Plans.

(ii) *Business and Health*   A monthly publication of Health Learning Systems, in consultation with the Washington Business Group on Health.

(iii) *Compensation & Benefits Management*   Quarterly journal of articles and columns directed to those in charge of designing or managing compensation programs; in mid-1980s, won award as outstanding new journal in business/social sciences/humanities category. Address:

Panel Publishers, Inc.
36 W. 44th Street
New York, NY 10036

(iv) *Compensation and Benefits Review*   Bimonthly published by the American Management Association. Address:

American Management Association
135 W. 50th Street
New York, NY 10020

(v) *Employee Benefits Journal*   Quarterly published by the International Foundation of Employee Benefit Plans; free to members of the IFEPB.

(vi) *Employee Benefit Plan Review*   Monthly digest of developments concerning employee benefits; summarizes legislation, speeches, consulting firms' studies, court cases, and trends. Address:

Charles D. Spencer & Associates, Inc.
222 West Adams Street
Chicago, IL 60606

(vii) *Pension World*   Monthly directed toward pension plan sponsors and investment mangers; understandable by people other than actuaries. Address:

Pension World
6255 Barfield Road
Atlanta, GA 30328

14.4   BENEFITS-RELATED TERMINOLOGY

Although this volume contains an extensive glossary, benefits-related terms are presented here for the reader's convenience. The entries have been selected to provide a basic working vocabulary, but by no means are they the only terms with which a benefits manager would have to be familiar.

accrual The accumulation and crediting of benefits to an employee by virtue of his or her participation in a compensation plan. Accrued benefits may be forfeited unless they are vested.

actuarial equivalent Amount of equal present value. An amount to be received in the future is the actuarial equivalent of another if they have the same present value, determined by using the same actuarial assumptions (such as rate of return and retirement age). See *present value*.

ADEA Age Discrimination in Employment Act, which prohibits discrimination in conditions or termination of employment because of age (protecting those over age 40). Mandatory retirement for employees eligible to receive pensions violates ADEA.

annuity A contract for the periodic payment of specified or objectively determinable amounts over a specified period or over the recipient's lifetime.

beneficiary The person eligible for benefits or payments upon the death of a plan participant.

bonus A lump-sum payment to an employee in recognition of some achievement. Because a bonus is not added to the employee's base pay, some employers use this approach to limit compensation and taxation growth as well as to recognize achievement.

break in service A year in which an employee is credited with no more than 500 hours of service. If an employee has such a break, he or she may lose credit for service before the break, unless he or she returns to service and works another year. A qualified maternity or paternity leave may not be counted as a break in service but may be treated as a neutral year.

cafeteria plan A plan in which participants can choose from among two or more options consisting either of tax-qualified benefits or of a combination of cash and tax-qualified benefits.

cliff vesting A schedule for vesting in which accrued benefits become nonforfeitable after a specified period of service, such as five years.

COBRA Consolidated Omnibus Budget Reconciliation Act of 1985.

CODA Cash or deferred tax arrangement, as a 401(k) plan.

coinsurance Payment by employees for part of the benefit being provided. A common approach is for a health insurer to pay 80 percent of a health service while the employee pays the remaining 20 percent.

contributory plan A plan to which contributions are made in part or whole by participants rather than (or in addition to) their employer.

coordination of benefits Procedure whereby two insurance companies share information to limit their individual liability for expenses. This may arise when spouses have insurance from different employers or when someone is covered by both Medicare and an employer-provided policy.

coverage test Requirement that a plan benefit a minimum number or percentage of employees, with the aim of avoiding discrimination in favor of highly compensated employees.

deductible Expense amount that an employee must pay before other sources (insurance company or employer) assume liability for payment. Deductibles are seen as cost-saving measures by employers and insurance companies.

defined benefit plan A pension plan that pays a specified benefit at retirement, often keyed to average salary over the last few years of employment and to years of service. Contributions to the plan vary according to the amount needed to provide the projected benefit. In this instance, the employer bears the risk and must set aside enough now to make the payments later.

defined contribution plan A pension or profit-sharing plan to which the contributions are specified amounts and the participants have a right to receive benefits contingent on the accumulated value of the total contributions. In other words, the benefits may vary according to the investment expertise of the plan's trustee; the employee, therefore, bears the risk under this plan.

dependent care assistance programs A plan whereby the employer helps employees with services for dependents, which the employee needs in order to earn a living. The employer may provide the needed services, pay the service provider directly, or reimburse the employee for the expenses incurred. If the employer gives the money to the employee, the funds are treated as regular compensation and the employee seeks tax relief under Internal Revenue Code Section 21, dependent care tax credit. If the employer provides or subsidizes the benefit, up to $5,000 per year may be excluded from gross income ($2,500 each, for married individuals filing separately).

direct compensation Pay received in the form of cash or cash equivalents (generally, wages and salaries).

discrimination Favoring of highly compensated employees, owners, or officers by the operation or terms of a plan.

disqualified person Someone who has a specified relationship to a plan, such as the fiduciary, the employer, and officers, directors, and highly compensated employees.

educational assistance program A plan whereby an employer provides instruction for or pays educational expenses of an employee. The plan must be written and must not discriminate in favor of officers, owners, highly compensated employees, or their dependents.

employee One who performs services for compensation and whose working conditions are set by the employer.

entry date The date on which an employee must be allowed to participate in a plan. The Internal Revenue Code requires that a tax-qualified plan admit an employee who has satisfied the age and length-of-service requirements no later than the earlier of these dates: (1) the first day of the first plan year beginning after the date on which the employee first satisfied the requirements; or (2) the date six months after the date on which the employee satisfied the requirements. Multiple dates (as many as 366 in a leap year) may be used when employers want to cover employees as soon as possible.

ERISA The Employee Retirement Income Security Act of 1974 (Public Law 93-403), the law that established the basic requirements for tax-qualified plans. ERISA covers pension and welfare plans, both of which must comply with provisions concerning reporting and disclosure, fiduciary responsibility, and enforcement. The former are also subject to detailed regulations concerning coverage, funding, and vesting. ERISA does not cover federal or state governmental plans for public workers, unemployment insurance, workers' compensation, church plans, excess benefit plans, or plans maintained outside the United States.

ERISA preemption   Explicit preemption by ERISA (in Section 514) of state laws concerning employee benefit plans, except those laws regulating insurance, banking, and securities.

excess benefit plan   A plan that provides benefits beyond those in a tax-qualified plan and therefore is not covered by ERISA.

executive perquisites ("perks")   Special benefits made available to top managerial employees. These are becoming more and more likely to represent taxable income to the employee receiving them.

Federal Insurance Contributions Act (FICA)   The source of social security withholding requirements.

forfeiture   Loss of benefits caused by leaving employment before all accrued benefits have been vested.

forward averaging   Procedure of computing tax on a lump-sum distribution whereby the tax is determined as if the money were received over a period of years. This application of Internal Revenue Code (IRC) Section 402(e) avoids combining the total distribution with the taxpayer's other income for a tax year, thereby lowering the overall effective tax rate.

401(k) plan   A CODA; a profit-sharing or stock bonus plan wherein an employee may choose to be paid in cash or through having the funds placed in a trust under the plan. Under the 1986 Tax Reform Act, tax-exempt organizations, as well as state and local governments, can no longer establish such plans, although any in existence before July 1986 could be continued.

403(b) plan   Tax-deferred annuity plan for retirement for employees of tax-exempt IRC Section 501(c) (3) organizations. The same nondiscrimination rules apply here as to Section 401(a) plans, including minimum participation rules. In addition, a Section 403(b) plan can be considered discriminatory in terms of elective deferrals unless *all* employees have an opportunity to make the deferrals. (These deferrals are amounts shielded from current taxation through a salary reduction agreement.) An employee's annual deferral is generally limited to $9,500 (with some possible additions), a limit higher than those for CODAs or SEPs.

frozen plan   A plan in which benefit accrual has stopped but existence continues to distribute assets to participants and beneficiaries.

graded vesting   A schedule whereby an increasing percentage of accrued benefits become vested, until 100 percent is reached. the 1986 Tax Reform Act replaced earlier forms with seven-year graded vesting: a plan must provide at least 20 percent vesting after three years, 40 percent after four, 60 percent after five, 80 percent after six, and 100 percent seven years.

highly compensated employee   One who, in the current or previous plan year, (1) was a 5 percent owner; (2) received $85,485 (in 1990) in compensation; (3) received $56,990 (in 1990 compensation) and was in the most highly paid fifth of employees of the organization, or (4) was an officer and received compensation more than 50 percent of the dollar limitation on annual benefits ($51,291 in 1990). (These figures are adjusted annually for inflation.) The 1986 Tax Reform Act created alternative tests for discrimination with regard to the percentage of compensation deferred in a year.

hour of service   An hour for which an employee is paid or entitled to be paid for performing duties, exercising excused absences, or meriting back pay.

indirect compensation   Pay received in the form of benefits or services.

integration   Reduction of pension benefits or contributions to take into account social security benefits to which a participant is entitled. Some pension plans are designed to yield a retiree a certain amount when combined with social security. In such cases, the contribution or benefits will vary according to the amount being paid into or received from social security.

IRA   Individual retirement account, a trust organized and created in the United States for the exclusive benefit of an individual and his or her beneficiaries. The limit on contributions for a tax year is $2,000, except for rollover contributions. An IRA may not be invested in insurance contracts or in "collectibles" (such as stamps or rare coins) and must provide for mandatory distributions. Under Internal Revenue Code Section 408(c), employers and employee associations may establish IRAs for employees. Distributions from both types are taxable in the year paid.

J & S   Joint-and-survivor annuity; upon the participant's retirement, a J & S lasts for his or her lifetime and then provides an annuity for the lifetime of the surviving spouse.

key employee   One who is an officer of the employer or who meets one of several ownership tests. "Key" and "highly compensated" are not synonymous.

leased employees   Someone who is not an employee yet provides services usually provided by an employee, but does so under contract with a leasing organization and on basically a full-time basis for over a year.

lump-sum distribution   Distribution of the entire balance of an employee's account within the same tax year as a triggering event (retirement, death, disability, termination of service, or reaching age 59½).

mandated insurance benefit   A benefit that a state requires in an insurance package or plan if the insurer is to operate within the state. The most commonly mandated benefit is mental health care within employee health plans.

minimum accrual standards   Established by ERISA's Section 204, these reinforce the vesting requirements. Section 204 describes three formulas to prevent backloading, or the limiting of generous accrual until later years. Accrued benefits may not be reduced because of increased age or years of service. Also, pension plan assets or liabilities cannot be transferred, merged, or consolidated unless each participant receives benefits at least equal to those to which he or she would have been entitled before the transaction. Still, someone may transfer enough assets to meet this stipulation and then keep the rest, a phenomenon increasing in recent years.

minimum funding standards   Guidelines for the minimum amount an employer must contribute to a plan, to cover all liabilities and operating costs. A plan is underfunded when the market value of its assets is less than the present value of vested deferred benefits. Sections 301 to 306 of ERISA specify funding requirements for pension plans.

minimum vesting standards Requirements for the points at which benefits become nonforfeitable. Benefits derived from employee contributions are fully vested immediately. Employer contributions may meet one of three standards: (1) 100 percent vesting after five years (cliff vesting), (2) seven-year graded vesting, or (3) ten-year cliff vesting under multiemployer, collectively bargained plans.

money purchase plan A defined contribution plan.

normal retirement age The earlier of (1) the age specified in the plan, or (2) the latest of (a) the participant's 65th birthday, (b) the fifth anniversary of plan participation, for someone who began participating within five years of the plan's stated normal retirement age, or (c) the tenth anniversary of someone's initial plan participation. Term does not refer to the age at which one falls asleep reading a benefits glossary.

participant Someone entitled to receive benefits under an ERISA plan. A former employee is a participant if he or she has been vested and has yet to receive all accrued benefits under a plan.

participation Taking part, or allowing one to take part, in a plan. Generally, the maximum required waiting period is one year if the employer wants to retain tax qualification; an employer may allow employees to participate immediately. The usual minimum age requirement is 21, although tax-exempt educational institutions may use age 26.

PBGC The Pension Benefit Guarantee Corporation, an entity operated under the Department of Labor to administer pension plan insurance and termination provisions. The PBGC may terminate a plan experiencing financial difficulty; it might also assert claims against an employer filing for bankruptcy.

pension plan A plan providing for definitely determinable retirement benefits over a period of years for participants or their beneficiaries. A tax-qualified plan must be in writing, be established by an employer, be communicated to employees, be a permanent rather than a temporary program, and exist for the exclusive benefit of covered employees and their beneficiaries.

plan year Any 12 consecutive months specified in a plan, not necessarily the calendar year or the employer's fiscal year.

present value Value in today's terms of money to be received in the future. Because money has a time value, a dollar today is not the same as a dollar received in a year. Present value calculations are used to translate future benefits or income to today's terms for ready comparison and to determine the amount of money one must put aside or invest to yield benefits of a certain amount in the future. Consider, for example, a sweepstakes awarding the winner $1 million to be paid at the rate of $25,000 a year for 40 years. Assuming a 6 percent inflation rate, that award is worth only $542,000 in today's dollars. Clearly, then, there is a substantial difference between a benefit promised in nominal dollars and one promised in current dollars.

prohibited group That group in favor of which a tax-qualified plan must not discriminate.

prohibited transaction One that is not allowed for a plan. For example, a plan fiduciary may not buy, sell, or exchange property or services with the plan; also, there must be an arm's-length relationship between the employer and the plan.

prototype plan   A master plan operated by a mutual fund or financial institution and adoptable by an employer upon execution of a participation agreement. (By using such an approach, an employer is saved the trauma of creating legally correct plan language.)

qualified plan   A plan that meets IRS requirements and therefore receives favorable tax treatment.

REA   Retirement Equity Act of 1984, noteworthy for requiring that married vested participants retiring under a plan must receive joint and survivor benefits (rather than having the employee exhaust all benefits and leave the surviving spouse without income) unless both participant and spouse consent in writing to a different option.

rollover   Reinvestment in a tax-qualified plan of funds or property received from a nonrequired distribution of another tax-qualified plan. If done within 60 days of the distribution, the transaction is not taxed.

simplified employee pension plan (SEP)   Essentially, an individual retirement account of annuity established by an employer, often under a model or prototype arrangement with a bank or other financial institution.

summary plan description (SPD)   Summary of each plan that must be given to all participants and beneficiaries. It must be written in language that the average participant can understand while at the same time covering the plan's provisions—not an easy task. ERISA requires that the plan administrator file the SPD with the Labor Department, and file an update every fifth year thereafter. (Employers adopting a prototype plan avoid this requirement because the operator of the master plan does the filing.) Among the items that must be included are the plan sponsor's name and administrative type; the name and address of the plan administrator; the requirements for eligibility, benefits, and vesting; the source of funding; the procedures for claiming benefits and redress; and the dates of the plan year. Failure to supply a participant or beneficiary with the SPD (or a summary of material modification when a major change is made) within a month of plan adoption or amendment can result in a fine of $100 a day.

tax-deferred annuity   An investment method used to fund retirement plans of tax-exempt employers or their employees. See *403(b) plans*.

TEFRA   Tax Equity and Fiscal Responsibility Act of 1982, regarded by some as the beginning of the trend toward nondiscrimination rules; this Act applied nondiscrimination rules to group term life insurance plans. When an employer pays the premium for more than $50,000 in group term life insurance for an employee, the amount in excess of the premium for $50,000 of coverage is taxable income to the employee.

top-heavy   Giving disproportionately more benefits to key employees.

unemployment insurance   Combined federal and state program (administered by each state) that is intended to provide financial security to jobless workers. Program is financed by an employer-paid tax on the first X dollars of each worker's pay; in a few states, a small employee contribution is required as well. Nonprofits may have the option of paying the tax (at a rate determined by employer age and experience) or of paying no tax but reimbursing the system for all unemployment benefits claimed. Such a choice can be made only once a year.

vesting   Acquiring the right to receive benefits; reaching the point at which benefits become nonforfeitable.

welfare benefit plan   Any plan or program to provide participants (and beneficiaries) with benefits for health care (medical, surgical, dental, hospital coverage), sickness, accidents, disability, death, unemployment, vacation, training, day care, educational assistance, or prepaid legal services.

workers' compensation   Employer-paid insurance program regulated by each state and designed to protect employees from financial loss as a consequence of a work-related injury or illness.

year of service   Any 12-month period during which an employee has at least 1,000 hours of service.

Compensation Management

Mark D. Michaels
People Technologies

CONTENTS

15.1 COMPONENTS OF AN EFFECTIVE PERFORMANCE-BASED SYSTEM

(a) ELEMENTS OF AN EFFECTIVE COMPENSATION SYSTEM In effective compensation systems, the internal worth of positions is balanced with compensation that is competitive when compared with rates paid and ranges utilized by those in other, similar positions. Balancing internal and market worth is the critical task in compensation management because it helps employees feel comfortable with answers to:

What is my job worth to the organization, compared with my co-workers?

What is my job worth to the organization, compared with what I can receive elsewhere?

When employees compare compensation, they generally think only in terms of their wages. Often, 35 percent or more of an employees's real compensation in nonprofit organizations is received as benefits. This high figure developed because nonprofits found it difficult to stay competitive with private-sector wages. To retain employees, nonprofits offered longer vacations, more holidays, more sick leave, and similar noncash benefits. Eventually, insurance policies were added; then state and federal law added requirements like social security for some nonprofits, and organizations that had started pension funds found their funds regulated by law. Quietly, the costs added up. Because of the high cost of benefits, as much as 30 percent of a labor-intensive nonprofit's annual operating budget can be spent on employee benefits. This expenditure forces the nonprofit executive into managing total compensation instead of wages alone.

Total compensation is the total cash value of all compensation received through wages and benefits. Determining the total compensation value requires computing the cash value of three types of costs: program benefits—both mandatory and voluntary—such as insurance, pension, unemployment, and workers' compensation; pay for time worked; and pay for time not worked, such as holidays, vacation, and sick leave.

It is almost impossible to calculate the exact total compensation amount, but any compensation study must find some way to consider all these factors when attempting to define a fair level of compensation. It is important that employees know the value that these benefits add to their compensation programs.

Workable compensation systems distinguish among a number of elements. All systems start with positions within organizations. *Positions* are the specific jobs held by employees. For instance, two registered nurses hold two positions; one works in department A and one works in department B.

A *job classification* is defined as the description of a group of positions in which employees perform similar, but not necessarily identical work. The positions share similar organizational responsibilities. They also require the same group of skills, knowledge, and abilities for successful performance of the work. The two registered nurses described above are in the same job classification, but their classification is different from, say, that of practical nurses.

A *pay classification* or *pay range* is a salary or salary range assigned to a group of job classifications. Registered nurses and human resource assistants may be in the same pay classification. Registered nurses would most likely be in a different pay classification than practical nurses.

The *classification system* is composed of all pay ranges. Along with benefits, it constitutes the complete compensation system.

(b) THE FOUNDATION OF EFFECTIVE PERFORMANCE-BASED COMPENSATION SYSTEMS

To meet both employee and employer needs, a performance-based compensation system must be considered fair by the employee and it must produce results for the employer in terms of increased organizational effectiveness,. The foundation of such systems includes four cornerstones: (1) job analysis; (2) salaries that are competitive in the marketplace while maintaining equity within the organization; (3) a valid performance management system; and (4) a policy guaranteeing that the greatest rewards go to the best performers.

Job analysis is the core function of all human resource management processes. For a compensation system to be effective, job analysis must identify the key contributions that each job makes to an organization's mission, plus the critical knowledge, skills, and abilities (KSAs) required to make such contributions. These are the data used for comparative analysis when establishing the salaries for the positions.

For instance, a supervisor in a sheltered workshop may be exposed to dangers associated with industrial equipment. At the same location, a social worker may be exposed to dangers associated with infectious diseases. The effective compensation system establishes a way to place a separate dollar value on each of these dangers.

How much is a job worth? Valuing contribution and skills in the organization requires balancing information from two often conflicting sources. The first source, the marketplace, is related to market worth. The second source, the pecking order, places the position's worth in a relationship with other positions within the agency to arrive at internal worth.

The market worth of a skill or position is the amount paid for that commodity or service by other employers with whom the agency competes when hiring and retaining employees. For some employees, such as social workers, this comparison can possibly be based on the whole job. The market worth of social work positions in a community is the average salary for social workers.

Nonprofits compete to recruit and retain social workers primarily within the nonprofit and public sectors. As a group, the market worth for social workers is depressed by the tight financial conditions experienced by nonprofit and public organizations. However, to recruit and retain a secretary, a nonprofit agency competes with both the public and private employment sectors. Current economic conditions can put an agency in the ticklish situation of paying a secretary the same salary as a social worker.

Before the 1970s, most organizations set their salaries as a function of budgetary ability and market conditions. This eventually led to charges of discrimination against women, because the marketplace paid lower salaries for female-dominated positions than for those held by males. The first response and attempt to remedy the problem was the Equal Pay Act of 1963, which required equal pay for equal work. Two positions whose jobs descriptions are highly similar are required to be given the same pay within the same establishment, or at least must be in the same pay range. For instance, men and women in computer programming jobs are placed in the same salary range, and the average salaries for males and females in similar positions should be equal. Job analysis is used to thwart attempts to evade the law by having two job titles, one filled by men the other by women, but with virtually the same duties.

Job analysis studies revealed a second, more insidious form of pay discrimination. It was discovered that an organization may value two different jobs or skill sets equally, or skills in a traditionally female position may even be valued more than a male-dominated skill set, but the marketplace values them differently because one is a traditionally female job. In a frequently cited example, a janitor is compared with a secretary. Because the salaries are set based on market value, the traditionally female jobs are kept as lower paying positions.

This finding resulted in demands to consider the internal, organizational worth of a position as part of the compensation formula. The demand for equal pay for comparable worth was born, and internal equity became an important part of the compensation process.

To date, the Supreme Court has rejected the comparable worth doctrine under both the Civil Rights Act of 1964 and the Equal Pay Act. However, many state governments have passed comparable worth laws, some of which cover local governments and state grant recipients. Unions, especially the American Federation of State, County, and Municipal Employees (AFSCME), are actively pushing comparable worth both politically and in negotiations. Nonprofits are quickly finding it strategically necessary, if not also motivationally valuable, to include internal worth in their compensation planning process.

The third cornerstone to a solid compensation system is a valid performance management system. To be valid, the performance management system must exhibit both validity and reliability. Validity means that the system measures what is claims to measure. Reliability means that, when two or more evaluators review the same performance against the same criteria, their evaluations will be very similar. (Strategies for developing valid and reliable performance management systems are discussed in Chapter 13.)

An effective performance-based compensation system will never be achieved without the fourth cornerstone. The system must guarantee that the best performers receive the highest awards. The need is logical and simple enough, but putting it into practice has been a nightmare, especially for merit systems.

The problem begins with a misuse of the bell curve as the controlling dynamic of the compensation system. Using the bell curve, or what some consultants call midpoint budgeting, assumes that, over time, the distribution of performance evaluations in an organization will look like the bell-shaped or standard curve. Because the curve is symmetrical, budgeting for performance increases only requires budgeting as if everyone received an average evaluation.

That average would be achieved over time, but as with any statistic, the concept "over time" means over a long time. In any given year, the probability exists that the majority of the evaluations will fall on one side of the line or the other. If the performance management system is invalid, the results will usually fall above midpoint. When these evaluations are linked to the compensation system, they cause salary increases to go over budget. Profit-making organizations can mange such overages in the short run, but nonprofits running on tight revenues can be devastated in just one year.

Traditional responses to the problem include arbitrarily lowering evaluations to fit the budget, reducing the amount available for reward for above-average evaluations during the second half of the year, and stopping pay increases totally at some point in the year. Each response destroys the integrity of the performance management system.

A second problem is "topping out"—reaching the top of a pay scale through exceptional performance and then not being able to go higher. At this point, the top performer no longer is rewarded for performance, or the policy is manipulated on an individual basis, slowly destroying the integrity of the compensation system.

Many organizations have tried a systemic response to the topping-out problem. When an employee is low in the pay scale, the percent of increase for top performance will be higher than for a person higher up on the scale. Employee A, who is currently paid below midpoint, receives an excellent evaluation, making her eligible for a 7 percent raise. Employee B's current salary is in the top quartile. With an excellent evaluation, he is only eligible for a 4 percent raise. The policy is justified with the learning curve, but Employee B's motivation quickly deteriorates in future years.

Piecework, commission, and other systems are all able to give the highest compensation to the best performer. Using methods described later in the chapter, merit systems can also achieve this goal.

(c) PAY-FOR-PERFORMANCE WORKS, SO WHAT'S THE PROBLEM? Merit pay, the strategy of providing annual pay increases based on a formula that relates the increase to one's annual performance review, is the most pervasive form of performance-based compensation in nonprofit organizations. Yet, numerous studies show that employees strongly dislike merit pay systems.

Ask just about any employee what should be the basis for pay and he or she will answer: "My performance." Is this some kind of schizophrenia? Or is it impossible to develop a workable pay-for-performance system?

Actually, neither situation is the case. Many workable pay-for-performance systems are found in for-profit and nonprofit organizations. They have been in existence since the industrial revolution, and probably before, in the form of piecework, commission, profit sharing, gain sharing, and achievement bonuses. (These successful programs are discussed in detail in a later section.)

Discussions with employees of nonprofits during consultations and seminars has shown a consistent pattern of problems with merit pay systems. Some of the problems are inherent with the compensation program; others are failures in the performance management system. The most frequently cited problems or complaints based on the compensation system and the performance management system are as follows:

COMPENSATION SYSTEM

Poorer workers and workers with less seniority can get greater increases.

Topping out occurs in the system (reaching the highest pay level means a restriction on further increases).

Merit increases are too small to be worth the effort.

The difference in increase between top workers and average workers is too small to be worth the extra effort.

The merit increase fund runs out before the evaluation period.

Everyone gets the same raise, regardless of evaluation, to fit the budget.

PERFORMANCE MANAGEMENT SYSTEM

The evaluations are biased.

The pay increase is based on the rank of the evaluation, even when two are very close together.

The pay increase comes 6 months after the evaluation.

With many human resource management issues, the problem is not with the baby, but with the bath water. Strategies exist for resolving the employees' legitimate complaints. Chapter 13 provides answers to performance management systems. This chapter addresses solutions to the compensation-based problems.

To avoid confusion, the rest of the chapter distinguishes between merit and performance-based compensation systems. Performance-based compensation systems include all methods for paying employees based on their work output, including merit pay. Merit pay is the type of system in which annual increases or bonuses are paid based on an annual performance evaluation review.

15.2   TYPES OF PERFORMANCE-BASED PAY

(a) PIECEWORK   Performance-based pay is as old as the world's oldest profession. Whether they pick bushels per day or build widgets per hour, individuals employed under piecework systems are paid for each piece produced.

Piecework systems are possible when workers have control over materials and work process. These systems require a defined product, such as total assembly of a product or completion of a series of repetitive tasks that form part of a total product. Pure piecework systems are now rare outside of agriculture. They have been banned to protect workers form the sweatshop conditions found in the garment industry early in this century.

An alternative and popular piecework approach is to establish a base salary and a baseline production level. An employee can earn additional income for each piece made above the baseline level. In some systems, the higher the workers' production, the greater the amount of the award per piece.

Piecework is almost nonexistent in nonprofit management. Piecework acts contrary to good service delivery, and most nonprofits are service providers. Admittedly, some governmental programs pay nonprofits under a piecework model. The performance-based contract under the Joint Training Partnership Act is an example.

(b) COMMISSION COMPENSATION   Commission is piecework for salespeople. Commission pays the employee a percentage of the sale price of an item when it is successfully sold. Pure commission systems, which also are not popular in nonprofits, pay only for the percentage of sales, with no other payment. Usually, the employee is allowed to take a draw (borrow) from expected future commissions until the sales level achieved is adequate for sustaining his or her livelihood.

Most commission systems combine base salary and commission. The base salary is recognition that the employee does not completely control the sales process. In most cases, the sale is dependent on the performance of various support staff. However, the base salary is lower than for comparable noncommission, salaried positions. The salary difference usually runs between 25 and 35 percent. The difference is expected to be made up in commissions.

Commission payments can be manipulated to support desired behaviors. Examples of motivational commission structures include:

- To increase the incidence of repeat clients, for whom the cost of sales is lower, pay a higher commission for repeat business over new sales.
- To increase sales of one stock over another, increase the commission on the desired stock.
- To increase sales volume per buyer, increase the commission rate for higher sales volume.

- To protect from overselling to one customer, use a graduated commission and decrease the commission rate after reaching the desired sales volume.

These types of modified commission programs frequently appear in nonprofit environments. Agencies with thrift stores provide commissions to managers, dependent on store volume. Agencies with sheltered workshops commission the employees responsible for selling the workshop goods. Fund raisers often receive a percentage of donations and grant income as part of their compensation. Membership recruiters, magazine subscription telemarketers, and advertising sales representatives are also prime candidates for commission programs.

(c) MANAGEMENT BY OBJECTIVES (MBO) The performance management system of management by objectives is frequently linked to the compensation system for managers. MBO was developed by Peter Drucker. If achieving objectives is viewed as production, MBO becomes a piecework system for managers.

In the 1980s, the popularity of MBO compensation systems decreased among the academic and consulting communities. W. Edwards Deming has suggested that MBO systems block development of a quality-focused organization. As described by Schneier (1979), MBO systems encourage achievement of the objectives at the expense of the process for achieving the objectives. A manager may achieve his or her objectives and, as a result of the manager's aggressive approach, lose an entire staff at the same time. When the manager's achievement of objectives is linked to compensation, that manger still gets rewarded. Objectives can also make managers inflexible or even blind to the need for change. Although MBO-based compensation has many critics, it remains one of the most popular systems for performance-based compensation in the United States.

A simple MBO system rewards a worker for meeting objectives established at the beginning of the evaluation period. The objectives are written in clear, quantifiable language. An example of an objective for a development director might be: "Increase donation income to 10 percent in 6 months." With clear objectives, evaluation is very simple.

The administrative structure for an MBO-based compensation system can become complex. As Exhibit 15.1 demonstrates, the final rating defining the percent-of-salary income can be the sum of a number of factors: timeliness in completing the objective, the priority of the objective, and so forth. The points given for each objective are added together, and the sum is matched against some external guideline. The guideline might read: "For a total score of 50 to 60, award a 3% raise. For a total score of 61 to 70, award a 4% raise."

(d) ACHIEVEMENT-BASED COMPENSATION PROGRAMS The fastest growing area of performance-based pay today is achievement-based compensation systems. These systems are particularly effective in organizations that offer few promotional opportunities and in connection with Total Quality Management (TQM) programs.

Achievement-based pay is simple to administer. The agency starts by establishing developmental opportunities for employees. For instance, secretaries might be encouraged to learn computer word processing, or employees might be encouraged to learn the skills needed for facilitating TQM teams. When an employee demonstrates learning and effective use of the new skill, the employee is given a predetermined raise as a reward.

One of the earliest of the modern achievement systems was the dual career ladder, which is a response to the Peter Principle (everyone is promoted to his or her own level

Exhibit 15.1.   Rating sheet for management by objectives (MBO).

MBO RATING SHEET

Goals	Weight (A)	Complete (B)	Effect (C)	Time (D)	Total
	100%	SCORE 1 to 3	SCORE 3 to 5	SCORE 2 to 5	A(B+C+D)

NOTE: Weightings and scores are for example only. Agencies should set their own standards establishing the importance of each criterion.

of incompetence). Dual career ladders reward individuals who want to remain producers by allowing another growth track or ladder as an alternative to the traditional ladder to management. At the same time, dual career ladders help organizations retain upwardly mobile employees where there are few promotional opportunities.

Exhibit 15.2 shows a dual ladder that provides two paths for development in the organization. On the right is the traditional path to supervision and management. The path on the left works like the Boy Scout merit system: the organization identifies additional skills that are needed within the job category. An employee who is happier as a service provider can go up the left-side ladder by completing the required development activities. A pay increase is given as each step is completed. This system is possible only in organizations that can set aside the money for such increases.

Many merit pay and MBO systems foster competition between individual employees, which tends to work against the group involvement approach inherent in TQM. Achievement-based systems are jumping in to fill the void.

At Ford Motor Company, as well as in many hospitals now promoting quality, Total Quality transformations eventually affect the entire work system. Work redesign leads to a breakdown of departmental differentiation of work and the creation of work cells involving the performance of multiple tasks in a team environment. This job expansion

Exhibit 15.2. Alternative paths on a sample pair of dual career ladders.

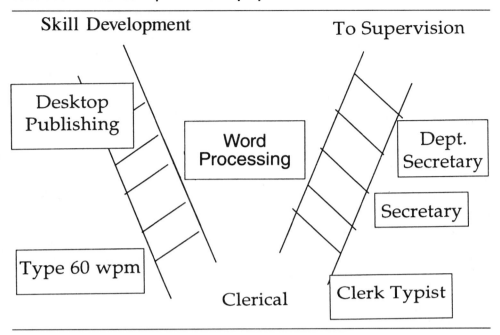

requires the development of team membership and technical skills. TQM program companies use the achievement-based system to encourage individual skill development and team collaboration.

(e) MERIT PAY SYSTEMS Merit pay is the catchall term for compensation systems that base part or all of their annual pay increase on the results of a formal evaluation of individual employee performance.

Merit pay was developed as a reward structure in situations where the task, the work process, or both are not clearly defined and easily assessed. This perceived lack of clarity is the basis for many of the problems with merit pay systems.

To function successfully, merit pay systems minimally require:

- A valid annual (or semiannual) evaluation of the employee's performance, using a system such as those discussed in Chapter 13.
- A compensation system based on salary ranges instead of flat salaries.
- An objective rule linking allowed salary increases to performance levels. The rule might read this way: "Excellent performers receive 5.5 to 7% increases, average performers receive 4.5 to 5.5% increases, below-average performers receive 3 to 4% increases, and poor performers receive no increases." The percentages may change each year as a function of the budget and market worth.
- Support for the objective rule, which ensures that the rule will be followed under all circumstances. If financial conditions are allowed to affect the rule, the result

is that the compensation system controls the performance system. The opposite is necessary for an effective performance-based compensation program.

(f) GAIN SHARING Gain-sharing compensation systems are group rewards programs that provide bonuses based on group and organizational success. They range from bonuses for successful suggestions to complex profit-sharing programs. Gain-sharing programs are becoming very popular as part of Total Quality transformations because they support team identity and achievement of organizational goals.

Gain sharing works in nonprofits, but with a catch. Private companies take a portion of their profits and distribute that portion to the employees. The distribution may be in cash, stock, or increased benefits. Nonprofits have no profits to share.

However, nonprofits can share money that is saved through a more efficient delivery of services. If, through continuous improvement efforts, employees develop techniques that save $5,000 over the budgeted expense—assuming revenues meet budget projections—a portion of those funds can be distributed to the employees as a bonus. The result is a win–win scenario for both the employees and the organization.

A typical gain-sharing program will start with some sort of problem solving, suggestion, or continuous improvement team system involved in organization problems. The decision-making process will work as follows:

1. The team recommends a change in equipment, procedure, or whatever, which it believes will save the organization some money.
2. Either a steering committee or management personnel review and approve the proposal.
3. The steering committee estimates the current budget costs associated with the problem.
4. The proposal is implemented and savings are tracked. After a set time period (usually either a quarter or a full year), the savings are computed. A portion of the savings is distributed to the employees as a bonus.
5. The bonus paid is based only on the initial savings from the change. The organization should experience ongoing savings as a result of the change.

The agency must decide to whom the bonuses are distributed. Some organizations distribute the bonuses to the team that developed and implemented the change. This supports team identity and can create competition among teams, a concept that has been institutionalized at corporations like Motorola.

Some organizations disagree with the value of interorganizational competition. They value large group identification with the organizational goals. Other organizations are too small for multiple teams. They distribute bonuses to the entire staff.

15.3 COMPENSATION PLANNING WITH EMPLOYEE PARTICIPATION

(a) AN OVERVIEW OF THE COMPENSATION STUDY Developing an effective compensation system is a complex process that requires a series of steps ranging from initial board policy development to detailed job and quantitative analysis. The project can take form 3 to 6 months in small to medium-size nonprofits. Some of the steps, like conducting a salary survey, must take no less than 1 month. For other processes, like job analysis, the time frame depends on the number of employees involved.

A qualified consultant skilled in conflict management should be used to guide the process. Even if, as suggested here, an employee participation strategy is used, it is still critical to use a consultant. Under the best of circumstances, there will be conflict during the project because it involves individuals' livelihoods and egos.

The project manager is the lightning rod for the project. If that person is an employee and the conflict is even slightly mishandled, it can take years to repair the relationships within the organization. Compensation study problems have seeded the termination of many professional executives who insisted on saving money by doing the work themselves. A good consultant deflects the criticism while effectively managing the project. A poor consultant can at least absorb the blame.

Because compensation studies take a great deal of time and effort, few compensation consultants are willing to perform the work for free. However, local retired executives are sometimes available through the local Chamber of Commerce. Larger United Way systems may have consulting resources, and some trade associations offer help to their members at below-consulting rates.

Compensation studies include eight basic steps, which are described briefly here. Each step is developed in greater detail throughout the chapter.

1. Establish policy direction. For the consultant to act effectively, the board must answer four questions: (a) Will we pay employees at, above, or below the market rate, to guide development of the salary ranges? (b) Against whom do we compete when recruiting and retaining our employees, to guide development of the salary survey? (The answer may differ for employees in various positions.) (c) What value do we want to give to market worth versus internal worth? (d) What is the relative value of the factors defining a given job's value (i.e., responsibility, skill, mental effort, physical effort, and so on)? Although consultants have their own answers to some of these questions, using them as policy questions helps achieve board approval of the final proposal.

2. Conduct a job analysis. This requires having employees complete self-analysis questionnaires, conducting bench audits (interviews) with a large percent of the employees, and writing the job descriptions.

3. Conduct a compensation survey, that is, send out, receive back, and evaluate a salary and benefits survey.

4. Perform a job evaluation study. This is the critical process of integrating salary survey and job analysis data to establish tentative midpoint salaries for each job classification. The three primary strategies for this task are factor comparison, the point factor system, and whole job comparison. (These are discussed later in the chapter.)

5. Combine positions with similar midpoint salaries into pay classifications. This task involves a regression analysis of the midpoint wages from step 4.

6. Adjust the benefit system to meet survey results and internal needs. It will be necessary to be aware of the benefits survey results at all times. Otherwise, wages can be over- or underestimated relative to the total compensation package.

7. Facilitate employee appeals of the classification decisions. Employee appeals provide accountability while helping to gain employee support for the project. Communication with and involvement of employees throughout the project reduce the conflict of a compensation study. However, mistakes are inevitable. Employees become more accepting of the results once they have had a chance to hear the reasoning behind the decisions affecting them.

8. Implement the plan.

The nonprofit agency can perform some of these steps under the guidance of the consultant, thereby saving consulting costs. In particular, the agency should be able to conduct the salary survey according to the consultant's survey strategy. Job analysis can also involve agency staff. Doing both tasks helps develop the in-house capacity for managing the system once the consultant is gone.

Whenever the client assists the consultant, the client must be careful to work within the consultant's research model. Each consultant has his or her own project strategy, which may not fit the nonprofit's initial strategy. For instance, job descriptions may not contain the information the consultant needs for making decisions in the job evaluation process. The consultant will still have to conduct a job analysis, and the agency's time will have been wasted.

Throughout, this chapter discusses ways to involve employees in the compensation process. When compensation planning became popular in the 1970s as the result of federal funds made available through the Intergovernmental Personal Act, most consultants acted as experts making all compensation decisions and recommendations to their clients. Conflict between management and staff in these agencies was very high, resulting in a high project rejection rate.

During the 1980s, a number of consultants began applying employee participation strategies to compensation planning. The employees did not set individual salaries, but they either rated positions on point-factor scales or ranked the positions through factor comparison, providing data from which consultants could derive the final compensation figures. Conflict has been reduced significantly when employee involvement is coupled with a strong communication program.

(b) CONDUCTING A JOB ANALYSIS Job analysis is the foundation of all human resource management functions, including designing effective compensation plans. It is also the starting point in involving employees in the compensation planning process.

Job analysis involves asking employees to describe their jobs, clarifying the employees' information through a bench audit, and writing and rewriting job descriptions.

Employees can prepare a written description of their duties using a standardized questionnaire. The questionnaire must be designed to elicit the information that will be needed to rate or rank the job.

The job analysis questionnaire (JAQ) shown in Exhibit 15.3 was designed to work with a factor-comparison job evaluation strategy. Its five main sections elicit information about each of the five factors in the factor comparison exercise.

Employees are given 1 to 2 weeks to complete the JAQ. It is then reviewed by the supervisor, who is allowed to comment about the information on a separate sheet. This two-step approach helps the consultant to quickly identify task and role conflicts and to thoughtfully plan the bench audit.

Bench audits are one-on-one interviews and job observations with individual employees. There are three reasons for conducting bench audits:

1. They help the analyst clarify vague responses in the JAQ. Responses to the questionnaire will differ, depending on employees' intelligence and attention to detail. It may be necessary to aid some employees in completing the form. Some employees think in terms of broad categories and objectives, providing brief responses. Others are so detail-oriented that they add multiple pages to their response. The bench audit allows the job analyst to standardize the information.

2. Some critical job information cannot be described in the questionnaire. Communication skill requirements like reading level, complexity of decision making, and working conditions can be difficult to understand from answers to the questionnaire. For example, in a study done by this author for a health district, one job had the simple title of Infectious Disease Investigator. The responses on the

Exhibit 15.3. Sample job analysis questionnaire.

ABC NONPROFIT
JOB ANALYSIS QUESTIONNAIRE

Instructions

This questionnaire is the key ingredient for preparing a new position description for your job, and in assigning your position to an appropriate salary classification.

Developing the position description will include a review of your responses by your supervisor. If necessary, we will discuss any major differences between your responses and your supervisor's review in a meeting with you. The consultant may also meet with you to gather additional information about your job. Later, you will also have the chance to review a draft of the position description and to make comments and suggestions. The final description will be reviewed by you and your supervisor.

The information you provide in this questionnaire will also be important in assigning your position to a pay classification. Those assignments will be based on a number of variables relating to the position's skill level; level of responsibility; level of physical and mental effort required to perform job tasks; and the job's working conditions, as these variables relate to other positions.

This questionnaire will not be used to evaluate your individual job performance. The assignment of positions to the pay classifications will be based on the requirements of the job, regardless of who the occupant is. Performance becomes a factor only when determining your actual salary within the assigned salary range. That issue will continue to be a matter among you, and your supervisor.

As you can see, it is important that you answer the questions as completely as possible. Please consider each question carefully and provide as much information as possible.

This questionnaire must be completed and passed on to your supervisor no later than close of business Friday, _____, to keep this project on schedule.

Thank you for your cooperation.

Position: _____

Name _____   Rate of Pay _____

Title _____   Date of Hire _____

Immediate supervisor _____

Supervisor's title _____

Exhibit 15.3.   *(Continued)*

I. **Job Responsibilities:** Please describe all your job responsibilities. Break broad responsibilities into duties and tasks, but try to avoid getting bogged down in detail. For tasks that are performed more than once per day, please include the average number of times the task is performed each day. (For example: "Type approximately 10 letters each day." "Check through approximately 50 books each day.")

A. Daily responsibilities (responsibilities you must achieve every day)   #Hrs/Day Rank

B. Weekly responsibilities (responsibilities you must achieve every week)   #Hrs/Wk Rank

C. Monthly responsibilities (responsibilities you must achieve every month) #Hrs/Mo Rank

D. Annual responsibilities (Responsibilities you must achieve annually)   #Hrs/Yr Rank

E. Choose from the above lists the responsibilities that you think are the 10 most important for the successful performance of your job. List them in their order of importance (1 = absolute highest, 10 = 10th highest):

1. _____   6. _____
2. _____   7. _____
3. _____   8. _____
4. _____   9. _____
5. _____   10. _____

Exhibit 15.3. (*Continued*)

II. **Job Relationships**

A. Draw a chart showing how you believe your position really fits into the organization. The chart should show your immediate supervisor(s) at the top, you and your co-workers (by name and title) on the next level, and the names and titles of those you supervise on lower levels.

B. Supervision Received

    1. Describe actions that you can perform and/or decisions you can make without approval from your supervisor.

    2. Describe work problems that you must review with your supervisor before taking action.

    3. For problems not needing a supervisor's review, indicate which of the following you consult or rely on for guidance.

_____ Established procedures such as:

_____ Manuals such as:

_____ Past training by a supervisor such as:

_____ Past technical training such as:

_____ Independent research and consultations such as:

_____ Past professional training such as:

C. Supervision Given

(If your position does not involve supervising any employee, please proceed to Section

D below.)

Check the appropriate responses to describe the nature of your supervision.

_____ Recommend applicants for hiring for vacant positions

_____ Recommend firing subordinates for rule infractions

_____ Suspend subordinates for rule infractions

_____ Recommend suspensions for rule infractions

_____ Give subordinates written and/or oral warnings for rule infractions

_____ Recommend written and/or oral warnings for rule infractions

_____ Conduct performance evaluations of subordinate employees

Exhibit 15.3. (*Continued*)

D. Fiduciary Responsibilities

Check the appropriate responses to describe your responsibilities, and fill in the approximate amounts.

_____ Receive cash and/or checks on behalf of the agency

Avg. amount per day: _____

_____ Prepare, authorize, and/or sign agency checks to pay agency expenses

Amount authorized to approve: _____

_____ Authorize the purchase of materials or equipment on behalf of the agency

Amount authorized to approve without higher approval: _____

_____ Handle materials of exceptional value, such as rare documents.

Examples: _____

_____

_____

E. Public Contacts

My job involves frequent contact with:

_____ 1. Executives in government, business, or other similar agencies

Purposes:

_____ To establish and maintain public contact

_____ To plan and/or negotiate cooperation, funding, or support

_____ To discuss, plan, or interpret policy

_____ To provide or request a specific service

_____ To ask or answer questions about agency practices

_____ 2. Representatives of outside organizations

Purposes:

_____ To establish and maintain public contact

_____ To plan and/or negotiate cooperation, funding, or support

_____ To discuss, plan, or interpret policy

_____ To provide or request a specific service

_____ To ask or answer questions about agency practices

_____ 3. The general public

Purposes:

_____ To establish and maintain public contact

_____ To plan and/or negotiate cooperation, funding, or support

_____ To discuss, plan, or interpret policy

_____ To provide or request a specific service

_____ To ask or answer questions about agency practices

III. **Working Conditions**

A. Describe the physical conditions under which this job is performed.

Exhibit 15.3.   (*Continued*)

B. Describe any unusual psychological demands connected with this job.

C. Describe any conditions under which the job is performed which make it unique.

D. Describe fully any health or safety hazards associated with this job.

E. Is any safety training or equipment required?

IV. **Tools**

A. Please describe any equipment that is necessary for completion of your job (automobile, typewriter, computer, etc.).

Equipment	Purpose	% Time Used	Alternative Method
_____	_____	_____	_____
_____	_____	_____	_____
_____	_____	_____	_____
_____	_____	_____	_____
_____	_____	_____	_____

V. **Special Requirements**

A. List any special certifications or licenses required by law for your position.

B. What level of education had you achieved before starting in this position?

C. How many years' experience did you have in your profession before starting in this position?

Certification of Employee

I hereby certify that the answers to the foregoing are my own, and that, to the best of my knowledge, they are complete and correct.

_____   _____

Signed   Date

Name (please print) _____

Exhibit 15.3. (*Continued*)

Supervisor's Review:

Comments on:
Section I

Section II

Section III

Section IV

Section V

Signed   Date

Name (please print) _____

---

questionnaire were brief but accurate, regarding report making and accountability. What did not show up was that persons in this position put their lives on the line daily as they visit dangerous housing projects to inform people that they may have contracted AIDS or other dangerous diseases. The position had taken on case management responsibilities as well.

3. Bench audits increase a sense of ownership and participation in the project for employees. Bench audits show employees that their input is important to the process and that the project is attempting to meet their needs. For this reason, when contracting with a consultant, the proposal should include requiring a minimum number of bench audits. For smaller agencies, the number should be high, from 50 percent to 75 percent of the resulting *job classifications* (not employees). For larger organizations, no less than 50 percent of the resulting job classifications should receive bench audits.

Specific items to consider during the bench audit, which are not well-defined in the questionnaire, include:

• Examples of how work is assigned to the employee, in written and/or oral form;
• Materials that the employee must read, to assess reading grade-level requirements;

- Forms and reports the employee completes, to assess writing skill levels;
- The complexity of special equipment that the employee uses, including diagnostic equipment, office equipment (for example, computers, and their associated software), and manufacturing equipment;
- Working conditions—inside or outside—and special dangers of exposure to environmental hazards;
- Any special conditions that the employee proposes for consideration.

The next job analysis step is writing the job description. Job descriptions are a by-product of the compensation process. Job evaluation is possible with the information gathered in the JAQ and bench audits, but properly prepared job descriptions are a valuable contribution to all management functions.

Exhibit 15.4 is an outline for a simple job description. For compensation planning purposes, nature of work, required knowledge, skills, and abilities, and required education and experience are the critical elements for the job evaluation process.

Draft job descriptions should be sent to employees and their supervisors for review and comment, as part of the participation process. Minor comments can easily be incorporated into the description. Major complaints may require a second bench audit and, possibly, mediation between the employee and the supervisor.

After the job descriptions are finalized, they should be subject to the grievance procedure that is established for the project.

Exhibit 15.4. Job description outline.

Nature of work:
A. The relationship of the position to the overall function of the organization, and the responsibilities incorporated in that job classification.
B. Extent of supervision received and from where.
C. Role in policy development.
D. Special responsibilities, such as for safeguarding funds.
E. Overall strategy for evaluation of performance for the position.

Examples of work
A. Examples of the types of tasks that are performed by members of the job classification covered by the description. Do not include all tasks performed by a given position covered by the description. Not all tasks listed will be performed by all positions covered by the description. Use those tasks that exemplify the knowledge, skills, and abilities listed in the next section.

Required knowledge, skills, and abilities (KSAs)
A. Describe the underlying performance requirements for satisfactory performance of this job.
B. Use a uniform rating system to define the levels of performance.

Required education and experience
A. Define the minimum education and experience levels needed for a person to be able to learn the KSAs for adequate performance of the job. There must be a relationship between this section and the KSAs.
B. Indicate the required licenses, certifications, and similar documents.

(c) CONDUCTING THE COMPENSATION SURVEY The goal of the compensation survey is to determine the average and range of wages and benefits paid for comparable positions within the local recruitment area. The questions that need to be answered include: Who should be surveyed? Which positions should be used? How many organizations should be included in the survey?

The persons surveyed are determined by the recruitment area for any given job classification in the survey. The organizations surveyed should be those with whom the agency competes when recruiting and retaining employees.

It may be easy technically to answer the question, but the problem can be complicated. A simple answer will come from the person responsible for advertising job openings, who knows what region is covered by the publications in which the ads are placed. That information is not enough, because disagreement among the board, the employees, and the surveyor can scuttle an entire project. Nonprofit employees will be concerned that the survey will include only other, low-paying nonprofits. At the same time, the board will be concerned with issues like the impact of including agencies from communities that have a higher cost-of-living index.

The problem is compounded when different positions are recruited from different areas. Nonprofessional positions may be recruited locally, but the agency may use a national search to fill top positions. The survey should be designed to cover the appropriate area, which can mean sending out multiple surveys.

Because of the potential for conflict, the board should consider these issues early in the project planning stages, and all parties should be made aware of the board's decision. The following can serve as guidelines:

1. Conduct a local survey for clerical positions and include for-profit companies.
2. Survey technical and professional positions that are specific to nonprofit services offered by comparable agencies within the local region. Include private-sector employers for technical and professional positions, like accountant, that are also found in the for-profit sector.
3. Survey similar organizations for executive position salaries within the recruitment areas (regional or national).

Job classifications included in the survey are called benchmark positions. Benchmark positions are chosen for their ease of comparison with positions in other organizations. For instance, the responsibilities, skill, and education for the job classification of Social Work Supervisor may be fairly standard among the surveyed organizations, which makes it an ideal benchmark position. On the other hand, there may be a great deal of difference in the work of secretaries: in one agency, the title may be reserved for department heads' secretaries, and in another agency it may designate the secretaries working in a pool. In this case, comparison is impossible and the position should not be used as a benchmark.

Classifications for benchmarking should be chosen from all levels of the existing salary scale. In this way, there will be adequate anchors for the job evaluation process.

During analysis of the survey, some of the results may prove useless for the job evaluation process. There may not be enough responses for a particular position, or there may not have been a standard description of that classification. For that reason, the survey should include more positions than may be needed for the job evaluation process.

How many organizations should be surveyed? The more organizations included in and responding to the survey, the more valid the results. Establishing a statistically representative sample is probably too cumbersome a job: 25 or more organizations would need to respond in each survey. In setting a survey goal, no more than a 50 percent survey return rate should be expected initially. If major competitors who are known to impact market rates are selected, a minimum survey return of 10 responses may be sufficient. That would require sending out at least 20 surveys.

Effective survey management can ensure higher returns and higher survey quality. The following steps can help improve the quality of survey results:

1. Include a brief description of each classification, including major responsibilities, critical job skills, and required education level. (See Exhibit 15.5 for a sample survey form.)
2. Establish a deadline of 1 month after mailing the surveys for return of the surveys. Include a stamped, return-addressed envelope with the survey. Offer

Exhibit 15.5. Sample survey of salary and benefits.

SAMPLE SALARY SURVEY

Occupation, Title, Description	Total No. Employees	Minimum/ Starting Wage/Hr.	Maximum Wage/Hr	Weighted Avg. (Actual)	Comments
Janitor/Porter/Cleaner Performs general custodial duties, including cleaning floors, facilities, washrooms, and trash removal.					
Receptionist/Telephone Operator Receives visitors, takes incoming phone calls, may handle plant/ factory paging system and outgoing calls. In addition, may perform simple clerical/typing duties.					
Secretary Serves as secretary for a department or division, sets up and maintains files and records and takes care of routine office functions without supervision. Meets and screens people, schedules appointments, handles correspondence not requiring a dictated reply, and allocates mail to subordinates.					
Administrative Assistant Serves as an assistant to an executive of the organization with regard to office management, personnel and fiscal management, allocation of work to others, and scheduling of meetings; makes decisions with regard to work flow assignments, and originates correspondence. Required: 4 years college and 4 years experience.					

Exhibit 15.5.   *(Continued)*

BENEFITS SURVEY

COMPANY _____   PREPARED BY _____

ADDRESS _____   TELEPHONE (___) ___ - _____

CITY _____ STATE _____ ZIP _____   Send results?   YES ____   NO ____

General Information

No. of employees: No. of hours in avg. work week:

    F/T hourly ____   Hourly ____

    P/T hourly ____   Salaried ____

    Salaried ____

    TOTAL ____

Are any employees unionized?   YES ____   NO ____

No. of unions: _____   No. of employees covered: _____

Present agreements from   _____ to _____

                               _____ to _____

Compensation Increase Policies

Do you grant across-the-board COLA increases?   YES ____   NO ____   Month ____

Do you grant market movement increases?   YES ____   NO ____   Month ____

Excluding the above, do you change salary ranges
at a scheduled time?   YES ____   NO ____   Month ____

Anticipated percent increase this year?   _____%

Do you grant individual "merit" increases?   YES ____   NO ____

Do you grant automatic longevity increases?   YES ____   NO ____

Paid Vacation: How long does an employee need to work, to earn a particular period of vacation leave?

    1 week: ____ years   3 weeks: ____ years   5 weeks: ____ years

    2 weeks: ____ years   4 weeks: ____ years

Sick Leave:

Does the organization offer paid sick leave?   YES ____   NO ____

Days per year? _____   Incentive Plan?   YES ____   NO ____

Holidays:

Number of paid holidays offered per year?   _____

Birthday as day off?   YES ____   NO ____

Number of floating or personal days off   _____

Overtime Pay Policy (indicate 1 (regular rate), 1½ (time-and-a-half), 2 (double-time), etc.):

Over 8 hrs/day ____   Over 40 hrs/week ____

Saturdays ____   Sundays ____   Holidays ____

Premium Pay Policies:

2nd shift $_____   3rd shift $_____   Work environment $_____

Variable by job title?   YES ____   NO ____

Call-in pay   Minimum hours _____   Rate of pay _____

Exhibit 15.5. *(Continued)*

Other Time Off:

Does your company offer paid funeral leave?   YES ____   NO ____

Days for immediate family ____   Days for others ____

Does your company offer paid leave for jury duty?   YES ____   NO ____

Does your company offer flex-time?   YES ____   NO ____

Does your company offer a compressed workweek? YES ____   NO ____

Insurance Programs: If your company offers different programs for different employees,

please report your policies as they cover your _____ employees.

Is weekly disability income insurance offered?   YES ____   NO ____

Duration of Coverage _____ weeks

Employer cost/employee $_____   Employee contribution $_____

Health Insurance:

Company's contribution/employee for:

    Individual coverage: $_____
    Dependent coverage: $_____

Employee's contribution for:

    Individual coverage: $_____

    Dependent coverage: $_____

Maximum amount covered: $_____   Deductible $_____

Does your company offer:

Prescription coverage?   YES ____   NO ____

Dental coverage?   YES ____   NO ____

Optical coverage: YES ____   NO ____

Other: _____

Life Insurance:

Company's contribution/employee $_____

Employee's contribution for basic amount $_____

Amount of death benefit $_____

Pension Plan:

Type: Earnings and service _____   Gain sharing _____   Other _____

Employee contribution: ____% of cost

Other Benefits:

Tuition refund?   YES ____   NO ____

% of reimbursement _____%

Other benefits?   YES ____   NO ____

Describe:

confidentiality of the respondent's form and transmittal of a copy of the aggregate survey results to the respondents upon completion of the study.

3. Call the respondents 2 weeks after the mailing to ensure that the survey was received and to check their intention for participation. This is the most critical step in ensuring a high return rate.

4. On the deadline date, call any respondents who indicated that they would participate but have not responded, and determine their response date. (Put 2 weeks' extra time into the project schedule, to allow for late returns.)

5. Call a sample (20% to 30%) of the respondents to discuss their survey responses. Discuss any comments that they made about any classifications, and review their job descriptions for a sample of the classifications. This will help to determine the validity of their responses. If the sample shows that the positions in the responses match the survey positions, all of the survey responses can be assumed to be valid.

Exhibit 15.5 presents a sample salary and benefits survey form. The form has been set up to simplify inputting the data into an electronic spreadsheet or database. Compensation survey software is available from a number of private sources. If a nonprofit is working with a consultant, the consultant may have developed software for this purpose. A copy should be requested for use in upgrading the compensation plan in future years.

Exhibit 15.6 shows the results of one survey of the position of Janitor/Porter/ Cleaner. The important information in the survey is at the bottom: an actual weighted average salary for all the survey participants, plus information about the range of salaries paid by the respondents for that classification. The survey weighted average

Exhibit 15.6. Example of salary survey results for one position.

| TYPE | Janitor/Porter/Cleaner | | | | |
Code	No.	Minimum	Maximum	Weighted Average	Comments
000	1	$9,000	$9,000	$9,000	
002	9	5,700	10,280	9,630	
003		4,250	7,700		
013	53	8,030	10,130	9,270	
014					
015					
016	1	8,950	8,950	8,950	
017	10	4,230	7,440	6,300	
018	27	4,250	6,160	5,210	
019					
020	9	4,540	6,140	4,740	
021	15	6,200	10,140	9,360	
022	17	4,000	6,360	5,360	
023	1	3,800	5,500	5,000	
MINIMUM		$3.80	$ 5.50		
AVERAGE		$5.72	$ 7.98	$7.54	
MAXIMUM		$9.00	$10.28		

salary is computed by averaging the weighted salaries in the individual responses. The individual weighted salaries are averages of actual salaries being paid, not of the midpoints of salary ranges in the reporting organizations. The weighted average is used to establish the preliminary midpoint for that position.

If the agency's policy will be to pay wages comparable to the market, the weighted average will be the preliminary midpoint. If the decision is to establish wages at the bottom of the range, or the first or third quartile, or the top of the range, the amounts are computed from this average and the minimum and maximum salary averages.

To the greatest extent possible, benefit survey results should be reported and analyzed in comparable dollars. For instance, the survey's average monthly contribution to health and life insurance premiums is more important for assessing total compensation than the benefit received. (The information may help to identify other survey participants who are getting greater benefits via their premiums. In that case, the agency should be contacted for more information.)

It is very difficult to compute time-off in dollar terms. Rather than taking the time to do so, the total time-off allocations between agencies should be compared.

Throughout the process, survey analysts should keep an eye on the relationship between the average cost of benefits and the average wage rates in the survey. If the agency shows generally lower salaries but higher benefits than the survey results, the value of the benchmark midpoints should be reduced before moving on to job evaluation to compensate for the difference. There will be less conflict when a lower wage is proposed than when attempting to equalize wages while taking away existing benefits.

(d) JOB EVALUATION

(i) Job evaluation strategies The core process for developing salary systems is job evaluation. Job evaluation combines *market worth,* as identified through a salary survey, *internal worth,* as identified through a ranking process, and *job analysis information* into a dollar value used to establish the midpoint salary for each position. There are three basic strategies for job evaluation: whole job comparison, the point factor system, and factor comparison. It is very important to distinguish among the three methodologies.

Whole job comparison determines the value of a position relative to all other positions in the organization, without reference to varying factors within that position. It is a ranking process that, in one sense, attempts to identify the pecking order within the organization and then establishes salaries accordingly.

Whole job comparison must be done by a highly experienced person who is sensitive to the organization's culture, organizational structure, and job analysis issues. The comparison is actually performed by taking completed job descriptions and shuffling them into an order that appears to match the needs of the organizational chart and culture, while conforming as closely as possible to salary survey information.

Whole job comparison is no longer a popular evaluation method. The decisions involved are usually based on the expertise of one or two individuals and are not easily validated.

The point factor system is the most popular evaluation strategy. The point factor process begins by breaking the job evaluation into constituent parts called factors. Examples of factors include knowledge, responsibility, and mental effort. The number of factors varies from one system to another and can range as high as 18.

Each job factor for a job classification is compared against an externally developed matrix of points assigned to that factor. For instance, under the Education factor, the system may give 50 points for a high school diploma, 75 points for a college associate degree, and 100 points for a four-year college degree.

Points represent dollars within the system. The final midpoint salary awarded to a job classification is derived form the weighted sum of points it receives.

The point/value relationship is usually established in a two-step process. First, the firm determines the weighting of each factor to the whole job. Exhibit 15.7 shows examples of weightings for various point factor schemes. The weighting results in identifying how many points should be assigned to a given factor. For instance, the system may award between 500 to 1,000 points on the responsibility factor scale, while only awarding between 50 and 100 points on the mental effort scale.

The second step, the actual assignment of a dollar value for each point, is done externally through regression analysis of large data bases of salary surveys.

Consulting firms that specialize in point-factor-based evaluation now involve employee groups in the rating process. An employee committee will, individually and then collectively, assign points to each job classification based on the matrix information assigned to any given factor.

The factor comparison methodology attempts to combine the strengths of both the whole job comparison and the point factor system. Like the whole job comparison, factor comparison allows for a ranking of positions based on internal, organizational realities instead of an external standard. Like the point factor system, factor comparison breaks down the job evaluation process to the factor level, allowing more information to be used in making ranking decisions.

Factor comparison enables a comparison of jobs on the basis of four to seven factors. Standard factors used include responsibility, skill, mental effort, physical effort, and working conditions. To ensure reliability in the ranking, these or other factors that are used are given specific definitions. An example of such definition is given in Exhibit 15.8.

Four steps comprise the factor comparison method:

1. Each factor is assigned a weighting relative to the other factors. These may come from other systems, such as in Exhibit 15.7, or may be defined by the organization.
2. Job classifications are ranked for each independent factor.
3. Benchmark classifications from the salary survey are assigned dollar values under each factor. The amounts come from multiplying the weighted average

Exhibit 15.7.   Factor comparison and point factor systems: Two alternative weighting systems.

Factor	NEMA–NMTA*	XEROX Corporation
Skill	50 %	55 %
Responsibility	20	40
Mental effort	7.5	—
Physical effort	7.5	2.5
Working conditions	15	2.5

* National Electrical Manufacturers Association-National Motels Trades Association

Exhibit 15.8.   Factor definitions.

SKILL: Measures the level of education needed to establish a base of understanding, common language, and professional or technical knowledge for performance of the job. Also measures the amount of experience that must be obtained from working in other positions to develop the knowledge, skills, and abilities necessary for the job, and the complexity of the problem-solving processes used in the job.

MENTAL EFFORT: Measures the amount of judgment and analysis, such as the amount of independent judgment required and how much leeway is available in decision making. Also measures the extent to which creative mental skills are required, such as the need for ingenuity, resourcefulness in adapting, and developing new solutions or methods; mental demands, such as the amount of attention needed (normal vs. continuous or close); and the duration and extent of concentration needed.

PHYSICAL EFFORT: Measures the amount of physical exertion necessary to perform the job, including type of exertion, extent of strain, and duration. Coordination and need for dexterity are also measured.

RESPONSIBILITY: Measures the extent to which supervision is needed: how much supervisory responsibility is in the position; the extent of and purpose for contact with others; the position's role in developing policies and procedures; and the effect of errors on the organization's ability to achieve its purpose. The amount of responsibility for safeguarding funds, valuables, or equipment should be considered. Also described as the amount of accountability in the position.

WORKING CONDITIONS: Measures the extent to which employees in the position are exposed to physical and environmental hazards that may affect their health or safety.

---

salary for the classifications in the salary survey by the percent weight for each factor.

4. Dollar amounts are awarded for each factor in each classification, according to its ranking in the factor relative to the benchmark positions.

The factor comparison method can be easily integrated into an employee participation process. The methodology and employee participation process are described in detail in a later section of this chapter.

(ii) Bringing employees into the job evaluation process   Both the point factor and factor comparison methods can be adjusted to include employee participation. When properly done, employee participation reduces organizational conflict while increasing client ownership of the compensation study results. When poorly done, employee participation results in politicization of the process while exposing the potential for unfair discrimination in the results.

Three keys to effective employee participation are: (1) selection of task forces from a representative group of employees; (2) group decision by consensus; and (3) final salary assignment for job classifications by non-task-force members.

Most small to medium-size nonprofits can perform the job evaluation task with one task force. The task force should include from 7 to 14 employees representing various constituencies within the organization. These numbers are effective for generating consensus-based decision making. The group can be selected from a combination of volunteers and recruits; however, it is not wise to force an individual onto the task force.

The obvious constituencies represented in the group are managers and nonmangers. Restricting the task force to managers meets the traditional concept of chain-of-command, but acts contrary to what the organization may be attempting in other areas of its Total Quality Management program. Attempts to use only managers makes it very difficult to establish a differentiated classification structure for managers. The group does fine when ranking nonmanagement positions, but the participants tend to smooth over real differences that exist among their own positions.

Other constituencies—clerical, technical, and professional employee groups—can also be represented. If the agency perceives that a problem exists for a particular job classification, it is wise to include that classification in the task force. There must also be a fair representation of minorities and women, especially because most compensation discrimination issues arise from an insensitivity to diversity issues.

The task force participants perform two critical functions in addition to completing the job evaluation process. Even though the consensus decision-making process removes the political nature of constituency representation, the participants are seen as representing the interest of their constituencies. This representative process results in more members of the organization feeling that they have had their say in the decisions, even if they did not get the results they wanted. This perspective establishes a sense of fairness within the process. At the same time, the members communicate task force achievements. The employees recognize the project as an organizational decision, not the decision of a "cold, disinterested, outside consultant."

As part of the organizational process for the task force, the group should agree that decisions will be made by consensus instead of by a vote. Averaging point spreads or voting on rankings brings about strange results. For instance, five task force members may give Job Classification A a rank of 3 in a 10-classification list; five other members may give the classification a rank of 7. Job Classification B, on the same list, may be ranked at 5 by all participants. If averaging is used, then both jobs are equal. Yet, none of the participants believes they are equal, and their constituencies won't believe it either. Consensus discussion resolves this conflict, producing a more credible outcome.

It must be made clear at the beginning that the task force will not assign final salaries to any job classification or employee. The task force product is a ranking that establishes a raw midpoint rating for each job classification. That assignment will be adjusted by the consultant as job classifications are grouped into pay ranges. Final position salaries will be determined based on identifying the position's current salary in relationship to the proposed salary range in a series of cost options available for plan implementation.

Task force members are usually relieved to know that they are not responsible for determining the final salaries of their peers and friends.

The employee participation strategy provides one other important benefit. After the project is finished, the task force remains available for job evaluations of new positions and requests for classification upgrades. Building such in-house capacity to manage the new compensation system should be a critical consideration for any compensation program.

(iii) Employee participation in a factor comparison evaluation The factor comparison job evaluation method mixes some of the best strategies from both the whole job and point factor methodologies. As with the whole job method, factor comparison is a ranking of positions. The difference is that whole ranking tends to reinforce an existing pecking order that is usually based on responsibility alone. Factor comparison, in ranking positions, uses from four to seven critical factors, including responsibility, working conditions, skill level, mental effort, and physical effort. Multiple rankings of this nature increase the objective nature of the results in a manner similar to the point factor system.

Employee task forces work through the following six steps, to complete their part in the factor comparison exercise:

1. **Task force orientation.** Task force participants are introduced to the job analysis methodology and information used by the consultant to create job descriptions. Strategies used to differentiate skill, knowledge, and responsibility levels within the job descriptions are clearly explained. The factors being used in the study are clearly defined and explained so that all members have the same information available to them.

2. **Individual ranking.** Task force members review job descriptions and job analysis information for each job classification. They then individually rank the job classifications for each of the evaluation factors. By separating factors, jobs like janitor should fall low on skill levels but high on the scale defining working conditions. If the factors are defined in the manner shown in Exhibit 15.8, it will be impossible for any one job to fall at the top or bottom of all factor scales.

3. **Development of group consensus rankings.** The consultant shares the individual ranking results on the factors one-by-one and facilitates a discussion to achieve a consensus ranking of job classifications for each factor. This is the hardest part of the process. A good facilitator will enable group members to share their reasoning. Usually, rankings change when individuals realize that they did not apply the factor descriptions in a consistent manner or that they missed job analysis information. Discussion leads to the group's developing a consistent use of the job analysis and factor definition information. It is useful to keep records of any group decisions regarding definitions, for use in analyzing new positions once the plan is implemented.

4. **Insertion of benchmark values into rankings.** The consultant converts salary survey information for usable benchmark positions into factor values based on the factor weightings established by the consultant or previously agreed to by the board. For instance, the survey weighted average for the position of nurse may be $10.45 per hour. After weighting the factors for percent of total salary and breaking down the salary in matching increments, the results might be:

Responsibility	45.0%	$4.70
Skill	45.0	4.70
Mental effort	2.5	0.26
Physical effort	2.5	0.26
Working conditions	5.0	0.52

These values are then inserted into the task forces values as shown in Exhibit 15.9. Some minor adjustments are made when a position that is generally ranked high has a low ranking for a specific factor.

5. **Assignment of values to nonbenchmark positions.** The task force then fills in the blanks with dollar values for the nonbenchmark positions. At this point, the

Exhibit 15.9.   Benchmark decision sheet.

SKILL FACTOR	
Position	Final Value ($)
Dir. of Dental Health I	_____
Dir. of Nursing	7.32
Dir. of Health Education	_____
Dir. of Envir. Health	_____
Dir. of Communicable Diseases	6.60
Dir. of Nutrition	_____
Dir. of Administration	_____
Program Consultant	_____
Public Health Nurse	5.88
Sanitarian I	_____
Nutritionist	5.45
Sanitarian II	_____
Assoc. Nutritionist	_____
Clinic Nurse I	_____
Communicable Diseases Investigator	_____
Dental Hygienist	4.60
Departmental Secretary	_____
Accounting Clerk	_____
Vision and Hearing Supervisor	_____
Intake Specialist	_____
Dental Assistant	2.13

rule is that the values assigned must maintain the ranking previously agreed to. This step establishes the distance between the job classifications within the ranking process. When this step is done, the task force has completed its role in the process; however, it is advisable to go back to the task force after step 6, to give the task force the chance to review the result of their work and consider adjustments.

6. Determination of raw midpoint rate. By adding together the values assigned to each position on each factor, the consultant arrives at the total value, or raw midpoint rate, for the position. The raw midpoint rate determines the final ranking of the positions.

After the raw midpoint rate is established, the consultant uses regression analysis to bring job classifications into pay classifications or pay ranges. The goal is to bring together, into single pay ranges, job classifications whose raw midpoint rates are close.

From this process, the consultant should be able to provide a compensation rule by which the agency can assign future positions into pay ranges. The rule will identify the cutoff points for range assignments from raw midpoint rate data. Exhibit 15.10 is an example of application of the decision rule.

The consultant should make sure that a position is not excluded from a higher pay range because its raw midpoint rate is a few cents off the required minimum for the next range. As with all job evaluation processes, there is some subjectivity to the process. Exclusion of a case of this nature from a higher range will probably be overturned in the grievance process through political pressure.

(iv) Establishing pay ranges Creation of competitive salary midpoints represents the critical step toward an effective compensation program. Expanding the system from the midpoints into salary ranges makes it possible to link the compensation and performance management systems.

The final midpoint position relative to market worth is a policy decision that should be decided by the board at the beginning of the project. The position of the midpoint has a major impact on the agency's ability to recruit and retain employees. This decision impacts most other human resource management issues in the organization.

There are three primary choices for the board:

1. Establish the midpoint above the market value. Establishing above market pay helps with both recruitment and retention of employees. Higher salaries will result in more qualified applicants. Selecting a more qualified applicant reduces training costs and start-up time. Reduction in turnover also reduces training costs. Larger agencies that recruit from smaller agencies must consider this option, realizing that their employees were pretrained in related agencies.

2. Establish the midpoint below market value. This choice reduces the quality of applicants because qualified applicants in other agencies will be less likely to apply. At the same time, turnover will be higher: employees will go on to better paying, and usually larger, agencies. Organizations selecting this option must

Exhibit 15.10. Example of range assignment rule.

UNADJUSTED SALARY		Range
Minimum	Maximum	Assignment
$20.10	$21.19	1
19.10	20.09	2
18.00	19.09	3
16.90	17.99	4
15.80	16.89	5
14.70	15.79	6
13.60	14.69	7
12.50	13.59	8
11.40	12.49	9
10.30	11.39	10
9.20	10.29	11
8.10	9.19	12
5.90	8.09	13

expect to offset the application loss and turnover with higher training costs, in order to maintain quality. Smaller agencies with less funding will frequently select this cash-saving strategy and accept the fact that they are a training ground for their employees' upward mobility.

3. Maintain the midpoint at market value. Assuming that the survey results are valid, this choice is halfway between the two previous options. It is most viable politically because employees and board members agree that employees are being recognized for their real worth.

Pay ranges can be any width desired. Traditional ranges run 10, 20, 25, or 30 percent above and below the midpoint. In other words, a range may have a 20 percent to 60 percent spread.

Some of the issues raised by the midpoint choices can be offset by the width of the salary range. A wide range on a below-average midpoint can help retain current employees. However, the starting salary rate, which is usually held to the first quartile of the range, may need to be extended to enable recruiting more qualified people. That decision would negate the reason for selecting a low midpoint value.

In like fashion, a wide range on an above-average salary can help bring in less qualified applicants for training while strengthening the retention rate. This may be the ideal situation for agencies with unique services that require training for all new employees.

The range spread can also be related to organizational structure. The wider the spread, the more likely one range will overlap another range (or other ranges). A problem generally arises when an overlap exists between supervisor and subordinate or when the two positions are on the same career path. Range overlaps should be allowed between subordinate and supervisory positions, if the organization includes limited chances for promotion or there is an achievement-based pay-for-performance system. In such a system, employees choosing not to become supervisors continue to have room and motivation for growth, thereby thwarting the Peter Principle, which suggests that everyone in the agency will rise to his or her greatest level of incompetence.

The impact of the overlap on promotion can be managed with a personnel policy, such as:

> The salary for an individual who is promoted will be within the first quartile of the salary range except when the employees's current salary already falls within or above the first quartile of the new position, in which case the employee will receive a raise of between 10 and 20 percent above his or her current salary.

When there is an overlap in career-ladder pay ranges, such as between two clerical positions, the confusion will be more frequent. Organizations should try to minimize the overlap in these cases, to provide ample motivation for pursuing promotions. Pay conflicts will then develop only for promotions onto a different career ladder.

Often, the final decision factor for range development is project implementation cost. Most compensation programs offer the board a choice of two implementation strategies: nonprobationary employees who are currently paid below the salary range can be brought up to the bottom of the range, or all employees below the midpoint of the range can be brought up to the midpoint. The first option presents a problem when long-term employees are brought up only to the bottom of the range. Long-term employees know that the midpoint represents the salary to the average performer, and they resent the idea of working with new employees hired in at the same salaries.

Bringing everyone up to the midpoint makes a statement that the study is not a judgement on individual performance, but the strategy can be three times as expensive to implement.

When a decision is made to bring people who are below the range up to the bottom limit, a link is made between range width and implementation costs. Assuming that a number of employees are being paid below the midpoint, the wider the range, the greater the number of those employees who will not require upgrading. Therefore, the wider the range, the less costly the implementation.

The pay range issue always raises the question of how to handle employees whom the study has identified as being paid above the range. The traditional response to the problem is to "red circle" the employee's pay. This is done in one of three ways:

1. Employees in red-circled positions receive no pay raises until their salary falls within the pay range. This is not a recommend strategy.

2. The red-circled employee's salary remains the same but the individual receives an annual bonus based on the pay-for-performance plan guidelines. When the position is vacated, the new hire is brought in at the appropriate rate for the position.

3. The employee receives a pay raise each year based on performance. When the position is vacated, the new hire is brought in at the appropriate rate for the position.

(d) MAINTAINING COMMUNICATION THROUGHOUT THE PROJECT Nothing is more stress-provoking to an employee than to know that his or her salary is being discussed behind closed doors. Images of smoke-filled rooms, political trades, and similar disheartening images immediately come to mind. The more the employee is faced with such images, the more distrustful he or she will become of the project.

The following communication strategies will reduce tension and conflict throughout the project time line:

1. Hold an employee orientation meeting at the beginning of the project. Discuss the project, employees' concerns and fears, and employees' expectations of the project results. Explain the project schedule, the nature of decision making, the grievance system, and employee participation strategies.

2. Until the task force is organized, send periodic notes to the employees to update them on the study.

3. Use the bench audit process as an additional method for communicating with employees.

4. Share draft job descriptions with the employees before they are carved in stone.

5. Have the task force take and disseminate minutes of their deliberations. Train the task force secretary to screen out sensitive information.

6. Send a note to each employee describing that employee's proposed salary range; include an explanation of where the position will fall into place in the system.

7. Hold employee debriefing sessions to explain results, and distribute contact information, in case questions arise from results. Include public recognition of the task force's work. Answer all questions during the session until employee concerns are exhausted. Enlist task force members to help with answers.

15.4 IMPLEMENTATION AND MANAGEMENT ISSUES

(a) MAINTAINING SYSTEM INTEGRITY USING THE TASK FORCE Many nonprofits have experienced this problem: A current employee who is given a new task complains that the new task adds responsibilities and should be compensated with a pay raise. The agency rule restricts raises within a job classification; only the annual performance increase is allowed. To placate the employee, the department head gives the employee a new title and starts politicking for the pay raise. If the budget allows it, the new job is created with a new salary. Otherwise, the employee gets disgruntled and refuses to do the new task. After one employee has successfully played the game, the rest join in. Within 2 years, a combined compensation system that cost $20,000 has, in practice, been discarded.

This does not have to be the outcome. A well-implemented system includes procedures that reject insidious "job creep" demands while providing employees with an objective strategy for assessing job changes. The same process also helps the organization integrate new positions into job and pay classifications. As a final benefit, the system supports the agency's budgeting proposals for fair wages for positions covered under governmental or other grants.

In larger organizations, these compensation management issues are traditionally left in the hands of the personnel department. However, the employee participation structure used in the compensation study leaves the organization with a well-trained group capable of making objective decisions that support maintenance of the system.

The following procedures on requests for pay classification changes institutionalize the task force process and reduce the politicization of the system:

1. Employees and supervisors may request a change in a job classification, and supervisors may request the establishment of new job classifications. The requests are made to the personnel director. Upon making such a request, the employee (for an existing position) or the supervisor requesting a new job classification completes a job analysis questionnaire (JAQ). The personnel director reviews the questionnaire and conducts a bench audit, if necessary. If, upon review of the JAQ and bench audit data, the personnel director believes that the position requires upgrading to a higher, existing job classification, that recommendation is made to the executive director. If, upon review of the information, the personnel director determines that a new job classification is needed for the position, a new job description is written and sent to the executive director with a recommendation for approval. If the personnel director determines from the information that a new job classification should not be established, a recommendation of that nature is sent to the executive director along with a copy of the JAQ and of the current job description. The decision of the executive director is subject to the grievance procedure.

2. Employees may request a change in pay classification after successfully receiving a change to a new job classification. Classification of newly established positions will follow this same procedure.

3. The salary classification task force, facilitated by the personnel director, will be responsible for proposing pay classification upgrades and assignment of new job classifications to the executive director.

4. The original membership of the task force was established during the classification study. The task force will develop rules for rotation and replacement of its members.

5. The task force will operate as follows:

    A. The task force will be called to order by the personnel director.

    B. The personnel director will facilitate individual and then joint consensus ranking of the position for each of the five factors used in the study, using the original ranking scale developed in the study. The ranking decision will be: Where does this job classification fit into the existing rankings for this factor?

    C. When consensus is reached on the rankings, the task force will assign a cash value under each factor for the position, through individual recommendation and consensus. The value must fall between the cash values for the positions just above and below the position, as ranked in that factor.

    D. The personnel director will add together the cash values for each factor and will consult the Rules of Classification Assignment to arrive at the tentative pay classification for that job classification.

    E. The personnel director will report the task force's results to the executive director, who will make a recommendation to the board concerning the reclassification request. If the recommendation differs from that of the task force, the task force's decision and a written explanation of the executive director's decision to differ will accompany the recommendation.

6. If the new pay classification for the job classification is lower than the one from which the job classification was created, the incumbent employee remains in the existing pay range, but new employees are hired in the new range.

7. Reclassification decisions can be processed through the agency's grievance system.

(b) HANDLING IMPLEMENTATION COMPLAINTS DURING SYSTEM IMPLEMENTATION
Many people will not be happy with the results of the compensation study; most employees believe they deserve higher salaries. Either because of survey results or the implementation strategy, these expected raises do not materialize. If there has been a strong communication program throughout the study, most employees will accept the results.

However, some employees will still believe that their pay is unfair in relation to others in the organization. These are the individuals who will take action against the study, most likely by politicizing their complaint to the board. The problem can be addressed by incorporating a complaint system into the study. The complaint process should be clear from the start; a written description should be handed to employees during the project orientation meetings.

Complaints are possible at two points: the assignment to a job classification, and the assignment to a pay range. Each can be handled differently.

Complaints about job classifications and job descriptions are generally easy to handle. After the complaining employee has reviewed the first-draft job description, the consultant will review requested changes. Usually, the consultant will either go ahead and make the changes or meet with the employee to discuss the request. A proposed final job description should be sent back to the employee.

The overwhelming majority of job classification complaints are resolved at this stage. For that reason, if the employee is still unhappy with the job description or the assignment to that classification, the employee should be allowed to use the agency's regular grievance system.

Complaints concerning pay classification (range) assignments are a little more complicated. The employee should be notified of the proposed pay range assignment upon completion of the assignment by the task force and consultant. The employee is not notified of any actual salary change at this time, although he or she is notified of the proposed rules for implementing the ranges. This is because the actual salary change will still be based, first, on bringing the employee's salary into range, and, second, on performance, as determined by the supervisor and not anyone involved in the study.

If one or more employees in a job classification have a complaint about their pay range, the task force is reconvened to hear the employees' reasoning. At the same time, the task force, through its chair, explains the reasoning used by the task force and reviews the ranking of the position on each factor. This description helps the employee better understand why the decision happened and facilitates focusing the employee's explanation into terms that may affect the task force's decision.

Following the meeting, the task force reconsiders its factor rankings for that position, based on the new information received. A report of its recommendations, showing either no change or the decision to change, is made in writing to the executive director, with a copy to the employee.

The overwhelming majority of complaints are resolved in meetings between the employee and the task force. The meetings are usually very productive. They help the task force to recognize when groupthink was a part of the decision process, and the employee can better recognize what is being valued by the agency, especially when the factor weightings are explained. When the issue is still not resolved, the employee should be directed to make use of the agency's grievance policy.

(c) THE ROLE OF THE BOARD IN COMPENSATION MANAGEMENT   The role of the nonprofit board is to develop the strategy of the agency and to ensure that the strategy is being implemented. The compensation program, representing as much as 80 percent of the agency's operating budget, is part of the strategic management of the organization. Consideration of the salaries of individuals, which places board members in the role of performance evaluators, is not a strategic endeavor.

The core strategic compensation issue is to determine the role played by market worth for agency positions. To what extent does the board feel it is necessary to compensate employees at, above, or below the market worth for the agency's positions? Market worth also establishes the issue of whether the market for comparison is the nonprofit industry or both nonprofit and for-profit organizations.

It is generally believed that an agency must pay above-market value if it wants to provide quality services and products. A more strategic view shows that quality can be achieved when paying lower entry-level wages and increasing available training funds. Low wages and little training are, of course, the deathbed of quality.

The corollary strategic issue is the agency's ability to pay. The decision to pay market value, instead of going for the cheapest available employee, requires increasing revenues or decreasing services. The systemic question is whether the agency's revenues will increase over time as a result of its improved quality as a service provider, thus offsetting the increased expenses.

The other major concern is proper implementation of the board-approved compensation system. This represents the board's role in quality control.

The board can perform the control function in two ways. First, as with most other human resource issues, the board acts as the last forum in the grievance procedure in most small to medium-size agencies. The information discussed in the grievance hearing enables the board to determine whether its wishes were actually carried out.

Its second action is to assess the quality of compensation information presented to it. Is the information strategic or operational? Operational information includes issues like individual pay raise requests, job descriptions, performance evaluations, and classification upgrade requests.

Strategic information includes comparison of competitors' salaries, budget impact statements, tracking of the number and disposition of grievances, career ladders, and pay classification assignment rules. When the board is planning staff pay increases, the board members will want to see the money available and the recommended organizationwide range changes. The board should also be looking at wage distributions based on race, sex, and so on, to ensure that the salaries are being paid out equitably.

15.5 INTEGRATING THE COMPENSATION PROGRAM INTO THE PERFORMANCE MANAGEMENT PROGRAM

Merit pay fails because the performance management program is not integrated into the compensation program. the result is that the compensation program runs the performance system. The opposite is necessary to make the system work.

The following system, Compensation for Excellence, resolves the major compensation-based complaints against merit pay. The system is designed to award top performers with the highest pay increases when computed on a cash basis. At the same time, the system ensures that funds are available for salary increases throughout the year and that individuals at the top of the scale cannot top out. Individuals whose performance lags behind find that, although they continue to get pay increases, their position falls in the salary range. As a side benefit, agencies using this system are able to build their fund balance over a period of years.

The system starts with the agency's determination of the annual increase to be awarded. In the ideal world, this would be determined solely on the basis of the amount by which the midpoints need to be raised to maintain market equity. In reality, the amount will be a trade-off between maintaining market equity and fulfilling budget considerations. A what-if exercise is performed between this and the budgeting strategy below, until the cash value of the annual increase equals the funds available for the increase.

The budget for increases in the salary schedule is computed as follows:

1. Determine the percentage increase for the salary system—how much to raise the midpoints of the system. That percent is applied to the midpoints of all ranges.

2. Compute new salary ranges by adding and subtracting the appropriate percent (width of range) of each new midpoint amount, to establish new minimum and maximum levels for the ranges.

3. Determine the budget for implementing the new ranges by computing the difference between the old and new maximum for each range and multiplying that amount by the number of employees in that salary range, regardless of where they fall in the range. Then add up the cost for each range to identify the total cost for increasing the system.

4. Do similar calculations for each range, and add up the total budgeted amounts for each range to determine the amount to be budgeted for raises that year.

Example.

• An agency decides to raise its midpoints 5 percent next year.
• The old midpoint for level 13 is $16,150, with the minimum at $12,920 and the maximum at $19,380.
• The new midpoint will be: $16,150 × 1.05 = $16,957. The new minimum will be: $16,957 × 0.8 = $13,565; the new maximum will be: $16,957 × 1.2 = $20,348.
• The amount budgeted for pay raises for this range is: $20,348 − $19,380 = $968, times the number of job positions at this pay classification (3), for a total budgeted amount of $2,604.

This budgeting strategy makes it possible for all employees to receive the highest possible merit increase for their pay classification. At the same time, the procedure results in a positive fund balance at the end of each year, unless everyone receives the top rating. That balance can be carried over to decrease the cost of management of this program in future years, or it can be applied to other agency needs, including improvement of the cash basis of the agency over time.

The second part of the system defines how individual pay increases are awarded:

1. Individual salary increases are based on individual performance, as identified through the organization's performance appraisal policies.

2. Each performance appraisal provides for an overall rating for the employee on a five-point scale ranging from "Excellent" to "Poor" performance. (This can be the average of the ratings on the performance standards, or some computation based on a weighting of the standards.)

3. Individual employee pay raises are computed according to the following schedule:

   a. An employee receiving a top rating receives a raise equal to the dollar amount by which the maximum of his or her range was raised in the budgeting process, regardless of where the employee is currently placed in his or her pay range.

   b. An employee receiving the middle rating receives a raise equal to the dollar amount by which the midpoint of his or her range was raised in the budgeting process, regardless of where the employee is currently placed in his or her pay range.

   c. An employee receiving a poor rating receives a raise equal to the dollar amount by which the minimum of his or her range was raised in the budgeting process, regardless of where the employee is currently placed in his or her pay range. (The organization may choose to give no raise to an employee receiving a poor rating. However, it should be noted that the proposed system acts to reduce a person's position in a range if performance is poor, without resulting in employees' being paid below the minimum of their range.)

d. Discretion can be used to compute increases for those employees falling between top and middle, or between middle and poor, if the discretion maintains the procedure in the previous three steps.

Example. Continuing the earlier example, an employee in this pay classification who receives the top rating would receive a pay increase of $20,348 - $19,380 = $968, regardless of where the employee presently falls on the range. This will move the top performers into the upper levels of the range, and continue to give them the top pay increases if they maintain top performance.

An employee in this pay classification who receives a middle rating will receive a pay increase of $16,957 - $16,150 = $807, regardless of where the employee presently falls on the range. This will keep average performers at the midpoint, will move former top performers whose work is no longer top quality slowly back to the midpoint, and will eventually move average performers who are at the bottom of the scale to the midpoint.

An employee in this pay classification who receives a poor rating will receive a pay increase of $13,565 - $12,920 = $645, regardless of where the person currently falls on the salary scale. This will keep a poor performer, already on the bottom, at the bottom, and will move others down toward the bottom of the scale over time.

An employee in this pay classification who receives a rating between top and middle performance can receive an increase between $968 and $807, and a rating between middle and poor performance can receive an increase between $807 and $645.

The first-year cost of implementing the Compensation for Excellence system can be high. The agency will not be used to putting aside what appears to be a large chunk of revenue in a single year. The carryover helps in future years until, like a self-insurance program, the fund begins to run itself.

15.6 CONCLUSION

Compensation management is intrinsically tied to Total Quality Management (TQM). It can also be assessed through Total Quality control methods. At Tellabs, Inc., a for-profit telecommunications company in Illinois, a TQM committee used traditional statistical methods to assess problems in their company's human resource management program. Using a Pareto analysis, the team began to focus on turnover. In their deliberations, they discovered that one group was the major cause of the high turnover rates for the company. The reason? The salary for that one classification was not competitive with the marketplace. Once the company established competitive wages, the turnover stopped (Jones, 1991).

Compensation management strategies are in flux as the Total Quality movement raises questions about the old procedures. What seems to be emerging is recognition that employees can participate in developing the system, and that a link between compensation and performance is a critical step in building high-quality organizations—especially if quality is the primary performance standard throughout the organization.

SOURCES AND SUGGESTED REFERENCES

Baird, Lloyd S., Beatty, Richard W., and Schneier, Craig E. 1985. *The Performance Appraisal Sourcebook.* Amherst, MA: Human Resource Development Press.

———. 1988. *The Strategic Human Resource Management Sourcebook.* Amherst, MA: Human Resource Development Press.

Deming, W. Edwards. 1986. *Out of the Crises.* Cambridge, MA: MIT Center for Advanced Engineering Study.

Jones, John W., Steffy, Brian D., and Bray, Douglas W. 1991. *Applying Psychology in Business: The Handbook for Managers and Human Resource Professionals.* Lexington, MA: Lexington Books, pp. 446–451.

Latham, Gary P., and Wexley, Kenneth N. 1981. *Increasing Productivity Through Performance Appraisal.* Reading, MA: Addison-Wesley.

Michaels, Mark. 1988. *The Performance Technologies Workbook.* Champaign, IL: People Technologies.

Mtazer, John, Jr. 1984. *Creative Personnel Practices: New Ideas for Local Government.* Washington, DC: International City Management Association.

Werther, William B., Jr., and Davis, Keith. 1985. *Personnel Management and Human Resources,* 2nd ed. New York: McGraw-Hill.

P A R T   F O U R

Fund-Raising

CHAPTER SIXTEEN

Fund-Raising Overview

James M. Greenfield
Hoag Memorial Hospital Presbyterian

CONTENTS

16.1 REVENUE SOURCES

Nonprofit organizations rely on charitable contributions as an essential source of revenue for their annual operations. A generous public will act on factual information and, possessing of confidence and trust, will give their money for good works to benefit others. This revenue enables nonprofit organizations to carry out their mission, purpose, goals, and objectives for public benefit.

Public solicitation is carried out by nonprofit organizations using several fund-raising methods and techniques, often in combination. Supervision of these interactive and interdependent activities begins with the board of directors because stewardship, the board's chief responsibility, includes developing revenue along with proper investment and management of funds raised. Policy and procedures for fund-raising begin with the board and flow to guidelines and operating rules for all elements of the fund-raising enterprise.

This chapter begins a series of presentations on fund-raising revenue sources. There is great breadth to fund development and, given the importance of each of the several forms of revenue it produces, a comprehensive policies and procedures manual for its successful conduct is highly necessary. Several additional guidelines and operating rules are offered throughout this Part IV of the *Handbook* (Chapters 17 to 26). These will explain direction and purpose for every phase of fund-raising, or fund development. The term "development" has several definitions, one being "the planned promotion of understanding, public participation and support" (Seymour, 1966).

A sample of a board-level policy and procedure manual for management of resource development is provided as the appendix of this chapter and has been written as a comprehensive guide to an overall fund development program. The several guidelines in the chapters that follow will fit well within this comprehensive manual. Their purpose is to provide added direction to the issues associated with operation of the individual methods used in an organization's fund-raising effort. These guidelines, prepared by several highly competent fund-raising professionals, will help to define how each solicitation method operates and how to guide its progress.

Other key areas in these chapters include the value of strategic planning, assessment plus audit and performance analysis, the use of fund-raising consultants, tax consequences, and computer assistance. Each author provides sample texts of specific policies and procedures, guidelines, exhibits, and other illustrations to assist the reader. Fund development is, of necessity, a highly coordinated and cooperative program designed to yield maximum public support for nonprofit organizations. The methods and techniques of fund-raising are usually segregated into three broad operating areas: annual giving, special-purpose giving, and planned giving. Each is built, in pyramid fashion, on the others' success. This structure permits each of the individual fund-raising methods in use to concentrate on three common fund-raising objectives: to acquire, to retain, and to maximize donors. Each fund-raising method, again for simplification, will make use of three common solicitation techniques for its communications: mail, telephone, and in-person solicitation. The purpose here is not to instruct the reader in detail on how each method of fund-raising performs. Descriptions are adequately explained so that fund-raising policies and procedures, guidelines, and operating rules can be better understood.

A brief description of the three broad operating areas of fund-raising follows.

(a) ANNUAL GIVING PROGRAMS Nearly every nonprofit organization engages in one or more active forms of solicitation each year. These annual programs have two main objectives: to ask for the money needed to support the current operating budget, and to find and retain more donors whose continued contributions will fund future programs with reliability. Annual giving serves as the backbone of resource development because it is designed to produce predictable amounts of gift revenues year after year. Sources for annual gifts include associations and societies, corporations, foundations, government, and individuals. Because the majority of gifts (an average of 80 to 85 percent) are made by individuals each year, solicitation programs for most organizations should concentrate on people most of the time. Each annual giving method is designed to acquire new donors while retaining as many prior donors as possible. Management of annual giving requires careful coordination of each separate method, whether during one year or as part of a multiyear effort, and is essential to increasing performance year after year. Directors and managers of nonprofit organizations who fail to understand the need for such coordination also may fail to understand the purpose of annual giving, which is to produce reliable revenue every year. Some may view an annual campaign only as a money-raising activity—a misleading perception that results in accepting quick fixes and easy money ideas for the apparent dollars they promise. These fund-raisers fail to appreciate the value of traditional annual giving methods; they have been tested a thousand times and proven to be reliable, cost-effective, and highly profitable because they work to build relationships.

Annual giving, the chief means to build relationships between donors and nonprofit organizations, will not succeed or long survive if thought of only as a money-raising activity. Donors result from annual investments; their value increases in direct proportion to the care and attention they receive over time. This also means that donor relations programs are an active part of every annual giving activity. Such attention will help ensure that each donor's interest and enthusiasm are retained and that his or her commitment to the organization grows and continues to produce faithful contributions for the future.

Nonprofit organizations can elect to use one or more annual giving methods during their operating year. The options include direct mail, for acquisition of first-time donors as well as for renewal of prior donors; telephone and public media channels; membership development; special and benefit events; support group organizations; donor clubs; volunteer solicitation committees; and more. The goal of each option is to achieve multiple gifts from the same donors during each year; one gift every 12 months is not likely to provide all the revenue needed to meet annual operating needs. Churches across America invite their members to give weekly; they also raise more money than any other type of nonprofit organization. These faithful, committed weekly/monthly/annual donors can and will provide the money needed for operations year after year. These same donors will become the patrons and benefactors of nonprofit organizations in the future, provided that the fund development program is designed to this end and not seen only as a money-raising activity within a single year.

A variety of skills are required to manage several annual giving activities at the same time. Coordination and cooperation will help to produce reliable results without causing confusion or "turning off" donors. Written procedures are needed to help guide the conduct of multiple methods of annual solicitation that are performed at the same time with the same audiences. The goals are: to increase the pool of suspects and prospects, to increase the number of donors, to retain most prior donors, to upgrade the gift level of current donors, to invite multiple gifts, to encourage active participation, to encourage volunteerism, to offer opportunities for leadership, and to recognize and reward everyone who steps forward to do more. The preservation of good will among all who become donors is essential; these same committed friends will faithfully support the priorities of the future with their "time, talent, and treasure."

(b) SPECIAL-PURPOSE PROGRAMS   When a solid base of annual giving activity is in full operation, nonprofit organizations are better prepared to engage in more complex forms of solicitation for significantly greater gifts, in size and in donor involvement and participation. Fewer donors will be engaged at this level as compared with annual givers, but their larger gifts will provide a greater majority of the funds required. The fund-raising techniques used in development of major gifts and grants are usually defined within the context of a special or capital campaign, which is possible only after years of successful annual giving activity. Some history of giving is always necessary before these expanded areas can begin to be successful.

Nonprofit organizations must prepare themselves for their own future, because their future plans will address the needs of more sophisticated donors. Long-range and strategic plans explain specific directions to be taken, timetables, steps required, estimated costs, opportunities for major gift support, reasoned outcomes, public benefits expected, and more. Major gifts can be solicited separately from annual giving, even in the absence of any institutional plans, in the same manner that government grants may be applied for once a program area is qualified. However, major gift solicitations always will be more successful when included as part of a visibly promoted, multi-year, institutional effort. This is true because the best sources of leadership, commitment, and enthusiasm are assembled in support of the organization to achieve such overall objectives.

The fund-raising method often employed to meet master plan objectives is a major campaign, usually designed to address only the most urgent of priorities. This means that new and higher levels of funding are essential to the organization's future. The campaign is the method to marshall attention to these priorities, presenting them as relevant, urgent, and to be met *now*. Special donor recognition opportunities are offered as added benefits for large gifts, to encourage donors in their generosity. Simply put, it is much more difficult to amass a winning combination for successful solicitation with a single project standing alone than to offer donors the biggest and best ideas the organization has to offer.

(c) PLANNED GIVING PROGRAMS Donors can be introduced to the special area of opportunity associated with planned giving at any time during annual giving, special-purpose, or capital campaign programs. In fact, through these communications the idea-seeds are planted early and lead to financial and estate-planning discussions. Planned giving is, by definition, a means whereby individuals plan to designate a portion of their estate to be delivered later to the nonprofit organizations of their choice. All that is required is a specific instruction written in their will or living trust. Planned gifts are major gifts involving significant assets, which is why they match up well with capital campaigns rather than annual giving programs. The technical complexity of planned giving requires close attention to appropriate policy and procedure by all who would consider this area of fund-raising. Planned giving also remains the preferred method to develop the endowment funds that are so essential to financial flexibility and security in every nonprofit organization's future.

Planned giving represents final decisions by donors who choose to make arrangements in advance to maintain their personal support of favorite organizations into the future, even after they are deceased. These decisions are guided by their estate plan, prepared alongside their personal financial plan for their retirement years. Planned gifts can be made now, either with (1) benefits from the transfer retained for the donor's lifetime and the asset transferred to the organization after death, or with (2) final assignment, via a will or living trust, of current assets that will flow to the organization after death. Because of their complex technical nature and the permanent obligations of the nonprofit organizations who accept them, estate planning and planned giving programs must be guided by clear and complete policies and procedures that address fully the fiduciary, legal, and stewardship responsibilities of the nonprofit organization for the life of the donor.

Throughout the following chapters dealing with fund-raising revenue sources, it is helpful to keep in mind three common ingredients. Success in fund-raising is always dependent on the interaction of: (1) leadership and voluntary action, (2) cultivation, solicitation, and donor relations, and (3) relationships built between donors and their choices of nonprofit organizations. Policies and procedures, guidelines, and operating rules must be designed to match each nonprofit organization's operating style, taking into account the need to support the professional conduct of fund-raising. Such guidelines are seldom a goal unto themselves, however, especially where they would impede fund development operations. These three ingredients for successful fund-raising are described briefly in the sections that follow.

(d) LEADERSHIP AND VOLUNTARY ACTION Nothing much happens in fund-raising until voluntary leadership takes charge and provides direction to all other volunteers and staff alike. Leadership, whether it comes from the board or from individuals appointed by the board, is much more than an appointment; it requires dedication, advocacy, personal sacrifice, and serving as an example to others. Among the qualities most often associated with effective fund-raising leaders are: they are rich, have "clout," are generous to lots of causes, are well liked, are true believers in the project, are well-organized, are good speakers, and are fearless (Warner, 1975). Leaders also have to be trained and aided toward a complete understanding of the mission and purpose, goals and objectives, personality and operating style of the nonprofit organization they serve. Professional staff can assist in many ways, but their chief purpose is to assure that each leader succeeds in the task he or she is assigned.

Leadership includes providing guidance and direction to others who volunteer their time and energy to the same cause. Volunteers can be asked to perform every task required for successful fund-raising; the trick is to pick the right people for the right task at the right time so that the entire program will run smoothly. Although this ideal is forever elusive, constant attention to volunteers' training and encouragement of their active support will help to achieve success every time. Volunteers are the "arms and legs" of fund-raising; no fund development program can expect to be successful without a host of men and women committed to the cause and willing to give of their personal "time, talent, and treasure" toward its fulfillment. Each volunteer must be given adequate time to learn an assignment, allowed to experiment with personal ideas measured against proven methods and prior successes, invited to do more rather than less, given opportunities for growth within the organization, asked for a personal gift early, recognized and rewarded for all that is accomplished, and considered for promotion to leadership assignments, including a seat on the board of directors.

(e) CULTIVATION, SOLICITATION, AND DONOR RELATIONS Donors and prospects, whether people or institutions, require attention and consideration. Each has potential to assist and, although some can give more money than others, each can give a share of time and a best effort to the cause. Annual giving, by its nature, invites thousands of donors and prospects to participate, and then asks them to do it again. It is not possible to give personal attention to all donors, so the focus must be on those whose prior giving history or potential volunteerism merits added consideration. Annual giving provides the best means to find and develop more qualified candidates. The use of mass communication techniques—for example, mail, telephone, and benefit events—is a bit impersonal, but careful analysis of the results is a means to identify those few-among-many who, by reason of gift size, pattern of support, effort, and commitment, justify more personal attention and further evaluation. Volunteers can help in these final evaluation steps leading to designation of those who will receive more active personal attention, all of which yields cultivation and solicitation of others who will follow.

Volunteer solicitors are pure gold to a fund development program. People who will ask their friends for money for an organization they believe in are indeed beautiful people. It is each organization's duty to train such volunteers in how best to approach others, how to be sensitive when mixing their enthusiasm for the cause with the prospects' potential for present and future support, and how to inform and invite prospects to joint worthy programs that will benefit others. Each form of solicitation, whether an impersonal letter, a telephone call, or a personal visit, is an important opportunity for the nonprofit organization to make friends. These initial few friends will invite others to join them and, over time, build a cadre of many friends who can be prepared to help the nonprofit organization realize its annual priorities and fulfill its long-term aspirations.

Relations with donors, as mentioned earlier, remain highly important for reasons other than just the next gift. As with friendships, time and effort are required of both parties to keep up the contact, show an honest interest in one another, share ideas and goals, and work together whenever possible. Formal recognition programs offer privileged communications for donors; they let them "inside" and include them in "family" discussions. Nonprofit organizations have an obligation to design donor communications programs and to include public recognition of those whose faithful service and generous contributions have made all the difference in achieving success.

(f) BUILDING RELATIONSHIPS   The entire purpose of fund development can be captured in the concept of good relations with a community of friends. Opportunities for friends' involvement and active participation exist alongside expectations that these faithful advocates and generous supporters stand ready to assist the organization in achieving its mission to the rest of society. Here, the true purpose of the fund development "process" come to term: it guides leadership and volunteerism, friend-raising and active solicitation, donor relations, and more; it unites *people* with the *purposes* of nonprofit organizations.

Relationships take time—often, lots of time—to develop. Multiple opportunities are included in the objectives of annual giving, special-purpose, and planned giving programs to nurture each individual who chooses to associate with a cause toward achieving the most satisfactory of outcomes for both parties, which can be repeated over many years.

16.2 GENERAL AREAS FOR POLICY AND PROCEDURES

Guidance for daily operations begins at the point of inception of the organization itself. Ownership, legal name, mission and purpose, authority, structure and organization, procedures for dissolution, and more, are all defined in the articles of incorporation. The next document, called the bylaws, states the operating rules and procedures for the organization. The bylaws define in detail the process for the election of officers and directors, and their job descriptions; the procedures for the conduct of all meetings; annual operations, including fiscal activities; the process to amend the bylaws; and much more. In combination, the articles of incorporation and the bylaws establish the board of directors as the supreme authority for ownership and operation of the nonprofit organization. Federal and state authorities, acting on these texts alone, will charter the organization as a voluntary nonprofit public benefit corporation under the law, by which it is forever bound. Out of these government approvals flow privileges of income, sales and property tax exemptions, and a charitable contribution deduction for all of the organization's donors.

Daily operations remain the responsibility of the board of directors. However, because the board's primary duty is to establish policy and supervise operations, day-to-day tasks are assigned to professional staff whom the board hires and directs through the president/CEO, who also evaluates their performance. Once routine operations are defined and implemented, including the accounting and reporting of all revenue received and spent, the board's attention shifts to supervision of daily activities against stated objectives. A mission statement, drawn from the articles of incorporation, completes the written interpretation of the purposes, goals, and objectives of the organization. Operations are guided through defined programs and services provided through the annual budget and, in time, through long-range and strategic plans designed to move the organization forward toward fulfilling the objectives stated in its articles of incorporation and mission statement.

All of these deliberate activities are necessary and must precede public solicitation activity. When complete, they also provide all the information needed to begin a successful fund-raising program. The board of directors appoints a committee on fund development and authorizes it to supervise all fund-raising activity, including setting annual and multiyear goals matched to the organization's plans and priority funding requirements. The objective is to raise, on schedule, the money for priority needs. The annual budget for fund-raising is prepared, reviewed, and approved by the administration and the board. Hiring practices, job descriptions, and evaluation procedures (for programs as well as employees) are used to recruit and supervise professional and support staff hired to conduct fund-raising activities as defined by the committee. Policies and procedures for fund-raising, the use of the institutional name in solicitation activities, accounting and reporting for all funds raised and budget expended, honors and recognition accorded to donors—all of these activities are defined, developed, and approved by the committee, administration, and the board. Everyone involved should receive complete information on how each of these activities will be performed and their relationship to all other aspects of the fund development program.

Because fund-raising programs produce cash and other forms of revenue for use by the organization, instructions on their proper disposition are required within the organization's fiscal policy and procedures. Other committees involved in the management of funds raised include the audit, finance, and investment management committees, which ensure accurate accounting for each gift and its appropriate use, investment of funds (including charitable trusts and endowments), and preparation of required audits and public fiscal reports in accordance with accounting standards and in fulfillment of state and federal requirements. Considerable coordination is required to ensure that the board's obligation for fiduciary stewardship of gift revenue is complete. The stewardship includes solicitation practices, fund accounting, budget and expenditures for fund-raising, and public reporting of the results.

The concluding segment of this overview gives an example of guidelines, operating rules, and procedures that must be prepared, to cover all aspects of the fund development program. Given the importance of the funds themselves and their value to the organization, the board of directors assigns its active responsibility for this entire area to the committee on fund development. This committee must define the programs of solicitation in the areas of annual giving, special programs, and planned giving, and then supervise their conduct each year according to policy and procedures. The result is a manual such as is shown in the appendix to the chapter.

In addition, direction for organizations that are related to the parent corporation and that also engage in fund-raising to support the mission of the parent is required from the committee on fund development. A related organization may be a subsidiary unit, such as a foundation, that is controlled by the parent or acts as its fund-raising arm. Related organizations may also be separate but affiliated groups whose existence, purpose, and franchise to exist originate from the parent corporation and whose own articles and by-laws establish, as their mission and purpose, the provision of financial and other support to the parent corporation. In each instance, operating rules and procedures are valuable and should include prescriptions (often in the form of bylaws) for the nomination and election of officers and directors, the approval of the fund-raising programs employed, the use of the parent organization's name, the accounting required for all funds raised in its name or expended for appropriate charitable purposes, and any other accounting and legal requirements associated with full and proper operation of related organizations.

When all these procedural necessities are in place and well-understood by all the participants, a program of fund development can proceed with confidence in its own excellent preparation and with the full support of the board of directors. The community of volunteers and active supporters will be secure in a sound design, will be prepared to follow the organization's leadership, and will be willing to work hard to provide the financial support so necessary to its success.

APPENDIX: A MANUAL OF FUND DEVELOPMENT POLICY AND PROCEDURE FOR NONPROFIT ORGANIZATIONS

CONTENTS

A. Authority for Fund Development
  1. The Importance of Philanthropy
  2. Board of Directors
  3. Board Committee on Fund Development
  4. Department of Fund Development
  5. Related Organizations
  6. The Role of Volunteers
  7. The Rights of Donors

B. Management of Fund Development Activities
  1. Priority Established by the Board of Directors
  2. Job Description for Director of Fund Development
  3. Public Solicitation Programs
  4. Priority and Project Management
  5. Procedures for Approval for Gift Solicitation
  6. Prospect Reservation
  7. Use of Consultants and Vendors

C. Public Solicitation Procedures
  1. Correct Legal Name
  2. Use of Organization Name for Fund-Raising
  3. Commercial Coventures and Charitable Sales Promotions
  4. Tax Laws and Public Reporting Requirements
  5. General Fund-Raising Guidelines
  6. Joint Fund-Raising Programs
  7. The Calendar for Solicitations

D. Forms of Contributions
  1. Types of Gifts
  2. Unrestricted and Restricted Gifts
  3. Appraisal Rules and Procedures
  4. Special Handling of Select Gifts
  5. Temporary Funds
  6. Gifts in Trust
  7. Income-Producing Properties
  8. Legacies and Bequests

E. Fund-Raising Methods and Techniques
  1. Procedures for Setting Goals
  2. Annual Giving Activities
  3. Procedures for Benefit Events
  4. Business, Corporation, and Foundation Relations
  5. Special-Project Campaigns
  6. Multiyear and Capital Campaigns
  7. Planned Giving Programs

F. Government Grants and Contracts Administration
  1. Authority and Supervision
  2. Office of Grants and Contracts
  3. Grants and Contracts Officer
  4. Institutional Review Committee
  5. Manuscripts and Articles
  6. Accounting, Reporting, and Audits
  7. Royalties, Copyrights, and Patents
  8. Nongovernment Grants and Contracts

G. Gift Processing Procedures
  1. Checks and Cash
  2. Gifts of Securities
  3. Gifts of Personal Property
  4. Gifts of Real Estate
  5. Gifts-in-Kind
  6. Employee Gifts and Payroll Deduction
  7. Fiscal and Calendar Year-End Procedures

H. Gift Acknowledgment Procedures
  1. Official Acknowledgment
  2. Additional Acknowledgments
  3. Time of Acknowledgment
  4. Donor Records and Recognition
  5. Tax Records and Public Disclosure
  6. Gifts Reports on Results

I. Accounting for Gift Revenue
  1. Fiduciary Responsibility
  2. Allocation to Restricted Funds

3. Expenditure Controls
4. Allocation to Endowment
5. Investment of Funds
6. Accounting Reports
7. Audits and Tax Returns

J. Honors and Recognition

1. Policy Concept
2. Guidelines
3. Qualifications
4. Procedure for Approval
5. Naming of Buildings or Space Therein
6. Naming of Endowed Chairs
7. Naming of Departments or Title Positions
8. Awards or Citations
9. Process for Recommendation
10. Public Notice
11. Forms of Recognition
12. Graphics Continuity
13. Renewed Solicitation
14. Donor Communications

K. Management of Planned Giving Programs

1. Programs for Solicitation
2. Acting as Trustee
3. Charitable Trust and Pooled Income Fund Management
4. Life Insurance Programs
5. Commissions Paid for Planned Gifts
6. Wills and Bequests: Probate Procedures

L. Investment and Endowment Operations

1. Obligation of the Board of Directors
2. Selecting Professional Management Services
3. Short-Term Money Management
4. Invested Funds Management
5. Endowment Fund Management
6. Purposes and Uses of Earnings

M. Corporate Member: The Separate Foundation

1. Corporate Member of the Foundation
2. Routine Operations and Information Reports
3. Review of Annual Goals and Objectives

4. Professional Staff Hiring Procedures
5. Transfer of Funds Raised and Held
6. Nominations Process for Foundation Directors
7. Honors and Recognition by the Foundation
8. Annual Meetings and Annual Reports
9. Annual Audit Review

N. Related Organizations: Support Groups

1. Authorization to Exist
2. Approval of Operating Rules and Procedures
3. Use of the Organization's Name
4. Review of Annual Goals and Objectives
5. Nominations Process for Officers and Members of the Board of Directors
6. Professional Staff Hiring Procedures
7. Control of Funds Raised and Held
8. Annual Meetings and Annual Reports
9. Annual Audit Review

O. Department of Fund Development

1. Areas of Management Responsibility
2. Approved Fund-Raising Programs
3. Donor Relations and Communications
4. Support Services
5. Job Descriptions and Hiring Practices
6. Budgets and Accountability
7. Records and Files

P. Public Reporting Requirements

1. Internal Revenue Service
2. State and Local Agencies
3. Public Requests for Information

Q. Approvals, Reviews, and Amendments

1. Authority of the Board of Directors
2. Periodic Review and Reissue
3. Process for Amendment

A. Authority for Fund Development

1. *The Importance of Philanthropy.* The several benefits enjoyed by [name of organization] under the law include active support and voluntary contributions from individuals, corporations, foundations, government, associations, and societies. The relations among all these parties are essential to the mission of this organization, especially its financial stability. Responsibility for preservation and enhancement of philanthropy shall be retained by the Board of Directors and carried out as it shall herein define.

2. *Board of Directors.* The Board holds authority and stewardship responsibility for all methods and techniques of fund-raising activity; for all forms of contributions received; for professional staff, consultants, and vendors hired; for investment and management of all funds raised; and for disbursement of contribution revenues in exclusive support of the mission of this organization.

3. *Board Committee on Fund Development.* This committee of the Board of Directors is charged with leadership and direction of fund-raising toward the objectives of: (a) defining and developing programs asking for public support, (b) active solicitation, and (c) maintaining positive relations with donors.

4. *Department of Fund Development.* Under the chief development officer, this department is responsible to the President/CEO and the Committee on Fund Development for day-to-day management of all fund-raising activities. Professional and support staff will provide professional assistance to fund-raising programs, the acknowledgment of all gifts and maintenance of donor records and recognition, deposit and accounting for all gifts received, supervision of the annual budget, and direction of all employees, consultants, and vendors hired.

5. *Related Organizations.* By authority of the Board of Directors, related organizations whose purpose is to develop gift revenue for this organization shall be authorized to use the name and tax-exempt privileges granted this organization, and shall be subject to the policies and procedures of the Committee on Fund Development. Accounting for all income of and expenses incurred by related organizations shall be made to the Office of Fund Development.

6. *The Role of Volunteers.* Active volunteer participation in the fund development program is essential to its success. The roles of volunteers shall be defined as to level of responsibility, period of service, reporting relationships, staff support, and other details as required. A volunteer recognition program shall also be provided to honor the service given by those who lead and assist this organization.

7. *The Rights of Donors.* The value of past, present, and future donors shall be preserved and respected at all times. The privileges and benefits accorded donors are defined in Honors and Recognition (Section J).

B. Management of Fund Development Activities

1. *Priority Established by the Board of Directors.* The priorities for public participation and support shall be established by the Board of Directors and carried out by the Committee on Fund Development through the Department of Fund Development.

2. *Job Description for Director of Fund Development.* The Committee on Fund Development and President/CEO shall define the duties and responsibilities of the Director of Fund Development and shall participate in the hiring and performance evaluation of occupants in this position.

3. *Public Solicitation Programs.* All fund-raising activities shall be approved by the Committee on Fund Development and the President/CEO for approved priorities only. Goals and budgets associated with their achievement shall be prepared in advance of active public solicitation.

4. *Priority and Project Management.* Each fund-raising priority shall be managed as a fund-raising project. The assistance of volunteers, staff, and budget shall be organized to meet project deadlines and objectives. Fund development volunteers, staff, time, and budget shall be authorized only for approved priorities. Overlapping priorities shall be resolved by the Committee on Fund Development.

5. *Procedures for Approval for Gift Solicitation.* All priorities for fund development shall be defined, within procedures established by the President/CEO, for submission to the Board of Directors for approval, including budgetary authorization. Those programs appropriate for fund-raising support shall be so identified, and evaluation shall be performed by the Committee on Fund Development to assess anticipated public support and budget and staff requirements for successful solicitation.

6. *Prospect Reservation.* Prospective candidates deserve considerate treatment at all times. When more than one approved project may qualify for the attention of the same prospect, the prospect reservation procedure shall guide resolution of the timing and period of reservation of each prospect. This procedure will ensure against duplicate solicitations of prospects already assigned to approved projects, which shall have priority.

7. *Use of Consultants and Vendors.* Professional assistance may be retained or purchased to support fund-raising activities. Each such association shall be guided by a written contract or memorandum of agreement, upon recommendation by the Committee on Fund Development and approval of the Board of Directors.

C. Public Solicitation Procedures

1. *Correct Legal Name.* All charitable contributions, regardless of value, form, or designated use, shall be made only to this organization, using the proper legal name of this corporation. Questions about methods of giving, timing, assignment, purpose, or use of gifts shall be directed to the Department of Fund Development, as shall all questions about legal forms for gifts, their tax consequences, and donor recognition.

2. *Use of Organization Name for Fund-Raising.* The use of the name of this organization for any fund-raising purpose by any other organization or entity shall require prior approval of the Committee on Fund Development, acting on recommendations from the Department of Fund Development.

3. *Commercial Coventures and Charitable Sales Promotions.* Joint ventures for public marketing and solicitation with business or commercial organizations shall be defined within applicable state and federal laws and regulations. Each such association shall be guided by a written contract or memorandum of agreement approved by the Board of Directors upon recommendation of the Committee on Fund Development and shall include disclosure by the commercial partner of all income and expenses associated with these promotions. The uses to be made of proceeds from each joint venture shall be in keeping with the mission statement of this organization.

4. *Tax Laws and Public Reporting Requirements.* Voluntary gift support of nonprofit organizations is endorsed by federal and state governments, which also permit substantial tax deductions for donors. The Board of Directors will, at all times, comply fully with its obligations to fulfill applicable tax laws and public reporting requirements. Public report documents shall be available within five days of receipt of a written request.

5. *General Fund-Raising Guidelines.* Donors and prospects shall be encouraged to support approved priorities and established programs at all times, in order that the most urgent requirements of this organization may be met to the greatest extent possible. Donor wishes will be considered to the extent possible, so long as their intended use of funds is in keeping with the mission statement. Resolution of donor wishes outside approved priorities and established programs shall be by the Board of Directors upon recommendation of the Committee on Fund Development.

6. *Joint Fund-Raising Programs.* Joint fund-raising activities between programs within this organization shall be encouraged because they provide donors more opportunities to meet approved priorities.

7. *The Calendar for Solicitations.* Each twelve-month period contains limited time available for fund-raising activities. Coordination and cooperation are required in planning each solicitation, to respect the rights of donors and to avoid creating the appearance of confusion and competition among the public. Each fund-raising program requires time for its own fulfillment and must also respect the preferred periods when other programs shall be scheduled. The calendar for solicitation shall be reviewed and approved by the Committee on Fund Development at the beginning of each fiscal year. Modifications to the calendar will be resolved by the Committee based on recommendations of the Department of Fund Development.

D. Forms of Contributions

1. *Types of Gifts.* Besides *monetary* gifts in the form of cash, checks, money orders, and the like, *nonmonetary gifts* may be accepted, such as: (a) bonds and securities, (b) real property, (c) tangible personal property, (d) gifts-in-kind to be used in the form in which they are given, (e) royalties, copyrights,

and trademark rights, and (f) insurance policies naming this organization as beneficiary in whole or in part.

2. *Unrestricted and Restricted Gifts.* Gifts with no stipulation by the donor as to their purpose or use are *unrestricted.* Gifts given for a specific purpose designated by the donor or so directed by this organization shall be *restricted,* and may be used only for the designated purpose. Gifts may be *expendable* (immediately usable for current purposes) or they may be *retained* for a period of time until release, or permanently held, during which period they may be invested, with use limited to a portion of earnings only.

3. *Appraisal Rules and Procedures.* Current Internal Revenue Service (IRS) regulations will be observed when calculating the charitable contribution deduction value of gifts of property, including advice to such donors regarding these regulations and the reporting obligations both parties must observe. A list of qualified professional appraisers will be offered each donor for his or her independent use. Donors are obliged to pay for professional appraisals of their property. The appraised value thus certified will be entered in the donor's gift record and reported in IRS Form 8282 if sold within two years of the date of the gift. Official gift acknowledgment documents will refer only to the appraised value.

4. *Special Handling of Select Gifts.* Commemorative gifts may be received in the form of "in memory of," "in honor of," or "on the occasion of" from any source. Separate gift acknowledgment procedures will reflect the special nature of these select gifts. Unless their use is specified by the donor or the person or family named, they shall be considered unrestricted gifts. Commemorative gifts that qualify for Honors and Recognition also will observe the procedures described in Section J herein.

5. *Temporary Funds.* A donor may deliver funds or property as a gift and specify a conditioned use over time. Such funds may be held for a fixed period and invested as directed by the Investment Committee, with a portion of earned income usable by this organization until conditions of time or maturation are achieved and the principal becomes available. In other cases, the use of principal also may be permitted at a fixed rate over a period of time, as specified by the donor.

6. *Gifts in Trust.* This organization may accept gifts in trust, agreeing to hold and manage a donor's principal resources and assets in exchange for life income, after which the principal and future income become the property of the organization for use as designated by the donor. A donor may deliver funds or property in a trust agreement to provide income for his or her lifetime and the lifetime of a spouse or other designated beneficiary, in accordance with the operating procedures of the Planned Giving Program (Section K). Specific details regarding trust documents, tax consequences, and income projections shall be reviewed by legal counsel prior to completion. If this organization acts as trustee, the selection of investment manager and custodian, performance evaluation, and administrative/accounting services shall be directed by the Investment Committee.

7. *Income-Producing Properties.* In instances where income-producing properties are gifted, the Investment Committee shall determine and report to

the Board of Directors, in advance of acceptance, several details including unrelated business income tax implications, environmental analysis and toxic waste potential, operations and maintenance expenses, and salability of the property. If accepted, the Investment Committee shall provide guidance on operations and disposition of the property to resolution.

8. *Legacies and Bequests.* A donor may arrange in a Will or Living Trust that this organization be designated as a beneficiary to receive a direct gift from the Estate. A donor may also arrange, after the death of a named beneficiary, that the principal or some of the surviving Estate shall become the property of this organization. Any restrictions on the use of such income as specified by the donor shall be in keeping with the mission statement. Unless otherwise specified, the Board of Directors, on advice of the Fund Development and Investment Committees, shall consider all other legacy and bequest income as unrestricted endowment.

E. Fund-Raising Methods and Techniques

1. *Procedures for Setting Goals.* Annual goals and multiyear campaign objectives shall be established by the Committee on Fund Development based on prior years' experience, established priorities of need, and budget appropriated, with approval by the Board of Directors. Fund development staff, time, and budget are reserved only for established priorities approved by the Board of Directors.

2. *Annual Giving Activities.* The several methods and techniques that solicit donors as well as prospects for support each year shall be coordinated by the Committee on Fund Development. A variety of solicitation programs may be offered, including direct mail, memberships, benefit events, telephone and media appeals, personal solicitation, and more.

3. *Procedures for Benefit Events.* Each special and benefit event shall be approved in advance by the Committee on Fund Development, based on the following criteria: (a) appropriate fit to the existing calendar of fund-raising activities, (b) recruitment of an adequate volunteer committee or sponsoring agency or organization, and (c) a budget reflecting income and expense plans projecting a minimum of 50 percent net proceeds as gift income to this organization. All event funds shall be administered by the Office of Fund Development; so also shall be all contracts and agreements for services required to support any event.

4. *Business, Corporation, and Foundation Relations.* These gift prospects are important resources and deserve careful consideration at all times. Direct contact with any business, corporation, or foundation for any purpose shall be only with prior approval of the Committee on Fund Development. Prospect reservation procedures shall apply at all times.

5. *Special-Project Campaigns.* Separate solicitation programs may be developed to meet urgent priorities or to take advantage of unusual opportunities offered by donors that match well with current fund-raising program objectives. Each such special-project campaign shall be approved by the

Committee on Fund Development prior to initiation, based on (a) appropriate fit to the existing calendar of fund-raising activities, (b) recruitment of an adequate volunteer committee or sponsoring agency or organization, and (c) a budget reflecting the expense required to achieve the income potential proposed with a minimum of 75 percent net proceeds as gift income to this organization.

6. *Multiyear and Capital Campaigns.* The Board of Directors may direct that a major fund-raising effort of a multiyear nature be conducted for urgent priorities, in keeping with long-range and strategic plans. Such plans shall be developed by the Committee on Fund Development in concert with the Finance and Investment Committees and with thorough analysis of leadership and volunteer support, gift potential, internal capability, time and expense required, and other preparations.

7. *Planned Giving Programs.* Public solicitation that offers forms of estate planning and planned giving shall be guided by the Planned Giving Policy (Section K) and administered by the Committee on Fund Development. This organization will act as trustee when accepting gifts in the form of charitable remainder trusts, charitable lead trusts, and pooled income funds, in accordance with state and federal regulations, subject to approval of each gift by the Board of Directors.

F. Government Grants and Contracts Administration

1. *Authority and Supervision.* The President/CEO and the Sponsored Research Administrator are authorized agents for all grant and contract agreements. Each grant or contract application shall be approved by the President/CEO and Sponsored Research Administrator prior to submission.

2. *Office of Grants and Contracts.* The Office of Grants and Contracts shall provide resource services including: details on application requirements, budget preparation with appropriate indirect costs and fringe benefits, application preparation and review, final signature approvals, and liaison to government agencies. Completed applications must be delivered to the Grants and Contracts Office at least five working days prior to the submission deadline.

3. *Grants and Contracts Officer.* The Grants and Contracts Officer is responsible for supervision of all grant and contract applications including budget review and approval, and for supervision of accounting for funds received and public reports required by these agreements.

4. *Institutional Review Committee (IRC).* An Institutional Review Committee shall be appointed by the President/CEO to be composed of nine members, three of whom shall be laypersons not employed by this organization. IRC duties include oversight and analysis of all work proposed and performed under grants and contracts as well as such other issues of ethics and professional conduct associated with any activity performed by this organization that is funded by government agencies and other revenue sources.

5. *Manuscripts and Articles.* Manuscripts, articles, and reports based on work performed under a grant or contract awarded this organization, or work

identified with this organization by name, shall be reviewed by the Grants and Contracts Officer prior to submission.

6. *Accounting, Reporting, and Audits.* The Chief Financial Officer will establish accounting procedures for administration of all funds received in a grant or contract agreement. Budget changes requested by the Principal Investigator shall be delivered to the Grants and Contracts Officer, who will negotiate with the agency for resolution. Requests for disbursement by the Principal Investigator first shall be directed to the Grants and Contracts Officer, who will verify the fund balance and expense to be in accordance with the approved budget. The Chief Financial Officer will supervise the preparation of all financial statements and public reports, including grant and contract audits, for submission to the granting or contract agency, in accordance with generally accepted accounting principles.

7. *Royalties, Copyrights, and Patents.* All royalties, copyrights, and patentable results from work performed under grant and contract agreements shall adhere to the Royalties, Copyrights, and Patents policy of this organization.

8. *Nongovernment Grants and Contracts.* Funds requested or received from nongovernment sources (e.g., corporations or foundations) that are, in fact, a formal agreement for specific work as defined in the application shall be administered by the Grants and Contracts Office in accordance with its operating policy and procedures, with support from the Fund Development Office as appropriate.

G. Gift Processing Procedures

1. *Checks and Cash.* All gifts in the form of checks, cash or credit cards received by any department shall be delivered *on the day they are received* to the Department of Fund Development, which will process the gift. In instances where the use specified by the donor is unclear, these details shall be brought to the immediate attention of the Department of Fund Development by telephone, because acceptance of any gift binds this organization to fulfilling the donor's wishes.

2. *Gifts of Securities.* The transfer of securities certificates or their ownership to the name of this organization is especially sensitive and may only be accomplished as follows: (a) Ask the donor and his or her broker to call the Department of Fund Development for instructions on transfer to our agent, setting up a brokers' account, board authorization action, and other details. In instances where prior securities transfers have occurred with the same broker, the Department of Fund Development will proceed with transfer instructions. (b) Certificates belonging to the donor will be delivered only by certified or registered mail, or by hand. A stock power form, signed by the donor and naming the organization as transferee, will be in a *separate* envelope using certified or registered mail. Disposition of the securities will be guided by policy from the Investment Committee.

3. *Gifts of Personal Property.* Personal property may be accepted when (a) the property can be sold, or (b) the property can be used in keeping with the

mission of this organization. Internal Revenue Service regulations require gifts other than money or publicly traded securities valued in excess of $5,000 to be appraised by a certified professional appraiser, and a copy of the appraisal must accompany the gift. Cost of the appraisal shall be the responsibility of the donor. The gift value shall be the appraised value at the time of the gift. If the property is sold within two years of its receipt, IRS Form 8282 will be completed and submitted to the IRS.

4. *Gifts of Real Estate.* Real estate in the form of a residence, business, commercial building, undeveloped land, etc., may be accepted when (a) the environmental and toxic waste review is completed, and (b) the property can be sold, or (c) the property can be used in keeping with the mission of this organization. A certified appraisal performed within 60 days of the gift date shall be provided by the donor. In most cases, real estate will be sold at current market prices through a broker hired by the organization. Properties with mortgages will not be accepted if the mortgage amounts to 50 percent or more of fair market value established in the appraisal.

5. *Gifts-in-Kind.* Gifts of material or products may be accepted when the form of the gift can be used immediately by the organization.

6. *Employee Gifts and Payroll Deduction.* Employees may make gifts at any time and may use payroll deduction to transfer their funds. Arrangements for the amount of the gift, frequency of deduction, and period when deductions are to begin and conclude are made by the employee, who shall be responsible for instructing the Payroll Office of these details in writing. The Department of Fund Development will provide sample language or a proper pledge card for these purposes.

7. *Fiscal and Calendar Year-End Procedures.* Gifts in any form received near the date ending the fiscal or calendar year may be credited to the prior reporting period if there is evidence that the donor intended to make the gift within this period, and the gift is received and processed within 10 days of the closing date for the fiscal or calendar year-end.

H. Gift Acknowledgment Procedures

1. *Official Acknowledgment.* All gifts, regardless of value, form, or designated use, shall be acknowledged by this organization with official correspondence. Acknowledgment represents to the donor this organization's acceptance of the gift along with its restrictions, and may also serve the donor as evidence to certify a possible tax-deductible event.

2. *Additional Acknowledgments.* Additional "thank you" messages by volunteers and staff are encouraged and are dependent on the donor, size of the gift, or purpose, as determined by the Department of Fund Development. Details about the gift will be provided by the Department of Fund Development; copies of additional acknowledgments shall be sent to the Department of Fund Development for retention in the donor file.

3. *Time of Acknowledgment.* Gifts must always be acknowledged as promptly as possible. Gift processing shall have as its first priority the timely acknowledgment of all gifts within 48 hours of receipt.

4. *Donor Records and Recognition.* The Department of Fund Development shall retain all correspondence regarding contributions, gift records, cumulative gift histories, and other data on donors' activity, which shall be confidential information for use only in support of fund-raising activities. All recognition and reward accorded to donors by reason of their frequency, amounts, or cumulative totals shall be in accordance with the Honors and Recognition guidelines (Section J).

5. *Tax Records and Public Disclosure.* Gift acknowledgment correspondence is useful to donors for tax submission purposes. Donors may request verification of previous gifts for any purpose, which will be documented and released only to donors. Public release of details surrounding individual gifts shall be made only with the express permission of the donor, who shall be appraised of the purpose for such disclosure and given prior approval of the language to be used.

6. *Gift Reports on Results.* Public reports of gift results will not disclose gift amounts for individual donors. Gift reports will tally results by revenue sources, purposes or use, and fund-raising programs employed. Distribution of gift reports shall be limited to those who need to know these results.

I. Accounting for Gift Revenue

1. *Fiduciary Responsibility.* Each gift, regardless of value, form, or designated use, shall be accounted for at the time of receipt until used as directed by the donor in support of the mission of this organization. During such time as funds are retained, they shall be actively invested in accordance with procedures of the Finance and Investment Management committees. The Department of Fund Development shall be responsible for any reports to donors on the use of their funds, to be accomplished in concert with operating managers and the fiscal/accounting department.

2. *Allocation to Restricted Funds.* Gifts received for restricted purposes shall be separately accounted for in order to maintain stewardship of these funds as donors direct. The segregation of these funds is to be performed by the fiscal/accounting department, who shall report to donors on their disposition and use by the departments and managers involved, through the Department of Fund Development.

3. *Expenditure Controls.* The uses of gift revenues, especially restricted gifts, shall be fully accounted for, beginning with their deposit to special-purpose fund accounts, stewardship, disposition reports, and with expenditures only as directed by the donor in keeping with the mission of this organization.

4. *Allocation to Endowment.* Funds restricted to endowment or so restricted by the Board of Directors shall be invested and accounted for in accord with policies of the Finance and Investment Management Committees.

5. *Investment of Funds.* All gifts received shall be invested until used in accord with donor wishes, using short-term or long-term investment plans as defined by the Finance and Investment Management Committees. Funds restricted to endowment or so restricted by the Board of Directors shall be invested and accounted for as directed by the Finance and Investment Management Committees. Investment earnings shall be used only for the purposes specified by

the donors or Board, with amounts as resolved by the Finance and Investment Management Committees.

6. *Accounting Reports.* Regular accounting reports will summarize the disposition of all gift money, illustrating their present disposition by source, purpose or use, and fund-raising program, which shall be prepared monthly and distributed to the Board of Directors and the Finance, Fund Development and Investment Management committees. Annual reports will be prepared as a summary of all fiscal-year activity.

7. *Audits and Tax Returns.* The Board of Directors will conduct an audit of all contributions received and held, which shall be conducted in accordance with generally accepted accounting principles. Public reports of financial details shall be prepared as required by federal and state regulations, which shall be available to the public within five days after receipt of a written request.

J. Honors and Recognition

1. *Policy Concept.* Formal recognition of distinguished service to this organization, in the forms of gift support and voluntary time and talent, shall receive official consideration by the Board of Directors. The qualifications, review and decision procedures, and methods of recognition to be followed in regard to gift support in its many forms, and as specified in this Section are: (a) the naming of buildings, property, or any space therein; (b) the naming of departments or titled positions, including chairs within this organization; and (c) the conferring of awards or citations on any individual, institution, association, or society for gift support or services rendered.

2. *Guidelines.* The Board of Directors, in concert with the Committee on Fund Development, shall assess each recommendation for honors and recognition. They shall consider the relationship between the honoree's qualifications and the size and scope of the project supported. Consideration in the conferral of honors and recognition will include (a) benefit to this organization, (b) visibility and prominence accorded to the honoree, and (c) use of honors and recognition to further the goals and objectives of this organization in financial gain and in public recognition and respect.

3. *Qualifications.* Individuals or institutions that make large contributions shall be qualified for honors and recognition. A gift of $25,000 or higher qualifies for such consideration and may include a single gift received, total giving over several years, or a pledge amount of fund-raising goal achieved. Each such donor may be offered an appropriate form of recognition to be placed in the area selected or in the main donor recognition area, or a suitable dedication ceremony with a tour of the area identified for recognition included whenever possible. Gifts valued under $25,000 shall be recognized at the discretion of the Committee on Fund Development.

4. *Procedure for Approval.* Recommendations for honors and recognition shall be made to the Board of Directors after review and approval by the Committee on Fund Development, with adequate details on the individual or institution to be honored and the reasons for such action by the Board of Directors.

5. *Naming of Buildings or Space Therein.* All areas of this organization are subject to naming. Such identification will be sensitive to function and location and shall be consistent with internal graphics and signage procedure. Buildings, floors, and areas may be named as donors prefer when the extent of service and contribution merits such recognition.

6. *Naming of Endowed Chairs.* Endowed chairs represent another means to recognize major contributions to this organization. Endowed chairs may be named in honor of a present or former staff member, the donor, or someone the donor wishes to honor, and may be either a memorial or a living tribute to the honoree. A financial goal shall be set for each endowed chair that is approved by this organization, and shall be based on a preliminary budget prepared for the use of a portion of the investment earnings.

7. *Naming of Departments or Title Positions.* Professional, scientific, and service departments and their administrative positions represent another means to honor a donor or someone the donor wishes to honor, or a present or former staff member. Such occasions occur especially when the personal contributions, service, and achievements of the honoree have been intimately associated with that department or its service or functional area.

8. *Awards or Citations.* This organization may establish and may confer at its pleasure such awards or citations on individuals or institutions in recognition for either or both their voluntary service and contributions. These awards or citations may be given at such time and on such occasions as the organization's Board of Directors may determine. Recommendations for conferring an award or citation shall be made as defined in paragraph 9 below.

9. *Process for Recommendation.* Recommendations for honors and recognition are directed to the Committee on Fund Development, who shall confer with the Chairperson of the Board of Directors and the President/CEO before action is taken. In those instances where a present or former employee is nominated or a department or title position is proposed, the President/CEO shall confer with the department head most closely associated with the candidate, or the department head most closely associated with the title position, for advice in advance of forwarding the recommendation to the Board of Directors for their decision. In addition, adequate consultation with the honoree or his or her family or their representative(s) shall be conducted at the same time as other internal consultations, to be concluded to their satisfaction prior to presentation of these recommendations to the Board of Directors for action.

10. *Public Notice.* Honors and recognition decisions represent opportunities for public announcement. Agreement for such public notice shall be requested of each honoree, or his or her family or representative(s), in advance. Honorees shall have the opportunity to notify family and friends, and to invite their participation with the organization in any dedication ceremonies and receptions conducted in connection with the conferring of honors and recognition. Responsibility for coordination of such public notice shall be by the President/CEO and Director of Fund Development.

11. *Forms of Recognition.* Various forms of recognition shall be available in accordance with the wishes of the donor and with the concurrence of the

Board of Directors. Details as to form shall be included in recommendations submitted to the Committee on Fund Development. Forms of recognition may be among the following: formal dinners, portraits, dedication ceremonies, receptions, plaques, gifts to donors and honorees, photo sessions, and other forms of recognition.

12. *Graphics Continuity.* Materials, type face, and presentation forms shall be consistent with graphics standards established by this organization. The application of overall visual aids, signage, and graphics utilization shall be in accordance with graphics standards established by this organization.

13. *Renewed Solicitation.* The resolicitation of donors who have been accorded honors and recognitions shall be reviewed in advance by the Committee on Fund Development, and shall be based on submission of a strategic action plan for continued donor relations and the master gift plan defined for each such donor prior to consideration of another gift that may qualify for added honors and recognition.

14. *Donor Communications.* The Office of Fund Development shall monitor relations with all individuals or institutions accorded honors and recognition, in order to provide continued communications with this organization at a level satisfactory to these donors.

K. Management of Planned Giving Programs

1. *Programs for Solicitation.* The types of planned gifts to be offered, minimum gift amount, range for percentage payout, assignment as trustee, and administrative services shall all be defined by the Committee on Fund Development and approved by the Board of Directors, and shall include procedures for preparation and review of performance of planned gifts in force.

2. *Acting as Trustee.* This organization will prefer to act as trustee of charitable trusts and pooled income funds with concurrence of the donor(s), and will provide (or arrange to provide) such investment, distribution, income tax, audit, and other administrative services as required of a trustee.

3. *Charitable Trust and Pooled Income Fund Management.* The Board of Directors, acting on recommendations of the Fund Development and Investment Management committees, will administer each charitable trust and pooled income fund in accordance with guidelines established by the trust document or pooled fund agreement, including investment strategies and payout rates. Investment managers will be selected by the Investment Management Committee, who will perform regular evaluations of investment performance and will report these results to the Board of Directors at least annually.

4. *Life Insurance Programs.* All life insurance programs offered as gift opportunities shall be defined by the Fund Development and Investment Management committees and approved by the Board of Directors. Selection of agents, performance of due diligence, and supervision of policies in force shall be the responsibility of the Investment Management Committee, acting on recommendations from the Committee on Fund Development. Other life insurance

gifts may be accepted, provided the policy is fully paid and designates this organization as owner and beneficiary. If partially paid, the donor will be required to submit a written pledge to complete premium payments within eight years and to provide the original policy to this organization.

5. *Commissions Paid for Planned Gifts.* It shall be the policy of this organization not to pay commissions or percentages associated with negotiation and acceptance of any form of planned gift. Further, the standards of professional conduct in this area shall be as published by the National Committee on Planned Giving.

6. *Wills and Bequests: Probate Procedures.* Sample texts shall be provided to all those who express an interest in naming this organization to receive a bequest. Donors who name this organization in their Will or Living Trust will be asked to provide a copy of their document or that section wherein this organization is named. It shall be the policy of this organization to closely follow to conclusion all probate proceedings where this organization is a named beneficiary.

L. Investment and Endowment Operations

1. *Obligation of the Board of Directors.* All gifts to be invested or funds held as endowment shall be managed with professional assistance at all times with the express approval of the Board of Directors. The objectives in management of such funds shall be to preserve their current value and to generate earnings for current use by this organization. Supervision shall be by the Investment Management Committee, who will establish investment guidelines, conduct performance evaluation, recommend distribution of earnings, and submit regular status reports on all invested funds.

2. *Selecting Professional Management Services.* The Investment Management Committee shall interview and recommend to the Board of Directors such professional managers, custodians and performance evaluation services for all invested and endowment funds as are required, and shall conduct performance evaluations at least semiannually.

3. *Short-Term Money Management (under two years).* The Investment Management Committee shall recommend to the Board in concert with the Finance Committee how funds to be held for a brief period (under two years) shall be invested and managed, including the selection of professional managers and setting their investment guidelines.

4. *Invested Funds Management (two to five years).* The Investment Management Committee shall recommend to the Board in concert with the Finance Committee how funds that may be held for a period of up to five years shall be invested and managed, including the selection of professional managers and setting their investment guidelines. Funds to be held for more than five years shall observe endowment fund management.

5. *Endowment Fund Management.* Funds restricted to endowment or designated by the Board to observe endowment management shall be invested with professional managers and may include commingling such funds together for

maximum benefit. Guidelines for investment shall consider current market conditions, preservation of principal, balanced fund strategies, and the annual income needs of this organization.

6. *Purposes and Uses of Earnings.* Investment earnings shall observe the use designated for any invested or endowment fund at its inception or may otherwise be used at the discretion of the Board of Directors. If a portion of earnings is not consumed or their use is not required, it shall be the policy of this organization to retain and reinvest all such funds.

M. Corporate Member: The Separate Foundation

1. *Corporate Member of the Foundation.* Any organization established in the form of a separate nonprofit corporation in foundation form, whose mission is to assist this parent corporation, shall be as a related organization. The Corporate Member shall be the Board of Directors of this organization, who shall approve the Articles of Incorporation and Bylaws and annually elect the Directors of each such related organization.

2. *Routine Operations and Information Reports.* The routine operations of the foundation shall be guided by its Articles of Incorporation and Bylaws. Information reports shall be made to this organization by the foundation President or other officer who shall be invited to regular meetings of the Board of Directors of the parent corporation. Reports shall include information about its activities in support of this organization, fund-raising programs, and financial results.

3. *Review of Annual Goals and Objectives.* The foundation shall prepare its annual goals and objectives in concert with the priority needs of this organization. These goals shall include projects identified for fund-raising, estimated income, and operating budget and staff required, to be submitted to the Board of Directors of this organization for review prior to inception.

4. *Professional Staff Hiring Procedures.* Professional employees of the foundation, including employees of this organization assigned to foundation work, shall include the Chairman of the Board, Chief Financial Officer, and the President/CEO in the interview and selection process. All employees shall observe the policies and procedures of the parent corporation at all times.

5. *Transfer of Funds Raised and Held.* The transfer of funds raised and held by the foundation shall be at the request of the President/CEO or Chief Financial Officer of the parent corporation or their delegates. Recommendations shall include the use or disposition of funds to be transferred for reports to donors. Each transfer shall be approved by the foundation board of directors and reported to the Board of the parent corporation.

6. *Nominations Process for Foundation Directors.* The Bylaws of the foundation specify that the Nominations Committee of the Board of Directors of the parent corporation shall identify, recruit, and nominate candidates for service on the Board of Directors of the foundation.

7. *Honors and Recognition by the Foundation.* Honors and recognition accorded to qualified donors and volunteers shall be conducted in concert

with the parent corporation at all times, including the naming of any part of facilities, named positions, and the placement of donor recognition materials in or on buildings owned by the parent corporation. Honors and recognition accorded by the foundation shall otherwise be guided by the Honors and Recognition policy of the parent corporation (see Section J above).

8. *Annual Meetings and Annual Reports.* The foundation shall conduct its annual meetings and issue its annual reports in concert with the parent corporation at all times. A selection of foundation directors, volunteers, and donors will be invited to attend annual meetings of the parent corporation. Annual reports prepared for the two organizations may be separate or combined, as the two Boards may determine.

9. *Annual Audit Review.* Audits prepared for the foundation shall be conducted in accordance with generally accepted accounting principles. Selection of the firm to conduct the audit shall be made by the parent corporation and the report delivered to the parent corporation. Further, as accounting guidelines may direct, the financial experience of the foundation may also be reported in the consolidated audit of the parent corporation as a related organization.

N. Related Organizations: Support Groups

1. *Authorization to Exist.* Support group organizations may be formed either by this organization or its subsidiary foundation only with the approval of the board of directors of both organizations. The purpose of any such support group shall be in keeping with the mission, purpose, goals, and objectives of the parent corporation. Support groups may not be established as separately incorporated associations except in the form of a subsidiary foundation as defined in Section M above.

2. *Approval of Operating Rules and Procedures.* Support group organizations formed for fund development purposes shall be guided in their activities by written operating rules and procedures, which shall be approved by the parent corporation or its subsidiary foundation. Their operating rules and procedures shall include text reporting their formal affiliation, purposes, members, Board of Directors, election of officers and their duties, powers, committees, meetings, receipt of funds and assets and their disposition, rules of order, limitations on political activities, insignia, amendments, and the like.

3. *Use of the Organization's Name.* Support groups may act only in the name of the parent corporation or its subsidiary foundation, use their name in their communications, solicit contributions only for support of their mission and priorities of need, and otherwise support their purposes, goals, and objectives.

4. *Review of Annual Goals and Objectives.* The annual goals and objectives of each support group organization shall be prepared in coordination and cooperation with the parent corporation or its subsidiary foundation. Preparation of annual goals and objectives shall be defined and approved by the Board of Directors of each support group and reported to the Board

of Directors of the parent corporation or its subsidiary foundation for review and approval.

5. *Nominations Process for Officers and Members of the Board of Directors.* A nominations committee shall be appointed by the Board of Directors of each support group who will conduct elections to its Board of Directors. Composition of each nominations committee will include the Chairman of the Board, Chairman of the Committee on Fund Development, and President/CEO of the parent corporation, along with similar representatives of its subsidiary foundation. Candidates for election shall be approved by the parent corporation and its subsidiary foundation in advance of their election.

6. *Professional Staff Hiring Procedures.* Professional staff hired to assist support group organizations shall be employees of the parent corporation or its subsidiary foundation. Representatives of each support group will be invited to serve on selection committees for the hiring of professional staff whose duties include staff management and support for these organizations.

7. *Control of Funds Raised and Held.* All funds raised and held by support groups shall be in the name of the parent corporation, or its subsidiary foundation, and shall be delivered to it upon receipt or following completion of the activity for which these funds were raised. Regular reports of funds raised and held shall be made to the Committee on Fund Development of the parent corporation or to the Board of Directors of its subsidiary foundation, which funds shall be included in their regular financial statements and annual audit report.

8. *Annual Meetings and Annual Reports.* Support groups shall conduct their annual meetings and prepare their annual reports as their Operating Rules and Procedures specify. Invitations to annual meetings shall include representatives of the parent corporation or its subsidiary foundation, who shall also receive their annual reports.

9. *Annual Audit Review.* Funds raised or held in the name of the parent corporation or its subsidiary foundation are the property of these organizations and shall be included in their financial statements and annual audit report. If support groups manage their own funds, their books and financial statements will be delivered annually to the parent corporation or its subsidiary foundation for review and to provide such information as is required for preparation of the annual audit statement and IRS return. A report of each review will be delivered to the President of each support group.

O. Department of Fund Development

1. *Areas of Management Responsibility.* The Department of Fund Development reports to the President/CEO and is charged with management and staff support to the entire fund development program, including all employees, annual budget, donor records, and files. The definition and direction of fund-raising activities, recruitment and training of volunteers, accounting for all funds raised, and public reports shall be with the approval of the Committee on Fund Development and the Board of Directors.

2. *Approved Fund-Raising Programs.* Only those fund-raising programs and activities approved by the Committee on Fund Development shall be performed by this Department with the use of its employees and their time and with such budget funds as are made available. Any other program must first receive full and formal approval by the Committee prior to its implementation.

3. *Donor Relations and Communications.* This Department is charged with responsibility for the complete supervision of all records, personal relations, and communications with donors, including honors and recognition. This Department shall act as a resource to this organization on its formal obligations to donors at all times.

4. *Support Services.* The organization shall provide this Department with normal and routine support services, such as accounting, financial management, personnel, employee health, engineering, housekeeping, etc., in the same manner as other Departments and assist in completion of its assigned duties, as appropriate.

5. *Job Descriptions and Hiring Practices.* All employees of this Department shall be guided in their daily duties by a written job description prepared for their position, as reviewed and approved by this organization. Salary levels, pay schedules, benefits, performance evaluations, and other matters relating to full- or part-time employment shall be consistent with personnel procedures of this organization, as shall be all hiring practices. Employees shall observe the same policies and procedures that apply to all other employees at all times.

6. *Budgets and Accountability.* Budget preparation and accountability for funds entrusted to the Department shall be performed by management staff of the Department in accordance with routine procedures of this organization. Departmental managers are responsible for the correct expense of all funds provided for operating purposes in accordance with organization policy, and for verifying these details to the finance division as required.

7. *Records and Files.* All records of correspondence, gift transactions, and their related details will be maintained by the Department as sensitive information for such periods of time and in such form as is appropriate. The use and disclosure of any of this information shall be restricted to Department employees and such others who have a need to know in order to carry out their assigned duties. Donor gift histories shall be preserved for the life of the donor. Any record destroyed shall protect the sensitive nature of the contents until destruction is complete.

P. Public Reporting Requirements

1. *Internal Revenue Service.* Preparation of Internal Revenue Service Form 990 and other IRS documents associated with the conduct of public solicitation and acceptance of gifts of any type and form shall be completed on schedules provided and in accordance with current IRS regulations.

2. *State and Local Agencies.* Such other reports as may be required by state, county, local community, or other agencies shall be completed on schedules

provided and in accordance with current regulations. Such permits, licenses, and fees that may be required along with public disclosure of tax-exempt certificates, audits, financial statements, etc., will be completed in accordance with current regulations.

3. *Public Requests for Information.* Any request in writing, asking for copies of public documents so defined by law, such as reports submitted to the IRS and local authorities, will be completed in accordance with current regulations and will be honored within five working days of receipt of the request.

Q. Approvals, Reviews, and Amendments

1. *Authority of the Board of Directors.* This Manual is authorized by the Board of Directors, acting on recommendation of the Committee on Fund Development. It is designed to provide guidance and direction to all areas of fund development activity of this organization. Its contents shall be followed by all who accept appointment to voluntary and staff positions of this organization.

2. *Periodic Review and Reissue.* A review of this entire Manual will be conducted by the Committee on Fund Development every other year, with results reported to the Board of Directors. The purpose of this review will be to maintain an accurate relationship between the current practices of operating programs and the contents of this Manual. Any section or subsection may be examined at any time, as appropriate, with changes and additions proposed in accordance with the amendment procedures.

3. *Process for Amendment.* Changes to this Manual must be approved by the Board of Directors, who will act only on formal recommendations from the Committee on Fund Development. Proposals for amendment may be submitted in writing, at any time, by any participant in the fund development program who shall utilize existing committees, related organizations, or other appropriate and standing leadership structure for prior reviews and approvals leading to submission by the Committee on Fund Development.

SOURCES AND SUGGESTED REFERENCES

Blazek, Jody. 1990. *Tax and Financial Planning for Tax-Exempt Organizations: Forms, Checklists, Procedures.* New York: John Wiley & Sons.

Brakeley, George A., Jr. 1980. *Tested Ways to Successful Fund Raising.* New York: AMACOM.

Broce, Thomas E. 1986. *Fund Raising: A Guide to Raising Money from Private Sources,* 2d Ed. Norman: University of Oklahoma Press.

Burlingame, Dwight F., and Hulse, Lamont J., Ed. 1991. *Taking Fund Raising Seriously.* San Francisco: Jossey-Bass.

Fink, Norman S., and Metzler, Howard C. 1982. *The Costs and Benefits of Deferred Giving.* New York: Columbia University Press.

Grasty, William K., and Sheinkopf, Kenneth G. 1983. *Successful Fund Raising: A Handbook of Proven Strategies and Techniques.* New York: Charles Scribner's Sons.

Greenfield, James M. 1991. *Fund Raising: Evaluating and Managing the Fund Development Process.* New York: John Wiley & Sons.

Gross, Malvern J., Jr., Warshauer, William, Jr., and Larkin, Robert F. 1991. *Financial and Accounting Guide for Nonprofit Organizations,* 4th Ed. New York: John Wiley & Sons.

Gurin, Maurice G. 1991. *What Volunteers Should Know for Successful Fund Raising.* New York: Stein & Day.

Hopkins, Bruce R. 1991. *The Law of Fund-Raising.* New York: John Wiley & Sons.

———. 1982. *The Law of Tax-Exempt Organizations.* New York: John Wiley & Sons.

———. 1989. *Starting and Managing a Nonprofit Organization: A Legal Guide.* New York: John Wiley & Sons.

Huntsinger, Jerald E. 1985. *Fund Raising Letters: A Comprehensive Study Guide to Raising Money by Direct Response Marketing.* Richmond, VA: Emerson Publishers.

Kotler, Philip, and Andreasen, Alan R. 1987. *Strategic Marketing for Nonprofit Organizations,* 3d Ed. Englewood Cliffs, NJ: Prentice-Hall.

Lautman, Kay, and Goldstein, Henry. 1991. *Dear Friend: Mastering the Art of Direct Mail Fund Raising,* 2d Ed. Washington, DC: The Taft Group.

Lord, James Gregory. 1982. *Philanthropy and Marketing.* Cleveland, OH: Third Sector Press.

O'Connell, Brian. 1983. *America's Voluntary Spirit.* New York: The Foundation Center.

Rosso, Henry A. and Associates. 1991. *Achieving Excellence in Fund Raising: A Comprehensive Guide to Principles, Strategies, and Methods.* San Francisco: Jossey-Bass.

Seymour, Harold J. 1988. *Designs for Fund Raising: Principles, Patterns, Techniques.* New York: McGraw-Hill.

Van Til, Jon and Associates. 1990. *Critical Issues in American Philanthropy.* San Francisco: Jossey-Bass.

Warner, Irving R. 1990. *The Art of Fund Raising,* 3d Ed. New York: Harper & Row.

CHAPTER SEVENTEEN

Direct Mail Fund-Raising

Constance Clark
Clark Communications

CONTENTS

17.1 THE BASICS: WHAT MAKES DIRECT MAIL WORK?

(a) THE AIDA THEORY OF DIRECT MARKETING Direct marketing got its start in America with mail-order catalogues, published and circulated by such giant retailers as Sears Roebuck and Montgomery Ward. Today, according to market researcher Arnold Fishman (as reported in the July 1992 of *Direct Marketing*), it accounts for $107.97 billion in sales of consumer products and services, and $49.03 billion in contributions to nonprofit organizations. Although consumers complain about the volume of mail they receive, they continue to buy and contribute through the mail in large numbers. What makes this medium work?

One of the classic theories behind the effectiveness of direct marketing is the AIDA concept:

Attention. Your direct marketing package must arouse the recipient's attention in order to get opened. Once the envelope is opened, the first lines of copy and the graphics must continue to hold the reader's attention so that the package does not get thrown away.

Interest. After grabbing the reader's attention, the package must present something that is of interest to the prospective buyer/contributor, something that touches on his or her ideals and feelings.

Desire. Now that the prospect's attention has been grabbed and his or her interest is piqued, the package must generate a *desire* for the product or transaction to be promoted.

Action. If the direct marketing package has done its job correctly, a small percentage of its recipients will have decided that they want to buy the product or make the contribution. Now the package must overcome the prospect's inertia, moving him or her to *action*—filling out the order card and returning it with payment or payment information in the envelope provided.

This chapter attempts to outline how the AIDA theory is successfully put to work for direct mail fund-raisers. It examines the creative strategies used by direct mail packagers who bring in millions of dollars for causes ranging from Alzheimer's disease research to zoos.

(b) BASIC COMPONENTS OF DIRECT MAIL FUND-RAISING PACKAGES Theoretically, anything can be added to a direct mail package, as long as it fits in the envelope; however, certain typical elements have evolved over decades of direct mail testing. Brief descriptions of these typical package components are given in the following subsections.

(i) The envelope Almost without exception, direct mail fund-raising efforts consist of a number of items within an envelope, rather than a self-mailer format such as a flyer or catalogue. The envelope package has repeatedly performed more effectively than less costly alternative formats.

The standard No. 10 window envelope is the workhorse of direct mail fund-raising, but many other envelope sizes and formats might be considered.

(ii) The letter The fund-raising letter is generally long—from two to four pages and sometimes longer—because direct mail tests have proven the effectiveness of this length of copy. The letter is the main vehicle for the "sales pitch" or case statement, and must include general information about the organization's needs as well as a strong call to action (e.g., a specific request for funds, instructions on how to give, and suggested gift amounts).

(iii) The reply device An order card, a memo-size sheet, a full page, or a small slip of paper can be enclosed for reply. It should bear the prospect's name and address (which often show through the envelope's window) and recap the fund-raising proposition: "Yes, I want to help save starving children in Ethiopia. Here is my contribution in the following amount," with a range of gift-size choices given. Specific instructions on how to complete the gift are also given.

(iv) The reply envelope A return-addressed reply envelope is usually enclosed. Often, but not always, the reply envelope is postage-paid.

(v) The brochure Sometimes a brochure or flyer is used to augment the fund-raising proposition detailed by the letter.

(vi) The lift note The tradition of the "lift note" or "publisher's letter" started in magazine subscription direct mail packages, when publishers found that enclosing a short note re-capping an aspect of the sales proposition lifted response, often by as much as 20 to 25 percent. In fund-raising, the lift often comes from a testimonial letter signed by a beneficiary of the organization or an endorsement from a well-known authority or celebrity.

(vii) Premiums   Fund-raising organizations often include inexpensive gifts in their direct mail packages. The most famous example of a direct mail fund-raising premium is probably Easter or Christmas seals, although today the range extends to personalized name-and-address labels, calendars, certificates of appreciation, membership cards, and even paperback books. For more on the use of premiums in donor mailings, see page 000.

(c) SEVENTEEN STEPS TO SUCCESSFUL DIRECT MAIL COPY   Whether you are planning a mailing to acquire new donors or to ask for gifts from existing donors, the following basic guidelines can help you develop a winning package concept and write effective direct mail copy.

(i) Ask people to give money in order to help other people   "People only give to people" is a ground rule of fund-raising. Your direct mail package must demonstrate how the donor's gift will help other people (or animals). Emphasize the people-to-people connection throughout your copy.

(ii) Be specific about what you need   Donors want to know exactly what good their hard-earned dollars will produce. Tell them, in detail, the results you hope to achieve with their money. Spell out the problem you hope to solve, and your method for solving it, to give credibility to your request for funds.

(iii) Convey a strong sense of urgency   Why give money if there's no good and immediate reason to do so? Provide that reason to your donors. Tell them why you need their money *today*.

(iv) Use a deadline whenever possible   Nothing gives a sense of urgency as effectively as a specific date. If potential threats to your organization's beneficiaries will become real on October 23, say so. Reiterate the date throughout the letter and on the reply form. Urge the donor to respond before that date passes.

(v) Help you donor identify with the people you help   Your appeal must forge an emotional bond between the potential donor and the recipient of that donor's largesse. A wealthy suburb dweller may not easily identify with the homeless person he or she overlooks on the street every day. But all human beings can understand pain. The fund-raiser's challenge is to portray the homeless person's pain in terms the donor can understand.

(vi) Write emotional copy   To forge an emotional bond, you must write emotionally inspiring copy. Avoid bureaucratic language, and speak simply and forcefully about the need your organization seeks to meet.

(vii) Use a case history   Use a compelling story in your fund-raising letter—a vivid, moving story of someone who needs your organization's help, or a before-and-after account of someone you have assisted. Such stories are your most valuable asset when you write a fund-raising letter. Use them whenever possible.

(viii) Make the outer ("carrier") envelope work for you   Getting the prospect to open the envelope is your most challenging task. People are most likely to open an envelope that closely resembles personal mail (hand-addressed, with a first-class stamp). Because this alternative is too expensive for most fund-raising mailings, envelope copy or "teaser" copy can be used to get the recipient's attention and draw him or her into the package. The envelope copy and design should make the carrier so intriguing, promising, or official-looking that the recipient cannot ignore it.

(ix) Drop your institutional brochure Your organization's standard brochure usually has no place in a fund-raising mailing. Direct mail tests have shown that packages *without* the "standard brochure" do *better* than those including it. Incorporate the basic information about your organization in the direct mail package letter instead.

(x) Develop exciting enclosures A special enclosure is not absolutely necessary, but is often increases response. You might include a premium, or something more directly tied to your fund-raising proposition—a "blueprint" of a new building; a photograph of a needy child, with your handwritten note on the back; a budget memo from your finance director to your president, spelling out why you urgently need money and what you will spend it on.

(xi) Use a "lift letter" to boost response Include a note from someone who needs the donor's help, from a celebrity, or from someone your organization has helped in the past. Make the note very brief, personal, and to the point.

(xii) Lavish attention on the reply device It is easy to overlook the reply device, but it is a critical element of your package: Without it, you will not get your gift! Make sure the basics are there:

> Your name, address, and telephone number;
> Space for the donor's name and address to be printed or supplied on a label;
> A restatement of your request and the gift amounts you hope to receive;
> Instructions on how to make out the check;
> Information on tax deductibility.

(xiii) Use participation devices to involve the donor When appropriate, ask the donor to sign a petition, return a postcard to a legislator, or fill out a survey.

(xiv) Write "I"/"thou" (not "we"/"you") copy Your letter should never sound like a business communication. It must be personal—written from one person to another, from one friend to another. If your writing style tends to be technical, journalistic, or bureaucratic, delegate the writing of the fund-raising letter to another staff member or a professional copywriter. Style is *critical* to the effectiveness of direct mail fund-raising copy.

(xv) Write long copy Although people claim they dislike receiving them, long letters almost always evoke a better response than short ones. This principle has been proven repeatedly, and it is unwise to ignore the findings of mailers who have spent millions of dollars to test these factors. Here are the rules for length:

> Letters to current donors: At least two pages (two sides of one 8½″ × 11″or monarch-size sheet).

Letters to prospective donors: At least four pages. (One notable exception is the "slip" mailing used by many medical charities, which is no more than a few sentences of copy; test this format very carefully.)

Letters to current donors asking them to increase their contribution substantially, or letters that are high-dollar invitations: At least four pages.

(xvi) Use short words, sentences, and paragraphs Your writing style should be simple. Many direct mail experts recommend using words no longer than two syllables, and paragraphs no longer than five lines. Remember that your prospect is looking for an excuse to throw away the letter. If he or she sees block after block of dense, difficult copy, it may well land in the trash can.

(xvii) Use a P.S. Studies have shown that recipients of direct mail letters often scan the letters. One of the first things they look at is the signature/P.S. area. Your P.S. should recap a key point of your fund-raising proposition and repeat the call to action.

(d) TWELVE STEPS TO SUCCESSFUL DIRECT MAIL FUND-RAISING DESIGN

(i) Send a letter that's first-class and personal Every step away from a fully personalized letter mailed in a handwritten and closed-face envelope bearing a first-class stamp is a compromise. This is the type of mailing that gets opened most often, but it is rarely affordable for fund-raising organizations. Compromises must be made, and that is where the challenge for the designer comes in.

(ii) Make the outer envelope as interesting as possible Here are some ways to create interest:

Mimic the first-class, personalized look by using a "live" third-class stamp and a window envelope designed to look as much as possible like the kind of mail a person cannot ignore.

Make the envelope look like official business. Use black ink only, on brown kraft stock, and use teaser copy that is official in nature—for example, copy echoing postal regulations.

Go the other way and pull the reader in with photos, illustrations, and/or fascinating and well-designed teaser copy.

Make the envelope look different from other items in the prospect's mailbox, using size, color, or other design elements to create a stand-out.

(iii) Make the letter look like a letter Some fund-raising organizations sprinkle photos throughout the pages of their letters. This can work, especially for human-interest-oriented packages, but, generally speaking, it is better to make the letter look like a real letter, and real letters don't have photographs on every page. Real letters are also typewritten, not typeset; do not go to the extra expense of typesetting your letters. Real letters are on letterhead, carry a single signature, and are printed in black on a white or very light pastel page.

(iv) Make the letter (and other package elements) easy to read The letter's long copy should be carefully laid out for readability, with adequate margins and a clear typewriter print style. Underlining in a second color helps guide the eye through the letter and leads the reader to key points.

(v) Make the reply device clear and easy to use   Avoid cluttering up the reply device with lots of photos or illustrations. Keep it simple and make sure it is easy to read.

(vi) On typeset elements, use serif typefaces   Serif typefaces are much easier to read than sans serif typefaces. In direct mail, readability is crucial. Make sure your designer knows, before designing the job, that you want a serif typeface.

(vii) Design for economy   Explain to your designer that you have a limited budget, and ask him or her for suggestions that will keep your expenses down. It is not necessary to use fancy paper, custom illustration, or more than two colors in a direct mail fund-raising package; these niceties do not increase response.

(viii) Look nice but not expensive   If your package looks *too* well-designed or richly produced, the prospective donor may conclude, even on an unconscious level, that you must not really need the money. You can mail a very inexpensive package—mostly black ink on white paper, without illustrations or photographs—and raise a great deal of money; it has been done many times. But you must be sure that the package is easy to read and not unpleasant to look at, and, above all, that the carrier envelope is compelling.

(ix) Avoid the indicia if possible   An indicia is the boxed-in third-class postal permit information in the upper right-hand corner of the carrier envelope. It is the least expensive way to use third-class postage, but it is a dead giveaway that this it *not* a personal communication of any kind. Consider instead using a postage meter or live third-class stamp, and ask your lettershop for quotes on each option.

(x) Use different colors on different package elements   Most people consider it elegant to carry a color theme throughout the different parts of a direct mail package. However, many experts recommend the opposite approach, on the theory that a different color might attract the person opening the package to a particular package element, even if he or she has already discarded the letter. If you are using color, try making the letter, reply device, enclosures, and reply envelope different shades, or use different shades of ink on each (though always use black for large blocks of text, like the letter and reply device).

(xi) Choose photographs that strongly convey your message   If you are using photographs, be sure they feature people (or animals, if your organization is a humane society) who are in need of your services, or people/animals who are benefiting from them. (Don't forget to obtain a release (permission in writing) for use of a subject's picture.) Pictures of buildings and staff people are usually irrelevant.

(xii) Keep the package simple   Direct mail fund-raising packages are not the milieu for fancy, state-of-the-art graphic design. They are the bread-and-butter of the design world, and should be designed to be simple and humble, but still pleasing.

(e) KEEPING COSTS LOW: BASIC RULES OF DIRECT MAIL PRODUCTION   Several volumes could be written on direct mail production. Presented here are some fundamental pointers for getting the best price and service from direct mail vendors, including printers, data processing houses, and lettershops.

(i) Take advantage of the industry's competitiveness　Many companies exist to serve the burgeoning direct mail industry. You need never feel restricted to using one particular printer, lettershop, or any other kind of vendor. Search out a number of experienced vendors by:

> Asking colleagues for referrals;
>
> Asking vendors themselves for referrals; e.g., ask a printer for names of quality lettershops or graphic artists;
>
> Visiting booths at direct mail shows, conventions, and local direct marketing club meetings;
>
> Consult direct marketing directories (e.g., *Direct Mail Marketplace*) and advertisements in magazines serving the direct mail industry (e.g., *DM News, Direct Marketing, Fund Raising Management*).

(ii) Consult experienced vendors　Printers, graphic designers, and related professionals are good sources for advice on the best ways to produce your fund-raising package. Once you have identified several potential vendors and reviewed their samples and references, talk with them about your package. They have a wealth of ideas at their fingertips about format possibilities, and they know how to keep costs down. Bring them in on the planning stages, to get the best results in execution.

(iii) Get at least three written bids　The competitive bidding process helps your organization get the lowest possible vendors' prices—a vital element for the success of your direct mail fund-raising program.

(iv) Issue a written purchase order for each job　Your purchase order should include all the specifications for the job, as well as the agreed-on price and terms of the sale.

(v) Stay involved　Be sure you will have the opportunity to check printer's bluelines and to sign off on any production process at critical turning points. Good vendors will want to make sure you are involved throughout. For both them and you, this helps ensure delivery of a quality product.

17.2　DONOR/MEMBER ACQUISITION THROUGH DIRECT MAIL

(a) CREATING SUCCESSFUL CONCEPTS FOR THE DIRECT MAIL ACQUISITION PACKAGE
The direct mail fund-raiser's biggest challenge is acquiring new donors (or members) for the nonprofit organization. Many factors come into play in this process: the wise selection of mailing lists; testing strategies; timing of mailings; and the creation of the right "offer" or message. This section attempts to give pointers on the creative aspects of the successful direct mail acquisition package, that is, the development and execution through copy and design of a package concept.

(i) Urgency and deadlines: Sounding the call to action   Your direct mail acquisition package is not going to be top priority for the recipient; he or she will have many good reasons to lay it aside and think about it later—which means never. Strike while the iron is hot: Ask for a response as soon as possible, and announce a deadline based on your urgent need for help. For example, a food distribution program for the homeless, focused on the Thanksgiving holiday, might state that families will go without holiday dinners unless the donor replies positively no later than November 10.

(ii) Finding and telling your organization's story   A direct mail letter is very different from your organization's case statement, standard brochure, or annual report. It should describe the organization's mission in terms of *stories,* using case histories and personal narratives wherever possible. Statistics and other facts can be used, but they should only buttress the personal view; they should not be a focus in themselves. The program people of your organization, as well as its beneficiaries, are the best sources for good stories.

(iii) Building credibility in the direct mail package   With the many recent scandals in the direct mail community, it is essential to establish your organization's credibility by:

Referring to the percentage of funds raised that goes directly to helping people—*if* that figure is very high;

Inviting the prospective donor to call or write the various charity watchdog agencies for information on you;

Claiming your organization's history as proof of your stability and good management (especially if it is more than 20 years old);

Pointing out (if true) that you operate on a shoestring budget, that your staff is underpaid or partially volunteer, and that your offices are anything but luxurious;

Using an endorsement from a prominent person who says, in effect, "I've checked out [your organization] thoroughly and I'm convinced they are a worthy, well-managed charity. I donate to them myself."

(iv) The use of personalization   Personalization—the use of computer-driven printers to spell out the prospect's name and address on the package elements—is a very expensive but very powerful tool. Generally, it is too expensive to use in acquisition mailings but very worthwhile for donor mailings. If your acquisition mailing program is healthy, test it against the nonpersonalized approach and see whether it is worth the extra expense for you.

(v) The use of premiums in acquisition mailings   Often, the inclusion of a premium, or gift, in an acquisition package can lift response. Because premiums also increase costs, their use must be carefully considered and tested in small quantities before a large mailing is undertaken. Some popular premiums include:

Membership or donor identification cards (cardboard or plastic) personalized by means of a computer-driven printer or left blank for the donor to fill in;

Labels personalized with the donor's name and address;

Stickers or seals bearing the organization's logo and/or a special message (e.g., Easter seals);

Bookmarks, mass or prayer cards, small reproductions of art, photographs;

Calendars (wallet-size cards, full-color wall calendars, or anything in between);

Pamphlets, booklets, or books on a subject matter related to the charity's cause (e.g., a collection of healthy recipes from a heart disease-related charity);

Greeting cards;

Decals or bumper stickers bearing the organization's logo.

The possibilities are limited only by the cost and size of the premium and its ability to withstand the machinery involved in the third-class mailing process.

(vi) A short roster of acquisition package concepts The following roster is, by necessity, far from inclusive; however, it offers successful package concepts for a variety of nonprofit organizations.

1. The *temporary membership card package* works well for membership groups like museums, symphony orchestras, and zoos. It involves sending a temporary ID card that entitles the bearer to a period of free membership (usually several months). The card will be activated and replaced with a permanent card once the new member's dues are received.

2. The *survey package* includes an opinion survey on a topic of extreme importance to the nonprofit organization. For example, an environmental group might send a survey asking for people's opinions on controversial legislation before Congress. The survey becomes an involvement device, important to the mailing not because it will be scientifically tabulated (it is not a statistically valid instrument), but because it draws people into the organization's cause. Related concepts include the petition package or enclosed postcards to be sent to the recipient's elected representatives or other officials. These packages strongly appeal to the prospect's desire to let his or her voice be heard on a matter of personal importance.

3. The *emergency package,* often used by hunger/medical relief organizations, states in starkest terms a threatening situation and asks for emergency assistance. This kind of package must be produced simply, without fancy design work; it should look as if it were dashed off at the last minute. Its success often hinges on the organization's credibility and the drama of the crisis.

4. The *"heavy premium" package* contains a premium that appears to have real financial value, rather than being simply an inexpensive addition to the package. "Heavy" premiums include a four-color wall calendar, a paperback book, or a packet of greeting cards. Such packages rely heavily on the premium as an attention-getting and guilt-inducing device. The organization's cause is explained in the accompanying letter, but the premium itself carries the effort. This is used successfully by many medical, religious, and social service charities.

5. The *heartstrings package* features sad stories of the actual or eventual fate of people or animals. The donor is told that this person's/animal's future is in the donor's hands. This package relies on very strong, emotional copy and often uses appealing or dramatic photographs of those in need.

To find additional acquisition package concepts that are working for nonprofit organizations, check your mailbox. Packages that turn up repeatedly are "control" packages—they have been proven to work well enough to justify their remailing.

(b) CREATING SUCCESSFUL DONOR AND RENEWAL DIRECT MAIL PACKAGES

Although packages mailed to an existing group of donors pose fewer creative challenges than acquisition packages, there are some rules of thumb that can prove extremely helpful.

(i) Ask for support for specific projects   Donors find requests for support for particular projects more appealing than requests to provide general operating support. They would greatly prefer funding a Christmas dinner for 400 homeless individuals to funding the salaries of the organization's staff or providing money to pay for any overhead expenses. As often as possible, frame your request in terms of a particular project or need, and provide as many details about the project and its costs as possible.

(ii) Use time-tested "institutional" approaches   Not every donor package can feature a specific project. The "institutional" package, focusing on the organization's overall needs, can be used occasionally to good effect when it is done correctly. An example of a typical institutional package is the year-end appeal, which recaps the organization's accomplishments over the past year, details plans for the year to come, and asks for the donor's continuing support. Other typical institutional packages include:

> The package announcing a major change or new program (e.g., the announcement that a new president has been selected for a university, or the launch of a major new research project by a medical charity);
>
> The upgrade package asking loyal donors to consider becoming major donors (e.g., asking a donor who is accustomed to giving $50 twice a year to become a $200-per-year donor); this package must make the case for the donor's increased involvement and support.

(iii) What your appeal package can and cannot do   The appeal package can:

> Bring in funds;
>
> Update your donors on events at your organization, thus enhancing their "family feeling";
>
> Pave the way for future contributions;
>
> Acknowledge the donor's past involvement (the package *must* do this!).

The appeal package cannot:

> Serve as a public relations piece; it is not a newsletter or press release, it is a personal and somewhat urgent communication, always from one individual to another individual, not from a committee or anonymous staff member to a wide audience;
>
> Compensate for controversy, bad feelings, or neglect; a direct mail letter cannot *by itself* take care of an image problem the organization is having, nor can it make up for a history of neglecting donors;
>
> Serve as its own thank-you letter; donors should always be thanked for their contributions *separately from* the appeal mailing. It is unwise to beg off from sending a receipt and thank-you, asking the donor to "understand that funds are short." People give because they feel an emotional connection to your cause. The least you can do is send them a stand-alone thank-you letter for every gift given.

(iv) To personalize or not to personalize   In donor mailings, the added cost of personalization is often overshadowed by the increased response personalization brings. However, many organizations find it most economical to "segment" their donor file, sending a personalized version of an appeal mailing to high-dollar donors and a non-personalized version to those below a certain gift amount threshold. There is no single guideline for how to segment; careful testing of your donor file is the only sure way to determine the right balance for your organization.

(v) The use of premiums in donor mailings   The premiums discussed above can all be added to donor mailings, and often produce excellent results. This is particularly true when your donors have been acquired through the use of premiums. It is effective to be able to say, "This premium has been produced exclusively for supporters like you, to thank you for all your help." Using a premium does not negate the need for a strong fund-raising proposition in the package's letter. Be sure that your letter could do at least marginally well without the premium.

(vi) Renewals vs. a series of appeals   Membership organizations may send a series of membership renewal notices in addition to, or in place of, the types of donor appeals used by nonmembership groups. Membership organizations that follow current events closely may find it better to use a series of appeal letters rather than renewals, because late-breaking events can be used to excellent advantage as topics of appeal mailings, whereas the renewal series is not based on minute-by-minute developments. Here are some basic pointers for a membership renewal series for a nonprofit group.

1. Mail at least five notices, and test more. The rule of thumb here is to keep sending renewal notices until the response no longer justifies it. Bear in mind that magazine publishers have sent as many as 23 renewal notices, because it is so much less expensive to renew an existing subscriber than to acquire a new one! The same holds true for members of and donors to nonprofit organizations.

2. Start well in advance of the expiration date—at least four months out. This gives you time to escalate from a gentle reminder to an urgent warning. Most groups find their highest response comes early in the series, even when notices come five or six months prior to expiration.

3. Continue to send renewals—at least one or two—*after* expiration. Give the person the chance to reactivate the membership. If membership benefits (such as a publication or free admission) are offered, remind the member that these will be reinstated immediately upon receipt of the renewal payment.

4. In terms of copy, increase the urgency with every notice. Start out low-key, recapping the organization's mission and plans. With each notice, add urgency. Often, the notice at expiration time comes in the form of a mock telegram, urging immediate action. A friendlier, more inviting tone returns in the notices after expiration.

5. Remind the member/donor what his/her money has accomplished, and what will happen without his/her support in the coming year.

6. Follow all the usual rules of direct mail copywriting and design. Letters can be somewhat shorter than for regular appeal mailings, but they do not have to be. Write copy long enough to tell your story and make your pitch.

7. If you have a special way of recognizing members/donors, appeal to their desire to be acknowledged in this way by pointing out that their names will appear in the Annual Report *only* if they renew. A variant on this is a reminder that they will receive a prized invitation to a special event only if the renewal is received by a particular date.

8. Avoid the use of premiums in the renewal series. Rewarding early renewers can be done profitably; however, this risks alienation and resentment from those who renew a bit later. It is definitely unwise to offer a premium to late renewers. This encourages members to "hold out" for the premium in subsequent years, costing the organization more money for sending the premium and for additional efforts to get the renewal gift.

Generally speaking, much creative attention should be lavished on the renewal series, which is too often taken for granted by nonprofit organizations.

(vii)   A short roster of successful appeal package concepts

1. The *crisis package* is built around a true emergency, such as "We will have to cancel our Christmas food distribution unless we receive XX,XXX by November 15." Use it sparingly, or you risk building an image of a poorly managed organization and straining your donors' credulity.

2. The *scholarship package* asks for funds to send a child to summer camp, a young person to college, or a college student to a special learning opportunity such as an internship. It works best when individual case histories can be detailed, when the amount of money needed is specified, and when a deadline date is given.

3. The *outrage package* is a good choice when an event has occurred that will infuriate your donors. An excellent example is the recent Medicare Catastrophic Coverage Expansion Act, passed by Congress in 1990, which would have required the payment of additional fees by individuals covered by Medicare. A number of senior citizens' groups decried this law as unfair to older Americans, and many successful packages were mailed asking for funds to help fight the Act. The groups collected a great deal of money and won their battle.

4. The *involvement package,* a close cousin of the outrage package, asks the donor to write to his or her Congressional representatives or other officials and often offers postcards or petitions to mail. There are a number of other variations on this theme. For this package to be successful, legislation or a ruling on a "hot" issue must be pending.

5. The *story package* characterizes most donor appeals. An especially compelling story about a beneficiary of the organization is told in detail. From this particular situation, the copy goes on to generalize about the need for the organization's services and to ask for financial support. The success of this package hinges on the appeal of the story or stories and the skill of the copywriter. This is a "no holds barred," emotional package.

In the life of most nonprofit organizations, many successful concepts for fundraising appeals will present themselves to staff members who seek them. For some groups, especially those whose mission does not involve direct service of some kind, the concepts can be more difficult to find. However, nearly every group can and should find an occasion to mail an appeal at least four times a year. With care and imagination, a strong direct mail program can be built for almost any organization.

SOURCES AND SUGGESTED REFERENCES

Benson, Richard V. 1987. *Secrets of Successful Direct Mail.* Savannah, GA: The Benson Organization.

Caples, John. 1974. *Tested Advertising Methods* (4th ed.). Englewood Cliffs, NJ: Prentice-Hall.

Himes, David P. 1982. *D.F.M.R. Sample Book.* Unpublished; used as text in course at George Washington University, Washington, DC.

Kuniholm, Roland. 1989. *Maximum Gifts by Return Mail.* Ambler, PA: Fund-Raising Institute.

Lautman, Kay Partney, and Goldstein, Henry. 1984. *Dear Friend: Mastering the Art of Direct Mail Fund Raising.* Rockville, MD: The Taft Group.

Throckmorton, Joan. 1987. *Winning Direct Response Advertising: How to Recognize It, Evaluate It, Inspire It, Create It.* Englewood Cliffs, NJ: Prentice-Hall.

Trenbeth, Richard P. 1986. *The Membership Mystique.* Ambler, PA: Fund-Raising Institute.

Warwick, Mal. 1990. *Revolution in the Mailbox.* Berkeley, CA: Strathmoor Press.

CHAPTER EIGHTEEN

Membership Development

Constance Clark
Clark Communications

CONTENTS

18.1 MEMBERS OR DONORS? DEFINING THE DIFFERENCE

People who support nonprofit organizations can be called friends, supporters, donors, sponsors, members, or any number of other names. They all connote one basic fact: An individual has given something of value, usually money, to the organization. The term *member* implies something else as well: The individual is *receiving certain benefits* and *holding certain responsibilities* as a result of having given a financial gift or paid annual dues.

(a) ADVANTAGES OF A MEMBERSHIP PROGRAM For some nonprofit organizations, conferring membership on supporters has a number of advantages over simply addressing them as donors:

- Membership builds loyalty. It gives people a greater sense of ownership or participation in the organization's mission and activities.
- Membership builds depth of commitment. People feel they are important beyond simply the amount of money they can give. Their volunteer help, opinions, and, sometimes, voting rights on policy and program matters are also important to the organization.
- Membership includes participation as part of the organization's action network. Members expect to be called on to take certain actions, such as participating in petition drives or writing to elected officials, especially as "hot" issues arise in the public arena.
- Membership conceptually prepares people to continue their support through annual membership renewals. When a person becomes a *donor* to an organization, he or she does not necessarily expect to be asked to renew the gift; a *member* knows or assumes that membership renewal will be an annual event.
- Membership programs solicit a higher-quality donor. Although it may be more difficult initially to solicit a membership dues gift rather than a one-time donation, supporters who do say "yes" to the membership option will usually stay with the organization longer. Members are also more likely to respond to appeals for larger gifts.

(b) TYPES OF ORGANIZATIONS BEST SUITED TO MEMBERSHIP PROGRAMS   Despite their advantages, membership programs may not work well in some organizations. They have been found to be best suited for:

1. Organizations promoting a political or social cause: an environmental advocacy group; a group of people wishing to promote patriotism; a group banding together to pass or defeat specific legislation;
2. Organizations representing the interests of a particular segment of society: a coalition of retired persons, like the American Association for Retired Persons; veterans' groups; groups promoting racial or gender equality;
3. Organizations with a cultural or academic mission: museums or galleries; zoos or botanical gardens; "think tanks" or academic institutes.

18.2 SETTING UP THE MEMBERSHIP PROGRAM

(a) MEMBERSHIP BENEFITS   Nearly every organization offering membership privileges in exchange for payment of dues (and possibly also requiring the meeting of other criteria) offers specific *benefits* to those who are accepted as members. In creating these benefits, the possibilities are limited only by the organization's budgetary concerns. However, a body of frequently offered benefits can be defined. Some of the most popular membership benefits offered by America's nonprofit membership groups are:

1. Periodicals: newsletters, magazines, or journals; typically a subscription to one or more of these is free once membership dues have been paid;
2. Directories: addresses of members, related organizations, or other types of resources;

3. Membership card: a plastic or cardboard card showing the member's name and address and identifying him or her as a member (often, a membership ID number and membership expiration date are included, and presenting this card may entitle the member to certain benefits, (such as a discount in a museum's shop); decals, bumper stickers, certificates, and other logo items identifying the owner as a member of the organization may also be offered;

4. Access to special programs, events, or services: an organization may make certain programs or services available only for members; for example, a botanical garden may offer a free telephone advice service to members who have gardening questions, or a museum may invite members to attend a new exhibit before the general public is admitted;

5. Discounts on programs, services, and products: members may receive a discount on courses, tours, seminars, information services, insurance programs, and any products an organization may sell; for example, members receive a 10 percent discount on all purchases from the Smithsonian Institution's museum shops and catalog;

6. Eligibility to serve as a volunteer or officer, and/or to have a vote in the organization's decisions and elections.

New membership benefits may be developed by surveying members for their wants and needs, brainstorming with staff and volunteer leadership, and simply looking at the marketplace. For example, when a gardening organization recognized that many of its members could not find a wide range of gardening books in their local bookstores, it arranged a mail-order book-buyer's service. Members were given a discount on purchases; nonmembers could use the service, but would not receive the discount. As a membership benefit, the book-buyer's service met several important criteria:

1. It provided a steady stream of additional income to the organization.

2. It provided a service that members could not find elsewhere. Although a gardening book club existed, it did not offer as wide a variety of books, the same level of personalized service, the implied "seal of approval" that the prestigious gardening organization placed on the books selected for the book-buyer's service, or the special discount to members.

3. It cost the organization very little to set up the book-buyer's service. The books could be ordered from publishers *after* members' orders were placed, thus obviating the need to keep an inventory on hand. Initially, the organization advertised the available books in its existing publications and provided an order coupon; no special catalog or mailing was needed. Because the organization's publications director was already reviewing books for its magazine, even selecting the initial list of books for sale did not present additional work!

When considering new or existing membership benefits, it is important to remember that *perceived value* can be a major factor in the members' evaluation of a benefit. A membership certificate of ID card that costs the organization pennies can be extremely important to members—sometimes even more important than an expensive four-color magazine. Indeed, the major benefit of membership for most people may be entirely intangible: a sense of belonging, or the satisfaction of being a contributor to an important cause or movement. Even though they might be inexpensive and

Exhibit 18.1.   Example of membership categories and benefits.

Category	Dues Amount	Benefits
Member	$ 25	Subscription to newsletter; 10% discount at museum shop; membership card.
Supporter	50	Basic benefits *plus* a free color catalog from a museum exhibit.
Benefactor	100	All of the above *plus* free advance admission to new museum exhibits.
Patron	500+	All of the above *plus* an invitation to the annual gala dinner.

inelegant, tangible benefits that represent these feelings to members may well be treasured by those who wish to belong or to identify themselves with a cause or a particular group of people.

(b) MEMBERSHIP CATEGORIES   Some organizations find it useful to create a system that includes several categories of membership. These categories may be created to accommodate different groups of people; for example, an academic or research institute might have *fellows,* who are scientists involved professionally but not directly in the organization's work; *members,* who support it through gifts of money and time; and *affiliates,* who are students or others involved peripherally with the organization's mission.

More commonly, nonprofit organizations set up categories according to the *size of donation* made by the member. These categories are sometimes referred to as "gift clubs." A typical group of membership categories for a museum is shown in Exhibit 18.1.

Organizations can use "stepped" categories like these to encourage members to give more money, or "upgrade" themselves from one level of commitment to the next. An effective way to encourage upgrades is to use the first letter of a membership renewal series as a special invitation to step up to the next category. This letter should be personalized and specific, letting the member know what additional benefits await in the next category (and in those further above the current level as well). An additional gift may be offered as an incentive to make the leap.

Membership categories or "gift clubs" work well for cultural organizations, alumni associations, parks, gardens, aquaria, and zoos, because these organizations offer high prestige by association and/or many popular and tangible benefits. Groups whose mission is more cause-oriented will probably not find membership categories as useful. For example, a humane society whose main goal is to promote spaying and neutering of pets will not be able to produce the attractive types of benefits that come naturally to an art gallery. In these cases, it is best to avoid membership categories keyed to donation size. Larger gifts can be solicited simply on the basis of urgent need, and a simple "thank you" is sufficient reward when the cause is emotionally compelling to the member.

18.3   RECRUITING NEW MEMBERS

The first task at hand for any membership organization is to build a body of members. For some, this task is easy; an alumni association, for example, will simply consider everyone who attended the school to be a member, although some members may be inactive. For most organizations, however, building a membership base is an expensive, time-consuming, and crucial challenge.

(a) DETERMINING YOUR POTENTIAL MEMBER UNIVERSE Before setting up a membership campaign, an organization needs to determine goals, and these goals should be based on a realistic assessment of the marketplace. Again, this can be fairly easy; for example, an association of returned Peace Corps volunteers can consult past membership records to estimate the number of prospective members. For most organizations, there is no single source of potential members. Sophisticated market research methods, such as scientifically valid surveys, can be undertaken; however, these are inexact and very expensive. Administrators can guess at their potential member universe by looking at the following information:

1. How many *competitor* organizations exist? How large are their membership rolls? How are they different? Can a smaller niche be carved from a larger organization by offering a more specialized group? Or can the organization serve as an umbrella, gathering members from several smaller groups?

2. How many individuals *share an interest* in the organization's mission? This cannot always be determined; however, figures available from a number of polls and surveys give an idea of how many Americans enjoy certain hobbies, like scuba diving or needlework, and how many are in various demographic categories (the number of parents with college-age children, for example).

3. How many names are available through *list rental or exchange?* A reputable list-brokerage firm can be consulted for information on mailing lists that have produced good direct-mail results for comparable organizations. Would colleague organizations be willing to exchange mailing lists, for purposes of membership solicitation?

With these figures in hand, the administrator can estimate, based on past experience or the experience of like organizations, what *percentage* of these individuals might respond positively to a membership offer. Given the vagaries of direct marketing and other forms of promotion, this is still an extremely rough estimate that can be verified only by actual testing; however, it gives the nonprofit organization's leadership an idea of what might be possible.

(b) MEMBER RECRUITMENT METHODS By far, the most widely used method of member recruitment in the United States today is *direct mail.* Groups of all sizes and with every type of purpose have learned to use direct mail economically and effectively, to build and enlarge their membership bases. (See Chapter 17 for more information on creating effective direct mail packages.) However, launching a major direct mail membership campaign can require a large initial investment that does not "pay off" until a year (or longer) after the new members are acquired. For this reason, direct mail membership acquisition campaigns must be carefully considered, planned, and financed. Smaller-scale direct mail campaigns can be undertaken at lower risk and expense, especially by local groups.

(i) Direct mail *Direct mail* package concepts that have been used successfully in membership promotion are described briefly in the following paragraphs.

1. The *nomination package* plays on the prestige of the organization and announces that the prospective member has been selected for membership by the board of trustees or nominated by a current member. The National Geographic Society and the Smithsonian Institution have used this approach with great success for a number of years.

2. The *trial membership package* offers a short-term free membership; a dues payment is not requested until after the trial membership has begun, at which time a series of invoices is sent to the new member. This is an inviting offer precisely because it offers something for nothing. Accepting the trial membership does not obligate the prospective member in any way; he or she may cancel at any time and pay nothing.

3. The *temporary membership card package* is really a variation on the trial membership package. The prospect is given an ID card good for a specified amount of time (often three months). A validated, permanent ID card is sent upon payment of dues. This package plays on the perceived value of a membership card; it is effective to show the member's name, printed on the ID card, through a window in the carrier envelope.

4. The *survey or petition package* is a means for advocacy organizations to recruit new members by asking for their opinion and/or help in promoting a specific cause. As an example, when Congress passed a law increasing Medicare premiums, retirees' groups mailed packages inviting people to "tell Congress what you think!" *and* to join their organization in order to fight the law and *future* threats to senior citizens' well-being. Many of these packages were extremely successful, and most asked the recipient either to (a) fill out an opinion survey and return it to the group, which would then tabulate the results and announce them to Congress, other officials, and the media; or to (b) sign and return to an elected official a petition or postcard stating displeasure with the new law. Known as "involvement devices," the petitions, postcards, and surveys work very well for groups with a political or social change agenda.

See Chapter 17 for other direct mail package concepts that may be adapted for use in membership promotion.

(ii) Telemarketing *Telemarketing* can be used by alumni or religious organizations to *activate* members who are on the rolls passively (e.g., simply by having attended a school or church at some time in the past). It is also effective in membership renewal (see below). However, it is not a cost-effective tool for outreach to individuals who are not already affiliated in some way with the ongoing group.

(iii) Members *Member-get-a-member campaigns* can work well for groups that have a fairly specific mission, like professional societies or hobby clubs, *if* there is a core group of highly motivated members who will participate in the effort. These campaigns tend to work best for local groups, not for large national coalitions where personal contact is at a minimum. A contest can be run to see who will bring in the highest number of new members, and a reward can be offered to the winner.

A variation on member-get-a-member campaigns is the *nomination campaign,* wherein current members are asked to nominate prospective members. The individuals nominated by current members then receive a letter of invitation from the organization's president, informing them of their nomination and offering them a special opportunity to join, often at a reduced dues rate or with a special gift for joining. Usually, current members are given a small gift for providing names; one wildlife organization offered its supporters a full-color calendar for providing five names and address of prospective members.

(iv)   Brochures   Distributing *flyers, package inserts, and "take-ones"* (small brochures placed in racks at stores and other public places) is an inexpensive way to supplement more aggressive membership recruitment methods. Putting the promotional piece in the right place is the key to success; for example, a brochure promoting membership in a local writers' club might produce good results when placed on a library, bookstore, or secretarial service counter but would glean *no* responses from a similar perch at a sports center. The venue must be chosen carefully, with an aim to "narrow-casting," not broadcasting.

(v)   Public relations   *Public relations and free publicity* can bring in new members for an organization; however, they usually do so indirectly. To illustrate this point, imagine that an organization's special event receives a great deal of free publicity, and that 100 people new to the organization attend. Out of those 100 individuals, only 10 have more than a casual interest in the organization's basic mission. Out of those 10, 5 pick up membership brochures and only 1 person actually joins. The membership administrator cannot count on large numbers of new members from such efforts. Still, public relations efforts are vital in supporting other membership recruitment methods such as direct mail. The more the organization's name is heard and its reputation is known, the more likely that people will respond to its solicitations positively.

(vi)   Advertising   *Paid advertising* for membership promotion in magazines and newspapers and on radio and television is usually prohibitively expensive compared with the results it garners. Even donated advertising space or time is better used to promote the organization's overall mission than to recruit members. The sale of a membership is a fairly complicated transaction; the prospect wants to know more about the group than can usually be presented in a small space or a brief amount of time, which is probably one reason why direct mail is effective in membership recruitment: more room is available to explain the group's purpose and to sell the benefits of membership.

(vii)   Gifts   Promoting *gift memberships* can be extremely profitable for organizations like museums, galleries, and zoos. They are easy to sell in a newsletter, magazine, or simple special mailing; they are inexpensive to process and fulfill; and, best of all, they are usually renewed at a very high rate. (After all, who wants to explain to Aunt Agatha that her gift membership in the local art gallery won't be renewed this year?) Membership program administrators need to review their data processing capabilities to make sure their computer records can handle gift membership donor and recipient information cleanly. Extra staff, volunteer or paid, may be needed to process gift membership in a timely manner during the Christmas holiday rush. These additional tasks are usually well repaid in the revenue a gift membership program generates.

18.4   RENEWING MEMBERS

Recruiting new members is usually so expensive and difficult that organizations often do not recoup their initial investment in membership promotion until membership renewal time. Compared to acquiring members, renewing members is easy. However, it is unwise to take renewals for granted; they provide the bulk of the membership income for most membership organizations.

To maximize membership renewals, the membership program administrator can consider the following efforts.

(a) EVALUATE MEMBER COMMUNICATIONS AND SERVICES   No matter how effective an organization's renewal letters may be, members will not renew if they are unhappy with the benefits and service they have received. Administrators can keep a finger on the pulse of member (customer) satisfaction by:

1. Reading notes and letters members send in with renewal checks and other correspondence;
2. Reviewing the process by which member complaints and problems are handled (Is service speedy, polite, and efficient?);
3. Surveying members, formally or informally. A market research firm can be retained to conduct a study of current and/or past members, or the organization's staff can create its own survey to be inserted in a newsletter or renewal mailing. Informal focus groups can also be convened, and the program administrator can receive a good deal of feedback simply by telephoning a few members occasionally to see how they feel about the organization.

(b) CREATE AN EFFECTIVE DIRECT MAIL RENEWAL SERIES   Many membership organizations fail to maximize their renewal potential because they neglect to *resolicit* their members effectively. Resoliciting is the task of the direct mail renewal series. The renewals must recap the sales propositions that initially convinced members to join, and they must do so persistently.

(i) How many efforts?   Each organization must determine, by trial and error, the right number of renewal letters to mail. The rule of thumb is to continue sending renewal efforts until the return no longer pays for the costs of the mailing. Generally speaking, organizations start with *too few* renewal notices. Five or six renewal letters is a good starting number for creating a renewal series; many organizations send more and do so profitably. Although this may seem excessive, it is important to remember that renewing an existing member is almost always less expensive than finding a new member to take his or her place!

(ii) What about timing?   Renewals should start early—at least four months before the member's expiration date. Most organizations send renewals on a monthly basis through the expiration date and even one month afterward, and follow up with a post-expiration "rejoin" mailing even later.

(iii) What should the copy tone and message be?   The copy for early efforts in the series should be friendly, appreciative, and relaxed, while reiterating the major reasons for renewing membership (benefits, prestige, the importance of the organization's mission). As the series continues, a sense of urgency should build, and the importance of maintaining membership continuously should be emphasized. Copy can be shorter in renewal letters than in membership acquisition efforts; a one-page letter is standard. However, some groups use longer letters to good effect in early efforts, especially if a membership upgrade is being solicited.

(c) TELEMARKETING IN RENEWALS Telemarketing is a highly effective tool in renewing members. Usually, it is used late in the renewal series, for example, immediately preceding or following the expiration date. A professional firm can be contracted to handle the telemarketing effort, or, for smaller organizations, a phone bank of volunteers can be assembled. In either case, a well-written script and thorough training of the telemarketers are essential.

(d) RECAPTURING LAPSED MEMBERSHIPS Organizations should not give up on members who have allowed their membership to lapse. Generally speaking, at least another 1 to 2 percent of them can be induced to rejoin within the year following their expiration date.

Lapsed members can be approached by phone or by mail. Some organizations offer a special gift for rejoiners, but this practice can encourage members to hold off on renewing to see what kind of reward they may receive—an outcome that is in no way beneficial to the organization! A reinstatement mailing might include a letter long enough to explain adequately the reasons for joining—in other words, to resell the membership. "We miss you and want you back" is an inviting, personal, and effective theme.

Those who do not respond to a reinstatement mailing can be put on a special list for future new-member acquisition campaigns. Often, these lapsed members respond as well (or better) to new-member solicitations as do individuals on rented or borrowed mailing lists. However, attempting aggressively to renew members is better than waiting and reinstating them, which is a more costly and less successful proposition.

Membership programs provide a vital source of income for major institutions (the Smithsonian, the Metropolitan Museum of Art, the National Geographic Society, The Wilderness Society, World Wildlife Fund—U.S., the American Society for Prevention of Cruelty to Animals, to name only a few). Smaller groups also benefit from the membership concept, as do individuals seeking a way to belong to something larger than themselves—a community of people who care about an idea, a group of people, or an institution. Well-run membership programs are advancing philanthropic organizations across the nation today. For this reason, every nonprofit organization can benefit from assessing the possibilities of a membership program, or enhancing an existing program, now and periodically in the future.

SOURCES AND SUGGESTED REFERENCES

Benson, Richard V. 1987. *Secrets of Successful Direct Mail.* Savannah, GA: The Benson Organization.

Caples, John. 1974. *Tested Advertising Methods* (4th ed.). Englewood Cliffs, NJ: Prentice-Hall.

Himes, David P. 1982. *D.F.M.R. Sample Book.* Unpublished; used as text in course at George Washington University, Washington, DC.

Kuniholm, Roland. 1989. *Maximum Gifts by Return Mail*. Ambler, PA: Fund-Raising Institute.

Lautman, Kay Partney, and Goldstein, Henry. 1984. *Dear Friend: Mastering the Art of Direct Mail Fund Raising*. Rockville, MD: The Taft Group.

Throckmorton, Joan. 1987. *Winning Direct Response Advertising: How to Recognize It, Evaluate It, Inspire It, Create It*. Englewood Cliffs, NJ: Prentice-Hall.

Trenbeth, Richard P. 1986. *The Membership Mystique*. Ambler, PA: Fund-Raising Institute.

Warwick, Mal. 1990. *Revolution in the Mailbox*. Berkeley, CA: Strathmoor Press.

Annual Giving Programs

Nan D. Doty
Doty & Cox

Barbara M. Cox
Doty & Cox

CONTENTS

19.1 ANNUAL VERSUS CAPITAL CAMPAIGNS

(a) ANNUAL CAMPAIGNS Annual campaigns are designed to provide funds for basic program operations and normal growth. They address relatively short-term needs (a year or less) and focus on individual giving, corporations, foundations, and civic groups.

Annual campaigns are, by their very nature, intended to be repeatable. Each campaign becomes the foundation for an expanded effort the following year. Donors understand that their support this year will be rewarded by a request for renewed and often increased support the year after. Volunteers know that succession planning is an important part of the organization's financial development.

Virtually any and every technique of fund-raising can be useful in an annual giving campaign. Phonathons, direct mail, one-on-one solicitations, and major or minor special events are some common options. Crafting an annual giving plan that makes the best use of agency human and fiscal resources is the key to effectiveness.

The public sector provides a large portion of the annual income for many nonprofit organizations, but public grant seeking is not ordinarily considered a component of annual giving.

(b) CAPITAL CAMPAIGNS   Capital campaigns are undertaken to achieve a major organizational goal for which an extraordinary investment is required. A local hospital wishes to establish a cancer treatment center. The YWCA demonstrates the need for a child care facility. The Girl Scout Council believes an endowment can be created to support programs that will serve low-income communities.

Instead of the thousands typically raised in annual giving campaigns, capital goals are often in the millions of dollars. Often, top corporate executives are enlisted to lead the effort. Wealthy individuals agree to give and to seek special gifts from other people who are in a position to make significant commitments. Big gifts are encouraged by utilizing multiyear pledges.

Prominent people are willing to get involved and to make extraordinary contributions because capital campaigns are rare events in the life of an organization. The defined goal and limited timetable also are attractive to volunteers.

Although special events, particularly *cultivation* events, can be part of a capital campaign, these campaigns rely primarily on face-to-face solicitation. Each request is carefully planned to match the strongest asker with the right prospect. The prospect universe is limited to major donors, in contrast to annual giving campaigns, which often emphasize small gifts from large numbers of people.

With the exception of the Kresge Foundation in Michigan, few professionally staffed foundations give to capital campaigns outside their own locality.

In recent years, a trend in capital campaigns has been the decision to precede the campaign with a feasibility study conducted by fund-raising consultants. (Most capital campaigns are themselves organized with the help of consultants who specialize in this area.) A feasibility study, a particular kind of market research, is designed to test potential donor support and to identify people who are ready, willing, and able to lead such an effort.

19.2   GETTING STARTED: DEVELOPING A FUND-RAISING PLAN

(a) EVALUATE PAST ACTIVITIES   Where an organization is going depends, at least initially, on where it has been. A good annual giving plan is a roadmap for a 12-month journey that will bring the organization home to as many different donors as possible. The plan begins with an analysis of contributions over the past three to five years:

1. What sources have been tapped?
2. How was the income obtained?
3. Is the income from a particular source growing, declining, or staying the same?
4. What are the direct (i.e., printing, postage, rental fees) and indirect (staff salaries, agency overhead) costs of raising these funds?

(b) IDENTIFY WHERE SUPPORT IS NEEDED   If the agency has multiple programs, which ones cover their own costs or break even? Which ones have a deficit? Who is served by each program? Can the program generate more income—by increasing fees, for example—thereby reducing the need for charitable contributions?

(c) IDENTIFY POTENTIAL FUND-RAISING MARKETS   This part of the plan has three phases. First, list the various sources of contributions and the techniques for obtaining them. (One technique may apply to a variety of sources.) Exhibit 19.1 shows a typical list.

Second, determine the answers to the following questions:

1. How much money might be anticipated from each sector?
2. What are the agency's strengths and weaknesses in terms of contacting each sector?
3. What will it cost in time (staff and volunteer) and direct expenditures to pursue each opportunity?

Finally, set supportable priorities. Where is the potentially biggest payoff, the maximum return on the investment of time and effort? What is expected to be the least productive source?

(d) ESTABLISH A DOLLAR GOAL   A realistic goal is important, and it can only be set after some careful analysis:

1. Look at the shortfall between anticipated revenue and desired program expenditures.

Exhibit 19.1.   List of potential contributors and proposed solicitation techniques.

Sources	Techniques
Individuals (major gifts)	Personal solicitation
Individuals (small gifts)	Direct mail
Individuals (bequests)	Phonathons
Foundations	Proposals
Corporations	Joint ventures
Civic groups	Raffles
	Special events (specify options)

2. Evaluate that figure in light of prior fund-raising results.

3. Consider what might be accomplished if a growth goal of x percent were established.

4. Ask whether this is realistic, based on an assessment of where contributions are likely to be obtained.

5. Take the total dollar goal and divide it among the different elements of the annual giving program: $x from the year-end mail appeal, $y from the dinner dance, $z from foundations, corporations, and civic groups.

(e) CREATE A CALENDAR AND PUT SOMEONE IN CHARGE OF EACH PROJECT Designate a person who is assigned specific responsibility for each element, and devise project timetables that can be used to match up actual events against the plan's schedule. Each plan should start with the completion date and build backward. As shown in Exhibit 19.2, the overall plan is the sum total of the particular activities.

(f) GIVE RECOGNITION It is just about impossible to say thank you too often. Every volunteer who works on any aspect of annual giving should receive a letter of thanks or a phone call from the chief volunteer officer (usually the president or chairperson of the board).

Work efforts should also be acknowledged publicly at board meetings, at membership meetings, and—with a tangible expression of thanks—at the annual meeting. Donors *and* annual giving volunteers should be saluted in agency newsletters.

The *primary* purpose of the annual report should be donor recognition. Keep the narrative lively (and brief!) and prominently list every donor within categories or "giving clubs" that signal large gifts.

These "giving clubs" should be listed on the gift information card included with the appeal (Exhibit 19.3). Each organization needs to determine appropriate target levels based on the history and potential of its donors.

Exhibit 19.2. Work plan for year-end appeal.

Completion Date	Activity	Responsibility
September 15	Gifts logged; "acknowledger" notified	Staff (specify)
	Acknowledgments sent, with copies to personal contacts	Staff or volunteers
October 1	Report generated for Appeal Committee	Staff or volunteers
October 15	Follow-up calls (phonathon)	Appeal Committee; board members
November 1	Letters mailed	Staff or volunteers
November 15	Personal notes added	Appeal Committee; board members
November 22–24	Appeal printed	Staff or volunteers
Daily, as gifts arrive	Appeal drafted and approved	Staff or volunteers; Appeal Committee
Weekly	List updated, expanded	All

Exhibit 19.3. Giving clubs.

The President's Circle	(Gifts of $5,000 and above)
Benefactors	(Gifts of $1,000 to $4,999)
Community Builders	(Gifts of $500 to $999)
Patrons	(Gifts of $100 to $499)
Sponsors	(All others)

Send *every* donor a copy of the annual report. Include a brief note of thanks and point out that the agency would not have accomplished all that it did "without your generosity."

19.3 FUND-RAISING MARKETS

(a) INDIVIDUALS Individual donors should receive the lion's share of attention in any annual giving plan. The numbers tell why: 80 percent of all giving comes from individuals. When planned giving and bequests are included, the total rises to nearly 90 percent.

Individuals who are close to the organization and who have the ability to make significant contributions should be solicited in person; others may be most efficiently contacted by mail. Volunteers and staff can create lists of people who, they believe, would be interested in agency programs. A special event that offers a fun experience or something of value may bring in people who have had no previous connection to the organization.

The annual giving plan should include the creation of lists that build on the agency's constituencies:

1. Present donors;
2. Prior donors;
3. Volunteers (they are giving their time, but they can be educated to give money, too);
4. Prior leadership (stay in touch with past board members, and not just as donors; too many organizations let them slip away without a ripple!);
5. Members (they are paying for a service, but they can be reminded that they are getting a bargain);
6. Friends of board and staff members (who will receive a personal note on the appeal).

(b) INSTITUTIONS

(i) Corporations For most organizations, scant income produced for basic operations will be produced from this sector. Overall, corporate giving accounts for less than 5 percent of total philanthropy. Most corporate gifts are small, even from giant companies. Significant corporate gifts are almost always elicited through personal relationships with top executives. It is virtually useless to send "cold" letters to a list of companies where no personal contacts exist.

Many large companies have, within their marketing budget, funds that can be made available to underwrite activities that may enhance their visibility in markets they value.

(ii) Foundations   Foundation giving accounts for another 5 percent (approximately) of total giving. Well-known, professionally staffed foundations rarely give to ongoing local programs. Directors of Development of major organizations spend countless hours trying to recast their proposals so that they are "innovative" and "national models."

Community foundations present the best opportunity for obtaining a significant grant for local or regional organizations. These foundations, formed by gifts from many unrelated individuals, will readily provide information about how to apply for a contribution and they like to fund new programs or programs that provide services to new populations. Most grants are for one year (occasionally, two). Applicants must be prepared with a good answer as to how the program will be funded after the grant money has been spent.

"Family foundations" can be a resource for local groups. There are thousands of these small, unstaffed foundations. Personal contacts are essential: "cold" requests will not even be acknowledged. *The National Data Book,* published by The Foundation Center and available in many libraries, lists family foundations by state, including information about assets and, usually, the name and address of an officer. Additional information about these small foundations appears in state foundation directories, available in most public libraries, or in the "990" (tax return) files maintained at branches of The Foundation Center. (See Section 19.8, "Resources.")

(iii) Service clubs   The Rotary, Kiwanis, Junior League, or Women's Club—every area has a host of service clubs that award financial grants among their other activities. Some like to support scholarships; others like to give equipment. Some sponsor specific program interests. With a little digging, a member can be found who will serve as guide and advocate for the request.

19.4   THE CASE FOR GIVING

Effective fund-raising is rooted in the organization's mission statement and the program priorities established through a long-range or strategic planning process. The term "case statement" comes from capital campaigns. Often presented in the form of a brochure, the case statement contains the rationale on which requests for support are based.

The case statement is a marketing or advocacy piece. It establishes that the need being addressed is important to potential donors by providing information about the people to be helped. It positions the organization as well-qualified to address the targeted problems.

A case statement for annual giving may only be one or two pages long. It should answer as many of these questions as possible:

1. What are the problems or opportunities?
2. Who is affected?
3. What is the proposed solution?
4. How will the problem be solved (what steps will be taken)?

5. Who will do the work?

6. What will be the result?

7. What difference will it make to the people with the problem? To the community?

8. Why is this organization uniquely qualified to address this problem?

9. What will it cost?

10. What's in it for the donor? (Good feelings, a healthier community, reduced crime, a more just society?)

Exhibit 19.4.   Sample case statement.

Meeting the Challenge

For four decades, AGENCY has been a lifeline for people with developmental and physical disabilities—and a bridge to friendship, work, and self-reliance.

During these years, we have wept together, laughed together, and celebrated small steps and large. Families with great wealth and families with little or none have found an understanding and supportive community dedicated to helping their special person be the best he or she can be.

Today, however, AGENCY itself must seek extraordinary help. Our ability to meet the needs of families in our community is in jeopardy. At a time when State funding has been cut back, AGENCY faces pressing demands for *increased* service:

- This year, AGENCY has been asked by area school systems to serve twenty graduates who have severe multiple disabilities;
- Our pioneering work with younger and younger infants is straining our resources;
- We have eliminated nine staff positions and have told the staff there will be no salary increases, in response to this year's budget.

A special campaign is being launched by board members, other volunteers, and staff, to strengthen AGENCY's financial resources. This effort is being greatly aided by a challenge gift made by an AGENCY family. They have pledged $25,000 if the campaign's donors will match that amount, to allow AGENCY to continue to serve all the children and adults who need our varied programs.

AGENCY's involvement sometimes begins prenatally, when a family anticipating the birth of an infant with Down's syndrome seeks information about the quality of life and community support that await their child.

- *Our Center for Infant and Child Development* provides integrated early intervention services through the age of five. These services enhance development and minimize developmental delay.
- *Employment Training* includes training and placement in competitive positions, employment as the member of a AGENCY work crew within a business, and placement in our sheltered workshop.
- *Senior Services* offer exercise, lectures, arts and crafts, and trips to stores, restaurants, parks, and nature centers.
- *Social Services* provide counseling, advocacy, assessment, and help in securing housing, financial, medical, and legal assistance.

From the youngest baby in our infant program to the oldest senior who comes to AGENCY to be with friends, everyone AGENCY touches, every family we support, and every employer who depends on a valued worker is a link strengthening a society that cares about the quality of life for every person. This is AGENCY's challenge and AGENCY's reward.

Reprinted by permission of Doty & Cox.

Exhibit 19.5. Sample list of giving opportunities.

WHAT YOUR GIFT CAN PROVIDE	
$500	One month of summer camp for an inner-city child.
250	Three months of hot breakfasts for a preschool child in the nursery program.
100	Four well-baby checkups.
50	Three nights in a "safe house" for a battered woman.
25	Four flu shots for homeless seniors.

The case material is designed to support the volunteer who will make the request in person. It should contain just enough information to give the volunteer confidence in making the presentation. The material should be attractive enough to leave with donors, to review while they are considering their contribution. An example of case material is given in Exhibit 19.4.

Donors respond best to appeals that allow them to see how their gifts help a person or a cause (Exhibit 19.5). Instead of a general request for "a gift for [name of agency]," the development of a table of giving opportunities enlivens or personalizes the appeal and covers a range of dollar amounts.

The list of opportunities can be included in the "case" material or printed on the gift response card.

19.5 RESPONSIBILITY FOR FUND-RAISING

(a) ROLE OF BOARD MEMBERS Responsibility for ensuring that the agency has the funding it needs to fulfill its commitments is one of the board members' most important functions. It is a dual responsibility: to give personally at a level commensurate with one's resources, and to get funds from outside sources. It is up to the Nominating Committee to communicate this responsibility fully and positively to candidates for the board of directors. When this does not occur, board members may feel they were recruited under false pretenses.

The role of board members in fund-raising is central to the success of the development program. Board members are unique and significant advocates for the organization; they must set the pace for other donors with their own contributions. As people giving not only money but time, they can elicit contributions that even the most experienced staff member cannot duplicate.

Board members can also be invaluable in extending an agency's outreach to other markets. They become ambassadors to the professions, to the business community, and to personal friends who are in a position to lend their support to a good cause. They can recruit additional leadership to strengthen the agency's network and experts to help with specialized tasks.

(b) FUND DEVELOPMENT COMMITTEE Although every board member should be involved in some aspect of annual giving, the work of the board should be organized through a Fund Development Committee. The board member who chairs this committee should present a report at every board meeting. Staff members should also be invited to work on the Fund Development Committee and on specific fund-raising projects.

The basic tasks of the Fund Development Committee are to develop the annual giving plan, to recruit people who will take responsibility for specific items in the plan, and to encourage other members of the board to give and to help. These tasks are incorporated into the board's charge for the committee (see Exhibit 19.6).

(c) ROLE OF THE STAFF Fund-raising staff work in two dimensions. First, they provide support and guidance for board members and other development volunteers, ensuring that the annual giving plan and calendar proceed on schedule. Second, they initiate and implement fund-raising activities that can be mostly accomplished at the staff level (Exhibit 19.7).

(i) Prospect research The goal of prospect research is to enable the organization to identify people who have major gift potential. A combination of science and diplomacy is required. The key questions are: How much can they give? Who should ask? The science part can be accomplished at the local library, where the following kinds

Exhibit 19.6. Sample charge for Fund Development Committee, from board of directors.

The Fund Development Committee is responsible for raising contributions to help support the work of AGENCY.

The Committee will develop an annual plan of work and a direct-expense budget. It will recommend a dollar goal to be adopted by the board. The Committee will recruit people to implement the plan and will keep the board informed of progress toward the goal.

The Committee will give input to the Nominating Committee to ensure the recruitment of board members able and willing to secure financial and other resources for AGENCY.

Exhibit 19.7. Job description: Director of Development.

- Design and implement an annual mail and telephone appeal.
- Identify and research major gift prospects.
- Provide training and support for AGENCY's president and other volunteers who will personally solicit people in a position to make gifts of $1,000, $5,000, and above.
- Organize annual Corporate Awards Breakfast.
- Seek special gifts and grants from foundations, corporations, civic groups, and other institutional givers.
- Develop a cultivation and solicitation program to reach out to the people who have benefited from AGENCY services.
- Produce a newsletter to be mailed twice a year to individual donors, corporations, families, and community leaders.
- Provide staff support for an ongoing bequest program to build AGENCY's endowment.
- Create and implement a donor recognition system to ensure timely expression of thanks, and activities to encourage continued support.
- Maintain donor records and provide periodic reports on income and expenses.
- Provide staff support to the Fund Development Committee.

Reproduced by permission of Doty & Cox.

of resources may shed light on prospects' interests, income, and business and social circles:

1. *Who's Who* (national, regional, or by specialization, e.g., "Finance and Industry");
2. *Who Was Who;*
3. *New York Times Index* (information on parents, family, other relatives; obituaries and wedding announcements can be especially helpful);
4. *New York Times Annual Index* (by person);
5. *Wall Street Journal Index* (by year, by person);
6. Local papers (if indexed).

Many good prospects will have only a brief (or no) entry in the above sources; "diplomacy" is often all one has to go on. Confidential discussions with knowledgeable board members or other volunteers who are active in community philanthropy are the next step.

The starting point is the organization's lists of present and former donors and volunteers. Auxiliaries can be excellent places to spot potential donors. A small group of people can be brought together to review the lists, to share any information that will be helpful in deciding potential levels of giving, and to provide advice on relationships with people associated with the agency who might be effective solicitors. This information should be discreetly recorded and brought to bear in the orchestration of personal solicitations.

(ii) Record keeping Data processing technology has made it relatively easy to maintain donor records and to tailor personal requests to a large number of people. A wide variety of off-the-shelf fund-raising management software is available, with varying degrees of flexibility and ease of utilization. Most agencies will find, however, that their needs can be well met by setting up their own system using standard data base and word processing programs. The following basic information should be collected:

Full name (and nickname, if any)
Home address and telephone
Employer's name, address, and telephone
Prospect's title
Spouse's name and occupation
Children: names, ages, schools
Prospect's relationship to agency
Committee assignments (past and present)
Programs of special interest
Giving history
Other community affiliations
Religious affiliation
Education
General comments

(iii) Reports Giving information should be captured in such a way as to make it easy to generate progress reports on individual gifts. Although information about specific contributions is confidential and should be limited to a small number of people, periodic summary reports help keep campaigns moving forward. The formats recommended for these reports are shown in Exhibit 19.8.

(d) ROLE OF CONSULTANTS Fund-raising consultants can be engaged to handle any and all of the work involved in planning and implementing a campaign *except* face-to-face solicitations of major donors and leadership recruitment. No matter what a consultant may suggest, there is no better solicitor than a volunteer who is giving his or her time and money in support of a valued organization.

There is a minor controversy in professional fund-raising circles as to whether it is ethical to pay fund-raisers on a contingency basis: Should they be compensated based on a percentage of the funds raised? Many experienced consultants believe contingency arrangements are unethical because they can encourage consultants to advocate high-pressure tactics that raise more money in the short term but end up alienating donors from future support.

Consultants are frequently used to handle specific pieces of an annual giving program—for example, organizing a corporate dinner. Some consultants specialize in identifying foundation or government sources and preparing written proposals; others provide advice on board development or train volunteers to solicit major gifts. Some consultants will analyze an agency's giving program, put together an overall plan, and provide periodic advice to the Executive Director or the Director of Development as the various activities take effect. Consultants write brochures and annual reports. Capital campaign consultants may place a member of their staff in the agency's offices to handle the day-to-day aspects of a complicated fund drive.

Most states regulate professional fund-raisers, especially those known as "professional solicitors," who actually ask for and may personally handle contributions. Copies of such regulations can ordinarily be obtained through the office of the State Attorney General.

Any relationship with a fund-raising consultant should be governed by a written contract specifying exactly what is to be done and at what cost. (See Exhibit 19.9 for an example.)

Exhibit 19.8. Sample report formats.

Individual Gifts Prospect Worksheet:

Prospect	Solicitor	Amount to Request	Status	Gift/ Pledge

Corporate Gifts Prospect Worksheet:

Company	Contact	Solicitor	Amount to Request	Status	Gift/ Pledge

Campaign Summary:

Team	Goal	Total Pledged	Percent of Goal	Requests Pending ($)	To Be Solicited ($)

Exhibit 19.9.   Sample consultant contract.

This letter is to confirm and constitute the understanding between WORTHY AGENCY and SUPERIOR CONSULTANTS, a __[name of state]__ partnership conducting the business of fund-raising consultation for not-for-profit organizations.

SUPERIOR CONSULTANTS will design and implement a fund-raising plan to increase contributions from individual donors.

__[Person's Name]__ will coordinate the delivery of service under this contract, with the support of SUPERIOR CONSULTANTS.

It will be SUPERIOR CONSULTANTS' responsibility to:

1. Direct the development of a contributions data base containing information about past and present giving. Train volunteers in basic research techniques.

2. Identify potential contributors to the "challenge fund." Prepare and assist the president and board members in soliciting selected individuals for this purpose.

3. Develop and implement both short-term and ongoing fund-raising strategies involving board members, parents, and friends of WORTHY AGENCY.

4. Review suggestions for fund-raising for WORTHY AGENCY. Help set priorities and advise on the implementation of the best ideas.

5. Outline the basic functions of a development office for WORTHY AGENCY and prepare a model job description for a Director of Development.

6. Develop a proposal for a feasibility study for an Endowment Campaign and advise on sources of underwriting for such a study.

It will be WORTHY AGENCY'S responsibility to:

1. Provide SUPERIOR CONSULTANTS with information on prior and ongoing fund-raising efforts and outreach.

2. Identify key volunteers, donors, and community leaders for fund-raising leadership, and help with involving them in the annual giving program.

3. Enable the Executive Director to work closely with the consultants to ensure full and timely communication.

4. Furnish whatever secretarial and other office services the contributions program requires.

5. Pay or reimburse any out-of-pocket expenses, such as printed materials, special-event costs, and recognition items. All expenditures will be subject to prior approval.

6. Receive all monies; log and collect gifts and pledges; and provide periodic reports on income and expenses.

7. Implement public relations aspects of the campaign, if any.

WORTHY AGENCY will not be billed for telephone, postage, photocopying, clerical, and similar expenses incurred by SUPERIOR CONSULTANTS in WORTHY AGENCY's offices, or for travel within Home County.

WORTHY AGENCY has the right to cancel this contract upon 30 days' written notice. WORTHY AGENCY is responsible for all authorized expenditures committed up to the date of notification and for the final 30 days' fee owed to SUPERIOR CONSULTANTS.

The period covered by this contracts is __[Date]__ through __[Date]__. The fee for these services is __[$X,000]__, payable monthly at the beginning of each service period. Should WORTHY AGENCY wish to continue to receive these services after __[Date]__, SUPERIOR CONSULTANTS will provide them at no increase in fee.

Exhibit 19.9. *(Continued)*

If this letter correctly expresses our mutual understanding, please signify approval by signing the original and the attached copy and returning the original to me at SUPERIOR CONSULTANTS.

AGREED

_____[Signature]_____	_____[Signature]_____
PRESIDENT	Partner
WORTHY AGENCY	SUPERIOR CONSULTANTS
Dated _____	

Reproduced by permission of Doty & Cox.

19.6 FUND-RAISING TECHNIQUES

(a) DONOR RELATIONS Careful cultivation, and attention to the individual dreams, fears, and needs of each major gift prospect, will reap huge rewards over the years. Let "the golden rule" be the guide: Treat all donors with the respect, honesty, and consideration that everyone appreciates.

Cultivation is the art of gradually developing personal links between the organization and its constituency. The first link might be a personal phone call of thanks from the president or chairperson, when a significant gift is received. An invitation to a small gathering in the private home of a board member, "to thank our special supporters and give them an advance look at important trends in our work," will coax some donors to draw closer.

Cultivation can be made a priority for top volunteers and the Executive Director. If three people commit themselves to having lunch twice a month with different major donors (or donors targeted for major upgrading), at the end of the first year 72 supporters will have been flattered and their commitment heightened.

Emphasis on cultivation is important: donors at all levels don't like being thought of only when money is involved. A twice-yearly newsletter, simple and attractive, is an efficient way to strengthen relationships with average donors. The newsletter can be used to recognize special gifts—memorials, bequests, and grants from local corporations.

The Executive Director should keep a list of actual and potential major donors on his or her desk. When there is a news article about an agency program or an issue of prime concern, a copy of the article should be sent to selected donors with a handwritten notation making a connection between the donors and the article—for example, "Thank you again for helping make this program possible. We're reaching even more kids than we had expected!"

Or, a phone call can be made: "I hope you saw today's editorial about . . . . I know you're interested in this and it's encouraging that other people are starting to pay attention, too."

Any agency representative who will be speaking at a community event should call and invite donors being cultivated. Most will not come, but they will be pleased to be remembered.

Recognizing and acting on these kinds of opportunities will be no trouble if they become part of one's regular way of work.

(b) PERSONAL SOLICITATION   The goal of cultivation is to pave the way for face-to-face solicitation of major donors. Personal solicitation is almost always the best way to elicit large gifts. Because it is also a very frightening prospect for many otherwise indomitable volunteers, the guidelines in Exhibit 19.10 will be helpful.

Volunteers who accept the responsibility for face-to-face solicitation need and deserve training and support. They need coaching in how to make a phone call to set up a solicitation appointment, often the toughest part of the entire transaction. They need to know as much as possible about the person they will solicit—his or her relationship with the agency; special program interests, if any; and what size gift is appropriate to request. They need an attractive brochure (the case material) and a pledge card.

Gathering this information is the job of the Director of Development or the Executive Director. If outside expertise is desired, people known to be effective fund-raisers should be asked to conduct a training session. Development directors from other organizations may be glad to help, or professional consultants might be retained for this specific purpose.

(c) FINDING NEW DONORS   Building a donor base works on the same principle as dropping a rock in a pool. Once the process begins, ripples create widening ripples and, gradually, outreach develops throughout the entire system. The key elements are described here.

1. Start with the *board of directors*. Ask each trustee to provide a list of people who are to receive a personalized letter emphasizing the sender's commitment to the work of the agency and asking the prospect to lend his or her support to this good cause. Involve as many nonmembers as possible on the Fund Development Committee and ask each of them to write to their friends and colleagues.

Exhibit 19.10.   Keys to successful solicitations.

- The $ XXXXX goal is attainable.
- Make your own gift first. Your personal commitment empowers you to ask for "stretch" gifts from others.
- Be familiar with your prospect's primary interest in the Agency.
- See your prospect in person.
- Work in teams.
- Express appreciation for prior contributions and indicate their importance to the organization.
- Use the case material and brochure to briefly describe Agency programs and the purpose of the request.
- Listen and respond to the prospect's questions and interests.
- Ask for a specific amount, mentioning your own commitment and that of other donors.
- Hold on to the pledge card if an immediate decision is not forthcoming.
- Send a follow-up letter.
- Report back to the appropriate person at the Agency.

DO IT TODAY!

Reproduced by permission of Doty & Cox.

As lists are provided, note any information that might be useful in building a donor record—particularly if there is the potential for significant support.

2. To stimulate *list creation,* collect donor and board lists from other organizations and have them reviewed by the Fund Development Committee. In many communities, the local hospital, library, or family service agency regularly lists donors in the annual report. "Cold" letters probably won't produce much, but volunteers can identify people they know when prodded by such a list.

3. Consider creating a *prestigious award* to be given annually to three or more prominent people whose association with the agency would be valuable. Be straightforward about the fact that this is a fund-raising event. Arrange a simple reception in a private home. Ask the honorees to provide invitation lists, and construct others based on information about their networks. Charge $100 a person and make it the responsibility of every board member to obtain 10 pledges and the use of the donor's name on the listing of the Award Committee. Print the names of the Award Committee on the invitation. Each year, expand the number of people charged with obtaining pledges. An organization that used exactly this technique raised $10,000 the first year (100 gifts at $100 each). Eight years later, the event netted $75,000 and the agency has made many new friends it would never otherwise have had.

4. Be willing to *start small.* Everybody else did.

(d) BEQUESTS Bequests are usually categorized with some highly specialized giving vehicles called "planned giving," as though the rest of fund-raising is the product of happy spontaneity. The subject of planned giving is often filled with daunting, technical discussions of "charitable remainder trusts" or "pooled income funds," and volunteers leave seminars convinced they have to become estate planning experts. Universities and major health and cultural institutions do secure impressive "planned gifts" by drawing on special professional expertise; however, for organizations that are just getting started in this area, the simplest and the most productive focus is on bequests.

A bequest, like any other special gift, must be solicited: donors must be told that the agency would like to be remembered in their wills. When a bequest is received, it should be highlighted in a newsletter, with information on what the gift will make possible. Mail solicitations should include a place on the gift card for a donor to indicate: "I have provided for [name of agency] in my will." A special mailing concentrating solely on bequests should be considered.

Because state laws differ, an attorney should draw up simple language to include in newsletters, in the annual report, and on pledge cards. For example:

After payment of all debts, taxes, and administration expenses, I leave _____ percent of my estate to [name of agency].

Donors can bequeath:

- A percentage of their estate;
- A specific amount of money
- A "contingent" bequest (comes to the organization only after other heirs have died);

- A "residuary" bequest: "I leave $1 million to my husband, Faithful Spouse. The rest and residue of my estate I leave to [name of agency]."

Bequests can also be a topic during the face-to-face discussions with major donors. It is important that the people soliciting bequests have, themselves, made such a commitment. This process needs to start with the board of directors. Even a young person or someone of relatively modest means can comfortably provide in a will that a percentage of his or her estate will go to the agency, and thus be in a position to ask someone else to do likewise.

When it becomes known, by whatever means, that someone has made a bequest, that person belongs high on the list for continuing cultivation.

19.7 SPECIAL EVENTS

It is no accident that special events is the final topic in a chapter on annual giving. A special event is often the first thing that comes to mind when people sit down to discuss fund-raising. However, for many organizations, it is the worst possible use of staff and volunteer energy, time, and commitment.

The annual giving plan must realistically evaluate every option under consideration. A special event has initial appeal: It sounds like fun, it may be glamorous, and it minimizes the sensitive (but almost always more productive) issues of personal solicitation.

But will the event raise money? How many hours and how many dollars will it cost to produce?

There are four questions to ask, when deciding whether a proposed special event makes sense:

1. What is the event's primary purpose? Is it fund-raising or something else? Be wary of trying to accomplish too many things with one event.

2. Is there an existing event to which a fund-raising component could be added, for example, an annual luncheon honoring businesses that employ people trained or rehabilitated by the agency? It will take nothing away from the existing event to overlay it with an appeal to major corporations in the area to purchase tables or make contributions.

3. Are there volunteers who are anxious to take responsibility? This is vital. The event will still need a good helping of staff support, but unless the event is "owned" by one or more volunteers—don't do it!

4. Will organizing the event foreclose the opportunity to do something more "profitable?" (Priorities again.)

There are hundreds (probably thousands) of formats for special events. They all work and they are all opportunities for disaster. Much depends on the culture of the community and the nature of the audience. In some places, gala dinner dances are popular. In other communities, auctions, bike-a-thons, golf or tennis tournaments, or concerts attract enthusiastic support.

Special events need not be ruled out, but they must fit firmly within the total development program.

19.8 RESOURCES

There are many very helpful books and periodicals about every aspect of fund-raising. The following are superior, in our opinion; at a minimum, they are good places to seek specific materials.

Chronicle of Philanthropy (biweekly magazine), 1255 23rd Street, NW, Washington, DC 20037. Invaluable (inexpensive source of information about trends and developments affecting all kinds and sizes of nonprofit organizations. Essential reading for development professionals and highly recommended for executive directors as well.

The Foundation Center, 79 Fifth Avenue, New York, NY (212) 620-4230. Maintains a free library, including at least the last 12 months of many publications. Information on many aspects of fund-raising, not just foundations. Microfiche copies of tax returns of all private foundations are available. Call for information about branches in other parts of the country. (This information can be obtained by phone by paying an annual membership fee.)

The Grantsmanship Center, P. O. Box 6210, Los Angeles, CA 90014. Publications catalog has many good articles and how-to pieces on fund-raising, public relations, and other aspects of nonprofit management. Provides information and advice on public funding.

National Center for Nonprofit Boards, 2000 L Street, NW, Suite 411, Washington, DC 20036. Established in 1988 by the Association of Governing Boards of Universities and Colleges and Independent Sector. Publications list and Nonprofit Governance Series booklets ($6.25 each) are especially worthwhile.

SOURCES AND SUGGESTED REFERENCES

American Association of Fund Raising Counsel. Annual. *Giving USA: The Annual Report of Philanthropy.* New York: Author.

Berendt, Robert, and Taft, J. Richard. 1984. *How to Rate Your Development Office.* Rockville, MD: Fund Raising Institute.

Brakeley, George A., Jr., 1980. *Tested Ways to Successful Fund Raising.* New York: AMACOM.

Brentlinger, Marilyn E. 1987. *The Ultimate Benefit Book: How To Raise $50,000-Plus for Your Organization.* Cleveland, OH: Octavia.

Gee, Ann D. (ed.). 1990. *Annual Giving Strategies: A Comprehensive Guide to Better Results.* Washington, DC: Council for Advancement and Support of Education.

Jenkins, Jeanne B., and Lucas, Marilyn. 1986. *Prospect Research Resource Directory.* Rockville, MD: Fund Raising Institute.

Klein, Kimberly. 1988. *Fundraising for Social Change.* Inverness, CA: Chardon Press.

Read, Patricia (ed.). 1986. *Foundation Fundamentals: Grantseekers.* New York: The Foundation Center.

Seltzer, Michael. 1991. *Securing Your Organization's Future: A Guide to Evaluating and Improving Your Fundraising.* New York: The Foundation Center.

Seymour, Harold J. 1988. *Designs for Fund-Raising.* Rockville, MD: Fund Raising Institute. (Originally published 1966.)

Sharpe, Robert F. 1986. *The Planned Giving Idea Book.* Memphis, TN: Sharpe & Whinney.

CHAPTER TWENTY

Planned Giving*

Lynda S. Moerschbaecher
Moerschbaecher & Dryburgh

Erik D. Dryburgh
Moerschbaecher & Dryburgh

CONTENTS

* Parts of this chapter are excerpted from *Plain English Planned Giving: Starting at Square One* and *Plain English Planned Giving: Working Effectively With Your Donors,* copyright © 1991 by Lynda S. Moerschbaecher. Both books are part of the *Plain English Planned Giving* series of books and tapes, and the excerpts are reprinted with permission.

20.1   DETERMINING WHAT THE PLANNED GIVING PROGRAM SHOULD BE

An assessment of the current development effort is the first step in determining what the planned giving program should be for an organization. The assessment can be viewed as having three parts:

1. The organization of the development effort must be viewed in its entirety and the role and sophistication of each part of the development office must be understood;
2. The gift history and the state of the donor records must be analyzed to determine the availability of immediate markets for planned giving;
3. The internal and external capabilities of the organization must be understood.

(a) ORGANIZATION OF THE CURRENT DEVELOPMENT FUNCTION

(i) Sources of revenue production   The development effort consists of various programs that are revenue sources for the organization. Although they may be called different names by different institutions, generally only a handful of programs are regularly used to generate fund-raising revenue. Before a planned giving program is established, an annual giving program, to which donors are encouraged to give on a regular and recurring basis, is in place. There may also be a major gift program, for the purpose of generating larger gifts, which donors would not make on a recurring basis. Typically, the organization will also have two types of special events: those that produce revenue and those that are held for the purpose of thanking or recognizing donors. The organization may also engage in special appeals by phone or by mail, which may or may not be part of the annual giving program. Finally, the organization will probably seek support from corporations and foundations (and, perhaps, the government).

These functions do not imply any particular organizational chart. One person may be doing all the functions, in a one-person development shop; or, a very large organization may have 100 people staffing the development office. No matter the size or structure, these are basic, generic, revenue-raising programs of a development office. Planned giving must fit into this development effort and coordinate with the other parts of the development office. From the point of view of adding another program and making it work, the most important factors are what it is designed to achieve and how it will fit with what is already in place.

To understand the coordination, we must focus specifically on two parts of the development office—annual giving and major gifts. The annual giving program is designed to attract continual, recurring, and, ideally, increasing support that is to be used for everyday, operating budgetary needs. Directly opposed in philosophy is the major gift program, which is designed to reach donors for a special-effort gift beyond the amount they could ordinarily give every year. There is an inherent possibility of tension between these two development roles. Major gifts might be viewed as "nonrecurring"; even though they may occasionally recur, they will not recur every year. If they did, the gift would be classified as an annual gift.

If major gifts are defined as nonrecurring larger transfers that a donor undertakes once or only a few times in his or her giving life, then, in large part, planned giving must fall within this definition because planned gifts are undertaken as a special effort on the donor's part. However, major gifts and planned gifts differ in an important way. Major gifts are generally in liquid form—cash, marketable securities, and the like. Planned gifts might be viewed as a subset of these major gifts: "planned" means that the gifts require structuring in a legal or accounting sense. Planned gifts must also be distinguished from deferred gifts. A planned gift may very well be an outright contribution, say, of closely held stock or real estate. It is a major gift from the donor's point of view, no matter the form or amount of gift structuring. Thus, definitionally, all planned gifts are major gifts, but not all major gifts are planned gifts. Planned giving is thus a subset of major giving.

In turn, some planned gifts are made without current receipt by the charity. These are *deferred* gifts, such as pooled income funds, charitable remainder trusts, and bequests. Some are irrevocable, others are revocable. Deferred gifts are, despite their name, made *currently* by the donor; it is the organization that views them as deferred. It would be more correct to call them deferred receipts. They are a major commitment by the donor, and are, therefore, major gifts that are planned and structured. As such, deferred gifts are a subset of planned gifts, because not all planned gifts are received later. Thus, deferred gifts are a subset of planned gifts, which are a subset of major gifts. Again, this definition does not necessarily imply organizational structure of the development office for management purposes.

(ii) Use of the revenue produced by various programs   These various fund-raising revenue sources produce spendable funds. How they may be spent falls within three categories: operational use, endowment, and capital spending. It is really quite simple on the expenditure side. However, what is less known is that revenue from any of the above sources may be used in any one of the three expenditure categories. Experience makes us believe that funds raised in an annual giving program are used for operational expenses. However, those funds may be restricted to endowment if the donor so designates. Often, it is assumed that major gifts feed into capital or endowment use, while bequests and other planned gifts generally feed into endowment; however, that is not necessarily true. Planned gifts may very well be used for any one of the three possible uses of fund-raising revenue.

It may be helpful to define endowment here. Endowment has meaning both in the law and in accounting. There are different types of endowment. If a donor places a restriction on a gift so that the income (or some percentage of the value of the assets of the endowment fund, where that type of endowment spending rule is adopted in lieu of true income) is to be spent but the principal is to be held and invested, that is true endowment, donor-restricted and respected in the law. That restriction may not be changed, other than in states that have adopted the Uniform Management of Institutional Funds Act, which permits the donor to release a written restriction by a later writing, or by petition to a court on a *cy pres* action (to change the purpose to another very similar). A board or other body may change the restriction where such discretion was expressly given to that body in writing by the donor.

Many organizations employ a different type of endowment in addition to true endowment. An endowment fund may be created by board resolution and then be held as if it were endowment. This type of endowment is called quasi-endowment or funds functioning as endowment. Where the board has designated funds as endowment, it may later undo the restriction. Some endowment funds are specified to be held for a definite term, after which they are to be spent. These are often called temporary endowments or term endowments.

Endowment is a word that is often used too loosely, and that may create problems. For example, if an organization promoted and publicized a gift-giving opportunity as one that "endows" a specific project or program, but it misused the term endow, it would find that donors could compel it to hold the funds as endowment. A contract or understanding and reliance by the donor may have been inadvertently created. Thus, proper use of the term is essential.

Endowment also has significance for accounting. It must be separately held from operational funds and, in fact, the true endowment must be accounted for separately from the quasi-endowment.

Capital projects may have some of the same problems as the use of the term endowment. If a donor has been led to believe that his or her gift is to be used for a capital project, a contract or detrimental reliance may have occurred, and the donor may be able to compel such usage.

The end uses of funds are important to understand, especially once the organization begins an even more complex program such as planned giving.

(b) ANALYSIS OF GIFT HISTORY AND STATE OF DONOR RECORDS   The second part of the assessment is to review the past support of the organization, to determine the strength of the major gift and annual giving efforts. This step is important in understanding whether the organization needs additional help in creating commitment equivalent to that required for planned gifts. Not every organization is ready to support a planned gift effort.

The donor base should be analyzed by gift level, by gift consistency (on a per-donor basis), and by the increase in giving by individual donors. This analysis can best be done with good, organized, computerized records. The process is similar to that of planning for a capital campaign. The goal is to ferret out early planned giving successes while also undertaking the planning and preparation for wider marketing.

From this study, a number of donors who have already given to the institution should become the first to be cultivated for planned gifts. If the organization finds few or no donors who have already committed support to the organization on a consistent and increasing basis, perhaps other work is necessary before attempting a planned giving program.

(c) INTERNAL AND EXTERNAL CAPABILITY   The third step in the assessment of the readiness of the current program involves a testing of the capability of the organization, internally and externally, to undertake a planned giving program. Internal readiness requires the ability of the development office and the finance and administration office to handle the program. Both offices must have staff time available. The development office must have a budget for planned giving, office space for the staff person, support staff assigned to the staff person, and a written understanding with the board, in the form of resolutions, guidelines, or whatever, indicating the board's willingness to give the new program time (and support) to succeed. Large capital transfers do not come to an institution without considerable cultivation. Boards and executive directors too often demand immediate dollar goals. In the early stages, goals should be set in terms of identifiable steps toward successful cultivation of prospective donors. Perhaps an initial number of prospects to be seen during the first year can be set. In any event, the board and executive director must understand the different nature of this program and guarantee their willingness to become actively involved.

The finance and administration office must be willing to learn the administration and record keeping required by the new gift vehicles. It may also need to learn specific rules of investment of property transferred outright or in trust, or how to undertake the sale and reinvestment of certain types of assets. Whether gifts such as pooled income funds, charitable gift annuities, charitable remainder and lead trusts are administered in-house or not, much new information must be processed regularly. Specific, written procedures must be developed so that gift acknowledgment, income checks, annual reports, and the like do not slip between the cracks.

How the organization conveys to the public its new program effort will set the tone for the program. External relations must be handled both by development and public relations. Planned giving requires the formation of new relationships with the outside world. The financial world can be a strong ally to the program. Relationships must be developed by the planned giving officer with trustees, investment advisers, CPAs, attorneys, CLUs, and CFPs. The public relations department must support the development office in its attempt to reach the right persons in the right way.

20.2 UNDERSTANDING THE PROPOSED PLANNED GIVING PROGRAM

(a) A PROGRAM IS MORE THAN THE SUM OF ITS VEHICLES A planned giving program is more than the sum of the various gift vehicles to be used. It includes the gift vehicles and the gift structuring to meet an individual donor's financial situation. The program, however, is the overall effort to bring prospective donors to the institution, to utilize life income gifts to their fullest advantage, and to organize, manage, and implement staff and volunteer efforts to bring gifts of a sophisticated nature to fruition. Is it something new? Not really. A Community Chest brochure dated 1948, and entitled "Looking Ahead," recited the need for long-range support and suggested ways to provide it: a bequest, a trust paying income to the donor, a trust paying income to the Community Chest, and a revocable trust. From this, it appears our current vehicles are hardly new. Only the rules are new (and ever changing).

If not new, is the program different from other fund-raising programs? In some respects, it is not. Planned giving is fund-raising and, therefore, involves general fund-raising principles. Many things are different, however. Planned giving is a highly technical, highly personalized, and highly structured area of development. It is different from other fund-raising programs because it is multifaceted. It requires significant planning and organizing in-house, it necessitates education or retraining of staff assigned to it, and it involves gift planning for prospective donors. New types of record keeping, reports to donors and governmental agencies, and choices of degree of institutional involvement are required. For example, the board must decide whether it will undertake the fiduciary responsibilities of handling the pooled income fund or being the trustee of charitable trusts, or whether it has sufficient in-house expertise to invest the funds entrusted to it.

The vehicles used are tax-oriented and require substantial time and effort to understand. A simple understanding of the gift vehicles does not mean one is capable of engaging in creative planning techniques with these vehicles. A depth of knowledge in financial and estate planning in general provides the framework for fully utilizing the charitable gift vehicles. Even with such knowledge, continual updating on events of significance is crucial. Thus, in addition to the organization, planning, and administration necessary for the development office, the planned giving officer and his or her outside advisers have continual educational needs.

Let us then attempt to define planned giving as it will be used here. It can be defined from either of two perspectives—that of the donor or that of the organization. From the donor's point of view, it is the thinking, the planning, the garnering of the best benefits for self, spouse, family, and others (generally in that order). From the perspective of the organization, it is the consistent *effort* at developing gifts that are "structured," are not recurring annually, and are designed to meet a donor's needs and objectives, which *effort* includes the planning, marketing, and delivery of appropriate gift structures and vehicles.

If planned giving from the organization's point of view is a consistent effort at achieving planned gifts, that effort will require certain other things, such as a budget, a staff, time, and a plan. It will need to be evaluated. Others, such as the board and the community professionals, will be asked to help. Central to the success of the effort is the choice of the planned giving officer. Each of these items is a concern to management.

(i) Budget   The amount an organization will have to budget will depend on the scope of the program to be undertaken, but the scope of the program may be limited at the outset by budgetary constraints. Thus, budget and scope of program must be dealt with simultaneously. There are many things to consider when setting the budget, and different organizations require different budget items to be picked up by departments that have the same name. For example, some offices may be required to put into their budgets an item for rent and office overhead; other institutions may not charge this item to departmental budgets. Thus, the budget model offered here (See Exhibit 20.1) is more of a checklist of items to consider in light of specific practices.

A planned giving program is a person-to-person, close-contact effort, and it will require some expenses other programs do not. The marketing and cultivation are indeed different.

(ii) Time commitment   Starting a planned giving program is not dissimilar to starting a new business. If you ask an entrepreneur about the start-up phase of the business, you will get insights that are definitely applicable to beginning a planned giving program. It will require a commitment of time on the part of the staff and on the part of the entity as a whole. The board and management must be prepared to fund the effort without expectation of immediate receipts. Even when gifts are closed, they are often in deferred form and the funds will not be available for many years. Thus, the organization starting a program must be secure enough financially to see the planned giving program through its start-up phase.

Exhibit 20.1. Budget items to consider.

Staff salaries
Employee benefits
Rent
Phone
Office overhead (indirect costs)
Office equipment:

typewriter	calculators
computer plus software	dictaphone
printer	transcriber
modem	fax machine

Fixtures and furnishings
Office supplies: paper, letterhead, labels, other
List rental
Expenses for mailings: graphics, typesetting, printing, label or mailing house
Postage
Brochures and newsletters in bulk (custom or purchased)
Consulting/Legal/Accounting
Continuing professional education and association membership for employees
Reimbursement for volunteers
Entertainment and meals
Travel and lodging
Library: books, newsletters, journals
Seminars: speakers, refreshments, room rental, audio-visual equipment, photocopies, postage, follow-up mailings, etc.
New program development
Marketing research/consultants
Advertisements

It is often said that it will take three to five years for a planned giving program to be up and running with a good flow of closed gifts. This is true not only because it is a start-up endeavor, but also because of the nature of what donors are being asked to do. A planned gift is often in the form of a bequest or a trust. To undertake such a gift, the donor must do his or her estate or financial planning. That process alone may take several months, and even years, for some people. For some donors, the thought of doing estate planning is something to put off because of the indication of finality and mortality. For these reasons, donors in this area of fund-raising cannot be pushed; the time constraints of capital campaign or annual giving do not apply.

The board and management must come to terms with this problem. Often, they are anxious to have a planned giving program, but, after a few months, they want to know where the money is and whether the funds they have already invested in the program have been wasted. This short-sighted attitude must be avoided if planned giving is to succeed. Management should satisfy itself that planned giving is feasible for the organization at the time it is proposed, and that the organizational efforts are proceeding at a normal pace. Projections and expectations can be a part of the plans, but the truth is that, at the beginning, dollar goals are nigh impossible to set. Later, after some experience with the particular donor base, goals may be established.

It may be wise to set out, in writing, the time commitment on the part of management and the development officer. This written understanding, while not at all binding, may serve to keep things on track. It should cover the commitment in terms of the dollars and years the board or CEO is willing to agree to. It should also cover the intended effort and time frame planned by the staff and should arrange for written evaluations to be submitted periodically, analyzing whether the program is on schedule.

(iii) Staff attention   No matter how many people are engaged in the planned giving effort, certain tasks must be accomplished. For example, a clerical support staff is necessary because of the volume of written materials, the amount of donor contact, and the preparation for donor and professional seminars. Legal help will no doubt be required at some point. Gift administration must be done correctly. Someone must make the actual contacts with the prospects. Finally, substantial marketing must be done to ensure continual donor acquisition. All these tasks either have to be done by or supervised by the person in charge of planned giving. If a part-time person is in charge, he or she will be very busy.

Several different models of staffing have been tried, from a CEO who does everything to an office with several planned gift officers. In between, there may be a one-person development office or a part-time or even a full-time person assigned to planned giving. If the staffing model assigns the staff person to multiple programs in the development office for which he or she is responsible, that person is often called away from the planned gift duties for more immediate chores. As a result, the planned gift effort never gets proper attention. However, it has been shown again and again that planned giving simply will not succeed without dedicated attention. With that kind of attention, even if given part-time, a planned giving program can succeed nicely.

(iv) Scope of the program   An important decision at the beginning of the program is how much to undertake all at once. This concern is interwoven with concerns of staffing and budget. A planned gift program may be as simple as a bequest program or as complex as sophisticated estate planning with closely held stock and several generations of the donor's family. Once again, between the extremes, there are many levels to choose from.

The decision regarding how much of a program to undertake must entail an honest examination of the numerous tasks involved in each gift vehicle selected. For example, if a pooled income fund is to be established, documents have to be prepared, an explanation for SEC purposes must be written, a trustee must be selected, marketing materials must be chosen or created, the donor base must be studied for suitable prospects, marketing must be implemented, response must be made to inquiries, proposals must be written, calculations must be performed, perhaps one or more visits must be made, assets must be transferred, files must be created, computer data bases must be updated, administration must be set up for the gift, and so on. Even these statements are set forth in cursory fashion; the actual job is much more detailed. When multiplied by the number of vehicles chosen, the number of tasks may become overwhelming for the time available by staff. Thus, some thought must be given to the size of the program. Too many gift vehicles undertaken at once may result in no success with any of them.

It should be made clear that selecting the scope of the program means choosing what the staff will consistently pursue and market. That does not prevent the organization from accepting a different type of gift offered "over the transom." Over time, of course, the organization can adopt other gift vehicles.

(v) Chronology of the creation of the program It is wise to write out a plan of action for the first year of the program, knowing that it will probably change during that year. It serves both as a guide and as a tool for evaluation of what has been achieved. Because, under the assessment described above, every program will have a different starting point, each chronology will be different. The scope of the program and the budget will also vary. Nevertheless, certain things have to be done in order to succeed at planned giving. Included in Exhibit 20.2 is a hypothetical chronology for an organization just starting its program with a new staff person. This is only a hypothetical example; each organization must create its own chronology, based on its needs.

(vi) Evaluating the progress When the chronology of action is set out month by month, the chronological steps serve as the best tool for evaluating the progress of the establishment of the program. At the beginning of the month, the planned giving officer has a set number of goals to accomplish. At the end of each month, he or she should use the same set of goals to report whether they have been accomplished, and, if not, what obstacle may have prevented the accomplishment. If the same problem keeps cropping up month after month, it will become evident and can be dealt with by management. After 6 months, a formal report should outline whether the program is on track. After 12 months, a new 12-month plan should be prepared.

(b) ROLE OF THE BOARD IN PLANNED GIVING Commitment is critical to the success of the program, but few people adequately address what that commitment really means. It means *owning* the concept, actually taking part and making it one's own. The board must undertake this type of commitment. No major program will take place or succeed without the board's understanding and support. That is a known and accepted fact for all types of programs undertaken by a corporate body.

Although most staff people understand that commitment is necessary, many misunderstand the feelings and motivations of the board members. The idea of getting board members involved is often overdone by organizations undertaking a planned giving program. Rather than getting a board member motivated and engaged, they bludgeon the board members with either the necessity of involvement in the program or by insisting on contributions to the program. *Neither of these tactics will result in board involvement or commitment.* Just as philanthropy has to be voluntary, so does commitment. Overbearing tactics have resulted in an attitude that "planned giving is just not right for us at this time."

The board has to be willing to participate in several policy decisions, among them a policy regarding the confidentiality of donor information, a decision to accept the fiduciary role that planned giving requires (not trusteeship), a policy concerning ethics in planned giving, policies and procedures for the acceptance of real estate in light of environmental liability, and others as they come up in the administration of the program. Generally, to make wise decisions regarding the liability of the institution and the board members' own liability, a committee of the board should study and

Exhibit 20.2.   Chronology of the creation of a planned giving program.

Month	Internal Work	External Work
Month 1	Budget Contract (understanding of employment), if not done prior Current fund-raising effort analysis Matrix Volunteers Study of organization Meet key people	Meet with consultants, interview, select Review computer systems—data Meet key people
Month 2	Board treaty Plan committees Confidentiality Ethics Committee action plan	Visit prospective members
Month 3	Marketing plan Begin planned giving Case Traditional guidelines	Meet with selected marketing advisers Survey of trustees; interview
Month 4	Define scope of program Board treaty approval Begin marketing brochure, funding opportunities Products	Meet with marketing committee Meet with volunteer committee Meet with board members Meet with technical advisers
Month 5	Marketing plan Internal training lunch Case Products Seminars to attend Volunteer book Begin legal work	Meet with marketing committee Assessment of finance and administration (F&A) unit Meet with lawyers; select
Month 6	Core group prospects; assign Brochures, newsletters Staff meetings Legal work	Meet with financial community F&A procedures Meet with public relations (PR) personnel Meet with volunteer committee
Month 7	Core group strategy Bequest plan Newsletter Proposals Legal work Plan donor seminars; board seminar	Meet with marketing community F&A procedures

Exhibit 20.2. *(Continued)*

Month 8	Bequest plan	Meet with volunteer committee
	Proposals	Meet with lawyer
	Donor seminar	
	Board seminar	
	Legal documents	
	Marketing brochure	
Month 9	Gift credit; recognition	Computer systems—financial
	Idea mailing	Meet with marketing committee
	Target seminars	Board thanks (personal) to volunteers
	Core group follow-up	
Month 10	Staff meeting	PR—media access
	Follow-up on idea mailing	Meet with volunteer committee
	Targeted seminars	
	Follow-up	
Month 11	Replace committee members	Meet with technical committee at institution
	Recognition mailing	Meet with board chairperson, others
	Idea mailing	
	Gift procedures	
Month 12	Follow-up on responses	Chat cultivation
	Elderly program	Visit financial advisers
	Recognition event	Volunteer committee's 12-month review

analyze the issues and make recommendations to the full board. Issues such as liability for hazardous waste cannot be addressed on a crisis basis. They must be thought through while the board is not faced with a problem that may cost thousands or, in some cases, millions of dollars. Thus, the planned giving officer will need the attention of some or all of the board to present these issues.

Board members can also play a vital role in opening doors and making contact with prospects for the planned giving officer. They should be asked to play a role they feel comfortable with, not many are comfortable with solicitations. Using a board member where he or she is comfortable will achieve better results and will not result in "burn-out" of the board member.

(c) PLANNED GIFT COMMITTEES For quite some time, the use of a planned giving committee has been in vogue. However, most often, it does not seem to work well and the committee members do not quite seem to know what their function is. The problem lies in part with the selection or mix of the committee members. The wrong mix of people results because the creator of the committee did not clearly focus on what the committee was supposed to accomplish. Because the committee is often not focused, the planned giving officer may begin to "make work" for the committee. Soon thereafter, the committee falls apart and members start to drop out of meetings.

One must ask whether there is a role at all for a "planned giving" committee. If so, perhaps the role or job description of the committee should be written out and discussed with each prospective committee member. In fact, committees may play several different roles, such as the board policy committee referred to above for issues the board must address. There may be a need for a technical or professional advisory committee and perhaps a marketing committee. Each then would be solely focused on its task and not burdened with other tasks the members may not be interested in or qualified for.

The most common problem occurs when a committee of attorneys and other professionals who have never before been involved with the organization is asked to address some serious planned giving issues, such as those the board policy committee should be addressing. Concerns that involve a board member's legal exposure should not be handed off to a committee of new people who have no experience with the organization; neither should issues that affect the entity's image or legal liability. These issues and recommendations should rest with a committee that is "close to the heart" of the organization.

Thus, forming a planned giving committee of professionals who may understand a donor's perspective in financial planning may not serve the institution effectively and may produce decisions that are not in accord with long-established policies and procedures for the organization. In addition, the greatest bulk of the work in planned giving is the marketing—both the research and the outreach to appropriate markets (not the technical side). Would a group of financial professionals really understand the long-term marketing needs of a fund-raising program? Committees can be made to be very effective, but their focus and purpose for existence must be clearly understood by all before they are created.

(d) USE OF CONSULTANTS   At the beginning of a program, the organization may need the help of a consultant. How to choose a consultant is always a question because many persons offer their services as "planned giving consultants." It is necessary to separate them into categories according to the expertise they offer. These categories are as follows:

1. Donor visits and solicitations. This type of consultant will participate in a program almost as an extended staff member, helping with specifically identified donor visits for the purpose of cultivation or solicitation. This person can be a beneficial extension of the current ability to carry on a planned giving program. Quite often, this consultant works with smaller organizations where either an executive director or a development director performs all the functions and there is no planned giving staff member.

2. Evaluations of donor records and feasibility of program. This type of consultant often works on a project basis as opposed to an ongoing consulting relationship. This service may be combined with other forms of consulting done on an ongoing basis. The purpose of using this consultant is to get a reading on whether the organization's donor history would support the beginnings of a planned giving program.

3. All duties—substitute for staff. Some smaller organizations wishing to undertake planned giving cannot afford to hire a full-time staff person. Some consultants work for those organizations one or two days per week, on an independent

contractor basis, and generally act as a planned giving staff person. Many of these consultants work for several organizations at the same time.

4. Technical support—tax and legal. Some consultants who are not attorneys or CPAs are nevertheless quite competent in the areas of providing technical support for a program. This support might include writing or reviewing brochures and newsletters and becoming involved with the organization in its gift structuring for prospects.

5. Marketing support. Marketing consultants are not used often enough in planned giving programs. They can perform marketing studies and help to identify target markets. With their help, markets can be expanded beyond those the organization thought existed. They can also work toward designing more effective methods of communications to reach those markets.

6. Internal structure, management, and funds administration. This type of consultant reviews the internal management structure for its strengths, weaknesses, needs for coordination, and readiness to undertake a planned giving program. At the initial stages of planned giving or when reviving a planned giving program, this consultant is absolutely necessary. Early coordination among the various offices, particularly those involving funds administration, is crucial to laying a good foundation for planned giving.

7. Board strengthening. Consultants working with nonprofit boards are not only known to planned giving consultants, but to development offices and nonprofit organizations in general. If there are extreme problems with the strength of the board, or with filling vacancies, this type of consultant can be very helpful.

The organization should carefully assess its own strengths and weaknesses and choose a consultant whose strengths are in the areas of the organization's weaknesses. In this way, the combination will form the best team. The purchaser may find that the consultants themselves have never considered their own strengths and weaknesses, or their areas of specialty. Very few consultants can be expert in all the areas listed above. It is critical to ferret out the level of expertise of a particular consultant and to get recommendations.

The organization should address the question of fees early in its conversations with consultants. Some staff at nonprofit organizations offer low-cost consultant services; they do not carry the overhead of a person or company in the consulting business full-time. On the other hand, those in the business full-time may have broader experience with different types of organizations and can carry the best and most successful ideas from one organization to the next.

In judging the qualifications of a consultant, the organization should consider these points:

1. General reputation;
2. Referral by other organizations;
3. Reputation among industry groups such as NSFRE (National Society of Fund Raising Executives), AHP (Association for Health Care Philanthropy), CASE (Council for Advancement and Support of Education), NCPG (National Committee on Planned Giving), and The Committee on Gift Annuities (which covers *all* planned giving vehicles now, even though its specialty is still gift annuities);

4. Length of time in field, and breadth of contact with different types of nonprofits;

5. Former or current fund-raising staff:

    i. Possible problem with ability to transfer skills;

    ii. Possible problem where planned giving staff member of an ongoing program becomes a consultant and has never created a planned giving program. A successful program at another organization does not necessarily make one a good consultant, particularly if the planned giving staff person came into an ongoing program.

    iii. Possible advantage of current, hands-on experience.

The consultant should also be asked to explain his or her policy regarding contracts. Some consultants require a noncancelable contract for a set period of time; others perform services on an at-will basis. (See Chapter 29, "Fund-Raising Consultants," for more information.)

(e) SELECTING AN ATTORNEY The process of planned giving will no doubt require the help of an attorney from time to time. It would be wise to choose this person ahead of time. Sometimes attorneys with experience in planned giving, especially from the organization's point of view, are hard to find. Consider these types of attorneys when selecting:

1. The fund-raising attorney. Certain attorneys specialize in working with fund-raisers and have knowledge of both fund-raising techniques and legal questions that arise during the fund-raising process, as well as funds administration, exempt organization matters, and related questions. It is especially helpful if this attorney has had staff experience either as in-house legal counsel or directly in fund-raising.

2. Exempt organization lawyer. This lawyer often has knowledge both in exempt organization legal and tax status matters as well as charitable giving. This specialist can be very helpful with a planned giving program, but will be almost as difficult to find as a fund-raising attorney.

3. The tax lawyer or estate planner. Many tax lawyers and estate planners have some degree of knowledge of charitable vehicles. However, even if they have a great deal of knowledge of charitable vehicles, they may not necessarily understand the donor/donee relationship or *the needs of the nonprofit itself.* These persons may be advocates or representatives of an individual client; nevertheless, they may be very knowledgeable in gift structures. The only caution for a nonprofit organization is that the structures they propose may be for the benefit of the individual client-donor as opposed to the best structure for the organization-donee.

4. The business lawyer. Business lawyers generally will not have a great knowledge of charitable giving, but if this is the only type of lawyer available, it may be worthwhile to undertake training him or her. A good business lawyer will try to work out creative solutions and help his or her client *make* things happen. That quality is invaluable in a charitable giving attorney as well.

5. General, large law firm. Large law firms almost always have expertise in the various traditional areas of law. A large law firm may or may not have a charitable giving specialist; the number of law firms with an in-house charitable giving specialist is small, but growing. If the firm does not have a specialist in this field, what happens when charitable giving questions arise? Sometimes, these are assigned to someone the partners feel either has time to learn it or is already working in an area that is closely aligned with the question asked. The nonprofit should follow the assignment closely because there have been many reports of organizations being charged for the learning curve of the attorney.

One advantage of a large law firm is that it offers many attorneys with expertise in different areas, so that when an unusual question comes up, perhaps regarding securities, contracts, patents, real estate, or the like, there will be someone in the law firm who can respond to that question—usually for an extra consulting fee. The advantages and disadvantages of the general large law firm should be carefully weighed.

6. Purchase of a name. Quite often, nonprofit boards are impressed with "big name" law firms and, for specific projects, they want to attach a "big name," regardless of whether that firm has any expertise in the subject matter in question. This is almost always disastrous and very costly to the organization. The law firm may not have expertise in charitable giving and may spend a lot of chargeable time and money researching the project. A very legal-sounding opinion letter will be issued, but the organization may have been much better off using a lawyer in any of the other categories listed above.

In considering what role the attorney might play with regard to the planned giving program, these are the key points:

1. Help in certain areas. The lawyer can help because he or she will have knowledge, either personally or conjointly with others in the firm, as to questions regarding special areas—real estate, corporate law, securities contracts, estates and trusts, exempt organization problems, unrelated business income, state laws regarding solicitation, endowments, and probate.

2. Need for independent judgment. It is human nature that when a fund-raiser works with a donor he or she will want to receive the gift. It is essential to have outside counsel review gift structures for their objectivity. Is this gift appropriate for the donee and for the donor? Simply said, the gift needs a second check.

3. Overcoming the reluctant adviser. The attorney selected should have or should be able to develop the ability to work with reluctant advisers, trying to persuade them to understand the charitable intent of the donor and the structure proposed. An attorney can be utilized as an "expert" who is offered to other advisers because of awareness that planned giving is an area of technical specialty.

4. Respect and credibility. In many situations, an attorney becomes a buffer or a shield, using the respect and credibility of the legal profession to advance the organization's position or to obtain things the organization needs.

(f) CHOOSING A TRUSTEE Because many of the gifts will be in the form of a trust, the organization must decide whether to act as trustee or whether to interview corporate trustees and recommend one or more to donors. The risk of the added liability of the organization and of individual board members when acting as trustee, plus the expertise required to handle trust matters correctly in-house, should be addressed at the board level. If the decision is to recommend corporate trustees, the planned giving officer will need to meet with the trustees available and assess their qualifications. A survey should be made of the trustees the organization may do business with. The following questions should be asked of all prospective trustees:

1. Does the trustee desire to handle charitable funds?
2. How long has the trustee been in the business and what kinds of charitable trusts is it managing?
3. How much money is under management?
4. How much charitable money is under management?
5. How much of that is in charitable trusts?
6. Who does charitable trust accounting and tax work?
7. Is there legal expertise on charitable matters in the general counsel's office?
8. How many trust officers are there with knowledge of charitable trusts?
9. Does the trustee provide other charitable services?
10. What are the fees?
11. What has been the investment performance?
12. What minimum levels have been established for trusts (i.e., what is the lowest fee and how does that relate to the size of the trust?)

Once a trustee is selected, its performance should be monitored regularly.

(g) CHOICE OF PERSON TO HIRE AS PLANNED GIVING OFFICER A nonprofit organization is created to carry out a specific function related to the needs of our society or culture. Quite often, the executive director has risen through the ranks of the substantive program as opposed to having been trained primarily as a manager, whether of a business, a governmental unit, or a nonprofit organization. The development office, on the other hand, generally attracts persons from the outside world, and they often have or develop an entrepreneurial attitude. The development office is a "profit center" within an organization not based on profits. Others in the institution quite often do not understand this mentality, which leads to conflicting cultures within the organizational structure. Development officers who come from the outside sometimes have little patience or understanding of the nonprofit bureaucratic process that prevents them from moving quickly to motivate donors or accept certain gifts (e.g., real estate). Whether or not the person is from the outside, the development office imposes a bottom-line mentality on a nonprofit organization. Values dear to most nonprofits—equity, fairness, avoidance of conflict—are often obstacles to entrepreneurial ventures. Thus, fund-raisers, and particularly planned giving officers, must exist in two worlds simultaneously: the money/business world of donors and the "nonmoney" world of nonprofits. The tension arising from this conflict causes more of the daily problems than we may realize at first.

Planned giving staff (in fact, all of the major gifts unit) deals with high dollar amounts and wealthy donors, from the crowded confines of a little office with indoor-outdoor carpeting and metal furniture down at the end of a narrow hall. Colleagues in other areas of the nonprofit cannot often understand the dichotomy or the stress it may produce. Often, the faculty of a school, the hospital personnel, the staff of an environmental organization, or a group of social workers may have no sympathy for the problems of the wealthy and may, in fact, disdain the very wealth that is the source of the gift. Meanwhile, the major gifts or planned gifts officer must maintain a balance between this attitude and the realities of dealing with a donor of wealth. Too often, the non-fund-raising staff feels it is the social responsibility of the wealthy to fund the nonprofit organization in question. Therefore, when the planned gifts officer wants special consideration in the gift structuring or gift acceptance process, cooperation is not always easy to come by.

In light of the potential for conflict and tension, who is inclined to accept a position as a planned giving officer? Realism about the job and its requirements will help the person seeking to work as a planned giving officer adjust and will perhaps lead to more job satisfaction and less job turnover. In addition, understanding the potential conflicts ahead of time will permit planning to avoid them, thereby creating an atmosphere conducive to a successful planned giving program.

From the organization's point of view, the choice of a planned giving officer is, needless to say, an important element in the success of the program. Organizations often ask: Which candidate is preferable, a marketing-oriented or a technically oriented person? Perhaps that question is irrelevant, and the following qualities should be sought. Generally, the person should understand philanthropy—the role it has played historically in building this country, the role it currently plays, and its future trends. Specifically, he or she must thoroughly understand the program the organization delivers and be committed to it. Commitment is always asked of board members, while staff persons, who are the backbone of the operation, are treated as "hired guns." This may be a factor in the high turnover rate of development office employees.

Personal characteristics and abilities to look for in a planned giving officer might include the following: someone who (1) is good-humored, pleasant, and determined; (2) does not let constant disruption, negativity, rejection, and shoestring budgets bother him or her; (3) while making $45,000–$65,000 per year, will try to understand what it means to part with a half-million dollars; (4) will try to understand the psychology of the wealthy without ever exhibiting jealousy or insensitivity to their special needs, and will never call a donor "Mrs. Gotrocks"; (5) is willing to learn large amounts of confusing information that will change just as soon as it is learned; and (6) has a "presence" that will be accepted by donors of wealth and professional advisers.

The job of a planned giving officer requires a willingness to learn. One must always be seeking a little more knowledge. Although many planned giving officers come from jobs and professions outside the world of fund-raising, it is important to remember that planned giving is just another form of fund-raising. Maybe a person with good fund-raising skills should be taught the field of planned giving, rather than teaching fund-raising skills to a person from the outside. Sometimes those who come in from the outside world just do not see the necessity of developing good fund-raising skills and of learning basic fund-raising principles. These are as important in planned giving as in any other function of the development office. Ultimately, the organization needs to determine which type of person will serve its needs best and will coordinate well with other staff members.

20.3 MARKETING THE PROGRAM

(a) THE MARKETING PLAN Too many organizations ignore the need for effective marketing plans. Just as the organization itself needs a long-term planning process to understand its goals and directions, the planned giving program needs a well-considered, written plan for approaching the marketplace for planned gifts. The program needs to know how to get from point A to point B. Many, or most, planned giving programs are started without an understanding of where the organization hopes to go in what time frame. Thus, a marketing plan can be the road map for a successful planned giving program.

Many books have been written on how to create a marketing plan, and each author has a different approach. This must say to the reader that nothing here is cast in stone, and each organization must ultimately determine its own best marketing plan. Nevertheless, as a starting point, these six steps in creating a marketing plan should be considered:

1. Understanding who the organization is in relation to the marketplace. This involves demographic and psychographic studies of the potential donor base, to determine what groups of people might realistically give to the planned giving program. Not every organization is willing to pay the cost of such a study, but those who have gone the extra step have found the study to be invaluable both for delivery of services and for fund-raising.

2. Segmenting the marketplace into target markets based on identities of wants and needs of the potential donors in each of the market segments.

3. Designing planned gift strategies that may be appealing to each target market and that meet the perceived wants and needs of that target market.

4. Checking similarly situated organizations to see what the competition is doing and what outreach programs they may be planning that may overlap or conflict.

5. Developing effective outreach efforts based on the market studies done in accordance with the above steps. These will no doubt include donor and professional seminars, bequest mailings, newsletters, advertisements (perhaps), and other sources of reaching people who may be willing to commit to the planned giving program.

6. Creating effective private communications, once an individual prospect is identified.

(b) IMPLEMENTING THE OUTREACH AND COMMUNICATIONS Once a marketing plan has been established, it must be implemented with the same diligence. The typical outreach and donor acquisition functions of planned giving include sponsoring seminars for donors and prospects on the subject of estate planning; presenting for the professionals in the community a seminar directly on the subject of the technical aspects of planned giving; and mailing brochures, bequest intention letters, and periodic newsletters. It is important to reach the same market in as many ways as possible and to keep the message straightforward and simple. The gift structuring phase can become complex quickly enough; in the early stages, motivation may be thwarted if the material is too complex.

20.4 PLANNED GIVING VEHICLES

No planned giving program can succeed without a good, basic understanding of the gift vehicles. What follows here is designed to give only a quick overview of some of the technical rules.

(a) CHARITABLE REMAINDER ANNUITY TRUST

(i) Definition Internal Revenue Code Section (IRC) § 664(d)(1) requires that a charitable remainder annuity trust ("CRAT") contain the following features (see Exhibit 20.3):

1. Payments to income beneficiaries of a fixed dollar amount or percentage of initial net fair market value (FMV), but at least 5 percent of initial net FMV;
2. One or more income beneficiaries, one of whom is not an IRC § 170(c) charity (otherwise it's a wholly charitable trust);
3. Annuity payments made for life or lives of income beneficiaries, or a term of years (not to exceed 20);
4. Remainder passes to IRC § 170(c) charitable organization(s);
5. Functions as CRAT from its "creation." Creation is the earliest time no person is treated as "owner" of the trust under subchapter J of the Internal Revenue Code and property is transferred to the trust.

(ii) Specific features Any person or persons may be the grantor of CRAT. The definition of "person" under IRC § 7701(a)(1) includes an individual, a trust, an estate, a partnership, an association, or a corporation.

Any person who does not make the CRAT a grantor trust may serve as trustee (see Revenue Ruling (Rev. Rul.) 77-285, 1977-2 Cumulative Bulletin (C.B.) 213). An independent trustee is needed, however, if the trust holds "hard-to-value" property (i.e., closely held stock, real estate) (see the 1969 Tax Reform Act Legislative History H.R. 91-413, 91st Cong., 1st Sess. 60 (1969)), or if the trust gives the trustee a "sprinkle power" (power to allocate the annuity amount among beneficiaries) (IRC § 674(c)). An independent trustee is a trustee or trustees, none of whom is the grantor, and no more than half of whom are "related or subordinate parties" within IRC § 672(c).

Exhibit 20.3. Charitable remainder annuity trust.

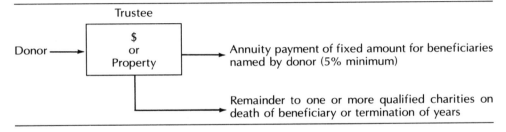

Permissible income beneficiaries include individuals, trusts, estates, partnerships, associations, and corporations. At least one income beneficiary must not be an IRC § 170(c) charity. In general, individual income beneficiaries must be living at the time the CRAT is created. If the income beneficiaries are a named class of individuals (e.g., "To my children living at my death"), all members of the class must be alive at the time the CRAT is created, unless the CRAT is for a term of years (Treasury Regulation (Treas. Reg.) § 1.664-2(a)(3)). The grantor may retain the power to revoke by will the interest of any beneficiary other than an IRC § 170(c) organization (Treas. Reg. § 1.664-2(a)(4)).

The remainder interest in a CRAT must be irrevocably contributed "to" or "for the use of" a charity. Alternative remaindermen must be named, in case the named beneficiary is not in existence or not qualified when the trust terminates. Remaindermen may be revocable if the remainder interest is irrevocably dedicated to qualified charities (Rev. Rul. 76-8, 1976-1 C.B. 179).

Unlike a charitable remainder unitrust, no additional contributions are permitted after the initial transfer.

No payments other than the annuity amount may be made to anyone except the charity, unless full and adequate consideration is given (e.g., trustee fees). The statute and the Treasury Regulations place no restrictions on trust investments, except that the trust provisions may not prevent the trustee from realizing both income and capital gains on an annual basis (Treas. Reg. § 1.664-1(a)(3)).

The trust document should define what is income and what is principal, both as to receipts and as to charges or expenses. The trust document should also include accurate, yet flexible, wording regarding use of the funds by the charity, to avoid a restricted gift that no longer meets the needs of the organization.

(b) CHARITABLE REMAINDER UNITRUST

(i) **Definition** Internal Revenue Code Section (IRC) § 664(d)(2) requires that a charitable remainder unitrust ("CRUT") contain the following features (see Exhibit 20.4):

1. Payments to income beneficiaries of a fixed percentage (minimum 5 percent) of the annual net fair market value (FMV) of the CRUT (the "unitrust payment" is not the same as "income"; the trust payments are based on the value of the trust assets, rather than income generated by those assets);

Exhibit 20.4. Charitable remainder unitrust.

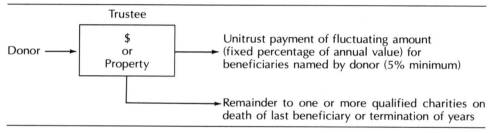

2. One or more income beneficiaries, one of whom is not an IRC § 170(c) charity (otherwise it's a wholly charitable trust);

3. Unitrust payments made for life or lives of income beneficiaries, or a term of years (not to exceed 20);

4. Remainder passes to IRC § 170(c) charitable organization(s);

5. Functions as a CRUT from its creation. Creation is the earliest time no person is treated as "owner" under subchapter J and property is transferred to the trust.

(ii) Specific features Any person or persons may be the grantor of a CRUT. The definition of "person" under IRC § 7701(a)(1) includes an individual, a trust, an estate, a partnership, an association, or a corporation.

Any person who does not make the CRUT a grantor trust may serve as trustee (see Rev. Rul. 77-285, 1977-2 C.B. 213). An independent trustee is needed, however, if the CRUT holds "hard-to-value" property (i.e., closely held stock, real estate) (see the 1969 Tax Reform Act Legislative History, H.R. 91-413, 91st Cong., 1st Sess. 60 (1969)), or if the trust gives the trustee a "sprinkle power" (power to allocate the unitrust amount among beneficiaries) (IRC § 674(c)). An independent trustee is a trustee or trustees, none of whom is the grantor, and no more than half of whom are "related or subordinate parties" within IRC § 672(c).

Permissible income beneficiaries include individuals, trusts, estates, partnerships, associations, and corporations. At least one income beneficiary must not be an IRC § 170(c) charity. In general, individual income beneficiaries must be living at the time the CRUT is created. If the income beneficiaries are a named class of individuals (e.g., "To my children living at my death"), all members of the class must be alive at the time the CRUT is created, unless the CRUT is for a term of years (Treas. Reg. § 1.664-3(a)(3)). The grantor may retain the power to revoke by will the interest of any beneficiary other than an IRC § 170(c) organization (Treas. Reg. § 1.664-3(a)(4)).

The remainder interest in a CRUT must be irrevocably contributed "to" or "for the use of" a charity. Alternative remainderman must be named, in case the named beneficiary is not in existence or not qualified when the trust terminates. Remaindermen may be revocable if the remainder interest is irrevocably transferred to qualified charities (Rev. Rul. 76-8, 1976-1 C.B. 179).

Unlike a CRAT, additional contributions are permitted *IF* the trust instrument provides for them *and* provides for (1) valuation of property at the time of contribution and (2) determination of a prorated unitrust payment. Otherwise, the trust instrument must prohibit additional contributions.

No payments other than the unitrust amount may be made to anyone except a charity, unless full and adequate consideration is given (e.g., trustee fees). The statute and Treasury Regulations place no restrictions on trust investments, except that the trust provisions may not prevent the trustee from realizing both income and capital gains on an annual basis (Treas. Reg. § 1.664-1(a)(3)).

The trust document should define what is income and what is principal, both as to receipts and as to charges or expenses. The trust document should also include accurate, yet flexible, wording regarding use of the funds by the charity, to avoid a restricted gift that no longer meets the needs of the organization.

(c) NET INCOME UNITRUST This variation of a CRUT has several names, including net income unitrust (NIU), IOU trust, and Income-only unitrust. The key differences from the standard CRUT are that the unitrust payment is one of the following:

1. The LESSER of trust income, as determined under state law, or the amount calculated using the fixed percentage of trust FMV. Thus, although the fixed percentage in the trust document may not be less than 5 percent, the trust payments will be less if the trust has insufficient earnings. This version is called the "net income" or "net income without deficiency make-up" CRUT;

OR

2. All of item 1 above PLUS trust income in excess of the amount calculated using the fixed percentage of trust FMV to the extent that trust income (and thus unitrust payments) in prior years (on an aggregate basis) was less than the amount determined by using the fixed percentage (on an aggregate basis). This is called the "net income unitrust with deficiency makeup," or "IOU" CRUT.

Property that is non-income-producing or low-income-producing and cannot meet a mandatory unitrust or annuity trust payment—such as real estate or closely held stock—is often transferred to a net income unitrust. A net income unitrust is appropriate because it allows the trust to pay the income beneficiary only the actual income earned by the trust asset. Absent such a net income provision, the trust would be required to return a portion of the contributed property to the income beneficiary in order to meet the mandatory unitrust payment. If a makeup provision is included (item 2 above), the deficiency amount can be paid to the income beneficiary once the trust generates income in excess of the fixed percentage.

(d) IRS PROTOTYPE DOCUMENTS The Internal Revenue Service (IRS) has published prototype, or sample, CRAT and CRUT trust instruments. The chart in Exhibit 20.5 describes these documents and sets out the Revenue Procedures in which they may be found. When reviewing these samples, it should be remembered that they are forms and most likely do not take into account the needs and wants of a donor. They also do not address nontax issues, such as the trustee's ability to hire agents, the grantor's ability to remove a trustee, and so on. (For a careful analysis of these samples, see Moerschbaecher, McCoy, and Simmons, August 1990.)

(e) POOLED INCOME FUND

(i) Specific features To date, individuals and corporations have been permitted to contribute to a pooled income fund ("PIF"). There is no guidance yet regarding trusts, partnerships, or other entities as donors (see Exhibit 20.6).

Tax-exempt securities may not be contributed to, or purchased by, a PIF. In addition, non-income-producing property will reduce the PIF's total return, thereby reducing income to all donor/beneficiary units. Generally, it is not advisable to accept such property unless the PIF can sell it quickly. Also, the PIF document must either prohibit the PIF from holding depreciable or depletable property (e.g., real estate) or require that a depreciation or depletion reserve be maintained in accordance with generally accepted

Exhibit 20.5. IRS prototype charitable remainder trust instruments.

	Intervivos	Testamentary	Revenue Procedure
Unitrusts	One life		89-20
	Two lives consecutive		90-30, Sec. 4
	Two lives consecutive and concurrent		90-30, Sec. 5
		One life	90-30, Sec. 6
		Two lives consecutive	90-30, Sec. 7
		Two lives consecutive and concurrent	90-30, Sec. 8
Net income unitrusts (with deficiency make-up)	One life		90-31, Sec. 4
	Two lives consecutive		90-31, Sec. 5
	Two lives consecutive and concurrent		90-31, Sec. 6
		One life	90-31, Sec. 7
		Two lives consecutive	90-31, Sec. 8
		Two lives consecutive and concurrent	90-31, Sec. 9
Annuity trusts	One life		89-21
	Two lives consecutive		90-32, Sec. 4
	Two lives consecutive and concurrent		90-32, Sec. 5
		One life	90-32, Sec. 6
		Two lives consecutive	90-32, Sec. 7
		Two lives consecutive and concurrent	90-32, Sec. 8

Exhibit 20.6. Pooled income fund.

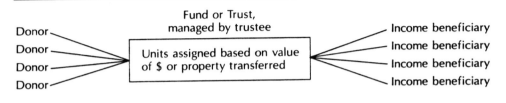

Remainderman—On death of beneficiary, value of units severed, given outright to charity.

accounting principles (GAAP) (unless state law already so provides) (Rev. Rul. 90-103, 1990-51 I.R.B. 14).

No donor or beneficiary (other than the charitable remainderman) may be trustee. However, if the charity is trustee, its officers, directors, or other officials may generally be donors or beneficiaries.

The income interest(s) retained by the donor and/or created for others must be for life. Thus, only individuals, not corporations, partnerships, trusts, and so on, may be income beneficiaries. Income beneficiaries must be living at the time of transfer. Income payments may be made to multiple income beneficiaries concurrently, consecutively, or concurrently and consecutively. The donor may retain the power to revoke an income beneficiary's interest by will.

Payments to income beneficiaries are of a share of net income after expenses of the fund. Net income is allocated based on the number of PIF units assigned to the value of the donor's transfer. PIF units are valued on periodic determination dates.

A PIF may have only one remainderman, which must be a public charity described in IRC § 509(a)(1). A parent entity can assign a remainder interest to its subordinate organizations, and national, regional, and other "umbrella" organizations can maintain a PIF for the benefit of their member groups. However, horizontal (or "brother–sister") organizations cannot share a PIF. The remainderman must "maintain" the PIF (i.e., be trustee or have the power to replace the trustee).

The property of the various donors is commingled and invested by the PIF. The assets of the PIF may be *jointly* invested with the trustee's other funds or endowments *if* the fund assets and income of the PIF are separately accounted for. At the death of an income beneficiary, the value of the donor's units is severed and made available to the charitable remainderman. In determining the amount severed, income is prorated to the date of death, or, where the trust provides for the last income payment to be on the last regular payment date prior to the date of death, the remainder is valued as of the last regular payment date.

The Securities and Exchange Commission has stated that a charity does not need to register its PIF (i.e., the SEC will not deem the PIF interests to be securities) IF there is full and fair *disclosure* of the operation of the PIF to the donor; gift solicitors do not receive compensation based on the amount of gifts made; and the PIF qualifies as a pooled income fund under IRC § 642(c)(5) (SEC Release No. 33-6175).

(ii) IRS prototype documents   The IRS has published a prototype, or sample, PIF trust document and gift agreements (Rev. Proc. 88-53, 1988-2 C.B. 712). These forms do *not* include the disclosure statement required by the SEC.

(f) CHARITABLE LEAD TRUST

(i) Definition   Very little discussion of the charitable lead trust ("CLT") appears in the Internal Revenue Code (see Exhibit 20.7). There are two types of CLTs: grantor and nongrantor. The grantor lead trust comes within the definition of a grantor trust in IRC §§ 671–679; the nongrantor version does not. See Exhibit 20.8 for a discussion of the differences.

The income payments to the charity can be in the form of an annuity or unitrust interest. With a charitable lead annuity trust, the charity has an irrevocable right to receive an annuity for a term of years or for the life of the donor or other individuals.

Exhibit 20.7.   Charitable lead trust.

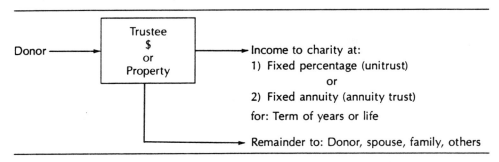

With a charitable lead unitrust, the charity has an irrevocable right to receive a fixed percentage of net FMV of assets, determined annually (no net income exception as with charitable remainder unitrusts), for a term of years or for the life of the donor or other individuals.

(ii) Specific features   Any person or persons may be the grantor of a CLT. The definition of "person" under IRC § 7701(a)(1) includes an individual, a trust, an estate, a partnership, an association, or a corporation. The property contributed to the CLT must be capable of generating income, because the payout to the charity is mandatory.

Anyone may be trustee of a CLT. However, the trust powers given to the trustee should not make the grantor the "owner" of trust assets where the grantor acts as the trustee (see IRC §§ 671–679), if a nongrantor lead trust is intended.

Any IRC § 501(c)(3) organization may be named as the income beneficiary. Private individuals may also be income beneficiaries, but only from segregated portions of the trust assets (Treas. Reg. § 1.170A-6(c)(2)(ii)(D)).

Exhibit 20.8.   Qualified charitable lead trusts.

	Annuity	Unitrust
Grantor	Grantor pays income tax on trust income	Same
	Grantor takes income tax deduction for present value of trust income*	Same
	Charity gets annuity for years or life	Charity gets unitrust amount for years or life
	Grantor (or grantor's estate) gets remainder	Same
Non-Grantor	Grantor parts with all ownership and control	Same
	Grantor gets no income tax deduction,** pays no tax on income	Same
	Charity gets annuity for years or life	Charity gets unitrust amount for years or life
	Others get remainder	Same

*Income and gift tax deduction.
**No income tax deduction, but gift/estate tax deductions available.

(g) LIFE INSURANCE POLICY A donor may make a "gift" of an insurance policy by merely changing the beneficiary designation. However, because the beneficiary designation is revocable, it is an incomplete gift and no income tax deduction is allowed. An income tax deduction for the value of the policy will be allowed if the ownership of the policy is changed to the charity. A policy's value for this purpose is generally its replacement value if the policy is paid up, and its interpolated terminal reserve value if it is not. Local law must be checked, however. In Private Letter Ruling 9110016, the IRS concluded that, under New York law (since changed), a charity did not have an insurable interest in its donor. Because the charity's rights to the policy proceeds were thus voidable, the donor's deductions were denied (Tidd, 1991).

(h) CHARITABLE GIFT ANNUITIES These gift vehicles are accomplished by means of a contract, not a trust. Because this gift is not in trust, it is actually an immediate, not a deferred, gift to charity. Each contract covers only one gift; future contributions require a new contract (see Exhibit 20.9).

A portion, determined by actuarial tables, of the amount transferred by the donor to the charity is deemed to be the value of the annuity and therefore for the benefit of the individual. The balance of the amount transferred is a deductible gift to the charity.

The annuity payment is an unsecured, general obligation of the issuing charity. The committee on Gift Annuities publishes uniform annuity rates for single- and joint-plus-survivor gift annuity contracts.

Some state insurance commissions regulate the issuance of gift annuities. The charity may have to maintain reserves to protect the annuitant's interest. State law should be checked to determine whether the charity must be certified or licensed to issue gift annuities and to ascertain audit and yearly filing requirements.

If certain restrictions are satisfied, the income earned by the contributed property is not unrelated business income to the charity. These conditions are: (1) one or two life contracts only; (2) the annuity portion must be worth less than 90 percent of the whole transfer; (3) the annuity must be the sole consideration issued for the property transferred; (4) there may be no guarantee of a minimum or maximum number of payments (i.e., no term-of-years annuity allowed); (5) there may be no adjustment of the annuity payment by reference to income received from the transferred property or any other property (Treas. Reg. § 1.514(c)-1(e)(1)).

In a deferred gift annuity, the first payment, as stated in the contract, is deferred at least one year. During the deferral period, the annuity rate is compounded. The Committee on Gift Annuities suggests uniform compounding rates. The effect of the deferral period is to reduce the value of the annuity and increase the charitable deduction.

(i) LIFE ESTATE—REMAINDERS IN RESIDENCE OR FARM A remainder interest is a future interest, given now and vested in ownership, where possession arises at a preset date or at the end of the life tenant's life (see Exhibit 20.10). An income tax deduction is available at the date of gift for the value of a remainder interest given to charity

Exhibit 20.9. Charitable gift annuities.

Donor — $ or property → Charity

Donor ← Annual Annuity — Charity

Exhibit 20.10. Gift of remainder interest.

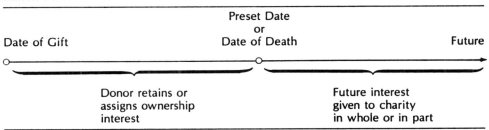

Date of Gift	Preset Date or Date of Death	Future
Donor retains or assigns ownership interest		Future interest given to charity in whole or in part

only with respect to remainder interests in: (1) a residence—any property used by the donor as a *personal* residence even though not the *principal* residence, including vacation homes, condos, and co-op apartments; and (2) a farm—any land, including improvements, used by the taxpayer or his or her tenant for the production of crops, fruit, or agricultural products, or for the sustenance of livestock.

Making a life estate-remainder gift creates joint ownership where the life tenant has possession. Certain issues must be addressed, such as which party is responsible for mortgage payments, taxes, insurance, and repairs. The laws of some states spell out some of the duties of a life tenant and the remainderman. Other major issues that should be covered in a contract are: (1) if there is a fire, flood, earthquake, or other casualty, whether the improvements will be rebuilt, and, if not, how the insurance proceeds will be split; and (2) whether the life tenant may lease the property, and whether the remainderman may review the lease and/or tenant.

20.5 AVOIDING PITFALLS

(a) STEP TRANSACTION OR COLLAPSIBLE GIFT RULE Often, a donor will contribute an asset to a trust (or charity) after having negotiated a sale of the asset. If the donor has fully negotiated the sale and there is a legal obligation on the part of the donee (trust or charity) to sell the asset to the buyer, the capital gain will be taxed to the donor. (See *Magnolia Development Corp. v. Commissioner,* T.C. Memo 1960-177.) To avoid this result, the trust (or charity) must have free reign to: (1) negotiate the sale, (2) change the terms of the deal, and (3) walk away from the deal entirely. (See *Martin v. Commissioner,* 251 F. Supp. 381 (1966).)

(b) TANGIBLE PERSONAL PROPERTY A charitable contribution of a future interest in tangible personal property is deductible for income tax purposes only when all intervening interests to the possession or enjoyment of the property have expired or are held by persons other than the taxpayer. Thus, a transfer of art to an organization, where a donor retains a life interest, results in no income tax deduction until the donor relinquishes the intervening life interest (IRC § 170(a)(3)). It is unclear whether this rule applies when tangible property is placed into a charitable remainder trust or pooled income fund in which the donor retains a life income interest, but the trustee sells the asset and reinvests in stocks or other assets paying a life income to the donor. Certain aggressive taxpayers have claimed that a deduction may be claimed once the art work or other tangible property is sold by the trustee.

Further, any gift of tangible personal property that is not used by the donee in a related use (related to the reason the organization exists—e.g., art to a museum) generates a deduction based only on the donor's tax basis in the property (IRC § 170(e)(1)(B)). If the property is gifted for a related use, the deduction is based on the property's fair market value.

(c) INTANGIBLES Intangible assets such as partnership interests, trademarks, patents, and copyrights are often proposed as possible gifts. Valuation of these assets is always a difficult question, and can be especially troublesome if the intangible is transferred to a CRT or PIF (as the income payable is based on the asset value).

As to partnership interests, the IRS employs either (or both) the aggregate theory and the entity theory. The aggregate theory states that each partner owns an undivided interest in each and every asset of the partnership; the entity theory holds that the partnership interest itself is the item of property. If the aggregate theory is employed with respect to a gift of a partnership interest, the donor will be deemed to have made a gift of each asset and liability held by the partnership. Thus, even though the partner may hold his or her partnership interest free-and-clear, the partner may be deemed to have given encumbered property if the partnership incurred debt (see Private Letter Ruling 7943062).

(d) MORTGAGED PROPERTY Transferring mortgaged property into a CRT raises several issues:

1. The transfer constitutes a bargain sale (i.e., part gift, part sale), because the donor is deemed to have received "sale proceeds" in the amount of the debt relieved (Treas. Reg. § 1.1011-2(a)(3));
2. The CRT may own debt-financed property generating unrelated business income (see below);
3. The transfer may constitute an act of self-dealing (see below);
4. If the donor remains personally liable on the debt after the transfer and the CRT makes a payment on the debt, the IRS has taken the position that the trust becomes a grantor trust and is therefore disqualified as a CRT (Private Letter Ruling 9015049).

(e) ALTERNATIVE MINIMUM TAX An in-depth discussion of the alternative minimum tax ("AMT") is beyond the scope of this chapter (see IRC § 55 et seq.). In brief, an individual pays the greater of his or her regular federal income tax or AMT. An individual's AMT is based on his or her regular taxable income, increased or decreased for certain adjustments and preferences. One preference that is added back is the amount by which the income tax charitable deduction would be reduced if capital gain property were taken into account at its tax basis (instead of FMV) (except for certain tangible personal property given in 1991 or the first half of 1992).

As a result, a large gift of highly appreciated property will reduce the donor's regular tax, but may not reduce his or her AMT, causing the donor to pay AMT. However, a donor (or his or her tax adviser) should not automatically reject a gift just because it would put the donor into an AMT situation. The donor's options should be evaluated:

1. Keep the asset (consider the income generated by the asset and the fact that the asset will be subject to estate tax at death);

2. Sell the asset (consider the capital gains tax and the fact that no deduction will be available);

3. Give the asset.

Even if a gift causes AMT, it may be the least costly alternative.

(f) UNRELATED BUSINESS INCOME The unrelated business income tax was enacted in the early 1950s to counteract complaints by businesses that exempt organizations were unfairly competing in business ventures because they paid no tax (see IRC § 5111 et seq.). The tax arises in two ways: operationally (running a business) and via "debt-financed property."

In its operational form, the tax is imposed on gross income from: (1) a trade or business; (2) regularly carried on; and (3) unrelated to the exempt purpose of the charity (IRC § 512). Deductions directly connected with the activity offset the gross income, and a specific deduction of $1,000 is permitted. Certain income is "passive" and thus exempt: dividends, interest, payments on securities loans, annuities, royalties, and rent from *certain types* of leases. Gains on the sale of property are generally excluded, except for gains on the sale of property held for sale to customers in the ordinary course of business.

The income (or a portion of the income) produced by "debt-financed property" may also be unrelated business income (IRC § 514). Debt-financed property is property held for the purpose of producing income on which there is "acquisition indebtedness" at any time during the taxable year. Acquisition indebtedness is defined as the unpaid amount of:

1. Debt incurred in acquiring or improving the property;

2. Debt incurred *before* the acquisition or improvement of the property, if the debt would not have been incurred other than for the acquisition or improvement;

3. Debt incurred *after* the acquisition or improvement, if the debt would not have been incurred other than for the acquisition or improvement *and* was "reasonably foreseeable when the property was acquired or improved."

If property is acquired subject to mortgage or certain liens, the debt or lien is considered acquisition indebtedness. However, if the property is received by bequest, the debt will not be acquisition indebtedness for 10 years. If the property is received by gift, the debt will not be acquisition indebtedness for 10 years, *if* the mortgage was placed over 5 years before the gift, and the donor held the property more than 5 years before the gift (IRC § 514(c)(2)). See Chapter 33 for more information.

(g) SELF-DEALING A tax is imposed on acts of self-dealing between a "disqualified person" and a "private foundation," by IRC § 4941. This section is made directly applicable to CRTs, CLTs, and PIFs (IRC § 4947(a)(2)). The first tier is 5 percent on the self-dealer and 2½ percent on the "foundation manager" (in this case, the trustee). If not corrected, a 200 percent tax is imposed on the self-dealer and 50 percent on the foundation manager (the maximum for the manager is $10,000 per act).

Self-dealing includes direct or indirect:

1. Sale, exchange, or leasing of property between a private foundation (trust) and a disqualified person;

2. Lending of money or extension of credit between a private foundation and a disqualified person;

3. Furnishing of goods, services, or facilities between a private foundation and a disqualified person;

4. Payment of compensation or reimbursement of expenses by a private foundation to a disqualified person;

5. Transfer to or use by a disqualified person of income or assets of the private foundation;

6. Agreement by the private foundation to make payment to a government official (other than for employment after termination of government services).

Certain special rules apply:

1. Real estate transferred subject to a mortgage assumed by the foundation or placed on the property within 10 years prior to transfer is considered a sale or exchange;

2. Loans to the foundation without interest are not self-dealing *if* used exclusively for charitable purposes;

3. Furnishing of goods, services, and so on, *to* a foundation is not self-dealing if without charge and exclusively for charitable purposes, and *from* the foundation if made on no more favorable a basis than to the general public;

4. Payment of compensation for personal services which are reasonable and necessary to achieving the exempt purpose is not self-dealing if the compensation is not excessive;

5. A liquidation, merger, redemption, or recapitalization involving a corporate disqualified person and the foundation is not self-dealing if all securities of the same class as the foundation holds are offered the same terms, and the foundation will receive fair market value for its stock.

Disqualified persons include:

1. A substantial contributor;

2. A foundation manager;

3. Someone who owns 20 percent or more of a corporation's voting power, a partnership's profit interest, or a trust's beneficial interest, where that entity is a substantial contributor;

4. A member of the family of a person described in items 1, 2, or 3;

5. A corporation, partnership, or trust in which persons described in items 1, 2, 3, or 4 own 35 percent or more (IRC § 4946(a)).

(h) ENVIRONMENTAL LIABILITY Environmental liability and hazardous waste have become major issues in gifts of real estate. Of particular concern is the extent to which a trustee's personal assets are exposed because the trustee holds legal title to property. Every charitable organization should adopt (at board level) a policy regarding the acceptance and review of gifts of real estate, both outright and in trust, addressing what level of environmental reviews are required and who should pay the cost of such review.

SOURCES AND SUGGESTED REFERENCES

Abbin, Byrle M., Cronwell, Diane, Helfand, Richard A., Janicki, Michael, and Nager, Ross W. 1984. *Tax Economics of Charitable Giving* (10th ed.). Chicago: Arthur Andersen & Co.

Ashton, Debra. 1990. *The Complete Guide to Planned Giving* (2nd ed.). Cambridge, MA: JLA Publications.

Charitable Giving Tax Service. 1977. Chicago: R&R Newkirk.

Donaldson, and Osteen. 1992. *The Harvard Manual on Tax Aspects of Charitable Giving* (7th ed.). Boston: Harvard University.

Hamlin, Petkun, and Bednarz. 1986. *Charitable Income Trusts.* Washington, DC: Bureau of National Affairs, Portfolio.

Moerschbaecher, Lynda. 1991. *Keep It To Yourself* (book and audio tapes). San Francisco: Author.

———. 1991. *Plain English Planned Giving: After the Gift Is Closed* (book and audio tapes). San Francisco: Author.

———. 1991. *Plain English Planned Giving: Starting at Square One* (book and audio tapes). San Francisco: Author.

Moerschbaecher, L., McCoy, and Simmons. 1990. *Charitable Gift Planning* (August).

Petkun, Hamlin, and Downing. 1986. *Charitable Remainder Trusts and Pooled Income Funds.* Washington, DC: Bureau of National Affairs, Portfolio.

R-Plan Manual. Los Angeles: Stanford University, Office of Planned Giving. Updated periodically.

Sharpe, Robert F. 1979. *Before You Give Another Dime.* Nashville, TN: Thomas Nelson.

———. 1980. *The Planned Giving Idea Book.* Nashville, TN: Thomas Nelson.

Stern, Schumacher, John L., and Martin, Patrick D. 1990. *Charitable Giving and Solicitation.* New York: Prentice-Hall/Maxwell MacMillan.

Teitell. 1991. *Deferred Giving.* Old Greenwich, CT: Taxwise Giving.

———. 1991. *Charitable Lead Trusts.* Old Greenwich, CT: Taxwise Giving.

Teuller, Alden B. 1991. *The Planned Giving Deskbook.* Rockville, MD: The Taft Group.

Tidd, Jonathan. 1991. "The Insurable Interest Rule and Charitable Gifts of Life Insurance." *Tax Management Estates, Gifts and Trusts Journal* (September–October).

RECOMMENDED PERIODICALS AND NEWSLETTERS

Brownell, Catherine (ed.). *Chronicle of Non Profit Enterprise.* Bainbridge Island, WA.

Hopkins, Bruce R. *The Nonprofit Counsel.* New York: John Wiley & Sons.

Meuhrcke, Jill (ed.). *Nonprofit World.* Madison, WI: Society for Nonprofit Organizations.

Moerschbaecher, L., McCoy, and Simmons, *Charitable Gift Planning News* (monthly) and *The Practical Gift Planner* (bimonthly, nontechnical). San Francisco (415-788-1414) Dallas.

Schoenhals, Roger. *Planned Giving Today.* Seattle, WA.

Stern, Larry (ed.). *Non-Profit Times.* Skillman, NJ.

Teitell, *Taxwise Giving.* Old Greenwich, CT.

Teuller, Alden B. *The Planned Gifts Counselor.* Washington, DC: The Taft Group.

Capital Fund Appeals

Charles E. Lawson
Brakeley, John Price Jones, Inc.

CONTENTS

21.1 DEFINITIONS

(a) ANNUAL VERSUS CAPITAL FUND DRIVES There are two main differences between annual and capital campaigns:

1. The impetus that drives them forward;
2. The level of gifts required for success.

In an annual campaign, time is the driving impetus and the timeline is finite. There is one year in which to reach the goal. If, by the end of that year, the organization has reached the goal, victory! Otherwise, something less than that.

Capital campaigns offer distinct benefits, as indicated in Exhibit 21.1. In both capital and annual campaigns, the gift level goals are proportionate to the overall goal. But annual goals do not have the magnitude of capital campaigns; therefore, the gifts given are generally much more modest. Annual gifts can be typified as coming from cash (the donor's wallet or checkbook); capital gifts tend to come from assets and are usually paid over several years.

(b) THE BIG GIFT: A RELATIVE TERM   The top tiers for giving in a capital campaign are much larger than in annual drives. Even within the capital fund arena, "the big gift" is a relative term. For a campaign goal of $100 million, for example, the lead gift sought might be $10 million (the lead gift should be at least 10 percent of the overall goal). In a campaign to raise $3.5 million, the top gift might be $350,000.

The sample gift-range tables shown in Exhibits 21.2 through 21.5 illustrate four separate capital campaigns, four separate goals, and four separate "big gifts" at the top.

(c) TOP DOWN/INSIDE OUT   The basis of successful capital campaigning is what we have come to refer to as "sequential solicitation," also known as the "top down/inside out approach."

Think of a pyramid, at the pinnacle of which sits a group of people (perhaps sipping tea) whom we will call "Leadership" (see Exhibit 21.6). Leadership people are the highest echelon of prospects—the people from whom the largest gifts are possible and should be expected, the people whose generosity will set the pattern for others. These are individuals who have a close relationship with your organization (board members and other constituencies closely related to the organization). These are the people you approach first and, figuratively speaking, you have tea with them.

The second tier can be envisioned as a group of people who are near the top of the pyramid—about three-fourths of the way up. These are prospects who are able to give major gifts—somewhat below those given by the leadership level, but nevertheless significant in amount and impact. *These are the people you approach second,* and, because of their giving potential, you should meet with them in personal, face-to-face appointments.

Exhibit 21.1.   Benefits of ongoing, periodic capital campaigns.

Accomplishing projects beyond the reach of the annual budget.

Developing volunteer spirit.

Putting the organization in the limelight with donors.

Building up the organization's image as a "winner"—especially if a study has been done to target strengths and weaknesses in the organization's case, leadership, and potential sources of support.

Cultivating new donors for ongoing annual support.

Enhancing (rather than conflicting with) the annual fund—even during the course of the capital campaign—though there is the need to coordinate the two tasks.

Exhibit 21.2. Gift-range table: a state university.

		Goal: $100,000,000		
Number of Gifts	Gift Range	Total in Range	Cumulative Number of Gifts	Cumulative Total
1	$10,000,000	$10,000,000	1	$ 10,000,000
2	5,000,000	10,000,000	3	20,000,000
2	2,500,000	5,000,000	5	25,000,000
4	1,000,000	4,000,000	9	29,000,000
*10 (endowed chairs)	1,000,000	10,000,000	19	39,000,000
•				
•				
•				
18	500,000	9,000,000	37	48,000,000
40	250,000	10,000,000	77	58,000,000
100	100,000	10,000,000	177	68,000,000
•				
•				
•				
200	50,000	10,000,000	377	78,000,000
360	25,000	9,000,000	737	87,000,000
600	10,000	6,000,000	1,337	93,000,000
1,000	5,000	5,000,000	2,337	98,000,000
1,500+	1,000–2,500	2,000,000	3,837+	100,000,000

*Endowed chairs: $600,000 private gift to be supplemented by $400,000 from state, through Eminent Scholars Act.

Exhibit 21.3. Pro forma gift-range table: a national women's organization.

	Goal: $17,000,000		
Gift Range	Number of Gifts	Total	Cumulative Total
$2,000,000+	1	$2,000,000	$ 2,000,000
1,000,000 to 1,900,000	2	2,000,000	4,000,000
500,000 to 900,000	4	2,500,000	6,500,000
250,000 to 500,000	5	2,000,000	8,500,000
100,000 to 250,000	20	2,500,000	11,000,000
50,000 to 100,000	30	1,500,000	12,500,000
25,000 to 50,000	40	1,500,000	14,000,000
Under $25,000	Many	3,000,000	17,000,000

Exhibit 21.4.   Pro forma gift-range table: a specialty hospital in New York City.

		Goal: $8,500,000				
Number of Gifts	Gift Range	Total	Number	Cumulative Gifts	Total Received	Dollars Received
Leadership						
1	$1,000,000 or more	$1,000,000	1	$1,000,000	2	$3,137,654
3	500,000 to 999,999	1,500,000	4	2,500,000		
6	250,000 to 499,999	1,500,000	11	4,000,000	3	850,000
12	100,000 to 249,999	1,200,000	23	5,200,000	25	2,862,252
Major						
18	50,000 to 99,999	900,000	41	6,100,000	17	901,250
35	25,000 to 49,999	875,000	76	6,975,000	34	891,561
Special						
40	15,000 to 24,999	600,000	116	7,575,000	27	454,098
45	10,000 to 14,999	450,000	161	8,025,000	31	338,422
55	5,000 to 9,999	275,000	216	8,300,000	33	190,551
General						
100+/−	4,999 and less	200,000	316+/−	8,500,000	398	216,733
						$9,842,520

Exhibit 21.5.   Pro forma gift-range table: a small Catholic college in Pennsylvania.

		Goal: $3,500,000		
Number of Gifts	Gift Range	Total	Cumulative Number of Gifts	Cumulative Total
1	$500,000	$500,000	1	$ 500,000
2	250,000 to 500,000	500,000	3	1,000,000
5	100,000 to 250,000	500,000	8	1,500,000
8	50,000 to 100,000	400,000	16	1,900,000
12	25,000 to 50,000	300,000	28	1,200,000
25	10,000 to 25,000	250,000	53	2,450,000
50	5,000 to 10,000	250,000	103	2,700,000
100	2,500 to 5,000	250,000	203	2,950,000
200	1,000 to 2,500	250,000	403	3,150,000
Many	Under 1,000	350,000	403+	3,500,000

Exhibit 21.6. The top down/inside out model.

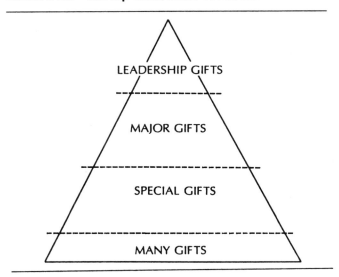

The final echelon can be pictured surrounding the pyramid, perhaps wearing climbing gear but not necessarily interested in scaling the walls. They represent a variety of potential donor categories, only some of whom warrant personal cultivation. Collectively, *they are the people you approach last* (generally by telephone and/or direct mail). They are very important: a broad base of support helps an organization demonstrate its impact on the larger community.

The pyramid amounts to a basic depiction of sequential fund-raising. Top prospects closest to the institution are solicited first, progressing gradually (and sometimes slowly) to those who are farthest removed and have the lowest giving potential. The pathway is top down/inside out.

A special note is needed regarding those board members who cannot make gifts at the leadership level. In the quiet phase prior to public announcement of the goal, 100 percent participation by board members is needed at levels that are a "stretch." Sometimes, outside leadership must be recruited to bring access to big gifts and productive connections, but the board's participation is always a telling factor—and savvy donors will ask about it. (See Exhibit 21.7.) Exhibit 21.8 transfers the pyramid categories to the format of the gift-range tables exhibited earlier.

Preparing a gift-range table helps to point out some of the general principles at work in sequential solicitation. These include the following:

- The lead gift should account for a minimum of 10 to 20 percent of the goal. Today's formula for successful campaigning is approximately 40/40/20 (at least 40 percent of the goal should be sought from not more than 10 gifts; the next 40 percent, from 100 gifts; and the remaining 20 percent, from hundreds or possibly

Exhibit 21.7. Board members' participation.

Ask for money, you'll get advice.
Ask for advice, you'll get money.

Establish an advisory board to involve top-level prospects in helping your organization:
1. Develop its case for support.
2. Enlist fund-raising volunteers.
3. Enhance its communication with the "movers and shakers" of the community.

---

thousands of gifts). Some campaigns can only succeed with a much greater percentage (55 or 60 percent) coming from the top 10 gifts.

- Ninety percent of the money given in this country comes from individuals, not corporations or foundations. Efforts should be focused on individuals in most capital campaigns.
- Today, it takes from 18 to 36 months to cultivate a big gift (almost triple the time it used to take). Sometimes, the cultivation/solicitation period can cover 5 or more years.
- The influence of the solicitor is a major factor in determining the level of the prospect's gift. The "case" is important, but, in the final analysis, people give to people. Donors often rise to the solicitor's level—or sink to it.
- Large gifts today are increasingly provided through deferred giving instruments. Solicitation strategies should be geared toward this approach, and staff and volunteers must be prepared to handle these opportunities.

(d) WHY SEQUENTIAL SOLICITATION WORKS Why is strict sequencing of solicitations, in order of gift potential, recommended for capital campaigning? Perhaps the reason is best illustrated by the following true tale:

A few years ago, Mr. and Mrs. Charles Woodruff were solicited by one of our clients for a pace-setting gift of between $5 and $10 million. When the solicitors arrived, the

Exhibit 21.8. Sample gift-range table.

	Goal: $17,000,000		
	Number of Gifts Needed	Average Gift	Total	Cumulative Total
Leadership	1	$2,000,000	$2,000,000	$ 2,000,000
	2	1,000,000	2,000,000	4,000,000
	4	625,000	2,500,000	6,500,000
	5	400,000	2,000,000	8,500,000
Major	20	125,000	2,500,000	11,000,000
	30	50,000	1,500,000	12,500,000
	40	35,000	1,500,000	14,000,000
Special	Many	25,000	3,000,000	17,000,000

philanthropically enlightened Woodruffs informed the solicitors that they had already made up their minds to pledge $100 million. At that moment, some fund-raisers became instant heroes and the campaign was a guaranteed success.

This story shows the truth of an old fund-raising maxim: Start with a prospect who could, conceivably, be persuaded to give the entire amount. Failing that, look to raise the total amount from two donors; failing that, from three; and so on.

The rationale for sequential solicitation is simple: It is the only way that works. Capital goals are sufficiently large to require extraordinary levels of giving, of which only a disproportionately few donors are capable. That is why half (at least) of any capital campaign goal is raised through just a handful of leadership gifts, and why even the second half depends on substantial ones. Only the last million or so are left to donors at the lower levels.

Deviating from sequential solicitation means potentially big donors can come in at lower levels, jeopardizing the entire goal. Many an organization has skipped merrily past the upper levels of the gift-range table, only to find themselves wishing for more gifts, more time, and more money to cover expenses.

Sequential solicitation does not work by accident, however. One key to success or failure is research capability (i.e., the ability to learn everything you can about each prospect). Research requires tremendous care, but it really pays off. Consider, for example, another true tale:

> At Columbia-Presbyterian Medical Center (CPMC), a gift from a prominent and wealthy family was considered implausible because they were known for their generosity to New York Hospital-Cornell Medical Center, not CPMC. After mounting an intensive research effort, it was discovered that 17 of the grandchildren had been born at CPMC; one daughter had graduated from the College of Physicians and Surgeons; another had graduated from Columbia's School of Nursing. Among the relatives, there was a fragmented but nonetheless comprehensive history of involvement with CPMC. That history helped to generate a series of gifts from family members that reached, in the aggregate, more than $1 million.

(e) THE SPECIAL CHALLENGES OF TOP DOWN/INSIDE OUT Sequential solicitation places a tremendous emphasis on personal, face-to-face visits by volunteer solicitors. Professional staff often accompany solicitors but are not the center of focus. Put yourself in the shoes of Mr. and Mrs. Prospect, capable of giving $500,000 to your organization. Wouldn't you be more convinced by a *peer's* belief in the cause than by that of a "hired hand" whose career may well hinge on the level of your pledge?

For most Mr. and Mrs. Prospects, the answer is yes, which means the selection of volunteer leadership is critical. Use extreme care in identifying and enlisting volunteers for the campaign—people who not only feel strongly about the worth of the organization but also are willing to give of their time, talent, and treasure. They should be people who are well-connected, who can either use their peer relationships to help the cause or open doors to the people who will.

Without a team of such volunteer leaders, even the most worthy organizations would be hard-pressed to achieve success in a capital campaign effort. Thus, it behooves professional staff to learn about the special "dos and don'ts" of managing volunteers—for example, the need to define, as precisely as possible, the job expected of each volunteer (even providing a written job description whenever possible). It is hard to "fire" a volunteer, but easy to clarify whether an individual volunteer feels suited to tackle a broadly prescribed set of objectives. Within the context of a capital campaign, several other "dos and don'ts" come into play in managing volunteers:

- Always remember, the volunteer gets the headlines.
- Bear in mind that the volunteer is always right in public—and always right, period.
- When confronted with a well-meaning suggestion from an overly enthusiastic volunteer, tread gently. Work around bad ideas without direct confrontation.
- The campaign will benefit if professional staff can manage to put some fun into fund-raising—and keep it there. Volunteers will continue to work in their spare time so long as they get some sense of satisfaction from it.

(f) THE SPECIAL ADVANTAGES OF TOP DOWN/INSIDE OUT Perhaps the overall advantage of using this approach is that it makes clear the precise *sequence* of your work, thereby expediting the completion of first things first. Take, for instance, three of the more pressing aspects of a major capital campaign: prospect research, the formation of strategies for cultivation and solicitation, and the actual asks:

1. *Prospect research* can be sequenced, restricting the "deep digging" to prospects you are approaching first, second, third, next. In even the most "mega" of capital campaigns, pace-setting gifts are targeted for just a handful of prospects. If you research (in detail) those people *first,* then you can set aside your second-tier research for later, third-tier for later still, and so forth. Your campaign priorities—and staff energies—will stay focused.
2. *Formation of strategies* can be similarly sequenced. Once the overall timetable is in place (including plans for the bottom-tier prospects and for campaign wrap-up), your priorities will become clear. Using completed research (a sample profile appears in Exhibit 21.10), a meeting with appropriate solicitors should produce at least one workable solicitation strategy—preferably two or even three!
3. *The actual asks.* Like strategies, "asks" often require a Plan B behind Plan A, and a Plan C in case Plan B fails. It is a good idea to work with solicitors to develop a *range* for each ask—an "ideal" gift for each prospect and an "acceptable" minimum that will not derail momentum. At times, it is actually preferable to defer accepting a gift if it is more appropriate to a lower tier of the giving pyramid.

There is always a question of how to track various campaign activities, in their various stages, throughout the several-year course of the campaign. My answer is based on the fundamental fact that most capital campaigns (even the most ambitious) live or die on the gifts of a few. The actual number of high-level prospects may be as small as 50 or as large as 500—but it is never as extensive as one might imagine.

Numbers like these can be managed manually, especially when sequential solicitation is adhered to strictly. If sophisticated computer programs are beyond an institution's financial reach, it is possible to manage the top end of a multimillion-dollar effort out of file boxes!

21.2 METHODOLOGY

(a) **IDENTIFYING LEADERSHIP GIFT PROSPECTS** More and more organizations are discovering that it is easier to get one $10,000 gift than it is to get 10 gifts of $1,000. Girl Scout councils, Red Cross chapters, local social service agencies, and other nonprofits of every size and shape, are starting to see the rewards of seeking "leadership" gifts even for annual funds.

To reap these rewards requires identifying leadership prospects, which can only result from taking at least three steps. These can be thought of as three separate phases, which, added together, can lead an organization to new heights in fundraising:

1. Change your mind set;
2. Look for prospective donors;
3. Know what to do next.

(b) **CHANGING YOUR MIND SET** It is fair to say that most small nonprofits are still oriented toward asking for 100 gifts of $100 than asking for one $10,000 gift. In part, this is because most organizations (both volunteers and boards) tend to be skeptical that a donor would *want* to give such a significant amount.

The first step in changing that mind set occurs within individuals. Each person involved with the appeal needs to be utterly convinced that the organization is worthy of significant, substantial, magnanimous gifts. The question is: How? The checklist in Exhibit 21.9 is directed at changing individuals' mind set *toward* positive convictions

Exhibit 21.9. Are you ready for a capital campaign?

Are you convinced personally that your organization deserves to ask for leadership gifts above and beyond those sought through annual giving?

Can you articulate that conviction to someone else?

Can you translate your commitment into a capital gift of your own?

Are you willing to become involved in evaluating donor potential within your organization's family?

Are you willing to take on the extra work (or hire extra short-term staff) to keep everything moving during the campaign?

Does your organization have or have access to the resources (books and personnel) needed to research background information on your prospects?

Are your volunteers willing to make personal visits to your prospects?

Do your volunteers have sufficient clout and/or access to open the doors you will need opened? If not, are they willing to approach such leadership for *ad hoc* involvement?

Is everyone involved (staff, volunteers, *and* various institutional departments) clear about each other's roles during the campaign process?

Does everyone understand who is to do what—and when?

If so, then you are ready for a capital campaign!

---

regarding a capital campaign. Your organization's "case" needs eloquent articulation. What is its work really all about? Who cares? Specifically, how much needs to be raised, for what, and why? What benefits will all this bring to the people of the larger community?

The answers to those questions are the reasons a donor will or will not choose to invest in your campaign. They constitute the basis for subsequent printed materials, brochures, and proposals—everything that is said about the program. In fund-raising, there is no such thing as organizational needs.

Once convinced, each person involved with the appeal should make his or her own gift decision and be able to articulate the reasons behind it. A solicitor's gift is more convincing than anything else that solicitor can say or do; it proves that the solicitor considers this appeal an investment, not just a nice idea.

With the mind set of the "inside family" thus shifted and demonstrated, the organization is fundamentally prepared to navigate the remaining potholes along the road to riches.

(c) LOOKING FOR PROSPECTIVE MAJOR DONORS   The "insiders" who have already committed themselves to leadership in the appeal are now your best solicitors. They are also your organization's best avenue to people who might have an interest in your organization. Members of your "inside family" should be asked to suggest potential volunteers. Widen your circle of prospects through them, looking for people who posses two characteristics: sympathy to your cause and the capability of giving "a big gift." Names of potential donors can be found in:

- Membership lists of other organizations;
- Publications related to the cause or to fund-raising;
- Service records of earlier campaigns;
- Real estate records;
- Foundation personnel and grants lists;
- Volunteer rosters;
- Reference books;
- Securities exchange membership lists;
- Personal inquiry among people who support the cause;
- Media coverage of other recent fund-raisers.

(d) KNOWING WHAT TO DO NEXT   Through your inside family and careful use of published source material, data on each prospect should begin to add up to information. Only the barest essentials are needed to determine a priority level for each prospect—whether that prospect will be solicited in the first tier, or the second, or the next, and so on.

Detailed research can then be sequenced. Do in-depth research first on those people who will be solicited first (those with the highest potential for giving to your organization). Research next those people who will be solicited next, and so on in alignment with the solicitations to be made.

Your goal is to provide each solicitor with as much information as possible about the prospect, before the solicitation is made. A sample "prospect profile" is shown in Exhibit 21.10.

(e) PERSUADING PEOPLE TO GIVE In addition to knowing *about* each prospect, your solicitors needs to know *how to visit* in a way that will be productive for solicitor and prospect alike. There will be a direct correlation between the "sales training" your organization can provide and your solicitors' level of success.

Persuading anyone of anything generally depends primarily on listening well. This is especially true in fund-raising; people do not typically give money away unless they

Exhibit 21.10. Leadership gift prospect profile.

---

99 Rumstick Point
Kennebunkport, Maine
Telephone: 207 447-1890

Giving History:	Over the past 50 years, Prospect has given more than $800,000 to the University. Of that total, nearly $300,000 has been given in the past 5 years. Prospect's gifts have generally been made for unrestricted purposes, thereby allowing the University to use them as it deemed best. Prospect's gifts, with the exception of a pledge to the last capital campaign, have been unsolicited.
Attitude Toward the University:	Prospect has been an exceptionally active and involved member of the board since 1949. Prospect's contributions were sufficient to serve as the basis for being the 1979 recipient of the Distinguished Service Award.
	The fact that only on one occasion was Prospect solicited for a gift to the University is further testimony to the extent and nature of involvement. Prospect has often spontaneously stepped forward and been responsive to the institution's needs.
Interests:	Prospect began as a lawyer and formed own partnership in 1940. Has served on the boards of the Legal Aid Society, the Civil Liberties Union, and the Legal Defense Fund. At the University, Prospect has always been interested in the visiting lecturers. In recognition of this interest, the board suggested an amphitheater as a commemorative giving option in the last campaign, and Prospect accepted the proposal with some modifications.
Finances:	We do not know the extent of Prospect's family resources. It is our best estimate that it runs to several tens of millions of dollars—possibly more. Prospect is related to the former ambassador to Sweden—a family that make its fortune in the shipping industry.
Strategy:	Prospect is rated at the top of our prospect pool with a gift potential of $5 million. Prospect is a natural leader and we must emphasize the need for leadership in this campaign.

---

are highly motivated to do so. Listening is the key to opening the door to insight as to what will motivate a particular donor prospect.

Your organization's solicitors need to look and listen for what makes a prospect tick—philanthropically, at least. If your team of volunteer leaders can determine what might motivate a prospect to give, a proposal can be created to specifically address those interests and concerns. Exhibit 21.11 gives a comprehensive list of donors' motivations for giving.

The goal is to find the intersection between the donor's desires and those of your organization. Linking the case to the prospect in this way is not possible, however, if everyone is too busy talking to hear what the prospect thinks. At the end of this chapter, three interactive scenarios are provided (along with outcomes) to give you some hands-on practice.

(f) HOW TO CONDUCT SUCCESSFUL SOLICITATIONS   The foundation of a successful solicitation is listening well. Establish that fact; brand it on the brain of each solicitor. Without it, all efforts to persuade will fail and all energy spent on soliciting gifts will be for naught.

The musical motif indicated in Exhibit 21.12 is not unintentional. Once your solicitors have found notes that will ring true to a particular prospect, the next thing they need is a song all their own—something to which the prospect will listen and will *want* to listen. A true, well-timed theme makes the prospect want to sing along. Exhibit 21.13 is a sample conversation, to help you learn the basic tune.

Exhibit 21.11.   **The reasons people give.**

Altruism
Ambition
Concern
Corporate responsibility
Corporate self-interest
Desire to belong/impress
Family custom
Fear
Generosity
Interest
Love
Loyalty
Pressure
Protection
Quid pro quo
Recognition
Religious principle
Respect
Respectability
Self-satisfaction
Sympathy
Tax advantages

Exhibit 21.12. The major motifs of big gift solicitation.

Taking the lead
Arranging the appointment
Conducting a successful solicitation
Fine-tuning
Performing in concert

Exhibit 21.13. How a solicitation actually sounds.

Solicitor (Anna):	John, we'd like you to consider a gift of $500,000 to endow that Herman Melville Lecture Series in Maritime Literature we discussed last March.
Prospect (John):	Heavens, Anna! I couldn't *possibly* consider a gift like that! Whatever makes you think I *can?*
Solicitor:	I'm not saying that you necessarily *can,* John. All we're asking is that you *consider* making a gift at that level . . . and with your sailing interests, the lecture series is something we thought would interest you.
Prospect:	Well . . . uh . . . I think it's a very good idea, Anna. I mean, you know where I stand on the whole maritime literature thing. I mean, wasn't it my idea in the first place? But $500,000! That's a great deal of *money!*
Solicitor:	Well, John, we are aiming high, but, as you said, you're the one who came up with the idea in the first place, and we felt you would want to make it your own. And you know a gift like this can be paid over a number of years. Remember, there are a lot of giving avenues—such as planned gift options—that are not dependent on your current income. After all, my own gift of $500,000 consists of $250,000 in cash and securities, and I've set up a life income trust arrangement for the balance.
Prospect:	I . . . I suppose Harriet and I could *think* about it. Why don't you let me have the pledge card and I'll mail it when we've made up our minds.
Solicitor:	Oh no, John. If I do that, I'll be breaking one of the cardinal rules of fund-raising. Tell you what, though. You and Harriet talk about this, and then let's get together again before you put anything on paper. Why don't we agree to meet in a week?

WHATEVER YOU DO, *DON'T* LEAVE THE PLEDGE CARD BEHIND!
THERE IS NOTHING WRONG WITH TWO VISITS (OR MORE)
TO FINALIZE SUCH A LARGE COMMITMENT.

21.3 NOTES FOR THE VOLUNTEER SOLICITOR

(a) TAKING THE LEAD Soliciting big gifts is not a science; it is an art. You will find yourself feeling graceful and accomplished in your solicitations if you:

- Believe in the institution;
- Understand something of the prospects's background, interests, and capabilities;
- Bring your own personality to the solicitation;

- Are unafraid to ask;
- Know how to listen and adapt;
- Prove, by your own example of generosity, that the campaign is worthy of support.

(b) ARRANGING THE APPOINTMENT Whether you write your prospect in advance or telephone directly, the following pointers are worth bearing in mind:

- Tell the prospect that it is your privilege to visit several people personally on behalf of the campaign;
- Emphasize that, while you don't intend to apply pressure, you would appreciate the chance to discuss, in person, why the campaign is important;
- Suggest a specific time;
- DO NOT simply mail a sample Letter of Intent; sending one, or leaving one behind after your visit, is far less effective than filling it out with the prospect.

(c) CONDUCTING A SUCCESSFUL SOLICITATION A good way to start your conversation is by talking about why you are personally involved in the campaign. Set an example by telling just how much you have given—either personally or through your company—as evidence of your commitment. You should also be prepared to talk about what others have given or pledged. This approach invites investment in the campaign by example instead of by advice, and will significantly influence the prospect's decision. Keep these pointers in mind:

- To avoid misunderstandings, listen carefully and then restate what you think you have heard. If there is any uncertainty about the donor's position, offer to return with a written proposal for the donor to consider and sign.
- It is often better to turn down a gift or postpone acceptance if a commitment is made that is considerably below expectation. If you accept, other leadership prospects could also fall by the wayside.
- If a donor is not responsive to the amount requested for a gift, be sure to suggest the possibilities of a planned gift.
- Even if you are turned down, know that you have left the prospect with a greater understanding of the institution and that you have opened the opportunity for a future solicitation.

(d) FINE TUNING Don't be concerned about closing a gift on the first visit. The first visit is just that—a first visit. A thoughtful gift is usually made on the second or third visit, after careful consideration of your earlier presentations. One way to make an appointment for a follow-up visit is to say: "I can appreciate that you will want to think this over before making a commitment. How about if I come back at this same time next week?" Coming back also gives you the opportunity to determine the right response to questions that remain unanswered. In essence, when you are fine-tuning:

- Don't leave the pledge card behind. Too often, leaving the unsigned letter or pledge card results in a much lower gift than anticipated or eventual loss of the prospect completely. All that should be left behind is the campaign brochure or other campaign material such as gift opportunity lists or planned giving brochures. Encourage the prospect to discuss the matter with family, business associates, and financial advisers.

- Do make the follow-up visit. On your subsequent visit, review how important the proposed gift is, and discuss the details of the gift. Try to secure the pledge verbally, and then use the Letter of Intent to record the pledge and the details of how it will be handled. Review it with the donor, and tell him or her that a confirming letter will be sent from the institution.

In soliciting a major gift, even the second visit may not close the commitment, but it should narrow the field in terms of the program interest and the general nature of the gift. Remember not to rush the gift. Closing a leadership gift can take a year or longer. Go back as many times as is necessary to obtain the gift.

(e) PERFORMING IN CONCERT Remember that you are working in concert with others on this campaign. Development staff can help with techniques, strategies, and approaches to your prospects; institutional administrators can accompany you on your first call to visit the prospect, or on follow-up visits if a situation warrants. Assistance is also available in the area of planned giving: you need only notify the campaign office to suggest that a planned giving expert is needed.

In summary, remember that successful solicitation, like playing good music, requires orchestration and rehearsals that concentrate on:

- *Tempo.* Timing is of the essence in big-gift solicitations. Allow sufficient time for at least two face-to-face, in-person appointments. When the time is right, ask for the gift in a specific dollar amount.

- *Learning your part.* It is important that you are completely facile as to the spirit of the campaign and the importance of philanthropic investments from donors like yourself. Learn as much as you can about each prospect you are assigned, and try to find the link between the campaign goals and the prospect's interests. Be prepared to ask for an appropriate dollar amount, but most important of all: DO ASK!

(f) YOUR ORGANIZATION'S GOAL: TRULY BIG GIFTS When all this is done—and done right—amazing things can happen. Some examples of amazingly big gifts follow, accompanied by brief-but-true stories to help make them memorable:

- *Gifts that are created out of necessity.* At Bayfront Medical Center, St. Petersburg, Florida, my firm counseled a $7 million campaign. We had no identifiable potential for top-level giving. What we did was establish the lead gift and its terms during the campaign planning study. The result was a $1 million lead gift which, in turn, leveraged a matching gift of $1 million and several other large gifts from $250,000 to $500,000. Without that first gift, however, the campaign would never have gotten off the ground. And it had to be created from absolute ground-zero *scratch.*

- *Gifts that are cultivated.* A vivid example of this occurred at Milton Academy, where an anonymous donor had once made a large gift through a 10-year trust of stock in a major corporation. When we were studying the feasibility of a capital campaign, none of the leadership wanted that donor to be contacted. After all, they said, the gift had been anonymous, and they wanted that anonymity protected. The headmaster, however, took it upon himself simply to visit the anonymous donor. He told the donor what the school was doing, what it hoped to do, and generally kept in touch. These visits resulted in the conversion of the trust to an outright gift of $1.5 million plus a bequest of an additional $3 million in Dow Jones stocks.

- *Gifts that are revived.* A disillusioned donor had once headed a particular board but was removed. The new leadership was fearful of cultivating him for a major gift; our recommendation was to keep him informed and involved. After two years, he responded at about 15 times his prior annual giving level with a five-figure gift.

- *Gifts that are enlarged.* This is a classic about a campaign led by George A. Brakeley, Jr. Apparently, the campaign chairman (and principal prospect) decided to take it upon himself to announce his gift unexpectedly at a board meeting. "I've decided on my contribution," he said. "It will be $4 million." To which George Brakeley replied, "That's not enough." Reportedly, the donor "blew out his fuse panel and left the premises." But the next day, he phoned George to say, "You're right. I've raised it to $6 million."

- *Gifts that are found almost by accident.* During Columbia-Presbyterian Medical Center's campaign for $133 million, the Dental School had been included in the program. We decided to apply the same principles of grateful patient solicitation to the Dental School as we did to the Medical School/Hospital. A Dental School professor cultivated a housekeeper (among others) who became a trustee of her employer's newly established foundation upon the employer's death. The result was receipt of the *first* fully endowed chair in Denistry.

- *Gifts that are "sleepers."* All successful campaigns attract "sleepers"—that is, large gifts that emerge from prospects not identified when the campaign is launched. My favorite is a $250,000 gift to Loyola Academy, in suburban Chicago, given by a former student who had been dismissed prior to graduation. Who could have predicted this fellow would become such a generous donor!

- *The stretch gift.* A "stretch gift" by one individual donor often determines success, but such gifts require creativity. In one case, we identified a $1 million prospect during the study. The organization needed a minimum of $2.5 million from him over 5 years. He declined. We knew, however, that he took great pride in managing monies for profit, so we asked him to pledge based on his managing an initial investment and personally guaranteeing the return-on-investment to meet his pledge total. The result? A gift of $5 million over 10 years!

- *Gifts that are loans.* Some imagination is needed for this type of gift. Consider, for example, a specialty hospital in New York City that asked a professionally administered foundation for $250,000 and was turned down. Our answer for the client was to suggest a 5-year, interest-free loan rather than a one-time, direct gift. It was granted!

- *The impossible gift.* The primary potential donor to a medical university in the East was overcommitted personally and had other philanthropic priorities. During the study, we told him he must commit to a pace-setting, $5 million gift from whatever resources available or the campaign would not be successful. As a board member of a large foundation, he was able to effect an exception to the existing policies and delivered a $5 million foundation gift rather than a personal gift.

- *The syndicated gift.* There are many examples of grouping a "united contribution" to overcome the lack of a single pace-setting gift. In this approach, a recipient organization accepts a group's dollar commitment to fill a need in the campaign gift chart. The most recent example I have experienced is a combined gift to a medical institution by a famous and affluent family. The family had been shown, by virtue of good research, the extent to which the institution had contributed to their health and well-being over the years. The result was a very significant family (i.e., syndicated) gift. Other syndicated gifts might be given by:

  Total board;

  Total medical staff;

  Total employees;

  Total response-to-a-challenge gift;

  Total gift from employees of a corporation (for example, the gift of $350,000 that Bear-Sterns gave to the Salvation Army of Greater New York, which resulted from one employee's soliciting other partners to come up with the total).

- *Turndowns that turn up after all.* At one of our nation's largest national charities, Shell Oil was persuaded to double its $100,000 gift and Xerox Corporation agreed to triple its initial $10,000 contribution. Our approach here is a three-part equation:

  First no   = ignore.

  Second no = start to take them seriously.

  Third no   = wait six months and then go back.

- *Gifts that should be rejected.* Another company solicited by that same large national charity did not want to give a penny. After three meetings, they agreed to a $20,000 grant for a specific program that would cost at least $50,000. We advised our client against accepting the grant because it would end up costing them money. We often advise clients to turn down gifts that are too expensive to accept. Beware of real estate gifts, for instance; the horror stories are almost endless.

Exhibit 21.14 will protect your efforts by headlining the worst mistakes any capital campaign can make.

(g) KEEPING TRACK OF THE WHOLE THING   There are many ways to manage a capital campaign. A "must," in my opinion, is the weekly staff meeting (or, in cases where the staff is only one person, the weekly staff report). Each of these should be identical in format, so that week-to-week progress can be readily assessed. Areas to track in most capital campaigns include:

- What was accomplished the preceding week, and by whom;
- What must be undertaken during the coming week, and who is responsible for what;
- Status of active solicitations and prospect cultivation activities;

Exhibit 21.14. The worst mistakes in capital campaigns.

Changing needs in the midst of the campaign.

Not asking for a gift.

Asking for too small a gift.

Poor campaign leadership.

Expecting the board to do more than it is capable of doing.

Using the wrong case.

Conducting a campaign without a study.

Having inexperienced development staff and/or professional counsel.

Using the wrong public relations message.

Not telling the story of the organization's achievements and potential for the community.

Overlooking the organization's heritage, previous donors, and past leadership.

Setting too low a goal.

Not knowing the membership or the potential for leadership and key gifts.

Wrong timing from one of two standpoints: either running into a competitive campaign or not allowing enough time to conduct the campaign.

Having a board that is not involved.

Concentrating only on corporations and foundations and not developing affluent individuals as prospects.

Presenting needs in terms of the organization rather than in light of needs and benefits of the community.

- Problems to be resolved, and by whom;
- Emerging problems to be addressed, and strategies for doing so;
- Checklist for reviewing status of leadership, budget, timetables, solicitations, prospect assignments, public relations, and research (the number of prospects, old and new; the number on whom primary research has been completed; the number on whom secondary research has been completed);
- Status of campaign gifts and pledges (in such categories as trustee gifts, staff gifts, leadership gifts, major gifts, etc.).

Whatever methods of management (and more detailed record-keeping) you devise, be careful not to overdesign. What you need is quick access to some very basic information: how a given area is progressing and where each prospect stands in the process. It should be possible for you to gain immediate, first-hand knowledge that Prospect A has moved from research to cultivation, or from cultivation to solicitation, or, finally—and more importantly—to *donor*. This brings us to what is perhaps the most important task of any capital campaign: donor recognition.

(h) DONOR RECOGNITION: PREAMBLE, NOT POSTMORTEM   I once heard a statistic that went like this: "A prospect, once converted into a donor, generally gives for the next 7 years." Let's assume, for the sake of argument, that it's true—that a prospect, once converted to a donor, gives for the next 7 years. Conversely, doesn't it mean that, if you lose a donor, you lose 7 years' worth of gifts?

That viewpoint suggests we ought to think of donor recognition, not as the end of the fund-raising process, but as the *beginning:* donor recognition should be treated as the preamble, not the postmortem. Done well, and done often, it should be the *beginning* of the next ask.

Then reality creeps in. The reality is that we professionals are often preoccupied with:

Plans for the upcoming meeting;

Follow-up of those plans;

Prospect research for the next solicitation;

Any number of other tasks related to the wealth and welfare of our organization.

Donor recognition is the *least* of our worries, which is why it tends to wind up at the end rather than the beginning. Let me give you *proof* that it is generally relegated to the end, using an example that comes from a country day school, where everyone was impeccably polite. No one ever forgot to write a thank-you note; the notes went out AS SOON AS a gift came in! However, that was the last time the donor heard from the solicitor until the end of the campaign. In most cases that I can recall, the solicitor went right into the next solicitation, rarely, if ever (and, I think, *never*) stopping to look back.

There are terrible ramifications of treating donors this way. One predictable outcome was that donors began asking whatever happened to the campaign? Was it over? Had it failed? (They hadn't read their printed newsletters, which proves that you can't rely on printed materials alone.)

Donor recognition, done right, means staying in touch with the donors *after* the gift is given. It means keeping them posted, visiting them for the sake of listening and conversation. Does that sound like cultivation? IT IS! Donor recognition is nothing less than the foundation of the next ask!

Perhaps an excerpt will buttress that important point. It comes from a letter written by a donor who was treated *right* (by which I mean that this person received a hand-written note whenever a major gift came in, was telephoned occasionally for advice, was invited to special events, and was generally made to feel a part of the IN crowd). Here is what this particular person wrote at the conclusion of the campaign:

> It was great having the personal touch with someone working closely with the current school activity. It made me—and I'm sure other alumnae—feel that they had some input into current and future developments—not just monetary input.

To me, that comment is proof of the depth of opportunity that becomes available to us *after* the gift is given! We should shift from thinking of donor recognition as the end and think of it instead as the preamble to subsequent solicitations—the foundation and beginning of the next ask. Exhibit 21.15 recommends four methods of giving donor recognition.

(i) CAMPAIGN WRAP-UP Concluding a campaign can be compared to a fine cognac: both should leave a pleasant taste, create a warm glow, and generate good feelings for the future.

Victory celebrations depend, of course, on bringing in the bottom levels of the giving pyramid. This is sometimes done through mailings; increasingly, it is done using phone/mail approaches in which a constituency first receives a written explanation of the campaign (with advance notice that a call will be forthcoming).

Exhibit 21.15. Four ways donor recognition can be done.

---

1. *Donors can be recognized through a systematic and speedy acknowledgment system.* Recently, some major corporate donors have had to call a medical center (unnamed) to ask whether their pledge payments had been received, how much is still owed, and whether the money is being used for the purpose designated. To make matters worse, this has often generated lengthy games of telephone tag to hospital officials, with no callbacks.

2. *Next (these are not necessarily in priority order), donor recognition can be done by giving visibility to donors* (that is, if they want it). Gift club categories, the proverbial photo/press release, a brochure on the life and times of a really high-level donor, or gala events, with all the attendant photography of dedicated volunteers, are all possible options.

3. *Incentives, like umbrellas, coffee mugs, and other forms of "bribes,"* might be awarded. One can easily go overboard, especially with respect to good taste, but there is a certain place for "geegaws" like bumper stickers, hats, pens, and so on.

4. *A higher form of incentives deserves its own category—named gift opportunities—which can also be used in annual appeals.* Commemorative gifts include *any* opportunities for donors to put their names on something—a building, a piece of a building, an academic chair, a scholarship, or an ongoing program. In annual giving, the options are more limited, but suppose Mr. Smith is giving $25,000 a year for three years, for immediate expenditure each year on scholarships. What's wrong with calling the recipients the Smith Scholars for those three years?

> Consistent policies are needed in any
> program of donor recognition.

One last responsibility comes with the end of a campaign: documenting it. Properly documented, the capital appeal can provide a valuable informational and public relations data base. My company prides itself on its "campaign case books" in which the following kinds of information are preserved:

Summary of the campaign;
Chronology;
The planning study;
The case statement(s);
Campaign design;
Campaign policies;
Executive committee;
Gifts by category;
Progress reports;
Proposals;
Sample letters;
Prospect research;
Printed materials.

(j) STRATEGIC PLANNING AND CAPITAL FUND APPEALS   Goethe once said, "Whatever you can do or dream you can do, begin it. Boldness has genius, power, and magic in it."

Yet boldness, in and of itself, is like a melody unchained. Loose, it is not sufficient—not, at least, in today's fiercely competitive philanthropic marketplace, and certainly not in the arena of capital campaigns.

For success, boldness must first be harnessed, defined, and tied to realities such as timeframes and budget lines.

In an ideal world, every nonprofit board would have a strategic planning committee that envisions, defines, and dreams. Once the strategic long-range plan is complete, its periodic review and updating would continue.

But this is not an ideal world. Many institutions simply arrive at a crisis—a critical crossroad—when capital needs, too long deferred, are either addressed or they are not. Out of crisis, a plan (of sorts) evolves—a backward sequence, but even this scenario can provide a good start on a strategic plan, so long as it is considered the beginning of the process and not its culmination.

What, specifically, is strategic planning? Simply put, it is the process through which dreams become reality. Every institution has its own unique purpose, its own set of aspirations, its own niche. However, not every institution has set them down, much less linked them to specific objectives and target dates or budget estimates. Strategic planning can help, through the following steps:

1. Define the institution's dreams (its mission, its values, its "raison d'être");
2. Determine the factors most critical to achieving the dreams set down in step 1;
3. Identify conditions that could adversely affect the institution's attainment of the dreams set down in step 1;
4. Set objectives (with action steps, deadlines, and budgets) that are required to achieve the dreams in step 1);
5. Track performance to ensure that the objectives stated in step 4 are being met.

Taking these steps helps an institution ascertain whether its development program is progressing on target, on time, and on budget. Problems do, inevitably, occur, and almost every campaign stalls at some point (or at least experiences a slowdown).

Should *your* campaign stall, for any reason, do not be disheartened. All that is called for is *more* creative methods of fund-raising. For example:

- In bad economic times, we generally encourage clients to continue the development process unabated. We believe that raising six- and seven-figure gifts is not severely affected by economic downturns.
- If the problem is solicitor burnout, our approach is never the same twice. Sometimes, we pull the *workers* into an especially prestigious body—named, perhaps, the "strategy group." In this way, members of the flagging committee are replaced without ever being overtly so. At other times, we try harder to underscore the *fun* in fund-raising—holding meetings in "fun" places or encouraging campaign leadership to employ "fun" gimmicks. One meeting was made unforgettable when it was started unforgivably late. But then entered the CEO, leading a full-fledged high school band playing a victory march.
- At times, attendance at meetings becomes an issue. Something as simple as changing to a business location can be effective; so can faxing the agenda on the day of the meeting. We have seen a very businesslike tone completely reverse a low-attendance situation.

An overall strategic plan is not affected by such slowdowns. In fact, slowdowns are a good reason for having one in the first place. Only if you know where you are headed can you see whether you are getting there! Can you imagine setting out from shore without a chart by which to navigate a ship? A capital campaign is no different; nor is it very different from the institution's overall strategic plan. It is just more specific. Exhibit 21.16 compares the principles that drive these two critical elements of a capital campaign.

Many campaign plans begin with a decision to conduct a professional planning study. The purpose of "The Study," as it is known in my firm, is to assess various key constituencies as to their views on the institution's case, leadership, and sources of support.

Negative as well as positive factors are considered in The Study. Weaknesses help to alert the institution to obstacles that will have to be overcome. Typically, these are misconceptions about the institution or a discovery that board development is needed to heighten fund-raising clout.

The Study looks for leaders, not workers. The idea is that, if you have the right generals, the other ranks will fall into place. Without the right generals at the right levels, workers cannot achieve the goal.

It also looks to establish a realistic fund-raising goal, based on the projected needs of the institution. Each study is, therefore, a tailor-made response to an institution's particular circumstances. However, certain common elements are generally included—a timetable for the campaign, a recommended organizational chart, and, in some cases, a set of pledge and cash flow projections. Samples of each are given in Exhibits 21.17, 21.18, and 21.19, respectively.

The need for your institution to get organized—and stay organized—throughout any capital fund appeal should be clear. One step to ensure success is to conduct The Study (just as a doctor consults an x-ray before performing surgery). Another step is to retain an experienced professional to manage the effort. Campaign management will be necessary, in some form, to succeed in the following functions (at the very least):

Keep meetings and solicitations on track;

Tend to the details of prospect research;

Develop strategies appropriate for each major solicitation;

Help prevent the campaign from stalling out or losing momentum;

Exhibit 21.16. Strategic planning principles as related to capital campaigns.

Strategic Plan	Campaign Plan
Mission	Mission
Future vision	Future vision
Needed to accomplish	Needs
Strengths/Weaknesses	Rationale
Issues, goals, objectives	Campaign goal
Timetable	Timetable
Budget	Budget

Exhibit 21.17. Campaign timetable.

Summary of campaign activity (by quarter)	Year 1			Year 2				Year 3				Year 4			
	2nd	3rd	4th	1st	2nd	3rd	4th	1st	2nd	3rd	4th	1st	2nd	3rd	4th

LEADERSHIP ENLISTMENT:
Enlist Chairperson of the Nucleus Fund
Enlist Nucleus Fund Committee
Enlist Chairperson of the Campaign
Enlist Honorary Chairpersons
Enlist Regional Screening Chairpersons/Committees
Enlist Leadership Gifts Division Chairperson
Enlist Chairperson for Individual Gifts
Enlist Chairperson for Corporate Gifts
Enlist Key leaders for selected colleges
Enlist Major Gifts Division Chairperson
Enlist Regional Major Gifts Chairpersons
Enlist Regional Major Gift Committees
Enlist Special Gifts Chairperson

PROSPECT SCREENING
Rate and assign the Board of Directors
Rate and assign Campaign Executive Committee
Research targets of opportunity
Rate and assign targets of opportunity
Screen leadership prospects
Screen regional prospects
Screen prospects in other states
Research prospects at $1,000,000 and above
Research prospects at $1,000,000 to $100,000
Research prospects at $100,000 to $10,000

REGIONAL ACTIVITY
Determine regional campaign goal(s)
Assign staff to regional offices
Schedule regional training for solicitors
Schedule regional cultivation

SPECIAL EVENTS AND PUBLICATIONS
Complete the case statement
Write campaign documents and audio-visual presentation
Produce campaign documents and audio-visual presentation
Schedule campaign kickoff announcement

Exhibit 21.18. Chart

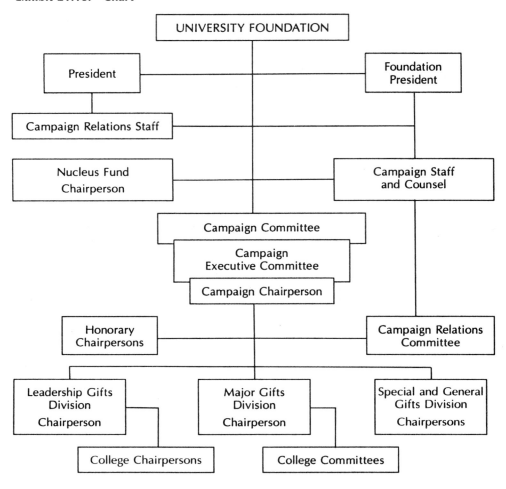

Not shown: Regional committees under Major Gifts.

Exhibit 21.19. Cash flow/pledge flow projections for a capital campaign.

Campaign Quarter Ending	Projected Cash	Actual Cash	Projected Cumulative Cash	Actual Cumulative Cash
12/31/84	—	$ 80,000	—	$ 80,000
03/31/85	—	78,767	—	158,767
06/30/85	$ 50,000	149,312	$ 50,000	308,079
09/30/85	75,000	115,843	125,000	423,922
12/31/85	385,000	677,561	510,000	1,101,483
03/31/86	100,000	133,086	610,000	1,234,569
06/30/86	525,000	249,308	1,135,000	1,483,877
09/30/86	500,000	716,380	1,635,000	2,200,257
12/31/86	900,000	1,222,034	2,535,000	3,422,291
03/31/87	450,000	191,688	2,985,000	3,613,979
06/30/87	750,000	1,057,337[1]	3,735,000	4,671,316[1]
09/30/87	850,000		4,585,000	

[1]Includes $916,000 payment through the buy-back of donated closely held stock anticipated in this quarter.

Handle gift receipts, acknowledgments, and giving records;

Orchestrate donor recognition (including publicity).

When such duties are added to the workload of existing staff, critical details can (and do) tend to slip through the cracks. A preferable alternative is to bring a person aboard who not only qualifies to direct the campaign but who might be considered for future openings in the development operation. Another alternative is to retain the services of a professional consultant to manage the effort for a specified period of time. There are three basic reasons why you might select a consultant:

1. *Objectivity.* Starting as early as The Study, counsel tends to be told things by donors and prospective donors that people inside the institution have not been told. This same objectivity ensures that "the case" of the institution is conveyed in a way that will communicate to outsiders.

2. *Instant expertise.* The experience of counsel is based on a variety of campaigns. Breadth, as well as depth, helps keep the campaign on course while preventing pitfalls along the way.

3. *Cost-effectiveness.* Counsel can provide campaign staff for a precise amount of time and in the precise area of expertise required, which avoids the costs of hiring, training, and carrying benefits and eliminates the need to suffer through an expensive learning curve.

The purpose of counsel is to be both active and reactive: *active* in offering new ideas and suggesting new initiatives, and *reactive* in observing, listening, analyzing, and responding to the circumstances of the moment. Ideally, client and counsel function as a partnership, not as a hierarchy. The "horizontal" approach to counsel maximizes the sense of teamwork that is so critical to success, with counsel used primarily for purposes of planning and strategy. Exhibit 21.20 lists the benefits of hiring campaign counsel.

For more on the benefits and use of campaign counsel, please refer to Chapter 29, "Fund-Raising Consultants."

Projected Cumulative Pledges	Actual Cumulative Pledges	Projected Cumulative Expenses	Actual Cumulative Expenses	Projected Net Income	Actual Net Income
—	$ 166,131	$ 100,000	$ 55,822	$ (100,000)	$ 24,278
—	264,931	190,000	119,979	(190,000)	38,788
—	1,124,931	295,000	203,014	(245,000)	105,065
$ 2,500,000	3,005,628	385,000	264,396	(260,000)	159,526
3,687,500	3,624,878	495,000	324,432	15,000	777,051
4,875,000	5,609,148	595,000	419,038	15,000	815,531
6,062,500	6,639,376	675,000	505,119	460,000	978,758
7,250,000	7,509,372	762,000	589,699	873,000	1,610,558
8,437,500	12,418,494	875,000	650,911	1,660,000	2,771,380
9,625,000	13,599,747	975,000	719,105	2,010,000	2,894,874
10,812,500	14,068,066[2]	1,075,000	N/A	2,660,000	N/A
12,000,000		1,182,200		3,402,800	

[2]Includes three gifts totaling $400,000 that will be confirmed in writing by the end of the quarter.

Exhibit 21.20   Benefits of campaign counsel.

Feasibility	Training
Planning	Expertise
Discipline	Sounding board
Ideas	Influence
Strategies and tactics	Publications
Resources	Research
Tracking systems	Guidance
Models	Enlistment of leadership
Solutions	Identification of new
Access	prospects

APPENDIX

CASE STUDY 1

Prospect: Civic-minded publishing firm in a community in which more than $3 million had never been raised through a capital campaign. Corporate giving limited largely to banks, utilities, and the prospect. Most corporate gifts to major campaigns ranged from $5,000 to $50,000.

Institution: One of two community hospitals among many proprietary hospitals serving the community. Serves the poor. Bad reputation among the upper and middle classes. Formerly owned by the City. Weak board of directors, i.e., no clout and no money. Fund-raising experience limited to an auxiliary-sponsored annual event. No donors of record on file; no development staff; no history of capital or annual campaigns. Little physician loyalty to the hospital.

Circumstances: The hospital undertook a mega-million-dollar capital campaign for construction, on advice of counsel. A minimum of three $1 million gifts was projected as necessary for success, as was a new level of allegiance and extraordinary giving by the medical staff.

Preliminary research disclosed that the publishing company had been editorially harsh in its treatment of the hospital and that its top management was generally dissatisfied with physician participation in community projects and charities. One hospital board member held a management position at the publishing company—number four or five on the management roster.

Strategy developed for approaching prospect

1. Ask for a $1 million gift from the publishing company, to be used to challenge a minimum of $1 million from the hospital medical staff and ultimately to help fund construction that would eliminate many of the hospital's weaknesses, which the publishing company was criticizing.

2. Persuade the publishing company that, by example, it could raise the entire standard of corporate giving in the community and, therefore, ultimately lessen the overall philanthropic burden, as well as directly provide more charitable dollars for the as yet unmet needs of the community.

3. Because the hospital board member on the publishing company's staff would not solicit the gift, and no other board member was a peer of the top management, it was decided to use an objective third party to approach the prospect.

Questions

1. Was the strategy sound?
2. What modifications in strategy would you have made, if any?
3. Did the strategy work?

Outcome   The publishing company responded with the $1 million challenge gift to the medical staff (the largest corporate gift in the community's history). The physicians surpassed their $1 million goal and then challenged the company to match an additional $250,000 in physician gifts, which the company did. The balance of the corporate community significantly increased its level of giving.

CASE STUDY 2

Institution:
Suburban 700-bed community teaching hospital;
$25 million capital campaign;
Target: A $4 million lead gift.
Prospective donor:
Well-known philanthropist;
Wife well cared for by hospital;
Husband enjoys recognition and likes to make pace-setting gifts.

The solicitation plan   Given the husband's preference for reserving areas in the family's name with his gifts, the plan called for offering the prospective donor the opportunity to name one of the hospital's seven-story buildings, which was to undergo renovation. The hospital assigned a gift value of $4 million to the building, roughly half the refurbishing costs.

The two co-chairs and another volunteer, who was an acquaintance and business associate of the prospect, made the call. They brought with them a proposal outlining the new programs and services the building would house and the remodeling plans. They also brought a framed photograph of the building's facade.

The negotiations   The solicitors reported that it was clear from the outset that the husband and wife intended to make a significant gift and were intrigued by the hospital's offer of extending them the honor of dedicating the building.

The solicitors then made the gift request, asking for $800,000 a year for five years ($4 million). They suggested the couple take a few weeks to consider their request. One of the co-chairs then called and arranged a second appointment. The husband indicated that he alone would be seeing the volunteers.

At the second meeting, the hospital was represented by the one co-chair who set up the appointment and the volunteer who was the husband's acquaintance.

The solicitors reported that the husband wasted little time in getting down to business (the husband and the two volunteers were all in the investment banking/stock brokerage business). The husband said he was very interested in funding the renovations and naming the building, and offered to make a *total* pledge of $750,000. After exchanging counteroffers, the husband said his final offer was a pledge of $2 million.

Question Did the solicitors accept or reject the husband's final offer to name the building for $2 million?

Outcome The volunteers accepted the husband's offer to pledge $2 million to dedicate the building [Editor's note: The $2 million pledge did end up being the Campaign's largest gift.]

Do you think this was the right decision?

Would you have handled the negotiations differently? How?

What do you see as the possible consequences of reserving the building for the $2 million gift?

CASE STUDY 3

Institution: A local community service organization serving women and their families is conducting its first capital campaign in over 25 years. The board of directors is all female, with no connections to the major corporations and prominent citizens residing in this wealthy suburban neighborhood.

The goal is $3 million to renovate the activities center to accommodate a day-care center and a new playground. The board approves the campaign plan, realizing they may be faced with a fiscal crisis if the building is not renovated. Yet, the board has not accepted responsibility for the success of the campaign. This is evidenced by their token gifts (far below their giving capability) and refusal to ask people for money: "It's not ladylike." A past president is essentially *the* board's campaign volunteer.

Prospect: The founder and chairman of a local family-owned manufacturer of beauty products (geared to males) with sales of $50 to $100 million. The company employs only 300 people (most area corporations employ thousands and have revenues in the billions of dollars).

The prospect is a regular $1,000 annual donor to the organization. Gifts come in response to year-end mailings. His secretary serves as his spokesperson on all communications. He has never granted a meeting to an Annual Fund volunteer, the current Executive Director, or the President. To everyone's surprise, three years ago he attended a retirement party for an Executive Director, who has since moved three states away.

The prospect has given two $10,000 gifts. The first was to the last capital campaign conducted 25 years ago. The second gift came unsolicited 5 years ago. The prospect has a small family foundation which gives away $75,000/year in gifts averaging $1,000. Unsolicited applications are not accepted.

His reputation with more "popular" local charities is: "He's a waste of time, and probably won't give, even if you do get to him." No volunteers know him well enough to evaluate his giving potential. Based on past giving history, his company's size, home address, and the absence of a peer-to-peer solicitation opportunity, the campaign director rates him conservatively at $100,000.

> *Circumstances:* The campaign has reached $2 million. A lead gift of $750,000 from a trust fund was given during counsel's planning study two years ago. The board has given a total of $250,000, and the corporate committee has reached their goal of $1 million from corporations. This leaves $1 million to come from individuals.

The top and bottom of the gift-range chart have been filled, with no gifts in between (in the $75,000 to $150,000 range). It is these 10 gifts that will ensure the campaign's success. Unfortunately, the prospect list is getting shorter; those who already have been solicited have given considerably less than their capability. The volunteer committees enlisted especially for the campaign are showing the typical signs of getting tired of the effort.

The campaign chairperson will not solicit the prospect. The past president says she will give it a try, but doesn't think he will respond. She had met the prospect briefly at the Executive Director's retirement party.

> *Need:* $100,000 gift to kick off the public phase of the campaign, and new volunteers who have peer-to-peer relationships with individual prospects in the $75,000 to $150,000 range.

The strategy set into action It's time for the campaign to go public, and a reception is planned (at the headquarters building of the largest corporate donor). The retired Executive Director agrees to personally invite the prospect, and to also attend the event. She is willing to cultivate—but not solicit—the prospect, provided the past president is with her. The past president gladly agrees. The prospect's secretary notifies the campaign office that the prospect will attend the kick-off reception.

To acquaint the prospect with the campaign, a plan is activated to cultivate him *before* he attends the reception. The past president immediately tries to schedule a meeting with the prospect. He refuses, asking that information be sent to him instead. A very general case description (not a proposal) with the subtle message, "This is why we want to meet with you," is sent. No request for a contribution is made.

The plan for the reception is to get the prospect to agree to tour the facility (the facility sells itself). Part of the strategy is to have everyone pay special attention to the prospect. The prospect attends the reception. Upon hearing the campaign chairman announce the most generous donors to date, he whispers to the retired Executive Director that he would like to do something big. She suggests that he tour the facility before making a decision so as to get a better understanding of the proposed plans. He agrees and asks that someone contact his secretary to set up a date.

The past president calls the secretary, and gets the usual cordial run-around. After two months and still no meeting, the past president says to the campaign director, "This guy is a waste of time. Let's forget about him." By now, it is December, and he has been pulled from the year-end appeal mailing for the annual fund.

Questions

  1. Should the campaign director "forget about him?" If yes, why?

  2. If no, what should the next steps be?

Outcome The campaign director refused to give up; there weren't enough prospects to ensure the campaign's success. In his own strange way, the prospect was showing discreet signs of interest. He had given to a capital campaign before, and the best solicitation tool available had yet to be used—the tour of the facility. A new plan was implemented:

1. The prospect was sent a list of named gift opportunities in the $75,000 to $150,000 range, to give him an idea of the kinds of projects available, and to have him think in that range.

2. The campaign director wrote a letter informing him of the new donors who had jointed the effort since the kick-off. A picture of the prospect talking to the Executive Director was put on the front page of the campaign's newsletter. The caption read: "Mr. ＿＿＿＿＿＿, a longtime friend of ＿＿＿＿＿＿, joins in the kick-off celebration."

3. Additional research was done. It was learned that the company's receptionist had resided at the organization's women's residence, and that the company employs a lot of single women and working mothers. The day-care center would be a great benefit to the prospect's employees.

4. The last week in December, the prospect sent a foundation check for $25,000.

5. Now that he is a donor, plans are made to see whether he can be further cultivated to be a volunteer for the campaign.

6. As part of the official opening of the day-care center, the prospect is invited to visit the facility. He declines. Two days later, the secretary delivers two checks for $50,000 each (one personal and one corporate). He is now the largest single individual donor to the capital campaign.

7. The past president contacts the prospect and gets him to agree to visit the facility.

8. Needing money to build a playground to complement the day-care center (government regulations), the "tour guides" decide ahead of time to emphasize the playground vs. the day-care center, which is already finished.

9. The prospect asks how much the playground will cost. Caught by surprise, the past president tells him the exact budgeted amount of $35,000. The guides also ask if he would like to participate in any of the named gift opportunities available for his gifts totalling $125,000. He replies that he is not really interested in having his name on a wall, but that he is flattered. Instead, if the organization would notify his employees of his generosity, he would appreciate it.

10. The next day, a $35,000 check is delivered.

11. Keeping in mind that a donor is a friend who can become a volunteer, the campaign director finds the ideal solicitation situation for this new major donor: an 82-year-old Forbes 400 businessman, another unreachable prospect. He wouldn't grant a meeting, and he asked for a written proposal. A proposal requesting $100,000 had been sent several months before, and there had been no word since.

12. The past president asks the donor if he would be willing to help with "just this one" prospect. He volunteers to call the prospect and to ask him to match his gift. He has since done this, and the organization is waiting for a response.

13. The infusion of this lead gift and a new volunteer has ignited the campaign's momentum and the volunteers' eagerness to see the campaign to its successful completion.

SOURCES AND SUGGESTED REFERENCES

Brakeley, George A., Jr. 1980. *Tested Ways to Successful Fund-Raising.* New York: AMACOM.

Council for the Advancement of Secondary Education. 1980. CASE Conference Presentation, Toronto, Canada (December).

Gurin, Maurice G. 1981. *What Volunteers Should Know for Successful Fund-Raising.* New York: Stein and Day.

Hutler, Albert A. 1977. *Guide to Successful Fund-Raising.* New York: Business Reports, Inc.

Kerness, Elton J. 1985. *Fund-Raising.* NJ: Cottage Press.

National Association of Hospital Development. 1980 *Effective Utilization of Fund-Raising Counsel.* Panel Presentation Report, NAHD Convention, Chicago.

Raybin, Arthur. 1985. *How to Hire the Right Fund-Raising Consultant.* Washington, DC: The Taft Group.

Seymour, Harold J. 1988. *Designs for Fund-Raising.* Ambler, PA: Fund-Raising Institute.

Soroker, Gerald S. 1974. *Fund-Raising for Philanthropy.* Pittsburgh, PA: Jewish Publication and Education Foundation.

Warner, Irving R. 1988. *The Art of Fund-Raising.* New York: Bantam Books.

Special Appeals

Sara H. Skolnick
American Society of Naval Engineers

CONTENTS

22.1 DEFINITION OF A SPECIAL APPEAL

A special appeal is a one-time special effort to raise funds for a unique and compelling need. By nature, a special appeal has a touch of passion, a note of nostalgia, and a ring of urgency about it. The fund-raising industry will tell the world that an appeal must have "heart" to achieve success. Money can't be raised for a party, at least not often and not easily. Money can be raised for serious, needed causes.

This chapter is devoted to management of a *unique* need to raise funds as opposed to periodic fund-raising activities that nonprofit organizations carry on to supplement dues or other revenue received from their regular activities. The one-of-a-kind nature of the special appeal makes it difficult for the volunteers or professional staffs of these organizations because they have little experience to do the job well and to optimize revenue against effort and costs expended. Help from a fund-raising counsel or development consultant can frequently overcome this handicap and more than make up for the fees involved by increasing the revenue realized; whether this is so in a particular case will require some trade-offs of expense versus energy expenditure and an assessment of the staying power of the volunteers and staff.

Special appeals don't—and shouldn't—have a tin-cup aura. Special appeals are important and serious business requiring smart business plans, tight budget processes, and careful implementation. On the other hand, they can be incredibly satisfying and rewarding.

Any nonprofit organization can conduct a special appeal. In the 1990s, revenues other than from dues income, exhibit fees, special service fees, sales, and similar sources, must be found to keep nonprofit organizations growing and improving their services.

(a) APPEALS THAT WORKED   Americans are generous with their time, talent, and money when they are touched by an appeal. The three projects described here illustrate three approaches using various mixes of issues, procedures, and methods; a manager should be able to infer from them a path for meeting specific objectives. They demonstrate that, when good leadership, good planning, and good implementation are applied to a good cause, the project will be successful. The three groups described are very different but, in each case, the community rallied together to accomplish something they all believed in. The sense of need, desire to "rally," and self-satisfaction from participating are set in place and stimulated by careful planning and implementation.

In the first situation, a religious meditation center in the United States needed money to erect a monastery in a ravaged foreign land. This narrative, from a personal interview, is an example of fund-raising based primarily on the dedication of the donors to the goals of the appeal. The head of the center asked one of the members, a volunteer, to design a flyer explaining the cause for which funds were needed. This individual, a language professor, was capable of producing a clear explanation of the appeal. The 8½-by-11-inch sheet he produced was the case statement. It was simple, but appropriately illustrated. The text explained that the funds were needed to build a monastery in a totalitarian-dominated region and to provide some support for some of the people who would be studying and practicing there. One thousand black-and-white copies were made by a resident of the center, also a volunteer.

The center has about 80 members, and its prospect mailing list has 500 names. A first-class mailing—the only mailing—was done by the one paid professional staff member. The remaining copies were posted and put out for people to pick up at the main center and at three or four affiliated centers.

A few people who had made large donations in the past were asked personally if they could help. Two gave $10,000 each, 10 gave $1,000 each, and $20,000 came from contributions of $300 and less from about 85 people. Because money goes a long way in underdeveloped countries, this amount was sufficient, especially when amplified by a few additional contributions received as the group from the center made their way across Europe to the Asian territories.

A unique element in this appeal is that those who asked for and collected the funds also personally completed or arranged the completion of the project described in the case statement. They purchased materials and supplies along the way, scheduled transport, and contracted the labor to build the monastery. I was told that most of the native population knows how to build in this peace-loving but unfortunate land, so building was the easy part. A "home video tape" was made of the trip and the many ceremonies that accompanied each stop along the way; this tape was shared with the donors and other volunteers when the group returned. One hundred percent of the funds collected went to the completion of the project. Receipts for materials and supplies were carefully collected and saved. The accountant told me that the financial report was an international jigsaw puzzle, with seven or eight languages and at least as many exchange rates involved. A letter was sent to all of the donors and the members of the center telling the story of the trip and the accomplishment of its mission.

I was told that whenever the center has a need for funds for a special project, this is the way the project is funded. Because the center is a religious organization, few federal or state regulations are involved. The center is extremely careful to disclose the full details about any project, to spend the money for the purpose for which it was collected, and keep the related expenses to a bare minimum. Its approach obviously has gained the trust and confidence of the donors, who receive the recognition and thanks appropriate to their generosity.

The next story, while equally successful, is more traditional. *Success Stories,* published by the American Library Association (1983), reported on the fund-raising projects of fifteen public libraries, submitted for the 1983 Gale Research Company Financial Development Award. The winner was the Altoona (Pennsylvania) Public Library which, after several years of belt tightening, erased a $28,000 deficit with a very special event. "One Saturday afternoon . . . a belly dancer, the symphony, vocalists, dance troupes, cheerleaders, stage bands, puppeteers, even Ronald McDonald, razzled and dazzled Altoona viewers out of $28,000 for their library." A committee of fifteen people representing various segments of the community ran the whole project. Many were media and public relations leaders who eventually obtained virtually everything needed for a six-hour telethon. A booth at a local shopping mall was staffed by volunteers who collected funds and pledges, all at no expense to the project. Other committee members, who were experts in pageant coordination or businesspeople active in the Chamber of Commerce, were able to get the necessary donations of equipment, advertising, and entertainment. The community became deeply involved, helped make the day a grand event, and then opened their pocketbooks to make it a financial success. Expenses: $107; income $28,538. The Gale awards jury commented: "This outstanding fund-raising endeavor proves that the success of a right idea is more a matter of inspiration and design than just good luck."

(b) A CENTENNIAL CELEBRATION   The third story is worth telling from start to finish. It describes an appeal that had many things going against it from the start, but overcame most of the obstacles by adopting principles and procedures that are critical to successful fund-raising. The planning was thorough and the volunteer leader, who had all the right qualities, was totally committed to the project and to the organization. He was determined to succeed and he did. I had the good fortune to be an eyewitness to the events as they occurred. I later discussed the details with John J. Nachtsheim, a past president of the American Society of Naval Engineers, who had accepted the task of raising funds for the Centennial Celebration of the Society. All of the best wisdom said "You can't raise money for a birthday party. Nobody will contribute to that." Nachtsheim proved them wrong, and he did it by carefully following the kind of advice he gave me in an interview in Crystal City, Virginia. "You have to define the product, and the product has to be something the membership believes in. If it's something that exists, but is falling apart or has lost its funding, it has to be something the prospective donor wants to keep." He cited as an example a symphony orchestra that adopted half a trombone as its fund-raising logo, symbolizing the fact that the orchestra couldn't function at all with only half of what it needed. People interested in the symphony understood and responded.

In the case of the Centennial, Nachtsheim was able to convince leadership that some unique and memorable things could be done to honor the 100th birthday. The Society commissioned an exquisite hand-crafted ship model to be presented to the President of the United States in recognition of the contribution of naval engineers to the maritime development and defense of the country over those 100 years. A special Centennial scholarship in the Society's Scholarship Program was established and funded that year, and an annual lecture series was inaugurated in honor of one of the country's early naval engineers. Finally, preparation of a history of naval engineering, with chapters contributed by members, was commissioned. Members had a reason to give—a series of programs that led to real achievement and would make members proud of their profession and its 100-year heritage. Nachtsheim now had a solid foundation for going to members and asking for support of the Society's Centennial observance. These were not easy tasks, but he pulled out every rabbit in his hat and made it all work.

"You have to make it easy to give and to provide reasons for giving." To include associate members in the drive, potential advertisers were offered packages of ads and registrations for the annual meeting which were good deals for them, and the association made money on the margin. Plaques were designed for each level of participation, and lists of givers were published in the Society's *Journal* for the entire year.

"If I had it to do over again," Nachtsheim said, "I would do part of the campaign differently. We should have identified senior people first and asked them for big contributions of $1,000 or more. We should have spent more time on the major givers and the smaller contributions would have been easier." As it was, a Century Club was formed of contributors of $100. Not until a couple of loyal members contributed $1,000 did Nachtsheim realize that this market existed, and he and the Society were able to go after it.

One of the local Society sections held a telethon—the most effective single event of the campaign. It was designed so that people talked to their peers. Its success was based on the fact that the best way to raise funds is for one person to ask another.

"What we did right was recognize all of the contributors in every *Journal* for the entire Centennial year, and give them a special ribbon to wear at the Annual Meeting that year."

In answer to a question about how to ensure the effectiveness of a fund-raising committee, Nachtsheim said, "The committee should first be a microcosm of the membership or the group it represents. In addition, each member should have special capabilities, such as writing well, having financial acumen, or being comfortable talking with people. And they should all be energetic, enthusiastic and capable. They need to be able to work together to plan and implement a solid, appealing program."

Staff support was the last element we discussed. "Very important," he said. "Someone has to do the paperwork and keep the records and make sure all the things the volunteer group promises get done. The staff has to be an intermediary, sometimes, when the phone call load gets too heavy. Good staff support can make all the difference in keeping a campaign moving along." John Nachtsheim and his committee made sure that the staff members who put in long hours making the Centennial a truly special event were duly recognized for their hard work. This celebration and the effort that went into raising the funds proved that, if people care about something, they will support it, even if it *is* only a birthday party.

(c) GETTING STARTED Causes within the mission of an exempt organization are suitable for special appeals. The first step is to define the cause for which the appeal is to be made, a cause that is in harmony with the mission of the organization. The idea must then be sold to both volunteer and staff leadership. When the cause has been identified and the leadership is behind it, a decision must be made on whether to hire a fund-raising counsel, a professional fund-raising company, and professional assistance for a telephone solicitation from a telemarketing service bureau, or to implement the program with volunteers with or without staff support. If the cause fits the mission statement of the organization; if the cause is compelling; if the leadership and the board of directors are 100 percent behind the cause; if there is no other source of funds, then it is time to proceed with a special appeal.

Exhibit 22.1 is a list of questions that need to be answered as a fund-raising program unfolds. The first four questions are the "getting started" or planning questions; they must be answered satisfactorily even before a fund-raising program can be authorized by the organization's governing body.

The next section outlines and elaborates on the important issues of special appeals fund-raising.

Exhibit 22.1. Checklist of questions guiding the planning process.

What makes you think you need a special appeal?

Are you ready to launch a special appeal?

Who is going to be responsible for the effort?

Who is going to do the work?

To whom are you going to address your appeal? (What, or who, is your market?)

How is the appeal to be conducted?

How are you going to approach your donors?

How are you going to thank your donors?

How will you make your donors feel good and be proud of their donations?

What is going to be done with the funds?

What kind of reporting must be done?

What state regulations will apply? What licenses or approvals will be required?

What evaluation system will you use when the appeal is over?

How will you thank your volunteers?

How well have you paved the way for the next time you will go out with a special appeal?

22.2 ISSUES

Mission relationship, the appeal or case statement, legal considerations, strategic planning, budgeting finance, and accounting, goal setting, volunteer selection, orientation and training, staff support and recognition are the issues involved in implementing a plan for a special appeal.

(a) **MISSION RELATIONSHIP** Before a special appeal program is undertaken, the mission of the organization should be carefully reviewed. The need for funds leading to the creation of a special appeal must directly relate to the mission of the organization. The organization must ask: Does the appeal fulfill the mission of our organization and contribute significantly to our progress and development? If it doesn't, the appeal is not compelling and should be rethought. Or, the mission is wrong and should be recast. Stewart R. Macdonald of Washington, DC, a fund-raising counsel, put his finger on the critical principle, as it applies to any nonprofit organization (1990): "An association foundation will be able to raise money successfully when its leadership holds a vision of a better future for its industry, its profession or its members." Macdonald introduced the element of vision, and vision requires a touch of passion—an important emotion in the very tough business of convincing others to give some of their money for a cause outside of their own everyday life. If the leadership does not believe in the cause, the effort will never get off the ground.

For a small organization, the idea for a special appeal usually arises within a small group of volunteer leaders or staff who see a need that their organization should meet and identify a special appeal as the way to meet it. If the goal does not relate to the mission of the organization, it will not be possible to sell the idea to the volunteers or donors. Macdonald (1990) reminded us that the reason for the appeal must be clear; a vague notion of "education programs" or "research programs" is not enough. Leadership must act as a check-and-balance, scrubbing the idea down and making sure that it is doable and compelling. Leaders must then enthusiastically and unqualifiedly support and advocate it.

(b) **CASE STATEMENT** If the appeal is in harmony with the mission of the organization, a definitive statement about the appeal can be drawn up. Fund-raisers call this the case statement. Essentially, it answers donors' questions: "How is my gift going to be spent?", "What is my money going to be used for?", "Why is this work important?" The statement must be short, clear, and direct. A well-designed brochure containing the case statement and other important information about the organization will be needed. The brochure must be understandable to laypersons and must capture the attention of potential supporters. Normally, a special appeal would be expected to supplement the operating budget of the organization. Often, however, a special appeal may be designed to raise a very substantial share of the organization's budget, as in the case of an endowment fund. If the appeal is well-defined and sharply focused, it can have minimal impact on other regular fund-raising activities that are scheduled or ongoing; a fine hand is needed to preclude negative interaction in these revenue streams.

Many appeals are philanthropic or charitable in nature, addressing the welfare of the sick, the needy, the hungry, or the undereducated. Some appeals are cultural or educational and most have broad appeal, but the winning case statements are optimistic and moving. Gloom, doom, and complaints never succeed. Exhibit 22.2 is based on an article by J.G. Lord (1991).

Exhibit 22.2. Ten elements of a winning case.

1. The case is an investment prospectus.
2. The case is larger than the institution; it has a broad, current, and universal appeal.
3. The case makes statements that are supportable and defensible.
4. The case shows that the project has been endorsed by respected leaders.
5. The most successful cases are both rational and emotional.
6. The case is optimistic.
7. The case is brief.
8. The case is easy to remember.
9. The case clearly relates to the mission of the institution and the benefits from the success of the campaign.
10. The case recognizes the need for a sense of urgency, to move people to act.

Based on Lord, 1991.

(c) LEGAL CONSIDERATIONS Whenever a group is raising funds, that is, collecting other people's money which will be spent in their behalf, care must be taken not to abuse that special trust. Usually, when soliciting among the membership of one's own organization, the requirements are that the solicitation be made only to the members and that they must be told what the solicitation is for. One of the principal legal issues in fund-raising is full disclosure. (See Chapter 35 for more information.) This means that the solicitation materials must clearly state, in very specific terms, what is being asked for, what funds are to be used for, and, if there are unusual twists, such as setting up a trust fund for later use, all of the particulars related to that action.

According to Alan Dye of Webster, Chamberlain and Bean in Washington, DC (personal conversation, July 1991), 37 states have some kind of state fund-raising regulation; some require registration of the appeal, others require a fee at the time of registration. At a time when states are losing much of their federal funding, many states are looking at tax-exempt organizations for any possible opportunity to generate tax or fee revenue. It behooves any organization planning a special appeal to check on the regulations in any state where funds are being raised, unless the solicitation is directed only to members of the nonprofit organization. Dye pointed out that the few dollars spent to ensure that the program is in compliance with state and federal regulations may save much grief later, and will allow the fund-raising committee to get on with the appeal or campaign without later facing legal difficulties. Dye suggested two principal references:

1. "Annual Survey: State Laws Regulating Charitable Solicitations" is prepared by the American Association of Fund-Raising Counsel, Inc. (AAFRC) as a special supplement of *Giving USA Update*. For every state that regulates charitable solicitations, the report gives particulars on the state regulatory agency, registration or licensing requirements, reporting dates, exemptions, limitations on use of funds raised, solicitation disclosure requirements and registration, and licensing and bonding requirements for fund-raising counsel and paid solicitors. Exhibit 22.3 is an excerpt from the 1991 Survey.

2. *The Philanthropy Monthly's* "Survey of State Laws Regulating Charitable Solicitations" is also useful. Most fund-raising consultants will make one, or both, of these references available to assist novice fund-raisers in sorting out the regulations that apply to their organization and its appeal.

Exhibit 22.3. Sample pages from AAFRC survey of state laws regulating charitable solicitations.

State/Regulatory Agency	Charitable Organizations — Registration or Licensing Requirements	Charitable Organizations — Reporting Dates and Requirements	Charitable Organizations — Monetary Exemptions	Solicitation Disclosure Requirements	Paid Solicitors — Registration/Licensing and Bonding Requirements	Fund-Raising Counsel — Registration/Licensing and Bonding Requirements
ALABAMA Attorney General Consumer Protection Div. 11 South Union Street Montgomery, AL 36130 205-242-7334	Registration requested (Not presently required by law).	Information provided should be updated annually.	None	Solicitors must disclose name, professional status, % of funds going to organization.	Registration requested (not required by law).	Registration requested (not required by law).
ALASKA Attorney General Dept. of Law 1301 W. 4th Avenue Anchorage, AK 99501 907-276-3550	None	None	None	None	None	None
ARIZONA Secretary of State 1700 West Washington, 7th Floor Phoenix, AZ 85007 602-542-4285 **Comment:** Legislation introduced in 1991.	Registration	None	None	None	None	None
ARKANSAS Secretary of State Trademarks Department Little Rock, AR 72201 501-682-1010	Registration	Financial report due March 31 or within 90 days after close of fiscal year.*	Maximum proceeds of $1,000, if all soliciting is done by volunteers.	Solicitors must disclose % of gross proceeds allocated to charity.	$50 registration fee and $5,000 bond. $10 registration for individuals employed by a paid solicitor.	$50 registration fee and $5,000 bond.

Glossary and notes

Registration and licensing: Most states require charities and fund-raising professionals to register with a regulatory agency before undertaking fund-raising campaigns. Because licensing provisions in North Carolina have been declared unconstitutional by the Supreme Court in *Riley v. North Carolina Federation of the Blind*, many states are expected to change their statutes accordingly in the next few years.

Reporting dates: Dates when financial or annual reports of charities must be filed with a regulatory agency. States accepting IRS 990 form in lieu of a state form are indicated by *.

Monetary exemptions: Charities with receipts and/or assets below a certain dollar amount are often excused from registering or filing reports.

Solicitation disclosure requirements: Disclosures that must be made to the prospective donor in an appeal for funds. The Supreme Court ruled unconstitutional requirements to disclose the percent of the donation that would go to pay for fund-raising costs.

Paid solicitors: Fund raisers—firms as well as individuals—employed to solicit contributions for a charity, and/or who have possession of contributions, must register and/or post bond in many states.

Fund-raising counsel: Fund-raising counsel, as defined in the Model Charitable Solicitation Act, does not solicit or retain custody of contributions. Therefore many states excuse counsel from filing bond, and in some cases, registering.

Excerpt published in AAFRC Trust for Philanthropy, 1991.

In preparing a mail-appeal piece, anything of value that will be provided to the donor as a result of a donation must be clearly stated. For example, if tickets to a charity dinner are sold for $200, and the cost of dinner is $40 a plate, the appeal brochure or letter must read "$160 of your $200 donation is tax-deductible." If the donor buys the $200 ticket but cannot attend, the entire $200 is tax-deductible.

As stated in Part VIII of this book, whenever there is doubt about the legality of an action, the staff should seek the advice of legal counsel. Smaller associations not able to afford counsel on retainer can contact the National Society of Fund Raising Executives for information on legal considerations in the organization's area.

(d) STRATEGIC PLANNING FOR A SPECIAL APPEAL The steps in the planning process are:

1. Formulate a goal that is in harmony with the mission.
2. Develop operational objectives, addressing the questions of who, what, when, where, how, and why.
3. Anticipate problems.
4. Develop strategies, including alternatives.
5. Develop policies to guide the plan's implementation.
6. Draw up a timetable or Plan of Action and Milestones (POA&M).
7. Develop a budget.
8. Prepare a monitoring system and evaluation process.

Leadership must be convinced that the cause is *their* cause; they must be willing to put their time and talent behind it. Strategic planning is a vital part of drawing up the special appeal program, because, once plans are set, endorsed by the leadership, and imbued with their enthusiasm, implementation of the program, although never easy, has a maximum opportunity for success.

Good planning requires time. In the Centennial Appeal described earlier, planning took almost a year. Planning should be done by the volunteers, with support from professional staff and facilitation by outside experts if possible. This does not have to be an expensive process. Nonprofit organizations can often find facilitators who will help at no charge or perhaps will seek only coverage of minor expenses. The resource list in section 22.6 includes organizations that are frequently willing to help locate needed persons. If the organization is on its own for planning, a timetable or schedule for planning meetings should be established, to help get the job done without overburdening the staff and volunteers. The planning team will need a leader who can keep things moving, give direction to the process, and protect the group from being diverted from its task. The leader should prepare for the first meeting by thinking through how the group will be guided to come to consensus. The checklist given in Exhibit 22.1 can be used to advantage during this planning phase.

(e) BUDGET, FINANCE, AND ACCOUNTING Every nonprofit organization and every special appeal should have a budget. The budgets for special appeals will vary from a simple pro forma to a detailed budget required in planning for a million-dollar endowment fund. The sample budget worksheet in Exhibit 22.4 provides a guide for small to medium-size organizations that do all or most of their work with volunteers and

Exhibit 22.4. Special appeal budget worksheet.

	Date _____		Draft _____
			Final _____
Program Name _____			

	Minimum	Maximum	Final
Expenses:			
Consultants' fees	_____	_____	_____
Design of case statement and advertising	_____	_____	_____
Office supplies	_____	_____	_____
Postage and shipping	_____	_____	_____
Telephone, fax	_____	_____	_____
Licenses, legal fees	_____	_____	_____
Computer rental	_____	_____	_____
Services	_____	_____	_____
Allowance for unrealized pledges	_____	_____	_____
Donor recognition	_____	_____	_____
Volunteer recognition	_____	_____	_____
Income:			
Corporate contributions	_____	_____	_____
Major individual contributions	_____	_____	_____
General contributions	_____	_____	_____

Copyright 1991, American Society of Naval Engineers. Reprinted by permission.

contributed staff support. If a consultant is part of the plan, his or her cost must be included in the budget. If a consultant is hired *and* a staff member has fund-raising experience, both must participate in the budgeting process. Volunteers would otherwise have to develop their budget "the hard way" with expert counsel.

There is no easy rule-of-thumb to estimate the overall cost per dollar raised, because many factors enter into the calculations. The checklist in Exhibit 22.5 includes some common guidelines, but the planning committee will want to add others that are specific to the organization, its mission, and its publics. Greene (1991) reported on a study by the Council for Advancement and Support of Education, which stated that colleges and universities, on average, spend 16 cents to raise one dollar. Stewart Macdonald provided the information that, in 1989, the American Red Cross reported that 11 cents of every dollar it collected went to fund-raising expenses; the Salvation Army reported spending 14 cents, and UNICEF, 35 cents. When they are conducting the entire program, the services of professional fund-raising firms can be costly. In big campaigns, hiring professionals is usually well worth the added expense. When, in the usual case, the firm serves as adviser and guide to the organization's staff and volunteers, the cost is considerably less. Most importantly, the organization needs to research the situation thoroughly and then make an informed decision. Small groups may find a good fit with an independent fund-raising counsel, acting in a planning and guidance mode. Frequently, the costs for the services of such an individual can be quite reasonable and his or her experience yields a much greater return than a neophyte group might achieve on a first appeal project. Both independent fund-raising professionals and large fund-raising

Exhibit 22.5. Checklist of factors to consider in estimating cost per dollar raised.

_____	Past experience on similar projects
_____	Estimates by fund-raising professionals
_____	Volunteer services
	_____ expected
	_____ promised
_____	Legal advice
	_____ to be paid for
	_____ pro bono
_____	Availability of contributions
	_____ supplies
	_____ equipment
	_____ space
	_____ radio or TV time
_____	Advertising
	_____ free
	_____ to be paid for
_____	Availability of corporate sponsors
_____	Cost of supplies needed
_____	Cost of equipment needed
_____	Cost for professional assistance

firms will provide proposals scaled to the needs of a particular group, including optional levels of their participation if requested.

The financial records of the revenues and expenses of the special appeal should truly reflect the costs and income of the program. Lawson (1988) stated that, although accurate reporting of cost figures may be difficult and some short-term benefits may seem to be derived from either over- or understating them, the long-term impact of inaccurate financial reporting can be devastating. The confidence of members and the public can quickly be undermined when discrepancies appear, and the ability to raise funds again may be damaged for years. The finance chairperson should be an individual who is skilled in keeping financial records and should be a person of the highest integrity.

A small organization or volunteer group can easily keep the records using three basic formats: two- or four-column ledger sheets, an income and expenses statement, and a simple balance sheet. Samples of the two financial statements are given in Exhibits 22.6 and 22.7. Ledger sheets are used to keep detailed records of cash receipts and outlays. The income and expenses statement should be based on the budget document, for easy transfer of information. A "Miscellaneous" or "Other" line can be used to take care of unexpected categories, which should then be explained in a footnote. The balance sheet will show the assets and liabilities and the fiscal balance of the project. Unless there is no activity, monthly financial reports are recommended. Their preparation should be looked on as an opportunity to review costs and receipts on a regular basis and to make adjustments in the program, if necessary.

Exhibit 22.6. Example of special program income and expense statement.

INCOME AND EXPENSE STATEMENT
As of 30 June 19XX

Income:
Interest	XXXXX.XX
Corporate contributions	XXXXX.XX
Major individual contributions	XXXXX.XX
General contributions	XXXXX.XX
Miscellaneous receipts	XXXXX.XX
TOTAL INCOME	XXXXX.XX

Expenses:
Advertising	XXXXX.XX
Office expenses	XXXXX.XX
Licenses, legal and consultant fees	XXXXX.XX
Recognition expenses	XXXXX.XX
Allowance for unrealized pledges	XXXXX.XX
Miscellaneous expenses	XXXXX.XX
TOTAL EXPENSES	XXXXX.XX
PROGRAM FUND BALANCE, Current Year	XXXXX.XX

Copyright 1991, American Society of Naval Engineers. Reprinted by permission.

Exhibit 22.7. Example of special program balance sheet.

BALANCE SHEET
30 June 19XX

Assets:
Cash	XXXXX.XX
Pledges, less allowance for unrealized pledges of xxxxx	XXXXX.XX
TOTAL ASSETS	XXXXX.XX

Liabilities and Fund Balance:
Allocation to program	XXXXX.XX
Less: Program expenditures	XXXXX.XX
Net available for program	XXXXX.XX
Less: Support expenditures	XXXXX.XX
TOTAL LIABILITIES	XXXXX.XX
Fund Balance	XXXXX.XX
TOTAL LIABILITIES AND FUND BALANCE	XXXXX.XX

Copyright 1991, American Society of Naval Engineers. Reprinted by permission.

Annual financial statements should be provided to the board and will be needed for preparation of the organization's Form 990 (Federal Return of Organization Exempt from Income Tax) and Form 990-T (Federal Organization Business Income Tax Return) for filing with the Internal Revenue Service. The subject of compliance with federal tax laws is covered in Chapter 34 of this volume, but it should be noted that fund-raising may require an organization to file these returns, when normally it does not have to do so. Gross and Warshauer (1983) warned:

> All exempt organizations except Churches and organizations with gross receipts of $25,000 or less must file tax returns with the Internal Revenue Service, and even churches and very small organizations may have to file returns under certain circumstances. For many, this is a traumatic experience because the principal forms which are used—Form 990, . . . and Form 990-T are written in technical language which requires expert knowledge. With few exceptions, exempt organizations are well advised to obtain competent tax advice . . . .

This reference by Gross and Warshauer includes a chapter on compliance with state regulations. However, it will be necessary to obtain up-to-date information for any state in which solicitation will be done, except when only members are included in the appeal.

(f) GOAL SETTING Setting a realistic goal for an appeal is essential. Goals must cover the amount of money the organization needs to carry out its mission and program. According to Tritsch (1987), "Sometimes enthusiasm runs away with common sense. This can be avoided by a careful analysis of previous history, a realistic look at the current economic climate, a reasonable projection of income and a detailed look at the investment necessary for success, in terms of time, money and people." If the organization cannot identify a goal that is reasonable, obvious and clear, such as the case of the library which had to raise a particular dollar amount to erase a deficit, it may be time to seek professional help. Options for both help and information are listed in section 22.6.

(g) VOLUNTEER SELECTION The next major step in the overall planning process is the selection of the chairperson or volunteer leader. It is desirable to find the very best person available. So often, good people are just waiting to be asked and would be honored to serve. The ideal fund-raising leader will stand out among peers in both the public and the private sectors, and sometimes will be found among those recently retired from active business or public service.

The ideal fund-raising leader is influential in the community, resourceful, creative, and ambitious; has a strong sense of order and is a good administrator; is interested in people and attentive to their ideas; gives others a feeling of involvement; delegates easily and wisely; has a contagious sense of commitment; possesses excellent communication skills; is accessible and discriminating; and is willing to take on a tough challenge for the right cause. These attributes are summarized in Exhibit 22.8.

Discussions about fund-raising leaders are widely available in the literature. (See, for example, Warner, 1991.)

Once the leader is chosen, he or she and the planning committee must work together to secure a team of able "lieutenants" under the chairperson's leadership.

Exhibit 22.9 shows how the responsibilities of the volunteer committee chair should be carefully delineated in the position description.

Exhibit 22.8.   The attributes of an ideal fund-raising leader.

Resourceful	Wise delegator
Creative	Strong sense of
Ambitious	commitment
Strong sense of order	Good communicator
Good organizer	Accessible
Interested in people	Discriminating
Good listener	Courageous

(h) ORIENTATION AND TRAINING   In Stewart Macdonald's view, formal training of volunteers is more often honored in the breach than in the observance. Formal training would be a valuable addition to the fund-raising program, but volunteer leaders in many big campaigns are frequently business executives who have considerable experience and limited time available for extensive training courses. Macdonald says:

> The usual practice is to set up a consultation committee or a development committee. During the meetings of this committee, guiding principles are set forth in a fashion to put the job into perspective. Fund raising counsel or staff development officer can provide or develop an appropriate training session for the volunteer solicitors. Written guidelines are helpful to volunteers who can then review them at their convenience.

Extensive materials have been developed telling people how to ask for money:

> For senior executives, a trained professional can give . . . the basic principles and a few words to say using "broad strokes." Sometimes, information can be transferred on the golf course or over the lunch table and that may have to be sufficient. Frequently, volunteer leaders will work with fund raising counsel to develop an orientation session for their committees. Some executives believe the best way to learn to solicit contributions is

Exhibit 22.9.   Sample position description: Fund-raising volunteer committee chair.

1. The Committee Chair of the Special Program Fund-Raising Committee is responsible to [the board] for planning and implementation of fund-raising for [the organization].

2. Duties:
   With the assistance of the Executive Director, select committee members.
   Develop fund-raising plan; present plan to Council
   With the assistance of the Executive Director, arrange for training of volunteers.
   Oversee implementation of fund-raising plan.
   Participate actively as senior fund-raising member.
   Present monthly financial statements to [the board].
   Conduct evaluation of program upon completion.

3. Staff support
   The Executive Director will provide the following staff support:
   Clerical support, mailing, printing
   Record keeping
   Preparation of financial statements
   Maintenance of up-to-date prospect lists
   Other support as required.

to use the "buddy" system—to go with a more experienced person and observe his technique and manner.

The character and mission of the organization will determine what training materials are appropriate for a particular group. A hard-sell approach will not go down well for some groups but will work well for others. Sources of further information on solicitation methods are listed in section 22.6.

(i) STAFF SUPPORT   If an organization has a professional development person on staff, that staff member will be the chief support to the committee chairperson and his or her team. In a small organization, half of the staff person's time may be allotted to the special project, and miscellaneous clerical functions, such as copying, typing, telephoning, fax service, publicity, and advertising in in-house publications may be provided. When the program is in full progress, the entire staff may be needed. A large organization is more likely to provide the same services on a larger scale, except that one person may be assigned in the beginning, with additional help added as needed later on. The paid staff serves a support role for the volunteer committee, which must lead the effort. Exhibit 22.10 gives a description of the staff support specialist's responsibilities.

It should always be made easy for staff members to volunteer assistance on their own time. Part of the planning process should include spelling out for volunteers what their tasks and duties are. Volunteers should not be asked to work unless they can be told precisely what they are being asked to do.

(j) RECOGNITION   When donors are treated right, they are an asset from the very beginning. People want to feel good about what they do; they want to feel appreciated. The Disabled American Veterans has used its famous red poppies for years, in the conduct of its annual public appeal. Volunteers appear in stores, at fire stations, and at

Exhibit 22.10.   Example of special program specialist's position description.

POSITION DESCRIPTION
STAFF SUPPORT SPECIALIST

1. This position is a paid staff position of [organization], under the supervision of the Administrative Director and the guidance of the Executive Director. This position may be half-time or full-time as needed for the specific program.

2. Duties:

   Provide clerical support to the chair and committee members of the Fund-Raising Committee.

   Arrange for typesetting and printing of advertising and other materials needed for implementation of the fund-raising plan.

   Act as liaison between staff and committee; arrange for committee meetings as requested by the chair.

   Take minutes of committee meetings; distribute correspondence as required.

   Keep financial records of activities within the special program.

   Prepare monthly and annual financial statements.

   Report to Administrative and Executive Directors as assigned.

   Provide other assistance as required.

---

places of public assembly to collect donations and dispense poppies. Thousands of people contribute small amounts of money and wear their poppies with pride. As the years have gone by, it has become hardly necessary to explain what the collections are for; the poppies' cause has become broadly accepted.

Gifts of highest value should be rewarded in proportion to that value. People who are in the public view are best rewarded by public recognition—special admittance to receptions, an identifying ribbon to be worn at an annual meeting or fund-raising event, a name engraved on a plaque in a public location, and so on. Very large donations can be rewarded by naming a room or even a building after the donor.

Throughout this chapter, pains have been taken to point out *important* issues and functions. I would be derelict if I did not make this next point in a most emphatic way: SPELL AND PRONOUNCE DONORS' NAMES CORRECTLY. Go to whatever trouble it takes to find out and verify the spelling of the donors' names. Find a person who is good at it, cares about it, and will commit the needed attention to the task. I have personally known people who have declined to give a second time because their name was misspelled on a list of contributors. The list of potential contributors is a valuable asset and should be treated with care and respect. The list then serves as an extra source for correct spelling for recognition.

Ten percent of a gift is not too much to pay for recognition. Certificates or mementos such as pens, cups, caps, T-shirts, desk accessories, coins, books are all appropriate; the list is endless. A good specialities firm can develop a package of recognition items suitable to the budget, the program, the donors, and the cause. The local Yellow Pages will yield some required suppliers if staff, professional fund-raising counsel, or committee members do not know of an appropriate company.

22.3 METHODS AND PROCEDURES

(a) DIRECT MAIL Everyone is familiar with direct mail advertising and solicitation. Our mail boxes brim over with every conceivable type of brochure, flyer, or envelope full of letters and product slips. Even with the cynicism usually displayed toward this method, enough people go through their mail every day (to be sure they aren't missing something) to make direct mail the most used form of solicitation by nonprofits today.

The end-of-chapter sources and references include several articles on direct mail. The subject is sufficiently detailed to be beyond the scope of this chapter; any public library will have numerous titles on the subject. When an organization decides to use direct mail, the professional staff will have or can get the necessary information to do the mailing. The current *U.S. Postal Service Domestic Mail Manual* is the official statement of current regulations and procedures. The rules in this "bible" must be followed *precisely,* to avoid costly mistakes.

Direct mail can reach large numbers of people. It is frequently requested by donors who want hard facts in their hands before giving. Direct mail works best if the organization's name is familiar. Care should be taken to capitalize on the warm feelings the target audience attaches to the organization by clearly identifying the outside envelope as coming from a friend. If the decision is made to use direct mail for even a part of the appeal, the lists should be "clean"—screened for duplicates, corrected for latest known address, and updated to ZIP + 4 codes if possible. A large organization will profit from the advice of Max Hart (1991).

(b) TELEMARKETING Telemarketing has the advantage of personal contact with the donor. However, great care must be given to how the campaign is conducted. A small organization planning to use telemarketing to its members can manage a good campaign by following basic rules of planning, volunteer selection, training, and organized implementation. Rappaport (1987) explored various ways to use telemarketing and has offered valuable advice. The public library is also a convenient and inexpensive repository for many sources of information on this subject.

(c) PERSONAL CONTACT Stewart Macdonald (1986) has said that people "make it happen" and has described how volunteers can and do just that. An organization should go for big donors; that's where the money is. Getting those donations must be done in a one-on-one personal visit, preferably by a peer of the prospect, by a person who has done homework on the prospect and the project. It helps if the volunteer knows the person, but that is not always essential. The volunteer and/or staff leader who conducts the visit must know the cause for which the donation is requested and must be skilled in "thinking on his (or her) feet." Most importantly, the donor must be asked for a specific dollar gift; otherwise, the prospect may give $500 when $50,000 should have been requested. "Fund raisers . . . report that 90 percent of funds raised today come from less than 10 percent of the donors. In a campaign with 1,000 prospects, less than 100 will give 90 percent of the money" (Macdonald, 1986).

Who makes the personal contact? Macdonald suggests:

> . . . volunteers are necessary for successful solicitation. . . . Professional staff or hired consultants, in some situations, may assist in making direct calls on prospects. However, volunteers are the backbone of successful fund raising; their value goes beyond their abilities as solicitors. Their involvement in the campaign makes them strong supporters and, often, leaders within the association itself.

Macdonald believes that major fund appeals benefit greatly from the services of a fund-raising consultant who can counsel leadership in obtaining influential and effective volunteers, and give these volunteers the information, guidance, and support they need to do the job. Professional assistance can ensure that the appeal is done right the first time, avoiding costly mistakes and even total failure.

22.4 BASIS FOR CHOOSING VARIOUS METHODS

During the planning process, the different possible ways to conduct the campaign will be discussed. The availability of certain services, budget, volunteer pool, mailing or prospect lists, the type of cause, time limitations, previous experience, and other factors unique to the organization will all enter into the decision. Professional advisers can help clarify issues and make recommendations, but, in the final analysis, the volunteers themselves will provide the basis for the choice of method for the appeal.

22.5 SIGNIFICANT IMPLEMENTATION PROBLEMS

(a) TIMING Discussions with Dr. Margaret New, a long-time professional fund-raising consultant in the Washington, DC, area, about some of the problems she thought were significant in the implementation of a special appeal, were revealing (personal interview, 1991). Timing is "everything," she said:

> Timing of the appeal should be set with great care. Remember that no one is home in August, and competing with the Christmas mail is almost always a mistake. If an event is part of the appeal, take the weather into consideration as well as what else is going on.

It is a good idea to try to find out whether some other appeal is going on simultaneously. If the causes are quite different and it would not be expected that the same donors would contribute to both, then the impact of the competition would be less important.

Dr. New said:

> The best times are October/November, January/February and May/June. Summer is vacation time and an attitude of less urgency prevails. March and April are tax months and people are distracted. December is holiday season and the mails are clogged with catalogs, sales brochures, cards and whatnot. People will not welcome more mail with much enthusiasm.

On the other hand, if an event is planned that takes advantage of the holiday season, the appeal should be all but finished by the first of December, with tickets sold and funds pretty much in hand, except for pledges to be collected later. The implementation phase for the event then occurs in December. A fund-raising event for children, the elderly, or the disadvantaged goes over well in December, especially if it provides an opportunity for parents to teach their children to help or give to others.

(b) INAPPROPRIATE LOOK OR SOUND   Another point Dr. New feels is important is the look of an appeal. What is its impact? Who is the audience? Is a slick, four-color mailing brochure going out from a group that is environmentally conscious? Recycled paper is readily available these days, with more and more people demanding conservation of resources.

> One instance where you can run into difficulty is when an event which is part of a special appeal is subsidized by a commercial organization. They may want to have their image portrayed in their usual way, and this may not be particularly compatible with your group. You may have to go along with their wishes, however, in order to benefit from their support.

This contingency should be considered during the planning process, and the potential impact assessed at that time.

> Another thing: use first-class mail, and include your return address on the envelope. Don't skimp on mailing. Think the whole procedure through, and think about how you would feel receiving the piece in your mail. You are trying to make it as easy as possible to give, so, give people options for different levels of gifts. Be sure to include a reply card and give them a postage-paid return envelope. And be sure the reply card fits into the envelope.

Why first-class mail? Because many people throw away unfamiliar bulk mail without even opening it. Why a reply card? People feel more comfortable if they know that their contribution is recorded on a card as well as on their check, which they know will be deposited and out of the hands of the recipients. Why a postage-paid return envelope? It just makes people feel better about the appeal, and they don't have to look for a stamp. Some samples of response media are shown in Exhibit 22.11.

(c) STALE MAILING LIST   A problem that haunts many groups is the "freshness" of their mailing list. A good address list must be updated regularly, with changes entered promptly. An organization that mails frequently to its members should request "address correction" service from the Postal Service at least four times a year, to keep its list current. Some people send in change-of-address cards, but in today's busy world, many count on the Postal Service to forward their mail. Dr. New reminds us

Exhibit 22.11.   Sample response statements.

XYZ EDUCATION FOUNDATION
   "a public/private partnership"

*I don't believe we can merely reform or restructure our schools . . .
we have to reinvent them. . .*

Robert E. Allen
Chairman, AT&T

Yes, America needs learning innovations.
And, yes, I want to help this venture as a founding member:

Enclosed is my donation as:

☐ Founding Member $ 1,000
☐ Founding Sponsor $ 5,000
☐ Founding Benefactor $10,000
☐ Founding Patron $50,000
☐ Friend of the Foundation $50 or more

Please send an invoice to my business address: _____

_____

I will make payments over _____ years with the first payment enclosed.

Name   _____

Address _____

          _____

Telephone Business _____   Home _____

For further information call (499) 999-9999; FAX (999) 999-9999
Please make checks payable to XYZ Education Foundation and mail to:

XYZ Education Foundation
P.O. Box 0000
Any City, ST 00000

Exhibit 22.11. (Continued)

A reception for Alistair Cooke and U.S. ENGLISH
Thursday April 13, 1989

Name _____

Address _____

City _____ State _____ Zip _____ Phone _____

☐ Enclosed is a check for _____ reservations at $125 per person. ($75 tax deductible)
☐ I am unable to attend, but wish to contribute $_____ to U.S. ENGLISH.

Please make checks payable to U.S. ENGLISH.

Limited space, reservations will be honored in order received.

— — — — — — — — — — — — — — — — — —

Trinity Episcopal Church Fashion Show
Saturday, September 29, 1990

NAME _____

ADDRESS _____

CITY/STATE/ZIP _____ _____ _____ TELEPHONE _____

I WISH TO BE INCLUDED AS A BENEFACTOR AT $250 (INCLUDES TWO RESERVATIONS)
I WISH TO BE INCLUDED AS A PATRON AT $100 (INCLUDES TWO RESERVATIONS)
I WISH TO INCLUDED AS A DONOR AT $30 PER PERSON

PLEASE FIND MY CHECK ENCLOSED FOR $_____ FOR _____ RESERVATIONS

SORRY, I AM UNABLE TO ATTEND. ENCLOSED IS A CONTRIBUTION OF $_____

BENEFACTORS AND PATRONS WILL BE LISTED IN THE PROGRAM
PLEASE MAKE CHECKS PAYABLE TO TRINITY EPISCOPAL CHURCH
DONATIONS ARE TAX DEDUCTIBLE AS ALLOWED BY LAW
RESERVATIONS ARE LIMITED AND WILL BE HONORED IN ORDER OF RECEIPT
PLEASE RESPOND BEFORE SEPTEMBER 15, 1990. GUEST LIST AT THE DOOR.

that "if any other organization's list is used, it should be paid for and approved for the purpose to which you intend to put it."

(d) INADEQUATE BUDGET Many elements can add up that ultimately result in an inadequate budget with which to implement a successful campaign. A problem that so many organizations overlook is the weight of a mail piece. "Don't let it go over an ounce, or your postage budget will suffer." Dr. New cautions about the selection of paper, to avoid both the weight problem and another, more obscure problem. "Paper with high rag content looks great and takes print beautifully, but you can't xerox it very well. It comes out grayish." There are many instances when a good copy of the materials mailed may be very important and you will want to provide for this. A good typesetter or your printer can give you advice on paper; good deals are sometimes available if some stock is left from another project. Be prepared to be flexible, and try to fit such an opportunity into your plans. A little extra time spent with professionals who know the business can save you precious funds.

"It takes money to make money" is an old adage that is sometimes hard to swallow when operating budgets are tight and earned revenues are hard to come by. Believe it! Pay for good professional advice; put on a first-class "show" and you will receive first-class contributions. People don't want to hear about your problems; they want to hear how great you are doing. They want to be a part of a winning team. Give them that role and they will give to your cause.

(e) DONOR NEGLECT OR FORGETTING THE PERSONAL TOUCH Never forget that *people* raise money. Direct mail solicitation works fine for up to 20 percent of the donors and serves as a reminder, but the bulk of the donations come in, from a small percentage of the total of donors, because a committed, enthusiastic leader personally asked the donors to become a part of a cause they believe in.

Don't neglect former donors. They are already halfway committed, and they will feel neglected and lose their enthusiasm if they are not made to feel they are an important part of the organization and the cause. Give them an opportunity to feel good about themselves.

A donor prospect list should be maintained by every organization that raises funds, and it should contain information about what appeals donors gave to previously, how much, and when. This information, as well as the prospects' vital statistics (addresses and phone numbers) should be carefully updated. (See Chapter 18.)

(f) INADEQUATE TRAINING OF VOLUNTEERS This stumbling block needs little amplification. If appropriate training is not possible within the organization, or if volunteer leaders are not sufficiently experienced to lead that effort, seek professional help. The cost will be returned many times over.

(g) MINDSET Stay positive and maintain a constructive attitude. Keep your cool even under trying circumstances; if others occasionally lose theirs, don't succumb to the siren song of an emotional reaction. The folks involved are friends and professional acquaintances whom you want to keep. If regrets are to be felt for heated words or other sharpness, let them be with others and not yourself. You will feel better about the incident later, and those who overreacted will think more highly of you and will continue to value your friendship and admire your equanimity.

SOURCES AND SUGGESTED REFERENCES

RESEARCH SOURCES

AAFRC Trust for Philanthropy, 25 West 43rd Street, New York, NY 10036. Annual survey: "State Laws Regulating Charitable Solicitations."

American Society of Association Executives, 1575 I Street, N.W., Washington, DC 20005; 202-626-2723.

Association for Healthcare Philanthropy (AHP), 313 Park Avenue, Room 400, Falls Church, VA 22045; 703-532-6243.

The Chronicle of Philanthropy, P.O. Box 1989, Marion, OH 43306-4089.

The Foundation Center, 1001 Connecticut Avenue, N.W., Room 938, Washington, DC 20036; 202-331-1400.

Fund Consultants Washington, Inc., 53 Main Street, P.O. Box 368, The Plains, VA 22171; 703-253-5800.

GWSAE (Greater Washington Society of Association Executives) Foundation, 1426 21st Street, N.W., Washington, DC 20036-5901.

Independent Sector, 1828 L Street, N.W., Washington, DC 20036; 202-223-8100.

Stewart R. Macdonald & Associates, 11619 Hunters Green Court, Reston, VA 22091; 703-860-1223.

The Middleburg Group, Dr. Margaret New, P.O. Box 1703, Middleburg, VA 22117; 703-687-3007.

National Society of Fund Raising Executives (NSFRE), 1101 King Street, Room 3000, Alexandria, VA 22314; 703-684-0410.

National Catholic Development Council (NCDC), 86 Front Street, Hempstead, NY 11550-3667; 516-481-6000.

The Philanthropy Monthly, 2 Bennitt Street, P.O. Box 989, New Milford, CT 06776. "Survey of State Laws Regulating Charitable Solicitations."

The Taft Group, 12300 Twinbrook Parkway, Room 450, Rockville, MD 20852; 301-816-0210.

REFERENCES

AAFRC Trust for Philanthropy. 1991. *Giving USA Update.* New York: Author.

American Library Association/Gale Research Company, Inc. 1983. *Success Stories.* Chicago, IL.

Greene, Stephen G. 1991. "It Costs the Average College 16 Cents to Raise a Dollar—a 525% Return." *The Chronicle of Philanthropy, 1991,* pp. 5, 10.

Gross, Malvern J., Jr., and Warshauer, William, Jr. 1991. *Financial and Accounting Guide for Not-for-Profit Organizations,* 4th ed. New York: John Wiley & Sons.

Hart, Max. 1991. "How to Improve the Bottom Line by Mailing Smarter." *The Nonprofit Times,* *5*(2): Vol. 5, No. 2, pp. 23–24..

Lawson, Charles E. 1988. "Institutional Integrity: A Prerequisite for Philanthropic Support." *The National Society of Fund Raising Executives Journal* (Winter): Vol. 16, No. 3, pp. 59–61.

Lord, J. G. 1991. "Building Your Case: How It Can Be Your Most Effective Marketing Tool." *Philanthropy and Marketing* (July 31).

Macdonald, Stewart R. 1986. "Fund Raising: People Make it Happen." *American Marketing News* (August); (October).

Macdonald, Stewart R. 1990. "How Do We Know When We're Ready to Raise Money?" Paper presented at 8th Management Conference, ASAE.

Rappaport, Stephen M. 1987. "Tackling Foundation Telemarketing." *Executive Update* (March): pp. 26–27.

Tritsch, Phyllis G. 1987. "Jumpstarting the Association Foundation." *Association Management, 39*(3): Vol. 39, No. 3, pp. 21–24.

Warner, Irving. 1991. "In Fund Raising, Leadership is Everything." *Contributions* (May–June): pp. 3, 6, 7.

CHAPTER TWENTY-THREE

The Corporate
Support Marketplace

Lester A. Picker
Pyramid Associates, Incorporated

CONTENTS

23.1 INTRODUCTION

Corporate charitable giving is as old as our nation. It is based on the belief that corporations have a stake in helping the communities in which they operate. Since the earliest times in our nation's history, American business has been concerned with the quality of the work force and the social conditions that have an impact on the business climate. In this context, one could view corporate charitable giving as self-serving.

In the quasi-capitalist system within which American business operates, corporations must be concerned with the bottom line; after all, no one in the community benefits if a legitimate business fails. The fallout from business closures goes far beyond the loss of income by the company's workers. A ripple effect is felt by suppliers, and the tax revenue to support critical social programs and community infrastructures like roads and schools is lost. Given the need to earn a profit, corporate charitable giving must be placed in its proper context. Despite its flaws, this quasi-capitalist system works and is lent credence by the recent events in Eastern Europe.

There are, however, other reasons for corporate giving programs. Many of these programs begin with self-serving interests and, over the years, evolve into a culture of caring. In these cases, giving is often divorced from the marketing interests of the business and exists to do good for its own sake. This caring attitude extends to the executive corps within the company, so that personal giving and volunteerism become norms of the business culture.

23.2 THE MARKETPLACE TODAY

(a) OVERVIEW The nonprofit field is an enormous enterprise in the United States. Annually, more than $350 *billion* flows through the books of the more than 1 million nonprofits recognized by the Internal Revenue Service. Collectively, these nonprofits control assets worth more than $1 trillion and employ between 11 percent and 15 percent of the total work force.

Corporate support of charities is also big business in the United States, but it is by no means the major source of charitable dollars. In 1990, corporations gave approximately $5.9 billion of the estimated total charitable giving of nearly $123 billion—a mere 4.8% of all charitable gifts.

Private foundations, another source of nonprofit revenues, play a larger role in charitable giving. In 1990, the nation's more than 30,000 private foundations contributed approximately $7.1 billion, or 5.8% of total charitable contributions. However, because of a variety of factors, the giving by foundations has a far greater impact on the nonprofit community than does corporate giving.

Private individuals donate the overwhelming preponderance of charitable dollars. In 1990, individual Americans gave more than 83% of charitable dollars, a total of more than $101 billion. Of interest to all nonprofit leaders is the fact that a sizable number of private givers are corporate executives or executive retirees, a group that tends to give larger gifts than the population at large. This fact should be calculated into a nonprofit's strategic plan for resource development. Specifically, the implications of giving by this market segment demonstrate that, once a relationship with rising stars in the corporate world is cemented, the nonprofit benefits not only from corporate support but from private dollars as well.

(b) PROGRAMS SUPPORTED The range of programs supported by corporate giving is as broad as philanthropy itself. Corporate gifts are applied to scholarships, endowments, capital campaigns, seed money for new program initiatives, operating support, and deficit reduction.

Although funding for some categories is undoubtedly easier to secure than for others, development officers can recount, for willing listeners, war stories of how traditional taboos against certain categories, deficit reduction in particular, have been overcome.

As one would expect, corporations are cautious about the programs they choose to support. Negative publicity can adversely affect the bottom line, especially in today's volatile stock market. It is not uncommon for a company to lose 10 percent of its value overnight because of negative press coverage. Therefore, it is considerably more difficult for controversial programs to receive corporate support than more traditional, conservative causes. Examples abound. Corporations regularly withdraw advertising support for television shows that may offend viewers, or choose not to advertise in publications that are considered offensive to sizable market segments. Often, these withdrawals draw as much attention and negative publicity as the controversial programming. This type of controversy is most evident in the highly charged, emotional, and polarized area of reproductive rights.

Many companies choose to support issues that directly affect their client marketers: a sneaker company may support youth programs or a pharmaceutical company may support population planning or other health-related programs.

(c) ATTITUDES The relationship between nonprofits and their for-profit counterparts is, and has always been, a tenuous one. Many factors are responsible for this shaky relationship, not the least of which is the widely different profiles of the individuals who have historically led the two types of institutions.

Nonprofit executives have traditionally been raised through the social caring network; in other words, they tend to be experts in their public service field, not necessarily in business management. They are typically caring individuals who place people's needs first, often at great cost to themselves. They frequently lack understanding of business needs and have a mistrust of businesspeople who are motivated by profit. This description represents a generalized and outdated stereotype. In recent years, the "Third Sector" has improved its management training and development.

Businesspeople, on the other hand, often have difficulty understanding the nonprofit environment. They almost universally recognize the good works that nonprofit organizations do, but they often do not speak the same language as nonprofit staff. Further, they are often in conflict between the desire to attend to the bottom line and the intense human needs that nonprofits address on a daily basis.

This mutual lack of understanding has several serious consequences. First, nonprofit executives are often reluctant to approach corporations for funding. When they do, they can be ill at ease and not terribly successful in terms of securing needed funds. Another consequence is that, through lack of understanding of the business environment, nonprofits are not particularly effective in designing strategies in which both parties benefit.

23.3 SEEKING CORPORATE SUPPORT

(a) THE NONPROFIT ORGANIZATION'S CASE *FOR* CORPORATE SUPPORT   The case for corporate support is a compelling one for many nonprofit organizations. Even during the best of times, there never seems to be enough money to support the ever increasing costs of operations. In today's turbulent economic climate, it is extremely hard to predict program fees, investment income, interest rates, and other financial vehicles on which nonprofits depend for revenues. As a result, most nonprofit organizations will at some time seek corporate support for their good works.

The following sections discuss management issues that are addressed by a nonprofit organization in achieving corporate support.

(i) Revenue for current operations   Corporate funding is one of several sources that nonprofits can approach to fund current operations. Admittedly, corporate funding is not the most likely source to cover this type of revenue need. Most corporate chiefs believe that nonprofits should develop detailed strategic plans, and accompanying budgets that will allow them to live within their means, much as the company's stockholders require. Therefore, raising corporate funds to support current operations is a difficult, but not impossible, sell.

The scenarios most likely to result in funding for current operations occur when a nonprofit has a long-time board member who is an influential position in a company. A nonprofit that supports an area that is critical interest to a company will have a greater chance for success, as when a science education program seeks support from a high-technology company. In most cases, though, support for current operations should be viewed as difficult to obtain and a temporary measure.

(ii) Predictable cash flow   Receiving a grant from a corporate source helps nonprofits plan better for the immediate future. Because most companies rarely commit to a funding initiative more than two or three years in advance, overly optimistic revenue assumptions based on this approach are dangerous. However, most nonprofits estimate budgets based on a mix of revenue sources, so a small percentage of anticipated corporate funding is healthy and frequently indicates a broad resource base.

(iii) Seed money for new programs   The likelihood of corporate support is increased when the request is for seed money for new programs. This is especially true when the program addresses social issues that have direct appeal to the business community such as improved science education, reform of public schools, university research, or health care initiatives designed to lower overall health care costs for the community.

Corporations tend to fund short-term projects, and most will require some evidence that the program will either be self-supporting or will attract new dollars after the seed period is over. No company leaders will agree to seed funding if they believe they will inherit a public relations nightmare when they stop the cash infusion and no one is able to pick it up.

(iv) Broadening of the resource base People like to support winners. Nowhere is this truer than in the nonprofit fundraising environment. How do corporate funders perceive winners? First and foremost, by their ability to attract donations from a diverse group of funding sources, including board members, private individuals, foundations, corporations, and government agencies. This broadened base also enables the nonprofit to weather economic storms by diversifying its revenue sources. In this case, corporate support can play a strong role by improving a nonprofit's ability to attract or leverage other revenue sources.

(v) Credibility and stature Receiving funds from corporate sources lends an air of credibility to a nonprofit organization. It is a vote of confidence from the business community. Rightly or wrongly, other donors view the support as an indication that the nonprofit has a track record and programs worthy of support.

As a result of intense competition for limited corporate dollars, nonprofits that are regularly funded by corporations gain additional stature and respect.

(vi) Entry to other funding Another major benefit from corporate funding is the leverage it provides to other funding. When a company with an established, reputable giving program decides to fund a nonprofit organization, it often accompanies the gift with additional resources, including volunteers and executive loans.

Often, corporations will help open doors to other corporations, believing that they have already made a significant investment and wishing to do whatever they can to ensure that the investment is successful.

(vii) Noncash contributions Another benefit of corporate support is the multitude of noncash resources that tend to flow, once trust and credibility are established. Such noncash resources include: volunteers; donations of depreciated assets and excess inventory; board members; executives-on-loan; and, other creative contributions. If the supported program(s) are successful, the leader of the nonprofit can augment their management resources with counsel from their for-profit counterparts. This has proved to be an invaluable asset to many nonprofit organizations.

(b) THE CASE *AGAINST* CORPORATE SUPPORT

(i) The odds are not good For every corporate donation to a charitable institution, there are often more than 100 requests. In today's competitive philanthropic environment, it is common for corporations with $1 million giving programs to exceed 1,000 requests for help per year. The odds of a particular nonprofit obtaining corporate funding are slim at best, even after absorbing the high costs to the nonprofit of staff time spent researching the company and soliciting the corporate decision makers.

There are many actions a nonprofit can take to improve dramatically the odds of obtaining corporate support and funding. But, even under the best of circumstances, sustained corporate funding is far from a sure thing.

(ii) It's a tough sell Many naïve or beginning nonprofit executives think that garnering corporate support is not very difficult. Some take a shotgun approach to funding, broadcasting hundreds of letters or proposals in the hope that one will find a receptive audience. That premature optimism is quickly extinguished.

Successful corporate solicitation processes involve: planning time; staff-consuming and painstaking research; cultivation of potential donors; writing and rewriting proposals; and meticulous follow-up. Often, even after extensive cultivation, the gift can dissolve under the pressures of declining corporate profits or may come in far lower than anticipated.

(iii) Integrity For many nonprofits, the "circus" of corporate solicitation is more a can't-make-any-misstep tightrope walk than the center ring attraction. Take a large environmental organization, for example. Should it accept gifts from corporations that have documented pollution histories? Should the American Cancer Society accept an offer of a large gift from a tobacco company? In these cases, the answers seem obvious. But every day, nonprofits face decisions involving corporate gifts and support that take them deep into ethical gray areas.

Integrity is the ethical foundation and "currency" of most nonprofit organizations. Many nonprofits therefore, consciously choose not to solicit corporations for fear of comprising this major asset.

(iv) It's not the real thing For many nonprofits, the search for the envisioned cornucopia of corporate support is undertaken to avoid dealing with major underlying problems, such as financial instability. There is simply no substitute for detailed strategic planning by the board and staff of a nonprofit, including financial planning. Most major corporate giving and support is contingent on a sound financial plan before any significant commitment is made.

23.4 CORPORATE SUPPORT FOR NONPROFIT ORGANIZATIONS

(a) THE CORPORATE CASE *FOR* SUPPORTING NONPROFIT ORGANIZATIONS All too often, nonprofit organizations imagine the corporate "pocket" as stuffed with cash, failing to realize that there is a dynamic rationale and process behind it. Corporations give away ("target," might be more accurate) their pretax profits for a variety of reasons, some of them more fully thought out than others. It is critical for the eventual success of a corporate solicitation program that nonprofit managers understand the rationale for corporate support *from the corporate perspective*. Some of the major reasons that corporations choose to invest in nonprofit causes are described in the following sections.

(i) Support business-related community infrastructure American business cannot gain a competitive edge in the long term if community infrastructures are not strong. Significant media attention has been devoted to documenting problems with public education, housing, drug abuse, and illiteracy. In one major United States automobile assembly plant, management has had to revert to instructions in sign language and graphics, to overcome the severe illiteracy problems it is facing.

By investing in public schools, affordable housing, and literacy programs, for example, the business community is ensuring its own survival.

(ii) Social investment Closely related to the issue of infrastructure is the issue of social investment. In the enlightened times in which we now find ourselves, corporations realize they have a responsibility to help address and solve social problems. Many social issues overlap (and at times, undermine) those that support the infrastructure of American business, Teenage pregnancy, for example, while not necessarily a direct problem for American business, imposes enormous drains on the tax base, removes needed workers from the labor pool, and perpetuates a cycle of poverty, all of which have significant implications for business.

Although no one would argue that the goal of any business is to earn a profit, many citizens advocate that part of a company's mission includes investing "social capital." Enlightened corporate executives understand the role that their company should play in the community and are prepared to exercise their responsibility in the area of social investment.

(iii) Doing good while doing well Doing social good while doing well in business is a value of long standing among corporations that have a strong history of charitable giving. These corporations produce and support a significant number of corporate senior leaders who are highly motivated to do good works for and within the community, whether local, national, or international.

(iv) Marketing Most corporations integrate their charitable support into the overall marketing strategy designed to increase market share. Some social activists attack this approach, but most philanthropy professionals understand, accept, and support it as entirely ethical within the context of a quasi-capitalist economic system.

There are countless examples of charitable giving and support provided in ways that boost marketing efforts. They include:

- Producers of products for youth supporting drug reduction programs;
- Computer makers donating inventories to schools;
- Manufacturers of house construction goods donating items for use by community development groups.

(v) Influencing public policy There is no doubt that strategically placed social investment can be part of an overall plan to affect public policy as it applies to the industry in question. Some companies develop plans that weave corporate giving, public relations, government relations, and community affairs into one fabric designed to achieve their public policy objectives. It is important for nonprofits to recognize when this motivation for giving is operating and to decide whether it is in their beset interests to participate. In some cases, there is no conflict; in others, there may be actual or perceived conflicts.

(b) THE CASE *AGAINST* CORPORATE SUPPORT OF NONPROFIT ORGANIZATIONS

(i) Profits Most large-company executives and directors understand the need for social investment, but the same cannot be said for small to medium-size businesses, especially in today's strongly entrepreneurial business climate. Many of these businesses were started by individuals who had little or no prior business experience, are family-owned and family-grown, or were created and then experienced explosive revenue growth within a few brief years.

These companies may not have a tradition or culture of giving. The individual who started the business is usually so focused on business goals that a giving program is the last thing on his or her mind. Finally, such people may be so caught up with their hard-won business success, and their history of fighting to stretch every dollar in their company's formative years, that they view handing out pretax profits as anathema.

Although this outlook could be a real problem for nonprofit resource development, it also presents an exciting opportunity to bring theses corporations into the philanthropic community. Then, as the company grows, a culture of giving and caring takes root and translates into strong programs of community investment.

(ii) Time In many companies, corporate giving is viewed as a waste of staff time and, in business, time translates into money. If anything characterizes business today as opposed to decades ago, it is executives' never ending search for more time to accomplish business goals.

As a result of this outlook, many businesses choose not to involve themselves in philanthropic activities or to delegate those responsibilities to lower management. Again, this situation is not all bad: a nonprofit can hitch itself to a rising corporate star and harvest the fruits of its efforts as the executive climbs the corporate ladder.

(iii) Philosophical orientation Although their viewpoint is less frequent today, some corporate CEOs see philanthropy as a private, individual activity, one not properly within the province of business. These people believe that they help the community best when they conduct a profitable business in such a way that jobs are created and taxes are paid, which in turn creates a better standard of living and supports services for those who cannot afford them.

(iv) Unfamiliarity It is a fact that many corporations do not participate in philanthropic activities simply because they have no history of doing so and are unfamiliar with how to get started. With the public service needs of nonprofit organizations at an all-time high, it is hard to accept this explanation; however, it is the most frequently cited reason among those small to mid-size corporate chiefs who are not involved in philanthropy. This sad state of affairs signals that nonprofits must do a far better job of educating and involving these businesses in charitable activities, through committee work, board memberships, and, eventually, donations of cash and assets.

(c) TYPES OF CORPORATE SUPPORT The types of corporate support available are even more varied than the reasons corporations choose to involve themselves in corporate philanthropy. Many nonprofit leaders, not fully appreciating the wide scope of help available from corporations, mistakenly ask only for cash assistance. Very often, that is entirely the wrong approach and will result in outright rejection or, if funded, minimal gifts.

Here are the broad categories of gifts and a brief discussion of when a nonprofit agency might choose to request each type of assistance.

(i) Cash Direct gifts of cash are obviously always welcome by nonprofit organizations. Cash gifts are the most sought-after and the most difficult to obtain. Cash gifts from corporate sources are most often requested to seed the start of new programs or for capital campaigns, but they also include requests for benefit events, such as sponsorship of a table at the annual dinner. Generally, corporations are not receptive to cash grants for operating support or deficit reduction.

(ii) In-kind services Corporations will often contribute in-kind services to help nonprofit organizations. In-kind services usually involve the donation of employee time and experience, which would otherwise contribute to overhead costs for the nonprofit. For example, a corporation may donate the services of its in-house accounting staff for tax preparation. Or, a corporation may donate the use of its four-color press to produce a capital campaign brochure, saving the nonprofit many thousands of dollars in printing costs.

(iii) Executive loan Throughout the country, large corporations have established executive loan programs in partnership with the nonprofit community. Competition is keen for the few available slots. These programs are effective for three basic reasons. First, they provide nonprofits with needed skills in such specialized areas as management, financing, or marketing. Second, they give corporate executives a more realistic understanding of the needs facing the nonprofit community, often followed by a deeper commitment to a cause, with all its resource development implications. Finally, the loan experience enables nonprofit leaders to gain more understanding of operations, issues, and policies within the corporate sector. Usually, such loan programs are the province of large corporations, which can better afford a temporary loss of some middle managers.

(iv) Employee matching Increasing numbers of corporations are establishing employee matching programs. In these programs, employee gifts to nonprofit agencies are matched by the corporation, thereby leveraging every dollar given. This has an immediate and long-lasting effect on employee morale and retention, while benefiting social causes.

(v) Gifts of inventory or depreciated assets This type of corporate giving is a boon to nonprofit organizations. Almost every manufacturing company in North America gives gifts of excess inventory or depreciated assets; most gain tax incentives or warehouse savings for doing so. In many locations throughout the country, specialized clearinghouses have been established to solicit, collect, and redistribute such gifts.

(vi) Cause-related marketing The term cause-related marketing (CRM) was coined by American Express in the early 1980s. In its most basic form, CRM is a way for a company to increase its market share by trading on the name and good works of a charity. For example, a company might offer a cents-off coupon for which, when redeemed, it will donate a specified amount of money to a nonprofit cause.

In the original American Express promotion, 10 cents was donated to the Statue of Liberty restoration fund each time its card was used. Results were impressive: American Express cardholders increased their card usage by more than 30 percent. More than $1.7 million was generated for the Statue's restoration fund.

CRM is an excellent vehicle for generating revenues for a nonprofit organization. It also enables the nonprofit to market its services to a wider audience because it enlists the efforts of the for-profit company to promote its products. On the down side, nonprofits must be very careful about lending their name to a for-profit marketing effort. Surveys, focus groups, or other appropriate data gathering, should be conducted by the nonprofit to ensure that client groups are comfortable with the proposed marketing relationship. Nonprofits should also ensure that he company is not embroiled in controversial causes that have a bearing on the same audiences served by the nonprofit. Prior to seeking a CRM agreement, a nonprofit must develop guidelines and policies that will enable it to make solid judgments regarding which CRM agreements to pursue.

Prudence is required on both sides of a CRM agreement, but the negatives are often overstated by those who have little experience in the corporate world. Most corporate executives do understand the implications of a CRM agreement entered into for spurious reasons—that ultimately this type of arrangement will backfire—with potentially disastrous consequences for the for-profit company.

The trend continues to be toward more CRM relationships between the corporate and nonprofit sectors, even extending to smaller businesses and nonprofits. The reasons for this center primarily around the fact that, following massive federal cutbacks, nonprofits are being expected to play an increasing role in resolving social issues. This expanded role provides corporations with the potential to reach significant new market segments through creative, mutually beneficial partnering with nonprofit organizations.

23.5 RESEARCHING POTENTIAL CORPORATE SOURCES

As with any fund-raising approach, potential corporate donors should be carefully researched, screened, and cultivated prior to requesting funds. No matter how compelling the need, gifts are invariably larger and extend over longer periods of support when a relationship has been carefully nurtured with corporate donors.

The odds of a nonprofit organization's receiving corporate support increase dramatically if the corporation being solicited is local or has a local operating division. The reasons for this are both obvious and subtle. Corporations understand that they must invest in the community's social infrastructure in order to promote a quality of life that will be attractive to new employees and will retain existing ones. They also recognize that, by investing in educational facilities, for example, they are ensuring a viable work force for their future business needs.

How does one begin the process of researching corporate sources close to home? Fortunately, many sources of information and methods are available to help nonprofits do the background research needed for corporate solicitation. However, as with any type of donor research, the entire process should be organized (so that priorities can be set), comparisons should be made between likely donors, and successful approaches in one category of companies should be tested with others in that category.

Exhibit 23.1 gives an example of a generic research organizer. Using a simplified systems approach to corporate research, a separate organizer sheet would be filled out for each corporate source. A corresponding file folder would be created with that company's name. All corporate sources should be identically color-coded (foundations, private individuals, federal, state, and local sources would each receive other color designations). Into the file folder would go news clippings relevant to that company or its industry, the annual report, marketing brochures, notes on meetings with executives, research on alumni working for the company, profiles of important executives, and other pertinent facts. Strong corporate potentials might have a separate, dedicated notebook. If the records are computerized (entered into a data base file), then reminders should be entered to request annual report updates.

(a) LOCAL CORPORATE SUPPORT Too often, nonprofit executives think in terms of national corporations and their large, highly visible gifts to nonprofit organizations. What are not readily apparent are the countless hours of cultivation that typically

Exhibit 23.1. Funding prospect.

Pyramid Associates, Incorporated

Keys _____
_____
_____

Name of Corporation _____

Name of Contact _____

Telephone No. ( ) _____

Address _____
_____
_____
_____

Deadline(s) _____

Assets _____ High _____ Average _____

Priorities _____
_____
_____

Notes

_____ 71 Balhon Circle ▲ Elkton, MD 21921 ▲ (410) 392-3160 _____

Reproduced with permission from Pyramid Associates, Incorporated.

precede such gifts. In most cases, *years* of relationship building and several incrementally larger gifts preceded a large donation. Relationship building today does not come cheap nor happen overnight. For example, there are (usually) travel and staff costs that must be incurred before gifts are received.

The fact is, the best means of securing corporate support is by carefully researching local support possibilities, then approaching, developing, and nurturing those relationships. Most nonprofits, in pursuit of the one large corporate gift, lose sight of the broad-base resource building they can accomplish by developing relationships with many smaller companies.

One of the most effective means of accessing local corporations is to obtain a list of members of the local, county, and state chambers of commerce. These lists can provide the names of corporate officers and the addresses, telephone numbers, and SIC codes of members.

SIC codes are an excellent way to determine the operating areas of a company. The eight-digit code classifies corporations into one of several increasingly finer categories. For example, the first four digits of a hypothetical company, 2542, reveals that the company is a manufacturer (25) of office fixtures (42). (The last four digits provide even more detail but are usually unnecessary for most nonprofits and can provide misleading data for mail campaigns.) Nonprofits should be sure that they enter the SIC codes into their data base, to allow for retrieval by industry affiliation when soliciting specialized program support. Lists of SIC code designations are available from the U.S. Department of Labor, mailing list vendors, or libraries.

Another way to secure local corporate support is by identifying rising corporate stars. This can be done through a thorough reading of the business section of local newspapers and regional business magazines. Concurrently, a nonprofit should request to be on the mailing list for corporate press releases, corporate newsletters, and annual reports for key companies in its service area.

The development function, as applied to corporate resource building, may involve many different levels and activities. Once a promising individual is identified, a nonprofit can ask that person to share his or her expertise and get involved—for example, serving on a committee researching some aspect of the nonprofit's work, including quality control, service delivery, client needs identification, or others. Or, a potential board member, volunteer leader, or advocate can be asked to serve on a committee developing a "white paper" on some significant social issue that involves the public service interests of the nonprofit organization. Businesspeople often willingly take such assignments; they are targeted in nature and have a finite time commitment. Still, the nonprofit must make expectations clear. *It is critical that the first assignments end in success.*

Once a businessperson is involved, and assuming an initial good experience, the nonprofit can ask the executive onto the board or, alternately, onto an advisory group. In either case, the organization should make certain that the individual receives challenging assignments. Many nonprofits, especially smaller ones, mistakenly believe that it is best to just name an important corporate executive to a committee without requiring him or her to work hard on an assignment. Nothing could be further from the truth. Challenging assignments help the corporate executive see that the nonprofit is serious about its mission and about meeting the needs of its clientele.

A good way to gain access to a corporate leader is through the nonprofit's board members and leading volunteers. If a professional or personal relationship already exists between a board member and a corporate leader, it will make the process of education and confidence building that much easier. The fund-raising maxim, "People give money to people," is particularly appropriate for corporate solicitations.

(b) NATIONAL CORPORATIONS Aside from local corporate support, including national corporations that have local operating locations or subsidiaries, there is a possibility of support from national corporations, outside the nonprofit's immediate locale. Corporate giants such as International Business Machines, American Telephone and Telegraph, and Xerox have national giving programs that distribute huge sums of money.

In general, national corporate giving programs are well-staffed and have carefully focused programs. The programs are frequently run by a corporate foundation or administered directly by the community affairs office.

There are many sources of information concerning national corporate giving programs. (Recommended research sources are listed in section 23.10. The first thing any nonprofit should do is request a copy of the guidelines and an annual report from the corporate giving program. This is most easily accomplished with a personal letter.

With the guidelines in hand, nonprofits should carefully determine whether their organization and/or programs qualify. The number-one reason that grant applications are rejected is that the requesting agency does not fit the published guidelines of the corporate program.

(c) FOREIGN CORPORATIONS There are millions of foreign corporations operating throughout the world, but those to which an American nonprofit will have access will be limited by two major factors: Does the corporation have a significant operating presence in the United States? Does the nonprofit have an operating presence in the corporation's homeland?

The major barrier to accessing foreign corporations is the culture gap that may exist, especially in the area of corporate involvement in social issues. A prime example is the influx of Japanese industry to the United States. For many years, it was very difficult for American nonprofits to access these corporations in terms of funding or volunteers. This was primarily traceable to an absence of corporate social programs in Japanese industrial culture. Only in recent years have Japanese companies doing business in the United States begun full-blown social investment programs.

Several reference works detail foreign corporations that operate in the United States. Most of the standard rules of approach apply to a nonprofit's search for foreign corporate support. One of the more interesting developments in foreign corporate support for American nonprofits has been in the area of corporate response time in the solicitation process. For example, Honda Corporation of America has published guidelines that pledge unusually quick turnaround time in evaluating and responding to query letters and telephone calls from program officers. It appears that corporate philanthropy is transferring to customer focus some of the attention emphasized in product sales and service.

23.6 PLANNING AND CULTIVATION

With the proper research materials, a strategic plan can be developed to guide the nonprofit organization in cultivating corporate sources and fostering enduring relationships. There is a distinct difference between cultivation and solicitation. Cultivation refers to the long-term, relationship-building process. This may entail several layers of involvement, during which time the corporate officers complete committee work and learn about the nonprofit and the needs of its clients. Cultivation may also include the nonprofit's performance of services for the corporation, ranging from breast cancer screenings at the corporate site to a string quartet in the corporate cafeteria. Solicitation generally refers to the actual process of asking for support for specific projects or programs.

Perhaps nowhere else in nonprofit management is relationship so important to meeting long-term objectives. In the corporate world, people in authority prefer to deal with other people they trust. This applies not only to agreements and deal making, but also the many occasions when business colleagues serve together on nonprofit boards or committees. Therefore, it is critical that a nonprofit have on its board several businesspersons with the ability (and credibility) to network to the larger business community.

Contrary to the perception of some who may be new to development, solicitation ideally begins with cultivation and an institutional commitment to keep potential donors informed about the organization. Even organizational failures can be used to advantage with potential corporate donors. If a nonprofit honors a corporate executive by asking for help in resolving an institutional problem, he or she will more often than not end up being a diehard supporter.

(a) THE APPROACH

(i) Personal meeting   In the actual solicitation process, creativity and persistence are prerequisites for success. In the solicitation approach itself, relationships are all-important. Corporate giving officers are continually barraged by well-meaning nonprofits seeking funding. Most requests for funding arrive through the mail and are rejected out of hand—in most cases, rightfully so. Cutting through barriers to obtain a face-to-face meeting with the corporative executives responsible for making the funding decisions should be a primary goal of any corporate solicitation process.

The personal meeting may concern or even frighten those new to the fund-seeking arena. Some people go to great lengths to avoid personal interviews, despite the fact that this is the single most effective way to secure funds for an agency. Some experts estimate that the chances of funding increase by 70% if the proposal is preceded by personal contacts. This is understandable on several grounds. First, corporate officers get to learn about the agency and its programs, staff, and board; that knowledge increases the comfort factor when close decisions on funding are made. Given the choice of funding a known versus an unknown entity, the known almost always prevails. Second, the nonprofit representatives learn what the latest priorities are; what lessons concerning other refunded projects have recently been learned by the corporate officers, which may impact the proposal being discussed; and what key issues, phrases, and concepts are frequently mentioned by the corporate officials and should be included in the proposal. Based on these data, all fund-and support-seeking efforts should be focused on obtaining a face-to-face meeting with carefully targeted corporate funding sources.

Many development officers use a form similar to the one shown in Figure 23.2, to organize the calling process. It should be noted, especially in these difficult economic times, that busy executives are often best reached *prior* to 9:00 A.M. and *after* 5:00 P.M. Calling at these times has the added advantage of frequently bypassing secretarial interference. Once the meeting is set, nonprofit representatives should:

1. Obtain all useful and appropriate information about the corporation before initiating any contact;
2. Dress according to accepted professional or business standards on the day of the meeting;
3. Shake hands firmly;
4. Act assured and behave assertively (no one feels comfortable handing over limited financial resources to a hesitant asker);
5. Be honest (no amount of money is worth compromising one's integrity; if there are questions that cannot be answered during the meeting, the nonprofit's representatives should promise to get back to the corporate executives with a response deadline date—and then do so);
6. Ask questions (What will be expected of the agency, if funded? Is continued funding a possibility, assuming all present program objectives have been met?

Exhibit 23.2.   Funding prospect follow-up calls.

Pyramid Associates, Incorporated

_____
Proposal

Week of _____

Day   _____

Date   _____

	Name	Corp/Agency/Fund	Tel #	Appointment Decision by Follow-Up Call
7:00				
7:30				
8:00				
8:30				
9:00				
9:30				
10:00				
10:30				
11:00				
11:30				
12:00				
12:30				
1:00				
1:30				
2:00				
2:30				
3:00				
3:30				
4:00				
4:30				
5:00				

71 Balhon Circle   ▲   Elkton, MD 21921   ▲   (410) 392-3160

Reproduced with permission from Pyramid Associates, Incorporated.

What materials need to be forwarded following this meeting? How will payments be made?);

7. Actively listen and not act defensively (if questions by the nonprofit representative are well-designed, the funding official will provide answers that can be incorporated into the formal proposal and will markedly increase chances of being funded);

8. Not mention a price tag (funding officials receive requests totaling many times what they can give; psychologically, funders look for ways to reject proposals quickly and cost is the most frequently cited reason—yet, when a project excites corporate officials, financial resources are almost never an obstacle;

9. Treat rejection graciously and look at it as an opportunity (perhaps the present request did not meet the funder's current objectives; however, such meetings help nonprofits understand the funding agency's priorities, establish rapport, and provide personal entry to their personnel);

10. Keep detailed notes;

11. Always follow up the meeting with a letter, thanking the funder for the opportunity to share the agency's aspirations and recounting any items agreed on;

12. Add the funding source representative to the agency's informational system mailing list.

(ii) Telephone contact   At the beginning of the solicitation process, a nonprofit executive may need to resort to the telephone, especially with the high costs associated with travel. In the process of telephone solicitation, the following points should be kept in mind;

1. Thoughts and questions should be organized and written down before the telephone is picked up. All relevant facts and figures should be at the fingertips of the nonprofit representative. Previous contacts with the funding source, collected in a file folder on the individual or company, should be thoroughly reviewed.

2. The highest ranking corporate contact person should be requested. Secondary sources should be avoided, unless absolutely necessary (e.g., the person is no longer with the company).

3. The nonprofit representative should speak clearly and authoritatively. He or she should state the agency's name and get directly to the point. The content of the conversation should not be summarized at the end. If the contact person has only a few minutes available, the nonprofit representative should arrange to call back.

4. If the funder asks a question that the nonprofit representative cannot answer. he or she should agree to get back to the corporate officer with the information and should be sure to follow through. Often, the opportunity to get back to the person with follow-up information actually increases a nonprofit's chances of being funded.

5. Rapport should be established by asking questions and advice of the funder.

6. The nonprofit representative should convey enthusiasm and a positive attitude for the agency and program.

7. Active listening skills are imperative. The nonprofit representative should not monopolize the conversation. Often, the representative will be able to suggest program or funding alternatives to a reluctant funder.

8. A secretary should never make the solicitation calls for the nonprofit representative; it degrades the funder.

9. Every attempt should be made to arrange for a person-to-person meeting to explain the project. As noted previously, a personal meeting increases chances for funding 70 percent, according to some estimates.

10. Good telephone etiquette is a prerequisite to telephone contact with funding sources.

11. Careful records of all pertinent details of conversations with funding sources should be logged.

12. If a follow-up meeting has been scheduled or the nonprofit representative agrees to send additional information, a one-page follow-up letter should be mailed (or faxed) within 24 hours. The main points of the conversation should be recounted and the letter should end by stating that the nonprofit representative is looking forward to a meeting regarding the agency's request.

13. Nonprofit representatives should try to avoid getting pigeon-holed regarding a price tag for the proposal. Beleaguered funding officers look for ways to reject proposals quickly, and the "too costly" label is the easiest to apply. Yet, if they like the concepts, they will often fund part of the project and help the agency to leverage that contribution to secure gifts from other sources. A good approach is for the nonprofit representative to tell the funding agency representative that his or her input is being sought and evaluated before finalizing the program and request. Following such a meeting, the agency can ask what the funder feels the realistic request range might be.

(b) PARTNERSHIPS Prior to requesting large sums of money, nonprofits have been successful in developing partnership arrangements with receptive corporations. As an example, health-related nonprofits can offer corporate site screenings for high blood pressure, breast cancer, or diabetes. Smoking cessation, stress reduction, and exercise classes are also popular with the corporate community. A key factor improving the chances for success is the perceived benefit to the corporation in terms of public perception or employee relations.

In the same vein, there are many case histories of corporations offering in-kind help to nonprofits, including accounting, marketing, public relations, or printing. These partnerships are vitally important; they attach a human involvement element to the partnership. These human partnerships are the best leverage a nonprofit has, to eventually obtain a commitment of financial support.

(c) SUBMITTING A FORMAL PROPOSAL Finally, after the cultivation and solicitation processes begin to bear fruit, the nonprofit may be asked to submit a formal proposal to the corporate giving committee. There is a strong tendency on the part of nonprofit organizations to throw at the corporate source every document the agency has ever produced, lengthy descriptions of the agency's history, rambling lists of programs, and program descriptions that are impossibly detailed. After all, according to this train of thought, this is the agency's chance to showcase itself to the corporation.

In reality, a formal proposal to a corporate source is the briefest of all formal proposals. A nonprofit agency should make every possible attempt to keep the proposal to under 5 single-spaced or 10 double-spaced pages, excluding cover letter and any appendices. Most giving committee executives simply do not have the time or inclination to give a thorough reading to lengthy proposals. Instead, they rely on the program officer's analysis and recommendations.

Corporate solicitation proposals are really supplemental follow-ups to the relationship-building that has preceded the submission by months or years. By then, the corporate source (a "critical mass" of corporate advocates) knows the essentials about the nonprofit and simply wants to know about the problem, the proposed solution, the methods of assessing success or failure, other funding sources, and the corporation's role.

In corporate solicitations, conciseness is the rule of the game. Be brief, make every word count, and use high-impact, simple graphics to make important points that would otherwise be buried in the narrative.

If supporting materials must be included, be highly selective about which ones are truly needed. Move cumbersome supporting materials, such as letters of support, to the appendices. This shows readers that you care about their time and effort and allows them to consult appendices only if and as needed.

Be sure to give the proposal to two or more naïve readers for comment. A naïve reader is someone who knows little or nothing about the problem being addressed, which is certain to be the case for many of the corporate decision makers. Ask businesspeople on the board or committees also to review and comment on the proposal before it is submitted.

A cover letter should *always* accompany a proposal, whether or not the funding contact expects the submission. The cover letter is critical; it must secure the reader's interest immediately. The cover letter should:

1. Summarize the request concisely;
2. Grab the reader's interest quickly (do not be afraid to use modifiers to make your concepts sparkle; however, avoid using words like "unique");
3. Link the nonprofit's request to the company's expressed interests (determine those interests through careful research, reading its published guidelines, telephone and personal contacts, and discussions with others familiar with those funding sources, especially agency board members);
4. Not ramble on any of the issues addressed in the proposal;
5. Be confined to one page and *never* exceed two;
6. *Always* be addressed to a person, not to "Dear Friend" or "Dear Corporate Director." (reference sources should be consulted to obtain the names of contacts *and* accuracy should be confirmed by telephone—(see Exhibit 23.3);
7. Reference previous telephone or personal contact with the addressee;
8. Be cleanly typed on agency letterhead, grammatically correct, and free of typos. If the agency letterhead does not include a telephone number, it must be included in the cover letter.

23.7 FOLLOW-UP

Too many nonprofit agencies tend to suffer from the take-the-money-and-run syndrome. Whether because of embarrassment, ignorance, or both, many agencies receive their corporate check, spend it on the intended purpose, and then avoid approaching that company again—until it is time to request new funding.

Once an agency secures funding for a project or capital campaign, it should redouble its efforts to maintain a positive relationship with the funder. Agencies show respect for their funders by providing ongoing communication. It should always be

Exhibit 23.3.   Sample letter seeking corporate support.

Mr. Jack Jones
Vice President
AB Corporation
100 Main Street
Hometown, MD 20001

Dear Mr. Jones,

Thank you again for taking the time to meet with us concerning the Arthritis Foundation of Maryland's upcoming Jingle Bell Run.

In follow-up to our meeting, we are submitting the enclosed request for support from AB Corporation. Specifically, we are requesting that AB serve as the exclusive statewide sponsor of the event for the next two years, which we estimate will involve costs not to exceed $20,000 each year.

As we discussed, sponsorship represents an extraordinary opportunity for a company to gain statewide visibility and advance its marketing goals. Our last exclusive sponsor, Maryland Financial Bank, exceeded its recognition goals by some 30% due to the joint promotion, a fact which its President, John Jacobs attributed to its success in opening branches statewide. Bank employee involvement in the event was highlighted on all three television networks and helped the Bank network into new communities. If it were not for a major corporate charitable initiative in homelessness and public housing, the Bank would certainly retain its sponsorship. Mr. Jacobs was kind enough to encourage any serious contenders for corporate sponsorship to contact him directly at (301) 333-3333.

The enclosed proposal provides the data you requested in terms of the number of scheduled public messages, media we use, types of promotional materials, and market segments.

We look forward to your response and to potentially working with you on the Jingle Bell Run to help prevent and treat arthritis.

Sincerely,

Janet Johnson
Executive Director

---

remembered that the ultimate goal is not to fund a single need, but to develop a consistent donor and supporter. Following are some suggestions for keeping an agency's funding base informed and involved.

- *Thank-you letters.* First and foremost, all funding must be acknowledged with a personal thank-you letter that accepts the support and briefly reiterates the need and intended use. This letter should be signed by both the board chairperson and the Executive Director. It should again state clearly and concisely what the funds will be used for; in many cases, the acknowledgment letter will be the first communication to a CEO on the specifics of the gift.

- *Press clippings.* Copies of local press clippings publicizing any aspect of the project and giving credit to funders should be forwarded to the funding agencies. Such clippings should be accompanied by a brief letter explaining the general content of the news article and how the gift made some of the newsworthy items possible. A handwritten personal note in the margins of such clippings is usually well received by corporate decision makers.

- *Committee work and progress reports.* The funder should be kept informed of work accomplished by the project. Agencies should be careful never to let their first communication with the funder be a request for continuance of funding! Funders should be asked for advice and/or to be on a working committee.
- *Personal visits.* Representatives of the funder should be invited to kick-off ceremonies and project openings. Notices of all important milestones should be mailed to funders, with follow-up calls inviting them to lunch when the board chairperson or Executive Director is in the funder's neighborhood.
- *Telephone calls.* Agency heads should be available to receive and to initiate telephone calls from and to the funding source and should be responsive to questions that show continued interest in the project.
- *Newsletters.* Funding agencies should be placed on the mailing lists for general organizational newsletters.
- *Donor recognition.* It is always a good idea to plan donor recognition events. One way to handle this is to use opportunities inherent in program milestones and newsworthy success stories. Linking a corporate donor to well-publicized successes in social programs is highly prized by corporate marketing departments.
- *Donor clubs.* Another excellent way to encourage relationships and future funding success is in the establishment of donor clubs. Corporate donors appreciate the opportunity to be viewed as community leaders and to rub elbows with others of influence in the community. In fact, donor clubs are an excellent way to get small to medium-size companies to stretch their gifts. The extra financial pain is often worth the gains in access to larger corporate decision makers.
- *Requests for continuing funds.* The request for continuing support is as important as the initial fund solicitation. Funded agencies should never simply send a letter asking for additional money. Instead, they should state the progress and accomplishments of the project and outline opportunities for continuance and expansion. In particular, funded agencies should detail for funders how their contributions made success possible. Funded agencies should ask funders for input on requests for continuing funds. If a funded agency has done its job properly, the road to continued funding will have already been paved.

23.8 HANDLING REJECTION

There is no such thing as rejection to a successful nonprofit executive or development officer; there are only situations where a company temporarily cannot fund a specific proposal. Development officers and top executives of nonprofits can spin many a yarn about initial project rejections that were subsequently turned into major gifts. The secret is wrapped in how one handles the initial rejection.

First, the nonprofit CEO should acknowledge the rejection and thank his or her corporate counterpart for taking the time to hear the request and making an effort to evaluate it. Next, by personal call or meeting, preferably the latter, the nonprofit representative should debrief the funding source as follows:

- What caused the proposal to fail?
- Was the proposal written clearly enough for the giving committee?

- In what ways could the proposal have been improved?
- Would the company entertain a modified request?
- What actions could the nonprofit take to bolster the chances for success in the next go-around?
- Given the nature of the program for which funding was requested, does the corporate contact know of any other corporations that would be more receptive to such a program? If so, would he or she agree to help in the initial contact?

In 90 percent of cases of corporate rejection of a funding request, corporate giving officers report never hearing from the agency again until the next round of requests. This is a strategic error. Instead, initial rejections should be viewed as the starting point for relationship and confidence building, which will result in larger corporate support in the future. If debriefing and other follow-up procedures are employed with a corporate funding source, the chances of future proposals being funded increase dramatically.

The fact is that, no matter how well written a proposal may be, no matter how well connected a nonprofit's board may be to the corporation, proposals will fail because a finite amount of funding is available. That means that a company may like a program, but be unable to fund it. Here lies an opportunity for a savvy nonprofit.

Are there ways that noncash involvement can substitute for program components? In the area of philanthropy, an old maxim says that involvement leads to commitment and commitment leads to a host of resources. Would the company agree to lend an officer to help with program committee work? Are there depreciated assets that can support the program, such as used furniture or excess product inventory?

Corporate officers must be kept abreast or the progress a nonprofit is making towards its stated goals. This includes placing receptive officers on mailing lists for newsletters and publicity releases, inviting them to key social functions, placing them on blue ribbon panels, assigning them committee work, requesting that they serve on boards—in essence, keeping them informed and involved. Only through such means can rejections be turned into gifts, and gifts into consistent donors.

23.9 LEVERAGING GIFTS

Corporate gifts can be used to secure other gifts. Corporate executives generally understand the concept of leveraging, where every dollar earns many times its value in results. Most people, given the choice between two worthwhile causes, would rather give to the one that will match their gift from other sources, thereby magnifying their gift. Corporations are no exception.

Leveraging works on both sides of the giving equation. First, during the solicitation phase, leveraging helps to secure corporate support. A company prefers to give knowing that it is not the only one that believes in the approach the nonprofit is taking. Call it security, confidence, aversion to risk taking, or whatever other words critics and supporters use; most corporate givers are swayed by the argument that others too, support the program.

After a corporate gift is secured, it can be used to secure other corporate gifts. In many cases, the corporate donor will work with the solicitation committee or its representative, to cull the list of other potential corporate givers. This is based on the premise that every dollar the donor gives will attract other dollars, thereby diversifying the resource pool. This has many consequences. For example, in cases where a particular industry is hard hit by economic trends, another industry group of companies can take up the slack. Diversity in funding sources also has the effect of making sure that the project is not undercapitalized, a situation to which any corporate donor is sensitive. Finally, a diverse resource pool offers the potential of many more people, with a wide range of experience and skills, for the nonprofit to draw from, thereby increasing the likelihood of program success.

SOURCES AND SUGGESTED REFERENCES

The following are excellent sources of information for researching corporate sources. However, keys to successful corporate solicitation include: keeping abreast of developments in the field of corporate giving; maintaining regular contact with likely corporate prospects; and developing a strategy that ties marketing efforts with fund-raising. This usually means that a nonprofit must dictate a staff position to these activities or, in a smaller nonprofit highly focus the corporate solicitation effort so that associated activities can be part of a staff position.

1. *Local Chambers of Commerce.* Find the listing in your local phone directory. Keep in mind that local chambers (town or city) are separate entities from statewide chambers of commerce. Each may have a role to play in your research. It may also be a good idea to join the local Chamber as an associate member.

2. *The Foundation Center.* 79 Fifth Avenue, New York, NY 10003. A nonprofit organization headquartered in New York City, with major branches throughout the United States and holdings in every state. Its main mission is to disseminate accurate and timely information concerning private foundations to the nonprofit community. It maintains a detailed data base on more than 30,000 private foundations in the United States, including corporate foundations.

   The Foundation Center issues annual publications that update earlier data bases, and bulletins that report on trends in private and corporate foundations. It also hosts training and informational seminars on foundation-related issues. Its entire data base is available for on-line computer retrievals. Retrieving the materials from an on-line source, such as DIALOG Information Services (3460 Hillview Avenue, Palo Alto, CA 94304; 1-800-3-DIALOG), has distinct advantages. A researcher can save the search parameters and simply request that the file be updated regularly, automatically.

   The Foundation Center also offers an Associates Program. For an annual fee, this program offers telephone help to researchers, data base searches, and printouts.

3. *The Taft Group,* 12300 Twinbrook Parkway, Suite 450, Rockville, MD 20852. A for-profit publishing company focusing on the largest private foundation and corporate giving programs. The materials (books, newsletters, and special-topic publications) are generally well researched and comprehensive, although the coverage is not as broad as The Foundation Center's materials. Data are updated annually.

4. *Publicly held corporations.* An excellent source of information for potential approaches by nonprofit organizations. You may request a copy of their corporations' annual 10-K report or quarterly 8-K update reports, which every publicly traded corporation must file with the Securities and Exchange Commission (SEC). The forms are also available from the SEC regional offices, from major libraries, and on-line through DIALOG. The 10-K forms give a great deal of information about the company, its executive compensation, board members, and other details that may help with your cultivation efforts.

A nonprofit organization should request to be placed on the public affairs mailing list of all potential corporate sources in its geographic area, including the national headquarters of firms with a local presence.

5. *Who's Who in Business and Industry.* (Marquis Who's WHO, Inc., 200 East Ohio Street, Chicago, IL 60611). This is one of several specialty publications by Marquis. They can be used to cross-match information on likely corporate prospects with their officers and directors. Also available on-line from DIALOG.

6. *Other reference sources.* Large libraries have a wealth of information about corporate sources, including: *Standard & Poor's Register of Corporations, Directors and Executives; Moody's Industrial Manual;* and *Dun and Bradstreet's Million-Dollar Directory.* In addition, nonprofit development officers and/or staff should read business publications regularly, including: *Forbes, Business Week, Fortune, The Wall Street Journal, Harvard Business Review,* and regional business publications.

SUGGESTED REFERENCES

AAFRC Trust for Philanthropy. 1991. *Giving USA,* New York: Author.

The Board Member's Guide to Fund Raising. 1990. San Francisco: Jossey-Bass Publishers.

Drucker, Peter. 1990. *Managing the Non-Profit Organization: Practices and Principles.* New York: HarperCollins.

Knauft, E. B. 1985. *Profiles of Effective Corporate Giving Programs.* Washington, DC: Independent Sector.

O' Connell, Brian. 1989. *Volunteers in Action.* New York: The Foundation Center.

Plinio, Alex, and Sanlon, Joanne. *Resource Raising: The Role of Non-Cash Assistance in Corporate Philanthropy.* Washington, DC: Independent Sector.

Shannon, James P. 1991. *The Corporate Contributions Handbook.* San Francisco: Jossey-Bass.

Stern, Gary, and Andrews, Rebecca. 1991. *Marketing Workbook for Non-Profit Organizations.* St. Paul, MN: Amherst H. Wilder Foundation.

Grant Proposal Writing

Lynn Lee
Pyramid Associates, Inc. and
Hartford Community College

CONTENTS

24.1   INTRODUCTION

Nonprofit organizations seldom have enough money to expand their operation or to develop and implement new programs. For this reason, the grant has become one of the chief sources of additional funding for many nonprofit organizations. The grant proposal is simply a written request and documentation for funding. The funding may be required to initiate a new program, hire an additional staff member, or aid in fulfilling a similar need. Whatever the purpose, a grant proposal is a vehicle for persuading a potential funder to sponsor the proposed spending.

Grant proposal writing today is one of the most competitive ways to obtain funding for a nonprofit organization. In this arena, organizations compete for federal, state, local, or private funding on several levels:

1. The competitors are other organizations that have similar missions;
2. The proposed program is in competition with other proposed programs;
3. Competition is based on the clarity of the proposal, the writing ability of the applicant, and the completeness of the grant package.

It is not uncommon for a federal grant to fund 200 proposals out of 900 applicants. It is imperative that the grant proposal present the program in the most comprehensive and accurate light, and that the grant package completely fulfill the requirements of the funding agency. The entire world may be aware that the organization is a nonprofit organization, but if a copy of the letter granting the nonprofit status is not included in the appendix of the proposal, the grant will not make it past the first review.

Grant proposal writing has become a science; a set of rules must be followed if the grant is to be funded. Although grant proposals may vary tremendously in length, documentation, and format, a number of common elements are found in all grant proposals.

24.2 GOVERNMENT VERSUS PRIVATE GRANT PROPOSALS

Grant proposals written for private sources, such as foundations or corporations, are usually less tedious than proposals submitted for government funding. Foundations and corporations will often require a brief cover letter explaining the request: the proposed program, the amount requested, and the contact person involved. This letter is accompanied by a brief proposal (one to six pages in length) that normally includes concise information about the organization and the project—how it will be accomplished and what it will cost. Each foundation or corporation will specify a length for the proposal. Normally, foundations and corporations will require only minimal materials in the form of appendices. Some foundations prefer that an applicant first call the foundation to discuss the project before sending a written proposal.

Grant proposals for government agencies are usually extensive and precise. Often, a government grant narrative will be 20 to 30 pages long and will be followed by complete budgetary information and numerous appendices. Because these types of proposals are major undertakings, this chapter is devoted to the development of a grant proposal for a government agency.

24.3 BACKGROUND AND CREDIBILITY

Prior to undertaking the writing of a grant for any project, the organization must develop, or review, and understand its own mission. Many organizations exist without ever having gone through the process of developing a mission statement. This must be the first step in the grant process, if it has not already occurred. No agency will fund a project that does not appear to be consistent with the nonprofit organization's mission. For instance, would it seem appropriate for a counseling agency to apply for a grant to fund a project to develop jobs for unemployed mothers with dependent children? The mission for a counseling center is not usually in the realm of job placement and career development.

Linked to the mission statement is the validity of the actual proposed project. Is it a project that is within the mission of the organization? Does it perpetuate the mission? Is it viable, given the background and leadership of the organization?

It is important for the nonprofit organization to develop credibility in the field. It must demonstrate that it is aware of what is being done in the area and that it has an excellent reputation. Its reputation may be derived from its key personnel; for example, the director may have published articles relating to the proposed project. Credibility also extends to the experience and accomplishments of the organization's individual board members. If the board includes an accountant, an attorney, and a marketing specialist, there is an indication of good guidance from the board.

Many grants are not funded simply because the applicants did not convince the funding agency of their competence in their own field. The task of selling an organization to the funder can be done through letters of support or news clippings displayed in the appendix. The organization must demonstrate to the potential funder that it is aware of what has already been tried with regard to the proposed project and of the results—what types of programs have been successful or unsuccessful. The funder must be assured that the organization will be in existence to follow the project through to evaluation.

24.4 LOCATING THE SOURCE FOR FUNDING

Many nonprofit organizations make the mistake of soliciting the wrong funding source. One of the most important tasks at the outset of the grant proposal writing is to research the funding sources. Most foundations, corporations, and government funding sources clearly state the types of proposals that they will fund. Government funding sources generally publish a Request for Proposals (RFP) which states the type of proposals being solicited and the precise format that each proposal must follow. Descriptions of funding guidelines for foundations are easily found in local libraries in such sources as *The Foundation Directory* and *Taft Foundation Reporter.* Sources of help in locating companies that have established giving programs are the *National Data Book* and the *Corporate Giving Yellow Pages.* Information regarding the actual giving policies of corporations can be found in *Source Book Profiles, Taft Corporate Giving Directory,* or *Corporate Foundation Profiles.* All of these sources can be found in local libraries. Often, a nonprofit agency will locate funding sources in its own backyard. A review of the major corporations located in the area may yield local funding sources, and a phone call may be all that is required to make the contact.

When seeking funds from a government agency, it is best to identify which agencies are concerned with the type of project that is being proposed. For example, if the project is a drug abuse prevention program, the following federal agencies would be potential funders:

Office of Substance Abuse Prevention:
    High-risk youth demonstration grants
    Pregnant and postpartum women and infants
    Substance Abuse Conference grants
    Community partnership demonstration grants
Department of Education:
    Drug-free schools and communities
    Training and demonstration grants to institutions of higher learning
    Federal activities grants programs

Funds for Improvement of Post-Secondary Education (FIPSE):
  National College Student Organization network program
  Approaches to Accountability in Prevention programs
U.S. Department of Housing and Urban Development (HUD):
  Public housing drug elimination program
  Youth sports clubs to combat drugs
  Resident manager clubs
  Comprehensive improvement assistance program
  Public housing child care demonstration grants
  Community development block grants
U.S. Department of Health and Human Services:
  National Institute on Drug Abuse
U.S. Department of Justice:
  National Institute of Justice
  Office of Juvenile Justice and Delinquency Prevention

In a similar vein, state governments often fund grants for specific types of programs, such as drug abuse prevention. After a few telephone calls, the applicant organization should be able to locate several potential funders on the state level.

24.5 UNDERSTANDING THE RFP

When working with government agencies, the Request for Proposals (RFP) becomes the basic tool in developing the grant proposal. The RFP may be called Invitation to Apply, Notice to Apply for New Awards, Program Announcement, or Grant Announcement. Whatever the name, the RFP is the means of communicating the vital information about the grant: how many grants will be awarded; what types of programs will be funded; what types of agencies should apply.

By law, all government grants are officially announced in a Request for Proposals or an Invitation to Apply. These announcements guarantee equal access to the federal funds and ensure that the competition for the funding will occur. Demonstration grants are often sponsored by government agencies. The purpose of a demonstration grant is to fund projects or programs that "demonstrate" new approaches to a certain problem, usually a social problem. The goal is to provide a model program that can be easily adapted to other communities with the anticipation of similar results. For this reason, the evaluation component of these grants is usually an important consideration in the awarding of the grant.

In approaching the RFP, it is important that the grant announcement match the mission and the proposed project of the nonprofit agency. The announcement should be carefully scrutinized to ascertain that the agency meets the applicant qualifications and that the proposed project is within the funding areas of the grant.

Most government RFPs are organized in the following pattern:

Introduction/Background: who is funding the grant, the purpose of the grant, what has been done in this area to date, what types of proposals will be considered, how the grant will be funded, and what the target populations will be.

Program Goals: the governmental agency's overriding program goal—the broad purposes of the agency. Any grant application must address the program goals of the governmental agency that is the potential funder.

Eligibility: what types of agencies and organizations are eligible to apply.

Letter of Intent: advance notification from organizations that are planning to submit an application in response to the grant announcement. The Letter of Intent usually must be submitted 30 days prior to the deadline for the grant application, so that the funding agency can plan appropriately for the review process. The Letter of Intent does not obligate the applicant to follow up with an official grant application or commit the applicant in any other way.

Application Characteristics: how the narrative section will be organized. Normally, the RFP will specifically define the contents of the application and the length of each section. It is important that careful attention be paid to this section. A grant will be automatically rejected for any incompleteness or inconsistency with the RFP requirements.

Abstract: a short, concise statement that includes the critical information about the grant: the who-what-when-where-how. The abstract should be well written and complete because it may be the only part of the grant that some reviewers read. Although the abstract is written last, it is placed before the grant narrative.

It is vital that the RFP be carefully reviewed. Most grant proposal writers outline the RFP so that important information is not overlooked. Additionally, the information found in the RFP will normally indicate the average size of the awards, how many awards will be made, what the anticipated competition will be, and the geographical distributions of the awards, if any. The RFP will also clearly indicate what types of organizations are eligible to apply and what types of proposals will be funded.

Many government grant sponsors offer Technical Assistance (TA) Workshops for potential applicants. If these are available, they are worth the effort and expense of attending. The TA Workshops elaborate on the RFP and provide additional information on the types of projects that the government agency is seeking, along with valuable tips on how to write the proposal. Information on developing the budget and completing the assurances and forms is also available.

Exhibit 24.1 suggests a 12-step sequence for developing an RFP into a grant application.

24.6 THE NARRATIVE

The crux of any grant application is the narrative. This is where all the vital information regarding the proposed project is located. The RFP or the grant announcement will clearly define the form that the narrative must follow. *Do not deviate from this form in any way.* If the RFP says that the introduction must be no longer than 2 pages, a 2½-page introduction will not be acceptable.

Writing the narrative is not an exercise in creative writing. If the proposed project is sound and well-developed, then it is not necessary to camouflage the information in jargon and prose. Grant writing is a task of presenting ideas in the format that the RFP requires.

Exhibit 24.1.   Steps for matching an RFP to a grant application.

1. Read the entire RFP first. Understand the goals of the funding agency.
2. Carefully review forms and assurances that are required.
3. Determine whether your organization meets the eligibility requirements.
4. Send a Letter of Intent, if required. Be brief. State your intent to apply and describe the problem you will address in your proposal.
5. Outline the narrative. Be specific in your outline so that you do not overlook any part of the narrative requirements.
6. Assign tasks for completing the narrative, timelines, and graphics.
7. Establish deadlines for completing the tasks.
8. Solicit letters of support. (You should have set the groundwork for this solicitation before you started your project.)
9. Write the abstract.
10. Proof the narrative. Proof it again with the RFP in one hand and the narrative in the other hand.
11. Complete the forms and necessary assurances.
12. Make copies of each page and then mail the original. *Hint:* The last two steps always take twice the amount of time planned for them.

Because most reviewers appreciate an application on which the information is not hidden, follow the narrative outline. Preface each section with a statement of what the RFP requested. For example, when describing the target population, preface the paragraph in bold letters with **Target Population.** This device will assist the reviewers in ascertaining the completeness of the application and will ensure that the grant writer will not omit required information.

The narrative will have a limit to the number of text pages for each section. Do not be afraid to use timelines or relevant graphs to conceptualize your project. These graphic aids can clarify the goals and objectives and support the thrust of the proposal.

If graphs or charts are used to supplement the text, be sure that they are clearly reproduced and easily understood. A rambling flow chart, such as the one shown in Exhibit 24.2, will both confuse the reader and detract from the quality and impression of the proposal.

On the other hand, a professionally developed graphic will enhance the proposal and clarify relationships or project goals. The graphic in Exhibit 24.3 demonstrates the agencies involved in a community partnership grant funded by the Office of Substance Abuse. The agencies and their relationship to the grantee are clearly depicted.

The use of time lines can illustrate the anticipated activities and accomplishment of goals over the period of the grant. A time line should include all of the activities designated in the proposal as means for accomplishing the goals, with the beginning and completion times clearly marked. The time line in Exhibit 24.4 provides a concise schedule for the designated program activities.

Normally, a grant proposal for government funding will follow a specified flow. The introduction generally includes the aims or goals of the proposed project. These objectives must fall into one of the categories of program goals listed in the RFP. Goals are usually statements of broad aims of the project, such as: "Participants' grades will be improved."

Exhibit 24.2.   Example of a confusing flow chart.

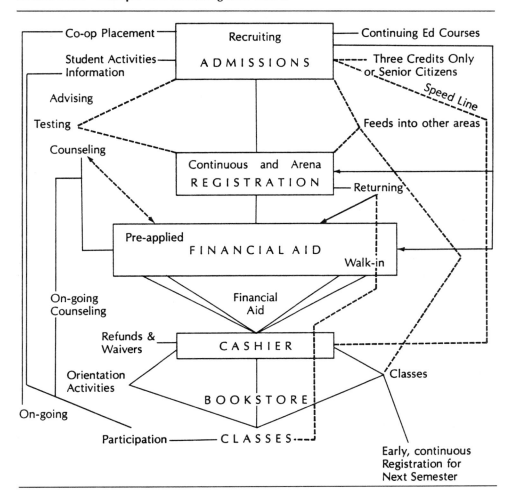

From the goals, the specific objectives are developed. In developing objectives, it is necessary to not only be specific but to state them in *measurable terms*. Use of a program model (U.S. Department of Health and Human Services, 1987) will force a logical flow, from objectives through activities to evaluation. Evaluation is a major component in grant writing, and this model will promote the evaluation concepts by setting objectives that are matched to specific activities. Exhibit 24.5 demonstrates a program model.

For the goal stated above (improving grades), the following specific objectives might be given:

Through a strong tutoring program with a summer component:

1. 60% will improve at least one letter grade, after one year, in the school subject(s) in which they are tutored, as measured by school report cards;

Exhibit 24.3.   Acceptable illustrative graphic showing how various community agencies will work with the central project management in a drug prevention program.

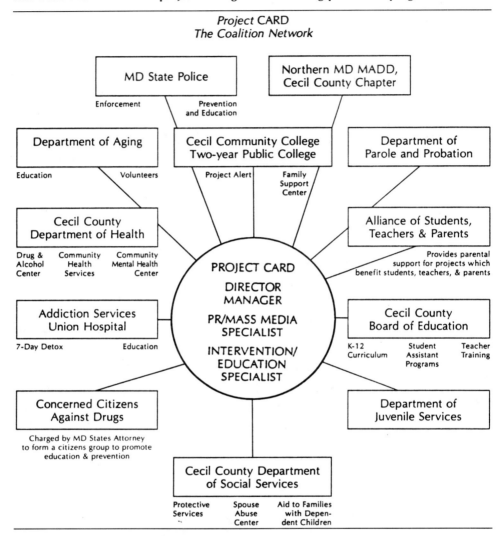

Project CARD
The Coalition Network

2. 25% will increase at least one grade level, after one year, in a minimum of one tutored subject, as measured by standardized tests and the Department of Public Instruction computer program.

As the objectives are developed, they must be measured in the evaluation plan. Too often, grants are not funded because the objectives are not measurable. The objectives should clearly state exactly what will be accomplished, when it will be accomplished, and how it will be measured.

The background and significance section allows applicants to demonstrate their knowledge of the problem. Here is where an applicant establishes credibility and describes the agency's experience with the targeted problem. The applicant must show

Exhibit 24.4. A project timeline.

Activity	Oct	Nov	Dec	Jan	Feb	Mar	Apr	May	Jun	Jul	Aug	Sept
Hire tutors												
Train tutors												
Meet with schools												
Identify students												
Conduct tutoring												
Implement summer program												
Review tests												
Review report cards												

Tutoring Program Timeline

Exhibit 24.5. A sample exhibit program model.

Resources	Program of Services	Immediate Results	Outcomes
3 Trainers 10 Tutors Curriculum package P.S. teacher assistance 4 Classrooms Vouchers for activities School supplies	Tutoring sessions offered weeknights in 4 area locations Summer tutoring offered 3 times per week in 4 locations Incentives given for summer tutoring	Students will: Learn study skills Improve reading ability Learn to budget time for homework Grow in self-esteem Experience bonding with school system Learn healthy leisure-time activities Report card grades will improve Scores on standardized tests will improve	The dropout rate will be reduced

an awareness of other successful and unsuccessful programs in the field or problem area, advocating the proposed project as one that is likely to be successful in solving the problem or helping the target population even though others may have failed. Much of the justification for the approach to the problem may be derived from research on prior program efforts in the field.

The background and significance section also allows the applicant to explain how society, or the field, will benefit from the knowledge obtained from the proposed project. The proposal should describe how the project will enhance, rather than duplicate, the knowledge base of the community.

The target population section will describe the community to be served by the project. Information about the population, location, demographic and socioeconomic characteristics, and ethnic minority composition will be included. There must be assurance that the target population is reasonably accessible and that the project can be easily implemented in the proposed target population.

In the approach or methods section, the applicant describes the actual proposed activities that will accomplish the objectives. Referring back to the program model, the explicit planned sequence of events is defined. The methods section, therefore, becomes the heart of the narrative. From a reviewer's perspective, it is important that a clear connection between the objective and the activities be defined. For this reason, some grant announcements will suggest that the program objective should be restated in this section, along with the subsequent activities planned to achieve it. For example, activities for the first objective stated earlier ("60% will improve at least one letter grade, . . .") might be:

1. Tutors who are culturally similar to the target population will be hired and trained by October 1.
2. Tutoring programs, developed in conjunction with the school teachers, will be offered Monday through Thursday after school in five neighborhood centers, beginning on October 15.
3. During the summer, tutoring will be offered in the neighborhood centers three times per week. To provide incentive to the participants, vouchers, which can be used as admittance to activities, will be given after the completion of each 5 hours of tutoring.
4. Subject-area grades will be compared at each marking period and evaluated after one year of tutoring for each student.

The method section must be specifically related to the goals and objectives that were originally established. This section will provide information about exactly what will be done with the project and how the desired results will be obtained. The activities described here should be realistic and achievable by the staff in the designated amount of time. Ambiguity in this section will typically leave the reviewers unsure of what the proposed project is trying to accomplish.

24.7   EVALUATION

In writing grants for government agencies, the evaluation section of the narrative has become more and more important to the success of the proposal. The trend toward demonstration grants and the desire of the government to provide models for other communities or agencies to duplicate has caused the evaluation to become a major component of the grant application.

Government grant reviewers indicate that about 60 percent of the grant applications received have inadequate or incomplete evaluation components. Some of the evaluation problems include inadequate detail, lack of expected outcomes, inappropriate measure, lack of consultant detail, lack of an evaluator, lack of planning for staff and resources to conduct the evaluation, and poor evaluation design.

The evaluation of the project is actually the collection and use of information, to determine whether the program has been successful in meeting the goals and objectives. By gathering such information, the organization is assuming a proactive position on problem solving and future planning. An objective evaluation is the only viable mode for assessing both the short- and long-term effectiveness of a project.

The evaluation must be planned as the goals, objectives, and activities are developed. As the objectives are established, they must be made measurable for the evaluation component. Using the program model will lead the applicant to the evaluation considerations. Exhibit 24.5 shows how the program model progresses to the evaluation phase of the project. This model provides information for the process component—the program of services or activity—as well as the short- and long-term outcomes.

Information for the Efficiency Evaluation can be ascertained from a review of the Resources.

The evaluation process will begin at the onset of the project. Data must be collected throughout the project, in order to determine the effectiveness of the program. For this reason, the evaluation plan must be fully developed, including the decisions on what data to collect and how they are to be collected and evaluated.

Many organizations contract for an outside evaluator to perform the evaluation component of the project. The outside evaluator will usually assist in writing the evaluation section of the narrative and will work with the program throughout its duration, to ensure that the appropriate data are collected and made available for analysis. Many colleges and universities have faculty or graduate assistants who can perform the evaluation and provide a statistical analysis of the results. The use of an outside evaluator can add credibility to the proposal and will indicate a sincere approach to the evaluation.

Among the numerous evaluation designs, three are most widely used: process evaluation, outcomes evaluation, and efficiency evaluation. It is very common for the evaluation component of a grant proposal to combine two or more of these designs.

In process evaluation, the implementation of the project is documented. The focus here is on the process of the program, rather than the long-term effects of the program. The evaluation is an assessment of whether the project was implemented according to the planned approach (activities) through the collection of quantitative and qualitative data. In essence, the process evaluation determines whether the objectives were accomplished and what specifically contributed to the attainment of the objectives.

For example, with the earlier objective ("60% of the participants will improve at least one letter grade . . .") the process evaluation would document: the number of tutoring sessions that each student participated in, whether the tutoring plan corresponded with the teaching plan of the school, and other designated activities for the accomplishment of this objective.

Many evaluators use program models as part of the process evaluation: for each activity, a program model form is completed and filed under the objective. This allows the evaluator to review and evaluate all the activities that supported the accomplishment of each objective. The process evaluation can occur only if the objectives are expressed in specific, quantifiable terms. Each objective should have a corresponding set of activities or methods for accomplishing the objective.

In planning for the process evaluation, consideration must be given to how the information will be collected, who will collect it, and when it will be collected. The process evaluation allows the project director to know who will do what, at each location, and in each segment of the time line. An ongoing data collection system that will serve as a tool for decision making and future planning must be created and maintained.

The outcomes evaluation will attempt to determine whether the project has made a difference in the target population and what this difference is. In essence, it answers the question: Did accomplishing the objectives help to achieve the goals of the project? The data obtained in the outcomes evaluation will provide the basis for the final conclusions that are drawn. Outcomes evaluations attempt to ask probing questions. For the example given earlier, the questions might be: Did the grades of the students improve? Was that improvement a result of the strong tutoring program?

In developing the evaluation plan for the outcomes evaluation, attention must be given to clearly articulating the goals of the program in both long- and short-term outcomes. Although many indexes of success may be long-term, it is sometimes necessary to develop short-term measurements that can be indicative of the attainment of the goal. For example, if the goal is to reduce the dropout rate in a high-risk target population via an elementary school reading enhancement program, the real measurement is long-term because it will occur when the students reach high school graduation. However, some short-term indicators of school success and completion, such as higher grades, would be appropriate measurements of attainment of the goal.

It is important to plan for and identify the measurement tools that will be used in the outcomes evaluation. Interviews, questionnaires, observation, tests, records and statistics, and surveys are among the means of measuring the outcome of the project. Similarly, the design itself could include the use of pretests and posttests, the use of a control group, or an evaluation of change over time.

Although the planning for the outcomes evaluation must occur at the design stage of the program, the actual performance of the outcomes evaluation will occur after the project has been implemented. With regard to the tutoring objective, it will be impossible to evaluate whether grades have improved until the tutoring activities have been implemented and grade reports have been compiled or testing has occurred.

The third type of evaluation, the efficiency evaluation, is used to assess whether the resources were used in the most efficient manner. A constant review of the procedures will highlight the ones that work most efficiently and will provide the best way to achieve the desired results. By means of the efficiency evaluation, the organization can review the activities and redirect them if they are not the most efficient manner of accomplishing the goals of the project. For example, it may be determined that producing and distributing 10,000 brochures was less cost-effective than purchasing one billboard on a main thoroughfare.

Whatever type of evaluation plan is used, it is most important that the evaluation become a part of the overall design of the program and that appropriate resources be budgeted to conduct the evaluation. The underlying reasons for conducting any evaluation are to determine whether a project has been successful and to develop ways for improving it and providing for program growth.

24.8 BUDGET

For any proposal for government funding, budget forms are usually included in the application packet. These forms must be completed accurately and usually must be accompanied by a budget narrative, to be located in an appendix.

Filling in the budget amounts is usually the last task in grant proposal writing, but thought must be given to the budget before the proposal is developed. Hints as to the average size of awards will be found in the grant announcement. If the project that is proposed cannot be implemented within the suggested budgetary range, it is wise to revamp the project activities. A realistic program with an appropriate budget will impress the grant reviewers more than a program consisting of objectives that cannot be reasonably attained with the proposed budget. For this reason, it is advisable to think in terms of cost when developing the objectives and activities of the program.

Some agencies require that the applicant organization provide some type of support, either budgetary or in-kind, to demonstrate the organization's commitment to the project. Most agencies will also require that the applicant organization provide information regarding the continuance of the project after the grant funding has ceased. Attention needs to be given, during the planning stages of the project, as to how the project will be funded in later years. At this point, the applicant may want to solicit a commitment for future funding from local entities or to devise a services fee schedule which will add to the support of the program.

Government grant budget forms normally include a budget summary, which delineates the government and nongovernment shares of the budget (if a match or in-kind support is present). The budget will be then broken into categories such as personnel and fringe benefits, travel, equipment and supplies, contractual or consultant costs, building or construction costs, miscellaneous costs, and indirect costs. Complete information regarding these budget items will be given in the budget narrative and must coincide with the data on the forms. If the project spans more than one year, the budget form may ask for the funding information for the balance of the project.

In developing the personnel section of the grant budget, costs for salaries and fringe benefits of grant employees must be considered. The number and types of personnel will relate to the activities of the program. The budget narrative should provide detailed information regarding the positions, the type of work that will be accomplished by the individuals in each position, the number of hours per week each position will work, and the anticipated salary for each position. In estimating benefits, the costs of social security, healthcare, disability insurance, and unemployment are among those that must be calculated. Normally, a grant employee will receive all of the benefits that a regular employee receives. Information and assistance in calculating the fringe benefits can be obtained from the organization's business office or from the payroll accountant.

Many grant proposals will require the inclusion of job descriptions for personnel who will be hired and résumés for incumbent personnel who will be involved with the project. These should be referenced in the narrative but located in a separate appendix.

The travel section of the budget will include the cost of all anticipated travel during the project period. Some government grants require that travel to government-sponsored meetings or workshops be included in the travel section. Costs of any other anticipated workshops or training opportunities for staff members should be included. If the project demands local travel, from project site to project site or for home visitations, a figure for local travel mileage reimbursement should be budgeted. All travel expenses must be justified and explained in the budget narrative section. Never say "Travel, $2,000" without itemizing how that money will be spent.

If the proposal calls for the purchase of equipment necessary to perform the activities, the cost should be included in the budget. For example, if computers are needed as a part of the tutoring program, the cost of the computers and necessary software should appear in the Equipment section, and the anticipated costs for supplies, such as computer paper and ribbons, should be recorded in the Supplies section. Cost estimates should always be accurate. For large items, actual estimates from vendors will ensure that the budget is realistic and accurate. Reviewers will easily spot unrealistic cost estimates and this will interpret them to mean that the applicant did not adequately prepare the budget.

Some proposals will require the use of contractual services or consultants. If the evaluation of the project is contracted to an expert, this should be reflected in the budget. An organization may hire consultants to train staff members or to implement an activity that is beyond the scope of the applicant organization. Sufficient detail must be provided in the budget narrative to explain who the consultant is and what the services will be.

If construction is a part of the proposal, information about permits, architectural design costs, and estimated construction costs is essential. Construction grants are usually separate grants, not normally linked with a service or activity grant. However, minor building renovations may be required for a service grant, in order to accommodate the proposed project. As an example, electrical wiring may have to be enhanced to support computers.

Indirect costs are the costs associated with general operation of the organization, such as the cost of preparing the payroll, heating the building, maintaining the equipment, or purchasing general supplies. Other examples of indirect costs are: administrative salaries, telephone expenses, equipment depreciation, and insurances and licenses. Indirect costs are normally costs that may not be identified with a proposed project, but are definitely associated with and integral to the overall operation of the organization.

Each organization receiving federal grant funds will negotiate an indirect cost rate through a regional office charged with that duty. This allowance is usually a percentage of the total direct costs of the proposal or simply a percentage of the personnel costs. This process should be completed prior to applying for federal funding, but, in some cases, can be negotiated after the grant is funded. For information regarding the indirect cost rate, contact the appropriate regional office listed in Exhibit 24.6.

Both state and private grantors will allow the inclusion of an indirect cost rate or administrative allowance. The method used should be similar to the calculation of the federal indirect cost rate.

As noted earlier, the budget forms supplied as a part of the application packet for federal grant allow room for only the figures for each category. It is recommended, if not required by the RFP, that a more complete budget narrative be included as an appendix. The budget narrative will allow the applicant to more fully justify each budget item and will ensure that the reviewers understand the need for the funding. Exhibits 24.7 and 24.8 show a typical budget form and the corresponding budget narrative giving detail to the figures. Use of the budget narrative to provide detail will also assist the applicant in developing a more realistic budget. By itemizing each activity cost, the organization is forced to obtain actual estimates and fares schedules, and build a realistic budget. If the grant be funded, the grantor will attempt to renegotiate some of the line

Exhibit 24.6. Regional offices for negotiating indirect costs.

Region	Address of Director, Division of Cost Allocation	For Applicants Located
I	J.F. Kennedy Federal Bldg. Government Center Boston, MA 02203 617/565-1485	Connecticut, Maine, Massachusetts, New Hampshire, Rhode Island, Vermont
II	Jacob K. Javits Federal Building 26 Federal Plaza New York, NY 10278 212/264-1823	New Jersey, New York, Puerto Rico, Virgin Islands
III	Federal Office Building 3535 Market Street P.O. Box 13716 Philadelphia, PA 19101 215/596-6423	Delaware, Maryland, Pennsylvania, Washington, DC, West Virginia, Virginia
IV	101 Marietta Tower, N.W. Atlanta, GA 30323 404/331-2455	Alabama, Florida, Georgia, Kentucky, Mississippi, North Carolina, South Carolina, Tennessee
V	Federal Office Building 300 South Wacker Drive Chicago, IL 60606 312/353-8330	Illinois, Indiana, Michigan, Minnesota, Ohio, Wisconsin
VI	Federal Office Building 1200 Main Tower Building Dallas, TX 75202 214/767-3261	Arkansas, Louisiana, Texas, New Mexico, Oklahoma
VII	Federal Office Building 601 East 12th Street Kansas City, MO 64106 816/374-2304	Iowa, Kansas, Missouri, Nebraska
VIII	Federal Office Building 1961 Stout Street Denver, CO 80294 303/844-5566	Colorado, Montana, North Dakota, South Dakota, Utah, Wyoming
IX	Federal Office Building 50 United Nations Plaza San Francisco, CA 94102 415/556-1704	American Samoa, Arizona, California, Guam, Hawaii, Nevada, Republic of the Marshall Islands, Republic of Palau, Federated States of Micronesia, Northern Marianas
X	2201 Sixth Avenue Mail Stop RX-04 Seattle, WA 98121 206/553-4390	Alaska, Idaho, Oregon, Washington

Exhibit 24.7. Completed budget form.

BUDGET INFORMATION — Non-Construction Programs   OMB Approval No. 0348-0044

SECTION A – BUDGET SUMMARY

Grant Program Function or Activity (a)	Catalog of Federal Domestic Assistance Number (b)	Estimated Unobligated Funds Federal (c)	Non-Federal (d)	New or Revised Budget Federal (e)	Non-Federal (f)	Total (g)
1. High Risk Youth	13,144	$	$	$ 327,791	$ 139,240	$ 467,031
2.						
3.						
4.						
5. TOTALS		$	$	$ 327,791	$ 139,240	$ 467,031

SECTION B – BUDGET CATEGORIES

6 Object Class Categories	GRANT PROGRAM, FUNCTION OR ACTIVITY (1)	(2)	(3)	(4)	Total (5)
a. Personnel	$ 121,000	$	$	$	$
b. Fringe Benefits	15,152				
c. Travel	5,200				
d. Equipment	34,260				
e. Supplies	24,700				
f. Contractual	112,364				
g. Construction	-0-				
h. Other Dues and Subscriptions	1,500				
i. Total Direct Charges (sum of 6a - 6h)	314,176				
j. Indirect Charges	13,615				
k. TOTALS (sum of 6i and 6j)	$ 327,791	$	$	$	$
7. Program Income	$ -0-	$	$	$	$

Standard Form 424A (4-88)
Prescribed by OMB Circular A-102

SECTION C - NON-FEDERAL RESOURCES

(a) Grant Program	(b) Applicant	(c) State	(d) Other Sources	(e) TOTALS
8. SAILS - Demonstration Grants for the Prevention, Treatment and Rehabilitation of Drug and Alcohol	$ 70,500	$ -0-	$ 68,740	$ 139,240
9. Abuse Among High-Risk Youth.				
10.				
11.				
12. TOTALS (sum of lines 8 and 11)	$	$	$	$

SECTION D - FORECASTED CASH NEEDS

	Total for 1st Year	1st Quarter	2nd Quarter	3rd Quarter	4th Quarter
13. Federal	$ 327,791	$ 152,880	$ 58,304	$ 58,303	$ 58,304
14. NonFederal	139,240	71,365	22,625	22,625	22,625
15. TOTAL (sum of lines 13 and 14)	$ 467,031	$ 224,245	$ 80,929	$ 80,928	$ 80,929

SECTION E - BUDGET ESTIMATES OF FEDERAL FUNDS NEEDED FOR BALANCE OF THE PROJECT

(a) Grant Program	FUTURE FUNDING PERIODS (Years) (b) First	(c) Second	(d) Third	(e) Fourth
16. SAILS - High Risk Youth	$ 269,100	$ 282,555	$ 296,682	$ 311,516
17.				
18.				
19.				
20. TOTALS (sum of lines 16 -19)	$	$	$	$

SECTION F - OTHER BUDGET INFORMATION
(Attach additional Sheets if Necessary)

21. Direct Charges:	22. Indirect Charges: 10% Wages, Salaries, Fringe

23. Remarks
     Budget narrative is attached.

SF 424A (4-88) Page 2
Prescribed by OMB Circular A-102

Exhibit 24.8. Example of budget narrative.

Budget Narrative

A. Personnel	
Project Director	(in-kind)
(20% time)	
Public Relations Director	(in-kind)
(10% time)	
Director of Tutoring/Dropout Prevention	(in-kind)
Rene Bryk will supervise the entire SAILS tutoring program in all 5 clubs.	
Directors of Tutoring 2 @ $20,000 ea	$40,000
Two fulltime directors will be hired from grant funds: one at the Rose Hill Club and one at the Claymont Club to supervise tutoring services and monitor school progress.	
The Boys Clubs will provide funds to hire Directors of tutoring at the Fraim, Brown and Jackson Clubs as an in-kind match.	(in-kind)
Tutors 5600 hours @ $10/hr	36,000
Tutors will provide individualized tutoring as per participant goals. The Clubs will match the tutoring costs with an additional $20,000.	
Computer Specialist Tutors will provide individualized assistance with DPI software and educational software programs.	
Five tutors-900 hours at $10/hour	45,000
Total personnel	$121,000
B. Fringe Benefits	
Fulltime (20%)	$ 8,000
Parttime(8.83%)	7,152
Total Fringes	$ 15,152
C. Travel	
Travel funds will be used to attend OSAP meetings, substance prevention conferences, COA workshops, etc. Staff travel will be used to reimburse staff for meetings at local schools, youth-oriented agencies, etc.	
5 staff auto travel	
.20/mi × 100 mi × 12 mos	$ 1,200
To work with schools, courts, and other referring agencies.	
5 conference attendance roundtrip travel @ $500 ea	2,500
10 days per diem travel @ $150/day	1,500
Total Travel	$ 5,200

item requests. If the organization has thoroughly researched the costs at the budget construction stage, it will be in a superior position to withstand the grantor's desire to negotiate some of the budgeted items.

24.9 THE FINAL PRODUCT

When the narrative is complete and the budget is developed and justified, the next steps are to complete the necessary forms and assurances, duplicate the grant proposal package, and mail or deliver it to the government agency. Each RFP or applicant package will contain a number of forms and assurances that must be completed and submitted with the written proposal. In a recent grant announcement for drug abuse prevention proposals, the Office of Substance Abuse required the following forms:

Application for Federal Assistance, Form 424

Budget Information—Nonconstruction Programs, Form 424A

Assurance—Nonconstruction Programs, Form 424B

Certificate Regarding Debarment and Suspension

Certificate Regarding Drug-Free Workplace Requirements

Civil Rights Assurance

Assurance Concerning the Handicapped

Assurance Concerning Sex Discrimination

As can be seen from the number of forms required, a sufficient amount of time should be allowed for the completion of this part of the grant writing project. It is not advisable to go to the final deadline with the proposal; delivering it one day late will eliminate it from consideration.

The grant announcement will indicate the specifics about the grant form, including the maximum number of narrative pages, the number of copies to be submitted, spacing requirements, and order of presentation. Some proposals will request a table of contents preceding the grant. Others will require certain information be provided in the appendixes, such as names and occupations of board members, résumés of key personnel, or certification of nonprofit status.

All grant proposals should include letters of support. These will not only establish the organization's credibility in the area, but will assure the reviewers that the proposed project has the endorsement of local agencies, particularly those agencies whose services normally complement the applicant's services. The applicant organization should begin the process of obtaining letters of support at the initiation of the proposal writing. Too often, supporting agencies procrastinate on writing a letter of support. They must be informed on exactly what the goals, objectives, and activities of the project will be and how they can interact with the activities, giving various forms of support.

When soliciting letters of support, it is advisable to give the project advocate an outline of the project and a summary of how each solicited agency can support the project. A sample letter of support will offer much appreciated guidance and will help guarantee strong letters of support that will fortify the proposal. For example, a letter of support for a drug abuse prevention program might include how many potential participants the supporting agency can refer to the program, how the two agencies have worked together in the past, and what accomplishments or successes the grant-seeking agency has had in the past. Because a weak letter of support can actually do harm to a proposal, it is vital that the champion receive guidance in how to compose a helpful letter.

Letters of support should be addressed to the applicant organization and included in a separate appendix to the proposal. Under no circumstances should they be sent separately to the funding agency. To ensure that they are credited to the proposal, they must be included in the proposal appendix.

24.10 THE ABSTRACT

The abstract, while written last, prefaces the proposal and may be the only opportunity to "sell" the project. Although brevity is mandated, the abstract must contain the essential information about the proposed project and explain to reviewers both the feasibility and the worth of the project.

24.11 THE REVIEW PROCESS

Whether the grant proposal is submitted to the federal government, a state government, or a foundation or corporation, the review process will involve a number of reviewers. Many foundations and corporations have a grant administrator who oversees the collection of grant applications and conducts a preliminary review for completeness and sufficient detail. The proposal is then presented to the foundation or corporate board for final review and approval.

When submitting a grant proposal to a state or federal agency, the review process differs dramatically. Generally, agency staff screen the grant applications upon receipt and return those that are incomplete, nonresponsive to the grant announcement (with regard to program), or nonconforming to the grant format (for example, too many pages). Applications that progress through the initial agency screening enter a multistage review process. In the first stage, the project may be assessed by nonfederal reviewers. Applications that are judged to be lacking in any of the required components will be considered noncompetitive and removed from further review. Surviving applications will then be reviewed for technical merit by peers in the field. The peer reviewers are selected for their technical expertise in the field or discipline of the grant. A point system of scoring the application is generally used. Potential scores and weights of each section of the narrative can be found in the RFP for a government grant. Written notification will be sent to those applicants who are judged to qualify in terms of completeness, competitiveness, and responsiveness upon final review.

For applications that are not selected for funding, most state and federal agencies will provide written information concerning how the application scored in the review process, and copies of the comments of the reviewers. This information is valuable if the agency is planning to resubmit the proposal at a future date, because it clearly identifies the weak areas in the application.

For grants submitted to foundations and corporations, the grant critique is easily obtained. Some grant administrators at foundations and corporations will even be willing to answer questions by telephone about weaknesses they perceived in the proposal.

Should the proposal not be funded, organizations are urged to obtain a copy of the proposal review and to revise the grant proposal for a future submission. The review process information is a valuable tool for all future grant proposal writing and should be considered part of a learning experience.

24.12 AFTER THE GRANT IS FUNDED

Perhaps even more difficult than writing the grant proposal is administering the grant after it is funded. This is the time when the nonprofit organization proves that it is a creditable agency and that it can produce what was promised in the grant proposal narrative.

Grant administration will vary from agency to agency. A small nonprofit agency's proposal writer might double as a project manager or the grant administrator. This person must develop the managerial skills necessary to implement the project and to manage the funding appropriately. Larger institutions may have the luxury of administrative staff to manage the fiscal end of the grant, leaving the grant writer to implement the project.

Once the grant is funded and the nonprofit enters into an agreement with the funding agency, it is responsible for producing the outcomes described in the narrative. This agreement between the funder and the nonprofit is, in essence, a legal contract to deliver promised goods. The importance of good grant administration becomes clear.

Project management is the actual implementation of the proposed activities that the organization hopes will produce the desired outcomes. Grant administration, however, goes beyond implementation to the accounting of the program. Most government agencies will require precise types of record keeping to account for the use of the funds. A yearly audit will be required, and some government agencies will conduct their own audit of the nonprofit agency.

The grant contract will clearly define the nonprofit's responsibilities as to the fiscal management of the funds. This document must be read carefully: it is legally binding. If the nonprofit is receiving funds from a number of agencies, each may have its own different fiscal requirements.

On a final note, the nonprofit may find that the needs have shifted slightly between the original proposal and the final funding, or that the cost of various items has changed. It is possible to realign the budget portion of the grant, but this must be done through the funding agency. An organization should never simply change the budget of a grant. The funding agency will provide guidance on budget adjustments.

24.13 FINAL ADVICE

Presentation plays a significant role in grant approval. Neatly typed, easy-to-follow narratives create a competent and professional impression. Good use of graphics can illustrate relationships, activities, and goals.

Organizational credibility is communicated in many ways: through the board members, through the organization's key personnel, and through letters of support. Credibility is also established through the completeness of the narrative, the demonstration that the organization is capable in the field, the feasibility of the project's goals and objectives, and the accuracy of the budget. The development of an evaluation plan aimed at a realistic assessment of the project will reinforce the credibility of the applicant. Organization credibility is important to the success of the proposal because it indicates to the funding source that the applicant organization has the capability of implementing and completing the project.

Grant proposal writing can become a major undertaking. In the nonprofit organization arena, grants provide a viable source of funding for program growth and the initiation of new thrusts in service. For this reason, the effort is certainly worth the expenditure of time and research. Government agencies fund more than four times the amount of money granted by foundations and corporations combined. Although these funds certainly require more in the way of preparation than do the shorter proposals for foundations and corporations, the monies may be more readily accessible.

SOURCES AND SUGGESTED REFERENCES

Corporate Foundation Profiles. New York: The Foundation Center. Provides giving profiles of 250 of the largest company-sponsored foundations.

Conrad. D. *The New Grants Planner.* San Francisco: Public Management Institute. Provides information about networking, developing ideas, researching, budget strategies, contacting funders, proposal review, proposal writing, and developing continued grant support.

Corporate Giving Yellow Pages. Washington, DC: The Taft Group.

Foundation Directory. New York: The Foundation Center. Provides a comprehensive listing of foundations in the United States, with information about number of awards, size of awards, funding preferences.

Funding Sources. Drug Information and Strategy Clearinghouse. Provides a list of agencies and foundations that fund proposals related to drug and alcohol abuse prevention.

Guide to U.S. Department of Education Programs. Washington, DC: U.S. Government Printing Office. Provides information necessary to begin the process of applying for funding from individual federal education programs. Lists the many grant opportunities available from the Department of Education.

National Data Book. New York: The Foundation Center. Provides assistance in identifying companies that have established giving programs.

Source Book Profiles. Quarterly. New York: The Foundation Center. Provides detailed descriptions of the 1,000 largest foundations.

Taft Corporate Giving Directory. Washington, DC: The Taft Group.

Taft Foundation Reporter. Provides comprehensive profiles and giving analyses of major private foundations.

U.S. Department of Health and Human Services. *Handbook for Evaluating Drug and Alcohol Prevention Programs.* Washington, DC: Author.

Note: In addition to the sources listed here, a number of computerized foundation and grant opportunity searches are available at local libraries for a nominal fee.

Fund-Raising Assessment

James M. Greenfield
Hoag Memorial Hospital Presbyterian

John P. Dreves
Staley/Robeson/Ryan/St. Lawrence, Inc.

CONTENTS

The assessment of nonprofit organizations remains underdeveloped, and evaluations have not often been performed. But times are changing. Whether because of the growth of the independent sector and the sheer magnitude of its presence, or unwanted focus as a result of public scandals and abuses, or financial pressures caused by negative economic conditions, attention to performance by nonprofit organizations increased substantially during the 1980s and will be increasingly enforced in the 1990s.

Nonprofit organizations entered the 1990s with more attention from the public and more internal resolve to evaluate their own performance. "Many opinions and assertions are put forth about the effectiveness and desirability of nonprofits, but evidence is scarce. Especially limited is information about whether nonprofits are better or worse at achieving certain goals than for-profit firms or government enterprises would be" (Weisbrod, 1988, p. 2).

Areas for assessment are broad; they include: institutional mission; public benefit; governance; management; fiscal accountability; strategic planning; resource allocations; and success in fund-raising.

Because fund-raising is only one measurable entity of a nonprofit organization's performance and because fund-raising results are inextricably tied to each of the other areas of internal operation, this chapter explores seven assessment areas:

1. Environmental audit on fund-raising;
2. Development department and program audit;
3. Development planning (feasibility) study;
4. Fund-raising productivity analysis;
5. Environmental audit for operations;
6. Mission;
7. Management.

The first four areas, beginning with an environmental audit for fund-raising readiness, relate directly to the fund-raising function. The remaining three areas focus on the nonprofit organization's self-evaluation and those factors that affect fund-raising through the fulfillment of mission and annual programs and the performance of management services. All seven assessment areas are framed against an audit of external environmental features, to help appreciate the degree to which external forces limit as well as assist success.

Together, these seven assessment areas demonstrate how institutional readiness and operating performance combine to stimulate the public support necessary to meet institutional goals and objectives. The use of productivity analysis helps to identify the sources of future contributions, the methods of securing them, the budget needed to achieve the organization's plans, and the priorities among various areas of public assistance.

Presentation of the seven assessment areas is coordinated to the seven major sections of the chapter.

25.1   ENVIRONMENTAL AUDIT ON FUND-RAISING

There is a growing conviction that nonprofit organizations need to demonstrate efficiency in fund-raising performance. Productivity analysis will do much more than justify the cost of raising money: it will develop an appreciation of the potential that fund development programs have as highly cost-effective profit centers. Each nonprofit organization has the potential to achieve some amount of public support and to grow up to its capacity for this support. However, only a few organizations know their potential, much less their capacity, because they use fund-raising only as a means to realizing a targeted amount of money.

> But a non-profit institution that becomes a prisoner of money-raising is in serious trouble and in a serious identity crisis. The purpose of a strategy for raising money is precisely to enable the nonprofit institution to carry out its mission without subordinating that mission to fund-raising. This is why nonprofit people have now changed the term they use from "fund-raising" to "fund development." Fund-raising is going around with a begging bowl, asking for money because the *need* is so great. Fund development is creating a constituency which supports the organization because it *deserves* it (Drucker, 1990, p. 56).

An understanding of fund-raising potential and capacity begins with an assessment of the immediate environment, which has an overriding influence on fund-raising performance. Exhibit 25.1 lists the factors that address both potential and capacity to raise money, and allows a ranking of each factor as low, medium, or high, in order to identify strengths and weaknesses, assets and liabilities, potential and capacity. There is no "passing grade" for this test. Assessment helps to increase awareness of the external factors that can affect annual and future fund-raising activities, and provides suggestions on how much impact these factors might have, what levels of reasonable gift expectations can be achieved, where attention to improvements will bear fruit, and similar information. Environmental audits on fund-raising should be conducted at least once every three years or even every two years as the pace of our world continues to accelerate. Organizations that do not anticipate change and are unable to execute decisions with speed, based on adequate assessments, will quickly fall behind.

The factors listed in Exhibit 25.1 are discussed in the following sections.

(a)   TYPE OF INSTITUTION OR AGENCY   There are seven separate classes of nonprofit organizations whose annual contributions data have been published by the American

Exhibit 25.1.   Environmental audit for fund-raising.

	Fund-Raising Score
Type of institution or agency	Low/Medium/High
Written long-range and strategic plan	Low/Medium/High
Board leadership, background, and attitude	Low/Medium/High
Geography	Low/Medium/High
Style	Low/Medium/High
Competition, image, and market position	Low/Medium/High
Tradition of fund-raising practice	Low/Medium/High
Volume and variety of fund-raising methods	Low/Medium/High
Availability of prospects	Low/Medium/High
Existing donors for renewal and upgrading	Low/Medium/High
Experienced and dedicated volunteers	Low/Medium/High
Access to wealth	Low/Medium/High
Focus on major gifts	Low/Medium/High
Professional staff and fund-raising counsel	Low/Medium/High
Development staff, space, budget, and systems	Low/Medium/High
Donor recognition	Low/Medium/High
Totals	Low = ____
	Medium = ____
	High = ____

Association of Fund-Raising Counsel for over 30 years, in their annual report, *Giving USA*. The dominant recipient of gifts in every year has been *religion,* with from 45 percent to 48 percent of all funds raised. The next level of support, with from 8 percent to 12 percent of all gifts each, is shared among *human services, education,* and *health. The arts* and *culture* receive from 6 percent to 8 percent annually, and *public and civic benefit causes* receive 2 percent to 4 percent (AAFRC, 1991, pp. 8–9). Based only on these data, an arts organization, for example, when setting its contributions goals, should appreciate the potential limitation in the extent of community support it may be able to achieve, compared with a college or university or the local United Way. Unrealized expectations, resulting in a board's loss of confidence in fund-raising as a viable source of revenue, can cripple any fund-raising program.

(b) WRITTEN LONG-RANGE AND STRATEGIC PLAN   The absence of a written plan for the future limits possible supporters to investigation of a single criterion: the annual operations budget performance. More important to donors, however, is the absence of any "vision" for the organization's future or any assessment suggesting its ability to continue to provide even present-day programs and services. This absence will inhibit their decision to make any sizable investment or commitment, whether of "time, talent or treasure," and thus prevents any significant progress.

(c) BOARD LEADERSHIP, BACKGROUND, AND ATTITUDE   Most board members come from business and industry and may arrive with preconceived attitudes about how to manage a nonprofit organization, derived from their for-profit training and experience. Organizations that provide their board members with well-prepared orientation and training activities will likely retain them and, with their help, grow. When board leadership is lacking, many good volunteers become frustrated and discouraged from future service.

(d) GEOGRAPHY Demographic studies help board members and management to see how location affects response to the programs and services offered, how they should be offered and to whom, what resources will be required to deliver them, and what potential for public support (volunteers and money) is available. Populations shift more quickly today than ever before; they are driven by age, economics, ethnic and cultural factors, and sheer numbers, and differing local influences accompany each shift.

(e) STYLE As the American landscape changes ever more rapidly, alertness to local community style, with its diversity of culture, tradition, and practice, will aid nonprofit organizations in determining where they "fit in" and how they may appear ("image is everything") in order to attract public support, volunteers, and contributions. Saturation with one fund-raising method (telephone calls by telemarketing professionals, or benefit-event ticket sales) can cause the public to build levels of resistance and even to reject solicitations, regardless of their legitimacy, the quality of their requests, or even their success only one year before.

(f) COMPETITION, IMAGE, AND MARKET POSITION Each organization should assess, as accurately as possible, where its mission, purposes, goals, and objectives match the needs of the community it serves. Competition exists for volunteers, clients, employees, resources, and public dollars. Those organizations serving less popular or less well-known causes will be working uphill to find people willing to share in its mission. Market research and other assessment tools greatly aid every organization to better understand public opinion and support potential.

(g) TRADITION OF FUND-RAISING PRACTICE The methods and techniques of public solicitation, although limited in number, are openly available to all to use equally. Some organizations use only one or two methods, limiting their capacity to develop funds by not using every means available. Results will vary with each method used, because causes and needs are different. Each organization's history of solicitation and breadth of methods used with success will guide it in how best to achieve consistent results and will help it to understand external realities such as the effects of environmental factors in an ever changing, ever more competitive marketplace. Determining what fund-raising methods to use or which combinations of methods will work best for each nonprofit organization, at what level of volunteer support and at what cost (budget), requires the new evaluation techniques provided in this chapter.

(h) VOLUME AND VARIETY OF FUND-RAISING METHODS Most nonprofit organizations begin with use of one or more annual solicitation methods, to produce the first donors and dollars. The same methods are used to renew these donors and to increase their numbers and dollars in the next year and the next. Several other methods can be added, once a base of donors and public support demonstrates a readiness or opportunity for acceptance. In time, an organization builds a broad base of fund-raising activities that will yield more predictable levels of cash for annual purposes;

special-project funds when necessary; major gifts for construction, renovation, and equipment projects (especially targeted in capital campaigns); and, eventually, endowment funds as a consequence of offering estate planning and planned giving programs. A nonprofit organization cannot expect to begin one day and achieve success the next, using only the planned giving method, nor should it expect every technique to succeed immediately and at maximum efficiency. Development has been aptly defined as "planned promotion of understanding, participation and support" (Seymour, 1966, p. 115), and it takes a lot of time. Each fund-raising method selected will develop to its own level of success, year after year, matched to the public's economic ability and personal conviction to support the organization. All methods in use must be integrated carefully, in a coordinated and cooperative manner. The audiences invited to participate are almost always the same people whom every other organization is soliciting at the same time. If an organization is to achieve the amount of financial and voluntary support that is adequate to meet its needs at any time, it must, at that same moment, match the capacity of its public to reply. The only limitation is the organization's own ability to ask for support with efficiency and effectiveness.

(i) AVAILABILITY OF PROSPECTS   Every fund-raising program has a geographic range or boundary within which it can effectively concentrate its search for prospects. This range is tied to the image and extent of the programs and services offered by the nonprofit organization. Time and budget invested in building relationships with those who are nearby, those who are served or will be served, and those who participate in the cause or programs offered will pay higher dividends because these groups are more likely to care about the organization and its future than groups who are not so committed. People who are far away, have never been clients, and are not involved in any way are much less likely to care and to give.

(j) EXISTING DONORS FOR RENEWAL AND UPGRADING   The best prospects are those who are already supporting the organization. They must not be taken for granted, despite their commitment; they must forever be cultivated, communicated with, and rewarded. Efforts to preserve and increase donors' personal participation and their potential for even greater support in alternate ways (time, talent, and treasure are all available) will always succeed.

(k) EXPERIENCED AND DEDICATED VOLUNTEERS   Although it is easy to count volunteers and to count the many areas and hours of their service, there can never be enough of them. Any expansion in community relations or philanthropic potential rests with the number of volunteers and the extent of their knowledge, experience, and commitment. The key to success in fund-raising, for every nonprofit organization, remains in the hands of its volunteers.

(l) ACCESS TO WEALTH   Attention to those few wealthy persons whose ability to participate is greater than that of others must be a priority for the board and for management. A defined program with specific objectives can be measured in terms of numbers of qualified prospects, a strategic plan for each, numbers of contacts made, and the results. People are not likely to make the biggest investment decision of their life in favor of any nonprofit organization before both parties engage in an extensive effort. Wealthy individuals must be available and within reach.

(m) FOCUS ON MAJOR GIFTS Success with annual giving programs is essential, but time and attention also must be given every year to the development of patrons and benefactors—those few best friends whose capacity for six-figure (and up) contributions is crucial for the present and the future of every nonprofit organization. Identification and invitation, recruitment and cultivation, solicitation and recognition of significant gifts from individuals, corporations, and foundations must be annual priorities. The attention of these donors must be directed toward the "vision" of the board of directors and management and the long-range plan they intend to help complete. They must know that each major gift will help bring that vision to life in a way that allows donor aspirations to be matched and fulfilled.

(n) PROFESSIONAL STAFF AND FUND-RAISING COUNSEL The use of competent fund-raising executives is essential to achieving success in public solicitation. Gone are the days when volunteers could provide the funds needed by staging a benefit event, or nonprofit organizations could rely on the board of directors to make up the difference needed to balance the budget at the end of each year. Potential for success can be enhanced by the use of professional fund-raising counsel. Counsel adds experienced and professional methods for staff recruitment and training, board and management involvement in solicitation, adequate levels of support systems, recognition programs, and other areas to improve performance. When best used, these expert advisers define specific programs with detailed plans, prepare everyone to conduct the effort, give supervision or "coaching" along the way, evaluate results, and demonstrate personal conviction on how to proceed with an expectation of success. Most important, their guidance helps everyone concentrate on the task of raising money, which helps to prevent distractions and misdirections and promotes success.

(o) DEVELOPMENT STAFF, SPACE, BUDGET, AND SYSTEMS Success in fund-raising is more likely to occur with an organized program led by a professional fund-raising executive who has adequate support in the form of office personnel, space, budget, and modern systems for managing all the data involved. Location is less important than competence. It costs money to raise money and, although reasonable cost levels can be targeted for each individual program, there are also costs for management functions, equipment, computers, research, support personnel, and continuing training programs, all necessary for continued success in the future.

(p) DONOR RECOGNITION Recognition is important to those so honored, no matter how they protest to the contrary. A program of recognition addresses how current donors are treated at *all* times, including after their gift has been received. Recognition must be visible so that donors (and those who aspire to increased giving) can see that their support is appreciated, is valuable, and has been visibly declared to have been significant and worthwhile. Hard evidence is needed to show how donors are treated, how their names will appear on buildings, plaques, or donors' walls, and how prominently their recognition will be displayed.

25.2 DEVELOPMENT DEPARTMENT AND PROGRAM AUDIT

External environments can exert a pervasive influence on fund-raising success. Completing an assessment of those factors (environments) prior to a review of the fund development department and its variety of solicitation programs will be useful but is not a necessity. Assessments can and should be performed when needed or when an extensive review can help to resolve current issues or aid operating decisions.

When should a decision be made to proceed with a departmental and program assessment? Any one of the questions listed below should suffice as a reason, and combinations of two or more questions will verify the urgency to begin:

How can I get my staff to be more productive?

How can I more effectively use my limited budget?

What additional resources do we need?

How can we increase our prospect pool?

How should our staff and volunteers be organized?

How can we get the board more involved in fund-raising?

How can we raise more money?

Before beginning, three guiding questions should be considered:

How will this review be used?

What should be measured and what criteria should be used?

Who should conduct the assessment? (Martin, 1990, p. 28)

When determining fund-raising performance, it may not be possible to separate the nonprofit organization from this same scrutiny, nor may it be advisable to do so. The ability to meet its mission is dependent, to a degree, on success in fund-raising, and success in fund-raising is dependent on a clear understanding of mission. As to when to do the assessment, there may never be an optimum time but there is likely to be time committed if the priority is high enough or when conditions recommend it. Biannual surveys should be adequate; annual reviews could be too strenuous and may lack sufficient time for recommendations from the last assessment to progress enough to allow for any measurable change. An opportune time to do an assessment is when a change in leadership occurs and a new board chairman, development committee chairman, or president or executive director takes office.

Areas to be assessed can be selected from the topics listed in Exhibit 25.2. Other areas open to review are: prior-year accomplishments against the mission statement; present size, scope, and number of clients served against demonstrated value of programs and services (outcomes for public good); written case statement for support against perceived public image and popularity; and measurements of public confidence and trust against compensation levels for staff. It may be true that nonprofit organizations are not the same in how they conduct fund-raising and that fund-raising does not perform the same for every organization, but there are many common criteria that justify self-analysis, objective measurements for any one organization, and comparisons with other organizations where possible.

Who does this work? Selection should follow the decision on what is to be assessed and the objective of the assessment. A study leader from among the employee pool outside the development staff may not be a suitable candidate because, generally speaking, few employees in nonprofit organizations have enough understanding of philanthropy

Exhibit 25.2. Areas for department and program assessment.

	Score
Comparison with prior year's results	Low/Medium/High
Growth in donor universe	Low/Medium/High
Penetration of new markets	Low/Medium/High
Quality of effort	Low/Medium/High
Leadership development	Low/Medium/High
Consistent messages and personalization	Low/Medium/High
Regular reports and analysis of results	Low/Medium/High
Staff training and development	Low/Medium/High
Matching institutional needs	Low/Medium/High
Forecasting future income	Low/Medium/High
Totals	Low = ____
	Medium = ____
	High = ____

and resource development to be prepared to be rigorous in the right areas. Development staff are not candidates either, but they should do the work of data gathering and can help interpret the data to the study leader.

If the assessment goal is a comprehensive review of current fund-raising programs (volunteer effectiveness, funding sources and gifts received, and analysis of the programs' interaction with the rest of the organization), an experienced and knowledgeable individual from outside the organization should be retained to conduct the process. Professional fund-raising consultants have first-hand experience from program audits conducted at numerous other nonprofit organizations in several parts of the country. Arrangements for their services should be by contract; voluntary or in-kind services should be avoided. A proper business relationship should be established and maintained, to aid credibility of the final product among board members, management, and the public.

One of the first areas to assess is readiness of the organization to engage in fund-raising. Exhibit 25.3 gives a few sample questions, excerpted from a more complete list (New, 1991), that address the question of preparations.

The basic ingredients for development department and program assessment are: documents, interviews, evaluation, and recommendations. Documents reveal results in hard-data form and bring together texts such as written policies and guidelines, gift reports, budgets, accounting reports, and audited financial statements. Private interviews with key people add information about attitudes, judgments, and other subjective details, along with their personal evaluations of program and staff performance. These data can be examined and arranged in comparative formats for analysis and comparison. The findings will include interpretation, specific recommendations and conclusions that address how the relationships among development programs are advancing the nonprofit organization in its mission and long-range plans, and progress achieved toward realization of fund-raising potential and capacity.

No development department stands or functions alone. Each is an integrated part of the larger nonprofit organization, and how it is attached can be instrumental to its

Exhibit 25.3. Assessment of readiness.

Readiness	Yes	No
Have you listed, in writing, the possible sources of support for your organization, including:		
a. individuals (kinds of people likely to be interested in and support what you do)?	[ ]	[ ]
b. civic groups such as Rotary, Lions, or Soroptimists?	[ ]	[ ]
c. religious institutions and auxiliaries?	[ ]	[ ]
d. social clubs?	[ ]	[ ]
e. corporations and foundations?	[ ]	[ ]
f. federated funding sources (United Way)?	[ ]	[ ]
g. local, county, state, and national government units?	[ ]	[ ]
Do you have evidence, such as formal endorsements, unsolicited letters, clippings, records of oral comments, indicating what people associated with the sources think of your organization?	[ ]	[ ]
Do you communicate regularly with these groups?	[ ]	[ ]
Do you have an annual fund-raising plan that is:		
a. written?	[ ]	[ ]
b. board-approved?	[ ]	[ ]
Fund-raising Action		
Last year, did the organization raise (or exceed) the amount it had budgeted for contributed income?	[ ]	[ ]
This year, have all parts of your fund-raising plan been carried out to date on schedule?	[ ]	[ ]
Have you set up a separate budget for each type of fund-raising you do?	[ ]	[ ]
Does each include projected results and projected net income form this type of fund-raising?	[ ]	[ ]

Source: Excerpted from New, 1991, pp. 7–8, 10–11, by permission. Reprinted with permission from *Raise More Money for Your Nonprofit Organization: A Guide to Evaluating and Improving Your Fundraising,* by Anne L. New, copyright © 1991 by the Foundation Center, 79 Fifth Ave., New York, NY 10008.

success. Access to the board of directors, president or executive director, and board-level committees for development, finance, and nominating should be open. Good relationships with employees whose duties include planning, marketing and communications, and public relations, plus those with investment and financial management assignments, can achieve maximum coordination, cooperation, and communication of the institutional priorities to be offered and explained to the community. Because development programs are conducted outside the organization, development staff can bring back information and experience-based insights about public attitudes and sensitivities, which can be valuable to others within management. Development programs will more often meet the expectations of the board and management when fully integrated into the current priorities and future goals of the organization. Without such access and integration, development programs are more likely to fall short in producing the support the organization needs.

Development assessments should review the organization's annual and long-range goals against the board's and management's expectations of fund-raising performance and its results. Individual appeal program performances, deadlines, and costs of time and money (budget) should be similarly reviewed. Each fund-raising method used should be measured for its results against forecasts, prior-year outcomes, and estimated future results, not as a single "bottom line" figure. (Several measurement tools are discussed in Section 25.4) Standards of performance and reasonable cost guidelines can be defined for every fund-raising method and used each year. Performance can then be evaluated against known criteria.

As an example, a decision to conduct a benefit event requires that an assistant fund-raising director and two clerical staff be assigned full-time to the project for three months. A goal of $25,000 net income is established. Assessment will measure gross income against expenses, beginning with all the direct costs to conduct the event. Added to this expense are all the indirect (overhead) charges—a percentage of staff salary and benefits; a portion of the lease, heat, light, telephone, postage, and other charges incurred over three months—to arrive at the total investment of time and money required to conduct the event and to achieve the goal. Next, the event should be evaluated for its ability to achieve other, "soft" objectives—the extra development opportunities this event will make possible. These include visibility and image enhancement for the organization, community participation, volunteer and leadership training, prospect and donor cultivation, public relations gains and press coverage, recognition of donors, and more. Total value from the event must include assessments of all these areas because $25,000 net proceeds alone may be judged to be an inadequate or inefficient gain for the cost involved, if measured only for profitability. A decision to continue or drop the event rests in part on its effectiveness to enhance the development process and its efficiency in maximizing net income. To use benefit events only as money-raising activities falls far short of their equal potential for aiding the organization and helping with several other development as well as institutional objectives.

Within the development program, another area that is worthy of assessment is departmental operations. These can be evaluated for their quality of performance, such as the effectiveness and extent of professional staff to provide leadership to the organization and the department; the training of volunteers and employees; communication of institutional priorities; efficiency in integrating planning, marketing and communications, and public relations goals; interpersonal relations with volunteers; and appropriate communications (frequency, timing, costs, effectiveness) with donors. Quantitative measurements of fund-raising will always include accurate and complete gift reports and financial statements, but should add: complying with government regulations and filing public reports on time; completing policies and procedures and gaining their approval and acceptance; setting up efficient and accurate procedures for timely gift acknowledgements and donor records systems; and similarly important measures. Solid departmental management is essential to the success of every fund-raising program offered. Abstract areas might be added, such as demands for nondevelopment work by development staff, stability of staff and fund-raising programs, public reputation of the department, and the like.

The operating success of the nonprofit organization has considerable influence on the potential for success of its fund-raising activities. Assessment of an organization's support of development work can be difficult to interpret in quantitative and qualitative terms. How does one express the value of advocacy of mission and nonprofit status; ethics in program fulfillment; measured public acceptance (popularity and respect) of the cause and the organization's overall performance; confidence and trust in the board of directors and top management; cultural diversity of the board of directors and the staff; board members' giving records and willingness to help to raise funds; correct use of funds raised; reporting of demonstrated outcomes of programs and services to the public; and the organization's willingness to disclose financial information?

The time period used in this assessment (fiscal year or calendar year) should, if possible, take into account the time and energy spent to identify, recruit, orient, and train volunteers. Time and money should be allotted to do prospect research, prospect cultivation, and donor relations, and to measure their outcomes. The payoff from these activities will occur later in time; no direct gift income from this work will show within the current fiscal period. A similar time frame applies to corporation and foundation proposals, which are submitted in one year for a decision in the next year; actual funding may be spread over the third and fourth years. Similar delays occur especially in planned giving, where it is common for charitable trusts and life insurance policies to "mature" in the form of legacies and bequests years later, following the death of the donor. Unsolicited gifts, unannounced bequests, unexpected memorial contributions, and even unwanted donations can happen at any time during the measurement period. These unpredictable results should be separated from program results that accrue from direct solicitation activities because they will easily distort the performance evaluation. Such gifts are unpredictable only to the extent that no one can forecast exactly how many, for how much money, will arrive in any one year. In reviewing these "extra" gifts, their value should be included in the total of gifts received, but, when setting goals for the next year, they should be separated to avoid any impression that unsolicited, unknown, unexpected, or unwanted gifts will continue to happen at a dependable level.

The areas of activity common to development departments and fund-raising programs are described in the sections that follow. (They can be scored using Exhibit 25.2). This assessment can also attempt to answer two overriding questions:

Did the department accomplish what it set out to do (that is, was it effective)?

Did the department accomplish this goal at an acceptable cost (that is, was it efficient, considering both monetary and nonmonetary costs)?

(Murray, 1987, p. 353)

(a) COMPARISON WITH PRIOR-YEAR RESULTS Given the short time interval between one year and the next, a review should begin with what happened last year (and the year before, if available). Program-by-program results should be compared, on a monthly basis, with results of the most recent year. Trends, which can be spotted quickly, allow timely decisions to change directions and to make program and budgetary revisions of estimated results and the costs to achieve them.

(b) GROWTH IN DONOR UNIVERSE The development department should always be engaged in finding new donors to replace those who leave the program. Nearly every organization wants to increase its results year after year, and, to gain the added gifts needed to meet higher goals, there must be a continuous effort to increase the numbers of donors. New donors can also be invited to participate in voluntary services, which will increase their involvement and enhance the prospect of repeated gifts from them. Acquisition of new donors is so routine to most annual giving activities that, if it is not found, in a close observation of performance (especially test results with new audiences), its absence can be the earliest sign of change in public affection, in project appeal, in message, or in package acceptance. Percentage of response and average gift size are indicators that reflect current public attitudes and quickly illustrate donors' judgment; the turnaround time for early decisions that implement corrective (and less costly) actions needs to be swift. Similar scrutiny should be given to programs that renew prior donors' gifts, to monitor the number who respond and the percentage who upgrade their gifts—both indicators of growing satisfaction and of more predictable dollars. Donors who are invited to join donor clubs and become active volunteers often demonstrate increased commitment and enthusiasm for the organization.

(c) PENETRATION OF NEW MARKETS Test mailings, telemarketing, and membership drives are used to reach out to new constituents, including new communities and demographic groups. Testing new mail packages containing various messages about the merits and needs of the organization will show which appeal will yield the best results. Alertness to the changing community will reveal opportunities to test old groups and to approach newly arrived prospects, and will help to create an awareness of when to solicit new corporations (*after* they achieve profitability) and when to submit proposals to foundations, matching a new need with their established priorities for grantmaking. Groups with declining responses can be dropped from further solicitation if appeals are likely to go unanswered and are thus unprofitable. Successful annual giving programs should be expanded to wider audiences after tests, market research, and demographic studies prove good response rates and forecast profitability. Such evidence, when matched to programs that can prove their profitability, will support requests for added budget.

(d) QUALITY OF EFFORT Although subjective, a review of solicitation materials to determine the time and cost of their preparation, the fulfillment of their deadlines, and their delivery costs, can influence success. These are hidden areas but they offer ways of increasing net results by improving quality of performance. The texts used in letters, brochures, and proposals can be evaluated for good English usage, brevity, clarity, contemporary design, completeness, and consistency with other materials and messages sent to these same audiences. The time spent drafting the text of appropriate "thank-you" letters and keeping the turnaround time to under 48 hours between receipt and response can affect public confidence and improve the potential for donor renewal. Assessment of operating areas can improve efficiency, effectiveness, and quality of the product, all leading to increased public acceptance and response (Berendt and Taft, 1983, pp. 70–73).

(e) LEADERSHIP DEVELOPMENT It is most valuable to track the development of volunteers into informed and competent leaders. The support activities that sustain them during their tenure of service are equally important. Board development should be highest on this list because board candidates often evolve within the fund development area. A systematic program to identify, recruit, orient, train, evaluate, and reward volunteers at all levels should be fully in operation. The nominating committee should maintain a sizable list of candidates whose progress they can observe. There is also a continuous need for board education on current issues, to help members in the decisions they are asked to make. Lastly, personal participation in giving should be part of the performance evaluation on all levels of leadership.

(f) CONSISTENT MESSAGES AND PERSONALIZATION   Several parts of the same organization are likely to be in constant communication with the general public throughout the year. Coordination and cooperation among those who communicate externally are necessary, for obvious reasons, not the least of which is the possibility that multiple and potentially conflicting messages will be sent to the same audience, with one message sender unaware of what the others are sending and when. For fund development to work well, the entire list of public communications of all kinds must be reviewed in detail: the appearance of the organization's physical plant (in videos and photographs), the materials used to describe programs and services, the consistency of style and appearance in all forms of mass communication and public relations, and other visible features. An honest sensitivity to individuals who are valuable to the organization, whether clients, employees, volunteers, or donors, results from attention to the personal relationships involved, to personalized forms of contact wherever possible, and to recognition. Nothing can beat a first-name greeting and a smile!

(g) REGULAR REPORTS AND ANALYSIS OF RESULTS   The results of fund-raising are of high interest to everyone. Donors want to know their money was received safely and was spent to do good works. Volunteers want to know whether their hard work was successful. Management wants to know how much money arrived, to allow them to proceed with programs and plans. Regular fund-raising reports should cover three basic areas:

Exhibit 25.4.   Report on sources of gifts.

Date: _____

Sources of Gifts	Number of Gifts	Gift Income	Average Gift Size
Trustees/Directors		$	$
Professional staff			
Employees			
Prior donors (renewal)			
New donors (acquisition)			
Corporations			
Foundations			
Associations/Societies			
Planned gifts written			
Legacies/Bequests received			
Unsolicited gifts			
Other gifts received	_____	_____	_____
Totals		$	$

sources of gifts, purposes or use of funds raised, and methods used to raise the money. (See Exhibits 25.4, 25.5, and 25.6 for examples.) Frequent reports help to demonstrate progress and success and to encourage volunteers and donors alike. These reports also help everyone to better understand the realities of fund-raising—how the various methods perform, and what can be expected of these methods based on results, not guesses or presumptions about what they should yield.

(h) STAFF TRAINING AND DEVELOPMENT Employees in the development office require training for more than the items listed in their job descriptions. They must understand something about the areas of program and service that use the money raised. They need to be shown how the several fund-raising methods they help support actually perform individually and together. They must have an appreciation for the value of clients, of volunteers, and of donors; must understand why thanking donors promptly for each and every gift is important; and must be capable of the need for accuracy *always* in mail lists, gift reports, and donor records. Funds assigned to train professional and support staff at conferences and workshops are a solid investment; these staff members can improve their skills along with their understanding of the development process they are so much a part of. Their own performance evaluations can assess their progress in understanding the purposes of their work, the fund-raising methods used, and their role in helping to accomplish goals and objectives for the development department and the nonprofit organization.

(i) MATCHING INSTITUTIONAL NEEDS There is more to fund-raising assessment than measuring amounts of money raised against the costs of raising it. Some boards and managers believe that high goals and firm deadlines encourage volunteers and staff to work harder. In reality, results are a function of those solicited being well prepared to receive the message asking for their support, just as much as their being well-asked by well-trained volunteers. Nevertheless, was all the necessary money raised in time for the purposes needed by the organization? Were those who were

Exhibit 25.5. Report on purposes or use of funds.

Date: _____			
Purposes or Use of Funds	Number of Gifts	Gift Income	Average Gift Size
Unrestricted cash		$	$
Capital and equipment funds			
Gifts restricted for:			
Programs			
Research			
Education			
Staff/Students			
Loan funds			
Unrestricted endowment			
Restricted endowment			
Other restricted purposes	_____	_____	_____
Totals		$	$

Exhibit 25.6.   Report on results of fund-raising programs.

Date: _____

Programs	Number of Gifts	Gift Income	Average Gift Size
Annual Giving Committee		$	$
Direct mail program			
1.			
2.			
3.			
4.			
Special and benefit events held			
1.			
2.			
3.			
Leadership gifts			
Trustees/Directors			
Major gifts program			
Support groups			
1.			
2.			
3.			
Corporate giving			
Corporate matching gifts			
Foundation giving			
Special project campaigns			
Planned gifts written			
Legacies/Bequests received			
Commemorative/Tribute gifts			
Other fund-raising programs			
1.			
2.			
3.			
Totals		$	$

asked to give ready to respond (prior marketing and public relations efforts), or were they uninformed and hesitant? Did they give the amount asked of them based on staff research and the rating and evaluation process? What other information and opinions did they express to the volunteer who called on them? Was this information reported back for evaluation and for future contact? Many details go into a solicitation, and all of them must be organized to produce happy donors, confident volunteers, and all the money needed—on time.

(j) FORECASTING FUTURE INCOME Assessment of the prior nine criteria encourages an organization to understand itself and its fund-raising programs better. It can now begin to forecast how fund-raising programs will continue to function, how they can react to changing circumstances and economic realities, and how their flexibility can be used to achieve the money when needed. Reliable analysis of external conditions measured against accurate results will increase the organization's ability to manage its public programs and services with increased confidence.

After the departmental study has been concluded, the results should be studied and interpreted in order to define recommendations for the future. Much has been learned and, before any more time passes, this knowledge should be shared with the board and management. Outcomes from analytical work are more frequently refinements of what is already known than they are surprises. Assessments are a way to document achievements and accomplishments as well as problems and shortcomings; both ways should be recognized for what they truly are—opportunities for attention, focus, challenge, and renewal.

Assessments of the development department provide the capability "to identify what is being done well and confer suitable rewards, to identify areas where improvement is possible and desirable, to assess the entire planning process and its critical assumptions, and to develop future plans, objectives, and standards" (Murray, 1987, p. 353).

25.3 DEVELOPMENT PLANNING (FEASIBILITY) STUDY

After departmental reviews, key areas of performance within each fund development program will be much better known. But what of the future? Another year or two may pass without any change in current priorities or financial needs of the organization. During that time, existing development programs may be most often challenged only to meet and exceed their present levels of annual performance. This should be considered good fortune! There is time to refine and improve areas such as volunteer and prospect identification, recruitment, and involvement; time to complete and implement donor recognition policies; time to train volunteers and office staff and improve office systems; time to improve present capabilities, achieve greater efficiency, and realize more cost-effective results for each program. This is the time to prepare for the future. A day will come, perhaps soon, when the organization will complete its own assessments and resolve to embark on a major surge forward, to expand its programs and services, to seize an unusual challenge or opportunity, or to respond to new options that were previously unseen (mergers or takeover proposals). When this day arrives, the fund development program will be challenged to extend its performance too, perhaps with significant new monetary objectives. A multiyear, major capital campaign frequently targets an amount five times current annual performance levels and more.

How prepared will the development program be to undertake such a challenge? Is the board of directors ready to accept its role of personal leadership in the campaign? Are enough volunteers trained and experienced with major gift solicitation? Have professional staff attended conferences and workshops on major-gifts research and capital campaign preparation and direction? The challenge of a capital campaign should not come as a total surprise to the development team. Ideally, they will have been actively involved in the planning process and will be well acquainted with the projects, their cost estimates, their priority, and the timetable set for their completion. Fund development participation in the planning process allows them to begin early to conduct their own assessments of how current and past fund-raising programs, messages, and public responses can be energized to a higher capability to meet future needs.

In the for-profit business world, market research is a well-developed science that provides hard evidence on which to base large decisions. One of the best known users of market research is the Procter and Gamble Company, which never introduces a new product without an extensive, thoroughly tested, and exhaustive assessment of that product's predictable success in the marketplace.

Nonprofit organizations are unlikely to commit themselves to market research to this extent, but board members and management, after some market analysis, can achieve a higher degree of confidence in their product (their "vision" of the future), in the accuracy of public needs, in delivery of their programs and services, and in their sales force (fund-raising). They need to accurately assess their internal strength of leadership, both volunteer and staff, plus the competence of departmental staff and proven systems.

It is now time for the final examination. What is the extent of the public's agreement with the urgency of the organization's plans? Will these plans test positive to those from whom financial support will have to come? This final exam is critical because the future of the organization is riding on the outcome. In assessing what is feasible, market research will test *everything:* the long-range plan and each of the defined projects for its priority of need, cost, and timetable for implementation. This exam will also test the financial goals, competency of leadership, campaign readiness, public concurrence with the plan, proposals to solve problems, and extent of public willingness (financial potential) to give of time, talent, and treasure to achieve the campaign goal.

The development planning study is an examination the organization must pass with high marks if it intends to go forward to fulfill its goals.

> One of the first questions to ask about a capital campaign is whether it is truly needed. This question deserves a compelling answer. Capital campaigns are not for raising significant numbers of gifts or significant numbers of large gifts, and not for achieving prestigious gifts or important objectives. A capital campaign is one means to financial security, but it should and, in most cases, it must, represent the studied conclusion that all traditional funding options have been exhausted and a capital fund drive is now required to raise most or all of the money needed by a certain date. (Greenfield, 1991, p. 171)

Plans must be well prepared to withstand tests of credibility, relevance, urgency, and practicality. The need for additional resources must be so convincing that those who are invited to participate will agree with the vision for the future, and its conclusions, not because of what their money will be spent on but because what their money will allow to happen is so necessary that the value of the objective compels them to act in support of it.

When a project holds such potential and value, it should not proceed without a comprehensive assessment of how it will be received. Equally important, it should not do such a critical study without experienced and professional guidance. The question is not how to do the study (a host of consulting firms are skilled in market research techniques), but who should lead the process. By every measure, objectivity is absolutely necessary, and only an experienced study director from outside the organization can perform this work with professional skill and credibility. Nearly every professional fund-raising consulting firm or seasoned fund-raising executive is experienced with a development planning study (or feasibility study) and the capital campaign that follow. If there is adequate talent to do this work, how should the study leader be identified, interviewed, and hired for the job?

To begin, the board of directors must concur there is a need to test their conclusions and convictions about their long-range plan on the public. The board committee on fund development, working with the chief development officer, should conduct the interview process and bring back to the board their recommendations for who will be the study leader, the cost of the services, and the time required to deliver the final report. Candidates are then invited to submit a proposal within 30 or 45 days. Board members and development staff should be available during this period for interviews and should fully disclose everything the study leader requires. The development committee should invite two or three of those who submit proposals for personal interviews, to verify their professional competence to determine answers to the questions the study must test. Reference checks on each firm and its staff are mandatory before final selection. The decision will be guided also by who will be the study leader, when the study can begin, the budget and fees required, and the timetable to completion. There should be absolute clarity about who is hiring the study leader and to whom the study team reports throughout the contract period. The answer can be any of the following, and everyone on this list must agree with the decision: chairman of the board, chairman of the development committee, president or executive director, or chief development officer. The development committee should review the written agreement for services and should understand all of its details, including payment dates and amounts, what expenses will be included, what study team members will be assigned, and similar arrangements.

Good chemistry between the study leader and the chief development officer is essential so that, working together, they can perform the maximum amount of work that can be accomplished during the study period. Development staff will be an active partner throughout, to identify and contact interview prospects, help draft the case statement to be tested, and secure appointments for the study team. The project should be managed so that the expertise of the study team is maximized and the information necessary to resolve how to proceed is readily available.

The conclusions and recommendations of the completed study will provide the board of directors and management with answers on their capability to proceed with their plans and on how much public support their future plans will inspire. Proposed goals will be tested and verified (or adjusted), just as the plan and its details (case statement) will be verified for their acceptance. Leadership availability, public confidence, access to volunteers and prospects, internal readiness, timing of when to start and when to end the campaign, and a campaign plan, including details of staffing, budget, materials, and support features, also will be provided (see Exhibit 25.7). In essence, study recommendations provide a complete road map to success from start to finish, with plenty of directions for each bend in the road along the way. The well-prepared, well-executed study should be a document in which the board and management can place full confidence and belief as a forecast of what will be required for optimal success in achieving their goals. The study will also identify the weaknesses that require attention and the process for their correction.

Martin Grenzebach, master of the feasibility study and the campaign plan it foretells, notes that a high-quality study and the answers it provides will spell out certain prerequisites that should be in place to enable the campaign to succeed. He summarized these prerequisites as follows:

> The institution must enjoy a *positive image* within its constituency and within the business, financial, and industrial community; there must be a clearly *perceived need,* well defined in the minds of those who know the institution best and which can be made

Exhibit 25.7.   What a feasibility study can reveal.

The response for campaign giving;

How much each audience might give;

The identity of major gift prospects;

The identity of leadership candidates;

Problem areas (case, timing, image, leadership, staff, systems, others);

An overall campaign objective;

Specific goals for each giving audience available;

A timetable and sequence for solicitation;

Elements of the case statement and all support documentation required;

Staffing and budget required;

Public relations support plan;

Where and how campaign counsel will be needed.

---

to inspire a sense of commitment in the thinking of those who are asked for financial support; there must be a *presence of available funds* ample enough in depth and breadth that, when properly motivated, those who hold the key to these resources will release enough of them to the institution in such measure as to meet its goal; there must be *capable leadership,* holding the complete respect of the community and willing to give the necessary time and talent to the institution and its causes; and there must be a generally *favorable economic climate* within the constituency and/or the community, such as is occasioned by a sound economic outlook and the reasonable absence of conflicting campaigns and competing enterprises. (Grenzebach and Associates, 1986, p. 1)

There can easily be failures in the best of plans. Their causes are known and are added here so as not to be missed. Errors can creep into any analysis and, as Dennis Murray (1987) states, in his excellent chapter on "Reviewing, Evaluating, and Rewarding the Development Effort," the potential for disaster can result.

An overly optimistic assessment, for example, can produce unattainable objectives. These, in turn, produce detailed but totally meaningless action plans. These action plans, when executed, do not produce the anticipated results. But the failure in this case was not in the action plans, much less with the individuals who tried to carry them out. The failure slipped in much earlier, in the assessment. This is why the evaluation must track back along the entire integrated model and examine each step for the causes of failure. Four common reasons for failing to meet objectives deserve special mention:

- Lack of top leadership
- Insufficient cultivation of prospects
- Lack of realism in assessments and objectives
- Lack of a tradition of giving.

(Murray, 1987, pp. 360–361)

How much more valuable is it to everyone, both inside and outside the organization, to enter and engage in this process with both eyes open? How much more valuable to avoid the hard lessons of those organizations which, having decided in advance all of their campaign objectives, use the feasibility study only to alert everyone that the campaign is coming? In their eagerness to get the money they need, they may fail to achieve even their income goal because they have not involved their potential best donors and campaign leaders in what can be accomplished with their help. They have failed to test their plan and its potential for public acceptance and have not used a proven market research technique to verify everything necessary to design their campaign for maximum success. They may achieve what they thought was possible, only to learn in the end that they could have achieved even greater goals; or, worse, they may fail to meet their goals and fulfill their plans while they incur a serious loss of confidence along with the public's resistance to provide support for years into the future.

25.4 FUND-RAISING PRODUCTIVITY ANALYSIS

This assessment area is not a summary of the first three nor is it the "big finish" wrapped up with a simple answer of what is the reasonable cost for fund-raising. As in the three prior sections, performance evaluation methods are offered to help demonstrate the productivity and "profitability" of fund development activities. This section will answer questions on what to measure, will show how efficient and how effective each solicitation program is, and will demonstrate the efficiency and effectiveness of volunteers in completing their assignments.

If fund-raising productivity were only a simple comparison of revenue received against cost to raise it (the "bottom line"), it would illustrate only a single money-raising ratio and would fail to show any amount of program effectiveness or efficiency. This oversimplified measurement also will fail to assess any progress toward the potential that may exist or the extent of the public's capacity for giving to the organization to satisfy its present needs and fulfill its future plans. There is much more to fund-raising than raising money, and there is much more to its productivity assessment than simple bottom-line analysis.

Fund-raising departments are engaged in a variety of methods and techniques to raise the money needed by their nonprofit organizations. They have goals and objectives that go beyond how much money is raised in a single fiscal or tax year. They employ these same fund-raising methods to communicate information, to cultivate positive relationships, and to solicit a variety of positive responses in addition to money. They produce ever larger numbers of suspects, prospects, and donors, stimulating their active participation as well as their fiscal support. They inform and enthuse, build confidence and trust, offer new and old friends important roles to play and valuable work to be done, and, using gifts as but one exchange medium, bond all these supporters ever more tightly to the organization and its mission, purposes, goals, and objectives.

Time and energy are necessary to support fund-raising, which must be understood to be an investment decision and a firm commitment. Each budget dollar spent and each gift received should be appreciated for its cost–benefit ratio and for its long-term return on investment, which helps enable the institution's own advancement. It will take years of investing in time and energy, plus budgeting, to build a successful development program that meets planned needs for the future. One year's budget and its results can and should be measured for direct performance; but they should also be measured for their contribution toward an increase or return on the next year's and future years' results as well.

Most professional fund-raising executives invite the image of a pyramid (see Exhibit 25.8) to illustrate the design for the overall fund development program. A pyramid shows each fund-raising method available, how each relates to the others, and at

Exhibit 25.8. The pyramid of giving.

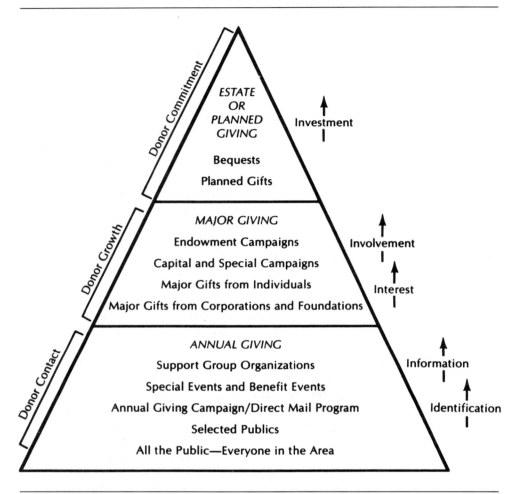

Source: James M. Greenfield, *Fund-Raising: Evaluating and Managing the Fund Development Process* (New York: John Wiley & Sons, 1991), p. 15. Reprinted by permission of John Wiley & Sons, Inc.

what levels performance should be measured. Management tools are available to measure each fund-raising activity. Murray (1987) identified the purposes for such evaluation as follows:

> Evaluation has four purposes:
> - To identify what is being done well and to confer suitable rewards
> - To identify areas where improvement is possible and desirable
> - To assess the entire planning process and its critical assumptions
> - To develop future plans, objectives, and standards.

(Murray, 1987, p. 47)

Murray also offered these methodologies for evaluating fund-raising programs:

- Opinions of professional consultants
- Outcomes measurement
- Cost–revenue ratios
- Solicitation effectiveness
- Congruence between predetermined objectives and outcomes
- Congruence between actual performance and standards of performance based on a systems approach.

(Murray, 1987, pp. 354–357)

Fund-raising productivity analysis is the means to examine how to measure, to explore what to measure, to explain how it should be performed, and to become educated in what the outcomes may mean. Fund-raising has been defined by Seymour as "the planned promotion of understanding, participation and support (Seymour, 1966, p. 115). Peter Drucker has stated that "Performance in the nonprofit institution must be *planned*. And this starts out with the mission . . . [f]or the mission defines what results are in this particular nonprofit institution" (Drucker, 1990, p. 109). Murray's definition adds that "fund-raising management . . . is proactive and results-oriented (Murray, 1987, p. 7). Each of these concepts (promotion, planning, results) can and should be measured. The results of their assessment will add a better understanding of their contribution to the overall success of a comprehensive fund development program and the nonprofit organization it serves.

Results measurement begins with adequate preparation to ensure (1) access to valid statistics and their fair comparison and (2) an easy-to-understand report format for every audience intended. Nick Costa, in his thorough study of fund-raising cost performance in health-care institutions, defined the following criteria for compiling and comparing statistics to ensure the integrity of their results:

- Establish clear and decisive standards for recording data for each of your reports
- Maintain the standards you establish
- Use the reports to simplify, clarify, and educate
- Seek a uniform standard of measurement when using external statistics.

(Costa, 1991, pp. 7–8)

(a) GIFT REPORTS Gift reports are creative ways to display numbers and illustrate results. Preparation depends on proper recordkeeping and consistent handling of all the data, which are then assembled for measurement. The value of gift reports is enhanced because fund-raising performance can be measured weekly, monthly, yearly, or whenever desired. The objectives in developing such reports, beyond being able to display results, are to show the level of performance at any time, to compare the results with those at the same time in the previous year or in other prior years, and to measure all areas of progress, program-by-program, toward this year's goals.

The three primary areas that should be displayed in gift reports are: sources of gifts, purposes or uses of the money raised, and results of each fund-raising program, as presented earlier in Exhibits 25.4, 25.5, and 25.6. The number of donors achieved and the amount of money raised in these three summaries are important data. The volume of people participating is as significant a sign of progress and program results as the dollars they provide; money follows people. When several fund-raising programs are being used at the same time, comparative analysis helps to determine which programs to emphasize during the year and which to postpone for emphasis in the following year. Programs whose financial results are not as productive as others, in terms of numbers of participants or dollars, may still have merit because they attract a number of faithful donors each time they are offered. Achieving an overall balance of results (people and dollars at reasonable cost) year after year, among all fund-raising programs offered, is more often the desired outcome. The health and vitality of each program will be important to long-term fund development growth because each depends on the success, efficiency, and effectiveness of its own activities, acting in concert with the others as well as on its own.

Public interests and moods can change rapidly with regard to charitable causes and issues. Regular analysis of results will help to track these changing patterns of response. Each nonprofit organization needs flexibility if it is to retain donor interest and faithful giving levels each year. It must allow for a shift in emphasis or a need to concentrate more budget and volunteer time on those methods currently having a greater or lesser success; again, the measurement of fund-raising performance goes beyond just counting net proceeds. Each method and its performance should be studied in detail, to gain insight in assessing the values and merits each can achieve as well as well as what it can contribute to the whole. The assessor might look for the following five areas; together they offer a broad measurement guide:

1. Percentage of participation. This is a clue to how prospects like what is being said to them. The percentage also can be an early signal of change of interests and moods during the year.

2. Renewal rates and average gift size. These will indicate donors' continued enthusiasm about the appeal method and the priority of the project or need that is "for sale." They also help with forecasts of what these same donors might be expected to do when asked again for their support.

3. Volunteers' personal performance. What percentage of assigned prospects did the volunteers actually see? What number and size of gifts did each bring in? What meetings did they attend? What contact reports did they submit? Who is ready to be promoted to a leadership position?

4. Special and benefit events. How well is the same event faring year after year? Are its sponsors, underwriters, and in-kind donors holding steady? Is the public willing to continue to attend? Should ticket prices be adjusted or the event's design or flavor changed? Is a new event needed to keep the public stimulated and active in its support?

5. Donors' response to recognition. Do donors attend recognition events? What was their response when invited to give higher amounts in order to gain more recognition privileges? Has the offer of privileged communications altered their behavior from year to year? Has any increase in other activity shown a desire to grow in involvement, beyond just total contributions? Do donors display any greater confidence and enthusiasm that might suggest they are ready for higher performance levels?

The first step is to study the immediate results of each fund-raising method used. Review of gift reports does not take much time and can be valuable to the decision making required throughout the operating year. Second, gift reports should be used to convert the results into a budget request that is tied directly to an estimate of next year's results. To convert gift results into a budget request, take the information prepared earlier using Exhibit 25.6 and add all the costs for each fund-raising method used in the current operating year. As a bonus, cost per dollar raised for each program is now provided (see Exhibit 25.9). With these data in hand, the final step is to complete a budget worksheet (Exhibit 25.10) arranged in traditional budget categories matched to the business office and Internal Revenue Service (IRS) Form 990 report formats.

Exhibit 25.9.   Fund-raising program performance analysis.

Date: _____

Programs	Gift Income	Estimated Budget	Actual Budget	Cost per Dollar Raised
Annual Giving Committee	$	$	$	$
Direct mail program				
1.				
2.				
3.				
Special and benefit events held				
1.				
2.				
3.				
Leadership gifts				
1. Trustees/Directors				
2. Major gifts program				
Support groups' results				
1.				
2.				
3.				
Corporate giving				
Corporate matching gifts				
Foundation giving				
Special project campaigns				
Planned gifts written				
Legacies/Bequests received				
Commemorative/Tribute gifts				
Other fund-raising programs				
1.				
2.				
3.				
Totals	$	$	$	$

Exhibit 25.10. Budget worksheet for fund development office.

Date: _____

	Estimated Budget	Actual Budget	Next Year's Estimated Budget
A. Salaries and Benefits			
Director of Development	$	$	$
Assistant Director			
Office support staff			
Part-time employees			
Temporary workers			
_____ Subtotal	$	$	$
Fringe benefits (_____%)			
Vacation/Holiday (PTO)			
Estimated salary increases			
_____ Subtotal	$____	$____	$____
Group A Total	$____	$____	$____
B. Office Operations			
Office supplies			
Telephone charges			
Telephone equipment			
Rental equipment			
List fees			
Postage fees			
Printing costs			
Books/Periodicals			
Travel (trips)			
Travel (local)			
Entertainment			
Awards/Plaques			
Dues/Memberships			
Conferences			
Insurance			
Office rental or lease			
New equipment			
Equipment maintenance			
Consultant fees			
Services purchased			
Other expenses			
Group B Total	$____	$____	$____
Grand Total (A + B)	$____	$____	$____

(b) VOLUNTEER PERFORMANCE   Fund-raising program measurement counts how and where time and money produce results. Next, the most essential ingredient for success, volunteer performance, should be assessed. Volunteers must be evaluated in ways that will encourage their continued participation. Assessments must demonstrate where they have been successful and where improvements are possible. Performance evaluation linked to their success in solicitation activities can include all of the following measurements of volunteer effectiveness and efficiency:

1. Number of qualified prospects available;
2. Number and percent of prospects assigned to volunteers;
3. Number and percent of solicitation calls made and gift results (by volunteer and group total);
4. Number of upgraded gifts requested, and results;
5. Number of prior donors renewed, and average gift size (by volunteer and group total);
6. Direct costs to support volunteer solicitation;
7. Average cost per gift received;
8. Cost to solicit any unassigned and unsolicited prospects, and results;
9. Total dollars raised, average gift size, and average cost per gift (by volunteer and group total);
10. Overall program costs and results comparison (cost per dollar raised this year and in prior years).

Fund-raising activity and results vary considerably among nonprofit organizations. Volunteer performances also vary and, among individuals, are hard to compare fairly. Years of experience in fund-raising teaches all of us that volunteers are successful in their commitments of time, energy, and talent. They also share their treasury with us, but their best performances are in seeking out other individuals whom they convert into faithful followers who will join and then succeed them. This function is much more valuable to the organization than their cost-effectiveness alone.

(c) OVERHEAD OR INDIRECT EXPENSES   A vital part of budget preparation is to include the indirect and overhead costs of fund development operations. Up to this point, assessment data have compared actual or direct costs for each fund-raising activity with their respective revenue results. There has been no mention of the indirect costs (most of which occur back at the development office), or other operating expenses for support activities. Typically, these costs are for gift processing, data processing, donor recordkeeping, donor recognition, and a portion of the expenses (salaries and benefits) for employees who do this work. These and other "soft" or "hidden" areas of the cost of fund-raising management may not show up on gift reports, but they should.

Fund-raising is a part of every organization's external affairs program to engage the general public. Fund development communications present the organization, its current programs and services, its future plans, and its need for "understanding, participation, and support." The fund development office shares management's goals and objectives for planning, marketing, communications, and public relations, all of which are joined together in the common cause of promoting and advocating the organization's mission. Assessing mission outcomes against overhead costs is not as simple as measuring newsprint copy or client satisfaction, but there are results that fund-raising certainly contributes to, in aiding these goals and objectives.

Murray (1987) defined several activities that are directly related to fund-raising but are not visible in the list of budget expenses. These include time and dollars spent on identification, screening, introduction, familiarization and understanding, appreciation and commitment, involvement, rating, solicitation, prospect reaction, and organizational reaction (Murray, 1987, pp. 266–270). After-gift activities of donor relations, recognition, and reward complete the list of non-income-producing but highly essential activities of any fund development program.

Indirect costs influence overall net results in such areas as:

Time and money spent with volunteers to prepare them to conduct the programs they lead as well as to identify, recruit, train and evaluate their results;

Time and money spent on prospect and donor research, on meetings and their planning, on gift processing and donor records, and on donor recognition;

Time and money spent on administrative work such as budget preparation and accounting, gift reports, personnel supervision, and personal and professional training of staff and volunteers;

Time and money spent on office equipment and its maintenance, lighting and heat, rent and lease costs, travel and meals for staff, and entertainment of prospects and donors as well as volunteers;

Time and money spent on community relations, friend-raising, overall visibility, and accessibility;

Time or money lost because of a lack of revenue, excessive demands on development staff for other management assignments, or vacations, holidays, and sick time.

How are all of these realities of time and money added to the direct costs of raising money? Professional management techniques are required to establish fair and equitable means to add back these "hidden" expense areas to each fund-raising activity and to assign their fair share of cost to every solicitation method, where appropriate. Only with total indirect and overhead costs understood and included in fund-raising assessment will the organization and its leadership fully understand fund development productivity.

(d) COST-EFFECTIVENESS MEASUREMENT   Nick Costa has advocated that each organization create its own comparative reports via these four steps:

1. Defining the purpose of the report and/or the area of fund-raising under study; . . .
2. Determining the data necessary to make the comparisons; . . .
3. Obtaining the data from internal sources and, as required, external sources such as outside surveys; . . .
4. Ensuring that all data is compiled according to a common standard so your comparisons are fair and have integrity.

(Costa, 1991, p. 5)

Costa also recommended that institutional plans, goals and objectives, and income forecasts be converted into "TARGET"™ goals that match the nonprofit organization and its environment to the purposes and direction of the fund development program, thus creating the basis for reports on activity as well as criteria for performance evaluation. These "TARGET"™ goals are:

T = Targeted to specific fund-raising programs for impact

A = Achievable, given the historical experience of your program

R = Results, or numbers, oriented, and name . . .

G = Group consensus or commitment by your volunteers

E = Executive approval

T = Timetable or deadline for completion.

(Costa, 1991, p. 5)

Five cost-effectiveness and productivity measurements should be applied to each fund-raising technique, to demonstrate its effectiveness, efficiency, and profitability, as shown in Exhibit 25.11. These five tools represent a uniform method to assess each fund-raising activity on its own results. It is commonly accepted today that direct-mail acquisition performs at a different cost–benefit level than do benefit events. Equally, capital campaigns should perform with different cost–benefit standards than corporate and foundation solicitations and planned giving programs. Each has its own standard of reasonable cost for cost–benefit measurement.

Exhibit 25.11. Example of cost-effectiveness and productivity assessments.

1. *Percentage rate of return:*

   Divide the number of responses received by the number of solicitations

   $$\frac{1,384}{125,000} = 01.1\%$$

2. *Average gift size:*

   Divide the total amount of contributions by the number of gifts received

   $$\frac{\$272,376}{1,384} = \$196.80$$

3. *Average cost per gift:*

   Divide the total fund-raising costs by the number of gifts received

   $$\frac{\$45,927}{1,384} = \$33.18$$

4. *Program cost percentage:*

   Divide the program's total costs by the total contributions received, then multiply by 100

   $$\frac{45,927}{\$272,376} = 0.168$$

   $$0.168 \times 100 = 16.86\%$$

5. *Overall "bottom line" cost percentage:*

   Divide the total fund-raising costs by total gift revenue, then multiply by 100

   $$\frac{\$325,440}{\$1,720,000} = 0.1892$$

   $$0.1892 \times 100 = 18.9\%$$

(e) REASONABLE COST GUIDELINES Experience has shown that cost guidelines should be defined for each method of fund-raising, to measure individual cost-effectiveness and to demonstrate how each has a capacity for increasing its own productivity. The reasonable cost guidelines shown in Exhibit 25.12 have been developed from the individual program results experienced at many nonprofit organizations across America and should be applied to programs after *at least three years* of active operation. The guidelines are considered to be the current levels of reasonable performance. They can be improved on when favorable conditions such as strong leadership, access to wealth, capable volunteers, positive economic conditions, well-managed nonprofit programs, and quality projects recognized as having significant public benefit all come together (Greenfield, 1988, 1989; Fink and Metzler, 1982, pp. 49–57).

Measurement of each fund-raising program also verifies how its results can aid other programs' performance; all contribute to one another in some fashion. Time and money required by volunteers and staff to support various annual giving programs year after year remain valid expenses because finding new donors and renewing and upgrading prior donors must continue. Bigger gifts are possible in time, but they are not likely to arrive unless time and money first are invested in developing qualified donors and prospects through effective and efficient annual giving programs.

What should be the bottom-line cost for total fund-raising performance? Because organizations are not the same in how they conduct fund-raising and because fund-raising does not perform the same for every organization, there is no single number or percentage for all to salute and observe. The Council of Better Business Bureaus, Inc. (1982) suggested that fund raising costs should not exceed 35% of related contributions. The United States Supreme Court, in the 1980s, delivered three major decisions (*Schaumburg v. Citizens for a Better Environment,* 444 U.S. 618 (1080); *Maryland Secretary of State v. Joseph H. Munson Co.,* 467 U.S. 947 (1984); *Riley v. National Federation of the Blind of North Carolina, Inc.,* 108. S. Ct. 2667 (1988)) on this question, prohibiting any enforcement of fund-raising based on an administrative percentage (Hopkins, 1991, pp. 45–46, 489).

Is there any answer? Yes. It is reasonable to compare the results of each fund-raising method with its own cost guidelines. The comparison is helpful for mature, well-balanced programs (those with several fund-raising methods in place for at least three years or more), but it is a bit unfair to expect such performance the very first time the method is used. It is reasonable to use an overall guideline of 35 percent (65 cents of every dollar given goes for charitable purposes), but that performance is not to be expected for a new organization or one that has just begun fund-raising. The best guideline may be: Too much emphasis on less efficient forms of fund-raising (direct mail and benefit events) will push average costs upward to 50 percent. What is recommended is a

Exhibit 25.12.   Reasonable fund-raising cost guidelines.

Direct mail acquisition	$1.00 to $1.25 per dollar raised
Direct mail renewal	$0.20 per dollar raised
Benefit events	50% of gross proceeds
Corporations and foundations	$0.20 per dollar raised
Planned giving	$0.25 per dollar raised
Capital campaigns	$0.05 to $0.10 per dollar raised

balanced program with some concentration on major gifts, to keep costs down while building a pyramid of future leaders and future donors of size.

The flip side to all these assessments is the use of these same measurement tools to forecast future gift revenue. Too much microanalysis of prior results can mask the results predicted as reliable future income. Fiscal planning should place high value on accurate forecasts of likely contributions revenue, especially when developed from uniform measurement tools with reasonable cost guidelines. When fund development results are added to the balance of data developed from all the other assessment areas presented in this chapter, including environment, development department operations, development planning (feasibility) study, mission, and management, the organization's path for the future can be drawn with much greater accuracy and confidence.

25.5 ENVIRONMENTAL AUDIT FOR OPERATIONS

Many of the annual operating areas of nonprofit organizations can be influenced by the external environment, which will also have an effect on fund-raising results. This section reviews 16 new environmental factors that affect management operations and provides a mix of qualitative and quantitative criteria for assessment of progress in meeting the mission, purposes, goals, and objectives of the nonprofit organization. Environmental audits paint a much different portrait for each nonprofit organization; each has a unique mission and is no more the same in how it performs daily operations than it is in how it conducts fund-raising. Operating areas do not perform the same for every organization. These 16 environmental criteria (arranged alphabetically, for convenience) can be scored as low, medium, or high (see Exhibit 25.13), to help identify those that may have a greater influence on the organization's potential to raise money and to fulfill its mission.

(a) AGING OF THE POPULATION Population growth impacts nearly every area of society, and older citizens are society's fastest growing segment. Older citizens require increased support from government, business, and community programs, and have high expectations for attention and service as well as for respect. Organizations whose programs and services for the elderly entitle them to financial reimbursement from government sources will find those sources of payment continually limited and shrinking, an experience already felt by the seniors themselves. Seniors are resources to nonprofit organizations for leadership, volunteerism, and gift support, but they are likely to give first of their "time, talent and treasure" where their relationships are strongest—the organizations they have supported throughout their lifetimes.

(b) DEBT FINANCING Financial pressure for daily operations requires nonprofit organizations examine every possible source of increased income while maximizing the use of funds held and containing expenses. Alternative revenue sources to help achieve fiscal stability include: (1) an excess of revenue over expenses from the operating budget; (2) entrepreneurial for-profit enterprises; (3) investment earnings from endowment; (4) cash from fund-raising; and (5) debt financing. Management should exhaust its use of the first four options before considering any borrowing decisions. Organizations that qualify for tax-exempt bond financing for major capital and equipment projects (a tempting solution) soon learn that debt financing increases annual operating costs and results in seriously limited financial flexibility for many years to come.

Exhibit 25.13.   Environmental audit for operations.

	Operations Score
Aging of the population	Low/Medium/High
Debt financing	Low/Medium/High
Coalitions, mergers, and acquisitions	Low/Medium/High
Costs of supplies and services	Low/Medium/High
Disclosure	Low/Medium/High
Ethics and professionalism	Low/Medium/High
Federal deficit	Low/Medium/High
Globalization	Low/Medium/High
Government regulation	Low/Medium/High
Leadership development	Low/Medium/High
Management competency	Low/Medium/High
Pressure for cash	Low/Medium/High
Profitability	Low/Medium/High
Public confidence	Low/Medium/High
Technology	Low/Medium/High
Wages and benefits	Low/Medium/High
Totals	Low = ____
	Medium = ____
	High = ____

(c) COALITIONS, MERGERS, AND ACQUISITIONS   The merits of joint ventures become all the more attractive when competition, fiscal limitations, market forces, and other factors close in and cause the board and management to be concerned with the viability of the organization itself. Mergers and acquisitions are management strategies that should be considered to achieve improvements in service rather than to ensure survival or control over market share. The public can be confused and even alarmed when too many duplicate services appear to be offered, especially when all of them are active in seeking public participation and support for what appear to be the same goals and objectives. Nonprofit organizations should coordinate and cooperate wherever possible; joint ventures without a threat of merger or acquisition will be well received by the public, who expect the leaders of nonprofit organizations to resolve community problems, not compound them.

(d) COSTS OF SUPPLIES AND SERVICES   The costs of the goods and services nonprofit organizations have to buy for day-to-day operations are increasing each year. With good management, delivery of programs and services can sometimes be contained within available resources, but rising expenses exert pressure on operating budgets and can cause reductions in the extent of programs and services offered. Hard decisions will be forced on boards and management as they try to balance their commitment to provide public services against fiscal restraints. Any reduction by one institution or agency only seems to transfer its burden to others who already share the same restraints.

(e) DISCLOSURE   Nonprofit organizations are public corporations. They are required to share information about programs and services offered (including their outcomes), management practices, and financial affairs. Several areas of operation are required by law to be included in reports made to federal, state, county, and city governments and to the public on request. Open and full disclosure should be the policy and attitude of every board and management, but many organizations are uncomfortable with this obligation—not because they are engaged in illegal or illicit practices, but because they believe their decisions, based on complex issues in areas largely unknown to the public, will not be understood or appreciated and therefore will be subject to criticism and the potential for withdrawn support. Those who cannot overcome their paranoia on the need for disclosure may next become targets of suspicion, with a decline in public confidence and support a distinct possibility.

(f) ETHICS AND PROFESSIONALISM Media reports of scandals and abuse harm public confidence and trust in every nonprofit organization. Ethical behavior should be inherent in the policies and decisions of the board and management, not a tactic to escape media attention or to evade public criticism. Nonprofit organizations are called to a higher standard of stewardship in order to merit the special privileges their tax-exempt status allows. Their actions should always meet or exceed these higher standards rather than only minimally satisfy the requirements that preserve tax status. Areas of behavior to be avoided include personal conflicts of interest by board members and employees, questionable investments, inhumane treatment of clients, improper use of funds raised (especially for personal inurement), expensive and inefficient fund-raising practices, failure to meet legal requirements, and similar offenses.

(g) FEDERAL DEFICIT The extent of governments' own financial situation will be the most influential driving force in the day-to-day decisions of every sector of the country during this decade. General economic condition could remain the dominant economic force into the next century and may have an ever expanding effect on the nation and the world. Until government spending at all levels can achieve a balance between public needs and public revenues, any relief measures will be short-term policy decisions. Their impact on every nonprofit organization will affect the extent of dependence on government funding, the continuation of the privileges of income, sales, and property tax exemptions, and the preservation of the charitable contribution deduction for donors.

(h) GLOBALIZATION Barriers between nations have all but disappeared in some parts of the world, suggesting that globalization is on its way to becoming a reality. How will this movement affect America's nonprofit organizations and their mission? The concept of philanthropy is spreading rapidly throughout the world as the merits of voluntary association to effect solutions are accepted and replicated. Nonprofit organizations will feel the effects of a changing world marketplace. Are they prepared for change as an opportunity? Change offers everyone the opportunity to reexamine the original mission statement.

(i) GOVERNMENT REGULATION Government law provides the tax-exempt privileges currently enjoyed by nonprofit organizations and legitimizes the actions of those who support them. Changing laws and regulations can have enormous impact on nonprofit organizations that the government now advocates and enhances. Some hold that nonprofit organizations are an extension of the government's own duty to provide public programs and services. Because of this opinion, any proposals to reduce tax-exempt benefits and privileges are considered a serious threat, even when disguised as a solution to government's own, larger problems, such as the deficit. Desperate times can produce desperate ideas and can challenge even well-established principles and traditions. Nonprofit organizations can protect themselves by organizing their supporters to respond to harmful proposals. New lobbying regulations may limit the extent of this action and may weaken the efforts of all who are threatened.

(j) LEADERSHIP DEVELOPMENT   Every nonprofit organization should assess its leadership strengths and resolve the size, talents, cultural diversity, and other components necessary for its maximum use of volunteers. Failure to attend to leadership development will limit success and progress. No one should expect that other organizations will identify, recruit, train, retain, and otherwise develop future leaders and then make them available to competitors. Leaders often are initiated into the life of an organization through active volunteerism in the fund-raising program, personal giving, willingness to recruit gifts from others, and other voluntary roles. Volunteers often have multiple experiences with many organizations, but they must learn their role anew each time they serve, because the needs for their services are likely to be as different as the several organizations they join.

(k) MANAGEMENT COMPETENCY   Nonprofit organizations require competent executives to lead and to supervise their operations. It is the duty of the board of directors to recruit, hire, supervise, evaluate, and dismiss senior managers. Gone are the days when individuals who were marginally successful in the business world could find a safe haven for their talents in the nonprofit world (although that image remains prevalent). Nonprofit management is different from other business management and requires different skills and training. Evaluation criteria can be traditional areas of planning, quality of services rendered, employment practices, and financial success. A few areas that are unique to nonprofit management—directing volunteers, advocacy, and engaging in fund-raising—also can be considered for measurement.

(l) PRESSURE FOR CASH   Every nonprofit organization must finance its annual operations as a first priority, which places the dominant pressure on its revenue sources to meet current expenses. Managers can achieve cost-effective success in providing programs and services, but there is constant pressure for extra cash for expansion renovation, equipment replacement, employee training, research, and much more. It may be true that nonprofit organizations can spend every dime they receive, but they are run by good financial managers who observe professional fiscal policies. The pressure for cash results more from the insistence of the public's needs for increased programs and services, for improved quality and quantity, and for the addition of new technology and modern facilities. Such pressured and hard choices affect long-range and strategic plans for programs and services as well as finances and facilities, which must remain flexible to meet the unseen and unmet needs of society.

(m) PROFITABILITY   Success in business is measured as profits. Nonprofit organizations can achieve "profits" in their operating budget but no person may enjoy any personal share in the excess; it can only be applied to further programs and services. Public understanding of both profits and deficits by nonprofit organizations is often limited and tends to be expressed as judgments of management ability, board competency, and the like. Assessment of profitability can evaluate management and financial expertise alongside quality of programs and quantity of services provided. Management and financial success comes from following professional management practices, including attention to alternate revenue sources such as fund-raising. "Excess of revenues over expenses" will often be used to improve programs and services provided to the public. These funds also can be applied to improve management capability, to fund depreciation, to improve physical plant and equipment, to conduct planning and market research, and to satisfy other essential decisions that will increase the organization's ability to manage for its future with increased competence and quality.

(n) PUBLIC CONFIDENCE The public's trust in an organization's name and reputation for commitment to its mission can and should be measured by its actions to achieve that mission. Failure in public confidence and trust will do more than damage reputation. The loss of public confidence in the quality of the public programs and services offered will cause people to hesitate to seek the organization's services, decline to serve on its board, and decide against making contributions.

(o) TECHNOLOGY As technological advances continue at a rapid pace, society expects to see modernization appropriately transferred to nonprofit organizations. The pressure to add technology brings higher costs for new equipment, new and more expensive employees, maintenance, space, and other necessities. One example of the effects of technology is seen in health care, where science and technology yield better medical care but at an increased cost to the consumer. To assess the impact of technology is to assess judgment in equipment selection, competitive pricing, group purchasing, maintenance contracts, alternative financial options, adjustments in charges after reimbursement analysis, and other business decisions.

(p) WAGES AND BENEFITS Employees are not volunteers; they require salaries, benefits, and retirement plans that are nearly competitive with private businesses. Management decisions on the extent and cost of employee benefits must meet full legal requirements and aid in recruitment and retention of individuals who have the expertise necessary to provide quality programs and services. Inflation, local cost-of-living adjustments, cost of facilities, and cost of equipment and systems are factors that affect success in employee relations.

25.6 MISSION

To be incorporated as a voluntary, nonprofit public benefit corporation, an institution or agency must fulfill both state and federal legal requirements. It must have appropriate legal form, fulfill a "charitable" purpose, receive tax-exempt status, conduct day-to-day operations within legal requirements, and complete annual public reporting requirements. It must also be well-run, "like a business" (Hopkins, 1989, p. 104). Several areas of mission assessment are readily available (see Exhibit 25.14); many of them have already been discussed earlier in this chapter.

Nonprofit organizations do not stand alone in their mission to provide programs and services for the public good, nor are they alone in their need to ask for and to receive a share of public support in the forms of time, talent, and treasure. Independent Sector, in

Exhibit 25.14. Assessment criteria for the mission.

	Mission Score
Fulfill a "charitable" purpose	Low/Medium/High
Complete annual public reporting requirements	Low/Medium/High
Provide high quality of service	Low/Medium/High
Offer accessibility to service	Low/Medium/High
Increase public awareness of the cause	Low/Medium/High
Address five advocacy measurements	Low/Medium/High
Adequately use audits and auditors	Low/Medium/High
Be financially accountable	Low/Medium/High
Stimulate innovative ideas	Low/Medium/High
Provide programs of value to the public	Low/Medium/High
Develop new leadership	Low/Medium/High
Be guided by written policies and procedures	Low/Medium/High

Totals   Low = _____

Medium =   _____

High =   _____

its mission to aid all nonprofit organizations to benefit the public good, has defined "measurable growth" as its current national objective. To this end, Independent Sector has developed the "Give Five" campaign, which defines what voluntary organizations can do and what benefits they can achieve from growth. The ten recommendations listed below can serve the board of directors as a checklist for performance of both mission achievement and organization management:

1. The Board should set fund raising goals for next year and five years that are realistic, but which stretch the Board and everyone else in the organization. . . .

2. The Board must commit a significant portion of the resources of the organization, including their own time, to the pursuit of the fund raising goals. For most organizations, it will take a minimum of 20 percent of the organization's time and money to develop significant fund raising thrust. This is fully justified if, in the long run, the organization will be able to do more in the fulfillment of its program mission. . . .

3. Similar goals and commitments should be made for increased volunteer participation. . . .

4. The Board should devote a portion of almost every meeting and at least one full meeting to evaluating progress toward the goals. It should resolve to make these goals central to everything the organization does. . . .

5. Make fund raising and the effective utilization of volunteers every bit as important and prestigious as the most important program activities of the organization. . . .

6. Encourage the Board and staff to participate in training efforts to improve fund raising skills and effectiveness in recruiting and involving volunteers. Where necessary, help create such training opportunities by working with experienced and successful volunteer and staff leaders from other organizations. . . .

7. The organization's communications to current volunteers, members, contributors and others should emphasize the message of "fiving" and the importance of all people being engaged in active citizenship and personal community service. Pay first attention to those who are already involved. They offer the greatest potential for increased participation. . . .

8. Help to develop a local coalition of churches, other volunteer organizations, funders, media and others to build interest and awareness of "fiving" and a spirit of

contributing back to the community through support of the causes of one's choice. . . .

9. Honor the strong contributors and volunteers. Make it clear that the organization is aware and appreciative how special they are. . . .

10. Elevate the good volunteers and fund raisers to the Board. Make it clear that their performance is what the organization respects.

(Independent Sector, 1986, pp. 11–12)

Beyond these assessment areas are hard questions that need solid answers, to determine the vitality of a nonprofit organization. "Building a non-profit's capacity to carry out its mission, develop leaders, insure accountability, handle conflicts of interest, recruit new and young staff members, maintain good relations with clients and community, and plan programs that will have a serious impact—these are the key issues that need scrutiny but have largely been ignored" (Eisenberg, 1991, pp. 37–38).

What standards against mission should nonprofit organizations observe? Should they be judged only by those criteria that allow them to retain their privileges of tax exemption? Should the organization be willing to be judged on how it has served its mission, whom it has served (and how many), and its public benefit (making a measurable difference)? Has it increased its accessibility beyond those to whom it provides services? Has it increased public awareness of the cause it represents and the value of its role to achieve results that are of benefit to the community? In response to these questions, five areas of mission, discussed in the following sections, are suggested.

(a) ADVOCACY Advocacy is an important assignment in every nonprofit organization, even if it conducts a self-serving program to enhance its own image and reputation and to inspire public gift support. Advocacy is measured by:

- Number of legislative and regulatory changes realized;
- Number and frequency of advertising pieces;
- Number and frequency of mass communications (public relations), messages, and materials circulated;
- Growth in number of members and their contributions;
- Market research to document altered public perceptions.

(b) FINANCIAL ACCOUNTABILITY Too often, boards of directors and management staff give attention only to financial measurements tied to budget reviews and to completion of the fiscal year with a break-even objective or a minimum deficit. Some nonprofit organizations' fiscal mission is to achieve an "excess of revenue over expenses" (profit) in order to secure greater financial stability and to fund current and future programs with these resources. Is that sufficient to preserve their privileged tax-exempt status?

The requirement to prepare, review, and approve the annual audit statement often is given only one brief period of scrutiny. After hearing the auditor's analysis, the audit is often set aside as an exercise of historical value rather than an instrument for continuous use in financial planning and performance evaluation.

Financial accountability is possibly the most frequently used method of assessment of nonprofit organizations, although others may serve as standards for comparison and self-analysis. The Council of Better Business Bureaus, in its "Standards for Charitable

Solicitations" (1982), concentrated on five areas: public accountability, use of funds, solicitations and information materials, fund-raising practices, and governance. The Council conducts evaluations of several nonprofit organizations each year in its "watchdog" capacity and publishes the results of its assessment. Failure to meet these criteria can mean disqualification for corporation and foundation grants as well as a potential for diminished giving from the general public.

Other areas of assessment merit mention to nonprofit organizations and the public. "Such matters as who benefits from philanthropy, equity in grant making, philanthropic access and accountability, ethical problems, governance, the financing of public policy and advocacy activities, innovation and risk taking in philanthropy, . . . have been, not surprisingly, overlooked or neglected" (Eisenberg, 1991, pp. 37–38).

(c) CHARITABLE PURPOSE   Charitable purpose, while always implied, can stand regular review. In 1985, the Supreme Court of Utah found the difference between a for-profit and a nonprofit hospital to be "indistinguishable" in making a determination whether the nonprofit hospital should pay any property taxes (*County Board of Equalization of Utah County v. Intermountain Health Care, Inc.,* 709 P.2d 265 (Sup. Ct. Utah 1985). Tax-exemption challenges and "commerciality tests" are complicated issues and already represent a serious threat to the nonprofit status of every institution and agency. Nonprofit organizations are, by nature, public understanding, and law, quite distinguishable from for-profit business corporations. Yet, if they must now prove in the courts their validity for retaining their exemptions, as it appears they must, these special privileges could be lost.

Part of the American tradition in fostering voluntary action has been as a substitute for direct government support. Given greater freedoms of expression and reinforced by tax-exempt privileges, nonprofit organizations have as their mission the implied duty to consider change, to stimulate and initiate innovative ideas, and to add programs of increased value and benefit to the public. How well have they fulfilled this duty? Boards of directors and management should evaluate their own performance in providing public leadership and innovation and should assess their ability to be an influence in meeting changing community needs.

(d) LEADERSHIP DEVELOPMENT   Although public participation and public support are obvious ingredients for the current and future success of every nonprofit organization, they are more vital than just part-time assistance where and when needed. The strength of each nonprofit organization is leadership, which is vested in the composition and membership of its board of directors. Without constant attention and a commitment to developing present and future leaders, the organization will soon stagnate and wither. Board members and other volunteers are proof to the public that they can entrust their money and their confidence to the organization. The role of volunteers must be well-defined, their time and expertise must be recognized and accepted, and their contributions must be rewarded. These are all easily measurable outcomes.

(e) WRITTEN POLICIES AND PROCEDURES   Much more than a book of rules, these are guidelines for daily operations that assist both volunteers and employees in their joint efforts to achieve the mission of the organization and to do so within well-defined and easily measurable purposes, goals, and objectives. Assessment of performance against policies and procedures is the easiest of measurements to accomplish with regularity.

Along with the work required to prepare and maintain such documents, the bonus often is a consensus that knits everyone together toward the common purposes defined in the mission statement. (See Ch. 16.2 for a Manual of Fund Development Policy.)

25.7 MANAGEMENT

Management skill within nonprofit organizations has grown extensively in the past two decades. No doubt there remain instances where boards and managers practice inefficiency, laxity, indifference, and complacency, but their numbers are shrinking. Any organization at any time may fall short in one or another management area, but most are increasingly alert to the need to improve their internal management skills and are committed to do so within their means. They also are more willing to acknowledge their weaknesses, an important step toward improvement.

Business executives often make up the majority of voluntary board members of nonprofit organizations. Trained to demonstrate success by measurement of corporate bottom-line profits, these individuals erroneously tend to use the same measurements for nonprofit organizations. One result has been criticism of the management ability of nonprofit executives, as in the following analysis:

> All organizations use inputs to produce outputs. An organization's effectiveness is measured by the extent to which outputs accomplish its objectives, and its efficiency is measured by the relationship between inputs and outputs. In a profit-orientated organization the amount of profit provides an overall measure of both effectiveness and efficiency. In many nonprofit organizations, however, outputs cannot be measured to quantitative terms. . . . The absence of a satisfactory, single, overall measure of performance that is comparable to the profit measure is the most serious management control problem in a nonprofit organization (Anthony and Herzlinger, 1984).

Several areas of assessment of the management function have universal standards for measurement (see Exhibit 25.15). Voluntary accreditation reviews are performed for several groups of nonprofit organizations, such as colleges and universities, hospitals, and museums. Standards of accounting used for audit preparation measure and report financial performance against criteria established by the Financial Accounting Standards Board (FASB) and the American Institute of Certified Public Accountants (AICPA). Equally known but without any comparative standard beyond compliance are the annual reports filed with the Internal Revenue Service and individual states. The IRS Form 990 is used by both federal and state authorities to monitor select areas of annual performance. These data are now being tabulated in a few states that publish summaries. A recent study led by Professor Frederick S. Lane at Baruch College/The City University of New York, found that, among nonprofit organizations that file IRS Form 990, the annual returns were "often incomplete and/or inaccurate," limiting their usefulness by nonprofit organizations as well as by regulators, policy makers, donors, and others. The study also found that inconsistent and inaccurate IRS Form 990 filings were caused by "different applications of accounting principles," and by "board member and manager unfamiliarity with nonprofit accounting in general and the requirements of Form 990 in particular" (Lane, 1991, p. 4).

The Baruch College project team offered three recommendations to assist nonprofit organizations in their public reporting:

Exhibit 25.15. Assessment criteria for management.

	Management Score
Computer technology application	Low/Medium/High
Successful accreditation review	Low/Medium/High
Compliance with current accounting standards	Low/Medium/High
Accurate IRS Form 990 submission	Low/Medium/High
Board checklist for liability	Low/Medium/High
Governance	Low/Medium/High
Accountability	Low/Medium/High
Financial management	Low/Medium/High
Planning	Low/Medium/High
Marketing and communications	Low/Medium/High
Community and client relations	Low/Medium/High
Human resource and employee benefits	Low/Medium/High
Totals	Low = _____
	Medium = _____
	High = _____

1. Raising the consciousness of nonprofit organizations regarding the importance of quality reporting of finances and programs . . .
2. Education of nonprofit organizations and those who advise them on accounting, financial management, and reporting . . .
3. Establishing and maintaining cooperative action for nonprofit quality reporting.

(Lane, 1991, p. 16)

Public reporting is important because it helps to build public confidence in the quality of the information provided and in interpretation of the documents' contents as a valid form of management performance evaluation. In this sense, nonprofit organizations resemble private businesses.

In this litigious age, liability has become a prominent issue to nonprofit board members. One result is that conservatism has escalated to the extent that willingness to innovate and to take risks has been greatly diminished. To overcome such hesitation, boards and management should take the steps necessary to avoid any conduct that might be the basis for a liability suit. In this way, they can regain their confidence in fulfilling their organization's mission. The following list of directors' responsibilities will, if adhered to, eliminate or at least minimize personal liability while allowing boards and management to think more boldly. These responsibilities also represent a good checklist for board assessment purposes:

- Make certain that all technical requirements of law have been met before the organization commences operations.
- Keep informed of the general activities of the organization and the general field of interest in which it functions.
- Ensure complete and accurate disclosure of the details of all transactions, such as the sale of securities.

- Avoid self-dealing in any matters relating to the organization's operations.
- Attend directors' meeting regularly; if meetings must be missed, be certain that the minutes reflect a valid reason for the absence.
- Register dissent when in disagreement with board action; be certain that it is made a matter of record in the minutes of the meeting and that the accuracy of the minutes is checked.
- Have a complete and competent knowledge of the duties of the office.
- Avoid any contract to serve personal interests or to assume any position that would bring personal interests into conflict or competition with the interests of the organization.
- Keep informed of the provisions of the documents creating the organization and setting forth its rules of operation, especially as they relate to the powers and duties of the directors.
- Exercise the utmost good faith in all deadlines with and for the organization, and be prepared to provide good faith if necessary.
- Obey all statutes and other forms of law that prescribe specific duties to be performed by directors.

(Webster, 1965, 2.07 [2])

Management standards apply to those areas of duty and responsibility that belong to voluntary members of the board of directors and hired executive officers. These men and women have a duty, directly and indirectly, to supervise the following seven areas of assessment, as a measurement of their own performance: governance, accountability, financial management, planning, marketing and communication, community and client relationships, and human resources and employee benefits. These criteria are the final assessment areas of this chapter.

(a) GOVERNANCE The ultimate responsibility for each nonprofit organization is vested in its board of directors. Their stewardship includes the quantity and quality of programs and services provided, financial accountability for all assets and funds, and fulfillment of all laws and regulations. Boards of directors share a degree of personal and collective liability in meeting these responsibilities and, although the nonprofit organization may be insured to protect them insofar as it can, their personal obligation remains.

Assessment of governance can be expanded from the list for board assessment presented earlier, beginning with the following standards:

1. Are the Board and staff set up to work effectively? . . .
2. How well defined are the needs served by the agency and its program for meeting these needs? . . .
3. Are adequate financial safeguards and sound controls maintained for fund-raising? . . .
4. Is the agency's work related to that of the national organization of other planning groups in the field? . . .
5. Is the agency doing a good job of what it is set up to do? . . .
6. How many other agencies are trying to do all or parts of the same job? . . .
7. Does the agency function in proper relationship to government agencies?

(Lippincott and Aannested, 1964, pp. 87–88)

Another method of self-evaluation is the well-established management by objectives (MBO) standard, which sets defined goals for measurable periods, such as the annual operating year, or for prepared three- or five-year strategic plans. An organization should be able to define specific goals for its public programs and services, based on its evaluation of current public needs and its ability to contribute to their fulfillment within its mission. Why else does it exist? In addition to public needs assessment, it should be able to assess specific internal goals based on current strengths and weaknesses, threats and opportunities, and should include areas of administrative competence and preparedness. For example, the goals set can be associated with the composition of the board of directors regarding size, sex, age, talents, cultural diversity, and rotation of its members. In this regard, assessment of its nominations process would include maintenance of a roster of qualified and qualifiable candidates whose development is being supervised on a regular schedule.

Does the board perform any self-evaluation and, if so, how often? What criteria are utilized? Caution may lead boards to be soft on themselves or to measure only hard data such as the volume of clients served, the fulfillment of budget objectives, and so on. The ability of the board to provide leadership and direction might be a more germane area of assessment. Criteria might be: routine educational presentations on advances in program and service areas; what similar organizations have achieved; workshops on liability issues, quality control, and long-range planning; or outside evaluations of legislative and regulatory directives that may influence current operations and future planning.

Another set of assessments might be framed as answers to the series of questions shown in Exhibit 25.16.

(b) ACCOUNTABILITY Accountability includes an assessment of programs and services as well as financial details. Activities easily can be counted but assessing their quality and the worth of their outcomes is more difficult. Performance measurement data do exist and can include, for example, comparative analysis of staff ratios to operating costs for each program, to discern cost per unit of client service. How are these data to be interpreted? Costs for a college to educate students are different from a hospital's cost to provide patient care or a museum's cost to be open daily for visitors. These data are more useful internally, to assist the board and management in cost–benefit analysis, such as the relation between staffing for service and income. The value or utility of these programs and services to the community served should also be assessed through market research methodologies.

Accountability also includes an assessment of the distribution of information about the nonprofit organization, usually in the form of an annual report, newsletters, brochures, and the like, to describe its programs and services and to report its financial affairs. An attitude of open and full disclosure is important for nonprofit organizations: Is there anything of significance that is honestly "private" about the management of a voluntary, nonprofit, public benefit organization?

Financial information is more tangible but its interpretation requires assistance. Nonprofit organizations have (at last count) four separate standards of accounting issued by the FASB and AICPA, depending on type of organization. The Internal Revenue Service requires all nonprofit organizations to follow the Health and Welfare audit guide in preparation of their annual IRS Form 990, which yields uniformity in presentation of financial information for every institution and agency—provided they know how to complete the form and do so with mathematic accuracy. Sources and

Exhibit 25.16. Assessment of leadership.

	Yes	No
Does the organization have records that enable it to document		
a. what it has achieved?	[ ]	[ ]
b. how it is continuing to carry out its mission?	[ ]	[ ]
Does the organization issue annual reports based on these records?	[ ]	[ ]
Do all board members have copies of		
a. the mission statement?	[ ]	[ ]
b. the long-range strategic plan?	[ ]	[ ]
c. the plan for the coming year?	[ ]	[ ]
d. the budget for the coming year?	[ ]	[ ]
Does the organization have a detailed, board-approved plan (including a plan for fund-raising) for the coming year?	[ ]	[ ]
Was the most recent auditor's report an "unqualified" report?	[ ]	[ ]

Source: Excerpted from New, 1991, pp. 5–6, by permission.

amounts of revenue are separated into several categories; expenses for programs and services are separated from costs of management and administration and from fund-raising expenses—all reasonable areas for assessment and performance evaluation.

(c) FINANCIAL MANAGEMENT Because most nonprofit organizations have limited assets to manage, financial data should be easy to measure, including the stewardship of these resources to gain full value during their period of use. Financial management requires expertise among the board and senior managers. The scope of fiscal activities is broad and requires sophisticated supervision even in smaller nonprofit organizations. Annual operating budgets report all the sources of revenue and categories of expense activity; their results are analyzed and reported in the annual audit statement. Liquid and fixed assets include property, buildings, and equipment; employee health and dental insurance, disability insurance, and pension and retirement programs must be supervised. Fund-raising is a active source of additional revenue both for daily operations and for capital and equipment, education, research, and other purposes. Categories for active capital management include cash, management of funded depreciation and reserves in short- and long-term investments, acting as trustee for charitable trusts, and investment management of endowment funds.

(d) PLANNING The mission statement establishes a grand design for every nonprofit organization. Annual operations implement the mission to the extent that present ability and resources allow. Planning is a discipline for looking beyond a current operating year and its limitations and defining a future direction that seeks to fulfill the mission of the organization. This plan or "vision" of the board and management reveals their commitment to specific and measurable goals that will achieve exciting and worthwhile activities and enterprises for the public good. Without a future plan, an organization will be more apt to wander aimlessly among daily threats and new (and untried) opportunities all likely to lead to hasty, ill-informed decisions that favor "quick fix" solutions. Such a plan is not likely to lead an organization in any future direction and may only allow it to survive perhaps a little while longer with minimal ability and effect; it should consider closing its doors and going out of its nonbusiness.

Whether called a master plan, a long-range plan, or a strategic plan, the "vision" for the future should be written to describe its orderly assessment of the present and its informed view of the direction it has set for itself. The board and management should next develop internal and external consensus and commitment to the goals and build enthusiasm for their accomplishment. Long-range plans include the three key areas of analysis and projection listed below. When completed, they serve as the road map to achieve that vision:

1. Sufficient details about current programs and services and their merits, plus new activities to be offered that will improve the quality and breadth of present programs and services;
2. A financial evaluation of existing resources and the extent of those required to pay for future programs and services;
3. A capital and equipment needs assessment that will support the planned programs and services to be carried out within adequate facilities.

(e) MARKETING AND COMMUNICATION   In prior years, the term "public relations" was adequate to cover the area of establishing and supervising public information and communications for nonprofit organizations. Different skills are required today, combining planning (both long-range and strategic) with market research and strategic marketing, all carried out through multimessage advertising and multimedia communications.

Assessment of the use and outcomes of these high-tech methods is as essential as assessment of other management areas. Volumes of analytical information are available on how market research can pinpoint different attitudes within segments of the public, or identify the medium to deliver the precise messages selected to those most likely to hear and reply, or measure results within a single organization in detail. The science of market research also measures progress against long-range and strategic plans, to enable early management intervention in their likely effect on current operations. Raw and uninterpreted intelligence is essential to keep pace with a changing world that can affect current management options and decisions.

Public communications channels are jammed with messages. The quality and cost of advertising production and distribution have skyrocketed so that only larger, more affluent organizations can afford their use. Public resentment toward mail and telephone invasion of privacy limits the ability of everyone to communicate, even with a select audience. The use of multimedia outlets reinforced with repeat messages has proven to be more effective but is also the most costly method. Added to this search for a means to gain people's attention is the competition with for-profit corporations whose larger budgets can outperform the best efforts and limited budgets of nonprofit organizations.

Assessment of merit, value, performance, and outcomes, using modern marketing and communications techniques, adds a wealth of helpful information for planning and decision making. However, limited management standards exist against which nonprofit organizations can measure their areas of activity as compared with the experience of others. Counting inches of newspaper space is only one indicator; others are needed. The cost of assessment itself has become a factor in budget decisions. The value of information has increased and may, for those organizations whose mission is advocacy, become more critical than analysis of routine operating programs that provide public services. Internal competition for operating dollars will increase because funds directed to marketing and communications can be proven to influence public perceptions about quality of service (attraction) and improve market position for continued expansion (growth).

(f) COMMUNITY AND CLIENT RELATIONSHIPS Nonprofit organizations have always been sensitive to their local community and its residents. Renewed attention to both is necessary because of rapid shifts in demographics, evolving attitudes, and direct changes introduced into the community through economic and government influence, all reinforced through mass marketing and communications techniques. People are more likely to relocate as a consequence of factors that influence their lives; they will even incur financial loss on jobs, housing, and life-style in order to achieve better opportunities. Demographic changes are widespread, and each community must pay increased attention to how culturally diverse groups influence its needs for government, business, and philanthropic support to meet basic community needs. Opening or closing a major plant or business can have overnight ramifications across the spectrum of community life and can affect everyone living there.

Nonprofit organizations should be active in community affairs to the extent possible, and for better reasons than preserving an inaccurate sense of corporate image. Programs and services provided by nonprofit organizations are often considered by community residents to be part of its basic fabric of essential public amenities available to every resident. Board members are uniquely qualified to bridge this gap, as are senior managers, who need to join civic, service, and social groups and be visible presences in community projects. They should also be active partners in discussions on community issues, especially when their own organization's expertise can help the resolution.

(g) HUMAN RESOURCES AND EMPLOYEE BENEFITS Whether in hard or prosperous economic times, nonprofit organizations must, by law, provide fair wages, comprehensive benefits, and safe working conditions for their employees. Their salaries and benefits often lag behind private business but, to their credit, many nonprofit employees bring to their job a sense of commitment to the cause and an honest concern for its clients. Given such favorable attitudes, the addition of a few privileges from among internal options (tuition remission, if a college or school; health care, if a hospital; tickets, if a museum or performing arts center) is valuable to employee relations. Aside from what is required, positive working conditions and benefits are needed to attract and retain competent managers, professional and technical staff, and trained employees at all levels. Their offerings will never match for-profit business packages, because shares of company stock, profit sharing, and other "perks" are unavailable, but nonprofit organizations can be quite competitive.

Comparative salary and benefits surveys also will keep each institution informed of what other organizations (both for-profit and nonprofit) provide, and an analysis of external conditions will help to keep current with issues that affect employment and employee satisfaction, such as union organizing activities. Access to public transportation, parking, local housing costs, child care, and other community indicators help to make employee benefit programs competitive. Well-designed employee relations programs that offer internal values can emerge as attractive alternatives to costly benefits. Organizing car pools and offering extra privileges and prizes for participants encourages employees to be environmentally sensitive, builds camaraderie, and may help to reduce highway and parking congestion.

The broad areas of management assessment briefly examined here offer numerous criteria for assessment. Each nonprofit organization can choose those most essential to its own success and measure their progress using the scorecard in Exhibit 25.14. Continued attention to these few areas, plus all those presented in this chapter, will aid the organization in carrying out its programs of public service and will help it to become even more capable of fulfilling its mission.

SOURCES AND SUGGESTED REFERENCES

American Association of Fund-Raising Counsel. 1991. *Giving USA*. New York: AAFRC Trust for Philanthropy.

Anthony, Robert M., and Herzlinger, Regina. 1984. *Management Control in Nonprofit Organizations*. Unpublished study, Harvard Graduate School of Business Administration, Cambridge, MA.

Berendt, Robert J., and Taft, J. Richard 1983. *How to Rate Your Development Office*. Washington, DC: Taft Corporation.

Costa, Nick B. 1991. *Measuring Progress and Success in Fund Raising: How to Use Comparative Statistics to Prove Your Effectiveness*. Falls Church, VA: Association for Healthcare Philanthropy.

Council of Better Business Bureaus, Inc. 1982. *Standards for Charitable Solicitations*. Arlington, VA: Author.

Drucker, Peter F. 1990. *Managing the Nonprofit Organization: Practices and Principles*. New York: HarperCollins.

Eisenberg, Pablo. 1991. "Why We Know So Little About Philanthropy." *Chronicle of Philanthropy* (December 17): 37–38.

Fink, Norman S. and Metzler, Howard C. 1982. *The Costs and Benefits of Deferred Giving*. New York: Columbia University Press.

Greenfield, James M. 1991. *Fund-Raising: Evaluating and Managing the Fund Development Process*. New York: John Wiley & Sons.

———. 1988. "Fund-Raising Costs and Credibility: What the Public Needs to Know," *NSFRE Journal* (Autumn): 45–53.

———. 1989. "Measuring Fund-Raising Success." *NAHD Journal* (Fall): 28–30.

Grenzebach, John, and Associates. 1986. *Prerequisites for Provable Campaign Success Investigated by a John Grenzebach and Associates Feasibility Development Study* (corporate report). Chicago, IL: Author.

Hopkins, Bruce R. 1991. *The Law of Fund Raising*. New York: John Wiley & Sons.

———. 1992. *The Law of Tax-Exempt Organizations* (6th ed.). New York: John Wiley & Sons.

———. 1989. *Starting and Managing a Nonprofit Organization: A Legal Guide*. New York: John Wiley & Sons.

Independent Sector. 1986. *Daring Goals for a Caring Society: A Blueprint for Substantial Growth in Giving and Volunteering in America*. Washington, DC.

Lane, Frederick S. 1991. "Enhancing the Quality of Public Reporting by Nonprofit Organizations." *The Philanthropy Monthly* (July): 3–38. Reprint of Report of the Nonprofit Quality Reporting Project, Baruch College/The City University of New York.

Lippincott, Earle, and Elling Aannestad. 1964. "Management of Voluntary Welfare Agencies." *Harvard Business Review* (November/December): 87–88.

Martin, Del. 1990. "The Development Audit: Providing the Blue Print for a Better Fund-Raising Program." *NSFRE Journal* (Autumn): 28.

Murray, Dennis J. 1987. *The Guaranteed Fund-Raising System: A Systems Approach to Planning and Controlling Fund Raising*. Boston: American Institute of Management.

New, Anne L., with Wilson C. Levis. 1991. *Raise More Money for Your Nonprofit Organization: A Guide to Evaluating and Improving Your Fundraising*. New York: The Foundation Center.

Seymour, Harold J. 1966. *Designs for Fund-Raising*. New York: McGraw-Hill. (Second edition (paperback): Ambler, PA: The Fund Raising Institute, 1988.)

Webster, George D. 1965. *The Law of Associations*. New York: Matthew Bender.

Weisbrod, Burton A. 1988. *The Nonprofit Economy*. Cambridge, MA: Harvard University Press.

CHAPTER TWENTY-SIX

Donor Software Management

Howard J. Rhine

CONTENTS

26.1 INTRODUCTION

Tracking donors, preparing fund reports, analyzing budgets, and planning campaign mailings are all functions that nonprofits perform daily. With a properly managed donor tracking system, an organization can operate more efficiently, improve its productivity, and provide an increase for its revenue base. For many years, most nonprofit organizations used manual systems to keep track of donors. As microcomputers became available and as the organizational structure became more complex, the need for data processing grew. Specialized software companies soon recognized and filled the

Exhibit 26.1.   How different departments within an organization interact.

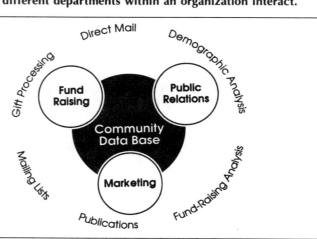

Reproduced by permission of Campagne Associates, Ltd.

need, producing programs that enabled organizations to perform their own fund-raising data management analyses. Software began to link functions formerly carried out by several departments and bring them together into one system (Exhibit 26.1). Organizations that had previously kept track of donors on index cards, using manual systems, now were able to track donors, create budgets and fund reports, and carry out all the data management functions of a fund-raising program by touching a few keys on a computer keyboard.

A number of multipurpose data-base programs currently on the market can be adapted and customized to fit nonprofits' needs. This chapter highlights the leading ready-made packages and accessories that are available. There generally is no need to invest precious resources in customized software when "generic" products are readily available to perform the necessary data management functions. It is important, however, to define the needs of an organization and shop for a system geared to those needs. A system suitable for a national, household-name organization may be overkill for a community-based organization. On the other hand, the community-based organization may need a lot of additional data for its local donors' profiles that the national organization does not require.

Ingenuity, creativity, and appropriate use of a computer and its programs can also help maximize the organization's investment and revenue base. This chapter reviews a number of the ways in which computers can enhance an organization's performance. It examines the steps to be taken before selecting a program and discusses some of the cautions involved in selecting and implementing a system.

26.2 SYSTEM FEATURES

What are some of the important features an organization will find in most nonprofit software packages? Each package will have its own unique approach in its presentation, but some standard features are universal. Here is how these standard features can be applied in day-to-day operations.

(a) DONOR PROFILES Most packages will use the donor profile screen as the backbone for the program. This screen contains basic information and background on the donor's name (Exhibit 26.2), beginning with the donor's, name mailing address, zip code, and telephone number. The donor profile can also include a "Demographics" section, with information on income, occupation, education, participation in prior events, outside interests, and philanthropic affiliations. (See Exhibit 26.3.) Using a sort feature built into the program, organizations can identify and target individuals by category—for example, those engaged in a specific occupation or those who share similar interests—to get these individuals involved in a specific campaign. The sort can be done by age, income, or any other attribute the user chooses.

Targeting specific groups of potential donors who have similar interests and backgrounds can increase the revenue base of an organization. In addition, organizations can focus on programs or services that a specific group might be likely to support, as a way of inviting this group to get involved. Special programs, fund drives, and phonathons all can assist in targeting new constituent groups. The nonprofit could develop a project or service that appeals to this group, and show the effect the project has had in helping the organization. By targeting specific individuals and groups that would be most likely to contribute to a specific campaign, the nonprofit might reduce or eliminate unnecessary mailings and avoid investing time in individuals who might not be interested. For example, if a national organization is conducting a fund-raising program specifically based in and benefiting the northeastern region of the United States, it would probably want to eliminate all prospects residing outside that region. Sorts can go well beyond zip codes and similar data. Many different and useful lists and sorts can be created and maintained in separate files for campaigns, dinners, and specialized fund drives.

Exhibit 26.2. Sample donor profile.

```
07/09/91        * CHANGE *      TIP$ MASTER RECORD MAINTENANCE        DM810S V 4.0.3
AF    105       RECORD #     F4 = CODES    F5 = ACTIVITY MENU    F8 = END    F10 = PRIOR
─────────────────────────────────────────────────────────────────────────────────────
          TITLE:   < DM >  Dr. and Mrs.      PROF TITLE:  < HPD >  Hospital Director
      ALT TITLE:   < DR >  Dr.
          NAME:   < Nathan K./Jones     > SALUTATION:  < Nat                      >
       ADDRESS:   < 2 East Ave.                        >
          CITY:   < Columbus     > STATE:  < OH >  ZIP:  < 02022-     >      ROUTE:  < 0000 >

     FIRM NAME:   < General Hospital              > ACCESS:  < GENERALHOSPI >
       ADDRESS:   < 1 Main St.              >
          CITY:   < Columbus     > State:  < OH >  ZIP:  < 02024-     >      ROUTE:  < 0000 >

 ◁ · · · · · · · TELEPHONE NUMBERS · · · · · · · ▷       SPOUSE:  < Janice          >
 AREA CODE       NUMBER        EXT     Home/Bus   SPOUSE TITLE:   < MZ >     Mrs.
   < 403 >     < 243-0024 >   < 1133 >    < B >
   < 403 >     < 243-0024 >   < 0033 >    < B >              SOLICITOR:   < JPM >  J. P. Morrigan
   < 403 >     < 577-0213 >   < 0000 >    < H >              SOL ONLY:   < N >
 STATUS (A/I):  < A >  MAIL TO (H/B/X):  < B >  STATEMENT(Y/N):  < Y >  RECEIPT(Y/N/H/B):  < N >
═══════════════════════════════════════════════════════════════════════════════════════
 F2 = NEXT RECORD        Next screen: 1/2/3/4/F(Financials)/N(Notes)/U(Update)/E(End)      .
```

Reproduced by permission of Autocomp Systems Corp.

Exhibit 26.3.   A donor screen showing interests, occupation, education, and philanthropic affiliations.

07/09/91	* DISPLAY *	TIP$ MASTER RECORD MAINTENANCE		DM813S V 4.0.0
AF 105	RECORD #	F4 = CODES F5 = ACTIVITY MENU	F8 = END	F10 = PRIOR

PROFILE CODES   Nathan K./Jones   General Hospital

1	Occupation	< MD >	PHYSICIAN	11	Send Raffle	< ALL >	ALL RAFFLES
2	Donor Club	< BEN >	BENEFACTOR	12	Parlor Meeting	< WTR >	WINTER MTG
3	Affiliation	< FF >	FORD FOUNDAT.	13	Luncheon	< YES >	YES
4	Grant Pref #1	< SCI >	SCIENCE	14	Luncheon Sol	< NRG >	NANCY REAGAN
5	Grant Pref #2	< >		15	CHAPTER	< 100 >	CHAPTER 100
6	Volunteer Type	< DIS >	DISASTER SRVCE	16	Member Type	< AMB >	AMBASSADOR
7	Vol Day Avail	< >		17	Member Status	< ACT >	ACTIVE MEMBER
8	Last Degree	< MD >	MD	18	.	< >	
9	Board affil.	< TRS >	TREASURER	19	.	< >	
10	Committee	< DVE >	DEVEL. COMM.	20	.	< >	

USER CODES

1	Newsletter	< Y >	YES	6	Board Member	< Y >	YES
2	Quality prosp.	< 1 >	HIGH	7	.	< >	
3	Marital Status	< M >	MARRIED	8	.	< >	
4	Journal Ad	< >		9	.	< >	
5	Attends Dinner	< Y >	YES	10	Source	< I >	INDIVIDUAL

F2 = NEXT RECORD	Next screen: 1/2/3/4/F(Financials)/N(Notes)/E(End) .

Reproduced by permission of Autocomp Systems Corp.

(b) RETRIEVAL Retrieval is a key function. Autocomp, a software company based in New York, has created a program called TIP$, which utilizes a mini-data base. Joseph Weinstein, President of Autocomp, has explained:

> The mini-data base is created from the master file and consists of a subset of records from the master file.

Let's say the Johnson Memorial Hospital wants to send out dinner invitations to a forthcoming dinner. It would like to select a group of 1,000 people from its master list of 10,000 names. The criteria must be set. The special events planners have chosen to send an invitation to everyone who attended and/or contributed to last year's dinner . . . 650 names. They also want to select their "high donors." To them, that includes everyone who contributed over $500 in the last year. The system then sorts and creates the mini data base, which will then be used for reporting, letter writing, and corresponding about the dinner.

> If the hospital were to honor a prominent doctor and lawyer from the community, the program could be configured to sort out all doctors from the master file and all lawyers from the master file. Each of the two lists could receive a special separate letter informing them of the impending honor to be extended to a fellow colleague.

In this case, the program would be able to generate a separate list and have each profession receive a specifically targeted letter. The list could further be broken down by geographic area or any subcriteria. Finding new ways to target groups could maximize the return on investment, not only from the software package but also from the donors.

In general, individuals "don't contribute to organizations they don't feel close to," Weinstein pointed out. Targeting specific groups and getting them involved could help maximize the revenue base and create long-term friends for an organization's future.

The donor profile screen might also list the organization's point of contact, perhaps a solicitor who has dealt with the donor in the past. Listing specific solicitors who have received donations from this individual can assist in future solicitations. One of these solicitors names would be the designated contact person for future requests for support; this person's guidance should be sought when reviewing the donor's file. Including solicitors in the profile could also assist an organization in reviewing their progress in a specific campaign. Suppose, during a summer fund drive, several volunteers are soliciting support for the drive. The organization can program the system, to allow the chairperson or other leaders to set targets, keep track of volunteers, monitor solicitor productivity, and use it as an important assessment and process management tool.

At the conclusion of the campaign, the next step would be to export the names of the solicitors and the total dollar amounts they have generated for the campaign to the report generators or word processing modules. Personalized letters of appreciation should be sent to all volunteers and staff, thanking them for a job well done.

26.3 CODE DRIVEN/MENU DRIVEN

Systems can be code driven, menu driven, or both. A code-driven system uses specific codes to bring up the files and screens; using alphabet-letter sequences the letters can

Exhibit 26.4. Donor profile screen—use of windows/menu.

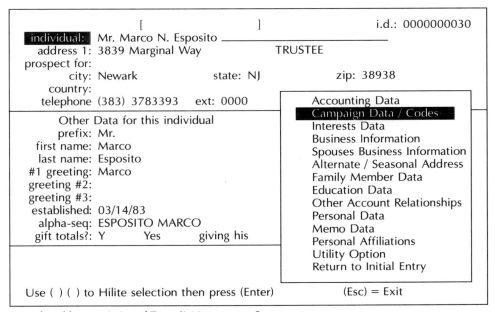

Reproduced by permission of Target/1 Management Systems.

represent a fund or appeal and can be used to call up a specific file. The letters "SPA" could represent the spring appeal and typically would be found in the general ledger next to the name of the donor who has contributed to the spring appeal. If an organization wanted to see all those who responded to the spring appeal, the sort mode could be selected. The system will search for "SPA" and generate a donor list, including the amount given for the spring appeal, and then prepare a report for the user. Some systems have pre-entered codes; others have user-defined codes. Weinstein pointed out that "user-defined codes will make your system much more flexible and easier to use." An example can be shown by considering the job description of a doctor. "M D" can indicate a medical doctor, but the letters "DR" could also be used. A user-defined code system allows the organization to create any letter sequence to represent any fund drive, interest code, or other function the system requires. An organization could also add different appeal codes that are relevant to its specific activities.

A menu-driven system could also be used and has its strong points (Exhibit 26.4). This program uses pulldown windows. The curser key is moved up and down to allow the user to select the screens he or she wishes to view. Many systems take advantage of both the menu and code systems, using them simultaneously. This flexibility gives the user the ability to "switch gears" and avoid fatigue during periods of extended use. Hours of data entry and looking at a computer screen can become monotonous and the "change of scenery" is always welcome.

26.4   FUND ACCOUNTING

Although nonprofits are similar in many respects to most business enterprises, important differences remain in key management areas. For example, nonprofits often require more detailed fund reporting. The ability to track restrictive funds is essential in order to ensure that funds are charged and credited to the proper accounts.

Many software vendors create special accounts, within the system, that can assist nonprofits in situations that they will most likely encounter. Software Services of Delaware includes in its software program a list of various funds, one of which is labeled "the restricted fund." Suppose a fund is to be used specifically for building a playground for a school. The fund currently has a balance of 10,000. A requirement is that this fund remain separate from the general ledger and have its own balance sheet. However, the board has authorized the accrued interest to be used for the school's general expenses. Using this system, the interest could be posted on the general ledger without touching the restricted fund. The restricted fund could have its own balance sheet, and reports could be produced for the restricted fund at any given time.

A nonprofit organization can set up its own accounting ledger with the use of a general-purpose software spread sheet. Although staff presumedly could do the work themselves, a ready-to-use nonprofit software program can save a great deal of time and expense in setting up and monitoring an organization's accounting ledger. In addition, purchased nonprofit software programs can save programming costs and include such extras as maintaining payroll accounts, check printing, fund reports, and foundation proposals. The system should include these features:

- The accounts receivable function of fund accounting will interface with the donor's profile screen and word processing module to print statements and manage the donor file.

• The accounts payable function will post statements and print checks for the organization. A software manufacturer may choose to interface the main software program with Lotus 1-2-3 (Exhibits 26.5 and 26.6) or choose to develop its own spread sheet to be used alongside its main program. The spread sheet can then be used as a general ledger and as an instrument campaign funds and assist in budget planning.

An important point to remember is: A software program, no matter how thorough the system may be, can never replace an accountant. J. Harry Feldman, Director of Client Relations for Software Services of Delaware, has warned: "Don't let the software company play accountant." Feldman advised: "Ensure your software program performs to its full capability, but as a "partner" with your accountant. This is the way to maximize your investment in a software program."

26.5 RECORD KEEPING

Interfacing both the donor profile screen and the fund accounting module will increase an organization's efficiency and productivity. Suppose "Mr. Robert Johnson" donates $1,000 to the Main Street Hospital. The user will type in the donor's name and, if Mr. Johnson has given in the past, his screen will appear. If he is a first-time donor, the user can then create a new file for Mr. Johnson. The user enters all data relevant to Mr. Johnson and enters the amount of the donation. The system enters the amount into both the donor file and the general ledger. The system could then interface with the word processing unit to prepare a personalized letter to the donor and print a receipt for $1,000. If a pledge was received, it can also be entered into the donor profile. The system will update the date and amount of the last payment, enter them in the file of the campaign that the donor has specified, and then calculate the current pledge balance. The chairperson or director of a specific campaign will be able to review specific pledges or the progress of the campaign as a whole, via the report generator. Reminder letters for outstanding pledges could then be sent out. The sort feature reviews pledges against payments and offers an option of including specific outstanding amounts (in dollars) in the letter if the organization or user wishes. Managing funds, creating budgets, and generating campaign reports are important management tools for nonprofit organizations.

26.6 REPORT GENERATORS/WORD PROCESSING

One of the most critical elements in the success of any nonprofit organization is its public image. How the community, foundations, and other nonprofit organizations and individuals perceive the professionalism of an organization and its projects can determine their future success. With the help of appropriate software, appeal and thank-you letters, receipts, foundation proposals, campaign reports, and many more documents can all be personalized. Additionally, they can be processed via the word processing module/report generator. Some software programs come with preprogrammed reports (Exhibit 26.7) to better enable an organization to communicate with the public (Exhibit 26.8). Most systems include a word processing module that allows an organization to develop its own letters and forms, receipts, and reports, and store them for future use. The word processing module can also be used to print mailing labels and membership cards. This module

Exhibit 26.5.   Internal reports interfacing with Lotus 1-2-3.

MICROPOLIS COMMUNITY CENTER
Annual Giving Analysis

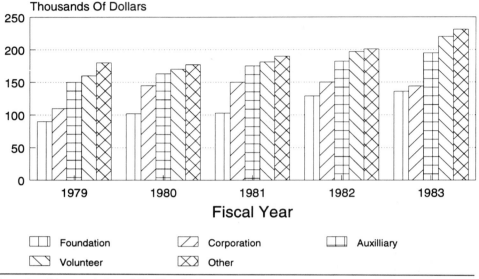

Reproduced by permission of Blackbaud Microsystems, Inc.

Exhibit 26.6.   Internal reports interfacing with Lotus 1-2-3.

MICROPOLIS COMMUNITY CENTER
H. F. Young Scholarship Fund

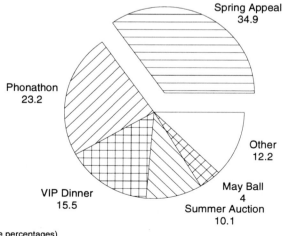

(Numbers shown are percentages)

Reproduced by permission of Blackbaud Microsystems, Inc.

Exhibit 26.7. Status report—Spring mail appeal.

```
05/05/90
                           Summary
                           Unaudited
           SM            SPRING MAIL APPEAL
                      Current Year    Last Year    2 Years Ago

Total Amount$          24075.00      37656.00      33547.00
Count                     335           674           450
Goal $                 40000.00      35000.00      23000.00
Number Prospects          600          1450          1600
Percent of $Goal          60.1         107.5         145.8
Response Rate             55.8          46.4          28.1
Average Pledge            71.86         55.86         74.54
New Gifts $            13517.00      23432.00
Renewed Gifts $        11358.00      13987.00

PRESS RETURN WHEN READY
```

Reproduced by permission of Target/1 Management Systems.

Exhibit 26.8. Foundation status report.

```
                                                     I.d.: 0000009660
   Foundation: The Acme Foundation
                         PROPOSAL TRACKING

   001 Symposium on Aids in Rural Areas      01/19/90   PENDING
   002 Foundation for a Future Campaign      02/14/86   REJECTED
   003 Library Expansion - Health References 10/02/88   FUNDED $250,000
   004 Medical School - Aids Research        07/13/87   FUNDED $58,000
   005 Management Courses for Non Profit Execs. 10/10/89  REJECTED
   006 Special Endowment Campaign            11/01/87   FUNDED $100,000

      (F7) = Add New Prop;    (Home) = View Again;    (Esc) = Exit
```

Reproduced by permission of Target/1 Management Systems.

can be very flexible in allowing the user to define such variables as label size and style and the selection of names to be printed. While interfacing with the accounting module, it can create graphs, project revenues for future years, and prepare a summary of any fund drive specified by the user. Properly used, this module will help project a positive public image for the nonprofit and will assist in its fund-raising efforts.

26.7   EVENT MANAGEMENT

The event management module is a unit that some packages offer as a part of the main software package; others offer it as an additional price. This module offers an organization important tools and the capability to manage a special event from start to finish alongside its donor profile screens, spread sheets, report screens, and form letters. Some systems can even disburse tickets, report event sales, and prepare seating charts. The module can export information to system spread sheets and can utilize the accounting function that may be required for dinner reservations and payments. It can send out confirmation notices and help staff prepare seating charts for all attendees. It can also prepare progress reports for the event committee. Properly used, this module can help make an event into the success its planners intended it to be.

26.8   EXTRAS

Some systems' little "extras" can be very helpful to an organization. However, improperly used, they can create distractions from the significant data or the information that is really needed.

(a) ALTERNATE ADDRESS SYSTEM   This system allows an option as to where the organization should send a donor's mail. Some donors will request that their mail be sent to their office; others want it sent to their home. Some alternate address systems allow the donor profile to handle home, office, and summer and winter residences, or they allow the user to override the system and authorize a specific mailing to the residence of the donor's choice. This feature can be helpful and an organization should decide if, how, and when it will take advantage of this extra."

(b) SPOUSE'S INTERESTS   Spouses often have chosen different careers, interests, and philanthropic affiliations than their mates. Some systems will reflect this separate path on the primary spouse's profile. Others will allow the user to utilize a "spouse cross reference" and create a separate profile linked to the primary file for the spouse.

(c) SECURITY   A security log-on found on some systems may often be bypassed. Log-on has many advantages. For example, if an organization has many people, volunteer and staff, using the main computer system, the leadership may not want un-authorized individuals to be privy to all donor information. This file could include such sensitive information as a donor's annual income or credit card numbers. The system might include a "lockout" feature, with the organization determining how much information each computer operator can use. Each operator's security code will send a signal to the system, specifying the fields of information to which the user should have access. This creates a challenge to determine who needs what information; however, it protects sensitive data or information. The organization, after weighing the pros and cons according to it's needs as a whole, and will need to determine what is best.

26.9 LOCAL AREA NETWORKS

Each computer work station need not stand alone; several can be connected to form a local area network (LAN). Networks have become more popular as organizations have realized their advantages. Local area networking is on the increase as a way to link several work stations. Many nonprofits can become more productive by using LANs, which offer the advantage that all the work stations on the LAN can share financial and other data, all with only the touch of a few buttons. According to J. Harry Feldman, by setting up a LAN, "you allow the director to check the giving history of a specific donor from his or her office." Several employees in the organization can enter data simultaneously. Cost-conscious nonprofits can purchase a quality laser printer and allow several users in one office to share the same printer, thereby eliminating the need for a laser printer for each work station. LANS can also allow messages to be sent and received at each person's individual work station, eliminating phone message slips or interoffice memos, which can be messy and can be easily lost. Many programs today allow themselves to becomes part of a stand-alone system, or to be eventually used within a LAN. Organizations planning to expand should investigate the advantages of a local area network and determine how it can be used to their benefit.

26.10 SERVICE AGREEMENT

When purchasing a system, a nonprofit organization faces a major investment in software, hardware, and the initial conversion and setup of the system. Another expense is involved in maintaining the system—keeping it "up" and in continuous running order. A service agreement can be the key to maximizing the system's capability and keeping it running productively.

One of the most important aspects of evaluating a software "package" is the review of the sale and service agreement. Although each contact and purchase agreement will differ, there are several important points to review before the purchase of any software package. A thorough review of the contract can help maximize the investment (gain an understanding of exactly what services the software company offers and under what conditions) and avoid future misunderstandings.

(a) INSTALLATION Many companies will come on-site to set up hardware, get the system running, and assist in transferring current records onto the system. An organization may be charged per day (for the on-site consultant) or given a flat rate for the system's setup.

(b) TRAINING Training sessions might be held either on-site or at the headquarters of the software vendor. Even if it is a bit more expensive, bringing a consultant on-site to tutor staff in the use of the program may be well worth the price. The consultant could review current operating procedures and offer suggestions as to how to incorporate them with the new system.

(c) UPGRADES   When purchasing a software package, an organization should not assume the package will get better with time. However, upgrades can enhance the system by offering additional tracking methods or fund reports not found in earlier versions. Some companies offer program upgrades and enhancements for a limited time after purchase; others charge a modest price for future upgrades. Systems often have new modules added after a request or suggestion has been received by users of the system. An enhancement passed on in an upgraded version of the system could be of use to the organization as well. A new owner should ask when the last release was and what it included. A company that has in the past offered upgrades may prove to be a company that is growing and developing better software.

26.11   CHOOSING A SYSTEM

Selecting a system can be an exciting step for any organization. This section details some areas that an organization will wish to explore before it selects a system. Time spent in researching a system that will best fit an organization's needs will be paid back in the future satisfaction with the system chosen.

It may be argued that a computer is only as smart as those operating it, but a well-run computer can be a considerable asset to any nonprofit organization. President John F. Kennedy, when presenting Astronaut Gordon Cooper with a distinguished service medal on May 21, 1963, remarked that "however extraordinary computers may be . . . man is still the most extraordinary computer of all." Success doesn't necessarily depend on the past experience the user has had with data processing or with programming; real success goes much further. The ingenuity and creativity of a user can help maximize the organization's investment and revenue base. For example, finding new ways to create different sorts and thereby target new constituents could help maximize both the investment in the software package and the response from donors.

A key to developing a successful organization's software program is employee retention. Losing an employee who has been trained on a specific software program can be devastating to a small organization. Just as backing up important data is always a priority, backup (alternate) trained users of the system are of major importance in any organization. In addition, the director of the nonprofit, or a designated individual, should fully understand the entire system. That person should inquire periodically about upgrades to the program and modifications in the system, in order to maximize use of the software. Although the "human element" in computer systems may seem small, it is a key to success in any organization's efforts to obtain maximum benefit from computer-related technology.

Information on companies offering computer packages for nonprofit organizations can be found in nonprofit newspapers, newsletters, and other periodicals (see section 26.14).

Any new purchaser should talk to colleagues in the nonprofit sector, especially at organizations that are close in size and have similar operating procedures. What systems do they use? What other systems have they had experience with, and what were their impressions, positive and negative? Current and former users of software could be the best advisers an organization could get. They can assist in choosing a package; they know which features are used and which features only add confusion and take up space.

Most software companies furnish a list of past customers. This list offers the advantage of benefiting from the experience of other users by *seeing the system in action!* These customers may be biased in favor of their package, but they could provide important insights if asked about the system. If a new purchaser proceeds objectively, these interviews can save time and money in the future.

Within a specific package, a user may encounter fancy graphics describing its use. It may also "welcome you" each time to a specific spot in the program with colors, diagrams, and more dazzle. The graphics on any system can be exciting and some users may be impressed with the dazzle of the software. However, the dazzle will wear off; the criterion for purchase is whether the system can be used productively in day-to-day operations.

An organization that has existing hardware (e.g. a computer, printer, disk drives) should find out how (and whether) it can be used with the new system. Will a high-quality printer be needed because of an increased capability (e.g., the computer will now be doing a mailing) and expanded functions. A printer that can handle a mailing of several hundred pieces and produce high-quality, professional-looking letters may now be needed.

Does the new package interface (with existing software packages) or have its own report generator, financial spread sheet, or word processor? Will the organization be able to operate all data processing functions under one system?

What is the general reputation of the company for product quality and service? Note: This may be difficult to project out 5 years, but a basic survey could save grief in the future.

Is on-site training available and at what price? An on-site training session can get the system up and running in a short time.

Many companies will do an initial conversion of all relevant data the organization currently has on software or on hard copy (e.g., paper, index cards). This can be a time-saving feature for any nonprofit.

How clear is the instruction manual? If it is written in computer jargon, can it be understood by the people in the organization who will be using the system? Do the prospective users concur in their assessment of the system?

Does the system meet the organization's requirements? Will it be needed to generate special reports or a report or record that is unique to the organization? Would a single-user or multi-user version be better? The organization may grow and will need a package that "grows" concurrently. Right now, a single-user version may be adequate. Is a multiuser or a local area network version available, and what would be involved in switching over?

What technical telephone assistance is available? Is it included in the price and how long will it be available to the staff? If there is a charge, how does the pricing work? Some companies charge per call, others charge a flat rate for 6 months or a year. Will an operator on a hotline give assistance or will someone call back later? An on-line operator could save valuable time and get a system up and running in less times.

Does the seller offer free upgrades? If not, what upgrades are available and at what prices? If a company has a history of offering upgrades, that company is interested in growing and developing better software. Updated versions may have more capabilities, but too many multiple releases may indicate repetitive problems with the software.

Switching from one system to another several years down the road can be costly in money, time, and retraining. The expense of re-entering data could also be substantial. An organization's requirements should be carefully analyzed before choosing any system. Those involved should look for a system that will increase revenue base as well as productivity. The time and energy spent in selecting a system will pay off handsomely in the future.

26.12   COMPUTERS AND BUDGETS

It may be obvious at the onset, or there may be a slow dawning; but the realization will be the same: Computer equipment and software are not cheap. Budgets may cause a well-meaning computerization program to be restrained or may even cause it to grind to a halt; yet, the project cannot merit a special fund-raising drive, for fear of interfering with ongoing programs.

Outside special-purpose funding should be considered. The *Directory of Computer and High Technology Grants* may be helpful in locating these funds. The *Directory,* which details foundation and corporate grants available for computers, software, and related technology, can be purchased from Research Grant Guides, P.O. Box 1214, Loxahatchee, FL 33470.

26.13   CONCLUSION

No one program is right for all situations, and there is no "best" program. Choice of the program will depend on the organization's specific requirements. Software programs can be as simple as a dBase program tailored to a nonprofit organization or a sophisticated program that handles donor profiles, fund accounting, word processing, specialized fund drives, and memorial funds. One such user ran a program on Blackbaud's Raiser's Edge. Tracey Becken, Director of Operations of Dartmouth-Hitchcock Medical Center, Hanover, New Hampshire, noted: "We were able to run the gift accounting, prospect tracking and report generation for a $55 million capital campaign, two $1 million annual funds, a $25 million major gifts initiative and over 300 memorial funds, all under one system." It not only increased overall efficiency, she pointed out, "but it brought together the many functions we encounter daily all under one roof." An organization needs to analyze and evaluate what its needs are and which software program will best meet them. Regardless of the system ultimately chosen, it is quite likely that the organization will be able to improve fund-raising results as well as overall operating efficiency.

26.14   PRODUCT LISTING

As an organization compiles its own list of software vendors, it may want to consult current professional nonprofit periodicals. These magazines often have listings and/or advertisements of current software vendors who cater to the nonprofit sector. One such magazine is *Fundraising Management,* published by Hoke Communications. A yearly nonprofit software directory that includes a listing of many software vendors is also available and can be of use in selecting potential vendors. These publications are available from Hoke Communications, Inc., 224 Seventh Street, Garden City, NY 11530; (516) 746-6700.

Following is a partial list of nonprofit software manufacturers and dealers. New products come on the market from time to time. This list includes manufacturers and dealers that have come to the author's attention as of mid-1992.

Acorn Data Systems, Inc.
529 South Second Avenue
Covina, CA 91723
(818) 967-0691

Autocomp Systems Corp.
21 Blauvelt Road
Monsey, NY 10952
(800) 727-4847

Blackbaud Microsystems
900 Johnnie Dodds Boulevard
Mount Pleasant, SC 29462
(803) 881-4700

Campagne Associates, Ltd.
491 Amherst Street
Nashua, NH 03063
(603) 595-8774

CM Systems
1904 East Meadowmere
Springfield, MO 65804
(417) 862-6500

Datafund Systems, Inc.
9348 Civic Center Drive
Suite 101
Beverly Hills, CA 90210
(213) 273-9689

Dynamic Programming, Inc.
650 South Shackleford Road
Suite 400
Little Rock, Arkansas 72211
(501) 224-9111

Echo Consulting Services, Inc.
P.O. Box 540
Main Street
Center Conway, New Hampshire 03813
(800) 635-8209

Executive Data Systems
1845 The Exchange
Suite 140
Atlanta, GA 30339
(800) 272-3374

Fundraising Toolbox
2221 East Lamar Boulevard
Suite 360
Arlington, TX 76006
(800) 458-4392

Fundware Systems, Ltd.
3114 Thompson Avenue
Des Moines, IA 50317
(515) 263-0817

GT National Computer Software
400 Center Street
P.O. Box 3008
Auburn, ME 04210
(207) 786-0195

Heritage Computer Systems, Inc.
4020 North 20th Street
Suite 101
P.O. Box 10779
Phoenix, AZ 85016
(800) 752-3100

Impact Systems, Inc.
21 Ray Avenue
Burlington, MA 01803
(617) 270-0099

Institutional Data Systems, Inc.
2 Hamilton Avenue
New Rochelle, NY 10801
(800) 322-4371

John Snow, Inc.
210 Lincoln Street
Boston, MA 02111
(800) 521-0132

Master Software
8604 Allisonville Road
Suite 309
Indianapolis, IN 46250
(317) 842-7020

Master Systems
1249 Pinole Valley Road
Pinole, CA 94564
(800) 827-7214

Metafile Information Systems, Inc.
421 First Avenue SW
Rochester, MN 55902
(800) 222-4096

Softrek
3729 Union Road
Buffalo, NY 14225
(800) 442-9211

Software Co-op, Inc.
1284 North Broad Street
Hillside, NJ 07205
(908) 355-7700

Software Services of Delaware
91 Lukens Drive
Suite D
New Castle, DE 19720
(302) 652-3370

Systems Support Services
8731 Red Oak Boulevard
Suite 140
Charlotte, NC 28217
(800) 548-6708

Zoller Data System
7525 Jefferson Highway
Baton Rouge, LA 70806
(504) 928-7169

SOURCES AND SUGGESTED REFERENCES

Bronson, Denise E., Pelz, Donald C., and Trzcinski, Eileen. 1988. *Computerizing Your Agency's Information System.* Newbury Park, CA: Sage.

MS-DOS Quick Start. 1990. Carmel, IN: QUE Corporation.

Muehrcke, Jill. 1991. *Computer and Information Systems, Leadership Series.* Madison, WI: The Society for Nonprofit Organizations.

Norton, Peter. 1992. *Inside the IBM PC and PS/2* (4th ed.). Carmel, IN: Brady Publishing.

Schildt, Herbert. 1987. *DOS Made Easy.* New York: Osborne/McGraw-Hill.

Sheldon, Tom. 1990. *Novel Netware: The Complete Reference.* New York: Osborne/McGraw-Hill.

Stephenson, Peter. 1992. *Introduction to Personal Computers STG.* New York: John Wiley & Sons.

Turley, James L. 1989. *PC's Made Easy.* New York: Osborne/McGraw-Hill.

PART FIVE

Marketing and Communications

Marketing

Eugene M. Johnson
University of Rhode Island

CONTENTS

There are no magic formulas for successful marketing. The principles and concepts presented in this chapter, however, will help nonprofit directors and managers plan, organize, and control their marketing activities. The key step for nonprofits are: to recognize the importance of marketing and to develop a marketing plan. Having a plan will help everyone within the organization focus on what is most important—identifying the needs of clients and supporters and determining the best ways to meet those needs.

27.1 INTRODUCTION

(a) MARKETING AFFECTS EVERYONE Marketing is an exciting, dynamic discipline that affects everyone's life in many ways. Everyone is a consumer, and many people are part of the marketing process, as salespeople, advertising executives, product managers, wholesalers, retailers, and so forth.

For most of its history, marketing has been viewed as strictly a for-profit business function. This is no longer true. Marketing has become a significant activity for nonprofit organizations with important contributions to make to overall quality improvement. Consider the following:

- A large midwestern hospital conducts inpatient surveys to determine the level of patient satisfaction and to identify suggestions for improved service.
- An art museum uses an "art-mobile" to bring famous works of art to a city's neighborhoods.
- A Roman Catholic religious order employs a national advertising campaign to recruit candidates for the priesthood.

- A public television station features a "900" number during program breaks to request contributions.

These are just a few examples of the many nonprofit organizations that have successfully applied marketing techniques during the past few years. The application of marketing research tools, advertising, personal selling skills, and the like has changed the way many nonprofit organizations operate.

(b) MARKETING INVOLVES EXCHANGE Most definitions of marketing refer to marketing as an exchange process. From a business standpoint, this process involves at least two parties—buyer and seller. Each party gives up something of value and receives something of value.

Because marketing activities bring about exchanges, marketing is an essential function in an economic system, especially a capitalistic system. In a free-enterprise system, resources are allocated by the interaction of supply and demand in the marketplace. Marketing activities and institutions provide the framework and mechanisms for this interaction and for the exchange that is taking place.

Although business aspects of marketing are very important, business-oriented definitions of marketing have been found lacking in recent years. Critics observe that marketing involves a wide range of activities and organizations and should be viewed from a broader perspective. They point out that marketing takes place in many nonprofit organizations, such as hospitals, universities, and social and government agencies. These new applications of marketing are further evidence of its growing importance in our society. Any definition must recognize that marketing is a fundamental human activity and that marketing decisions affect everyone's welfare.

The definition of the American Marketing Association provides a description of marketing in its broader context:

> Marketing is the process of planning and executing the conception, pricing, promotion, and distribution of ideas, goods, and services to create exchanges that satisfy individual and organizational goals.

While it includes exchange as a key part, this definition expands the marketing process to include all types of organizations. This has been termed the "broadened" or "generic" view of marketing. The importance and application of marketing to nonprofit organizations and problems are recognized. As in business, a carefully planned, coordinated marketing program can help a nonprofit organization reach its goals, whether they are to attract more members, to increase donations, or to provide better client service.

27.2 BROADENING THE SCOPE OF MARKETING

(a) EARLY VIEWS OF MARKETING The earliest forms of marketing started in primitive economic systems. Specialization and division of labor allowed early economies to achieve a production surplus. This necessitated an exchange process. For example, one person's surplus of farm produce might be traded for another's surplus of clothing items. This process of a face-to-face exchange of goods and services is known as bartering. It still characterizes some types of transactions.

The development of monetary systems permitted the emergence of selling, by which goods and services were exchanged for some form of currency. Later, selling on credit further expanded the selling process. For most of history, selling has dominated marketing thought. From the first widespread use of money to the advent of the marketing concept following World War II—a span of several thousands of years—selling was the basic thrust of marketing thought and activity.

Marketing as we know it today began to emerge when marketing support activities were recognized. Staff activities such as advertising, marketing research, and product management were acknowledged to be important segments of the total marketing program. The marketing concept's emphasis on *customer satisfaction* as the organization's prime objective signalled the acceptance of marketing as a major function within a business enterprise. The marketing concept was widely accepted by industry, and customer orientation became the basic premise for most business philosophies.

(b) MARKETING THOUGHT TODAY Concern for customer satisfaction will certainly remain a critical ingredient of sales and marketing thought. However, since widespread adoption of the marketing concept, several proposals have been suggested that advance or extend the concept of marketing beyond the traditional limits of a business organization. These and earlier changes in sales and marketing are shown in Exhibit 27.1.

(i) Broadening concept This view sees marketing as a pervasive societal activity that goes well beyond the selling of toothpaste, soap, or steel. First proposed by Kotler and Levy (1979), the broadening concept views marketing as being an important activity of nonbusiness, as well as business, organizations. The ideas, philosophies, and concepts espoused by museums, government agencies, labor unions, colleges and universities, hospitals, charitable organizations, and other nonprofit entities can also be marketed. In

Exhibit 27.1.　Advancement of marketing thought.

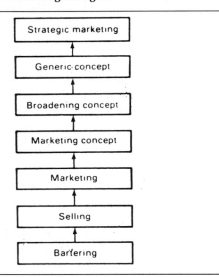

Source: Eugene M. Johnson, David L. Kurtz, and Eberhard E. Scheuing, *Sales Management* (New York: McGraw-Hill, 1986), p. 518.

fact, it has been argued that many worthwhile social projects have failed simply because they were not marketed effectively.

Although some have disagreed with this contention, the broadening concept has been generally accepted by marketing scholars and practitioners. Marketing will continue to play an increasingly larger role in the administration and operation of non-business enterprises.

(ii) Generic concept   The broadening concept of marketing has been taken even further to include *any* transaction between an organization and its publics. The generic concept of marketing proposes that marketing applies to any social unit that seeks to exchange values with other social units. Products include organizations, persons, places, and ideas, in addition to goods and services. These products are marketed by a wide variety of business, political, social, religious, cultural, and knowledge organizations. Thus, all marketers face the same tasks in all forms of marketing.

A further aspect of generic marketing is the concept of social marketing, which is described as the use of marketing principles and techniques to advance a social cause, idea, or pattern of behavior. Also suggested by this approach to marketing are ethical and social concerns related to marketing practices. This means that both business and nonprofit organizations may be marketing the same cause or social issue. For instance, Anheuser-Busch, Miller Brewing Company, Seagram's, and other firms have begun to point out the dangers of underage drinking and of drinking and driving, in their promotional efforts. At the same time, the primary mission of MADD (Mothers Against Drunk Driving) is to prevent drinking and driving.

As marketing thought has changed to include nonprofit organizations and social concerns, the need for marketing in nonprofit organizations has become very clear. A recent article (Schwartz, 1989) in *Marketing News,* the news magazine of the American Marketing Association, put it this way:

> High ideals, mission statements, and dedicated volunteers may not be enough for non-profit organizations in the 1990s.
>
> Faced with pursuing lofty goals and paying the rent in a crowded world of service, charitable, and educational groups, competing for the same dollars, many nonprofit organizations— without marketing plans—soon may be taking unwelcome baths in vats of red ink.

(iii) Strategic marketing   In recent years, the focus of business management has shifted to strategic planning. Limited resources, changes in world markets, intense competitive pressures, and other forces have caused senior management to reexamine the role of marketing. Nonprofit managers have also turned to strategic planning, in their effort to adapt to rapidly changing conditions (Laycock, 1990).

Although some executives and scholars have questioned the validity of a marketing orientation, it has been suggested that the shift to strategic planning presents an opportunity for marketing to assert is traditional influence. This thrust, which has been termed strategic marketing, has been described by Day and Wensley (1983):

> The strategic decision process requires a dialogue between the corporate and business unit levels to develop individual strategies based on the specifics of market segments and competitive positions. Such a dialogue can only be effective if marketing management reasserts its role in providing strategic direction at the product-market level.

(c) IMPLICATIONS FOR NONPROFIT ORGANIZATIONS The changes in marketing thought emphasize that marketing is applicable to all forms of nonprofit organizations. Effective marketing does not just happen, however; there are no magical formulas or secrets to marketing. Nor will nonprofit managers be able to adapt business marketing concepts and practices to their organizations without some difficulty. Like all management activities, marketing must be planned, organized, and controlled. Further, because marketing is new to most nonprofit organizations, it is even more critical that a carefully thought-out, customer-focused marketing strategy be developed and carried out (Miaoulis, 1985).

27.3 MARKETING CONCEPT

(a) ORGANIZATIONAL PHILOSOPHY Most businesses—and some organizations—have adopted what has become known as the marketing concept. This philosophy, or conceptual framework, has given marketing a much more important role in all forms of organizations, for-profit and nonprofit alike.

Kotler and Andreasen (1991) call this the "marketing mindset." They point out that a nonprofit organization's directors and managers must have a clear appreciation of what marketing is and what it can do for the organization. Most importantly, they must put the customer, or client, at the center of everything the organization does.

(b) MAJOR PROPOSITIONS As applied to a nonprofit organization, the marketing concept is based on three major propositions: client orientation, coordination of all client-related activities, and goal direction.

(i) Client orientation As noted above, this is the key to the marketing concept. Nonprofit managers must shift from an internal organizational perspective to the client's viewpoint. Successful marketing in a nonprofit organization requires a complete understanding of an organization's clients—their needs, attitudes, and buying behavior. For instance, a community agency that provides services to the elderly must know exactly what the needs of the elderly in its community are and must develop programs that meet these needs. *A nonprofit organization must never forget that it exists to serve the needs of its clients.*

When a nonprofit organization does not understand or heed the needs of its clients, marketing can be a dismal failure. The U.S. Treasury Department's introduction of the Susan B. Anthony dollar clearly made this point. Despite research studies that suggested little enthusiasm for a small dollar among bankers and business executives and likely rejection by consumers, Treasury Department officials went ahead with their plan to introduce the Anthony dollar. Almost a million dollars was spent to promote and publicize the new dollar, but consumers rejected it. Why? The major reason was that the Anthony dollar was designed poorly and did not meet the needs of businesses and consumers. It was too similar to a quarter in size and appearance. The Treasury Department's promotion effort could not overcome the product's design weakness.

(ii) Coordination For marketing to be effective in a nonprofit organization, there must be coordination of all elements of the marketing program. Because these elements, known as the "marketing mix," constitute an interrelated system, the program must be viewed and planned as a whole. Marketing itself must be closely interrelated with other activities of a nonprofit organization.

To achieve the desired coordination, there must be close cooperation among all components of an organization. For instance, if the executive director of a health care agency commits the agency to participate in a community health education program, the director must be sure that the agency's education committee supports this activity and that the agency has the resources available to participate.

(iii) Goal direction The marketing concept stresses that *the only way an organization can achieve its own goals is by satisfying the needs of its clients (customers)*. For example, a college wishing to increase the level of funding provided by the business community must demonstrate to business executives that it is meeting the business education needs of the community. This may require the development of special educational programs and activities for local businesses and their employees.

(c) IMPLEMENTING THE MARKETING CONCEPT Nonprofit directors and managers must shift their focus from an internal organizational perspective to the clients' viewpoint. Exhibit 27.2 suggests how some nonprofit organizations have redefined their orientation to reflect the clients' viewpoint.

A marketing success story illustrates how a coordinated marketing plan based on meeting clearly understood needs will work. Several years ago, the Dallas Museum of Fine Arts was faced with an urgent need to develop an effective marketing program after its goal of expansion was thwarted. The defeat of a bond referendum for a new museum forced the Dallas Museum's administrators to redefine the museum's goals and its relation to the public. They decided to emphasize that "a great city deserves a great art museum." Through a carefully planned marketing program, they informed the people of Dallas that an art museum is more than a place to store art treasures. They stressed the educational values and the economic benefits from tourists attracted by exhibits and special shows. They developed a model showing the key features, and the corresponding benefits for the public, of the proposed building. Museum officials used this model when they met with public groups. These marketing efforts succeeded, and the second bond referendum passed.

(d) INVOLVING THE SALES AND MARKETING PEOPLE To develop and implement the required marketing orientation, nonprofit organizations must include sales and marketing managers on their boards and on appropriate committees and teams. According

Exhibit 27.2. Organizational versus marketing orientation.

Nonprofit Organization	Organizational Orientation	Marketing Orientation
Urban transit authority	We run a bus system.	We provide transportation services.
Art museum	We display art objects.	We offer artistic experiences.
Child-care center	We take care of children.	We provide security for children and their parents.
Community theater	We put on plays.	We offer entertainment.
Family planning center	We give family-planning information.	We offer solutions to family-planning problems.

to Fram (1991), board members with sales and marketing backgrounds will help non-profit organizations view their operations from their customers' viewpoint. They will also help to identify changes in the market for an organization's services, to assess how well an organization is meeting the needs of its clients, and to develop a strategic plan to meet future needs.

Recruiting sales and marketing people for nonprofit boards is not easy. They travel frequently, and board membership may not fit their career needs and life-styles. Aggressive recruiting efforts and strong network building will be required to attract people who have the desired sales and marketing expertise.

27.4 UNIQUE ASPECTS OF NONPROFIT MARKETING

(a) **MULTIPLE PUBLICS** The marketing efforts of business organizations are concentrated on the firm's customers. This is not the case with nonprofit organizations, which must market to multiple publics. As defined by Kotler and Andreasen (1991), a public is "a distinct group of people, organizations or both whose actual or potential needs must in some sense be served." Four types of publics are identified for nonprofit organizations by Kotler and Andreasen:

- Input publics (e.g., donors and suppliers) provide resources;
- Internal publics (e.g., staff and volunteers) convert resources into useful goods and services;
- Intermediary publics (e.g., agents and facilitators) deliver goods and services;
- Consuming publics (e.g., clients and local residents) gain satisfaction from the goods and services provided.

From a marketing standpoint, the key publics are supporters and clients. Supporters (donors and volunteers) provide the key resources to a nonprofit organization, through either their monetary contributions or their time and personal expertise. Clients, who are the primary customers of a nonprofit organization, benefit from its services.

In addition to clients and supporters, a specific nonprofit organization's publics will include many other types of people and groups. A brief review of the important publics of a community hospital illustrates this fast. Its publics include:

- Patients and their families and friends;
- Members of the community who aid the hospital through donations, volunteer services, and other forms of support;
- Suppliers of goods and services;
- Doctors, nurses, administrators, and other employees;
- Trustees of the hospital;
- Regulatory agencies;
- The general public.

Because members of each of these publics have different needs and attitudes, marketing concepts must be applied differently.

(b) MULTIPLE OBJECTIVES Business firms have long-run profitability as their over-riding objective. Because they must serve multiple publics, nonprofit organizations have multiple objectives. Sometimes, these objectives may not be consistent with one another. For instance, a community center may wish to provide free family-planning counseling to its clients, but it is limited because a major portion of its funding comes from donors who are opposed to certain forms of birth control.

For many nonprofit organizations, the process of formulating objectives involves compromise and consensus building. This makes marketing more difficult than in business because more time must be spent in involving board members, staff, and volunteers, and convincing them to accept the objectives.

(c) PRODUCTS ARE SERVICES The products of most nonprofit organizations are services, not tangible goods. A service is an activity performed for another person or organization. Johnson, Scheuing, and Gaida (1986) have identified several characteristics that set services apart from goods and make their marketing more challenging.

(i) Intangibility Services go out of existence at the very moment they are rendered (e.g., counseling session), although their effects may last for some time. Because of the lack of tangibility, marketers of services find it quite difficult to differentiate their offerings. Their clients see intangible services as abstract and thus difficult to describe and understand.

(ii) Perishability Services cannot be stored; they have to be produced on demand. Marketers of services, unlike goods marketers, are unable to manufacture for inventory during slow times and draw on inventory during periods of peak demand. Excess capacity not used in services production is lost forever—for example, empty beds in a hospital or vacant seats in a classroom.

(iii) Simultaneity Services are produced and consumed at the same time, in contrast to goods, which are generally produced, then purchased, and then consumed. As a result, a service performer and service buyer usually have to interact and, accordingly, be in the same place at the same time.

(iv) Heterogeneity The quality of service performance varies from one service organization to another, from one service performer to another, and from one occasion to another. This variability of service output makes it difficult for a nonprofit service organization to establish and maintain performance standards and thus guarantee quality continuously.

(d) PUBLIC SCRUTINY Many nonprofit organizations provide vital services for society. Because of this, they are often subsidized by government and are given tax-exempt status by government. Their activities are closely watched by government officials, news media, and the general public.

One particular concern is public criticism of the administrative and marketing costs incurred to raise funds. For instance, a newspaper article reported that a charitable organization raised $9 million in 1988 and 1989. After deducting marketing and administrative expenses, about $650,000—less than 8 cents of every dollar raised—was left to assist the needy.

From a marketing perspective, this type of media coverage is harmful to all nonprofit organizations that rely on contributions for a portion of their funding. The negative publicity and possible government intervention related to this situation increase the public pressure on nonprofit organizations. Accordingly, they must be very careful to conduct their affairs in a way that does not result in public displeasure.

27.5 MARKETS AND BUYER BEHAVIOR

(a) DEFINING A MARKET Marketers view the term "market' in a very specific way. To them, a market is a group of people or organizations who have a common need or share a common problem. Their common need or problem requires them to seek a product or service to satisfy their need or to resolve their problem.

In some cases, almost everyone is part of the market for a particular nonprofit organization. For example, there are very few people who have not been affected in some way by the dreaded impact of cancer. As a result, the American Cancer Society finds widespread interest in its activities and programs. In contrast, the market for a local church is limited to the people in a community who have similar religious beliefs.

(b) BUYER BEHAVIOR Human behavior, especially buyer behavior, and its causes are complex. In attempting to understand and predict buyer behavior, marketers have turned to the behavioral sciences: psychology, sociology, social psychology, and anthropology. Behavioral concepts can help a nonprofit manager understand the "whys" and "hows" of behavior.

For most people, the buying process involves a series of steps, as shown in Exhibit 27.3. The starting point is *need recognition,* which may result from internal or external stimuli. For instance, a mother notices that her teenage daughter is showing signs of behavioral difficulties that may be caused by drug abuse.

After recognizing the need, a buyer begins a *search for purchase alternatives.* This step usually involves a search for information about various ways to satisfy the need. The mother may talk to the high school guidance counselor, a priest, a social worker, and others, to find out more about her daughter's problem. She may also read books, pamphlets, and other published information on teenage drug problems.

Nonprofit organizations may be called on to play an important role in these first two steps of the buying process. They can assist people like this mother in recognizing a problem and identifying alternatives. In fact, the dissemination of information about social issues and problems is one of the major marketing tasks of many nonprofit organizations.

Exhibit 27.3. Buying process model.

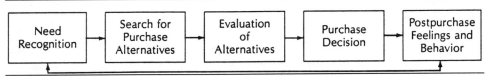

Source: Eugene M. Johnson, *Fundamentals of Marketing from Product to Profit* (Boston: American Management Association, 1990), p. 21.

Evaluation of alternatives comes next. Again, a nonprofit organization can assist the buyer. Advice on treatment options, costs, and other relevant concerns will be important to the mother. Her actual choice may involve comparing several options; for instance, a community-funded drug abuse center, a church-affiliated drug counseling program, or a health care facility.

An important *purchase decision* like the one this mother must make will require careful deliberation. Even after making the decision, she will have doubts. The final step in the buying process involves *postpurchase feelings and behavior.* Postpurchase doubt, which has been called purchase dissonance, is not unusual. It is important, therefore, for marketers to follow up important purchase decisions in a supportive manner. The model of the buying process also shows how feedback from the decision will affect future buying decisions.

This aspect of buying behavior is especially important to nonprofit organizations. Contributions must be acknowledged promptly, and donors must receive feedback about how their money is used. Nonprofit organizations must also use surveys and other forms of communication to obtain feedback from their clients. They cannot neglect the postpurchase feelings and behavior of their donors and clients.

(c) NEEDS AND MOTIVES People act in response to a need or a combination of needs. Behavioral scientists suggest that buyer behavior is multimotivated; a decision to buy is normally the result of a number of different needs or motives, not merely one. What the nonprofit marketer must determine is the priority donors and clients give to their various, sometimes conflicting needs.

Guy and Patton (1988) have studied donor behavior from the perspective of buying motivation and behavior. They concluded that the strongest motivating force for giving to a nonprofit organization is the "very basic, deep-seated need to help others." Their study also assessed the behavioral process that results in a decision to make a contribution. Nonprofit marketers must make sure that potential donors are aware that a need exists, that they have a personal responsibility to help, and that their contribution can help others in need.

(d) GROUP INFLUENCES ON BEHAVIOR Buyers do not live in isolation. As social beings, they belong to various groups or social units. These groups may play a significant role in influencing buyer behavior. The various groups include members of a person's social class, peers, family, friends, business associates, members of social clubs, and so forth. How closely a person identifies with a group determines the influence of that group on the person's behavior.

Nonprofit organizations themselves are groups and, therefore, are a factor in determining buyer behavior. People will be influenced to join a nonprofit organization, contribute money, or volunteer their time based on the organization's current membership. They will become clients of the organization if they feel that it reflects their social values. For example, an urban church that wants to increase participation by teenagers in its recreational activities will improve its chance for success if it attracts peer group leaders as participants.

Some nonprofit organizations use famous people to influence buyer behavior. Because they are well-known and serve as role models, professional athletes, motion picture and television performers, and other celebrities will influence the behavior of young people and other consumers. Featuring Chicago Bulls' basketball star Michael Jordan in a TV advertisement to prevent alcohol abuse by teenagers has more impact because he is recognized and admired by teenage viewers.

(e) MARKET SEGMENTATION   In recent years, marketing theorists and practitioners have learned much about buyers' behavior. This new knowledge has led to the emergence of market segmentation as a significant marketing planning and management tool. Market segmentation is the process of dividing a market into separate subsets, or segments, of buyers. The organization can concentrate its marketing efforts on a distinct subset of the market, or it can develop different marketing strategies for each market segment. For instance:

- A college offers classes during the day for its full-time students and at night for its part-time students who work during the day.
- A hospital offers outpatient surgery options for minor operations and traditional inpatient surgery for more serious conditions.
- A nonprofit theater offers matinee performances for senior citizens and school children and evening performances for working people.
- A library provides large-print books for the visually impaired and Saturday morning reading sessions for preschool children.

The most frequently used bases for segmenting consumer markets are demographic, geographic, behavioral, and purchase volume characteristics.

(i) Demographic   A market is subdivided on the basis of age, gender, occupation, income, education, marital status, and other demographic variables. For example, a health-care agency might want to concentrate on services for the elderly.

(ii) Geographic   A market is subdivided into different locations, such as states, counties, urban versus rural areas, and so on. For instance, public libraries in rural areas must often use bookmobiles to take books to their distant clients; urban libraries are more accessible to their clients, who may be within walking distance of a branch.

(iii) Behavioral   A market is subdivided on the basis of life-style, personality, social class, attitudes, and other behavioral characteristics. Organizations that build housing complexes for the elderly use behavioral characteristics to segment the housing market and develop appropriate facilities. Social service agencies that cater to single parents use life-style characteristics to reach those in need of their services.

(iv) Volume   A market is subdivided on the basis of usage. Heavy, medium, and light users are studied, to determine whether they have similar demographic or behavioral characteristics. For example, it has been shown that certain segments of the population are most likely to abuse alcohol and other drugs and are therefore the prime target market for rehabilitation programs.

(f) BUSINESS MARKETS   Many nonprofit organizations seek support from businesses, and some may offer services in cooperation with businesses. For example, many large companies have charitable foundations that provide funds for the arts, education, health care, and other types of nonprofit programs. Usually, the support of businesses is driven by the interests of management and the goals of the business. Thus, nonprofit managers and directors must understand how businesses function and make resource allocation decisions.

Business managers are professional decision makers. They are trained to make deliberate, informed decisions. They will give careful consideration to objective factors when deciding whether to support a nonprofit organization. Of particular concern is whether the nonprofit organization's mission and activities are compatible with the mission and goals of the business. Business managers tend to support causes that fit their company's image and are not controversial.

In the past few years, American Express, Kimberly-Clark, Johnson & Johnson, and many other firms have turned to cause-related marketing as a promotion approach that provides funding for nonprofit organizations (Williams, 1986; Kelly 1991). Perhaps the best known is the widely publicized Statue of Liberty restoration effort by American Express.

Corporate sponsorship of a fund-raising event can be good for business and for a nonprofit organization. The charity receives a fixed amount of money for the use of its name during the promotion, a fee for coupons redeemed by consumers, or a percentage of the sales of the product or service promoted. The Children's Miracle Network, American Heart Association, and Shelter-Aid are causes that have benefited from corporate marketing programs.

Another aspect of business markets that may offer marketing opportunities for nonprofit organizations is the needs of employees. For instance, many businesses are beginning to recognize the growing need for safe, affordable child-care centers at business locations. Other business needs include alcohol and drug abuse counseling, advice, on caring for the elderly parents of employees, and continuing education. Each of these needs represents a potential market for nonprofits with experience in these areas.

27.6 INFORMATION FOR MARKETING

(a) MARKETING INTELLIGENCE Marketing intelligence is a broad term used to describe the information-gathering function of marketing. This function may involve informal information gathering, such as conversations with clients in waiting rooms or discussions between nonprofit managers at seminars and conferences. Most often, however, marketing intelligence refers to formal, organized information-gathering activities and subsequent analysis.

The purpose of marketing research and other marketing intelligence activities is to provide information for marketing planning, decision making, and control. For instance, a community service agency carried out a market survey of the attitudes and practices of employers toward hiring people with a mental handicap (Tomes and Harrison, 1991). The results of the survey were used to develop a marketing program, which involved a job trainer at no cost to the hiring firm, and a promotional program, which emphasized the dependable job performance of employees with a mental handicap.

(b) MARKETING INFORMATION SYSTEM A marketing information system (MIS) is a set of procedures and methods that provides an orderly flow of relevant information to marketing decision makers. Two types of information are gathered, processed, and analyzed by an effective MIS: secondary data and primary data.

Secondary data are data that have been or are being collected for another purpose and are already in existence. Frequently available from both outside and inside sources, secondary data save a manager time and money. Data from publications, government reports, university studies, and other published sources often provide the information needed for nonprofit marketing planning. Also needed, however, are data about clients and donors, and other relevant data from sources within the nonprofit organization. In particular, a current data base of clients and donors is essential to follow up other marketing activities.

Primary data involve the collection of information by the nonprofit organization for a specific purpose. Primary data are needed to fill the information gaps left by lacking, outdated, or otherwise inadequate secondary data. For example, a Chamber of Commerce knew from its internal records that members were canceling faster than new ones were enrolling. However, there was no information on why the Chamber was losing members. To find out, primary data collection was needed. A survey of members who had canceled led to the development of a marketing program to involve inactive members, provide added benefits to members, and offer after-sale service (Nald and Dimsdale, 1985).

(c) MARKETING RESEARCH As part of an organization's marketing information system, marketing research is used to collect, process, and analyze primary data. Because marketing research is concerned with helping managers find solutions to marketing problems, there are almost as many uses to marketing research as there are problems.

Many nonprofit marketing research studies are concerned with clients and donors—who they are and what they need; their attitudes and behavior patterns; and so forth. Other projects study marketing activities, such as pricing, service policies, advertising, and public relations. Control and reappraisal of marketing costs, such as promotion expenditures and delivery costs, are the subject of other research efforts. Finally, many nonprofit organizations are concerned with the overall marketing strategy considerations, such as the organization's image, marketing policies, and objectives.

Marketing researchers use a number of different techniques and tools to obtain the desired information. Among those that might be used by nonprofit organizations are:

- Informed opinion interviews—asking people with special expertise or knowledge to discuss a problem or to suggest other sources of information;
- Focus groups—exploring the feelings and ideas of a small group of people who have similar backgrounds and interests;
- Case studies—reviewing, in depth, a few selected situations in order to identify key factors and relationships;
- Observation—noting objects or actions through the senses, primarily sight and hearing;
- Surveys—obtaining information by asking questions of people (clients or donors, for example) who are affected by marketing activities.

27.7 MARKETING MANAGEMENT

(a) ROLE OF THE EXECUTIVE DIRECTOR The long-term success of any organization is determined by the capabilities of its management. In a nonprofit organization, the

Executive Director must assume responsibility for marketing management. When the Executive Director is innovative and customer-driven, a nonprofit organization will prosper and grow ("Profiting from the Nonprofits," 1990).

Frances Hesselbein became Executive Director of the Girl Scouts of America in 1976. She took over an organization that had seen its membership fall for 8 straight years. When she retired 13 years later, the Girl Scouts had grown to a healthy 2.3 million members. She accomplished this growth by using marketing strategies and programs to adapt to changes occurring in girls' interests and motivations.

Hesselbein had market studies conducted, to find out how to attract more members and retain the interest of teenage girls. Based on these studies, greater emphasis was placed on girls' growing interests in science, the environment, and business, and less on cooking, sewing, and traditional household skills. Fashion designers developed a modern line of uniforms. Special programs for girls in low-income neighborhoods were developed. The Girl Scout handbook was revised to reflect changing interests and racial and cultural patterns. Through these and many other activities, Hesselbein changed her nonprofit organization to meet the needs of its customers. Some other innovative, customer-driven Executive Directors are Faye Wattleton of Planned Parenthood, James A. Osborne of the Salvation Army, and Gail L. Warden of the Henry Ford Health Care Corporation ("Profiting from the Nonprofits," 1990).

(b) MARKETING MANAGEMENT IN NONPROFIT ORGANIZATIONS Management is defined as the process necessary to bring the most return from a particular commitment of an organization's resources (technical, financial, human, and so on) when other alternative commitments are possible. The information on which the commitment is made is always incomplete, and the conditions under which the decision will be carried out are uncertain.

Nonprofit organizations feel special pressure because they have limited resources. Cutbacks in assistance from federal, state and local governments, changes in tax laws that hurt gift giving, and limited growth in corporate giving have combined to place added financial pressure on directors and managers of nonprofit organizations. They must learn to use marketing concepts and techniques to focus their efforts on the needs of their clients.

An overview of the marketing management process is presented in Exhibit 27.4. As suggested by the marketing concept, marketing management is an integrated, interrelated process. The first, very important step is to analyze the marketing situation.

Exhibit 27.4. Marketing management process.

Source: Eugene M. Johnson, "Marketing Planning for Nonprofit Organizations," *Nonprofit World,* May–June, 1986, p. 21.

This is part of marketing planning, as are the next three steps shown in Exhibit 27.4. In summary form, the critical marketing management tasks are:

- Planning: analyzing the marketing situation, selecting marketing objectives, identifying target markets, and developing a marketing strategy program, and organization;
- Organization: developing a marketing structure;
- Control: selecting activities that will make sure that the objectives are achieved.

The description of the marketing management process highlights the importance of marketing planning and suggests that marketing planning is a continuous process. Even the most thorough marketing planner realizes that plans cannot be cast in stone. Flexibility is needed. Changes must be made in marketing plans, in order to meet unanticipated market changes, competitive actions, and similar environmental changes. This is why Exhibit 27.4 contains a feedback path from marketing control to the beginning of the marketing management process.

(c) STRATEGIC MARKETING PLANNING Strategic marketing planning is an essential activity for all nonprofit organizations, regardless of size, location, or function. As shown in Exhibit 27.5, the strategic marketing planning process can be divided into four major steps:

Exhibit 27.5. Strategic marketing planning process.

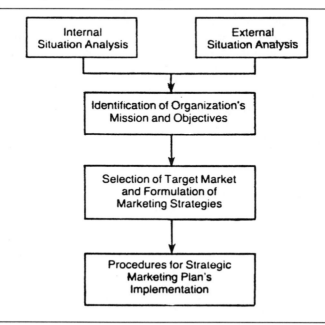

Source: Eugene M. Johnson, "Situation Analysis for Nonprofit Marketing Planning," *Nonprofit World,* July–August, 1986, p. 26.

1. *Situation analysis* answers the question "Where are you?" by providing a realistic view of the organization's environment, marketing opportunities, and internal strengths and weaknesses.

2. *Identification of an organization's mission* and objectives provides an answer to a second question: "Where do we want to go?"

3. *Formulation of marketing strategies* is the third step. These strategies answer the question "How do you want to get there?" The answer to this question is dependent primarily on the target market that the organization wishes to serve.

4. Procedures for *implementation of the marketing plan* provide the schedule ("When do you want to arrive?"), organization ("Who is responsible?"), and budget ("How much will it cost?") for carrying out the market plan.

27.8 MARKETING SITUATION ANALYSIS

(a) COMPONENTS OF SITUATION ANALYSIS Situation analysis is an assessment of an organization's present position in its current environment. Before establishing its marketing objectives and plans, a nonprofit organization must have a clear understanding of its present situation. This involves the identification of present and potential problems and opportunities. There are two parts to this analysis:

*   External analysis: evaluating an organization's markets and publics, market segments, competitors, environmental trends and issues;
*   Internal analysis: evaluating critical measures of an organization's performance, resources, strengths, and weaknesses.

(b) MARKETING AUDIT Some organizations use a marketing audit to review their marketing resources and activities and to carry out the situation analysis. Just as a nonprofit organization's financial position is regularly and systematically reviewed, so should its marketing efforts be subjected to regular and systematic evaluation to determine whether the marketing efforts are appropriate and whether they are being properly executed.

A marketing audit is sweeping and comprehensive. Kotler and Andreasen (1991) provide a complete guide to the kinds of questions that a marketing audit should consider, as do Lovelock and Weinberg (1989). The nonprofit organization's environment is studied; its policies, organization, methods, and marketing philosophy are reviewed; its programs for reaching its goals are assessed; and its procedures for determining and controlling its marketing efforts are analyzed.

Even the most successful nonprofit organizations should carry out regular marketing audits. Seldom is any organization so good that it cannot be improved. Also, past success may breed complacency and carelessness. Audits that can be conducted easily and inexpensively on certain aspects of the marketing program should be undertaken frequently. In some situations, a checklist can be used to provide a flexible, inexpensive self-study tool (Van Doren and Smith, 1985).

(c) EXTERNAL ANALYSIS External situation analysis concentrates on a nonprofit organization's environment. It focuses on external factors that can influence funding and participation.

(i) Clients and supporters The external situation analysis should begin with an assessment of an organization's clients. The key questions are:

- Who are they?
- Who should they be?
- What are they "buying"?
- What could cause this situation to change?
- Why do they "buy" or participate?
- When do they "buy" or participate?
- How do they make decisions to "buy" or participate?
- Where do they "buy" or participate?

The next step is to consider the nonprofit organization's supporters. Unlike business organizations, which are mainly concerned with customer analysis, nonprofit organizations depend on others for support. In particular, a nonprofit organization must answer similar questions about its funders and volunteers.

- Who are they?
- What are they supporting?
- What could cause this situation to change?
- Why do they provide support?
- When do they provide support?
- How do they make decisions to provide support?

Based on the analysis of clients and supporters, several key issues will emerge, including:

1. Market size and growth. The primary concern here is to determine how large the market is and what potential growth opportunities exist, based on estimates of (a) the potential number of clients and supporters, and (b) the potential rate of participation and/or support.
2. Client/Supporter decision making. An organization must try to understand how clients and supporters (or potential clients and supporters) make decisions regarding the organization; specifically, how do they decide whether to "buy" service and which organization to "buy" from?
3. Market segments. The organization must identify groups of clients and supporters who are similar in terms of decision making and who might represent specific targets for specialized marketing efforts.

Thorough analysis of clients and supporters will help an organization identify marketing opportunities. This requires taking a broad view of the market and avoiding the limitations of "marketing myopia."

Theodore Levitt (1975), in his classic article "Marketing Myopia," pointed to the shortcomings of major firms and industries that failed to analyze their marketing opportunities correctly. His contention was that top executives in many industries have unnecessarily taken a limited view of the scope of their businesses. They have been product-oriented rather than customer-oriented. Because of their limited views of marketing, executives in these industries, such as dry cleaning, railroads, electric utilities, and motion pictures, missed marketing opportunities based on changing customers' needs.

Levitt's admonishment is as applicable to nonprofits as it is to businesses. A public library that fails to provide its clients with videotapes, computer software, and other recently developed techniques for making knowledge and entertainment available will soon lose many clients. In contrast, an organization that successfully changed was the March of Dimes. After polio ceased to be a major health concern, this organization switched to birth defects and prenatal care as causes that needed a focal point.

(ii) Publics In addition to clients and supporters, a nonprofit organization must assess the impact of its other publics. As noted earlier, a nonprofit organization's publics will include many types of people, organizations, and groups.

Key questions that should be asked are:

- Who are the people and/or entities that have an impact on the organization?
- Which are most influential?
- Why do they have an impact on the organization?
- What are their objectives and the reasons for their concern with the organization?
- In what ways do they affect the organization?
- What could cause this situation to change?
- What impact will changes have on an organization's publics and their relationship with it?

(iii) Competition In recent years, competition has become an important concern for most nonprofit organizations. Not only must an organization be concerned about competition from other nonprofits, but it is also likely to be facing competitive challenges from business organizations. For example: public hospitals compete with for-profit hospitals for patients, staff, and financial support; private and public colleges compete with profit-oriented trade schools, correspondence programs, and business educational services for students; the United States Postal Service competes with United Parcel Service, Federal Express, and other businesses for customers.

The key questions to be asked as part of the competitive analysis are:

- Who are the major competitors?
- How do they compete?
- What are their strengths and weaknesses that will pose problems and opportunities? These may include:
  —costs and fees;
  —access to clients and supporters;
  —image;
  —type of client base;
  —personnel;
  —marketing budgets and other resources.

(iv) Other external factors Nonprofit directors and managers make marketing decisions in a dynamic environment. There are many other external factors over which they have little or no control. Some specific questions that must be considered are:

- What economic factors might influence the attainment of the organization's objectives?
- What national, state, and local regulations affect the organization?
- What are the demographic, social, technological, and other external factors that may affect the organization?

(d) INTERNAL ANALYSIS The internal situation analysis will help a nonprofit organization identify the internal problems and opportunities that can affect the organization's performance. In particular, what are the organization's marketing strengths and weaknesses? This portion of the situation analysis concentrates on those aspects of the organization that affect its ability to satisfy the clients' needs and influence participation and support.

To assess the marketing performance of their organizations, nonprofit directors and managers must ask themselves questions relating to the following critical areas of performance:

1. Trends. What are the significant trends in the organization's programs, services, participation, and support?
2. Share of market. How much of the market does the organization have in relation to competitive organizations?
3. Stability. Has the organization demonstrated "staying power"?
4. Efficiency. Has the organization been cost-effective in its utilization of facilities, personnel, and other resources?
5. Flexibility. Has the organization been able to adapt to market and environmental changes?

A second part of the internal situation analysis involves an assessment of the nonprofit organization's marketing efforts (that is, its marketing objectives, programs, personnel, and practices). The organization must examine its physical, financial, personnel, and other resources used to provide services to clients. The two critical questions are:

- What key competitive advantages and disadvantages does the organization have?
- How can the organization maintain its competitive advantages and overcome its competitive disadvantages?

After completing this assessment, marketing planners will have an understanding of what sort of marketing their organization can and cannot do. They will know which of the marketing opportunities can be pursued.

27.9 MARKETING PLANNING

The three strategic marketing planning steps are: selecting marketing objectives, identifying the target market, and developing a marketing strategy. The planning steps are then implemented through the preparation of an action plan.

(a) SELECTING MARKETING OBJECTIVES   Objectives provide the direction for a nonprofit organization's activities; they answer the question: "Where do we want to go?"

(i) Marketing objectives and mission   A nonprofit organization's marketing objectives must be consistent with its mission. If they are not, marketing activities may work against what the nonprofit wants to accomplish.

For example, a medium-size university located in a resort area wanted to upgrade its image as a quality institution with high academic standards. However, the advertising theme used to promote the university to potential students continued to emphasize "sun and fun." Unfortunately, the advertising efforts conflicted with the university's goal.

(ii) Marketing objectives and organizational goals   It is not easy to coordinate marketing objectives and activities with the goals of a nonprofit organization. Unlike a business, which is dominated by the profit motive, nonprofits tend to have multiple goals, such as survival, growth, and social change. As a result, marketing objectives may require modification to adapt them to the varied goals of a nonprofit organization.

(iii) Guidelines for setting marketing objectives   When formulating marketing objectives, there are several guidelines to follow. Most important, marketing objectives must be specific; an objective must be a precise statement of what is to be accomplished by the organization's marketing efforts. Objectives should be stated in simple, understandable terms so that everyone involved in marketing knows exactly what is to be done. Further, objectives should be measurable; that is, they should be stated in quantitative terms. Finally, marketing objectives should be related to time, so that everyone knows when the objectives should be achieved. Examples of marketing objectives that meet these criteria include the following:

- Church: "To increase average attendance at the Sunday morning worship service from 130 to 150 by the end of one year."
- Senior citizens' center: "To raise $250,000 for a new recreation facility in two years."
- Private college: "To increase enrollment by 10 percent for next year's fall class."

(b) IDENTIFYING THE TARGET MARKET   After formulating its marketing objectives, a nonprofit organization will choose its target market—the specific group of clients and supporters to whom it wishes to appeal. Selection of a target market depends on a careful review of potential clients' and supporters' needs, attitudes, and buying behavior. This analysis will provide nonprofit marketers with the insights needed to develop an appropriate marketing strategy.

There are two prime marketing strategy options: concentrated marketing and differentiated marketing.

Concentrated marketing, also called targeted marketing or niche marketing, involves focusing on a single, easily defined market segment. This approach is especially appropriate for organizations with limited resources. For instance, a small private college might concentrate its efforts on providing a quality liberal arts education for students from students from its region of the country.

When a nonprofit organization defines its target market in terms of several market segments, it is employing a differentiated marketing approach. A large state university will offer professional as well as liberal arts courses and programs. It may have several campus locations and will schedule classes at many times of the day and evening. It may offer special courses and seminars to businesses and government agencies for their managers and professional employers.

(c) DEVELOPING A MARKETING STRATEGY   Strategy, the "how" of marketing planning, is the overall design for achieving a nonprofit organization's marketing objectives. Development of a marketing strategy depends on the target market chosen. The nonprofit marketing planner formulates a marketing approach that will best satisfy the needs of the target market.

(i) Creating a differential advantage   When developing its marketing strategy, a nonprofit organization must strive to achieve a differential advantage. This is the "something extra" that makes an organization's marketing efforts just a little better than those of its competitors. Consequently, a particular group of clients (the target market) prefers the organization's services.

A differential advantage can be the result of any part of the marketing effort—price, service uniqueness or quality, psychological benefits created by promotion, and so forth. Consider, for example, the prestigious image of certain colleges and universities, such as Harvard, Yale, and Stanford. When people think of the nation's top academic institutions, they usually think of these universities. As a result, these schools have an advantage when recruiting students and faculty or seeking financial support.

(ii) Growth strategies   Because clients' needs are changing rapidly and competition is increasing for traditional nonprofit services and programs, many nonprofit organizations are searching for growth opportunities. Exhibit 27.6 suggests four growth strategy options: market penetration, market development, service development, and diversification.

Market penetration involves an organization's efforts to increase sales and support of its present services to its present markets. The organization may do so by persuading present clients to use more of its services or by attracting clients and supporters from competitors. Aggressive promotion is the approach used most often by nonprofits to increase their market penetration. For instance, college admissions officers are using direct mail, telemarketing, and personal selling to recruit students. On a smaller scale, a minister, priest, or rabbi can increase attendance at religious services and other activities by visiting members and potential members in their homes.

Market development involves selling present services to new markets. This is often done by moving into new geographic markets. Boston's Northeastern University is drawing new students for its specialized, nondegree courses by offering night classes to high-tech engineers and computer scientists in California's Silicon Valley—over 3,000 miles away!

Service development involves creating new services for present markets. In this approach, an organization identifies an unsatisfied need that can be met by introducing a new or modified service. Many hospitals, for instance, are developing community "wellness" programs, designed to prevent illness rather than to provide treatment. These hospitals are serving the same clients but in a different way. Another example of service development by nonprofits is the emergence of Christian schools. Sensing a need for a different approach to education, many fundamentalist churches have established their own elementary and secondary schools. Thus, they provide a new service to their present members.

Exhibit 27.6.   Growth strategy options.

	Present Services	New Services
PRESENT MARKETS	Market Penetration	Service Development
NEW MARKETS	Market Development	Diversification

Source: Eugene M. Johnson, "Developing a Marketing Plan for a Nonprofit Organization," *Nonprofit World,* September–October, 1986, p. 30. Reprinted by permission of Society for Nonprofit Organizations, 6314 Odana Road Suite 1, Madison, WI 53719 (1-800-424-7367).

Diversification involves developing new services for new markets. An example is a community service agency that decides to market its internal management development seminars to other local nonprofit organizations. This approach carries the most risk, because diversification opportunities are difficult to evaluate. A nonprofit organization must be sure it understands the new markets it wants to pursue.

(d) PREPARING AN ACTION PLAN   Implementing marketing strategies ("How do we get there?") requires the preparation of a marketing action plan. The development of schedules and budgets will answer the questions: "When do we want to arrive?" and "How much will it cost?" Marketing organization and implementation plans are also needed.

(i) Schedule   As noted in the discussion of marketing objectives, a marketing plan must have a time frame, a schedule for achieving the plan's objectives. The plan must also include priorities, or a statement of which objectives are to be given the most attention. Marketing planners develop three types of schedules for marketing plans: short-range plans cover a period of one year or less, medium-range plans cover a period of up to 5 years, and long-range plans are developed for 5 years or more. Long-range plans are the most difficult to prepare because long-range forecasts of rapidly changing markets and environmental conditions are unpredictable.

(ii) Budget   Because marketing resources are limited, especially in nonprofit organizations, budgets are needed to allocate resources to the desired marketing activities. The budgeted amount for an activity should match its importance to the organization's marketing strategy. For instance, as the number of college-age students has declined in recent years, colleges and universities are spending more of their budgets on direct mail and other techniques to attract students. This reflects the increased importance of recruiting to the growth—and even the survival—of many colleges and universities.

The objective and task approach has become the preferred method for budgeting marketing expenditures. This approach begins with the formulation of specific, measurable marketing objectives. Then the marketing activities, or tasks, required to achieve the objectives are determined. The marketing budget will be the total amount of money needed to accomplish the required activities. The strength of this budgeting approach is its close relationship to the nonprofit organization's marketing objectives.

(iii) Organization   A structure must be established to achieve the nonprofit organization's marketing objectives. If the marketing concept is accepted as a philosophy, the organization must focus itself to reflect its commitment to is supporters and clients. The result will be an expanded policy-making role for marketing personnel.

Because the board of directors is the policy-making body for most nonprofit organizations, its members must include people who have marketing knowledge and experience (Fram, 1991). It may be wise to establish a marketing committee and to designate specific staff persons to perform marketing tasks such as market research and promotion. Larger nonprofit organizations have created marketing departments with a director or vice president of marketing charged with overseeing all customer-related activities (Lovelock and Weinberg, 1989).

(iv) Implementation   Finally, the nonprofit marketing planner must transmit marketing objectives, strategies, schedules, and budgets to the people who will carry them out. However, communication of marketing plans involves more than informing people of the plans. Nonprofit managers will have to "sell" people on accepting and implementing the marketing plans. People tend to resist change, even a change that may benefit them. They anticipate that new marketing plans and programs will mean more work for them. Management must convince skeptical members of the nonprofit organization that the success of a plan will help them achieve their personal goals.

27.10   MARKETING MIX

A convenient concept for explaining a nonprofit organization's marketing activities and the decisions made by marketing managers is the marketing mix. Just as a cook prepares a mix of ingredients for a favorite recipe, a marketing manager combines marketing activities to form a satisfactory marketing mix.

The major components of the marketing mix (Exhibit 27.7) are:

- Product: the "bundle of satisfactions" provided; the services and ideas marketed to clients and supporters;
- Price: what is charged for the services and ideas provided; a "price" may be money, time, or something else of value;

Exhibit 27.7.   The marketing mix.

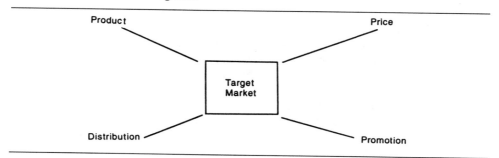

- Distribution: where and how services are provided; the delivery systems responsible for getting services to clients;
- Promotion: the organization's efforts to inform and persuade clients and supporters; promotional techniques include advertising, personal selling, public relations, and sales promotion.

These four elements are blended together to create a total package that will best satisfy the target market's needs.

(a) PRODUCT The product component of most nonprofit organizations consists of services, ideas, experiences, and, in some cases, complementary goods. Albrecht and Zemke (1985) called this the service package—"the sum total of the goods, services and experiences offered to the customer." They and others (Lovelock (1991) for example) pointed out that the service package consists of a core service or idea plus a cluster of supplementary goods and services. The core service or idea is the specific benefit the nonprofit customers want. For example, a church member will seek spiritual inspiration and guidance. Supplementary goods and services support, complement, and add value to the core service. Examples include a church's newsletter, nursery care during services, and recreational activities for young adults. Developing the appropriate service package requires a clear understanding of the nonprofit organization's mission and the needs of its clients and supporters.

(i) Product life cycle Products, like people and other living things, have life cycles. An important managerial planning and control tool, the product life cycle, follows a product from birth (introduction) to death. It provides a conceptual framework for developing marketing strategies and programs for different stages of a product's life. As shown in Exhibit 27.8, the life cycle of a product can be divided into four major stages: introduction, growth, maturity, and decline.

Lovelock and Weinberg (1989), in describing the role of the product life cycle in nonprofit marketing management, noted that public and nonprofit organizations are

Exhibit 27.8. Product life cycle.

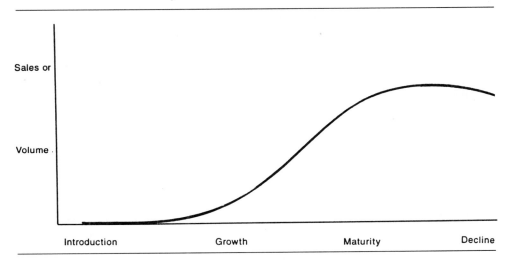

frequently involved with a product for only a portion of its life cycle. For instance, a nonprofit agency may raise public awareness of a social issue, such as the dangers of smoking or the need for environmental protection, during the early stages of the life cycle. As awareness grows, legislation is passed, public agencies become more involved, and responsibility for the issue shifts to them.

At the other extreme are services that have reached the decline stage of the life cycle in the private sector and are then taken over by public or nonprofit organizations. Passenger rail service and urban public transit are historical examples. More recently, it appears that some form of government health insurance may soon replace private coverage, which is not meeting the needs of many Americans.

During the introductory portion of the product life cycle, the marketer's major task is to create demand. Potential clients and supporters must be told about the cause or service, the need must be demonstrated, and they must be persuaded to make a commitment. In the growth stage, these efforts begin to take effect as support for the nonprofit cause or service increases. However, competitors also emerge during the growth stage.

As the product moves into maturity, support begins to level off as competition becomes more intense. Finally, as the decline stage is reached, the nonprofit cause or service will become out-of-date and may be eliminated. Some organizations will shift their cause, as the March of Dimes did; others may alter their services, as the Girl Scouts did.

(ii) New service development The needs of a nonprofit organization's supporters and clients are constantly changing. Responding to these changing needs involves the development of new services. This process should be similar to the new product development procedures used by service businesses (Johnson, Scheuing, and Gaida, 1986).

Ideas for new services can come from a variety of sources. Volunteers and staff members may have insights into emerging needs of clients; client surveys, focus groups, and other forms of market research may provide guidance; secondary sources of information may suggest new service opportunities. For instance, the rapid growth of personal computer sales and use has stimulated many educational institutions to offer new courses and programs to teach people how to use the new technology.

Once an idea for a new service has been suggested, it should be subjected to careful screening and evaluation. This is essential, because taking the idea further will usually require significant time and monetary investments. Most ideas are rejected at this point, for reasons of limited resources, unacceptable market potential, inappropriate fit with the organization's mission and objectives, and potentially strong competition.

If the idea passes the assessment step, the development process begins in earnest. The idea is further tested and refined, and the overall marketing strategy is formulated. Frequently, a new service idea is test marketed: it is introduced to a limited market prior to full-scale introduction. This process is very much like a dress rehearsal before a new theater production opens.

Gail L. Warden, chief executive officer of Detroit's Henry Ford Health Care Corporation, has proposed a new-product strategy to provide more facilities for inner-city people ("Profiting from the Nonprofits," 1990). The "Urban Initiatives Program" may include such innovations as storefront clinics to provide health care at lower costs. Warden has been meting with community leaders and other constituents to test the new program idea.

(iii) Product differentiation Many nonprofit organizations use various marketing techniques to differentiate their service offerings. The development of a unique name, symbol, or design, a process known as branding, is one approach. United Way, March of Dimes, college mascots, like the University of Michigan's wolverine, and American Medical Association are widely recognized examples. Like business brands, these provide a means of identifying and differentiating one service or non-profit agency from another.

Services may also be modified, or supplementary goods and services may be provided to differentiate one organization's product from others. A church's special services feature unique forms of music; a public TV station offers local cultural shows to compete with network programs; a civic club sponsors a long-distance bike race. Sometimes tangible goods are used to differentiate. T-shirts displaying the nonprofit organization's name and logo, reproductions of a museum's most famous artwork, and souvenir programs are examples.

Finally, the nonprofit organization's clients or supporters may receive added value from the "packaging" of several services. A community theater offers major donors preferred seating and parking, tickets to social events, and other amenities. A museum includes free parking and a guided tour as part of its program for selected visitors. A university offers married student housing, a campus child-care center, and a family health-care program for its students with families. These and many other examples represent ways in which nonprofit organizations can distinguish themselves through product differentiation.

(b) PRICE Everything has a price, whether price is called "dues," "fare," "tuition," "admission fee," or something else. All nonprofit organizations must raise revenue to support their activities. More and more, these revenues must come from clients and donors because government sources of funding are becoming restricted.

(i) Fees Many nonprofit organizations have moved to a membership-based structure. If this is done, it is important that membership fees be reasonably priced for the marketplace (Temper, 1990). This can be accomplished by establishing several categories of membership, with different fees for various levels of participation and support. Other nonprofit organizations choose to charge program or activity fees above and beyond membership fees. For instance, a YMCA may charge its members for swimming lessons.

(ii) Donations Most nonprofit organizations receive money, time, and personal effort in the form of donations from members, volunteers, and other supporters. The donation is the price paid by the supporter. Sometimes, the level of donation is set—tithing to a church, or a "suggested" donation to a museum when entering. In many other cases, however, the donor sets the level of monetary support and volunteered assistance. To encourage that assistance, it may be wise to provide guidance by suggesting desired levels of support.

(iii) Service charges Faced with rising costs and diminished government support, many nonprofit organizations are charging for services that were once free. This brings up the question: "How much can we charge?"

Ellis (1990) has suggested two ways to establish prices for nonprofit services. Both of these approaches require that a nonprofit organization accurately estimate its expenses before establishing a price for an activity or event:

- The recovery of costs approach involves determining what the organization's expenses will be and charging whatever is necessary to recover these expenses.
- The revenue-producing approach covers all expenses and provides additional revenue for the organization.

Ellis feels that the revenue-producing approach makes more sense because excess revenues from one activity and event may be needed to offset losses from others. To establish a reasonable charge, the nonprofit organization must consider demand and competitive market conditions, in addition to costs. Further, like all other marketing decisions, the decisions concerning price should be based on the target market selected and the organization's objectives.

(c) DISTRIBUTION Business marketing theory and practice stress the importance of establishing an integrated network, known as a channel of distribution, to transfer goods and services from producers to consumers.

(i) Utilities provided Taken together, the components of a channel of distribution comprise a delivery system that makes goods and services available to buyers and creates time, place, and possession utilities, as follows:

- Time utility refers to making goods and services available when buyers want them. Examples: Hospital emergency rooms remain open 24 hours a day; colleges offer classes during the evening and weekend hours; community centers remain open late in the evening to provide activities for young adults.
- Place utility refers to making goods and services available where buyers want them. Examples: Storefront clinics and counseling centers provide services in local neighborhoods; emergency hotlines allow people with problems to reach counselors from their homes; colleges have satellite campuses.
- Possession utility refers to the transfer of ownership from the producer to the buyer. Examples: A college student "owns" the professor's time and knowledge during a class; a patient "owns" a doctor's expertise during a visit; a group of teenagers "own" a community center's playground during a game.

(ii) Service delivery systems Because nonprofit organizations deal mainly in ideas and services, goods distribution concepts and strategies must be modified. Lovelock (1991) has suggested that two major questions must be considered, in order to understand service delivery systems:

- Must the customer be in direct physical contact with the service organization or can transactions be completed at arm's length?
- Should a service organization maintain only a single outlet or should it serve customers through multiple outlets at different sites?

Answers to these questions will help a nonprofit organization develop its distribution approach. For example, community medical care can be provided at a single location (hospital) or at several (storefront clinics). A community visiting nurses association can visit the elderly and others who need medical attention but are unable to leave their homes for treatment.

For some nonprofit services and ideas, the contact can be at arm's length through mailings, written materials, or electronic media. For example, a public TV station's contacts with its clients and donors is usually accomplished through its broadcasts. Likewise, many nonprofit organizations use radio, television, and other nonpersonal media to deliver educational messages to the public.

(iii) Intermediaries Although intermediaries, or "middlemen," as they were formerly called, are primarily involved in the marketing of goods, they are also becoming important in service and nonprofit marketing. Intermediaries make the distribution process more efficient by reducing the number of contacts between producers and their customers. They also perform a number of distribution tasks, such as communication and resource allocation. Applying the concept of intermediaries to nonprofit marketing yields several intriguing possibilities. Some nonprofit organizations, such as United Way, can serve as clearinghouses for other agencies. They can raise and distribute funds, provide information about other agencies and their services, and suggest appropriate agencies to potential clients. A social worker can serve as an intermediary, guiding needy clients to specific nonprofit agencies and services. This role can also be played by the clergy, doctors, community action agencies, and others. It is important, therefore, that nonprofit organizations establish and maintain relationships with people and organizations that can serve as intermediaries for them.

(iv) Direct marketing By far, the fastest growing form of distribution is direct marketing. As a special kind of delivery system, direct marketing bypasses established distribution channels to deliver goods and services directly from sellers to buyers. The two major forms of direct marketing are direct mail and telemarketing.

Like businesses, many nonprofit organizations have turned to direct marketing for its efficiency as a sales and marketing approach. To date, the major applications have involved fund-raising. Direct mail appeals and telemarketing have become commonplace as fund-raising techniques. Organizations as diverse as the American Cancer Society, college alumni associations, and local Chambers of Commerce use direct marketing to solicit members and contributions.

Direct marketing has the potential to deliver services to clients. Interactive communication (mail, telephone, or electronic media) can be used to establish direct relationships with targeted clients. For instance, prenatal information and an invitation to visit a prenatal clinic can be sent to young women identified as expectant mothers. Follow-up telephone calls can verify receipt of the information and schedule appointments at a clinic. A video illustrating proper diet, exercise, and personal care programs could be provided.

Another direct marketing tool for delivering nonprofit services and ideas is the advanced telephone technology, specifically "800" and "900" numbers. These relatively new services offer convenient access to a nonprofit organization's staff, information, and expertise. They can be used to provide time and place utility to clients who are unable to visit the organization in person. An example is a university's "answer center" for gardeners and other people who have questions related to their homes, lawns, and gardens.

(d) PROMOTION　No matter how excellent a nonprofit organization may be, or how worthwhile its purpose and services, or how dedicated its staff and volunteers, all effort will be wasted unless people are informed and reminded about its availability and persuaded to use its services and support its activities. This is the task of promotion, which involves communication with a nonprofit organization's publics.

The three primary goals of promotion are:

1. To inform. As a method of communication, promotion informs people about a nonprofit organization's existence, purpose, services, and capabilities. This is an especially important goal for new agencies, programs, and services. For example, a civic association has decided to offer a late-night basketball program to inner-city youth. To obtain participation in the new program, the association must use promotion to inform the community's young people of the program's availability, time, and location.

2. To persuade. Promotion attempts to influence people to do something—support the Easter Seal Society, don't drink and drive, fight illiteracy. Persuasion becomes an important promotional goal as an agency or service enters the growth stage of its life cycle.

3. To remind. Promotion is often used to keep an idea, service, or nonprofit organization's name in people's minds. This goal is important during the maturity stage of the life cycle. The Salvation Army, American Red Cross, and United Way are organizations that stress reminder promotion.

To accomplish these goals, advertising, personal selling, sales promotion, and public relations are combined to form the promotional mix. It is especially important that the promotional mix elements be properly coordinated so that they work together to achieve the same goals.

(i) Advertising　This is the dominant form of nonpersonal promotion. Promotional messages are carried to the public by mass communications media—newspapers, television, and outdoor signs.

There are many forms of advertising and many purposes for which advertising may be used. Product and institutional advertising, the two major forms, are described as follows:

- Advertising designed to stimulate sales of a specific product or service, or participation in a specific activity, is called product advertising. Nonprofit organizations use this form of advertising when they feature a specific program or activity—for example, a fund-raising event, a blood donors' day, or a special museum exhibit.

- Institutional advertising promotes a concept, idea, image, or philosophy of a nonprofit organization or cause. Anyone who may have an impact on the advertiser, such as legislators, business leaders, or the general public, can be a target of institutional advertising. Much of the advertising done by nonprofit organizations is institutional advertising—for example, the promotion of values and beliefs by the Mormon Church.

(ii) Personal selling   In contrast to the impersonal approach of advertising, in personal selling the promotional message is carried by someone who normally communicates with the potential client or supporter face-to-face. As a result, personal selling can be a highly individualized process that involves complex interpersonal relations.

Kotler and Andreasen (1991) observed that almost everyone in a nonprofit organization is likely to have personal contact with persons outside the organization. Salespeople, whose job is to actively influence the behavior of others, will have the most extensive contacts with outsiders. College recruiters, development officers, community organizers, and lobbyists are all contact persons. Service personnel who provide assistance to clients and members of the public will also have personal contacts and must understand the nature of personal selling. Service personnel include receptionists, museum guards, ticket takers, librarians, and the like.

Many observers of service marketing have emphasized the importance of personal contacts to customer satisfaction. Gronroos (1982) suggested that service organizations require a different organizational structure, one that integrates the simultaneous production and marketing of a service. This has been called "interactive marketing." As shown in Exhibit 27.9, the focus is on client–organization interactions.

These points of interaction have been termed the "moments of truth." To make sure that its clients are truly satisfied, a nonprofit organization must manage these moments of truth from start to finish. For instance, the receptionist in a health-care clinic must greet clients warmly; health-care professionals must be friendly and professional; billing and other follow-up activities must be handled effectively. In short, all the contacts with the clinic must make the client feel good about having come there.

Exhibit 27.9.   Interactive marketing

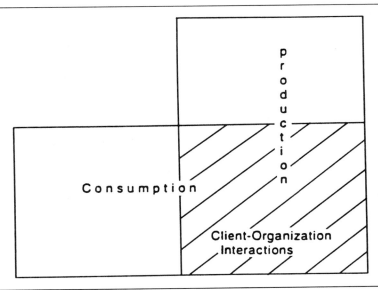

Source: Adapted from Christian Gronroos, *Strategic Management and Marketing in the Service Sector* (Helsingfors: Swedish School of Economics and Business Administration, 1982), p. 137.

(iii) Public relations These promotion activities play an important role in the marketing programs of most nonprofit organizations. Public relations activities and programs are used to create a favorable impression for the organization and its efforts. Further, effective public relations complement a nonprofit organization's other promotion activities by building credibility. As a result, potential supporters and clients will be more receptive to the organization's ideas and services.

Many nonprofit organizations plan, manage, and coordinate their public relations activities through a director of public relations. This manager is responsible for communicating with an organization's various publics. The media and form of public relations will be adapted to each specific public. Some of the techniques used are press releases, speeches by executives, facility tours, annual reports, and community events. The goal of public relations management is to ensure that all contacts with a nonprofit organization's publics support and reinforce the desired image.

Harrison (1991) suggested that the most important public relations development for nonprofits is the concept of issue-oriented public relations. This involves positioning an organization as an authority on an issue and as an important part of the solution to the problem. The key, according to Harrison, is to focus on one or two issues that are "hot." By doing this, a nonprofit organization will create an environment in which people are more inclined to respond to its appeals for funds and volunteers, to attend its events, and to support its cause.

(iv) Sales promotion A variety of promotion activities—other than personal selling, advertising, and public relations—can be used to achieve specific short-term objectives. Business examples include samples, premiums, coupons, demonstrations, contests, sweepstakes, and games.

Because they provide services, many nonprofit organizations are limited in their use of sales promotion techniques, but there are some examples. Fund-raising programs sometimes include a contest or sweepstakes to generate interest and excitement. Contributors may receive tokens of appreciation, and large contributors may be given special gifts. Even clients or customers can be stimulated with sales promotion techniques. For instance, a public transit authority rewards its one-millionth passenger; a museum gives a free bumper sticker to the first 5,000 visitors; a college recruiter gives prospective students a pen with the college logo. The possibilities are endless and so, it is hoped, are the results.

SOURCES AND SUGGESTED REFERENCES

Albrecht, Karl, and Zemke, Ron. 1985. *Service America!* Homewood, IL: Dow Jones-Irwin.

Bateson, John E.G. 1989. *Managing Services Marketing.* Chicago: Dryden Press.

Coffman, Larry L. 1986. *Public Sector Marketing.* New York: John Wiley & Sons.

Day, George S., and Wensley, Robin. 1983. "Marketing Theory with a Strategic Orientation." *Journal of Marketing.* (Fall).

De los Santos, Gilberto. 1986. "Universities Offer Marketing Research Key." *Nonprofit World* (January–February).

DeVos, Karen. 1986. "Manufacturing Support Through Marketing." *Nonprofit World.* (March–April).

Dickson, John P., and Dickson, Sarah S. 1984/1985. Four-part marketing research series. *Nonprofit World* (November–December, 1984 through May–June, 1985).

Drucker, Peter F. 1989. "What Business Can Learn from Nonprofits." *Harvard Business Review* (July–August).

Ellis, Susan J. 1990. "What Should We Charge for Our Services?" *Nonprofit World* (May–June).

Fram, Eugene H. 1991. "Nonprofit Boards Would Profit with Marketers Aboard." *Marketing News,* April 29.

Gronroos, Christian. 1982. *Strategic Management and Marketing in the Service Sector.* Helsingfors: Swedish School of Economics and Business Administration.

Guy, Bonnie S., and Patton, Wesley E. 1988. "The Marketing of Altruistic Causes: Understanding Why People Help." *Journal of Services Marketing* (Winter).

Harrison, Thomas A. 1991. "Six PR Trends That Will Shape Your Future." *Nonprofit World* (March–April).

Johnson, Eugene M., Scheuing, Eberhard E., and Gaida, Kathleen A. 1986. *Profitable Service Marketing.* Homewood, IL: Dow Jones-Irwin.

Kelly, Bill. 1991. "Cause-Related Marketing: Doing Well While Doing Good." *Sales & Marketing Management* (March).

Kotler, Philip, and Andreasen, Alan. 1991. *Strategic Marketing for Nonprofit Organizations* (4th ed.). Englewood Cliffs, NJ: Prentice-Hall.

Kotler, Philip, Ferrell, O.C., and Lamb, Charles. (Eds.). 1987. *Strategic Marketing for Nonprofit Organizations: Cases and Readings.* Englewood Cliffs, NJ: Prentice-Hall.

Kotler, Philip, and Levy, Sidney J. 1979. "Broadening the Concept of Marketing." *Journal of Marketing* (January).

Lancome, Claude. 1985. "Strategic Marketing for Nonprofit Organizations." *Nonprofit World* (July–August).

Lauffer, Armand. 1984. *Strategic Marketing for Not-for-Profit Organizations.* New York: Free Press.

Laycock, D. Kerry. 1990. "Are You Ready for Strategic Planning?" *Nonprofit World* (September–October).

Levitt, Theodore. 1975. "Marketing Myopia" (With Retrospective Commentary). *Harvard Business Review* (September–October).

Lovelock, Christopher H. 1991. *Services Marketing* (2nd ed.). Englewood Cliffs, NJ: Prentice-Hall.

Lovelock, Christopher H., and Weinberg, Charles B. 1989. *Public and Nonprofit Marketing* (2nd ed.). Redwood City, CA: Scientific Press.

Miaoulis, George. 1985. "Nonprofits' Marketing Strategies Begin with Customer Satisfaction." *Marketing News,* March 15.

Muehrcke, Jill (Ed.) 1989. *Marketing: The Society for Nonprofit Organizations' Leadership Series,* Madison, Wi: The Society for Nonprofit Organizations.

Nall, Janice R., and Dimsdale, Parks B. 1985. "Civic Group Adopts Marketing Technique." *Marketing News,* June 21.

"Profiting from the Nonprofits." 1990. *Business Week,* March 26.

Schwartz, Karen. 1989. "Nonprofits' Bottomline: They Mix Lofty Goals and Gutsy Survival Strategies." *Marketing News,* February 13.

Temper, Roy H. 1991. "Donations Versus Dues." *Nonprofit World* (January–February).

Tomes, Anne E., and Hamilton, Barbara. 1991. "The Marketing of a Community Service." *Journal of Marketing Management.* April, 1991.

Williams, Monci Jo. 1986. "How To Cash in on Do-Good Pitches." *Fortune,* June 9.

Developing a Customer Focus

Michael E. Knight
Kean College of New Jersey

Denise Gallaro
Kean College of New Jersey

CONTENTS

A customer is the most important visitor to our premises. He is not dependent on us; we are dependent on him. He is not an interruption on our work; he is the purpose of it. He is not an outsider in our business; he is part of it. We are not doing him a favor by giving us an opportunity to do so.

Mahatma Ghandi

Developing a customer focus is not intended as a solution to every problem an organization may confront. The purposes of developing such a focus are to create an environment in which existing talent and skill may be utilized with a clearer understanding of how each person contributes to the effectiveness of the organization, and to allow the release of the creativity of the people who will develop this environment. A secondary benefit is a realization that the success of the organization is the success of the individual.

28.1 WHO ARE OUR CUSTOMERS?

The term customer frequently creates extreme resistance when used outside of the "business" environment. The intention in using the word customer is not to suggest that any organization will become more effective by simply becoming more "businesslike." By using the word customer, providers initiate an exploration of the relationships, associations, and interactions that influence the ability of people (individuals and teams) to accomplish the tasks comprising their work in a manner that is more effective, more satisfying, and more reinforcing to those who are engaged in the work. In other words, the implementation of a quality system requires us to know the people whom we serve and how we serve them.

Terms such as client, recipient, case, patron, constituent, consumer, or patient may be more acceptable, but the particular term used in the initial stages of developing a new focus is probably best left undetermined. Through a systematic examination of how both the specific and the general, the narrow and the broad, goals of a particular work group, office staff,or team can best be accomplished, it is likely that the appropriate term or terms will be forthcoming. Prior to these determinations of labels, it is necessary to engage in discussions and resolution of several primary questions. (Readers can substitute any word they choose, for customer.)

How will the organization decide that a customer focus is appropriate and necessary?
Who will be involved in these discussions?
If the decision is made to develop such a focus, how will it be implemented?
How is customer defined?

Organizations that have been successful in changing their primary focus from internal satisfaction to external satisfaction have experienced similar paths to their goal. Yet, despite the fact that there are many similarities, each group experiences the process in a unique way. Common conclusions that can be drawn through an analysis of these organizations include the following:

Emphasis must be moved from competitive to collaborative goals.

A redefining of successful performance is necessary. These definitions have consistently moved from the view of the provider to the view of the recipient.

Involvement of all the people contributing to a particular goal is required.

All change creates resistance. It must be demonstrated to everyone that a new way of doing things will not place them in jeopardy.

Keeping people informed is essential. If good information is not disseminated, rumors will fill the vacuum.

(See Chapter 6, "Empowerment and Teamwork in the Quality Organization.")

When management has addressed these questions and has developed an understanding of the experiences of others in developing a customer focus, it is possible to return to the question: Who are our customers? In order to expand the definition of customer, it may be helpful to analyze the customer relationship between employers and employees. In what circumstances might an employee in the organization also be a customer?

There are probably many quick answers to this question, but a deeper analysis will lead to an expanded view of relationships and activities that describes employees as customers of their own organizations. The number of employers providing child care to their employees has nearly tripled in the past 6 years. After an analysis of personnel needs, many employers determined that the only way to attract the people necessary to fill their needs was to respond to the needs of potential employees. It seems logical to describe this process as the organization responding to the needs of its customers. The exact fit of the term customer is not necessary. What has been described is an examination of the means to achieve a goal and a changed relationship as a result of this examination. It is probable that most organizations will engage in an even broader analysis of employee needs, to address the concerns created by turnover rates and the shrinking pool of potential employees. This example of the changing relationship between employers and employees provides a foundation for examining and creating other views.

(a) EVERYONE HAS NUMEROUS CUSTOMERS, INTERNAL AND EXTERNAL

Who are my customers?
Whose customer am I?

The purpose of these questions is not only to assign responsibility and accountability, but also to understand the structure of a system that allows accomplishment of the goals of the team, so that flaws or problems within the system can be identified and resolved. The mission, objective, goal or assignment of any unit not only proscribes the activities of that unit. In addition to these assigned activities, an expectation of intention is communicated. Through an analysis of some of the following questions, the relationship of each unit to every other and to the goals of the total organization can be defined. A significant aspect of these definitions is the intention of management for this team or individual. The focus on customers places the emphasis on significant outcomes, as opposed to process analysis or simplistic tallies.

What do I really want this team to accomplish?
Who are the customers of a purchasing department?
Who are the customers of a complaint department?
Who are the customers of a library?
Who are the customers of a receptionist?

This list of questions could be expanded to include every individual, office, work unit, or team in any organization. Some investigation can provide us with the basis for a broader perspective, for example, on how people in a purchasing department spend their time and, therefore, whom they serve and how they serve them. This process can serve as a model of how anyone can address "customer" questions.

(b) EVERYONE IN THE ORGANIZATION IS EVERYONE ELSE'S CUSTOMER Selecting an office or team that may appear to be less central to the mission of the organization can provide an illustrative example of the reciprocal support encouraged in successful workplaces and the solution of systematic problems.

If the purchasing department's objective is simply to process the purchase orders they receive, are they not fulfilling their obligation to the organization if they efficiently process orders and obtain the items quickly and at the best possible price? If this is the intention of management, then success has been clearly defined and will be easily measured. It is understood that the customer of the purchasing department is the individual or office placing the order, and delivery of the item completes the particular task. A specific item, such as a secretary's chair, may be ordered for numerous offices over a year's time. How will anyone know whether these chairs are functioning in the way that was anticipated? If they break and are returned to the manufacturer, or if they are repaired by maintenance personnel, there will probably be no record of the chairs' failure. The purchasing department would probably like to know what is happening with these chairs. The costs associated with their return or repair would certainly seem of interest to a number of people. A more significant issue than these costs may be the number of sick days taken because the chairs are not providing proper back support. The human resources office should know whether this is the case, or whether additional compensation claims are being made. The costs of recruiting temporary or long-term replacements may make human resources one of the many customers of the purchasing department.

> Who are my customers?
> Whose customer am I?

Involvement of the employees of any purchasing department in answering these questions will provide a long list of answers that will demonstrate the need for a systemwide view, an understanding of the reciprocal support relationships that exist in organizations, and the need to collect information about the significant objectives of every work unit.

The registrar's office in a college provides an example of the reciprocal interrelationships that exist between internal customers (see Exhibit 28.1):

> Whom does the registrar's office serve?
> Who are its customers?
> Who serves the registrar's office?

Exhibit 28.1 indicates several distinct units on the college campus that could be customers of the registrar's office, while at the same time acting as providers to that office. The financial aid office would have to know from the registrar how many full-time students are enrolled for each semester, in order to prepare the budget and allocation of monies to individual students. The financial aid office must, in turn, supply to the registrar's office the names of those students who have applied for and been granted financial aid, so that these students' names can be forwarded to the bursar.

In addition to faculty, students, staff, the campus bookstore, the campus police, the financial aid office, and health services, the registrar's office serves such customers

Exhibit 28.1.   Reciprocal support relationships.

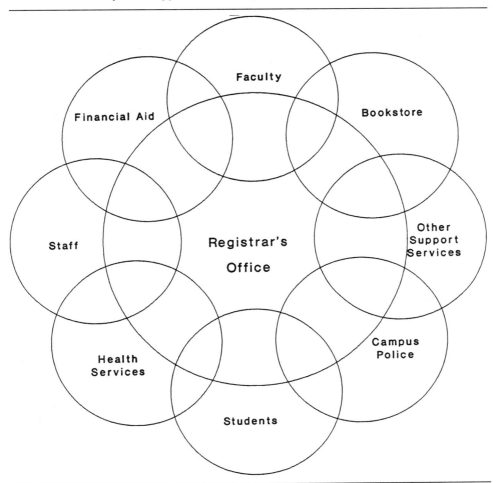

as the library (enrollment numbers and academic majors declared would be essential information to the library when placing orders with publishers), the housing office (dormitory space is always a scarce commodity; planning for each semester is essential and must be based on information on enrollment), and food services (snack bars, cafeterias, extracurricular events, student organization meetings, and so on), which, in turn, can be served by information from the registrar. The college newspaper, student activities, the parking office, and others are all elements of the customer support system found on a college campus.

The customers of a public lending library could be defined in a similar manner. Who are the customers of a free public library? Does a library serve township residents? Can it also be considered a customer?

To effectively service the community and identify those materials that will be placed inside the library, a municipal free public library must know whom it serves—who its customers are. Reciprocally, it must have channels available for feedback from its customers as well as from its supporters or providers. The library will receive support and backing from the community when it serves its residents well.

Customers of a public library can be categorized by age, by type of activity, and other characteristics. Based on age, those customers served might include: preschoolers, who come to "reading hours" in the children's section, and the mothers of those preschoolers, who utilize the services of the library as a baby-sitting service while they catch up on errands; students, whether in junior high, high school, college, or graduate school; professional researchers, who utilize the library's resources; or senior citizens, who use the facility to meet old friends and find conversation and companionship with others.

Activities of nonprofit organizations, such as the Girl Scouts, boards of education, or charitable associations, may utilize the meeting rooms available in the library during the day or evening hours. Political action committees, the township's library board, and local elementary and high school teachers are a few examples of other nonprofit stakeholders in a local library.

These examples, which have focused on the identification of internal customers, have been based on the belief that external customers are usually easier to identify.

(i) Understanding who the external customers are and what they want

"Everyone knows . . . ."
"My experience tells me . . . ."
"It's obvious that . . . ."

The difficulty of applying successful past experiences to current problems is that there have probably been numerous changes in the context between the application of the old solutions and the development of the new problem. It is also risky to believe that we know the full extent of any problem, including the needs and motivations of other people.

(c) WHAT ASSUMPTIONS DO WE MAKE ABOUT OUR CUSTOMERS? "Everyone knows . . . ." Exploring the following exercises may provide some insights about how we all make assumptions based on our own experience and beliefs. Before you begin, try to anticipate possible responses and then compare the reasons given with your own reasons.

Ask 10 college freshmen why they chose to attend their particular institution.
Ask 10 people coming out of a museum why they had visited it.
Ask 10 employees to identify the one thing they would like to change if they had the authority.

In each of these circumstances, and in innumerable others that have *direct effect on your organization's work,* you will find that your anticipated responses will frequently have no relationship to the actual responses. Not knowing the beliefs and assumptions your employees have about their work, and the beliefs and assumptions they have about the intentions and expectations of management, will create conflicts when none actually exists and will detract from the effectiveness of their work. Exhibit 28.2 can be enlisted for information gathering.

Exhibit 28.2.   An activity for examining changes in the workplace.

Ask any employee to respond to the following:

Describe how the world has changed in the past three years.

Describe how your family life has changed in the past three years.

Describe how your organization has changed in the past three years.

Describe how your work has changed in the past three years.

Identify the causes of the changes listed in the two previous items.

If an employee can respond more easily to the first two items than to the second two, this probably indicates a lack of appropriate employee involvement.

If an employee cannot respond to the final item, it is *unlikely* that he or she:

1. Knows the customers;
2. Understands how he or she contributes to the effectiveness of the organization and the accomplishment of its goals;
3. Is encouraged to identify problems;
4. Is encouraged to use creativity;
5. Is encouraged to assume responsibility and authority.

These items, begun from a negative perspective, in fact describe an organization that has both empowered its employees and developed a customer focus. (See Chapter 6, "Empowerment and Teamwork in Quality Organizations.")

The following suggestions can begin the process of quality improvement through a customer focus:

Ask the user. Whether regarding furniture, counseling services, reimbursement for travel, the organization's newsletter, or recruiting efforts, the person who is using the item or service is in an excellent position to describe the results.

Encourage the contributions and creativity of every employee.

Identify your "customers" and listen to them with no preconceived notions of their responses. Don't guess what they are thinking. If your customer is dissatisfied, how will you know? If your customer is dissatisfied, what will you do?

Ask the person who is doing the work. That person understands the work best.

(d) ADDITIONAL BENEFITS FOR THE INDIVIDUAL AND THE ORGANIZATION   The effects of involving employees and encouraging them to use their talents with greater autonomy are benefits to both the individual and the organization at the same time and in the same ways. These benefits describe both the successful individual and the successful organization, and they remain as continuing goals:

1. Cohesion with the team and organization;
2. A job well done;
3. Job fulfillment and satisfaction;
4. Increased self-esteem;
5. A cycle of success.

28.2   A MATRIX OF CUSTOMER RELATIONSHIPS

(a) SEEKING A COMMON VOCABULARY   Some observations related to the selection of a particular term to replace customer have already been made. The process of selecting the term and determining the customer relationships both contributes to the building of group cohesion and answers the prior questions. The particular vocabulary identified does not seem to have any great significance; however, participation in determining the appropriate vocabulary plays a crucial role in building unity and commitment to an idea. A broad understanding of the terms selected is crucial to their acceptance and application. There is little doubt that numerous organizations will struggle with a different view of those they provide with their services. The available terms are:

Customer	Case
Client	Patron
Recipient	Patient
Beneficiary	Constituent
Consumer	

If none of these terms describes the relationship, you will find one that does!

(b) IDENTIFYING CUSTOMER RELATIONSHIPS   A pilot study is suggested, to initiate the first attempt at developing the process. Seek out individuals and groups who have demonstrated interest in quality efforts and a consumer focus, or who generally are interested in innovations. Recruit these "volunteers" with the clearest set of expectations that can be provided, along with an explanation of the types and level of support that will be available. Pilot approaches contain an element of trial-and-error. Expectations of false starts, mistakes, and other errors should be clearly communicated.

The three primary objectives of the pilot study are:

1. Have we identified those we serve, those who depend on the quality of our work?

   They are our customers!

2. Have we identified those who serve us, those whom we depend on for the quality of their work?

   We are their customers!

3. Have we developed a system to collect information that will ensure improvement in our work of satisfying our customers, and will inform those who serve us of our needs?

   Goal attainment!

(c) DEVELOPING A CUSTOMER RELATIONSHIP MATRIX   Exhibit 28.3 can be used as a beginning point to identify both internal and external customers. Each employee can complete this matrix by placing a check in each box that identifies internal and external people who will contribute to the achievement of team objectives. By tabulating the individual responses, the team manager will begin to see a pattern of relationships

Exhibit 28.3. Customer relationship matrix.

Table _____

Identifying Customers

	Organizational Objectives	Team Objectives						
	Quality Service to "X" Clients per Month	Your Team	Human Resources	Management	Accounting	Purchasing	Community Relations	Others
Your Team								
Human Resources								
Management								
Accounting								
Purchasing								
Community Relations								
Others								

emerging. This pattern should be presented for discussion at a team meeting, for the purposes of clarifying and confirming the common view of the pattern.

Having identified those who must be involved in achieving each team's objectives, the next step is to define the various teams' contributions toward achieving each other's objectives and, therefore, the organizational objectives. Surveys, interviews, and focus groups are some methods of clarifying the needs of external customers. (See Chapter 4, "Problem Solving with Information and Analysis.")

An extended intergroup meeting of the teams provides a further opportunity for clarifying and confirming the relationship and expectations of the groups. By having each team take the role of customer, the necessary objectives will be identified for each of them with the necessary understanding and commitment. The facilitator responsible for guiding this effort can either be a person external to the organization or an internal person who has established credibility and respect with the people involved.

Using the objectives developed at this session, each team engages in the specific planning necessary to assign responsibility and to design the methods and activities required for achieving each of the objectives. As part of the process, a system for collecting information to assess the level of success in reaching the objective (customer satisfaction) should be developed. This approach will focus data collection on objectives and will minimize data glut.

Completing the cycle requires a review process examining interteam functioning. The timing of these reviews will vary by type of organization and objective. The purpose of this review is not evaluation, but providing feedback to the individual and team on how they might improve. This step completes the cycle, but it does not complete the process. After a period of time (best determined by each organization), a return to the first step may be seen as appropriate.

This effort will create an environment in which each employee participates in defining his or her work with appropriate responsibility and authority. Participation, commitment, and empowerment provide opportunity to enhance the quality of work and the quality of the workplace.

28.3 IMPLEMENTING A QUALITY CULTURE

The application guidelines for the Malcolm Baldrige National Quality Awards provide a comprehensive series of goals, objectives, and research areas, including the category of customer satisfaction. (A complete set of guidelines can be obtained from The Malcolm Baldrige National Quality Award Consortium, Inc., P.O. Box 443, Milwaukee, WI 53201-0443.)

Recognition of the way an organization must change is needed in order to become customer-focused. The success of any organization will depend on how well that organization stays in touch with and serves both its internal and external customers. Listening to customers, treating them as individuals instead of components in an assembly line, and accommodating their wants and needs are changes that can lead to a quality organization.

Developing an atmosphere of employee involvement and empowerment plays an important role in building a customer-focused organization. Employee use of creative and innovative ways to satisfy customers can make the difference. Workers who are given the power to solve customer problems on the spot can build positive relationships with customers and can communicate the organization's commitment to quality service. Not only success but sheer survival may depend on how well an organization serves its customers.

Internal customers and external customers should be treated equally. Organizations can learn to improve service to all their customers by listening to them. Any information a customer may give to an organization, whether in the form of praise or criticism, should be viewed as positive. The use of information in the interest of change and/or improvement is a positive result of both good and bad news.

All customers should be treated with respect. Promises may sometimes be broken. Taking responsibility for broken promises or mistakes is a sign of a quality organization. Customer demands should be viewed as requests or business opportunities, and every effort should be made to meet these requests. Acting in concert with customers demonstrates a commitment to the customer's as well as the organization's success.

Every organization that hopes to implement a quality culture should be aware that the commitment to being customer-focused must start at the top and be instilled at all levels. Organizations must aggressively seek and *use* customer input. Employees should be given the training and authority to solve problems on the spot. Organizations should listen to their customers and to their competitor's customers, and should be accessible in order to serve their needs.

Developing a strong customer focus is an essential step in obtaining quality. Knowledge of customer requirements and expectations, customer relationship management, customer satisfaction determination, customer satisfaction results, and customer satisfaction comparison leads to quality in organizations. The lists in Exhibit 28.4 are based on the Malcolm Baldrige National Quality Award's guidelines and are provided by the authors to reduce an intensive, organizationwide process to a more practical series of questions applicable to a team as well as an organization.

28.4 DYNAMIC INTERACTION BETWEEN CUSTOMER AND PROVIDER

Many organizations will attempt to systematically implement a variety of strategies along a well-charted course of action, in order to achieve a truly customer-focused environment. Developing such a climate involves dynamic interaction between customer and provider, and among information-gathering strategies, communication strategies, and training issues. An awareness that plans must be flexible will become apparent as customer needs are identified and as interactions change.

The dynamic interaction between a customer and a provider is not a linear occurrence; which strategy is implemented first should not be of utmost concern. The fact that there is interaction between the two entities is the critical aspect.

28.5 STRATEGIC SYNERGISM—A PLAN FOR QUALITY

(a) INFORMATION-GATHERING STRATEGIES The intention to move decision-making capabilities into direct contact with customers is the reasoning behind an organization's use of information-gathering strategies. Some obvious information-gathering strategies include:

Exhibit 28.4. Developing a customer focus.

General Questions

How do you identify customers and potential customers?

How do you determine their expectations?

How do you ensure the internal communication of customer requirements?

How do you ensure ease of communication between customers and employees?

How do you ensure employee involvement in creating objectives?

Do you communicate performance-based organizational effectiveness to your customers?

Do you determine training needs based on customer expectations?

Do you have a system to gather and analyze data on each of the preceeding items, with the focus on problem resolution?

Do you empower employees to act?

Specific Questions

Is there a process for identifying market segments, customer and potential customer groups, including customers of competitors, and their requirements and expectations?

Is there a process for identifying product and service quality features and the relative importance of these features to customers?

Can the organization make cross-comparisons with other key data and information, such as complaints, losses and gains of customers, and performance data?

Can the organization evaluate and improve the effectiveness of its processes for determining customer requirements and expectations?

Does the organization have a process for ensuring that customer service requirements are understood throughout the organization?

Does the organization have means for ensuring easy access for customers to comment, seek assistance, and complain?

Does the organization follow up with customers on products and services, to determine satisfaction?

How does the organization follow up with customers to gain information for improvement?

Does the organization engage in special hiring requirements, attitudinal and other training, recognition, and attitude/morale determination of customer-contact employees?

Does the organization's infrastructure support employees to provide effective and timely customer service?

Does the organization have a process for analysis of complaint information, gains and losses of customers, and lost orders, to assess costs and market consequences?

Does the organization have a process for evaluating and improving services to customers?

Does the organization know how satisfaction is divided by customer groups and how satisfaction relative to competitors is determined?

Does the organization know the correlation between satisfaction results and satisfaction indicators, such as complaints and gains and losses of customers?

Does the organization know how to use customer satisfaction information in quality improvement?

Is the organization aware of trends in customer satisfaction?

Is the organization aware of trends in major adverse indicators, such as complaints, claims, refunds, mandatory recalls, returns, repeat services, replacements, downgrades, repairs, warranty costs, and warranty work?

Does the organization systematically compare customer satisfaction results with those of competitors?

Is the organization aware of trends in gaining or losing customers?

---

1. Empowering employees, thereby giving them decision-making authority when they are listening to and interacting with customers. As the people in the organization who are closest to the customer, they can be a valuable resource for gathering information.
2. Customer satisfaction surveys will give an organization an indication of what is right or wrong with the organization, product, or service.
3. Customer participation in the development or redevelopment of the organization will avoid costly mistakes.
4. Talking to competitors' customers will give an organization a clear indication of why these customers do business elsewhere.
5. Working partnerships with customers, in the form of feedback systems, will lead to continuous improvement and quality.

There are costs involved in *not* gathering pertinent information concerning an organization's customers. They include:

The cost of conformance;
The cost of nonconformance;
The cost of lost opportunities;
The cost of quality.

Data that are hidden, ignored, not collected, or not taken seriously by organizations can lead to stagnation and customer dissatisfaction.

Organizations must ask themselves questions similar to the following, in order to ensure that the use of this strategy will bear benefits and lead to quality improvement:

Exhibit 28.5. Chart for strategic synergism.

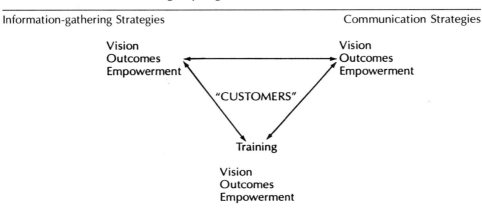

Information-gathering Strategies		Communication Strategies
Vision		Vision
Outcomes		Outcomes
Empowerment	"CUSTOMERS"	Empowerment
	Training	
	Vision	
	Outcomes	
	Empowerment	

Vision:	What are we like?
	What is our mission?
Outcomes:	What do our customers need?
	What do our customers want?
Empowerment:	Do I understand my contribution to our success?
	Do I have the authority to act?

How have we ensured that all volunteers, leaders, and employees are made aware of customer needs and expectations?

What effective and innovative methods have we employed in obtaining both internal and external customer feedback?

Have we empowered employees to resolve customer problems?

Have we implemented systems that link customer feedback, including comments, recommendations, and complaints, to those who can act on the information?

Do we have processes for evaluating these feedback systems?

(b) COMMUNICATION STRATEGIES   An organization's climate and mission can affect the communication process. If the mission is the pursuit of quality and excellence regarding all aspects of operation, including the attainment of a customer focus, effective communication can become a means for decision making, obtaining consumer feedback, and fulfilling the organization's goals and objectives.

Effective communication, a vital link in any interaction, is especially meaningful when dealing with both internal and external customers. Communication strategies can be classified into three categories; interpersonal, intraorganizational, and interorganizational, as shown in Exhibit 28.6.

If you are keeping in mind a customer focus, what questions will *you* have in this type of setting?

Open communication—a supervisor's willingness to act on subordinates' ideas, or an organization's willingness to listen to and act on customer feedback—can create a climate conducive to attaining the organizational goals.

Nonverbal communication, or the messages communicated without the use of words, can alter the climate of an organization. This type of communication can also be a powerful indicator of the organizational climate. Perceptions of distortions or half-truths can lead a customer (whether internal or external) to believe that he or she has been misled or is a victim, and can result in low satisfaction with job, workplace, relationships (internal), or service or product (external).

Organizations must ask themselves the following questions, to ensure a clear and unobstructed flow of information between customer and provider:

Have we recruited employees with the understanding that a main goal of our organization is harmonious customer relations?

In training our employees, have we communicated the aspect of customer focus?

Have we communicated to both our internal and external customers the fact that employees are empowered to resolve customer problems?

Are we accessible to our customers?

Do customer concerns and complaints lead to change and improvement?

Is both good and bad information, in the form of customer communication and feedback, used positively?

Are the methods of communicating with customers effective?

(c) TRAINING ISSUES   Training refers to the formal procedures an organization uses to change the behavior (learning) of its employees, so that the organization's goals and objectives may be realized. Training should be purposeful, systematic, and intentional.

Exhibit 28.6. Chart of communication strategies.

Type of Communication	Who Is the Customer?	Who Needs to Know?
Interpersonal	Whom will you communicate with? Internal: 1. _____ 2. _____ 3. _____ External: 1. _____ 2. _____ 3. _____	Customer: 1. _____ 2. _____ 3. _____ Provider: 1. _____ 2. _____ 3. _____ Subordinate: 1. _____ 2. _____ 3. _____ Superior: 1. _____ 2. _____ 3. _____
Intraorganizational	Internal: 1. _____ 2. _____ 3. _____ External: 1. _____ 2. _____ 3. _____	Groups: 1. _____ 2. _____ 3. _____ Units: 1. _____ 2. _____ 3. _____
Interorganizational	External: 1. _____ 2. _____ 3. _____	Agencies: 1. _____ 2. _____ 3. _____ Organization: 1. _____ 2. _____ 3. _____

Altering employees' behavior through training and the acquisition of skills from this training will contribute to the overall effectiveness of the organization, the individual, and, ultimately, the consumers of services or products.

Communication is an important aspect of developing and implementing a successful training program. The goals of the training itself should be clearly expressed. Organizations must also train their employees to become better communicators. Verbal and listening skills are behaviors that can be learned or acquired with practice.

A key element of an organization's survival and success is the quality of its employees. Training can enhance that quality.

Interactions with customers rest mainly with the employees of an organization. Training of employees, therefore, should reflect the organization's concern for customer service and quality. These are key criteria:

Has employee training been designed with a customer focus?

Have employees been empowered to resolve customer problems?

Are employees trained to not only meet but to exceed customer expectations?

Have employees been trained to give priority attention to those processes requiring improvement based on customer needs?

Have employees been given the training necessary to evaluate customer feedback systems?

28.6 AFFIRMATIONS OF A SUCCESSFUL CUSTOMER-FOCUSED ORGANIZATION

We will be successful because we have a clear understanding of what we are going to do.

We will be successful because we will provide the support and training everyone needs to improve the development of the individual, the team, and the organization.

We will be successful because we take pride in our work.

We will be successful because we each have the responsibility and authority to act on improving service to our customers.

We will be successful because we know our customers, what they need, and what they want.

SOURCES AND SUGGESTED REFERENCES

Application Guidelines, Malcolm Baldrige National Quality Award. 1990. Milwaukee, WI: The Malcolm Baldrige National Quality Award Consortium, Inc.

Chaffee, Ellen E. 1990. *Quality: Key to the Future.* Keynote address, annual meeting of the American Association of Colleges of Pharmacy, Salt Lake City, Utah, July 8.

Consultants

CHAPTER TWENTY-NINE

Fund-Raising Consultants

Henry Goldstein
The Oram Group, Inc.

CONTENTS

29.1 WHEN TO USE A CONSULTANT

Among the most important decisions a nonprofit makes is whether to work with a fund-raising consultant. A firm or an individual might be initially employed for the following reasons:

1. The nature of the fund-raising project is beyond the agency's experience. Example: A human services agency wants to expand into its own building and will have to raise $3 million in a capital campaign. No one on the board or staff has ever been through this type of campaign.
2. The staff is technically inexperienced or cannot undertake additional work. Example: One member of the development staff has conducted a capital campaign

previously but feels her effort should be devoted to annual giving and government grants, which produce the bulk of the agency's annual income. She does not think it wise to be diverted from this top priority.

3. The feasibility and prospects of fund-raising success are uncertain or undetermined; an objective analysis is desired. Example: The board is not convinced a capital campaign can produce $3 million. Having never been through one before, the development committee strongly feels an objective study of community attitudes, the case for philanthropic support, likely campaign leadership, and potential major gifts should be undertaken to ascertain the likelihood of success.

4. A specific fund-raising task is to be accomplished. Example: Having determined to run a capital campaign in-house, the development director has decided to use a consultant to prepare the case statement, train the solicitors, and provide strategic advice.

29.2 THE FUND-RAISING ASSIGNMENT

The decision to retain a consultant should rest on a clear understanding of the fund-raising assignment, why a consultant is sought, who in the nonprofit board or staff structure wants (or doesn't want) a consultant, and realistic expectations. Whether a nonprofit is large or small, and irrespective of the size of the development office, a consultant supplements but does not replace (except temporarily) agency resources. The board and staff members involved need to agree that this option is worthwhile and workable. The selection process often provides clarity.

Fund-raising consultants offer an array of services (see Exhibit 29.1). As with other professionals, some are generalists, others concentrate on specific areas. An agency should select only those services that are required.

A consultant may see an assignment differently than the client. For example, a nonprofit wants to raise endowment funds but is a new organization with a very small donor base. The consultant advises that endowment funds are generated internally and recommends developing a broad-based annual giving program directed primarily to individuals and family foundations.

Exhibit 29.1.   Principal fund-raising consulting services.

Alumni giving	List brokerage
Annual giving	List management
Board development	Planned giving programs
Capital campaign counsel	Printed materials
Capital campaign management	Proposal writing
Case development	Public relations
Computer systems, hardware and software	Recruitment of fund-raising executives
Corporate campaigns	Research
Direct mail	Special events
Endowment campaign counsel	Strategic planning
Endowment campaign management	Telemarketing
Foundation grants	Training for board and staff
Feasibility studies and surveys	Video production
Government funding	

29.3 INITIATING A SEARCH

In most nonprofits, hiring a consultant is a committee affair. Four to six people, staff and board, should be sufficient to encompass a variety of opinions and concerns. A typical group will include the chief executive, a board officer or two, the development director, and perhaps a major donor or someone else with a specific interest in fund-raising.

Successful fund-raising depends on involvement. Choosing a consultant is educational for volunteers and staff, especially when a campaign, or employment of an outsider, is a new experience.

(a) WHAT THE CONSULTANT NEEDS TO KNOW ABOUT POTENTIAL CLIENTS The staff should prepare an information packet. The first enclosure, a short paper of no more than a few pages, should describe the fund-raising program. Most consultants will depend on it to gauge the organization's potential and their interest in accepting employment. Some organizations that are familiar with the governmental grant and contract process issue formal "RFPs" (requests for proposals). However, consultants are often reluctant to respond to an RFP from an unknown organization unless it is preceded, or followed up, by personal contact. General information—a brochure or fund-raising materials—a board list (including the members' business affiliations), a recent audit, and other financial information should be added to complete the packet delivered to the prospective consultant.

(b) FINDING CONSULTANTS The initial objective of the search should be to identify three to five consultants who will be invited to personal interviews with the hiring committee. Individual consultants, small firms, or the industry leaders might all be considered. A mixed group is a good idea, for their differences in style, perspective, and experience.

The best source for finding a consultant is word-of-mouth. The board and staff, other nonprofits in the same field, and sources in the geographic area and among professional colleagues should all be asked for names and a critique of services. The assignment and the services sought should be specifically detailed.

Second, the American Association of Fund Raising Counsel (AAFRC), the National Society of Fund Raising Executives (NSFRE), or the Association of Healthcare Professionals (AHP) will provide lists of firms that offer services in various locales. The AAFRC is a trade association of consulting firms; the NSFRE and AHP enroll individual fund-raisers. All set ethical fund-raising standards to which their members agree to adhere. (See Exhibit 29.2.)

Not all major firms belong to AAFRC. Those reputable firms who choose not to belong accept the same ethical standards as those who do. Others offer services so specialized they do not qualify for membership. Many small firms and part-time consultants do not belong to AAFRC.

Not all individual professionals belong to NSFRE, but experienced people with a track record accept and abide by NSFRE's ethical standards.

The third step is to scan the trade press. Consultants advertise and often write for the trades. The principal media are *Nonprofit Times, The Chronicle of Philanthropy, Foundation News, NSFRE Journal, Giving USA,* and *Fundraising Management.*

Consultants advertise in the Yellow Pages as well. However, letting "your fingers do the walking" is chancy. The publishers' occupational classifications include under "Fund

Exhibit 29.2. Key sources for information on consultants.

AMERICAN ASSOCIATION OF FUND-RAISING COUNSEL
25 West 43rd Street
New York, NY 10036
212-354-5799   Fax: 212-768-1795

Ms. Joanne Hayes, President/CEO

NATIONAL SOCIETY OF FUND-RAISING EXECUTIVES
1101 King Street
Alexandria, VA 22314
703-684-0410   Fax: 703-684-0540

Ms. Pat Lewis, President/CEO

ASSOCIATION FOR HEALTHCARE PHILANTHROPY
313 Park Avenue, Suite 400
Falls Church, VA 22046
703-532-6243   Fax: 703-532-7170

Mr. William McGinly, President

Raising" a mix of businesses whose relationship to fund-raising consulting is distant at best.

(c) CONTACTING POTENTIAL CONSULTANTS   A starting list of 10, or even 15 consultants is a good field. For the rest of this chapter, we'll assume that the hiring committee has given you its list and asked you to "take it from there." You can write to each name on the list, enclosing the information packet. On the other hand, unless you are experienced, you are learning nothing about the consultants and, of course, you have to wait for their responses.

Most development people agree that the feedback provided by an introductory telephone call is very useful for both parties. Your gut reaction may well be "These people sound like we might be able to work together," or it may be "This is not a fit." The consultant may have exactly the same reaction toward you.

The first few telephone calls will sharpen your presentation to the rest of the list. Keep a record of your first impressions. When you send along the cover letter and information packet, include a deadline for responses.

These actions are especially recommended:

- *Ask to speak to the top person.* Even in large firms, you will find that the CEO is happy to talk to a prospective client. If you can't reach him or her, ask for the next person down. The firm's decision to take you on as a client is made at the top, not the bottom.

- *Be as specific as possible.* You will be asked how much money you hope to raise, how large your organization is (in staff and budget), how long you have been in business, and so on. Even though this is all in the information packet, the exchange is important in classifying your circumstances.

- *Ask if the consultant's experience fits your needs.* A quick rundown of the consultant's experience, size of operation, other clients served, one or two local references, the range of fees, who might be assigned to your account, and length of time in business is basic.

- *Ask for a brief written response, a list of the consultant's current and recent clients, and information about the firm.* Many consultants are employed full-time by non-profits but their arrangements permit outside consulting. Be sure that the consultant (unless an independent) has such permission, and that the scope of your assignment will fit the consultant's availability and competence.

Don't:

- *Expect a consultant to submit a formal proposal on the basis of a phone call or a letter.* The preparation of proposals is time-consuming and, without fairly detailed information, meaningless. Most consultants won't do it.

- *Expect a consultant to set a fee over the telephone.* It is reasonable to discuss fees and it is helpful to both parties if this discussion takes place up front. Consultants will respond to a preliminary question about fees, usually by providing a range of fees for the services offered. This should suffice for immediate comparative purposes.

- *Expect a consultant to respond well to an unrealistic deadline.* A request for detailed information, even if well short of a formal proposal, still takes time to prepare properly. The more you expect, the longer the time. As a guide, a routine request for a brochure and a client list can be attended to immediately. For a more complete response, which considers the uniqueness of a given situation, allow at least two weeks, longer if convenient.

29.4 SELECTING A CONSULTANT

Having developed a list of possibilities, it is now time to make the initial cuts. As the person principally responsible for the process thus far, you have a sense of who's out there. You may have a preferential order. You, your chief executive, and the chairperson of the selection committee should shorten the list to no more than five consultants who will be invited to personal interviews.

Some organizations like to meet the consultants informally before inviting three finalists to meet with the full committee; others prefer different courses. The interaction between the parties is the most important aspect of the relationship to come. Therefore, the interview is critical.

Consultants normally do not charge a fee for an initial consultation, or even two. In most instances, the consultant's expenses incidental to the selection process are absorbed. Someone based in your city incurs little expense in visiting your premises.

However, long distances pose a problem. Consultants have differing policies on speculative travel. Some will travel at no apparent expense to the potential client: expenses are recouped later, as an overhead factor in the fees charged all clients. Others will ask for reimbursement. Still others will judge how badly they want the client and act accordingly. As an example, a southern college in a small city called three national firms and sent information. Each firm was invited to travel many hundreds of miles at its own expense to a destination that has spotty airline service. For each, the round trip represented the better part of two billable days' time. Each consultant was to be allotted 30 minutes to appear before the trustees' development committee. Given this scenario, two firms agreed to appear; the other declined.

(a) HOW TO CONDUCT AN INTERVIEW   Allow at least 60 minutes for each interview. A 15- or 20-minute break between interviews gives everyone a chance to relax and permits a bit of feedback. It is also a courtesy to the consultants not to have them stacked up like air traffic over O'Hare.

Ideally, the full selection committee will participate. However, not every person can attend every meeting. If consultants are coming a distance and repeat visits are therefore impractical, an extra effort should be made to ensure that everyone attends.

The atmosphere should be purposeful but relaxed enough to permit lively exchange among the participants. The easy way to begin is to invite the consultant to describe his or her background, the firm's experience, and why it should be selected for the assignment. The consultant should also be encouraged to ask questions of the committee.

Next, zero in on the specifics related to the assignment, and close by asking the consultant if he or she is interested in offering a written proposal.

(b) EIGHT CRITICAL QUESTIONS TO ASK A CONSULTANT

1. How long have you been in business?
2. Who in the firm will work on our account, and who will supervise?
3. How are you specifically qualified to handle this assignment?
4. What is your fee?
5. What is your estimate of reimbursable expenses?
6. How long will it take to complete this work?
7. Who are your current and recent clients, especially those for whom you accomplished a similar task?
8. Why do you want to work for us?

(c) HOW TO READ A PROPOSAL   Although the formats vary, a proposal addresses nine elements. If all are included, and if at the end an acceptance clause, a place for an authorizing signature, and a request for a retainer are included, the executed document is considered a binding agreement.

If no authorizing action is required on your part, the proposal is nonbinding. It is ultimately attached to a shorter, binding letter of agreement (sometimes called a letter of engagement). The nonbinding proposal is useful when one party or the other has not yet made a decision. Consultants will also submit nonbinding proposals when they feel they do not yet know enough about a potential client's requirements to commit themselves.

An agreement is effective when it is signed by both parties and the retainer is paid (usually the first month's fee or 25 to 33 percent of a project fee).

Elements of a proposal or letter of engagement

1. *Presenting information.* The consultant's understanding of the work to be done.
2. *Basic agreement.* The work to be performed by the consultant to complete the assignment addressed in the proposal.

3. *Objectives of the assignment.* A description of each element to be considered. A feasibility study, for example, will usually focus on case, constituency, leadership, staffing, cost, and duration of a campaign.

4. *Methodology.* The techniques the consultant will use to complete the assignment. These may include a specified number of interviews among defined constituents, focus groups, analysis of records, plans and materials; or the completion of a specific task: a mailing, a special event, installation of a customized computer software program; a telemarketing test, and so on.

5. *Work product.* The deliverable: it may be a written report, a test analysis, or money in the bank!

6. *Timetable.* An estimate of the time required to complete the assignment, usually presented week by week, month by month, or quarterly.

7. *Personnel.* The consultant's staff to be assigned to your account. You may ask for bios to be included on the people to be assigned; the consultant may include a clause prohibiting you from offering employment to any of his or her staff members for a specified period of time.

8. *Fees and expenses.* In the fund-raising field, it is considered unethical for consultants to work on speculation or commission, or on a percentage of fees raised. Expect a fixed fee. Reimbursable out-of-pocket expenses include telephone, fax, travel, lodging, and other than routine administrative expenses, e.g., reproduction of a lengthy report, or extensive research. Expenses should be agreed on in advance.

9. *References.* It is extremely important to insist on references and equally important to check them carefully. Current and former clients will be the most helpful. References should be obtained by telephone; no one will say anything negative on paper. On the other hand, do not expect all accolades. Otherwise top-notch consultants occasionally do poorly, and not very good ones sometimes get lucky. Time after time, the principal reasons for client dissatisfaction are first, the personality or, second, the competence of the staff assigned to the account.

In checking references, obtain the answers to these six key questions, and be sure to talk with someone who has direct, first-hand knowledge:

1. What services did the consultant perform?
2. Were you satisfied?
3. Who was assigned to your account?
4. Did you have regular access to a senior member of the consultant's staff?
5. Would you employ this consultant again?
6. What was the fee?

Staff and volunteers often see things differently. In checking references, try to include a few board members or other volunteers in the mix.

29.5 FEES, EXPENSES, REGISTRATION

Fees are a multiple of time and personnel and cover the consultant's salary costs, overhead, and profit margin. They are quoted on an hourly, daily, monthly, annual, or project basis.

There is nothing illegal about working on contingency, commission, or percentage. The professional associations discourage it but the National Council of Better Business Bureaus holds that contingency fund-raising might work to a nonprofit's economic advantage. The debate has been going on for some time and is unlikely to be satisfactorily resolved anytime soon.

For new, small, impecunious nonprofits, a contingency arrangement may look good. If you are tempted, check carefully with others who have tried it; the results have generally been poor.

(a) WHAT IS A "FAIR" FEE?   Fund-raising consultants operate in a free market. Theoretically, they can charge whatever they wish—in fact, they are bound by competitive forces. The best way to determine whether a fee is "fair" is to ask others what they paid for the services they received, and to compare the fees various consultants propose. A low fee is not always the best choice, and a high fee does not ensure superior service.

(b) EXPENSES   Unless you otherwise agree, out-of-pocket expenses are not included in the fee. It is possible for both parties to estimate out-of-pocket expenses in advance and to "cap" the agreement.

(c) REGISTRATION   A thicket of state, and sometimes local, ordinances govern the relationship between consultants and clients. Whether an agreement must be registered with a government agency depends mainly on the jurisdiction and the services to be performed. Religious groups are generally exempt from all registration requirements.

29.6   A HAPPY RELATIONSHIP

More than anything else, a productive relationship between a consultant and a client derives from mutual respect, shared vision, open communication, and hard work all around.

If the client–consultant relationship is working well, you will perhaps wonder why you need a written agreement. If it is not working well, a piece of paper will not save it.

SOURCES AND SUGGESTED REFERENCES

Bailey, Willard. 1991. "Confessions of a Fundraising Consultant." *The NSFRE Journal* (Summer): 20–26.
Hall, Holly. 1991. "Choosing the Right Consultant." *The Chronicle of Philanthropy,* 3 (February 26): 22–27.
Raybin, Arthur D. 1985. *How to Hire the Right Fund Raising Consultant.* Washington, DC: The Taft Group.

Consulting for Total Quality Improvement: Beyond the Expert Role to Empowerment

Kenneth L. Murrell
The University of West Florida and
Empowerment Leadership Systems

CONTENTS

30.1 INTRODUCTION

As organizations in all sectors are instituting quality improvement programs, thousands of new consultants are emerging on the scene to offer their services. Unfortunately, in the basic nature of these consulting relationships, there is an inherent bias built from tradition, habit, and social expectations. That bias is that the consultant is the expert—the hired gun or the charismatic problem solver. The consultant is expected to operate in the role of the hero just at the time when the literature is stressing how bankrupt that model is for the individual manager. Beyond the hero or the postheroic manager (as Bradford and Cohen (1984) described so well in *Managing for Excellence*) is the manager as developer. This is the path the educated manager is pursuing, but the consulting world in many ways has not kept pace. It is incumbent on managers, particularly in the nonprofit sector, to carefully allocate their limited consulting budgets to activities that empower the organization to create and achieve its own strategic vision rather than follow a prescriptive path laid out by an external expert.

With the tremendous pressures put on nonprofit managers to improve their organizations, what is essentially at work is that both the client and the consultant find many reasons to perpetuate the mystique of the consultant as expert or hero. In these days of total quality management (TQM), the role of consultant as a wise and all-knowing guru has influenced much of the manner in which organizational reform has been introduced. It may be too early to express any evaluative comments as to the success or failure of this approach, except to say that even organization development in its most active years seldom produced as much messianic faith in a single guru as has the TQM movement. In the terms of a religious movement, the consultant as expert is carried to near-sainthood in TQM. The result is that an increasingly recognizable backlash is occurring among those who are feeling coerced into accepting a major change program they may feel little or no involvement in creating.

As an alternative change model, the process model seems to be much closer to the *Kaizen* concept of constant improvement and it is one of the underlying philosophical foundations of TQM. The *Kaizen* philosophy represents why Japanese management practices have been leading the world in what is basically a revolution of thought about what good management is. *Kaizen* is a way of life and, as practiced by managers, it is a philosophy of continuous incremental improvement. The process approach is built on a similar set of assumptions; if not in conflict with the traditional belief of consultant as expert or guru, they are at least very different from it. The process model is based on employee involvement and may be seen as change moving both up and across the organization. Management operates in a more facilitative manner to create change leadership in the organization. The process is one of transforming the organization from within, versus top-down and often forced structural change.

Exhibit 30.1 identifies the role differences between the expert and the process model. In the process approach, the total system depends on the client and it focuses on long-term and sustainable effectiveness. This type of consultancy results in a customized process of change that involves local leadership. The major difference from the expert approach is that the process model created is more implementable: it is not an imposed solution; instead, it is a set of change strategies developed by those who can operationalize them.

Exhibit 30.2 explains basically what a manager needs to know about which consultants have process skills, where to find them, and how to evaluate their credentials.

In process consulting contracting (see Exhibit 30.3), the essential issue is relationship building, with the manager as client and with the change leadership within the organization. The consultant needs to be informed clearly on who the client is, and all parties to the process should basically be in agreement with that contract. Where the client is more than an individual manager, the client system (group, team, committee, or whatever it is labelled) must all be in agreement with the client–consultant relationship proposed.

30.2 DEVELOPING THE PROCESS SKILLS: A, B, C, AND D

A consultant needs a number of requisite skills to operate in a process model. Critical is a level of expertise and credibility; but this is only the beginning. Process consultants have developed expertise in the behavioral sciences ranging from psychology to anthro-

Exhibit 30.1. Process versus expert consulting roles.

Expert Role	Process Role
Engages client organization from authority position and uses technical expertise as power base.	Works with client system and other stakeholders to determine where opportunities to make progress are based.
Primarily asks for information from reports in order to diagnose problems as viewed from the technical perspective of the specific expert engaged.	Sets out to develop an internal team, to create a diagnostic process with emphasis on finding opportunities for positive change.
Determines from limited data gathered the nature of problems and how they should be solved using primarily external resources.	Provides action team with useful information and other experiences as they work together to develop plans of action and priorities based on the organization's values.
Emphasis is on task and technical side of development, less on an understanding and appreciation for organizational dynamics.	Focus is on facilitative role, to help empower team to face the issues and appreciate the organizational context as well as the technical challenges.
Evaluation is conducted externally and beneficiaries are involved more as passive receptors than as active and equal participants.	Evaluation is ongoing and involves real-time processing of strengths and limitations of teams' work. Emphasis on project or program evaluation is to discover ways and means of using successful experiences to achieve future goals.
Preplanned, rigid, and blueprint models of organizational improvement are used to logically direct change in a highly structured manner. The consultant-as-guru approach.	Organic and constantly changing models are created jointly and used within the team in order to energize positive forces for change and to fully engage local stakeholders in implementation. Continuous follow-up is designed in.

Exhibit 30.2. Process consultants: Who, where, how much, and how to evaluate.

WHO: Process expertise is a rare but growing commodity. Consultants in the fields of Organizational Development (OD) and Community Development have skills and experiences in developing effective relationships with clients in order to assist the organization.

WHERE: These consultants are not always well-known, but any university program in OD or its related fields can be a source of recommendations. National networks of OD consultants exist; the three largest are the OD Institute, the OD Network, and the American Society for Training and Development's OD Group. Regional and local groups also exist in every large urban area and in the South, in the form of the Southern OD Interest Group.

HOW MUCH: Consulting fees range from several hundred dollars a day upward to several thousand. For the nonprofit sector, pro-bono work is a possibility. Calling a university-based professional and offering an honorarium is another alternative.

HOW TO EVALUATE: The credentials of a competent process consultant would almost always reflect significant graduate level work in the applied behavioral sciences as well as years of successful application of the process model. Asking any consultant to furnish a list of references is perfectly appropriate. The most common referral process is word-of-mouth. A consultant's reputation is highly correlated with impressionistic data, so it's wise to ask for more data. To ask a process consultant for a self-evaluation in terms of strengths and weaknesses is an acceptable inquiry and one that can be expected from the consultant as well. What is being evaluated is not the traditional notion of expertise but the ability to develop effective relationships in order to help the organization empower itself and develop its own change strategy.

Exhibit 30.3.   Sample contract guidelines for process consultation.

Because of the unique nature of the relationship of client and consultant when using a process approach, rather than an expert or doctor–patient model, the following guidelines are offered:

1. The nature of the relationship is primarily interpersonal and, if the mutual feelings of attraction and respect are not there at the beginning, the process may be jeopardized or considerably slower in developing.

2. A period of mutual exploration should occur, so that the parties to the contract can establish some basis of a human relationship prior to an agreement on the nature of the task. In a Western culture setting, this may occur in a number of hours; in other, more affiliation-based cultures, this process may take weeks or even months.

3. As an initial trust is being developed, a frank and open discussion should follow as to the expectations each party has for the other in the following areas:

   a. amount of time per week or month available for meeting;

   b. environments mutually agreed to as best for conducting initial meetings;

   c. type of information each party needs and desires about the other party in order to work effectively;

   d. a tentative timeline for acting together in order to begin a diagnostic or appreciative process where information about the client system can be generated and tested;

   e. amount, type, and form of payment for services that each party can agree to with an understanding of what these services represent;

   f. a sharing of expectations for both the worst- and best-case scenarios, in terms of the phases of the consulting relationship. The phases at this initial point represent simply a beginning plan, an action phase, and a concluding phase.

4. As appropriate, the contract can be formalized and recorded for future review. A signed and dated contract can also be used, but contracting in this type of relationship should represent the current state of agreement. With each step in the process, the contract should be reviewed and modified where appropriate.

5. A substantial change in the contract or an ending of the relationship is not prohibited. If it is necessary, a joint discussion of the reasons for it are expected and an agreement should be reached that each party feels is fair, given the circumstances.

pology and even economics, if the consultancy has that dimension to it. The difference is that, as opposed to a narrowly trained and programmed expert, the process consultant is a generalist with an intellectual and experiential broad base of expertise. This is the starting point. The process consultant has highly developed and refined interpersonal and group skills that enable him or her to function effectively with others. These skills are based on both high levels of self-awareness and an ability to ground oneself emotionally prior to working with a client. High self-acceptance and an ability to listen are fundamental skills that process consultants should be seen to possess.

The As, Bs, Cs, and Ds of the process approach can be described as shown in Exhibits 30.4 through 30.8. The A is for ACTION, ALIGNMENT, and APPRECIATION. A consultant who is not aligned with the elements of the organization that desires change is not going to operate well in a process mode. Alignment is not necessarily limited to a few individuals. As more and more of the organization truly desires change, then alignment and acceptance of these individuals and groups will speed the process approach. Those forces nonaligned should not be assumed to be opposing forces but, rather, interested forces; their active appreciation must be developed. Appreciation in this case means knowledge at a deeper level, a full understanding. This alignment, having allies and an appreciation for all the forces at work, is a prerequisite for a successful

Exhibit 30.4.   The As of process consulting.

A
ACTION, ALIGNMENT, APPRECIATION

ACTION	Moving beyond rhetoric to real movement; the words are being spoken; now the action and effort at the operational level follow.
ALIGNMENT	Coalescing of the forces working for change and representational teams identified for leading the empowerment changes.
APPRECIATION	Developing a deep level of understanding of the organization and the forces working both for and against change. Learning to appreciate and fully know all the elements of the organization and its environment.

Exhibit 30.5.   The Bs of process consulting.

B
BELIEF IN SYSTEM, BELIEF IN PEOPLE, BELIEF IN PROCESS

BELIEF IN SYSTEM	The acceptance of where the organization is and a respect for what it has taken to develop it to that point.
BELIEF IN PEOPLE	Faith in and respect for each and every individual in the organization, with an appreciation of their differences.
BELIEF IN PROCESS	Trust that a positive process for change (empowerment) will eventually prevail and that organizational development is a reality.

Exhibit 30.6.   The Cs of process consulting.

C
PSYCHOLOGICAL CONTRACTS, STRATEGIC CONTRACTS, EMPOWERMENT AGREEMENTS

PSYCHOLOGICAL CONTRACTS	Formalized processes to identify mutual expectations and assumptions that working teams have about each other and about how they best work together.
STRATEGIC CONTRACTS	The agreement in principle of the philosophy and approach used in the organization to create and develop empowerment changes.
EMPOWERMENT AGREEMENTS	Acceptance of the depoliticizing of the process in order to develop the creation of power versus the competition over power and the infighting that too often result.

Exhibit 30.7.   The Ds of process consulting.

D
DEVELOPMENT AS CONSTANT IMPROVEMENT

Short-term measures of organizational success—profit and loss, budget compliance, and sales growth, for example—are used relative to . . .

Medium-term measures of improvements in quality of products or services produced that are to be considered in terms of . . .

Long-term measures of constant improvement or a developmental perspective that indicates cultural change creating an empowered organization constantly learning how to improve!

Exhibit 30.8.   The E-to-Z span of process consulting.

E-to-Z

E-to-Z EMPOWERMENT creates the human energy and capacity to develop the organization and take it through the entire alphabet of terms on its way to reaching its full potential.

The E-to-Z steps are anything but easy. A leadership style that is empowering creates the essential components of:

- Enhanced information flow and education;
- Supportive and encouraging relationships;
- Structures and empowering alignments;
- Rewards and resources for quality output;
- Leadership and followership skills;
- An actualized work environment where people *want* to contribute and the organizational culture is empowering them to do it!

---

process consultancy. The nonprofit manager as client is expected to help develop this appreciation of the organization in the consultant.

The B factor stands for the development of a BELIEF in the client system as well as a faith or belief in the process approach. This is the old adage, "Trust the process," and accept the clients where they are and not where they should be. This takes considerable patience and trust; if that's not possible, a process approach can't be built. This highly interpersonal relationship must be built on belief and trust in the client and in self. If it's not there, it can't be faked. Again, the manager working with the process consultant is instrumental in developing this relationship of trust. If it's not there, the process will falter.

The C factor is the CRITICAL dimension of developing at first a psychological and then a strategic CONTRACT. The psychological contract is based on shared and mutually acceptable expectations; the strategic contract is a set of change principles everyone can believe in. These two contracts are time-consuming and difficult, but, if they are not developed effectively, there may be significant problems later in the consultancy. These contracts are attempts to put everything on the table and should deal with both personal and ethical concerns about working together. The individual manager and the other change leaders involved must all work together to develop the agreements on how they will interact and how they think the organization will improve.

The final factor D is for the DEVELOPMENT process itself. It is the real activity of working to develop and improve the system. This D for development follows the spirit of the Japanese *Kaizen* philosophy, in which constant improvement is the goal while fear and humiliation are removed from the process. The development goal is a process consulting hallmark because the ethical and professional stance of the process consultant is to help develop the system's own capacity for improvement and not to allow for a dependence on the consultant. This is one of the most difficult challenges for the process consultant; yet, the success of any process model depends on the client's capacity for self-improvement. Clients should not be dependent on an outside consultant for development. Constant improvement becomes part of the culture, and the impact is much broader than in just how people work together. *Kaizen* as constant improvement has become a way of life in some of the world's most successful organizations (notably Toyota) and is one of the best explanations of the Japanese economic miracle. As a typical example, an illustrative case is offered in the next section, to show how this longer-term developmental goal can be actualized.

30.3 CASE ILLUSTRATION

For three years now, I have been working with an independent nonprofit agency of 200 professionals in the field of aging. During these three years as a process consultant, I have been involved in roughly a dozen luncheon meetings, several short planning meetings, numerous phone conferences, and three very successful off-site annual weekend retreats. During this period, the agency has expanded its staff, programs, and facilities on a regular basis, and has developed a strategic planning approach and design where none existed before. As an outside consultant, my goal has been to work with the Executive Director and his top assistant in creating for the agency an action planning process that has full board involvement and an empowered staff leading its implementation. As a process consultant, I have helped to create this model, but the desire for it and the ownership of it have been 100 percent the agency's and the board's. Repeatedly, I have backed away from the expert strategic planning consultant role and, instead, have encouraged the Executive Director and his assistant to create and develop the planning process they value.

So many times, I've been tempted to provide all of my own models and theories, but I've maintained my trust and respect for my clients to know better what they think will work.

As a team, the executives and the board chair have, for the past two years, taken nearly total responsibility for planning the off-site retreat. My consulting input has been more and more one of encouragement and support. Every year, the board's involvement in the process expands and the ownership of the strategic process grows. In the years to come, my services will be less needed but my support and assistance will remain as close as the nearest telephone. During the three-year period, I have phased myself out of being critical to the process. In the first two years, I seemed overly central to what was occurring; in the most recent third annual retreat, I felt my presence more symbolic than substantive. The system has empowered itself and the staff has developed new and impressive skills. The board is more involved, and even the public is more aware of the important role the agency plays in the community.

The development of the agency is a most impressive sight and, as the population ages, its services increase in importance. The agency also sees itself in a new role as both a nonprofit service agency and a proactive organization that must try to stay one step ahead of the coming trends. Its identity is blurring between the public service image previously promoted and that of the rapid response organization that can charge for its offerings in order to subsidize delivery of services to those without any means to pay. The self-image is one of a "learning organization" that is empowered to create its own future and not just exist on the available institutional funding.

These developments are surely not due to my involvement as a process consultant. But, as I have been able to act as a catalyst and a facilitator, previously untapped potential has emerged and is now being managed by the organization itself. The significant rewards for a consultant in a case like this one are not so much in the tangible form but in the satisfaction of helping people who are providing critical social services. The joy is in seeing them achieve the professional goals they have set for themselves and their agency. The other reward offered is to be able to observe how much easier it is for people to work successfully together when they are supported and appreciated rather than instructed on how they should improve. The expert consultant provides answers; the process consultant facilitates growth and, from that growth, answers continue to emerge long after the consultant leaves.

30.4   EXPANDING INTO ACTION RESEARCH

As the process consulting approach is expanded, it moves to a continuous research activity known as "action research." This research methodology is developed within the client system through constant self-appraisal and reflection, creating a culture where the organization itself is learning. This organizational learning occurs in a myriad of ways. Its most distinguishing features are experimentation and reflection. Quality as a culture fosters this continuous improvement in all that the organization does. For that to be developmental, the organization must be constantly scanning its environment and learning from others, as well as improving internally. It is the responsibility of the process consultant to leave behind these process skills so that managers in the organization, particularly its leadership, can continue learning from experience and experimentation. The A, B, C, and D principles are necessary here in order for everyone to work and learn effectively together. Process consultants do not create dependency relationships; instead, they foster organizational growth that allows them to assist organizations that are less developed in their learning skills. Action research is simply the ability of the organization to continuously reflect on the processes it uses to learn and develop, and to strive for a better understanding of those process dynamics and for use of that knowledge to improve the organization.

30.5   ACTION EMPOWERMENT AS
ORGANIZATION DEVELOPMENT

As the process unfolds and the action research/organizational learning skills improve, what occurs is an empowerment of the total organization. Power is created, not just distributed or transformed. Power from knowledge and information is expanded because of the learning capacities the organization has developed. Contracting facilitates better team and interpersonal agreements, giving everyone more support and encouragement. Structures are developed to assist in improving work flows and moving information more effectively. Leadership is developed and supported by more assertive and safe followers who don't fear giving or receiving feedback. The reward systems and the recognition given expand everyone's appreciation of what is possible and what their efforts contribute to the success of the whole. Finally, an empowerment ethic encourages self-actualization so that people are assisted in finding what they truly do best and in helping others to discover the unique talents they possess. Cross-training and job sharing increase the attention to constant improvement. As the organizational learning capacities expand, so also do the individual capacities.

All of this results in organizational development where the evaluation of success is not based solely on short-term gain, or medium-term quality improvements, but on a longer-term capacity to develop and sustain that ethic and philosophy over the life of the organization.

30.6   CONCLUSION: THE PROCESS PERSPECTIVE

The process consultant is brought in to function as a catalyst who focuses attention on the processes of learning and organizational development. The manager is expected to be responsible with, as opposed to dependent on, the outside expert. The alignment and appreciation element starts by building alliances for those inside the organization who want change to occur. The belief or faith in the system, and in self, starts a positive process wherein trust is established. From trust come valid data in order to contract honestly and clearly with others to develop shared expectations and a strategic philosophy of change. Finally, a development culture emerges which, based on empowering and not controlling, facilitates organizational learning and actualization at the individual level. The E to Z process of empowerment (Exhibit 30.8) is built on the theory that the following conditions are essential: enhanced information flow, supportive relationships, structures that liberate, resources for quality output, leadership and followership skills, and an actualized work environment.

All of these conditions evolve from respect and mutual interdependence modeled by the consultant. The consulting process is intended to empower and not to build a long-term dependency relationship. The relationship with a process consultant may be very short or may last years, but proof of how well the process approach is working is directly related to how well the organization is working. As the organization learns, the consultant is successful. Even if this is a very limited relationship, the modeling of a process behavior can be a long-term intervention where the payoff is for both the individual and the organization.

The nonprofit manager must be self-educated in understanding these process approaches to change, or he or she will risk the future of the organization. In these turbulent times, with organizations failing by the thousands, the manager's job as a leader demands exceptional new talents and abilities. There are process consultants willing and able to help educated managers in how to take advantage of the opportunity they face. The following suggested readings are only a few of the more commonly referenced materials that successful managers are familiar with. The management field is developing so fast that there is little room for those who are not developing their individual skills at an equal pace. What is happening with IBM, Ford, Rockwell, Eastman Chemicals, and Toyota is reflected in these pages, and there is not one successful manager resting on his or her past education and experience. The best private-sector managers and organization leaders fully understand the importance of a total quality improvement process built around the action empowerment perspective described here. Managers and leaders of nonprofit organizations are encouraged to move ever further in this direction and to take advantage of the process consulting assistance available. As the world of management goes through fundamental changes, it is essential not just to catch up with these changes, but to stay ahead of them.

SOURCES AND SUGGESTED REFERENCES

Argyris, Chris. 1970. *Intervention Theory and Method: A Behavioral Sciences View.* Reading, MA: Addison-Wesley.

————. 1990. *Overcoming Organizational Defenses: Facilitating Organizational Learning.* Boston, MA: Allyn & Bacon.

Bellman, Geofrey. 1990. *The Consultant's Calling: Bringing Who You Are to What You Do.* San Francisco: Jossey-Bass.

Bradford, David, and Cohen, Allan. 1990. *Managing for Excellence.* New York: John Wiley & Sons.

French, Wendell L., and Bell, Cecil H. 1990. "Action Research and Organizational Development." In *Organizational Development: Behavioral Science Interventions for Organization Improvement* (4th ed.), Chapter 8. Englewood Cliffs, NJ: Prentice-Hall.

Gibb, Jack. 1978. *Trust: A New Way of Personal and Organizational Development.* New York: The Guild of Tutors Press.

Goodstein, Leonard D. 1978. *Consulting with Human Service Systems.* Reading, MA: Addison-Wesley.

Imai, Masaaki. 1986. *Kaizen: The Key to Japan's Competitive Success.* New York: McGraw-Hill.

Lippitt, Gordon, and Lippitt, Ronald. 1986. *The Consulting Process in Action* (2nd ed.). San Diego, CA: University Associates.

Murrell, Kenneth L., and Valsan, E.H. 1985. "A Team-Building Workshop as an OD Intervention." *Leadership and Organization Development Journal,* 6 (2): —————.

Schein, Edgar H. 1969. *Process Consultation: Its Role in Organization Development.* Reading, MA: Addison-Wesley.

Vogt, Judith, and Murrell, Kenneth L. 1990. *Empowerment in Organizations: How to Spark Exceptional Performance.* San Diego, CA: University Associates.

Whyte, William Foote. 1984. *Learning from the Field: A Guide from Experience.* Newbury Park, CA: Sage Publications.

Financial Management

CHAPTER THIRTY-ONE

Accounting

Richard F. Larkin
Price Waterhouse

CONTENTS

A sound accounting and financial management function is important for every not-for-profit organization. Good financial practices by themselves will not ensure program success, but they will greatly facilitate it. On the other hand, poor financial practices are a certain recipe for organization failure.

Responsibility for sound financial management, as for all other operating functions, rests squarely on the senior executive staff. There may be others involved, such

Based on chapters from *Financial and Accounting Guide for Not-for-Profit Organizations, Fourth edition* by Malvern J. Gross, Jr., William Warshauer, Jr., and Richard F. Larkin (Wiley, 1991).

as a treasurer/board member, an outside CPA, and paid or volunteer controller and bookkeeping staff. However, the Executive Director controls the process.

Specifically, the Executive Director must determine the kinds of accounting functions the organization needs, hire the senior financial staff, supervise the financial activities on an ongoing basis, ensure that adequate controls are in effect, know when to take action and what action is needed if problems arise, ensure that financial information is received by those who need it (in useful form and on a timely basis), and coordinate the budget process (see Chapter 32).

All of this sounds like it requires a person with a lot of financial savvy; it does. Yet, very often in the not-for-profit sector, senior executives and (most) board members hold the positions they occupy not as a result of extensive training in management or finance, but because of knowledge of and dedication to the program activities of the organization. Thus, these managers (and trustees) have a special responsibility to learn what they need to know to effectively discharge their financial duties.

31.1 DUTIES OF THE CHIEF EXECUTIVE

(a) FINANCIAL RECORDS   The Executive Director is charged with seeing that the organization's financial records are maintained in an appropriate manner. If the organization is very small, the treasurer will keep the records. If the organization is somewhat larger, a part-time employee—perhaps a secretary—may, among other duties, keep simple records. If the organization is still larger, there may be a full-time bookkeeper, or perhaps even a full-time accounting staff reporting to the Executive Director. Regardless of size, the ultimate responsibility for seeing that adequate and complete financial records are kept is clearly that of the Executive Director. This means that, to some extent, this person must know what is involved in elementary bookkeeping and accounting, although not at the level of a bookkeeper or a CPA.

(b) FINANCIAL STATEMENTS   One of the important responsibilities of the Executive Director is to see that complete and straightforward financial reports are prepared for the board and membership, to tell clearly what has happened during the period. To be meaningful, these statements should have the following characteristics:

1. They should be easily comprehensible so that any person taking the time to study them will understand the financial picture. This characteristic is the one most frequently absent.

2. They should be concise so that the person studying them will not get lost in detail.

3. They should be all-inclusive in scope and should embrace all activities of the organization. If there are two or three funds, the statements should clearly show the relationship among the funds without a lot of confusing detail involving transfers and appropriations.

4. They should have a focal point for comparison so that the person reading them will have some basis for making a judgment. In most instances, this will be a comparison with a budget or with figures from the corresponding period of the previous year.

5. They should be prepared on a timely basis. The longer the delay after the end of the period, the longer the period before corrective action can be taken.

These statements must represent straightforward and candid reporting—that is, the statements must show exactly what has happened. This means that income or assets should not be arbitrarily buried in some subsidiary fund or activity in such a way that the reader is not likely to be aware that the income or assets have been received. It means that if the organization has a number of "funds," the total income and expenses of all funds should be shown in the financial statements in such a manner that no one has to wonder whether all of the activities for the period are included. In short, the statements have to communicate accurately what has happened. If the statement format is confusing and the reader doesn't understand what it is trying to communicate, then it is not accomplishing its principal objective.

It will be noted that the characteristics listed above would apply equally to the statements of almost any type of organization or business. Unfortunately, financial statements for not-for-profit organizations frequently fail to meet these characteristics.

(c) PROTECTING ORGANIZATION ASSETS Unless the organization is very small, there will be a number of assets requiring safeguarding and, again, it is the responsibility of the Executive Director to be sure that there are both adequate physical controls and accounting controls over these assets.

Physical controls involve making sure that the assets are protected against unauthorized use or theft, and seeing that adequate insurance is provided. Internal accounting controls involve division of duties and record-keeping functions that will ensure control over these assets and adequate reporting of deviations from authorized procedures.

Another responsibility of the Executive Director is to see that the organization's excess cash is properly invested to ensure maximum financial return.

(d) GOVERNMENT REPORTING REQUIREMENTS The Executive Director is also charged with complying with the various federal and state reporting requirements. Most larger tax-exempt organizations, other than churches, are required to file annual information returns with the Internal Revenue Service, and some are even required to pay federal taxes. In addition, certain organizations must register and file information returns with certain of the state governments even though they are not resident in the state. All of these requirements taken together pose a serious problem for a person who is not familiar with either the laws involved or the reporting forms used. Chapters 34 and 35 discuss these requirements in detail.

31.2 UNDERSTANDING NOT-FOR-PROFIT ACCOUNTING

Many businesspersons, as well as many accountants, approach not-for-profit accounting with a certain amount of trepidation because of a lack of familiarity with such accounting. There is no real reason for this uneasiness because, except for a few troublesome areas, not-for-profit accounting follows many of the same principles followed by commercial enterprises.

One of the principal differences between not-for-profit and commercial organizations is that they have different reasons for their existence. In oversimplified terms, it might be said that the ultimate objective of a commercial organization is to realize net profit for its owners through the performance of some service wanted by other people; the ultimate objective of a not-for-profit organization is to meet some socially desirable need of the community or its members.

So long as the not-for-profit organization has sufficient resources to carry out its objectives, there is no real need or justification for "making a profit" or having an excess of income over expense. Although a prudent board may want to have a "profit" in order to provide for a rainy day or to be able to respond to a new opportunity in the future, the principal objective of the board is to fulfill the functions for which the organization was founded.

Instead of profit, many not-for-profit organizations are concerned with the size of their cash balance. They can continue to exist only so long as they have sufficient cash to provide for their program. Thus, the financial statements of not-for-profit organizations often emphasize the cash position. Commercial organizations are, of course, also concerned with cash, but if they are profitable they will probably be able to finance their cash needs through loans or from investors.

Not-for-profit organizations have a responsibility to account for resources that they have received. This responsibility includes accounting for certain specific funds that have been given for use in a particular project, as well as a general obligation to employ the organization's resources effectively. Emphasis, thus, is placed on accountability and stewardship. To the extent that the organization has received gifts restricted for a specific purpose, it may segregate those assets and report separately on their receipt and disposition. This separate accounting for restricted assets is called fund accounting. As a result, the financial statements of not-for-profit organizations can often be voluminous and complex because each restricted fund grouping may have its own set of financial statements.

There are five areas where the accounting principles followed by not-for-profit organizations often differ from the accounting principles followed by commercial organizations. The accounting significance of these five areas should not be minimized, but it is also important to note that, once the significance of each is understood, the reader will have a good understanding of the major accounting principles followed by not-for-profit organizations. The five areas are discussed in the sections that follow.

(a) CASH VERSUS ACCRUAL ACCOUNTING   In commercial organizations, the records are almost always kept on an accrual basis. The accrual basis simply means keeping records so that, in addition to recording transactions resulting from the receipt and disbursement of cash, there is also a record of the amounts owed to and by others. In not-for-profit organizations, the cash basis of accounting is frequently used instead. Cash basis accounting means reflecting only transactions where cash has been involved. No attempt is made to record unpaid bills owed or amounts due. Most small not-for-profit organizations use the cash basis, although, more and more, the medium and larger organizations are now using the accrual basis.

The accrual basis usually gives a more accurate picture of an organization's financial condition. Why, then, is the cash basis frequently used for not-for-profit organizations? Principally, because it is simpler to keep records on a cash basis than on an accrual basis. Everyone has had experience keeping a checkbook. This is cash basis accounting. A nonaccountant can learn to keep a checkbook but is not likely to comprehend readily how to keep a double-entry set of books on the accrual basis. Furthermore, the cash basis is often used when the nature of the organization's activities is such that there are no material amounts owed to others, or vice versa, and so there is little meaningful difference between the cash and accrual basis.

Some not-for-profit organizations follow a modified form of cash basis accounting: certain items are recorded on an accrual basis and certain items on a cash basis. Other organizations keep their records on a cash basis but at the end of the year convert to the accrual basis by recording obligations and receivables. The important thing is that the records kept are appropriate to the nature of the organization and its needs.

(b) FUND ACCOUNTING   Although commercial enterprises often do a separate accounting for departments or branches, fund accounting is a term that is not used by most businesspersons. In fund accounting, assets are segregated into categories according to the restrictions that donors place on their use. All completely unrestricted assets are in one fund, all endowment funds in another, all building funds in a third, and so forth. Typically, in reporting, an organization using fund accounting presents separate financial statements for each "fund." Fund accounting is widely used by not-for-profit organizations because it provides stewardship reporting. This concept of separate funds in itself is not particularly difficult, but it does cause problems in presenting financial statements that are straightforward enough to be understood by most readers.

(c) TRANSFERS AND APPROPRIATIONS   In not-for-profit organizations, transfers are frequently made between "funds." Unless carefully disclosed, such transfers tend to confuse the reader of the financial statements. Some organizations make "appropriations" for specific future projects (i.e., set aside a part of the fund balance for a designated purpose). Often, these appropriations are shown, incorrectly, as an expense in arriving at the excess of income over expenses. This also tends to confuse. Transfers and appropriations are not accounting terms used by commercial enterprises.

(d) TREATMENT OF FIXED ASSETS   In commercial enterprises, fixed assets are almost always recorded as assets on the balance sheet, and are depreciated over their expected useful lives. In not-for-profit accounting, fixed assets may or may not be recorded. Some organizations "write off" or expense the asset when purchased; others record fixed assets purchased at cost and depreciate them over their estimated useful life in the same manner as commercial enterprises. Still others "write off" their fixed asset purchases, and then turn around and capitalize them on their balance sheet. Some depreciate; some do not.

(e) CONTRIBUTIONS, PLEDGES, AND NONCASH CONTRIBUTIONS   In commercial or business enterprises there is no such thing as a "pledge." If the business is legally owed money, the amount is recorded as an account receivable. A pledge to a not-for-profit organization may or may not be legally enforceable. Some not-for-profit organizations record pledges because they know from experience that they will collect them. Others do not because they feel they have no legally enforceable claim. A related problem is where and how to report both restricted and unrestricted contributions in the financial statements.

Noncash contributions include donations of securities, equipment, supplies, and services. Commercial enterprises seldom are recipients of such "income."

31.3 AVOIDING FINANCIAL PROBLEMS

Some people have the mistaken idea that bankruptcy only happens to businesses. Not-for-profits are not immune, and management must work to avoid financial problems that could cause the organization to be unable to carry on its activities. Although final responsibility is the board's, the Executive Director is the person who must watch both the day-to-day and long-term financial pictures. The treasurer, controller, and other financially oriented persons are important resources for management, but they are often either not around every day or do not have the broad perspective of the Executive Director.

The Executive Director must monitor the financial progress of the organization with respect to the budget, both as to whether revenue is keeping up with projections and whether expenses are being kept within limits. In particular, the current and forecasted cash position must be watched carefully for any trend that indicates possible future shortages. This monitoring must occur regularly during the year; the more delicate the organization's financial position, the more frequently a "reading" must be taken.

If problems occur or appear imminent, the Executive Director must alert others in the organization, especially other members of management and key board members, so that a plan of action to deal with the problems can be implemented. It is, however, management's responsibility to decide what needs to be done, and do it, whether more revenue is needed or expenses must be cut, or some other action is required.

Some possible ways to respond to financial problems include:

- Increasing contributions. This is often more easily said than done. It usually requires an up-front outlay of money and/or time, and the results may not be seen for a while, or at all. An organization in or approaching financial difficulty has an especially hard time convincing donors to support what some may see as a sinking ship.

- Raising service fees. By the laws of supply and demand, this may or may not result in an overall revenue increase. Some "customers" will be lost, especially if the organization serves an economically disadvantaged population.

- Reducing expenses. This is also easier said than done, because many expenses are relatively fixed, at least in the short term. It is not easy for dedicated staff and volunteers to make decisions that may reduce the entity's services.

- Borrowing. This is quick (if a willing lender can be found), but expensive (interest cost). Further, it may merely postpone an ultimate day of reckoning. Borrowing should be undertaken only for long-term projects such as capital assets, where the debt can be repaid over the life of the assets, or as a very temporary short-term measure, when receipts to repay the borrowing are assured in the near future. A grant may be awarded but not yet received, or a firm pledge may have arrived from a reliable donor.

- Considering whether the needs of the organization's service beneficiaries would be better met by other organizations that have greater financial resources. This is a euphemism for one of two actions: merging with another entity, or going out of business and turning the organization's remaining resources and clients over to another service provider. These are never easy choices, but are sometimes the only feasible alternatives. If one of these options is to be chosen, the decision should be made quickly so that the transfer of services will occur smoothly, before cash is totally depleted and operations become disrupted.

31.4 STAFFING THE ACCOUNTING FUNCTION IN A SMALL ORGANIZATION[1]

Obtaining the right kind of accounting staff is important to the smooth running of this function. The Executive Director usually has no training, time, or inclination to do the bookkeeping. Competent professional assistance is needed.

The problem of finding the right bookkeeper is compounded for not-for-profit organizations because, traditionally, such organizations pay low salaries to all of their staff, including the bookkeeper. The salary level frequently results in the organization's getting someone with only minimum qualifications, which appears to be a false economy. A good bookkeeper can help the organization save money and can free the time of other staff and volunteers.

Often, the other staff members in the organization are extremely dedicated individuals who are interested in the particular program of the organization and willing to accept a lower-than-normal salary. Bookkeepers may not be dedicated to the programs of the organization in the same way. They have been hired to provide bookkeeping services and often have no special interest in the program of the organization.

(a) FINDING A BOOKKEEPER The first step in obtaining a bookkeeper is to determine what bookkeeping services are needed. Depending on the size of the organization, there are a number of possibilities. If the organization is very small and fewer than 25 checks are issued per month, a "checkbook" type set of records will likely be all that is required. If so, the treasurer may very well keep the records and not try to find someone to help.

For many organizations, the number of transactions is too large for the treasurer to handle but not large enough to justify a full-time bookkeeper. If the organization has a paid full- or part-time secretary, often some of the bookkeeping duties are delegated to the secretary. Usually, this means keeping the "checkbook" or perhaps a simple cash receipts and cash disbursements ledger. At the end of the month, the treasurer will summarize these cash records and prepare the financial statements.

Another possibility for the small organization is to find a volunteer within the organization who will help keep the records. While this can occasionally be effective, it often turns out to be less than satisfactory. Keeping a set of books is work, and although a volunteer bookkeeper's enthusiasm may be great at the beginning, it tends to diminish in time. The result is that there are often delays, clerical errors, and, eventually, the need to get another bookkeeper.

Another possibility is a part-time bookkeeper. Some of the best potential may be found among parents with school children, who were full-time bookkeepers at one time, or, if the organization wants someone at its office for a full day each week or during hours not suitable for a parent with school children, then perhaps a retired bookkeeper or accountant will be the next best bet.

For larger or growing organizations, there is a point when a full-time bookkeeper is needed.

An advertisement in the newspaper is probably the best approach. Alternatively, an employment agency can be used. The principal advantage is a saving of time and effort. The agency will place the ad in the paper and will do the initial weeding out of the

---

[1] This section deals only with the bookkeeping problems of relatively small organizations. Larger organizations are not discussed because, to a very large extent, they are run like commercial organizations.

obvious misfits before forwarding the potential candidates to the organization for review. Agencies also know the job market and will probably be in a good position to advise on the "going" salary. They should also be able to help in checking references.

If the organization has outside auditors, they may be able to help. Their advice should be requested and, before actually hiring a bookkeeper, they should talk with the candidates.

(b) ALTERNATIVES TO BOOKKEEPERS   One thing that can be done to reduce the burden on the bookkeeper is to let a bank or a service bureau handle the payroll. This is particularly effective where employees are paid the same amount each payroll period.

Responsibility for bookkeeping, however, cannot be delegated outside the organization. An employee of the organization must continuously monitor and review the work of an outside bookkeeper.

Some banks will handle the complete payroll function. Most will prepare the payroll tax reports. Banks usually have a minimum fee for each payroll. If there are more than about 20 employees, this amount increases. The charge may seem high, but the time saved can be considerable. In addition to the payroll preparation, the bank will keep cumulative records of salary paid to each employee and will prepare the various payroll tax returns, W-2 forms, and similar documents.

Another possibility is to have a service bureau keep all the bookkeeping records. If there is any volume of activity, a service bureau can often keep the records at less cost to an organization than hiring a bookkeeper. For example, some service bureaus will keypunch information from original documents, such as the check stubs, invoices, and so on. They can then prepare a cash receipts book, cash disbursement book, general ledger, and financial statements, all automatically. The organization only has to provide the basic information.

It is also possible to hire an outside accounting service to perform the actual bookkeeping. Many CPAs and public accountants provide bookkeeping services for their clients. Under this arrangement, the accountant has one of the staff do all of the bookkeeping but takes the responsibility for reviewing the work and seeing that it is properly done. The accountant usually prepares financial statements monthly or quarterly.

There are still some functions the organization itself usually must perform. The organization will normally still have to prepare its own checks, vouchers, payroll, depositing of receipts, and billings. This means that normally it cannot delegate 100 percent of the bookkeeping to an outside accounting service.

31.5   PROVIDING INTERNAL CONTROL

"Employee admits embezzlement of ten thousand dollars."
"Trusted clerk steals $50,000."

These headlines are all too common, and many tell a similar story—a trusted and respected employee in a position of financial responsibility is overcome by temptation and "borrows" a few dollars until payday to meet some unexpected cash need. When payday comes, some other cash need prevents repayment. Somehow the employee just never catches up, and borrows a few more dollars, and a few more and a few more.

The reader's reaction may be, "Thank goodness, this kind of thing could never happen to my organization. After all, I know everyone and they are all honest, and besides who would think of stealing from a not-for-profit organization?" This is not the point. Very few people who end up as embezzlers start out with this intent. Rather, they find themselves in a position of trust and opportunity and, when personal crises arise, the temptation is too much. Not-for-profit organizations are not exempt, regardless of size. There is always a risk when a person is put in a position to be tempted.

The purpose of this section is to outline some of the practical procedures that a small organization can establish to help minimize this risk and thus safeguard the organization's physical assets. For purposes of this discussion, the emphasis is on smaller organizations (those with one or two persons handling all the bookkeeping). This would include many churches, country clubs, local fund-raising groups, YMCAs, and other agencies. Internal control for larger organizations is not discussed here because controls for such organizations can become very complicated and would require many chapters. The principles, however, are essentially the same.

Internal control is a system of procedures and cross-checking which, in the absence of collusion, minimizes the likelihood of misappropriation of assets or misstatement of the accounts, and maximizes the likelihood of detection if embezzlement occurs. For the most part, internal control does not prevent embezzlement but should ensure that, if committed, it will be promptly discovered. This likelihood of discovery usually persuades most workers not to allow temptation to get the better of them. Internal control also includes a system of checks and balances over all paperwork, to ensure that there was no intentional or unintentional misstatement of financial data.

There are several reasons for having a good system of internal controls. The first, obviously, is to prevent the loss through theft of some of the assets. A second reason, equally important, is to prevent "honest" employees from making a mistake that could ruin their lives.

Aside from this moral responsibility of the employer, there is a responsibility of the board, to the membership and to the general public, to safeguard the assets of the organization. If a large sum were stolen and not recovered, it could jeopardize the program of the organization. Furthermore, even if only a small amount were stolen, it would be embarrassing to the members of the board. In either case, the membership or the public would certainly want to know why internal control procedures had not been followed.

One of the most effective internal controls is the use of a budget which is compared to actual figures on a monthly basis. If deviations from the budget are carefully followed up by the controller or Executive Director, the likelihood of a large misappropriation taking place without being detected fairly quickly is reduced considerably. This type of overall review of the financial statements is very important, and every member of the board should ask questions about any item that appears out of line either with the budget or with what would have been expected to be the actual figures. Many times, this type of probing for reasons for deviations from the expected has uncovered problems.

A number of other basic internal controls are probably applicable to many, if not most, small not-for-profit organizations; these controls are discussed below. However, it must be emphasized that these are only basic controls and should not be considered all-inclusive. Establishing an effective system of internal control requires knowledge of the particular organization and its operations.

In this discussion, we will be considering the division of duties for a small organization, The Center for World Peace. This organization sponsors seminars and retreats and has a paid staff to run its affairs. The office staff consists of an Executive Director, the Executive Director's secretary, a program director, and a bookkeeper.

The officers of the Center are all volunteers and usually are at the Center only at irregular times. The Executive Director, treasurer, president, and vice president are check signers. With this background, let us now look at each of eleven controls in detail and see how they apply to this organization.

(a) CONTROLS OVER RECEIPTS   The basic objective in establishing internal control over receipts is to obtain control over the amounts received at the time of receipt. Once this control is established, procedures must be followed to ensure that these amounts get deposited in the organization's bank account. Establishing this control is particularly difficult for small organizations because of the small number of persons usually involved.

   1. *Prenumbered receipts should be issued for all money at the time first received. A duplicate copy should be accounted for and a comparison eventually made between the aggregate of the receipts issued and the amount deposited in the bank.*

   The purpose of this control is to create a written record of the cash received. The original of the receipt should be given to the person from whom the money was received; the duplicate copy should be kept permanently. Periodically, the aggregate receipts issued should be compared with the amount deposited. The receipts can be issued at the organization's office, or, if door-to-door collections are made, a prenumbered receipt can be issued for each amount received by the collector.

   In our illustration, the Center receives cash at its seminars and retreats on weekends, when the bookkeeper and treasurer are not available. One of the participants, designated as the fee collector for that session, collects the fees and issues the receipts. After all of the fees are collected, they are turned over, with the duplicate copy of the receipts (along with all unused receipt forms), to the program director. A summary report of the cash collected is prepared and signed in duplicate. One copy of this report is mailed directly to the treasurer's home in an envelope provided, and the duplicate is turned over to the program director. The program director counts the money, agreeing the total received with the total of the duplicate receipts and with the summary report. The program director puts the money in the safe for the weekend and, on Monday morning, gives the money, the duplicate receipts, and the copy of the summary report to the bookkeeper for depositing. The bookkeeper deposits the money from each program separately, and files the duplicate receipts and summary report for future reference. Once a month, the treasurer compares the copy of each summary report with the deposits shown on the bank statement.

   2. *Cash collections should be under the control of two people wherever possible, particularly where it is not practicable to issue receipts.*

   In the illustration in the previous paragraph, control was established over cash collections by having the person collecting at each seminar issue receipts and prepare a summary report. The program director also had some control through knowledge of how many persons attended and comparison of the amount collected with the amount that should have been collected. This provided dual control.

   There are many instances, however, where cash collections are received when it is not appropriate to give a receipt. Two examples are church "plate" collections during worship services, and coin canisters placed in stores and public places throughout the community for public support. To the extent that only one person handles this money, there is always a risk. The risk is not only that some of it will be misappropriated, but also that someone may erroneously think it has been. This is why it is recommended that two people be involved.

With respect to church plate collections, as soon as the money has been collected, it should be locked up until it can be counted by two people together. Perhaps the head usher and a vestryman will count it after the last service. Once the counting is completed, both should sign a cash collection report. This report should be given to the treasurer for subsequent comparison with the deposit on the bank statement. The cash should be turned over to the bookkeeper for depositing intact.

This procedure will not guard against an usher's dipping a hand into the "plate" before it is initially locked up or counted, but the ushers' duties are usually rotated and the cumulative risk is low. The bookkeeper and treasurer normally have access to such funds on a regular and recurring basis. This is why their function of counting these cash receipts should be controlled by having a second person involved. It is not because they are not trusted; it is to ensure that no one can think of accusing one of them.

Canisters containing cash, which are placed in public places, should be sealed so that the only way to get access to the cash is to break the canister open. Someone could take the entire canister, but if the canister is placed in a conspicuous place—near the cash register, for example—this risk is fairly low. These canisters should be serially numbered so that all canisters can be accounted for. When the canisters are eventually opened, they should be counted by two people using the same procedures as with plate collections.

3. *Two persons should open all mail and make a list of all receipts for each day. This list should subsequently be compared to the bank deposit by someone not handling the money. Receipts in the form of checks should be restrictively endorsed promptly upon receipt.*

Two persons should open the mail; otherwise, there is a risk that the mail opener may misappropriate part of the receipts. This imposes a heavy burden on the small organization with only a few employees, but it is necessary if good internal control is desired.[2] One alternative is to have mail receipts go to a bank lock box and let the bank do the actual opening of the mail.

The purpose of making a list of all checks received is to ensure that a record is made of the amount that was received. This makes it possible for the treasurer to later check to see whether the bookkeeper has deposited all amounts promptly.

Checks should be promptly endorsed because, once endorsed, there is less likelihood of misappropriation. The endorsement should be placed on the check by the person first opening the mail.

In theory, if the check has been made out in the name of the organization, no one can cash it. But experience has shown that a clever enough person can find a way to cash it or deposit it in a "personal" bank account opened for the purpose. On the other hand, once the check is endorsed with the name of the bank and the organization's account number it is very difficult for the embezzler to convert the check to personal use.

In our illustration, the secretary to the Executive Director of the Center, together with the bookkeeper, jointly open all mail and place the rubber-stamp endorsement on the check. They then make a list, in duplicate, of all checks received; one copy of the

---

[2] Organizations that have their financial statements audited by CPAs will find that the CPA cannot give an unqualified opinion if internal control is considered inadequate.

list goes to the bookkeeper with the checks for depositing. They both sign the original of the list, which goes to the Executive Director. The Executive Director obtains the copy, to see what amounts have been received. At the end of the month, all of these lists are turned over to the treasurer, who then compares each day's lists with the respective credit on the bank statement.

4. *All receipts should be deposited in the bank, intact and on a timely basis.*

The purpose of this control is to ensure that there is a complete record of all receipts and disbursements. If an organization receives "cash" receipts, no part of this cash should be used to pay its bills. The receipts should be deposited, and checks issued to pay expenses. In this way there will be a record of the total receipts and expenses of the organization on the bank statements.

This procedure does not prevent someone from stealing money but it does mean that a check must be used to get access to the money. This leaves a record of the theft and makes it more difficult for a person to cover up.

(b) CONTROLS OVER DISBURSEMENTS The basic objective in establishing internal controls over disbursements is to ensure that a record of all disbursements is made and that only authorized persons are in a position to withdraw funds. The risk of misappropriation can be significantly reduced if procedures are established to minimize the possibility that an expenditure can be made without leaving a trail, or that an unauthorized person can withdraw money.

5. *All disbursements should be made by check, and supporting documentation should be kept for each disbursement.*

This control is to ensure that there will be a permanent record of how much and to whom money was paid. No amounts should be paid by cash, with the exception of minor petty cash items. For the same reason, no checks should be made payable to "cash." Checks should always be payable to a specific person, including checks for petty cash reimbursement. This makes it more difficult to fraudulently disburse funds.

At the Center, the bookkeeper is the one who prepares all checks for payment of bills. Before a check is prepared, however, the vendor's invoice must be approved by the Executive Director. If the purchases involved goods that have been received at the Center, the person who received the goods must indicate their receipt, right on the vendor's invoice.

The bookkeeper is not a check signer. If this were the case, this person could fraudulently disburse funds to himself or herself and then cover up the fraud in the books. The check signers are the Executive Director, the treasurer, the president, and the vice president. Normally, the Executive Director signs all checks. Checks of more than $1,000 require two signatures, but these are very infrequent. The Executive Director carefully examines all supporting invoices, making sure that someone has signed for receipt of the goods before signing the check. After signing the check, each invoice is marked "paid" so that it won't inadvertently be paid twice. The secretary mails all checks to the vendors as an added control over the bookkeeper. By not letting the bookkeeper have access to the signed checks, the bookkeeper is not in a position to profit from preparing a fraudulent check to a nonexistent vendor.

6. *If the treasurer or check signer is also the bookkeeper, two signatures should be required on all checks.*

The purpose of this control is to ensure that no one person is in a position to disburse funds and then cover up an improper disbursement in the records. In part, this recommendation is designed to protect the organization, and in part, to protect the treasurer.

Two signatures on a check provide additional control only so long as the second check signer also examines the invoices or supporting bills behind the disbursement before signing the check. The real risk of having dual signatures is that both check signers will rely on the other and will review the supporting bills in such a perfunctory manner that there is less control than if only one person signed but assumed full responsibility.

7. *A person other than the bookkeeper should receive bank statements directly from the bank and should reconcile them.*

This control is to prevent the bookkeeper from fraudulently issuing a check for personal use and, as bookkeeper, covering up this disbursement in the books. The bookkeeper may not be a check signer, but experience has shown that banks often do not catch forged check signatures. The bookkeeper usually has access to blank checks and could forge the check signer's signature. If the bookkeeper were to receive the bank statements, the fraudulent and forged cancelled checks could be removed and then destroyed, with the fraud covered up through the books.

In most smaller organizations, the bank statement and cancelled checks should go directly to the treasurer, who should prepare the bank reconciliation.[3] In those situations where the treasurer is also the bookkeeper, the bank statements should go directly to another officer to reconcile. The treasurer should insist on this procedures as a protection from any suspicions of wrongdoing.

In the Center's case, the bank statement and cancelled checks are mailed directly to the treasurer's home each month. After receiving the bank statement, the treasurer usually spends half a day at the Center's offices preparing the complete bank reconciliation and comparing the lists of mail and program receipts received throughout the month to the deposits shown on the bank statement.

(c) OTHER CONTROLS

8. *Someone other than the bookkeeper should authorize all write-offs of accounts receivable or other assets.*

This control is to ensure that a bookkeeper who has embezzled accounts receivable or some other assets will not also be in a position to cover up the theft by writing-off the receivable or asset. If the bookkeeper is unable to write such amounts off, someone will eventually ask why the "receivable" has not been paid and this should trigger correspondence that would result in the fraud's being discovered.

Generally, write-offs of small receivables should be approved by the treasurer (provided the treasurer is not also the bookkeeper), but if they are large in amount they should be submitted to the board for approval. Before any amount is written off, the treasurer should make certain that all appropriate efforts have been made, including, possibly, legal action. The treasurer must constantly keep in mind the fiduciary responsibility to take all reasonable steps to make collection.

---

[3] In large organizations, the control can be even more effective where the division of duties is such that an employee who is not a check signer *or* bookkeeper can prepare the bank reconciliation. It is possible for check signers to fraudulently make out a check to themselves and then, if they have access to the returned checks, to remove the cancelled check. However, if they don't also have a means of covering up the disbursement, soon or later the shortage will come out. The person reconciling the bank account is not in a position to permanently "cover up" a shortage, although it could be hidden for several months. For this reason, it is preferable to have neither a check signer nor the bookkeeper prepare the reconciliation.

The Center only very rarely has accounts receivable. It does have, however, many pledges receivable. Although the Center would not think of taking legal action to enforce collection, it does record those pledges as though they were receivables. Occasionally, the bookkeeper has to call the treasurer's attention to a delinquent pledge. The treasurer, in turn, usually calls the delinquent pledgor in an effort to evaluate the likelihood of future collection. Once a year, a written report is submitted to the board advising it of delinquent pledges, and requesting formal approval to write them off. The board discusses each such delinquent pledge before giving its approval.

9. *Marketable securities should be kept in a bank safe deposit box or held by a custodian in an account in the name of the organization.*

This control is to ensure that securities are protected against loss by fire or theft or from bankruptcy of a brokerage house. Safeguarding investments is discussed more fully on pages 802–804.

10. *Fixed asset records should be maintained and an inventory taken periodically.*

These procedures ensure that the organization has a complete record of its assets. The permanent record should contain a description of the asset, cost, date acquired, location, serial number, and similar information. Such information will provide a record of the assets that the employees are responsible for. This is particularly important in not-for-profit organizations where turnover of employees and officers is often high. It also provides fire insurance records.

11. *Excess cash should be maintained in a separate bank or investment account. Withdrawals from this account should require two signatures.*

Where an organization has excess cash that will not be needed for current operations in the immediate future, it should be placed in a separate account to provide an added safeguard. Frequently, this separate account will be an interest-bearing savings account. The bank or investment manager should be advised that the signatures of two officers are required for all withdrawals. Normally, in such situations, withdrawals are infrequent; when they are made, the funds withdrawn are deposited intact in the regular current checking account. In this way, all disbursements are made from the regular checking account.

In this situation, the officers involved in authorizing a withdrawal should not do so without being fully aware of the reasons for the need of these funds. Approval should not be perfunctorily given.

One final recommendation. Fidelity insurance should be carried. The purpose of fidelity insurance is to ensure that, if a loss from embezzlement occurs, the organization will recover the loss. This insurance does not cover theft or burglary by an outside person; it provides protection only against an employee's dishonesty. Having fidelity insurance also acts as a deterrent because the employees know that the insurance company is more likely to press charges against a dishonest employee than would a "soft-hearted" and embarrassed employer.

There is only one "catch" to this type of coverage. The organization has to have good enough records to prove that an embezzlement has taken place. This means that this coverage is not a substitute for other internal controls. If the theft occurs but the employer doesn't know it or if there is no proof of the loss, fidelity insurance will not help.

Sometimes, employees feel that a lack of confidence in them is being expressed if the organization has fidelity insurance. The treasurer should assure them that this is not the case, and that fidelity insurance is similar to fire insurance. All prudent organizations carry such coverage.

Even the smallest organization should be able to apply the internal controls that have been recommended in this section. The board should insist that these and similar controls be established. It has a responsibility to insist that all practical measures be taken to protect the organization's assets. Otherwise, the board would be subject to severe criticism if an embezzlement were to occur.

The controls discussed in this section are basic ones and should not be considered all-inclusive. A complete system of internal control encompasses all of the procedures of the organization. If the organization is large or complex, or if it has peculiar problems or procedures, the board will want to retain the services of a professional to help set up and monitor the effectiveness of internal control. The next section discusses the services that the certified public accountant can provide, including assistance in establishing internal controls.

31.6 INDEPENDENT AUDITS

Related to the internal controls discussed in the preceding section is the question of whether the books and records should be audited. Like many other decisions the board has to make, this is a value judgment for which there are no absolute answers. Audits cost time and money, and therefore the values to be derived must be considered carefully.

An audit is a series of procedures followed by an experienced professional accountant to test, on a selective basis, transactions and internal controls in effect, all with a view to forming an opinion on the fairness of the presentation of the financial statements.

Several things should be underscored. Auditors do not examine all transactions. If they were to do so, the cost would be prohibitive. They do look at what they believe is a representative sample of the transactions. In looking at these selected transactions, they are as concerned with the internal control and procedures that were followed as they are with the legitimacy of the transaction itself. If internal controls are good, the extent of the testing can be limited. If controls are weak, the auditors will have to examine many more transactions to be satisfied. In smaller organizations, where internal controls are often less effective, auditors must examine proportionately more transactions.

Another point is that, for the most part, the auditors can only examine and test transactions that have been recorded. If a contribution has been received but not deposited in the bank or recorded in the books, there is little likelihood that it will be discovered. This is why the preceding section emphasized that controls should be established over all receipts at the point of receipt and all disbursements should be made by check. In this way, a record is made and the auditor has a chance of testing the transaction.

The end product of the audit is not a "certificate" that every transaction has been properly recorded, but an expression of an opinion by the auditor on the fairness of the presentation of the financial statements. The auditor does not guarantee accuracy; the bookkeeper may have stolen $100, but unless this $100 is material in relation to the financial statements as a whole, the auditor is not likely to discover it.

(a) WHY HAVE AN AUDIT? Audits are not free. This means that the board has to evaluate the benefits to be derived from an audit, and its cost. What are the benefits that can be expected from an audit? There are four: credibility of the financial statements; professional assistance in developing meaningful financial statements; professional advice on internal control, administrative efficiency, and other business matters; and assistance in tax reporting and compliance requirements.

Credibility is the principal benefit of having an independent CPA express an opinion on the financial statements. Unfortunately, over the years, there have been many instances where not-for-profit organizations have been mismanaged and the results have been buried in the financial statements in a manner that made it difficult, if not impossible, for the readers of the statements to discern them.

It has been noted that the purpose of financial statements is to communicate in a straightforward manner what has happened. The presence of an auditor's opinion helps in this communication process because an independent expert, after an examination, tells the reader that the financial statements present fairly what has happened. Not-for-profit organizations are competing with other organizations for the money of their members or of the general public. If an organization can tell its financial story accurately and completely and it is accepted at face value, the potential contributor is more likely to feel that the organization is well managed.

Another benefit of having professional help is that the auditor is an expert at preparing financial statements in a format that will be most clear to the reader. All too often, financial statements are poorly organized and hard to understand. The CPA has experience in helping organizations to prepare financial statements in clear and understandable language.

Another benefit is that the CPA will be in a position to advise the board on how to strengthen internal controls and simplify the bookkeeping procedures. The CPA can also assist the board in evaluating the organization's bookkeeper and can help the organization hire someone for this position.

The CPA has had experience in dealing with different types of organizations and is likely to have a number of general business suggestions. Typically, periodic meetings with senior staff or board members will be held to discuss the problems of the organization and business conditions in general. Many boards arrange annual meetings to ask questions and to be sure that the organization has picked the CPA's brain. This meeting also provides the CPA with an opportunity to call any potential problems to the board's attention.

As is discussed in Chapters 34 and 35, most not-for-profit organizations are required to submit some form of report to one or more agencies of a state government and the IRS. These reports are technical in format and, unless the treasurer is an accountant, the assistance of an expert will probably be required. The CPA is an expert, and can either offer advice on how to prepare the returns or can actually prepare them.

(b) FINDING AN AUDITOR   When it comes time to choose a CPA, discussion should include the organization's banker, attorney, and members of the board. The chances are that collectively they will know many CPAs practicing in the locality and will know of their reputations. Officers of other not-for-profit organizations should be consulted. They will probably have had some experience that may be of help. One significant criterion in the selection should be the CPA's familiarity with not-for-profit entities.

As in any professional relationship, the CPA's interest and willingness to serve the organization are among the most important factors to consider when making a selection. It is always difficult to judge which of several CPAs has the greatest interest in helping the organization. In large part, the board will have to make the decision from impressions formed in personal interviews.

During this personal interview, the CPA should be asked to take a look at the records, to get a general impression of the amount of time that will be necessary, and thus the fee. For the most part, the judgment should not be swayed significantly by the fee range estimated, unless it is out of line with other CPA fees. Like a doctor or lawyer, the accountant expects to receive a fair fee for services. The organization is largely dependent on the honesty and professional reputation of the accountant to charge a fair fee.

What does it cost to have an audit? This is a difficult question to answer because most CPAs charge on an hourly basis. If the organization's records are in good shape, the time will be less. There is no way to know how much time will be involved without looking at the records and knowing something about the organization.

Sometimes an organization will shop around in an effort to find the CPA that will charge it the least. Because the treasurer is not likely to be in a position to judge the quality of the work, there is a risk in choosing a professional accountant solely on the basis of an estimated fee. Choosing a CPA should be on the basis of reputation, expertise, and willingness to serve the organization.

(c) REVIEW SERVICES A possible alternative to an audit, for an organization that does not have to submit audited financial statements to a state, a funding source, or another organization, is to have its financial statements "reviewed" by a CPA. A review requires less time, hence incurs less cost; however, it results in a lesser degree of assurance by the CPA. Instead of saying that the financial statements "present fairly," the CPA does only enough work to be able to say, "I am not aware of any material modifications that should be made in order for the financial statements to be in conformity." This is called "negative assurance" and does not give as much credibility to the financial statements as an audit does. Nevertheless, a review may meet the needs of some smaller organizations.

(d) AUDIT COMMITTEES Many smaller organizations do not feel they can afford a CPA and yet want some assurance that accounting matters are being adequately managed, and especially that disbursements have been made for proper purposes. One solution to this is to set up an "audit committee" consisting of several members of the board or of the membership. The committee may meet on a monthly or bimonthly basis and review transactions since the last meeting. It may also review bank reconciliations, marketable securities bought, sold, and on hand, and any other matter that could be "sensitive."

The advantage of an audit committee is that it strengthens internal control significantly, with little cost. This is particularly important where internal control is weak because it is not practical to segregate duties as much as might be desired.

The institution of external audit committees has now become a common practice for not-for-profit organizations. A properly functioning audit committee goes a long way toward demonstrating that the board of trustees has taken prudent steps to perform its administrative and control functions. Thus, with regard to audit committees, the author recommends that:

- Every not-for-profit organization that raises funds from the general public or that receives grants or membership dues should have an active and functioning audit committee.
- For most effective operation, audit committees should be composed of three to five directors, with the majority (including the chairperson) being trustees who are not employees.
- Audit committees should be responsible for recommending the appointment of the independent accountants and for discussion of their work with them.
- Audit committees should be responsible for the review and evaluation of reports prepared by the independent accountants that contain recommendations for improvements in controls. Audit committees should determine whether management has taken appropriate action on these recommendations.
- Audit committees should be delegated the responsibility to review the annual financial statements with the independent accountants.

31.7 INVESTMENTS

Some not-for-profit organizations have an investment program to manage, as a result of receipt of endowment funds and other restricted gifts. Some organizations also have excess cash in their unrestricted general fund, which can be invested. Sometimes, all of these investment funds can be very sizable. They are usually invested in publicly traded securities, although occasionally a partial amount is invested in real estate or in mortgages.

Where should an organization go to get good investment advice? The answer is clear: to a professional; to someone who knows the market and is in the business of advising others.

Sometimes, a nonprofit's board, recognizing its fiduciary responsibilities, will tend to be too conservative in its investment policy, and will purchase high-grade, low-interest-bearing bonds. This conservatism can be almost as risky as purchasing a highly volatile stock, as many holders of bonds discovered in recent years when high interest rates depressed bond prices. This is why professional advice is needed.

There are a number of places to go for professional advice. If the total investments are relatively small in size (say, under $100,000), many organizations find that a no-load mutual fund or a bank common stock fund is the answer.[4] In both cases, the organization is purchasing expertise while it pools its funds with those of many other people. Mutual funds offer a convenient way to obtain investment management when the organization has a minimum amount to invest.

Bank-commingled or common stock investment funds are a form of mutual fund. One of the advantages of using a bank fund is that the reputation of the bank is involved and the bank will pay close attention to the investments made. Banks are often more conservative than mutual funds in their investment decisions, but this may be appropriate when one considers the fiduciary responsibility of not-for-profit organizations.

---

[4] If an organization has under $100,000 to invest, the board should carefully consider the nature of the funds being invested before buying common stocks. If the funds available are to be invested for only a short period of time, or if investment income is essential, then the organization should not be investing in common stocks. Instead, a savings account or money-market instrument is probably more appropriate.

If the investment fund is large in size, the organization may prefer to select a professional to advise on specific stocks and bonds to purchase for its own portfolio. Most brokers are pleased to offer this service. On the other hand, many not-for-profit organizations are reluctant to entrust investment decisions to the brokers who handle the actual purchasing, because they are "wearing two hats." This can be avoided by going to one of the many available investment advisory services that does not handle the actual purchasing or selling.

Investment professionals can also offer advice on a type of investment that is frequently not given the attention it warrants by not-for-profit organizations—short-term investments. Short-term investments are investments in interest-bearing instruments of that portion of an organization's cash balances which is currently inactive but will be needed to fund programs and activities in the near future.

An ordinary savings account is one type of short-term investment of cash balances that are temporarily not deployed. Often, however, it is possible to improve on the interest rate available in savings accounts, without substantially increasing risk, by purchasing "money-market" instruments. These vary in interest rate, risk, minimum denomination available, time to maturity, and marketability prior to redemption; included are U.S. Treasury Bills, "agencies," certificates of deposit, and repurchase agreements.

Treasury Bills are the most marketable money-market instrument. The smallest denomination currently available is $10,000 and the shortest maturity is 13 weeks.

"Agencies" are federally sponsored debt instruments issued by federal agencies or quasi-governmental organizations. Some are explicitly guaranteed by the full faith and credit of the United States Government but others are not.

Certificates of deposit (CDs) are available directly from commercial or savings banks, or through securities dealers. Only large CDs (over $100,000) are negotiable, and all bear substantial penalties for redemption prior to maturity.

Repurchase agreements are agreements under which a bank or securities dealer agrees to repurchase at a specific date and at a specific premium securities sold earlier to an investor. Interest rates on repurchase agreements are often attractive, and a wide range of maturities is usually available.

A list of investment advisory services can usually be found in the classified telephone directory. As with all professionals, the investment adviser's reputation should be carefully checked. The bank's trust department is usually also happy to give advice on investment decisions. The point to emphasize is that investment decisions should be made by professionals in the investment business and not by amateurs (this is as true of investments as it is of medicine!). Even professionals can make errors in judgment, but the risk is lower.

The professional adviser will charge a fee, generally calculated on the basis of a percentage of the monies invested. The larger the investment fund, the lower the rate charged.

The physical safeguarding of an organization's investment securities is as important as making the right decision as to which stocks to buy or sell. This is often overlooked. The board of directors or the finance committee of the board has general responsibility for all investment instruments owned by the organization. Periodic verification of the existence of the securities should be made, either by independent accountants or the board itself. Verification usually involves a physical counting of the securities at the location where they are deposited. Three areas warrant special attention. The first is that stock certificates aren't lost or misplaced through carelessness or poor handling. The second is that they are not lost through misappropriation by an employee. The third is that the stockbroker doesn't lose the certificates or, worse yet, go bankrupt.

If the organization keeps the certificates in its possession, the certificates should be kept in a bank safe deposit box. They should be registered in the name of the organization. The organization should also maintain an investment register that shows the certificate number as well as the cost and other financial information. There should be limited access to the safe deposit box, and it is wise to require the presence of two persons (preferably officers) whenever the box is opened.[5]

An organization must always be concerned that someone having access to stock certificates may be tempted to steal them. Although the certificates may be registered in the organization's name, there is an underworld market for stolen certificates. Furthermore, if the loss is not discovered promptly and the transfer agent advised to "stop transfer," the organization's rights may be jeopardized.

The best control is to have the broker deliver the stock certificate directly to a custodian for safekeeping. When the stock is sold, the custodian is then instructed to deliver the certificate to the broker. In this way, the organization never handles the certificate.

Some organizations leave their certificates in the custody of their broker. This has certain risks. One is that the broker will temporarily lose track of the certificates if the back office falls behind in its paperwork or incorrectly records the certificates.

The other risk is the broker's going bankrupt while holding the stock. Provided the broker has not fraudulently hypothecated the stock, bankruptcy should not result in a loss to an organization. However, there could be considerable delay before the stock is released by a court. On the other hand, if the broker has, without the consent of the organization, pledged the stock for personal borrowings, there is a possibility of actual loss. While the organization might be able to take both civil and criminal action against the broker, this would be of little consolation in bankruptcy. The first $500,000 of such losses, however, would be recovered from the federally chartered Securities Investor Protection Corporation.

While these risks might be relatively small, a not-for-profit organization has a fiduciary responsibility to act with more than ordinary care and judgment. Accordingly, it would be prudent for an organization to have the broker deliver the stock certificates in the organization's name, either to an independent custodian or to the organization.

SOURCES AND SUGGESTED REFERENCES

American Institute of Certified Public Accountants, Committee on College and University Accounting and Auditing. 1975. "Audits of Colleges and Universities, Including Statement of Position Issued by the Accounting Standards Division." *Industry Audit Guide* (2nd ed.). New York: AICPA.

————. Committee on Voluntary Health and Welfare Organizations. 1988. "Audits of Voluntary Health and Welfare Organizations." *Industry Audit Guide* (2nd ed.). New York: AICPA.

---

[5] It is also wise for the board to establish an investment committee charged with the responsibility for authorizing all investment transactions. If an outside adviser is retained, this committee should still review the outside adviser's recommendations before they are accepted. It is not wise to delegate authority to an outside adviser to act except in accordance with an investment policy approved by the investment committee.

————. Health Care Committee. 1990. "Audits of Providers of Health Care Services, Including Statement of Position Issued by the Accounting Standards Division." *Industry Audit Guide*. New York: AICPA.

————. Subcommittee on Nonprofit Organizations. 1988. "Audits of Certain Nonprofit Organizations," including "Accounting Principles and Reporting Practices for Certain Nonprofit Organizations." *Statement of Position No. 78-10* (2nd ed.). New York: AICPA.

Anthony, R. N. 1978. *Financial Accounting in Nonbusiness Organizations: An Exploratory Study of Conceptual Issues*. Norwalk, CT: Financial Accounting Standards Board.

Anthony, R. N., and Young, D. W. 1984. *Management Control in Nonprofit Organizations* (3rd ed.). Homewood, IL: Richard D. Irwin.

Blazek, J. 1990. *Tax and Financial Planning for Tax-Exempt Organizations: Forms, Checklists, Procedures*. New York: John Wiley & Sons.

Daughtrey, W. H., Jr., and Gross, M. J., Jr. 1978. *Museum Accounting Handbook*. Washington, DC: American Association of Museums.

Evangelical Joint Accounting Committee. 1987. "Accounting and Financial Reporting Guide for Christian Ministries." Diamond Bar, CA: Christian Ministries Management Association.

Financial Accounting Standards Board, Statements of Financial Accounting Concepts. 1980/1985. No. 4, "Objectives of Financial Reporting by Nonbusiness Organizations" (1980); No. 6, "Elements of Financial Statements" (1985). Norwalk, CT: FASB.

————. 1990. "Accounting for Contributions Received and Contributions Made and Capitalization of Works of Art, Historical Treasures, and Similar Assets" (exposure draft). Norwalk, CT: FASB.

Gross, M. J., Jr., Warshauer, W., Jr., and Larkin, R. F. 1991. *Financial and Accounting Guide for Not-for-Profit Organizations* (4th ed.). New York: John Wiley & Sons.

Holck, M., Jr., and Holck, M., Sr. 1978. *Complete Handbook of Church Accounting*. Englewood Cliffs, NJ: Prentice-Hall.

Hummel, J. 1980. *Starting and Running a Nonprofit Organization*. Minneapolis: University of Minnesota Press.

National Association of College and University Business Officers. 1990. *Financial Accounting and Reporting Manual for Higher Education*. Washington, DC: Author.

National Health Council, National Assembly for Social Policy and Development, Inc., and United Way of America. 1988. *Standards of Accounting and Financial Reporting for Voluntary Health and Welfare Organizations* (3rd ed.). New York: Authors.

Price Waterhouse. 1992. *The Audit Committee, the Board of Trustees of Not-for-Profit Organizations and the Independent Accountant*. New York: Author.

————. 1988. *Effective Internal Accounting Control for Nonprofit Organizations*. New York: Author.

United Way of America. 1989. *Accounting and Financial Reporting: A Guide for United Ways and Not-For-Profit Human Service Organizations* (2nd ed.). Alexandria, VA: Author.

————. 1975. *Budgeting: A Guide for United Ways and Not-for-Profit Human Service Organizations*. Alexandria, VA: Author.

Wacht, R. F. 1984. *Financial Management in Nonprofit Organizations*. Atlanta: Georgia State University.

Warshauer, W., Jr., and Larkin, R. F. 1990. "Not-for-Profit Organizations," In D. R. Carmichael, S. B. Lilien, and M. Mellman. (Eds.), *Accountants' Handbook* (7th ed.), ch. 25. New York: John Wiley & Sons.

Budgeting

Ruthie G. Reynolds
Howard University

CONTENTS

32.1 INTRODUCTION

Budgeting is an important aspect of an enterprise's operations. It is a process that consumes a significant part of management's time, but the time spent is well worth the effort. Although budgets are used for many purposes in the nonprofit sector, the primary ones are planning, programming, and control.

Budgeting may be defined as the process of projecting future resources to be received and future resources to be used by an organization. The process may be viewed as the development of a master plan that is used to guide the members of the organization through operations. Whereas many people think of budgets in only quantitative terms, budgets of nonprofit organizations contain a great deal of nonquantitative information. Examples of qualitative information included in their budgets are: job descriptions of key personnel, number of volunteers needed, and listing of potential supporters.

The purpose of this chapter is to describe in detail the budgeting process. The discussion includes the various budgeting techniques, the basic types of budgets, and the steps in preparing a budget. The appendix contains sample budgeting forms recommended by United Way of America for use by small human-service organizations.

32.2 PURPOSES OF BUDGETING

As mentioned above, the primary purposes of budgeting are planning, programming, and control. These functions are discussed in this section.

(a) PLANNING The planning phase of budgeting encompasses the setting of goals and objectives for a specified period of time. The period of time is usually 12 months; however, longer or shorter periods are not uncommon.

Balancing is the key in planning, because strategies must be developed to make the objectives consistent with the goals. Furthermore, it is necessary to make sure goals complement the established mission of the organization. The mission sets forth the vision of the organization and generally is formulated by the founding members. It may, however, be altered or completely replaced over the years. The goals set forth the manner in which the mission is to be accomplished, and the objectives are operational statements of the goals. Exhibit 32.1 shows an example of the relationship among the mission, goals, and objectives of a hypothetical human-service organization called American Centers.

Planning requires cooperation among all members of the organization. The Executive Director and the board of directors must work together to ensure successful planning. Some top managers prefer a management style in which directives are handed down from the top; others favor a management style in which directives are developed from the bottom up. The latter approach is called participative management, and the related budgeting style is called participative budgeting. In participative budgeting, the top-level managers bring lower-level employees into the planning phase. Their ideas and opinions are solicited and incorporated into the final budget plans, in an effort to make everyone feel like a member of the team. Participative management and budgeting are outgrowths of the behavioral approach to management.

Exhibit 32.1.   Example of mission/goals/objectives interrelationship.

	American Centers
	Statement of Mission, Goals and Objectives
Mission:	To provide program services as needed to the citizens of American City, regardless of their ability to pay.
Goals:	To assist the citizens in improving the quality of their lives by providing community services, day care, and recreation.
Objectives:	To provide community services through an adult tutoring service; to provide day-care services for 20 children and 10 senior citizens; and to provide after-school and summer recreation activities for children.

During the planning phase, administrators must take a new look at the needs and desires of the group or groups to be served. They should look at past performance and take note of the changes that have occurred since the last budgeting period. This review is necessary to determine changes in approaches and strategies. One of the ways to gather this information is to conduct community need surveys.

Economic and social changes may make it necessary to change the mission, goals, and objectives. For example, 20 years ago, day care was not a major issue in society because fewer mothers worked and the extended family was relied on for assistance. Today, however, there is a substantial increase in the number of mothers working outside the home, and there has been deterioration of the family unit. Consequently, day care for children and senior citizens is an important issue in today's society. Accordingly, an agency with a mission that includes the provision of day-care services may find it necessary to change its goals and objectives in order to deliver the services intended.

(b) PROGRAMMING Programming as it relates to budgeting within the nonprofit organization refers to the execution of the plans developed in the planning phase. During this phase, programs and the staffing of the program positions are the major considerations. Another name for this phase of budgeting is called management.

Programming connects the goals and objectives into programs or activity units. The balancing process continues as management attempts to design specific programs within the constraints given. Naturally, resource availability is important; however, management should attempt to concentrate not on the availability of funds, but on the desired results if sufficient resources were made available. In fact, the "desired results approach" is quite beneficial to management because management may use its planned programs as a basis for soliciting funding.

The programming phase begins with a review of the proposed goals and objectives and an evaluation of the existing programs. Old programs are continued, revised, or abandoned. Next, new programs are developed and evaluated as alternatives to existing programs. Finally, the program or programs that best meet the objectives, goals, and mission of the organization are selected. Programs should be the result of fact-finding procedures, not guesswork. This calls for not only a knowledge of the needs of the community, but a knowledge of how those needs are currently being addressed.

(c) CONTROL Control deals with making provisions for the adherence to goals and objectives. It is the monitoring of actual activity to ensure that budgeted activity is accomplished in an efficient and effective manner.

One of the most common ways to use budgets as a control measure is variance analysis. A report is prepared showing actual performance compared with budgeted performance. The resulting differences are called variances. When variances are isolated, they are labeled as favorable or unfavorable. Each variance is analyzed to determine its source and cause.

A common misconception in variance analysis is that only unfavorable variances should be investigated. For several reasons, favorable variances should be investigated with equal attention. For example, a favorable expense variance may be the result of the use of inferior goods. A favorable revenue variance may be the result of poor forecasting or indicative of poor management. For effective control, all factors underlying the variance, both external and internal, must be isolated and investigated.

Another common misconception about budget variances is that the manager should be "blamed" for unfavorable variances. To do so would destroy the purpose of isolation of variances—finding explanations for deviations. "Blame fixing" can be unduly penalizing to managers and may reduce motivation. There may very well be acceptable explanations for the variances, and the manager should be given the opportunity to explain. In the final analysis, managers should be held responsible only for those variances that are controllable at the management level.

32.3 BUDGETING ROLES

Successful budgeting is the result of a coordinated effort. In light of decreasing sources of revenue and increasing demands for services, an organization's board members, managers, and employees must work together to develop a set of planned programs that will efficiently and effectively utilize the entrusted resources.

Generally, there are five participants in the budgeting process:

1. Board of directors;
2. Executive Director;
3. Controller;
4. Program managers;
5. Employees.

The board of directors sets the organization's mission, from which goals and objectives are developed. The Executive Director acts as the coordinator of the budgeting process and, with the assistance of the controller and within the constraints handed down by the board, develops the revenue estimates. The program managers are required to develop expense budgets for their programs. Employee input is solicited as to daily performance expectations. The controller provides historical data that are used by program managers and the Executive Director to transform the projections into dollar amounts.

In many organizations, a budget committee is formed to take on the responsibility for overseeing the entire budgeting process. The committee is composed of selected board members, the Executive Director, the controller, and key program managers. The Executive Director represents the committee on a day-to-day basis.

After all revenue and expense estimates are gathered, the information and data are combined into the final budget documents: the operations budget, the cash budget, the capital budget, and the pro forma statement of financial position. The final budget is presented to the board—and, possibly, to funding sources—for approval.

32.4 BUDGETING VERSUS ACCOUNTING

Budgeting was defined in the introductory section as the process of projecting future sources and uses of resources. Accounting may be defined as the financial reporting of the historical events of an entity. Accounting provides for the recording, classifying, summarizing, analyzing, and reporting of past financial transactions. Budgeting is future-oriented and accounting is past-oriented. In addition, budgeting in a nonprofit organization involves qualitative reporting, but accounting deals with quantitative reporting only.

In profit-oriented organizations, budgeting and accounting are quite separate; each is a distinct function. That is not the case in nonprofits. It is not uncommon to see the operations budget as part of the formal accounting reporting system. For example, some agencies show a comparison of actual operations and budgeted operations as part of their periodic accounting report.

Accounting reports are also used to forecast future expenses and revenues. Regardless of the approach used in budgeting, past financial reports should be examined for historical trends and patterns. This method of estimating expenses may be combined with other methods for maximum benefit.

32.5 BUDGETING TECHNIQUES

Numerous techniques have been developed to plan program expenses. Some of the most commonly used approaches in budgeting for nonprofit organizations are:

1. Line-item budgeting (LIB);
2. Zero-base budgeting (ZBB);
3. Planned-programming-budgeting system (PPBS).

All three approaches deal with the estimation of *expenses* because revenue estimation generally does not call for a specific technique. It is based largely on historical costs.

(a) LINE-ITEM BUDGETING (LIB)   The distinguishing characteristic of LIB is its emphasis on the past. Preparers of the budget look at amounts expended for various programs and program activities in the past. Then an attempt is made to adjust the amounts upward using a predetermined rate.

A source of expense increase, such as inflation, may be used to adjust each budget line item upward. Top management provides these figures. The projected increases are called increments. Thus, LIB is commonly referred to as incremental budgeting. The upwardly adjusted figures are used as estimates of the upcoming year's expenses. The increment adjustment may differ for each line item or it may be consistently applied to some or all line-item amounts.

Exhibit 32.2 shows a line-item budget for a day-care program. The given percentages, representing the increase adjustments, are applied to each line item to arrive at the budgeted amounts for the upcoming year.

The advantage of LIB is simplicity. Once the percentages are determined, the new budget results from mere mathematical computations. The major disadvantage is that ineffective programs, along with their related costs, are maintained in the budget year after year because of the heavy reliance on historical costs.

In spite of the major disadvantage, LIB is still widely used in budgeting for the nonprofit sector. When used in conjunction with other techniques, the benefits are retained while the effects of the disadvantages are minimized.

Exhibit 32.2.   Example of line-item budget.

	American Centers		
	Line-Item Expense Budget for Day-Care Program		
	Budget Year 19X2		
Expense	Actual 19X1	Percent of Increase	Budget 19X2
Salaries	$155,327	7	$166,200
Employee benefits	7,766	7	8,310
Payroll taxes	15,532	7	16,620
Supplies	62,891	6	66,665
Telephone	2,596	4	2,700
Occupancy	15,472	10	17,020
Total	$259,584		$277,515

(b) ZERO-BASED BUDGETING (ZBB)   The ZBB technique became popular during Jimmy Carter's tenure as governor of the State of Georgia. Later, when he became president, he took the technique to the White House where it was implemented in the federal government.

The initial appeal of the technique was centered on the fact that, under ZBB, each program had to justify its existence each year. There was complete disregard for historical costs. As a result, only those programs that were "productive" in satisfying the organization's goals and objectives survived. In a sense, program managers had to "fight" for their programs' existence each time a budget was prepared.

The federal government's experience, as well as the experiences of nonprofits, proved to be unfavorable, primarily because of the time required to implement the technique. Today, ZBB is not as widely used as it was during the 1970s, but certain aspects of the procedures still have possible benefits in the budgeting process for nonprofits.

Exhibit 32.3 presents the steps in the ZBB technique. Notice that the emphasis in ZBB is on a fresh start each year, disregarding actual performance of past years. The decision packages require a considerable amount of preparation time. Each program manager is required to prepare projections of expenses at various levels of effort. These estimates are proposed as alternative ways of accomplishing the goals and objectives of that particular program. Therefore, one program manager's set of decision packages may resemble a complete traditional budget for an entire organization because of the massive volumes of paper work involved.

The greatest time effort, however, is spent in ranking the decision packages. Because ZBB requires handling literally thousands of decision packages each year, rarely is there sufficient time in the normal budgeting cycle to accommodate a proper evaluation. Furthermore, it may be necessary to go through the ranking procedures more than once, or even more than twice, which will place additional time pressure on the preparers. The resulting demands on time and resources can be overwhelming.

(c) PLANNED-PROGRAMMING-BUDGETING SYSTEM (PPBS)   ZBB became popular in the 1970s; PPBS was a product of the 1960s. The popularity of the PPBS technique was an outgrowth of its use in the Department of Defense. It was abandoned in the early

Exhibit 32.3. Zero-base budgeting steps.

1. Define the decision center (program or activity).
2. Assume that each line item in each program has a zero balance.
3. Develop decision packages for each decision unit.
4. Rank each decision package, first within the decision unit, then within the organization.
5. Allocate the resources to the decision packages.

1970s when ZBB was introduced. However, many of its elements still linger in the budgeting process of many organizations today.

Exhibit 32.4 shows the steps in the PPBS technique. The center of focus in PPBS is the program. This technique is often confused with the programming phase of the general budgeting process, discussed in an earlier section. As the steps indicate, PPBS is more extensive than the programming phase of the budgeting process. The latter deals exclusively with the establishment of programs needed to meet the goals and objectives of the nonprofit. PPBS deals not only with the establishment of programs, but with the evaluation of those programs in terms of cost effectiveness.

The advantages of PPBS are:

1. It provides an integrated approach to management control;
2. It is somewhat scientific in that it leads to effective and efficient use of resources.

The disadvantages of PPBS are:

1. Good coordination of efforts is mandatory;
2. It is political in nature;
3. It is costly to implement, both in terms of resources and time.

(d) INTEGRATED APPROACH Although LIB, ZBB, and PPBS are often thought of as individual budgeting techniques, there is no reason these methods cannot be combined. The integrated approach to budgeting takes the benefits and advantages of all of the common budgeting techniques and formulates an approach to budgeting that is tailor-made for the specific organization involved. In reality, this is an ideal approach for nonprofits because the unfavorable attributes of the individual methods can be abandoned while preserving the favorable attributes. Therefore, ZBB may be used for some program expense estimates while LIB or PPBS may be used for others. The obvious benefit of this approach is that the organization gets the best of all worlds.

Exhibit 32.4. PPBS steps.

1. Define the program.
2. Set program priorities.
3. Allocate cost to programs.
4. Evaluate programs in term of cost effectiveness.
5. Select most cost-effective programs.

32.6 THE BUDGET PROCESS

Once a technique has been selected, the budget documents are prepared and presented to the board for approval.

Generally, the first phase of the process is the dissemination of the guidelines that govern the budgeting process. If a nonprofit establishes a budget committee to oversee the budgeting function, the committee will be responsible for distributing the guidelines to the appropriate members. This is often accomplished through the Executive Director.

Guidelines are formulated by top management, and they are passed on to program managers to act as floors and ceilings on programs and program activities. The guidelines set forth all constraints—those on spending and hiring, and government regulations. Other matters covered include budget format, timetable, and feasible assumptions.

Top management estimates revenues, and the program managers estimate the expenses. These figures may go through several revisions before they are accepted. Program estimates are gathered and reviewed. There are usually negotiations between upper management and lower management, and the success of these negotiations is of utmost importance in the overall success of the budgeting process. Even if estimates are in agreement with guidelines, they may be challenged. If so, all or selected budget items may require justification. This procedures strengthens the budgeting process because it increases the probability that only worthy programs survive. The revised data and information are compiled into a single document that has several interrelated parts.

(a) TYPES OF BUDGETS There are at least four component parts of the overall budget: operations budget, cash budget, capital budget, and the pro forma statement of financial position.

(i) Operations budget The operations budget is probably the most widely used of all types of budgets. It contains the estimates of revenues from all sources and the estimates of expenses for all programs. In summary, it projects the financial operating activities of the organization for a specified period of time.

In the appendix, which contains sample budget forms, the operations budget form is labeled Budget Form 1. There are two major sections of an operations budget: revenues and expenses. On Budget Form 1, the specific titles of these sections are Public Support and Revenue, and Expenses. The form shows that United Way agencies, which are human-service organizations, receive their support from the sources appearing on lines 1 through 12.

Sources of revenue differ, depending on the type of nonprofit. A human-service organization such as a neighborhood center may receive contributions, legacies, bequests, and so on; a governmental agency receives revenue from various types of taxes such as income tax and sales tax.

The starting point for the estimation of revenues is prior-year sources. It is not unusual for top management to get commitments from former revenue supporters prior to the estimating phase. Grant approval or special allocations from related organizations may be received months before the budgeting process begins. It is an advantage for organizations to receive revenue commitments prior to preparing the budget. Governmental agencies have a different type of advantage. In order to meet revenue requirements, increases in taxes and assessments can be imposed. Therefore, revenue estimation for governmental units may occur before expense estimates are finalized.

When services and products are sold to the public by nonprofit organizations, the procedure for estimating revenues to some extent resembles the estimation activity of profit-making enterprises. The number of service units or products to be sold is estimated, an estimated sale price or rate is applied, and gross revenue is calculated. For example, a neighborhood center may be licensed to provide day care for 20 children. Top management estimates an average operating capacity of 90 percent throughout the budget year. Assuming that a sliding scale will be used to charge clients and that the average hourly rate is determined to be $2, the estimate of the revenue to be earned by the day-care program can be determined as follows:

$$90\% \text{ capacity} = 18 \text{ children}$$

$$18 \text{ clients} \times 52 \text{ weeks} \times 40 \text{ hours} \times \$2 \text{ per hour} = \$74,880$$

The day-care service fees earned are not likely to be the only source of revenue for this program. Additional sources of revenue may include grants or contributions.

Other forms of revenue can be estimated, also. Investment income, for example, can be estimated by applying an expected rate of return to the investment amount. If an organization has a portfolio of stocks and bonds of $80,000 and its financial adviser estimates an annual return of 9 percent, the revenue estimate from the investment can be determined as follows:

$$\text{Investment} \times \text{Expected return} = \text{Estimated investment income}$$

$$\$80,000 \quad \times \quad 9\% \quad = \quad \$ 7,200$$

Governmental agencies can estimate revenues by applying the tax rate to the tax base. For example, in estimating revenue from property taxes, assume the assessment base is $10 million and the assessment rate is 15 mills per $1:

$$\text{Assessment base} \times \text{Assessment rate} = \text{Estimated revenue}$$

$$(\$10,000,000) \quad (15 \text{ mills per } \$1)$$

$$\$10,000,000 \quad \times \quad .015 \quad = \quad \$ 150,000$$

If the governmental agency needs to increase the tax assessments to balance its budgets, it may do so by raising the tax base or the assessment rate. The increase must be approved by the appropriate governmental bodies, but this is an option that no other nonprofit organizations enjoy.

Budget Form 1, in the appendix, shows the proposed expenses for a human-service organization on lines 14 through 29. A sample program expense budget is presented in Exhibit 32.5. The organization, American Centers, has three programs. Most of the expenses shown are common to all types of nonprofits. One of the largest expense categories in nonprofit budgeting is compensation expense, which is the sum of salaries, employee benefits, and payroll taxes. These expenses appear on lines 14, 15, and 16 on Budget Form 1 and appear as the first three line items in Exhibit 32.5.

Exhibit 32.5.   Example of program expense budget.

American Centers
Program Expense Budget
For the Year Ending December 31, 19X2

	Day-Care Services	Recreation Services	Community Services	Management and General	Total
Salaries	$166,200	$124,000	$ 7,200	$40,315	$337,715
Employee benefits	8,310	6,200	360	2,015	16,885
Payroll taxes	16,620	12,400	720	4,030	33,770
Total compensation	191,130	142,600	8,280	46,360	388,370
Professional fees	—	—	—	3,335	3,335
Supplies	66,665	12,500	1,300	7,280	87,745
Telephone	2,700	1,300	400	8,450	12,850
Postage	—	—	—	1,350	1,350
Occupancy	17,020	12,160	2,100	1,475	32,755
Equipment rental	—	11,600	—	—	11,600
Total	$277,515	$180,160	$12,080	68,250	$538,005

The estimation of a compensation package requires a personnel budget. Optional Budget Form 5, which lists personnel positions and the related salaries, should be optional only for small agencies. This particular personnel form requires the past and present years' data to be presented along with the projected data for the budget year.

The personnel budget is usually prepared during the programming phase, when the objectives and goals are defined in terms of programs. Optional Budget Form 5 does not provide for program information; however, the "Account No. Charged" column serves the same purpose. Programs are assigned specific account numbers in the accounting system, to allow each program to be identified individually.

Employee benefits and payroll taxes are usually stated as percentages of salaries. Therefore, if a day-care program's annual salaries expense is estimated at $166,200, the employee benefits expense at 5 percent of salaries, and payroll taxes expense at 10 percent of salaries, compensation expense can be projected as shown in Exhibit 32.6.

Salaries expense and other compensation costs for a particular employee may be assigned to one individual program or they may be prorated to two or more programs based on expected time devoted to each program. Consider the salary and related costs

Exhibit 32.6.   Projection of compensation expense.

American Centers
Estimation of Compensation Expense
Budget Year 19X2

Salaries expense	$166,200
Employee benefits (5%)	8,310
Payroll taxes (10%)	16,620
Total Compensation Expense	$191,130

for an Executive Director. In addition to the management of the entire organization, assume the position calls for the Executive Director to tutor adults in reading through its community service program. If 30 percent of the Executive Director's time is expected to be devoted to tutoring, 30 percent of the salary and related employee benefits and payroll taxes should be allocated to the Community Service Program. The remaining time is prorated to other programs and to the management and general function.

An important aspect of expense budgeting is making estimates as specific as possible. The type and quality of goods and services to be used should be considered. Future price increases should be anticipated, as well as technological changes that may positively or negatively affect future operations.

Equally important in preparing the operations budget is the need to prepare estimates by months, as well as by years. Too often, operations budgets are prepared for the budget year, then divided by 12 months. This approach bears the erroneous assumption that each month will have the same operational level. Nothing could be further from the truth. Rarely will an organization's revenues and expenses be the same each month. Consider an organization that provides recreational services for youth. Because most students do not attend school during the summer months, the recreational services are likely to be in more demand during this time. Thus, the budgets for the summer months of June, July, and August should have provisions for greater operating cost than other months.

Estimating Techniques. Various techniques are used in estimating revenues and expenses for program activity. A single individual technique may be used or a combination of several.

A commonly used technique for estimating revenue and expenses for the upcoming budget year is market survey. A nonprofit may hire a professional marketing team or may develop its own. A market survey begins with a survey of the community needs and includes an investigation into the availability of resources to meet the needs.

Other expense estimation techniques include statistical methods such as regression analysis, probability theory, and modeling. Some preparers have found statistical methods to be reliable; others have not. Generally, the more homogeneous the data used and the larger the data base, the more reliable the results. Traditional methods such as informed judgment and analysis of historical data are still preferred by some agencies.

(ii) Cash budget The cash budget should begin with an estimate of the beginning cash balance for the budget year. Estimated cash receipts are added to the estimated beginning cash balance, resulting in the total cash available for use during the budget year. Cash disbursements expected during the year are estimated and subtracted from the estimated total cash available, resulting in the estimated ending cash balance for the budget year.

The cash budget allows management to plan ahead for expected cash shortages. In addition, expected cash overages can be more adequately managed.

Estimated cash receipts may approximate estimated revenues, and estimated cash disbursements may approximate estimated expenses. This is especially true if the nonprofit operates on a cash basis. Cash basis is an accounting procedure that results in the recognition of revenues when cash is received and the recognition of expenses when cash is paid. In contrast, in accrual basis accounting, revenues are recognized when earned, and expenses are recognized when incurred. Differences will result, regardless of the method used, when a nonprofit experiences cash transactions that do not involve operations. Differences will always occur when accrual basis accounting is used. It should be noted that only accrual basis accounting qualifies as a generally accepted accounting principle; thus, it is required by most nonprofits. Some organizations, however, still may use cash basis accounting.

(iii) Capital budget The capital budget provides for acquisition and disposal of property, equipment, and other types of fixed assets. If an asset is to be purchased, the specifications and the funding source are outlined in the capital budget. If an asset is to be disposed of, the selling price and replacement information are also included. Therefore, the capital budget may contain as much nonquantitative data as it does quantitative data.

(iv) Pro forma statement of financial position The pro forma statement of financial position (referred to as a pro forma balance sheet, in profit-making enterprises) estimates the financial status of the nonprofit at the end of the budget year. All estimated assets and liabilities are presented. The difference between the two categories is the projected fund (equity) balance. The cash balance appearing under the asset category is the same estimated ending cash balance from the cash budget, and the fixed assets are the same fixed assets provided for in the capital balance.

32.7 SUMMARY

Budgeting is an important but time-consuming part of management. It is used primarily for planning, programming, and control. Coordination plays a key role in the process because of the desirability to gather estimates from all levels of the organization. The key figures in the process are the board of directors, the Executive Director, the controller, and the program managers.

Unfortunately, there is no perfect budgeting technique. The recommended approach is referred to as an integrated approach where elements of commonly used techniques, such as LIB, ZBB, and PPBS, are combined. The benefit of this approach is that the disadvantages of the individual techniques are minimized.

The four types of budgets discussed are the operations budget, the cash budget, the capital budget, and the pro forma statement of financial position. These budgets together form a master plan used to guide the organization through the process of achieving its goals and objectives.

SOURCES AND SUGGESTED REFERENCES

Brownwell, Peter. 1983. "Leadership Style, Budgetary Participation and Managerial Behavior." *Accounting, Organizations and Society* (August): 307–321.

Covaleski, Mark A., and Dirsmith, Mark W. 1988. "The Use of Budgetary Symbols in the Political Arena: A Historical Informed Field Study." *Accounting, Organizations and Society* (November 1): 1–24.

Haines, David G., and Listro, John P. 1988. "Gain Control of Your Organization's Finances. Financial Management in Nonprofit Organization (Part 1)." *Nonprofit World* (November/December): 14–18.

Hayes, Robert D., and Millar, James A. 1990. "Measuring Production Efficiency in a Not-for-Profit Setting." *Accounting Review* (July): 505–519.

Merchant, Kenneth A. 1985. "Budgeting and the Propensity to Create Budgetary Slack." *Accounting, Organizations and Society* (May): 201–210.

Phaup, Marvin. 1990. "Federal Financial Reporting: Some Views of R. K. Mautz." *Public Budgeting & Finance* (Summer): 21–25.

Schick, Allen G. 1985. "University Budgeting: Administrative Perspective, Budget Structure, and Budget Process." *The Academy of Management Review* (October): 794–802.

United Way of America. 1989. *Accounting and Financial Reporting: A Guide for United Ways and Not-for-Profit Human Service Organizations* (2nd ed. rev.). Alexandria, VA: United Way of America.

————. 1975. *Budgeting: A Guide for United Ways and Not-for-Profit Human Service Organizations.* Alexandria, VA: United Way of America.

United Way of America. 1982. *Simplified Budget Forms for United Ways in Smaller Communities.* Alexandria, VA: Author.

Ziebell, Mary T., and Decosta, Don T. 1991. *Management Control System in Nonprofit Organizations* (pp. 210–271). New York: Harcourt Brace Jovanovich.

APPENDIX

The appendix to this chapter contains a set of simplified Budget forms prepared by United Way of America for use by United Way-funded agencies. All of the forms and chart are presented with the permission of United Way of America, Alexandria, VA.

The set contains:

- Summary Information Form—A 2-page outline of the agency's mission, services, budgetary requests, and audit comments.
- Budget Form 1—This is the Support Revenue and Expense Form which, together with the Summary Information Form, can be used as the basic budget forms for those United Ways not using function accounting.
- Budget Form 2—This optional "spread sheet" details the income and expense by function. It provides a total agency picture and unit costs of programs where appropriate.
- Budget Form 3—This is an optional form that describes funds that have restrictions placed on their use by the donor.
- Budget Form 4—This is also an optional form. It describes reserve funds designated by the agency's board.
- Budget Form 5—An optional form that lists the personnel positions and salaries of the agency.

Exhibit 32.7.   United Way fianancial reporting forms.

UNITED WAY FINANCIAL REPORTING FORMS

AGENCY:_____

Mailing Address: _____

City, State, Zip: _____

Telephone: (   ) _____

For the Fiscal Year

_____To_____

Presented _____ on _____
　　　　　　　　　　(Name of Funding Body)　　　　　　　　　　　　　　　(Date)

This budget was considered and approved for submission at the Board of Directors Meeting on _____
　　　　　　　　　　　　　　　　　　　　　　　　　　　　　　　　　　　　(Date)

_____　　　_____
Chief Professional Officer　　　　　　　　　President or Other Authorized Official

---

Reproduced by permission, United Way of America.

Exhibit 32.7. *(Continued)*

AGENCY: DATE:

I. SUMMARY INFORMATION

A. Program Data

1. What is the agency's mission?

2. What programs/services did your agency provide this year?

3. Target population served: (age, sex, special interest, etc.)

4. Number of unduplicated individual units served in United Way area: (3 yrs. ago _____   2 yrs. ago_____   last yr._____)

5. Geographic area covered:

6. How are agency programs/services assessed for effectiveness?

7. What are the specific objectives?

(Continued on Back)

Exhibit 32.7. *(Continued)*

8. What new or different programs/services does your agency contemplate providing next year?

9. How will these new or different programs/services be financed?

10. What supplementary fund-raising activities does the agency conduct?

Activity	Net$ Results	Area Covered	Month Conducted

B. Financial Highlights

Financial Highlights	Last Year	This Year	Next Year
Total Expenses (BF 1: Line 35)			
Total Support & Revenue—All Sources (BF 1: Line 13)			
Excess (Deficit)			
Allocation From This United Way Direct to Agency Matching Government Grant Total			
Allocation From Other United Ways to Agency			

FOR UNITED WAY USE ONLY

Audit report has been received by the United Way for the year ending _____

This audit report was: ( ) Unqualified   ( ) Qualified

If Qualified, explain: _____

_____

(Signature of Chairman of Audit Committee)

c United Way of America 1982

Exhibit 32.7. *(Continued)*

AGENCY:

Budget Form: 1

Support Revenue & Expenses	Fiscal 19 Last Year Actual	Fiscal 19 This Year Budgeted	Fiscal 19 Next Year Proposed
Public Support & Revenue— All Sources [4000-6999]			
1 0000 **Allocation From This United Way**			
2 4000 Contributions			
3 4200 Special Events			
4 4300 Legacies & Bequests (Unrestricted)			
5 4600 Contributed by Associated Organizations			
6 4700 Allocated by Other United Ways			
7 5000 Fees & Grants From Government Agencies			
8 6000 Membership Dues			
9 6200 Program Services Fees & Net Incidental Revenue			
10 6300 Sales of Materials			
11 6500 Investment Income			
12 6900 Miscellaneous Revenue			
13 TOTAL SUPPORT & REVENUE (Add 1 thru 12)			
Expenses [7000-9999]			
14 7000 Salaries			
15 7100 Employee Benefits			
16 7200 Payroll Taxes, etc.			
17 8000 Professional Fees			
18 8100 Supplies			
19 8200 Telephone			
20 8300 Postage & Shipping			
21 8400 Occupancy			
22 8500 Rental & Maintenance of Equipment			
23 8600 Printing & Publications			
24 8700 Travel			
25 8800 Conferences, Conventions & Meetings			
26 8900 Specific Assistance to Individuals			
27 9000 Membership Dues			
28 9100 Awards & Grants			
29 9400 Miscellaneous			
30 TOTAL EXPENSES (Add 14 thru 29)			
31 9691 Payments to Affiliated Organizations			
32 Board Designations for Specified Activities for Future Years			
33 TOTAL EXPENSES FOR BUDGET PERIOD FOR ALL ACTIVITIES (30 + 31 + 32)			
34 TOTAL EXPENSES FOR ACTIVITIES FINANCED BY RESTRICTED FUNDS			
35 TOTAL EXPENSES FOR ACTIVITIES FINANCED BY UNRESTRICTED FUNDS (33 − 34)			
36 EXCESS (DEFICIT) OF TOTAL SUPPORT & REVENUE OVER EXPENSES (13 − 35)			
37 9500 Depreciation of Buildings & Equipment			
38 9900 Major Property & Equipment Acquisition ($ __1000__ +)			

All Financial Information Rounded to Nearest Dollar

© United Way of America 1982

Exhibit 32.7.   *(Continued)*

AGENCY:

Proposed Budget for Fiscal 19 ____ By Program & Supporting Functions	Grand Total (2 · 5)	Total Supporting (3 · 4)	Supporting Services		Total Program Services 6 through 12
			Management & General	Fund Raising	
	1	2	3	4	5
Public Support & Revenue— All Sources [4000-6999]					
1 0000 **Allocation From This United Way**					
2 4000 Contributions					
3 4200 Special Events					
4 4300 Legacies & Bequests (Unrestricted)					
5 4600 Contributed by Associated Organizations					
6 4700 Allocated by Other United Ways					
7 5000 Fees & Grants From Government Agencies					
8 6000 Membership Dues					
9 6200 Program Services Fees & Net Incidental Revenue					
10 6300 Sales of Materials					
11 6500 Investment Income					
12 6900 Miscellaneous Revenue					
13 TOTAL SUPPORT & REVENUE (Add 1 thru 12)					
Expenses [7000-9999]					
14 7000 Salaries					
15 7100 Employee Benefits					
16 7200 Payroll Taxes, etc.					
17 8000 Professional Fees					
18 8100 Supplies					
19 8200 Telephone					
20 8300 Postage & Shipping					
21 8400 Occupancy					
22 8500 Rental & Maintenance of Equipment					
23 8600 Printing & Publications					
24 8700 Travel					
25 8800 Conferences, Conventions & Meetings					
26 8900 Specific Assistance to Individuals					
27 9000 Membership Dues					
28 9100 Awards & Grants					
29 9400 Miscellaneous					
30 TOTAL EXPENSES (Add 14 thru 29)					
31 9691 Payments to Affiliated Organizations					
32 Board Designations for Specified Activities for Future Years					
33 TOTAL EXPENSES FOR BUDGET PERIOD FOR ALL ACTIVITIES (30 + 31 + 32)					
34 TOTAL EXPENSES FOR ACTIVITIES FINANCED BY RESTRICTED FUNDS					
35 TOTAL EXPENSES FOR ACTIVITIES FINANCED BY UNRESTRICTED FUNDS (33 − 34)					
36 EXCESS (DEFICIT) OF TOTAL SUPPORT & REVENUE OVER EXPENSES (13 − 35)					
37 9500 Depreciation of Buildings & Equipment					
38 9900 Major Property & Equipment Acquisition ($ _1000_ +)					

Summary of Program Cost Analysis	
Computation of Per Unit Cost of Agency's Programs	1 Total Program Services Expenses Direct (from Line 33) 2 Total Supporting Services Expenses (Line 33, Column 2 proportionally distributed) 3 Payments to Affiliated Organizations (Line 31, Column 1, proportionally distributed) 4 **TOTAL PROGRAM** (1 + 2 + 3) **PROGRAM VOLUME & UNIT COST** 5 Total Number Program Units 6 Direct Cost Per Unit (Line 1 Line 5) 7 Total Cost Per Unit (Line 4 Line 5) 8 Unit Description

All Financial Information Rounded to Nearest Dollar

Exhibit 32.7. *(Continued)*

Budget Form: **2**

Program Services						
6	7	8	9	10	11	12

c United Way of America 1982

Exhibit 32.7. *(Continued)*

Optional Budget Form: 3

AGENCY:

EXPLANATION OF RESTRICTED FUNDS
(Source Restricted Only—Exclude Board Restricted)

A. Name of Restricted Fund _____ Amount: $ _____

    1. Restricted by: _____

    2. Source of fund: _____

    3. Purpose for which restricted: _____

    4. Are investment earnings available for current unrestricted expenses?
       _____Yes _____No   If Yes, what amount: _____

    5. Date when restriction became effective: _____

    6. Date when restriction expires: _____

B. Name of Restricted Fund _____ Amount: $ _____

    1. Restricted by: _____

    2. Source of fund: _____

    3. Purpose for which restricted: _____

    4. Are investment earnings available for current unrestricted expenses?
       _____Yes _____No   If Yes, what amount: _____

    5. Date when restriction became effective: _____

    6. Date when restriction expires: _____

C. Name of Restricted Fund _____ Amount: $ _____

    1. Restricted by: _____

    2. Source of fund: _____

    3. Purpose for which restricted: _____

    4. Are investment earnings available for current unrestricted expenses?
       _____Yes _____No   If Yes, what amount: _____

    5. Date when restriction became effective: _____

    6. Date when restriction expires: _____

©United Way of America 1982

Exhibit 32.7.   *(Continued)*

AGENCY: **Optional Budget Form: 4**

EXPLANATION OF BOARD DESIGNATED RESERVES
(For Funds Which Are Not Donor Restricted)

A. Name of Board Designated Reserve:_____ Amount: $ _____

    1. Date of board meeting at which designation was made: _____

    2. Source of funds:_____

    3. Purpose for which designated: _____

        _____

    4. Are the investment earnings available for current unrestricted expenses?
        ____Yes ____No   If Yes, what amount: _____

    5. Date when board designation became effective: _____

    6. Date when board designation expires: _____

B. Name of Board Designated Reserve:_____ Amount: $ _____

    1. Date of board meeting at which designation was made: _____

    2. Source of funds:_____

    3. Purpose for which designated: _____

        _____

    4. Are the investment earnings available for current unrestricted expenses?
        ____Yes ____No   If Yes, what amount: _____

    5. Date when board designation became effective: _____

    6. Date when board designation expires: _____

C. Name of Board Designated Reserve:_____ Amount: $ _____

    1. Date of board meeting at which designation was made: _____

    2. Source of funds:_____

    3. Purpose for which designated: _____

        _____

    4. Are the investment earnings available for current unrestricted expenses?
        ____Yes ____No   If Yes, what amount: _____

    5. Date when board designation became effective: _____

    6. Date when board designation expires: _____

©United Way of America 1982

Exhibit 32.7. *(Continued)*

AGENCY: **Optional Budget Form: 5**

Account No. Charged	Position Title and/or Employee Name*	Full-Time Equiva-lent**	19___ Last Year Actual	19___ This Year Budgeted	19___ Next Year Proposed
	TOTAL				

*Denotes position vacant.
**Full-time staff will be noted as 1:00: Halftime as 0.50: Quartertime as 0.25, and so on.
All Financial Information Rounded to Nearest Dollar.

©United Way of America 1982

CHAPTER THIRTY-THREE

Unrelated Business Income

Jody Blazek
Blazek, Rogers & Vetterling

CONTENTS

Based on material from *Tax and Financial Planning for Tax-Exempt Organizations: Forms, Checklists, Procedures* by Jody Blazek (Wiley, 1990).

Exempt organizations (EOs) receive two types of income: earned and unearned. Unearned income—income for which the EO gives nothing in return—comes from grants, membership fees, and donations. Think of it as "one-way-street" money. The motivation for giving the money is gratuitous and/or of a nonprofit character with no expectation of gain on the part of the giver; there is donative intent.

In contrast, an EO furnishes services/goods or invests its capital in return for earned income: an opera is seen, classes are attended, hospital care is provided, or credit counseling is given, for example. The purchasers of the EO's goods and services do intend to receive something in return; they expect the street to be "two-way." An investment company holding the EO's money expects to have to pay reasonable return to the EO for using the funds. In these examples, the EO receives earned income. The important issue this chapter considers is when earned income becomes unrelated business income subject to income tax.

There are complex rules that govern when an EO's earned income becomes unrelated business income (UBI). The concepts of UBI are vague and contain many exceptions carved out by special interest groups. The House of Representatives Subcommittee on

Oversight held hearings and drafted revisions over a four-year period during 1987 to 1990 and still has not proposed tax legislation (see list of proposals on page 860).

33.1 IRS SCRUTINY FOCUSED ON UNRELATED BUSINESS INCOME (UBI)

Beginning in 1989 with the addition of a new page 5 to Form 990, the IRS is studying the UBI issue. Until page 5, with its "Analysis of Revenue-Producing Activities," was added to the annual EO reporting requirements, UBI was not identified in any special way on Form 990; the income was simply included with related income of the same character. Both the Congressional representatives and the IRS agreed there was insufficient information to propose changes to the existing UBI rules.

Now, EOs filing Internal Revenue Service (IRS) Form 990 (not including Form 990EZ filers whose gross income is less than $100,000) complete the new page 5 to separate income into three categories:

1. Unrelated income (identified with a business code from Form 990T that describes its nature),
2. Unrelated income identified by the specific Internal Revenue Code section by which the income is excluded from UBI, and
3. Related or exempt function income, along with a description of the relationship of the income-producing activity to the accomplishment of exempt purposes.

This statistical information is being gathered to evaluate the consequences of proposed changes to the UBIT rules. Marcus Owens of the IRS National Office announced, in May 1991, the initiation of a compliance program with a public educational effort and emphasis on large case examinations. The exams started in 1992 and the results may be known in 1993.

33.2 HISTORY OF THE UNRELATED BUSINESS INCOME TAX (UBIT)

A historical note helps to understand how the rules have evolved. Before 1950, an EO could conduct any income-producing activity and, in fact, did operate businesses without paying income tax. Using a "destination of income" test, as long as the income earned from the business was totally expended for grants and other exempt activities, any amount of business activity was permissible. One famous tax case involved New York University Law School's operation of a highly successful spaghetti factory.[1] In view of the extensive profits and businesslike manner in which the factory was operated, the IRS tried to impose an income tax on the profits. The courts decided, however, that no tax could be imposed under the then existing tax code as long as the profits were used to operate the school.

In response to pressure from businesses, Congress established the unrelated business income tax (UBIT) with the intention of eliminating the unfair competition

---

[1] *C.F. Mueller Co. v. Commissioner*, 190 F.2d 120 (3d Cir. 1951).

charitable businesses represented, but it did not prohibit its receipt. The Congressional committee thought that the:

> tax free status of exemption section 501 organizations enables them to use their profits tax free to expand operations, while their competitors can expand only with profits remaining after taxes. The problem. . . . is primarily that of unfair competition.[2]

The key questions in finding UBI are, then, whether the activity that produces earned income competes with commercial businesses and whether the method of operation is distinguishable from that of businesses. Another way to ask the question is, "Does it serve an exempt purpose and therefore it is related?" The distinction between for-profits and nonprofits has narrowed over the years as organizations have searched for creative ways to pay for program services. Consider what the difference between a museum bookstore and a commercial one is, other than the absence of private ownership. Privately owned for-profit theaters operate alongside nonprofit ones. Magazines owned by nonprofits, such as *National Geographic* and *Harper's,* contain advertising and appear indistinguishable from Condé Nast's *Traveler* or *Life Magazine.* The health-care profession is also full of indistinguishable examples.

33.3   CONSEQUENCES OF RECEIVING UNRELATED INCOME

There are potentially several unpleasant consequences of earning unrelated income.

- *Payment of unrelated income tax.* Unrelated net income may be taxed at corporate or trust rates with estimated tax payments required. Social clubs, homeowners' associations, and political organizations also pay the UBI tax on their passive investment income in addition to the business income.

- *Exempt status revocation.* Exempt status could be revoked. Separate and apart from the UBI rules, the basic exemption statute under Section 501 of the Internal Revenue Code[3] requires that an organization be organized and operated *exclusively* for exempt purpose, although "exclusively" has not been construed to mean 100 percent. Some commentators say any amount of UBI under 50 percent of the EO's gross income is permissible, although many others recommend no more UBI than 15 to 20 percent. The courts have allowed higher amounts; the IRS tends to vote for lower amounts in measuring whether the EO is operating "exclusively" for exempt purposes rather than for business purposes. An organization can run a business as a secondary purpose, but not as a primary purpose.

  In evaluating the amount of unrelated business activity that is permissible, not only the amount of gross revenue but other factors may be taken into consideration. Nonrevenue aspects of the activity, such as staff time devoted or value of donated services, are factors in determining whether UBI is substantial.

  A complex of nonexempt activity caused the IRS to revoke the exemption of the *Orange County Agricultural Society.*[4] The unrelated business revenues represented

---

[2] House of Representatives No. 2319, 81st Cong., 2d Sess. (1950) at 36, 37.

[3] Throughout the chapter, references to "Section" will mean a Section of the Internal Revenue Code, unless otherwise stated.

[4] *Orange County Agricultural Society,* 90.1 USTC ¶ 50.076 (2d Cir. 1990), *aff'g* 55 T.C.M. 1602 (1988).

between 29 to 34 percent of the gross revenue; although troublesome, they were not the sole factor in the decision of the Tax Court to uphold the IRS's revocation. The presence of private inurement in doing business with the Society's board of directors influenced the decision.

- *All income taxed.* Income from all sources will be taxed if exempt status is lost.
- *Private foundation issue.* Private foundations' ownership of unrelated businesses would likely trigger "excess business holdings" tax and cause loss of exemption.

33.4 DEFINITION OF TRADE OR BUSINESS

To have UBI, the EO must first be found to be engaging in a trade or business. *Trade or business* is defined to include any activity carried on for the production of income from the sale of goods or performance of services.[5] This is a very broad, sweeping definition. The language seems pretty straightforward and, as a safe rule-of-thumb, would literally mean that any activity for which the exempt receives revenues constitutes a business. Unfortunately, this is an area where the tax rules are very gray and the statutory history is difficult to follow. The word "income" does not mean receipts or revenue and also doesn't necessarily mean net income. Section 513(c) provides: "Where an activity carried on for profit constitutes an unrelated trade or business, no part of such trade or business shall be excluded from such classification merely because it does not result in profit."

If one delves deeper into the Internal Revenue Code ("the Code") and the Treasury Regulations ("the Regulations"), it becomes more difficult to find what is meant by "trade or business." The Regulations couch the definition in the context of unfair competition with commercial businesses, saying that "when an activity does not possess the characteristics of a trade or business within the meaning of Section 162," the unrelated business income tax (UBIT) will not apply. These Regulations, however, were written before the Section 513(c) profit motive language was added to the Code, and they are the subject of continuing arguments between taxpayers and the IRS.

(a) PROFIT MOTIVE TEST   The confusion has produced two tests: profit motive and commerciality. Under the profit motive test, an activity conducted simply to produce some revenue but without an expectation of producing a profit (similar to the hobby loss rules) is not a business.[6] This test is used by the IRS in situations where an EO has more than one unrelated business. Losses from the hobby cannot be offset against profits from other businesses. Likewise, the excess expenses (losses) generated in fundamentally exempt activity, such as an educational publication undertaken without the intention of making a profit, cannot be deducted against the profits from a profit-motivated project.

(b) COMMERCIALITY TEST   The commerciality test looks instead to the type of operation: if the activity is carried on in a manner similar to a commercial business, it

---

[5] Treas. Reg. § 1.513-1(b).

[6] *West Virginia State Medical Association, aff'd*, 89-2 U.S.T.C. § 9491 (4th Cir. 1989); 91 T.C. 651 (1988), *Commissioner v. Groetzinger*, 480 U.S. 23 (1987).

Exhibit 33.1.   Components of unrelated business income.

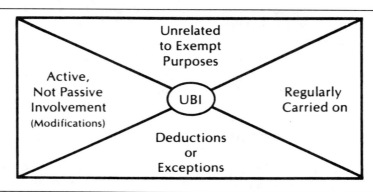

constitutes a trade or business.[7] This test poses serious problems for the unsuspecting because there are no statutory or regulatory parameters to follow. A broad range of UBI cases where the scope of sales or service activity was beyond that normally found in the exempt setting have been decided by examining the commercial taint of the activity.

(c) FRAGMENTATION RULE   Further evidence of the overreaching scope of the term 'trade or business" is found in the *fragmentation rule*.[8] This rule carves out an activity carried on alongside an exempt one and provides that unrelated business does not lose its identity and taxability when it is earned in a related setting. Take, for example, a museum shop. The shop itself is clearly a trade or business, often established with a profit motive and operated in a commercial manner. Items sold in such shops, however, often include both educational items, such as books and reproductions of art works, and souvenirs. The fragmentation rule requires that all items sold be analyzed to identify the equational, or related, items the profit from which is not taxable and the unrelated souvenir items that do produce taxable income. (See "Special Interest Topic—Museums," later in the chapter, for more information about museums.)

33.5   WHAT IS UNRELATED BUSINESS INCOME (UBI)?

UBI is defined as the gross income derived from any *unrelated trade or business regularly carried on,* less the *deductions* connected with the carrying on of such trade or business, computed with *modifications* and *exceptions*.[9] These terms are key to identifying UBI. Exhibit 33.1 shows them graphically. All the prongs of the circle

---

[7] *Better Business Bureau v. United States,* 326 U.S. 279, 283 (1945); *United States National Water Well Association, Inc. v. Commissioner,* 92 T.C. 7 (1989); *Scripture Press Foundation v United States,* 285 F.2d 800 (Ct. Cl. 1961), *cert. denied, Greater United Navajo Development Enterprises, Inc. v. Commissioner,* 74 T.C. 69 (1980).

[8] Section 513(c).

[9] Section 512(a)(1).

surrounding the circle must be considered, to determine what earned income is to be classified as UBI.

33.6 REGULARLY CARRIED ON

A trade or business regularly carried on is considered to compete unfairly with commercial business and is fair game for classification as a taxable business. In determining whether an activity is regularly carried on, the IRS looks at the *frequency and continuity* of an activity when examined by comparison to commercial enterprises. The normal time span of comparable commercial activities can also be determinative.[10] Compare the following:

Irregular	Regular
Sandwich stand at annual county fair.	Cafe open daily.
Annual golf tournament.	Racetrack operated during racing "season."
Nine-day antique show.	Antique store.
Gala Ball held annually.	Monthly dance.
Program ads for annual fund-raising event.	Advertisements in quarterly magazine.

(a) MEANING OF IRREGULAR Intermittent activities may be deemed "regularly carried on" or commercial unless they are discontinuous or periodic. For example, the revenue from a weekly dance would be more likely to be taxed than the profits from an annual fund-raising event. By the same token, ads sold for a monthly newsletter would more likely be classed as commercial than program ads sold for an annual ball. Where the planning and sales effort of a special event or athletic tournament is conducted over a long span of time, the IRS may argue that the activity itself becomes regularly carried on despite the fact that the event occurs infrequently. (See the NCAA advertising sales discussion following under "Agency theory," page 842.)

In a 1981 case, the IRS lost in arguing that the engagement of professionals to stage the show and produce a program guide containing advertising caused a patrolmen's fund-raising event profits to be UBI.[11] The fact that the solicitors worked for 16 weeks in preparing and organizing the event made the activity regular in the IRS eyes; the Tax Court disagreed.

(b) SEASON ACTIVITY Activities conducted during a period traditionally identified as seasonal, such as Christmas, if conducted during the "season," will be considered regular and the income will not qualify to be excluded from UBIT. Christmas card

---

[10] Treas. Reg. § 1.513-1(c).
[11] *Suffolk County Patrolmen's Benevolent Association, Inc. v. Commissioner,* 77 T.C. 1314 (1981), *acq.* 1984-1 C.B. 2.

sales during October or November, or Independence Day balloons sold in June/July, would be "regular."

33.7 SUBSTANTIALLY RELATED

"Any business the conduct of which is not substantially related (aside from need to make money) to the performance of an organization's charitable, educational, or other purposes or function constituting the basis of its exemption is defined as unrelated," according to the Regulations.[12]

An activity is substantially related only when it has a causal relationship to the achievement of an EO's exempt purpose (that is, the purpose for which the EO was granted exemption according to its Form 1023 or 1024 or subsequent Form 990 filings). The Regulations suggest that the presence of this requirement necessitates an examination of the relationship between the business activities (of producing or distributing goods or performing services) that generate the particular income in question and the accomplishment of the organization's exempt purposes.[13]

The size and extent of the activity itself and its contribution to exempt purposes are determinative. The "nexus" (association, connection, or linkage) between the activity and accomplishment of exempt purposes is examined to find "relatedness." The best way to illustrate the concept is with examples.

(a) EXAMPLES OF RELATED ACTIVITY *Related income-producing* activities include:

- Admission tickets for performances or lectures;
- Student or member tuition or class fees;
- Symphony society sale of symphonic musical recordings;
- Products made by handicapped workers or trainees;[14]
- Hospital room, drug, and other patient charges;
- Agriculture college sale of produce or student work;
- Sale of educational materials;
- Secretarial and telephone answering service training program for indigent and homeless;[15]
- Operation of diagnostic health devices, such as CAT scans or magnetic imaging machines by a hospital or health-care organization;[16]
- Sale of online bibliographic data from EO's central data bases;[17]
- "Public entertainment activities," or agricultural and educational fair or exposition;
- "Qualified conventions and trade shows."[18]
- Producing tapes of endangered ethnic music.

---

[12] Treas. Reg. § 1.513-1(a).
[13] Treas. Reg. § 1.513-1(d).
[14] Rev. Rul. 73.128, 1973-1, C.B. 222 and Priv. Ltr. Rul. 9152039.
[15] Priv. Ltr. Rul. 9009038.
[16] Tech. Adv. Mem. 8932004.
[17] Priv. Ltr. Rul. 9017028.
[18] Priv. Ltr. Rul. 9210026.

33.8 UNRELATED ACTIVITIES

Potentially unrelated categories of UBI are numerous, as the following controversial types of income illustrate. The examples don't always follow a logical pattern because courts and the IRS don't always agree and the IRS has not always been consistent in its rulings.

(a) RENTALS *Rentals of equipment and other personal property* (for example, computer or phone systems) to others are specifically listed in Section 512(b)(3) for inclusion in UBI. Such rental presumably is undertaken only to earn revenue and cover costs, with no direct connection to the EO's own exempt purposes; it "exploits" the exempt holding of the property. However, the following situations should be noted:

- Renting to (or sharing with) another EO (or, conceivably, an individual or a for-profit business) is related if the rental expressly serves the landlord's exempt purposes, such as a museum's rental of art works—that would otherwise be kept in its storage—to other institutions to ensure maximum public viewing of the work.
- Mailing list rentals produce UBI except for narrow exceptions allowed to Section 501(c)(3) organizations ("501(c)(3)s").[19] For business leagues and other EOs that are not 501(c)(3)s, revenues from the exchange or rental of mailing lists produce UBI. The Disabled American Veterans fought a valiant battle in the tax courts to avoid this tax. Twice—in 1982, and again in July 1991—they lost in the Tenth Circuit court their attempts to characterize their mailing list sales as royalty income. (Refer to "The Royalty Dilemma" on page 858, for more information.)
- Whether rental charges are at, below, or above cost can be determinative in evaluating relatedness. A full fair market value rental arrangement does not evidence exempt purposes (although the taint can be overcome by other reasons for the rental, such as dissemination of specialized educational information).
- Real estate revenues may also be excluded from UBI under the passive exceptions, but only if the property is unencumbered (see later discussion of debt-financed property).[20]

(b) SERVICES *Providing services* (such as billing, technical assistance, administrative support) to other EOs doesn't serve the exempt purposes of the furnishing EO and is unrelated, according to the IRS. The fact that sharing services creates efficiencies that allow all the EOs involved to save money doesn't necessarily sway the IRS. Only where the services themselves represent substantive programs better accomplished by selling the services to other EOs has the IRS classified the revenue as related. The services themselves must be exempt in nature. Selling computer time to enable another EO to maintain its accounting records would create UBI, but selling computer time to analyze scientific information might be related. Where an organization is created to serve a consortia of organizations with a common building or pooled investment funds, the IRS has generally allowed its exemption where the new organization itself is partly supported by independent donations.

---

[19] Section 513(h).
[20] Section 512(b)(3).

- Certain cooperative service organizations have been specifically exempted, by Congress, to avoid the IRS position that such rendering of services was a taxable business activity. Section 501(e) grants exempt status to cooperative hospital organizations that are formed to provide on a group basis specified services including data processing, purchasing (including the purchase of insurance on a group basis), warehousing, billing and collection, food, clinical, industrial engineering, laboratory, printing, communications, record center, and personnel (including selection, testing, training, and education of personnel services). Note that laundry is not on the list.

Cooperative services organizations established to "hold, commingle, and collectively invest" stocks and securities of educational institutions are also provided a special exempt category under Section 501(f).

Section 513(e) allows a special exclusion from UBI for the income earned by a hospital providing the types of services listed in Section 501(e) to another hospital that has facilities to serve fewer than 100 patients, provided the price for such services is rendered at cost plus a "reasonable amount of return on the capital goods used" in providing the service.

The IRS recently considered "related services" being rendered by a Section 501(c)(6) tourist and convention organization for the local government. Their memo discusses a broad range of services provided to businesses planning conventions in the city (which the EO was organized to benefit) and finds them related activity. Commissions received from hotels in return for referring groups and conventions for reservations, however, were deemed unrelated.[21]

(c) SALE OF NAME *Sale of the organization's name* normally is accomplished by a licensing contract permitting use of the EO's intangible property—their name—with the compensation constituting royalty income that is excluded from UBI under concepts discussed later. However, in the IRS's view, such arrangements usually constitute commercial exploitation of an exempt asset. Since issuing a Revenue Ruling in 1981, the IRS has been trying to tax EOs on the sale of their names in connection with insurance programs, affinity sales, and other commercial marketing schemes.[22]

To add flavor to the problem, in April 1990, the IRS reversed its position that a "royalty arrangement" licensing an EO's name, logo, and mailing list to an insurance agent (to promote life insurance to its membership) didn't produce UBI for the exempt.[23] Because of the extensive involvement (active, not passive) of the exempt in servicing the membership lists, Section 513(h)(1)(B)'s narrow exemption of mailing lists, and the agency theory (discussed below), the IRS ruled the supposed "royalty arrangement" produced UBI. The American Bar Association lost a similar battle in 1986, although their case was made more complicated by an arrangement whereby their members made substantial donations of the program profits.[24]

Where the sale of the organization's name or logo is accompanied by any additional requirements on the part of the EO, such as servicing the mailing list as discussed

---

[21] Tech. Adv. Mem. 9032005.
[22] Rev. Rul. 81-178, 1981-2 C.B. 135.
[23] Priv. Ltr. Rul. 9029047.
[24] *United States v. American Bar Endowment*, 477 U.S. 105 (1986).

above or endorsing a product or performing any other services for the purchaser, the IRS has made it very clear they consider such arrangements to produce unrelated income. Also suspect would be contracts where the "royalty" amount paid for use of the name is tied to the number of times it is used in solicitations all of which are mailed to the separately purchased mailing list of the EO.

Affinity card revenues are in the same category as far as the IRS is concerned and do not qualify for the "royalty" exception. When first ruling on affinity cards, the IRS allowed royalty exclusion for a fraternal order's card income.[25] By 1988, they had reversed the initial position.[26] While use of the EO's name and logo alone can produce royalty income, the credit card arrangements often depend on an accompanying sale of the organization's mailing list and, in some cases, endorsements and promotion by the EO in its publications and member/donor correspondence. The IRS therefore again applies an "agency-type" theory to deem that the EO itself, rather than the intermediary organization, performed valuable services that produced unrelated income. Some organizations try to avoid this problem by bifurcating the royalty and mailing list aspects of the contract. The IRS has commented that "they are probably going to see them as one transaction, in reality, one contract, and apply UBIT."

(d) ADVERTISING *Sale of advertising* in an otherwise exempt publication is almost always considered unrelated business income by the IRS. The basic theory is that the advertisements promote the interests of the individual advertiser and cannot therefore be related to the charitable purposes of the organization. The following examples are indicative:

- The American College of Physicians was unsuccessful in arguing with the IRS that the drug company ads in their health journal published for physicians educated the doctors. The College argued that the ads provided the reader with a comprehensive and systematic presentation of goods and services needed in the profession and informed physicians about new drug discoveries; but the court disagreed.[27]

- A college newspaper training program for journalism students enrolled in an advertising course produced related income.[28]

- Institutional or sponsor ads produce UBI if they are presented in a commercial fashion with a business logo, product description, or other sales information. Only where sponsors are listed without typical advertising copy can the money given for the listing be considered a donation. Different sizes for different amounts of money may not cause the ad to be classified as commercial.[29]

- Despite classification of ad revenues as UBI, the formula for calculating the taxable UBI yields surprising results, however, enabling some ad sale programs to escape tax. (A more thorough discussion of advertising and the formula appears later in the chapter.)

---

[25] Priv. Ltr. Rul. 8747066.

[26] Priv. Ltr. Rul. 8823109.

[27] *American College of Physicians vs. United States,* 457 U.S. 836 (1986).

[28] Treas. Reg. 1.513-1(d)(4)(iv) Example 5.

[29] *Fraternal Order of Police, Illinois State Troopers Lodge No. 41 v. Commissioner,* 833 F.2d 717 (7th Cir. 1987), *aff'g* 87 T.C. 747 (1986); Priv. Ltr. Rul. 8640007.

(e) SPONSORSHIPS *Corporate sponsorships* of a wide variety of events—golf tournaments, fun runs, football bowl games, public television, art exhibitions and so on—are a favorite form of corporate support for exempt organizations. The appeal of wide public exposure for sponsoring worthy causes and cultural programs has gained extensive popularity. *The Wall Street Journal* ran a series of articles during 1991 discussing the extent of such support and why it made good business sense.

Under examination and now in a heavily edited Private Letter Ruling 9147007, the IRS said the Cotton Bowl's payments from Mobil Oil Company are taxable, essentially because the Cotton Bowl was rendering services for Mobil. Substantial benefit in the form of advertising was given to Mobil and such revenue was business income, not a contribution. Legislation has been introduced to carve out a special exemption for such revenues, but, until then, caution is advised. Even if such arrangements create UBI, the EO may be able to argue that the event or activity is irregularly carried on, although, as the NCAA found out, the IRS may not agree.

The IRS announced in early 1992 that "Tax exempt organizations can publicly acknowledge donors for their contributions, but if the organizations conduct advertising for donors, the payments are taxable income, not tax exempt contributions." The following examination guidelines were proposed and public comments solicited:[30]

- In analyzing corporate sponsored events, the contract or arrangements (either written or oral) are reviewed to determine whether the agreement requires the exempt organization to perform any services.
- Copies of the organization's meetings and correspondence or other written statements between the EO and the sponsor must be reviewed. It was noted that it "may be beneficial to review films, videotapes or photographs of the event over the years to determine the extent the corporate sponsor's name is mentioned or depicted."
- Factors to consider in evaluating the provision of services or other benefits in return for the payment received were enumerated. Those factors "tending to indicate an unrelated business" include:

  —Inclusion of the corporate sponsor's name or logo in the official event title;

  —Prominent placement of the sponsor's name or logo throughout the stadium, arena, or other site where the event is held;

  —Printing the sponsor's name or logo on materials related to the event;

  —Placement of the sponsor's name or logo on participant or other support personnel uniforms;

  —Reference to the sponsorship in corporate advertisements during the course of the contract;

  —Making participants available to the sponsor for personal appearances and endorsements;

  —Special seating, accommodations, transportation, and hospitality facilities at the event provided to sponsors;

  —Requirement of media coverage for the event.

---

[30] IRS Announcement 92-15, IRB 92.5.

The IRS has announced an "audit tolerance" and says it will not apply the guidelines to organizations of a purely local nature, such as Little League baseball and soccer teams (no mention of basketball, football, or any other sport), and local theaters and youth orchestras (presumably, intentionally excluding ballet companies or symphony orchestras).

Providing "mere name recognition" will "normally" continue to be considered "incidental benefit" to the sponsor and not of sufficient value to the contributor to convert the funds to UBI. Specific examples cited in the announcement include naming a university professorship, scholarship, or building after the corporation; acknowledging the underwriting of a public radio or television program or museum exhibition; and listing a contributor's name in a fund-raising event or performing arts program. The issue is whether *quid pro quo* services are rendered by the charity to the sponsor. Legislation exempting public sporting and cultural event sponsorship revenues were under consideration in the summer of 1992. Hearing about the IRS audit guidelines raised many questions and were inconclusive. Watch for new developments.

(f) MEMBER SERVICES *Services to members* will be scrutinized carefully by IRS. Note especially the following:

- Sale of legal forms by a bar association, billing and credit services for members, and testing fees have all been argued with decisions for and against the organizations. EOs considering this type of income-producing activity should research this question thoroughly.[31]
- Free bus service provided to a particular shopping center versus a downtown area of a city was ruled to produce unrelated income for a chamber of commerce.

The question to watch for is whether services rendered to members constitute private inurement or private benefit for the members versus the general public or the profession (for a business league).

(g) INSURANCE *Group insurance programs* have been a subject of active litigation among trade unions, business leagues, and the IRS, with the IRS currently prevailing in classifying revenues produced in an insurance program for members as UBI. The American Bar Endowment lost its battle to classify the dividends assigned to it by members participating in its group insurance plan as donations. Here again, careful planning in view of the most recent rulings and court decisions is in order to avoid UBI.[32]

(h) REAL ESTATE *Real estate development* projects can be characterized as related (low-income or elderly housing), as a trade or business (subdivision, debt-financed rental, hotel), as an investment (unindebted rental), or sometimes as a combination of all three.

Any EO anticipating such a program should study Private Letter Ruling 8950072 in which the IRS outlines the UBI consequences of four different methods of developing a piece of raw land owned by an exempt. Leasing or selling raw land unquestionably produced no UBI because of the passive income modifications. Completion of the preliminary development work of obtaining permits and approval prior to the property's sale

---

[31] *San Antonio Bar Association v. United States,* 80-2 U.S.T.C. § 9594 (W.D. Tex. 1980).
[32] *Louisiana Credit Union League v. United States,* 693 F.2d 525 (5th Cir. 1982), *aff'g* 501 F. Supp. 934 (E.D. La. 1980).

did not convert the sale into a business transaction. But total development of the property prior to the sale converts the property into a business asset and produces UBI.

Development of an apartment building and parking garage as a part of an urban renewal effort is a related business for an organization whose purpose it is to combat community deterioration. The organization operates to assist the city by encouraging revitalization of its downtown area. While the activity would result in UBI if conducted for investment, in this case the activity served the EO's exempt purposes.[33]

(i) AGENCY THEORY   An *agency theory* may be applied to look through certain arrangements. To avoid UBI classification for potentially unrelated activities listed above, an organization might engage an independent party to conduct the activity in return for a royalty or a rental payment. Inherently "passive" activities for which compensation is paid in the form of rent or royalty are not subject to UBIT, even if the activity is deemed unrelated. The question is, however, whether the IRS can look through the transactions and attribute the activity of the independent party back to the organization, as they did in the following example.

The National Collegiate Athletic Association (NCAA) hires an unrelated commercial publishing company to produce its tournament programs. NCAA gives the publisher a "free hand" in soliciting the advertisements, designing the copy, and distributing the programs, in return for a percentage of the advertising and direct sales revenues. Because they have little or no involvement in the activity, the NCAA treats the income as a passive and irregularly carried on activity not subject to the unrelated business income tax. There is no argument that selling the program itself produces related income; nor is there any question that the advertising income is unrelated. The tournament lasts only three weeks.

The issue considered by the Tax Court[34] was whether the NCAA had sufficiently disengaged itself under the contract. Did it sell the right to use its name or did it engage in the activity itself? The Tax Court adopted an "agency" theory, stipulating that because the publisher acted as the NCAA's agent, the activity was totally attributable to the NCAA. The Tenth Circuit Court agreed with the Tax Court but reversed the decision (because the activity was irregularly carried on and not in competition with business); the agency theory was not disputed. The IRS disagrees with the decision.

Another athletic tournament-sponsoring organization also failed the agency test. The independently hired promoter's efforts during a 15-month ad campaign were attributed to the organization.[35] The agency theory was escaped, however, by an organization who turned over the publication of its monthly journal to a commercial company, retaining one-third of the net revenues from subscriptions and reprints. All advertising income, two-thirds of the circulation revenues, and all the risk of publication expenses were borne by the company. So, the IRS decided, under the circumstances, that the company was acting on its own behalf, not as agent for the charity. No advertising revenue was allocated to the charity.[36]

---

[33] Priv. Ltr. Rul. 9208033.

[34] *National Collegiate Athletic Association v. Commissioner,* 90-2 U.S.T.C. § 50513 (10th Cir. 1990), *rev'd,* 92 T.C. No. 27 (1989). See also Priv. Ltr. Rul. 9137002.

[35] Tech. Adv. Mem. 8932004.

[36] Tech. Adv. Mem. 9023003.

33.9 THE EXCEPTIONS

Despite their literal inclusion in the "unrelated" prong of the UBI rules, certain types of revenue-raising activities are not subject to UBIT presumably because they are not businesslike and do not compete with commercial businesses.[37] Charitable Section 501(c)(3)s qualify for all of the following exceptions. Certain exceptions do not apply to non-501(c)(3) organizations, as noted under the particular exception.

(a) VOLUNTEERS Any business where substantially all the work is performed without compensation is excluded from UBI. "Substantially" means at least 80 to 85 percent of the total work performed, measured normally by the total hours worked. A paid manager or executive, administrative personnel, and all sorts of support staff can operate the business if most of the work is performed by volunteers.

In most cases the number of hours worked, rather than relative value of the work, is used to measure the 85 percent test. This means that the value of volunteer time need not necessarily be quantified for comparison to monetary compensation paid. In the case of a group of volunteer singing doctors, the value of the doctors' time was considered. Because the doctors were the stars of the records producing the income, their time was counted by the court at a premium and allowed to offset administrative personnel whose time was paid.[38]

Expense reimbursements, in-kind benefits, and prizes are not necessarily treated as compensation unless they are compensatory in nature. Particularly where the expenses enable the volunteers to work longer hours and serve the convenience of the EO, the payments need not be counted in measuring this exception. Where food, lodging, and total sustenance were furnished to sustain members of a religious group, the members working for the group's businesses were not treated as volunteers.[39]

(b) DONATED GOODS The selling of merchandise substantially all of which is received as gifts or contributions is not subject to the UBIT. Thrift and resale shops selling donated goods do not report UBI on donated goods they sell. A shop selling goods on consignment as well as donated goods would have to distinguish between the two types of goods. UBI would be earned for the consigned goods, but might escape tax if the shop is run by volunteers.

(c) BINGO GAMES Bingo games not conducted in violation of any state or local law are excluded. Section 513(f) defines bingo as any game of bingo of a type in which usually (1) wagers are placed, (2) winners are determined, and (3) distribution of prizes or other property is made, in the presence of all persons placing wagers in such game.

The Regulations expand the definition by explicitly saying:

> A bingo game is a game of chance played with cards that are generally printed with five rows of five squares each. Participants place markers over randomly called numbers on the cards in an attempt to form a preselected pattern such as a horizontal, vertical, or diagonal line, or all four corners. The first participant to form the preselected pattern

---

[37] Section 513(a).

[38] *Greene County Medical Society Foundation v. United States*, 345 F. Supp. 900 (W.D. Mo. 1972).

[39] *Shiloh Youth Revival Centers v. Commissioner*, 88 T.C. 579 (1987).

wins the game. Any other game of chance including but not limited to, keno, dice, cards, and lotteries, is not bingo [and will create UBI].[40]

Pull-tabs and other forms of "instant bingo" are not bingo in the IRS's opinion and produce unrelated business income despite the fact that such variations of the bingo game are so classified by the state bingo authority. During 1990, the IRS aggressively examined EOs in the Southwest District and assessed tax on any bingo variations not strictly meeting the Code and Regulation definitions.

(d) PUBLIC ENTERTAINMENT ACTIVITIES Public entertainment is defined as traditionally conducted at fairs or expositions promoting agricultural and educational purposes (including but not limited to animals or products and equipment) and does not produce UBI for Section 501(c)(3), (4), or (5) organizations. Section 513(d)(2) requires that the event be held in conjunction with an international, national, state, regional, or local fair or be in accordance with provisions of state law that permits such a fair.

(e) QUALIFIED CONVENTIONS AND TRADE SHOWS A convention and trade show is one intended to attract persons in an industry generally (without regard to membership in the sponsoring organization), as well as members of the public, to the show for the purpose of displaying industry products or stimulating interest in and demand for industry products or services, or educating persons engaged in the industry in the development of new products and services or new rules and regulations affecting the industry. A "qualified" show is one conducted by Section 501(c)(3), (4), (5), or (6) organizations in conjunction with an international, national, state, regional, or local convention, annual meeting, or show. Exhibitors are permitted to sell products or services and the organization can charge for the display space.

33.10 APPLY ONLY TO 501(c)(3)s AND VETERAN POSTS

(a) LOW-COST ARTICLES Gift premiums costing (not fair market value) the organization no more than $6.01 (during 1992—indexed annually for inflation) and distributed with no obligation to purchase in connection with the solicitations of contributions are not treated as a sale of the gift premium. The gift must be part of a fund-raising campaign.

The recipient of the premium must not request or consent to receive the premium. Literature requesting a donation must accompany the premium and a statement that the recipient may keep the low-cost article regardless of whether a charitable donation is made. If the donation is less than $30.09 (during 1992—indexed annually), the fair market value of the premium reduces the deductible portion of the donor's gift.[41]

(b) MAILING LISTS A business involving the exchange or renting of mailing lists between two organizations eligible to receive charitable donations under Section 170(c)(2) or (3) is excluded from UBI classification. In other words, a charitable organization exempt under Section 501(c)(3) and veteran organizations qualify for this

---

[40] Treas. Reg. § 1.513-5.
[41] Rev. Proc. 90-12 (Feb. 1990), updated in Rev. Proc. 92-58, 1992-2 IRB 10.

special treatment added by Congress in 1986.[42] Sale or exchange of mailing lists by all other types of 501(c) organizations now create UBI.

33.11 501(c)(3)s ONLY EXCEPTIONS

(a) CONVENIENCE A cafeteria, bookstore, residence, or similar facility used in the EO's programs and operated for the convenience of patients, visitors, employees, or students is specifically excepted from UBI classification by Section 513(a)(2) for 501(c)(3) organizations only. Presumably, it benefits hospital patients to have family and friends visiting or staying with them in the hospital, and the cafeteria facilitates the visits. Museum visitors can spend more time viewing art if they can stop to rest their feet and have a cup of coffee. Parking lots for the exclusive use of participants in an exempt organization's activities also produce related income.

When the cafe, shop, dorm, or parking lot is also open to the general public, the revenue produced by public use is unrelated income. Some commentators suggest the whole facility becomes subject to UBIT, particularly where the facility has an entrance to a public street. At best, the income from a facility used by both qualified visitors and the disinterested public off the street is fragmented. The taxable and non-taxable revenues are identified and tabulated and the net taxable portion is calculated under the dual use rules discussed later under "Calculating the Taxable Income."

Where the unrelated income produced is rental income, there is still a possible escape route from application of the UBIT. The technical question then becomes whether the lot rentals are excludable UBI under the "Passive Income Modifications."

The IRS admits it has issued unclear and conflicting positions on the matter. Their memo states unequivocally that revenue from direct lot operation never produces rent, and refers to the Regulations.[43] Only where the lot is operated by an independent party under a lease arrangement in which the organization performs no services can the revenue be classified as passive rental income excludable from UBI.

33.12 PASSIVE INCOME MODIFICATIONS

Income earned from passive investment activities is not included in UBI unless the underlying property is subject to debt. Social clubs, voluntary employee benefit associations, supplemental unemployment plans, and veterans' groups are taxed on such income. Types of passive income excluded from UBI under Section 512(b) include "all dividends, interest, royalties, rents, payments with respect to security loans, and annuities, and all deductions connected with such income." It is important to note from the outset that passive income of a sort not specifically listed is not necessarily modified or excluded from UBI.

(a) DIVIDENDS AND INTEREST *Dividends and interest* are paid on amounts invested in savings accounts, certificates of deposit, money market accounts, bonds, loans, preferred or common stocks, and payments in respect to security loans and annuities, along with any allocable deductions.

---

[42] Section 513(h).
[43] Gen. Couns. Mem. 39825.

- In 1978, the general exclusion of interest and dividends was expanded to include the words "payments in respect of security loans." Since then, there has been uncertainty regarding sophisticated techniques such as "strips," interest rate swaps, and currency hedges. After two Private Letter Rulings were issued in 1991, Proposed Regulations were announced in September 1991, to recognize that such investments were "ordinary and routine" and to make it clear that income earned from such transactions in security portfolios would be considered as investment income for Section 512 purposes.[44]

- Such securities acquired with indebtedness are swept back into UBI by Section 514, and an EO must be careful to use new money to acquire each element of investment in its portfolio. A recent Tax Court case provides a good example. A pension fund, stuck with five-year certificates of deposit in 1979 when the interest rates shot up over five points, negotiated a plan to purchase new CDs using its old CDs as collateral, thereby escaping an early withdrawal penalty and receiving a higher rate of interest. The court found that, despite the fact that the transaction was not abusive, it fell squarely within the literal definition of a debt-financed asset purchase. The CD switch was not a "payment in respect of a security loan" within the meaning of Section 512(b)(1). Such a loan involves allowing a broker to use the EO's securities in return for a fee, not a loan against which the securities are used as collateral. Thus, the fund's original CD produced "modified" or non-taxable income and the new higher-rate CD acquired with the loan proceeds was held to be taxable as unrelated debt-financed income.[45]

(b) CAPITAL GAINS *Gains or losses* from sale, exchange, or other disposition of property generally is not UBI.

- Gains on lapse or termination of covered and uncovered operations, if written as a part of investment activity, are not taxable according to Section 512(b)(5), added to the Code in 1976.
- Sales of stock in trade or other inventory-type property or property held for sale to customers in the ordinary course of trade or business do produce UBI.

(c) RENTALS *Rentals* are excluded, except:

- Personal property rentals are taxable unless they are rented incidentally (not more than 10 percent of rent) with real property.
- Net profit (versus gross revenue) interests produce UBI.
- Where substantial services are rendered, such as the rental of a theater complete with staff, the rental will not be considered passive.

(d) ROYALTIES *Royalties,* whether measured by production or by the gross or taxable income from the property, are excluded. Oil and gas working interest income would not be excluded. (See discussion at 33.23(d)).

---

[44] Prop. Reg. §§ 1.509(a)-3, 1.512(b)-1, and 53.4940-1.
[45] *Kern County Electrical Pension Fund v. Commissioner,* 96 T.C. No. 41 (1991).

(e) SUBSIDIARY PAYMENTS *Controlled subsidiary* payments for interest, rents, roy-alties, or annuities, however, are includable in UBI. Control exists when one organi-zation owns stock possessing at least 80 percent of the total combined voting power of all classes of stock entitled to vote and at least 80 percent of all other classes of stock of another organization (exempt or nonexempt). A nonstock organization mea-sures control by quantifying its interlocking directors. If at least 80 percent of the directors of one organization are members of the second organization or have the right to appoint or control the board of the second, control exists according to the Regulations.

That portion of a controlled organization's income which would have been taxed as UBI to the parent EO if the income had been earned by it is includable (whether or not regularly carried on). Thus, payments from a subsidiary corporation conducting a re-lated activity would qualify as a modification and not be UBI.

(f) RESEARCH *Research* income is not taxable if the research is performed for the United States, its agencies, or a state or political subdivision thereof by any EO. In addition:

- A college, university, or hospital can exclude all research income from private or governmental contractors.
- An EO performing fundamental research, the results of which are freely avail-able to the general public, can also exclude all research income.

33.13 CALCULATING THE TAXABLE INCOME

Gross unrelated business income, minus expenses and exemption (listed below), is subject to tax. As long as the percentage of revenues from UBI is modest in relation to the organization's overall revenues, the only problem UBIT presents is the reduction in profit because of the income tax paid. Tax planning of the sort practiced by a good businessperson is in order. Maximizing deductions to calculate the income is impor-tant. The income tax sections of the Internal Revenue Code of 1986 govern, and the same concepts apply, including:

- *Tax rates.* The income tax is calculated using the normal tables for all taxpayers: Section 1(e) for trusts or Section 11 for corporations. For controlled groups of exempt organizations (also including 80-percent-owned for-profit subsidiaries), the corporate tax bracket must be calculated on a consolidated basis under the rules of Section 1561.
- *Alternative minimum tax.* Accelerated depreciation, percentage depletion, and other similar tax benefits are subject to the alternative minimum tax just as for-profit taxpayers.
- *"Ordinary and necessary" criteria.* Deductions claimed against the unrelated in-come must be "ordinary and necessary" to conducting the activity and must meet the other standards of Section 162 for business deductions. Ordinary means com-mon and accepted for the type of business operated; necessary means helpful and

appropriate, not indispensable. The activity for which the expenditure is incurred must also be operated with profit motive.[46]

- *Profit motive.* To be deductible, an expenditure must also be paid for the production of income, or in a business operated for the purpose of making a profit. Section 183 specifically prohibits the deduction of "hobby losses," or those activities losing money for more than two years out of every five. The IRS will challenge the deduction for UBI purposes of any expenditures not paid for the purposes of producing the profit.[47]

- *Depreciation.* Equipment, buildings, vehicles, furniture, and other properties that have a useful life to the business are deductible theoretically over their life. As a simple example, one-third of the total cost of a computer that is expected to be obsolete in three years would be deductible during each year the computer is used in the business, under a system called "depreciation." Unfortunately, Congress uses these calculation rates and methods as political and economic tools, and the Code proscribes rates and methods that are not so simple. Sections 167, 168, and 179 apply and must be studied to properly calculate allowable deductions for depreciation.

- *Inventory.* If the EO keeps an inventory of items for sale, such as books, drugs, or merchandise of any sort, it must use the inventory methods to deduct the cost of such goods. The concept is one of matching the cost of the item sold with its sales proceeds. If the EO buys ten widgets for sale and, as of the end of a year, only five have been sold, the cost of the five is deductible and the remaining five are "capitalized" as an asset to be deducted when in fact they are sold. Again, the system is far more complicated than this simple example and an accountant should be consulted to ensure use of proper reporting and tabulation methods. Sections 263A and 471–474 apply.

- *Capital and nondeductibles.* A host of nondeductible items contained in Sections 261 to 280H might apply to disallow deductions either by total disallowance or required capitalization of permanent assets. Again, all the rules applicable to for-profit businesses apply, such as the luxury automobile limits, travel and entertainment substantiation requirements, and 20 percent disallowance for meals.

- *Dividend deduction.* The dividends received deduction provided by Sections 243 to 245 for taxable nonexempt corporations is not allowed. As a general rule, a corporation is allowed to exclude 70 percent of the dividends it receives on its investments; exempts are not. This rule only presents a problem for dividends received from investments that are debt-financed. Most dividends received by exempts are excluded from the UBI under the "Modifications" previously discussed.

33.14 SPECIFIC CATEGORIES OF DEDUCTIBLE COSTS

As a general rule, there are two categories of expenses allowed as deductions for purposes of calculating UBIT: direct and dual use expenses. No portion of the organization's

---

[46] Treas. Reg. 1.512(a)-1(a).

[47] *Iowa State University of Science and Technology v. United States,* 500 F.2d 508 (Ct. Cl. 1974); *Commissioner v. Groetzinger,* 480 U.S. 23 (1987), Treas. Reg. § 1.513-1(4)(d)(iii).

basic operating expense theoretically is deductible against UBI because of the exploitation rules discussed below. However, where there is an ongoing plan to produce UBI and such revenue is part of the justification affording a particular exempt activity, allocation of overhead is permitted, although technically challenging.

(a) DIRECTLY RELATED Those expenses attributable solely to the production of unrelated gross income are fully deductible. According to the IRS, a "proximate and primary relationship" between the expense and the activity is the standard for full deduction. Proximate means near, close, or immediate. A "but for" test can be applied by asking the question, "Would the expense be incurred if the unrelated activity was not carried on?"[48]

(b) DUALLY USED FACILITIES OR PERSONNEL A portion of the cost of so-called "dual use," or shared, employees and facilities, is deductible. An allocation between the two types of activities is made on "a reasonable basis." The only example given in the Regulations allocates 10 percent of an EO president's salary to an unrelated business activity to which he or she devotes 10 percent of his or her time. Where actual time records are maintained to evidence effort devoted to related versus unrelated activities, deduction of the applicable personal costs is ensured. In the IRS *Manual,* examining agents are instructed that any reasonable method resulting in identifying a relationship of the expenses to revenue produced is acceptable. There is no particular approved method that must be followed.[49]

Absent time records, an allocation based on relative gross income produced might be used if the exempt activity reaps income. Take, for example, a museum bookstore that sells both related and unrelated items. Sales in this case could be used as the allocation base. Where an income-producing activity is carried out alongside one that is not producing revenue, time records must be maintained.

Where a portion of the building is devoted totally to unrelated activity, building costs, including utilities, insurance, depreciation of the cost, interest on mortgage, and maintenance, are allocated based on total square footage of the building used for the UBI activity. Where UBI space is shared with related space, again a reasonable method is used. For a publication project, the lineage devoted to advertising could be calculated for its relationship to the total publication.

Taxpayers and the IRS have argued about allocation methods, and there are differences of opinion. An EO with this question should be sure to determine the current situation. For hospitals, the Medicare cost allocations methods "usually fail to accurately reflect UBI," in the IRS's opinion.[50]

(c) DIRECT VS. INDIRECT EXPENSES A subset of the expense allocation problem is the application of different methods for direct and indirect expenses. Direct expenses are those that increase proportionately with the usage of a facility or the volume of activity; they are also called variable. The number of persons attending an event influences the number of ushers or security guards needed, and represents a direct cost; in

---

[48] *Supra* note 42.
[49] *Exempt Organization Examination Guidelines Handbook,* Section 720(7) of Internal Revenue Manual 7(10)69.
[50] Gen. Couns. Mem. 39,843.

other words, the cost is attributable to that specific use that would not have been incurred except for the particular event.

Indirect costs, on the other hand, are incurred without regard to usage or frequency of participation and are usually called the fixed expenses of the organization. Building costs are an example. The presumption is that the organization's underlying building costs, for example, do not vary with usage.

(d) FORMULA DENOMINATOR QUESTION The denominator of the fraction used to calculate costs allocable to UBI is significant in reducing or increasing allowable deductions. The question must be considered in view of the exploitation rules, and the point is again whether the EO would conduct the related activity without the unrelated revenue stream. Arguably, no fixed costs of an exempt institution should be allocated to UBI, but to date the courts have chosen to allow allocation among both the exempt and nonexempt functions that benefit from building use.

In allocating fixed facility costs, the courts haven't agreed on whether the total number of hours a facility is used versus the total number of hours in the year is the appropriate denominator. To anyone grasping mathematics, it is easy to see each factor yields vastly different results. Watch for new legislation or Regulations; more complicated and varied formulas have been proposed.

- The Second Circuit of the federal courts[51] in a college football stadium case allowed:

$$\frac{\text{number of hours or days used for unrelated purposes}}{\text{total number of hours or days in USE}}$$

- The IRS argues that fixed costs were to be allocated by:

$$\frac{\text{number of hours or days used for unrelated purposes}}{\text{total number of hours of days in YEAR}}$$

(e) GROSS-TO-GROSS METHOD The gross-to-gross method of cost allocation is applied where costs bear a relationship to the revenue produced from exempt and nonexempt factors. For example, where students and members are charged one fee and nonmembers and nonstudents are charged another (usually higher) fee, an allocation using the total revenue from each different category would not be reflective of the true cost to produce the revenue. A proration based on the overall number of individuals in each group might better reflect reality and ostensibly be more accurate. This type of formula is often used in calculating allocations for social clubs or publications serving all participants at the same price.

(f) EXPLOITATION When a fundamentally exempt activity, such as a publication or a bookstore, produces some UBI from advertising or sales of unrelated items, the Regulations provide a limitation on the deduction of underlying exempt activity cost against the UBI. This limitation presents a classic "chicken and egg" or "tail wagging the dog" situation. Is the UBI activity an afterthought? Probably the best question is whether the exempt activity would be carried on regardless of the UBI funds. It is

---

[51] *Rensselaer Polytechnic Institute v. Commissioner,* 732 F.2d 1058 (2d Cir. 1984), *aff'g* 79 T.C. 967 (1982).

curious that the football stadium case cited above allows allocation of expenses despite the obvious assumption that a college must have a sports facility and without regard to its ability to rent it during the down time, a seemingly classic "exploitation." Nonetheless, where an EO chooses to consider UBI as produced in connection with an exploited activity, deduction limitations are based on income.

- Expenses of an exploited activity are allowable as a general rule only to the extent of the gross unrelated income they produce.
- Exempt function expenses related to the activity are first reduced by any related revenues, then the excess expenses are allocated to the unrelated income to the extent of the unrelated income. No loss resulting from an excess of exempt function plus unrelated activity expenses over total revenues can be used to offset other UBI.
- See the calculation of deductible expenses on an exploited publication later in the chapter.

(g) CHARITABLE DEDUCTION   Up to 10 percent of an exempt corporation's UBI and 100 percent of a charitable trust's UBI is deductible for contributions paid to a charitable organization. The deduction is not allowed for internal project expenditures of the organization itself. Excess contributions are eligible for the normal five-year carryover allowed for-profit tax-payers. Social clubs, voluntary employee business associations, unemployment benefit trusts, and group legal service plans can take a 100 percent deduction for direct charitable gifts and "qualified set asides" for charitable purposes.

(h) ADMINISTRATIVE OVERHEAD   It bears separate note that a portion of the organization's administrative expenses may be deductible against UBI and substantially reduces the tax burden from unrelated activity. Adequate proof of the allocation methods and escape of the exploitation rule discussed above is important to support an EO's overhead deduction against UBI.

(i) $1,000 EXEMPTION   A specific exemption of $1,000 ($5,000 under Congressional Select Committee Proposals) is allowed.

33.15   ACCOUNTING METHOD CONSIDERATIONS

(a) IN-KIND GIFTS   Donated goods and services properly recorded under accounting principles promulgated by the Accounting Principles Board (APB 78-10) should be booked and deducted.

(b) DOCUMENTATION   To correctly calculate the EO's expenses that are allocable to UBI, documentation is critical. Time records, expense identification, departmental approval systems, and similar internal control techniques will allow the organization to compute maximum allowable deductions against UBI. Particularly for staff time allocations and administrative expense items, such as printing and supplies, capturing the information is simple once documentation methods are installed.

(c) ACCRUAL METHOD   If the EO's gross income from UBI exceeds $5 million annually, the accrual method of accounting must be used. If an inventory of goods and products for sale is maintained and is a "material" income-producing factor, the accrual method must be utilized.

(d) NET OPERATING LOSSES   A loss realized in operating an unrelated business in one year may be carried back for 3 years and forward for 15 years, for offset against another year's operating income. Gains and losses for different types of UBI earned within any single EO are netted against profits from the various business activities of the organization, including acquisition of indebted investment property. Tax years in which no UBI activity is realized are counted in calculating the number of years for permissible carryovers. Conversely, net operating losses are not reduced by related income.

A social club cannot offset losses on serving nonmembers against income from its other investments, according to the Supreme Court, which sided with the IRS in the *Portland Golf Club* case decided in 1990.[52] There has been a conflict of decisions in the U.S. Circuit Courts for several years, and clubs claiming such losses must now consider filing amended returns to report tax resulting from the loss disallowance.

It is extremely important for an EO to file Form 990T despite the fact that it incurs a loss. Reporting the loss allows for carryback or carryover of the loss to offset past or future income. An election is available to carry losses forward and forgo any carryback in situations where the EO has not previously earned UBI.

33.16   ESTIMATED TAX

Income tax liability for UBI is payable in advance during the year, as the income is earned, similar to for-profit businesses and individuals.

33.17   DEBT-FINANCED INCOME

The *modifications* exempting passive investment income from the UBIT, such as dividends and interest, do not apply to the extent the investment is made with borrowed funds. Debt-financed property is defined by Section 514 as including property held for the production of income that was acquired with borrowed funds and has a balance of acquisition indebtedness attributable to it during the year. The classic examples are a margin account held against the EO's endowment funds or a mortgage financing a rental building purchase.

(a) PROPERTIES EXCLUDED FROM DEBT-FINANCED RULES   Real or other tangible or intangible property used 85 percent or more of the time when it is actually devoted to such purpose, and used directly in the EO's exempt or related activities, is exempt from these rules. If a university borrows money and builds an office tower for its projected staff needs over a 20-year period, and if less than 85 percent of the building

---

[52] *Portland Golf Club v. Commissioner,* 90-1 U.S.T.C. § 50,332 (Sup. Ct. 1990); *Iowa State University of Science and Technology v. United States,* 500 F.2d (Ct. Cl. 1974); *Commissioner v. Groetzinger, supra* note 6.

is used by its staff and net profit is earned, the non-university-use portion of the building income is taxable as UBI.

- Property the income of which is included in UBI for some other reason is specifically excluded by the Code and need not be counted twice for this reason.
- Future-use property acquired and held for use by the organization within 10 years from the date it is acquired and located in the neighborhood in which the EO carries out a project is exempt from this provision.
- A "life estate" does not constitute a debt. Where some other individual or organization is entitled to income from the property for life or another period of time, a remainder interest in the property is not considered to be indebted.
- Debt placed on property by a donor will be attributed to the organization where the EO assumes and agrees to pay all or part of the debt OR makes any payments on the equity.

  Property that is encumbered and subject to existing debt at the time it is received by bequest or devise is not treated as acquisition indebted-property for 10 years from its acquisition, if there is no assumption or payment on the debt by the exempt.
- Gifted property is similarly excluded if the donee placed the mortgage on the property over 5 years prior to gift and had owned the property over 5 years unless there is an assumption or payment by the EO on the mortgage.
- A property used in unrelated activities of an EO, the income of which is excepted from UBI because it is run by volunteers, for the convenience of members, or sale of donated goods, can be indebted and still not be subject to this classification.
- Research property producing income otherwise excluded from the UBIT also is not subject to the acquisition indebtedness taint.

(b) WHAT IS "ACQUISITION INDEBTEDNESS?" Acquisition indebtedness is the unpaid amount of any debt incurred to purchase or improve property or any debt "reasonably foreseen" at the time of acquisition which would not have been incurred otherwise.

- Securities purchased on margin are debt-financed; payments for loan of securities already owned are not.
- The formula for calculation of income subject to tax is:

$$\text{income from property} \times \frac{\text{average acquisition indebtedness}}{\text{average adjusted basis}}$$

The average acquisition indebtedness equals the arithmetic average of each month or partial month of the tax year. The average adjusted basis is similarly calculated, and only straight-line depreciation is allowed.

(c) CALCULATION OF TAXABLE PORTION Only that portion of the net income of debt-financed property attributable to the debt is classified as UBI. Each property subject to debt is calculated separately with the resulting net income or loss netted to arrive at the portion includable in UBI. Expenses directly connected with the property are deducted from gross revenues in the same proportion.

The capital gain or loss formula is different in one respect: highest amount of indebtedness during the year preceding sales is used as the numerator.

33.18 PLANNING IDEAS

The first rule in reducing UBIT is to keep good records. The accounting system must support the desired allocation of deductions for personnel and facilities with time records, expense usage reports, auto logs, documentation reports, and so on. Aggressive avoidance of the "exploitation rule" must be backed up with proof.

Minutes of meetings of the board of directors or trustees should reflect discussion of relatedness of any project claimed to accomplish an exempt purpose where it could appear the activity is unrelated. For example, contracts and other documents concerning activities the organization wants to prove are related to its exempt purposes should contain appropriate language to reflect the project's exempt purposes.

An organization's original purposes can be expanded and redefined to broaden the scope of activities or to justify some proposed activity as related. Such altered or expanded purpose can be reported to the IRS to justify the relatedness of a new activity.

Where dual-use facilities can be partly debt-financed and partly paid for, the EO could purposefully buy the nontaxable exempt function property with debt and buy the unrelated part of the facility with cash available. Or, separate notes could be executed with the taxable and unrelated property's debt being paid off first.

If loss of exemption is a strong possibility because of the extent and amount of unrelated business activity planned, a separate for-profit organization can be formed to shield the EO from a possible loss of exemption due to excessive business activity.

33.19 SPECIAL INTEREST TOPIC—MUSEUMS

Museum gift shop sales and related income-producing activities are governed by the "fragmentation" and "exploitation" rules discussed earlier. Since 1973, when it published a ruling concern greeting cards,[53] the IRS has formally agreed that items printed with reproductions of images in a museum's collection are educational, related to the exempt purposes, and their sale produces UBI. The ruling expressed two different reasons: (1) the cards stimulated and enhanced the public awareness, interest in, and appreciation of art; and (2) a self-advertising theory stating that a "broader segment of the public may be encouraged to visit the museum itself to share in its educational functions and programs as a result of seeing the cards."

Another 1973 ruling[54] explored the fragmentation rule and expanded its outlook to trinkets and actual copies of objects and distinguished items. The IRS felt that educational merit could be gained from utilitarian items with souvenir value. Since that time, it has been clearly established that a museum shop often contains both related and unrelated items and the museum must keep exacting records to identify the two.

---

[53] Rev. Rul. 73-104, 1973-1 C.B. 263.
[54] Rev. Rul. 73-105, 1973-1 C.B. 265.

(a) IDENTIFYING RELATED AND UNRELATED OBJECTS After the IRS and museums argued for 10 years about the relatedness of a wide variety of objects sold, four exhaustive private rulings were issued in 1983 and are still followed (Fall, 1992).[55] The primary concern for a museum is to identify the "relatedness" of each object sold in its shops and segregate any unrelated sales. The connection between the item sold and achievement of the museum's exempt purpose is evidenced by the facts and circumstances of each object and the policy of the curatorial department in identifying, labeling, and categorizing objects on public view.

IRS rulings direct the *"facts and circumstances"* of each object to be examined, to prove the objects being sold have educational value, and list the following factors to consider in designating an item:

- "Interpretive material" describing artistic, cultural, or historical relationship to the museum's collection or exhibits.
- Nature, scope, and motivation for the sales activity.
- Are sales solely for production of income or are they an activity to enhance visitor awareness of art?
- Curatorial supervision in choosing related items.
- Reproductions of objects in the particular museum or other collections, including prints, slides, posters, post or greeting cards, are generally exempt.
- Adaptations, including imprinted utilitarian objects such as dishes, ashtrays, and clothing, must be accompanied by interpretive materials and must depict objects or identify an exhibition. Objects printed with logos were deemed unrelated.
- Souvenirs and convenience items are generally unrelated unless imprinted with reproductions or promoting a particular event or exhibition. Souvenirs promoting the town in which the museum is located are not considered related to the museum's purposes.
- Toys and other teaching items for children are deemed inherently educational and therefore deemed related in IRS rulings.

(b) ORIGINAL WORKS OF ART Original works of art created by living artists and sold by museums are considered unrelated by the IRS. "It is inconsistent with the purpose of exhibiting art for public benefit to deprive [the] public the opportunity of viewing the art by selling it to an individual." This policy can apply as well to deceased artists.

- A cooperative art gallery established to encourage individual "emerging artists" was not allowed to qualify as an exempt organization because, in the IRS's opinion, the interests of the general public were not served by promoting the careers of individual artists. The art sales served no exempt purpose and constituted unrelated business income. Because the organization was supported entirely by unrelated business income from the sales of art of the artists, it was not exempt.[56]
- A community art center located in an isolated area with no commercial galleries obtained exemption and the Tax Court decided its sales of original art were

---

[55] Priv. Ltr. Rul. 8303013, 8326003, 8236008, and 8328009.
[56] Priv. Ltr. Rul. 8032028.

related to exempt purposes. The decision was based on the fact that no other cultural center existed in the county, the art sales were not the center's sole source of support, and a complex of other activities were conducted.[57]

- An unrelated gallery managed by volunteers and/or selling donated works of art produces unrelated income but the income is not taxable, because of exceptions. Exempt status depends on whether the gallery is a substantial part of the EO's activities.

(c) STUDY TOURS Museums and other types of exempt organizations sponsor study tours as promotional, educational, and fund-raising tools. The issue is whether such tours compete with travel agents and commercial tour guides and thus produce UBI. A study tour led by professionals and qualifying for university credit qualifies as related to a museum's educational purposes. Generally, the IRS looks carefully and will scrutinize:

- The "bona fide" educational methodology of the tour, including the professional status of leaders and the educational content of the program. The amount of advance preparation, such as reading lists, can be a factor. The actual amount of time spent in formal classes, mandatory participation in the lectures, or opportunity for university credit are other attributes evidencing the educational nature of a tour.[58]
- Conversely, the amount of recreational time allowed to participants, the resort-taint of the places the tour visits, and holiday scheduling will suggest predominantly personal pleasure purposes and cause the tour to not qualify as educational.[59]

Not only the profit from the tour itself, but the "additional donation" requested as an organizational gift by all participants in a travel tour program, may be classed as unrelated income if the tour is not considered as educational.[60]

33.20 SPECIAL INTEREST TOPIC—PUBLISHING

EO publications present two very different exposures to trouble: the unrelated income tax and potential revocation of exemption. As discussed earlier, the most universal problem is that publication advertising sales create UBIT in most cases. A less common, but more dangerous, situation occurs where the underlying exemption is challenged because the publication itself is a business.

(a) ADVERTISING Revenue received from the sale of advertising in an otherwise exempt publication is considered business income by the IRS, and is taxed unless:

- The publication schedule or ad sale activity is irregularly carried on.
- The advertising is sold by volunteers.

---

[57] *Goldsboro Art League, Inc. v. Commissioner*, 75 T.C. 337 (1980).
[58] Rev. Rul. 70-534, 1970-2 C.B. 113.
[59] Rev. Rul. 77-366, 1977-2 C.B. 192.
[60] Tech. Adv. Mem. 9027003.

- The advertising activity is related to one of the organization's underlying exempt purposes, such as ads sold by college students or trainees.
- The ads do not contain commercial material, appear essentially as a listing without significant distinction among those listed, and represent acknowledgment of contributors or sponsors.

The IRS has continually taken the position that advertising sold using the EO's name is unrelated activity despite the creative contracts attributing the activity to an independent commercial firm. See agency theory discussion at 33.8(i).[61]

(b) READERSHIP VS. AD LINEAGE COSTS Even if ad revenue is classified as UBI, the tax consequence is limited by the portion of the readership and editorial costs allowed as deductions against the ad revenue. The important question is what portion of the expense of producing and distributing the publication can be allocated against the revenue.[62] It is helpful first to study the *Calculation of Taxable Portion of Advertising Revenue,* a worksheet reflecting the order in which readership and editorial costs versus advertising costs are allocated.

What the formula accomplishes is to prorate deductions in arriving at taxable advertising income. Publication costs are first divided into two categories: direct advertising and readership. Because readership costs are exempt function costs, under the "exploitation rule" discussed later they theoretically shouldn't be deductible at all against the UBI income. In a limited exception, the Regulations allow readership costs, if any, in excess of readership income to be deducted against advertising income. In other words, advertising revenues can be offset with a readership loss.

Arriving at a readership loss, however, means the publication's underlying production costs must be more than its revenues.

(c) CIRCULATION INCOME The term *circulation income* means the income attributable to the production, distribution or circulation of a periodical (other than advertising revenue) including sale of reprints and back issues.[63] Where members receive an EO's publication as a part of their basic membership fee, a portion of the member dues is allocated to circulation income. Other types of member income, such as educational program fees or convention registration, are not allocated.[64] Where the publication is given free to members but sold to nonmembers, a portion of the members' dues is allocated to readership revenue. The IRS formulas require that an allocation of a hypothetical portion of the dues be made as described in the calculation.

1. Free copies given to nonmembers are subject to controversy with IRS (check latest decisions).
2. If the EO has more than one publication, the IRS and the courts disagree on the denominator of the fraction for calculation of allocable exempt function costs.[65]

---

[61]Rev. Rul. 73-424, 1973-2 C.B. 190 and Tech. Adv. Mem. 9222001.
[62]Treas. Reg. § 1.512(a)-1(f)(6).
[63]Reg § 1.512(a)-r(f)(3)(iii).
[64]Tech. Adv. Memo. 9204007.
[65]*North Carolina Citizens for Business and Industry v. United States,* 89-2 U.S.T.C. § 9507 (Cl. Ct. 1989).

(d) COMMERCIAL PUBLICATION PROGRAMS The overall publication program can be considered a commercial venture, despite its educational content. Distinguishing characteristics, according to the IRS, are found by examining the EO's management decisions.

The characteristics deemed commercial by the IRS include:

- *Presence of substantial profits.* Accumulation of profits over a number of years evidences a commercial purpose. The mere presence of profits, by itself, will not bar exemption,[66] but other factors will be considered. Among the questions asked would be: For what purpose are profits being accumulated? Do the reserves represent a savings account for future expansion plans?
- *Pricing methods.* The method of pricing books or magazines sold yields significant evidence of commercial taint. Pricing at or below an amount calculated to cover costs shows nonprofit motive. Pricing below comparable commercial publications is not required but certainly can evidence an intention to encourage readership and educate, rather than to produce a profit.
- *Other factors.* Other factors can show commerciality:
  —Aggressive commercial practices resembling those undertaken by commercial publishers;[67]
  —Substantial salaries or royalties paid to individuals;
  —Distribution by commercial licensers, such as "est."
- *Nonprofit publications.* By contrast, nonprofit and noncommercial publications:[68]
  —Rely on volunteers and/or modest wages;
  —Sell some books/magazines that are unprofitable;
  —Prepare and choose materials according to educational methods, not commercial appeal;
  —Donate part of press run to other EOs or members;
  —Balance deficit budgets with contributions.

(e) THE ROYALTY DILEMMA It is the IRS's opinion that Section 512(b)(2), which say royalty income is not unrelated business income, does not apply to certain types of "royalties," including particularly those received in return for the sale of an organization's mailing list and the EO's name or logo.[69] While agreeing that mailing lists are intangible property the use of which produces royalty income, the IRS argues that royalties are inherently passive. In the IRS view, when the royalty income is produced in an active, commercial manner in competition with tax-paying businesses, it is contrary to the underlying scheme of the UBIT to allow such royalties to escape taxation.

Among the UBIT changes proposed by the House Oversight Committee (discussed in the next Section), royalties received for licensing property created by the EO, or property involving substantial services and costs on the part of the EO, would be subject to UBIT—a rule the IRS is essentially now applying without statutory authority.

---

[66] *Scripture Press Foundation v. United States,* 285 F.2d 800 (Ct. Cl. 1961), *cert. denied,* 368 U.S. 985 (1982).
[67] *American Institute for Economic Research v. United States,* 302 F.2d 934 (Ct. Cl. 1962).
[68] *Presbyterian and Reformed Publishing Co. v. Commissioner,* 70 T.C. 1070, 1087, 1083 (1982).
[69] Gen. Couns. Mem. 39827 (Aug. 20, 1990); Priv. Ltr. Rul. 9029047.

After its success in the DAV case discussed below, the IRS may turn its "active" argument to other types of licensing arrangements as it pursues its UBI Compliance Program. The issue is very unsettled and the details of the history may be useful.

Unfortunately, the term "royalties" is not defined under the Code or Regulations concerning unrelated income. In response to objections by large charities whom the IRS was subjecting to UBIT on their list revenues, Section 513(h)(1)(B) was added to provide special exception only for organizations eligible to receive charitable contributions, primarily 501(c)(3)s, to exclude from UBI any mailing list sales and exchanges with other similar organizations. By reference, mailing list sales by all other categories of tax-exempts would be includable in UBI.

In an interesting case, the Sixth Circuit Court[70] in July 1991 reversed the Tax Court and said the Disabled American Veterans (DAV)'s mailing list revenues were taxable unrelated business income. DAV (a 501(c)(4) organization) was arguing in the courts to escape tax deficiencies of over $4 million based on $279 million of revenue. The IRS partly based its position on the active business principle, contending that the level of active business involvement in servicing the list rental activity prevented the revenue from being classified as passive and, thereby, excludable from the UBIT.

The DAV admitted the revenue was from an unrelated business activity. There was no argument that DAV managed the activity in a businesslike manner. Among the stipulations were the fact that DAV had several personnel working full-time to keep the list current (not a volunteer operation), placed conditions on the name usage, required advanced approval of the client copy, had a complicated rate structure printed and widely circulated on rate cards, and belonged to Direct Mail Marketing Association (DMMA), a trade association composed of organizations using direct mail techniques in their operations.

The DAV argued that the revenue was a royalty excepted from UBI. The Tax Court had decided that it was up to Congress to cause "active" royalties to be taxed when the Code plainly says all royalties are excluded. They found nothing in the policy of the statute to offer any basis for characterizing royalties earned by a tax-exempt organization differently from royalties earned by a commercial organization. This issue is of particular interest in the scientific and medical fields, where considerable sums are earned from royalties paid for the licensing of patented devices and methods.

The DAV case is complicated by the fact that the Court of Claims had already decided in 1981 that DAV's mailing list sale income was taxable (it specifically declined to decide about exchanges). What the Sixth Circuit decided in overruling the Tax Court was that DAV was collaterally estopped by the 1981 decision from bringing the argument again to court, not that mailing lists sales were necessarily taxable. Thus, although the DAV lost on a technicality, the Tax Court decision still stands as to sales and no decision has ever been made about list changes.

What appear from the facts to be the Interscholastic League also failed in its effort to turn advertising revenues in to royalties. Under the licensing agreements with sporting goods manufacturers and insurance providers, the league was required to perform services and provide free advertising for the commercial concerns.[71]

---

[70] *Disabled American Veterans v. Commissioner, rev'd,* 91-2 U.S.T.C. § 50,336 (6th Cir. 1991), 94 T.C. 60 (1990).
[71] Tech. Adv. Memo. 9211004.

Look for a new decision on the subject. Rumor has it that the Sierra Club filed a suit with the Tax Court in May 1991 but no decision has been published as this book went to press.

Given the present economic climate, with Congress responding to revenue-raising possibilities, it is reasonable to expect future changes to occur to narrow the royalty exception, particularly as it relates to mailing lists and other types of name or logo sales. The proposals for UBI changes have contained several different versions as regards royalties, since first being proposed in 1987.

33.21 HOUSE SUBCOMMITTEE ON OVERSIGHT HEARING PROPOSALS

In June 1987, under the leadership of Congressman Jake Pickle of Texas, the House of Representatives Subcommittee on Oversight held hearings on the Unrelated Business Income Tax. The hearings were in response to pressure brought by a wide variety of small business owners complaining that exempt organizations are allowed unfair advantage by the existing UBI tax laws.

Actual legislative proposals weren't introduced by the subcommittee because of insufficient data as discussed in 33.1. The issues of concern and possible changes to the existing rules listed in suggested versions of proposed legislation are outlined below:

- Proposal would tax categories of income deemed to unfairly compete with business:
  —Off-premises (mail order or telephone) sales taxable;
  —Affinity card (credit cards imprinted with an EO's logo) revenue;
  —Food sales (except for members, patients, students);
  —Hotels, condominiums, theme and amusement parks;
  —Sales and rental of medical devices.
- Definitions narrowed for the following:
  —Only royalties measured by gross income or expressed as a fixed amount excluded;
  —Deductions from advertising revenue limited to direct costs;
  —General administrative costs and depreciation not deductible against rents from joint-use property.
- Form 990 expanded to report details of revenue sources. Special studies to evaluate "unfair competition" mandated.
- Allocation formula for dual-use facilities costs used in both related and unrelated activities would be revised.
- Exemption raised to $5,000 from $1,000.
- For-profit subsidiary income is attributed to the nonprofit parent when ownership is 50 percent or more (now must be 80 percent).
- The House subcommittee proposed an "aggregation rule" to combine all subsidiary activities with the exempt parent for purposes of measuring ongoing qualification for exemption. The subcommittee wants some method for measuring the extent of the EO's involvement in the subsidiary's actual operations. Under existing rules, there is no cross-attribution between controlled subsidiaries

of an exempt. Stock owned by one EO subsidiary in another subsidiary is not attributed to the parent EO. The intention is to view a controlled group as an integrated enterprise to ensure that the parent exempt's primary purpose comprises a significant portion of the whole. This proposal was not included in the Treasury Department's report.

As of fall 1992, none of the proposed changes to the unrelated business income tax provisions has been made and it appears no changes will be proposed until after the IRS completes its study of the UBI using the new page 5 of Form 990 in 1993 or 1994.

33.22 CALCULATION OF TAXABLE PORTION OF ADVERTISING REVENUE

(a) BASIC FORMULA

$$A - B - (C - D) = \text{Net taxable advertising income or loss}$$

where $A =$ Gross sales of advertising
$B =$ Direct costs of advertising
$C - D =$ Readership costs in excess of readership revenue

(b) DEFINITIONS

$B =$ Direct costs of advertising:

Occupancy, supplies, and other administrative expense	$_____
Commissions or salary costs for ad salespeople	_____
Clerical or management salary cost directly allocable	_____
Artwork, photography, color separations, etc.	_____
Portion of printing, typesetting, mailing, and other direct publication costs allocable in the ratio of total lineage in the publication to ad lineage	_____
	$_____

$C =$ Readership costs:

Occupancy, supplies, and other administrative expense	_____
Editors, writers, and salary for editorial content	_____
Travel, photos, other direct editorial expenses	_____
Portion of printing, typesetting, mailing, and other direct publication costs allocable in ratio of total lineage in publication to editorial lineage (in general, all direct publication costs not allocable to advertising lineage)	_____
	$_____

$D =$ Readership (or circulation) revenues:

If publication sold to all for a fixed price, then readership revenue equals total subscription sales.	_____

If 20 percent of total circulation is from paid nonmember subscriptions, then price charged to nonmembers times number of issues circulated to members plus nonmember revenue equals readership revenues.

      ———

or

If members receiving publication pay a higher membership fee, readership revenue equals excess dues times number of members receiving publication, plus nonmember revenue.

      ———

or

If over 80 percent of issues distributed to members free, readership revenue is the membership receipts times the ratio of publication costs over the total exempt activities cost including the publication costs.

      ———

SOURCES AND SUGGESTED REFERENCES

American Institute of Certified Public Accountants. 1981. *Audits of Certain Nonprofit Organizations, Including Statement of Position Issued by the Accounting Standards Board.* New York: Author.

Blazek, Jody. 1993. *Tax and Financial Planning for Tax Exempt Organizations: Forms, Checklists, Procedures.* (2nd ed.) New York: John Wiley & Sons.

Desiderio, R. J., and Taylor, S. A. 1988. *Planning Tax-Exempt Organizations.* New York: Shepard's/McGraw-Hill.

Gross, M. J., Jr., Warshauer, W., Jr., and Larkin, R. F. 1991. *Financial and Accounting Guide for Not-for-Profit Organizations* (4th ed.). New York: John Wiley & Sons.

Hopkins, Bruce. 1992. *The Law of Tax-Exempt Organizations* (6th ed.). New York: John Wiley & Sons.

———. 1989. *Starting and Managing a Nonprofit Organization—A Legal Guide.* New York: John Wiley & Sons.

———. 1992. *Charity, Advocacy, and the Law.* New York: John Wiley & Sons.

———. 1991. *The Law of Fund-Raising.* New York: John Wiley & Sons.

New York University Conferences on Tax Planning for 501(c)(3) Organizations. Annual. New York: Matthew Bender. Published Annually.

Oleck, Howard L. 1992. *Nonprofit Corporations, Organizations, and Associations* (5th ed.). Englewood Cliffs, NJ: Prentice-Hall.

Tax-Exempt Organizations. Englewood Cliffs, NJ: Prentice-Hall (loose leaf service).

U.S. Department of the Treasury, Internal Revenue Service. Annual. *Exempt Organizations Continuing Professional Education Technical Instruction Programs.* Washington, DC: Author. (Available from IRS Reading Room, Washington, DC.)

———. *Exempt Organizations Handbook.* 1992. IR Manual 7751. Washington, DC: Author.

———. *The Exempt Organization Tax Review, Tax Analysts.* Arlington, VA. Monthly journal.

———. *The Journal of Taxation of Exempt Organizations.* Faulkner & Gray, Inc. New York, NY. Quarterly journal.

———. *The Nonprofit Counsel.* John Wiley & Sons, New York, NY. Monthly journal.

———. *Private Foundations Handbook.* 1992. IR Manual 7752. Washington, DC: Author.

United Way of America. 1989. *Accounting and Financial Reporting, A Guide for United Ways and Not-for-Profit Organizations* (2d ed. rev.). Alexandria, VA: United Way Institute.

Laws and Regulations Governing Nonprofit Organizations

Law and Taxation

Bruce R. Hopkins
Powers, Pyles & Sutter

CONTENTS

Nonprofit organizations in the United States are regulated at both the federal and state levels of government. The purpose of this chapter is to summarize this body of law, which largely is federal tax law.[1]

Each segment of this chapter is followed by a brief checklist, enabling an organization to review its status under and compliance with this body of law. An organization may wish to photocopy these checklists, complete them, and keep the information as part of its minutebook or other organization document file.

34.1 NONPROFIT ORGANIZATIONS: THE LEGAL DEFINITION

United States society is comprised of three sectors. In one sector are the federal, state, and local governments. For-profit entities comprise the business sector. Nonprofit organizations constitute the third of these sectors, which is often referred to as the "independent sector" or the "voluntary sector."

The concept, in the law, of a "nonprofit" organization is best understood through a comparison with a for-profit organization.

In many respects, the characteristics of these two categories of organizations are identical; both require a legal form, have a board of directors and officers, pay compensation, face essentially the same expenses, are able to receive a profit, make investments, and produce goods and services.

However, a for-profit organization has owners—those who hold the equity in the enterprise, such as stockholders of a corporation. The for-profit organization is operated for the benefit of its owners; the profits of the enterprise are passed through to them, perhaps as the payment of dividends on shares of stock. This is what is meant by the term "for-profit" organization; it is one that is intended to generate a profit for its owners. The transfer of the profits from the organization to its owners is considered the inurement of net earnings to the owners.

Unlike the for-profit organization, a nonprofit organization generally is not permitted to distribute its profits (net earnings) to those who control and/or financially support it. A nonprofit organization usually does not have any owners (equity holders). Consequently, the private inurement doctrine is the substantive dividing line that differentiates, for law purposes, between nonprofit organizations and for-profit organizations. (The private inurement doctrine is discussed further below.)

A "tax-exempt" organization is a subset of nonprofit organizations; that is, not all nonprofit organizations are tax-exempt organizations. The concept of a nonprofit organization usually is a matter of state law; the concept of a tax-exempt organization is principally a matter of the federal tax law.

34.2 ROLE OF STATE LAW

The rules concerning the creation of nonprofit organizations are essentially a subject for state laws. A few nonprofit organizations are chartered by the U.S. Congress, but

---

[1] This body of law is summarized in greater detail in Bruce R. Hopkins, *The Law of Tax-Exempt Organizations,* 6th ed. (New York: John Wiley & Sons, Inc., 1992).

most are formed under state law. A nonprofit organization will be created as a corporation, an unincorporated association, or a trust. The document by which these organizations are formed is termed the "articles of organization."

In contemporary times, most nonprofit organizations are established as corporations. This is the case because of the limitation on personal liability that the corporate form generally provides and because of the substantial body of law that defines the operations and duties of the organization and its directors and officers. A corporation is formed by filing articles of incorporation; the document containing its rules of operation is termed the bylaws. (See Exhibit 34.1.)

An unincorporated association is formed by the execution of a constitution. Again, its rules of operation are contained in bylaws. A trust is created by the execution of a trust agreement or a declaration of trust. A trust can, but infrequently does, have bylaws.

A nonprofit organization's articles of organization and/or operational rules should contain provisions addressing the organization's structure and administration (Exhibit 34.2.).

State law also addresses matters such as the extent of personal liability for the directors and officers of nonprofit organizations, the deductibility of charitable contributions (under state law), the imposition of or exemption from several taxes (such as income, sales, and property taxes), and the extent to which fund-raising by the organization is regulated (Exhibit 34.3.). As to the latter, see Chapter 35.

State law may require an annual report. If an organization is "doing business" in another state, it must comply with the corporate and other laws of that state. (See Exhibit 34.4.)

Exhibit 34.1. Checklist.

Form of organization:

_____   Corporation

_____   Unincorporated association

_____   Trust

_____   Other

Types of articles of organization:

_____   Articles of incorporation

_____   Constitution

_____   Declaration of trust

_____   Trust agreement

Date organization formed _____

Place organization formed _____

Date(s) of amendment of articles _____

Date operational rules (e.g., bylaws) formed _____

Date(s) of amendment of rules _____

Exhibit 34.2.   Checklist.

Fiscal year _____

Membership   Yes _____ No _____

   If yes, annual meeting date _____

   Notice requirement _____

Chapters   Yes _____ No_____

Affiliated organizations _____

Board of directors (or trustees):

   Origin _____

   Number _____

   Quorum _____

   Voting power _____

   Terms of office _____

   Annual meeting date _____

   Notice requirement _____

Officers:

   Origin _____

   Titles:

      _____President

      _____Vice President

      _____Treasurer

      _____Secretary

      _____Other: _____

      _____Other: _____

   Terms of office _____

Committees:

      _____   Executive

      _____   Nominating

      _____   Development

      _____   Finance

      _____   Long-Range Planning

      _____   Other

Registered agent (if incorporated) _____

Exhibit 34.3. Checklist.

Does organization have officers' and directors' liability insurance?	Yes _____ No _____
Is organization eligible to receive contributions that are deductible under state law?	Yes _____ No _____
Is organization exempt from state taxation?	
Income tax	Yes _____ No _____
Sales tax	Yes _____ No _____
Use tax	Yes _____ No _____
Tangible personal property tax	Yes _____ No _____
Intangible personal property tax	Yes _____ No _____
Real property tax	Yes _____ No _____

Exhibit 34.4. Checklist.

State annual report due	_____
State in which organization is qualified to "do business"	_____
Registered agent(s) in other states(s)	_____

34.3 FEDERAL TAXATION SYSTEM

Generally, every person is subject to income taxation. The term "person" includes individuals and entities (corporations, unincorporated associations, trusts, some partnerships, and estates).

Some organizations are exempt from federal and state income taxation; these are known, as noted, as tax-exempt organizations. The categories of organizations that are eligible for tax exemption include those that are charitable, educational, scientific, and religious, as defined under the Internal Revenue Code section ("IRS § ") 501(c)(3).

Charitable organizations include those that have the following purposes:

- Relief of the poor and distressed or of the underprivileged;
- Advancement of religion;
- Advancement of education;
- Advancement of science;
- Lessening the burdens of government;
- Community beautification and maintenance;
- Promotion of health;
- Promotion of social welfare;
- Promotion of the arts.

Educational organizations include:

- Formal educational institutions, such as schools, colleges, universities, and museums;
- Organizations that instruct individuals for the purpose of improving or developing their capabilities;
- Instruction of the public on subjects useful to the individual and beneficial to the community.

The concept of education does not include propagandizing, which is the propagation of particular ideas or doctrines without presentation of them in any reasonably objective or balanced manner. The Internal Revenue Service (IRS) utilizes a "methodology test" to differentiate between "educational" activities and propagandizing.

Scientific organizations include:

- Research organizations;
- Publishing organizations.

Religious organizations include:

- Churches;
- Conventions and associations of churches;
- Integrated auxiliaries of churches;
- Religious orders.

However, tax-exempt organizations include organizations other than those that are charitable and the like. Other types of organizations that are exempt from federal income taxation include:

- Title-holding organizations (IRC § 501(c)(1)).
- Social welfare organizations (IRC § 501(c)(4));
- Labor organizations (IRC § 501(c)(5));
- Professional, business, and trade associations (IRC § 501(c)(6));
- Social clubs (IRC § 501(c)(7));
- Employee benefit funds (IRC §§ 501(c)(9), (17), and (20));
- Farmers' cooperatives (IRC § 521);
- Political organizations (IRC § 527);

The concept of "tax exemption" does not necessarily mean a total exemption from taxes. Thus, nearly all forms of tax-exempt organizations are taxable on their unrelated business income (see below).

Charitable, educational, and like organizations can become taxed if they engage in an excessive amount of lobbying activity (see below) or in any political campaign activity (see below). These taxes, which are technically cast as "excise" taxes, can also be imposed on the directors and officers of these organizations.

Private foundations (see below) are taxed on their net investment income. Private foundations can also be taxed, again in the form of excise taxation, if they engage in "self-dealing" with "disqualified persons," fail to make adequate grants and other distributions for charitable purposes, have "excess business holdings," make "jeopardizing investments," or make "taxable expenditures" (such as lobbying or political expenditures, or certain grants to individuals).

34.4 APPLYING FOR RECOGNITION OF TAX EXEMPTION

To be exempt from federal income taxation, a nonprofit organization must fit within at least one of the categories of tax-exempt organizations (see above). Once this classification is achieved, and assuming it is maintained, the organization generally is tax-exempt by operation of law.

However, four categories of nonprofit organizations, to be tax-exempt, are required to have their tax exemption "recognized" by the IRS. These categories of organizations are subject to this "notice" requirement:

- Charitable, educational, scientific, religious, and like organizations;
- Three types of employee benefit funds:
  —Voluntary employees' beneficiary associations;
  —Supplemental unemployment benefit trusts;
  —Group legal service organizations.

The other types of nonprofit organizations may apply for recognition of tax-exempt status if they wish. Charitable and like organizations make application for recognition of tax-exempt status on IRS Form 1023. Other nonprofit organizations make this application on Form 1024.

Certain organizations are exempt from the general rule of mandatory application for recognition of tax-exempt status. These organizations are churches, associations and conventions of churches, integrated auxiliaries of churches, and charitable and like organizations (other than private foundations) the gross receipts of which do not normally exceed $5,000.

When a nonprofit organization seeks to be recognized as a tax-exempt charitable or like organization, it also seeks to be classified as a charitable organization for purposes of the income, estate, and gift tax charitable deduction. Moreover, if the organization has a basis for avoiding classification as a private foundation (see below), it makes this claim as part of this filing. All three of these statuses are retroactive to the date the organization was formed, if the application is filed within 15 months of the end of the month in which the organization was created. See Exhibit 34.5.)

Exhibit 34.5. Checklist.

Tax-exempt (federal)	Yes _____	No _____
IRC § _____		
Has organization received IRS recognition of tax exemption?	Yes _____	No _____
If yes, date of determination letter _____		
Descriptive IRC section	IRC § 501(c) _____	
Other IRC section	IRC § _____	

34.5   ORGANIZATIONAL TEST

Most forms of tax-exempt organizations must meet an "organizational test." This test is a set of rules containing certain requirements as to the contents of the document by which the organization was created. As noted above, this document will be articles of incorporation, a constitution, a trust agreement, or a declaration of trust. The organizational test requirements are the most refined in the case of charitable, educational, scientific, religious, and like organizations.

The organizational test for charitable and like organizations requires that the articles of organization limit the organization's purposes to one or more exempt purposes (see above) and do not expressly empower it to engage (other than unsubstantially) in activities that are not in furtherance of exempt purposes. These articles of organization may not authorize the organization to devote a substantial part of its activities to legislative purposes or any of its activities to political campaign purposes (see below). Moreover, these articles of organization must provide that, upon dissolution, the organization's assets and net income will be distributed for exempt purposes.

Additional requirements are imposed for the governing instruments of private foundations (see below).

34.6   OPERATIONAL TEST

Most forms of tax-exempt organizations must meet an "operational test." This test is a set of rules containing certain requirements as to the nature of the activities in which the organization can engage. Basically, the operational test requires that a tax-exempt organization engage primarily in exempt purposes. The operational test requirements are the most refined in the case of charitable, educational, scientific, religious, and like organizations.

The operational test for charitable and like organizations, because it focuses on the activities of these organizations in relation to their stated purposes, embraces the proscriptions on private inurement, substantial legislative activities, and political campaign activities (see below). Organizations that engage in excessive lobbying activities or any political campaign activities are considered "action" organizations and, for that reason alone, cannot qualify as tax-exempt charitable organizations.

The federal tax law provides that a nonprofit organization, to be tax-exempt as a charitable or like organization, must be organized and operated "exclusively" for exempt purposes. The courts have converted the term "exclusively" to the term "primarily," with the Supreme Court stating that the "presence of a single . . . [nonexempt] purpose, if substantial in nature, will destroy the exemption regardless of the number or importance of truly . . . [exempt] purposes." The term must be interpreted in this manner, if only to accommodate the existence of some unrelated business activity (see below).

34.7   PRIVATE INUREMENT DOCTRINE

A nonprofit organization, to be tax-exempt as a charitable, educational, scientific, religious, or like organization, must be organized and operated so that "no part of . . . [its] net earnings . . . inures to the benefit of any private shareholder or individual." This is known as the "private inurement doctrine." This doctrine applies with respect to other categories of tax-exempt organizations.

The concept of private inurement is broad and wide-ranging. Essentially, the doctrine forbids ways of causing the income or assets of a tax-exempt organization (that is subject to it) to flow away from the organization and to one or more persons who are related to the organization ("insiders"), for nonexempt purposes. The Office of Chief Counsel of the IRS once stated the doctrine quite bluntly: "The inurement prohibition serves to prevent anyone in a position to do so from siphoning off any of a charity's income or assets for personal use."

The essence of this concept is to ensure that a tax-exempt organization is serving a public interest and not a private interest. That is, to be tax-exempt, it is necessary for an organization subject to the doctrine to establish that it is not organized and operated for the benefit of private interests such as designated individuals, the creator of the organization or his or her family, shareholders of the organization, persons controlled (directly or indirectly) by such private interests, or any other persons having a personal and private interest in the activities of the organization.

In determining the presence of any proscribed private inurement, the law looks to the ultimate purpose of the organization. If the basic purpose of the organization subject to the doctrine is to benefit private individuals, then it cannot be tax-exempt even though exempt activities are also performed. Conversely, incidental benefits to private individuals will usually not defeat the exemption if the organization otherwise qualifies under the appropriate exemption provision.

The IRS and the courts have recognized a variety of forms of private inurement. These include:

- Excessive or unreasonable compensation;
- Unreasonable or unfair rental arrangements;
- Unreasonable or unfair lending arrangements;
- Provision of services to persons in their private capacity;
- Certain assumptions of liability;
- Certain sales of assets to insiders;
- Certain participation in partnerships;
- Certain percentage payment arrangements;
- Varieties of tax avoidance schemes.

There is a separate but analogous doctrine termed the "private benefit" doctrine. This doctrine is a derivative of the operational test (see above) and is applicable with respect to persons who are not "insiders." Thus, it is broader than the private inurement

Exhibit 34.6. Checklist.

Has organization identified its "insiders"?	Yes ____	No ____
If yes, identify them _____		
Is organization engaging in transactions with these persons?	Yes ____	No ____

doctrine and, in many respects, subsumes that doctrine. The private benefit doctrine essentially prevents a charitable or like organization from benefiting private interests in any way, other than to an insubstantial extent.

More specific rules are applicable to private foundations (see below) in the form of prohibitions on self-dealing. (See Exhibit 34.6.)

34.8   LEGISLATIVE ACTIVITIES LIMITATION

Nonprofit organizations, to qualify as charitable or like organizations, are subject to a rule of federal tax law, which is that "no substantial part of the activities" of the organizations may constitute "carrying on propaganda, or otherwise attempting, to influence legislation."

The term "legislation" is quite broad, and includes bills, resolutions, appropriations measures, treaties, and Senate consideration of presidential nominations. The term "propaganda" is discussed above, in the context of educational activities.

Legislative activities—or lobbying—are of two types. One is "direct" lobbying, which includes the presentation of testimony at public hearings held by legislative committees, correspondence and meetings with legislators and their staffs, and publication of documents advocating specific legislative action. The other is "grass-roots" lobbying, which consists of appeals to the general public, or segments of the general public, to contact legislators or take other specific action as regards legislative matters.

As to the meaning of the term "substantial" in this context, there are two sets of rules. One is termed the "substantial part test," which is a vague requirement limiting allowable lobbying (both direct and grass-roots) to "insubstantial" lobbying. Insubstantiality in this setting can be measured in terms of expenditures, time, or influence. A charitable or like organization that exceeds the bounds of "insubstantiality" is considered an "action" organization (see above) and may lose its tax-exempt status as a result.

Organizations that are under the substantial part test and lose their tax-exempt status because of excessive lobbying are subject to an excise tax in the amount of 5 percent of the excessive lobbying expenditures. A like tax may be imposed on the directors and officers of an organization who agreed to the making of the excess lobbying expenditures, unless the agreement was not willful and was due to reasonable cause.

The other set of rules, which is termed the "expenditure test," must be affirmatively elected by eligible charitable and like organizations. These rules measure allowable lobbying in terms of percentages of total expenditures (other than certain fund-raising expenses). Direct lobbying expenditures may be up to 20 percent of the first $500,000 of expenditures, 15 percent of the next $500,000, 10 percent of the next $500,000, and 5 percent of the balance, with no more than $1 million expended for lobbying in any one year. These percentages are measured over a four-year average. Maximum allowable expenditures for grass-roots lobbying are 25 percent of the allowable expenditures for direct lobbying.

An organization that exceeds the lobbying expenses tolerated by the expenditure test is subject to a 25 percent excise tax on the excess lobbying expenditures. Where the lobbying expenditures exceed 150 percent of allowable lobbying expenditures, the organization may well lose its tax-exempt status.

Exhibit 34.7. Checklist.

Does organization engage in lobbying?	Yes _____	No _____
Percentage of funds devoted to lobbying	_____	
Has expenditure test been elected?	Yes _____	No _____

Private foundations (see below) are essentially prohibited from engaging in any lobbying activities.

Most other categories of tax-exempt organizations—such as social welfare organizations, membership associations, and veterans' organizations—may freely lobby without concern as to their tax-exempt status. (See Exhibit 34.7.)

34.9 POLITICAL CAMPAIGN ACTIVITIES LIMITATION

Nonprofit organizations, to qualify as charitable or like organizations, are subject to a rule of federal tax law, which is that they must "not participate in, or intervene in (including the publishing or distributing of statements) any political campaign on behalf of (or in opposition to) any candidate for public office."

This prohibition is deemed by the IRS to be "absolute," that is, it is not underlain with an "insubstantiality" threshold. However, some court opinions suggest some form of de miminis standard in this context. In general, this rule of federal tax law is considerably undefined.

The political campaign activities prohibition embodies four elements, all of which must be present for the limitation to become operative. These elements are:

1. A charitable or like organization may not "participate" or "intervene" in a political campaign;
2. The political activity that is involved must be a "political campaign";
3. The campaign must be with respect to an individual who is a "candidate";
4. The individual must be a candidate for a "public office."

A charitable or like organization may not establish and maintain a "political action committee" to engage in political campaign activities.

There are a variety of activities that may be considered "political" but are not political campaign activities. These activities include lobbying, action on behalf of or in opposition to the confirmation of presidential nominees, litigation, boycotts, demonstrations, strikes, and picketing. However, tax-exempt organizations may not engage in activities that promote violence, other forms of law-breaking, or other activities that are contrary to "public policy."

A tax-exempt organization (other than a political organization) that engages in the type of "political" activity embraced by attempts to influence the selection, nomination, election, or appointment of any individual to any federal, state, or local public office will not lose its tax exemption but will become subject to a special tax.

Exhibit 34.8. Checklist.

Does organization engage in political campaign activities?	Yes _____	No _____
Does organization have a political action committee?	Yes _____	No _____
Does organization engage in any advocacy activities?	Yes _____	No _____

Charitable and like organizations that lose their tax-exempt status because of political campaign activities are subject to an initial excise tax in the amount of 10 percent of the political campaign expenditures and perhaps an additional 100 percent tax. Like taxes, in the amounts of 2½ and 50 percent, may be imposed on the directors and officers of an organization who agreed to the making of the political campaign expenditures, unless the agreement was not willful and was due to reasonable cause.

Private foundations (see below) are essentially prohibited from engaging in political campaign activities.

Most other categories of tax-exempt organizations—such as social welfare organizations, membership associations, and veterans' organizations—do not directly engage in political campaign activities but utilize political action committees for that purpose. (See Exhibit 34.8.)

34.10 PUBLIC CHARITIES AND PRIVATE FOUNDATIONS

Federal tax law differentiates between charitable, educational, scientific, and religious organizations that are "public" and those that are "private." The latter type of organization is termed a "private foundation." Because there is no advantage to being a private foundation, charitable and like organizations strive to be classified as "public" entities. The private foundation distinction does not apply with respect to any other categories of tax-exempt organizations.

The law does not define what a private foundation is; it defines what it is not. Generically, however, a private foundation essentially is a charitable or like organization that is funded from one source (usually, one individual, family, or corporation), that receives its ongoing funding from investment income (rather than a consistent flow of charitable contributions), and that makes grants for charitable purposes to other persons rather than conduct its own programs.

In defining what a private foundation is not, the federal tax law presumes that all charitable and like organizations are private foundations. It is, therefore, the responsibility of the organization to (if it can) rebut this presumption by showing that it is a "public" organization. There are four basic categories of public organizations:

- Institutions, such as churches, universities, colleges, schools, hospitals, and medical research organizations;
- Organizations that are publicly supported, because the support is substantially in the form of contributions and grants;
- Organizations that are publicly supported, because the support is substantially in the form of contributions, grants, and revenue from the performance of exempt functions;

- Organizations that are organized and operated exclusively for the benefit of, to perform the functions of, or to carry out the purposes of one or more public organizations (so-called "supporting organizations").

Organizations that are classified as private foundations are subject to a battery of rules and requirements. These are:

- A private foundation must, at all times, know the identity of persons who have special relationships to it (such as directors, officers, and their family members; and major ("substantial") contributors); these persons are termed "disqualified persons";
- A private foundation may not engage in acts of "self-dealing" (such as sales, rental, or lending transactions, or the payment of excessive compensation) with one or more disqualified persons;
- A private foundation must annually pay out, in the form of grants for charitable purposes (termed "qualifying distributions"), an amount equal to at least 5 percent of its investment assets (termed "minimum investment return");
- A private foundation may not hold more than 20 percent (sometimes 35 percent) of an active interest in a commercial business (termed "excess business holdings");
- A private foundation may not invest its income or assets in speculative investments (termed "jeopardizing investments");
- A private foundation may not make expenditures for purposes that are noncharitable, lobbying, or political, nor make grants to individuals or nonpublic charities without complying with certain rules (termed "taxable expenditures");
- A private foundation generally must pay a 2 percent tax on its net investment income;
- A private foundation must file an annual information return (see below) that is more complex than that required of other charitable and like organizations;
- Contributions to private foundations may be less deductible than contributions to public charities.

There are some organizations that are not "standard" private foundations and thus are treated differently under the federal tax law. A private foundation that conducts its own programs is termed a "private operating foundation" and is treated in certain ways as a public charity. Private foundations that are exempt from the investment income tax and that have only a 1 percent payout requirement are "exempt operating foundations." "Foundations" that are supportive of governmental colleges and universities are regarded as public charities. A "conduit" private foundation is one that makes qualifying distributions, which are treated as distributions out of its assets, in an amount equal to 100 percent of all contributions received in the year involved. So-called "community foundations" are publicly supported organizations.

A private foundation may convert to one of the four forms of public charities. To do this, it must "terminate" its private foundation status, following one of a variety of procedures.

As noted, a charitable organization is classified as a public or private charity as part of the process of applying for recognition of tax-exempt status. An organization that qualifies as an institutional public charity or a supporting organization is categorized as

Exhibit 34.9.   Checklist.

If IRC § 501(c)(3) organization:

    Public _____   Private _____

If public IRC § 501(c)(3) organization:

    Church _____

    University _____

    College _____

    School _____

    Hospital _____

    Medical research organization _____

    Donative publicly supported charity _____

    Fee-based publicly supported charity _____

    Supporting organization _____

    Other _____

If private IRC § 501(c)(3) organization:

    Standard private foundation _____

    Private operating foundation _____

    Exempt operating foundation _____

    Other _____

If publicly supported organization:

    Date advance ruling period (if any) ends/ended _____

    Date definitive ruling issued _____

---

a nonprivate foundation by a "definitive ruling" from the IRS. If an organization is seeking to be categorized as one of the two types of publicly supported charities, and it has been in existence for at least one full tax year, it may acquire nonprivate foundation status by means of a definitive ruling; otherwise, it will receive an "advance ruling" during a period when it obtains the requisite public support (if it can), with that ruling subsequently ripening into a definitive ruling. (See Exhibit 34.9.)

34.11   FILING REQUIREMENTS

Nearly every organization that is exempt from federal income taxation must file an annual information return. This return generally is one of the following:

- Most tax-exempt organizations—Form 990;
- "Small" tax-exempt organizations—Form 990EZ;
- Private foundations—Form 990-PF;
- Black lung benefit trusts—Form 990-BL.

The annual information return filed by charitable and like organizations must include the following items:

1. The organization's gross income for the year;
2. Its expenses attributable to income and incurred during the year;
3. Its disbursements during the year for exempt purposes;
4. A balance sheet showing its assets, liabilities, and net worth as of the beginning of the year;
5. The total of the contributions received by it during the year, and the names and addresses of all "substantial contributors";
6. The names and addresses of its managers and highly compensated employees;
7. The compensation and other payments made during the year to each of its managers and highly compensated employees;
8. Certain information concerning lobbying activities by those organizations that have elected to come within the expenditure test (see above);
9. Information with respect to direct or indirect transfers to, and other direct or indirect transactions and relationships with, other tax-exempt organizations (other than charitable and like organizations, and political organizations).

(a) FORM 990 The annual information return that is required to be filed by most tax-exempt organizations is the Form 990. The general contents of this return are stated in the preceding paragraph. In addition, an organization must describe its "program service accomplishments." Expenses must be reported on a functional basis, that is, allocated to program, management, and fund-raising. Revenue-producing activities must be detailed. Business activities must be categorized using various "business codes."

A tax-exempt organization must report certain other information, including information concerning:

- Taxable subsidiaries;
- Changes made in organizing or governing instruments;
- Receipt of unrelated income;
- Ownership of an interest in a partnership;
- Liquidations, dissolutions, terminations, or substantial contractions;
- Relationships with other organizations;
- Political expenditures;
- Receipt of nondeductible gifts;
- Requests to see an annual information return or application for recognition of tax exemption (see below);
- Grass-roots lobbying (see above) by labor organizations and business leagues;
- Public interest law firm activities.

In addition to filing the annual information return, a charitable or like organization must file an accompanying schedule requiring additional information. This is Schedule A of Form 990.

Schedule A is the document by which charitable and like organizations report on the compensation of the five highest paid employees, the compensation of the five highest paid persons for professional services, eligibility for nonprivate foundation status (see above), and on information regarding transfers, transactions, and relationships with other organizations.

Charitable organizations that elected the expenditure test with respect to their lobbying activities (see above) must report their lobbying expenses, including those over the four-year averaging period. Organizations that have not made this election, and thus remain subject to the substantial part test (see above), are subject to other reporting requirements.

(b) FORM 990EZ The annual information return for "smaller" tax-exempt organizations is the two-page Form 990EZ. This return may be used by tax-exempt organizations that have gross receipts of less than $100,000 and total assets of less than $250,000 at the end of the reporting year.

An organization can use this annual information return in any year in which it meets these two criteria, even though it was, and/or is, required to file a Form 990 in other years. The Form 990EZ cannot be filed by private foundations (see below). A charitable or like organization filing a Form 990EZ must also file a Schedule A (see above).

(c) FORM 990-PF Private foundations (see above) must file an annual information return. This return is on Form 990-PF.

On this return, private foundations must report their revenue and expenses, assets and liabilities, fund balances, and information about trustees, directors, officers, other foundation managers, highly paid employees, and contractors. Private foundations must report on qualifying distributions, calculation of the minimum investment return, computation of the distributable amount, undistributed income, and grants programs and other activities (see above).

A private foundation must calculate the tax on its investment income (unless it is an exempt operating foundation) and its qualification for the reduced payout amount. A private foundation must provide certain information regarding foundation managers, loan and scholarship programs, grants and contributions paid during the year or approved for future payment, transfers, transactions, and relationships with other organizations, and compliance with the public inspection requirements (see below).

In addition to reporting on its activities in general, like nearly all tax-exempt organizations (see above), a private foundation must also report on any self-dealing transactions, failure to distribute income as required, excess business holdings, investments that jeopardize charitable purposes, taxable expenditures, political expenditures, and substantial contributions (see above). Additional reporting requirements are applicable to private operating foundations (see above).

(d) DUE DATES The Form 990, 990EZ, or 990-PF is due on or before the 15th day of the fifth month following the close of the tax year. Thus, the return for a calendar-year organization should be filed by May 15 of each year. Extensions of time for filing can be obtained.

The filing date for an annual information return may fall due while the organization's application for recognition of tax exemption is pending with the IRS. In that instance, the organization should nontheless file the information return (rather than a tax return) and indicate on it that the application is pending.

Exhibit 34.10. Checklist.

Is organization required to file return with IRS?	Yes _____	No _____
If yes, identify form	Form _____	
Date annual return due	_____	
Is Form 990-T required (see below)?	Yes _____	No _____

(e) PENALTIES Failure to file the appropriate information return, or failure to include any information required to be shown on the return (or failure to show the correct information), absent reasonable cause, can give rise to a $10 penalty, payable by the organization, for each day the failure continues, with a maximum penalty for any one return not to exceed the lesser of $5,000 or 5 percent of the gross receipts of the organization for one year. An additional penalty may be imposed, at the same rate and maximum of $5,000, on the individual(s) responsible for the failure to file, absent reasonable cause, where the return remains unfiled following demand for the return by the IRS. An addition to tax for failure to timely file a federal tax return may also be imposed.

(f) EXCEPTIONS Certain categories of organizations are excused from the filing of an annual information return with the IRS (Exhibit 34.10.). These include:

- Churches and associations, conventions, and integrated auxiliaries of churches;
- Religious orders;
- Organizations (other than private foundations) the gross receipts of which in each year are normally not more than $5,000;
- Certain state institutions.

34.12 CERTAIN DISCLOSURE REQUIREMENTS

The annual information returns and application for recognition of tax exemption of a tax-exempt organization (other than a private foundation) must be made available during regular business hours for public inspection.

The penalty for failure to provide access to copies of the annual return is $10 per day, absent reasonable cause, with a maximum penalty per return of $5,000. The penalty for failure to provide access to copies of the exemption application, payable by the person failing to meet the requirements, is $10 per day, absent reasonable cause, without any limitation. Any person who willfully fails to comply with these inspection requirements is subject to a $1,000 penalty with respect to each return or application.

The application for recognition of tax exemption and any supporting documents filed by most tax-exempt organizations are open to public inspection at the National Office of the IRS.

A tax-exempt organization must pay a penalty if it fails to disclose that information or services it is offering are available without charge from the federal government. The penalty, which is applicable for each day on which the failure occurred, is the greater of $1,000 or 50 percent of the aggregate cost of the offers and solicitations that occurred on any day on which the failure occurred and with respect to which there was this type of failure.

Exhibit 34.11.   Checklist.

Does organization make its annual return available to the public?	Yes _____	No _____
Does organization make disclosure concerning information or services?	Yes _____	No _____
If private foundation, is return availability published?	Yes _____	No _____

A copy of a private foundation's annual information return must be made available to any citizen for inspection at the foundation's principal office during regular business hours for at least 180 days of its availability. Notice of the availability of this annual return must be published in a newspaper having general circulation in the county in which the principal office of the foundation is located (Exhibit 34.11).

34.13   COMMERCIALITY DOCTRINE

The courts have engrafted onto the rules, found in the Internal Revenue Code and the accompanying Treasury Regulations, concerning eligibility of nonprofit organizations for tax-exempt status additional requirements for obtaining and maintaining exempt status. These rules are largely embraced by the "commerciality doctrine."

In essence, the doctrine holds that a tax-exempt organization is engaged in a nonexempt activity when that activity is engaged in in a manner that is considered "commercial." An act is a commercial one if it has a direct counterpart in the world of for-profit organizations. If an activity is, or combinations of activities are, nonexempt in nature, the organization cannot be tax-exempt. Otherwise, the nonexempt activity is treated as an unrelated activity (see below).

There are several factors that can trigger application of the commerciality doctrine. They include:

- Sales of goods or services to the general public;
- Operation in direct competition with for-profit organizations;
- Setting of prices using a formula that is common in the realm of commercial business;
- Actual profit margins;
- Utilization of promotional materials and other forms of advertising to induce sales;
- Hours of operation;
- Lack of use of volunteers;
- Absence of charitable contributions as part of the revenue base.

Somewhat related to the commerciality doctrine is the "commensurate test." This is a standard articulated by the IRS in 1964 and not vigorously applied until the late 1980s. The commensurate test basically is used to determine whether a tax-exempt organization (particularly a charitable one) is engaging in an appropriate amount of exempt activity in relation to its available resources (Exhibit 34.12).

Exhibit 34.12. Checklist.

Does organization have for-profit counterpart?	Yes _____	No _____
Does organization operate in "commercial" manner, using above criteria?	Yes _____	No _____
Does organization satisfy the "commensurate test"?	Yes _____	No _____

34.14 UNRELATED INCOME TAXATION

The unrelated business income rules are an integral part of the law of tax-exempt organizations. While discussed more fully in Chapter 33, a brief overview is warranted here.

(a) OVERVIEW Taxation of a tax-exempt organization's unrelated business income is based on the concept that the approach is a more effective and workable sanction for authentic enforcement of this aspect of the law than denial or revocation of tax-exempt status. This body of law is fundamentally simple: the unrelated business tax only applies to active business income that arises from activities—technically known as "trades or businesses"—that are "unrelated" to the organization's tax-exempt purposes. The purpose of the unrelated business income tax is to place tax-exempt organization business activities on the same tax basis as the nonexempt business endeavors with which they compete.

The term "unrelated trade or business" means any trade or business, the conduct of which is not substantially related to the exercise or performance, by the tax-exempt organization carrying on the trade or business, of the exempt purpose or function. The conduct of a trade or business is not substantially related to an organization's tax-exempt purpose solely because the organization may need the income or because of the use the organization makes of the profits derived from the business.

Absent one or more exceptions, gross income of a tax-exempt organization subject to the tax on unrelated income (and most tax-exempt organizations are) is includable in the computation of unrelated business taxable income if three factors are present:

- The income is from a "trade or business";
- The trade or business is "regularly carried on";
- The conduct of the business is not "substantially related" to the organization's performance of its tax-exempt purposes.

(b) "TRADE OR BUSINESS" Generally, any activity that is carried on for the production of income from the sale of goods or the performance of services is a trade or business for purposes of the unrelated income tax. The courts are adding another criterion, which is that an activity, to be considered a "business" for tax purposes, must be conducted with a "profit motive."

The IRS is empowered to fragment a tax-exempt organization's operations, run as an integrated whole, into its component parts in search of an unrelated business. This "fragmentation rule" enables the IRS to ferret out unrelated business activity that is conducted with, or as a part of, related business activity.

(c) "REGULARLY CARRIED ON" In determining whether a trade or business from which a particular amount of gross income is derived by a tax-exempt organization is regularly carried on, regard must be had to the frequency and continuity with which the activities that are productive of the income are conducted and the manner in which they are pursued. This requirement is applied in light of the purpose of the unrelated business income tax which, as noted, is to place tax-exempt organization business activities on the same tax basis as the non-exempt business endeavors with which they compete. Thus, specific business activities of a tax-exempt organization will ordinarily be deemed to be "regularly carried on" if they manifest a frequency and continuity and are pursued in a manner generally similar to comparable commercial activities of nonexempt organizations.

Where income-producing activities are of a kind normally conducted by nonexempt commercial organizations on a year-round basis, the conduct of the activities by a tax-exempt organization over a period of only a few weeks does not constitute the regular carrying on of a trade or business. Where income-producing activities are of a kind normally undertaken by nonexempt commercial organizations only on a seasonal basis, the conduct of the activities by a tax-exempt organization during a significant part of the season ordinarily constitutes the regular conduct of trade or business.

(d) "SUBSTANTIALLY RELATED" Gross income derives from "unrelated trade or business" if the conduct of the trade or business that produces the income is not substantially related to the purposes for which tax exemption is granted. The presence of this requirement necessitates an examination of the relationship between the business activities that generate the particular income in question—the activities, that is, of producing or distributing the goods or performing the services involved—and the accomplishment of the organization's tax-exempt purposes.

Trade or business is "related" to tax-exempt purposes only where the conduct of the business activity has a causal relationship to the achievement of a tax-exempt purpose, and it is "substantially related" only if the causal relationship is a substantial one. Thus, for the conduct of a trade or business from which a particular amount of gross income is derived to be substantially related to the purposes for which tax exemption is granted, the production or distribution of the goods or the performance of the services from which the gross income is derived must contribute importantly to the accomplishment of these purposes. Where the production or distribution of the goods or the performance of the services does not contribute importantly to the accomplishment of the tax-exempt purposes of an organization, the income from the sale of the goods or the performance of the services does not derive from the conduct of related trade or business.

Whether activities productive of gross income contribute importantly to the accomplishment of any purpose for which an organization is granted tax exemption depends in each case on the facts and circumstances involved.

In determining whether activities contribute importantly to the accomplishment of a tax-exempt purpose, the size and extent of the activities involved must be considered in relation to the nature and extent of the tax-exempt function that they purport to serve. Thus, where income is realized by a tax-exempt organization from activities that are in part related to the performance of its exempt functions but that are conducted on a larger scale than is reasonably necessary for performance of the functions, the gross income attributable to that portion of the activities in excess of the needs of tax-exempt functions constitutes gross income from the conduct of unrelated trade or business. This type of income is not derived from the production or distribution of goods or the performance of services that contribute importantly to the accomplishment of any tax-exempt purpose of the organization.

Ordinarily, gross income from the sale of products that result from the performance of tax-exempt functions does not constitute gross income from the conduct of unrelated business if the product is sold in substantially the same state it is in upon completion of the exempt functions. However, if a product resulting from a tax-exempt function is utilized or exploited in further business endeavors beyond that reasonably appropriate or necessary for disposition in the state it is in upon completion of tax-exempt functions, the gross income derived from these endeavors would be from the conduct of unrelated business.

An asset or facility necessary to the conduct of tax-exempt functions may also be utilized in a commercial manner. This is a "dual use" arrangement. In these cases, the mere fact of the use of the asset or facility in exempt functions does not, by itself, make the income from the commercial endeavor gross income from related business. The test, instead, is whether the activities productive of the income in question contribute importantly to the accomplishment of tax-exempt purposes.

Certain types of income or activities are exempt from taxation under these rules. These exemptions include:

- Passive income, such as interest, dividends, royalties, rents, annuities, and capital gains;
- Income derived from research for government;
- Income derived from research performed by a college, university, or hospital;
- Income derived from a business in which substantially all of the work is performed by volunteers;
- Income from a business conducted by a charitable or like organization primarily for the convenience of its members, students, patients, officers, or employees;
- Income from a business that is the sale of merchandise, substantially all of which has been received by the organizations as contributions;
- Income from the conduct of entertainment at certain fairs and expositions;
- Income from the conduct of certain trade shows;
- Income from the provision of certain services to small tax-exempt hospitals;
- Income from the distribution of certain low-cost articles incidental to the solicitation of charitable contributions;
- Income from the exchange or rental of mailing lists with or to charitable organizations.

In computing a tax-exempt organization's unrelated business taxable income, there must be included with respect to each debt-financed property that is unrelated to the organization's exempt function—as an item of gross income derived from an unrelated trade or business—an amount of income from the property, subject to tax in the proportion in which the property is financed by the debt.

Unrelated business taxable income is reported to the IRS on Form 990-T. In computing taxable unrelated income, an organization can utilize all related deductions and is entitled to a specific deduction of $1,000 (Exhibit 34.13.).

Exhibit 34.13. Checklist.

Does organization engage in any unrelated business activities?	Yes _____	No _____
If yes, identify activities _____		
Does organization rely on any exceptions from unrelated income taxation	Yes _____	No _____
If yes, identify exceptions _____		
Does organization have unrelated debt-financed income?	Yes _____	No _____

34.15 COMBINATIONS OF TAX-EXEMPT AND NONEXEMPT ORGANIZATIONS

One of the most striking and significant practices of contemporary tax-exempt organizations is the structuring of activities, which in an earlier era were or would have been in a single tax-exempt entity, so that they are undertaken by two or more related organizations, either tax-exempt or taxable.

For example, there are several common categories of combinations of tax-exempt organizations. These include a tax-exempt organization that utilizes a tax-exempt title-holding organization, a tax-exempt charitable organization that has an affiliated tax-exempt social welfare organization that engages in substantial lobbying, a professional association with a related foundation, and a business association with a related political action committee. Another illustration of this type of bifurcation is the use of a supporting organization (see above). Hospital systems represent the larger of clusters of related tax-exempt organizations.

There are combinations of tax-exempt organizations and nonexempt organizations as well. Thus, tax-exempt organizations often utilize taxable subsidiaries. Where this relationship is properly structured, the activities of the subsidiary will not be attributed to the parent tax-exempt organization. Revenues from the subsidiary to the parent tax-exempt organization will likely be taxable as unrelated business income (see above).

Another combination of exempt and nonexempt entities involves a partnership. However, it is the position of the IRS that a charitable or like organization will lose its federal income tax exemption if it participates as the, or a, general partner in a limited partnership, unless the principal purpose of the limited partnership itself is to further charitable purposes. Even where the partnership can so qualify, the exemption may be revoked if the charitable organization/general partner is not adequately insulated from the day-to-day management responsibilities of the partnership and/or if the limited partners are to receive an undue return.

Tax-exempt organizations may enter into a joint venture with a for-profit organization without adversely affecting their tax-exempt status. The only situation where tax exemption would be revoked for participation in such a joint venture is likely to be where the primary purpose of the exempt organization is to participate in the venture and if the function of the venture is unrelated to the exempt purposes of the tax-exempt organization (Exhibit 34.14.).

Exhibit 34.14. Checklist.

If organization has any of the following, identify:

Taxable subsidiary _____

Participation in partnership as general partner _____

Participation in partnership as limited partner _____

Participation in joint venture _____

Other affiliations with other organizations _____

Exhibit 34.15. Checklist.

County tax exemption information _____

City tax exemption information _____

Tax returns due:

State _____

County _____

City _____

Other _____

Payroll taxes filings _____

Lobbying registration(s) (nontax) _____

Insurance (other than D & O) information _____

Leases _____

Other contracts _____

Names and addresses of:

Accountant

_____

_____

_____

Executive Director

_____

_____

_____

Fund-raiser[1]

_____

_____

_____

_____

[1] A separate checklist in the fund-raising context is in Chapter 35.

Exhibit 34.15.   *(Continued)*

Lawyer

Insurance representative

President

Registered agent(s)

34.16   OTHER LEGAL MATTERS

There are a variety of other matters of law that a nonprofit organization should be concerned with. Some of these are referenced in Exhibit 34.15.

SOURCES AND SUGGESTED REFERENCES

Blazek, Jody. 1990. *Tax and Financial Planning for Tax Exempt Organizations: Forms, Checklists, Procedures.* New York: John Wiley & Sons.

Gross, Malvern J., Jr. Marshaver, William, Jr., and Lavkin, Richard F. 1991. *Financial and Accounting Guide for Not-for-Profit Organizations* (4th ed.). New York: John Wiley & Sons.

Hopkins, Bruce R. 1992. *The Law of Tax-Exempt Organizations* (6th ed.). New York: John Wiley & Sons.

————. 1989. *Starting and Managing a Nonprofit Organization: A Legal Guide.* New York: John Wiley & Sons.

Fund-Raising
Rules and Regulations

Bruce R. Hopkins
Powers, Pyles & Sutter

CONTENTS

The solicitation of charitable contributions in the United States involves practices that are recognized as being forms of free speech protected by federal and state constitutional law. Thus, there are limitations on the extent to which fund-raising for charitable, educational, scientific, religious, and like organizations can be regulated by government. Nevertheless, nonprofit organizations in the United States face considerable regulatory requirements at the federal and state levels when they solicit contributions for charitable purposes. The purpose of this chapter is to summarize this body of law.[1]

Each segment of this chapter is followed by a brief checklist, enabling an organization to review its status under and compliance with this body of law. An organization may wish to photocopy these checklists, complete them, and keep the information as part of its minutebook or other organization document file.

---

[1] This body of law is summarized in greater detail in Bruce R. Hopkins, *The Law of Fund-Raising* (New York: John Wiley & Sons, 1991, 1992 Supp.).

35.1 STATE LAW REGULATION

The process of raising funds for charitable purposes is heavily regulated by the states. At this time, all but eight states have some form of statutory structure by which the fund-raising process is regulated.[2] Of these states, 30 have formal charitable solicitation acts.

(a) STATE REGULATION IN GENERAL The various state charitable solicitation acts generally contain certain features. These are:

- A process by which a charitable organization registers or otherwise secures a permit to raise funds for charitable purposes in the state;
- Requirements for reporting information (usually annually) about an organization's fund-raising program;
- A series of organizations or activities that are exempt from some or all of the statutory requirements;
- A process by which a professional fund-raiser, professional solicitor, and/or commercial co-venturer registers with, and reports to, the state;
- Record-keeping requirements, applicable to charitable organizations, professional fund-raisers, professional solicitors, and/or commercial co-venturers;
- Rules concerning the contents of contracts between a charitable organization and a professional fund-raiser, professional solicitor, and/or a commercial co-venturer;
- A series of so-called "prohibited acts";
- Provision for reciprocal agreements among the states as to coordinated regulation in this field;
- A summary of the powers of the governmental official having regulatory authority (usually the attorney general or secretary of state);
- A statement of the various sanctions that can be imposed for failure to comply with this law (such as injunctions, fines, and imprisonment).

These elements of the law are generally applicable to the fund-raising charitable organization. Yet there are several provisions of law that are directed at the fund-raising professional or the professional solicitor, and/or that go beyond traditional fund-raising regulation.

(b) HISTORICAL PERSPECTIVE Until the mid-1950s, the matter of fund-raising practices was not addressed by state law. At that time, there was not much attention to those practices from an ethical perspective. Some counties had adopted some fund-raising regulation ordinances but there was not any state or federal law on the subject.

This began to change in the mid-1950s, as part of the disclosure and consumer protection movements. North Carolina was the first state to enact a fund-raising regulation law. However, others soon followed, generating a series of laws that came to be known as "charitable solicitation acts." New York was the second state to enact one of these acts, and this law became the prototype for the many that were to follow.

---

[2] The states that have no statutory or other regulatory law in this regard are Alaska, Arizona, Delaware, Idaho, Mississippi, Montana, Vermont, and Wyoming.

The New York law and its progeny involved a statutory scheme based on registration and reporting. Charitable organizations were required to register in advance of solicitation and to annually report; bond requirements came later. Subsequently, forms of regulation involving professional fund-raisers and professional solicitors were developed. Exceptions evolved, disclosure requirements expanded, and a variety of "prohibited acts" (see below) developed.

Today's typical charitable solicitation statute is far more extensive than its forebears of decades ago.

When charitable solicitation acts began to develop (as noted, beginning in the mid-1950s), the principal features were registration and annual reporting requirements. These laws were basically licensing statutes. They gave the states essential information about the fund-raising to be conducted, so that they would have a basis for investigation and review should there be suspicion of some abuse.

Time passed. Some states decided to go beyond the concept of licensing and began to affirmatively regulate charitable solicitations. This was done in part because of citizens' complaints; another part was political grandstanding. The regulation worked its way into the realm of attempting to prevent the "less qualified" (including out-of-the-mainstream) charities from soliciting in the states.

Structurally, the typical charitable solicitation statute originally did not have much to do with actual regulation of the efforts of either the fund-raising institution or the fund-raising professional. Rather, the emphasis was on information gathering and disclosure of it to desiring donors. As noted, its requirements were based on the submission of written information (registration statements, reports, and the like) by charitable organizations and their fund-raising advisers, bond requirements, and enforcement authority granted to the attorneys general, secretaries of state, or other governmental officials charged with administering and enforcing the law.

Later, however, law requirements began to creep in that sounded more like ethical precepts. These requirements were more than just mechanics—they went beyond registration requirements, filing due dates, and accounting principles. They went beyond telling the charity and the professional fund-raisers when to do something, and entered the realm of telling them how they must conduct the solicitation and what they cannot do in that regard.

From the regulators' viewpoint, the high point of this form of regulation came when the states could ban charitable organizations with "high" fund-raising costs. (As noted below, this form of regulation ultimately was found to be unconstitutional.) This application of constitutional law rights to charitable solicitation acts left the state regulators without their principal weapon. In frustration, they turned to other forms of law, these based on the principle of "disclosure" (see below).

In this aftermath, more state fund-raising law developed. The registration and annual reports became more extensive. The states tried, with limited success, to force charities and solicitors into various forms of point-of-solicitation disclosure of various pieces of information. Some states dictated the contents of the scripts of telephone solicitors. This disclosure approach failed to satisfy the regulatory impulse. More frustration ensued.

The regulators turned to even more ways to have a role in the charitable fund-raising process. They started to micro-manage charitable fund-raising. They began to substitute their judgment for that of donors, charities, and professional fund-raisers. Thus, they engendered laws that beefed up the record-keeping requirements, spelled out the contents of contracts between charities and fund-raising consultants and solicitors, stepped into commercial co-ventures, and even injected themselves into matters such as the sale of tickets for charitable events and solicitations by fire and police personnel.

The regulatory appetite still remained unsatisfied. Having accomplished the imposition of just about all of the "law" they could think of, they turned to principles of "ethics." Now, for example, in one state, charities that solicit charitable gifts and their professional fund-raisers and solicitors are "fiduciaries." This is a role historically confined to trustees of charitable trusts and more recently to directors of charitable corporations.

(c) THE POLICE POWER Prior to a fuller analysis of state law regulation in this field, it is necessary to briefly reference the underlying legal basis for this body of law: the so-called "police power."

Each state (and local unit of government) inherently possesses the "police power." This power enables a state or other political subdivision of government to regulate— within the bounds of constitutional law principles (see below)—the conduct of its citizens and others, so as to protect the safety, health, and welfare of its people.

Generally, it is clear that a state can enact and enforce, in the exercise of its police power, a charitable solicitation act that requires a charity planning on fund-raising in the jurisdiction to first register with (or secure a license or permit from) the appropriate regulatory authorities and subsequently to render periodic reports about the results of the solicitation. There is nothing inherently unlawful about this type of law. It may also require professional fund-raisers and professional solicitors to register and report, or empower the regulatory authorities to investigate the activities of charitable organizations in the presence of reasonable cause to do so, and impose injunctive remedies, fines, and imprisonment for violation of the statute. It appears clear that a state can regulate charitable fund-raising notwithstanding the fact that the solicitation utilizes the federal postal system, uses television and radio broadcasts, or otherwise occurs in interstate commerce.

The rationale is that charitable solicitations may be reasonably regulated to protect the public from deceit, fraud, or the unscrupulous obtaining of money under a pretense that the money is being collected and expended for a charitable purpose.

However, despite the inherent police power lodged in the states (and local jurisdictions) to regulate the charitable solicitation process, and the general scope of the power, principles of law operate to confine its reach. Most of these principles are based on constitutional law precepts, such as freedom of speech, procedural and substantive due process, and equal protection of the laws, as well as the standards usually imposed by statutory law, which bars the exercise of the police power in a manner that is arbitrary.

(d) SOME DEFINITIONS State law regulation of fund-raising of this nature pertains to fund-raising for "charitable" purposes. However, the use of the term "charitable" in this setting refers to a range of activities and organizations that are much broader than those embraced by the term as used in the federal tax context (see Chapter 34). That is, while the term includes organizations that are charitable, educational, scientific, and religious, as those terms are used for federal purposes, it also includes (absent specific exemption) organizations that are civic, social welfare, recreational, and fraternal. Indeed, the general definition is so encompassing as to cause some of these statutes to expressly exclude fund-raising by political action committees, labor organizations, and trade organizations.

Some of this regulation is applicable to a "professional fund-raiser" (or similar term). The majority of the states define a professional fund-raiser as one who, for a fixed fee under a written agreement, plans, conducts, advises, or acts as a consultant, whether directly or indirectly, in connection with soliciting contributions for, or on behalf of, a charitable organization. This definition usually excludes those who actually solicit contributions. Other terms used throughout the states include "professional fund-raising counsel," "professional fund-raiser consultant," and "independent fund-raiser."

Much of this regulation is applicable to those who are "professional solicitors." Most of the states that use this term define this type of person as one who, for compensation, solicits contributions for or on behalf of a charitable organization, whether directly or through others, or a person involved in the fund-raising process who does not qualify as a professional fund-raiser. A minority of states define the term as a person who is employed or retained for compensation by a professional fund-raiser to solicit contributions for charitable purposes.

There is considerable confusion in the law as to the appropriate line of demarcation between these two terms. Because the extent of regulation can be far more intense for a professional solicitor, it is often very important for an individual or company to be classified as a professional fund-raiser rather than a professional solicitor.

Some states impose disclosure requirements with respect to the process known as "commercial co-venturing." This process occurs when a business announces to the general public that a portion (a specific amount or a specific percentage) of the purchase price of a product or service will, during a stated period, be paid to a charitable organization. This activity results in a payment by the business to a charitable organization, the amount of which is dependent on consumer response to the promotion by, and positive publicity for, the business sponsor (Exhibit 35.1.).

(e) REGISTRATION REQUIREMENTS A cornerstone of each state's charitable solicitation law is the requirement that a charitable organization (as defined in that law and not exempt from the obligation (see below)) that intends to solicit—by any means—contributions from persons in that state must first apply for and acquire permission to undertake the solicitation. This permission is usually characterized as a "registration"; some states denominate it as a "license" or a "permit." If successful, the result is authorization to conduct the solicitation. These permits are usually valid for one year.

These state laws apply to fund-raising within the borders of each state involved. Thus, a charitable or like organization soliciting in more than one state must register under

Exhibit 35.1. Checklist.

Does organization consider itself a "charitable" organization?	Yes _____	No _____
Does organization solicit contributions?	Yes _____	No _____
Does organization utilize services of a professional fund-raiser?	Yes _____	No _____
Does organization utilize services of a professional solicitor?	Yes _____	No _____
Does organization participate in one or more commercial co-ventures?	Yes _____	No _____

(and otherwise comply with) not only the law of the state in which it is located but also the law of each of the states in which it will be fund-raising. Moreover, many counties, townships, cities, and similar jurisdictions throughout the United States have ordinances that attempt to regulate charitable fund-raising within their borders.

As noted below, most states' charitable solicitation acts require a soliciting charity (unless exempt) to annually file information with the appropriate governmental agency. This is done either by an annual updating of the registration or the like, or by the filing of a separate annual report.

In many states, professional fund-raisers and professional solicitors are required to register with the state (Exhibit 35.2.).

(f) REPORTING REQUIREMENTS   Nearly all of the state charitable solicitation acts mandate annual reporting to the state by registered charitable organizations, professional fund-raisers, and professional solicitors. This form of reporting can be extensive and may entail the provision of information concerning gifts received, funds expended for program and fund-raising, payments to service providers, and a battery of other information.

These reports are made on forms provided by the states. These forms, and the rules and instructions that accompany them, vary considerably in content. Underlying definitions and accounting principles can differ. There is no uniformity with respect to due dates for these reports.

In many states, professional fund-raisers and professional solicitors are required to file annual reports with the state (Exhibit 35.3.).

Exhibit 35.2.   Checklist.

If organization solicits contributions, is it registered under the laws of the state in which it is headquartered?	Yes _____ No _____
If yes, date registration expires	_____
Does organization solicit contributions in one or more states other than the one in which it is headquartered?	Yes _____ No _____
If yes, is it registered under the laws of each of these states?	Yes _____ No _____
If yes, identify these states (attach sheet of paper for these and other questions if necessary)	_____
Date(s) registration(s) expire	_____
Counties, cities, etc. where registered	_____
Date(s) registration(s) expire	_____
Is organization in compliance with reporting requirements of one or more applicable states?	Yes _____ No _____

Exhibit 35.3   Checklist.

State(s) in which organization files annual report(s)	_____
Date(s) report(s) due	_____
Counties, cities, etc., where report(s) are due	_____
Date(s) report(s) due	_____

(g) EXEMPTIONS FROM REGULATIONS   Many of the states exempt one or more categories of charitable organization from the ambit of their charitable solicitation statute. The basic rationale for these exemptions is that the exempted organizations are not part of the objective—the protection of its citizens from fund-raising fraud and other abuse— the state is endeavoring to achieve through this type of regulation. (Other rationales are the constitutional law limitations involved in the case of churches and the ability of one or more categories of organization to persuade the legislature to exempt them.)

The most common exemption in this context is for churches and their closely related entities. These entities include conventions of churches and associations of churches. Some states broadly exempt religious organizations. These exemptions are rooted in constitutional law principles, barring government from regulating religious practices and beliefs. Some states have run into successful constitutional law challenges when they have attempted to narrowly define the concept of "religion" for this purpose.

Some states exempt at least certain types of educational institutions from the entirety of their charitable solicitation acts. Usually, this exemption applies where the educational institution is accredited. The more common practice is to exempt educational institutions from only the registration or licensing, and reporting, requirements.

Some states, either as an alternative or in addition to the foregoing approach, exempt from the registration and reporting requirements educational institutions that confine their solicitations to their "constituency." That is, this type of exemption extends to the solicitation of contributions by an educational institution to its student body, alumni, faculty, and trustees, and their families. A few states exempt solicitations by educational institutions of their constituency from the entirety of their charitable solicitation laws.

Many educational institutions undertake some or all of their fund-raising by means of related "foundations." Some states expressly provide exemption, in tandem with whatever exemption their laws extend to educational institutions, to these supporting foundations. A few states exempt, from the registration requirements, alumni associations.

The rationale for exempting educational institutions from coverage under these laws is the general rationale articulated above. These institutions do not solicit the general public, there have not been any instances of abuses by these institutions of the fund-raising process, these institutions already adequately report to state agencies, and the inclusion of these institutions under the charitable solicitation statute would impose an unnecessary burden on the regulatory process.

Some states exempt hospitals (and, in some instances, their related foundations) and other categories of health-care entities. Again, the exemption can be from the entirety of the statute or from its registration and reporting requirements. Other exemptions for organizations embrace veterans' organizations, police and firefighters' organizations, fraternal organizations, and, in a few states, organizations identified by name. Exemptions are also often available for membership organizations, "small" solicitations (ranging from $1,000 to $10,000), and solicitations for specified individuals.

Some of these exemptions are available as a matter of law. Others must be applied for, sometimes on an annual basis. Some exemptions are not available or are lost if the organization utilizes the services of a professional fund-raiser or professional solicitor (Exhibit 35.4.).

(h) FUND-RAISING COST LIMITATIONS   Once, the chief weapon for state regulators in this regard was laws that prohibited charitable organizations with "high" fund-raising costs from soliciting in the states. Allegedly "high" fund-raising expenses were defined in terms of percentages of gifts received. These laws proliferated, with percentage limitations extended to the compensation of professional fund-raising consultants and professional solicitors. The issue found its way to the U.S. Supreme Court, where all of these percentage limitations were struck down as violating the charities' free speech rights. This application of the First and Fourteenth Amendments to the U.S. Constitution stands as the single most important bar to more stringent government regulation of the process of soliciting charitable contributions.

As noted, the states possess the "police power" to regulate the process of soliciting contributions for charitable purposes. However, the states cannot exercise this power in a manner that unduly intrudes on the rights of free speech of the soliciting charitable organizations and their fund-raising consultants and solicitors.

First, the Supreme Court held that a state cannot use the level of a charitable organization's fund-raising costs as a basis for determining whether a charity may lawfully solicit funds in a jurisdiction. Four years later, the Court held that the free speech principles apply, even though the state offers a charitable organization an opportunity to show that its fund-raising costs are "reasonable," despite the presumption that costs in excess of a specific ceiling are "excessive." Another four years later, the Court held that these free speech principles applied when the limitation was not on a charity's fund-raising costs but on the amount or extent of fees paid by a charitable organization to professional fund-raisers or professional solicitors. Subsequent litigation suggests that the courts are consistently reinforcing the legal principles so articulately promulgated by the Supreme Court during the 1980s (Exhibit 35.5).

(i) PROHIBITED ACTS   Most of the state's charitable solicitation acts contain a list of one or more acts in which a charitable organization (and perhaps a professional fund-

---

Exhibit 35.4. Checklist.

Is organization exempt from fund-raising regulation laws of any state?	Yes _____ No _____
If yes, identify state(s) where exemption is total.	_____
If yes, identify state(s) where exemption is partial.	_____
Identify state(s) where exemption must be applied for.	_____
As to each of these states, identify date this application is due.	_____
Date(s) state exemption determination(s) expire.	_____

Exhibit 35.5. Checklist.

Is organization restricted from fund-raising in any jurisdiction because of level of its fund-raising expenses?	Yes _____	No _____
If yes, organization should advise government agency that the rule is unconstitutional and refuse to comply with it; jurisdiction(s) where this type of dispute is continuing		_____

raiser and/or professional solicitor) may not lawfully engage. These acts may be some or all of the following:

- A person may not, for the purpose of soliciting contributions, use the name of another person (except that of an officer, director, or trustee of the charitable organization by or for which contributions are solicited) without the consent of the other person. This prohibition usually extends to the use of an individual's name on stationery or in an advertisement or brochure, or as one who has contributed to, sponsored, or endorsed the organization.

- A person may not, for the purpose of soliciting contributions, use a name, symbol, or statement so closely related or similar to that used by another charitable organization or governmental agency that it would tend to confuse or mislead the public.

- A person may not use or exploit the fact of registration with the state so as to lead the public to believe that the registration in any manner constitutes an endorsement or approval by the state.

- A person may not represent to or mislead anyone, by any manner, means, practice, or device, to believe that the organization on behalf of which the solicitation is being conducted is a charitable organization or that the proceeds of the solicitation will be used for charitable purposes, when that is not the case.

- A person may not represent that the solicitation for charitable gifts is for or no behalf of a charitable organization or otherwise induce contributions from the public without proper authorization from the charitable organization.

In one state, it is a prohibited act to represent that a charitable organization will receive a fixed or estimated percentage of the gross revenue from a solicitation in an amount greater than that identified to the donor. In another state, it is a prohibited act for an individual to solicit charitable contributions if the individual has been convicted of a crime involving the obtaining of money or property by false pretenses, unless the public is informed of the conviction in advance of the solicitation.

In still another state, the following are prohibited acts for a charitable organization (or, in some instances, a person acting on its behalf):

- Misrepresent the purpose of a solicitation;
- Misrepresent the purpose or nature of a charitable organization;
- Engage in a financial transaction that is not related to the accomplishment of the charitable organization's exempt purpose;
- Jeopardize or interfere with the ability of a charitable organization to accomplish its charitable purpose;
- Expend an "unreasonable amount of money" for fund-raising or for management.

Some states make violation of a separate law concerning "unfair or deceptive acts and practices" a violation of the charitable solicitation act as well. Identify acts that an organization is prohibited from engaging in for each state.

(j) CONTRACTUAL REQUIREMENTS Many of the state charitable solicitation acts require that the relationship between a charitable organization and a professional fund-raiser, and/or between a charitable organization and a professional solicitor, be evidenced in a written agreement. This agreement is required to be filed with the state soon after the contract is executed. These types of requirements are clearly "law" and are not particularly unusual.

However, a few states have enacted requirements—some of them rather patronizing—that dictate to the charitable organization the contents of the contract. For example, under one state's law, a contract between a charitable organization and a fund-raising counsel must contain sufficient information "as will enable the department to identify the services the fund-raising counsel is to provide and the manner of his compensation." Another provision of the same law mandates that the agreement "clearly state the respective obligations of the parties."

The law in another state requires a contract between a charitable organization and a fund-raising counsel to contain provisions addressing the services to be provided, the number of persons to be involved in providing the services, the time period over which the services are to be provided, and the method and formula for compensation for the services.

Under another state's law, whenever a charitable organization contracts with a professional fund-raiser or other type of fund-raising consultant, the charitable organization has the right to cancel the contract, without cost or penalty, for a period of 15 days. Again, this type of law seems predicated on the assumption that charitable organizations are somehow not quite capable of developing their own contracts and tend to do so impetuously.

It can be argued that these laws are forms of overreaching, in terms of scope and detail, on the part of government, and that charitable organizations ought to be mature enough to formulate their own contracts (Exhibit 35.6.).

(k) DISCLOSURE REQUIREMENTS Many of the states that were forced to abandon or forgo the use of the percentage mechanism as a basis for preventing fund-raising for charity (see above) utilize the percentage approach in a disclosure setting. Several states, for example, require charitable organizations to make an annual reporting, either to update a registration or as part of a separate report, to the authorities as to their fund-raising activities in the prior year, including a statement of their fund-raising

Exhibit 35.6. Checklist.

Does organization have a contract with one or more professional fund-raisers?	Yes _____	No _____
Does organization have a contract with one or more professional solicitors?	Yes _____	No _____
Identify state(s) where these contracts must be filed.	_____	
Identify state(s) that have laws dictating contents of these contracts.	_____	
Is organization in compliance with these laws?	Yes _____	No _____

expenses. Some states require a disclosure of a charity's fund-raising costs, stated as a percentage, to donors at the time of the solicitation—although this requirement is of dubious constitutionality. In a few states, solicitation literature used by a charitable organization must include a statement that, upon request, financial and other information about the soliciting charity may be obtained directly from the state.

Some states require a statement as to any percentage compensation in the contract between the charitable organization and the professional fund-raiser and/or the professional solicitor. A few states require the compensation of a paid solicitor to be stated in the contract as a percentage of gross revenue; another state has a similar provision with respect to a professional fund-raiser. One state wants a charitable organization's fund-raising cost percentage to be stated in its registration statement.

An example of this type of law is a statute that imposed on the individual who raises funds for a charitable organization the responsibility to "deal with" the contributions in an "appropriate fiduciary manner." Thus, an individual in these circumstances owes a fiduciary duty to the public. These persons are subject to a surcharge for any funds wasted or not accounted for. A presumption exists in this law that funds not adequately documented and disclosed by records were not properly spent.

By direction of this law, all solicitations must "fully and accurately" identify the purposes of the charitable organization to prospective donors. Use of funds, to an extent of more than 50 percent, for "public education" must be disclosed under this law. Every contract with a professional fund-raiser must be approved by the charitable organization's governing board. Some of the provisions of this law probably are unconstitutional, such as the requirement that professional fund-raisers or solicitors must disclose to those being solicited the percentage of their compensation in relation to gifts received.

Another example is some of the provisions of another state's law, which makes an "unlawful practice" the failure of a person soliciting funds to "truthfully" recite, upon request, the percentage of funds raised to be paid to the solicitor. This state, like many other states, is using the concept of "prohibited acts" (see above) to impose a sort of "code of ethics" on all who seek to raise funds for charity.

Under one state's law, any person who solicits contributions for a charitable purpose and who receives compensation for the service must inform each person being solicited, in writing, that the solicitation is a "paid solicitation." In another state, where a solicitation is made by "direct personal contact," certain information must be "predominantly" disclosed in writing at the point of solicitation. In another state, the solicitation material and the "general promotional plan" for a solicitation may not be false, misleading, or deceptive, and must afford a "full and fair" disclosure (Exhibit 35.7.).

Exhibit 35.7. Checklist.

Identify state(s) that impose disclosure requirements on organization, in connection with the following types of solicitations:	
Written materials	_____
Telephone scripts	_____
Television and/or radio statements	_____
Other	_____
Is organization in compliance with these laws?	Yes _____ No _____

35.2 FEDERAL LAW REGULATION

Despite the absence of a specific statute on the point, fund-raising regulation at the federal level is immense. Nearly all of this form of regulation is administered by the Internal Revenue Service.

The IRS regulates the practice of fund-raising for charitable purposes in the following ways:

- It is engaged in a program of education and examination of charitable organizations that engage in fund-raising, to encourage them to disclose the portions of payments that are not considered "charitable gifts";
- It applies the unrelated business income rules in a variety of ways, to cause certain "fund-raising" practices to be characterized as unrelated businesses;
- It requires a charitable organization to summarize its fund-raising program at the time it applies for recognition of tax-exempt status;
- It requires an organization to report the receipts of its fund-raising activities, and to report its fund-raising expenses, on an annual basis;
- It applies the rules concerning private inurement in such a fashion as to discourage fund-raising compensation arrangements that are based on percentages or otherwise involve commissions;
- It applies the rules embodying limitations on lobbying by, and calculation of the public support of, public charities in a way that defines and encourages certain forms of fund-raising;
- It "regulates" the fund-raising process by its interpretations and enforcement of the rules involving deductible charitable contributions.

A brief summary of some of these forms of federal regulation of fund-raising for charitable purposes follows.

(a) DISCLOSURE REQUIREMENTS   It is the perception of the IRS that some charitable organizations are misleading persons, sometimes deliberately, into believing that a payment to a charitable organization is a deductible gift when in fact the transaction does not involve a gift at all or is only partially a gift. It is a matter that has concerned the IRS since 1967, when it issued guidelines directing charities to advise "donors" of circumstances where their "gifts" are not deductible at all (where the payors receive something from the charity of approximately equal value for the payment) or are only partially deductible (where the donor received something in return for the gift of a value that is less than the amount of the gift). The 1967 guidelines describe these rules in some detail and provide examples as to how the rules apply in common situations. These situations include theater parties, sports tournaments, and similar special events. In 1988, a congressional committee expressed dismay over continuation of, if not increase in, these practices and demanded that the IRS act to resolve the problem. Later in the year, the Commissioner of Internal Revenue sent a special message on this subject to the nation's charities.

This matter concerns a variety of practices. Some are relatively obvious and easy to resolve, such as tuition payments to schools and patient payments to hospitals. Although these are payments to "charitable" organizations, they are purchases of services and are not "gifts." Other payments to charitable organizations that are not gifts are payments for winning bids at auctions and purchases of tickets for games of chance (such as raffles and lotteries).

Other practices that entail partial gifts are special event programs, where the patron receives something of value (such as a ticket to a theater performance or a dinner, or the opportunity to play in a sports tournament), yet makes a payment in excess of that value amount. In these circumstances, the amount paid that is in excess of the value received is a deductible charitable gift.

Thus, for example, the IRS ruled that contributions to athletic scholarship programs are not deductible as charitable gifts where the donors are provided the preferential opportunity to purchase tickets to athletic events hosted by the educational institution providing the scholarships. (However, this ruling was largely overruled by Congress, when it wrote a tax law providing that 80 percent of the value of this type of "gift" is deductible as a charitable contribution.)

The IRS also held that payments by corporate sponsors of college and university bowl games are not charitable gifts to the bowl game associations but must be treated by the association as forms of unrelated business income because the corporate sponsors received a valuable package of advertising services. This, in turn, led to the issuance of more general donor recognition guidelines, to enable charitable organizations to distinguish between instances of "mere recognition" and situations where payors are provided a substantial return benefit.

In the view of the IRS, a charitable organization has the obligation to inform the payor of the extent (if any) to which a portion of the payment is not deductible (Exhibit 35.8.).

(b) THE CSCI STUDY The IRS is of the belief that many charitable organizations are not adequately complying with these disclosure rules. This view has led the IRS to further explore these types of fund-raising, and many others. These explorations have led the IRS to conclude that charitable organizations are engaging in "questionable" fund-raising practices, with some solicitations "appear[ing] to" mislead donors about the deductibility of their donations.

The IRS launched an attack on these forms of fund-raising misperformance by inaugurating a "Special Emphasis Program." This program entails a "Charitable Solicitations Compliance Improvement [CSCI] Study." The program has two phases. One, which ended September 30, 1990, was an educational phase, where the IRS endeavored to disseminate information about the law in this regard to the nation's public charities. This was accomplished by means of speeches, review of the practices of a variety of

Exhibit 35.8. Checklist.

Does organization solicit payments that are partially deductible gifts?	Yes ____	No ____
Does organization solicit payments, none of which is a deductible gift?	Yes ____	No ____
If either answer is yes, does organization so notify the payors?	Yes ____	No ____
Is organization in compliance with IRS donor recognition guidelines (if applicable)?	Yes ____ No ____	NA ____

charitable organizations, and the establishment of a special telephone number at which individuals could reach the IRS for advice and interpretations on the subject.

The intent of Phase I of the CSCI Study was to determine the "extent to which charities furnished accurate and sufficient information to their donors concerning the deductibility of their contributions." The IRS is assessing the nature of the "voluntary compliance level." It is also attempting to learn the amount of the "revenue loss from erroneous charitable deductions."

The IRS says that there is a presumption that the total amount paid by the "donor" in these circumstances represents the fair market value of substantial benefits received in return. Thus, the presumption is that there is no charitable contribution deduction in this setting.

The second phase of the program is the examination phase. Agents of the IRS are examining the fund-raising practices of public charities, using an 82-question checksheet. (This checksheet is titled "Exempt Organizations Charitable Solicitations Compliance Improvement Program Checksheet" (IRS Form 9215).) The IRS is intent in ferreting out instances of what it terms "abusive" fund-raising. The National Office of the IRS has sent to its examining agents across the country instructions and guidance as to the CSCI Study. The IRS has told these agents that "[t]here is evidence to suggest that taxpayers, in the absence of clear disclosure of the deductible amount by the charities, claim a deduction for their donation in excess of the amount permitted by law." Indeed, it is the fundamental assertion of the IRS that the "charities have an obligation to both know the rules and to properly inform donors about the deductibility of their donations."

In using the term "abusive" fund-raising, the IRS includes the following:

- [M]isleading statements in solicitations literature that imply deductibility of contributions, where none probably exists; . . .
- [C]ontracts with professional for-profit fundraisers, who themselves use questionable fund-raising methods to solicit funds from the general public; . . .
- [S]ituations where other expenses, such as administrative and fundraising costs [,] constitute an unusually high portion of the solicited funds or noncash contributions; . . .
- [F]und raising activities that result in other tax consequences, i.e., generating taxable income, resulting in additional filing requirements, etc.

The above-noted checksheet explores all forms of fund-raising: annual solicitations; membership drives; awards ceremonies; bingo and other forms of gambling; charity balls; sporting events; raffles, lotteries, and sweepstakes; luncheons, dinners, and banquets; and cultural exhibitions.

The checksheet searches for information about property gifts, use of professional fund-raisers, use of games of chance, travel tours, thrift stores and like activities, provision of goods or services in exchange for "gifts", and noncash contributions. It suggests a battery of penalties that might be assessed against a charity for failure to comply with these rules, including the promotion of abusive tax shelters, aiding and abetting understatements of tax liability, and failure to file certain returns.

The IRS Exempt Organizations Division is referring returns of donors for examination where the records of the charity indicate that the individual taxpayer made a donation meeting certain (unstated) dollar threshold criteria and that he or she received goods, services, or benefits in exchange for the donation.

The IRS National Office has cautioned its agents that the "scope and depth of the examination should be sufficient to fully disclose the nature of abusive situations involving fundraising activities that mislead donors to claim the incorrect charitable contribution deduction; misrepresent the use of the solicited funds; engage in questionable fundraising practices or techniques, etc." The instructions state that "[w]orkpapers and responses to checksheet items must fully describe these abuses and provide copies of supporting evidence of the abuse."

The results of the CSCI Study will be used to accumulate case-oriented statistical data and other data on the fund-raising methods and practices conducted by charitable organizations. This information will be provided to the Department of the Treasury and Congress for their consideration for legislative action.

Because of this end-use of the Study results, the IRS guidance states that it is "essential that the examinations be thorough." The examiner is importuned to "pursue the examination to the point where he/she can conclude that all areas and data concerning fundraising activities have been considered." It is possible that the outcome will be legislation mandating certain disclosures to prospective donors, along the lines of existing legislation requiring this type of disclosure by tax-exempt, noncharitable organizations.

In the meantime, the IRS has conceded that it cannot impose any sanctions for violation of these disclosure rules. Thus, these rules are less "law" and more in the nature of "cajoling." The IRS has advised its examining agents that "the charities have an *obligation* to both know the rules and to properly inform donors about the deductibility of their donations."

This, then, is a form of fund-raising regulation that, as a function of current statutory law, is murky at best. The IRS is hoping that its activities under the Special Emphasis Program will spur charitable organizations into "voluntary" compliance—to, in effect, act on their own without benefit of statutory legal sanctions. If this approach fails to satisfy the IRS, it can be assumed that the agency will encourage Congress to write these rules into law (Exhibit 35.9.).

(c) THE UNRELATED INCOME RULES   The IRS is applying the unrelated income rules as a means of regulating the process of raising funds for charitable purposes. These rules are discussed in greater detail in Chapter 33, but a brief review of these rules is warranted.

For an activity to be taxed as an "unrelated trade or business," the general rule is that it must have these characteristics:

- It must be a "business," that is, be an activity that is carried on to produce revenue;
- The business must be "regularly carried on"; and
- The activity must not be substantially related to the achievement of tax-exempt purposes.

Many fund-raising activities are "businesses" in this sense. This is particularly true with respect to special-event fund-raising. Nearly all fund-raising activities are

Exhibit 35.9.   Checklist.

Was organization contacted by the IRS during Phase I?	Yes _____	No _____
Was organization contacted by the IRS during Phase II?	Yes _____	No _____
Identify outcome(s) of either contact.		_____

not inherently charitable or other tax-exempt undertakings. Thus, when a church sponsors a bingo game to generate funds for its programs, the bingo game is a business and it is not a religious activity. (An activity is not a related one solely because the net monies from it are applied to exempt purposes.)

Many fund-raising activities escape treatment as taxable businesses on the ground that they are not regularly carried on. Thus, an annual charity ball, golf tournament, auction, car wash, bake sale, and the like are not taxable events because they are infrequently carried on and thus are not competitive with for-profit operations.

There are some exceptions to unrelated income taxation (discussed in Chapter 33) that also help protect various fund-raising activities from tax. These include:

- Businesses in which substantially all of the work is performed by volunteers;
- Businesses carried on primarily for the convenience of the organization's members, students, patients, officers, or employees;
- Businesses that consist of the sale of merchandise, substantially all of which has been received by the organization as gifts;
- Certain bingo games;
- Certain fairs and expositions;
- Certain practices involving mailing lists rented to and exchanged with charitable organizations;
- The offering of certain low-cost premiums as inducements to charitable giving.

Nonetheless, a variety of fund-raising techniques and practices have been subject to litigation as to whether they are taxable business. Recent issues include the extent to which a revenue-producing activity can be structured so that the revenue to the tax-exempt organization can be regarded as a nontaxable royalty; whether the distribution of greeting cards is a sale of the cards to the public or a use of premiums to stimulate charitable giving; and the provision of group insurance policy coverage.

Current popular fund-raising techniques that are beginning to raise questions about application of the unrelated business rules are forms of "commercial co-venturing" and "cause-related marketing." The former involves situations in which a charitable organization consents to be a donee under circumstances where a commercial business agrees to make a payment to the organization, with that agreement advertised, of an amount predicated on the extent of products sold or services provided by the business to the public during a particular time period. Cause-related marketing involves the public marketing of products or services by or on behalf of a tax-exempt organization, or some similar use of an organization's resources.

A manifestation of cause-related marketing can be seen in the participation by exempt organizations in affinity card programs, in which an exempt organization is paid a portion of the revenues derived from the use of the cards by consumers who make up the affinity group. The position of the IRS is that the revenues from affinity card programs are taxable because they arise from the exploitation of mailing lists, and that the special exception for these lists (see above) is not available because the lists are provided to noncharitable organizations (Exhibit 35.10.).

(d) EXEMPTION APPLICATION PROCESS   A charitable or like organization generally must secure recognition of its tax-exempt status from the IRS. This application process requires the organization to reveal some information about its fund-raising program.

Exhibit 35.10. Checklist.

Does organization treat one or more fund-raising activities as unrelated businesses?	Yes _____ No _____
If yes, identify these activities	_____

In this application, the organization must describe its actual and planned fund-raising program. In this context, the applicant organization must summarize its actual use of, or plans to use (if any), selective mailings, fund-raising committees, professional fund-raisers, and the like. The organization must identify, in order of size, its sources of financial support.

The application for recognition of tax exemption, if properly completed, amounts to a rather complete portrait of the programs, fund-raising plans, and other aspects of the applicant organization. It is a public document and thus, during the course of its existence, the organization probably will be called on to supply copies of the application. Because those who inspect the document are likely to be prospective donors or grantors, it is particularly important that it be properly prepared.

(e) REPORTING REQUIREMENTS As discussed in Chapter 34, nearly every tax-exempt organization must file an annual information return with the IRS. This is usually a Form 990. This return solicits considerable information about an organization's fund-raising efforts.

A principal component of the Form 990, which consists of an extensive reporting of income-producing activities. The information sought is designed to provide Congress with data needed to assess the impact of current or future unrelated business income rules and to enable the IRS to better administer the present unrelated income laws.

On this form, a tax-exempt organization must identify each income-producing activity. These activities include various forms of program service revenue, membership dues and assessments, investment income, sales of assets, and special fund-raising events. The revenue from each reported activity must be categorized as unrelated business income, exempt function (related) income, or income excluded from taxation by a particular provision of the Internal Revenue Code. The IRS has devised a system of codes to use in classifying unrelated (taxable) business income and income excludable from taxation because of a particular Code section. When an exempt organization classifies an item of income as related, it must explain how the associated activity contributed importantly to the accomplishment of exempt purposes.

An organization is required to report all amounts received as contributions or grants. An organization must attach a schedule listing contributors during the year who gave the organization, directly or indirectly, money or property worth at least $5,000. Separate reporting is required for program service revenue, membership dues and assessments, investment income, asset sales, revenue from special fund-raising events, and other revenue.

Although revenue from special fund-raising activities generally is (as noted) separately reported, when the payment is part a purchase for the event or activity and part a contribution, the gift portion is reported separately from the purchase portion. Direct expenses associated with special fund-raising events are subtracted on the face of the return. A schedule must be attached to the return listing the three largest (in terms of gross receipts) special events conducted by the organization.

Exhibit 35.11.   Checklist.

Does organization pay a fund-raising professional on a percentage basis?	Yes _____ No _____
If yes, identify the arrangement	_____

Revenue, for these purposes, does not include the value of services donated to an organization or the free use of materials, equipment, or facilities. However, these items may be reported elsewhere on the return.

In general, expenses must be totaled, and also allocated to three categories: program, management, and fund-raising. This is known as the "functional method of accounting." Proper compliance with the requirements of the functional method of accounting obligates organizations to maintain detailed records as to their fund-raising and other expenses, because the fund-raising component of each line-item expenditure must be separately identified and reported.

(f) FUND-RAISING COMPENSATION ARRANGEMENTS   Charitable and like organizations must be operated so that they do not cause any inurement of their net earnings to certain individuals in their private capacity or otherwise cause private benefit (see Chapter 34). The private inurement and private benefit doctrines can be triggered when a charitable organization pays excessive or otherwise unreasonable compensation for services. Therefore, a charitable organization may not, without endangering its tax-exempt status, pay a fund-raising professional an amount that is excessive or unreasonable.

Questions about the propriety of compensation of a fund-raising professional may not have as much to do with the amount being paid as the manner in which it is determined. This is particularly true with respect to compensation that is ascertained on the basis of a commission or percentage. However, although the IRS is rather suspicious of fund-raising compensation that is based on percentages of contributions received, the courts have been rather tolerant of the practice (Exhibit 35.11.).

35.3   CONCLUSION

The giving public is deserving of protection against fraud and other abuse in charitable giving. But, the process of raising money for charitable purposes in the United States is becoming heavily weighed down with a swirl of inconsistent and unnecessary procedures and other burdens, as the state regulators endeavor to outdo each other in the development of "tougher" laws.

For a nation that has a tradition of a healthy and productive nonprofit sector, this slow but steady imposition of additional burdens on the good works of nonprofit organizations is becoming a drain on charitable resources. One of the challenges for the nonprofit community in the years ahead will be to minimize these burdens while simultaneously protecting the charitable giving public.

SOURCES AND SUGGESTED REFERENCES

Hopkins, Bruce R. 1991. *The Law of Fund-Raising.* New York: John Wiley & Sons.

Legal Issues in the Involvement of Volunteers

Jeffrey D. Kahn
Schnader, Harrison, Segal & Lewis

CONTENTS

36.1 INTRODUCTION

(a) SCOPE OF THE CHAPTER What is the liability of a meals-on-wheels program for a car accident caused by one of its volunteers? Are injuries to volunteer naturalists covered by a nature center's insurance policy? Can volunteers bring lawsuits alleging discriminatory "hiring"? Can a hospital be held liable for not paying a minimum wage to volunteers who work in the gift shop? These are some of the questions that are addressed in this chapter.

Volunteers are part of an organization's staff, and their presence, like that of salaried employees, raises legal questions. Both volunteers and employees work diligently on the organization's behalf, and both may accidentally cause injury to some third party in the course of their work, or may be injured themselves. Although volunteers are not paid, their relationship with an organization bears many of the characteristics of an employment relationship: volunteers apply for positions, agree to perform certain work, may be given increased responsibilities if they perform well, and may be terminated if the organization is dissatisfied with their performance. Volunteers, like employees, represent the organization to the public, and may enter into agreements on behalf of the organization. Volunteers may even enter into service agreements with the organization, akin to employment agreements. Legal questions may arise in connection with all of these aspects of volunteering.

This chapter outlines some of the ways in which tort liability, contract, and employment laws apply to volunteers. This material is not intended to provide specific legal advice, because relevant laws vary from state to state, change over time, and may apply differently to the situations of different organizations. Organization leaders should consult with legal counsel for guidance as to how the laws apply to their volunteer programs. To facilitate that discussion, this chapter contains a series of checklists to help organization leaders focus their thoughts and questions with regard to these legal issues. The chapter also contains legal summaries following discussions of important legal points.

(b) WHY NOT LEAVE LEGAL QUESTIONS TO THE LAWYERS? Even though lawyers are the best source of information on how to protect an organization from legal exposure, there are several reasons why it is also important for leaders of organizations to understand the basic legal issues relating to volunteers.

First, an organization's leaders have the ultimate power to take steps to help the organization avoid potential liabilities. Any discussion of legal issues relating to volunteers conjures up images of accidents, expensive lawsuits, bad publicity, and attorneys' fees. Nonprofit organization leaders who are informed about possible grounds for lawsuits against an organization can work to minimize the likelihood of such legal actions. Organization leaders need to know when to consult an attorney, what questions to ask, and the importance of resolving open legal issues regarding the use of volunteers.

The second reason for nonprofit organization leaders to understand the legal issues relating to volunteers is that the process of considering these issues may have beneficial effects on the overall operation of the volunteer program. For example, implementing a risk management program to reduce the chances of injuries by volunteers to third parties may result in better trained and supervised volunteers who are not only less likely to cause accidents, but are also better equipped to carry out their duties effectively. An expansion of volunteers' roles is often opposed on the vague grounds of "liability," without anyone fully probing what that means. Many people believe that volunteers are inherently riskier than salaried workers, less reliable, and harder to control.

An advocate for maximum volunteer participation can combat these myths when armed with the facts about liability and an understanding of the value of risk management. If an organization conducts an examination of its volunteers' status as "employees," and then shares that information with its volunteers, the organization has the opportunity to communicate respect for the volunteers as well as legal information.

36.2 VOLUNTEERS AND TORT LIABILITY

(a) WHAT IS A "TORT"? An organization may be liable for injuries caused by its volunteers under the law of "torts." A "tort" occurs when one person violates a legal duty owed to another person and causes an injury to that other person. Most civil lawsuits (that is, lawsuits involving two private parties), except those alleging breach of contract, are tort actions. Common examples include actions for damages resulting from a car accident or a "slip and fall" on an icy sidewalk. In order to understand the possible tort liabilities relating to volunteers and how to avoid and carry proper insurance for those liabilities, it is necessary to understand the basic principles of tort law. Those principles are not complicated, and the following discussion includes only a single Latin phrase.

(b) COMMON LAW RULES The starting point for an analysis of tort liability rules as they apply to volunteers is the so-called "common law." The common law is the body of case law that has been developed through judicial decisions over the years. It is the law that applies unless there is a special statute overriding or changing it.

(i) Liability of individuals The basic common law liability rule applies to all people, including volunteers and employees: A person is liable for the damages caused by his or her negligent or intentional conduct. Each of the key words in that basic rule has a particular legal meaning. "Damages," under the law, must be measurable but may encompass harm beyond physical injury, such as economic loss, or pain and suffering. "Cause" has a complex legal meaning but essentially connotes the event that leads to the damages. "Negligence" is a deviation from the standard of care a reasonable person would exercise in the circumstances. Finally, "intentional" conduct is engaged in willfully or deliberately.

Consider the common law liabilities of the motorist in the following scenario. The driver is proceeding on a street in a residential neighborhood and fails to slow down when a ball rolls into the street. The young child running after the ball is injured in the ensuing accident. Under the common law, the driver is liable for the child's injuries if the child (or the adults acting on the child's behalf) can establish, first, that a reasonable person would have slowed down when the ball rolled into the street, and therefore that the driver was negligent; and second, that this negligence caused the child's injuries.

(ii) Liability of an employer What if, at the time of the accident, the driver was carrying out duties for his or her employer? The employee/driver's liability does not change; the basic common law rule still applies. In addition, the employer may *also* be vicariously liable under the common law doctrine of *"respondeat superior."* (There's the one

Latin phrase.) Under *respondeat superior,* the "master" (such as the employer) is vicariously liable for the acts of its servant (such as the employee) if the following requirements are met: (1) the master was benefiting from and had a right of control over the servant's activities; (2) the servant was acting within the scope of his or her employment, that is, he or she was carrying out assigned duties at the time of the accident; and (3) the servant acted negligently or intentionally.

If the driver in the above example was traveling from one business meeting to another and was doing so in the proper scope of his or her employment, then the employer would be liable for the full amount of the resulting damages. The child's family could maintain a cause of action against the driver or the employer, or (most likely) both. Injured parties often look to employers as "deep pockets" that will yield large amounts of damages. Note that the employer's liability does not depend on a finding of negligence or fault on the part of the employer.

(iii) Liability of an organization for acts of volunteers Suppose the driver described above was a volunteer and was traveling in the course of carrying out his or her volunteer duties. The same common law liability rules apply. The volunteer would be personally liable for the damages caused by his or her negligence. The organization for which the volunteer was working would also be fully liable for the damages caused by the volunteer's negligence, if the above criteria for vicarious liability are established.

In addition, the organization might be directly liable for its own negligence in operating the volunteer program, such as for the failure to properly screen or supervise volunteers. This liability would be in addition to the possible vicarious liability.

(iv) Injuries to volunteers There is one final situation to consider under common law: What happens if the volunteer suffers the injury? Absent any statutory restrictions, the basic common law liability rule would apply. The organization would be liable if the accident was caused by its negligent or intentional conduct, or that of one of its "servants." In some states, workers' compensation laws may provide the exclusive remedy for an injured volunteer, depending on how those laws define the "workers" they cover.

(c) VOLUNTEER PROTECTION STATUTES In recent years, about half of the states have enacted "volunteer protection statutes" that change the common law liability rules for acts of direct service volunteers. In addition, all of the states have enacted laws that give some protection to volunteers serving as officers and directors of certain categories of nonprofit organizations. Although these laws vary greatly in their terms, in general they make it more difficult to recover against a volunteer who caused an injury while performing volunteer work.

There are two primary variations among these statutes. First, the statutes use differing definitions of the "volunteers" to which they apply. Most of the statutes define "volunteer" as someone working without monetary compensation for a particular type of organization. Some statutes, for example, apply only to volunteers working for an organization exempt from federal income taxes; other statutes apply to the volunteers of more broadly defined "charitable organizations."

Second, the volunteer protection statutes vary in the degree of protection given to volunteers. The statutes change what an injured party must prove before recovering against a volunteer; there must be proof of something more than negligence. Some statutes require proof of willful or wanton conduct; others condition recovery on proof of gross negligence. The statutes may contain exceptions for volunteers driving automobiles or volunteers working for organizations that do not maintain adequate insurance. Despite these varying formulations, none of the volunteer protection statutes completely immunizes volunteers from liability. Nor do most of the statutes make any change in the possible liability of the organization.

Legal Summary

1. Basic common law rules

   a. A person is liable for the damages caused by his or her negligent or intentional conduct.

   b. An organization is liable (as "master") for the damages caused by the negligent or intentional conduct of one of its volunteers (as "servant"), if the organization was benefiting from and had a right to control the volunteer's activities, and the volunteer was acting in the scope of his or her volunteer assignment at the time of the injury.

   c. The organization may also be liable for injuries *to* one of its volunteers if such injuries are caused by the negligent or intentional conduct of one of its volunteers or employees.

2. Effect of state statutes

   a. State volunteer protection statutes may change the common law negligence standard for recovery from volunteers.

   b. Some statutes may also change the liability rules for an organization's liability for accidents caused by a volunteer.

   c. State workers' compensation rules may, depending on the "workers" to whom they apply, limit the volunteer's recovery of damages for an injury suffered while performing volunteer work. (See Exhibit 36.1.)

Exhibit 36.1. Checklist.

1. Has your state made any changes in the common law liability of volunteers? Has your state made any changes in the common law liability of nonprofit organizations for injuries caused by volunteers?

2. Under the current law in your state, what does an injured party have to prove to recover damages from a volunteer for an injury caused by the volunteer? What does an injured party have to prove to recover damages from an organization for an injury caused by a volunteer? Are there any limits on such liabilities?

3. Does your state's workers' compensation law apply to volunteers?

36.3 RISK MANAGEMENT

(a) IMPORTANCE OF RISK MANAGEMENT The bottom line is that, although these new volunteer protection statutes change the personal liability of volunteers in some states, the statutes do not, in general, alter the common law scheme under which organizations (as "masters") may be vicariously liable for the acts of both volunteers and employees (as "servants"). Nor do the statutes remove the possibility that organizations may be liable for injuries suffered by volunteers. Just as the potential liabilities are largely the same for volunteers as for employees, so too should the organization's response be the same. The organization should take reasonable steps to limit the possibility that accidents will occur, through a program of risk management and maintenance of liability insurance, discussed below.

(b) STEPS IN RISK MANAGEMENT Risk management consists of essentially three steps, which are best performed by a risk management committee.

(i) Identify and evaluate risks The first step is to identify and evaluate potential risks. The risk management committee should examine the activities of each volunteer position and list all of the ways the volunteer could cause an injury to someone else, and all of the ways the volunteer could be personally injured. Next, the committee should evaluate which of these accidents is most likely to result in liability for the organization under prevailing law, which accidents are likely to occur often, and which accidents would result in especially severe harm. This is an intricate process during which the risk management committee will need to consult with people throughout the organization.

(ii) Develop strategies for reducing risk The second step is to develop appropriate strategies for reducing the chances that accidents will occur. The challenge in this step is finding *appropriate* strategies. Risk management carried to an extreme can reduce the effectiveness of an organization's volunteer program. Examples of risk management strategies include establishing rules for how certain activities are to be conducted, holding training programs for staff and volunteers, screening staff and volunteers for certain skills, and deciding whether there are some activities that create so much risk that they should be avoided completely.

For example, suppose the risk management committee is concerned about the frequency of automobile accidents involving volunteers. One way to reduce the chances of such accidents is to require all volunteers who drive to have perfect driving records, without even a single speeding ticket. This may reduce the chances of car accidents, but it might also greatly reduce the pool of potential volunteers. It may be desirable, and more appropriate, for the organization to examine the driving records of volunteers who drive and to set some more reasonable standard.

A volunteer job description is an invaluable risk management tool. A good job description specifies the duties of each volunteer position, the skills required for the job, and the training the new volunteers must receive before starting work. The job description should also list the on-the-job training the volunteer will receive, and the procedures for supervising and evaluating the volunteer. All of this information serves multiple functions. Ensuring that the position will be filled by properly qualified volunteers not only helps prevent accidents, but also helps ensure that the volunteer in the position will perform as effectively as possible. All of the other parts of a volunteer job description have the same far-reaching benefits.

(iii) Implementing a risk management program The third risk management step, after identifying and evaluating risks and developing risk reduction strategies, is implementation. Successful implementation depends on the full support of the organization at all levels. If representatives of all departments of the organization participate in the formulation of the risk management program, and if they all believe that the program will help to reduce the chances of liability and also improve the overall operation of the volunteer program, then the risk management program is more likely to be accepted by everyone. There is no reason why the risk management program should be restricted to volunteers. The same steps should be followed for all members of the organization's staff.

Another key element of implementation is a periodic assessment of the risk management program's effectiveness. For example, when accidents do occur (and they may occur even with the best risk management program), the organization should consider whether additional risk management steps are appropriate to prevent that type of accident or occurrence in the future.

Legal Summary

Steps in risk management:

a. Identify and evaluate risks.

b. Develop strategies for reducing risks.

c. Implement and make periodic assessments of the risk management program.

36.4 INSURANCE

(a) EVALUATING INSURANCE COVERAGE Every nonprofit organization should not only take reasonable steps to limit risks associated with volunteers' work, but should also maintain adequate insurance coverage. In evaluating insurance coverage, an organization should go back to the list of potential risks involving volunteers and be sure those events are covered by the organization's insurance. A professional risk manager or insurance broker can provide the best assistance in assessing an organization's insurance needs.

The place to start is the organization's general liability insurance—the policy that covers the organization for a broad category of claims brought against it. Are claims based on acts of volunteers covered by this policy? A policy might, for example, only provide coverage for claims arising out of the acts of "employees," and this may in effect exclude volunteers. It is also possible that the policy may specifically exclude coverage for the acts of volunteers. Some organizations maintain separate policies to cover acts of volunteers, as an alternative to coverage under the general liability policy.

Insurance carriers tend to be wary of volunteers, and may believe that volunteers are more likely to cause accidents than salaried employees. An organization may have

Exhibit 36.2.   Checklist.

---

1. What is your organization's insurance coverage for injuries to volunteers while they are performing volunteer services?

2. What is your organization's insurance coverage for claims against the organization for acts of its volunteers?

3. If volunteers are driving vehicles, is their adequate insurance to cover the organization in the event of accidents?

4. Does the organization's insurance policy provide any coverage to the volunteers themselves for liabilities they may have for their actions?

---

to convince the insurance representative otherwise. Evidence that the organization has a risk management program in place may be very helpful in that effort.

Some categories of claims, such as those involving automobile accidents, may not be covered by the general liability policy. It is important to evaluate the organization's automobile insurance policy to be sure there is coverage for accidents caused by volunteers if they drive in the course of their volunteer work. Special, large-scale events, such as a large walkathon, also may not be covered by the regular liability policy, and an organization may have to purchase separate coverage. Again, that coverage should include claims arising out of volunteers' work.

In evaluating coverage for injuries to volunteers, it will be important to know the application of state workers' compensation laws to volunteers, and to analyze the organization's workers' compensation policy in that light.

(b) ALTERNATIVES TO COMMERCIAL INSURANCE   To the extent that coverage for acts of volunteers is either unavailable or unduly expensive through the commercial insurance market, an organization may wish to consider alternatives. For example, in some states, there are nonprofit risk pools that function similarly to insurance companies but provide insurance only to nonprofit organizations. Such pools may be able to provide cost-effective liability insurance for the organization as a whole, including coverage for damages caused by volunteers (Exhibit 36.2.).

36.5   VOLUNTEERS AND THE LAW OF CONTRACTS

(a) BASIC REQUIREMENTS OF CONTRACTS   A contract is a legally binding agreement between two parties. Some "consideration"—some valuable thing or right—must pass between the parties in order for the contract to be valid. A contract does not necessarily have to be in writing to be valid, although certain types of contracts, such as those for the sale of goods in excess of specified amounts or certain kinds of employment contracts, do have to be written. Requirements for the enforcement of contracts are a matter of state law, and may vary somewhat from state to state. The basic principles of contract law, however, are relatively uniform among the states.

(b) CONTRACTS FOR VOLUNTEER SERVICE   Some organizations formalize their obligations and those of volunteers in volunteer service contracts, which are analogous to employment contracts. There is no legal barrier to such service contracts between an organization and a volunteer. The organization receives the volunteer's services as consideration; the consideration to the volunteer does not, of course, consist of money, but may include training, career development, or the opportunity to participate in the program. A contract for volunteer services may have to be in writing to be valid, depending on state law and the period of service agreed on.

The primary purposes of most contracts are to clarify the obligations of two parties with respect to each other, and to provide the basis for a legal remedy in case of a breach of the contract. Contracts for volunteers' services are more likely to serve only the former purpose, although a lawsuit for breach of the volunteer service contract is theoretically possible.

Contracts between volunteers and an organization typically enumerate the duties and benefits of volunteer service. These contracts may specify, for example, the hours a volunteer must work, the requirement that volunteers follow particular organization procedures, and the training that volunteers will receive. This same information may be contained in the volunteer job description.

Some organizations believe that listing these requirements in a written document signed by both parties will increase the chances that the volunteers will follow the specified rules. Contracts may be desirable if there is a particular rule or policy which the organization wants to be sure is followed to the letter. A duty embodied in a contract is more likely to be taken seriously, in the view of some organizations.

A written understanding of the obligations of both the organization and the volunteer is undoubtedly desirable, but there may be some disadvantages to the formality of a contract. Volunteers may perceive the requirement that they sign a contract as indicating a lack of trust on the part of the organization. A contract may be deemed too formal and restrictive, and inconsistent with the spontaneity and spirit of a good volunteer program.

(c) VOLUNTEERS AS AGENTS OF THE ORGANIZATION Organizations enter into contracts through the actions of individuals, who are the "agents" of organizations. An agent is someone authorized to act on behalf of another person or entity. Volunteers may certainly be legal agents of organizations and can bind organizations to perform obligations under contracts.

Even if an organization does not explicitly authorize a volunteer to act as its agent, the organization may follow procedures that make it appear that the volunteer has such authorization. In that case, the organization may be legally barred from denying that the volunteer lacked authority to enter into a contract on behalf of the organization. Under this doctrine of "apparent authority," a volunteer may thus commit the organization to

Exhibit 36.3. Checklist.

1. Is there any policy or rule in your organization that is especially important and would make it desirable to have written volunteer service contracts? What are the advantages and disadvantages of requiring volunteers to sign such an agreement?

2. What are limits on volunteers' authority to enter into contracts on behalf of the organization?

3. Does the organization take any steps to make it appear that volunteers have more authority than they actually have?

perform contractual obligations even if that commitment may be beyond the scope of the volunteer's actual duties.

Organizations in which volunteers interact with vendors, other organizations, or service providers should be conscious of the extent of volunteers' authority to enter into contracts on behalf of the organization, and may wish to set some limits on that authority. The organizations should also be aware of the possibility that third parties will believe that the authority of a volunteer is greater than is actually the case (Exhibit 36.3.).

36.6 VOLUNTEERS AND EMPLOYMENT LAW

(a) SOURCES OF EMPLOYMENT LAW The relationship between employees and their employers is governed by a complex system of federal, state, and local laws. These laws govern, for example, the extent to which employers can make decisions to hire or promote certain employees based on the employees' race, gender, or age, and the ability of an employer to terminate an employee who speaks out against the employer. A full review of all of the legal doctrines relating to the employment relationship, and the application of those doctrines to volunteers, is beyond the scope of this chapter. The following paragraphs instead give a sample of how some of these laws may apply to volunteers.

The relevant employment law statutes certain specific definitions of the "employees" and "employers" to which they apply. It may be unclear from the wording of the statutes whether volunteers are considered "employees" and whether a given nonprofit organization constitutes an "employer." In that case, court decisions interpreting the statute may give either an explicit answer or guidance as to how the question would likely be answered.

Even if such statutes do not literally apply to volunteers, there may be good policy reasons for nonprofit organizations to treat their volunteers as if they were protected by those statutes. If an organization is in any doubt as to whether particular employment statutes apply to volunteers, the safest policy is to proceed as if volunteers were considered employees for all purposes.

(b) DISCRIMINATION The extent to which employers can make employment decisions based on the race, religion, sex, national origin, age, or other characteristics of individuals has been the subject of much legislation and litigation in recent years. In applying the legal principles relating to employment discrimination to service by volunteers, courts engage in a close analysis of the governing statutes.

The federal law prohibiting discrimination based on race, color, religion, sex, or national origin is contained in Title VII of the Civil Rights Act of 1964 (42 U.S.C. § 2000(e) et seq.). The few courts that have examined the application of Title VII to volunteers have concluded that volunteers are not "employees" within the meaning of Title VII. Those courts have stated that there is an implicit requirement that "employees" covered by Title VII be paid. Another court reached a similar conclusion with respect to the federal law relating to employment discrimination based on age, the Age Discrimination in Employment Act of 1967 ("ADEA"; 29 U.S.C. § 621 et seq.).

However, most states and even many municipalities have their own discrimination laws, and some of these may in fact apply to nonprofit organizations and their volunteers. For example, the Pennsylvania Human Relations Act (43 P.S. § 955(a)) prohibits discrimination by an employer against an employee on the basis of various characteristics, including the individual's sex. For purposes of this statute, the definition of "employer" with respect to discriminatory practices specifically includes religious, fraternal, charitable, and sectarian corporations and associations that employ four or more persons (43 P.S. § 954(b)). The Act does not define "employee" except to state that it includes certain categories of workers; none of those exclusions relates to volunteers. Therefore, the Act has been applied to volunteer fire companies that have rejected membership applications from women because of their sex.

(c) TERMINATION Organizations sometimes believe that a volunteer should be terminated. This conclusion may be based on a particular incident or pattern of misconduct, on the volunteer's inability to perform in accordance with the organization's standards, or on a variety of other valid and important grounds. These are the same types of reasons underlying decisions to terminate employees.

The termination of an employee may be governed by several bodies of law, which might also apply to the termination of a volunteer. State laws vary as to whether an employer may only terminate an employee "for cause," or whether the employer can terminate an employee "at will." These state requirements could conceivably also apply to the termination of volunteers. The various antidiscrimination laws also relate to the termination of employees, and, depending on the statute, to volunteers as well.

Volunteers or employees who are terminated after speaking out against an organization's policy may claim a violation of a law protecting "whistleblowers," or even a violation of the First Amendment right to freedom of speech.

For an employee or a volunteer to establish that an employer has violated the rights of one of its staff under the U.S. Constitution, it must be first established that the employer's action constitutes "state action." The protections of the Constitution do not relate to exclusively private organizations whose actions are not considered state action. However, just because an organization is a nonprofit does not mean that its action would definitely not be considered state action. In such cases, the organization's acts with respect to its volunteers could be subject to constitutional scrutiny.

For example, the acts of local volunteer firefighting companies have been held to constitute state action. Courts have upheld the right of volunteer firefighters who were terminated because they publicly complained about policy decisions to maintain actions for violation of their free speech rights.

Like the termination of an employee, the termination of a volunteer, may, in fact, have severe legal consequences. Volunteers have a stake in their positions and are sometimes willing to incur legal expenses to rectify what they believe has been an unjust termination. It is therefore prudent for an organization to carefully document its reasons for terminating volunteers, just as it would for termination of its salaried staff.

(d) FAIR LABOR STANDARDS ACT The Fair Labor Standards Act ("FLSA"; 29 U.S.C. § 201 et seq.) sets minimum wage, overtime, and recordkeeping requirements for the "enterprises" covered by the Act. The FLSA only applies to enterprises that "engage in commerce or in the production of goods for commerce" (29 U.S.C. § 203(s)). It also only applies to individuals who are "employees" within the meaning of the Act. However, just because an organization is not for profit and just because its workers are not paid does not mean that there is no liability under the FLSA.

Exhibit 36.4. Checklist.

---

1. Do the federal laws relating to employment discrimination apply to our organization? If so, to what extent do they apply to the relations between our organization and its volunteers?

2. To what extent do the applicable state and local employment discrimination laws apply to our organization? To what extent do they apply to the relations between our organization and its volunteers?

3. Would our organization's acts constitute "state action" for purposes of a suit alleging violations of constitutional rights?

4. Does our organization engage in any activities that would make the organization an "enterprise" for purposes of the FLSA? If so, and if we involve volunteers in those activities, do the volunteers perform without any expectation of compensation?

The Supreme Court, in *Tony and Susan Alamo Foundation v. Secretary of Labor* (471 U.S. 290 (1985)), found FLSA liability on the part of a nonprofit religious organization that derived income from the operation of commercial businesses staffed by "associates," most of whom had been "drug addicts, derelicts or criminals before their conversion and rehabilitation by the Foundation" (471 U.S. at 292). Although these workers did not receive any cash salaries, they were given food, clothing, and shelter by the Foundation. The Supreme Court determined that the Foundation did constitute an "enterprise" within the meaning of the FLSA because it engaged in essentially commercial activities. The Court also found that the "associates" were "employees" within the meaning of the Act because they worked in expectation of some compensation, even though that compensation did not take the form of cash salaries. The FLSA would only apply to the "ordinary commercial activities" of religious organizations and only to individuals who engaged in those activities with the expectation of compensation. The Court concluded that "ordinary volunteerism is not threatened by this interpretation of the statute" (471 U.S. at 302–303).

As nonprofit organizations increasingly engage in various commercial activities to raise funds, the FLSA may be of great importance to them. It appears that organizations could nonetheless avoid the application of the FLSA to their volunteers if it was clear that the volunteers were serving without any expectation of compensation (Exhibit 36.4.).

36.7 CONCLUSION

Volunteers provide valuable skills and energy to the organizations they serve, but their involvement may create some potential legal liabilities for the organizations. The recognition of the legal issues relating to the involvement of volunteers should lead an organization to be careful, but not to stop using volunteers. Appropriate planning, consultation with an attorney, and the maintenance of adequate insurance will all help to protect the organization and enable it to continue to benefit from the time and effort of volunteers.

SOURCES AND SUGGESTED REFERENCES

Kahn, Jeffrey D. 1986. "Legal Issues." In *From the Top Down: The Executive Role in Volunteer Program Success,* chap. 9. Energize Books. Philadelphia, PA.

————. 1985. "Organizations' Liability for Torts of Volunteers." *University of Pennsylvania Law Review* (July), 133: 1433.

National Center for Community Risk Management & Insurance. Washington, D.C. 1991. *State Liability Laws for Charitable Organizations and Volunteers.*

Stone, Byron, and North, Carol. 1988. *Risk Management and Insurance for Nonprofit Managers.* First Non Profit Risk Pooling Trust.

Tremper, Charles. 1991. "Compensation for Harm From Charitable Activity." Cornell Law Review (January), 76: 401.

Tremper, Charles, and Goldberg, James. 1991. *Hiring and Firing Within the Law: A Guide for Nonprofit Organizations.* Pittsburgh: National Union Fire Insurance Company of Pittsburgh.

United Way of America. 1987. *Risk Management Guide for Nonprofits.* Alexandria, VA.

Index